THE ASIAN MARKETING CASEBOOK

Noel Capon
Wilfried R. Vanhonacker

Pearson
Education

PRENTICE HALL

Singapore   New York   London   Toronto   Sydney   Mexico City

Published in 1999 by
Prentice Hall
Simon & Schuster (Asia) Pte Ltd
317 Alexandra Road
#04-01 IKEA Building
Singapore 159965

Prentice Hall, Simon & Schuster offices in Asia: *Bangkok, Beijing, Hong Kong, Jakarta, Kuala Lumpur, Manila, New Delhi, Seoul, Singapore, Taipei, Tokyo*

Printed in Singapore

5 4 3 2 1
02 01 00 99

ISBN 0-13-795550-2

Simon & Schuster (Asia) Pte Ltd, *Singapore*
Prentice Hall, Inc., *Upper Saddle River, New Jersey*
Prentice Hall Europe, *London*
Prentice Hall Canada Inc., *Toronto*
Prentice Hall Of Australia Pty Limited, *Sydney*
Prentice Hall Hispanoamericana, S.A., *Mexico*

Contents

VIETNAM

Preface

This is a marketing book about Asia, a compilation of case studies that demonstrates the diversity of marketing problems faced by organizations operating in Asia. The book does not pretend to be exhaustive, but certainly is illustrative of the challenges faced by both domestic Asian and foreign corporations operating in Asian markets.

In preparing the material for this book, we have attempted to cover a broad span of marketing problems set in Asia, represented in the 60 cases. The cases are based in 16 countries (plus countries in the Middle East); they focus on industrial and consumer marketing issues, they are concerned with products and with services, they deal with intra-country as well as inter-country problems; some focus on broad scale marketing strategy development, others concern specific implementation issues such as distribution, promotion or pricing; some focus on new and emerging markets, others are concerned with more mature markets; most concern private sector organizations, but some public and non-profit marketing situations are also included; some cases concern European or American companies doing business in Asia, others focus on local firms.

Several motivations underlay the development of this book. First, many business students and institutions around the world tend to exhibit at least some degree of ethnocentrism, ranging to xenophobia in some cases. In a world in which globalization is an increasing trend, such a view is not only excessively narrow, in the long run (and maybe in the short and medium run also) it will certainly lead to business failure. Taking the position that knowledge about different countries and dealing with issues in those countries are ways to open minds, this casebook can hopefully lead to increased global thinking. Second, the focus of this book is Asia, a region of the world that for those outside, and many inside, is much less well-known than the countries of Europe and North America. Third, day-by-day, Asia is becoming an increasingly important part of the world economy and marketing students the world over should be provided with some experience of doing business in Asia. Fourth, the late 1997 Asian financial crisis and its continuing impact exemplifies Asia's global importance. Fifth, Asia provides a group of especially interesting countries to study inasmuch as organizations may face many different environments, from extremely rich to extremely poor, and from democratic to authoritarian societies. Sixth, the preparation of this book marks the first major collaborative effort among the major schools of business and management in Asia, and between two western schools that have major global reputations, Columbia Business School in New York and INSEAD in France.

Finally, the set of readily available contemporary marketing cases written on Asian organizations from which teachers may draw is rather limited. Of course, Harvard Business School has for many years been the major source of marketing case studies but, although it has moved to develop more European and Asian cases in recent years, its major focus is North America. In addition, although some Asian cases are finding their way into the European case clearing house (ECCHo) at

Cranfield University in the U.K. and Babson College in the U.S., and into international marketing books, the numbers are limited and the cases are frequently not contemporary.

When this case writing project started, the goal was limited, just to write a few cases for use in courses at The Hong Kong University of Science and Technology (HKUST) and Columbia Business School. As work commenced, however, it became clear that the supply of Asian cases was greater than we had thought. Several leading business and management schools in Asia had ongoing case-writing projects but these cases were typically used for internal purposes and were not generally available. When it was suggested to these institutions that they cooperate with a project that would lead to the development of a book of Asian cases they were quite enthusiastic.

Thus, the cases in this book come from a variety of sources. The largest group are those written especially for this book at HKUST and Columbia but others were provided by: Asian Institute of Management (AIM), the Philippines; Indian Institute of Management, Ahmedabad, India; INSEAD, France; Korea University, South Korea; Institute for Management Development (IMD), Switzerland; Lahore University of Management Studies (LUMS), Pakistan; Stanford Business School; National University of Singapore, Singapore; and University of Western Ontario.

The choice of countries did not proceed in any scientific manner. Basically, we selected those countries where extant cases were available or where we thought we would identify interesting issues. In two instances we selected "typical" countries that we thought might face issues similar to their neighbors: Vietnam for Laos and Cambodia, and Kazakstan as an exemplar of the Central Asian Republics; we omitted Myanmar (Burma).

Although the focus of this book is a set of Asian marketing cases, for each of the countries in which the cases are based we provide a map of each country and brief overview to a standard template. This template focuses on the country's background, its political, social, economic and financial environments and its infrastructure. A set of basic statistics is also provided. These descriptions are not meant to be exhaustive but they do form a valuable background for those unfamiliar with specific countries and should be read in conjunction with the cases themselves. Finally, to provide a background for the casebook as a whole, the introductory section provides an overview of Asia.

Acknowledgments

Many individuals and organizations played a part in the development of this book. In particular, the School of Business and Management at The Hong Kong University of Science and Technology (HKUST), the Chazen Institute and the Center on Japanese Economy and Business at the Graduate School of Business, Columbia University provided financing for the project. The organizations noted in the Preface graciously agreed to allow us to select from among their cases for inclusion in the book; we thank them, the case authors and the individuals who helped smooth the way for positive organizational decisions. Included in this latter set are Professor Ehsan ul Haque, Lahore University of Management Sciences (LUMS), Pakistan, and Professor Jacinto C. Gavino, Jr., Asian Institute of Management (AIM), the Philippines. We also thank the organizations that provided the case sites and the many managers who believed sufficiently in the value of management education that they gave freely of their time for preparation of case studies.

At HKUST, students in Services Marketing classes in spring 1995 provided the basis for several of the local case studies and stimulated the case writing effort because of the high quality of their work. We single out for special attention, Ho Man Kap Alex who worked on the country summaries and the case writing team of Samina Seth, Ho Yuen Ching Michelle, Leung Wang Kei Terence and Shamza Khan; Michelle and Samina were critical to development of the Sri Lanka cases, and the China and Kazakstan cases respectively. In addition, we applaud the special efforts of Samina who played a critical role; not only was she heavily involved in case writing, she served as a prolific idea generator, an inspiration (and task mistress) to all involved (students and faculty) and was project manager during the early phases of the project. When she graduated into the world of high finance, she was most ably succeeded by Shamza Khan who was largely responsible for managing development of the final manuscript. This book would not have been possible without their efforts. Thank you, Samina and Shamza.

Finally, we thank Deborah Evans of Columbia for her heroic efforts with such a large manuscript, the ever helpful Dorothy McIvor and our editors, Christine Chua Poi Kian, Lam Wai Ling and Ang Lee Ming.

Dedication

To our students – past, current and future – for whom the opportunities in Asia are as exciting, but challenging, as they are to us.

About the Authors

Noel Capon is a tenured full professor at Columbia Business School; during the initial stages of the development of this book he was Visiting Professor at HKUST. Professor Capon earned Ph.D.s in chemistry from London University and marketing from Columbia University.

The recipient of teaching awards at both UCLA and Columbia, Professor Capon has also taught at INSEAD; University of Hawaii; Monash University, Melbourne, Australia; and HKUST. Before joining the Columbia faculty in 1979; he taught at the Graduate School of Management, UCLA and Harvard Business School. He teaches at the China-Europe International Business School (CEIBS) in Shanghai, PRC and regularly directs and teaches executive seminars at Columbia's executive training center, Arden House, and teaches and consults for major corporations throughout the world.

Professor Capon's works are widely published. His 40-plus articles have appeared in: *Annals of Operations Research; Columbia Journal of World Business; Communication Research; Developmental Psychology; Harvard Business Review; Industrial Marketing Management; Journal of Advertising Research; Journal of Applied Developmental Psychology; Journal of Applied Psychology; Journal of Business Administration; Journal of Consumer Research; Journal of Financial Services Research; Journal of International Business Studies; Journal of International Forecasting; Journal of Management Studies; Journal of Marketing; Journal of Marketing Research; Lending for the Commercial Banker; Management Decision; Management Science; Public Opinion Quarterly; Strategic Management Journal.* In addition, he has contributed to numerous edited books.

Professor Capon has published four books: *Corporate Strategic Planning* (1988), a major study of the planning practices of major U.S. manufacturing corporations; *The Marketing of Financial Services: A Book of Cases* (1992); *Why Some Firms Perform Better than Others: Towards a More Integrative Explanation* (1997), on the underpinnings of superior corporate financial performance; and *Planning the Development of Builders, Leaders and Managers for 21st Century Business* (1997), on business school curriculum development. He is editor for sections on *Marketing*, and *Sales Management and Distribution*, in the *AMA Management Handbook* (1994) and is currently completing a graduate-level marketing text and a book on Key Account Management.

Wilfried R. Vanhonacker is recognized worldwide as a leading scholar in the field of marketing science. He gained a Ph.D. in Management from Purdue University (Indiana, U.S.) in 1979. Before joining INSEAD, Professor Vanhonacker spent nine years on the faculty at Columbia Business School; he also taught at UCLA and Cornell University. At INSEAD, he has been Marketing Area Coordinator and Director of the Ph.D. Program. He is currently on partial leave from INSEAD and is Professor of Marketing and Department Head at HKUST in Hong Kong. In the early 1990s, he played a key role in developing and establishing the China-Europe International Business School (CEIBS) in Shanghai, PRC. He was Visiting Professor, Executive Program Director, and Acting Dean at the China-Europe Management Institute (CEMI), CEIBS's predecessor in Beijing. He is currently the Academic Advisor at

CEIBS and represents INSEAD on the Academic Council of CEIBS. Prior to his involvement with CEMI in Beijing, he was a Visiting Professor in the Management Colleges of the Ministry of Electronics and the former Ministry of Machine Building (both in Beijing). He is currently an Honorary Advisor to the Hong Kong Institute of Marketing.

Professor Vanhonacker's research interests include analytic modeling of marketing phenomena and marketing research. His publications include two books and numerous papers in academic journals such as *Journal of Marketing Research, Marketing Science, Marketing Letters, Journal of Global Marketing, Journal of International Consumer Marketing, Management Science, Journal of Business and Economic Statistics, Journal of Business Research, Managerial and Decision Economics, Journal of Statistical Computation and Simulation, International Journal of Human Resource Management, and Applied Stochastic Models and Data Analysis.* He also serves on the editorial boards of academic journals. He has taught in executive programs in Europe, the U.S. and East Asia and has been a consultant to various corporations and governments.

Having been involved extensively with foreign corporations operating in and doing business with China since 1985, Professor Vanhonacker has developed extensive experience and expertise in setting up and operating businesses in the PRC, and recently completed an extensive field study on operating equity JVs in that country. He is a partner in a Hong Kong-registered consulting company specializing in investment strategies in the PRC. Professor Vanhonacker is a Belgian national, resident in France and Hong Kong.

Synopsis of the Cases by Country

Asia

1. **Holiday Inn Worldwide Asia Pacific.** Holiday Inn Asia Pacific has ambitious expansion plans. In light of these plans management is considering how to measure service quality and human resource performance. The problem is exacerbated by the fact that many of its current properties are, and much of its anticipated expansion will be, franchise operations. A consultant group has made a series of recommendations to senior management; these must be evaluated and next steps determined.

2. **Waste Management International PLC: Strategy for Asia.** Waste Management International is the international division of U.S.-based WMX Technologies, a company specializing in offering comprehensive environmental services to industry, government and residential consumers. In late 1993, having successfully secured a contract for an advanced treatment facility in Hong Kong, Waste Management International is in the process of developing a strategic plan for Asia.

Bangladesh

3. **Social Marketing Company, Bangladesh.** In early 1995, key Population Services Inc. representatives at Social Marketing Company (SMC) in Bangladesh are evaluating the performance of the SMC's brands of condoms, contraceptive pills, oral dehydration therapy and sanitary napkins. Performance is mixed and although several brands have found considerable acceptance in Bangladesh a donor change means that several established contraceptive pill brand names must be discontinued. SMC has to decide how to manage this brand transition and how to improve overall cost recovery, possibly by expanding the product line.

Hong Kong

4. **City Telecom (HK) Ltd.** Historically, long distance telephone service in Hong Kong was provided by the monopoly supplier, Hong Kong Telecom. City Telecom (HK), the Hong Kong subsidiary of a Canadian company, has identified a regulatory loophole and is providing long distance "call back" service by routing international calls through Canada. In April 1995, City Telecom (HK) has to devise a marketing strategy for enhancing its market position in the face of likely actions by Hong Kong Telecom, the entry of new suppliers and gradual deregulation of the Hong Kong market. Correspondingly, Hong Kong Telecom must devise a strategy to protect its entrenched position.

5. **Hair-Works.** One of Hong Kong's leading entrepreneurs is contemplating entry into the upper tier of the hair care market. In September 1995, he has given

his assistant the task of developing a market entry strategy. A considerable amount of data is available about the hair care industry in general and about potential direct competitors in particular.

6. **Jimmy Lai and Daily Newspapers in Hong Kong.** Controversial founder and owner of Giordano, a highly successful retail clothing chain based in Hong Kong, Jimmy Lai is contemplating entry into the mature, Chinese-speaking Hong Kong newspaper market. Lai has to evaluate whether such an entry is viable; if so, he must develop a complete marketing strategy for entry. He has to consider not only the short term but must contemplate the impact of any plans in light of the impending transition of Hong Kong from British rule to the PRC in June 1997.

7, 8, 9. **Jimmy Lai: Apple Daily (B), (C), (D).** The subsequent cases in the series detail the events that occurred after entry and pose many decisions both for Jimmy Lai and publishers of other newspapers currently competing in Hong Kong.

10. **The Mass Transit Railway in Hong Kong.** In March 1995, the Mass Transit Railway (MTR) faces a severe imbalance of supply and demand on its important "Nathan Road Corridor" in rush hour leading to unsafe traveling conditions. It has to devise a strategy, or series of strategies, to even out the imbalance, in part by identifying critical de-marketing options.

India

11. **Allwyn.** This once successful state-owned manufacturer of refrigerators was unable to respond to increased competition when economic liberalization allowed competitors to enter the Indian market. In mid-1993, Allwyn has been closed for over a year and management is contemplating possible options for relaunching the Allwyn brand.

12. **National Publishing Company: Marketing of Children's Fortnightly Magazine.** Although it is the market leader in children's magazines, *Titli* has experienced a downward trend in circulation. In November 1990, the marketing manager has commissioned an extensive market study and must analyze the data in an attempt to develop a strategy to reverse this serious trend.

13. **Nims Apparel.** A successful Indian decorative shirt manufacturer with its strong "Double Bull" brand, Nims is facing increased competition from new entrant multinational shirt manufacturers offering formal-wear shirts. In recent years, Nims' sales of non-promoted, unbranded formal-wear shirts have also increased; management is trying to decide whether or not to brand its formal-wear shirts and, if so, whether to use the "Double Bull" name or introduce a new shirt brand. Regardless, a strategy and implementation plan must be developed.

14. **Splendor Decorative Laminates India Ltd.: Evaluating Market Research Proposals and Selecting a Market Research Agency.** In November 1993, the marketing manager of Splendor Decorative Laminates is in the process of setting up facilities to manufacture decorative laminates. He is studying market

research proposals from three well-known market research companies. He must decide what criteria to use to evaluate the proposals and what processes he should employ to make a decision on which company to choose.

Indonesia

15. **PT Indocipta Pangan Makmur: Snack Food Manufacturing Company.** In late 1990, this leading snack food company is facing increased competitive threats. Although its "Chiki" brand is the industry leader, the marketing manager is considering a repositioning strategy as one of several options to take advantage of new opportunities.

16. **Sumber Tehnik.** In July 1992, the CEO of Sumber Tehnik, the largest dealership for reconditioned cars in East Java's capital city, Surabaya, is evaluating his marketing strategy. Although Surabaya has benefitted from Indonesia's economic boom, Sumber's unit monthly sales have not increased for at least three years. A strategy is needed both to retain market leadership and to increase sales and profits.

Japan

17. **Club Med, Japan.** The secret of Club Med's success in Japan was considered to be pioneering new ideas. Its first village, opened in 1987, was a ski resort; currently, it is developing City Club for corporate use and making alliances with major private companies in resort areas development. In December 1989, Mr. Agnello, Chairman of Club Med Asia-Pacific-Indian Ocean, is attempting to prepare Club Med for the anticipated boom in leisure and travel consumption in the face of anticipated competition from non-traditional competitors with deep pockets.

18. **Delissa in Japan.** Agria, Sweden's leading dairy products cooperative, has successfully penetrated 13 foreign markets via know-how transfer ventures, whereby a local licensee manufactures yogurt using Swedish technology, then markets and distributes products with its own distribution network. In contrast to these successes, Agria's "Delissa" brand has fared poorly in Japan. Senior management is evaluating the reasons for failure and trying to identify alternative courses of action.

19. **Levi Strauss Japan K.K.** Levi Strauss is the market leader in Japan's jeans market. However, market growth has slowed and competitors are offering broader product lines through a wider range of distribution outlets. Levi's management is considering alternative courses of action to resume growth and maintain and enhance Levi's market position.

20. **Lussman-Shizuka Corporation.** The Japanese authorities have arrested three of Lussman-Shizuka's employees accused of bribing university professors to win orders for the company's pharmaceutical products. The German CEO of the Sino-German joint venture is being hounded by the Japanese press and has to decide what actions to take.

21. **See's Candies: Japanese Market Entry.** See's Candies, a successful U.S. West Coast confectionery manufacturer, is facing demographic changes in its core market. In the 1970s it entered and failed in the Japanese market; in the 1980s it entered and failed in the U.S. Midwest market. It is examining three alternatives for re-entering the Japanese market.

Kazakstan

22. **Arthur Andersen, Kazakstan.** In August 1995, the major U.S. accounting and consulting organization is developing a marketing strategy. Initially targeting U.S. multinationals, it is contemplating trying to secure business from local Kazak companies.
23. **Astana Foods, Kazakstan.** Entrepreneur Alexander Garber has successfully developed a food-importing business in Kazakstan. He is considering how to improve operations to increase revenues and profits.
24. **Kazak Enterprises.** Kazak Enterprises is a successful importer of consumer goods that, in just a few years, has developed extensive wholesale and distribution operations in Kazakstan. A recently returned native Kazakh is examining Kazak Enterprises' success to see what can be learned for a possible entry into the distribution industry in Kazakstan.
25. **Philips N.V.: Representative Office in Kazakstan.** Philips, a major multinational company with a broad product range of consumer and industrial goods, entered the Kazakstan market in 1994 several years behind major international competitors. Long-term planning is difficult because of highly unstable sociopolitical and economic environments. Philips must identify which of its many products are best suited to the Kazak market and which market segments should be addressed. Philips must formulate product/market segment strategies in the face of an underdeveloped infrastructure that is different from most other countries in which Philips does business.

Malaysia

26. **Edaran Otomobil Nasional Berhad: Challenge of the 1990s.** Partly owned by the Malaysian Ministry of Finance, Edaran Otomobil Nasional Berhad (EON) is sole distributor for Proton Saga, Malaysia's national car. By 1994, EON achieved almost 75% market share. In September 1994, the second national car, the Perodua minicar, a joint venture between the Malaysian government and Japan's Daihatsu Motor, was launched. EON must decide how to respond.
27. **Malaysia Airlines: Landing Gear Shop.** Malaysia Airlines is contemplating transforming its landing gear shop into a profit center. Rather than just service and repair landing gear for its own planes, the new profit center would solicit business from other airlines. Management must decide whether or not this growth path is viable in light of other business pressures faced by the airline.

28. **Prime Pharmaceuticals Malaysia (M) Sdn. Bhd.** Prime Pharmaceuticals, the subsidiary of a U.S. pharmaceutical company, distributes its products through one of three major Malaysian distributors. In early 1991, it is trying to decide whether to continue its exclusive arrangements or to discontinue them in favor of self-distribution.

Middle East (Bahrain, Egypt, Israel, Jordan, Kuwait, Lebanon, Oman, Qatar, Saudi Arabia, United Arab Emirates)

29. **Star TV.** Star TV, owned and operated by a listed Hong Kong company, is a regional satellite TV station beaming a large footprint encompassing over 40 countries between Japan and the Middle East, reaching 70% of the world's population. In June 1993, having operated for almost 18 months, Star TV is evaluating the market attractiveness of ten Middle East countries. Country information is limited, often outdated, yet tough choices must be made quickly and market entry prioritized.

Pakistan

30. **Allied Marketing (Private) Ltd., Lahore.** In June 1992, one of three distributors for the Pakistan Tobacco Company Ltd., Allied is under pressure to increase sales volume in the face of strong competition from other cigarette manufacturers and their distributors. Critical issues for Allied are identifying optimal sales force size and salesperson compensation. Allied must also decide on the retailer/wholesaler distribution mix, taking into account problems of cross territory sales, unofficial discounted sales to retailers, high excise taxes and cigarette smuggling.

31. **Atlas Honda Ltd.: Communication Plan 1993.** Atlas Honda's former CEO has defected to major competitor Suzuki, taking with him information on Atlas Honda's future strategy. Atlas Honda management is considering its communication strategy for 1993; in particular, it is concerned with allocations to consumer and dealer promotions and print versus television advertising. Management is concerned that customers in some markets seem unconvinced of the benefits of Honda's four-stroke engine technology versus competitors' two-stroke engines.

32. **Excel Engineering: Accelerating into the Future.** Since entering the market in 1981, Excel Engineering has become a successful tractor component supplier. However, in December 1994, its two major customers face severe competitive threats as the result of the government's Awami Tractor Scheme, intended to open up the tractor market to foreign competition. Reductions in sales of domestic tractors would severely affect Excel. Adil Mansoor, CEO and founder of Excel, is considering a variety of strategic alternatives, including broadening the tractor component line, adding automotive parts, entering other metal working applications and further diversifying within the engineering industry.

33. **Pearl Continental Hotel, Lahore.** In early 1990, Syed Qasim Jafri, general manager of the 200-room Pearl Continental Hotel, one of the top-ranked hotels in Lahore, faces three critical pricing decisions. First, what, if any, quotation should he make to a sports tour group wishing to book significant hotel capacity for an 11-day period in February. Second, what room rates should he offer to contract customers (e.g., Pakistan International Airlines, foreign tour groups). Third, what overall room rate recommendations should he make for 1991; in particular, should a change be made in Pearl's historic strategy of a fixed percent price increase each year.

People's Republic of China (PRC)

34. **Shanghai Chlor-Alkali Chemical Company Ltd.: PVC.** The largest chlor-alkali producer in the Far East, in July 1994, SCAC is a major player in the PVC market. However, demand greatly exceeds supply and SCAC must decide how to allocate scarce production capacity among many current and potential customers.

35. **Shanghai Chlor-Alkali Chemical Company Ltd.: F12 (A).** In September 1994, the giant Shanghai chemical producer faced severe competition from rivals selling fluoro products F12 and F22. As the PRC government moved from centralized planning to embrace market-oriented reforms, this former state-owned enterprise and market share leader in fluoro products lost its former advantages and market share to more flexibly managed new entrants. Management must decide whether to attempt to regain lost market share and if so, through what strategies. The decision is further complicated by environmental concerns and the PRC government's embracing of the Montreal Protocol banning ozone-depleting substances.

36. **Shanghai Chlor-Alkali Chemical Company Ltd.: F12 (B).** A chemical product in decline is revived through introduction of an innovative marketing strategy based on distribution and service. The shrinking market for F12 is stimulated but significant environmental concerns remain.

37. **Shanghai Honggong Advanced Instrument Co. Ltd. (SHAIC): Marketing Electromagnetic Flowmeters in China.** SHAIC, a successful Sino-German joint venture located in the Minhang ETDZ of Shanghai, uses advanced German technology to manufacture magnetic inductive flowmeters for process control functions in such industries as steel, water supply, sewage treatment, chemicals and paper. SHAIC has no domestic competition and in four years has captured 60% market share; 40% is supplied by foreign competitors, including SHAIC's German parent. SHAIC faces many challenging questions in further developing the Chinese market given the complexity and divergence of these, primarily state-owned, sectors.

38. **Shanghai Zheng Zhang Textiles Factory.** Shanghai Zheng Zhang, the largest patchwork quilt exporter in the PRC, has paid relatively little attention to the domestic China market. Paradoxically, Shanghai Zheng Zhang views its domestic market as high risk and export markets as low risk. Given its lack of

domestic experience and government supervision of prices and quality, management faces the challenges of building brand recognition, brand equity and a distribution system to merchandise its products. In July 1995, six months after its domestic entry, management is evaluating performance and planning future actions.

The Philippines

39. **Barclay International Manufacturing Corporation: Gruff Aircon Maintenance Fluid.** Barclay International manufactures and distributes a variety of consumable products to consumer and institutional customers. It uses a distribution system similar to "Amway" whereby products are neither advertised nor distributed at retail, but sold by many thousands of individual distributors. Sales of Gruff Aircon Maintenance Fluid, launched one year earlier, are disappointing. Many complex issues are involved in Barclay Management's decision of how to proceed.

40. **Basic/Black Zale Youngman Advertising, Inc.** In recent years, the agency has participated in the successful growth of several Colgate-Palmolive brands. However, it has just been informed that Colgate-Palmolive has decided to concentrate all advertising, worldwide, with just two agencies. Although the parent U.S. company is one of these agencies, the product groups Basic/Black Zale Youngman (BZY) will lose are those in which it has been most successful. BZY's share of Colgate-Palmolive's Philippine billings will drop from 60% to about 6%.

41. **J&J (Philippines), Inc.: Johnson's Face Powder.** J&J (Philippines) is under pressure to increase revenues and profits. It is about to launch a new "face powder" product. Production is in place, advertising has been produced and the trade has reacted positively. The marketing VP has just received an urgent telephone call from a senior manager at J&J's International Division in New Jersey telling him the launch must be canceled.

42. **SAE Products Marketing Corporation: The Air Compressor Company.** The CEO is reviewing reports from the sales and marketing director that its chief competitor is gaining market share as a result of innovative promotional schemes. SAE must decide how to respond to this competitive threat.

Singapore

43. **Haw Par Villa Dragon World.** Opened in 1990, Haw Par Villa Dragon World, a first class theme park in Singapore consisting of nine major attractions, competes with such established sites as Tang Dynasty Village, Bugis Square, Sentosa and Jurong Bird Park. In May 1991, management is considering long-term strategies to increase park visitors, targeting both residents and short stay visitors. Among possible actions are: modifying the attractions to make Haw Par Villa more like an amusement park (e.g., by adding more rides) and using a variety of promotional strategies.

44. **Procter and Gamble:** *Always/Whisper.* The global manufacturer and marketer of many household products has decided to change the brand name of its feminine sanitary napkin products in Singapore. The name change from Always to Whisper aims to achieve marketing synergy in Asia. In early 1988, the company is evaluating three alternative strategies to implement the name change. It must select one strategy and develop an implementation plan.

45. **Singapore Airlines.** This leading international carrier is facing ever increasing competitive pressure from international carriers such as Cathay Pacific, United Airlines, British Airways, Qantas and JAL; industry over-capacity is increasing and budgets are tight. No longer does flight and ground service excellence guarantee superior market share. Furthermore, Singapore Airlines has diversified into related industries (e.g., catering, airport services, cargo handling, tourism, hotels, aircraft engineering). In light of the changing environment, in October 1992, Singapore Airlines must find new ways of differentiating itself from competition.

South Korea

46. **A President is Made: The Three Parties' Political Marketing in the Presidential Election.** This case details strategies employed by candidates in the 1992 Korean presidential campaign. Five days before the election, each of the three candidates must make key decisions on how to use the remaining time most effectively.

47. **Cheil Jedang Corporation's Seasoning.** Mi-Won was well established as the MSG market leader when Cheil Jedang introduced natural seasoning. By 1992, Cheil Jedang is the clear leader in natural seasoning; Mi-Won the leader in chemical seasonings. Management is reviewing Cheil Jedang's strategy and performance to identify what lessons, if any, can be gleaned for its new "instant food" product.

48. **Super Miracle CC: Marketing and Advertising for the Large-screen TV Market.** Three major Korean electronics companies, Samsung, Daewoo and GoldStar, entered the Korean market for large-screen TV sets. Although GoldStar, which entered after Samsung, was initially less well positioned, recent marketing efforts have improved its share. Management is evaluating GoldStar's actions and performance and contemplating future strategy.

Sri Lanka

49. **Keells Food Products Ltd.** The food products division of John Keells Holdings offers several successful "Keell" packaged meat products to the Sri Lankan market; it enjoys a high level of brand equity. Corporate management operates under the philosophy that all Keell offerings, embracing such products as computer services, agricultural products and tourism, should carry the company name. Food Products division management is concerned about long-run brand dilution and is contemplating introducing new food products under different brand names.

50. **Mackinnon & Keells Financial Services Ltd.** At end 1994, Mackinnon & Keells Financial Services Ltd. (MK) is a diversified financial services organization offering limited numbers of products with limited success. Management believes its moderate performance is due in part to a negative association with Keells Food Groups (in some circles, MK is perceived as the "Sausage Financial Group") and that MK should be re-named after broadening its investment product offerings. By October 1994, the committee supervising all Keells' financial services activities has to create a comprehensive marketing strategy to build and establish brand equity for Keells' financial services operations.

51. **Waldock Mackenzie.** Mackinnon & Keells Financial Services Ltd. was relaunched as Waldock Mackenzie; by mid-1995, the first stage brand equity campaign was successfully completed. The advertising themes generated widespread response in the investment banking community, target markets and general public, and won the 1994 advertising award. Management is concerned to keep up the momentum in a second advertising campaign but copycat commercials have been aired by several competitors and others are using print and TV to strike at the core of Waldock Mackenzie's message. The Management Committee must assess the impact of competitors' efforts and evaluate advertising agency suggestions for a new campaign.

52. **Richard Pieris Distributors Ltd., Sri Lanka.** In July 1995, Jeremy Ferriera, Senior Marketing Manager for the latex foam mattress manufacturer is evaluating his new sales targets. Although Pieris is market leader in the local mattress market, management believes low customer awareness and incorrect product positioning has impeded growth. Mr. Ferriera must propose a new marketing strategy to the Board of Directors and recommend short-term actions to improve sales in both the near and long term.

Taiwan

53. **Carrefour in Asia (A) Taiwan: A Bridgehead to Asia.**[1] The major French mass retailer entered the Taiwanese market on the basis of its original principles: one-stop shopping, self-service, discount, quality products and free car parking. However, this concept was adapted to local circumstances regarding supplier and human resource management and volatile customer needs. From 1986 to 1993, five successful stores were built from scratch and two new stores were contemplated. Competition was increasing from major supermarket chains, Taiwan hypermarket leader, Makro, and other domestic entrants. In June 1993, new strategies are needed; Carrefour is contemplating operating through membership sales at larger new stores as a means of circumventing regulations on selling in "industrial" suburban areas.

54. **Retailing in Taiwan.** This note details recent developments in the retail system in Taiwan. It serves as a rich example of retail distribution development in an emerging economy and background for discussion of Carrefour (A).

---

[1] This case won the European Management Development Foundation prize in *International Business*, 1995.

55. **Carrefour in Asia (B): The Expansion in Asia.** Based on its Taiwanese experience, Carrefour is considering entering other countries in Asia, in particular, Malaysia, Thailand and China. In June 1993, it plans to continue its global strategy but make adaptations to local conditions in new potential markets.

Thailand

56. **Gilman Office Automation, Bangkok, Thailand.** Since assuming the distributing contract for Ricoh copiers in 1986, Gilman Office Automation has successfully re-captured market share (14%) for the Japanese manufacturer. By 1990, the Thai copier market has doubled and Gilman faces severe challenges from major international players, Fuji-Xerox, Mita and Canon. In planning for growth, Gilman is considering becoming an integrated office equipment supplier with a potential product mix of typewriters, printers, computers, key telephones and office furniture.

57. **Maverick Bank.** In December 1994, Maverick Bank is contemplating expanding credit card operations into either the PRC or Thailand. In the near term, Maverick has sufficient resources for one new market entry. Management must compare the PRC and Thailand options, make a recommendation and devise an entry strategy.

58. **RAA (Thailand).** A Thai graduate of the Asian Institute of Management (the Philippines) has noticed that the Classified Advertisements section of Bangkok daily newspapers are crammed with advertisements, many of which look very similar and, she believes, are insufficiently creative to attract attention. Having learned of a successful recruitment advertising agency in Malaysia, in fall 1990, she contemplates opening a similar agency in Thailand.

Vietnam

59. **European Liquors, Vietnam.** Because of high tariffs on liquor imports, few cases of the firm's products are imported to Vietnam. However, most hotels catering to westerners, and significant numbers of stores, offer European's products to customers. Market demand is filled by smugglers who actively supply liquor products. Alcohol advertisements are banned in the media and billboards and other forms of outdoor advertising are expected to be banned shortly. European has to decide whether to continue and, if so, how to approach the Vietnamese market.

60. **Vinataxi.** In 1991, Vinataxi, a joint venture between a Hong Kong company and the investment arm of the Vietnamese government, was the first modern taxi fleet to commence taxi service in Ho Chi Minh City; it captured roughly 75% market share. In July 1995, it faces two new entrants following strategies similar to Vinataxi. In addition to this new competition, Vinataxi has effectively been barred from picking up passengers at the airport, a substantial source of potential business. Vinataxi must devise a strategy to secure and enhance its position in Ho Chi Minh City and consider whether to expand service to other cities such as Hanoi, Hue and Haiphong.

Cases: Key Words

Template: Company, product category, nationality of company, key words

Asia

1. **Holiday Inn Worldwide Asia Pacific:** Hotels, U.S., Asian regional strategy, service quality, human resource management, multiple branding, positioning strategy, comparative hotel market analysis, brand identify profiling, brand mapping, projective techniques, quality service delivery.
2. **Waste Management International PLC: Strategy for Asia:** Waste treatment, U.S., Asian regional strategy, market entry choices, growth opportunities, strategy implementation, service expansion, government participation, environmental waste management, partnering.

Bangladesh

3. **Social Marketing Company, Bangladesh:** Contraceptives, Bangladesh, forced brand name changes, product line strategy, retail distribution, advertising, social marketing, entrepreneurs.

Hong Kong

4. **City Telecom (HK) Ltd.:** Long-distance telephone service, Canada, new product entry, deregulation, competitive strategy, market growth, strategic planning, technological change, integrated customer service, telecommunications industry.
5. **Hair-Works:** Hair-care, Hong Kong, evaluation of potential market entry, differentiation and positioning, human resource management of creative employees, service management/control, hair-cut industry.
6, 7, 8, 9. **Jimmy Lai and Daily Newspapers in Hong Kong; Jimmy Lai: Apple Daily (B), (C), (D):** Newspapers, Hong Kong, evaluation of potential market entry, industry cartel, customer satisfaction, price war, pricing policy, product differentiation, marketing strategy and implementation, competitive response.
10. **The Mass Transit Railway in Hong Kong:** Mass transit, Hong Kong, supply/demand imbalance, demarketing, customer service, core product benefits, inter-modal coordination, commuter flow.

India

11. **Allwyn:** Refrigerators, India, state-owned enterprise, market liberalization, foreign and domestic competitive threats, regional fragmentation, poor performance, turnaround options.
12. **National Publishing Company: Marketing of Children's Fortnightly Magazine:** Children's magazine, India, market decline, consumer decision system, market segmentation, marketing strategy, product positioning, focus group

discussions, life cycle stages, active promotion, passive approval, image perception.

13. **Nims Apparel:** Men's shirts, India, market evolution, consumer attitudes, foreign competitive threats, market leadership, branding.
14. **Splendor Decorative Laminates India Ltd.: Evaluating Market Research Proposals and Selecting a Market Research Agency:** Laminates, India, evaluation and selection of marketing research supplier, market segmentation, customer needs, market segmentation and targeting, product positioning decision.

Indonesia

15. **PT Indocipta Pangan Makmur: Snack Food Manufacturing Company:** Snack food, Indonesia, sustaining performance, market segmentation, marketing strategy, product positioning, advertising, market leadership goal, distributor system, wholesaler system.
16. **Sumber Tehnik:** Used automobiles, Indonesia, competitive advantage, retail distribution, promotion, pricing, display, sales force motivation, customer perception.

Japan

17. **Club Med, Japan.** Resorts, France, seasonal demand, travel trends, product differentiation, customer satisfaction, service delivery.
18. **Delissa in Japan:** Yogurt, Sweden, franchise system, consumption habits, distribution, retail fragmentation, culture barriers.
19. **Levi Strauss Japan K.K.:** Clothing, U.S., market trends, changing retail distribution, market leadership, brand perceptions, pricing.
20. **Lussman-Shizuka Corporation:** Pharmaceuticals, Germany, illegal conduct, employees in jail, cultural understanding, aggressive foreign entrant, managerial decision making.
21. **See's Candies: Japanese Market Entry:** Candies, U.S., market re-entry, partnership selection, brand saliency, managing perishable goods.

Kazakstan

22. **Arthur Andersen, Kazakstan:** Professional services, U.S., market selection, marketing strategy, international accounting, tax avoidance, market penetration.
23. **Astana Foods, Kazakstan:** Wholesale food distribution, Kazakstan, domestic infrastructure, retail structure, foodstuffs promotion, consumer products launch.
24. **Kazak Enterprises:** Wholesale/retail distribution, Kazakstan, privatization, product selection, marketing strategy, sales management.
25. **Philips N.V.: Representative Office in Kazakstan:** Industrial/consumer durable products, Holland, market penetration, product portfolio, infrastructure support, low budgets, black market substitutes, multiple product lines.

Malaysia

Middle East (Bahrain, Egypt, Israel, Jordan, Kuwait, Lebanon, Oman, Qatar, Saudi Arabia, United Arab Emirates)

Pakistan

People's Republic of China (PRC)

38. **Shanghai Zheng Zhang Textiles Factory:** Handmade quilts, PRC, domestic market risk, distribution, product, design, learning effects, poor market data, production process, market segmentation, sales force management.
(**Maverick Bank:** See Thailand)

The Philippines

39. **Barclay International Manufacturing Corporation: Gruff Aircon Maintenance Fluid:** Air-conditioning fluid, the Philippines, market selection, distribution, sales force, product line strategy, advertising prohibition, benchmarking, distribution, training.
40. **Basic/Black Zale Youngman Advertising, Inc.:** Advertising services, the Philippines, global advertising centralization by client headquarters, major business loss, market targets, employee empowerment, organizational structure, organizational feedback mechanism, foxhole organizational structure.
41. **J&J (Philippines), Inc.: Johnson's Face Powder:** Face powder, U.S., new product development, launch strategy, relationship to headquarters, organizational change, strategic product groups, company image.
42. **SAE Products Marketing Corporation: The Air Compressor Company:** Air compressors, the Philippines, aggressive competitors, scarce resources, promotion mix, counter-strategies, sales force reorganization.

Singapore

43. **Haw Par Villa Dragon World:** Theme park, Singapore, target markets, service positioning, service quality, communication and distribution strategy.
44. **Procter and Gamble:** *Always/Whisper:* Sanitary napkins, U.S., brand equity, name change, "personal" product, customer confusion.
45. **Singapore Airlines:** Airline service, Singapore, service quality, service positioning, increasing competition, cost control, working committees, airline management.

South Korea

46. **A President is Made: The Three Parties' Political Marketing in the Presidential Election:** Presidential election, South Korea, political marketing, marketing strategy, segmentation, short-term promotional strategy.
47. **Cheil Jedang Corporation's Seasoning:** MSG, South Korea, market evolution, duopoly strategies, new product introduction.
48. **Super Miracle CC: Marketing and Advertising for the Large-screen TV Market:** Television sets, South Korea, competition, new products, advertising strategy.

Sri Lanka

49. **Keells Food Products Ltd.:** Food, Sri Lanka, umbrella branding, brand strategy, religious sensitivities, consumption patterns, quality control, multiple distribution channels.

Map of Asia

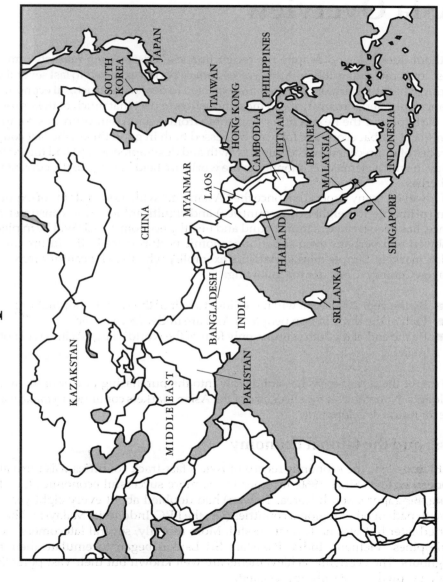

Asia Overview

Without question, and despite the recent financial crisis, Asian markets remain on most corporate radars today. After a recessionary period expected to last several years, during which the various countries are expected to deal with structural economic and financial problems, many firms in most industries expect that much of their growth in the early part of the next century will come from Asia. Asian countries comprise a significant global economic force as witnessed both in good times (the last couple of decades of unprecedented economic growth and development) and bad times such as today in which all major economies in the world are held hostage to the current financial crisis.

However, many expect that once the "Asian flu," with its symptoms of export erosion (primarily to neighboring countries) and significant losses in consumer confidence, has been treated, a more sound and healthy economic basis will be in place for renewed and perhaps even superior economic performance in the future for some Asian markets. Simple market statistics exemplify why the 21st century remains the Dragon Century. Consider the following:

- By the year 2000, Asia will have close to half of the world's population;
- Half of the three billion people in Asia are under 25 years old;
- By the end of the 20th century, only four of the world's largest cities will not be in Asia.

No doubt the recent crisis has cut deeply into the purchasing power of many Asian residents. Nonetheless, the sheer size of the Asian markets continues to make it attractive for future development.

Asia and the Global Economy

Until mid-1997, the economic record of Asia's fast-track countries was unrivaled in modern history. Since 1960, incomes in the more successful economies (i.e., Hong Kong, Singapore, South Korea, Taiwan) had doubled about every eight years. The growth path of other regional countries (i.e., the PRC, Indonesia, Malaysia, Thailand) started later but was no less successful. More recently, several latecomers (i.e., the Philippines, Vietnam, India, Pakistan, Sri Lanka) began to emulate their richer neighbors. The economic achievements are well known but their vast potential for further growth is not fully appreciated.

In the last 15 years, many Asian nations had had annual average GDP growth rates over twice the OECD rate. Table 1 summarizes the economic record of the 16 countries whose companies contributed to this book. Much progress in Asia's economic development in the 1980s and early 1990s could be attributed to economic advances in the PRC and the region's "newly industrializing economies" (i.e., Hong Kong, Singapore, South Korea, Taiwan). The PRC's slowdown in economic growth, due to government policies (1993) designed to combat inflation, should be short-lived although the government's failure to tackle the high levels of indebtedness among state-owned enterprises could lead to a resurgence of inflationary pressures.

However, these economies faced several fundamental problems: the loss of comparative advantage based on cheap labor as wage increases overtook productivity growth (especially in South Korea and Malaysia); lagging technological development and management skills required for industrial upgrading; continued economic inefficiencies resulting from widespread corruption and resistance to economic liberalization (especially in the PRC, Vietnam and Indonesia); and excess regional as well as global capacity in industries like automobiles, semiconductors, steel and petrochemicals (especially in South Korea).[1] Increased competition for capital and export markets from other economically emerging regions (e.g., Latin America, Eastern Europe) also put pressure on the Asian economies. These structural impediments were aggravated by global downturns, currency issues and political risk factors (e.g., South–North Korea and the PRC, Taiwan tensions, rising crime and corruption scandals) that determined the willingness and ability of governments to undertake the domestic policy reforms necessary to ensure that growth was based on real productivity increases rather than simply on inputs of cheap land, labor and capital. Furthermore, the large family- and state-owned companies became less able to rely on government patronage, protected markets and the exploitation of cheap resources for continued success.

Starting in summer 1997, Southeast Asia went through a financial crisis triggered by the July 2 devaluation of the Thai baht; the crisis quickly rippled through many Asian countries leading to widespread currency devaluations and huge stock market losses. By year end, about US$100 billion was pledged to shore up Asian economies, especially Thailand, Indonesia and South Korea.

Rock-bottomed interest rates in Japan and low interest rates in the US had led banks, insurers and investment houses to borrow heavily in yen and U.S. dollar for investment in short-term notes paying higher rates in Southeast Asia. Since Southeast Asian currencies were relatively stable this was an attractive investment.

The first sign of the "Asian flu" came in May when Japanese officials, concerned about the yen's decline relative to the U.S. dollar, hinted at possibly raising interest rates. With this Japanese threat, investors started unwinding their investments. As local currencies started weakening, foreign firms hedged their positions, and local banks and other companies which had borrowed heavily at low rates abroad (U.S. dollars and yen) to finance expansion (and real estate investment) rushed into U.S.

---

[1] Lim, L. (1997), "Asia 2000," *The China Business Review*, 8–13.

Table 1: Domestic Economic Strength

Countries	GDP (1994) US$ billions	GNP per capita (PPP) $ 1993	Real GDP growth (1990–94) CAG%	Gross domestic Total investment 1994 avg. %	Gross domestic Savings (1993) %	Consumer price inflation (1994) %	Cost of living comparisons (NYC=100) 1994 Index
Bangladesh	n/a	n/a	n/a	n/a	n/a	n/a	n/a
Hong Kong	130.7	21,670	5.66	27.19	30.20	8.10	105.27
India	257.9	1,250	3.56	21.68	22.00	11.00	75.58
Indonesia	148.7	3,140	6.70	35.66	23.00	9.24	86.05
Japan	4,509.9	21,090	1.56	30.57	34.70	0.80	161.49
Kazakhstan	n/a	n/a	n/a	n/a	n/a	n/a	n/a
Malaysia	70.6	8,630	8.35	35.30	38.30	3.80	79.38
Pakistan	n/a	n/a	n/a	n/a	n/a	n/a	n/a
PRC	508.2	2,120	9.97	39.29	41.19	24.10	84.85
Singapore	69.0	20,470	8.17	36.22	48.30	4.50	100.39
South Korea	379.6	9,810	7.07	36.68	34.80	6.20	92.22
Sri Lanka	n/a	n/a	n/a	n/a	n/a	n/a	n/a
Taiwan	241.1	n/a	6.46	23.01	28.29	4.09	118.09
Thailand	143.2	6,390	8.08	33.56	35.00	5.00	79.33
Philippines	63.9	2,660	1.53	23.09	14.60	9.00	76.87
Vietnam	n/a	n/a	n/a	n/a	n/a	n/a	n/a
Comparison							
U.S.	6,738.4	24,750	2.31	13.77	14.50	2.20	88.66
Germany	2,047.5	20,980	4.15	22.38	20.40	2.60	108.90

Table 1 (cont'd)

Countries	Selected consumer price indices (1993) (1980 = 100)					Real growth in industrial production index	Retail sales (1993) US$ per capita	1989–93 real growth %
	Food indices	Clothing indices	Rent indices	Fuel & light indices	Global indices			
Bangladesh	n/a	n/a	n/a	n/a	n/a	n/a	n/a	n/a
Hong Kong	282	293	289	167	289	184	4892.20	4.16
India	278	284	329	253	310	223	13.90	2.05
Indonesia	134	136	166	153	139	324	271.90	7.86
Japan	130	143	146	99	130	135	8748.70	0.09
Kazakstan	n/a	n/a	n/a	n/a	n/a	n/a	n/a	n/a
Malaysia	156	141	141	122	156	312	767.00	8.40
Pakistan	n/a	n/a	n/a	n/a	n/a	n/a	n/a	n/a
PRC	276	168	203	335	232	418	199.00	6.56
Singapore	123	109	125	75	135	232	4229.90	1.43
South Korea	236	210	266	182	223	366	1655.70	9.83
Sri Lanka	n/a	n/a	n/a	n/a	n/a	n/a	n/a	n/a
Taiwan	169	148	162	153	n/a	211	1729.20	-0.03
Thailand	166	183	163	169	175	n/a	554.70	5.35
Philippines	460	489	550	531	487	540	446.90	5.50
Vietnam	n/a	n/a	n/a	n/a	n/a	n/a	n/a	n/a
Comparison								
U.S.	163	147	186	149	175	132	5641.00	-0.30
Germany	104	103	162	136	121	115	4755.90	0.88

• GDP (1994): US$ billions at current prices and exchange rates; • GNP per capita (ppp) 1993: International $ at current prices and purchasing power parity (ppp); • Real GDP growth (1990–94): Annual compound percent change, computed on a local currency basis at 1990 prices; • Total gross domestic investment 1990–94 average: Gross fixed capital formation as a percentage of GDP; • Gross domestic savings (1993): Gross domestic savings (residents + non-residents) as a percent of GDP; • Consumer price inflation (1994): Average annual rate; • Cost-of-living comparisons 1994 (NY = 100): Cost index of basket of goods in major cities, excluding housing (New York City = 100); • Selected consumer price indices (1993) (1980 = 100); • Real growth in industrial production: Seasonably adjusted, 1980 = 100; • Retail sales (1993): US$ per capita; • Real growth in retail sales (1989–93): Annual compound real percent change in local currency.

Source: Derived from *The World Competitiveness Report 1995* (IMD).

dollars/yen to make payments. These moves sent Asian currencies tumbling. Hedge funds (speculators), trying to profit from the tumble, aggravated currency losses. By end 1997, relative to the beginning of the year, Thailand, Indonesia, the Philippines, Malaysia and South Korea all saw their currencies fall over 35% against the U.S. dollar, and each was grappling with erosions of investor confidence. Weathering this currency crisis were Taiwan, Hong Kong, Singapore, India and China, although general deflationary pressures also affected their currencies. The crisis affected equity markets worldwide; the Hong Kong stock market crashed in late October and the Dow Jones Index experienced a record 554 points loss in one day. At end 1997, Asian currencies remained quite weak and volatile making equity investments unattractive. Only Taiwan and India showed leading benchmark index gains for 1997; all other markets were down, declines ranging from 31% in Singapore to 55% in Thailand.

The financial crisis revealed weaknesses in the Asian economies; over-regulated, heavily burdened with bank debt and cluttered with troubled financial institutions. Thailand, Indonesia, the Philippines and South Korea were forced to seek financial assistance both from the IMF and individual nations; many were busy rescheduling short-term debt repayments with overseas banks to secure temporary relief. On December 22, Moody's Investors Service Inc. downgraded the worst-hit economies, Thailand, Indonesia, South Korea, to junk-bond status, raising the possibility that debt moratoriums might be imposed.

At end 1997, the short-term outlook for Asia was not healthy and most economists were revising growth figures downward (to less than half previously expected in many Southeast Asian countries). Observers believed that central banks would be forced to lower interest rates to absorb the shock and attempt to reverse the decline in growth. Many corporate and bank bankruptcies were anticipated in Asia, especially in South Korea and Japan; anxious western banks might pull credit lines. Exports to the region were expected to fall; Asian investments in factories abroad were also expected to decline. Observers predicted that a tidal wave of surplus products from South Korea, Japan, Taiwan, and to a lesser extent from other Southeast Asian countries (trying to export out of trouble) would collide head-on in North America, Europe and even mainland China. General deflationary pressures and currency adjustments in Asia were expected as countries attempted to remain competitive.

One result of the crisis was that Southeast Asian countries were expected to modernize their financial markets and banking systems to allocate capital more efficiently. The critical question was whether they had the political will and ability to make the changes. Elections, weak coalition governments, health of presidents and the emergence of newly-aligned opposition parties might undermine economic stability. In recent years from South Korea to Malaysia, politicians and business leaders had staked their prestige on the ability to deliver unending high growth. Backward steps would be seen as a great loss of face. Nonetheless, observers believed that each country had an opportunity to strengthen its economy and might well emerge stronger than before.

Trade, Investment and Regional Interdependence

To a large extent, in recent years, the world's industrialized nations created their wealth through the development of huge industries (e.g., chemicals, automobiles, computers, computer software, aerospace). The path Asian countries have followed is different inasmuch as they have largely relied on export-led growth to generate income and wealth. Their success is due less to mastery of new and rapidly growing industries/technologies than to an ability to make mature and standardized products more cheaply and reliably than overseas competitors. (See Table 2 for the degree of internationalization of the Asian countries.)

Table 2: Internationalization

Countries	Balance of trade 1994 US$B	% of GDP	Trade to GDP ratio (1993)	Exports of goods and commercial services US$B 1993	Growth % (1991–93)	Imports of goods and commercial services US$B 1993	Growth % (1991–93)
Bangladesh	n/a	5.51	n/a	n/a	n/a	n/a	n/a
Hong Kong	−10.40	−7.96	139.85	164.33	17.32	157.53	17.04
India	−1.07	−0.41	8.58	22.62	n/a	29.60	12.73
Indonesia	8.20	n/a	27.74	36.91	13.92	37.13	7.40
Japan	121.60	2.65	9.01	414.12	7.17	341.40	1.91
Kazakstan	n/a	n/a	n/a	n/a	n/a	n/a	n/a
Malaysia	−0.10	−0.14	82.73	52.96	16.54	53.67	10.98
Pakistan	n/a	n/a	n/a	n/a	n/a	n/a	n/a
PRC	5.30	1.04	20.03	102.64	14.15	115.56	30.62
Singapore	−6.00	−8.70	167.59	94.81	11.88	96.74	12.77
South Korea	−6.00	−1.58	29.73	97.59	7.76	100.32	2.88
Sri Lanka	n/a	n/a	n/a	n/a	n/a	n/a	n/a
Taiwan	−7.70	3.19	44.41	99.32	8.11	98.43	11.18
Thailand	−10.20	−7.12	42.61	48.37	14.99	58.04	12.94
Philippines	−7.80	−12.21	37.34	18.27	15.89	21.86	22.45
Vietnam	n/a	n/a	n/a	n/a	n/a	n/a	n/a
Comparison							
U.S.	−176.50	−2.62	10.63	623.26	5.26	716.55	8.54
Germany	45.30	2.21	23.45	441.88	−2.44	454.43	−3.52

Balance of trade 1994: US$ billions (minus sign = deficit).
Trade to GDP ratio 1993: Exports + Imports divided by GDP × 2.
Growth in exports of goods and commercial services (1991–93): Annual compound percent change based on US$ export values.
Source: Derived from *The World Competitiveness Report 1995* (IMD).

Subtle changes in the region's engines of growth are taking place as standards of living rise. For example, a larger proportion of Asian exports is now being sold to neighboring countries. This trend, reflecting the region's growing prosperity and increased number of middle-class households, means that exporters' dependence on European and U.S. markets is reducing. A second key change is that whereas Asia has long been a favored target for investors from industrialized countries, a larger share of capital inflow now comes from within the region as locals have capital to invest. Furthermore, as production costs rise in Hong Kong, Korea, Singapore and Taiwan, businesses are setting up operations in other low-cost Asian economies.

As regional interdependence increases and industry shifts from labor-intensive to more capital- and technology-intensive, it is crucial that an effective multilateral framework is developed for trade regulation. One of the first steps was the establishment of the APEC Forum. The organization's 18 members (Table 3) have set a goal of "free and open trade and investment" by 2010 for the industrialized nations, by 2020 for the remainder; in the short run, APEC will probably concentrate on matters of trade liberalization. Several countries are under constant attack from exporters in the U.S. and EU citing a systematic pattern of Asian regulations and restrictive business practices that limit trade.

Table 3: Membership in the Asia-Pacific Economic Cooperation Forum

Industrialized countries	Developing countries in Asia		Other members	Applicants*
Australia	Brunei	Papua New Guinea	Chile	India
Canada	PRC	Philippines	Mexico	Russia
Japan	Hong Kong	Singapore	Vietnam	
New Zealand	Indonesia	South Korea		
U.S.	Malaysia	Taiwan		
	Thailand			

*APEC currently has a moratorium on accepting new members.

Inter- and intra-regional investment is at a much earlier stage of development. Globally, industrialized countries continue to absorb the bulk of investment funds although East Asian countries (particularly the PRC) have become the major recipients of foreign direct investment (FDI) in the developing world. Countries on the Indian subcontinent lag far behind. One reason for the uneven dispersion of FDI is the economic record of Asia's "fast-track" economies. Investors from industrialized countries focused on these countries in the 1980s and early 1990s; initial investments led to subsequent commitments as foreign firms became more familiar with local economies. Interest in other parts of the region only emerged in recent years as cost differentials among countries widened.

Another reason for Asia's skewed FDI distribution is the influence of the Chinese Diaspora (Table 4); the overseas Chinese community is extremely important in some Asian countries. Indian subcontinent countries have no comparable investor group and their ability to attract FDI from within the region is affected accordingly. Around 40% of all FDI in Asia now originates within the region; the bulk of these funds is from the overseas Chinese community.

Although the growth record of fast-track performers and preferences of overseas Chinese contribute to a more concentrated foreign investment pattern, changing political attitudes are encouraging a wider dispersion of FDI funds. In the past, foreign firms were often pressurized for FDI to gain access to a country's markets. Today, competitive pressures within the region, particularly the opening of the PRC and India to foreign investors, leave governments less able to act in this manner. Foreign firms have more freedom to choose where to locate; frequently they select sites in less developed, low-cost countries.

Table 4: Overseas Chinese Community in Selected Asian Countries (1996)

		Population (millions) as % of locals	Business output as % of local economy	Contribution to GDP*
Hong Kong	6	98	80	120
Indonesia	8	4	50	98
Malaysia	6	32	60	48
Philippines	1	1	40	30
Singapore	2	76	76	62
Taiwan	21	99	95	255
Thailand	6	10	50	80
Vietnam	1	1	20	4
Total	51			

*In US$ billion.
Source: *Consumer Asia 1997*, Euromonitor.

Demographic Trends and Forecasts

By 2000, Asia will account for about 45% of the world population (Table 5). The PRC will still be the most populous country but the number of people in South Asia (i.e., India, Pakistan, Sri Lanka) will be nearly as great by 2010. Activity rates (i.e., economically active population as a share of the total) are expected to rise in most countries (except the PRC). Especially large increases are forecast for ASEAN countries as more women enter the workforce. Dependency rates should also fall, with especially sharp declines in South Asia and in ASEAN countries.

Before the crisis, economic success was creating severe problems in most Asian countries' labor markets. The demand for unskilled and semi-skilled workers typically exceeded supply, but the shortage of skilled workers was far more acute. Turnover rates for locally recruited engineers, accountants and managers were high as they job-hopped for better pay. More recently, the picture has changed dramatically as labor shortages have given place to previously unknown high unemployment levels with severe social implications. Rising costs of living and increased unemployment levels will put politicians under pressure and magnify concerns that stayed beneath the surface in good economic times. For example, in Indonesia where 40% of the population is living below the poverty line, ethnic Chinese have been targets in social disturbances.

At the other end of the labor market, armies of migrant workers are likely to be a regional feature for some time to come. For home countries, these workers are a valuable export as they typically repatriate a large percent of earnings. Labor migration has a long history in Asia but the numbers involved today are unprecedented; the use/abuse of migrant labor is a constant source of tension between states. Governments try to regulate the inflow strictly but high economic growth rates make their efforts generally futile. A vast subterranean industry moves people wherever they can afford to go and corruption is widespread. Migration experts argue that governmental systems unwittingly have a very exploitative aspect and that a lighter hand may be a better option.

Table 5: People

Countries	Population 1994 (million)	Inhabitants per sq. km.	Population growth 1986–94 (%)	Population Under 15 years 1994 (%)	Population Over 65 years 1994 (%)	Life expectancy at birth 1990–95 age	Labor force 1994 % of population	Unemployment 1994: % of labor force	Illiteracy 1990 (%)
Bangladesh	n/a	n/a	n/a	n/a	n/a	n/a	n/a	n/a	n/a
Hong Kong	6.01	6010.00	1.05	19.10	10.10	77.60	50.33	2.00	11.90
India	910.00	276.76	2.17	34.80	4.90	60.40	35.22	n/a	51.80
Indonesia	193.10	101.36	1.73	33.40	4.50	62.70	42.93	2.80	18.40
Japan	124.90	330.42	0.35	17.00	13.90	78.70	50.20	2.90	n/a
Kazakhstan	n/a	n/a	n/a	n/a	n/a	n/a	n/a	n/a	n/a
Malaysia	19.20	58.18	2.22	37.90	3.90	70.80	40.79	2.90	21.60
Pakistan	n/a	n/a	n/a	n/a	n/a	n/a	n/a	n/a	n/a
PRC	1200.00	125.51	1.48	27.30	6.30	70.90	51.17	2.90	22.60
Singapore	2.92	2920.00	1.51	22.70	6.40	74.50	57.98	2.60	13.90
South Korea	44.50	449.49	0.97	23.40	5.40	70.80	45.67	2.40	3.70
Sri Lanka	n/a	n/a	n/a	n/a	n/a	n/a	n/a	n/a	n/a
Taiwan	21.00	583.33	1.03	25.10	7.10	73.70	43.24	1.56	6.80
Thailand	59.40	115.79	1.52	29.20	4.50	69.30	54.83	0.40	7.00
Philippines	67.18	223.93	2.30	38.40	3.30	65.00	41.17	9.40	10.30
Vietnam	n/a	n/a	n/a	n/a	n/a	n/a	n/a	n/a	n/a
Comparison									
U.S.	261.30	27.88	1.03	21.90	12.60	75.90	50.70	6.00	0.50
Germany	81.10	227.17	3.62	16.30	15.00	76.00	47.71	9.60	1.00

Source: Derived from *The World Competitiveness Report 1995* (IMD).

Megatrends in Asia

With their rapidly developing economies and changing societies, several trends have been identified in Asia. John Naisbitt identified eight basic axes of change before the recent crisis, most of which are still relevant:[2]

- *From nation-states to networks*: The power of Japan as a nation-state is giving way to dynamic collaboration of the overseas Chinese network.
- *From export-led to consumer-driven*: Built on exports, Asian economies will increasingly be fueled by consumer spending and the emerging middle class.
- *From western influence to the Asian way*: The most significant development of the 1990s and the following few decades will be Asia's modernization.
- *From government-driven to market-driven*: Central government control of economies has shifted to market economies, fueling an explosion of economic growth.
- *From villages to supercities*: Migration from rural areas to the cities is transforming Asian societies into those where the information age will dominate.
- *From labor intensive to high technology*: We are witnessing a dramatic shift from labor intensive agriculture and manufacturing to state-of-the-art technology.
- *From male dominance to the emergence of women*: Women are participating in all aspects of Asian life in unprecedented ways, as voters, consumers and members of the workforce.
- *From West to East*: The global axis of influence has shifted from West to East. Asia was once the center of the world; now the center is returning to Asia.

Consumer Behavior in Asia[3]

Do Asian consumers behave as their western counterparts? Casual observation indicates they do not. Values, norms and culture differ; since these influence consumer behavior, they are likely to form a basis for disparate purchasing behavior and, hence, a requirement for different marketing approaches. The objective in this section is to point out some fundamental differences between Asia and the West. However, we must recognize that although Asia is different at a macro level, it is not homogeneous; at a more micro level, important and relevant heterogeneity in culture, religion, heritage, values and norms exists among Asian nations. Thus, Asian subcultures might require marketing adaptations.

The focus in this section is on Southeast Asia that, through its Confucian tradition, is easier to characterize in an East–West macro comparison. The Indian subcontinent (South Asia), probably comprising the most heterogeneous and complex society on earth, is not directly addressed; its social structure (caste hierarchy and extended family system), the role of religion (both as a spiritual doctrine and as a way of life) and the

---

[2] Naisbitt, J. (1995), *Megatrends Asia: The Eight Asian Megatrends That are Changing the World*, Nicholas Brealy Publishing Ltd.: London (U.K.).

[3] Part of the discussion is based on "Consumer Behaviour in Asia," by Schutte, H. and V. Vanier, EAC Research Series No. 33 (February 1995), EAC/INSEAD (France).

cosmic role of the individual, and pluralism in life patterns and experiences make it very difficult to characterize a uniform basic cultural code of life; from a western point of view that emphasizes material order, and in contrast to Southeast Asia, Indian society appears to be full of contradictions, juxtapositions and irreconcilable differences.

Social behavior. Group conformity is central to social behavior in Asian societies. Acting in ways prescribed by society is a highly valued behavioral characteristic. To be different from other people and do things differently from other people (i.e., not prescribed) make Asians feel uncomfortable. Social expectations require a person's behavior to be consistent with situational requirements. Asians generally feel strong social pressure to comply with group norms regardless of their own private views. If a person's social behavior deviates from group norms, s/he may be treated as an outsider who cannot adjust to the group; social acceptability is at stake.

The concept, and maintenance, of face is one of the most prevalent factors determining social behavior; it enforces social control and discourages expression of individual differences. In Chinese society, for example, losing face often makes an individual feel incapable of leading a normal social life and thus of being a human being.

Whereas the concept of face in understanding interpersonal behavior is a human universal, Asians have a much more sophisticated and developed understanding than virtually any other group. Use of face as a reference in behavior guides the high degree of interpersonal sensitivity in Asian societies.

Face, a concept of central importance because of its pervasive influence on interpersonal relations, may be classified into two types, *lien* and *mien-tsu*. *Lien* represents the confidence of society in the integrity of ego's moral character; loss makes it impossible to function properly in the community. Everyone is entitled to *lien* by virtue of societal membership; a person needs *lien* to have influence over others. It can only be lost through misconduct; for example, thieves renounce their concern for *lien*. When *lien* is completely lost, suicide may be a final resort. Even today in Chinese society, women who are raped often commit suicide to demonstrate their innocence.[4]

By contrast, *mien-tsu* stands for "the kind of prestige that is emphasized ... a reputation achieved through getting on in life through success and ostentation."[5] *Mien-tsu* can be obtained through personal qualities or derived from non-personal characteristics (e.g., wealth, social status, education level, occupation and authority). It may be lost when conduct falls below the minimum acceptable standard or when essential requirements corresponding to social position are not met. Since the standards are social expectations held by the relevant group, *mien-tsu* may be lost not only by behavior, but from the expectations of others regarding expected behavior or treatment. Chinese, in particular, are under strong constraints to meet the expectations of others to maintain their *mien-tsu*, as well as reciprocating a due regard for others'

[4] Yau, O.H.M. (1988), "Chinese Cultural Values: Their Dimensions and Marketing Implications," *European Journal of Marketing*, 22(5), 44–57.

[5] Hu, H.C. (1944), "The Chinese Concept of Face," *American Anthropologist*, 46, 45–64.

mien-tsu. Thus, they try avoid causing others to lose face, regarded as an aggressive act by those whose face has been discredited; rather, protecting against loss is an act of consideration.[6] Before behaving, a person should assess the effects of his action on people's face; this may influence the decision and way of acting. Common strategies for saving others' face include: avoiding criticizing others, especially superiors, in public; using circumlocution and equivocation in any criticism of others' performance; accord greater social rewards to those skilled at preserving face for others. All these techniques are frequently used in managing modern social organizations.

To a large extent, the Chinese face-saving norm is similar to the shame notion in Japanese culture. Japanese parents' emphasis on empathy-oriented discipline, by showing how a child's misbehavior hurts another's feelings, reinforces a sense of inter-relatedness. Similar cultural traits are found in other Asian countries. In the Philippines, a parallel social force of *pakikisama*, the ethic of smooth interpersonal relations, combined with a heightened (to a westerner) sense of personal pride and high sensitivity to shame instilled from childhood, produces behavior that, as in China, appears conciliatory, docile and free from open conflict. In Indonesia, dignity and smoothness of behavior is highly valued and a key source of respect. Not to lose face is more important than material losses. To be forced by someone to lose face in front of other people is seen as a deep insult; as a result, free discussions do not occur very often. Among the Malays, a person is judged primarily by his social sensitivity, comprising courtesy and a permanent concern for harmony. In Thailand, a key rule of social behavior is to maintain smooth interpersonal relations.

In sum, an almost universal Asian characteristic is a high degree of interpersonal sensitivity. Although descriptive terms and the exact way it operates vary from country to country, the underlying dimensions are the same.

Interpersonal relations. Within the group consciousness and social orientation of Asian societies, the nature and role of interpersonal relationships are very important as they give rise to shared cultural values. Confucianism, still deeply rooted in many Asian societies (especially Chinese), plays a central role in orchestrating interpersonal relationships.

Central to Confucianism are five cardinal human relationships (i.e., ruler/subject, father/son, older/younger brother, husband/wife, older/younger friend) that effectively control social behavior in society; correct observance of these relationships is regarded as integral to proper functioning of society.[7] Social harmony is achieved via cultural norms established to guide day-to-day behavior. One such norm is the principle of *li*. Li means rite; practicing *li* was first prescribed by Confucius as a means to achieve *jen*, the essence of his humanistic philosophy.[8] *Jen* literally means human being in Chinese, but Chinese conceive this differently from westerners. The Chinese

---

[6] Yau, O.H.M. (1988), ibidem.

[7] Yau, O.H.M. (1988), ibidem.

[8] Hsu, F.L.K. (1971), "Psychosocial Homeostasis and Jen: Conceptual Tools for Advancing Psychological Anthropology," *American Anthropologist*, 23–44, 73.

conception is based on the individual's transactions with fellow human beings; every person thinks of him/herself in relation to other people and the way they are connected. *Jen* represents an ideal state under which an individual's social relationships with fellow human beings are harmonious. The principles of *li* state the proper way to behave in various social situations and with various individuals with whom one forms interpersonal relationships. These principles require an individual to follow ritualistic prescriptions rather than behaving according to his/her desires or for selfish reasons. They require an individual to be constantly on guard to monitor his/her behavior to ensure its social acceptability. This is especially visible in achievement motivation: achievement goals are for group benefit (e.g., family, the state) rather than for the individual; furthermore, others, not the individual, often define the standards against which achievement is measured.

The reciprocity norm in interpersonal relations is universal; it has long been accepted as a basic moral rule of social cohesion in most cultures; social relationships among human beings cannot be effectively established without the reciprocity norm. However, Asian societies follow rules that differ from the West. Westerners assume that individuals act in their own self-interest, make decisions rationally and are in control of their own destiny. By contrast, Asians perceive one's existence in society as largely influenced by relationships with others that one cannot change; rather, one must harmonize with the environment. Asians maintain that to survive and cope in competitive and hostile environments, as many friends as possible are necessary for support; these friends should be protected against adversity. Reciprocity norms tend to persist for cultural reasons; for example, the Chinese have an elaborate vocabulary for interpersonal obligations and rules regarding how they may be won or lost. They also persist for structural reasons. Historically, and even in modern contexts, many Chinese lived in hierarchically organized, encapsulated communities in which major economic and other resources were controlled by a few powerful figures. In these settings, it was imperative to be sensitive to one's social position and to the kinds of resources one could elicit and be forced to give up through obligations incurred over long periods of time.[9]

Chinese flexibility in managing interpersonal relations comes from the principle of *pao*, "doing favors," literally signifying one's honor to another. Favors done for others are often considered as social investments for which returns are expected. The application of this principle has tremendous influence on social and business behavior.[10]

In Chinese societies, the unit involved in the principle of *pao* is mostly family, not the individual. The return of a favor need not be directed to the original individual giver; it may be directed to family members or even close associates. In a typical Chinese family, social exchange also follows the norm of reciprocity. The proverb "foster your children to prevent misery in old age and hoard grain to prevent death," implies that parents expect children to repay parental care. The exchange of favors and acceptance of wide

---

[9] Huang, K.H. (1987), "Face and Favor: the Chinese Power Game," *American Journal of Sociology*, 92 (January), 944–74.

[10] Yau, O.H.M. (1988), ibidem.

responsibilities for relatives lead to extended families. These networks have much greater power than in western family units; they are used to reduce uncertainties.[11]

Clan and family affiliation networks provide stability, or at least trust and reliability, in otherwise uncertain business environments. The development of *guanxi* (literally "connections"), cultivation of special relations, is very important for Chinese businessmen. These relationships are not impersonal but require dealing warmly with people; they involve reciprocal obligations, the essential feature of *guanxi*.

The concept of "fraternity" is the closest analog in the West; two or more persons join together to attain common objectives, mostly social in nature. Through close association, members develop mutual respect and each is expected to act in the best interests of the fraternal members. However, the sense of reciprocal obligation is not present to the degree evident in *guanxi*. Furthermore, unequal treatment in *guanxi* distinguishes it from a comrade relationship. China is a world in which what counts is not only whom one knows but also who owes whom a favor.[12]

The concept of *on* in Japanese culture implies a similar reciprocal exchange: a benefactor may generate an *on* relationship by giving a benefit; the receiver is obligated to repay *on* to restore balance.

Extended family orientation. In western societies, individual goals typically have primacy over group goals. In most Asian societies, the group to which a person belongs involves special patterns of obligation and behavior. As a result, what applies inside the group does not necessarily apply outside the group. In China, the group is primarily the extended family, secondly the clan or region of origin. In Japan, the primary group is the *ie* or "house," represented today by the corporation. In Indonesia, Malaysia and the Philippines, it is the village community or extended family.[13]

The family unit is important to all Chinese.[14] Children develop a sense of connection to family via a myriad of daily exchanges with parents: circular tables, shared bedrooms, late night outings with parents, homework supervision by an elder sibling, daily phone calls to mother after marriage and so forth. The Chinese child is raised to regard home as a refuge against the indifference, rigors and arbitrariness of life outside. S/he is taught to put family members before her/himself, to share their pride and fame, sadness and joy. Since family is the central Confucian institution, from an early age, a person is constantly reminded not to allow one's family to lose face, rather face should be gained, for the family by accumulating wealth, prestige, status and power.

In Japan, child rearing is characterized as fostering a blurring of the boundary between mother and child. Children are raised by promoting satisfaction experiences

---

[11] Redding, G. (1982), "Cultural Effects on the Marketing Process in Southeast Asia," *Journal of the Marketing Research Society*, 24(2), 98–114.

[12] Brunner, J.A., J. Chen, C. Sun, and N. Zhou (1989), "The Role of Guanxi in Negotiations in the Pacific Basin," *Journal of Global Marketing*, 3(2), 7–23.

[13] Redding, G. (1982), ibidem.

[14] Bond, M.H. (1991), *Beyond the Chinese Face*, Oxford University Press: Oxford U.K.

through physical and psychological relatedness with parents and siblings. Skin-to-skin relations, even beyond feeding, are much more extensive than in the West. Infants share beds with mothers and the limited housing situation requires the children to accommodate other family members. Japanese children's dependency on the mother in early childhood years exists later in life as a sense of obligation. The Japanese family binds individuals for life; each member is encouraged to view relationships with other family members as of continuing mutual support and participation in common goals. Whereas the western literature on family change notes the growing centrality of husband-wife (versus parent-child) bonds, despite some weakening of old patterns, in Japan, most parents live with adult sons and financial flows (cash and in-kind gifts) continue from adult children to parents.

One consequence of the Asian emphasis on familism is that individual behavior reflects less the person's own preferences and will than it does a consensus or compromise with family members, or an assumption of the family's (most often parents) preferences or will. In contrast to joint husband-wife decisions in the West, Asians always consider other family members. The major motivation is to achieve (extended) family or group goals rather than individualized self-fulfillment.

Social pressure and behavior. Social interdependence, group conformity pressures and face saving have significant behavioral implications. First, the importance of social context makes Asians' behavior quite situation-dependent; this affects both involvement and perception.

Western analysis of the involvement concept, dichotomized into product attributes and situational factors, is not applicable to Chinese consumers; they are more concerned with social risk than physical or monetary risk. The Chinese see product attributes in the context of situational factors; a product is perceived along with the consumption situation and situational factors play as important a role as the product itself. Often, the product is evaluated not on its merits universal to all users and for all occasions, but on its appropriateness for the particular use situation: by whom, with whom and for what purpose. Involvement relates the product's capacity to give the correct social signals according to accepted norms and standards. When products are for private use, involvement is usually low; when for social consumption (e.g., reflect social status, maintain and advance social relationships, seek social approval), involvement is high.

The Japanese philosopher, Hajime Nakamura, wrote of the Chinese: "One of the most important characteristics of Chinese philosophy is its reliance on sense-perception. They reluctantly dwell on that which is beyond the immediately perceived. For the purposes of instruction and persuasion, they resort to images that have the appeal of direct perceptions." Comparative research supports this assertion. Chinese are more concrete and practical than westerners in the objects they choose to draw and more pragmatic in their tendency to evaluate ideas in terms of their immediate application. Chinese show a tendency toward non-abstract thought; their thinking is more pragmatic, has greater immediacy and, as such, they adopt a more utilitarian posture toward products.

Social pressure also affects the need structure motivating behavior. Maslow's motivation theory ranks psychogenic needs (self-actualization, ego) as the most important.[15] However, in Confucianism (also Buddhism and Taoism), man is judged by his consideration for, and service to, others, rather than by self-aggrandizement achievements and self-actualization. Emphasis on the self is more common in the West; in Asia, behavior that outwardly shows excessive concern with the self is generally considered coarse and uncivilized.

Self-fulfillment is a less acceptable goal in collectivistic cultures, even in modernized ones. For example, researchers have identified a cluster of "post-materialistic" values (including a shift toward greater expression of self-actualization needs) characterizing the transition to modernity in North American and European cultures. However, a similar change has not been found in Japan, one of the world's most highly industrialized countries. Rather, a combination of attitudes has been detected that appears inconsistent with western views of modernity. "Strong traditional values such as group solidarities, interpersonal harmony, paternalism and familism are co-existing with quite modern values such as achievement and competition."[16]

Conflict avoidance and fate. Besides social pressures of group conformity and face saving, two other principles guide Chinese behavior: *chung-yung* (the Confucian principle of moderation) and *yuan* (fate). Moderation is described as "being without inclination to either side." Confucians do not believe in suppression of passions and impulses but in their regulation to achieve internal harmony. Chinese are taught neither to completely repress nor unrestrictedly satisfy primitive passions and impulses; the result is high degrees of moral self-control (at least publicly).

Chinese believe that initiation of any kind of dispute is an invitation to chaos. Consequently, if possible, they avoid direct confrontation, preferring indirect means if necessary. Japanese avoid confrontation, embarrassing situations and direct rejection by use of indirect language. For example, they have seven ways of saying "yes"; depending on pronunciation, the same word can mean anything from "yes" to "may be" to "no." Thais can smile their way out of almost any situation, carefully avoiding words or actions that might be regretted later.

The concept of *yuan*, fate, is deeply rooted in most Chinese. Resembling *karma* in Buddhism, it refers to predestination, especially in interpersonal matters; Chinese use it to explain social events. Both sides in an ephemeral relationship may regard their meeting as a predestined occurrence that will lead to happy results. As *yuan* is an external factor, it serves a protective function in "explaining away" negative exchanges with others. In contrast, westerners are combative with fate, regarding it as a measure of ignorance and inability to bend nature to their wills. They struggle against fate's dictates and often respond to failure with depression. The Chinese believe that

---

[15] Maslow, A.H. (1964), "A Theory of Human Motivation," in *Readings in Managerial Psychology*, H.J. Levitt and L.R. Pondy (eds.), University of Chicago Press: Chicago (U.S.), 6–24.

[16] Yang, K.S. (1981), "Social Orientation and Individual Modernity Among Chinese Students in Taiwan," *The Journal of Social Psychology*, 113, 159–70.

life comprises a much larger element of unpredictability, uncontrollability and predestination. An acceptance of *yuan* provides a ready explanation for both propitious and calamitous social outcomes, thereby buffering people from intense feelings of elation or regret. *Yuan* also explains the pervasive value of luck in Chinese culture and a general Asian belief in the supernatural (e.g., ghosts [Japan], card-reading and *feng-shui* [China], healing techniques [Philippines]).

The need to maintain face in public, together with values of conflict avoidance and belief in fate, serve as negative forces for complaint behavior and dissatisfaction expression. Not to achieve a satisfactory result from complaining means losing face in front of others. The principle of moderation elevates levels of tolerance; belief in fate prevents taking direct action.

Tradition and hierarchy. Two additional beliefs color Asian behavior: history (or tradition) and need of hierarchy. Chinese have a strong preference for past-time orientation; they are very historically-minded and have a strong admiration for their thousands-of-years-old culture. Besides, they believe that relations with others and objects are continuous. Because of their emphasis on tradition, experimentation and creativity are not encouraged; they raise the dreaded specter of *luan*, or chaos. Indeed, in Chinese culture, risk taking is considered thoughtless and reckless; Chinese are the least likely to change just for the sake of change.

Asian cultures are marked by strong differences in power and status. Chinese believe that an efficient society requires a broadly accepted ordering of people. They believe in the naturalness, necessity and inevitability of hierarchy and have a general tendency to defer to persons in positions of power, status or control. Deference to authority is perceived as upright, prudent and to the benefit of society. In Chinese culture, the basic rule is "honor the hierarchy first, your vision of truth second." The superior must always be accorded face.

Exchange Rates

Table 6 gives a concise overview of exchange rates in the 16 countries covered as well as some reference currencies.

Asian Cyberspace

An overview of a number of Web sites where updated information on Asia and some Asian countries can be obtained is given below:

General

CIA World Factbook: *http://www.odci.gov/cia/publications* Offers good background information on every country in the world.

Hong Kong-based Political and Economic Risk Consultancy Ltd. (PERC): *http://www.asiarisk.com/* Allows free access to "risk reports" on each of the countries in the region, together with key economic indicators.

Countries

Many of these Web sites are government-sponsored.

Bangladesh: *http://www.tuns.ca/~abidmr/bdesh.html* Information, statistics and economic news.

Hong Kong Home Page: *http://www.hongkong.org/* History, shopping and travel from the Hong Kong government.

India Home Page: *http://mathlab.sunysb.edu/~cpandya/india.html* Links to many sites throughout India.

India Online: *http://indiaonline.com/* Information about India and its neighbors.

Indonesia Home Page: *http://mawar.inn.bppt.go.id/in-dex.html* Information on Indonesian government, business and communications.

Japan – The Japan Economic Planning Agency: *http://www.epa.go.jp/* Annual economic survey of Japan and links to economics-related servers in Japan.

Japanese Trade: *http://www.aist.go.jp* Tracks Japan's imports and exports.

Malaysia Information Network: *http://www.jaring.my/* Offers information on research and development, the economy, statistics and the Malaysian Legal Code.

People's Republic of China Trade Center: *http://www.netchina.com/trade/main1.html* Listing of the top 100 companies trading abroad; detailed list of contracts awarded in China, divided by category.

Taiwan: *http://tradepoint.anjes.com.tw/* Trade opportunities, trade shows, a comprehensive business directory and other business information.

Thailand – Thai Government Online: *http://www.nectec.or.th/bureaux.index* Business information and links to more than a dozen ministries, research organizations, export bodies and the Board of Investment.

Financial Information

Asian Development Bank (ADB): *http://www.asiandevbank.org/* The home page of Asia's principal development-finance institution offers a wide range of documents, including project profiles, law and development, links to international organizations and environment-impact assessment reports for the region's countries.

Asian Stock Market Closings: *http://www.asia-inc.com/finance/index.html* Operated by Asia-Inc. and Lippo Industries, this site offers Asian business and financial news from Knight-Ridder, stock market closings and a daily analysis of currency markets.

On-line Publications

Asia, Inc. Online: *http://www.asia-inc.com/* An on-line magazine to which one can subscribe. It also offers interesting free services like "Net Resources for Asia," a superb starting point for finding everything you need. It is like a search engine, placing items in two categories: country and subject.

Trade Directories

ABC Trade Directory: *http//asiabiz.com/*Listings and links for Asian businesses (e.g., business services, shopping, manufacturers and exporters, travel and leisure.

Asia Trade: *http://www.asiadir.com/* An on-line directory for Asian business (e.g., business services, conventions, trade bulletins).

Hong Kong Exporters Directory: *http://www.stw.com/hk/hk.htm* Lists 10,000 products manufactured in Hong Kong or available from suppliers in China.

For more information on countries in Southeast Asia, see Anthony Pecotich and Clifford J. Shultz II, *Marketing and Consumer Behavior in East and South-East Asia*, Sydney, Australia: McGraw-Hill Australia, 1998.

Table 6: Currencies (January 1, 1998)

One unit of	Is worth	U.S. dollar	Japan yen	Hong Kong dollar	Singapore dollar	Malaysia ringgit	Philippines peso	Thailand baht	Indonesia rupiah	South Korea won	Taiwan N.T. dollar	China renminbi	Vietnam dong
U.S.	dollar	1	130	7.75	1.61	3.80	39.45	40.30	10,100	1,462	32.44	8.28	12,998
Japan	100 yen	0.77	100	5.79	1.24	2.92	30.40	31.05	7,783	1,126	25.00	6.38	10,001
Hong Kong	dollar	0.13	17	1	0.21	0.49	5.09	5.20	1,304	189	4.19	1.07	1,696
Singapore	dollar	0.62	80	4.80	1	2.35	24.46	24.98	6,262	906	20.11	5.13	8,046
Malaysia	ringgit	0.26	34	2.04	0.43	1	10.40	10.62	2,661	385	8.55	2.18	3,420
Philippines	peso	0.03	3	0.20	0.04	0.10	1	1.02	256	37	0.82	0.21	329
Thailand	baht	0.02	3	0.19	0.04	0.09	0.98	1	251	36	0.81	0.21	322
Indonesia	100 rupiah	0.01	1	0.08	0.02	0.04	0.39	0.40	100	14	0.32	0.08	128
South Korea	100 won	0.07	9	0.53	0.11	0.26	2.70	2.76	691	100	2.22	0.57	888
Taiwan	N.T. dollar	0.03	4	0.24	0.05	0.12	1.22	1.24	311	45	1	0.26	400
China	renminbi	0.12	16	0.94	0.19	0.46	4.76	4.87	1,220	177	3.92	1	1,568
Vietnam	1,000 dong	0.08	10	0.60	0.12	0.29	3.04	3.11	778	113	2.50	0.64	1,000
India	rupee	0.03	3	0.20	0.04	0.10	1.00	1.02	256	37	0.82	0.21	328
Pakistan	rupee	0.02	3	0.18	0.04	0.09	0.90	0.92	230	33	0.74	0.19	295
Sri Lanka	rupee	0.02	2	0.13	0.03	0.06	0.64	0.65	164	24	0.53	0.13	211
Bangladesh	taka	0.02	3	0.17	0.03	0.08	0.68	0.87	218	32	0.70	0.18	280
Australia	dollar	0.67	87	5.19	1.08	2.54	26.41	26.98	6,762	978	21.72	5.54	8,688
New Zealand	dollar	0.58	75	4.60	0.94	2.20	22.91	26.41	5,867	849	18.84	4.81	7,538
Canada	dollar	0.71	92	5.48	1.14	2.68	27.89	28.49	7,141	1,033	22.94	5.85	9,176
Britain	pound	1.67	217	12.92	2.69	6.33	65.83	67.25	6,853	2,439	54.13	13.81	21,655
France	franc	0.16	21	1.27	0.26	0.62	6.46	6.60	1,654	239	5.31	1.36	2,125
Germany	mark	0.55	71	4.25	0.89	2.08	21.66	22.13	5,545	802	17.81	4.55	7,126
Europe	ECU	1.09	141	8.43	1.76	4.13	42.96	43.89	10,999	1,592	35.33	9.02	14,133

Table 6 (cont'd)

One unit of	Is worth	India rupee	Pakistan rupee	Sri Lanka rupee	Bangladesh taka	Australia dollar	New Zealand dollar	Canada dollar	Britain pound	France franc	Germany mark	Europe ECU
U.S.	dollar	39.52	44.00	61.65	46.30	1.49	1.72	1.41	0.80	6.11	1.82	0.92
Japan	100 yen	30.45	33.91	47.51	35.68	1.15	1.33	1.09	0.46	4.71	1.40	0.71
Hong Kong	dollar	5.10	5.68	7.96	5.98	0.19	0.22	0.18	0.08	0.79	0.24	0.12
Singapore	dollar	24.50	27.28	38.22	38.22	0.93	1.07	0.88	0.37	3.79	1.13	0.57
Malaysia	ringgit	10.41	11.59	16.25	12.20	0.39	0.45	0.37	0.16	1.61	0.48	0.24
Philippines	peso	1.00	1.12	1.56	1.17	0.04	0.04	0.04	0.02	0.15	0.05	0.00
Thailand	baht	0.98	1.09	1.53	1.15	0.04	0.04	0.04	0.01	0.15	0.05	0.02
Indonesia	100 rupiah	0.39	0.44	0.61	0.46	0.01	0.02	0.01	0.01	0.06	0.02	0.01
South Korea	100 won	2.70	3.01	4.22	3.17	0.10	0.12	0.10	0.04	0.42	0.12	0.06
Taiwan	N.T. dollar	1.22	1.36	1.90	1.43	0.05	0.05	0.04	0.02	0.19	0.06	0.02
China	renminbi	4.77	5.31	7.45	5.59	0.18	0.21	0.17	0.07	0.74	0.22	0.11
Vietnam	1,000 dong	3.04	3.39	4.75	3.57	0.12	0.13	0.11	0.05	0.47	0.14	0.07
India	rupee	1	1.11	1.56	1.17	0.04	0.04	0.04	0.02	0.15	0.05	0.02
Pakistan	rupee	0.90	1	1.40	1.05	0.03	0.04	0.03	0.01	0.14	0.04	0.02
Sri Lanka	rupee	0.64	0.71	1	0.75	0.02	0.03	0.02	0.01	0.10	0.03	0.01
Bangladesh	taka	0.85	0.95	1.33	1	0.03	0.04	0.03	0.01	0.13	0.04	0.02
Australia	dollar	26.46	29.46	41.27	31.00	1	1.15	0.95	0.40	4.09	1.22	0.61
New Zealand	dollar	22.95	25.56	35.81	26.89	0.87	1	0.82	0.35	3.55	1.06	0.53
Canada	dollar	27.94	31.11	43.59	32.74	1.06	1.22	1	0.42	4.32	1.29	0.65
Britain	pound	65.94	73.42	102.87	77.26	2.49	2.87	2.36	1	10.19	3.04	1.53
France	franc	6.47	7.21	10.10	7.58	0.24	0.28	0.23	0.10	1	0.30	0.15
Germany	mark	21.70	24.16	33.85	25.42	0.82	0.95	0.78	0.33	3.35	1	0.50
Europe	ECU	43.03	47.91	67.13	50.42	1.63	1.87	1.54	0.65	6.65	1.98	1

Source: *Asiaweek.*

Case 1

Holiday Inn Worldwide Asia Pacific

Noel Capon[1]
Graduate School of Business, Columbia University

Bill Chan, Sammy Chan, Geoffrey Cheng, Kin Sang Chow, Sau Chiu Ho, Estella Ng
The Hong Kong University of Science and Technology

In July 1995, Steven Parker, Vice President Strategic Management at Holiday Inn Worldwide Asia Pacific (HIWAP) was contemplating the consulting report recently delivered by Synergy, a six-member student consulting organization from the Hong Kong University of Science and Technology. Synergy addressed a series of issues concerning HIWAP's measurement of brand identity and customer and employee satisfaction. Parker knew that HIWAP's aggressive growth goals would only be successfully accomplished if both brand identity and customer and employee satisfaction attained consistently high levels. As he considered the alternatives suggested by Synergy he wondered how much weight to place on these recommendations, which, if any, should be implemented, whether other alternatives were viable or whether current systems were adequate.

↾☍↽

Company Background[2]

In 1952, Kemmons Wilson opened the first Holiday Inn in Memphis, Tennessee. After financing and building several hotels, he decided to sell investors rights to use the Holiday Inn name on properties they would build and operate. Franchising is now used by almost all hotel chains worldwide. Holiday Inn opened its first overseas hotel in Europe in 1968; its first Asian property in 1973.

---

[1] Assisted by Evelyn Creachy.
[2] Several figures relating to Holiday Inn Worldwide operations are disguised.

23

Holiday Inn traditionally served the middle market, but in the mid- to late 1970s it was squeezed by competition from lower-price hotel chains and from higher-end chains that aggressively lowered prices. In response to these pressures, Holiday Inn developed new brands targeted at specific markets. For example, in 1983, Holiday Inn Crowne Plaza Hotels were inaugurated to compete in the fast-growing upscale market. Several difficult years followed, and in 1989 the entire Holiday Inn brand was sold to Bass PLC, a publicly-held, $7.9 billion British conglomerate, for $2.2 billion. The sale included the North American Holiday Inn franchise system, 122 company-owned properties, the Hotel Service Division and the Holidex information/reservation system; at the time, 95% of the chain's distribution was in the U.S.

Bass had ambitious plans for Holiday Inn. Chairman Ian Prosser's vision was: "To be the preferred hotel brand system and lodging franchise in the world." This goal was deceptively simple since Bass had limited experience running a hotel chain and competition was growing. Nonetheless, an early action was a move into new markets. In 1990, the chain's name was officially changed to Holiday Inn Worldwide (HIW) and it began aggressive expansion into Asia Pacific: $200 million was allocated for the development of 57 hotels in China, 10 in Thailand and 7 in Indonesia by 1995 (including five Crowne Plaza properties). In 1992, HIW announced a $60 million investment in information technology, including the Holiday Inn Reservation Optimizer (HIRO), used for yield management and demand forecasting; this system would be located in every property worldwide.

By end 1995, almost 2,000 Holiday Inn hotels, targeting mainly the middle-market, were operating around the world: 1,700 in the U.S., 200 in Europe, 70 in Asia. The hotels comprised five individual brands: high-end, Crowne Plaza Hotels and Crowne Plaza Resorts; middle-market, Holiday Inn Hotels and Holiday Inn Resorts; and Holiday Inn Express (Table 1).

Table 1: Holiday Inn Brand Portfolio

Brand	Positioning
Holiday Inn Express	Budget; upper economy occasions
Holiday Inn Garden Court	Low mid-market; less expensive compact hotel
Holiday Inn	Mid-market; full-service properties
Holiday Inn SunSpree Resorts	Upper mid-market; activity-rich; serves middle-market leisure traveler
Holiday Inn Crowne Plaza Hotels and Resorts	Deluxe; upper tier of middle market

Holiday Inn Worldwide Asia Pacific

Holiday Inn Worldwide Asia Pacific (HIWAP), based in Hong Kong, was the regional headquarters for Holiday Inn Worldwide (HIW). HIWAP recently surpassed Sheraton as the largest international chain in the region; at end 1994, Holiday Inn's 70 hotels (20,639 rooms) surpassed Sheraton's 45 hotels (18,300 rooms). HIWAP's mission was "to build a profitable long-term business in Asia Pacific through being the largest mid-market chain in the region with a comprehensive presence in international destinations and, where appropriate, participation in the domestic market." HIWAP sought to increase the ratio of business travelers in its customer mix. Asia Pacific was divided into five regions, each led by a regional vice president: China, the Indian sub-continent, Southeast Asia, Japan and Australasia. The vice president for China had been in place for several years; the others were recently appointed.

Reflecting Chairman Prosser's vision, HIWAP's five-year goals (1995 to 2000) were ambitious: 245 hotels (end 1995, 91), mainly in larger cities; profit US$77.3 million (1994/95 US$19.6 million). From 1995/96 to 1998/99, HIWAP planned 55 hotels in China (mostly greenfield construction); 51 in the Indian sub-continent; 20 in Japan; 61 in Southeast Asia (Indonesia, Malaysia, Thailand, the Philippines, Vietnam); 13 in Australasia.

HIWAP's properties were operated as franchises, joint ventures (managed by HIWAP) or management contracts. Franchising was the preferred expansion method in more mature economies (e.g., Japan, Australasia) and in Malaysia; growing economies (e.g., India, Thailand) would be served primarily by joint ventures;[3] Indonesia, the Philippines, Vietnam and China would be mainly HIWAP managed properties. Hotel investment in joint ventures (and frequently in directly-managed hotels) was wholly funded internally. HIWAP had little involvement in franchised hotels and regularly received only financial information for calculating franchise fees. Holiday Inn franchise contracts were typically for ten years; frequently these were renewed but, from time to time, HIWAP lost a franchise contract to a competitor.[4] (Competitors fared similarly.)

HIWAP faced two major obstacles in achieving its goals: first, the current revenue base was quite narrow, five hotels accounted for 30% of revenue, the next five for an additional 13%; second, convertible hotels were in short supply, as was labor at all levels. Training for staff was critical but required significant outlay for each employee hired.

HIW's information technology has long been seen as a competitive advantage, in particular the powerful Holidex reservation system.[5] However, in Asia Pacific, the variety of languages, cultures, sophistication levels, literacy rates and market maturities demanded information systems tailored to each country. Such systems were not yet developed and, like hiring and staffing, required significant investment. In addition, HIW enjoyed widespread brand recognition by U.S. travelers. However, just as intra-Asian travelers were much less aware of the Holiday Inn name and its connotations, HIWAP's customers were comparative strangers to HIWAP as it had much less data on customer needs and segmentation than its U.S. counterpart. HIWAP historically allocated sales and marketing expenditures to markets and individual properties on the basis of revenue generated.

---

[3] HIWAP's interest in joint ventures ranged widely: for example, 24% in India, 80% in Thailand.

[4] Competitor franchise contracts ranged in length from 5 to 20 years.

[5] 300,000 reservation terminals around the world provided direct reservation service to HIW customers. New hotels were guaranteed access to this system.

HIWAP's marketing organization comprised five functional areas: Brand Marketing, Frequency Marketing, Field Marketing, PR and Communications, and Worldwide Reservations; each reported to the Vice President of Marketing. Marketing programs were organized at three levels: pan-regional, country and hotel. (See Figures 1A, 1B for organization charts.)

Figure 1A: HIWAP Organization Chart

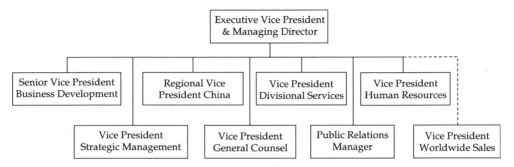

Figure 1B: HIWAP Marketing Department

At the pan-regional level, Brand Marketing worked with counterparts in the U.S. and Europe, Middle East and Africa (EMEA) on global advertising, worldwide marketing programs and promotions and branding issues such as corporate identity and collateral (promotion) items (annual global budget, approximately $100 million).[6] Brand Marketing produced manuals and guidelines to assist hotels with their own campaigns and created collateral materials (e.g., bathroom products).

Frequency Marketing, managed at the pan-regional level, focused on loyalty and repetitive purchase marketing. HIW's Priority Club had over 4.5 million members glo-

---

[6] HIW appointed Dentsu, Young and Rubicam as its global agency; pan-regional promotional campaigns were corporate funded but company-managed; franchised hotels were typically asked to contribute a $1,000 participation fee.

bally (60,000 Asia Pacific), generating 15% annual global occupancy; 8% of revenue generated, paid to HIW as commission, was used to finance marketing activities and settle redemption of awarded benefits (Exhibit 1). Cooperative marketing programs were in place with leading multinational travel industry firms (e.g., Northwest Airlines, Qantas) for cross-selling customers. Priority Club members received special recognition at the hotels; however, HIWAP's training burden to deal with these customers was heavy. Attracting new members (via point-of-sale at hotels, advertising, direct mail, airline frequent flyer programs) was costly; HIWAP focused most effort on recruiting members at the hotel level and activating current members.

Field Marketing facilitated Country Marketing Committees (CMCs). Each country had a CMC (some countries were grouped into a single CMC [e.g., Singapore, Thailand, Malaysia, Indonesia]) that pooled funds to launch advertising, promotions and collateral events promoting all hotels in the country. HIWAP paid Field Marketing Managers (FMMs) (stationed in the countries).[7] Currently, several countries were without CMCs; slots were budgeted for China, Japan, Singapore (Thailand, Malaysia, Indonesia), Australia (Australia and New Zealand). FMMs liaised frequently with Brand Marketing, Frequency Marketing and PR and Communications; the FMMs communicated initiatives to the CMCs and fed back responses from the CMCs and hotels.

At the hotel level, each hotel had its own sales and marketing team that focused on room sales and hotel events (e.g., food festivals, special discount packages).

The Asian Hotel Market

The Asian market for mid-price accommodations, as reflected in current room availability, was historically underserved despite mid-market properties traditionally outperforming luxury hotels in occupancy rates. One industry observer stated: "Past building booms have catered almost exclusively to the five-star business traveler. The middle range has been ignored in the region. No matter which country you look at, there is a shortfall." For example, in Hong Kong, mid-priced hotels accounted for 21% of available rooms; luxury hotels for 75%; the same disparity was found in Jakarta, a somewhat less cosmopolitan city; of 6,900 available rooms, only 16% were mid-priced.

Industry observers said that when mid-market rooms became available, demand tended to be strong. The economic emergence of many local economies (e.g., Malaysia, Thailand, Indonesia) coupled with the continued strength of Hong Kong, South Korea and Singapore increased intra-Asian business and leisure travel substantially. Intra-Asian travel was expected to comprise 85% of total visitors and 50% of room nights by 2000. Travel into Asia from other regions was also robust. From 1987 to 1991, visitor arrivals to the region grew on average 10.2% p.a.; over 70% of travelers in Asia were in the mid-priced category.

Customer behavior in Asia differed from North America and Europe along several key dimensions: family travel was less, even on vacations children typically did not

---

[7] CMC members were general managers from the various hotels (company-managed and franchise); one member was elected chairman.

accompany adults, nearly all travel was by air, most popular vacation activities were shopping and eating out, a typical vacation involved stops in more than one country. The business traveler segment, comprising primarily males, was growing in tandem with the regional economies; it shared features with business traveler requirements worldwide (e.g., high use of auxiliary services, relative price insensitivity, higher yields). However, leisure travel was expected to grow faster than business travel as disposable income increased and countries such as Taiwan and South Korea relaxed travel restrictions.

Foreign hotels were at some disadvantage in Asia as brand awareness had to be built in a new customer group. In addition, they faced operating problems. Said one observer: "These foreign-driven hotels have coffee shops when they should have karaoke lounges. They have hamburgers on the menu when they should be serving noodles. They need to focus more on the wishes of the Asian guest."

Competition

HIWAP faced competition from both international and Asian chains. The largest international competitors were previous leader Sheraton (recently lost contracts on several hotels) and Hyatt. Hyatt pursued a methodical, relatively slow growth strategy (1992 to 1994, two to three new hotels), concentrating on high cash flow properties.

According to industry observers, the prospects for regional chains were mixed. Accor Asia Pacific experienced strong growth, especially in Australia, Thailand and Indonesia but, apart from Indonesia, growth was expected to slow. Accor had weak brand recognition, even in Asia, and suffered from the same shortage of qualified labor plaguing other chains. Southern Pacific Hotel Corp. Ltd. (SPHC) had mixed success but appeared more healthy after a recent restructuring; however, insufficient access to capital would retard growth. Shangri-La was perhaps the best performer, in part because of vertical integration and extensive financial resources; its recently changed focus from China to the rest of the region was expected to slow growth in the short term.

Overall, the hotel room supply was extremely fragmented; even the largest chains supplied a small fraction (< 1%) of total rooms. As capital became available in areas such as China and India, fragmentation was expected to increase. Regional chains with local connections, recognition, and market knowledge would have some advantages, but the expertise and access to capital of international chains would remain formidable.

The Hotel Management Business

Opening a hotel in Asia Pacific was considerably different than in the U.S., Europe or Australia; as for regional business development in general, relationship building was a key component, especially with local government officials for operating licenses. Said one observer: "What this culture really does is make you work on relationships." Development deals often moved more slowly in Asia than the U.S. due to time spent in negotiations and securing financing; lawyers played a far less prominent role but although this expedited closing deals many difficulties were present for the unwary. Said one observer: "There are a lot of traps and banana peels out there."

Once the hotel was opened, positioning and staffing became critical. Said one observer: "A formula-driven hotel can't be brought into Asia in the same way it's done in North America or Europe. A hotel that goes into a small town in, say, India or Indonesia has a social function in a city ... you must flex your product with the market." As a rule, Asian customers demanded more and better public facilities in hotels than U.S. customers, similar amenities and service to those at luxury hotels; concessions at midprice hotels usually came from location and room size.

Staffing at all levels was critical and difficult. As Asian economies developed, labor became more expensive and, other than Australia, all countries in the region demanded higher staff-to-guest ratios than in the U.S. These factors combined to drive up labor costs, over 25% of total costs for some luxury hotels. To compound the problem, scarce qualified staff led to high turnover throughout the region. Hotel management faced the same market pressures. Said one industry insider: "I'm ashamed to say that the international hotel companies haven't done a very good job in developing Asian managers."

In addition to difficulties in attracting, retaining and developing front line managers, the sheer distance of top management from the Asian market created problems for managers and franchisees. Said one hotel executive: "How can you remotely control a market that starts at the dateline in the east, India in the west, Russia in the north, and New Zealand in the south? The distances are mind-boggling." Asian hotel owners' and partners' demonstrated desire to deal directly with top management posed logistical difficulties.

The Consulting Project: Current Measurements

The student team examined internal documents (e.g., 1995 to 2000 Strategic Plan, Divisional Training Plan) and conducted numerous interviews with HIWAP senior management including Director of Training & Development, Vice President of Human Resources and Vice President of Marketing. Three key requirements were identified for HIWAP to achieve its goals:

- A clear brand image and high awareness among existing and potential HIWAP customers;
- A consistently high level of customer satisfaction;
- A dedicated team of employees that delivered a high, consistent, level of service to HIWAP customers.

The team believed it identified service gaps in these areas that would inhibit HIWAP's ability to compete in the fragmented and competitive hotel market (Figure 2). HIWAP's ambitious expansion plan required both growth in number of properties and growth in revenue yield; these would be impossible to achieve without superior positioning and customer service.

Figure 2: Service Quality Gap Model

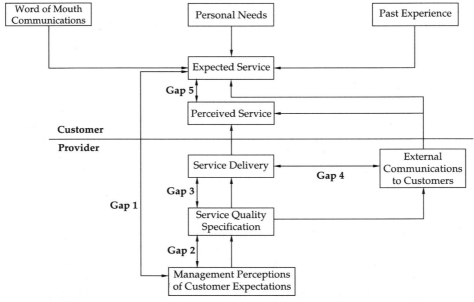

Source: Zeithaml, Parasuraman and Berry, "Delivering Quality Service," *The Free Press*, New York, 1990.

Brand Image

In recent years, HIWAP used two ad hoc approaches to measure brand image: Pan Asian Syndicated Hotel Survey (PASHS) and Brand Asset Valuator.

Pan Asian Syndicated Hotel Survey (PASHS). In 1990 and 1992, HIWAP participated in PASHS with nine other international hotel chains. In 1992, PASHS objectives were to provide sponsors with feedback on products and services from frequent hotel users (FHUs) in Hong Kong, South Korea, Taiwan, the Philippines, China, Thailand, Malaysia, Singapore and Indonesia and to report behavioral and attitudinal changes to the sponsors since the prior survey.[8] In 1992, 1,801 FHUs were interviewed in Tokyo, Seoul, Taipei, Hong Kong, Bangkok, Kuala Lumpur, Singapore, Jakarta and Manila. Key data collected were factors influencing hotel choice, food/beverage requirements, brand awareness, advertising awareness, hotel chain images and relative strength/weakness of images.

Results from the 1992 survey showed that, across the region, HIWAP was second in brand awareness to Hilton; Hyatt was third. On an individual country basis, HIWAP was leader in Hong Kong, Japan, Singapore and Thailand. Holiday Inn was closely

---

[8] An FHU was a person who traveled to other Asian countries (excluding Japan) and spent a minimum of 22 nights in the previous 12 months spread over at least three trips.

associated with "value for money" and consistent quality; no other hotel came close on "value for money." HIWAP rated very highly as a family hotel; it was less highly rated as a business hotel. This survey also showed that only 55% of hotel booking decisions were made by guests.

HIWAP management said that PASHS provided valuable information on brand awareness and customer satisfaction. However, the interest level of participants decreased and a proposed 1994 study was abandoned.

Brand Asset Valuator. Conducted mainly in the U.S. (but also in Australia and Japan) by HIW's advertising agency, Holiday Inn was rated more highly on familiarity, popularity and esteem than any of the 18 other hotel brands surveyed. Holiday Inn's image was exceptionally strong: it was perceived as "more friendly" than 99% of 1,000 consumer brands in the study, more trustworthy (greater than 91%) and more caring about customers (greater than 91%).

Customer Satisfaction

In-room guest questionnaire (GIS). HIWAP collected customer satisfaction information via a voluntary in-room guest questionnaire. The GIS form comprised eight questions concerning satisfaction with physical facilities and services (Exhibit 2). Survey results were consolidated at the hotel level. HIWAP management said the response rate to GIS was generally unsatisfactory.

Other systems. In the U.S., a Guest Satisfaction Tracking System (GSTS) was in place. HIWAP did not implement this system since it believed it would be expensive to do so; hotel owners would have to mail back questionnaires and a database would have to be developed. HIWAP conducted periodic product surveys (to a standard checklist) on facility quality standards by experienced engineers / auditors. This survey did not attempt to measure customer services provided to guests.

Human Resources

HIWAP's Human Resources Division (HRD) was organized by traditional human resource areas: recruitment, compensation and benefits, training and development. HIWAP coordinated the performance appraisal system for graded staff (executive and important staff) of company-managed hotels (CMHs) in the region. Its long-term plan was to install a regional human resource structure in each of the five sub-regions; currently China was the only region with a regional director and regional training manager. Other CMHs were mostly self-sufficient in day-to-day human resource operations; these accorded with HIWAP guidelines. Each CMH filed a monthly human resources report.

HIWAP employed sophisticated human resource systems (i.e., job evaluation, staff grading, salary systems) and training programs designed at HIW's Atlanta headquarters. Training comprised two levels: basic training for frontline junior staff, supervisory training for more senior departmental managers. CMHs adhered to recommended training routines, but training in franchised hotels was highly variable across owners/operators.

For new hotels, the management team had a compulsory nine-day training program; after opening, many technical and managerial skills training were offered on an as-requested basis by individual hotels. HIWAP training staff believed its hotel training materials were the best in the region; currently, these were being translated into local languages. More established CMHs (e.g., Holiday Inn Golden Mile Hong Kong) had their own training managers; however, in most cases, HIWAP provided instructors. Participants' satisfaction with courses, focusing on course materials and trainers' effectiveness, was measured by post-course evaluations; no system measured the impact of training on participants' performance.

HIWAP recruited three key posts in CMHs: general manager, resident manager (the general manager's deputy) and financial controller. Hotels recruited local staff but found this difficult in fast-developing countries (e.g., China). The limited supply of quality local staff proficient in spoken English, and competitive hiring by non-hospitality institutions, led HIWAP to experience high staff turnover. HRD administered the Executrack database that maintained records of graded staff (e.g., chefs) and potential candidates for executive positions; this system enhanced visibility of senior staff and cut down lead times for filling vacant positions. Promotions were based on recommendations from potential promotes' managers.

The Consulting Project: Recommendations

The consulting team presented recommendations in three key success areas: brand marketing, customer satisfaction and service delivery.

Brand Image

Three structured techniques were recommended for measuring HIWAP's brand image: brand identify profiling, projective techniques for assessing brand image and personality and brand mapping. HIWAP's image as determined by these techniques could be profiled against the desired image to assess the success of HIWAP's communication campaigns.

Brand identify profiling. This technique was designed to assess a brand's perceptual inventory, the imagery, feelings, associations about the brand in the respondent's mind. Synergy recommended collecting a complete perceptual inventory for HIWAP in a series of in-depth interviews or focus groups by means of such questions as: What do you think of Holiday Inn? What comes to mind? What images or feelings do you associate with Holiday Inn? To provide structure, these questions would be asked of four areas: the product/service itself, product usage, product users, product values/benefits. Once an exhaustive list of images, associations and feeling was developed, respondents would be asked to rank them in terms of the degree to which they connoted Holiday-Inn-ness. In this manner, Holiday Inn's brand image would be captured.

Projective techniques. Respondents would be asked to personify the brand (Holiday Inn) by means of such questions as:

- What would Holiday Inn be like if it were a person?
- Would it be male or female? Young or mature?
- How would the personified brand be dressed?
- What are its hobbies and interests?

- Where would it most likely go on vacation?
- What would its occupation be?
- How does it spend its time?
- What kind of car does it drive?
- What kind of music does it listen to?

Based on responses, the average image of HIWAP could be profiled.

Brand mapping. This method focused on comparing the brand with its competitors. Key dimensions representing product attributes and benefits would be identified and respondents asked to rank various brands on these dimensions. Respondent perceptions would be plotted on a perceptual map to see how the various brands were positioned relative to one another. Results from this approach would allow HIWAP to design marketing activities to reposition Holiday Inn as required.

Implementation. Synergy recommended that HIWAP select one or more of these methods and that surveys be conducted on a continuous basis to track the results of managerial actions. It recommended that regional headquarters take a leading role in brand measurement and that this be coordinated by Field Marketing in the five sub-regions (i.e., Singapore, China, Australia, Hong Kong, Tokyo). In favor of this approach were: no capital investment required; maximum flexibility in budgeting by outsourcing survey work (budget would be a function of sophistication of information required); ability of FMMs to have more direct contact with existing and potential customers. HIWAP would train FMMs on survey methodology and implementation of corrective actions; FMMs as a team would be responsible for the selection of research firm, questionnaire design and analysis of results. The first cycle was expected to take nine months; subsequent cycles would be much shorter.

Synergy gave several reasons why the function should be totally funded by HIWAP: HIWAP owned the Holiday Inn brand name; individual hotel owners could not influence survey results through manipulation; sufficient investment would be placed in fast-developing countries where current sales contribution was low; HIWAP could fully control the survey process and need not compromise with survey partners.

Synergy recommended surveying both existing and potential customers. (Customer satisfaction surveys would only cover existing customers.) Existing customers could be extracted from the Priority Club members database, Worldwide Corporate Account (WWCA) database or the Travel Agent Commission Program (TACP) customer list. Since some Holiday Inn customers were also customers of other hotels, Holiday Inn's brand position versus competitors could be found in the same survey. In an effort to ensure that response rates were high, Synergy suggested offering incentives to respondents (e.g., donations to favorite charities). Potential customers would be secured from customer lists of firms with which HIWAP had collateral marketing arrangements (e.g., Visa, American Express, AT&T, Time Magazine). Finally, Synergy recommended data collection by both mail and telephone; telephone response rates were likely to be higher, non-response bias would be lower, but this method would be more expensive.

Customer Satisfaction

Synergy recommended that the GSTS form be used for customer satisfaction measurement inasmuch as it covered 22 aspects of a guest's stay at a Holiday Inn (Exhibit 3). HIWAP management did not consider this instrument applicable to HIWAP in part because it believed response rates were inappropriate for serious customer satisfaction measurement. Synergy recommended three new data collection methods: In-hotel Customer Survey Officer (CSO); Touch-Screen (Electronic) Survey System (TSSS) and Focus Group Dinner (FGD).

In-hotel Customer Survey Officer (CSO). Under this approach each CMC would form a team of customer survey officers (CSOs) to conduct face-to-face customer satisfaction surveys in hotel lobbies; these CSOs would rotate among different hotels in the same country. CSOs would be based at a counter in the hotel lobby to attract guests on a voluntary basis; incentives (e.g., drinks, fruit baskets) would be provided. Synergy recommended that hiring criteria be "nice-looking, presentable young women"; it believed such candidates would likely be enthusiastic and physically fit for the demanding face-to-face interviewing work and meeting the job rotation schedule among different hotels. Synergy believed five to nine CSOs should be hired initially; costs would be salary, travel, room and board and incentives. It estimated six months to have fully trained CSOs in the field.

Touch-Screen (Electronic) Survey System (TSSS). This unit, a touch-screen color monitor and simple micro-computer (estimated purchase cost approximately $1,200, annual maintenance cost 20% of capital cost), would be housed in hotel lobbies to attract guests who were waiting for whatever reason. Participants would identify themselves via room numbers, period of stay or registered guest names before answering the survey; incentives would be offered as above. Discs could be retrieved on a daily basis; TSSS units, under FMM supervision in individual countries, would be rotated among hotels in the same country. Synergy estimated nine months to develop the system and conduct a trial run.[9]

Focus Group Dinner (FGD). A selected group of guests, preferably frequent hotel users, would be invited by HIWAP's marketing team or by local hotel management staff to a Holiday Inn dinner party. Hotel staff would ask satisfaction and expectation type questions. Costs would be confined to the direct cost of the dinner and incentives.

---

[9] Fairfield Inns (U.S.) had a similar system.

Analysis. Synergy believed the three indices being computed from the GSTS results, General Product Index (GPI), General Service Index (GSI), Overall Satisfaction Index (OSI) could be adopted by HIWAP as benchmarking measures to track customer satisfaction over time. These indices were computed as follows:

- General Product Index (GPI): outside appearance (15%), lobby appearance (5%), amenities (5%), temperature control, lighting, etc. (10%), bed/pillow comfort (10%), TV/radio, etc. (10%), condition of furnishings (25%), overall physical conditions (20%).
- General Service Index (GSI): service at check-in (10%), room cleanliness (15%), responsiveness to needs (15%), friendliness of staff (10%), professional attitude and appearance (20%), service at check-out (10%), overall service received (20%).
- Overall Satisfaction Index (OSI). This index was a weighted average of GPI and GSI; Synergy believed HIWAP should decide on the relative weightings.

Use. Synergy believed the results of the survey could be used in two ways, to highlight specific problems and improvement areas and to quantify continuous improvement in customer satisfaction over time. It developed two flowcharts (Figures 3A, 3B) to describe the processes.

Implementation. Synergy recommended that HIWAP fund the surveys, in part to minimize resistance from franchised hotels. The CSO and TSSS methods would be managed by FMMs; schedules of surveys would be proposed by FMMs and agreed by CMCs. A small team at HIWAP headquarters would coordinate guest surveys on brand equity and customer satisfaction. This team would collate and consolidate survey results, perform statistical analyses and compute index trends.

Priority group members. Synergy also recommended that HIWAP conduct a bi-annual survey of Priority Club members offering incentives (e.g., bonus points) for completion and return of questionnaires. (The first cycle was estimated at six months; subsequent cycles would be shorter.) Members were classified as active and inactive; active members included customers that: sometimes stayed at Holiday Inns; regularly stayed at Holiday Inns; told others how good Holiday Inn was. Inactive members might be prospects interested in staying at Holiday Inns or who stayed at least once.

Synergy believed that the main purpose of surveying active members should be to measure the effectiveness of individual benefits to attract repeat purchase; it identified some "must ask" questions:

- If there were no Priority Club program, would the member still use Holiday Inn? Why?
- What benefits attract the member to use Holiday Inn? (Members would rate the importance of a series of benefits.)
- What additional benefits would attract members to use Holiday Inn more frequently? (Members would rate the importance of these benefits.)
- Will the member recommend the program to his/her friends? Why?

Figure 3A: Problem Identification and Solution Process

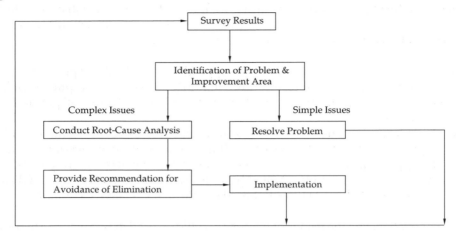

Figure 3B: Continuous Customer Satisfaction Process

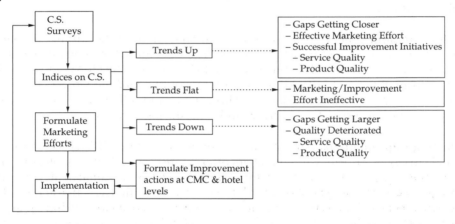

The purpose of surveying inactive members would be to measure the attractiveness of benefits and members' awareness of the program. "Must ask" questions were:

- Why is the member inactive? Tentative questions included brand image, service standards, price, facilities, program incentives/benefits, food and beverage. Respondents would rank responses in order of importance.
- What extra benefits would make the member active? These would be weighted by importance.

Synergy believed these survey results would enable HIWAP to highlight areas of improvement to increase attractiveness of the Priority Club program; it would then be able to monitor the effectiveness of new benefits. In addition to the surveys, Synergy believed HIWAP should monitor the activity of active members and contact by letter those whose activity level dropped to identify the cause.

Quality Service Delivery

Synergy identified three focus areas to improve human resource effectiveness: recruitment, development, retention. It believed its recommendations would mostly be applicable to CMHs but that the training element would also be applicable to franchised hotels.

Recruitment. Synergy identified two potential effectiveness approaches: quantitative and qualitative. It believed that because high staff turnover and supply shortages of quality staff at the hotel level were mostly due to circumstances beyond HIWAP's control (e.g., tight labor markets, local regulations on staff employment), quantitative measure would be of little help for improving recruitment effectiveness.

Qualitative measures would focus on whether staff of the right quality were being recruited; measurement would focus on the relationship between post-entry job performance and required competencies specified in job descriptions. Synergy believed that since many other factors affected job performance (e.g., cultural fit, peer relationships, management leadership, training and development), such measures would not produce reliable results for recruitment effectiveness. In sum, Synergy recommended that recruitment effectiveness not be measured.

Training. Synergy identified training planning (what to train and who to train) and training implementation (effect of training on individual performance) as two areas for measuring effectiveness. Quantitative training planning effectiveness would focus on comparing the number of people trained versus the number of people planned to be trained. However, because of rapid development and changing demand for training, Synergy did not believe such quantitative measures would prove very useful. Qualitative measurements of training planning effectiveness would monitor whether the right staff were getting the right training. Synergy believed there were significant definitional problems in identifying the "right" staff and the "right" training. It also noted that, in some countries, training was provided as a reward or recognition for good performance rather than because a specific training need might exist. It concluded that practical problems were sufficiently severe that qualitative measures of training planning should not be attempted.

Synergy believed performance improvement was the best way to measure training effectiveness. It noted that standard forms were in place for annual performance appraisal but that no training effectiveness measures were taken. Synergy recommended that the performance appraisal form be redesigned to incorporate details of training received. For interpersonal skills training, it recommended evaluation based on frequency and proper exercise of new behavioral skills acquired from training. In addition, Synergy recommended focus groups for identifying problems with individual training courses.

Staff retention. Staff retention was a critical problem for HIWAP; Synergy recommended staff satisfaction surveys for those key areas that helped retain staff. It believed questionnaire items should be relevant to management efforts to retain staff and that a common questionnaire be used to facilitate inter-temporal and inter-country comparisons. Synergy recommended the survey be conducted annually just before the annual performance appraisal. Hotels owned and managed by HIWAP would be prime targets for the survey, but Synergy encouraged HIWAP to persuade franchised hotels to participate to benchmark the different hotel types. The first cycle was expected to take nine months (subsequent cycles shorter); HIWAP would fund the surveys.

Decisions

Parker completed reading the report. He felt Synergy had hit on critical areas; brand identity, customer satisfaction and employee satisfaction were of considerable concern to him and to HIWAP senior management in general. However, he was not sure how much faith to put in the group's ideas; individual members were clearly well-trained but they had little experience in the hospitality industry. As he opened the report to re-read the recommendations he knew that decisions would have to be taken about these critical areas.

Exhibit 1: Excerpts from Priority Club Brochure

You're Our First Priority.

As a Priority Club™ member, you're a very important person whenever you stay at a Holiday Inn® hotel. You will receive a host of special extras and personal services...and at the same time you'll earn points which will bring you free hotel stays at beautiful tropical resorts, exciting capital cities, centres of cultural interest, or sporting meccas. You can even receive frequent flyer credits!

Holiday Inn offers dependable, friendly service and attractive facilities, as well as excellent value for money. And for every US$1 you spend at the Qualifying Room Rate* (most business and leisure rates) at any Holiday Inn hotel, you'll earn one Priority Club point.

You can take advantage of this programme at more than 2,000 Holiday Inn hotels around the world, including over 75 in the Asia Pacific region — more choices than any other hotel chain offers you.

*Points may not be awarded on deeply discounted rates. You will receive 25 Priority Club points per night for stays at Holiday Inn Express™ hotels in all countries except Japan, where you will receive 75 points per night.

The Rewards of Priority Club™ Membership

As a Priority Club member, you'll be entitled to a variety of exclusive member benefits, privileges and promotions. And once you have earned 400 Priority Club points, you will receive your permanent Membership Card and Member Guide with full details of all Priority Club awards and how to claim them.

When you begin to earn Priority Club points, you can treat yourself to some of the little luxuries that will make your stay even more enjoyable, like room upgrades or free in-room movies.

You can also use your Priority Club points to enjoy free room nights at your favourite Holiday Inn hotels around the world — from exciting capital cities to exotic resorts.

There's a whole range of exciting Priority Club awards to choose from. Enjoy extended shopping sprees in some of the world's most exciting cities.

If adventure's more your style, what about white water rafting on the Colorado river? Trekking in Lhasa? Or diving off Hamilton Island?

Play golf on the shores of Malaysia's beautiful Pedu Lake...or play the tables at Macau's leading casinos. Tour the cultural wonders of Beijing...or the scenic wonders of West Coast America.

Frequent Flyer Options

As a Priority Club member, you may choose to accumulate your Priority Club points until you are ready to enjoy one of our awards.

On the other hand, you may opt to have all your Priority Club points converted automatically into frequent flyer credits with any of these leading airlines. (Priority Club gives you the widest choice of airlines, too!) Simply indicate your choice of frequent flyer programme when you complete the application form.

You're Our Most Valued Guest.

As a Priority Club™ member, stay at any Holiday Inn® hotel around the world and you'll enjoy:
- Guaranteed single corporate room rate every time you stay
- Free weekday newspaper
- Express reservations
- Express check-in/check-out
- Extended check-out till 2 p.m. upon request
- Family stays for free (in the same room)

In addition, whenever you stay at Holiday Inn hotels in Asia Pacific, you will also enjoy:
- A welcome drink of your choice
- Room upgrades when available (excluding Executive Floors and Suites)
- Complimentary morning tea or coffee
- Extended check-out until 4.30 p.m. when available
- 20% discount on selected Business Centre services

Exhibit 2:   HIWAP In-room Guest Questionnaire

1. How do you rate this Holiday Inn hotel?

VERY GOOD ☐   GOOD ☐   SATISFACTORY ☐   POOR ☐   VERY POOR ☐

2. How do you rate this hotel's service?

	VERY GOOD	GOOD	SATISFACTORY	POOR	VERY POOR
Friendliness	☐	☐	☐	☐	☐
Helpfulness	☐	☐	☐	☐	☐
Attentiveness	☐	☐	☐	☐	☐
Efficiency	☐	☐	☐	☐	☐
Discretion	☐	☐	☐	☐	☐

3. Please rate the following:

a) YOUR ROOM

	VERY GOOD	GOOD	SATISFACTORY	POOR	VERY POOR
Value for money	☐	☐	☐	☐	☐
Appearance	☐	☐	☐	☐	☐
Furnishing	☐	☐	☐	☐	☐
Cleanliness	☐	☐	☐	☐	☐
Functioning of facilities	☐	☐	☐	☐	☐
Bathroom	☐	☐	☐	☐	☐
Room service	☐	☐	☐	☐	☐
Overall impression	☐	☐	☐	☐	☐

b) THE RESTAURANTS

	VERY GOOD	GOOD	SATISFACTORY	POOR	VERY POOR
Quality of food	☐	☐	☐	☐	☐
Value	☐	☐	☐	☐	☐
Service	☐	☐	☐	☐	☐
Overall impression	☐	☐	☐	☐	☐

Which meal(s) did you have?
Breakfast ☐   Lunch ☐   Dinner ☐

c) THE BARS

	VERY GOOD	GOOD	SATISFACTORY	POOR	VERY POOR
Overall impression	☐	☐	☐	☐	☐
Beverage quality	☐	☐	☐	☐	☐
Value for money	☐	☐	☐	☐	☐
Service	☐	☐	☐	☐	☐

Which bars were used ? _____

d) THE RECEPTION/FRONT DESK

	VERY GOOD	GOOD	SATISFACTORY	POOR	VERY POOR
Handling of check-in/check-out	☐	☐	☐	☐	☐
Efficiency	☐	☐	☐	☐	☐
Friendliness	☐	☐	☐	☐	☐

e) CONFERENCE FACILITIES

	VERY GOOD	GOOD	SATISFACTORY	POOR	VERY POOR
Comfort	☐	☐	☐	☐	☐
Lighting	☐	☐	☐	☐	☐
Temperature	☐	☐	☐	☐	☐
Service	☐	☐	☐	☐	☐

f) HOTEL APPEARANCE

	VERY GOOD	GOOD	SATISFACTORY	POOR	VERY POOR
Building exterior	☐	☐	☐	☐	☐
Lobby/public areas	☐	☐	☐	☐	☐

4. Did you use our leisure facilities?
YES ☐   NO ☐

5. Have you stayed at any Holiday Inn hotel in the last 12 months?
YES ☐   NO ☐

6. If you return to this area, will you stay at this hotel again?
YES ☐   NO ☐

7. Which was the most important factor in choosing this hotel?

Location ☐
Standard of service ☐
Friendliness of staff ☐
Leisure facilities ☐
General standards of Holiday Inn hotels ☐
I did not choose this hotel ☐
Other ☐
(e.g. price/advertising/special offer)

8. We would appreciate receiving any other comments you wish to make (please write in block capitals)

_____
_____
_____
_____

Mr/Mrs/Miss _____
Name _____
Company _____
Address _____

Country _____
Room no. _____ Date of arrival _____
Reason for stay: Business ☐   Pleasure ☐   Meeting ☐
Please place this questionnaire in the box provided in the Reception area.

HOLIDEX ☐☐☐☐☐

Asking All The Right Question

Please Tell Us What You Think!

Holiday Inn
WORLDWIDE

Did you recently stay at the Holiday Inn Express McMinnville, TN?
If so, please let us know how well we served you.

1. During this stay, how satisfied were you with the:	Very Satisfied	Somewhat Satisfied	Neither Satisfied Nor Dissatisfied	Somewhat Dissatisfied	Very Dissatisfied
Outside Appearance of Hotel *(curb appeal, grounds, building, etc.)*	☐	☐	☐	☐	☐
Lobby Condition/Attractiveness	☐	☐	☐	☐	☐
Service at Check-In *(friendly, efficient, prompt)*	☐	☐	☐	☐	☐
Guestroom/Guestbath:					
• Overall Cleanliness	☐	☐	☐	☐	☐
• Guestbath Facilities *(amenities, hot water, etc.)*	☐	☐	☐	☐	☐
• Heating/Air Conditioning *(quiet, efficient, etc.)*	☐	☐	☐	☐	☐
• Bed/Pillow Comfort	☐	☐	☐	☐	☐
• Television/Radio/Remote Control	☐	☐	☐	☐	☐
• Condition of Furniture *(dresser, chairs, table, etc.)*	☐	☐	☐	☐	☐
• Condition of Bedspread/Drapes/Carpet	☐	☐	☐	☐	☐
Service of Hotel Staff:					
• Responsiveness to Your Needs	☐	☐	☐	☐	☐
• Friendliness of Staff	☐	☐	☐	☐	☐
• Professional Attitude & Appearance	☐	☐	☐	☐	☐
Restaurant/Breakfast Bar: Did not use ☐					
• Quality of Food/Beverage	☐	☐	☐	☐	☐
• Restaurant Cleanliness	☐	☐	☐	☐	☐
• Quality of Service	☐	☐	☐	☐	☐
Telephone Services *(wake-up calls, messages, long distance/local services)*	☐	☐	☐	☐	☐
Lighting *(brightness, good working order, etc.)*	☐	☐	☐	☐	☐
Hotel Safety & Security	☐	☐	☐	☐	☐
Accuracy of Billing	☐	☐	☐	☐	☐
Service at Check-Out *(friendly, efficient, prompt)*	☐	☐	☐	☐	☐
Value Received for Price Paid	☐	☐	☐	☐	☐
2. REGARDLESS OF WHAT YOU PAID, how satisfied were you with the:					
• Overall Physical Condition of this Hotel	☐	☐	☐	☐	☐
• Overall Service Received at this Hotel	☐	☐	☐	☐	☐
3. All things considered, please rate your OVERALL SATISFACTION with this hotel.	☐	☐	☐	☐	☐

4. Would you recommend THIS hotel to a friend or business associate?	Definitely	Probably	Might or Might Not	Probably Not	Definitely Not
	☐	☐	☐	☐	☐

123456789012345678

Scale: 100 60 40 20 0

Case 2

Waste Management International PLC: Strategy for Asia

Kristiaan Helsen
The Hong Kong University of Science and Technology

In late 1993, several questions concerned Edwin G. Falkman, CEO of Waste Management International (WMI). With a recession in Europe, he wondered if WMI should temporarily postpone its European expansion and focus investment in faster growing regions. Gregory Fertile, senior VP for Asia and the Pacific Rim, claimed that, given conditions in developed countries, "Asia was the perfect substitute." Even though great successes such as the Hong Kong project could be achieved, Falkman knew developing Asian business was time consuming and costly. Besides, since needs differed from one country to another, he was unsure if he could create a global strategy. Conscious of his superior's concerns, Fertile contemplated a strategic plan for Asia.

ଚ୦୯ଔ

Company Background

WMX Technologies, Inc. (formerly Waste Management), founded in 1968, grew steadily at high rates into a $8.66 billion firm while maintaining profitability (Exhibits 1, 2). This rapid expansion resulted in significant changes in company activities including addition of new technological skills. Traditional solid waste management currently accounted for only half of the firm's revenues as new services grew quickly. In particular, from 1990 to 1992, energy, environmental and related services grew by 256%, in part by acquisition of majority ownership in an American company, WTI; this business accounted for 17% of total revenues. By pursuing acquisitions, especially in Western Europe, international waste management services grew by 78%. More strikingly, profits generated by WMI doubled; income from energy and environmental services quintupled (see Table 1 for 1992 distribution of revenues and income).

42

Table 1:   WMI Distribution of Revenues and Income in 1992 (US$ '000)

Diversification*	Revenues	Income	Internationalization	Revenues	Income
Solid waste	4,310	807	U.S.	6,974	1,161
Hazardous waste	755	138	Europe	1,143	151
Engineering and related	1,441	32	Other foreign	544	58
Environmental	1,441	197	Total	8,661	1,370
International	1,446	202			

*Figures do not sum to totals; corporate eliminations not included.

Although the U.S. was its major market, WMX Technologies, Inc. diversified geographically; revenue and income grew faster internationally as it gradually became global. CEO Dean L. Buntrock proudly said WMX was:

> the acknowledged worldwide leader in providing comprehensive environmental, waste management and related services of the highest quality to industry, government and customers using state-of-the-art systems responsive to customer need, sound environmental policy with highest standards of corporate citizenship.

Nevertheless, recession brought corporate identity and organizational problems into sharp focus. Among the most important decisions was adoption of the umbrella name WMX Technologies, Inc. (Waste Management, Inc. now characterized the traditional solid waste services business.) The new name conveyed the idea of an unequaled collection of technological and scientific resources. Subsidiaries Chemical Waste Management, Wheelabrator Technologies, Inc. and Waste Management International (Table 2) retained their identities but benefited technologically from the entire group.[1] Another major strategic decision was creation of Rust International, Inc. By combining environmental consulting, construction and engineering resources, previously in several different subsidiaries, Rust became an overnight leader with 13,900 employees. As a result, the whole Waste Management group gained synergy effects, for example, by receiving more efficient technical support. (See Exhibit 3 for services by industry.)

To foster rapid growth, WMX Technology introduced the Expanded Management System (EMS). This program put emphasis on the customer, WMX employees, the environment and shareholders. Together with development of 14 environmental principles (Table 3), EMS increased employee motivation to comply with the firm's mission of providing remarkable services for a clean environment while making profit.

---

[1] Waste Management International's ownership structure was: Waste Management, 56%; Rust International, 12%; Wheelabrator Technologies, 12%; public (20%).

Table 2: WMX Family of Companies

Waste Management, Inc.

Solid Waste Reduction; Recycling; Materials Recovery; Residential and Commercial Waste Collection; Processing; Transfer; Disposal; Medical Waste Services; Portable Sanitation Relocatable Office Structures; Special Events Services

Wheelabrator Technologies, Inc.

Trash-to-Energy; Cogeneration; Water and Waste Water Treatment; Biosolids Management; Composting; Clean Air Technologies and Services; Industrial Material Design Services

Rust International, Inc.

Environmental/Infrastructure/Process Consulting; Environmental/Infrastructure/Process Engineering; Marine/Infrastructure/Industrial Construction; Project Management; Demolition; Hazardous/Nuclear Remediation; On-site Waste Treatment Technologies; Industrial Cleaning/Maintenance; Nuclear Products/Services; Scaffolding

Chemical Waste Management, Inc.

Hazardous Waste Reduction; Recycling/Recover; Collection; Transportation; Treatment; Identification; Thermal Destruction; Disposal; Low-level Radioactive Waste Services

Waste Management International, Plc

Solid Waste Reduction; Recycling; Waste Collection; Waste Transfer; Waste Disposal; Trash-to-Energy; Comprehensive Hazardous Waste Services; City Cleaning; Special Events Services

Waste Management International

Waste Management International (WMI), a leading provider of solid and hazardous waste management services, including collection, recycling, transportation, storage, treatment, incineration and disposal, also operated waste-to-energy facilities and related services. WMI was in nine European countries (i.e., Britain, Denmark, Finland, France, Germany, Italy, the Netherlands, Spain, Sweden) as well as Argentina, Venezuela, Australia, New Zealand, Hong Kong, Brunei and the Middle East.

In April 1992, WMI raised $700 million in a global public offering, among the most successful of its kind. Less than 90 days later, WMI successfully achieved significant

Table 3: WMX Environmental Principles

1. Environmental protection and enhancement
2. Waste reduction, recycling, treatment and disposal
3. Biodiversity
4. Sustainable use of natural resources
5. Wise use of energy
6. Compliance with all legal requirements
7. Reduction of environmental, health and safety risk
8. Damage compensation
9. Research and development for integrated waste management
10. Public policy
11. Public education
12. Participation in environmental organizations
13. Environmental policy assessment
14. Annual environmental report

gains in existing and new international markets. In the first half of 1992, WMI's profit increased 51% over the comparable 1991 period.

Europe

Western Europe (population, 400 million) was historically the main focus of WMI activities. A key growth factor was the trend towards increasingly rigorous and harmonized environmental legislation and standards set by the European Union. WMI's European operations served over three million households through approximately 1,600 municipal contracts; hazardous waste management services were provided to approximately 16,000 customers.

WMI grew by acquisition. In 1991, it purchased a solid waste business. In May 1992, U.K. Waste Management (UKWM) acquired Marvin Ltd., a storage, handling and chemical waste treatment facility in Great Yarmouth that had a broad permit for storage, transfer and treatment of hazardous and industrial waste, complementing UKWM's existing disposal capabilities. In France, acquisition of SPAT gave WMI eight operating landfills in the Paris area. In Germany, WMI contracted to construct and operate a second waste-to-energy facility at Gutersloh (first, Hamm), the second privately-owned facility of its kind in Germany. Projected to start operations in 1997, it could convert a minimum of 180,000 tons solid waste and 25,000 tons sewage sludge annually into useful energy.

Swedish subsidiary WMI Sellbergs signed a preliminary agreement with the Swedish Ministry for the Environment to acquire 90.1% of government-owned SAKAB, the foremost hazardous waste treatment facility in Sweden with incineration capacity of 33,000 tons yearly. Sellbergs also acquired Servi Jatehuolto OY, the leading solid waste management company in Finland. Said Falkman: "We are very excited by the number and range of opportunities we are currently pursuing in all our markets, some of which could be realized in the second half of this financial year." The scope of these opportunities ranged from full-blown acquisitions to state-of-the-art treatment facilities.

Asia

WMI had long been aware of growing Asian needs for environmental services. Nonetheless, current operations were limited to Brunei and Hong Kong, where the most sophisticated waste treatment plant of its kind had just been built. WMI expected to start operating its US$304 million SENT Hong Kong landfill project in late 1994.

In May 1993, WMI announced a joint venture with Bimantara, a leading Indonesian firm, to develop a solid and hazardous waste business. Indonesia had the world's fourth largest population and a government that had expressed a commitment to safely managing waste. WMI and Bimantara would identify other projects involving waste water treatment, waste-to-energy systems, waste reduction, recycling and remediation activities, as well as the collection, treatment and disposal of municipal (solid and chemical) waste. Said a WMI executive: "WMI's excellent reputation means we are a favored choice to benefit from increased governmental privatization projects, as shown by our success in Gutersloh and Indonesia."

Reasons for Concern

WMI's 1993 financial results were troubling: third quarter pre-tax profits slipped to US$58.32 million from US$60.12 million. In October 1993, WMI announced a message of confidence in earnings growth to calm shareholders. WMI management believed it could maintain its earnings per share record and that investors realized new opportunities had to be pursued. Having grown steadily by acquisition, it was looking for more purchases.

Europe. Europe was the main cause of financial distress. Because economic recovery had not occurred in Western Europe, WMI commenced extensive cost reduction and productivity improvement programs. Nonetheless, profitability was hampered and "the results were achieved in the face of difficult European trading and fewer acquisitions than anticipated." Delay in securing landfill permit extensions in Italy also hurt revenues and earnings.

Asia. By contrast, WMI made major progress in several markets. It was bidding on several waste-to-energy projects in Taiwan with a joint-venture partner, and exploring opportunities in other countries (e.g., Thailand, Malaysia, Taiwan [Appendix]).

The Environmental Situation

Internationally

Recently, international concern about the environment had grown rapidly. Increased awareness of air, soil and water pollution by chemical plants, and of hazardous and solid waste, created new market opportunities. Although still young, by 1992, the worldwide environmental technology industry was a US$200 billion market: air purification, 15%; waste purification, 30%; refuse disposal, 20%; general services, 24%; other systems, 11%. The most dynamic sectors were waste management, sewage treatment, air pollution control, water purification and conservation.

In developed countries, the focus increasingly shifted from combating damage caused by pollution and disposal of industrial waste to pollution prevention during production processes. As a result, competition in "end-of-pipe" technologies was very fierce. Until recently, these firms dominated the industry but their significance was declining. Recently, several takeovers and mergers led to industry concentration: driving factors were rapidly rising break-even levels for firms producing pollution control and energy-conservation equipment and large amounts of equity capital required to finance major investments.

In Asia

In recent decades, Asian countries experienced significant population growth; many suffered from overpopulation. High population levels, rapid industrialization and increased urbanization sharply increased household and industrial waste. As land became scarce, especially in smaller countries such as Hong Kong and Singapore, environmental harm was increasingly visible. In major Asian cities many stifled in garbage stench and breathed contaminated air.

Governments were increasingly willing to enact tighter pollution controls and make political commitments to environmental safeguards. Furthermore, as Asian economies boomed, governments received more tax revenues to invest in environmental clean-up. Asian countries could also secure support from several multinational institutions; besides the World Bank and IMF, the United Nations Center on Transnational Corporation (UNCTC) investigated measures to encourage and mobilize transnational development. Major concerns were protection of the atmosphere, land resources and conservation of biological diversity. Environmental policies and programs were as sophisticated as those dealing with health and safety issues. In an alert report, ASEAN stressed the importance of air quality in Asia; it recommended that the Pollutant Standards Index (PSI), developed by the U.S. Environmental Protection Agency, be adopted by all member countries. The Asian Development Bank established an ad hoc program (1992–94) to remedy environmental damage. Support was provided as loans, standby loans, technical assistance programs for water pollution control, river cleaning, urban water supply and sewerage and waste water treatment projects in Southeast Asian countries.

Waste Management's Market Entry Strategies in Asia

WMI was pursuing Asian opportunities from a strong foothold in Western Europe. In developed countries it sought to acquire well-established players and continue to provide services under their names. However, in developing Asian countries, such companies did not exist; local competitors were typically small and offered few environmental services. WMI essentially had to start from scratch.

Key Issues

WMI's Asian focus was motivated by rapid regional growth. Waste Management's first international project (1970s), was a unique investment opportunity in Saudi Arabia. Highly positive cash flows from that project helped finance acquisitions in the U.S. "Our strategy is not country specific, but region specific," said Gregory Fertile. "We respond to opportunities with the highest profit potential." Nevertheless, WMI considered itself a conservative company. Despite alluring profit potential, it only entered markets fulfilling certain criteria set by top management.

First, the project had to be large. Since WMI would operate mainly in the public sector in Asia, governments were principal customers. Vying for new government contracts required significant investment of time and money, so the effort was only worthwhile if the expected return was substantial.

Second, WMI must identify a suitable local partner. Local partners (e.g., construction companies, influential members of the ruling family) typically had no knowledge or expertise in waste management, but brought valuable contacts with government authorities and potential industrial customers; they were also familiar with local business practices. In addition, local company involvement was often required by Asian governments. WMI only aligned with a local partner when WMI was majority owner and reaped the majority of profits to compensate for the risks of technology transfer. If these requirements were not fulfilled, WMI did not participate.

Third, the regulatory environment in a specific country must be suitable: environmental laws had to be established and strictly enforced. "If companies were not forced to take care of their waste, they would simply dump it into the next river or ocean," said Fertile.

Fourth, the environment for developing new business had to be attractive. WMI was not contemplating the Russian or Eastern European markets. Although Eastern Europe's pollution problem would make it an attractive market in the future, WMI believed that, in the near term, the region would be unable to support business development or generate sufficient finance for environmental clean-up.

Finally, convertibility of the local currency was of primary importance. Restrictions on profit repatriation or high socio-economic country risk were unacceptable to WMI.

Getting the Contract

Once Waste Management decided to enter a new market, it might win contracts in two ways. First, Asian governments might ask WMI to bid for a particular project. However, since Asian authorities were inexperienced with environmental issues, project requirements were often insufficient. Consequently, WMI spent significant time counseling and giving advice to governments on how to improve environmental protection efforts. Similar activities were undertaken by WMI's international competitors. Local governments selected issues from various proposals to form a new public offer and asked companies to rebid. This process usually took two to three years. If the project was very sophisticated and only WMI had the expertise to provide all required services, it could set almost any price. If, however, the project could be completed by several companies, competitive pricing was crucial. Actual bidding was divided into two steps: Step 1 prequalified and screened interested companies based on the match between their skills and needed services; Step 2 awarded the project to the lowest bidder.

Second, WMI might set up a local development office, staffed with one or two people, to establish contacts with government authorities and potential industrial customers. To foster the basis for environmentally friendly legislation and behavior, WMI tried to educate governments, major polluters, waste producers and the general public. Marketing persons set up contacts; when the opportunity for a new project arose, a management team was called in. This process was time consuming; for example, it took several years to win a chemical waste project, then five to seven years to build. Observers estimated 80% of public offers were won by foreign companies; WMI won about 50%. However, it had to pay salespeople and incur costs of submitting proposals, up to US$8–10 million for the most complicated projects. A project's duration varied according to type (e.g., garbage collection, chemical waste plant, landfill). Elapsed time contract extension bid was also case specific.

Once a contract was won, WMI often trained local people to make them familiar with the technology. This U.S.-based on-the-job training was expensive. Frequently, newly highly qualified people were wooed away by competitors. To diminish turnover, WMI established a lucrative incentive system; it also increasingly pursued decentralization, transferring country responsibilities to local management who decided on WMI expansion.

Financing the Project

Since large projects needed significant capital, bank financing via loans was fairly difficult for WMI to secure. Although WMI helped Third World countries cope with environmental problems, it received no funding from the World Bank or IMF. Projects were primarily financed from existing cash flow or through public stock offers and bonds; local partners occasionally participated in the investment.

Competition

The future East Asian market for environmental clean-up technology was estimated at US$300 billion. Although attractive to many players, few dedicated environmental service companies had the technology and resources to expand to Asia. However, many engineering, heavy industry, construction and power firms had significant experience in large scale undertakings; they were trying to leverage this experience into waste management. Others attempted to expand environmental niches developed elsewhere. Still others formed alliances to offer more encompassing services. Local competitors were present, but lack of technology minimized their influence.

American companies had a distinct advantage in global markets since they had most experience with environmental regulations. However, increased environmental concerns in Mexico and South and Central America, offered significant opportunities closer to home. European firms had experience but were battling recession and exploring Eastern European opportunities. Australian firms had proximity advantages and regulatory experience but were in a deep recession since 1988. WMI had difficulty securing specific data on waste management companies operating in Asia; the market was so new and most competitors only revealed information required by law. Furthermore, many organizations in waste management were subsidiaries of larger corporations (Table 4).

The Hong Kong Model

The Hong Kong project was the largest of its kind that WMI had undertaken. When asked: Why choose Hong Kong to break into Asia? Gregory Fertile emphatically stated:

> A country must meet three criteria before Waste Management will enter its market: strong economy, stable government and a currency freely convertible into hard currencies and easy to be repatriated. Economically, Hong Kong has sustained tremendous growth in the past 15 years; GDP has grown 300%, population increased by 30%. In 1997, the territory will be unified with China. Politically, Hong Kong's situation was questionable in 1989 with turmoil in Beijing and union with China only eight years away. But China is committed to gradual reforms; so, the transition will likely be smooth. The Hong Kong dollar is pegged at 7.78 to the U.S. dollar, has fluctuated little since inception of the linked rate policy (1983) and is freely convertible; no regulations hamper inward or outward remittance of capital or profits.

Table 4: Competitive Environment

Country	Company	Activities
Australia	Cleanaway	– diverse waste management services – largest in Europe and Australia
Canada	Laidlaw	– diverse waste management services – one of the largest in North America – recent involvement in Asia
France	Bouygues	– civil engineering – experienced in waste water – established internationally – much Asian experience
	Generate	– very experienced in waste water – large presence in Asia
Germany	Edelhoff	– diverse waste management services – large European player – focus on former East Germany and Eastern Europe
	Otto	– diverse waste management services – large European player – focus on former East Germany and Eastern Europe
U.K.	Attwoods	– diverse waste management services – large in U.K. and Europe – recent involvement in Asia
U.S.	Bechtel	– environment engineering – largest in the U.S. – presently involved in Asia
	Browning-Ferris	– diverse waste management services – one of the largest in North America – recent involvement in Asia
	WMX	– diverse waste management services – largest in the world – recent involvement in Asia

High demand for environmental services is also evident. The territory's industrial and other wastes have increased by 500% in the past 15 years. Two industries Hong Kong relies on, manufacturing and shipping, are two of the largest polluters. No government regulations governed hazardous waste disposal. Firms disposed of chemical waste by dumping it into sewers or directly in the sea. Victoria Harbor, surrounding nearly all of Hong Kong, has become a toxic waste dumping ground. Hong Kong also has geographic advantages; it is easily accessible and borders China. As an international hub, it is highly visible. Massive environmental problems and small size make it perfect showcasing WMI's many services.

How WMI Established Itself in Hong Kong?

Fertile explained: "The key to success in our overseas business is to take time and choose the right local partner. The partner must be an established company with a solid reputation and, most importantly, must have the knowledge and experience of working with the local government."

After searching for a year, WMI chose Citic Pacific and Kin Change Besser as partners. Citic Pacific, an arm of the Chinese government based in Hong Kong, acquired a 20% interest. Kin Change Besser, a Hong Kong-based group, took 10%. WMI renamed its Asian group, Pacific Waste Management, and retained 70%. Fertile said:

> The group needed a name, easily translated into Cantonese, that conveyed commitment to Hong Kong's environment. This was a major concern because a previous project in Saudi Arabia named its subsidiary, "Waste Management – Saudi Pritchard." In Arabic this meant, Saudi Pritchard the waste management company. Enviropace was chosen. In Cantonese and English, it conveyed environmental commitment.

How Enviropace Sold the Idea?

Fertile noted: "Victoria Harbor surrounds Hong Kong. The people and its government had to be made aware of the magnitude of this environmental problem. We had to assist in making people aware of the dangers around them and how these dangers could be avoided." The first step was pinpointing the magnitude of the problem and developing a solution to counter the environmental devastation. Next came an education campaign. Pamphlets were distributed to government officials, firms creating hazardous waste and the general public. Dialogue was established with government officials. Partly as a result, in 1989 the government drew up an environmental plan to stop gross pollution. Pollution control ordinances and regulations were enacted and would be enforced rigorously.

The new government focus was best described by Chris Patten, Governor of Hong Kong:

> By Hong Kong's normal standards of success, the environment is the one striking failure. We may have the tallest and finest buildings in Asia, but right next to them, we have a harbor into which we discharge 1.5 million cubic meters of untreated sewage and industrial waste every day. We may have some of the best natural parks in the world, but we dump 1,200 cubic meters of livestock waste into our rivers and streams each day. This daily discharge of filth has poisoned rivers and streams; almost extinguished marine life in the harbor; and become a serious hazard to public health. It has to stop.

The framework was established; Enviropace had to demonstrate to the government it possessed the savvy and know-how to tackle this enormous challenge.

The Facility and Operation

Explained Fertile: "This will be the most comprehensive waste management facility in the world and will be completed in a two-year time frame, January 1993." The plan called for construction of a US$130 million integrated waste treatment plant on Tsing Yi island. The contract ran for 15 years; it spanned Hong Kong's transfer from Britain to China. The facility broke down chemicals by burning, separating and adding neutralizing agents. Its purpose-built high temperature incinerator destroyed organic wastes (e.g., spent polymers, solvents) that could not be recycled. Oily waste was treated in an oil-water separator; reclaimed oil was used as fuel for the incinerator. Chemical and physical processes (lime dosing and filters) treated inorganic matter accounting for 70% of waste. Whenever possible, materials were recycled and recovered. Prime candidates for recycling were copper etching solutions from printed circuit board factories and organic solvents from the electronics industry.

One of the greatest challenges facing Enviropace was waste collection and transportation. Unlike the U.S. and most European countries, where waste was generally produced by large facilities and transported on adequate road systems for disposal, waste producers in Hong Kong tended to be small companies located in cramped, congested areas. Enviropace developed a quasi just-in-time pick-up system. It delivered empty containers (20–200 liters) to factories and picked them up a few days later. Enviropace used a purpose-built 650-ton barge to pick up oil-contaminated and chemical-contaminated water from container ships in Victoria Harbor and delivered waste direct to the facility. Initially, costing US$25 million annually to operate (increasing with volume), the waste center was designed to evolve as Hong Kong's industry changed. Enviropace was incentivized by the government based on hazardous material treated. The government estimated it would pay on average US$25–65 million each year for the contract's duration.

Avoiding the Fatal Flaw

Said Fertile: "If we want this technologically unique project to succeed we must do everything possible to avoid the fatal flaw; this has been our philosophy during the entire project." He explained some of the problems:

> We had to take our time throughout; from choosing a partner to planning the facility. This is the only comprehensive hazardous waste management facility of its kind in the world. So, there could be no room for error in planning and all segments had to be completed on schedule. The task sequencing system worked remarkably well. As one group accomplished its unique mission, another would join and perform its specialty and so on. The marketing team evaluated the problem, devised the solution and won the contract. The construction team built the facility to specification on budget and on time. We had to ensure the government would create and enforce environmental regulations. What is the use of having the most technologically advanced facility in the world if no one uses it?

So far about 9,000 chemical waste producers have registered with the Environmental Protection Department as required by law. The maximum penalty for failing to register is a US$25,000 fine and six months in jail. The Enviropace consortium will be the first licensed waste collector/transporter. We needed qualified personnel to operate the facility. Because it was the first facility of its kind in Asia, individuals with the necessary operating experience were not available. We sent all new management personnel to the U.S. for specific training. Back in Hong Kong, they were being lured away by other companies realizing the value of their training. Enviropace constructed an incentive pay structure which stopped defections.

Fertile now pondered his problem. Where should WMI go now? Asia sounded very promising, but:

- Which Asian countries should he choose? What do the various countries need?
- What should be Waste Management's competitive advantage to make it successful in Asia?
- Were there any ways to pursue a global strategy?

Exhibit 1: Waste Management – Consolidated Income Statement, 1990–92 (US$)

	1990	1991	1992
Revenue	6,034,406	7,550,914	8,661,027
Operating expenses	3,997,720	5,165,319	5,945,762
Special charges	296,000	219,900	
Selling and administrative expenses	821,202	910,935	1,048,047
Goodwill amortization	47,460	61,682	77,144
Gains from stock transactions of subsidiaries	12,755	(38,046)	(263,489)
Interest expense	(40,193)	(15,470)	(191)
Interest income	110,782	168,558	223,052
Minority interest and sundry (income) expense, net	(17,209)	29,837	70,083
Income before income taxes	1,173,174	1,027,899	1,398,412
Provision for income taxes	463,865	421,576	477,237
Income before extraordinary item and cumulative effect of accounting changes	709,309	606,323	921,175
Net income	684,762	606,323	850,036

Exhibit 2:   Waste Management – Consolidated Balance Sheet, 1991, 1992 (US$)

	1991	1992
Current assets		
Cash	101,999	6,473
Short-term investments	120,149	61,599
Accounts receivable, less reserves	1,434,442	1,574,798
Employee receivable	12,691	16,396
Parts and supplies	114,522	126,594
Cost and estimated earnings in excess of billings on uncompleted contracts	111,541	379,841
Prepaid expenses	249,300	342,841
Total current assets	2,144,644	2,508,372
Property and equipment, at cost		
Land, primarily disposal sites	2,748,758	3,048,834
Buildings	959,199	1,101,827
Vehicles and equipment	5,322,665	6,141,322
Leasehold improvements	86,081	90,692
Less – accumulated depreciation	(2,147,228)	(2,624,472)
Total property and equipment, net	6,699,475	7,758,203
Other assets	3,728,191	3,847,605
Total assets	12,572,310	14,114,180
Current liabilities		
Portion of long-term debt payable within one year	512,126	597,674
Accounts payable	668,983	724,418
Accrued expenses	688,404	852,436
Unearned revenue	244,484	205,044
Total current liabilities	2,113,997	2,379,572
Deferred items (income taxes, investment credit, other)	1,663,543	1,823,565
Long-term debt, less portion payable within one year	3,782,973	4,312,511
Minority interest in subsidiaries	878,697	1,278,887
Stockholder's equity		
Common stock	493,621	496,203
Additional paid-in capital	722,351	708,296
Retained earnings	2,957,667	3,354,624
Less – treasury stock	–	204,490
1988 employee stock ownership plan	40,539	34,988
Total stockholders' equity	4,133,100	4,319,645
Total liabilities and stockholders' equity	12,572,310	14,114,180

Exhibit 3: WMX Technologies – Array of Services by Industry

	Res.	Const.	Comm.	Inst.	Agri.	Gov.	Ind.	Util.	Trans.	WP
Ash treatment and reuse		X	X			X	X			X
Biosolids management	X		X		X	X	X			X
City cleaning	X	X	X	X		X	X	X	X	X
Clean air technologies and services		X	X	X		X	X	X		X
Cogenerations		X	X	X		X	X	X		X
Composing	X	X	X	X	X	X	X	X		X
Demolition		X	X	X		X	X	X	X	X
Disposal of solid, hazardous and special wastes	X	X	X	X	X	X	X	X	X	X
Environmental/infrastructure/process consulting		X	X	X		X	X	X	X	X
Environmental/infrastructure/process engineering		X	X	X		X	X	X	X	X
Hazardous/nuclear remediation	X	X	X		X	X	X	X	X	X
Hazardous waste identification	X	X	X	X	X	X	X	X	X	X
Hazardous waste reduction	X		X		X	X	X	X	X	
Hazardous waste services and treatment	X	X	X	X	X	X	X	X	X	X
Industrial cleaning		X	X	X		X	X	X	X	X
Marine/infrastructure/industrial construction		X	X	X	X	X	X	X	X	X
Materials recovery/hazardous and non-hazardous	X	X	X	X	X	X	X	X	X	X
Medical waste services			X	X		X	X	X		
Nuclear products/services			X		X	X	X	X	X	X
On-site waste treatment technologies		X	X	X	X	X	X	X	X	X
Plant maintenance		X	X			X	X	X		
Portable sanitation	X	X	X	X	X	X	X	X	X	X
Project management		X	X	X	X	X	X	X	X	X
Radioactive waste processing		X				X	X	X		
Recyling; residential and commercial collection	X	X	X	X	X	X	X	X	X	X
Scaffolding	X	X	X	X		X	X	X	X	X
Solid waste reduction	X	X	X	X	X	X	X	X	X	X
Special event services	X	X	X	X		X		X		X
Specialty nuclear services						X	X	X		
Street sweeping; temporary fencing; transfer	X	X	X	X	X	X	X	X	X	X
Thermal destruction	X	X		X	X	X	X	X	X	X
Transportation	X		X	X		X	X	X		
Trash-to-energy	X		X	X	X	X	X	X	X	X
Waste minimization	X	X	X	X	X	X	X	X	X	X
Water and waste water treatment	X	X	X	X	X	X	X	X	X	X

Legend: Res. = Residential; Const. = Construction; Comm. = Commercial; Inst. = Institutional; Agri. = Agriculture; Gov. = Government; Ind. = Industrial; Util. = Utilities; Trans. = Transportation; WP = Waste Processing

Asian Country Profiles[2]

India

Environmental situation and needs. The environmental situation continues to deteriorate due to rapid population, industrial and economic growth. Concern with and commitment to environmental issues is growing, in government and industry. The market for industrial waste treatment equipment (1991: US$100 million) is estimated to expand (1995: US$245 million). Three-year estimated average annual total market real growth rate is 30%.

Competition. Local companies are numerous but small; they lack capabilities for more advanced waste treatments; these must be imported. American companies have already established a strong foothold in the Indian market.

Legislation. The Indian government recently established several new environmental protection regulations. Main legal instruments for pollution control are: Water (Prevention and Control of Pollution) Act, 1974; Air (Prevention and Control of Pollution) Act, 1981; Environment Protection Act, 1986; Hazardous Chemical Rules, 1989; and Hazardous Wastes (Management and Handling) Rules. The Government's Central Pollution Control Board has established Minimum National Standards (MINAS) for various polluting industries. To help companies comply with these regulations, the government is receptive to industry pleas for fiscal incentives for installation of pollution control equipment and waste disposal. Within the scope of the Asian Development Bank Operational Program (1992–94) US$600,000 is provided for a river clean-up action plan to finance technical assistance.

Economic and political situation. The government has recently restructured and liberalized India's investment, trade and economic policies; the rupee is now convertible. The business climate is more favorable to foreign firms.

Indonesia

Environmental situation and needs. One side-effect of Indonesia's growth is a negative environmental impact, in particular in cities with high population densities and/or regions with substantial manufacturing. Demand for pollution control has increased substantially since 1990, in part because of implementation of the Clean River Program (PROKASIH) in eight provinces, including 17 rivers. This program concentrates on decreasing pollution from industries that contribute seriously to decreased river quality. Demand for water pollution equipment in 1991 was estimated at US$340 million, 60% up from 1990. A new air pollution control program, "Langit Biru" (blue sky), scheduled to begin in late 1993, will "crack down" on pollution from private

---

[2] Source: National Trade Data Bank.

motor vehicles and industry. Total environmental equipment imports increased from US$22.1 million (1990) to US$44.6 million (1991).

Competition. Local companies are now capable of providing approximately 60% of equipment for air and water pollution control; the remainder is imported. Technological capabilities of local Indonesian manufacturers have increased considerably through technology transfer from the U.S., Europe, Japan and other foreign partners. Examples include P.T. Basuki with Keller Lufttechnik (Germany); C.V. Lunto Prima with Farr (U.S.). Although technology levels of local firms are rising, they remain heavily dependent on engineering support from foreign partners.

Legislation. Since 1982, the government issued various regulations to control, or achieve sustainable development of, the environment. The most recent is decree No. 03/MenKLH/11/1991 from the Minister of Population and the Environment; limits on pollution levels for industry are clearly defined. In June 1990, the New Environmental Impact Management Agency (BAPEDAL) was formed by Presidental decree No. 23 as an implementation agency for pollution control. BAPEDAL assumed responsibility for programs related to environmental pollution, environmental destruction, hazardous waste management and environmental impact assessment.

Economic and political situation. Indonesia is growing rapidly. In 1991, GDP was US$115 billion; it was expected to grow 6% in 1992. Governmental implementation of deregulation and debureaucratization reforms (1987) is improving the environment for foreign business interests.

Korea

Environmental situation and needs. Korea's solid waste is 89% landfilled, only 2% is incinerated. Disposal of solid, municipal, industrial and hazardous waste is a major priority in the re-energized environmental field. The government considers at least six more hazardous solid waste treatment plants should be constructed by 1996. Korea is particularly aware of medical waste treatment; medical refuse has grown exponentially as disposables are used to limit spread of infectious diseases. Korea's 603 hospitals, 107,720 beds and 12,137 doctor's offices/clinics, produce 1,200 tons of medical waste monthly; large volumes have been illegally landfilled, stirring public concern.

Competition. U.S. firms have an enormous competitive advantage because of traditional ties. A high official of the Environmental Management Corporation (EMC) stated it is eagerly seeking U.S. technologies in waste tire recycling, advancement treatment (third stage) of industrial waste water and hazardous solid waste treatment. This would also decrease the chronic trade deficit with Japan. Besides efforts to acquire U.S. technologies, EMC is considering sending engineers to the U.S.

Legislation. To monitor environmental policy, the government set up EMC; it constructs and operates industrial waste water and hazardous solid waste treatment plants. But laws do not force firms to take their waste back. Korean land use and management law prohibits construction of medical incineration plants to deal with medical waste, but an amendment is about to be passed.

Economic and political situation. Korea's economic expansion is among the most rapid in the world; its stable government encourages foreign firms to do business in Korea.

Malaysia

Environmental situation and needs. As the Malaysian government tightens enforcement of pollution control regulations, the market for related products and services will grow rapidly. Currently, pollution control equipment and services center on air and water pollution and disposal of solid and hazardous waste. The market for pollution control equipment and services is expanding quickly with increased requirements for sophisticated products and higher levels of technology. Estimated average annual total market real growth rate is 27% over the next three years.

Competition. Many foreign suppliers are in the pollution control industry and competition is keen. The largest foreign suppliers are from Singapore and Japan; others are from Germany, Italy, Denmark, Switzerland, Canada, Belgium, Korea and France. Some are entering joint ventures. For example, Biotem (Belgium) has a joint venture on anaerobic digestion technology with a Malaysian firm.

Legislation. Since 1989, regulations to control pollution have become stricter, especially water and air pollution. However, the government has been criticized for poor enforcement; in the past ten years, an average of only 40 citations yearly was issued by the Department of Environment (DOE). Growing pressure from a better informed and more environmentally aware public will lead to change; tougher enforcement is expected in the next three years. The government is investing large sums in pollution control. In 1991, local authorities spent about US$68 million on solid waste disposal, almost 80% of some local councils' operating revenues. In addition, the federal government allocated over US$10 million for research on solid waste disposal and training local authorities. Beginning 1992, it will invest over US$180 million in sewerage projects.

Economic and political situation. Since independence (1957), Malaysia has become a role model for developing countries. Good political stability has created an environment where economic forces have flourished. The next five-year plan (1991–96) calls for an annual growth rate of 7.5% to raise Malaysia's nominal output from US$42 billion to US$75 billion by 1996.

The Philippines

Environmental situation and needs. In the last few years, the government has turned serious attention to the environment. Its Medium Term Development Plan (1987–92) explicitly states government environmental policies; the recent Philippine Strategy for Sustainable Development stresses the need to view economic growth and environmental protection as interdependent and mutually compatible.

Competition. Many local companies are active, but small. The infrastructure is not present for the locals to build more sophisticated waste treatments. American companies already dominate the market.

Legislation. The responsibility for implementing governmental environment strategies and policies rests with the Department of Environment and Natural Resources (DENR). DENR's Environmental Management Bureau spearheads the government's efforts to protect its people and resources from the growing menace of environmental degradation. Aside from DENR, other government agencies concerned with environmental protection and management are Laguna Lake Development Authority, Department of Health, Philippine Coast Guard, Human Settlements Development Corporation and the National Water Resources Council. Although several agencies are involved in environmental protection, compliance with environmental regulations is low due to lack of technically qualified personnel, laboratory facilities, pollution monitoring equipment and enforcement mechanisms. This deficiency has led to rapid growth of non-governmental organizations (NGOs) concerned with the environment. NGOs are very active in raising environmental issues, leading protests against polluting firms and planned projects with polluting effects, and monitoring the environmental impact of projects. These developments augur well for purchases of pollution control equipment and services.

Economic and political situation. Assuming daily power outages are reduced by third quarter 1993 as predicted, the economy may experience a modest turnaround after two years of stagnant growth. Philippine economic fundamentals have improved due to control of the fiscal deficit, reduction of inflation to single digit and interest rate moderation. President Ramos appears investor-friendly and reform-oriented but has had difficulty securing support for his economic agenda in the Senate. Reconciliation efforts have helped reduce political unrest but law and order remains unsettled; chronic power shortages and inadequate infrastructure restrain industrial expansion. These factors are key obstacles in attracting more foreign investment and achieving sustainable economic growth.

Singapore

Environmental situation and needs. Singapore's small land area, high population density and rapid industrialization brought environmental issues to the national consciousness. Although environmental awareness is prevalent, Singapore is still at least five years behind the U.S. in environmental technology. The most promising subsectors (estimated 1993 total market size [US$]) are: filters, $25 million; pollution control equipment, $50 million; solid waste management equipment, $40 million.

Competition. Domestic production of industrial waste treatment equipment is relatively small. Few firms produce environmental equipment and these are so small they represent minimal competition. Total environmental product imports increased US$36 million from 1990 to 1991; U.S. imports increased in the past two years. Singapore's private and public sectors are still actively seeking foreign partners to join forces with local firms to meet environmental control needs, products and services. Local importers look to the U.S. as their main supply source. Several companies in Singapore deal with industrial waste equipment. Usually, equipment is imported by distributors who sell directly to factories or dealers. Obviously, the middleman can be eliminated and U.S. firms could sell directly to factories or regionally-based MNCs, or even set up their own distribution.

Legislation. To combat growing pollution, in 1972 the Singapore government established the Ministry of the Environment (ENV). ENV acts as environmental authority, regulatory body and source of contract tenders for odor control, sludge treatment and incineration. Subsequent legislation for industrial waste was Trade Effluent Regulations (1976) and Environmental Public Health Regulations (Toxic Industrial Waste) (1988). According to the Ministry of the Environment Annual Report (1990), factories discharging acid trade effluent are required to install continuous pH monitoring and recording systems. Singapore is a duty free port; only 4% of all goods imported are taxed. There are no trade barriers; the Singapore government does not interfere in relationships between U.S. manufacturers and Singapore agents and/or distributors. The Pollution Control Department (PCD) must evaluate and approve new environmental control equipment. The PCD is also responsible for reviewing factory plans of new industries that might produce waste or pollution.

Economic and political situation. Strong and stable government.

Thailand

Environmental situation and needs. Recent double-digit growth of industrial output is expected to continue into the 21st century; already, industry's share of GDP is over twice agriculture's. Thailand is becoming a NIC. Traffic congestion, water shortages, solid waste, air, water and noise pollution problems have noticeably worsened during the last few years of rapid industrialization. The growth rate of industrial pollution follows the rate of industrial growth: 1970, 8%; early 1980s, 10%; late 1980s, 13%. Thai industry's high profitability suggests a degree of affordability for pollution-control expenditures without significant loss of international competitiveness.

The Bangkok area contains 52% of industry (76% of GDP); such concentration of industrial waste in a limited space overloads the environment's natural assimilative capacity. However, this concentration implies economies of scale in pollution control and treatment. Engineering Science Inc. has projected (1989) that hazardous waste generated by the manufacturing sector will reach 1.9 million tons in 1991, 5.7 million tons by 2010.

Competition. Virtually no environmental services are provided in Thailand. Bangkok does not even have a sewer system; household waste is dumped at Soi Onnuch where a waste mountain grows bigger every day. Only local companies have tried offering waste management services. General Finance and Securities spent 10 million baht on two pilot projects to manage home waste in Chiang Mai and Phuket. So far, neither project is commercially viable since the firm cannot get big enough concessions. Besides, public awareness must be created since no one is ready to pay for environmental services. Foreign companies are dissuaded from intervening.

Legislation. Both environmental awareness and environmental legislation (setting of standards) have advanced considerably in recent years, but enforcement is lagging. In choosing an appropriate pollution-control instrument, the government has considered the type of industrial waste and the scale and geographic distribution of industry.

Economic and political situation. According to the U.S. Embassy, U.S. investors are very positive about their operations and are generally reinvesting heavily. The government implemented several reform measures (e.g., trade tariff reductions, corporate tax reduction). Obstacles to sustained rapid growth are infrastructure constraints (e.g., telecommunications, roadway, electricity generators) and shortages of engineers and skilled personnel.

Taiwan

Environmental situation and needs. Taiwan has one of the world's highest population densities (573 people per sq. km.) and is increasingly urban and industrial. This evolution has resulted in rapid increase in solid waste; environmental damage to the island is now visible. According to Environmental Protection Administration (EPA) estimates, municipal waste will increase by 6% p.a. from 7.6m metric tons (MTs) (1991) to 9.7m MTs (1996). Industrial waste is likely to grow at 3% to 5% p.a. Industrial waste amounts to 30m MTs p.a., 10% hazardous. About 60% of waste is disposed by regular means: 85% landfills; 4% incinerators; 1% composting sites; 10% other disposal forms. Owing to increased waste, Taiwan is running out of available land for burial. The EPA has developed a five-year target plan (July 1, 1992 to December 1996, Green Plan): 23 new incinerators built; 722 collection and disposal vehicles purchased; 60 landfills constructed; one compost site developed. Areas with strongest growth potential in waste include hospitals and the petrochemical and pulp and paper industries.

Competition. Taiwan has 370 firms in pollution control equipment; however, most of the waste market is covered by foreign suppliers. American firms dominate the public sector; Japanese equipment is preferred by private firms because of lower prices, geographic proximity and better customer service. Major active American firms include Westinghouse, Foster Wheeler, Agden Martin and American Ref-Suel. Principal Japanese firms are Mitsubishi, Takuma, Hitachi, Yamamoto and Toshiba. Germany is represented by Fichtner, Schench and Katec.

Legislation. The EPA is currently completing a legislative framework embracing 19 laws and 53 regulations for control of air, water, noise and soil pollution, toxic chemicals, vibration and waste disposal; inspections and law enforcement are becoming more rigorous. The EPA has developed a blacklist of 15,000 air and water polluting plants. If these factories do not install proper control facilities within four years, daily penalties will be NTD 60,000. Government policy is to privatize the industrial waste treatment industry. To encourage private investment in pollution control, Taiwanese authorities provide attractive incentives and financial supports to polluting companies. Incentives comprise free import duties, investment tax reductions and low interest loans.

Economic and political situation. Taiwan is politically stable and economically booming.

Appendix Table: Market for Environmental Products

India (US$ millions)	1990	1991	1992	Est. 3-year real growth (p.a.)
Import market	27	30	29	20%
Local production	70	78	75	–
Exports	7	8	7	–
Total market	90	100	97	30%
Imports from U.S.	7	8	10	20%

Indonesia (US$ millions)	1990	1991	1992	Est. 3-year real growth (p.a.)
Import market	73.6	84.1	146.6	35%
Local production	153.4	180.2	304.6	–
Exports	0.4	0.6	0.8	–
Total market	226.36	263.7	450.7	30%
Imports from U.S.	25.5	25.6	36.7	30%

Korea (US$ millions)	1990	1991		Est. 3-year real growth (p.a.)
Import market	n/a	n/a		n/a
Local production	n/a	n/a		
Exports	n/a	n/a		
Total market	n/a	n/a		n/a
Imports from U.S.	60.5	67.1		9%

Malaysia (US$ millions)	1990	1991	1992	Est. 3-year real growth (p.a.)
Import market	27.8	42.4	61.5	30%
Local production	0	0	0	–
Exports	1.4	2.8	4	25%
Total market	26.4	39.6	57.5	27%
Imports from U.S.	8.9	10.9	12.8	17%

Philippines (US$ millions)	1992	1993 (est.)		Est. 3-year real growth (p.a.)
Import market	11.7	14.0		30%
Local production	0	0		–
Exports	0	0		–
Total market	11.7	14.0		20%
Imports from U.S.	1.9	2.1		15%

Singapore (US$ millions)	1990	1991	1992	Est. 3-year real growth (p.a.)
Import market	228	275	144	–
Local production	20	33	19	–
Exports	87	113	61	–
Total market	161	195	102	–
Imports from U.S.	68	79	43	7%

Taiwan (US$ millions)	1990	1991	1992	Est. 3-year real growth (p.a.)
Import market	36.0	49.6	88.4	25%
Local production	2.1	4.5	11.1	–
Exports	0.7	1.2	1.3	–
Total market	37.4	52.9	98.2	20–25%
Imports from U.S.	10.7	15.7	47.9	23%

Map of Bangladesh

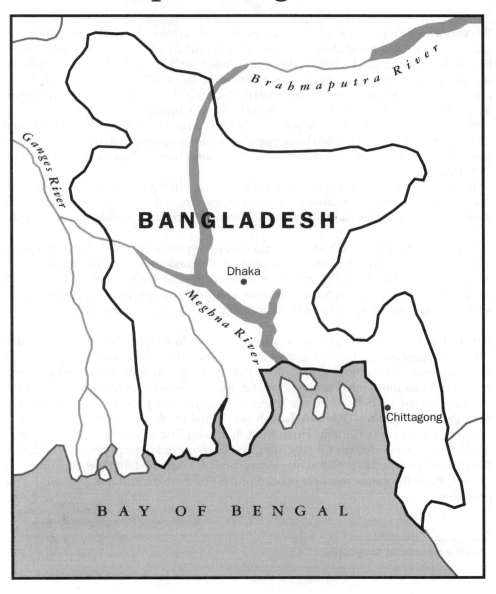

Bangladesh Overview[1]

Background. Situated in southern Asia, Bangladesh is almost entirely surrounded by India, apart from a small shared border with Myanmar and a southern coast on the Bay of Bengal. The 123.1 million (1996) population (98% Bengali), living on a 144,000 sq. km. land area (about the size of Wisconsin, U.S.) (67% arable), coastline 580 kilometers, speak mainly Bengla (official) (95%); English is widely spoken. The majority are Muslim (85%), Hindu (10%); Buddhist and Christian (1%) are minorities. In 1998, Islam became the state religion. Only Dhaka (capital) (3.6 million) (1991) and Chittagong (1.6 million) (1996) have populations over one million. Bangladesh has a tropical monsoon climate, average temperatures range from 19°C (October to March) to 29°C (May to September).

Bangladesh is mostly a wide, low plain carved out by five major river systems (including the Ganges). Because of its location and tropical monsoon climate, Bangladesh is frequently the victim of natural disasters including floods, cyclones, tidal waves and droughts.

The country is governed by a prime minister (five-year term) and Cabinet; the president (five-year term) is nominal head of state. The unicameral Jatiya Sangsad comprises 300 directly elected members and 30 additional seats reserved for women elected by parliamentary vote. The judiciary comprises a Supreme Court composed of a High Court and an Appellate Division that hears High Court appeals.

Political. Britain ruled Bangladesh as part of Imperial India from the 18th century until 1947 when East Bengal became part of Pakistan. Bangladesh became independent in 1971 following a rebellion against West Pakistan's dominance that developed into civil war; India intervened against Pakistan forces. Three years of parliamentary democracy ended in 1975 when the national founder and president, Sheik Mujibar Rahman, was assassinated. Bangladesh was ruled by the military for the next 15 years; in a 1982 coup, General Hussain Mohammed Ershad seized power, imposed martial law, suspended the Constitution, and pronounced himself president. In 1991, Bangladesh returned to parliamentary government. The president is the constitutional head of state; the prime minister is head of the government and is appointed by the president.

---

[1] People's Republic of Bangladesh.

In recent years, women have assumed powerful leadership roles in Bangladesh, a highly unusual situation for a predominantly Muslim country. In 1991, the Bangladesh National Party (BNP) came to power under the leadership of Mrs. Begum Khaleda Zia. This government brought a measure of democratic stability but faced strong challenges from opposition parties and Muslim fundamentalists. A political impasse created by allegations of corruption and incompetence by the opposition led to Zia's resignation on March 30, 1996; a caretaker government under Mohammed Habibur Rahman governed until the June 1996 general elections. In these elections, the most peaceful in Bangladesh's history, the left-leaning Awami League, led by Sheik Rahman's daughter, Mrs. Wazed, gained power; nearly three quarters of eligible voters went to the polls.

Social. Bangladesh is one of the most densely populated countries in the world. Approximately 84% of the population lives in rural areas; village life has been important in shaping the culture and lifestyle, with family playing a central role. In 1996, life expectancy at birth was 56 years; birth rate was 28 per 1,000. About 40% (1996) of the population was 0–15 years. Family planning agencies are active in Bangladesh. In 1992, over 70% of the population attended primary school; only 2% had any post-secondary education.

Economy. Bangladesh is a member of the United Nations (UN), World Bank (WB), International Monetary Fund (IMF), World Trade Organization (WTO), Asian Development Bank (ADB) and Islamic Development Bank (IDB). Bangladesh is one of the poorest countries in the world (GNP per capita, US$230 [June 1995]). It is the world's largest exporter of jute but has recently seen difficult times in this vital industry (13% of GDP) because of the decline of jute as a world commodity. Bangladesh is burdened by a high foreign debt load, primarily owed to multilateral aid agencies (over US$20 billion since 1970; US$2.1 billion in 1994/1995). In 1993, external public debt was over US$13 billion, slightly less than half of the US$30 billion GDP (1994). Bangladesh relies heavily on foreign aid; US$2.1 billion was pledged by international aid donors in 1994/1995. In recent years, the government has tried to open up the economy by emphasizing private enterprise, encouraging foreign investment and setting up an export processing zone at Chittagong.

Agriculture (including forestry and fishery) accounts for 30.4% of GDP (66% labor force), manufacturing 9.9% (15% labor force), services 50.2% (21% labor force). Major export destinations (1993) are U.S. (33%), Germany (8%), Italy (6%); major import origins (1993) are Hong Kong (8%), Japan (7%).

The national currency, the taka (Tk), has been appreciating against the U.S. dollar since the late 1980s; in mid-1996, the exchange rate was around 42Tk = US$1. In October 1993, Bangladesh Bank (the central bank) declared the taka convertible for international payments on current account.

Bangladesh has 39 licensed banks, nationalized commercial banks, government-owned banks, private commercial banks (incorporated in Bangladesh), government-owned specialized banks (industry, agriculture, agricultural development) and foreign private banks. The small Dhaka Stock Exchange (DSE) traded just over US$1 billion in 1994. To encourage foreign direct investment, foreign investors can own 100% of equity; there are no restrictions on repatriation of profits.

Infrastructure. In 1993, electricity generating capacity was 2.4 million kWh; electricity generation reached 9 billion kWh, a very low 75 kWh per capita. Bangladesh has 6,240 kilometers of roads, 3,840 kilometers paved. In 1986, it had 2,892 kilometers of railroads. Telecommunications is underdeveloped, less than 3 telephones per 1,000 population.

Bangladesh suffers whenever India unilaterally withdraws water from the Ganges during drought seasons or releases excess water during rainy seasons. India has promised (1992) to take "positive steps" towards sharing the Ganges water.

Statistics*	June 1991	June 1997	Statistics*	June 1991	June 1997
Per capita GNP	US$179	US$283	Infant mortality/1,000	108	102
GDP growth	6.2%	4.7%	Life expectancy (yrs)	n/a	56
Savings (GNP)	n/a	8%	Literacy rate	33.1%	38.0%
Inflation (CPI)	9.3%	5.7%	People per tel.	n/a	435
Foreign debt (in billion)	US$10.8	US$16.4	People per doctor	6,219	5,264
Pop. (million)	116	123.1	People per TV	n/a	336
Urban pop.	n/a	16%	Calorie intake (cals)	n/a	2,246
Pop. growth	2.7%	2.2%			

*Secured from *Asiaweek*.

Case 3

Social Marketing Company, Bangladesh

Noel Capon
Graduate School of Business, Columbia University

In early 1995, Bob Karam, Population Services International's (PSI) country representative in Bangladesh met with Waliur (Wally) Rahman, managing director of Social Marketing Company (SMC), to discuss a series of critical decisions facing SMC. In particular they were concerned about impending brand name changes for SMC's three established oral contraceptive products and increased direct marketing competition from the Bangladesh government for contraceptives and ORSaline, SMC's anti-diarrhea rehydration product, versus SMC's retailer distribution system. Decisions also had to be made both about possible back-integration into contraceptive and ORSaline manufacture and a variety of new product opportunities.

ଚେଠଷ

Company Background[1]

Social Marketing Company, formed in 1990, was an outgrowth of the Family Planning Social Marketing Project (FPSMP) initiated in Bangladesh in 1974 by Population Services International (PSI), a Washington-based organization involved in family planning and AIDS prevention projects in several developing countries.

Founded in 1970 by Philip Harvey and Timothy Black, then graduate students in the University of North Carolina's Public Health Program, PSI's original objective was to disseminate "family planning information and marketing birth control products to people who needed to avert births but did not know where to seek the information or products." PSI's perspective was that modern, effective marketing techniques could supplement scarce medical skills and that none of the developing countries, whose

---

[1] Much of the background for this case, some verbatim, is drawn from *Population Services International: The Social Marketing Project in Bangladesh*, Harvard Business School, 9-586-013 by Professor V. Kasturi Rangan.

67

population growths posed severe economic and social problems, had sufficient medical personnel to treat the many diseases afflicting their people, let alone the resources to address birth control. Harvey, still active on PSI's board, believed that: "if contraceptive products such as pills and condoms are made the leading vehicles of family planning, the entire society would be better off."

By 1995, PSI was involved in social marketing programs in over 30 countries (e.g., Bangladesh, India, Nigeria, U.S.); in other cases PSI had handed over successful programs and infrastructure to local organizations (e.g., Sri Lanka). The FPSMP in Bangladesh was one of PSI's more successful programs; however, at end 1996, PSI's contract with SMC would terminate. In anticipation of the conclusion of PSI's contract, in 1990 SMC was incorporated as a private non-profit corporation, the largest such enterprise in the world. (See Figure 1 for SMC's organization chart.[2])

Figure 1: SMC Organization Chart

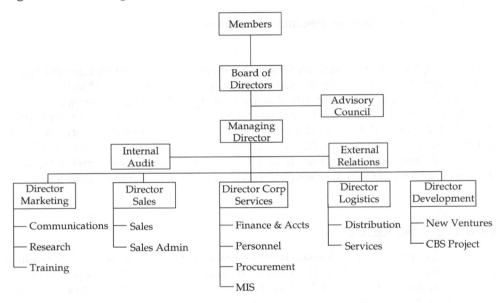

According to SMC's annual report:

Social marketing is defined as marketing products or services for social benefit rather than for profit motive. Social marketing uses the techniques for commercial marketing to secure a change in behavior that can benefit the whole society. Generally, social marketing has two components, (a) motivating people to behave in a

---

[2] The SMC board rejected an Arthur D. Little recommendation that sales and marketing be split into two separate functions.

way that benefits family, society and the nation, and (b) providing products through normal marketing channels so people can practice the desired behavior using those products.

For many years, PSI's efforts in Bangladesh focused on condoms and contraceptive pills. However, in recent years it added anti-diarrhea rehydration[3] and hygiene products (Exhibit 1). Typically, SMC received both product and operating cost subsidies from donors. Since its inception, the FPSMP was supported by USAID, a U.S. government arm. USAID supplied contraceptives (purchased from U.S. suppliers), paid PSI a fee for providing management services and subsidized a significant portion of operating expenses.[4] In 1995, USAID was in the process of reducing program support; the slack was being taken up by the European Commission (EC) and possibly the British Overseas Development Authority. One result of this donor shift was that contraceptives would now be supplied by European manufacturers rather than from the U.S. This supplier shift posed several problems for SMC.

Historically, SMC's financial performance was measured in part by the cost recovery percent, a measure of gross revenues versus product and operating costs. Cost recovery was low for both condoms and pills; it was significantly higher for ORSaline (Exhibit 2). SMC management was somewhat concerned about low cost recovery inasmuch as it competed in the market for donor funds and donors were concerned about this issue. Although 100% self-sufficiency was not possible in such a low income market, management believed that SMC should strive to cover operating costs.

More recently, SMC shifted to measuring net profit rather than cost recovery.[5] Relatedly, PSI executives argued that the only correct efficiency measure for the various contraceptive programs in Bangladesh was cost per couple year protection (CYP); on this basis SMC programs compared favorably with government programs.

Country Background

Retail Distribution

The Bangladesh economy comprised an intense network of local retail outlets owned by small scale entrepreneurs. Marketing and distribution were greatly influenced by these retailers who preferred quick inventory turns to high margins (but wanted both). Although it was difficult to secure precise numbers, in 1995, SMC products were handled by approximately 10,000 stockists and 124,000 retail outlets (approximately, pharmacies 20%, general stores (half grocery stores) 45%, "pan" kiosks 35%).

---

[3] SMC's product reversed an important symptom, dehydration; it did not cure or prevent diarrhea.
[4] Operating expenses included a substantial research budget. For 1995, SMC budgeted Tk 3.05 million (US$78,000) for several studies: product and market share, product diagnostic, consumer brand awareness audit, non-practicing couples, exploratory research and communication testing.
[5] Contraceptive costs were set at zero (products were donated); for ORSaline, product cost was set at SMC's purchase price.

Pharmacies. Located mostly in urban areas, pharmacies typically occupied 300–400 sq. ft. of space and sold an assortment of pharmaceuticals, drugs and local medicinal preparations. Most items (e.g., birth control pills) did not require a doctor's prescription. The consumer usually went to the sales counter and either asked for the product by name or described the symptoms; the salesperson often recommended a particular product or brand. After the consumer had made a decision, the salesperson (not the consumer) filled the order.

General stores. Although larger in size than the pharmacies, general stores were mostly small, independent, family-owned operations with no more than four employees (including the owner). A typical store (approximately 400–500 sq. ft.) carried 50 to 100 items. (Larger general stores were found in cities.) Store personnel assembled, measured and bagged all products. Consumers were rarely allowed into the shelf areas.

Pan kiosks. Typically 20 to 40 sq. ft., operated by one person, pan kiosks were very basic temporary enclosures at street corners or other busy locations in rural areas. Pan kiosks sold convenience items (e.g., soft drinks, aspirin, candy, cigarettes), typically 25–30 products the seller could reach from a sitting position. One of the fastest moving items was the pan, an assortment of spices wrapped in a betel leaf. Among Bangladeshi men, pan consumption was more commonplace and frequent than drinking tea or smoking cigarettes. Unlike pharmacies and general stores, pan kiosks were open until late at night; they were convenient socializing spots for men.

The Medical Care System

In 1995 Bangladesh had about 150,000 doctors; about 10,000 had formal medical education. Most of these 10,000 doctors had graduate degrees from western countries, excellent credentials, spoke fluent English and practiced in urban areas. In addition to western-trained doctors, 20,000 spiritual doctors practiced in villages. These practitioners scribbled down secret formulas, uttered hymns and asserted they invoked the power of God to treat ailments. Although unscientific in their approach, spiritual doctors were valued by their patients.

Patients were also treated by 100,000 rural medical practitioners (RMPs). Although not trained in western medicine, RMPs maintained contact with professional doctors and hospitals through a system of patient referrals. They had a practical, working knowledge of common illnesses and drugs mainly through the influence of professional doctors they respected. RMPs recommended and dispensed either local, indigenous medications or western drugs, depending on their diagnosis. Mostly making house calls, RMPs participated in village community activities and were respected and regarded as friend, philosopher and guide by their patients. Consultation was usually free, but patients were expected to buy medications from the RMP's inventory of medicines generally carried on their rounds; payment terms were flexible.

Family Planning Activity in Bangladesh

The Bangladesh government (BDG) oversaw all family planning activities. Except for directly sponsored programs, it had no financial commitment to private programs. Several programs communicated and distributed family planning products.

- The government employed 40,000 field workers who encouraged family planning through home visits; they distributed condoms and contraceptive pills for a nominal fee. Field workers were usually educated and literate; they were compensated by the government agency that employed them. Their advice and recommendations were usually strong enough to affect consumption decisions. In recent years, substantial numbers of workers were added and this "direct" distribution system started surpassing the efforts of private vendors such as SMC. In 1993, field workers visited 38% of Married Women of Reproductive Age (MWRAs), evenly split by urban and rural residence, up from 25% (23% rural, 28% urban) in 1989.
- The government provided cash incentives for the country's 10,000 trained doctors to perform clinical birth control procedures. Each sterilization procedure or IUD insertion was fully subsidized: in 1995, doctors received about US$10 for each clinical procedure; incentives to field workers were another $10.
- Volunteer organizations with 10,000 field workers, mostly promoted family planning, sponsored education and communication programs. Some organizations offered free contraceptives to the public and/or referred eligible couples to the appropriate medical facility.
- Private pharmaceutical firms marketed brands of oral contraceptive pills through licensing agreements and collaborations with European and U.S. firms; products were distributed mainly through pharmacies. To secure testimonials from professional doctors, sales forces made systematic presentations to encourage prescriptions (not legally necessary), or advice, for clients to use specific brands of oral contraceptives.
- SMC used a social marketing approach to achieve family planning. SMC had been very effective in creating awareness of birth control and a large demand for its products.

The Contraceptive Market

Population. In the 1970s, Bangladesh had a high population growth rate (mid-1970s, 2.5%).[6] Although still substantial, family planning programs were largely responsible for reducing growth rates (1991, 2.7%). Concurrently, female fertility rates were also dropping (1989–91, 4.3%; 1993–94, 3.4%).[7] In 1995, total population was 119 million; about 30 million women were capable of child bearing (Table 1). At the current growth

---

[6] This birth rate was less than the 3.5% in many African nations.
[7] Fertility rate is number of children per woman. Data from Directorate of Family Planning, Government of Bangladesh.

rate, 2030 population was expected to reach over 200 million people; the government's objective was zero population growth. Per capita income (1994) in Bangladesh was $212; economists considered it one of the poorest countries in the world. Although GNP growth was about 3% to 4% p.a., the standard of living for many Bangladeshis hovered around subsistence. About 75% of Bangladeshis lived in rural areas; the overall literacy rate was 35%, three to four times greater for males than females. In general, women were more knowledgeable about family planning than men, but men made most family purchases.

Table 1: Population Statistics

	1981	1985	1990	1995
Population (millions)	89.9	100.5	112.8	119.0
% women (15 to 49 years of age)	21.5	22.1	22.8	26.0
% married women (15 to 49 years of age)	82.5	83.0	82.0	80.8
MWRA* (millions)	15.9	18.4	21.1	25.0

*Married women of reproductive age (15–49).

Although many Bangladeshis understood the desirability of family planning, social customs (e.g., importance of sons for agricultural labor, old age care [Bangladesh did not provide for social security or state pensions for its elderly], balancing out of dowries for daughters, concern for epidemics and natural calamities [e.g., floods, tidal waves {on average 100,000 people died each year}]) and religious dogma (83% of the population were conservative Muslims) posed significant obstacles to the success and cost-effectiveness of family planning programs.[8]

Distribution. SMC's major contraceptive efforts were through traditional retail channels. Competition for condoms was minimal but not so for pills. Several commercial brands were selling well. For example, Organon was the largest selling competitor brand, priced three times higher than SMC's most expensive brand (Tk 36 versus Tk 12 per cycle).[9] In addition to retail distribution, condoms and pills were distributed direct to consumers by government and non-profit entities; government distribution of pills was more successful than for condoms.

SMC operated almost exclusively in retail distribution; it had a small direct distribution pilot project in three thanas in eastern Bangladesh, near the Indian border, 100 kilometers from Dhaka.[10] Rather than use salaried field workers, the SMC approach involved household-level distribution of SMC products (condoms, oral con-

---

[8] Muslims practice Islam based on the Koran. Although some Islamic scholars have argued that the Koran does not take a position on family planning, many Bangladeshi mullahs (holy priests) believe family planning is an act against the will of God.

[9] Tk was the standard abbreviation for the currency unit, taka.

[10] A "thana" was the smallest administrative region in Bangladesh (the equivalent of a U.S. county); 489 thanas in total.

traceptive pills, ORSaline) by rural housewives. This female "sales force" was paid incentives for sales to friends, neighbors and village acquaintances. Although insignificant in terms of volume, SMC executives believed the project was more efficient than the much larger government efforts; it was contemplating expansion to 58 thanas.

Products. Several different product forms, typically classified as clinical and non-clinical were used for birth control. Non-clinical methods included condoms, contraceptive pills and injectables; clinical methods included sterilization and IUDs. Although each method offered birth control benefits, each had drawbacks. For example, lapsed users of condoms complained of bursting, lack of sexual satisfaction, inconvenience, bad smell (of latex/lubricant) and disposal problems. For pills, side effects dominated the reasons for lack of adoption and discontinuance; for some women they were totally unsuitable. Several pills of differing estrogen and progestin quantities were available; women might try more than one before settling on a brand with minimum side effects.

Although most distribution of condoms focused on birth control, it was becoming increasingly clear that a market existed in Bangladesh for prevention of sexually transmitted diseases (STD).[11] Although good data was difficult to secure, SMC executives believed that as many as 25% of condoms sold were used for extra- and pre-marital sex.

Measurement of contraceptive effect. Population control experts used two measures of contraceptive effectiveness, couple year protection (CYP) and contraceptive prevalence rate (CPR). Based on studies in Bangladesh, it was estimated that one CYP was provided by 100 condoms or 13 oral pill cycles; one IUD insertion was equivalent to 2.5 CYP, one sterilization to 7.75 CYP.[12] In 1994, SMC contraceptive products provided 2.43 million CYPs: 1.54 million from condoms, 0.89 million from pills.

Contraceptive prevalence rate was defined as the number of Married Women of Reproductive Age (MWRA) using family planning (i.e., modern methods [e.g., condoms, pills] and traditional methods [e.g., rhythm and withdrawal]). In Bangladesh, this rose from 6.5% in 1975 to about 45% in 1993–94 (Table 2).

SMC Businesses

In late 1993, SMC completed its first five-year (1994–98) strategic plan.[13] SMC's mission statement was developed as part of the planning exercise:

> Social marketing is the application of commercial management techniques to maximize the sales volume of products and services which offer clear social benefits –

---

[11] Official statistics indicated an HIV positive rate of <1% sexually active adults; a 1993 study estimated 3% of women and 5% of men (15–49) had sexually transmitted diseases or reproductive tract infections.

[12] USAID in Bangladesh insisted on a conversion of 150 condoms = 1 CYP; PSI executives were adamant that 100 condoms = 1 CYP was the correct factor.

[13] With guidance from Arthur D. Little International.

Table 2:   Contraceptive Prevalence Rate

	1979	1981	1983	1986	1989	1991	1993–94
Total CPR (%)	12.7	18.6	19.1	25.3	31.4	39.9	44.6
Total % modern	n/a	n/a	13.8	18.4	24.4	31.2	36.2
Condom	1.5	1.6	1.5	1.8	1.9	2.5	3.0
Oral pill	3.6	3.5	3.3	5.1	9.1	13.9	17.4
Injectables	0.2	0.4	0.2	0.5	1.1	2.6	4.5
IUD	n/a	n/a	1.0	1.4	1.7	1.8	2.2
Vaginal methods	n/a	n/a	0.3	0.2	0.2	n/a	n/a
Female sterilization	n/a	n/a	6.2	7.9	9.0	9.1	8.1
Male sterilization	n/a	n/a	1.2	1.5	1.5	1.2	1.1
Total % traditional	n/a	n/a	5.4	6.9	7.0	8.7	8.4
Periodic abstinence	n/a	n/a	2.4	3.8	3.8	4.7	4.8
Withdrawal	n/a	n/a	1.3	0.9	1.2	2.0	2.5
Other methods	n/a	n/a	1.8	2.2	2.9	2.0	1.1
Total % rural	n/a	n/a	17.3	23.2	29.1	38.5	43.3
Total % urban	n/a	n/a	35.7	44.2	44.8	48.0	54.4

but which are sold in markets that offer little prospect of full cost recovery in the long term.

SMC's purpose is to use social marketing and supportive information, education and motivation programs to enhance the quality of life of the people of Bangladesh – while maximizing the cost effectiveness of our use of funds from donors. We shall engage in manufacturing, marketing and distribution and our focus will be on consumer products and services which offer improved health and welfare benefits to the less privileged members of society. We are prepared to commit a proportion of our total resources to profitable products in order to improve the long-term sustainability of our social marketing programs.

For planning purposes, SMC comprised three strategic business units, contraceptives, health care, and hygiene.

Contraceptives

SMC offered two types of non-clinical contraceptive products: three condom brands (Raja, Panther, Sensation) and three birth control pill brands (Maya, Ovacon, Norquest).[14] (SMC was not involved in clinical birth control methods). These products

---

[14] Contraceptive pill brands differed based on the concentration of estrogen and progestin. In general, lower dosage pills were considered safer with less side effects; however, some women experienced spotting or break through bleeding and might require higher dosage pills.

were distributed through retail outlets and advertised widely throughout Bangladesh. SMC was the largest consumer advertiser in Bangladesh.

Product distribution. Donor organizations (USAID, European Commission [EC]) purchased contraceptives in bulk from North American and European manufacturers and shipped them to the port city of Chittagong. SMC transported products to a central warehouse at Dhaka for repackaging and colorful labeling. Maya was packed 28 pills to a cycle (21 birth control pills and 7 iron tablets). Products were sent to seven subwarehouses to be distributed to pharmacies, large general stores, and about 10,000 semi-wholesalers or stockists by SMC's sales force. Stockists broke bulk and resold in smaller lots to pan kiosks and small general stores. Wholesalers primarily distributed either grain and rice, cigarettes or pharmaceuticals. Semi-wholesalers had greater product variety, including such items as soap, tea, biscuits, toothpaste, newspapers and magazines. Condoms had the broadest distribution; contraceptive pills were distributed only through pharmacies. (See Tables 3A, 3B for condom sales and market share; see Tables 4A, 4B for pill sales and market share; see Table 5 for retail prices.)

Raja. Raja condoms, first introduced in 1975, had several positive associations inasmuch as, in Bengali, the word raja meant king or emperor implying masculinity, bravery and power. In addition, the choice of the King of Spades as the Raja symbol provided instant recognition for Bangladeshi men, many of whom were enthusiastic card players, but also illiterate. Backed by extensive promotional efforts, Raja was widely available across the country; sales of Raja increased through the 1980s and 1990s; it was the most widely used condom brand in Bangladesh. Raja was targeted at the lower and lower-middle economic segment (regardless of residence) in particular to about-to-be-married young men, and married couples where: the husband worked out-of-town and was an occasional visitor to his wife; the wife was a nursing mother; other methods of contraception were contra-indicated and the rhythm method was the primary contraceptive.

Raja was distributed widely through stockists, pharmacists, grocery shops and kiosks. Recently Raja packaging was improved from polythene to silver-colored aluminum foil with an attractive Raja logo. On average, retailers sold Raja contraceptives at 25 paisa (Tk 0.25) per piece. Raja was available singly or in three-item packs; retailers could purchase disposable dispensers containing, for example, 32 packs of three condoms (Raja-3).[15] To some extent, Raja sales were negatively affected by condom leakage from government-sponsored distribution to commercial outlets.[16]

Raja was advertised mainly on radio (national and in regional dialects), on large billboards and through a one-minute film; various promotions (e.g., calendars, pads, give-aways, sponsoring special programs) were also employed. SMC's inability to advertise Raja and other condoms on television was believed to lead to improper use in some cases. (See Exhibit 3 for the 1995 consolidated advertising and promotion sched-

---

[15] Raja-3 was mainly distributed in pharmacies.
[16] This resale effect also occurred for Maya brand oral contraceptives.

Table 3A: SMC Condom Sales

| | Unit sales (millions) (average price to traders [Tk]) sales revenue (Tk million) | | | | |
	Raja	Panther	Sensation	Total unit sales[1] (millions)	Total CYP[1] (millions)
1976	8	–	–	8	0.08
1977	14	–	–	14	0.14
1979	29	–	–	29	0.29
1981	51	–	–	51	0.51
1983	81	2.3	–	84	0.84
1985	75	3.7	–	85	0.85
1987	88	4.5	–	99	0.99
1989	107	3.5	–	115	1.15
1990	76 (0.21) 16.3[2]	7.4 (0.54) 4.0[3]	–	84	0.84
1991	72 (0.22) 16.3	10.3 (0.58) 6.0	–	83	0.83
1992	104 (0.15) 16.2	11.1 (0.58) 6.4	1.3 (1.04) 1.3	117	1.17
1993	125 (0.17) 21.9	10.9 (0.58) 7.0	2.3 (1.04) 2.4	138	1.38
1994	135 (0.18) 23.3	16.1 (0.62) 10.0[4]	no stock	151	1.51
1995 target	135 (0.18) 23.4	16.0 (0.80) 12.8	3.0 (2.0) 6.0	154	1.54

[1] Includes sales for Majestic (1985, 6.3; 1987, 6.1; 1989, 4.7) and Carex (1991, 0.3; 1992, 0.7).
[2] 1990 unit sales represented a 29% decrease from 1989 caused primarily by a 66% price increase to traders passed onto consumers.
[3] Sales doubled from 1989 in part due to withdrawal of the Majestic brand.
[4] Sales growth due in part to absence of Sensation brand.

Table 3B: Condom Sales Volume (million) and Market Shares (%)

| | 1989 | | 1990 | | 1991 | | 1992 | | 1993 | | 1994 | | 1995 (est.) | |
	Vol.	MS	Vol.	MS	Vol.	MS	Vol.	MS	Vol.	MS	Vol.	MS	Vol.	MS
Retail condoms														
SMC	115	100	84	100	83	100	117	100	138	100	151	100	154	100
Others/private	0	0	0	0	0	0	0	0	0	0	0	0	1	0
Total	115	100	84	100	83	100	117	100	138	100	151	100	155	100
Direct condoms														
SMC	0	0	0	0	0	0	0	0	0	0	0	0	0	0
BDG[1]	58	71	63	79	44	72	51	74	39	58	45	69	50	79
NGOs[2]	24	29	17	21	17	28	18	26	28	42	20	31	13	20
Total	82	100	80	100	61	100	69	100	67	100	65	100	63	100
Total condoms	197		164		144		186		205		216		218	
SMC MS		58		51		58		63		67		68		71

[1] Bangladesh government.   [2] Non-government organizations.

Table 4A: SMC Pill Sales

| | Pill sales (millions cycles) (average price to traders per cycle [Tk]) sales revenue (Tk million) | | | | |
	Maya	Oracon	Norquest	Total cycles (mil)	Total CYP (mil)
1976	0.4	–		0.4	0.03
1977	0.8	–		0.8	0.06
1979	0.8	–		0.8	0.06
1981	0.7	0.2		1.0	0.07
1983	1.1	0.5		1.6	0.12
1985	1.3	1.1		2.3	0.18
1987	1.4	1.9		3.4	0.26
1989	2.7	4.8		6.7	0.51
1990	2.6 (2.4) 5.4[1]	3.6 (4.3) 15.5	–	6.2	0.48
1991	2.7 (2.4) 6.1	4.8 (4.6) 22.4	0.4 (10) 4.4	7.9	0.61
1992	6.6 (2.4, 0.7) 4.7[2]	3.0 (4.6) 14.0[4]	0.7 (10) 7.0	10.3	0.79
1993	4.5 (0.7) 3.1	4.2 (4.6) 19.7	1.3 (10) 13.0	10.0	0.77
1994	4.9 (1.0) 4.8[3]	4.8 (4.6) 23.1	1.9 (10) 20.4	11.8	0.89
1995 target	3.0 (1.0) 3.0	6.0 (4.6) 27.8	2.5 (10) 28	11.5	0.88

[1] Price increased 50% in April 1990.
[2] Price reduced 71% and traders compensated.
[3] Target with 43% price increase.
[4] Maya price reduction affected traders' purchases.

Table 4B: Contraceptive Pill Sales Volume (million) and Market Shares (%)

| | 1989 | | 1990 | | 1991 | | 1992 | | 1993 | | 1994 | | 1995 (est.) | |
	Vol.	MS	Vol.	MS	Vol.	MS	Vol.	MS	Vol.	MS	Vol.	MS	Vol.	MS
Retail pills														
SMC	6.7	74	6.2	74	7.9	75	10.3	82	11.0	83	11.8	83	11.5	82
Organon	2.4	26	2.7	26	2.6	25	2.4	18	2.3	17	2.4	17	2.5	16
Total	9.1	100	8.9	100	10.5	100	12.7	100	13.3	100	14.2	100	14.1	100
Direct pills														
SMC	0	0	0	0	0	0	0	0	0	0	0	0	0.2	0
BDG[1]	17.0	79	28.0	79	31.5	83	38.8	74	32.4	58	42.0	71	60.5	91
NGOs[2]	4.5	21	4.8	21	6.2	16	6.9	26	19.8	42	17.0	29	5.9	9
Total	21.5	100	32.8	100	37.7	100	45.7	100	52.2	100	59.0	100	66.6	100
Total pills	30.6		41.7		48.2		58.4		65.5		75.2		80.7	
SMC MS	22		15		16		16		17		16		15	

[1] Bangladesh government.   [2] Non-government organizations.

Table 5: Consumer Prices for SMC Contraceptive Products (Tk)

Brand	Raja-100	Raja-3	Panther	Sensation	Norquest	Femicon	Ovacon	Maya
Consumer pack	Loose pieces	3-piece pack	5-piece pack	4-piece pack	1 cycle	1 cycle	1 cycle	2 cycles
Consumer price (Tk)	0.25	1.0 per pack	5.0 per pack	10.0 per pack	12.0 per pack	10.0 per pack	6.0 per pack	3.0 per pack

ule; see Exhibit 4 for print advertisements.) SMC executives were concerned that product uniformity might deteriorate with EC procurement from multiple suppliers.

Panther. Panther was introduced in the mid-1980s. Panther was targeted at married young men, appealing to their sense of responsibility at the beginning of family life. Priced above Raja, it was an upmarket product with good brand image; packaging was recently improved. Panther was available through stockists, pharmacies, grocery shops and kiosks; distribution was especially strong at pharmacies. On average, Panther was sold to consumers at Tk 5 per five-pack; retailers purchased disposable dispensers containing 15 five-packs. Panther, promoted similarly as Raja, was advertised also in national and regional newspapers and in magazines. SMC executives were concerned that EC procurement would lead to lack of product uniformity.

Sensation. Sensation was introduced in June 1992 for the upper-end of the condom market, in particular, men who were 20–45 years of age, with higher educational and socio-economic background, who wanted more out of life and lived in urban and semi-urban areas. Despite its high price, Sensation was quickly established as a popular upmarket product; however, it was out-of-stock in 1994. Reintroduced with new packaging, Sensation, the only ribbed condom available in Bangladesh (the original Sensation product was plain) was promoted as highly reliable and providing high satisfaction; users expressed highly positive attitudes towards ribbed condoms inasmuch as it created "friction" during intercourse. Sensation was targeted for pharmacies and general stores, particularly in urban and semi-urban areas, with a retail price of Tk 10 per four-pack. Advertising was planned for radio, newspapers and magazines; promotional items included calendars, mobiles, give-aways and sponsoring special events.

Maya. Maya, literally meaning affection in Bengali, commonly meant beauty in cultural translation; its choice as brand name was to create a positive feeling and sense of optimism about the product. Introduced in the mid-1970s, it had a checkered sales history: sales increased to 1.1 million cycles p.a. in 1980 but dropped to scarcely half that amount a few years later. In the mid-1980s, PSI made a strategic targeting switch in promoting to rural medical practitioners; sales recovered and reached a maximum of 6.6 million cycles in 1992 (up from 2.7 million, 1991) following a dramatic 73% price reduction and trade compensation. However, sales at retail did not increase as dramatically and SMC's sales dropped considerably in 1993, leading to a product relaunch in 1994. Heavy trade promotion was necessary to overcome traders' reluctance to stock Maya.

Maya pills served around 200,000 women aged 30 to 40 years (mostly married) with at least two children, across all economic segments throughout the country; SMC efforts were focused on repeat purchase. Maya was available in rural and urban pharmacies and from rural medical practitioners; retail price was Tk 3 per twin-cycle pack. Maya was advertised on radio, television and on an electronic outdoor display; numerous promotions (e.g., calendars, pads, give-aways) were also conducted. Recent research showed Maya's image at its lowest ever level; lapsed and potential users believed negative side effects could be overcome only with continuous intake of nutritious food.

Ovacon. Ovacon pills were the most widely distributed in rural and urban pharmacies. Its lower progestin and estrogen (0.035 mg Ethinyl Estradiol) levels reduced side effects and made it attractive to new pill users; since 1980, it had been positioned as the "genuine low dose pill" for new pill users. In recent years, Ovacon sales suffered as traders hoarded Maya following the dramatic price reduction and neglected Ovacon, but sales growth was recovering. Retail price of Ovacon was Tk 6 per cycle; retailers purchased 40-cycle disposable dispensers. Ovacon was advertised on radio, television, magazines, outdoor advertisements and through a film; various promotional items (e.g., calendars, pads, give-aways, information leaflets, key rings, pens) were provided to the trade.

Norquest. Norquest pills, introduced in January 1990 and targeted at an upmarket audience, were designed to generate revenues and fill the wide price gap between commercial and social marketing brands. Norquest's progestin level, between Maya and Ovacon (but similar estrogen level to Ovacon), might be suitable for women encountering side effects from other pills. SMC currently had a large stock of Norquest approaching the expiry date; the retail price of Tk 12 per cycle would rise to Tk 15 per cycle when this stock was exhausted. Retailers purchased 20-cycle dispensers. Norquest was advertised on radio, television, magazines, outdoor advertisements and through a film; various promotional items (e.g., calendars, pads, give-aways, information leaflets, hanging mobiles) were provided to the trade.

Pill supply issues. All SMC's pills were manufactured by Syntex Laboratories under contract to USAID. However, USAID's contract with Syntex expired in December 1994; as a result, when residual stocks were used up, SMC would lose its three brand names, Maya, Ovacon and Norquest. Maya was likely to be exhausted in 1996, Ovacon in 1997. Norquest stocks would be exhausted in April/May 1995 but SMC executives believed there was a reasonable chance that a new donor, ODA would provide a similar pill for sale in early 1995 to end 1997 allowing the brand name to be retained; however, there was a strong possibility that the Norquest brand would also be lost. SMC executives learned that by end 1996, the BDG pill would also be replaced; the new pill, with a new brand name, would have a much lower dosage of estrogen [0.03 mg. versus 0.05 mg. Ethinyl Estradiol].

Femicon. Femicon, the chosen local brand name for a new contraceptive pill from Wyeth Laboratories, shortly to be introduced by SMC, had progestin and estrogen levels (0.03 mg. Ethinyl Estradiol) lower than Ovacon. It was targeted at the middle and upper-middle class and would be priced somewhat lower than Norquest. Femicon's exact positioning was not yet decided but SMC executives said this would depend upon whether the new ODA pill would retain the Norquest brand name or be launched with a new name.

Health Care

In 1986, SMC launched the ORSaline (ORS) brand of oral dehydration salts under USAID's Child Survival Program.[17] The goal was to reduce child mortality and morbidity due to diarrhea related dehydration. Unlike Raja and Maya, ORS was self-financed from sales to the trade (not including promotional expenses) (using the maximum retail price authorized by the government). USAID funded research, promotion and marketing of ORS. SMC secured product from the government-owned Essential Drug Company Ltd. and a charitable organization, Ganasastha Pharmaceutical Ltd. Another commercial organization sold oral rehydration therapy (ORT) products through retailers, sometimes identical to ORS's formulation, in deceptively imitative packaging, often at lower prices.

SMC's objectives were to motivate parents of children under five years (21 million) to use ORS by providing education and information, and by prevention and management of diarrhea-related diseases; ORS was sold through urban and rural pharmacies and grocery shops. ORS, supported by the Pharmacists Training Program and the School ORT Education Program, was credited with saving the lives of countless children dehydrated by water-borne diseases prevalent in Bangladesh. Since 1986, over 25,000 pharmacists had attended a one-day program on diarrhea diseases (6,500 planned for 1995); over 350,000 secondary school children were trained on hygiene, sanitation and administration of ORS (60,000 planned for 1995) by special teams that traveled around Bangladesh.[18]

On average a Bangladeshi child had 3.5 diarrhea episodes annually, typically, four ORS sachets were required per episode. In addition to young children, older persons (>55 years) were at high risk from death due to diarrhea but little effort had been placed on this group by either SMC or its competitors. Recent studies found that although ORS achieved over 95% distribution in urban and rural pharmacies, availability in grocery stores was less than 10%. Although knowledge of oral rehydration therapy (ORT) was almost universal, only about 28% used packaged ORS, another 16% used

---

[17] Product ingredients of ORSaline were 1.75 grams of sodium chloride, 0.75 grams of potassium chloride, 1.45 grams of tri-sodium citrate dihydrate, and 10 grams of glucose anhydrous per sachet. This citrate formulation had significant advantages over the previously-used bicarbonate formulation. Each package of ORSaline had to be mixed with 500 cc. of pure drinking water.

[18] SMC's 1995 budget for training teams and ORSaline related materials for rural medical practitioner (RMP) meets was Tk 4.37 million (US$112,000). Executives were concerned that this effort was insufficient for repeat training.

homemade fluids. The major reason for not using ORT was that "it does not stop loose motion." Some mothers used drugs as they believed they would stop diarrhea more quickly.

Sales of ORS increased dramatically in recent years (Table 6); it commanded 83% market share in rural pharmacies and 88% in urban outlets. In addition, the Bangladesh government distributed packaged ORT free through hospitals and field workers.

Table 6: ORT Distribution (million sachets) and Market Shares*

	1987		1994	
	Volume (million)	Market share (%)	Volume (million)	Market share (%)
SMC (ORSaline)	4.6	12	32.6	35
Other commercial	0.0	0	15.2	17
BDG	35.4	88	44.7	48
Total	40.0	100	93.0	100

*Other years' ORSaline sales were: 1989, 6.9; 1990, 7.2; 1991, 15.8 (after tidal bore); 1992, 16.6; 1993, 24.7 (disruption in competitor supply).

SMC executives were concerned that current suppliers were also competitors that could offer better margins to retailers; they might also raise input prices while, since ORSaline was classified as a drug, the retail price was fixed by the government. In addition, SMC had no buffer supplies in case of an emergency (e.g., 1991 cyclone). Because of these concerns SMC was considering both self-manufacture and contracts with other suppliers.

ORSaline was promoted by advertising on radio, television, newspapers and magazines, outdoor displays (billboards and water tanks), a film and sponsoring special events. Promotional items included children's book covers and stickers, pads, detailing cards, calendars, ball point pens, measuring glasses and hanging mobiles. In addition, in 1994, UNICEF launched a nationwide campaign to raise awareness of ORT. SMC advertising urged mothers to keep an inventory of three ORS sachets, the minimum for dehydration prevention. (See Table 7 for 1995 advertising and promotion budget.) The maximum retail price (MRP) for ORSaline was Tk 3.16 per sachet; SMC sold 20-sachet dispensers to the trade at Tk 2.75 per dispenser.[19]

SMC was contemplating introduction of flavored ORSaline to counteract children's reluctance to drink the fluid. Although the possibility of hypernatremia (high concentration of sodium chloride in the blood, especially in infants) would be present, SMC executives believed that advantages far outweighed this disadvantage.[20] In addition it would be available before similar products from other organizations.

---

[19] SMC's raw material cost was currently Tk 2.01 per sachet.
[20] Health-care workers typically suggested that children be given fruit juice to make ORT more palatable.

Hygiene. SMC offered a pulp-based sanitary napkin product for the female menstrual cycle. Products based on both pulp (about two thirds) and cotton (about one third) were available from various suppliers. SMC's Femme product had a 5% share of the pulp portion of the market. Although cost recovery was high for Femme, numerous problems including irregular supply of product, current flattening of demand and competitors' strong positions led SMC managers to consider discontinuing the product.

Table 7: ORSaline Advertising and Promotion Budget 1995*

Medium	Budget (Tk '000)	% of budget
Radio	3,623	19
Television	7,266	39
Press	951	5
Outdoor	1,842	10
Film	2,090	11
Promotional materials	2,986	16
Total	18,762**	100

*In addition to advertising and promotion, SMC budgeted Tk 4,200,000 (US$108,000) for various marketing research studies (e.g., retail price monitoring, health-care providers' attitudes to ORSaline, consumer brand awareness, testing communication and training materials [40%], and a major diarrhea morbidity and treatment study [60%]).
**US$481,000 @ US$1 = Tk 40.

Sales Force

SMC employed a geographically organized sales force comprising 85 salespeople, eight area managers and five zone managers (zone offices supplemented area offices). Salespeople called on larger retail outlets carrying SMC products and on stockists that served smaller retail outlets, often in rural areas that were frequently difficult to reach. Salespeople were supposed to make on average 15 effective sales calls per day (about three to stockists); in 1994, the sales force made 60,000 effective calls on stockists and 400,000 calls on retailers. Salespeople traveled in vans, motorcycles and boats; they carried inventory of SMC products which were sold for cash; in most cases salespeople were responsible for banking payments. SMC did not offer credit to any customer. Retailers received margins; stockists received no margins but resold products to retailers at slightly higher prices; they also received the packaging cases from which they derived a small income. In 1994, 53% of all condom sales by volume were through stockists (47% direct to retailers); exactly 50% of contraceptive pill sales were to stockists.

In addition, the sales force held meetings with rural medical practitioners. Typically each RMP meeting (one to two hours) would be attended by 15 to 20 RMPs; the advantages and disadvantages of different family planning methods would be presented, with information on diarrhea-related diseases and ORSaline. In 1994, 15,000 RMPs were covered in this manner; 12,000 were targeted for 1995. The sales force also detailed trained physicians; however, SMC executives believed this effort was less successful than Organon's sales efforts which used a dedicated detailing force.

The sales force was compensated by salary and an increasing bonus incentive on a per product basis. Bonuses commenced at 95% of targeted volume and increased at 100%, 110% and 120% of target; no additional bonuses were paid above 130% of target. A separate department operated 17 mobile film units that criss-crossed Bangladesh showing films describing the use of SMC products.

New Ventures

SMC management was considering offering a flavored version of ORSaline as well as several other new ventures:

Flavored ORSaline. Despite the advantages of offering this product and its use in neighboring countries, management was concerned that the World Health Organization and UNICEF were not in favor of this. These organizations considered ORSaline an essential drug that should be available at an affordable price; adding flavoring would increase the price.

Injectable contraceptives. This contraceptive method was being increasingly used in Bangladesh. Two brands were available: Depo-Provera (Upjohn, FDA-approved) and Noristerat (Schering) had three-month and two-month efficacy, respectively. SMC would require medical establishment approval to sell injectables; the establishment was concerned that SMC had inadequate safeguards for side effects, needle re-use and counseling.

Low dose vitamin A. Malnutrition was a significant problem in Bangladesh. Although vitamin A supplements had been available for over 20 years, coverage (20% to 25%) was low. Although health workers administered a high potency dose (200,000 international units [IU]) twice yearly, SMC believed that a social marketing approach would be viable based on a low weekly dose of 10,000 IU. At present, a small commercial business of 50,000 IU pills existed, mainly as treatment for ophthalmic and other diseases. Preliminary planning efforts suggested that 88% cost recovery should be possible five years after introduction if 10% of unserved under fives consumed the product.

Manufacturing. SMC executives were contemplating manufacturing of condoms, oral contraceptives and ORSaline as a means to improve cost recovery. In terms of manufacturing complexity, ORSaline, essentially a mixing and packaging operation, would be the simplest product to manufacture; for a capital investment of Tk 70 million (US$2 million) a plant with annual capacity 100 million sachets could be built. Exploration of condom and pill manufacture was far less advanced.

Social marketing products. Options under consideration were: operation of a medical clinic, distribution of school supplies on behalf of the government (e.g., pencils, slates);

marketing of weaning foods, marketing of high protein biscuits and distribution of agricultural seeds.

Commercial products. Among other suggestions were marketing of other companies' products (e.g., cosmetics, soap, over-the-counter (OTC) pharmaceuticals, school books/ supplies, light bulbs), property development (single building for SMC and others), operation of a medical diagnostic laboratory, advertising agency and/or commission agency for overseas manufacturers.

Decisions

As Karam and Rahman contemplated their task it seemed there were several interrelated strands. First, USAID's withdrawal affected both funds for SMC activities and raised questions of product uniformity. Uniformity was a concern for condoms, but for oral contraceptives, two and possibly all of SMC's brand names would have to be dropped. They had to decide on the relative level of resources placed on the various condom and oral contraceptive brands, whether injectable contraceptives should be introduced and whether manufacture of either or both condoms and contraceptive pills should be undertaken. In addition, the increasing success of government-sponsored direct distribution was a cause of concern.

They also had to make decisions on a variety of other new product opportunities, in particular a brand extension of flavored ORSaline, manufacture of ORSaline and introduction of a vitamin A nutritional supplement; the long-term viability of efforts in the hygiene market was also an issue. USAID's withdrawal caused a variety of operational problems but a more serious global issue concerned future funding from donors. SMC competed in the international donor fund market and had to demonstrate effective performance. In part to build in more organizational flexibility, a variety of new venture opportunities had been identified.

Finally, PSI's management contract would terminate at end 1996. Karam and Rahman had to make some serious decisions and develop a successful strategy and action plan that would long outlast PSI's direct SMC involvement.

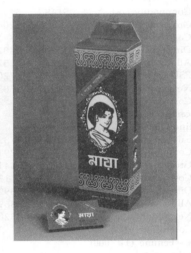

Exhibit 2: SMC Financial Performance

Summary – retail Condoms (Tk '000)		Business unit: contraceptives case: base						
		1989	1990	1991	1992	1993	1994	1995
	Sales revenue	27686	22524	23174	26057	26749	29765	32356
less:	Commodity cost	176496	140315	146511	219339	223033	111422	128869
	Gross margin	−148810	−117790	−123337	−193281	−196284	−81658	−96513
	Cost recovery (%)	16	16	16	12	12	27	25
less:	Direct cost	45143	42003	46900	62526	73934	73980	81850
	Allocated overhead	3312	2952	2886	3339	4435	4662	4733
	PSI expenses	9951	8425	8265	9341	16098	14082	11995
	Net margin	−207217	−171170	−181388	−268488	−290752	−174382	−195090
	Cost recovery (%)	12	12	11	9	8	15	14

Summary – retail Pills (Tk '000)

		1989	1990	1991	1992	1993	1994	1995
	Sales revenue	24650	22876	32768	30295	32639	36293	37600
less:	Commodity cost	51485	54925	77965	111793	123906	157642	188874
	Gross margin	−26835	−32049	−45197	−85498	−91267	−121350	−151274
	Cost recovery (%)	48	42	42	27	26	23	20
less:	Direct cost	39216	44076	64450	79089	97255	105039	120132
	Allocated overhead	2217	2524	3195	3372	4536	5303	5588
	PSI expenses	6647	7202	9151	9424	16453	16031	14161
	Net margin	−74915	−85851	−121993	−173383	−209515	−247723	−291156
	Cost recovery (%)	25	21	21	15	13	13	11

Health care – ORSaline (Tk '000)

		1989	1990	1991	1992	1993	1994	1995
	Sales revenue	16703	17327	37944	42543	51041	70315	87170
less:	Commodity cost	12449	12912	29073	31427	37704	51466	64659
	Gross margin	4254	4415	8871	11116	13337	18849	22511
	Cost recovery (%)	134	134	131	135	135	137	135
	Direct cost	16349	33929	40957	43141	50302	54929	59379
less:	Allocated overhead	8265	8690	10503	11420	13820	15220	15398
	Net margin	−20360	−38204	−42589	−43445	−50785	−51300	−52266
	Cost recovery (%)	45	31	47	49	50	58	63

Hygiene – Femme (Tk '000)

		1989	1990	1991	1992	1993	1994	1995
	Sales revenue	0	0	304	2239	2100	2800	3500
less:	Commodity cost	0	0	239	1759	1650	2200	2750
	Gross margin	0	0	65	480	450	600	750
	Cost recovery (%)	0	0	127	127	127	127	127
	Direct cost	0	0	91	839	1074	954	1110
less:	Allocated overhead	0	0	7	36	68	81	89
	Net margin	0	0	−33	−395	−692	−435	−449
	Cost recovery (%)	0	0	90	85	75	87	89

SMC Total (Tk '000)

		1989	1990	1991	1992	1993	1994	1995
	Sales revenue	69039	62738	94256	101257	112660	139372	161122
less:	Commodity cost	240432	208189	253932	364652	386754	323415	387017
	Gross margin	−171393	−145451	−159676	−263395	−274094	−184043	−225895
	Cost recovery (%)	29	30	37	28	29	43	42
	Direct cost	100709	121453	154602	188893	225058	240079	268084
less:	Allocated overhead	30394	29826	34172	37098	55575	55544	52136
	Net margin	−302496	−296730	−348450	−489386	−554727	−479666	−546115
	Cost recovery (%)	19	17	21	17	17	23	23

Exhibit 3: Contraceptive Advertising and Promotion Budget

Media	Raja	Panther	Sensation	Sub-total	Maya	Ovacon	Norquest/ODA	Femicon	Sub-total	Grand total	%
Radio	879	702	429	2,011	938	634	1,159	1,159	3,890	5,901	17
TV	0	0	0	0	548	2,830	3,147	3,147	9,672	9,672	28
Press	0	715	735	1,450	0	300	955	955	2,210	3,661	11
Outdoor	300	600	300	1,200	120	670	420	420	1,630	2,830	8
Film production	0	0	600	600	0	0	600	600	1,200	1,800	5
Duplication and release	0	1,350	1,350	2,700	0	90	90	90	270	2,970	9
Total mass media	1,179	3,368	3,414	7,961	1,606	4,524	6,371	6,371	18,872	26,833	78
Promotional Items	1,225	925	875	3,025	760	800	900	900	3,360	6,385	19
Pop materials	0	0	140	140	0	0	175	80	255	395	1
Sponsorship	100	100	200	400	0	100	100	100	300	700	2
Total other	1,325	1,025	1,215	3,565	760	900	1,175	1,080	3,915	7,480	22
Grand total (Tk)	2,504	4,393	4,629	11,526	2,366	5,424	7,546	7,451	22,787	34,313	100
%	7	13	13	34	7	16	22	22	66	100	
Total US$ (@Tk 39)	64	113	119	296	61	139	193	191	584	880	
Grand total 1994 (Tk)	4,966	3,763	2,877	11,586	5,989	6,820	5,810		18,619	30,205	
Percent change 1994/1995 (%)	-50	17	61	-1	-60	-20	30		22	14	

Exhibit 4: Selected SMC Contraceptive Print Advertisements (in Bengali with translation)

RAJA Condoms

RAJA condoms এখন নতুন আকর্ষণীয় প্যাকেটে

Now in new attractive packets

It's not just novelty of packaging. For your convenience, the new packets of three condoms contain a visual users instruction

RAJA condom is packed in aluminium foil – which preserves the quality of the condom inside for a longer time.

RAJA — The foreign made 'high quality' condoms.

Are you thinking of tomorrow?
আপনি কি আগামীদিনের কথা ভাবছেন ?

Times are changing Women's values are changing. Now you can plan your life according to your own choice. You can express your desires in various ways. Your life can become enjoyable amidst your busy moments.

Therefore make every moment successful. Your every activity will express your originality and elegance. Let Ovacon be your everyday companion. Ovacon – The birth spacing pill made with such care that it inspires your future plans to become successful.

Ovacon — genuine low dose birth – spacing pills.
Suits your life style.
আপনার জীবন যাত্রা মানানসই।

Exhibit 4 (cont'd)

Map of Hong Kong

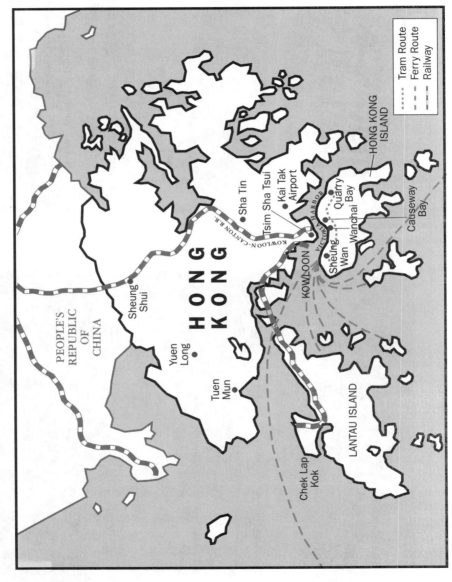

Hong Kong Overview

Background. Hong Kong has a land area of only 1,070 sq. km., coastline 733 kilometers population is 6.4 million (1997), growing at 2.1% p.a. Official languages are Cantonese and English, but residents also speak a variety of Chinese dialects. Hong Kong comprises three major inhabited areas: Hong Kong Island, Kowloon and the New Territories. The main business areas are concentrated in southern Kowloon and the northern coastal section of Hong Kong Island. Weather is tropical monsoon: cool and humid in winter, hot and rainy in spring and summer, warm and sunny in fall. Hong Kong's major natural resource is its deep-water Victoria Harbor, a major factor in Hong Kong's successful growth since 1950. Until July 1, 1997, when it was returned to China, Hong Kong was a British colony, ruled by a governor assisted by an appointed Executive Council (EXCO) and a Legislative Council (LEGCO), comprising both directly and indirectly elected members. The Chinese government has scrapped LEGCO, replacing it with an appointed body comprising over 400 members. Under British rule, the government traditionally pursued a non-intervention style of administration, but there is considerable uncertainty regarding the role the Chinese government will play as Hong Kong assumes its new status. The legal system, based on British Common Law, will continue after 1997: the Basic Law (mini-constitution) was enacted by the National People's Congress following the Joint Declaration negotiated by the governments of Great Britain and the People's Republic of China (PRC).

Political. Hong Kong Island (1842) and Kowloon (1860) were ceded to Britain after the Sino-British Opium Wars; the New Territories were leased in 1898 for 99 years. As a result of agreements (Joint Declaration, 1984) with the British government, sovereignty over the entire territory reverted to the PRC on July 1, 1997. In the waning years of British rule, Britain and China had several disputes, notably concerning the degree of democratization, the Court of Final Appeal and financing major infrastructure projects. The PRC has agreed to maintain Hong Kong as a capitalist society with a high degree of autonomy for 50 years under a one-country-two-systems policy, rather than pursue full integration with the rest of China.

Social. In 1997, life expectancy was 76.2 years for males and 81.8 years for females; the number of people aged 65 or over increased from an estimated 389,600 in 1984 to 560,000 in 1994; it is projected to increase to one million by 2016. Unless the government continues to allow entry to immigrants and foreign workers, falling birth rates will lead to an aging population and increased pensioner dependency ratio (1996,

16%; 2036, 47% estimated). This potentially aging population makes pensions a crucial issue.

Significant social structure changes occurred after the signing of the Joint Declaration; in particular much emigration occurred (averaging roughly 60,000 p.a. in the early 1990s), largely to Canada and Australia; as a result, population growth was low (1991, 0.9%). However, in recent years, owing to an influx of mainland Chinese (both construction workers and executives for mainland enterprises [by 1994, 750 had offices in Hong Kong]) and expatriate managers (by October 1994, 7,714 international companies had regional headquarters in Hong Kong; 1992, 588), the population growth rate increased (1994, 2.4%). Over half a million Hong Kong residents travel to the mainland each week, mainly to Guangdong, to work for Hong Kong-owned firms. In 1995, an estimated 12% of Hong Kong permanent residents held foreign passports. In anticipation of the sovereignty change, Hong Kong residents of Chinese extraction born in Hong Kong were able to secure British National Overseas (BNO) passports; they maintain British nationality and the right of unlimited stay in Great Britain. Many minority residents, largely of Indian and Pakistani extraction, born in Hong Kong and holding BNO or British Dependent Territories citizenship have been given right of abode in Britain.

Economy. Hong Kong is a member of the World Trade Organization (WTO), Asian Development Bank (ADB) and the Asia-Pacific Economic Cooperation (APEC) Forum. Since 1992, Hong Kong's GNP and per capita exports have been in the world's top ten. GNP per capita, US$24,455 (1997), grew at well over 10% p.a.; exports, US$180 billion (1996), grew at a similar rate. China is Hong Kong's largest trading partner for both exports and imports; re-exports from China account for roughly 80% of total exports. Hong Kong tax rates are among the lowest in the world: personal tax rate 15%, corporate tax rate 16.5% (1995). In recent years, inflation has been in the single digits and real interest rates have been low. In recent years, *Fortune* ranked Hong Kong as the best city for business in the world.

Until recently, labor shortages were a serious matter for Hong Kong-based businesses; unemployment rates in 1987 and 1989 were 1.7% and 1.1%, respectively; "brain drain" following the Joint Declaration is partly responsible. To deal with this problem, a significant part of the labor force is "imported" from China and the Philippines. In addition, labor-intensive manufacturing plants have moved from Hong Kong to southern China, mainly to the Shenzhen Special Economic Zone in Guangdong Province, just across the border. As a result, by the mid-1990s concern was expressed at the growing rate of unemployment, over 3.2% in 1995. Tourism is Hong Kong's second largest foreign exchange earner accounting for 7% of GDP (1993) with 8 million arrivals (1.7 million from the PRC); in 1994, arrivals jumped to 9 million.

Hong Kong's banking system is regulated by the Hong Kong Monetary Authority. The banking structure comprises a three-tier system: licensed banks, restricted licensed banks and deposit-taking banks, differing in paid-up capital requirements and minimum deposit sizes. In 1994, deposit interest restrictions were removed, leading to increased inter-bank competition for depositors. Also, interest rates on deposits exceeding HK$30,000 are now subject to discretion between depositor and bank.

Continuing deregulation will affect interest rates on demand deposits (1996) and saving deposits (1997). Bank notes were traditionally issued by two private banks: the Hong Kong & Shanghai Banking Corporation (HKSC) and Standard Chartered Bank; in January 1995, the Bank of China became the third note-issuing bank.

Because the Hong Kong dollar is pegged (within a narrow band) to the U.S. dollar (HK$7.8 = US$1) (the only remaining Southeast Asian currency), and capital controls are completely absent, Hong Kong interest rates are hostage to U.S. rate movements. Since property and finance are important sectors in Hong Kong, the economy is very sensitive to interest rate changes, and hence, to political uncertainties and changing conditions in world markets.

In recent years, capitalization of the Hong Kong stock market (end 1994: US$270 billion) has grown significantly. Hong Kong's stock market is the world's eighth largest and Asia's second largest in terms of capitalization; over 500 companies are listed. However, in 1995, a major Hong Kong company, Jardine Matheson, delisted in anticipation of the sovereignty change. In recent years, the Hong Kong property market has surged dramatically, making Hong Kong property some of the most expensive in the world; however, by 1995 prices stabilized.

In fall 1997, the Asian currency crisis led to several speculative currency attacks. The Hong Kong stock market came under pressure and, on October 27, the Hang Seng Index crashed, setting off a worldwide collapse in equity markets. During 1997, the market lost just over 20% of capitalization; real estate was down 30%–35%. Although the monetary authority (with extensive foreign exchange reserves and support pledges from the Bank of China) deflected the speculative attacks, the extensive devaluations in neighboring countries raised the question of Hong Kong's continued competitiveness if it maintained the peg.

Infrastructure. By international standards, Hong Kong has good infrastructure development; rail transportation is particularly strong following completion of the Mass Transit Railway (MTR). Hong Kong has 1,717 kilometers of highways (1996), 94 kilometers paved. Electricity capacity was 9,566,000 kWh in 1992, per capita production 4,980 kWh. Several major projects are being pursued to further upgrade the system: a new airport at Chek Lap Kok (Lantau Island; completion date 1998, estimated cost about US$20 billion) designed to handle 87 million passengers p.a. and associated ground transportation; new container terminals at Kwai Chung (estimated cost US$2 billion); and major new road construction (estimated cost US$4 billion). Hong Kong Telecom, one of the world's most expensive carriers, is investing heavily in fiber optic systems but has lost monopoly status for both local and domestic calls.

Statistics*	June 1991	June 1995	Statistics*	June 1991	June 1995
Per capita GNP	US$12,069	US$24,455	Infant mortality/1,000	6	5
GDP growth	2.4%	6.0%	Life expectancy (yrs)	n/a	79
Savings (GNP)	n/a	35%	Literacy rate	88.1%	90.0%
Inflation (CPI)	11.9%	5.2%	People per tel.	2.1	1.5
Foreign debt (in US$ billion)	0	0	People per doctor	1,024	772
Pop. (million)	5.7	6.4	People per TV	n/a	3.0
Urban pop.	n/a	95%	Calorie intake (cals)	n/a	3,144
Pop. growth	0.9%	2.1%			

*Secured from *Asiaweek*.

Case 4

City Telecom (HK) Ltd.

Noel Capon
Graduate School of Business, Columbia University

Kong Man Din, Lee Chi Shing, Leung Tat Pui, Wong Mei Keung, Shamza Khan, Samina Seth
The Hong Kong University of Science and Technology

On April 17, 1995, Ricky Wong, Regional Director of City Telecom (Hong Kong) Ltd., expressed his views regarding future competition and telecommunications opportunities in Hong Kong and the PRC to four MBA students from The Hong Kong University of Science and Technology. He told them the time was fast approaching to make some serious decisions on how to maintain and improve City Telecom's position in the Hong Kong international calls market and how to enter the PRC.

༄༅

The Long Distance Telecommunications Market

The Regulatory Framework

Hong Kong had one of the highest telephone densities in Southeast Asia. At year-end 1994, 3.8 million telephones were served by three million exchange lines, 65 telephones per 100 people. In 1995, Hong Kong Telecom (HKT) reported an installed base of 3,149,280 lines, more than one line for every two people. During 1994, more than 18,000 kilometers of new fiber optic cable was added, increasing HKT's total to 78,780 kilometers.

In Hong Kong, basic public telecommunication services were provided under franchise. Under the Telephone Ordinance, the Hong Kong Telephone Company Ltd. had the exclusive right until June 30, 1995 to provide public voice telephone service by wire within Hong Kong. Hong Kong Telecom International Ltd. (HKTI) was granted an exclusive license, until September 30, 2006, to provide a range of public international telecommunications services, including telephone, telex, telegram and leased circuits for data and facsimile traffic. Any companies wishing to offer telecommunications services were required to apply for a license to the Public Non-Exclusive Telecommunications Services (PNETS) of the Telecommunications Authority.

On July 1, 1994, a new telecommunications regulatory body, the Office of the Telecommunications Authority (OFTA) was established. OFTA was headed by the Director-General of Telecommunications (DGT), concurrently the Governor as the Telecommunications Authority. The DGT administered the Telecommunications Ordinance and the Telephone Ordinance governing the establishment and operation of all telecommunications services.

Deregulation Trends

Following a decision to liberalize the telecommunications industry, in November 1993 the Hong Kong government announced its intention to license three new fixed telecommunications networks to provide local competition to HKT – initially for data and facsimile services, but for voice telephony beyond June 1995. Furthermore, companies and organizations might also be licensed to provide their own external telecommunications links. Notwithstanding these formal deregulatory moves, several companies entered the international telephone calling market by identifying loopholes in the government's agreements with HKTI.

Commenting on these liberalization moves, Wong said:

> In Hong Kong, no real changes were made in regulations and ordinances relating to long distance telecommunications service. Observed changes concerned interpretation of regulations and the government's attitude. The government seems to want more competition but subject to current regulations. Actually, I don't think the government will make a big move to change the telecommunications ordinances or already signed contracts, especially during the transition period to 1997. It is a reputation and recognition issue.

Alex Arena, Director of OFTA, said the services CTI (HK) sold were allowed by existing regulations.

Hong Kong Telecom

> Hong Kong Telecom has a clear vision and ambitious goals. Naturally, developing the business locally and regionally will be of key importance. However, we will also diversify into promising new areas such as interactive multi-media services. This initiative and others like it will be repeated many times over as we develop even closer ties with China and increase our presence throughout the region. In line with our belief that 'What can be imagined can be achieved,' we aim for nothing less than to be the most successful telecommunications company in Asia. (Hong Kong Telecom 1995 annual report, p. 12.)

Background

Hong Kong Telecom, the founder of Hong Kong's telecommunications industry in the 1870s, was the holding company of Hong Kong's principal telecommunications group. Incorporated in 1988, HKT had several subsidiaries and associated companies providing ancillary telecommunications services and products (Table 1). In January 1988, HKT had 16,300 employees; it was one of the colony's largest employers. However, as part of a cost cutting and efficiency effort, HKT was downsizing: 2,000 employees left the company in 1994; in the next three years, workforce reductions of 2,500 were planned.

Table 1: HKT's Subsidiaries and Associated Companies (% ownership)

Name	Principal activities
Subsidiaries	
Hong Kong Telephone Company Ltd. (100%)	Telecom. services
Hong Kong Telecom International Ltd. (100%)	Telecom. services
Hong Kong Telecom CSL Ltd. (100%)	Telecom. products and services
Computasia Ltd. (100%)	Computer services
Monance Ltd. (100%)	Property development
Hong Kong Telecom Finance Ltd. (100%)	Financing
Mobile One Ltd. (60%)	Telecom. products and services
CSL United Personalcom Ltd. (67%)	Telecom. products and services
Hong Kong Telecom (Pacific) Ltd. (100%)	Telecom. services
Associated companies	
Great Eastern Telecommunications Ltd. (49%)	Investment
Telecom Directories Ltd. (51%)	Provision of directories
Unitel Communication Ltd. (40%)	Telecom. products and services
Abacus Distribution Systems (Hong Kong) Ltd. (37%)	Computerized airline reservations system

Technology

Beginning in 1987, satellite communication facilities were provided HKT from five satellites situated over the Indian and Pacific oceans, one of the largest commercial satellite facilities in the world. In 1990, HKT's CSL subsidiary was established to develop sophisticated paging and mobile radio telephone equipment and services. By 1994, Hong Kong had an all-digital telephone network; HKT planned to spend HK$4 billion developing telecommunications services in Hong Kong. By end 1996, HKT planned to increase the number of satellite dishes from 14 to 17.

Besides providing traditional telephone service, HKT was planning many other services (e.g., home shopping, distance learning, video games, electronic banking). If Video-on-Demand was launched as planned in mid-1996, HKT would be one of the world's first companies to deliver interactive multi-media applications direct to users. HKT had applied for government permission to provide cable television service.

Awards and Community Services

Named in the 1994 *Asian Business* survey as one of Asia's *Most Admired Companies*, HKT was placed first in the telecommunications industry and first in Asia for contribution to the local economy. The Asian Institute of Management (the Philippines) honored HKT with its Award for Financial Management; the Oriental Press Group recognized HKT by presenting the Golden Bridge Award for good customer services. HKT's CSL 1010 division captured the Hong Kong Management Association and Television Broadcast award for marketing excellence.

HKT was very active in the community; it committed HK$100 million each year to social, cultural and educational programs. For example, the newly opened "Open Learning Institute" was solely sponsored by HKT. Such sponsorship activities kept HKT's reputation as a well-established and respected company. It promoted the image of supporting Hong Kong and showed its loyalty to the colony by continuous investment despite growing political tension between Britain and China.

Customer Service

HKT was widely perceived as having paid little attention to customer service before competition arrived. Beginning April 1995, it pledged to increase focus on customer needs and to provide more value for money. Deputy CEO Howell Davies stated: "We have good experience in operating in a competitive environment. We are now about to see competition in the local telephony market but we have had quite a while to restructure Telecom to meet competition. We are much more customer focused."

HKT was attempting to upgrade service quality; its Customer Service Commitment. In addition, it received ISO 9000 certification for some key operations. To implement its new customer-oriented culture, HKT set up various customer focus groups to assess customer needs, then modified services to meet individual requirements. However, HKT insisted it would not be positioned as the cheapest telephone company. Said Allen Ma, Director of Marketing: "We are going to position ourselves as the company with the best value for money. It is our objective to make sure the customers choose Hong Kong Telecom over other companies."

HKT's integrated customer service system, Dragon, provided employees with technological support for improved customer service. The Customer Front Office unit (1995) gave customers a single point of contact. Also in 1995, HKT launched a service guarantee plan, G-Force. Customers received compensation if HKT failed to meet high service standards: install new lines within seven days, repair faults the next day, restore telephone service and connect new mobile telephones and pagers promptly.

China Telecommunications Services

HKT's China commitment was demonstrated by its strong relationship with the Chinese government. CEO Linus Cheung expressed in the 1994 *Chief Executive Review:* "HK Telecom continues to strengthen its ties with the mainland. We enjoy an excellent working relationship with the Ministry of Posts and Telecommunications, as well as the various provincial and municipal telecommunications authorities."

HKT opened offices in Beijing, Shanghai and Guangzhou. Despite new local and international competition, HKT was the unrivaled supplier for calls to China. In August 1994, HKT announced it was working with the Chinese government to investigate the construction of a HK$1 billion, 3,000 kilometers optical fiber cable system linking Hong Kong and Beijing. This project was the first important cooperative venture between the Chinese telecommunication industry and a foreign telecommunication corporation in China. The mid-1994 launch of International Private Leased Circuits from Hong Kong to Fujian province (including provincial capital Fuzhou and the Xiamen Special Economic Zone) was another milestone in HKT's China operations.

By March 1995, China accounted for about 34% of HKT's total international revenues and almost half the total IDD traffic. Growth in China business was expected to increase at a lower rate than previous years. In 1994, high Chinese inflation forced the government to slow economic growth; telephone traffic growth moderated to 18% (1994 to 1995). Unification of exchange rates in China led to an increase in the real cost of China to Hong Kong calls.

Financial Results

In 1994, HKT reported HK$26,910 million revenues, up from HK$24,280 million (1993) (Exhibit 1). Sources comprised: international telephone service, 60.6%; local telephone service, 13.6%; other telecommunications services, 16.5%; equipment sales and rental, 6.1%; computer, engineering and other services, 3.2%. Significantly, incoming call revenues increased by 7%; outgoing grew by 9%. Lines in service increased by 5.3% to 3,149,280; business lines grew by 8%, residential lines by 4%.

International Telecommunications

HKTI was market leader in international telephone service. Its key strengths included: monopoly protection under the current legislation, strong relations with the Hong Kong and Chinese governments, strong financial position, and commitment to the telecommunications industry through continual advances in technology. In 1975, HKT's franchise for domestic service was extended for another 20 years, expiring ahead of Hong Kong's reversion to China's control in mid-1997. Chairman, Lord Young of Graffham, expressed confidence that its sheer size, quality of facilities and services justified the renewal.

Despite advantages firmly established through this extension, HKT faced competition from three new licensees for local business (out of seven applications). Regarding international calls, competitors were able to enter the telecommunication business via legal loopholes in HKTI/government agreements such that calls from Hong Kong were actually made to originate in a foreign country via a "call back" system. Significant participants for international call services included: AIC Telecom Ltd., City Telecom, Elephant Talk Ltd., Grand Tel International Ltd., APT Telekom Ltd., USA Global Link and AT&T. (See Tables 2A, 2B for price comparisons.)

Actual procedures to make "call back" international calls could be classified into two main categories (Table 3):

Personal Identification Number (PIN): A user dialed the telephone company's access number, then entered the PIN. When checked and approved, the user dialed the long distance telephone number to communicate with the overseas party. Companies in

Table 2A: Price Comparisons between CTI and HKT (HK$ per min.)

		HKT SureFax	CTI G-Fax	CTI Discount
	Canada	8.5	6.09	28%
Apr-94	U.K.	9.3	6.71	28%
	U.S.	9.3	6.71	28%
	Canada	7.5	6.09	19%
Aug-94	U.K.	8.4	6.71	20%
	U.S.	8.2	6.71	18%

Table 2B: Price Comparisons between Various Competitors on Long Distance Calls (HK$ per min.)

			HKT IDD	CTI	AIC	Grand Tel
	Canada	Peak hour	7.9	6.72	5.99	6.25
		Non-peak hour	6.9	6.07	5.52	5.85
Apr-95	U.K.	Peak hour	8.8	7.48	7.45	7.42
		Non-peak hour	8.2	7.48	7.45	7.42
	U.S.	Peak hour	8.6	7.31	6.85	6.8
		Non-peak hour	6.9	6.07	5.99	5.85

this category were CTI (HK), AIC Telecom Ltd., AT&T, Elephant Talk Ltd. and Grand Tel International Ltd.[1]

Table 3: Comparisons between International Call Systems

Category	Pros	Cons
PIN (CTI)	Use at any telephone; pay later; input no PIN with Auto Dialer	More expensive than Call Back
Call Back*	Pay later; cheaper than PIN and calling card	Use at pre-assigned telephones; longer time to wait before dialing; phone to home country if problems

*Technically, Call Back calls were considered originated from the home country rather than from the country where the caller made his/her call. Currently, Call Back was not permitted in China; all IDD calls from China had to go through China's official Post and Telecommunications network.

Call back: A user with a pre-assigned telephone entered an assigned "passport number" to connect with the company's origin country (e.g., U.S.). S/he replaced the

---

[1] Calling cards could be both "pay later" or prepaid "stored-value." Both CTI (HK) (Global link) and HKT (Hello) offered stored-value cards.

phone; when it rang after a short interval (< ten seconds), s/he picked up the receiver and dialed the international phone number. APT Telekom Ltd. and USA Global Link were classified under this category.

Market Growth

Because of fast economic growth in the Asia-Pacific region, high quality and efficient international message transmission was critical. Healthy annual growth rates of international telephone traffic (Table 4) were also fueled by Hong Kong's evolution from manufacturing to the world's third largest financial center (Exhibit 2). Large numbers of émigrés[2] and Hong Kong students departing for Canada and Australia were also significant factors in the growth of calls to these regions.

Table 4: Growth of International Telephone Traffic

Year	Million minutes	Growth rate (%)
1993	2522	24
1992	2025	26
1991	1609	23
1990	1312	24
1989	970	32

Price Reductions for International Calls

Following the agreement between the government and HKTI, an overall 8% reduction in international direct dialing (IDD) charges was effective on August 1, 1993; further price reductions, 2% annually, would continue through 1995. Wong believed price was critical in choosing an international calls carrier. For U.S. and Canada calls, CTI (HK) decreased price over 20% in the previous 12 months; HKTI's IDD rates were reduced by over 30%.

Price competition was fierce. Almost all competitors claimed their services were cheaper during certain time periods for certain countries. On average, CTI (HK) calls were cheaper than IDD by about 15%–20%. However, price comparisons depended on the particular route and time dialed. Calls to the U.K. or Australia were about 15% cheaper than IDD, but for some routes, IDD was cheaper than CTI (HK). "Call Back" companies offered even lower prices. Referring to competition, Wong observed:

> In this market, business is like a war game. You never know what will happen tomorrow! Things are changing so rapidly, our predictions are always off. Three giants are entering the telecommunications industry (i.e., Hutchison, New World and New T&T).[3] In the U.S., there are over 300 long distance telephone companies.

---

[2] In particular to Canada, U.S., U.K., Australia and New Zealand.
[3] These companies were financially secure Hong Kong-based firms. The Hutchison group was highly diversified; it had major investments in property, container terminals and telecommunications and

When will they come to provide service like ours? ... Unknown. Right now, our strategy on the competition is to take the First Mover Advantage. We want to stand out and say loudly that CTI (HK) is one of the biggest players in the market. We try to mimic the success of Star Paging ten years ago.[4]

International competitors primarily competed on price, but each adopted differentiation strategies reflected in distribution channels, promotion strategies and customer services (Exhibit 3).

Effects of Call Back Services

Hong Kong Telecom filed complaints with OFTA, claiming CTI (HK) was in breach of the Telecom Ordinance; it also threatened a law suit. However, besides reducing prices as required by its license agreements, HKTI took few market-based actions to counteract its recent market share deterioration. Rather, it emphasized cost control.

Initially the public believed HKT was losing international business and investors feared HKT share devaluation as competition increased. Many believed competitive call back services would reduce HKTI's future profits significantly. However, some market analysts disagreed; Fredson Bowers, Associate Director of Nomura Research Institute stated that: "There's some evidence that call back is slightly beneficial to Hong Kong Telecom."

Bowers' reasoning was based on HKT's handling of calls that came to the territory from call back companies. Under a decade-old international accounting system, HKTI received a fee for handling its half of an international call, currently negotiated at US$0.50 per minute for calls originating in the U.S. Conversely, for a call to the U.S. via Hong Kong Telecom, HKTI paid US$0.50 per minute to the U.S. company delivering the call. After the July 30, 1995 price cuts, HKTI would charge customers HK$6.80 per minute to the U.S., and pay HK$3.90 per minute to the U.S. call deliverer.

Observers predicted that call back services would begin offering cheap rates to some parts of China; HKTI might then do even better. If a call was sent to the U.S. and then to China, HKTI would receive the standard HK$3.90 a minute from the U.S. call back firm – up to ten times the amount it would keep if the call was sent directly. Thus, with call back services, the Hong Kong customer wins, HKT wins and of course the call back company wins. Who loses? According to Bowers: "AT&T loses. The logic is complex, but if a Hong Kong customer uses call back to get a cheap call to Britain, it is the U.S. phone giant that ends up worse off."

(cont'd)

was a leading paging company. New World's major business was property development; it had recently entered the paging business. Wharf was the only company offering Cable Television in Hong Kong; the Wharf group also had significant business in container terminals and real estate.

[4] Star Paging Ltd. (STL) was one of five early entrants in the Hong Kong paging business. In the mid-1980s, when Hutchison bought out these early entrants, STL remained independent. In 1995, STL was still in the top three; it diversified into telecommunications and entertainment.

Local Telecommunications

Domestically, the window for competition was small since local HKT calls were free. The challenge for new competitors was to launch basic phone service with a monthly charge (home users: HK$62 per month; commercial users: HK$90).[5] So far the three new entrants had not made heavy infrastructure investments.

Said Dan Taylor, telecommunications consultant for Andersen Consulting: "The challenge for the three licensees – Hutchison Communications, New T&T Hong Kong and New World Telephone – is finding ways to differentiate their services, given the existing system where the local calls are free." Another analyst observed: "What is going to differentiate them (competitors) is customer services and billing; basically, interfaces with the customer."

Industry observers believed that Hutchison Communications and New T&T (Wharf) would offer high speed data communications lines, which HKT lacked, to attract commercial sector firms. New World Telephone was focusing on Interactive Services. Both New T&T and New World might offer cable TV; New T&T might offer multimedia.[6]

On the eve of deregulation, the battle between the phone companies became very public; New T&T directly attacked HKT's key advertising campaign, launched in October 1994. Based on the brand positioning slogan "What can be imagined can be achieved," HKT advertisements featured John Lennon's "Imagine" sound-track. As HKT explained:

> The commercial pays tribute to people whose imaginations and achievements have enriched the lives of millions over the years. The underlying message is that by constantly harnessing our imagination, anything is possible.

In response, New T&T's commercials declared: "You can stop imagining," using as a main theme the Beatles' song "Revolution." This "attack" set New T&T as the most openly competitive company with HKT. Although New T&T's president stated room existed for all competitors, he was determined New T&T be in the forefront of publicity. In addition to the controversial advertisements, New T&T launched many promotions and road shows. Distribution outlets were located in prominent districts throughout Hong Kong and were heavily advertised.

City Telecom (HK)

Background

City Telecom Inc. was established in Toronto, Canada following deregulation of the North American telecommunications industry. Following successful market entry as a

---

[5] The exchange rate was US$1 = HK$7.75.
[6] Estimated investments were (HK$): Hutchison $3.5 billion; New T&T $6 billion; New World $2 billion.

re-seller of international telecommunication services in the Vancouver area, CTI recognized the large international telecommunication business in Hong Kong; in September 1992, CTI (HK) was formed. Wong was questioned about his decision to enter the Hong Kong market:

> The international telephone market is so huge. Revenues were over HK$10 billion in 1992; and business is expected to grow at over 20% p.a. By year-end 1995, it will be in the range of HK$15–16 billion. Lucrative profits are there. And, most importantly, there is only one player – Hong Kong Telecom. In fact, there is a franchise agreement between Hong Kong Telecom and the Hong Kong government for providing international service in Hong Kong. We sought legal advice before we came. We asked about regulations from the Secretary for Economic Services and the Office of the Telecommunications Authority (OFTA) to see if we could identify any contradictions in the franchise agreement. Eventually, we identified the possibility of offering service in Hong Kong. So long as no equipment was installed in Hong Kong, offering long distance service was perfectly legal. That was the rationale for our move to Hong Kong and probably to the People's Republic of China (PRC) in the future.

Mission Statement

In 1992, prior to Hong Kong entry, some part-time MBA students at Chinese University of Hong Kong prepared a consulting report for CTI (HK). The report recommended that CTI (HK) define a mission statement as soon as possible. Wong believed this was a good idea, for a clear mission could help guide employees in directions the company wished to pursue. However, due to time and other constraints, CTI (HK) had not worked on the content of a mission statement and consequently had none.

Organization Structure

Since its establishment, CTI (HK) had made many changes. Between April 1994 and April 1995, the headquarters office was moved three times. In April 1995, CTI (HK) was stationed in one of the most expensive business areas in Hong Kong, Tsim Sha Tsui, in the business district of southern Kowloon; office size was over 56,000 sq. ft. CTI (HK)'s sales force efforts had increased from four persons in 1993 to over 20. As Wong recalled: "The marketing team at the very beginning was led by myself only. Now I am working closely with marketing executives outside my office on all marketing planning and analysis." CTI (HK) was run by two executive directors, Ricky Wong (Regional Director) and Paul Cheung (Admin. Technical Director) (Figures 1A, 1B). Wong reported to an eight-person Board of Directors that included Wong and Cheung.

CTI (HK)'s System

Operationally, CTI's system was quite complex but could be described simply. When a Hong Kong resident used CTI's service, the first connection was from the user's phone to the switch box in CTI (HK)'s office. When this connection was made, it was redirected to CTI in Canada through a leased line from Hong Kong Telecom. The final

Figure 1A: CTI Organization Chart

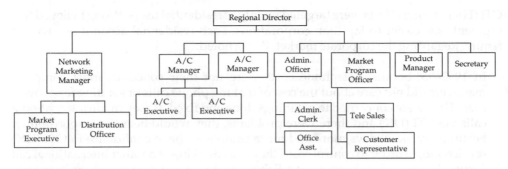

Figure 1B: CTI Organization Chart

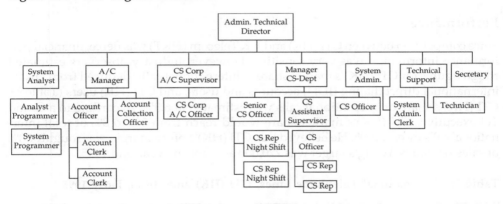

connection was from the Canadian switch box to the destination country. CTI (HK)'s costs were two-fold: a fixed monthly charge for Hong Kong Telecom's leased line connecting Hong Kong to Canada, and a variable charge to CTI for the Canada-to-destination country connection; the initial connection was at no cost.

CTI (HK) assembled one of the most advanced digital telecommunications network platforms using Northern Telecom and Newbridge Network's state-of-the-art technologies with switches in Buffalo, Montreal, Toronto and Vancouver. In January 1994, CTI (HK) leased a number of lines from HKT. Initially, CTI (HK) used an analog switch but this system provided poor voice quality (i.e., weak voice, interference). After several user complaints, CTI (HK) changed the system to digital in 1995. Transmission quality improved, complaints dropped dramatically.

CTI (HK) performed quality control on international calls, outgoing and incoming. Twenty-four hours a day, traffic control staff in Hong Kong and Canada monitored the numbers of incoming and outgoing calls to each country where CTI (HK) service was available. If call volume was low or zero, technical and computer system officers would check the switching system and fix problems.

Customer Profile

CTI (HK)'s initial efforts were targeted mainly at residential users; Wong believed this segment was easier to tap than corporations. Each residential account served one family. Regarding the corporate market, Wong noted:

> In 1992–93, because telephone costs were not their concerns, most company managers did not care about the cost of making phone calls or sending faxes overseas. They were concerned to get things done and fixed. If they made international calls via CTI (HK) and there were problems, they would bear the responsibility. Fortunately, nowadays more and more companies have confidence in CTI (HK) service and, in order to control costs, they start thinking of another international call carrier that provides cheaper but reliable service. So, our business in the corporate segment is improving.

Performance

Since competition between CTI (HK) and HK Telecom (HKT) was fierce, financial performance information was very sensitive. However, industry observers estimated rough figures for CTI (HK)'s market share in international calls, deduced from HKT's international direct dialing (IDD) accounts and users, and CTI (HK) users (Table 5). CTI (HK)'s share of international calls was estimated at 6.3%. According to a Grand Tel executive, CTI (HK)'s market share would reach from 5% to 8% of total international calls by end 1995. He believed that CTI (HK)'s profit margin was roughly 30% of sales revenues. Wong's target was 220,000 accounts by year-end 1995.

Table 5: International Telephone Lines, CTI (HK) and HKTI, Early 1995

Telephone lines connected with	Corporate	Residential
International Direct Dialing (IDD)*	611,559	1,593,494
CTI (HK)	10,000	130,000

*Hong Kong Telecom's service. Corporate and residential figures for IDD were adjusted upwards by 15% and 7% respectively for comparison purposes.

Regardless of actual market share, Wong asserted subscribers were growing rapidly (Table 6); he said each day hundreds of new customers signed up. Around 20 staff worked full time inputting new customer data.

Table 6: Growth in CTI (HK) User Accounts (June 1994–March 1995)

Month, Year	Number of accounts
March 1995	140,000
December 1994	110,000
June 1994	72,000

Although CTI (HK) competed directly with HKTI for international business, it did not compete for PRC business. HKTI provided the cheapest international calls to China; Wong said the cost of the Canada to China connection for CTI (HK) was simply too high. However, he believed China could not be neglected as the relative importance of calls to China was increasing (Table 7). For CTI (HK), the most important markets were the U.S. and Canada. CTI (HK) claimed to carry 15% of calls to North America implying a HK$1.5 billion business.

Table 7: Percent of Outgoing Traffic from Hong Kong

	1994	1993	1992	1991	1990		1994	1993	1992	1991	1990
China	50	47	42	36	31	U.K.	4	4	5	5	6
U.S.	7	7	8	9	11	Macau	3	3	4	4	4
Taiwan	6	6	7	8	9	Singapore	3	3	4	4	4
Canada	4	5	5	5	5	Australia	3	3	3	4	4
Japan	4	4	5	6	7	Philippines	3	3	3	3	3
						Others	13	15	14	16	16

Source: HK Telecom 1994 annual report.

Strategic Planning

Long-term objectives. Although CTI (HK) had not defined long-term objectives, Wong said business was highly unpredictable and full of challenges. In 1994, he and a few CTI (HK) executives went to a Hong Kong resort to discuss future directions for CTI (HK). After eight hours the group developed detailed directions and actions. However, after a few months, the market reality turned out to be totally different from their predictions.

We want to go ahead. Like a soldier in the war, he has no time to think. CTI (HK) just goes ahead and tries to reach the top as soon as possible. Things are difficult for us because there are no precedents in Hong Kong. We are the pioneer. If we win, others will follow. If we fail, others will avoid doing the same stupid things. What we do is to try everything that is new and probably feasible. Do you guys think that it is feasible to pick up a phone and ask for someone to give you the information required for filling in the CTI (HK) account application form? You know, you need to get the guy's Hong Kong identity card number, credit card number, bank account, address and contact numbers. But remember, the guy doesn't know whether you are the staff of CTI (HK) or not. You tell him that you are, however, he may not trust you. My marketing executives said in a meeting such approach would not work. I agreed, but asked why we didn't try. Just last night, we got positive feedback. Each staff member working on the job got eight applications in three hours. It proves that "Trying and Learning from Experience" is very important to us and it could be one of our philosophies.

Wong said his aim was to increase the client base as much as possible; as a result, CTI (HK)'s initial strategy was to keep prices 25% below Hong Kong Telecom's.[7]

Target segment and market positioning. In its early years (1992–93), CTI (HK)'s major target segment was residential users. However, since corporate accounts showed satisfactory growth, more resources were placed in this segment; in early 1995 a corporate accounts team was set up. CTI (HK) was also considering strategies and timing for entering China. Beyond Hong Kong and China, its major focus would be the Asia-Pacific region; Wong believed economic growth would lead to sufficient demand for future investments to be profitable. Wong said CTI (HK)'s positioning in the Hong Kong market was: "To be the second largest company providing international telephone service." CTI (HK) did not expect to replace HKTI, even over ten years. Nonetheless, he wanted Hong Kong people to know CTI (HK) was the best company in the international telephone business, exclusive of HKTI.

Marketing strategy. Since mid-1993, CTI (HK) invested significantly in advertising (Table 8). CTI (HK)'s instruction to the advertising agency was: "Make everyone in the street know what CTI (HK) is." The agency was responsible for above-the-line promotion;[8] CTI (HK) was responsible for below-the-line promotion (Table 9). In the previous 12 months, CTI (HK) conducted two research studies (June 1994, January 1995) to assess CTI (HK)'s awareness level and secure other market information.[9] The January 1995 study (150 valid interviews) showed a 66% awareness level, up from 60.3% in June 1994.

In June 1994, main sources of knowledge about CTI (HK) were: the press (32%), referrals (19%), TV (13%). For those aware of CTI (HK), over 65% were unsure if CTI (HK) was cheaper than IDD. A full 25% "knew" CTI (HK)'s service was cheaper. In January 1995, 54% of interviewees said price was the most important factor in choosing an international telephone carrier; coverage area ranked second (43%). Off-peak discounts were third.

Table 8: CTI (HK) Advertising Expenditures*

Period of year	HK$ million
December 1993–April 1994	3
August 1994–December 1994	7
February 1995–August 1995	10

*Mostly in Cantonese.

---

[7] According to a U.S. survey, a 15% price reduction was sufficient for international telephone users to switch telephone carriers.

[8] This term, used by the advertising agency, subsumed all media advertising including TV, press and radio.

[9] For the June research report: 829 calls made, 209 questionnaires completed, 180 valid. For the January research report, 150 valid interviews.

Table 9: Advertising Budget Allocations, 1994–95

Media	% of total budget
TV	65
Press	27
Others	6

In addition to "above-the-line" advertising, CTI (HK) engaged in aggressive "below-the-line" activities: direct calling, road show exhibitions, drop-mail to all major private estates and coupons at 200 CTI (HK) phone booths in urban areas. CTI (HK) also located telephone-installed vans in urban districts so residents could try its service for a three-minute free call. CTI (HK) provided phone booths for store owners to install their own phones; at these phone booths, CTI (HK)'s logo and other information were prominently displayed and application forms were available.

CTI (HK) had over 5,000 network marketing distributors; freelance and part-time, in addition to 20 full-time salesmen and 50 part-time salespeople. Salespeople (corporate customers only) were paid a basic salary and 5% to 10% commissions. The marketing distributor system operated similarly to "Amway"; distributors (mainly residential but corporate customers permitted) both sold CTI (HK) service to long-distance telephone users and signed up "downline" distributors.[10] CTI (HK) allocated 8% of revenues to distributors; sales by first level distributors earned 2% commission; if a second level distributor made a sale, she received 2% commission, the first level distributor received 1%; if a third level distributor made a sale, each distributor level received 1% commission. The chain ceased at the seventh level; distributors did not receive a salary. Commission payments (with no time limit) were based on CTI revenues per customer.

Marketing implementation. Wong kept the price difference between CTI (HK) and HKTI service at around 15%–20%. Call Back companies (APT Telekom Ltd., USA Global Link) provided international telephone service cheaper than CTI (HK), about 50% of IDD rates. However, Wong believed these companies' awareness was low and their dialing procedures inconvenient.

For CTI (HK) service, a user had to dial over 15 digits before she could dial the overseas number. To enhance convenience, CTI (HK) provided customers with Auto-Dialers (criteria: monthly revenues HK$500 to HK$1,000 and a "gut feel" the customer was worth providing the device) and Smartphones to reduce the inconvenience of inputting so many digits. With these devices, dialing procedures were identical to IDD. Moreover, users could switch back to IDD conveniently if required.

Wong said that since international telephone service was invisible, it was difficult for customers to assess service quality without trial. As a result, CTI (HK) tried to visualize its corporate image and service; its logo was a satellite in white color against

---

[10]Amway was an U.S. firm that sold household products directly to consumers through a multi-tiered, pyramid-type distribution system.

a blue background (Exhibit 4). Almost all published materials were in eye-catching orange; orange color telephones were shown in most publications; the Smartphone was also orange. TV commercials and other advertising were mainly in Cantonese. In addition, CTI (HK) cooperated with credit card companies to promote its service; application forms were sent together with credit card payment statements.

The Future for City Telecom (Hong Kong)

Reminiscing about CTI (HK)'s early days, Wong said:

> I am one who wants action. I did not plan thoroughly when I started my business. About three years ago, on June 3, 1992, I was in Canada. I said to my friends that I wanted to go to Hong Kong to start a telecommunications business. One week later, on June 10, I was in Hong Kong contemplating applying for a license to compete with HK Telecom. In October, I opened my office. One month later, we provided service. On the third day after opening, we received over 3,000 applications to use CTI (HK) service.

The CTI (HK) culture was described by Wong:

> I can tell you, I am not a good boss. I don't know much about how to appreciate and motivate others, or how to communicate with staff. Very often, my employees misunderstand what I say. My instructions are always unclear, I think. And these are the things I need to learn in the coming years. I understand that the success of CTI (HK) will no longer rely on myself only. I need others' help. I find my efforts and time are so limited. Fortunately, many people are working very hard in CTI (HK). They have the spirit to strive for success, to win and overcome the competition. The motivation is brought by the prospects of the firm. They all can see the company growth and feel the opportunities at CTI (HK) are much greater than outside.

Wong believed CTI (HK) had been lucky. It faced little competition at the outset, though more competition was evolving. He believed the market was sufficiently fluid for CTI (HK) to try new things; it could afford to make errors. Regarding price reductions by new entrants, Wong claimed:

> As long as we continue to gain customers from HKTI, we do not care much about the others. If HKTI reduces prices, we shall follow; otherwise, we are happy with the current situation. I do not think HKTI will make a big price move. What we will do is build up brand loyalty.

Wong said he could not predict the future. CTI (HK) would continue to move forward and work hard on those aspects where it had potential. As he set off for the badminton court, Wong said he had to make two important decisions: how to gain more market share, especially in the corporate market, and how to compete in China. Regardless, CTI (HK) would continue to improve its products and services to establish a strong position as the second largest international telephone company in Hong Kong.

Exhibit 1: Hong Kong Telecom – Ten-year Financial Review (HK$ million)

	1995 $	1994 $	1993 $	1992 $	1991 $	1990 $	1989 $	1988 $	1987 $	1986 $
Profit & Loss Account										
Turnover										
Intl' telephone services	16,310.5	15,164.8	13,588.9	11,083.9	9,610.7	7,963.0	6,452.1	4,848.0	3,526.8	2,543.9
Local telephone services	3,668.7	3,281.4	2,890.9	2,664.0	2,310.8	2,049.0	1,739.0	1,572.5	1,451.1	1,319.1
Other telecom. services	4,443.2	3,587.9	3,045.2	2,751.3	2,442.4	2,303.9	2,161.9	2,164.2	2,171.3	2,022.2
Equipment sales and rental	1624.5	1405.8	1280.5	1212.3	1212.3	1202.9	1048.7	927.4	698.9	635.3
Computer, eng. & other services	862.7	839.9	839.8	659.6	689.9	610.5	435.4	403.3	361.3	265.3
Total turnover	26,909.6	24,279.8	21645.3	18,370.8	16,266.1	14,134.3	11,837.1	9,915.4	8,209.4	6,785.8
Operating costs										
Allocations to other administrations										
– Intl' telephone services	7,367.8	6,780.8	6,100.0	4,996.6	4,551.7	3,745.5	3,129.3	2,307.5	1,558.6	1,076.9
– Others	298.7	324.5	372.0	401.4	477.7	528.5	579.2	644.8	672.5	616.0
Salaries and related costs	3,661.5	3,228.6	3,159.9	2,722.2	2,696.1	2,277.9	1,880.0	1,610.7	1,425.3	1,323.4
Depreciation and amortization	1,710.4	1,468.9	1,332.1	1,034.9	961.4	779.0	670.1	635.6	581.0	575.7
Cost of sales	888.6	925.8	808.4	654.7	583.2	604.3	420.5	301.9	179.1	156.5
Rent, rates and utilities	565.8	516.7	538.7	455.2	445.0	352.2	244.2	187.0	161.1	150.5
Royalty to H.K. government	543.8	495.1	438.9	370.6	319.5	284.4	216.6	171.3	155.9	127.2
Mgt. fees to Cable & Wireless Plc	217.2	306.3	306.3	267.3	233.2	204.7	176.3	156.0	138.9	117.1
Other operating costs	1,894.6	1,624.3	1,334.0	1,129.6	852.7	916.6	754.1	658.3	655.3	605.7
Total operating costs	17,148.4	15,671.0	14,390.3	12,032.5	11,120.5	9,693.1	8,070.3	6,673.1	5,527.7	4,749.0
Operating profit	9,761.2	8,608.8	7,255.0	6,338.3	5,145.6	4,441.2	3,766.8	3,242.3	2,681.7	2,036.8
Net interest and other income	276.2	151.6	194.0	160.9	226.8	201.9	187.3	115.0	104.4	80.3
Profit before taxation	10,037.4	8,760.4	7,449.0	6,499.2	5,372.4	4,643.1	3,954.1	3,357.3	2,786.1	2,117.1
Taxation	1,338.7	1,202.8	1,018.9	833.4	420.0	351.5	289.2	317.9	402.4	258.2
Profit after taxation	8,698.7	7,557.6	6,430.1	5,665.8	4,952.4	4,291.6	3,664.9	3,039.4	2,383.7	1,858.9
Minority interests	–	0.1	(0.2)	7.4	5.7	2.0	(4.5)	(4.2)	(3.2)	–
Development fund transfer	–	–	–	–	110.4	66.5	(29.9)	(43.4)	(11.5)	7.6

Exhibit 1 (cont'd)

		1995 $	1994 $	1993 $	1992 $	1991 $	1990 $	1989 $	1988 $	1987 $	1986 $
Profit before extraordinary item		8,698.7	7,557.7	6,429.9	5,673.2	5,068.5	4,360.1	3,630.5	2,991.8	2,369.0	1,866.5
Extraordinary item		–	–	–	–	(729.9)	–	–	–	–	–
Profit attribute to shareholders		8,698.7	7,557.7	6,429.9	5,673.2	4,338.6	4,360.1	3,630.5	2,991.8	2,369.0	1,866.5
Balance Sheet											
Current assets		9,590.1	8,696.0	7,021.0	5,782.8	4,926.7	4,845.0	4,136.9	3,698.3	2,834.9	2,406.0
Total assets		29,906.1	26,656.0	22,952.4	19,593.5	17,600.4	15,496.0	12,995.5	10,605.3	8,825.7	7,739.7
Current liab.		11,437.1	10,190.5	8,240.9	6,093.1	5,498.0	4,654.4	3,777.2	2,776.5	2,183.4	2,198.4
Long-term liab.		39.9	119.4	200.7	516.1	632.2	647.3	206.3	412.0	47.6	126.3
Shareholders' funds		17,718.0	15,632.9	13,763.1	12,173.5	10,738.4	10,080.2	8,840.1	7,282.8	6,513.1	5,360.6
Total liab. and shareholders' funds		29,906.1	26,656.0	22,952.4	19,593.5	17,600.4	15,496.0	12,995.5	10,605.3	8,825.7	7,739.7
Capital expenditure	$M	4,045	3,532	3,620	2,204	3,018	2,676	2,387	1,576	1,280	1,167
Leasehold land buildings	$M	396	342	876	71	205	144	224	148	124	96
Exchange equipment	$M	1,007	888	886	830	1,420	1,273	1,152	903	562	315
Intl' transmission plant	$M	393	604	457	299	248	419	413	118	205	472
Local transmission plant	$M	1,010	838	771	356	335	285	185	152	141	133
Other plant and equipment	$M	1,239	860	630	648	810	535	413	255	248	151
Earnings per share	cents	78.0	67.8	57.7	50.9	45.4	39.1	32.7	27.1	21.4	16.9
Inc. in earnings per share	%	15.1	17.5	13.3	11.9	16.1	19.6	20.7	26.6	26.6	37.4
Dividend per share	cents	59.3	51.0	43.4	38.0	33.0	28.0	22.7	5.0	n/a	n/a
Shareholders		20,104	19,953	25,439	27,679	29,293	39,560	48,273	25,274	15,165	13,619
Staff		16,054	16,039	15,888	15,449	16,279	17,800	17,261	16,755	16,201	15,793

Exhibit 2: Telecommunication Traffic Statistics

	1995	1994	1993	1992	1991	1990	1989	1988	1987	1986
Intl' telephone ('000 minutes)										
Outgoing voice										
IDD	1,267,268	1,091,190	892,507	715,690	564,578	437,507	326,582	234,549	162,122	118,510
Operator-assisted	86,244	87,760	77,456	55,847	48,057	49,201	47,999	40,207	36,594	32,770
Outgoing fax and data	224,910	197,908	166,685	141,638	116,723	95,460	66,874	42,095	21,974	9,007
Total outgoing	1,578,422	1,376,858	1,136,648	913,175	729,358	582,168	441,455	316,851	220,690	160,287
Total incoming	1,446,350	1,260,325	1,009,375	782,989	645,527	537,776	427,259	315,387	243,103	182,011
Total	3,024,772	2,637,183	2,146,023	1,696,164	1,374,885	1,119,944	868,714	632,238	463,793	342,298
Growth in total outgoing (%)	14.6	21.1	24.5	25.2	25.3	31.9	39.3	43.6	37.7	30.2
Growth in total incoming (%)	14.8	24.9	28.9	21.3	20.0	25.9	35.5	29.7	33.6	27.4
Percent of outgoing traffic										
China	52	50	47	42	36	31	29	25	20	18
U.S.	6	7	7	8	9	11	12	13	14	15
Taiwan	5	6	6	7	8	9	9	9	9	9
Canada	4	4	5	5	5	5	5	4	4	4
Japan	4	4	4	5	6	7	8	9	9	10
U.K.	4	4	4	5	5	6	6	7	8	8
Macau	3	3	3	4	4	4	4	5	5	8
Singapore	3	3	3	4	4	4	4	4	5	5
Australia	3	3	3	3	4	4	4	4	4	5
Philippines	3	3	3	3	3	3	3	3	3	4
Others	13	13	15	14	16	16	16	17	19	19
Telex ('000 minutes)										
Local	20,749	21,202	21,506	23,917	26,195	29,697	32,109	37,828	37,952	32,488
Intl' outgoing	25,178	28,776	30,562	34,682	37,435	41,548	46,526	51,743	55,237	51,552
Intl' incoming	14,158	17,689	19,376	22,714	26,572	31,401	38,340	44,756	48,910	46,580
Intl' telegram ('000 messages)										
Outgoing	113	153	212	277	360	529	711	784	904	1,102
Incoming	100	150	217	286	379	534	744	819	933	1,080

Exhibit 2 (cont'd)

	1995	1994	1993	1992	1991	1990	1989	1988	1987	1986
Exch. capacity	3,294,472	3,175,298	3,026,869	2,841,161	2,729,922	2,519,630	2,396,886	2,226,759	2,096,327	2,002,812
Exch. lines in service										
Business lines	991,803	926,159	854,673	773,015	698,593	659,338	607,183	541,068	490,253	451,118
Datel lines	50,705	41,900	34,064	27,159	23,950	19,497	15,595	11,993	7,999	4,970
Business fax lines	186,290	173,919	153,951	126,755	111,239	88,550	65,384	38,411	15,135	5,639
	1,228,798	1,141,978	1,042,688	926,929	833,782	767,385	688,162	591,472	513,387	461,727
Residential lines	1,896,592	1,828,796	1,758,892	1,703,624	1,641,216	1,577,851	1,502,835	1,429,922	1,363,935	1,302,611
Residential fax lines	23,890	21,282	18,217	11,861	0#	0#	0#	0#	0#	0#
Total exch. lines in service	1,920,482	1,850,078	1,777,109	1,715,485	1,641,216	1,577,851	1,502,835	1,429,922	1,363,935	1,302,611
	3,149,281	2,992,056	2,819,797	2,642,414	2,474,998	2,345,236	2,190,997	2,021,394	1,877,322	1,764,338
Growth in exch. lines in service (%)										
Business lines	7.1	8.4	10.6	10.7	6.0	8.6	12.2	10.4	8.7	6.8
Datel lines	21.0	23.0	25.4	13.4	22.8	25.0	30.0	49.9	60.9	67.4
Business fax lines	7.1	13.0	21.5	13.9	25.6	35.4	70.2	153.8	168.4	195.9
Residential lines	3.7	4.0	3.2	3.8	4.0	5.0	5.1	4.8	4.7	5.3
Telephones in service	4,094,200	3,898,800	3,694,000	3,508,500	3,314,100	3,157,400	2,944,000	2,708,000	2,507,100	2,347,800
Telephones per 100 pop.	66.6	65.9	63.6	61.0	57.1	54.3	51.3	48.3	45.3	43.0
IDD connection	2,136,040	2,021,037	1,849,325	1,636,388	1,417,235	1,151,219	875,084	321,884	406,506	269,488
Business	576,624	531,790	462,434	388,014	327,584	276,284	215,571	147,258	97,318	71,441
Residential	1,559,416	1,489,247	1,386,891	1,248,374	1,089,651	874,935	659,513	474,626	309,188	198,047
Home fax 2 connections	46,777	38,345	24,704	0	0	0	0	0	0	0
Telex lines	11,870	15,052	17,700	19,859	21,502	23,075	26,757	29,316	29,102	27,370
Datapak lines	69,349	58,243	45,756	37,333	29,568	19,831	11,359	5,985	2,956	560
Intl. leased circuits capacity (MBPS)	186.1	130.4	87.9	67.0	41.8	26.1	17.7	11.3	7.4	5.7

Exhibit 3: Comparison of CTI with Competitors

(I) Product:	CTI	HK Telecom	AIC	UTI	Grand Tel
Calling card	i) CTI calling card – HK to overseas; – Overseas to HK	i) HK Telecom calling card: – IDD200 (HK to overseas) – Auto HK direct (overseas to HK) – HK direct through operator (overseas to HK) – Global calling – Int'l conference call – Int'l interpreter services	i) AIC Int'l calling card – HK to overseas – Overseas to HK	i) UTI Long distance service – HK to overseas ii) Sprint fon card – Overseas to HK & cross country	i) Grand Tel Int'l calling card
Prepaid card	ii) Global Link (prepaid phonecard)	ii) Hello phone card (prepaid)		iii) Uniglobe prepaid phone card iv) Sprint prepaid phone card- Overseas to HK; cross country v) UTI countdown card	ii) Grand Tel prepaid phone card
Other card				– shopping discount card	

(II) Services:	CTI	HK Telecom	AIC	UTI	Grand Tel
IDD coverage countries					
1) HK to overseas	194	>200	148	80	194
2) Overseas to HK	30	most countries	21	89	26
3) Cheaper than IDD	125		54	>70	97
Cross country		i) IDD calling card			
Fax 002 services	Yes	Yes	Yes	Yes	Yes
Store & forward fax	003 Fax	Sure Fax			
Stored-value coupon	Price $500 => Face value $525		Price $1000 => Face value $1050		$500/1000/2000
Prepaid card	i) Global Link; Based on IDD rate; Price $200 of face value $240	i) Hello phone card; Price $100/200/300		i) Uniglobe prepaid card; Price $780 per 4pcs ii) Sprint prepaid calling card; 10 units/$46; 20 units/$92; 40 units/$186; 50 units/$230	i) Grand Tel Int'l prepaid calling card; Based on IDD rate

Exhibit 3 (cont'd)

(II) Services (cont'd):	CTI	HK Telecom	AIC	UTI	Grand Tel
Auto-dialer	Price: $480				
Tone dialer	"Little smart" at $65	Over $100, available at CSL			
Joint-venture services	CTI-Chase Visa/Master Card			UNI countdown card – discounts $300/yr.	
Other services		TIMEWATCH = Duration of calls – advised within 15 mins after the call – $4 per call TIMEWATCH PLUS = Duration + charge – advised within 15 mins after the call – $4 per call TELETAPES = world information – various languages – same rate as IDD		UNI number: One person one number concept – individuals assigned unique numbers which allow being reached when desired only – call management take down all messages when not free – monthly fee $200 – buy will get one month free plus $60 long distance cash coupon	TIMEWATCHER – press ## after finishing the call CHECK BILLING INFORMATION POT

(III) Calling Procedures:	CTI	HK Telecom	AIC	UTI	Grand Tel
001/002 services	1) Dial 3003-3888/ 3002-188 2) Input pin (10): 5 on card and 5 delivered separately 3) 001 + country code + area code + phone no. + #	1) Dial 200 2) Calling card 8 digits + pin (4 digits) 3) country code + area code + phone no. + #	1) Dial 3003-3777 2) a/c no. (6) + (changeable) Pin no. 8 3) country code + area code + phone no. + #	1) Dial 3002-3777 2) a/c no. (6) + (changeable) Pin no. (8) 3) country code + area code + phone no. + #	1) Dial 3003-8008 2) Pin (11): 6 ID no. + 5 delivered separately 3) 001 + country code + area code + phone no. + #
Store & forward fax	1) Dial 3002-8228 2) Pin 3) 003 + country code + area code+fax no. + #				

Exhibit 3 (cont'd)

(IV) Charges and Rates:	CTI	HK Telecom	AIC	UTI	Grand Tel
Charges:					
i) Application fee	Nil	Nil (must be current customers of HK Telecom)	Nil	Nil	Nil
ii) Others		Timewatch: $4/call; Timewatch Plus: $4/call		UNI-No. Service: $200/mth; UNI-countdown: $300/yr.	GT Jetso discount card: $280/yr.

(V) Promotion:	CTI	HK Telecom	AIC	UTI	Grand Tel
Rates:					
i) Peak/off-peak	Peak: Mon–Sat (0700–0000) for 001/002; Flat rate for 003	Peak: Mon–Fri (0700–0000); Sat (0700–1300)	Peak: Mon–Fri (0700–0000); Sat (0700–1300)	Flat rate	Peak: Mon–Fri (0700–0000); Sat (0700–1300)
ii) Charging unit					
a. HK to overseas (peak)	6 sec	6 sec	6 sec	1 min	6 sec
HK to overseas (Off-)	6 sec (started from 2nd min)	6 sec	6 sec	ditto	6 sec (started from 2nd min)
b. Overseas to HK	1 min	6 sec min (through operator, after 3 min)	1 min	1 min	1 min
c. Others			Basic rate & discount rate (monthly bill over $1000)		
Campaigns	1) Store-value coupon, price lower than face value by 23.5% 2) Prepaid $500 to entitle to get autodialler 3) CTI-Chase: a) $200 call coupon + $88 discount for Telelink CT2 handset to new customers (10/9/94–31/12/94)	1) Lucky draw	1) Volume discount rate for monthly rate >$1000 2) Double-saving, i.e., (1) + stored value coupon 3) Extra savings (37% discount) for calls to U.S. made in July and Aug. '94 4) GrandMart members get 5% discount stored-value coupon and $50 call coupon 5) Macau promotion	1) UTI lucky draw	1) Press briefing on 28/3/94 2) Free gift in promotion month 3) Volume discount rate for monthly bill > $1000 4) Pre-value coupon save additional 5% 5) Credits accumulated for each call, gifts given up to certain credits

Exhibit 3 (cont'd)

(V) Promotion (cont'd):	CTI	HK Telecom	AIC	UTI	Grand Tel
	b) Free gifts such as autodialler, $200 call coupon, exemption of 1st year annual fee for Chase Visa/Master card (31/3-31/12/94 4) CTI-P&G: (Mid-Jan to May 31) CTI appl. form attached to Head & Shoulder; $50 free call by response in this before 30/6/95 5) Sponsored ATV in related programs 6) Estates Introduction Programs in mid-June including TV ads and phone in registration. 7) Roadshows in shopping arcades, public estates and MTR				6) VIP package 7) Roadshows in shopping arcades, public estates, MTR, institutes
Promotion channels	– Direct mail – Press: Newspaper and magazines – TV: Advertising magazine on TVB, commercial spots on prime and fringe time – Radio: Station CRI – Leaflets through distributors and MTR stores – Others: Joint promotion with Chase Manhattan Bank	– Direct mail – Press: Newspaper and magazines – TV: Regular commercial spots on TVB	– Press – Asia TV, TV magazine commercial spots at fringe time – Leaflets through ABC paging and MTR stores	– Leaflets through distributors	– Direct mail to institutes, gov't. hospitals, attached with coupons – Press: Newspaper and magazines; press conference – Radio: Station CRI – Leaflets through distributors – Others: Joint venture with Jetso discount card

(VI) Other Information:	CTI	HK Telecom	AIC	UTI	Grand Tel
Establishment year	92	Long history	94	–	95
Number of accounts	140,000	3,000,000	40,000	10,000	10,000

Source: Adapted from *Hong Kong Economics Daily*, April 12, 1995.

Case 5

Hair-Works

Noel Capon
Graduate School of Business, Columbia University

Li Mei Mei, Chau Man Kuen, Wong Tze Shan, Ho Yuen Ling, Lee Ching Yee
The Hong Kong University of Science and Technology

In September 1995, Eddie Wong, one of Hong Kong's wealthy real estate barons, was contemplating his latest business venture: the hair care industry. Wong recalled the incident when Ned Johnson, owner of Boston-based mutual fund company, Fidelity Investments, purchased a limousine company after he missed a flight because of a late limousine pick-up. Correspondingly, Mrs. Naomi Wong recently had a couple of unfortunate experiences with hair salons, so Mr. Wong, together with some business acquaintances, decided to enter the hair care business. However, the venture was much more serious than simply a device for making his wife happy; Wong demanded that all his ventures be based on a sound marketing strategy and reach a minimum ROI. As he paged through the consultant's report on the upper end of the hair care industry, he began to consider how to break into the top tier.

8003

Industry Background

Until the 1960s and 1970s, Hong Kong residents secured hairdressing service at "Shanghai" barber shops (Figure 1). Simple services like hair cutting, hair washing and beard shaving were provided by traditional barbers, "Shi-fu." In the 1970s, many up-to-date hair salons opened offering a wide variety of hair care services. Old style "Shanghai" barber shops began to be replaced by these emerging hair salons. By 1995, a wide range of hair salons targeted many different customer groups.

Middle and upper-class Hong Kong residents, both local Chinese ("tai-tais") and expatriate women, were renowned for the attention they paid to looking good.[1] For

---

[1] "Tai-tai" was a Cantonese word literally meaning "wife"; however, colloquially, it referred to rich married women, mainly socialites, who spent a majority of their time improving their appearance.

120

Figure 1: Shanghai Pao Barber Shop in Hong Kong

many married Hong Kong women at the high-end of the income scale, life involved a succession of weddings and other social gatherings. Balls were popular before Christmas; cocktail parties and formal dinners took place throughout the year. For many more women, annual dinners were regularly held before the Lunar New Year (December to February).[2] Hong Kong was also very traditional despite its modernity and the numerous traditional festivals were an important facet of Hong Kong life.

In addition, the many independent and luxury hotel-based restaurants reflected the fact that "going out" was a regular event, not only reserved for special occasions. Moreover, Hong Kong's continued economic success allowed large numbers of highly educated women to secure executive positions, especially in the lucrative services sector.[3] Furthermore, in the early 1990s, a significant influx of expatriates occurred; Chinese who left Hong Kong in the mid-1980s returned to join its robust economy. These new sources of demand, added to Hong Kong's dizzying social and professional whirl, meant that hairdressing was a big and fast-growing business.

In 1990, over 4,725 hair salons operated in Hong Kong, employing over 24,000 personnel; by 1994, there were over 5,000 salons catering to a potential six million Hong Kong scalps (Table 1). However, despite so many salons in such a small terri-

---

[2] Typically, Chinese employers held dinners for their employees; these symbolized reunion and gratitude. Many restaurants and hotel ballrooms in Hong Kong were reserved for this purpose.

[3] In first quarter 1995, the age distribution of the female labor force was ('000s): "Never Married" 15 to 19, 32.1; 20 to 29, 312.9; 30 to 39, 117.8; 40 and over, 26.8. The distribution for "Ever Married" was: under 29, 93; 20 to 29, 92.7; 30 to 39, 261.2; 40 and over, 285.9. The age distribution of the total labor force (male and female) was ('000s): 15 to 19, 68.9; 20 to 29, 795.3; 30 to 39, 978.9; 40 to 49, 636.9; 50 to 59, 294.2; 60 and over, 126.2.

tory, the number of elite salons was limited, and only a handful catered to the high-income segment. In addition, around 80% of the salons mainly served women; the concept of specialized hair care for men had little penetrated the traditional Asian culture of salons serving foremost a "feminine" need.

Table 1: Hair Salon and Beauty Shop Information

		Number of persons engaged		
Year	Number of establishments	Male	Female	Total
1990	4,725	16,866	7,496	24,362
1992	5,006	16,218	8,317	24,535
1994	5,068	13,885	8,621	22,506

Sources: *Employments & Vacancies Statistics* (1990, 1992 and 1994), Census and Statistics Department, Hong Kong.

	Estimate of high class hair salons and beauty shop openings	
Year	Number of new establishments*	Estimated number of high class barber shops opened**
1990–92	281	22
1992–94	62	5

*281 = 5006 − 4725 (no. of establishments in 1992 less no. of establishments in 1990);
62 = 5068 − 5006 (no. of establishments in 1994 less no. of establishments in 1992).
**22 = 281 × 8% (% estimate of high income group); 5 = 62 × 8%.
Note: The figure does not include the new branches of existing establishments.

The hairdressing industry was characterized by stylists who frequently switched allegiances between salons, or branched out on their own after gaining a group of loyal customers and raising sufficient capital. Stylist mobility was enhanced since Hong Kong's hairdressing industry had minimal regulations; the only formality to open a salon was to register the business. Some salons tried to place stylists under contract to restrict this movement; loyalty might be enhanced by offering further training, in the salon's own school or abroad to hairdressing academies. However, many hairstylist entrepreneurs believed that once the technique and skill of hair styling was acquired, they should open their own salons. A new and growing trend was individual stylists providing hair care service at clients' residences. Clients were typically secured through local advertising and personal contacts (Table 2).

Hair Trends

Chinese movies of the 1950s and 1960s reflected Chinese people's hair trends. An astute observer would notice the uniformity of styles in men and women; hair was cut simply with no particular style; for women sporting long hair, braids were the norm. This lack of style-consciousness was due in part to a void in hair styling expertise, but mostly to a culturally-based desire of not wanting to stand out (e.g., with perms and

Table 2:   Advertisements in *Dollar Saver* by Individual Stylists

PRIVATE HAIRDRESSER, INSTRUCTOR AND SESSION STYLIST. Trained in London by Alan International W1 Academy. All services available including Tin-Foil Highlights using western colours and products. Also serving Asian clients including cutting, colouring and perming. Paul Cooklin 2547 6562.

HAIR BY PAUL GERRARD – I am offering a professional home service, 6 days a week, Foil H/L from $450, cut finish from $250, colour from $300. Please try to allow 1 week's notice for appointment. For more information, please phone or fax, 2869 4408, page 1168886/9272.

FACIAL AT HOME: Pamper yourself at home with a relaxing facial by an experienced beauty therapist. Please call Miss Li for details. Tel: 2549 7927 Pager: 138 330 236.

non-black hair colors). Chinese had strong cultural ties and lack of flexibility in this respect. However, Hong Kong's prosperity and increased western influence infiltrated all business sectors, especially fashion apparel and aesthetics; and hair trends evolved. One newspaper reported: "Some hairstylists call it a 'hair color revolution' but to others it is a "natural progression."

To some, hair style fashion, similar to apparel, had distinctive trends that changed continuously and endlessly; from long hair to short hair, from single length to layer cut, from short hair to extended hair.[4] Sometimes apparel and hair style fashion walked hand-in-hand to suit the same overall trend. One observer commented:

> With increasing overall purchasing power and living standards, people, nowa-days, are concerned with how they look. They are more willing to spend on beauty-related products/services, especially, hairdressing. All major salons offer more or less the same kind of services to customers. However, they are widely differentiated in terms of various quality dimensions such as shampoo quality, shop decoration, professionalism and attitude of stylists. More explicitly, quality is closely correlated with price.

Andre Frezouls, director of the Rever chain observed:[5]

> Coloring has existed for men who want to cover all their gray hair because they think it looks as if they have business problems or bad luck – that's a cultural thing. But with the younger generation coming up, and people wanting to show they are big spenders, you are seeing a little coloring in men. Old stereotypes still prevail for men: they might agree to perm their hair, but are afraid to try coloring because of appearing feminine or vain. Not a lot, but a little. It's going to take time.

---

[4] Human hair extended with artificial hair by the use of wax.
[5] Kavita Daswani, "Colorful approach to hair necessities," *South China Morning Post*, June 8, 1994, p. 23.

An increasing number of Chinese women are coloring their hair in a way they would never have done a few years ago, and realizing they can get away with it – without looking "cheap." Before, if a woman had any form of colored hair, it was thought that she was working in the wrong sort of place. Now it is completely different and far more accepted. Over the past year, the trendiness of hair coloring had increased steadily, and salons in Hong Kong are looking at different ways of combining colors and highlighting techniques to create unusual yet wearable effects.

For a long time perming has been predominant because all women like to see a change in their hair. But now, as fashion continues to change, coloring has become very popular and there has been an evolution between a consumer's understanding of coloring and the range of products available. It is an educational process for the hairdresser to come up with a form of color acceptable to Asians.

According to Kim Robinson of Le Salon Orient, 80% of clients were requesting hair color. He stated: "It was previously a taboo in the upper Asian circles, but it has now become a norm; the shift towards colored hair was the first major hair trend since the wash-and-wear perm craze of the 1980s."

This heightened demand resulted in the need for Hong Kong stylists to create new techniques; for example, multi-shading, a new form of highlighting. Frezouls, who introduced hair extension services stated: "That is something we're pushing so we can encourage clients to have that fun, strong aspect in their hair like cyclamen-violet and aubergine, which they can then take out when they go to work, but that really is the extreme of it."

Frezouls believed hair coloring services were irreversible:

But the public is ready to experiment with more. As stylists, we're all dreaming of being able to give people highlights, and it certainly is popular with the trendier, upmarket and more outgoing people. And if a client enjoys the new look, she won't mind paying for it. You walk around the streets of Hong Kong and you see all kinds of fashion, and this is another form of it. It's starting through the 16 to 20-year-olds.

However, hair treatment per se was not the only issue that concerned customers. Said one observer:

Among customers of leading salons, about 80% are women who really care very much about their looks. However, they are not just concerned about service quality, they also care about their "emotional experience" in the chair. Customer experience is a huge factor in a shop's success. Customers dislike sitting too close to in waiting areas and hate being kept waiting for long periods.

Top salons' clientele were willing to spend money and wanted salons where they could be pampered and indulged. Many working women led high pressured lives coping with careers and family; visits to salons were often "outlets" or precious moments of limited private time. It was important they got more than a haircut! As one stylist at a leading salon stated: "Customers don't just experience our lavish decoration, they begin their day with freshly prepared lemon tea or cappuccino, and either whole grain toast or a slice of carrot/banana cake. We offer music and the top international magazines."

Some salons provided the latest fashion and other videos for customers to watch during their visits, together with well-appointed VIP rooms, designed for maximum privacy, provided on request.

The Hair Care Experience at Top Salons

Although visual differences were evident among salons, high class salons followed similar operating procedures. Entering the salon, the client would be asked to wait while the receptionist paged the stylist. The client might be offered refreshments (free or paid depending on the salon), examine hair care and accessory products or read a magazine.[6] An apprentice escorted the client into the salon; if special services (e.g., perms or coloring) were required, the stylist would examine the client's hair before the apprentice performed hair washing and combing. The apprentice might comment on the client's hair, suggesting a hair care product the client might purchase at the salon.

The stylist, meanwhile, would typically be working with another client. When work on that client was completed, the stylist would move to the client who had been prepared by the apprentice. Some stylists worked fast and might serve as many as five clients in one appointment slot (0.75 to 1.25 hours). Others engaged in more conversation and opted for lesser throughput. As a result, some stylists had more apprentices than others. In general, a stylist's pay was related to prices charged for various services. Typically stylists were paid a low base salary and a percent of revenues generated. Industry observers believed these averaged around 30%.

When work on a client was completed, the apprentice escorted him/her to the receptionist for payment and any hair care purchases. Apprentices received relatively low salaries depending on knowledge and experience; as a result, they relied on sales commissions and tips for supplementary income. In Hong Kong, serious tipping was becoming the norm. Kim Robinson of Le Salon Orient reported HK$500 to HK$1,000 might be slipped in his pocked by an appreciative client; even junior staff could expect some red bills (HK$100) by the end of the day; Robinson elaborated: "It's the average person who is really happy with the service and thinks the staff have gone out of their way who will tip well." Since stylists generally took a paternal interest in their apprentices; they accepted and sometimes encouraged commission- and tip-seeking behavior.

Before clients left the salon, the receptionist might suggest they purchase displayed products. This would most likely occur if the apprentice failed to suggest hair care products or if the client had to wait for the appointment.[7] For various accessory sales, around 10% of the retail value was typically earned by the employee initiating the sale.

---

[6] Some salons had a tendency to overbook at holiday times and waits might be significant.

[7] In several salons, the products available for purchase were supplied on consignment. The salon may earn a 40% margin: sales commissions averaged 10%.

The Hair Industry Environment at Top Salons

Personnel. Major salons had relatively simple organizational structures comprising three levels. The Shop Manager (senior person) was responsible for supervising and controlling all business and staff in a specific outlet. Shop Managers dealt with many issues occurring in day-to-day store operations, including, but not limited to, employing staff, re-stocking supplies, personnel management, shop decoration and customer complaints.

Stylists were the salons' core resources; they played the key role in providing hair styling services to customers. Some salons hired experienced stylists; others relied mainly on internal promotion and in-house training. Some salons sent senior stylists for advanced training in Great Britain; knowledge acquired from such courses was provided to trainees under the stylists' supervision. Compensation varied with employment grade, closely related to years of experience. One leading salon had three grades; commission rates ranged from 23% to 75% of revenues generated. This salon also guaranteed monthly compensation: stylist grade (< 3 years' experience) $4,500; senior stylist (3 to 5 years) $5,000; top stylist (> 5 years) $5,500. Top stylists with solid / affluent client bases could easily earn over $100,000 per month.

Trainees learned and practiced hair styling skills in salons and were responsible for simple tasks (e.g., washing and drying customers' hair). Monthly salaries ranged from $4,000 to $7,000. (By comparison, full-time live-in maids received $3,750 plus room and board.) In addition to providing customer experience, many salons offered trainees the opportunity to practice hair cutting skills at vastly reduced prices (sometimes free).[8] Training periods were not fixed in time; rather they depended on the individual's talent and ability. Usually, salons took great precautions when hiring trainees since acquiring a hairdressing certificate in Hong Kong was a simple matter and few prerequisites were set for those taking courses. As a result, top tier salons tended to favor candidates qualified overseas since these courses were more comprehensive and candidates typically had more practical and diverse talents.

In some salons, the dominant stylist set the tone for type of styling; in others, stylists were allowed a great deal of latitude and individual freedom in performing their work. Stylists were encouraged to learn about new hair trends, to evaluate new styles from foreign countries and, if appropriate, modify these to fit the local market. Industry observers believed that hairstylists tended to be self-oriented rather than customer-oriented, focusing more on style and haircut than paying much attention to related factors such as the clients' face, color or personality. Another common phenomenon was that many stylists did not like to arrive at work punctually; this created problems for customers who had to wait or reschedule their appointments.

The Consumer Council (consumer watchdog) reported 87 complaints against the hairdressing industry in 1993; 53 for unsatisfactory service, the others for price misrepresentation. In 1994, complaints nearly doubled to 143. Over 100 concerned poor

---

[8] "Model Nights" were organized for trainees to practice hair styling techniques. Trainees invited models, mostly friends, for free hair styling.

service; the remainder, distortion of prices. When confronted with this increased number of complaints, stylists claimed their customers were overly discriminating people! One stylist at a prominent salon stated: "I hate those troublesome guys who don't know what is 'fashion' and don't respect my opinion. I will kick them out!"

Some salons employed manicurists; most employed receptionists whose duties included answering inquiries, making reservations and generally serving customers. A former employee of a leading salon said that because receptionists played an important role in salons, job pressure often led to high turnover. Their functions, depending on store policy, included: greeting clients and setting the hair care experience in motion, allocating new clients to stylists (a role involving salon politics), being exemplars of the salon's services inasmuch as their hair was styled in the salon, preparation of raw data for statistical reports (e.g., number of different types of services performed, revenue earned per stylist, visits per customer), and collection of hair care related client data.[9]

Few salons systematically managed human resources; staff benefits (e.g., pension fund, life and health insurance) were atypical. In general, long-term commitments were not expected since job-hopping was common. Incentives were not generally provided to secure long-term commitments; commissions formed 60% to 80% of take-home pay.

Operations. Most top salons were open Monday to Saturday, closed on Sunday. Working hours were 9:00 am to 6:00 pm, although variations occurred among salons. Typically, customer throughput on Fridays and Saturdays was double the rest of the week; in addition, annual festivals (e.g., Christmas, Chinese New Year [February]) produced exceptionally heavy demand. In peak periods, when stylists were fully booked, walk-in customers were frequently turned away. Many salons followed the Chinese barbershop tradition and doubled prices on these occasions.

Locations. Although hair salons were located all over Hong Kong, preferred locations for top-of-the-line salons were in Central (Hong Kong Island) and Tsim Sha Tsui (Kowloon). These locations were convenient for executives, yuppies and affluent consumers. Both locations were in commercial business districts frequented by high spending power shoppers. Correspondingly, salons paid heavy rents (Exhibit 1). Some industry observers believed that, in the near future, a branch of a major salon would be opened in Causeway Bay, a popular shopping area on Hong Kong Island, two miles from Central and the site of several high class Japanese department stores.

Services and products. In addition to providing hairdressing services (e.g., permanent waving, highlighting, coloring, other forms of hair treatment) many salons offered supplementary services and products: manicure, pedicure, French manicure (varnish only the nail's outer edge), sold-only-in-shop shampoo, conditioner and other hair

---

[9] This data was sent to salon headquarters daily for consolidation and analysis. Advertising and promotion decisions used this analysis.

care accessories. Specialty shampoos and conditioners included herbal, high protein and ultraviolet protection products. Shampoos and conditioners, containing different types and amounts of ingredients, might be offered for different types of hair. Several salons offered accessories such as faux and semi-precious jewelry, designer watches, hair ornaments, silk scarves and trendy satin ribbons.

Pricing. Although most superior salons followed premium price strategies (Exhibits 2A, 2B, 2C), the price setting process differed among salons. In one salon, stylists met individually with management annually to discuss, and negotiate, prices for various services. Stylists might be given a high degree of latitude in determining their prices. Many stylists decided prices by evaluating customer spending power, data secured from close relationships formed with customers. For similar haircuts, in the same salon, different stylists typically charged different prices. Prices ranged significantly among top stylists, less so for trainees. Management might set prices for a stylist trainee; on promotion to stylist, s/he set prices for her/his services. Of course, if a stylist's prices were too high and delivered service was inconsistent with customer expectations, dissatisfaction and loss of business might occur.

Advertising and promotions. Advertising philosophies differed among salons. Some salons advertised in local fashion-oriented magazines; others relied on events such as beauty pageants, fashion shows and hair design competitions (e.g., Asian Hair Show Competition) that they might sponsor (Table 3). Many stylists firmly believed that evidence of good service based on hair styles spread through word-of-mouth and that it was not necessary to behave pro-actively to promote a salon. Said Felix, a senior stylist at a major salon: "The customer is our company's most important advertiser. When customers are satisfied with our personalized service, they will spread our goodwill instantaneously."

Hair care was serious matter! For most socialites, superstars and singers in Hong Kong, choosing a salon was a serious business issue since it reflected on their personalities, where they lived and the cars they drove. The whole image was an important consideration. One columnist, humorously summarized the hair care industry as follows:[10]

Topic: The Hairdressing Industry
Hairstylists: Dean, Lee, Warren or Lope, Homond, Dingo, Boffie (an artistic approximation of names that never existed in the first place).
Nationality: Either expatriate Brits and Australians or local Chinese whose English came from a study trip to Vidal Sassoon in London.
Age: Only their IDs can say.

---

[10] Source: Anonymous, "Icons of Our Time: The Hong Kong Hairdresser," Sunday Magazine, *South China Morning Post*.

Money: Pots of it. But the trouble is their pay comes in irregular chunks and can often lead to barren spells during which your man may need a little assistance with a bill here, a pint there.

Distinguishing Marks: Either skinhead or luxuriating in hair, often pony-tailed. Given the amount of time they and colleagues have to spend on their hair, they can get away with hair styles that otherwise swiftly become unmanageable on members of the general public.

Brief History: Warren Beatty single-handedly teased the hairdresser-as-icon into the public's consciousness with his 1972 movie Shampoo. Suddenly hairdressers shed their "barber" tag and became budding Lotharios, Casanovas of the curling tong, boulevarding bob-cats. The international hairdresser has been an icon for nearly as long: all those Chelsea crimpers from the swinging 1960s like Twiggy's boyfriend Justin de Villeneuve whose real name is apparently Bert. Local hairdressers became cool a lot later when they started changing their names and charging a fortune too.

Hong Kong Sub-division: The Mongkok chopper. These salons, usually in insalubrious areas and carrying an air of menace are staffed by threatening looking gents called Ricky and Ah Ming. They sport dyed brown hair in footballer cuts and look as if they'd be happier cutting off a hand during a dispute at a foodstall than giving you a Soho crop!

Favorite Films: Shampoo, The Hairdresser's Husband and Edward Scissorhands.

Table 3: Rates of Popular Fashion Magazines and Television

Average rate per page				Average rate during prime time			
Magazines	HK$	Magazines	HK$	Television	HK$	Television	HK$
Cosmopolitan	40,000	Boutique	12,000	120 second	52,080	60 second	26,040
Bazaar	36,800	Couture	31,300	90 second	39,060	55 second	24,720
Elle	34,000	Orient Beauty	25,000	75 second	33,780	50 second	23,000
Eve	27,700	Marie Clarie	30,900	70 second	31,950	45 second	20,760
Mode	28,470	Amobe	20,000	65 second	29,790	40 second	18,930
						35 second	16,770

Industry Structure

The hair care industry in Hong Kong could be divided into four basic segments. First, street snippers provided simple haircuts at reasonable prices (HK$30 to HK$60); second, most salons targeted the middle to upper-middle class; third, Ocean Wave, A&B and Mona Lisa Hair Shop, the largest hairdressing organizations in terms of scale, number of employees and outlets, mostly targeted middle to high-income consumers. Top salons such as "aristocratic" segment leader – Headquarters, targeted the high income market (over HK$20,000 per month) and serviced those favoring trendy and modish hair styles.

Many salons competed in the high income market segment: Andre Norman Haircutting Salon, Le Salon Orient, Bella Donna Hair, Le Coupe Hair Avant Garde, Philip George Hair Salon, Pixie's, Rever, Salon de Coiffure Clare, Mandarin Oriental Hair, TaliJessie and Roger Craig International Hair Salon. These salons were mainly independent outlets with average staff rosters between eight and 20 but Le Salon Orient and Rever were well-organized chain operations with solid business volumes (Table 4, Exhibit 3). A factor distinguishing Le Salon and Rever was that they operated their own academies. As a result, these two salons wielded substantial industry power; they attracted the best employees and chose the best candidates from their schools. Graduates not only served as live advertisements for their schools; their creativity could be molded to suit the culture of the hair salons they joined.

Rever. Established and based in Tsim Sha Tsui in Kowloon by two foreign stylists, Andre Ouellette and Norman McLeod, in 1970. Rever had six outlets targeting mainly

Table 4: Competitor Profiles

	Headquarters	Le Salon	Rever
Working hours	9:30–7:00	8:00–8:00	10:00–7:00
	Mon–Sat	Mon–Sat	7 Days
Advertising			
– TV	None	None	None
– Newspaper	Yes	Yes	Yes
– Fashion magazine*	Yes	Yes	Yes
No. of locations	2	4	6
Areas	Central	Central	Central (1)
	Tsim Sha Tsui	Tsim Sha Tsui (2)	Kowloon (2)
		Repulse Bay	Wanchai
			Causeway Bay (2)
No. of employees	80	250	200
No. of stylist levels	1	3	3
Division of stylists	Junior stylist	Intl' creative director	Artistic director
	Senior stylist	Creative director	Leading stylist
		Top stylist	Top stylist
Promotions/discounts	None	None	10%–15% disc. for Cathay Pacific Staff
Comp. beauty service	None	None	None
Beauty school facilities	None	Yes	Yes

*These fashion magazines were usually bi-lingual; ads were in both English and Cantonese.

high class customers.[11] (One salon focused on a younger market and offered lower price services.) Rever's stores were located mainly in hotels and commercial areas: Central, Wanchai and Causeway Bay on Hong Kong Island, Tsim Sha Tsui in Kowloon. Each store was staffed with at least 20 personnel (eight stylists, 12 trainees). Industry gossip anticipated Rever would open more stores in the near future. Prices for standard services were fixed, in part a function of the grade/level of stylist; hair cutting at Rever salons ranged from HK$300 to HK$500. It did not compete on price with other salons.

Rever's well-organized training school provided intensive training for potential hairstylists. To subsidize the school, customers paying highly reduced Rever prices were worked on by students. After school training, an apprenticeship program allowed trainees to learn in-field hair styling skills in stores. However, a good student could bypass the trainee and apprentice stage. Usually, promotion to senior stylist was determined by store managers based on examination results, revenues earned and performance appraisals by senior stylists. Rever set up a special program to place academy graduates in its branches. It periodically invited foreign professionals to conduct seminars for stylists on latest hair styling skills and offered magazines and videos about modern hair styling trends.

In the past, Rever used a variety of promotion strategies; it offered employees of some large companies (e.g., airlines and hotels) 20% discounts on weekdays, 10% on weekends. It sponsored fashion shows and offered short-period trial customer vouchers to employees of firms like MasterCard and Esprit. Hair care accessories were sold in Rever stores; the salesperson, hairstylist or receptionist, was paid 10% commission.

Rever's consumer awareness was believed to have decreased in recent years because of retrenched promotional spending. Observers management planned to increase awareness and competitiveness by investing more in promotion. Rever usually advertised in fashion magazines such as Eve (Exhibit 4) and recently aired several television commercials. A senior Rever executive recently visited several foreign countries; he returned with information on the latest trends and new skills such as hair extension for which Rever was registered as the sole Asian agent. (Rever offered to sub-license other competitors although it was unclear how much demand existed.) Rever planned to optimize profit levels, in part by increasing supplementary services.

Le Salon Orient. Founded by the well-known Australian hairstylist Kim Robinson in the mid-1980s, Le Salon Orient, targeting high income mature customers, achieved market leader status by 1987. Le Salon Orient, with four stores, was the most respected hair salon in Hong Kong; it also operated a training school providing various hair related courses (Exhibit 5). In its major store, Le Salon employed 45 stylists. Le Salon was known for the attention it paid to physical facilities. Each store was decorated similarly in an 18th century classic baroque style and clients, whose hair was being washed, could contemplate angels on the muraled ceiling. As one regular customer

---

[11] Ouellette and McLeod sold Rever in 1993; McLeod begun another salon in the renowned Mandarin Oriental Hotel located in the heart of Central District.

stated: "Using a red, white and black color scheme accented with gold, the store's ambiance effectively captures a mixture of the 18th and 21st century!"

In addition to hairdressing, Le Salon Orient offered beauty and body care treatment in its spas (Exhibit 6), believing that as customers' social values and lifestyles changed they tended to become more concerned with their looks and body care. Robinson's reputation allowed him to attract many superstars and performing artists. Their patronage secured favorable publicity in magazines. Le Salon sponsored beauty pageants and in the past offered discounted hair service coupons to first-class ticket holders for an Anita Mui concert.[12]

All new clients filled out forms, requesting extensive personal information, before beginning their hair care experience. In return, Le Salon mailed an in-house produced bi-annual newsletter "Orient Vision," launched in November 1994 to keep customers informed on the latest in hair, beauty and fashion trends. This magazine was strictly for Asian women. Robinson stated "There'll be no blue eyes and blond hair in its pages." Robinson was also reported to have said his ambition was to "satisfy every woman in Asia." According to industry sources, in 1996, "Le Salon" would open new branches in Singapore and Malaysia.

Headquarters. Headquarters was founded in the early 1980s when several foreign stylists (from Australia, Britain, U.S.) joined to open a family-size hair salon as a partnership in Kowloon Tong, two miles from commercial downtown Kowloon. Operating at street level, while the partners lived on the upper floors, Headquarters served mainly expatriates and neighborhood clients; it secured a reputation for offering artistic and fashionable hair styles. Partners came and went; in 1987 the remaining local partner added new partners from among his customers. On lease expiration, Headquarters moved to a new location in Tsim Sha Tsui. In 1992, Headquarters was purchased by a diversified conglomerate operating jewelry shops, boutiques, coaching, catering and entertainment services.

By 1994, Headquarters operated two stores in highly accessible commercial areas, Tsim Sha Tsui (Kowloon) and Sheung Wan (Hong Kong Island). In March 1995, the Sheung Wan store closed; Headquarters moved to the Entertainment Building in Central, occupying a whole floor (roughly 6,500 sq. ft.) and became the largest scale hair salon in Hong Kong. The lavish, deluxe, magnificent style was incorporated in decoration, display and stylists' apparel. Set-up cost, including equipment replacement and decoration, was reputed to be HK$4 million.

Headquarters employed over 60 stylists (30 senior, 33 junior) and somewhat more trainees at its two store locations. A special group of customers was artists and superstars such as Faye Wong (Figure 2) and Anita Mui who had new, modish, noticeable images in the entertainment business. These customers' high-profile exposure served as walking advertisements for hair styles created at Headquarters. Headquarters also

---

[12] Anita Mui was a Cantonese pop star, very popular among the local and overseas Chinese populations.

gained free publicity in high class fashion magazines (e.g., Eve, Elle, Cosmopolitan, Mode, Bride, Vogue). It was official hairdresser for Miss Hong Kong.

Figure 2:   Superstar Faye Wong's Haircut by Headquarters

Market Entry

Eddie Wong put down the consultants' report. There seemed so many questions to answer. Should he open a new salon or try to buy an existing salon and upgrade it? He knew that neither Rever, Le Salon Orient nor Headquarters were for sale, but several solid, if not super top tier, salons might be available. If he purchased one of these, many changes would be necessary.

On the other hand, if he opened a new salon, he would have to be concerned with many matters: where to locate, how to secure stylists; what and how to pay, what service(s) to offer, how to price, what means of communication to use and so forth. Beyond this, Eddie wondered if there were more strategic questions he should ask. He called in Shamza Khan, his newly hired marketing manager:

Shamza, you used to be in the hair care industry; I need a strategy to make "Hair-Works" a major player in the top echelon of hair salons. Take a couple of weeks' break and have a marketing plan on my desk by October 1. I know those marketing professors at HKUST taught you how to analyze industries and markets, and develop strategies and action programs. Now, let's see if they are any good!

Exhibit 1: Retail Rental and Retail Capital Value Index

OFFICE RENTAL INDEX 寫字樓租值指數 オフイス賃貸価格指數

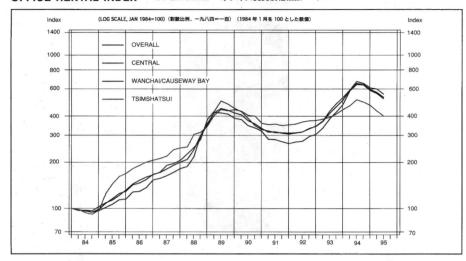

OFFICE CAPITAL VALUE INDEX 寫字樓資本值指數 オフイス資産価値指數

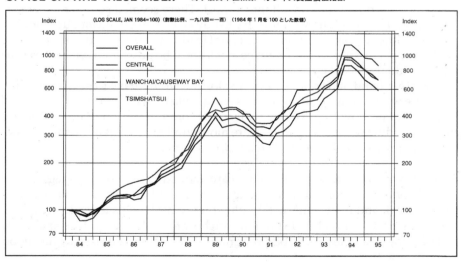

Exhibit 2A: Le Salon Orient Price List

Method Jeanne Piaubert – Face	Time	HK$ Price	HK$ Price
Clarifying deep cleansing problem skin	1 hr	440	3,960 × 10
Rehydrating and moisturising	1 hr	480	4,320 × 10
Adv. facial with rejuvenating treatment	1½ hr	900	8,120 × 10
Special eye treatment	½ hr	300	2,706 × 10
Neck and decollete treatment	½ hr	275	2,470 × 10
Advanced facial	1¼ hr	545	4,900 × 10
Acne treatment	1 hr	475	4,270 × 10
Le Salon Basics – Face			
Basic facial	½ hr	340	3,060 × 10
Hydrolise treatment	1¼ hr	590	5,300 × 10
De-pigmentation treatment face	1½ hr	715	6,430 × 10
Glycolic acid treatment face (including deep cleansing facial)	1 hr	475	4,270 × 10
Intensive collagen treatments	1¾ hr	1,350	6,075 × 5
Method Jeanne Piaubert – Body			
Lymphatic drainage & slimming	¾ hr	610	5,490 × 10
Stretch mark treatment	½ hr	380	3,420 × 10
Back deep cleansing	¾ hr	525	4,720 × 10
Post natal treatment	1 hr	630	5,670 × 10
Bust firming	¾ hr	525	4,720 × 10
Waxing face			
Upper lip	5 min	105	
Upper lip and chin	10 min	150	
Eyebrow arching	15 min	110	
Eyebrow tint	5 min	180	
Eyelash perm	1 hr	350	
Eyelash tint	½ hr	260	

Le Salon Basic – Body	Time	HK$ Price	HK$ Price
Firming and toning	¾ hr	550	4,950 × 10
Relaxing massage	½ hr	330	2,970 × 10
Wholistic massage	1 hr	495	4,450 × 10
Aromatherapy massage	1 hr	495	4,450 × 10
	1½ hr	660	5,940 × 10
Swedish massage	½ hr	360	3,240 × 10
	1 hr	495	4,450 × 10
	1½ hr	660	5,940 × 10
Foot reflexology	¾ hr	420	3,780 × 10
Face massage	½ hr	360	3,240 × 10
Le Salon Basics – Hands & Feet			
De-pigmentation treatment hands	½ hr	325	2,920 × 10
Hands and lower arms	½ hr	495	4,450 × 10
Hand treatment	½ hr	350	3,150 × 10
Glycolic acid treatment hands	½ hr	325	
Feet	½ hr	360	
Le Salon Basics			
Half day spa	3 hr	1,435	
Waxing body			
Full leg	45 min	480	
Thigh	20 min	330	
Lower leg/bikini line	15 min	265/220	
Under arm	15 min	180	
Full arm	30 min	350	
Half arm	15 min	240	
Back/chest	30 min	390/290	
Back and chest	45 min	550	
Electrolysis (min. 20 mins)	20 min	410	1,845 × 5
(Additional 10 mins)		280	

Exhibit 2B: Headquarters Price List

Cut & finishing
$450 $500 $600 $700 $800
$350 (Children under 12 years old)
Shampoo blowdrying/finishing Highlights
$250 $300 $350 $400
Headquarters setting
Permanent waving

Touch perm	$650
Hair straightening	$1,200
Permanent waving	$1,100
Technical perm	$1,300

Hair treatment

Protection treatment	$400
Damage care	
Short	$550
Medium	$600
Long	$650
Anti-dandruff	$600–800

Course treatment
Short $1,200   Medium $2,200   Long $2,400

Highlight with tinting
Half-head $1,200   Short $1,400
Medium $1,550   Long $1,900

Half-head highlights		$900
Whole-head highlights	Short	$1,100
Medium $1,200	Long	$1,300

Color
Short $600   Medium $700   Long $800

Nail treatment

Revarnish		
Manicure	$100	$140
Pedicure	$190	$280
Nail buffing		$170
French manicure		$170

*All chemical work not including shampoo blowdry.

Exhibit 2C: Rever Price List

Styling for ladies	HK$
Cut, shampoo and blowdry / set	
These services include conditioner & setting lotion	
By top stylist / senior stylist / stylist	415 / 340 / 300
Shampoo blowdry / setting	130 to 165 / 140 to 198
Long hair partial braiding, special dress up *(quotation at consultation)*	190 to 490

Technical services for ladies	
Perming – including pre-perm treatment	
Normal, body wave & directional wind	695 to 830
Partial perm	225 to 700
Technical perming – spiral, root, pincurl, stack, rag, double wind, weave & braid *(quotation at consultation)*	780 to 1255
Highlights or lowlights (cap)	
Tinfoil highlights or lowlights	
Special effects, color changes *(quotation at consultation)*	690 to 1310
Permanent color, fashion color or color glossing	375 to 450
Hair clinic	220 to 460

These technical services exclude cut, shampoo and blowdry

Styling for men	HK$	Styling for men	HK$
Cut, shampoo and blowdry		Coloring*	345 to 400
By top stylist	340	Highlights and lowlights*	520 to 615
By senior stylist	315	Perming*	520 to 620
By stylist	290	Partial perming	210 to 460
Shampoo blowdry	115 to 140	Beard trim*	90 to 105

These technical services exclude cut, shampoo and blowdry

Real hair extensions	22 per strand
Styling for children (under 12 years old) – Cut, blowdry by stylist only	240

Exhibit 2C (cont'd)

Nail beauty	HK$	Nail beauty	HK$
Manicure/nail buffing	95	Oil manicure	160
French manicure	150	Oil pedicure	300
Manicure revarnish	70	Eyebrow shaping	78
Pedicure	240	Nail mend or tip (per nail)	35
Pedicure revarnish	75	Hand massage	120

Exhibit 3: Average Estimated Income of Top Tier Salons

	1992	1993	1994
Revenues	HK$	HK$	HK$
Hairdressing[1]	51,155,846	55,555,249[2]	60,333,000
Supplementary[3] products	–	445,475	631,255
Costs & expenses:			
Cost of sales & services[4]	17,904,546	19,600,253	21,337,489
Stylists' salaries[5]	15,346,754	16,666,575	18,099,900
Selling and admin. expense	832,000	903,552	981,257
Rent	5,280,000	5,280,000	5,280,000
Total income before taxes	11,792,546	13,550,344	15,265,608
Income taxes[6]	2,063,696	2,371,310	2,518,825
Net income	9,728,850	11,179,034	12,746,783

[1] Estimated revenues from hairdressing (1994):
- Haircut = HK$ (350 + 800)/2 * 52 stylists * 4 people/day/stylist * days * 52 weeks/year = 37,315,200
- Shampoo blow-drying/finishing = HK$ (250 + 400)/2 * 5 2 stylists * 2 people/day/stylist * 6 days * 52 weeks = 10,545,600
- Permanent waving = HK$ (650 + 1300)/2 * 9 people/day * 6 days * 52 weeks = 2,737,800
- Hair treatment = HK$ (400 + 800)/2 * 8 people/day * 6 days * 52 weeks = 1,497,600
- Course treatment = HK$ (1200 + 2400)/2 * 3 people/day * 6 days * 52 weeks = 1,684,800
- Highlight with tinting = HK$ (1200 + 1900)/2 * 5 people/day * 6 days * 52 weeks = 2,418,000
- Highlights = HK$ (900 + 1300)/2 * 6 people/day * 6 days * 52 weeks = 2,059,200
- Color = HK$ (600 + 800)/2 * 5 people/day * 6 days * 52 weeks = 1,092,000
- Nail treatment = HK$ (100 + 190 + 170 + 170) * 5 people/nail treatment type/day * 6 days * 52 weeks = 982,800

Total revenues = HK$60,333,000.

[2] Assumed sales in 1993 are the same as in 1994. Price of each type of service is deflated at (1 + 8.6%), where 8.6% is the average growth rate of hairdressing prices, e.g., revenues from haircut = HK$ (350 + 800)/2/1.086 * 52 stylists * 4 people/day/stylist * 6 days * 52 weeks = HK$34,360,221.

[3] Estimate.

[4] Cost of sales and services is estimated as 35% of total revenues.

[5] Revenues divided in the proportion of 3:7, so salaries = total revenue from hairdressing * 30%.

[6] Profit tax rate is 17.5%, 17.5% and 16.5% in 1992, 1993 and 1994 respectively.

Exhibit 4:   Rêver's Advertisement in *Eve* Magazine

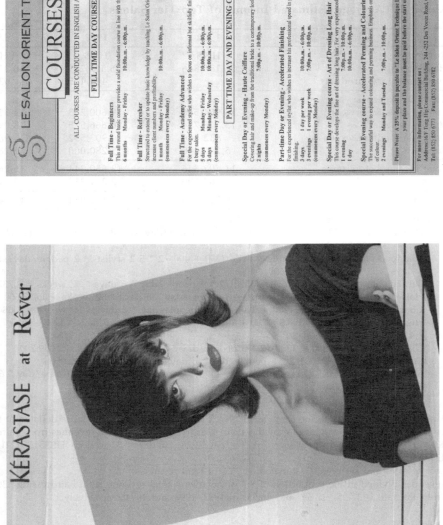

KÉRASTASE at Rêver

Exhibit 5:   Courses Provided in Le Salon's Academy

LE SALON ORIENT TECHNIQUE

COURSES

ALL COURSES ARE CONDUCTED IN ENGLISH AND CANTONESE

FULL TIME DAY COURSES

Full Time - Beginners
This all round basic course provides a solid foundation course in line with the EEC system.
6 months   Monday - Friday   10:00a.m. - 6:00p.m.   HK$30,500

Full Time - Refresher
Structured to extend or to update basic knowledge by teaching Le Salon Orient's creative techniques to increase client numbers and profitability.
1 month   Monday - Friday   10:00a.m. - 6:00p.m.   HK$ 7,800
(commences every Monday)

Full Time - Academy Advanced
For the experienced stylist who wishes to focus on informal but skilfully finished styles at speeds suitable for a busy salon.
5 days   Monday - Friday   10:00a.m. - 6:00p.m.   HK$ 4,500
3 days   Monday - Wednesday   10:00a.m. - 6:00p.m.   HK$ 3,100
(commences every Monday)

PART TIME DAY AND EVENING COURSES

Special Day or Evening - Haute Coiffure
Covering hair and make-up from the traditional bride to a contemporary look for photographic week.
2 nights   7:00p.m. - 10:00p.m.   HK$ 2,000
(commences every Monday)

Part-time Day or Evening - Accelerated Finishing
For the experienced stylist who wishes to increase his professional speed in perming, colouring, cutting and finishing.
3 days   1 day per week   10:00a.m. - 6:00p.m.   HK$ 3,000
3 evenings   1 evening per week   7:00p.m. - 10:00p.m.   HK$ 1,650
(commences every Monday)

Special Day or Evening course - Art of Dressing Long Hair
This course develops the fine art of dressing long hair. For very experienced stylists only.
1 evening   7:00p.m. - 10:00p.m.   HK$ 2,000
1 day   10:00a.m. - 6:00p.m.   HK$ 4,000

Special Evening course - Accelerated Perming and Colouring
The successful way to expand colouring and perming business. Emphasis on speed perms and all aspects of colour.
2 evenings   Monday and Tuesday   7:00p.m. - 10:00p.m.   HK$ 1,500

Please Note: A 25% deposit is payable to "Le Salon Orient Technique Ltd." on enrolment to guarantee your place and the balance must be paid before the start of the course.

For more information, please contact us:
Address: 16/F Tung Hip Commercial Building, 244-252 Des Voeux Road, Central, Hong Kong.
Tel: (852) 850 6777   Fax: (852) 850 6782

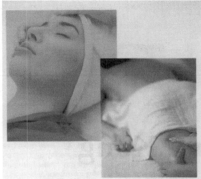

SAVING FACE

From the original health spa set in acres of landscaped countryside to the compact, efficient city "day spa". A natural transition to cater for the urban executive whose chief concern is how to maximize every moment.

Every major city in the world now has day spa facilities located in hotels, hair salons and department stores.

由傳統的郊外health spa走到繁華鬧市式的day spa，過中轉變反映出人類在生活上的變化；今天的都市人面對無重壓力，工作緊張，生活節奏匆迫，甚至休息鬆弛的時間也分秒必爭，絕不浪費，day spa便是這種生活模式下的產物。

Day Spa在很多大城市已經很普遍，在酒店、高級髮廊，甚至大型百貨公司等都有Day Spa的設備。

PHOTO: RAYMOND CHAN

HALF DAY SPA AT LE SALON ORIENT

In surroundings of quiet luxury, professionally trained masseurs and asetheticiennes treat clients with various techniques depending on individual requirements. With proven century old treatments using essential oils known as aromatherapy. With wholistic massage to ease an aching lower back or chronically tense shoulder muscles. With Oriental massage for those who prefer deep muscle release. The half day spa is a way of releasing tension and associated problems usually resulting from sedentary lifestyle, pressure jobs and all the associated stresses that go hand in hand with 1990's urban living.

在法國高雅的環境中，專業的按摩師及美容師為顧客提供最細心的服務，顧客按不同的需要，採用不同的按摩法，包括香芬精華按摩、wholistic按摩、東方穴位按摩。Le Salon Orient的半天Day Spa是都市人的另一喜訊。置身其中，可忘卻工作和生活帶來的壓力和痛楚，進入百分百鬆馳的世界。

A Gift of Beauty

A new perspective is being offered by Le Salon Orient to the eternal question of what gift to give that special person in our lives.

A Gift of Beauty is a beautifully packaged promise of a morning, an afternoon or a whole day of luxurious pampering.

Miracle Morning combines a facial, light make up, morning tea, hairstyling and manicure. **Afternoon Allure** offers a massage, full day or evening make up, afternoon tea, hairstyling and manicure. **The Day Affair** puts together a complete experience of facial, massage, full day or evening make up, morning and afternoon tea and lunch, hair treatment, hairstyling, manicure and pedicure. Or the customer can make up their own package.

This unique gift is available at the Central Salon 13 Duddell Street, Telephone 524 7153   Fax 877 2896

「美」學成就禮品系列，給禮物的定義，重新詮釋。三款禮貼週全的個人服務，讓你的至愛親朋，在不同的時間，感受煥然一新。

「晨曦倩影」包括皮膚護理、淡粧、怡神小食、髮型修飾及修甲(手)、早上兩小時的服務。

「黃昏誘惑」三小時的服務包括全身按摩、化粧、下午茶點、髮型修飾及修甲(手)。

「濃凝魅力」整天五小時的享受，包括皮膚護理、全身按摩、化粧、午餐、髮型修飾、Rene Furterer頭髮護理及修甲(手和腳)。

我們也可按你的要求，特別設計一款禮品咭。

「美」學成就禮品系列，在中環都爹利街13號的Le Salon Orient有售，可致電或傳真索取資料(電：5247153 傳真：8772896)

Case 6

Jimmy Lai and Daily Newspapers in Hong Kong

Noel Capon
Graduate School of Business, Columbia University

Ho Yuen Ching, Michelle
The Hong Kong University of Science and Technology

In February 1995, successful Hong Kong entrepreneur Jimmy Lai was contemplating launching a Chinese language newspaper in Hong Kong. Jimmy Lai was best known in Hong Kong and elsewhere in Southeast Asia as the driving force behind Giordano, a successful retail chain of casual wear for young people. In addition, his publication group was a leader in Hong Kong's weekly magazine market. Despite these successes, launching a daily newspaper in the saturated Hong Kong market would be an enormous challenge. Lai had to decide whether or not to market and if so, what entry strategy would be most appropriate.

⟡

Background

In less than two and a half years (July 1, 1997), British-administered Hong Kong would be returned to Chinese rule. Under British rule, Hong Kong had grown from a minor fishing port to one of the world's major financial and service centers. It was widely heralded as a model of capitalist development whose success was generated largely by industrious local entrepreneurs driven by the profit motive. By contrast, although it had adopted many capitalistic practices in recent years, China was the world's largest socialist economy. Under the Basic Law, agreed between the British and Chinese governments, after the hand-over Hong Kong would be administered as a Special Administrative Region enjoying a high degree of autonomy and maintaining its current capitalistic system for 50 years under the "one-country-two-systems" doctrine.

The impending hand-over generated considerable anxiety in the British colony. This anxiety reached a high point in June 1989 when the Chinese government used military force to put down a large scale student demonstration in Beijing. A significant

140

number of native Hong Kongers emigrated (e.g., to Canada, Australia); others secured additional passports as insurance.

Many in Hong Kong debated the likely effect of the transfer of power to the Chinese government. Some believed that Hong Kong would be forever changed, that the Chinese government would be unable to avoid interfering in Hong Kong affairs, that confidence would plummet, that many multinationals headquartered in Hong Kong would relocate to elsewhere in Southeast Asia and that the economy would spiral downwards. Others argued that Hong Kong was such a success story that the Chinese government would largely maintain a hands-off policy to ensure that Hong Kong's economy continued to surge ahead. These observers argued that the Chinese government ministers would be crazy to interfere with such economic success for any reason, even political. Many in the former group accepted this argument but retorted: "They might just be that crazy."

Jimmy Lai

In 1961, as a 12-year-old boy, relatives helped Jimmy Lai evade border controls and enter Hong Kong from mainland China. Starting out as a poor textile factory worker, by age 20 his industrious efforts earned him a factory manager position. In 1973–74, when the Hong Kong stock market soared, Lai used capital gains to launch his first company, in the textile industry. Lai's major entrepreneurial breakthrough came with the launch of Giordano in the mid-1980s.

Giordano

Giordano was a retail chain of basic casual wear that astutely and systematically outperformed existing players in the relatively untapped clothing market in Asia. By mid-1995, Giordano had over 280 stores in 11 Asian and Middle East countries; 60 stores in China were operated by Tiger Enterprises Ltd., a company formed (1992) to establish a retail network in China. Giordano's success (Exhibits 1A,1B) transformed Lai into a billionaire.

Lai (46) was well-known for his fervent anti-communism. In 1989, when the student democracy movement in Tiananmen Square was ruthlessly suppressed, Lai funded demonstrating students via pro-democracy T-shirt sales in Hong Kong. This action resulted in significant positive publicity for Giordano. The bloody, violent confrontation between army and students, graphically televised in Hong Kong, caused great concern; Lai, realizing Hong Kong's special informational needs in sustaining the city-state's role as an entrepôt and financial center, identified the media industry as a business opportunity, while realizing a personal ambition to own a publication.

Publications

Lai's first publication venture, Next magazine (flagship of Next Media Group), was launched in March 1990. Next was a weekly magazine containing "sensitive" political issues, local crimes and "insider" stories from the "less exposed side" of high society. These controversial stories were skilfully blended with the latest information on entertainment, consumer news and gossip. The first magazine of its type in Hong Kong, Next competed with magazines that targeted either the more educated segment demanding business information or the non-professional group (largely housewives) who were more interested in gossip than news. Next magazine successfully satisfied the diverse interests of both groups in a single publication.

In Next editorials Lai wrote about his political views, frequently taking extreme critical stances towards the Chinese communist government. In July 1994, he stated that China's premier was a "turtle's egg with a zero IQ"; he was referring to the premier's display of disgust and anger during a visit to Germany when anti-communist protesters appeared at a public engagement. Lai believed the premier's unprofessional behavior was inappropriate and embarrassing to the Chinese people. The subsequent closure of three Giordano stores in Beijing was rumored to be the result of Lai's outspoken criticism of, and insults towards, the Chinese government. Lai, stepped down as Giordano's chairman (retaining his 36% ownership), stating he did not want Giordano to suffer financially from his political views; Giordano's stock immediately rose by 10%. In 1991, Lai introduced a second weekly magazine, EasyFinder, combining popular fashion trends, consumer news and recruitment advertisements in a single volume.

Despite the launch of copycat publications, by 1994, both Next and EasyFinder had established stable market positions as leaders in Hong Kong's weekly magazine market. According to the Audit Bureau of Circulation (ABC), an independent survey agency for Hong Kong's print media, Next's circulation was 188,000; EasyFinder's was over 140,000. In addition, the Next group published leisure books and comics; Lai authored several books, including *Fact and Prejudice* in which he stated his business and life philosophies.

As a private company, the Next Group did not publish detailed financial statements. Nevertheless, profit and loss data issued by the group indicated a steadily improving financial picture (Exhibit 2). In 1995, the Next Group planned to list on the Hong Kong Stock Exchange.

Lai had always dreamed of owning a newspaper; his successful launch of Next and EasyFinder intensified this obsession. In late 1994, after an analysis of Hong Kong newspapers and the Hong Kong newspaper market, Lai made a bid for Ming Pao Daily, a newspaper targeting the more sophisticated consumer segment; his offer was refused. Lai was unwilling to purchase any other newspaper as he considered them low quality. Lai reasoned that: "A handicapped person is still handicapped even though he has been rehabilitated."

The Hong Kong Print Media Industry

Hong Kong's six million population supported 43 local Chinese and two English newspapers (Table 1); the industry was often described as highly competitive and saturated. Competition for shelf space was intense as newspapers fought for readership and circulation. Of the Chinese newspapers, about 30 were considered general newspapers reporting local and world news with roughly equal emphasis; five focused specifically on financial, economic and business news (e.g., Hong Kong

Table 1: Hong Kong Newspapers: Number and Advertising Revenues (US$ billion)*

Year	Chinese	English	Others	Year	Chinese	English	Others	Revenues
1984**	51	12	3	1989	50	14	2	1.3
1985	50	13	3	1990	53	14	2	2.0
1986	51	15	4	1991	45	14	3	2.1
1987	52	14	2	1992	51	12	4	2.9
1988	46	14	2	1993	57	14	3	4.1
				1994***	56	13	2	5.0

*Chinese dailies only. **Advertising revenues 1984 to 1988 is not available. ***Until November 1994. Source: Hong Kong Government Statistics Bureau.

Economic Journal, Hong Kong Economic Times); still others specialized in reporting entertainment news.

Total revenue for all Chinese language dailies (1994) was HK$5.9 billion (US$0.76 billion), roughly two thirds from advertising, the remainder from the cover price (Survey Research Hong Kong [SRH]). Circulation was defined as number of copies sold; readership referred to the number of people who read the newspaper. Typically, readership was two to three times higher than circulation. The SRH Audit Bureau of Circulation monitored readership and readers' profiles of all newspapers with circulation over 1% of population. Interested publishers and advertising agencies making media buying decisions might subscribe to semi-annual reports (SRH Media Index) to secure market information.

Newspaper Distribution

Everyday, soon after midnight, employees of over 30 newspaper distribution agents gathered in different areas in Central (heart of Hong Kong's business district) to begin work, piling newspapers and assembling supplements. Before 7:00 am, distributors would deliver quantities of ordered newspapers to over 5,000 newspaper stands in their servicing territories. A subsidiary distribution system involved 60 "dai-zhis"[1] who took papers from distributors and distributed to news-stands in their service areas. (See Table 2 for share of revenues in newspaper distribution systems in various Asian countries: Table 2A for two-level systems; Table 2B for three-level systems as in Hong Kong.)

According to industry practice, newspaper publishers usually approached distribution agents. Choi, Director of Choi Kee Books and Newspapers Agency, said that newspaper publishers and distributors maintained contractual relationships. Newspaper publishers had the freedom to select distributors; distributors could accept or reject an arrangement. Typically, each distribution agent represented seven or eight newspapers; most newspapers had more than one distribution agent.

---

[1] Translation: "People who bring the paper."

Table 2A: Revenue Shares in Two-level Newspaper Distribution Systems

Country	First level	Share of total revenue	Second level	Share of total receipts
Taiwan	Publisher	70%	Distributing agencies: direct to subscribers	30%
			Convenience stores (over 9,000)	30%
			Vending machines	Not applicable
China	Publisher	about 60%	Post offices directly distributing to subscribers	about 40%
		75%	Distributing agencies: (non-govt.) direct to subscribers	25%
Singapore	Publisher	70%	Newspaper agencies: direct to subscribers	30%

Table 2B: Revenue Shares in Three-level Newspaper Distribution Systems

Country	First level	Share of total revenue	Second level	Share of total revenue	Third level	Share of total receipts
HK	Publisher	58.5%	Distributors	6.50%	News-stands, convenience stores, supermarkets	35%
U.K.	Publisher	65%	Distributors Oil stations, supermarkets, etc.	8.50%	Small stores that sell newspapers	26.5%
Singapore	Publisher	70%	Distributing agencies	20%	Retail shops and stores	10%

Major Players

The top five newspapers in Hong Kong (circulation/readership) were Chinese language publications: Oriental Daily News (ODN), Sing Pao, Tin Tin Daily News, Ming Pao and Hong Kong Daily News (Exhibits 3A, 3B). The highest average daily circulation (sales) was recorded by ODN, approximately 400,000 copies.

As a means of protecting profits (Exhibit 3C), 28 industry players (Chinese and English language) belonged to a cartel (founded 1954), the Newspaper Society of Hong Kong (NSHK). The society was empowered to discuss and act to protect members' common interests, including setting cover prices. (See Table 3 for historic price changes; see Table 4 for Society objectives.) Despite claims that their price agreements were voluntary and non-binding, members admitted all Chinese papers tended to comply.

Table 3: Newspaper Price Changes in Hong Kong

Date	Original price (HK$)	New price (HK$)	Increase (HK$)	%
Nov 1, 1983	0.8	1	0.2	25
Nov 1, 1986	1	1.5	0.5	50
Nov 1, 1988	1.5	2	0.5	33
Oct 1, 1990	2	2.5	0.5	25
Oct 1, 1991	2.5	3	0.5	20
Oct 1, 1992	3	3.5	0.5	17
Oct 1, 1993	3.5	4	0.5	14
Oct 1, 1994	4	5	1	25

Table 4: The Newspaper Society of Hong Kong – Principal Objectives

The principal objectives of the society are as follows:
  (a) To act as a central organization of the newspapers of Hong Kong.
  (b) To promote cooperation in all matters affecting the common interest of newspapers.
  (c) To do or concur in doing anything conducive to the interests of Hong Kong newspapers in general, or of the Society; or of any of its Members, where such interest does not run contrary to the common good of the Hong Kong press.
  (d) To promote and safeguard local newspaper interests in matters relating to the Hong Kong Government Administration, and all municipal and other local affairs.
  (e) To encourage and enhance communication, liaison or affiliation with newspaper societies or the like and the press in Hong Kong, mainland China, Taiwan and other places in the world.

Costs and Revenues

In recent years, surges in raw paper prices and staff salaries placed many newspapers in financial difficulties. In 1994, two papers closed due to escalating costs and unsatisfactory circulation:

Wah Kiu Yat Po originally focused on the informative and educational values of news reporting. After suffering substantial losses for several years, the paper shifted to more business-oriented reporting and cultivating a younger image by revising content and style. Circulation increased by 60% (30,000) but the paper was still losing an estimated HK$30 million (US$3.9 million) annually when the owner finally decided to close.

Hong Kong Today, launched by the Ming Pao Group, targeted the youth and white collar segments. It folded after one year's operations; circulation was only 3,000 to 4,000 copies.

Generally, the percent breakdown of operating expenses was similar for most publications (Exhibit 4); a particularly critical issue in Hong Kong was paper prices since all paper was imported. In 1993, raw paper costs were approximately US$500 per ton; in 1994, US$650 to US$700 per ton; 1995 estimates were US$800 to US$850 per ton. In addition to soaring paper costs, editorial and reporters' salaries were rising fast, 50% in the past five years, accounting for around 40% of operating costs. Color pages cost double black and white pages. Hong Kong newspapers averaged 40 to 60 pages (larger papers had more advertisements); on average the print cost was HK$3.

Revenues were generated from two sources: cover prices paid by consumers and advertising revenues. For major players (e.g., ODN) circulation revenues averaged 25% of total revenues. For smaller newspapers (e.g., Tin Tin Daily News) circulation revenues ranged from 30% to 40%. As a rule of thumb, newspapers with circulation revenue over 40% were believed to be in imminent danger of closing down.

Advertising charges, listed in newspapers' rate cards, varied with column inches of space and placement. In the 1990s, a slowdown in Hong Kong's economy reduced company advertising budgets and active advertisers; newspaper advertising revenues fell. A contributing phenomenon was the government's successful action to curb speculation in the residential property market. Real estate advertising, historically 30% to 50% of newspaper advertising, declined. In early 1995, China's property market declined significantly; newspaper income derived from real estate rental and sales advertisements decreased (year-to-year) 15% in the first half of 1995.

Consumer Trends in Hong Kong

During the 1980s, newspaper readership behavior changed as prices rose. In the early 1980s, approximately one third of the population read more than one newspaper; by 1990, this dropped to 13% as readers stopped buying multiple papers. At the same time, to capture wider readership, some newspapers offered more comprehensive coverage.

Lai believed newspapers did not really evolve with consumer tastes and preferences. Rather, he thought price fixing and dominance by several major players led to overall industry complacency and a lack of motivation to improve product offerings by most publishers. He said newspaper layout and content were unchanged over 10 to 15 years and that many papers comprised dull black and white pictures and densely packed text, causing sore eyes for some. Newspapers, he said, were not customer focused; they ignored readers' perspectives and continued "doing things the way they were used to." Despite Hong Kong's increasing affluence, reports indicated a decline in buying intentions. Lai believed this was due less to consumer desires to save for protection against political uncertainty, than because consumers lacked adequate consumer news and information "advising" them how to spend. He believed an opportunity existed to provide better news value to customers.

Lai did not test these beliefs through consumer research; he preferred to act instinctively and quickly. One evening he gathered several friends, experienced media professionals, and discussed options to capture the unfilled market potential. Several major attributes were suggested for a new newspaper:

Revolutionary layout. Hong Kong's greatest purchasing power was among the 18 to 45-age group, the TV generation, for whom color was important. Lai's group observed that when color TV became popular, black and white TVs were discarded; once hooked on color, viewers did not easily revert to black and white. Newspapers were similar; he thought that once consumers became accustomed to a more colorful newspaper (e.g., USA Today) they would be locked into the format. To pursue this thrust, colorful illustrations and photos of news events and high-quality computer professionals and photographers would be essential.

Amount of consumer news. A preliminary study conducted by one business partner showed readers could digest up to 12 pages of consumer news per day.

Content. Information on consumption, entertainment and travel would initially be a competitive advantage. However, Lai believed top quality editorials and articles would be necessary for long-run survival: "Consumers could be fooled, but they could not be fooled for continuous periods of time." For excellent content, Lai would need high-quality staff; he would have to pay premium salaries for respected veteran writers from competing newspapers.

Competitors

Since he was not considering a financially-focused newspaper, such publications as Hong Kong Economic Times would not be direct competitors. Rather, Lai's competitive focus was the largest circulation players offering mass market appeal. He considered it unwise to copy competitors; an over-emphasis on matching competitors would divert attention from focusing on consumers. As a result, the Next Group intentionally did no competitor scanning and little competitive information was known. It merely maintained a news cutting book focused on competitors' promotional activities.

Oriental Daily News. Founded in 1968 by the Oriental Press Group (OPG), Oriental Daily employed over 1,200 people; by mid-1995, it had Hong Kong's highest circulation and readership. The group also printed several magazines including Eastern Sunday, EastWeek (a Next imitator) and EastTouch (similar to EasyFinder in style and content). OPG, a publicly listed company, also published Eastern Express, an English-language newspaper targeted against the leading publication, South China Morning Post (SCMP). Oriental Daily News' target customers were the general public; it offered wide ranging content including economic, social and entertainment news.

Ming Pao. Generally recognized as a high-quality paper, Ming Pao typically received various awards in Hong Kong's annual "Best Press Articles of the Year," organized by NSHK. Although profiles were not released, readers were perceived as more educated and affluent. In a recent effort (March 1995) to provide more lifestyle information, Sunday Ming Pao launched three color pages, including celebrity profiles, information on new publications, consumer products and the latest entertainment events in Hong Kong. Ming Pao recognized consumer desires for more in-depth news analysis;

its "Local News" section concentrated on "investigative reporting" of issues of public concern.

Sing Pao. Similar to ODN, Sing Pao sought mass appeal by combining local and international news, entertainment and gossip in a single publication.

Tin Tin Daily News. Tin Tin Daily News (founded 1960) was the first Hong Kong newspaper to use color printing. It ranked second in circulation, was similar in style to ODN and targeted the general public.

Hong Kong Daily News. The Hong Kong Daily News finalized an agreement (November 1994) to acquire two new offset printing machines. This equipment, to be fully operational by spring 1996, would add to the newspaper's strength for long-term development.

Sing Tao Daily. Established in 1938, Sing Tao Daily's objective was to provide readers with up-to-the-minute news coverage on local and international affairs with a special emphasis on objective, extensive, in-depth and authoritative news reporting. Balancing coverage between economic, political and social news of Hong Kong and China, it was thought to appeal mainly to students.

Decisions

Lai believed that if he were to start a newspaper; the current period was ideal since Hong Kong would return to China in only 18 months. He believed many local newspapers were exercising self-censorship in reporting politically sensitive news; he believed this was "kowtowing" to the Chinese government. As he commented during one interview: "The allure of the China market and the fear of Communists have made guys who own other papers dance to new music before the music even starts. That leaves a vacuum for us to fill."

Lai believed that in the critical transition period, Hong Kong people needed unbiased, reliable and objective information to resolve the various uncertainties they faced; they wanted truth, not euphemism. Lai elaborated that if he entered, "I would be in a business that delivers information and information is freedom ... my mission would be to battle the fear and uncertainty that grows daily in Hong Kong ... People are very uncertain about the future; and the more intensified people's minds are about the future, the more they want to know about it."

Lai mused about the hand-over to China: "In light of Hong Kong's high transparency, China can't really take full control of the media, otherwise, China would be subject to loss of credibility, international investors, and the used-to-be free-market practitioners would flee away, in flocks." Nonetheless, the impact of a change to Chinese rule on the news media could not be ignored.

Notwithstanding his personal ambitions in publishing, Jimmy Lai knew that any entry into the daily newspaper business in Hong Kong would have to be well thought out with realistic and achievable circulation and financial targets. First he had to decide whether or not to enter; if he decided to go ahead, he would have to develop a strategy and implementation plan.

Exhibit 1A: Giordano Financial Highlights (amounts in HK$ '000)

	1994	1993	1992	1991
Turnover	2,863,762	2,334,135	1,661,364	1,169,622
Turnover increase (%)	22.7	40.5	42	31.1
Profit after tax and minority interests	195,347	137,632	115,091	85130
Profit after tax and minority interests increase (%)	41.9	19.6	35.2	87.1
Shareholders' funds	544,521	454,697	361,667	283,239
Working capital	361,952	297,379	238,905	219,262
Total debt to equity ratio	0.9	0.8	1.1	0.6
Bank borrowings to equity ratio	0.1	0.1	0	0
Current ratio	1.8	1.8	1.6	2.2
Inventory turnover on sales (days)	53	59	86	76
Return on total assets (%)	18.8	16.7	15.4	18.3
Return on average equity (%)	39.1	33.7	35.7	49.8
Return on sales (%)	6.8	5.9	6.9	7.3
Earnings per share (cents)	30.9	22	19	15.8
Cash dividend per share (cents)	11	9	7.5	5

Exhibit 1B: Giordano Operations Highlights (figures at year-end unless specified)

	1994	1993	1992	1991
No. of retail outlets directly managed	283	257	191	160
Total no. of retail outlets (excl. Aoyama)	360	278	203	168
Retail floor areas directly managed (sq. ft.)	2,822,700	209,500	139,500	99,800
Sales per square foot (HK$) (Note 1)	10,600	12,600	12,200	10,900
No. of employees	6,863	2,330	2,104	1,477
Comparable store sales increase/ decrease (%) (Note 2)	−9	15	25	25
No. of sales associates	1,928	1,502	1,207	794

Notes:
1. On weighted average basis.
2. Outlets open for the full 12 months in each of the two financial years under comparison.

Exhibit 2: Next Media Group: Profit and Loss (year ending March 31)

Year	Loss		Profit	
	HK$	US$	HK$	US$
1989–90	17,375,000	2,227,564		
1990–91	44,987,000	5,767,564		
1991–92	16,496,000	2,114,872		
1992–93	8,252,000	1,057,949		
1993–94			41,968,000	5,380,513
1994–95			60,758,000	7,789,487

Exhibit 3A: Leading HK Newspapers: Daily Circulation ('000s)

	1992	1993	1994*
Oriental Daily News	425	390	410
Sing Pao	220	215	210
Tin Tin Daily News	200	200	180
Ming Pao	115	120	115
South China Morning Post**	102	106	99
Hong Kong Daily News	75	80	105
Express News	50	50	62
Sing Tao	60	65	75

*Until June 1994.   **English language.   Source: ABC Report.

Exhibit 3B: Leading HK Newspapers: Readership and Advertising Revenues

Newspapers	Readership Dec 1993–May 1994	Advertising revenue (US$ million) Dec 1993–May 1994
Oriental Daily News	1,664,000	78.66
Sing Pao	690,000	45.01
Tin Tin Daily News	649,000	15.48
Ming Pao	442,000	31.59
Hong Kong Daily News	258,000	6.27

Note: Average issue readership (read yesterday) for ages 9+.
Sources: Readership–SRH Media Index; Ad revenue–SRG Adex, Survey Research Group.

Exhibit 3C: Leading HK Newspapers: Financial Performance (Apr 1 to Dec 31, 1994)

		ODN	Sing Tao	Ming Pao	SCMP	Tin Tin
Revenues	US$ million	104.6	129.0	82.1	80.9	39.7
Profit before tax	US$ million	33.3	22.2	13.3	46.5	5.0
Operating profit margin		31.8%	17.2%	16.2%	57.4%	12.7%
Profit after tax	US$ million	27.8	25.2	11.6	38.5	2.7

Exhibit 4: Leading HK Newspapers: Operating Expense Breakdown (%)

Item/company	ODN	Sing Tao	Ming Pao	SCMP	Average
Paper	35	20	35	20	27.5
Infor. gathering and news editing	40	40	30	36	36.5
Others (admin., promo. and dpn.)	25	40	35	44	36
Months inventory of paper	3–3.5	1.5–2	3	1–1.5	2.5

Case 7

Jimmy Lai: Apple Daily (B)

Noel Capon
Graduate School of Business, Columbia University

Ho Yuen Ching, Michelle
The Hong Kong University of Science and Technology

On June 20, 1995, successful Hong Kong entrepreneur Jimmy Lai launched Apple Daily, a controversial Chinese language newspaper in Hong Kong. As part of the promotional launch campaign, Lai was featured in the first television commercial. Seated in an armchair in the center of a darkly lit office, the rather stout Lai was shot and struck by arrows darting from all directions (Figure 1). At the end of the 30-second episode, a narrator calmly stated in Cantonese, "An apple a day keeps the lies away!" The advertisement illustrated Apple Daily's primary mission: to report the "truth" rather than follow competitors that, according to Lai, self-censored news by bowing to political pressures.

Two weeks after the launch, Apple Daily was distributed through approximately 1,500 news-stands and 300 convenience stores territory-wide. Responses to the newcomer varied: readers were talking about it, competitors were angry about it, the Chinese government was cautious about it, Jimmy Lai was confident about it. By July 4, 1995, printing almost 210,000 copies daily, Apply Daily often sold out before noon. This success had not come easily; spending had been substantial and Lai foresaw more obstacles from the newspaper cartel. Lai gave Apple Daily's newly hired marketing staff five days to prepare a flexible marketing plan to overcome potential problems.

ℰⱮℭᏏ

The Launch of Apple Daily

Lai knew that launching Apple Daily would consume significant time and financial investment. Because of the uncertain political future (Hong Kong would return to Chinese rule on July 1, 1997), many observers believed Lai was placing a substantial bet with poor odds. However, Lai saw the political uncertainties as opportunities; he was betting on politics: "In the light of Hong Kong's high transparency, China can't really take full control of the media, otherwise, China would be subject to loss of

152

Figure 1: Portrait of Jimmy Lai

credibility, international investors, and the used-to-be free-market practitioners would flee away, in flocks."

Apple Daily was launched on June 20, 1995. The name "Apple" was inspired by Campbell's soup. As Lai put it: "If Andy Warhol can call a soup Campbell, why can't I call a newspaper an Apple?" To make the entry more interesting, Lai developed the launch into an "Adam and Eve" theme; "if Eve hadn't eaten the apple there would be no news!"

At the launch, Lai set Apple Daily's survival as his major focus. The operational goal was to sustain a 200,000 circulation for the first five years. To attract advertising agencies and advertisers, newspaper readership as audited by a recognized agency (e.g., SRH) had to be high; however, audited half-yearly circulation figures would not be released until February 1996. Although Lai believed significant market impact would cause advertisers to come to Apple Daily, initially, circulation income would be the sole revenue source; for several months it would be the major source.

By launch, Lai had invested roughly HK$100 million in Apple Daily; currently HK$1 million (US$128,205) per day was sustaining the paper. First month operational expenses were expected to be HK$29 million (US$3,718,000). However, Lai believed Apple Daily had established credibility through observable market impact; substantial price advantages should soon attract advertisers. Operational break-even was expected by mid-1996. Apple Daily's initial print-run was 190,000 copies; two weeks later production was running at 210,000 copies.[1] The printing subcontractor's capacity was about 300,000 copies.

---

[1] In a rash moment, Lai offered to cut off one of his fingers if Apple Daily's circulation failed to average 200,000.

Organization

At launch, Apple Daily's production staff was about 300. Lai hired the best people in the industry by offering lucrative compensation packages. Before launch, newly recruited journalists were promised a three-month bonus regardless of circulation. Senior journalists would reportedly earn annual salaries of HK$675,000 (US$86,538); section heads would receive up to HK$1.5 million (US$192,308). The five major papers pressured some of Apple's new journalists to quit Apple Daily before launch under threat from being blackballed in the newspaper industry, but none resigned. Since Lai abhorred formal hierarchy the organization was very flat (Figure 2). Morris Ho, Apple Daily's managing director, a J. Walter Thompson alumnus with substantial advertising experience, came from the Next Group with five advertising and sales personnel. The Accounting and Human Resource departments maintained very lean staff. In production, staff were organized by sections (e.g., local crimes, social news, sports, horse-racing, international news); all were supervised by the editor-in-chief.

Figure 2:   Apple Daily Organization Chart

Product

Color and paper: Consistent with ideas proposed at a consumer trends strategy meeting, Apple Daily was a colorful paper. To ensure distinctive print quality, superior quality paper (up to 20% higher cost than competitors) was purchased from the Netherlands. For 300,000 Apple Daily copies, paper cost per sheet (four newspaper pages) averaged HK$90,000 (US$11,500) to HK$100,000 (US$12,800). Total production cost per paper was estimated at HK$8.40 (US$1.08) versus Oriental Daily News, HK$5 to HK$6 (US$0.64 to US$0.77).

Important local news was supplemented by in-depth analysis and eye-catching illustrations for quick and easy assimilation. As one industry expert commented, Apple offered remarkably higher quality in both paper and printing than other newspapers. Since photographers were paid the highest salaries in the industry, photos had especially high quality.[2] "It is a nicely presented newspaper, appealing to lower-end and popular-class readers. Its content is popular to the mass public. Whether Apple can sustain its competitive advantage or not depends on content and its continuous credibility in keeping up and digging out special and insider news."

Crime news. A team of 20 young enthusiastic photographers worked in the city crime section; they rushed to crime scenes on company-supplied motorcycles. The concentration of 90 reporters and photographers working around the clock on city crime reflected Apple Daily's dedication, competence and commitment to report in-depth timely news.

Political issues. Apple Daily took firm political stances; it promised readers impartial news and a refusal to bow to the upcoming new government.

Consumer focus groups: Lai believed Apple Daily could not create competitive advantage simply via paper and print quality. With even deeper pockets, competitors could replicate these moves at lower costs via economy-of-scale purchases. Rather, Lai believed continuously monitoring consumer preferences was crucial: Apple would compete on versatility and flexibility, typified by changing the Apple logo each day for the first month. Nightly, Apple Daily conducted consumer focus groups; five consumers (paid HK$100 [US$13]) were randomly selected off the street. In the hour and a half group session, participants were required to read that day's Apple Daily edition and provide comments on each page. Lai considered these sessions a cost-effective approach to collect timely consumer feedback. Suggested improvements were immediately passed on for staff discussion enabling changes to be made in the next day's paper.

Price

To break consumer loyalty to existing newspapers and encourage trial, Lai broke the newspaper cartel's "golden rule" by setting Apple Daily's price, for the first month, at HK$2.00 (US$0.26); the cartel's uniform news-stand price was HK$5.00 (US$0.64). Lai felt intuitively that a one-month price reduction period should be enough to establish a core loyalty group for Apple Daily. He had no concrete support for this belief but was concerned that a too long discount period would cause readers to take it for granted, making later price rises more painful.

---

[2] Total Apple Daily production cost was estimated at HK$8.40 (US$1.08) versus HK$5 to HK$6 for its major competitor, Oriental Daily News. Distribution costs were additional.

Advertising prices were listed on newspaper rate cards. At launch, Apple Daily based its rates on rate cards of Oriental Daily News, Sing Pao and Ming Pao. To account for being new to the market, substantial discounts (30% to 50%) were factored into Apple's rates. Promotion to advertisers and advertising agencies started one month before actual launch. Positive responses were only received one week before launch. In Apple's advertising package, advertisers were guaranteed 200,000 circulation for rates paid. If circulation was under 200,000 copies, only 50% of the rate was payable. If circulation was below 120,000 copies, no fees would be charged.

Promotion

Apple Daily was promoted in TV commercials, magazines (in Next and EasyFinder [Exhibit 1]) and on radio; publicity was also secured via Lai as a controversial figure (Exhibit 2). On launch day, Apple Daily handed out 200,000 apples to people on the streets in Hong Kong Island and Kowloon. Apple Daily's launch received significant media attention, especially on television; Jimmy Lai was interviewed on several talk shows. The first month's promotional budget, including price cut subsidies (from the HK$5.00 cartel price) were HK$7 million (US$900,000). Lai was considering other promotions to please existing readers and attract others. One staff reporter suggested printing posters as gifts to readers (HK$3.00 [US$0.38] cost per copy). Lai asked staff for other alternatives; he was willing to conduct several promotions simultaneously. He told his staff: "Be creative."

Distribution

News-stands. After two weeks, Apple Daily was distributed at about 1,500 news-stands. Unhappy at Apple Daily's entry, especially the low entry price, competitors made distribution difficult for Lai. Distributors were rumored to have been threatened by major players; their contracts would be canceled if they carried Apple Daily. Only one distributor, Tak Keung Kee, agreed to distribute Apple Daily in Hong Kong. Shum Tak Keung, head of Tak Keung Kee, was expelled from the Hong Kong and Kowloon Hawkers Association days before Apple Daily's launch. Some news-stands claimed to have been threatened if they sold Apple Daily; for the first few days, Lai hired 40 part-time and 60 temporary staff to sell Apple Daily adjacent to these news-stands. Since the major players forbade Tak Keung Kee to carry Apple Daily in the same delivery vehicles as their papers, Apple Daily provided a fleet of 12 vans solely for delivery of its paper. To assist 200 Tak Keung Kee staff, then exclusively distributing Apple Daily, the so-called "independent distribution team," Apple Daily paid for 20 additional Tak Keung Kee staff as monitors and assistants to ensure smooth delivery to Hong Kong news-stands.

Since Apple Daily's price was significantly lower than competing newspapers, Lai had to ensure that the distributor and news-stands received sufficient mark-ups. He was currently subsidizing the distribution channel HK$3.50 per paper sold: HK$1 for the distributor, HK$2.50 for news-stands. News-stands thus received HK$4.50 per paper sold, compared to HK$1.50 for competing newspapers (Figure 3).

Figure 3: Newspaper Distribution in Hong Kong, the Launch of Apple Daily

Distribution of Apple Daily

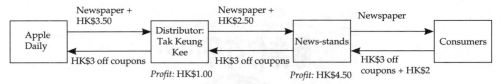

Distribution of other newspapers

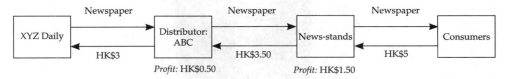

Convenience stores. Apple Daily vans also serviced over 439 round-the-clock convenience stores. This channel accounted for about 20,000 copies daily.

An added difficulty was that Apple Daily's printing facilities were located in Yuen Long, New Territories, about one hour's drive from Central. Apple Daily used this printer because of its advanced printing technology and high quality product.[3] Compared with more strategically located competitors, Apple Daily's transportation time could result in less up-to-minute reporting. Lai was considering alternative distribution means, even helicopters.

Decisions

Lai knew he was at the most critical stage of launching his newspaper; each decision would affect Apple Daily's ability to survive. During the past few weeks he had developed a real feel for the media industry and was prepared to take new strategic initiatives to ensure success. His initial idea was to raise prices in two weeks' time after one month on the market; he wondered if he should follow through, how much the price should be raised and what would be the impact on circulation. He was also concerned whether his promotional expenditures were optimal and was contemplating extending distribution, possibly to restaurants and supermarkets. Lai demanded a set of firm proposals backed up by rigorous analysis. These proposals, next best alternatives and requests for research budgets were to be presented to him by Friday, just five working days away.

---

[3] Printing machines cost HK$50 to HK$60 million; competitors used older machines at about half the cost. However, Apple Daily's quality was significantly higher.

Exhibit 1 (cont'd)

你咬咗未？ June 30, '95
277

咬吧！

蘋果日報
經已出版

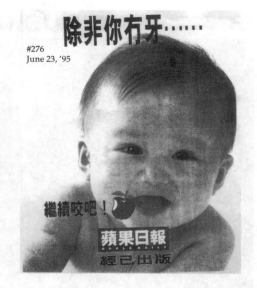

#276
June 23, '95
除非你冇牙……

繼續咬吧！

蘋果日報
經已出版

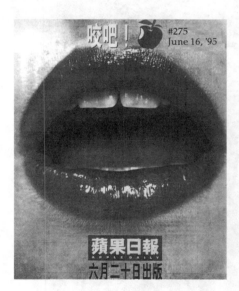

咬吧！ #275
June 16, '95

蘋果日報
六月二十日出版

肥佬黎智英又黐咗佢話……

#275
June 16, '95
Fat Boy "Lai" goes crazy.
He said "the newspaper
costs $2".

Jimmy Lai launches his newspaper amidst a sea of apples and complaints from industry rivals.

Jimmy is not their darling

Case 8

Jimmy Lai: Apple Daily (C)

Noel Capon
Graduate School of Business, Columbia University

Ho Yuen Ching, Michelle
The Hong Kong University of Science and Technology

On December 8, 1995, five and one half months after the launch of controversial newspaper Apple Daily, Jimmy Lai proudly announced the newly audited circulation figures to his staff. Apple Daily had met its 200,000 daily circulation objective, readership was rising and aware-ness and trial targets were being met. However, led by industry leader, Oriental Daily News (ODN), many newspapers were intensifying promotional campaigns. Lai wondered what other moves competitors might take and how Apple Daily should respond.

ℝℝℝ

Apple Daily's First Six Months

Results

According to independent auditor ABC, from January to June 1995, prior to Apple Daily's launch, Sing Pao was market leader averaging 187,000 daily sales copies. In reality, Sing Pao was second to Oriental Daily News (ODN); however, as ODN's results were not independently audited, it was excluded from this analysis. From August to October 1995, Apple Daily claimed to be lead seller, average daily sales over 272,000 (Exhibit 1); Sing Pao's semi-annual (July to December) results would be avail-able in January 1996. Because of Apple Daily's strength, advertisers were increasingly placing advertisements in Apple Daily.

At launch, Apple Daily was losing HK$1 million (US$128,200) daily; by November daily losses were HK$0.5 million. Lai expected to reach operating break-even (not including start-up expenses) by end March 1996. Apple Daily significantly impacted rival newspapers' sales. (See Table 1 for estimates by "dai-zhi," industry experts and distributors; see Exhibit 2 for articles on Apple Daily.) An unofficial survey released in

161

Table 1: **Estimated Impact of Apple Daily on Sales of Other Newspapers**

Newspaper	Daizhi's estimate Before Apple / After Apple (Number of piles*)		Ind. expt's estimate Decrease in sales %	Distributors' estimate Before Apple '000 copies / After Apple '000 copies / %		
	Before Apple	After Apple		Before Apple '000 copies	After Apple '000 copies	%
Oriental Daily News	3 to 6	3 to 5	7 to 10	320	–50	–20
Tin Tin Daily News	2 to 3	2	10 to 15	170 to 180	–20	–15
Sing Pao	4	2 to 3	20 to 30	200 to 240	–40	–18
Express News	4 to 6	2	30	60	–40	–67
Ming Pao	–	–	–	110 to 120	–1 to –2	–7 to –8
H.K. Daily News	–	–	–	–	–	–10
Sing Tao Daily News	7 to 8	6	–	–	–	–

*1 pile = 40 papers.

August reported that circulation of several established Chinese newspapers dropped by 5% to 20% since Apple Daily was launched.

However, not everything ran smoothly. To maintain maximum autonomy for Apple Daily's journalists and editors, Lai exercised little control over published material. Apple Daily was subject to much public criticism for publishing a graphic photograph of a mother and son after a 30-floor suicide jump and a photograph of a 19-year-old girl immediately after she was raped. Apple Daily publicly apologized.

Marketing Programs

Pricing. On July 20, one month after the launch and following much internal debate, Lai increased Apple Daily's price from HK$2 (US$0.26) to the cartel price, HK$5 (US$0.64). Lai planned to offer other incentives to secure and reinforce what he considered "fragile loyalty." Lai compared building loyal customers with chasing a desirable woman: "You bring her to nice restaurants every day and shower her with gifts. Then she'll be yours." Before the price increase, daily sales averaged 236,000 copies; after July 20, circulation dropped to 210,000 copies, then increased by 10,000 copies per week, quickly reaching maximum daily printing capacity of 300,000 copies.

Distribution. Apple Daily's distribution network expanded to 2,500 news-stands: 325 7-Eleven outlets, 114 Circle K convenience stores, 46 mini-store outlets, 10 Fairwood Fast Food outlets, and one Mannings (pharmaceutical retail chain) store.

Promotional activities. Apple Daily used several incentive schemes to boost circulation. As soon as Apple Daily increased its price it offered give-aways, free "Apple Target" T-shirts, to readers who collected six Apple logos from the cover page (multiple logos for a single day were allowed); these could be redeemed at convenience stores selling the newspaper. During the week-long campaign, 140,000 T-shirts (HK$20 [US$2.56] each) were distributed. On July 27, Apple Daily gave posters to readers (Exhibit 3); this promotion lasted one month.

Beginning August 6, Apple Daily enclosed free supplements of Sudden Weekly on Saturdays; daily sales increased to over 240,000 copies.[1] At 200,000 copies, Sudden Weekly's production cost was about HK$2.5 million (US$320,500) per issue; annual production costs would be HK$100 million (US$12.82 million). Lai believed this was too heavy a financial burden for Apple Daily; after a couple of months Sudden Weekly was spun off as a separate magazine targeted mainly at housewives.

Lai broke new ground with an advertising rule; no advertising space on Apple Daily's front page; the front page was reserved for consumer value-adding news. Competitors' daily front page advertising revenues averaged HK$200,000 (US$25,600).

Political Harassment

Despite protests by local politicians, Apple Daily's political reporters were refused permission to cover the Preliminary Working Committee (on Hong Kong's reunification) meeting in Beijing, as well as Liberal Party and Education Commission visits to the Chinese capital. Chinese officials did not explain these decisions but internal documents were said to have labeled Apple Daily as "anti-China" and stirring up trouble in Hong Kong.

Competitors

Financial results. Oriental Press Group announced net profits for the six months ended September 30, 1995 were HK$138.2 million, 36% down from 1994. Sing Tao reported six-month interim profits at HK$20.45 million, 89.6% down; Ming Pao Enterprise Corporation reported half year profits of HK$53.9 million, down 40%, citing higher newsprint costs and tougher competition.

Reaction to Apple Daily

Competitors' reaction to Apple Daily was two-fold. First, most newspapers improved their formats and, many employed aggressive promotional campaigns. ODN organized lucky draws every week; prizes were residential flats worth over HK$1 million (US$128,200). Other newspapers also offered give-aways; for example, Sing Pao provided coupons redeemable for free goose noodles at certain restaurants.

On December 3, ODN announced a new promotional plan. For five consecutive Sundays (December 3 to 31) readers buying the Group's entertainment magazine, Oriental Sundae, could redeem coupons for a free copy of ODN that day. This promotion targeted Apple Daily's rich Sunday sections.

Decisions

Lai contemplated both long-run and short-run problems. In the long run he had to decide how to ensure that consumers continually enjoyed Apple Daily; in the short run he had to anticipate rival newspapers' actions and decide how to respond.

---

[1] Sudden Weekly contained gossip, celebrity coverage and entertainment. It included many photographs, predominately of "stars," together with their opinions on various topics.

Exhibit 1: Average Daily Circulation of Apple Daily by Week

Date	News-stand sales	7-Eleven sales	OK stores sales	DeiLeiDim sales	Eastwood Fast Food sales	Airport Manning Shop sales	Company used	British Airways sales	Delivered for circulation	Total sales
Aug 26, 95	224,137	15,276	6,126	6,217	99	103	1,080	65	277,688	251,921
Sept 2, 95	233,046	17,481	7,073	6,322	100	100	1,080	65	282,544	264,086
Sept 9, 95	248,766	13,607	6,789	6,154	100	100	1,000	65	296,697	275,481
Sept 16, 95	259,398	13,135	6,621	6,802	86	100	1,000	65	297,648	286,107
Sept 23, 95	261,805	12,850	6,689	6,801	–	100	1,000	65	297,649	288,209
Sept 30, 95	263,984	13,035	6,912	6,947	–	100	1,100	65	300,537	290,943
Oct 7, 95	261,978	13,595	7,116	6,367	–	89	1,100	65	292,689	288,439
Oct 14, 95	268,351	12,641	6,866	7,157	–	82	1,100	65	292,813	294,405
Oct 21, 95	270,989	13,337	7,051	7,267	–	94	1,060	65	292,725	298,090
Oct 28, 95	276,541	12,479	6,790	7,140	–	92	950	65	299,809	303,022
Nov 4, 95	279,276	13,014	7,028	6,920	–	84	950	65	307,898	306,354
Nov 11, 95	278,843	34,274	6,987	7,358	–	68	840	65	307,758	327,587
Nov 18, 95	278,243	12,906	6,958	7,312	–	70	840	65	307,758	305,553
Nov 25, 95	278,959	13,085	7,022	7,373	–	69	840	65	307,758	306,544
Dec 2, 95	279,039	13,048	7,007	7,345	–	70	840	65	307,758	306,630

Apple Daily Succeeds in Cutting into Share of Rival Newspapers

Apple Daily is estimated to have grabbed at least a 10 to 15 per cent share of Hong Kong's Chinese language newspaper market in its first two months in operation. Media analysts described the industry as being in its most competitive phase in years with all players engaged in trench warfare.

But they told *MEDIA* that garment and publishing tycoon Jimmy Lai's newspaper is still a long way off from mounting an effective challenge on the long-established market leader, *Oriental Daily*.

Figures from accounting firm Coopers & Lybrand said *Apple*'s circulation in early August stood at just over 200,000 at a market price of HK$5 a copy. This is down from 220,000 achieved in the launch period in June/July when the paper was being sold off news-stands at $2 each. But while the media analysts said the launch circulation number looks accurate, the latest figure appears to have been inflated. They said the real figure would likely be between 100,000 and 150,000 because "the novelty value of *Apple* has worn off."

One analyst said, "When *Eastern Express* launched last year, they were claiming a circulation of 50,000 to 100,000 and that might have been true, but the circulation rapidly dropped after that because the initial euphoria had died out."

Despite this, however, another analyst said, "*Apple* has taken at least a 10 per cent share from everybody. But it has its work cut out to cause a mass defection of readers from the top three [*Oriental*, which claims a circulation of 450,000, *Sing Pao* and *Tin Tin*] because long-time readers aren't likely to be in a hurry to switch papers."

The analysts also said that while *Oriental* might have lost some of its share to *Apple,* it would not mind its circulation settling at between 400,000 and 450,000. They explained that *Oriental* is widely believed to be the most effective advertising medium in Hong Kong and that as long as it maintains its number one position it will be able to charge premium advertising rates.

Meanwhile, *Apple* has launched a Sunday glossy magazine but unlike the magazines published by *Oriental* or *Ming Pao*, it is free of charge. Mr. Morris Ho, managing director of Next Media Group, which publishes *Apple*, said, "No charge was put on the magazine because we wanted to give more value to customers."

Oriental's salvo in the newspaper was to give rate protection to advertisers. It raised its rate card by an average nine per cent, the first such hike in 14 months.

However, advertisers who commit their budgets before the new rates take effect this month will enjoy rate protection until next March.

Oriental Press Group deputy publisher Simon Lai denied that the move was an attempt to lock in advertisers away from *Apple*. "If we wanted to lock in advertisers, we would have done this a long time ago."

"Our main consideration was to offset higher operating and materials costs, including newsprint."

"We also did not increase the rates by too much because adspend appears to be softening from a year ago," he said.

Source: *MEDIA*, August 18, 1995

Exhibit 2 (cont'd)

Apple Scores Strong Circulation Gains as Bid to be No. 1 Grows

Apple Daily has said it is now Hong Kong's second most popular newspaper and that it could be within striking distance by early next year to challenge *Oriental Daily* for the number one spot.

Morris Ho, managing director of Next Media Group which publishes *Apple Daily* as well as hugely successful Next magazine, told *MEDIA*, "We want to be number two for at least six months.

"By next Chinese New Year, we will likely be in a position to take the top spot, provided the current situation remains constant."

His optimism is reflected by *Apple's* tremendous growth since its launch just a few months ago.

According to figures provided by Coopers & Lybrand, *Apple* has been posting weekly circulation increases since near the end of July when the publication's news-stand price reverted to HK$5 following a month long promotional campaign.

For last week, Coopers & Lybrand reported that *Apple* sold an average of 242,000 copies daily, up a strong 28.7% per cent from 188,000 in the final week of July.

In order to cope with the rising demand, the print-run has also been increased from 223,000 to 259,000 in the same period, while the print-run currently stands at more than 272,000.

Mr. Ho said media analysts (quoted in the August 18 edition of *MEDIA*) who speculated that *Apple's* circulation might have been lower were merely making observations and that the actual circulation figure is provided by a leading accounting firm and cannot be disputed.

He added that he estimated one million Chinese language newspaper copies are circulating in Hong Kong every day, giving *Apple* a 25 per cent share.

Apple has already set in motion a plan to try to realise its aim of being Hong Kong's top selling newspaper.

"To increase our printing capacity, we will be paying for and installing a fourth printing machine worth HK$50 million in Robert Chow's Premier Printing Group," said Mr. Ho.

He said *Apple* would be picking up the tab for the new machine because the newspaper group takes up the capacity for the existing three machines.

"After we get the new printer, we will have a chance to become number one since that will give us a printing capacity of more than 300,000," he said.

Mr. Ho explained that *Apple's* success lies in it addressing the needs of the young to middle age group, who has been neglected by the established papers.

"You can see Hong Kong is changing, especially over the past 10 years. People are getting more affluent, more educated and what they want is something of their own.

"But the established publications have not been changing to fit their needs."

He said other factors include *Apple* having the most color, up to 60 per cent, compared with its rivals as well as its offering of a wide range of news coverage.

"We have detailed news, quick news and on the entertainment section, we have our own story style instead of matching with other newspapers."

Mr. Ho also pointed to the fact that *Apple* is continually testing the market so that it can respond to "the fast changing needs and tastes of readers."

Exhibit 2 (cont'd)

He said that the company organises three focus groups a week to make sure it is keeping up with market expectations.

"We randomly pick up 10 people per group who buy *Apple Daily* at the news-stands and then invite them by giving them a $400 transport allowance to have a chat with us for an hour."

"When we listen to our readers, we could find we might have missed something, or maybe something could be done better, or perhaps adding or even cutting columns," Mr. Ho said.

Source: *MEDIA*, Sept 1, 1995

Exhibit 3:   Free Posters Given Out by Apple Daily

Case 9

Jimmy Lai: Apple Daily (D)

Noel Capon
Graduate School of Business, Columbia University

Ho Yuen Ching, Michelle
The Hong Kong University of Science and Technology

In December 1995, industry leader Oriental Daily News initiated a price war by reducing its cover price from HK$5 to HK$2. In the ensuing weeks, many Chinese language newspapers closed. Concurrently, overall industry circulation increased. Although Apple Daily was less affected than some other newspapers, the events of the previous three months had taken their toll. On March 1, 1996, almost three months after the price war started and over half a year since Apple Daily launch, Lai had to decide how to proceed.

࿇ఠ౪ఠ࿇

The Price War Commences

On December 9, 1995, ODN reduced its cover price from HK$5 to HK$2 as "a reward for reader loyalty on the paper's 28th anniversary." Since there was no prior announcement of the price-cut to distributors or readers, some confusion ensued. Industry observers said it was ironic ODN should instigate such a price-cut. Six months earlier, ODN took the lead in defending the newspaper cartel's HK$5 price in response to Apple Daily's HK$2 launch price. Apple Daily's HK$2 campaign lasted one month.

One observer believed ODN's HK$2 strategy was planned to coincide with the paper's face-lift: content and layout changes were accompanied by introduction of a daily financial supplement. Another observer believed ODN planned for an extended (three to six month) battle by building up a $600 million "war chest."

Industry Response

Newspaper Society of Hong Kong

Shum Choi-sang, consultant with the Newspaper Society of Hong Kong (NSHK), said the public should realize most newspapers could not break-even from cover prices

168

because revenue from sales did not even cover newsprint costs. For most papers, the more copies sold, the more money lost, unless rising circulation was accompanied by increased advertising. He said the absence of price-fixing could be disastrous; he noted the now-defunct Kung Sheung Daily's decision (late 1970s) to maintain a 20-cent price when all other papers decided to sell at 30 cents. Other industry members believed price-fixing was ideal because it prevented publishers with deep pockets from aggressively attacking weaker rivals; rather, it encouraged competition based on quality. The NSHK issued a press release regarding ODN's action:

> The Newspaper Society of Hong Kong regrets the possible igniting of an industry price war by this event (ODN's price-cut to HK$2), because this action does not help the long-run development of the newspaper industry in Hong Kong. Nevertheless, as Hong Kong is a free trade community, the Newspaper Society of Hong Kong may not attempt to influence pricing decisions of individual newspapers. The Newspaper Society of Hong Kong agrees that member newspapers may, depending on their individual situations, adopt corresponding plans and take appropriate actions.

Chairman Tang Lap-yan emphasized that the Society had no legally-binding power on actions of member newspapers and no power to require members give prior notice of their activities to the Society.

According to a respected economist, price wars could squeeze out weak competitors; demand elasticity was fairly strong and 60% to 80% price-cuts might increase newspaper sales by 100% to 200%. Since newspapers lost most value the day after they were printed, predatory pricing could eliminate small competitors effectively and instantly. He said the critical success factor in this price war would be effective entry barriers; the critical question was: "Who had the financial power to sustain the price war?"

Apple Daily. In August 1995, Jimmy Lai's net worth was estimated at over HK$2.5 billion (US$320.5 million). He claimed to own HK$1.5 billion (US$192.3 million) in Giordano, HK$1 billion (US$128.2 million) in Next magazine and US$100 million in Apple Daily. He also owned various properties in Paris and Niagara Falls.

Sing Pao. Sing Pao owners, the Ho family, were known to have deep pockets. According to ABC, Sing Pao's average daily circulation in the first half of 1995 was 187,000. If it chose to follow ODN's price-cut to HK$2, and sustained its pre-Apple Daily circulation, it would lose at least HK$370,000 per day.

Hong Kong Daily News claimed full support from its owner (Emperor Group) in sustaining operations for a prolonged fight. ABC reported circulation at 110,000 prior to Apple Daily's launch.

Ming Pao appealed to middle-class households; audited (ABC) daily circulation was 107,000 during the first half of 1995; it was rumored to be wary of price reductions.

The Price War

In immediate response to Oriental Daily News' price reduction, several major newspapers lowered prices (Table 1); many actions were taken on December 11. For example, Hong Kong Daily News dropped price to HK$1 (charged 12 years previously) surprising both the industry and the public. Director Lun Shiu-ming explained the final decision was made the previous afternoon but that management devised the price-cuts much earlier. He was unsure how long the price war would last, but hoped the "investment" would generate a reasonable return, and that volume could be maintained or even increased. Editor-in-Chief Fung Kam-Fei said the newspaper had to fight hard to survive; at present, the greater the sales, the more money lost. He said Hong Kong Daily News supported uniform prices but was forced to cut price because it had "lost its position." Some industry observers believed the HK$1 price was very dangerous; production costs for newspapers with more than 13 pages were about HK$3 per copy plus a HK$2 handling fee paid to distributors. Thus, HK$4 per copy was lost on a HK$1 priced newspaper.

Apple Daily also reduced its price on December 11, to HK$4, promising this price would be maintained until July 1, 1997; Apple Daily's promise was reiterated to readers each day on the cover page, just under the Apple Daily logo (Exhibit 1). In addition, sufficient HK$1-off coupons for Apple Daily were printed in each copy of Next magazine and EasyFinder, reducing the effective price of Apple Daily for these readers to HK$3; Apple Daily continued to provide HK$3.50 per newspaper to the distribution system. Also on December 11, Express News organized a game asking readers to guess the price ranges of ten Hong Kong stocks over the week; the prize was an apartment valued at HK$12 million (Exhibit 2).

Several newspapers folded (e.g., TV Daily News [December 13], Express News [December 16], Hong Kong United Daily News [December 16], Huanan Jingji Journal[1] and Leisure News (Table 2); a recent casualty was the Hong Kong Economic Journal (January 1, 1996).[2] Survivors' stock prices plunged substantially (Table 3). The Newspaper Society estimated damage from the price war at 590 jobs lost in closures and HK$110 million lost revenues due to lower cover prices. Despite reductions in number of newspapers, total daily circulation rose from 1.3 million copies to between 1.6 million to 2 million as people bought multiple newspapers.

On January 17, ODN claimed 800,000 copies were distributed for circulation, a doubling from the 300,000 to 400,000 pre-price war level (Table 4). On January 21, ODN published a special interview with Group Chairman, Ma Ching-kwan; he said

---

[1] Culturecom Holdings Ltd. closed this unprofitable financial newspaper reporting on southern China business to concentrate on the more established Tin Tin Daily News.

[2] Express News claimed that under the "malicious" competitive conditions of the Hong Kong newspaper industry, management decided to "temporarily" stop publishing; the paper lost over HK$100 million in the previous three years. Hong Kong United Daily reported estimated cumulative losses of HK$6 million since establishment; in the previous week, circulation declined 25% per day and was 20,000 at closing.

Table 1: Immediate Newspaper Reactions to the Price War (December 11, 1995)

Newspaper	Price (HK$)	Claimed strategy
Hong Kong Daily News	1	To confront the price war, there is no other choice
Oriental Daily News	2	Unwilling to comment further on price. Will change strategy depending on future competitors' move
Sing Pao	2	New price will be maintained through July 1997 when Hong Kong would be returned to China
Apple Daily	4	Maintain original price for today
Tin Tin Daily News	5	High-end positioning, if enter price war it would have no hope. Also expected certain newspapers would fold in the war
Express News	5	Price to be maintained for the time being
Ming Pao	5	Targeted reader base different from those of price-reducing newspapers
United News	5	Expected little influence of price war on United News
Sing Tao Daily News	5	No price reduction plan for the time being
Hong Kong Economic Daily	5	Stable reader base, no price reduction plan for the time being, expected little influence of price war on the paper
Hong Kong Economic News	–	Still under discussion that morning
Hong Kong Commercial News	5	Will consider whether to reduce price at a later stage
Wen Wei Pao	5	Price reduction is only the action of other newspapers
Da Gong Pao	5	Cannot disclose commercial decisions to competitors. Will inform readers once the decision to cut price is made

Table 2: Newspapers Closing Early in the Price War (as of December 17, 1995)

Newspaper	Date established	Estimated daily circulation before closing	Number of employees
TV Daily	1968	5,000	40
Hong Kong United News	May 4, 1992	20,000	150
Express News	March 1, 1963	90,000	400

Table 3: Impact of the Price War on Newspaper Stock Prices

Newspaper publishing corporation	Closing previous Friday HK$	Closing Dec 11 HK$	Decrease HK$	%	Drop in firm market value HK$ million	Trading volume ('000 shares)	Trading amount (HK$ '000)
Oriental Daily News	3.2	2.675	−0.525	−16	762.9	10,160	28,167
Sing Tao Daily News	4.175	3.5	−0.675	−16	287.1	518.6	1,872
CultureCom (Tin Tin Daily News)	0.234	0.196	−0.038	−16	41.3	78,093	1,642
H.K. Daily News	1.13	0.98	−0.15	−13	40.0	811	785
Ming Pao Group Co.	3.8	3.7	−0.1	−3	35.6	0	0
South China Morning Post	4.675	4.6	−0.075	−2	112.5	2,411	10,958
Nam Wah Holdings (Express News)	1.63	1.63	0	0	0	0	0

daily target sales were one million copies. He promised to deliver readers a "cheap, beautiful and good" newspaper. (See Exhibit 3 for ODN's promotion of its face-lift; it claimed ODN would include more colors and high-quality content.)

Price-reduced newspapers (e.g., ODN, Sing Pao, Apple Daily) were often sold out before 10:00 am. News-stands earned more money through increased volumes since the HK$1.75 margin under the $5 cartel price was sustained by publishers. Nevertheless, many proprietors and retailers complained about complexities caused by different prices; never had the newspaper industry been so chaotic!

On January 4, 1996, the Newspaper Society of Hong Kong (NSHK) attempted to end the price war. It established a special committee urging "renegade" publishers to reintroduce a uniform price for the Chinese-language press. The committee appointed Simon Lun, Managing Director of Hong Kong Daily News as chairman; his newspaper had introduced the deepest price cut, to HK$1. The Society's spokesperson said a "recommended price (was) necessary for newspapers to compete on an equal footing and (that) price cuts threatened smaller publications." Lai said he would meet with the committee, despite previously promising readers a fixed price of HK$4 until July 1, 1997.

Industry analyst Andy Ho spoke about the future of the price war: "Those engaged in the price war are the five best selling papers in town; it seems inconceivable that any of them could be driven out of the market in the next year or so." Edward Chen, Chairman of Hong Kong's Consumer Council, urged the government to intervene: "A few newspapers are setting prices below cost to put competitors out of business."

Magazines

The newspaper price war spread to magazines; two primary rivals were involved: Next Group and Oriental Press Group (OPG). In the previous three years, OPG published new magazines to compete directly with Next publications. In 1992, OPG launched a weekly magazine, EastWeek, similar to Next's format and style (i.e.,

Table 4: Apple Daily and Oriental Daily News Circulation Since the Price War Started

Date	Apple Daily*	Oriental Daily News
December 10, 1995 (Sun)	307,086	481,684
December 11, 1995 (Mon)	297,101	543,734
December 12, 1995 (Tue)	291,161	771,254
December 13, 1995 (Wed)	291,524	773,319
December 14, 1995 (Thu)	269,344	754,769
December 15, 1995 (Fri)	273,017	749,133
December 16, 1995 (Sat)	288,459	838,487
December 17, 1995 (Sun)	271,567	732,070
December 18, 1995 (Mon)	266,758	775,539
December 19, 1995 (Tue)	274,671	779,526
December 20, 1995 (Wed)	289,759	756,194
December 21, 1995 (Thu)	265,604	
December 22, 1995 (Fri)	270,289	
December 23, 1995 (Sat)	271,233	
December 24, 1995 (Sun)	258,539	
December 25, 1995 (Mon)	260,259	
December 26, 1995 (Tue)	262,454	
December 27, 1995 (Wed)	264,277	

*Each day, Apple Daily distributed around 2,000 copies free for promotional purposes.

gossipy, investigative, sensational stories). On December 20, OPG cut the cover price of EastWeek from HK$18 (US$2.3) to HK$8 (US$1.3); analysts believed this action sought to damage Next Group's prospects for a 1996 London Stock Market listing. Next responded by cutting price from HK$18 to HK$12. Lai claimed Next circulation rose to over 180,000 copies per week from the pre-price cut 167,000.

In January, OPG announced a preferential package of advertising rates; advertisers in EastWeek could place free advertisements in other OPG publications. This deal was only available to advertisers that chose OPG publications as their sole print medium for a six-month period. Although it was too soon to say how effective this action would be, one industry observer said although small advertisers might be tempted, the exclusivity provision might be too onerous for large advertisers that needed the demographic diversity from multiple publications: "Next is indispensable to many advertisers," he said. In late February (just prior to Chinese New Year), ODN slashed 50% off its rate card on Sundays and public holidays. Apple Daily replied with a buy-one-take-one deal to run from February 20 to March 31;[3] in early February, Apple Daily had launched a classified advertising section.

---

[3] Overall, newspaper advertising's share of total advertising was falling: 1994 35.2%, 1995 29.1%. From 1994 to 1995, TV increased from 44.1% to 49.2%; magazines increased slightly from 11.6% to 11.9%.

Decisions

Opinions on the effects of the price war on consumer welfare were mixed. Some claimed competitive pressures would benefit readers (Exhibit 4); others believed the likely result would be a shake-out of small players leading to an industry structure with two dominant players, ODN and Apple Daily. This group claimed readers' choices would be limited and make it easier for the autocratic Chinese government to control the Hong Kong media industry. (See Figure 1 for a cartoon on this theme.)

Figure 1: Cartoon on Hong Kong Newspaper Industry

Characters: Left – Ma, Oriental Daily News; Center – Chairman Jiang Zemin; Right – Lai, Apple Daily.
Chairman Jiang: "Finally, only you two are left. It's easier for me to control now."

Apple Daily's managing director, Morris Ho, expected the price war to last a long time. He said, "Some newspapers with a lot of cash will push this conflict for as long as they can." He also said:

> We would be happy to discuss the issue with the Society and give them our thoughts and opinions. But if the Society is doing things simply to protect themselves, then no way. Go back to a $5 cover price? No way. There is one exception: if they follow Apple to HK$4.

ODN's actions had rocked the entire newspaper industry and Jimmy Lai had to decide what further action to take. His pricing actions would impact both Apple Daily and other competitors. He believed he had numerous options: continue on his current course, follow the price leader, or make bold aggressive moves to seize leadership. Perhaps he should join the cartel he helped collapse!

"Even after 1997, the price will remain $4"

"Apple Daily costs $4"

Exhibit 2: Express News Promotional Campaign – The Stock Price Game

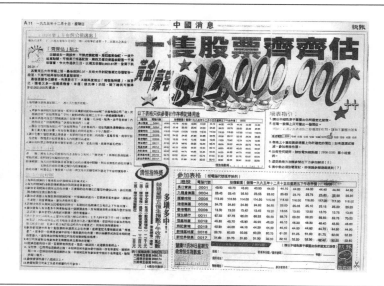

Exhibit 3: ODN's Advertisement of its New Face-lift

Review and Outlook

Paper Warriors

As Hong Kong's newspaper war heads toward it second month, the corpses are beginning to pile up. Three Chinese-language dailies, a handful of magazines and even a racing tip sheet have now been impaled on the price slashing spike. Hundreds of journalists are out of a job, and stocks of various affected newsgroups have lost a lot of their value. There's not a white flag in sight, either. Like gamblers on a losing streak, newspaper owners can't seem to tear themselves away from the grim contest.

We say: Go for it. Because when the smoke clears, Hong Kong will probably have a stronger press, and its citizens a better choice than is the case now. In the meantime, the colony and the rest of us will have learned another valuable lesson in how free markets work.

What's going on in Hong Kong now is actually the death throes of a distorted system. It's easy to understand why one of the local press moguls should be whining that competition has suddenly turned "unfriendly." Until recently, a newspaper cartel-in-all-but-name openly agreed on a recommended price of HK$5 per paper. Publisher Jimmy Lai busted a hole in that arrangement when he launched his spectacularly successful Apple Daily last year at an initial price of $2. In December, facing unprecedented pressure from Mr. Lai's now full-priced paper, the Oriental Daily News broke cartel ranks and dropped its price to $2.

At first, the reading public had a wonderful time, devouring two or even three local papers for what it used to cost them to buy just one. Once some blood was on the floor, though, the jitters set in. Some anxiety is being fed by Hong Kong's Newspaper Association, which wants the government or the local legislative council to "monitor" the war, and perhaps enact laws against "predatory pricing."

So far no one important is listening, and let's hope it stays that way. The people clamoring for government intervention say their noble goal is to make sure the quality press is not squashed by more popular, populist giants. More credible is Hong Kong Chinese Press Association leader Hue Peu-ying, who blamed everything on the Apple Daily which "did not play by our price setting rules."

Good, because there's almost no way consumers can fail to benefit from the current shakeout. Take the scare mongers' claim that the price war will rob consumers of choice. Who says they have much choice now? Readers who are getting what they want from their newspaper will not abandon it just because another rag lowers its price by a few cents. If Hong Kongers are comparison shopping for their papers by price, it means there is little else to distinguish between them. The papers that survive will be the ones with content and formats – girlie photos and all – that people like. It's that simple.

People who have lost their jobs have little time for free market mantras. Yet the fact that many had work for this long was pretty remarkable. Only a few years ago, for instance, Hong Kong had some 90 publications. Since then, a number have dropped off their perches almost unnoticed and due to natural causes – like the rising cost of newsprint. Why should anyone mourn the demise now of the Taiwanese owned United News Daily? It didn't make a penny, and if anything its closure represents a victory for political accountability in Taiwan, where the ruling Kuomintang can no longer afford to subsidize an organ with no readers.

Of Hong Kong's remaining 20-odd papers, many grew up entirely on the life support system of ad revenue from the cross-border property boom and other products of the market opening in China. As an executive of one relatively unread daily admitted when his paper closed last month, though, "To get by on advertising alone is not healthy."

With so many newspapers, and sponsors representing every shade of local and foreign Chinese political interests, Hong Kong offers an enormous smorgasbord of opinion. When the current war ends, the menu will almost certainly be smaller. But it should also be changed in ways that reflect the needs – and tastes – of Hong Kong people.

Case 10

The Mass Transit Railway in Hong Kong

Noel Capon
Graduate School of Business, Columbia University

Lai Riana, Lee Sze Lai, Ng Yuek, Kuk, Sam Wai Kin
The Hong Kong University of Science and Technology

Standing close to the platform edge as the train approached Mong Kok station at 8:30 am on a Tuesday morning in January 1994, Sam Wai Kin, having failed to enter the two previous trains, suddenly found himself propelled towards the opening doors by passengers behind him seeking to board. Sam vainly attempted to avoid bumping into exiting passengers and, as the train left the station heading south down the Nathan Road corridor, found himself wedged between other commuters. Just as the train gathered up speed in the tunnel, his cellular telephone started to ring. As he reached for his pocket, Sam felt a sharp kick in his shins from the attractive 25-year-old business suit jammed next to him. Murmuring an apology to the young woman, he hastily disposed of his caller and gritted his teeth in anticipation of the trip to Central, the main business district of Hong Kong.

∞∞∞

The Mass Transit Railway Corporation (MTR), operator of a predominately underground rail system in Hong Kong, was considering ways to solve the morning bottleneck problem. Problem sources were intra-daily demand cyclicality and the special commuting needs of Hong Kong residents. MTR previously tried several measures to alleviate the situation and was engaged in a comprehensive review; it was also attempting to identify other alternatives. Management wondered which measures were likely to improve customer service levels and what marketing actions could be employed for effective implementation.

The Overcrowding Problem

In particular, the MTR faced a severe bottleneck problem from Prince Edward station on Kowloon Peninsula to Admiralty station on Hong Kong Island on weekday mornings between 8:00 am to 9:00 am.[1] Most commuters traveled north to south, hoping to report punctually to work, either in southern Kowloon or across Victoria Harbor in northern Hong Kong Island. The MTR was concerned about overcrowding and wished to institute measures to reduce commuters to the tolerable safety level of 77,500 per hour (1993). Though many passengers really "suffered" in the morning rush hour, they were reluctant to switch to transportation modes that were slower and less reliable. To reach Hong Kong Island from Kowloon, alternative road transportation modes had to pass through one of two crowded cross-harbor tunnels. Currently the tunnel toll was $10 but a government study group was investigating a possible increase to $30 in an attempt to alleviate road congestion.

Hong Kong

Hong Kong, a surviving remnant of Britain's colonial empire, had a 6 million population mostly living in Hong Kong Island, Kowloon and the New Territories; 78% lived in Kowloon and the New Territories. With total land area only 1,076 sq. km., Hong Kong was one of the most densely populated places in the world. It was an important center of trade, finance and business in the Asia-Pacific region and one of mainland China's largest trading partners. Service industries accounted for 60% of GDP and employed 70% of the working population.

MTR Background

History

In response to rapid population growth and economic development, in the early 1970s, the Hong Kong Government decided a comprehensive underground rail network was needed to ease heavy road traffic. The Transport Department wanted to provide fast, comfortable, reliable public transportation to the increasingly affluent, time-conscious Hong Kong commuters. The MTR was established in 1975 primarily to construct and operate a mass transit railway system.

Construction of the Mass Transit Railway System posed enormous challenges for the MTR; the system had very tight construction schedules and was built in varying ground conditions in a densely populated urban environment. Constructed first, the Modified Initial System was fully completed in 1980 serving stations from Kwun Tong to Central, followed by the Tsuen Wan Extension (1982) running from Tsuen Wan to Prince Edward. In 1986, the Island Line started operation from Chai Wan to Sheung Wan. The Eastern Harbor Crossing, extending the Kwun Tong Line across Victoria Harbor to an interchange station at Quarry Bay on the Island Line, commenced service in 1989. The total system, which cost $26 billion to construct, was built on schedule and under budget (Exhibit 1).[2]

---

[1] The Kowloon segment, running down Nathan Road, was termed the Nathan Road Corridor.
[2] All monetary amounts are in Hong Kong dollars. At the time of the case, HK$1 = US$0.1285.

In conjunction with railway construction and operation, the MTR engaged in joint-venture development and management of key residential and commercial properties above its stations and depots. Ownership of commercial properties provided investment opportunities and commercial exploitation of real estate assets and skills. The MTR was also involved in engineering evaluation, financial appraisal and transport planning studies for possible provision of new rail lines to meet Hong Kong's future public transportation requirements.

Finance

MTR management believed financial performance was quite satisfactory. Fare revenue in 1993 was $3,824 million, up 12.8% from 1992. Recurring revenue from sources other than property development made a real contribution. Estate management and rental income rose to $414 million (up 17.9%); and advertising, kiosk rental and other income was $290 million (up 15.1%). Concurrently, operating costs increased to $1,970, up 16.2%.

In 1993, the MTR earned profits before interest and finance charges of $2,558 million, up 16.3%. At $1,251 million, interest and finance charges were 4.5% lower than 1992; net profit was $735 million, up from $403 million. Total MTR borrowings were $18,591 million at year-end 1993; cumulative losses, mainly incurred in start-up, would be recouped by 1996. (See Exhibit 2 for nine-year statistics.)

The MTR System

The 43.2-kilometer route included 38 stations: 28 underground, the others overhead or at ground level. The three lines, Kwun Tong Line (Quarry Bay to Yau Ma Tei), Tsuen Wan Line (Tsuen Wan to Central) and Island Line (Chai Wan to Sheung Wan) ran through the most densely populated residential and commercial areas of Hong Kong Island and Kowloon Peninsula, Tsuen Wan and Kwai Chung.

During 1993, the system carried 779 million passengers, up 3.7% from 1992.[3] The trains were supported by efficient automatic train control and ticketing systems and other station facilities (Table 1). The MTR provided safe, reliable and efficient passenger service. Stations and trains were air-conditioned to provide an acceptable environment in the context of Hong Kong's high temperatures and oppressive humidity, notably in summer.

A majority of passengers (87%)[4] used Common Stored Value Tickets (CSVTs) rather than single journey tickets. CSVTs saved passengers time; they need not seek change and buy a ticket for each journey. CSVTs were sold at a small discount to single journey fares, were valid for nine months and could be used on the MTR, the Kowloon-Canton Railway Corporation (KCR) and specific routes of Kowloon Motor Bus (KMB) and Citybus (Citybus). CSVTs could be purchased at station ticket offices

---

[3] Intra-Hong Kong Island 15%; intra-Kowloon 47%; cross-harbor 39%.
[4] Adult 73%; child/student 10%; senior citizen 4%.

Table 1: MTR System Specifics (1993)

	Tsuen Wan Line (Tsuen Wan to Central)	Kwun Tong Line (Quarry Bay to Yau Ma Tei)	Island Line (Chai Wan to Sheung Wan)
Number of trains			
Morning peak	31	23	23
Evening peak	28	23	22
Frequency			
Morning peak (sec.)	116	144	135
Evening peak (sec.)	135	150	150
Journey times (min)	Tsuen Wan to Central: 28	Kwun Tong to Yau Ma Tei: 20	Sheung Wan to Chai Wan: 23
	Tsuen Wan to Tsim Sha Tsui: 23	Kwun Tong to Central: 21	Sheung Wan to Tsuen Wan: 32
	Tsuen Wan to Kwun Tong: 24	Kwun Tong to Chai Wan: 18	Chai Wan to Tsuen Wan: 46
Entrances	81	58	83
Ticket offices	21	13	23
Entry/exit/reversible gates	368	253	404
Ticket issuing machines			
Single ride	181	117	143
Common stored value	7	4	9
Ticket checkers	29	20	23
Change machines	32	22	29
Escalators	121	90	225
Closed circuit TVs	72	39	97
Kiosks/shops	65	42	98
Mini-banks	14	10	19
Poster panels	5,992	2,530	6,156
Length of train	8 cars (each 22.5 meters × 3.2 meters)		
Car capacity	48 seated and up to 265 standing		
Speed			
Scheduled	33 kph	Maximum	80 kph

and at Hang Seng Bank branches located in all stations. Passengers could buy single journey tickets from Ticket Issuing Machines (with money changers), use money change machines and check remaining ticket values at Ticket Checking Machines. All machines were easily accessible at station concourses and were user-friendly.

All tickets (CSVT and single journey) were used at automatic turnstiles twice per journey, for entry and exit.[5] When passengers exited, the automatic LED turnstile display showed the amount remaining on the CSVT. If a single journey ticket was

---

[5] Both CSVTs and single journey tickets were made of plastic, were reusable and were the size of a credit card.

used, or the beginning CSVT value was less than or equal to the journey fare, the turnstile retained the ticket. As a result, CSVT users received a last journey bonus. In 1993, adult stored value fares ranged from $3.10 to $8.90, depending on journey length; average fare revenue per passenger was $4.91.

MTR concourses contained kiosks offering many services: banking, cake shops, convenience stores, dry-cleaning, florists, laundry, news-stands and travel agents. In addition, facilities such as "Payphones," "Photo Booths," "Payment Express Terminals" for paying utility bills and a free classified job openings publication, "Recruit," were available. Cordless and mobile telephones could be used in concourses and on many stretches of track.

Personnel

Day-to-day MTR operations were overseen by chairman, Hamish Mathers, and seven executive directors (Finance, Legal and Contracts, Operations, Human Resource and Administration, Property, Marketing and Planning, Projects); they reported to a Board comprising local business personalities and government representatives. Total MTR staff was 5,500 in 1993. The MTR adopted three core values: "Customer Service," "Respect for the Individual," and "On Time and Within Budget" as guiding principles of behavior to maintain service levels and motivate staff.

Market Performance

The MTR's advertising message, "Hong Kong cannot do without the MTR," was not simply propaganda; it was a reflection of life in the crowded colony. Since its inaugural trip on October 1, 1979, the MTR successfully won over the people of Hong Kong. From 1983 to 1992, the MTR's average annual passenger growth was 6.9% p.a. (See Table 2 for System Information.) Prior to opening the Eastern Harbor Crossing on August 5, 1989, the average daily passenger load was 1.9 million; in 1993, daily patronage increased to 2.3 million. Market share of the total Hong Kong transport market was 27.8%.[6]

MTR fare revenue grew in parallel with increase patronage; fares increased with inflation. During 15 years' service, MTR's overall average fare increased by 7.8% p.a., slightly less than the Consumer Price Index (CPI) (A),[7] 8.6% p.a., and significantly below worker payroll increase, 14% p.a.

The MTR system was the most technologically advanced of all transportation modes. Not only were its cars comfortable (apart from rush hour) and suitable for all-weathers, the MTR provided speedy, yet, safe service. To demonstrate MTR's

---

[6] Buses in total had 45% market share; ferries in total <3%; other rail modes 16%; minibuses 9%; taxis not included.

[7] The CPI (A) was based on a bundle of goods (e.g., food, housing, fuel, alcohol, tobacco, miscellaneous durables, clothes and shoes) purchased by the lowest 50% income population.

Table 2: MTR System Information

Railway operation data	1993	1992
Total route length	43.2 km	43.2 km
Number of rail cars	671	671
Number of station kiosks and mini-banks at stations	242	232
Number of poster advertising panels at stations	12,552	11,715
Daily hours of operation	19	19
Minimum train headways in seconds		
Tsuen Wan Line	116	120
Kwun Tong Line	144	135
Island Line	135	135
Average weekday ridership in December	2.4M	2.3M
Highest daily ridership in year (Christmas Eve)	2.9M	2.8M

Avg. weekday peak hour passengers carried at critical section for the summer months

	1993	1992
Morning peak		
Nathan Road Corridor towards Central	77,400	72,900
Causeway Bay Section towards Central	53,500	51,600
Skek Kip Mei Section towards Yau Ma Tei	54,500	51,700
Evening peak		
Nathan Road Corridor towards Tsuen Wan	60,400	56,500
Causeway Bay Section towards Chai Wan	39,200	36,800
Skek Kip Mei Section towards Quarry Bay	39,200	37,600

Highest peak hour passenger flow at key stations on a particular day

	1993		1992	
	Incoming	Outgoing	Incoming	Outgoing
Central	31,100	34,600	34,800	33,300
Tsim Sha Tsui	20,000	23,700	17,700	23,400
Mong Kok	12,900	21,200	12,100	20,500
Kowloon Tong	20,600	20,000	21,000	18,500
Kwun Tong	11,400	12,700	11,800	14,000

continuing commitment to customer service, openness and accountability to the traveling public, three Customer Service Reports were published.[8] Moreover, the MTR's core product benefits (i.e., speed, reliability) were demonstrated in thematic advertising campaigns including TV commercials, scenic tracked posters and poems on trains. To improve service, the MTR sought and received many suggestions and

---

[8] Publication of customer service reports was a recent innovation in Hong Kong following Governor-General Chris Patten's urging of many public service organizations to take this step to become more customer focused. Among the organizations involved were: Kowloon-Canton Railway (KCR), Hong Kong Telecom, The Hong Kong and China Gas Company Ltd. (Towngas) and the Hong Kong Housing Authority.

complaints from passengers through many channels (e.g., Coffee Evenings [Figure 1], Telephone Hotline, Suggestion Boxes in stations and reply coupons in advertisements): in 1993, 930 complaints and 2,180 suggestions were received. The MTR took actions against specific problems like crowding and fares (Table 3).

Figure 1: Advertisement for "Coffee Evenings" in Newspapers and MTR Stations

AT OUR MTR COFFEETIME THE CHOICE IS ALWAYS YOURS. Welcome to the MTR Coffeetime, where you can chat face to face with our management and tell us what you think about any aspect of the MTR service over a cup of tea or coffee. To make things even easier for you, we've extended the Coffeetime from evenings to lunchtimes as well. Drop by for a drink and a chat, we're always delighted to see you.

The Public Transport System in Hong Kong

Hong Kong had a diverse multi-modal public transport system. Apart from the MTR, it had two electrified railways, several franchised bus systems and ferries, two tramways, public light buses and taxis. Each provided complementary as well as competing services to people in Hong Kong.

Kowloon-Canton Railway

The Kowloon-Canton Railway Corporation (KCR) ran a 34-kilometer electrified railway system providing fast public transport to people in new towns in the eastern New Territories. (Beyond Hong Kong, the line extended to Guangzhou [Canton] in mainland China.) Within Hong Kong, 13 stations spanned the route from Kowloon station to border town, Lo Wu. The KCR had an extended line to the racecourse near Sha Tin. KCR fares comprised two types: local Hong Kong travel from Kowloon Station to Sheung Shui ($3 to $7.50); and from all stations to Lo Wu for cross-border travel ($16.50 to $27). As increasing numbers of people moved to the New Territories, demand for rail service increased. In 1993, KCR's market share was 5.7% (Exhibit 3); it was expected to rise.

Table 3: Complaints and Suggestions Collected by the MTR

Concerns	Actions being taken
Level of crowding	• Improved with system-wide platform queuing scheme • More uniformly loaded trains with Automatic Train Regulation system • Train capacity down Nathan Road section to increase to 85,000 by 1996
Air-conditioning/ ventilation	• Station temperatures improved by 2°C • Tsuen Wan station concourse air-conditioned with 4°C improvement
Fares	• Rationale for fare changes to be explained • Peak surcharges eliminated on a trial basis • Senior citizen fares introduced
Passenger behavior	• To be reinforced through annual Courtesy Campaigns
Ticket malfunction	• Magnet-proof wallets offered • Introduction of more reliable stored value tickets on October 1, 1993
Public announcements	• Digital pre-recorded public train announcements to be introduced
Train service	• Improved train headway on Tsuen Wan Line during morning peak • 11 new trains being purchased • Commitment to performing even better on train reliability
Station facilities	• Feasibility on toilets being re-examined • Ticket checkers and note change machines installed • Platform screen doors for Airport Railway stations. Feasibility study of retrofitting on existing system
Staff	• Close monitoring on manpower allocation at stations • Skills training for front-line staff
Slippery seats	• Fire services requirement and easy to maintain
No scenery	• Common phenomenon on any underground system • In-train poems to create a more relaxing atmosphere
More payphones	• Additional payphones on concourses and some platforms
Seats on platforms	• A trial at Kwai Fong station later this year
Station mail boxes	• To pursue with post office
Music on trains	• Thought to be against the interest of majority of customers
Radio reception in trains	• Further surveys to be undertaken
More escalators	• Demand being closely monitored
Insufficient signage	• Specific cases to be studied
Walks too long at Quarry Bay	• More explanation to be given on design constraints

Light Rail Transit

The Light Rail Transit (LRT) was operated by the KCR to provide fast and comfortable rail transport to residents living in new towns in the northwestern New Territories. It formed the backbone of public transport in Tuen Mun and Yuen Long; total length, 30.4 kilometers LRT fares ranged from $3 to $4.30; market share approximated 2.9%. As with the KCR, demand was expected to rise in the next decade.

Franchised Bus Services

Despite increasing rail links, franchised buses remained a major passenger carrier. They offered scheduled service relatively cheaply and were the main modes of public transport in areas not served by rail. Franchised bus companies were: Kowloon Motor Bus (1933) (KMB), China Motor Bus (CMB), New Lantao Bus (1973) (NLB), and Citybus. To a large extent, each served different geographies.

Kowloon Motor Bus. KMB (344 routes) was the largest operator of franchised bus service in Hong Kong. It mainly served the Kowloon Peninsula and New Territories. In addition to intra-Kowloon and New Territories service (297 routes), KMB provided cross-harbor bus service (47 routes) from Kowloon/New Territories to Hong Kong Island. In recent years, KMB upgraded service; it introduced air-conditioned buses at premium fares on some routes. KMB fares ranged from $0.70 to $14.50 for intra-territories routes; $5.30 to $25.50 for cross-harbor routes. Although KMB fares were cheaper than the MTR, market share, currently 26.2%, was decreasing.

China Motor Bus. CMB, the second largest franchised bus system, operated 91 routes on Hong Kong Island; it also offered cross-harbor bus service (38 routes) to Kowloon. In recent years, as CMB service declined relative to other bus companies, some franchise routes were reassigned to Citybus (see below). To compensate for these losses, CMB opened routes in newly-developed residential areas; it also introduced air-conditioned buses on selected routes. CMB fares ranged from $1.80 to $9 for intra-island routes; $5.30 to $25.50 for cross-harbor routes. In recent years CMB experienced declining market share; 1993, 6.4%.

New Lantao Bus. NLB provided service on sparsely populated Lantau Island. Eight routes connected different areas to the ferry pier at Mui Wo. (Ferries ran from Central [Hong Kong Island] to Mui Wo.) Fares ranged from $2.40 to $19. Most passengers were weekend tourists. Because of its geographic constraint, NLB's market share was less than 1%.

Citybus. Citybus was launched to provide premium commuter bus travel (including breakfast and newspapers) for long-haul routes at bargain prices (e.g., Sha Tin to Central, $15 including newspaper.) More recently, the government gave Citybus limited franchised routes on Hong Kong Island, directly competitive with CMB. Citybus had 29 franchised routes including two cross-harbor routes. Compared to KMB and CMB, Citybus was perceived as a pioneer in providing high level passenger service, including air-conditioned buses and express routes. Citybus fares ranged from $1.80 to $6.40 for Hong Kong Island routes, $3.50 to $12 for cross-harbor services. Although Citybus' market share was small, observers expected it would be awarded new routes as KMB and CMB services were at lower levels; consequently, market share would increase.

Ferries

Ferries both provided an essential link to the outlying islands and supplemented cross-harbor rail and bus service. Ferry services were mainly provided by the Star Ferry (SF) and Hong Kong and Yaumati Ferry (HYF) companies.

Star Ferry. Star Ferry operated three cross-harbor routes between Hong Kong Island and Kowloon: Tsim Sha Tsui to Central, Tsim Sha Tsui to Wan Chai, Hunghom to Central. In addition to commuter use, frequent and relatively comfortable service across Victoria Harbor made Star Ferry popular with tourists. Star Ferry fares, $1.20 to $1.80, were much cheaper than most competitors. Market share, about 1%, decreased steadily since the mid-1980s.

Hong Kong and Yaumati Ferry. HYF provided both cross-harbor ferry service and service to the outlying islands (e.g., Lantau, Lamma, Cheung Chau). HYF also operated special licensed ferry routes between Central and New Territories new towns (e.g., Tuen Mun, Tsuen Wan [four hoverferry routes]), as well as cross-harbor service for vehicles. Fares ranged from $3.30 to $4.80 for cross-harbor passenger service; ($4 to $120 [depending on size] for cross-harbor vehicles); $5 to $20 from Central to the new towns; $4.5 to $23 for trips to outlying islands. Market share was about 1.1%. In the previous decade, HYF lost significant business to tunnel bus and MTR services, notably on completion of the initial MTR stage and the Eastern Harbor Crossing. Tactics to attract passengers included higher ferry frequency and improved bus service to ferry piers.

Public Light Buses/Minibuses

Public Light Buses were licensed to carry a maximum of 16 seated passengers. These minibuses supplemented other public transportation modes and were substitutes for private cars and taxis. They tended to serve areas without higher capacity transport modes or where road terrain posed limitations. Two types of minibus operated in Hong Kong: green and red. Green minibuses provided scheduled service at a fixed official fare; red minibuses provided non-scheduled service at variable and higher fares, but were more flexible; pick-up and drop-off was by request.

Trams

Trams, operated by Hong Kong Tramways, provided slow but inexpensive service, east to west, on northern Hong Kong Island. The fixed fare for the 13-kilometer system was $1.20; market share, 3.4%. A tramway also ran to "The Peak", an upscale residential area and tourist attraction on Hong Kong Island overlooking Victoria Harbor.

Taxis

Three types of taxi provided door-to-door service 24 hours per day: red taxis served all Hong Kong except outlying islands; green taxis were only in the New Territories;

blue taxis only on Lantau Island. Taxi fares were a fixed fare flag drop, $13 for two kilometers, $1 per 200 meters subsequently. Market share was 12.6% and increasing.

Inter-modal Coordination

Although the various public transport modes competed with each other, an inter-modal coordination policy was designed to provide more efficient transportation in Hong Kong. For example, an interchange station at Kowloon Tong allowed MTR and KCR passengers to shift from one mode to the other. Franchised buses and minibuses cooperated with MTR and KCR by providing feeder bus services; bus routes terminated at ferry piers.

Environmental Changes

Road Congestion

Road congestion, caused by land scarcity and hilly terrain leading to narrow and insufficient numbers of roads, and rapid economic development (low unemployment) leading to soaring numbers of private cars and goods vehicles, was a serious Hong Kong problem. Between the mid-1980s and mid-1990s, vehicles more than doubled. (From 1991 and 1992, the number of licensed cars increased by 7.16%.) Completion of the Eastern Harbor Crossing, Tate's Cairn Tunnel and other highways relieved some pressure on highly congested areas such as the Cross Harbor Tunnel.[9] However, government policy of unlimited increase in road users was expected to exacerbate congestion. It was predicted that peak hour driving speed would slow from 25.5 kilometers per hour (kph) in 1991 to 15 kph in 2001.

Changes in Land Use

In recent years, Hong Kong property prices rose enormously; residential areas on Hong Kong Island and Kowloon were cost prohibitive for many people. This economic pressure, combined with increasing population, led to new towns being established in the eastern and northwestern New Territories (e.g., Sha Tin, Sheung Shui, Yuen Long, Tuen Mun) where large populations were concentrated. Furthermore, Hong Kong's commercial area was expanding eastwards beyond Central to Causeway Bay and even Quarry Bay. Completing the reclamation project and opening the new airport at Chek Lap Kok on Lantau Island were expected to make large tracts of land in eastern and western Kowloon, in and around the current Kai Tak airport (to be closed), available for development. On the airport site a mixture of residential, hotel, commercial and parkland use was envisaged and new MTR stations planned.

---

[9] Discussions were proceeding in the Hong Kong government as to the advisability of raising the one-way toll from HK$10 to HK$30.

Economic Performance

Hong Kong's economy was expanding rapidly; 1992 per capita GDP was $111,630. Average income increased significantly as an increasing proportion of residents were engaged in professional, technical, administrative or managerial jobs. These people were willing to pay for higher quality transportation.

Government Policy

Government intervention was an important factor shaping traffic flow. Its inter-modal coordination policy gave priority to off-street modes and economic road users, and minimized wasteful competition. Future application would be based on demand changes, traveling public convenience, capacity of competing modes, availability of suitable curbside and terminus facilities, road congestion, and financial viability of proposed new routes.

The government took several actions. It increased the Cross Harbor tunnel toll (1984); for a short period the number of private cars and taxis was reduced, but traffic soon returned to its original level. Electronic mileage billing designed for private car users was tested but abolished because of public discontent. The Government raised registration taxes and license fees for private cars and imposed high taxes on gasoline. Regardless, the number of private cars rose; car park capacity was insufficient in commercial areas due to competition for land use.

Overcrowding on the MTR

As increasing numbers of commuters shifted to the MTR, overcrowding problems became evident, especially during rush hour. MTR average weekday ridership was 2.4 million, making it the busiest underground rail systems (per route kilometer) of the six most densely populated cities in the world (i.e., London, Sao Paulo, Seoul, Singapore, Tokyo). In Hong Kong, most people started work at 9:00 am; severe overcrowding occurred from 8:00 am to 9:00 am. The most difficult problems were at interchange and other stations located on the "Nathan Road Corridor." Problems were most severe at Kowloon Tong, Prince Edward, Mong Kok, Yau Ma Tei, Jordan, Tsim Sha Tsui, Admiralty, Central and Quarry Bay. Other heavily congested stations were Wan Chai and Causeway Bay.

From customer feedback, MTR management determined that rush hour congestion was a major issue where passengers wanted improvement. Some effects created by overcrowding were:

Uncomfortable traveling environment. Overcrowding led to deterioration of service since too many people were pushed into train cars. Passengers were confined in a small standing space in uncomfortable conditions. Such high passenger density also created a stuffy environment; ventilation was a problem.

Schedule delays. During rush hour, many passengers tried to board the first arriving train; they rudely squeezed into cars and often stopped doors from closing. Since trains spent longer periods at stations, total traveling time was lengthened. In addition, an extra burden was placed on the control system.

Safety. As some passengers pushed through train doors at the expense of fellow passengers, safety could be compromised. Such accidents as stepping on others or falling on the live rail might occur.

Measures Taken by the MTR to Alleviate Congestion

Among measures taken and / or considered by the MTR to alleviate congestion were:

Peak-hour surcharge. The MTR imposed a surcharge policy in May 1988 to spread the load from peak hours to reduce congestion and enhance safety. A 50-cent surcharge was in effect, Monday to Saturday,[10] from 8:00 am to 9:00 am for travelers alighting at Jordan and Tsim Sha Tsui; and for those alighting at stations from Sheung Wan to Causeway Bay who boarded at stations west of Kowloon Bay and north of Jordan. Between 5,000 and 6,000 passengers were expected to change travel schedules or switch to other transport modes. When first introduced, most passengers at Mong Kok station could board the first Central-bound train.

Public discontent was aroused. Some pressure groups stated that fare increases in rush hours would not relieve Nathan Road Corridor overloading in long run. According to MTR statistics, although passenger traffic fell in the first month, it quickly returned to previous levels. Many passengers resented paying extra fees when no alternatives for punctual economical transport were available. In response, Hamish Mathers said if only 3% of travelers stopped using the MTR, passenger loads would reduce to a tolerable level, under 77,500 per hour.

Early bird pass. In conjunction with the surcharge policy, the MTR introduced a 20% discount for commuters using the MTR before 7:45 am. The "Early Bird Pass" was a flat-fee monthly ticket for commuters traveling during specified times within set fare zones. Tickets could be used an unlimited number of times monthly and commuters could reduce fare expenditures by 30% to 45% of the new peak fares. Over 24,000 Early Bird Passes were sold in the first four days, but a passenger surge to board MTR trains before the 7:45 am deadline was not observed.

Eastern Harbor Crossing. In August 1989, a second tunnel crossing Victoria Harbor opened. The new Lam Tin station, between Kwun Tong and Quarry Bay, was designed to accommodate 250,000 passengers daily, rising to 300,000 in five years. However, after a few months, only 23% of 780,000 MTR passengers crossing the harbor used this new link. The immediate impact was a slight relaxation of traffic (about 7,000 passengers per hour) on the Nathan Road Corridor at its busiest time. An incentive program was launched to attract more passengers to use the Eastern

---

[10] Many Hong Kong residents worked a five-and-a-half or six-day week.

Harbor Crossing (EHC) during rush hour. Adult passenger fares from the first morning train to 9:30 am were 80 cents less than normal fares; further, the 8:00 am to 9:00 am surcharge was waived for EHC commuters.

Staggered working hours. In 1990, the MTR encouraged firms in Central, Tsim Sha Tsui and Wan Chai to introduce staggered working hours. Since many passengers traveling the Nathan Road Corridor worked in these areas, the MTR believed its policy would assist keeping peak-hour passenger traffic on the corridor under the 77,500 safety limit. The relief effort combined additional bus routes, a staggered working hours campaign and pricing policy. It was expected that 3,000 to 4,000 passengers would no longer travel the MTR in peak periods.

Four major transport operators, MTR, KCR, KMB, HYF, spent HK$3 million on a promotional campaign advocating staggered working hours (Figure 2) mainly to firms with over 100 employees. The campaign included television and newspaper advertisements, direct mail and seminars. Rob Noble, MTR's marketing and planning director, said:

> The campaign was to increase public awareness of the benefits of staggered working hours and to encourage wider adoption by the business community.... For employers, adoption can bring benefits of better recruitment and retention of staff, extension of business hours, raising morale and loyalty of staff and improving punctuality.... All these would contribute to increased company productivity.

Three options were proposed by transport operators:

- Adopt staggered working hours between 8:30 am and 4:30 pm instead of 9:00 am to 5:00 pm.
- Allow staff to choose from alternative but fixed working hours.
- Allow employees to decide on individual arrival and departure times day by day so long as they started work between 8:00 am and 10:00 am, and left between 4:00 pm and 6:00 pm.

Hamish Mathers said the MTR worked hard to encourage staggered working hours. The campaign was supported by a member of the Transport Advisory Committee who believed it would reduce the MTR's operating costs and stabilize ticket fares. Rob Noble said that the initial stage of the campaign was successful: 90% of those surveyed were aware of the campaign. However, only 10% of Hong Kong firms joined, compared to 30% or 40% in overseas cities. Of 1,000 target companies surveyed, 36 had staggered hours, 14 were new participants.

Waiving concessionary fares during rush hour. Children, students and senior citizens' concessionary fares were waived for 8:00 am to 9:00 am journeys, Monday to Friday. Students accounted for 12% of daily traffic.

Platform assistant and platform queuing. In April 1989, the MTR hired 120 part-

Figure 2: Advertisement for "Staggered Working Hours"

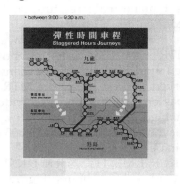

time platform assistants to streamline traffic at interchanging stations Prince Edward, Mong Kok and Yau Ma Tei during peak morning hours. Commuters were persuaded not to board crowded cars so the trains could depart quickly and on-time.

In January 1991, two all-day crowd control pilot schemes were introduced at interchange stations to train passengers in appropriate train boarding behavior, in addition to the 120 morning peak hour platform assistants. At the Kowloon Tong MTR/KCR interchange station, passengers waiting to board were asked to avoid standing in yellow box areas painted on the platform: these were for alighting passengers. At Prince Edward, passengers were asked to wait inside yellow queuing lines and board trains only after all departing passengers had alighted.

The Prince Edward scheme was judged successful; by April 1991 additional platform assistants were hired to introduce similar systems for all stations from Mong Kok to Admiralty. To increase passenger awareness and persuade them to follow instructions, a promotional campaign including posters in MTR stations, pamphlets, broadcasts in concourse and platform areas and specifically designed slogans was used. (See Exhibit 4 for Tokyo's solution.)

Modifying the signaling system. Each eight-car train had a capacity of 2,500; station departure could occur at two-minute intervals. Upgrading the signaling system could increase train frequency from 30 to 32 trains per hour.

Construction of Western Harbor Crossing. Many passengers traveled from Tuen Mun, Tsuen Wan and western Kowloon to work on northern Hong Kong Island. Some considered a new tunnel between western Kowloon and Central, currently being planned, to be a solution to overcrowding in the Nathan Road Corridor.

Actions Taken by Other Transportation Modes

Kowloon-Canton Railway Corporation. The KCR offered discount fares for passengers traveling before 7:45 am, Monday to Friday; savings of 70 cents to $1.60 were possible depending on distance traveled. In January 1991, the KCR introduced a free feeder bus service from Kowloon station to Tsim Sha Tsui. Departure frequency was eight times per hour from 7:00 am to 10:00 am, six times per hour from 4:00 pm to 10:00 pm, Mondays to Saturdays. In 1991, a free route was introduced from Mong Kok station to Tsim Sha Tsui;[11] it operated daily every 20 minutes from 7:00 am to 8:00 pm. The buses were air-conditioned; they accommodated 136 passengers.

Hong Kong and Yaumati ferry. Passenger and vehicular traffic across the harbor decreased year by year. To combat competition, ferry frequency was increased and bus service to ferry piers improved. The MTR's surcharge policy (1988) caused HYF traffic to increase by 750 persons daily (25% increase), mainly on the Jordan to Central ferry, 7:00 am to 10:00 am. Traffic increased by 18% on major Central-bound ferry routes from two other West Kowloon piers. HYF also improved hoverferry service to Central from Tuen Mun and Tsuen Wan.

Kowloon Motor Bus and China Motor Bus. According to KMB, the MTR surcharge led 500 extra passengers to wait for buses at the Cross Harbor Tunnel entrance during morning rush hour. Both KMB and CMB deployed extra buses and introduced new cross harbor bus routes from Kwun Tong to Central. In April 1991, the Transport Department asked the two firms to offer 50-cent discounts to passengers traveling on four cross harbor routes from 8:00 am to 9:00 am. This discount increased the price differential between MTR and cross harbor bus travel to $3.20.

In June 1991, the Transport Department made agreements with the KMB and CMB for new air-conditioned bus routes: Prince Edward station to Central via Mong Kok station; KCR Kowloon station to Central. These express routes had only two to three pick-up points on Kowloon, yet stopped at major commercial buildings from Causeway Bay to Central. To ease traffic for franchised tunnel buses in peak periods, special traffic lights, dedicated bus lanes and special toll lanes for tunnel buses were introduced. The new bus line fares (cheaper than MTR) were $5.50 in peak hours, $6 off peak. Capacity on the two routes was over 5,000 passengers per hour. According to KMB statistics, the two air-conditioned bus lines attracted 2,400 original MTR commuters, reducing MTR peak time travelers to 73,000. Introduced later were seven additional routes terminating in Central and Sheung Wan, mainly serving areas in western and central Kowloon and satellite towns Sha Tin and Tai Po.

Decisions

MTR executives had to determine which current measures the MTR should maintain; and which, if any, new measures should be introduced. Furthermore, an action plan was needed to alleviate the congestion problem.

---

[11] The MTR Mong Kok station was located about half a mile from the Mong Kok KCR station.

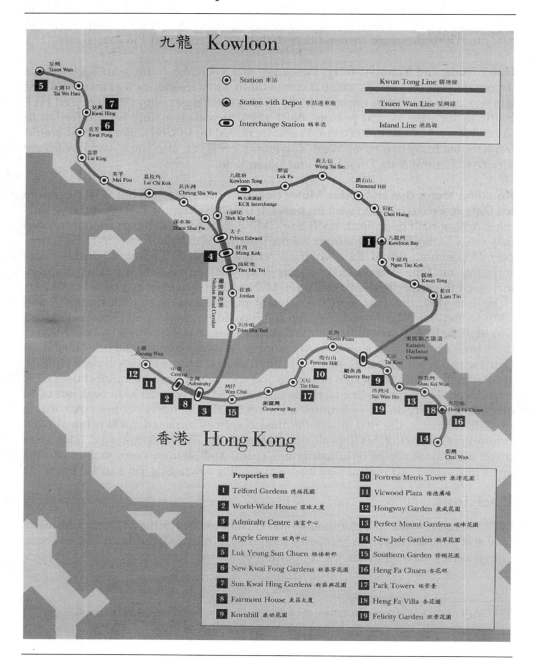

Exhibit 2: MTR Nine-year Statistics

Financial	1992	1991	1990	1989	1988	1987	1986	1985	1984
Profit and Loss Account (HK$ million)									
Total revenue	3,994	3,553	3,164	2,734	2,307	2,062	1,750	1,440	1,168
Operating profit	2,299	2,080	1,846	1,637	1,362	1,179	983	789	647
Interest and finance charges	1,310	1,454	1,578	1,572	1,359	1,449	1,424	1,199	806
Property development profit	4	2	204	579	722	720	482	33	133
Profit/(loss)	403	67	(108)	56	200	(78)	(470)	(794)	(355)
Balance Sheet (HK$ million)									
Assets	25,917	25,175	25,251	25,600	24,480	22,915	23,687	23,906	22,870
Net current liabilities	2,754	2,782	5,131	2,938	3,885	4,827	5,514	5,676	5,073
Long-term liabilities	15,231	15,504	13,576	16,198	14,280	14,686	14,797	14,437	14,954
Shareholders' funds	7,932	6,889	6,544	6,464	6,315	3,402	3,376	3,793	2,843
Financial Ratios									
Operating profit as a percent of revenue	57.6	58.6	58.4	59.9	59.0	57.2	56.2	54.8	55.4
Profit before interest and finance charges (% of revenue)	42.8	42.8	40.0	38.4	36.3	31.6	27.0	25.8	27.2
Debt/equity ratio	2.3:1	2.7:1	2.8:1	2.9:1	2.8:1	5.3:1	5.7:1	4.9:1	6.4:1
Debt/equity ratio (excluding revaluation reserve)	3.4:1	3.7:1	3.8:1	3.9:1	3.7:1	5.3:1	5.7:1	4.9:1	6.4:1
Employees									
Corporation management and service departments	938	819	778	730	713	678	703	713	743
Operations	4,033	3,852	3,655	3,543	3,498	3,444	3,484	3,395	2,947
Engineering and project	296	111	102	90	84	86	211	502	1,084
Estate management and property development	335	321	327	330	338	317	256	232	247
Total	5,602	5,103	4,862	4,693	4,633	4,525	4,654	4,842	5,021

Exhibit 2 (cont'd)

Railway operation	1992	1991	1990	1989	1988	1987	1986	1985	1984
Revenue car km operated ('000s)	76,566	76,357	75,371	69,817	65,870	65,027	60,105	53,102	43,262
Total number of passengers ('000s)	751,005	725,966	719,117	687,606	629,875	592,912	532,073	462,894	410,556
Average number of weekday passengers, December figures ('000s)	2,258	2,156	2,134	2,083	1,916	1,790	1,606	1,431	1,152
Average passenger km traveled	7.5	4.6	7.6	7.6	7.6	7.7	7.8	7.5	7.1
Average car occupancy	73	72	73	75	73	70	69	66	68
Proportion of franchised public transport boardings									
– All movements (%)	27.1	26.6	26.5	25.5	23.5	22.9	21.3	19.2	17.7
– Cross harbor movements (%)	63.4	61.3	59.2	54.9	52.1	51.6	48.8	41.8	35.5
HK$ per car km operated									
– Fare revenue	44.28	39.82	36.26	34.11	31.37	28.60	26.32	24.48	24.59
– Railway operating costs	21.49	18.70	16.98	15.25	14.03	13.30	12.48	11.96	11.81
– Railway operating profit	26.09	23.96	21.54	20.82	18.92	16.67	15.07	13.65	13.78
HK$ per passenger carried									
– Fare revenue	4.51	4.19	3.80	3.46	3.28	3.14	2.97	2.81	2.60
– Railway operating costs	2.19	1.97	1.78	1.55	1.47	1.46	1.41	1.37	1.24
– Railway operating profit	2.66	2.52	2.26	2.11	1.98	1.83	1.70	1.57	1.45
Safety performance									
Number of incidents	725	808	901	922	875	722	634	575	488
Incidents per million passengers carried	0.97	1.11	1.25	1.34	1.39	1.22	1.19	1.24	1.19

Exhibit 3: Public Transport Passenger Journeys by Operator Group, 1983–93

Year/Month	Kowloon Motor Bus	China Motor Bus	City-bus	Mass Transit Railway	Heavy Rail	KCRC # Light Rail	Bus	Hongkong Tramways	Green Mini-bus @	Hong Kong & Yaumati Ferry	Star Ferry	Fixed Route Sub-total	PLB #	Taxi @	TOTAL
1983	981,823	348,084	—	441,955	48,110	—	—	131,093	104,082	100,132	37,406	2,176,405	416,114	401,179	2,993,698
1984	1,069,322	362,633	—	410,556	79,973	—	—	122,502	138,349	90,511	41,593	2,329,856	363,566	404,210	3,097,632
1985	1,079,045	344,031	—	462,894	103,270	—	—	120,831	170,418	83,727	43,285	2,424,023	369,742	422,091	3,215,856
1986	1,108,286	318,397	—	532,074	115,866	—	—	120,245	189,511	76,474	40,808	2,521,017	362,906	437,119	3,321,042
1987	1,088,363	318,396	—	592,912	136,352	—	1,403	128,677	212,802	74,966	39,911	2,611,858	356,616	441,923	3,410,396
1988	1,081,832	317,607	—	629,857	154,615	16,112	10,143	131,917	228,408	75,691	41,707	2,707,844	351,259	445,056	3,504,159
1989	973,886	298,813	—	687,598	173,094	62,596	27,081	127,562	241,978	70,531	39,808	2,727,080	394,584	445,198	3,566,862
1990	965,858	280,884	—	719,111	181,077	73,149	27,972	127,643	249,003	55,202	37,907	2,748,503	387,232	451,670	3,587,404
1991	968,082	267,145	182	725,966	190,668	82,061	33,984	123,247	250,634	50,960	36,602	2,767,807	378,746	455,825	3,602,377
1992	970,653	262,430	957	751,005	199,905	92,273	33,933	124,087	259,888	44,368	35,884	2,816,606 *	371,905	463,595	3,652,106
1993	965,849	235,665	22,203	778,519	208,863	106,555	32,005	125,211	254,398 *	41,107	35,723	2,853,121 *	367,311	464,950	3,685,383
1993 Jan	79,941	21,554	83	62,350	16,981	8,484	2,718	10,292	21,246*	3,278	2,820	233,361*	31,465	39,463	304,289
Feb	76,598	21,175	77	58,377	15,802	8,017	2,641	9,712	20,304*	3,097	2,765	222,003*	28,420	35,656	286,079
Mar	83,853	23,363	75	64,667	17,678	8,825	2,903	10,792	21,691*	3,391	3,059	244,037*	31,432	39,435	314,905
Apr	78,947	20,772	64	59,668	16,930	8,549	2,536	10,284	20,488*	3,544	2,940	228,449*	30,265	38,126	296,839
May	82,517	21,578	73	63,258	17,032	9,286	2,733	10,782	22,146*	3,425	3,041	239,658*	31,114	39,407	310,179
June	75,327	19,330	73	61,810	16,106	8,805	2,462	9,793	20,185*	3,161	2,686	223,443*	29,909	38,152	291,503
July	80,349	20,467	78	69,994	17,993	8,619	2,812	10,654	20,499*	3,750	3,115	242,539*	30,884	39,417	312,840
Aug	78,464	19,392	74	67,739	17,954	8,081	2,582	10,439	21,541*	3,806	3,011	237,380*	30,977	39,453	307,811
Sept	77,010	15,707	5,208	65,370	16,921	9,163	2,613	9,894	20,674*	3,135	2,656	232,269*	30,121	38,264	300,655
Oct	84,055	17,405	5,508	67,388	18,473	9,535	2,607	11,064	21,479*	3,670	3,235	248,693*	31,229	39,588	319,511
Nov	82,583	17,304	5,328	66,793	17,938	9,592	2,724	10,524	21,931*	3,313	3,027	245,057*	30,270	38,337	313,664
Dec	86,205	17,618	5,563	71,105	19,055	9,601	2,674	10,981	22,205*	3,537	3,367	256,231*	31,224	39,653	327,108
1993 Total	965,849	235,665	22,203	778,519	208,863	106,555	32,005	125,211	254,389*	41,107	35,723	2,853,121 *	367,311	464,950	3,685,383
Average per day in 1993	2,646	646	61	2,133	572	292	88	343	697*	113	98	7,817*	1,006	1,274	10,097

†New Lantao Bus, Peak Tramways, Residential Coach Services and Minor Ferry Services omitted but included in Totals. #Estimated figure is based on the average daily extracted from TTSD survey report multiplied by the number of licensed PLBs (other than GMBs) and number of days in the month. @Estimated figure is based on the Taxi Surveys, having regard to the number of taxis licensed. *Provisional figure.

Map of India

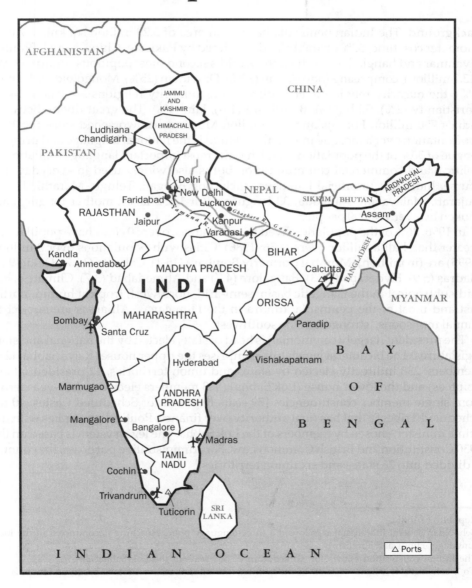

India Overview[1]

Background. The Indian peninsula has a land area of 3.29 million sq. km., a 7,000-kilometer coastline; 52% of arable land. Bordered by Pakistan, China, Nepal, Bhutan, Myanmar and Bangladesh, India is the world's second most populous country (1996: 913.2 million), comprising Indo-Aryan (72%), Dravidian (25%), Mongoloid and others (3%); the majority religion is Hinduism (80%); minority religions are Islam (14%), Christianity (2%), Sikh (2%), Buddhism (1%), Jain (1%). The great divide between India's 750 million Hindus and 120 million Muslims has worsened since the 1992 confrontation over a mosque in Ayodhya. Hindi is the national language and primary tongue of 30% of the population; English is the most important language for national, political and commercial communication but is also widely used in everyday discourse. India has 15 official languages including Bengali, Telugu, Marathi, Tamil, Gujarati, Malayalam, Kannada; 33 languages (of 1,652 listed mother tongues) are spoken by over 100,000 people.[2]

In 1996, 26% of the population lived in urban areas; over 50 cities have populations greater than half a million (versus 36: 1986). Cities with populations over 3 million (1995) are (in million): Mumbai (formerly Bombay) (15.1), Calcutta (11.7), Delhi (9.9), Madras (5.9), Hyderabad (5.3), Bangalore (4.7) and Ahmedabad (3.7). Climate is humid-subtropical in the Gangetic basin; semi-arid, northwest; tropical humid, northeast and most of the peninsula; tundra in the Himalayas. All areas are subject to annual monsoons, strongest in the southwest.

The president (largely ceremonial) is head of state, elected by the national and state legislatures. The bicameral legislature comprises the upper house (Rajya Sabha) (250 members: 238 indirectly elected by states and union territories, 12 presidential appointees) and the lower house (Lok Sabha) (543 members elected to five-year terms from single-member constituencies [79 seats reserved for Scheduled Castes, 40 for Scheduled Tribes])[3] that has final authority over finance. Political power lies with the prime minister, chosen by members of the Lok Sabha. The legal system is based on the 1950 Constitution and British Common Law. For administrative purposes, the country is divided into 26 states and six union territories.[4]

---

[1] Republic of India.
[2] Schools in several Indian states followed a three-language policy: teaching is conducted in the local language, Hindi and English.
[3] The Indian constitution allows for a maximum of 552 seats in the Lok Sabha.
[4] To a considerable extent, division of the country into administrative units is based on language.

Political. Operating as the East India Company, the British gained control of most of the Indian subcontinent; company rule ended with the great revolt (1857–58) in northern India; power was ceded to the British crown. Nationalism grew rapidly after World War I; the Indian National Congress and the Muslim League demanded constitutional reform. In 1930, peace-loving leader Mahatma Gandhi advocated self-rule, non-violence and removal of "untouchability"; he launched a "civil disobedience" campaign including a boycott of British goods and rejection of taxation without representation. Independence was proclaimed on August 15, 1947, though the British government partitioned British India into India and Pakistan. India became a democratic republic in 1950 but the unresolved status of Kashmir was the immediate cause of war between India and Pakistan; its end marked the start of a still-tense territory division along the truce line. (Other wars followed [1965 and 1971].)

Jawaharlal Nehru (first prime minister) initiated India's international non-aligned stance. The Congress Party ruled more or less continuously from independence until 1996. Nonetheless, there was considerable political instability: prime minister Indira Gandhi (Nehru's daughter) was murdered by Sikh bodyguards (1984) and her son and successor, Rajiv Gandhi was assassinated during the 1991 elections. Prime Minister Rao's government, formed in 1991, initiated widespread economic reforms but scandals and defections of senior Congress figures rocked the party and it lost power in 1996. Following elections in early 1998, the Hindu Nationalist Bharatiya Janata Party (BJP) formed the government. In May, India tested nuclear weapons causing much consternation around the world, especially in Pakistan. As the result of U.S. pressure, World Bank assistance to India was delayed indefinitely. Pakistan subsequently responded with tests of its own.

Social. Population control is a top government priority. Unless family planning succeeds (target growth, 1.2%), population will reach one billion by 2000 and surpass China by about 2030. Regional income disparities and poverty in many parts of India are serious social problems. Despite advances in living standards, 30% of the population lives in poverty. Education is another problem; adult literacy is 48% (1995). Social security is provided for by various laws (e.g., health insurance, provident fund, family pension, deposit-linked insurance, superannuation and retirement payments). Both employers and employees are required to contribute to the Employees Provident Fund at rates dependent on wage levels, starting at 8% of employee's basic salary. India has the world's third largest pool of scientists and engineers; mainly English-speaking, they have attracted software and high-tech companies to India.

The Hindu caste system is a complicated aspect of modern Indian life. It evolved over 3,000 years into a formalized system of four distinct classes, comprising many subdivisions based on such factors as region, each with prescribed sets of rules for conduct. Historically, the lowest caste (the Dalits) had little or no opportunity for education and advancement, thus ensuring an inability to break free from their social level. Government programs have sought to rectify this imbalance by providing special quotas for "untouchables," but these policies have provoked a widespread backlash.

Economy. India is a member of the United Nations (UN), World Bank (WB), International Monetary Fund (IMF), World Trade Organization (WTO) and Asian Development Bank (ADB). India is an agricultural country; the agricultural sector (including forestry, fisheries) accounts for 28% of GDP and employs 65% of the labor force. India is self-sufficient in food and exports processed foods; it is the world's leading tea producer. Industry (including manufacturing, construction, utilities) accounts for 26% GDP (1960s: 18%). India's economy is the world's 14th largest but estimated per capita income of US$310 makes it one of the world's poorest nations. In June 1995, foreign debt was US$85.2 billion, quite large for a developing country. Between 1993–94, foreign direct investment stood at US$4.7 billion.

In the early 1990s, real GDP growth averaged 4%; the eighth five-year plan (1992–97) targeted annual GDP growth at 5.6%, estimated at 6.8% in 1996/97. The plan aimed to expand and diversify agriculture, transport and communication and irrigation and develop India's infrastructure, especially in energy. To achieve its targets, the industrialization process is regulated through a comprehensive licensing system and several statutes (notably the Monopolies and Restrictive Trade Practices Act; and the Foreign Exchange Regulation Act) that enable the government to channel investment to areas considered beneficial to national development. Major export destinations (1994) are: U.S. (20%), Japan (8.1%), Germany (7%). Major import origins (1994) are: U.S. (10%), Japan (8%), Germany (8%).

Introduction of unified exchange rates and abolition of export subsidies (1991) spurred export growth (1991/92, 35%; 1992/93, 22%); in 1994/95, the top customs duty rate was cut from 85% to 65% and corporate tax rates (for closely- and widely-held firms) were lowered to 40%; the top bracket marginal income tax rate is 40%. Enterprises manufacturing goods primarily for export may be set up in one of seven export processing zones (EPZs) (Cochin, Kerala; Falta, West Bengal; Kandla, Gujarat; Madras, Tamil Nadu; Noida near New Delhi; Santa Cruz near Mumbai; Visakhapatnam, Andhra Pradesh); 100% for export units (EOUs) may be set up anywhere in the country.

India has a strong financial system comprising a network of commercial banks, financial institutions and small financial service firms. Over 60,000 bank branches are scattered across the country, many located in villages. In 1994, the banking sector comprised eight banks in the State Bank of India Group, 19 nationalized banks, 23 private sector banks, 27 foreign banks with full licenses, 23 foreign banks with representative offices, and 66 cooperative banks. The Reserve Bank of India (RBI) regulates a predominantly state-owned banking industry. In 1993, the State Bank of India (98% owned by RBI), the largest commercial bank, raised capital in the stock market.

There are no restrictions on bringing foreign currency into India, but no more than the amount brought in can be taken out. All transactions involving foreign currency conversion to Indian rupees must be made with authorized banks or foreign exchange dealers. In August 1994, the rupee became convertible on current account subject to RBI "indicative limits" on outward remittances. Expatriates temporarily residing in India may remit 50% of net income after tax to home countries; applications for higher amounts are reviewed by RBI. Because of a recent surge in foreign investment, the rupee was expected to appreciate against the U.S. dollar (June 1996, US$1 = 34.06 rupees).

The five major stock exchanges (among 23 total) (Mumbai, New Delhi, Calcutta, Ahmedabad, Madras) account for over 90% of listed stocks and market capitalization (6,500 companies; estimated market capitalization Rs 2,994 billion) (1994). The Bombay Stock Exchange, Asia's oldest (1857), accounts for two thirds total securities' turnover, averaging 90,000 trades per day. Foreign investors may invest in stocks directly; in 1993/94, US$2 billion flowed into the Indian market.

India weathered the Asian financial crisis well, in part because its currency was not fully convertible. Given the extensive currency devaluations in Southeast Asia at end 1997, the competitiveness of India's products was questioned. A slowdown in economic growth to about 5.5% was expected for 1998.

Infrastructure. India's rail and postal systems are quite impressive: ports, air service and telecommunications are improving but the road system is unsuited to modern requirements. Of about 2 million kilometers of roads, only 1 million kilometers are surfaced; 34,000 kilometers of national highways carry 40% of total traffic. Over one third of villages have no road link; 70% have no all-weather link. Only 3.8 million cars and 2 million commercial vehicles (trucks, buses) are in use. The greatest vehicular expansion is two-wheelers; India is the world's largest producer of mopeds, motorcycles and scooters (annual output 2 million [1995/96]). Because of lack of capital for road building, the government is considering allowing privately-constructed toll roads on a build-operate-transfer (BOT) basis.

India has the world's most extensive railway system, total route length 62,570 kilometers. The railways are government-owned, employing 1.6 million people (India's largest employer). Trains carry two thirds of goods traffic, 40% passenger traffic, an estimated 311 billion passenger-kilometer p.a. (1994/95). India has 11 major ports: five on the east coast (Calcutta-Haldia, Paradip, Visakhapatnam, Madras, Tuticorin); six on the west coast (Kandla, Mumbai, Jawaharlal Nehru, Mormugao, New Mangalore, Cochin). India has six international airports (Mumbai, Calcutta, New Delhi, Madras, Trivandrum, Varanasi) and 100 domestic airports. National carrier, Air India, and several international airlines operate regular direct services between India and major Asian, European and American cities. Sanctioning of private airlines (including some international routes), led Air India's domestic market share to drop to 65%.

Telecommunications has expanded rapidly to meet demand for switching capacity to service telephone connections; these grew 8.5% p.a. in the 1980s, 15% to 20% in the 1990s. However, demand still outpaces supply and most Indians have to wait several months (or even years) before securing a new telephone connection. The private sector plays a key role, on a franchise or license basis, for cellular mobile telephones and electronic mail systems. In 1993, electricity production stood at 43.6 billion kWh; in 1994, total energy production equalled 344 billion kWh (368 kWh per capita).

Statistics*	June 1991	June 1997	Statistics*	June 1991	June 1997
Per capita GNP	US$350	US$360	Infant mortality/1,000	88	79
GDP growth	4.5%	6.8%	Life expectancy (yrs)	n/a	61
Savings (GNP)	n/a	2.8%	Literacy rate	40.8%	52.1%
Inflation (CPI)	10.0%	10.0%	People per tel.	180	77.6
Foreign debt (in billion)	US$69.8	US$93.8	People per doctor	2,522	2,165
Pop. (million)	843	948.7	People per TV	n/a	18.6
Urban pop.	27%**	26%	Calorie intake (cals)	n/a	2,243
Pop. growth	2.1%	2.1%			

*Secured from *Asiaweek*.
**From "A report of the INSEAD Euro-Asia Centre," J. Probert (Sept. 1994), INSEAD.

Case 11

Allwyn

Shamza Khan
The Hong Kong University of Science and Technology

Noel Capon
Graduate School of Business, Columbia University

In July 1993, Mr. Sunil Gupta contentedly recalled the good old days in the late 1950s when state-owned Allwyn was India's sole refrigerator manufacturer; it had a good reputation for advanced technology and quality products. However, when competitors entered the market in the late 1970s, Allwyn lost ground to become a marginal player. Although Allwyn experimented with several marketing plans in the 1980s, Gupta realized its repositioning was ineffective and that it should have been less passive in marketing. Nonetheless, he believed Allwyn's long-run decline was inevitable in face of inefficiencies caused by over-employment.

Since India's market liberalization in the past couple of years, new competitors had entered the market; in particular, multinationals formed joint ventures with local firms. Now, Allwyn had been shut down for over 14 months and Gupta wondered if Allwyn could be relaunched. "If we decide to give it a try, marketing will have to play a vital role," he mused. Possible revival could be sought by selling off the refrigerator division or forming a joint venture with an overseas or local firm; or, the business could simply be written off.

⧢⧣

Country Background

In Allwyn's early days, India was radically different from the more modernized country of the 1990s. In the 1950s and 1960s, the Indian government followed socialist policies; all major industries were state-owned and products were manufactured according to government quotas. Many observers pointed to systemic problems (e.g., inefficiencies from over-spending; mismanagement of funds); many federal and state controls existed on land and labor. In this period, India pursued a national economic policy of consuming locally produced goods. The "Being Indian, buying Indian" attitude protected domestic industries from overseas competition; product variety was limited and many foreign goods were banned. Private sector growth was constrained and companies expanded only with government permission.

Company Background

Allwyn, inaugurated in 1957, was a division of Hyderabad Allwyn Ltd., a state-owned enterprise located in the southern state of Andra Pradesh, run by the Andra Pradesh government. Hyderabad Allwyn Ltd. comprised many divisions producing various products (e.g., gas cylinders, bus bodies). Compared to other state-owned enterprises, the organization structure was relatively flat and individual divisions had significant autonomy. Allwyn was the first Indian firm to manufacture refrigerators. The launch was a national affair; Prime Minister Nehru opened the plant, claiming a victory for socialism.

Although the common perception of products and services produced by state-owned enterprises was largely negative, Allwyn pursued aggressive, sophisticated R&D. Compared to consumer durables produced by other state-owned enterprises, refrigerator technology was relatively advanced. Allwyn regularly introduced new developments (e.g., different colors, long-lasting paint finishes) and maintained a pioneering reputation long after competitive entry.

Among its landmark successes, in 1972–73 Allwyn won a huge order to export refrigerators to Poland. As a result of continued product improvement, in 1974–75, Allwyn received the ISI mark (Indian version of ISO 9000) for its models "Snow" and "Queen." In 1979–80, Allwyn entered a collaborative agreement with Hitachi for compressors. Allwyn's various milestones earned it significant respect and strengthened its reputation as a technologically advanced, progressive and dynamic unit of a state-owned enterprise.[1] Despite these successes, increasing competition and other economic changes ultimately caused Allwyn to close its factory. (See Exhibits 1A, 1B for financials.)

Industry Analysis

Until the late 1970s, India's refrigerator market was very small; owning a refrigerator was a major status symbol. Since India was a poor society in the 1960s, only an elite segment of the population, mainly successful businessmen and established politicians, owned refrigerators. These customers were generally satisfied with Allwyn products since they were long-lasting, sturdy and performed well. A 20-year life-span was expected; refrigerators rarely needed repairs so long as they were well maintained. Allwyn also appealed to locals because of its "made in India" stature.

In the 1960s, much domestic infrastructure, including distribution networks, was primitive; electricity supply was non-existent in most villages and scarce in many cities. Demand for large consumer durables (e.g., televisions, refrigerators) was low and emanated mainly from major cities (e.g., Bombay, Delhi). Retail distribution in these cities was more sophisticated than smaller cities; consumers could locate many

---

[1] In 1981, the R&D center experimented with, but later abandoned, polyurethane foam (PUF) technology.

products in a single household goods outlet. Allwyn's marketing efforts focused on securing distribution in a limited number of appliance stores in a few major cities; Allwyn conducted little print and no television advertising. Until the late 1960s, the market was state controlled with no competition. One government official commented:

> Private competition was not encouraged, therefore there were few goods in the market. It was not unusual for customers to happily buy whatever was available during the 1960s. In any case, the ability to own an electrical product was a big deal in those days!

Allwyn's market dominance ended in 1967 with the entry of local manufacturer, Godrej; U.S.-based, Kelvinator, arrived in 1970. These entries radically changed and shaped the refrigerator industry. Indian firm, Voltas, entered in the early 1980s but was not prominent until the late 1980s. Competitive entry increased product choice and reduced prices. Early refrigerators, generally large (e.g., 300 liter), single-doored and unwieldy, were treated by the government as luxury products. The high excise taxes were based on capacity; 165L models taxed at Rs 500; 240L taxed at Rs 750. Lower capacity models became popular; by 1981, 81% of refrigerators sold were 165L. These refrigerators were adequate for middle-class families; larger sizes were unpopular since most women did not work and preferred to prepare freshly cooked meals. In the late 1980s, excise duties were somewhat reduced and sales of larger models picked up. Although Allwyn continued to produce good quality refrigerators and lead in innovation, consumers became less concerned with technological advances.

From 1980 to 1992, about 9.5 million refrigerators were sold. Refrigerator sales grew substantially: 320,000 units (1981), 650,000 units (1986), 1.25 million (1991) (Table 1). Sales dropped in 1991–92, in part due to closure of the Kelvinator factory, and in part due to the recession and increased excise taxes. Projected market size for 1994 was 15 lakh (1.5 million) units. An important trend commencing in the early 1990s was refrigerator replacement. Consumer research indicated that one million owners of pre-1980 refrigerators would soon be in the replacement market. Refrigerator exports were minimal as a result of both the duty structure and high freight rates.

Table 1: Growth of Refrigerator Market (million units)

Year	Millions	Year	Millions
1986	0.65	1989	0.88
1987	0.60	1990	1.10
1988	0.75	1991	1.25

Economic Reform

Changes in the Indian economy were generally associated with changes of political leadership. When Prime Minister Indira Gandhi was assassinated (1987) her son Rajiv Gandhi succeeded her. He slowly reduced restrictions on business and commenced deregulation in some industries. However, foreign investment was still barred in dozens of key sectors; when foreign investment was permitted, technology transfer was a prerequisite. Foreign ownership was limited to 39.9% maximum and firms could only repatriate $1 for $5 export sales. These policies protected local firms from foreign competition but were also believed to be the cause of India's mid-1991 foreign exchange crisis.

The "reform-by-storm" (1991) initiated major changes in government economic management; several long-existing barriers to growth were removed. Liberalization of the Indian economy led to a boom for consumer durables. The "permit-raj," by which Indian bureaucrats regulated and restricted business activity, was dismantled. The government no longer determined if businesses could build new plants/diversify into new businesses:

- Trade barriers were lowered. Tariffs, frequently approaching 300%, were trimmed, some to less than half; further reductions were promised gradually.
- The Indian rupee was devalued; partial convertibility was pledged on the capital account as an interim step to full convertibility within three years.
- Privatization of state enterprises was pledged.
- Bans on foreign investment were lifted.
- Industry was de-licensed.
- The quota system for most goods, including refrigerators, was abolished.
- The government pledged to lift all restrictions on consumer goods imports by 1998.
- The government proposed significant changes and reductions on refrigerator duty structure in the future.

These liberalization measures were expected to aid the refrigerator industry. By early 1992, refrigerator firms were discovering a new segment of consumers; low income, poorly educated, not previous refrigerator purchasers who were being lifted out of poverty by economic growth. These people wanted to buy durable, reputable products; their main concerns were product life and smooth functioning of the refrigerator. In addition, demand for durables (e.g., refrigerators, air-conditioners) was expected to grow for offices and industrial establishments particularly in the long run.[2] On the supply side, by mid-1992, industry production capacity was 2–2.5 million units (approximately 50% to 60% capacity utilization). Godrej was believed operating at over 100% capacity; Voltas' utilization was around 40%. Industry experts believed installed capacity would increase to around 6.5 million units in the next few years.

The Indian refrigerator market had several other distinct features:

---

[2] The industrial refrigeration market was completely separate from the consumer market. Major sellers were small unorganized firms offering stripped down cheap models; major brands were not unsuccessful in penetrating this market.

- Refrigerators were much cheaper (up to 20%) in the north; it was a large, price sensitive market. Products were sold as economy models.
- Prices varied from city to city in part because sales taxes varied (e.g., Bombay 12%–13%, Calcutta 20%, most other markets 10%).
- The refrigerator market in general was very price sensitive. Brand switches occurred for small price differences (e.g., Rs 200), leading to parity prices.

Market Factors in 1992

India comprised 23 major cities (Exhibit 2A) and 580,702 villages; the market was so large that few brands in any industry had national coverage. The distribution system was complex and choice of areas to concentrate was a tedious but important process. Highest refrigerator penetration was in the northern and western states (e.g., Maharashtra, Uttar Pradesh, Gujarat), poorest penetration was in the south, reflecting higher purchases in hot, dry cities; Delhi, Chandigarh and Lucknow had comparatively high sales volumes relative to population. (The east and south accounted for 30% of the total refrigerator market.) Historically, sales were highly seasonal, displaying sharp increases in summer, decreases in winter. However, all companies conducted major winter promotions, causing winter sales peaks to exceed those in summer. Sales decreases in monsoon season (month-to-month) were uniform across brands.

Since local governments had different attitudes/policies to economic liberalization, economic performance and incomes varied markedly across states (Exhibit 2B). The northern region had a high concentration of upper-middle and high income households; eastern states were dominated by middle-income households. Income distribution was consistent with purchasing behavior inasmuch the north dominated purchase of many consumer durables (Exhibit 3); purchase of refrigerators was greatest in the northern and southern regions.

The 1991 economic changes caused rippling social effects. Consumers began voicing complaints of being deprived of foreign goods for too long; they displayed intolerance with the climate of exploitative indigenous monopolies providing substandard goods and services. Many foreign products became available (e.g., Coke, IBM computers) for the growing middle class.

Economists believed per capita income statistics did not accurately reflect Indians' real purchasing power. Rather, a more accurate reflection was believed to be the purchasing-power-parity (PPP) model. This model showed that India would be the world's fifth largest economy by 1992, PPP-adjusted per capita income, $1,255. Per capita incomes in some western (e.g., Gujarat, Maharashtra) and northern (e.g., the Punjab, Haryana) states were being compared to newly industrialized nations (e.g., Malaysia). In 1991, the National Council of Applied Economic Research estimated that 20 million households had annual incomes over Rs 25,000; 38 million households Rs 12,500 to Rs 25,000. This data suggested that India's middle class was between 100 million and 350 million, and expected to grow at 12% p.a.

India's rising affluence was apparent in consumer purchasing behavior. Spending on household appliances, consumer goods and services rose 14% p.a. in the 1980s; consumer electronics spending increased 30% p.a. (Table 2). Consumption also increased due to changing attitudes toward spending money versus saving for the next generation; consumer finance schemes, many evident by mid-1992, encouraged spending. Said one observer: "Rajiv Gandhi and color televisions had a startling effect on consumer habits in the 1980s. That trend has infiltrated and today, keeping up with the Joshis (the Indian Jones) is the accepted middle-class norm."

Table 2:   Ratio of Household Owning Durables to Total Number of Households[3]

	1987–88 (%)	1992–93 (%)
Color TV	27	55
Motorcycle	15	23
VCR	5	12
Refrigerator	32	62
Washing machine	6	18

Immediately after liberalization, observers noted definite preferences for foreign goods but no clear consensus was reached on the impact of foreign brands on the Indian market. In some cases, international giants (e.g., Pepsi, Gillette, Tang) were embroiled in major battles with local firms. By and large, domestic brands more than held their own in low-cost, mass consumption products but for high-cost consumer durables, international brand names lent prestige and encouraged consumer confidence. It was generally believed that, after the initial burst of preference for foreign goods, most Indians had a simple desire for quality products, local or foreign.

Purchase of consumer durables became an important part of people's lives; consumers were able to spend on goods the earlier generation could only dream of. Customers took purchases seriously and much thought was given to brand choice. A SSC&B Lintas survey showed that refrigerator purchasers had a specific decision-making pattern inasmuch as consumers took certain issues into consideration while making refrigerator purchases (Exhibit 4).

Problems for rural penetration of consumer durables were widespread; nearly one third of villages had no bus connection; a comparable proportion were not connected by modern roads. Nevertheless, rural India was projected to account for two thirds of retail consumption expenditures by 1996; up-market products did well close to major cities that received spill-over from media and marketing activities. A well-regarded survey suggested the number of rural rich was not significantly lower than the urban figure but consumer attitudes seemed markedly different. Industry observers said firms entering the rural market now would reap huge benefits as rural income increased over the next 10 to 15 years. However, servicing and distributing to rural consumers would be critical considering the poor infrastructure and low density of

---

[3] Based on a sample of middle and upper class Indian households. Study conducted by National Council of Applied Economic Research.

well-off inhabitants. There was some evidence suggesting reach was less an issue for durable products since consumers would mostly plan trips to nearby towns to make purchases.

Promotion

Not only did refrigerators gain in popularity, overall consumption patterns changed post-liberalization; spending on clothing, kitchen gadgets, refrigerators, watches and personal accessories surged by eight to ten times the population increase. Simultaneously, advertising expenditures rose; from 1984 to 1990, total advertising more than tripled to Rs 15 billion and was expected to grow by 10% to 15% p.a. through the 1990s.

Said a spokesman for Modi Olivetti, makers of hybrid-name micro computers: "Quality alone, without a brand name, takes longer to establish itself in the market. Having a foreign tie-up in consumer goods will benefit the Indian partner a hell of a lot." However, Titu Alhuwalia, managing director of MARG cautioned:[4] "A well-known brand name and a big advertising budget are no guarantee for success in the Indian market anymore; price, quality and market niche are equally important."

Other observers noted exposure to western ideas, many Indians watched international television via Star TV, a Hong Kong-based satellite network, and read international magazines; films and multinationals brought western influence and a strengthened consumerism concept. One observer noted: "During the pre-liberalization period, there was no such thing as consumerism. People were just fulfilling their needs. Consumerism is a troublesome idea for a country whose hero liberated his country wearing a loin-cloth and spent his leisure hours toiling at a spinning-wheel."

Some observers pointed to the Indian market's complexity, noting that India was regionally and culturally fragmented. In addition, India had a large underclass: around 50% were illiterate, and 30% lived below the poverty line. Said one industry analyst: "India still has a long way to go. You're dealing with a country where the poverty level is intense. There's a large underclass of people that can't imagine purchasing products."

However, an integrating factor was the national obsession with movies; an account manager with SSC&B Lintas said: "Bombay is one of the biggest film businesses in the world. The reality of life in India is so miserable that the people just want to escape into the movies." Another change was the advent of television choice. Until 1991, Indians had access only to Doordarshan, the state-owned channel, still India's only terrestrial broadcaster. Then, Star TV arrived along with Zee TV, a Hindi channel. In 1991, 330,000 homes in India received satellite or cable channels; 12 million people were projected to have access by 1992 (Exhibit 5). Radio was a popular method of communication, especially for targeting housewives; the number of sets in use was 110 million. To counter the threat from television, newspapers were increasingly becoming

---

[4] MARG was the Marketing and Research Group; based in India, it conducted much research for the government and private corporations.

"viewspapers," re-orienting their style to include in-depth analysis, backgrounders and features that television could not provide. Said one dealer: "If you don't stock what people see on television, you lose customers. It's a real nuisance."

Advertising outdoors was also a very effective promotion medium but the outdoor industry was highly fragmented with numerous small operators and few controls; rates were not standardized. Billboards made up a large percent of India's outdoor advertising. There were at least 100,000 billboards in the country, 60% in towns and cities. They were increasingly expensive in cities due to limited availability of sites and government restrictions on new sites.

Competition

Increasing refrigerator sales and predicted volume growth encouraged entry in the refrigerator business. Major competitors to Allwyn were Godrej, Kelvinator and Voltas; their changing industry positions were apparent in sales volume fluctuations (Table 3).

Table 3: Sales Volume ('000 units)

	1985–86	1986–87	1987–88	1988–89	1989–90	1990–91
Godrej	240	150	180	496	498	510
Kelvinator	310	300	380	238	265	219
Voltas	70	100	100	52	223	369
Allwyn	10	50	87	94	69	107

Godrej

Like most of India's large private industrial enterprises, the huge Godrej company was a family concern (owned and managed by three brothers) combining the feudal style of maharajahs with 19th century capitalism and 20th century technology. In 1992, Godrej had over 10,000 employees; it manufactured typewriters, refrigerators, forklift trucks, shampoo, animal feed and many other products.

Ardeshir Godrej began his firm in 1897 as a lock-producing workshop. Godrej knew and admired Gandhi and coupled his interest in profit with a desire to compete effectively with protected British-manufactured products in British-ruled India. The alliance between the fledgling industrialist and Gandhi's freedom movement, with its emphasis on *swadeshi* (indigenous production), provided the firm with some patriotic validity. A second boost came in World War II when Britain encouraged Indian entrepreneurs to increase production for the war effort. On the eve of independence, Godrej was a modest company making locks, safes and office furniture; it received a contract to produce five million ballot boxes for independent India's first election.

Seated in his mahogany paneled office in the Godrej Building (Bombay), the eldest brother, S.P. Godrej speculated about the future. He distrusted offering shares to the public: "Once you do that, all your stockholders become interested in is maximizing profits; they forget about such things as responsibility to the workers." He said his father once visited an old employee and was so appalled by the man's living conditions that he began a system of subsidized housing; two-bedroom apartments with kitchens and bathrooms were provided to white-collar workers for 10% of salary, and factory hands for $6 per month. "No, I don't think we'll ever relinquish family control. But, of course, as we grow more and more sophisticated we will have to rely more and more on professional managers."

Godrej began producing refrigerators in 1967 but only became a significant force in the late 1970s. In the early 1970s, Godrej was unable to match Allwyn's highly developed R&D team and could not compete on product attributes. Through much of the 1970s, Godrej experimented with products and manufacturing operations; it secured second place in the mid-1980s via a series of concerted attempts at new product introductions and forceful marketing. In 1988, it shut down its entire operations for two months for a total overhaul of production and introduction of PUF technology.

Re-entering the market with PUF technology, Godrej established itself as a premium brand by investing heavily in promotion. Godrej's marketing had a profound impact on people. Said one industry analyst: "Every kid and grown-up today can tell you about Godrej PUF! It was such a high profile campaign that everyone started associating PUF technology with Godrej. PUF wasn't advertised as a technology, it was advertised as a super-human character who did wonders for your refrigerator. Everyone wanted PUF technology. Refrigerators were not seen as technology products, so when Godrej launched PUF all consumers wanted it because it fulfilled their desire for value-addedness. It was something new, something which enticed them to spend their savings on."

Since PUF introduction, Godrej continued to outperform competitors in features and attributes; its products were seen as more attractive with a wide range of designs and colors. Promotional activities were especially aggressive in winter when sales were traditionally slow. Godrej conducted semi-annual promotions (summer, winter); price reductions were much steeper than competitors during these promotions. Godrej's success was also due to savvy selection of regional markets.

Prior to PUF, Godrej targeted products at housewives, appealing to their sense of aesthetics and creating the atmosphere of a happy home. Post-PUF promotions appealed to men; most advertisements focused on two dimensions; super-technology and PUF. Later, once PUF was established, advertising shifted back to emotion in focusing on how Superpower PUF brought happiness to many homes.

In 1992, Godrej's major refrigerator line was "Cold Gold." Following extensive customer research, "Cold Gold" boasted several new features: the ability to modify cabinet and door storage arrangements and automatic defrosting with a draining facility; the door could be opened to left or right. "Cold Gold" was available in seven different colors and three different sizes (i.e., 165, 230, 300 liters); the 230-liter model had double doors (Table 4). (Refrigerators comprised three rough categories: small, 165L and premium, including additional features such as frost free, three-door, and power-saving.)

Kelvinator

Kelvinator India Ltd. was a publicly listed firm offering a diversified product line (e.g., refrigerators, scooters, laminations). It entered the refrigerator market in 1964.

Table 4: Refrigerator Product Ranges

Size (liters)	Price (rupees)	Brand
100	5,000 to 5,500	Kelvinator
165 single-door	8,000	All brands
165 double-door	8,000	Allwyn
230 double-door	12,000	Godrej
300	15,000	Godrej, Kelvinator, Voltas

However, Kelvinator faced significant difficulties; on June 25, 1989, the Customs and Excise Department issued two show cause notices alleging fraudulent excise evasion of Rs 332.5 million by the refrigerator division.

Although Kelvinator was perceived as a technology laggard it became more aggressive in the late 1980s. In 1989, it introduced a new refrigerator model designed for energy conservation, and then opened a new fully automated plant in Faridabad to produce PUF refrigerators. It signed an agreement with Zanussi (Italy) to develop a new generation of refrigerators, Sterling; meanwhile a planned increase in compressor manufacturing capacity resulted in a South Korean order for 10,000 compressors. Kelvinator claimed its Sterling refrigerators, based on sophisticated Zanussi technology, would revolutionize the market. Sterling had 100% polyurethane foam insulation, a feature long since introduced by Allwyn and specialized by Godrej.

Industry observers said that despite relatively weak products, Kelvinator had high saliency and was perceived as an inexpensive brand. Similar to competitors, Kelvinator used promotions extensively during the winter, including its famous "Kelvinator Khazzana"[5] during which free gifts were given away. Kelvinator was the only significant player in the small refrigerator market; also, the 330L model was the largest selling large refrigerator. Kelvinator sales peaked in summer, coinciding with promotional activity.

Kelvinator's advertising budget was similar to Voltas' but the content was quite different. Advertisements were strongly based on features; for example, compressors were shown with steel bodies and refrigerators as masculine men who could perform indefinitely.

In April 1991, the Kelvinator's factory was shut down for two and a half months because of the corruption charges and continuing labor difficulties. Employees demanded higher wages and reinstatement of all but 15 workers previously suspended on disciplinary charges. There were also disputes over production targets and union representation.

In the previous few years, Kelvinator lost significant market share. The instability affected company performance and it was unable to keep up with technological developments. In 1992, the excise evasion charges were dropped; Kelvinator planned to upgrade refrigerator quality and penetrate the national market with a more aggressive marketing strategy.

---

[5] Khazanna is a Hindi word meaning "treasures."

Voltas

Voltas was formed in 1954 when Tata Sons and Volkart Brothers[6] decided to collaborate ("Vol" for Volkart, "Tas" for Tatas). Voltas was highly diversified; it gained strength in "cooling" since inception. Besides air-conditioners, washing machines and refrigerators, Voltas divisions made industrial chemicals, textile machinery, materials handling equipment, machine tools and water management systems.

In 1984, Voltas entered the refrigerator industry; profit margins were high on introduction even though initially its products had quality problems. However, in the late 1980s, Voltas sales increased markedly, in all regions, in part the result of competitors' problems and in part due to distribution expansion related to broader market targeting. Voltas sold products at premium prices, justified in terms of product features. Initially, Voltas focused on small refrigerators where its products achieved a good reputation. However, as a result of Kelvinator's problems, focus shifted to 165L models resulting in increasing market share post-1989. Future strategy involved increasing production capacity and introducing a wide range of "Soft Look" refrigerators.

A Voltas spokesman commented: "Radical efficiency improvements in Indian refrigerators may be impossible until the country's power quality improves. We are forced to use oversized compressors to compensate for voltage fluctuations. As a result, we cannot always satisfy consumer's evolving tastes in refrigerator aesthetics, quality, etc." Voltas advertising employed the two bursts per annum similar to competitors, mainly targeted at women, depicting convenience and comfort; products were also advertised as having the best features.

Allwyn

Allwyn's high profile market entry in 1957 left a lasting impression; management believed it enjoyed high consumer awareness despite weak, non-aggressive marketing. However, Allwyn drifted to marginal status, consistently retaining a no. 4 position; the highest post-1980 market share was 14%.

Allwyn's sales were mainly concentrated in the south, largely because it was based in the southern state of Andra Pradesh; it was known as a "South Indian" brand. As Allwyn lost market share, sales declined more slowly in the south (Table 5) because its distributor network was stronger than elsewhere.

Through the years, Allwyn continued to produce good quality products; it even remained aggressive technologically and was first to launch a double-door refrigerator. In general, it focused on lower capacity refrigerators. Observers said that Allwyn's advertising created little interest; it lacked focus and did not promote technological and customer benefits, one of its key strengths. For example, after the installation of Hitachi compressors, message themes were:

---

[6] Tata Sons was a large conglomerate, one of the largest companies in India; Volkart was a Swiss firm operating in India since 1851.

Table 5: Allwyn Sales ('000 units)

Year	North	South	East	West
1988	17	28	14	28
1989	16	35	16	27
1990	9	32	11	17

Year	Campaign	Medium
1985–86	"Why the Allwyn is like Kawasaki, Canon"	Press
1986–89	"The refrigerator makes no sound"	TV
1986–87	"The best in life is worth more"	Press
1987–88	"Never compare an apple with an orange (chicken for the price of an egg)"	Press

The first and second campaigns associated Allwyn's quality and performance with Japanese products perceived as high quality and durable; they had little impact on sales.

Conversely, the quality of competitors' advertising and promotions rose and attracted attention. Refrigerator advertising expenditures rose significantly, reaching an all time high in 1991 (Table 6); consumers were bombarded with information on quality, innovation and modernization. Ultimately, Allwyn failed to establish a position and messages were lost in the cluttered media environment. In addition, Allwyn was premium priced, an increasing problem as competition got tougher. Observers said consumers were willing to pay for good quality products but Allywn's products as communicated in advertising did not justify the premium. A dealer explained: "Refrigerators are almost like a commodity product in terms of margins. Margins are very tight, and to support large R&D expenditures, Allwyn had to price its products slightly higher."

Table 6: Advertising Expenditure for Press and TV (Rs '000)

	1989	1990	1991
Godrej	32,761	47,421	52,515
Kelvinator	32,689	40,858	44,849
Voltas	9,999	14,798	15,952
Allwyn	8,348	16,227	18,933

Allwyn distributed refrigerators through multi-brand dealers in major cities; previously, Allwyn considered targeting fast expanding rural markets but never made any serious attempts at rural distribution. Historically, it had little difficulty securing distribution since limited goods were available, but this changed as competition intensified, especially after liberalization. Godrej was opening exclusive outlets. Allwyn considered distribution coverage satisfactory in the south and east, but less so in regions far from its plants. Prospective dealers were approached by Allwyn's head office which negotiated margins; these were very tight, around Rs 600 on a Rs 8,000 product.

Impact of Economic Liberalization

The government's liberalization program did not favor state-owned enterprises like Allwyn. Unable to face challenges from foreign and local competition, many public sector enterprises began to struggle; Allwyn's operations were adversely affected. Observers believed Allwyn's management initially spent frivolously; cash-flow problems were dealt with by pumping money into the refrigerator division rather than forcing major changes; as a result, it was insufficiently flexible to adapt to the changing environment. According to one industry observer: "Where competitors were using 700 people to produce 500 refrigerators, Allwyn had 5,000! The fact that it was a state-owned division allowed all the politicians and ministers to manipulate the organization. The usual political theme was to gain brownie points by adding to employment, and swaying public opinion in favor of a candidate."

Although, for a while, revenues were sufficient to cover operating expenses, funds were not available for investment. The situation was little better in other Allwyn divisions (e.g., watches, automotive bodies, appliances, industrial products). In June 1991, the Allwyn refrigerator factory closed, putting its 11,500 workforce out of work.

Allwyn's exit created market confusion and frustration among distributors and owners. Loyal customers could not have refrigerators serviced as dealers could not secure spare parts. Observers said Allwyn received bad word-of-mouth; some customers were ashamed to tell family and friends they owned Allwyn refrigerators.

By mid-1992, competition gained strength and several new participants were entering the market. Godrej retained its leadership position; its strong performance and high brand equity had attracted many proposals. The corporate world was talking about recent joint-venture discussions between General Electric (U.S.) and Godrej. If consummated, GE would inherit Godrej refrigerator business and become market leader before introducing any of its own products. In addition, the successful electronics company, BPL, was about to produce its first refrigerators.[7]

Decisions

Allwyn had several possible options to re-enter the refrigerator market. Some existing players (e.g., Voltas) had shown an interest in purchasing the government-owned company and executives wondered about possible joint ventures. For either option, the new entity would have to take on around 3,000 employees who would need retraining and re-orientation. All other staff had been offered, and most had taken, voluntary retirement when the company closed down. If he pursued the first option, Gupta knew he would have to identify the firm for whom a purchase would make the most sense, convince it about the purchase, then negotiate terms. Alternatively, Allwyn could

---

[7] BPL was a Rs 10 billion Indian consumer electronics group with huge financial resources; it was a major industry player.

liquidate its assets; these included considerable inventory since Allwyn had manufactured to quotas, often unrelated to demand. Indeed, dealers were continuing to sell Allwyn products.

Exhibit 1A: Allwyn's Profit and Loss Account

	Year ended 31.3.1993 Rupees	Year ended 31.3.1992 Rupees
Income		
Sales	402,415,707	1,409,280,812
Goods capitalized for internal use	252,248	1,636,610
Sale of scrap	16,187,250	41,415,798
Jobs done for internal use	3,399,418	9,338,824
Other income	55,123,341	86,332,523
	477,377,964	1,548,004,367
Expenditure		
Raw materials and components consumed	105,912,085	592,116,625
Purchase of trading goods	1,847,352	9,750
Payments and benefits to employees	418,899,351	396,576,713
Other expenses	245,114,016	591,288,818
Depreciation	75,193,817	73,144,290
Interest	476,562,070	371,576,557
Increase in stock other than raw materials	83,137,947	157,920,532
Total	**1,406,666,638**	**2,182,632,995**
Profit/loss before adjustments	(–)929,288,674	(–)634,628,428
Adjustment relating to prior years	(–)7,102,126	(–)20,059,577
Profit/loss before appropriation	(–)936,390,800	(–)654,688,005
Investment allowance reserve written back	0	46,400,000
Profit/loss before tax	(–)936,390,800	(–)608,288,305
Provision for taxation	0	0
Profit/loss after tax	(–)936,390,800	(–)608,288,305
Balance of loss brought forward	(–)911,159,279	(–)302,870,974
Loss transferred to Balance Sheet	(–)1,847,550,079	(–)911,159,279

Exhibit 1B: Allwyn's Balance Sheet

	As at 31.3.1993 Rupees		As at 31.3.1992 Rupees	
Sources of funds				
Shareholders' funds				
Capital	276,462,010		276,453,266	
Reserves & surplus	52,414,259	328,876,269	52,412,383	328,865,649
Loan funds				
Secured loans	2,566,994,225		2,200,316,970	
Unsecured loans	595,583,977	3,162,578,202	436,874,703	2,637,191,673
Optional warranty charges		24,912,575		52,719,976
Total		3,516,367,046		3,018,777,298
Application of funds				
Fixed assets				
Gross block	1,672,467,391		1,652,298,032	
less: depreciation	415,169,078		338,125,759	
Net block		1,257,298,313		1,314,172,273
Capital work-in-progress		53,319,667		64,150,299
Financial expenses pending allocation		20,856,971		10,879,798
Technical know-how fee		18,155,422		14,229,983
Investments		20,627,990		20,627,990
Current assets				
Loans & advances				
Inventories	675,963,443		774,887,605	
Sundry debtors	38,633,064		136,283,419	
Cash & bank balances	8,875,263		67,022,910	
Other current assets	927,027		1,400,531	
Loans and advances	56,984,807		100,739,411	
	781,383,604		1,080,333,876	
Less current liabilities & provision	493,631,785		422,183,652	
	493,631,785		422,183,652	
Net current assets		287,751,819		658,150,224
Miscellaneous expenditure		10,816,805		25,407,452
Profit and Loss account		1,847,550,059		911,159,279
		3,516,367,046		3,018,777,298

Exhibit 2A: The Top 23 Cities

West	Popn. ('000)	South	Popn. ('000)	North	Popn. ('000)	East	Popn. ('000)
Bombay	12,572	Madras	5,361	Delhi	8,375	Calcutta	10,916
Ahmedabad	3,298	Hyderabad	4,280	Kanpur	2,111	Patna	1,099
Pune	2,485	Bangalore	4,087	Lucknow	1,642		
Nagpur	1,661	Cochin	1,140	Jaipur	1,514		
Surat	1,517	Coimbatore	1,136	Varanasi	1,026		
Vadodara	1,115	Madurai	1,094	Ludhiana	1,012		
Indore	1,104	Vishakapatnam	1,052				
Bhopal	1,064						

Source: 1991 Indian Census.

Exhibit 2B: Per Capita Income and Urbanization by State

States	Per. cap. inc. (Rs)	% urbanization	States	Per. cap. inc. (Rs)	% urbanization
Andra Pradesh	5,348	27.09	Madhya Pradesh	4,793	24.08
Arunchal Pradesh	6,955	11.08	Maharashtra	10,299	39.84
Assam	5,294	12.10	Manipur	5,832	13.00
Bihar	3,534	13.38	Meghalaya	5,413	n/a
Goa	11,556	n/a	Orissa	5,106	13.92
Gujarat	9,000	35.39	Punjab	11,793	30.33
Haryana	10,434	25.66	Rajasthan	4,868	23.43
Himachal Pradesh	6,670	9.20	Tamil Nadu	6,485	34.58
Jammu & Kashmir	5,696	23.80	Uttar Pradesh	5,116	20.47
Karnataka	6,787	31.52	West Bengal	6,600	27.67
Kerala	5,644	28.75			

Exhibit 3: Penetration by Income and Consumption (%)

Penetration by income (Rs 4,000+)

North		South		East		West	
Delhi	90.4	Hyderabad	74.6	Calcutta	59.8	Bombay	81.5
Kanpur	80.4	Madras	71.3	Nagpur	71.4	Ahmedabad	83.7
Lucknow	86.7	Bangalore	70.7			Jaipur	93.2

Penetration by goods ownership*

North		South		East		West	
Delhi	44.3	Hyderabad	16.7	Calcutta	14.9	Bombay	33.7
Kanpur	20.3	Madras	13.4	Nagpur	14.1	Ahmedabad	21.6
Lucknow	28.2	Bangalore	17.7			Jaipur	19.4

*Goods include T.V., refrigerators, mixer, scooter, VCR, washing machine. (This was also the hierarchy of purchase.)

Exhibit 4: Factors Influencing Purchase of Refrigerators

Determining factors	Percent	Determining factors	Percent
Reputation of brand	25.5	Storage space	6.5
Availability of desired color	12.5	PUF	6.1
Guarantee periods	10.3	Service	4.1
Auto defrost	9.5	Dealer reputation	3.8
Recommendation of friends/relatives	8.4	Size of freezer	3.8
Capacity	6.8	Price	2.7

Source: Survey conducted by SSC&B Lintas.

Exhibit 5: Satellite TV Penetration Projected for 1993

State/zone	TV HH ('000)	SAT HH ('000)	Penetration %	Contribution %
North	10,126	3,538	34.9	28.8
Uttar Pradesh	4,338	1,249	29.8	10.5
Rajasthan	1,415	504	35.6	4.1
Delhi	1,686	658	39.0	5.4
Haryana	2,687	1,082	40.3	8.8
East	7,875	1,051	13.3	8.6
West Bengal	3,740	339	9.1	2.8
Bihar	2,379	372	15.6	3.0
Orissa	828	165	19.9	1.3
NESA	928	175	18.9	1.4
West	11,047	5,106	46.2	41.6
Maharashtra	5,927	2,423	40.9	19.7
Gujarat	2,526	1,646	64.2	13.4
Madhya Pradesh	2,558	1,037	40.5	8.4
South	11,289	2,585	22.9	21.1
Andra Pradesh	3,580	816	22.8	6.6
Tamil Nadu	3,800	964	25.4	7.9
Karnataka	2,500	671	26.8	5.5
Kerala	1,409	134	9.5	1.1

Source: Lintas Media Guide – India.

Case 12

National Publishing Company: Marketing of Children's Fortnightly Magazine

Abraham Koshy
Indian Institute of Management, Ahmedabad

In November 1990, Mr. R. Saxena, marketing manager of National Publishing Company (NPC), was considering alternative strategies to improve sales of "Titli,"[1] a children's fortnightly vernacular magazine, in Venad,[2] one of India's 26 states. Titli was market leader in children's periodicals but its circulation decline was serious. First, Titli's circulation declined by 40% from peak sales in 1987; second, despite an active advertisement campaign, coinciding with market withdrawal of direct competitor Children's Delight, highlighting Titli's inclusion of some of its popular cartoon serials, circulation gains were minimal; third, although promotional schemes (e.g., time-table cards, name slips, animal face-masks, mythological characters given free with purchase), might increase circulation by 10%, significant numbers of additional buyers were not retained. Saxena contracted for a consumer study to gain deeper market insight.

જ૦૯૪

The Company

NPC was a leader with several years' experience in printing and publishing. Its several publications included a daily newspaper and weekly, fortnightly, monthly and annual journals; many were market leaders in their product categories. NPC had a team of competent editors and managers.

---

[1] The name and language of the magazine, the name of the company, the state and similar identifying data have been disguised to maintain confidentiality; no other data have been changed.
[2] The term "vernacular" refers to the "local" language.

NPC publications were distributed through a network of 3,000 agents and sub-agents located in all important places in Venad. A high proportion of most periodicals' sales was door-to-door delivery at subscribers' premises. Periodicals were also distributed to shops carrying magazines and other assorted products. These shops (usually, paan-beedi) catered mainly to occasional readers.[3]

The Product

Titli, published in Venad, carried various features of interest to 5- to 12-year-old children. A typical issue comprised two or three short two-page stories, three or four longer stories, one (or at the most two) serialized stories, two or three short poems, about seven or eight regular cartoon features (including two serialized cartoons), titbits and fun and games. For new readers, Titli carried one story written in simple language, printed in bolder letters. For not-yet-good readers, Titli carried another "read aloud" short story written in rhyming language. The magazine (12 cm × 20 cm) was printed in multiple colors and liberally illustrated. Titli was priced at Rs 2 per copy; all other children's fortnightly publications were in the same price range. (See Appendix 1 for summary of a typical Titli issue.)

Market and Competition

In 1990, the number of households in Venad was 52.35 lakh;[4] three to five member households comprised 68% of total households (Table 1). A majority of households (81%) were in the annual income category, up to Rs 12,500; this proportion was lower in urban (67%) than rural areas (Table 2).

Titli was targeted at 5- to 12-year-old children but experience indicated that children up to 14 years read and enjoyed Titli. In 1986–87, the number of children studying in classes I to X (corresponding to ages of the target readers) was estimated at 60 lakh, divided somewhat equally among the various classes, but slightly higher enrollment at the lower end. Around 40% of children were in primary classes (standards I to IV); 60% were equally divided between middle (standards V to VII) and high school (standards VIII to X). Enrollment in schools (average increase about 1% p.a.) did not increase significantly from 1984 to 1987.

Recently, the competitive situation in children's magazines underwent several changes. For example, in 1985, about 20 children's periodicals/magazines, fortnightly/monthly, were published in the vernacular language; in 1986, 31 publications, reduced to nine by 1989. Current monthly circulation of all children's publications was estimated at 16 lakh copies. In 1986, total circulation of children's periodicals increased by 25% over 1985; by 1989, total circulation declined by 56% from 1986.

---

[3] Paan-beedi shops were small retail outlets (5 to 6 sq. m.) located at busy places (e.g., bus stops, road junctions) carrying limited assortments of convenience products (e.g., cigarettes, candy) in addition to paan (made for chewing from several ingredients [e.g., chewing tobacco, betel nut], wrapped in a betel leaf and beedi, a hand-rolled substitute for cigarettes made from tobacco rolled in a tendu leaf. Many such shops, often without fixed locations, carried popular periodicals and magazines.
[4] 1 lakh = 100,000.

Table 1: Estimated Number and Percentage of Households by Household Size in 1990

Household size	Urban	Rural	Total	Urban	Rural	Total
	No. in '000s			%		
1–2	36	8	44	3.2	0.2	0.8
3–5	674	2,901	3,575	60.3	70.4	68.3
6–8	265	802	1,067	23.8	19.5	20.4
More than 8	141	407	548	12.7	9.9	10.5
	1,116	4,119	5,235	100.0	100.0	100.0

Table 2: Estimated Number and Percentage of Households by Income

Annual household income	Urban	Rural	Total	Urban	Rural	Total
	No. in '000s			%		
Up to Rs. 12,500	750	3,481	4,232	67.2	84.5	80.8
Rs. 12,501–25,000	230	511	741	20.6	12.4	14.2
Rs. 25,001–40,000	90	105	195	8.1	2.6	3.7
Rs. 40,001–56,000	25	19	44	2.3	0.5	0.8
More than Rs. 56,000	21	3	23	1.9	0.1	0.4
	1,116	4,119	5,235	100.0	100.0	100.0

Source: For Tables 1 and 2. Rao, S. L. (ed), *Consumer Market Demographics in India*, NCAER, Delhi, 1993.

Titli was market leader in children's periodicals. In 1985, Titli and Children's Delight each had 30% market share: 1986 – Titli 26%, Children's Delight – 23%. In 1989, Children's Delight ceased publishing; Titli's share rose to 47%. The closest follower had about 14% share; the other publications shared the remainder.

By and large, all publications targeted at children 15 years and under followed a similar format (e.g., stories, cartoons, titbits), although some concentrated on mythological and historical stories. In addition to such children's publications, other magazines (e.g., family, women's, political) were published in Venad (Appendix 2).

Salient Findings from the Market Research Study

Saxena found several important items of information in the market research agency's report. The study comprised two phases. The objective of the first (survey) phase was to understand the profile and reading habits of magazine readers, especially Titli readers. The second phase comprised a series of focus group discussions to understand the attitudes, needs and expectations of children and parents regarding children's magazines. The survey was conducted among households with monthly incomes above Rs 750 and children 3 to 14 years. Respondents were mothers or guardians of children. Survey sample size was 3,500 from various regions of Venad. The focus group comprised 16 groups of children and five groups of parents. Major findings included:

Awareness of children's magazines among parents. Seventy-six percent of respondents mentioned Titli spontaneously; competitor scores were Petals – 31%, Little Flowers – 19%. Aided awareness of all three publications, including Titli, was 85%.

Current purchase pattern of children's magazines. The study indicated 51% of households purchased either a vernacular or English children's magazine; 49% purchased at least one vernacular magazine (Table 3). (A current magazine buyer was defined as a household buying at least one of the last six issues; for Titli, a purchase was required in the last three months.) The study indicated 70% of Titli buyers were regular buyers; 30%, occasional buyers. Regular purchase levels of other magazines ranged from 20% to 60%: Petals – 50%, Chand aur Suraji – 32%, Guiding Light – 23%.

On average, 1.7 magazines were bought by each buyer household; 55% of Titli buyers purchased no other magazine, but among all other magazine buyers, over 80% also bought Titli. For households with children in the target age group, 60% read Titli; 45%, purchasers; 15% borrowed from neighbors/friends.

Purchase of children's magazines based on monthly household income. The study indicated 33% of households with monthly income up to Rs 1,000 purchased at least one vernacular magazine; 61% of households with a monthly income over Rs 4,000. The purchase pattern differed for English magazines (Table 4).

Table 3: Current Purchase of Children's Magazines (%)

Name of magazine	% household buying	Name of magazine	% household buying
Titli (fornightly)	45	Guilding Light (F)	3
Petals (F)	11	Others	1
Little Flowers (Monthly)	5	Vernacular	49
Chand aur Suraji (F)	5	Children's stories (English)	4
Dadima (F)	3	Sun & Star (E)	2
Little Master (M)	3	Any English	9
		Any vernacular/English	51

Table 4: Current Purchase of Children's Magazines by Monthly Household Income (%)

Name of magazine	Monthly household income				
	Up to Rs 1,000	Rs 1,001 – Rs 1,500	Rs 1,501 – Rs 2,500	Rs 2,501 – Rs 4,000	Above Rs 4,000
Titli	29	48	55	58	59
Petals	9	11	13	13	12
Any vernacular children's periodical	33	51	59	63	61
Any English magazine	4	7	12	19	29

Profile of Titli readers. Children aged 6 to 11 years comprised about 50% of children's magazine readership; 54% for Titli. Children from 6 to 14 years comprised 75% of readers of children's magazine; 90% for Titli (Table 5). Titli's readership base was similar to major competing publications on other dimensions.

Table 5: Profile of Titli Readers (%)

Age	Readers of children's magazines	Readers of Titli	Index of relative penetration*
3 years	6	2	33
4–5 years	18	8	44
6–7 years	17	14	82
8–9 years	16	20	125
10–11 years	17	24	141
12 years	9	13	144
13 years	9	11	122
14 years	7	9	129
	100	100	
Sex			
Male	52	51	98
Female	48	49	102
	100	100	
Monthly household income			
Up to Rs 1,000	36	24	67
Rs 1,001–1,500	26	26	100
Rs 1,501–2,500	22	27	123
Rs 2,501–4,000	11	15	136
Above Rs 4,000	5	7	140
	100	100	

*Ratio of penetration of readership in each segment to penetration of readership in all segments.

Lapsed purchase of Titli. Among past buyers of Titli, 45% discontinued in the past two to three years. These lapsed buyers comprised households with children in the target age group (Table 6). However, few lapsed Titli buyers purchased other magazines; when they discontinued buying Titli, they gave up buying all children's magazines rather than shift to a competitor. Major reasons for discontinuing were:

- Affects studies, busy with school work (50%);
- Easy to borrow from neighbors/library (16%);
- Expensive (9%);
- Not interested/interested in other areas like sports/English magazines (7%);
- Outgrown children's magazine (3%);
- Availability problems (1%);
- Other magazines better than Titli (1%).

Table 6: Lapsed Readership Rates by Age

Age of lapsing	Lapse rate (% of past readers)	Age of lapsing	Lapse rate (% of past readers)
6–7 years	36	12 years	49
8–9 years	40	13 years	47
10–11 years	46	14 years	56

Features most liked. The parent survey provided insight into Titli's features preferred by children. Parents said picture stories like "Friendly Ghost," "Magic Monkey," and "Detective stories" were most popular (Table 7).

Table 7: Relative Preference of Various Titli Features Assessed by Parents (%)

	All children	Up to 5 years	6–9 years	10–12 years	13–14 years
Friendly Ghost*	80	79	83	83	77
Magic Monkey*	51	46	54	50	45
Detective Stories*	25	17	26	31	27
Clever Crow*	21	17	21	21	18
Clumsy Hunter*	17	20	19	19	20
Short Stories	28	31	29	28	35
Boy with Magic Power*	12	10	13	11	12
Read Aloud Stories	2	5	2	1	–
Quiz	1	1	2	1	1

*Cartoon stories.

Children's leisure habits. Uniformly across age groups, 90% of children watched television. Regular viewing was also uniform, 65%; both total duration and programs were monitored and controlled by parents. Children three to five years primarily played with toys; reading had hardly any relevance. From six to eight years, playing and watching television were the main activities; reading was becoming a major activity, although at a low key. For children 10 to 14 years, book and magazine reading was a dominant activity, second only to watching television (Table 8).

Table 8: Children's Main Leisure Activities (%)

	All ages	3–5 years	6–9 years	10–12 years	13–14 years
Indoor games/toys	54	85	61	36	27
Outdoor games/sports	33	25	34	37	37
Reading books/magazines	37	6	33	54	59
Watching TV/video	64	65	63	65	68
Art/music/dance	5	4	6	6	6
Listening to stories	5	15	3	–	–

Major findings of focus group discussion. Focus group research provided insight into children and parents' attitudes to reading, expectations from children's magazines and predisposition towards children's periodicals in general, Titli in particular.

This phase of the study identified three "life cycle" stages of magazine reading, each characterized by different attitudes, interests and expectations from reading.

Active promotion. Most children started reading children's magazines on their own in classes III to V. Parents actively promoted reading habits and magazine purchase was mostly initiated by parents.

Children's main interest was playing with other children their own age, frequently with siblings (since they were not allowed out of the house). Although children watched TV, they had little interest or involvement. For most children, interest in reading was secondary to playing. However, parents encouraged reading habits since they believed reading would lead to interest in studies. Magazine purchase was at parental discretion and occasional rather than regular; children's brand loyalty was low.

Children and parents expected entertainment rather than information from reading. Children looked for picture stories, short stories, games and coloring. The magazine's appeal was as much through "window dressing" as content; purchase was heavily influenced by gift, prize and poster offers.

Passive approval. Children, typically 10 to 12 years (classes VI to VIII), showed a high interest in reading. Parental attitudes to reading had "cooled down" to passive approval. Reading was mainly guided by children's insistence and choice; they purchased magazines more regularly and were more loyal to specific magazines. In addition to children's magazines, some children started reading science magazines, often prompted by parents and teachers, and genuinely began to like them.

Despite the fact that playing was still of great interest to children, reading enjoyed a distinct preference and was becoming the most liked activity. Parents were careful to ensure that reading magazines did not distract children from studying. Watching television was also of considerable interest. Many children started hobbies (e.g., collecting stamps, coins, matchbox labels, car/motorcycle posters and keeping pets), thus demonstrating varied interests and activities.

Because of relatively high interest in reading, children exchanged magazines and books and even discussed popular stories and features. The main features interesting to children were stories, general knowledge and sports information. Parents expected children to read stories providing moral values and articles with scientific and general information/knowledge. Parental attitudes improved when children displayed information acquired by reading.

Stage of active control. These children (classes IX and X) derived much enjoyment from reading and "relished" it even more than TV. However, leisure time was less due to increased study load and tuition. Parents exhibited a strong tendency to control children's leisure activities including enforcing TV-bans and restricting time for playing/reading. Parents were concerned about children's studies and character building, and kept a close watch over what the child saw, read and did in his/her spare time.

Children started exhibiting preferences for features in magazines. They preferred stories that inspired and motivated; stories that made them think. They were also interested in "thought provoking" articles on general and/or social issues and had a greater desire to seek exposure to the adult world and look for "realistic" values. Parents expected reading to inculcate responsibility values and to develop personality and self-confidence. Reading had a high impact on character and behavior.

The main reading materials for children were magazines like Titli and science magazines. They also indicated growing penetration of general interest magazines targeted at grown-ups (e.g., India Today); such magazines were highly favored by parents as suitable reading material. Readership of story books/novels (e.g., those written by Enid Blyton, Nancy Drew by Carolyn Keene) was low. Children regularly "scanned" newspaper headlines and sports.

Image Perceptions of Titli

Focus group discussions indicated that Titli was perceived as a superior magazine by children because it contained more interesting and diverse stories, more picture stories and more color. In general, Titli was perceived as appealing mostly to 8- to 12-year-old children and, to a lesser extent, 13- to 14-year-old children. Although younger children were eager to associate with Titli, several older children were embarrassed to be seen reading it, as if it were "childish" for their age.

Among parents, Titli's image was as a source of "good, harmless entertainment." Some parents were appreciative of its usefulness/informative value, but in general Titli was dismissed as "light reading." This tendency was less pronounced among parents who read Titli. Parents of older children in particular perceived Titli as offering little value, believing it more appropriate for younger children. Frequently, this perception led to discontinuing Titli as children got older.

Children who seldom bought Titli or any similar magazine had relatively low exposure to any reading. Their parents did not read magazines, attached little value to reading and were generally passive/unconcerned about it.

Marketing Manager's Concerns

Saxena was aware that Titli had a significant role to play in children's publishing. Should it be repositioned? If so, how? Should the target segment(s) for this publication be redefined? If so, which segment(s) should he concentrate on? He wondered how best to increase Titli sales in the short and long run. His decisions would have major implications on NPC's current and future fortunes.

Appendix 1: Features Published in One Sample Issue of Titli in Sequential Order

1. Cover: Color.
2. Inside cover: Advertisement.
3. Pages 3 and 4: Title page, small editorial.
4. Page 5: Short story of a generous trader from whom the neighbor tried to steal a beautiful horse and finally how generosity made the neighbor feel ashamed and sorry about his act. Color, illustration.
5. Pages 5–9: Cartoon/picture story (Magic Monkey).
6. Page 10: Puzzle story to be solved by the reader (correct answer given on a different page). Color, illustration.
7. Pages 11–14: Short story of a thief who tried to take revenge on the person who spoiled his plans of stealing and how he finally fell prey to his own schemes. Color, illustration.
8. Page 15: Cartoon story – occasional feature. Color.
9. Pages 16–19: Feature on 'hormones' – describes in very simple, story telling style as to what hormones are and what their functions are. Also, titbits and additional information about hormones (for example, are there hormones in plants, etc).
10. Pages 20–21: Titbits, puzzles, things to do like join-the-dots, find-the-way, etc. No color.
11. Pages 22–25: Serialized story from mythology. Illustrated. Color.
12. Pages 26–27: Advertisements.
13. Pages 28–29: Illustrated picture and brief description of wild animals.
14. Page 30: Cartoon, humor. Occasional feature.
15. Page 31: Advertisement.
16. Pages 32–36: Serialized novel. Gives summary of previous issues. Illustrated. Color.
17. Pages 37–41: Cartoon – serialized, but stand alone story, humor (Boy with Magic Power).
18. Pages 42–43: Titli quiz including answers to quiz in the previous issue.
19. Pages 44–46: Story – illustrated. Two colors.
20. Pages 47–52: Cartoon story based on Indian history – serialized, continuous story.
21. Pages 53–54: Short story – illustration. Black and white.
22. Pages 55–58: Short story – illustration. Black and white.
23. Pages 59–62: Short story – illustration. Black and white.
24. Pages 63–68: Cartoon – serialized, but stand alone story (Friendly Ghost).
25. Pages 69–70: Short story – illustrated. Black and white.
26. Pages 71–73: "Read-aloud" story written in rhyming language.
27. Page 74: Letters to the editor.
28. Pages 75–76: Story for beginners – bigger type, illustrated. Color.
29. Pages 77–79: Cartoon – serialized, but stand alone story, humor (Clumsy Hunter). Color.
30. Page 80: Strange facts. Titbits. Illustrated. Color.
31. Page 81: Interesting questions and prize-winning answers from readers.
32. Page 82: Cartoon, humor.
33. Inside back cover advertisement.
34. Back cover advertisement (color).

Appendix 2: A Brief Description of Major Magazines Published in Venad

General Interest Magazines
This group of magazines constituted the largest segment, both in terms of the total circulation as well as the number of publications. This group can further be divided into the following sub-categories:

Magazines of Interest to the General Public
These magazines carried features interesting to the grown-up – stories, serialized novels, theme articles on social issues, jokes, "ask-the-doctor" features, etc. These magazines were read by most adult members of the family and were considered "family magazines." Stories and features were written in simple, easy to understand style.

"High-brow" Magazines
In addition to the above category, there were other magazines which were positioned as magazines for the intellectually more sophisticated readers. This was because they carried stories which were more abstract and philosophical and were written in a more literary style.

Social Magazines
These were magazines which emphasized social and political (both local, national and international) issues, news analysis, and some information on business and industry.

Political Magazines
These were published by groups or persons who had specific ideological inclinations and carried features most of which concerned political issues. Some of these were published by the arms of the political parties themselves.

Specialized Magazines
Broadly, there were three types of magazines in this category. In the first category, there were women's magazines which carried features interesting and appealing to women. The second category consisted of film based magazines. The third consisted of magazines which specialized in topics like 'psychology' ('popular' psychology), competitive examinations, and such other issues. In addition to these, there were also several children's magazines in this category.

Case 13

Nims Apparel

Shamza Khan
The Hong Kong University of Science and Technology

Noel Capon
Graduate School of Business, Columbia University

Ram Thadani, owner of the famous Double Bull brand (Nims Apparel) had made a huge impact on India's ready-made shirt industry. Over the years, his mid-1970s entry of a fancy-wear line featuring bold and vivacious designs became extremely popular. In addition to its major designer-wear business, Nims also manufactured formal-wear shirts but sales in this category were modest until the entrance of international brands Van Heusen and Louis Philippe in 1988. However, these entries, together with India's economic liberalization (1991), led to rapid expansion of the ready-made market and a shift in male preferences from fancy wear to formal wear.

Despite the fact that Nims had never advertised formal wear nor made this activity a central focus of the organization, sales of formal-wear shirts were responsible for an increasing proportion of Nims sales. Notwithstanding these increases, in 1994, Thadani concluded that Double Bull was losing out to the new international formal-wear market players.

In September 1994, the debate within Nims Apparel centered on the decision of whether to retain the Double Bull brand, now well-entrenched in consumers' minds, for formal-wear shirts or launch an entirely new brand. Thadani asked his advertising agency, SSC&B Lintas to develop alternatives, and make a recommendation.

୫୦୧୫

Evolution of the Ready-made Shirt Industry

India's ready-made garment industry could be traced to the early 1940s during British rule. At the time, the majority of Indians could only afford garments from the neighborhood tailor; typically they would purchase cloth from a merchant and have it made into a garment. British residents were the main customers for ready-made garments since only a few privileged Indians (e.g., doctors, lawyers, professionals) could afford them.

Ready-made shirts were mostly imported from Britain and sold through British department stores (e.g., Army and Navy, Whiteways, Evans Fraser). At the time, local ready-made shirt manufacturers (e.g., Liberty Shirts [started 1940 in Parel, a Bombay suburb]) made little headway as British residents preferred imported garments. After independence (1947), Liberty Shirts became the first local brand to establish a domestic presence. Despite the emergence of competitors (e.g., Wingswear, Armour) in the 1950s, Liberty Shirts emerged as ready-made shirt and garment leader with outlets in south Bombay, Delhi and Madras.

The 1960s was a tumultuous period for the ready-made shirt industry, marked by many entrants, amalgamations and highly visible advertising wars. For example, Armour and Liberty Shirts engaged in extensive (and expensive) advertising in the *Times of India* newspaper, publishing full page color ads with aggressive predatory promotional offers. Rumors abounded of under-the-table dealings with top local newspapers. Liberty Shirts was rumored to have used media connections to gain access to Armour's media schedule; it was alleged that Liberty then placed advertisements slightly in advance of Armour in attempts to restrain its growing popularity.

By the 1970s, the ready-made shirt market had grown significantly enough to sustain several competitors. A number of local men's shirting brands were well-entrenched (e.g., Raymond's, Vimal, Bombay Dye), but local tailoring was still the main route to securing shirts for most Indians.[1]

Government Intervention

The government closely monitored 1960s developments in the garment industry and in 1972 placed substantial taxes on the industry; it was rumored that the highly visible Liberty Shirts versus Armour advertising wars, implying a very profitable industry, was a major spur to action. The Finance Minister, Y. Bichawan, announced multiple levels of taxation:

- Ad valorem on yarn;
- Sales tax for converting yarn to shirts;
- Release tax for yarn stitching;
- 10% excise duty on registered trademarks (e.g., Armour, Liberty) and ready-made garment factories with turnover greater than Rs 5 lakhs.

The taxation process was especially difficult for garment manufacturers inasmuch as excise duty inspectors collected tax from manufacturers on factory premises before shipment of goods. As a direct result, the locally produced ready-made garment industry went into rapid decline and was eviscerated within a couple of months. Major brand names withdrew, companies disbanded and directors set up their own export units creating somewhat of an export boom. Local tailors strengthened their positions.

---

[1] The shift to ready-made also encompassed other garments (e.g., trousers, suits).

Simultaneously, small, regional ready-made shirt manufacturers mushroomed to fill the void. For example, brands such as Dash and Sero became popular in the south. In Bombay, Dunhill, Aristo and Envoy were regional players that gained popularity; Charagh Din, another popular shirt-maker, opened a major store. In 1974, realizing its mistake, the government withdrew the entire taxation system. The only remaining restrictions were on import of foreign brands and entry barriers for foreign companies, applicable to all industries. However, the damage was done and from 1975 to 1982, the ready-made shirt industry sported no national brands.

The Ready-made Shirt Industry

The ready-made shirt industry was characterized by low entry and exit barriers. Several elements characterized the industry:

Regionally fragmented market:[2] Viable markets for ready-made shirts in the "organized" sector (i.e., branded) were few and limited to India's major cities (e.g., Bombay, Calcutta, Delhi, Madras, Bangalore). The scattered "unorganized" sector, with varying quality standards, comprised 85% of ready-mades.[3]

Weather: Geographic issues were a critical factor inasmuch as India's two major seasons (i.e., winter, summer) limited the scope of fabrics and styles. Since the degree of hot and cold varied by region, shirt construction had to consider local weather conditions. In general, since pure cotton shirts tended to be uncomfortable in the summer, blended materials prevailed.

National brands: Only a handful of brands were advertised nationally and/or targeted at the entire market. The difficulty of developing, cultivating and sustaining a national brand in such a large, diverse country allowed the presence of several thousand regional brands, encompassing many entrants but also many exits. Many regional brands were particularly strong in their respective regions where national brands had limited presence.

Products: By the early 1990s, two distinct types of shirts could be identified: casual and formal. Formal shirt manufacturers competed largely on the basis of quality; casual shirts competed largely on design.

Price: Price was an important competitive weapon throughout the ready-made shirt industry. Only at the top end of the market where some firms had developed strong brand recognition was this pressure lessened. In addition, since brands attempting national distribution had to operate with an inefficient national infrastructure, profit margins were low.

---

[2] The regional segmentation made it difficult to gather information on market positions.
[3] The unorganized segment referred to small shirt manufacturing units whose products were either not branded or not advertised. Typically, they were produced and sold locally.

Segments: By 1993, industry observers identified three tiers in the organized sector: premium (mainly foreign brands), medium range (mainly regional brands) and low-priced (regional brands). These observers believed that sales of premium shirts were smallest of the three, followed by the medium range, but were unable to offer specific figures.

Shirt market: Only about 5% of the adult male population, roughly 22.5 million, wore ready-made shirts; major markets were limited to major cities. Seventy percent of ready-made shirts were purchased in urban areas.

Retail: There were no department stores in India; thus economy of scale benefits in distribution, taken for granted in many western countries, did not exist. Even the largest stores carrying shirts had only a limited inventory of shirt designs.

Culture: Each region of the country had its distinct culture and style of dress. In the north, western dress became more popular after economic liberalization (early 1990s); previously, only the affluent or those traveling abroad wore western dress. In the south, it was unusual to wear western clothes; traditional garments were accepted even at the official level.

Market trends: In the 1980s, the convenience of purchasing ready-made caught on and increasing numbers of Indians began purchasing ready-made garments. With liberalization and greater exposure to foreign habits and products, Indian tastes modified significantly; by 1992, a definite preference for ready-made shirts could be discerned. As ready-made shirt sales increased, some Indian brands achieved market success. In addition, introduction of internationally branded shirts encouraged local manufacturers to be more cost-effective and quality conscious.

Largely because of excessive industry fragmentation, accurate data on ready-made shirt industry sales was impossible to secure. However, industry observers believed that sales of national and major regional brands were growing at 30% to 40% p.a. Sales of ready-made shirts in total were predicted to grow at 10% p.a. for the next five years. These trends implied that at the top end of the market purchases of tailor-made shirts were decreasing rapidly (Table 1); one observer estimated that fewer than 10% of men buying these shirts used a local tailor versus 75% in the late 1980s.

Table 1: Competing Ready-made Shirt Brands

	1989	1990	1991	1992	1993	1994 est.
Ready-made garments (Rs crore)*	254	320	490	514	540	600
Shirt market (Rs crore)	152	192	299	329	362	398
Ready-made shirts	25%	44%	50%	63%	78%	93%
Tailor-made shirts	75%	66%	50%	37%	22%	7%
Premium shirts (Rs crore)	–	–	–	–	51	67

*Most other ready-made garments were jeans and trousers.

Foreign Brands

By 1993, competitors in ready-made shirts comprised both foreign and local firms. Gradual liberalization of the Indian economy created a wave of mergers and joint ventures in many industry sectors. In 1988, Madura Coats (now British-owned Coats Viyella) started importing the major international brand, Van Heusen, known for its style, elegance and fit.[4] After a few months, when a shirt factory opened in Bangalore, the Louis Philippe brand was launched alongside Van Heusen.

Together, the Van Heusen and Louis Philippe brands created a new market; prior to their entry, no manufacturer had offered such high quality shirts nor commanded such high prices. Over the years, they did a thorough job of educating consumers about ready-made shirts and arousing awareness in quality and brand positioning. Both Louis Philippe and Van Heusen were popular items with visiting Non-Resident Indians (NRIs), businessmen and foreign tourists.[5] However, even members of lower income-level groups were not deterred by the price or Louis Philippe's elegance from purchasing these shirts. Said one customer:

> It is impeccably stitched and fits beautifully. The shirt has a very crisp look and it's impressive to be in a Louis Philippe shirt while meeting a client. A Louis Philippe shirt will never lose its shine no matter how long one owns it. Therefore, it is better to invest in one or two shirts for special occasions than to buy many cheap shirts.

Once Louis Philippe and Van Heusen were established, Madura Coats introduced a new brand, "Allen Solly," as a relaxed alternative to formal wear. Each brand had a strong market position. Louis Philippe led in national brand market share of ready-made shirts, followed by Van Heusen and Double Bull.

Not all foreign entrants were successful. In 1993, Arrow was introduced by the Arvind (U.S.) Group following establishment of India's most modern shirt manufacturing plant in Bangalore (cost, Rs 13 crore). Unlike other producers, 75% of sales were dedicated for overseas markets, 25% for local sales. Arrow shirts were available at a few select franchise outlets; sales reportedly remained low despite several marketing strategies. Initially, Arrow spent large promotional sums educating prospective consumers on the "corporate" way of dressing – right collar, correct sleeve length but did not gain in popularity.

Similarly, in 1992, Pierre Cardin's market entry, with foreign-made shirts at prices significantly in excess of Van Heusen and Louis Philippe and attended with hype, media attention and paparazzi, was generally perceived as a huge flop. Explained Rusi Jasawallah of Double Bull:

---

[4] Coats Viyella India Ltd. was a leading composite textile mill, manufacturing fabrics, threads and accessories.
[5] NRIs were generally known as wealthy individuals; they had strong global networks and were desirable members of Indian society.

They were not successful because consumers are still price-conscious and some foreign companies have the wrong marketing strategy. Ready-made garments are such that you must know the pulse of the markets, where to locate, which bazaars to go into. Before launching a product, one needs to get a feel for the market. For example, the main buyers have been NRIs; due to the dollar's appreciation it's cheaper for them.

Industry experts also pointed to the use by some international brands of local fabric from the best Indian mills and local expertise to produce shirts. Thus, they said, there was no reason for consumers to prefer high-priced imported international brands over quality Indian ready-made shirts unless a distinct positioning could be achieved. They asserted that Pierre Cardin's failure could be attributed to this cause: similar quality and high prices in a fairly price elastic market.

In general, foreign brands offered limited product ranges; for example, in 1994, Arrow had just 15 shades and designs.

Upper Segment Opportunity

Sales of high priced, high quality ready-made shirts expanded significantly in the post-liberalization period; competing companies were launching new shirt ranges of every few months. By 1993, sales of premium shirts, estimated by industry observers at roughly one million p.a. (Rs 50 crore) were growing by 25% p.a. Meenakshi Iyer, head of sales and marketing at Sunray Textiles, a regional shirt brand, said industry experts failed to anticipate the rapid growth in demand and that conversion to ready-mades was much faster than expected. Explained Iyer:

> The premium market needs to be handled with more care. Its sanctity lies in its exclusivity. The moment you tamper with that exclusivity, the brand loses its credibility. Of the six to eight million buyers of ready-made shirts in the country, about 70% buy shirts that cost less than Rs 200 a piece; only 15% purchase more expensive shirts. Ultimately, the customer seeks a brand where the product matches the price. You cannot sustain a brand on just image; you need volumes to drive a brand. To generate volumes, other shirt manufacturers had to create larger distribution networks, which was expensive in terms of working capital and real estate costs. In addition, heavy investment was needed to create a brand image.

According to Dilshad Desai, client service controller at the advertising agency for Stripes, a regional shirt brand:

> The premium category has two distinct class of buyers; the businessman and the executive. The business class mostly buys a price tag. They would like to wear a shirt that is perceived as a Rs 1,000 shirt. If six months after launch, a new brand were launched at a higher price, that brand would become the reference brand. Executives and professionals, on the other hand are more likely to assess their purchase for product delivery against price.

Observers detected definite bias toward foreign brands in the premium segments inasmuch as they offered exclusivity, international style and quality. Consumers were increasingly attracted to the premium segment where competitors were creating new offers through style, fabric and price variations. However, local manufacturers had a cost advantage because they did not have to pay royalties like foreign brands. (See Table 2 for data on competing brands.)

Table 2: Partial Information on Competing Ready-made Shirt Brands

Brands	Image	Price (Rs)	Distribution Outlets	Regions
Low range				
Ambassador	Economic, but stylish	130–240	Distributors/ 3 multi-brand outlets*	North
Snow White	Low budget, slick	130–150	Distributors/ 7 multi-brand outlets	North
Stencil	Easily available	120–200	Distributors/ 10 multi-brand outlets	North
Medium range				
Zodiac	Casual elegance	150–250	Franchise agents	Regional
Vivaldi	Continental image/ upmarket	150–250	18 exclusive	North/ South
Dash	Youthful flair	150–200	Agents	South
Cambridge	Formal yet comfortable and reasonable	200–250	30 cities agents	North
Dunhill	Designer wear	200–250	20 satellite towns/ agents	South
Liberty	Industry pioneer, quality	200–600	Franchise/outlets	National
Premium range				
Louis Philippe	Designer wear, office wear	350–850	50 franchises; 400 dealers	National
Van Heusen	Premium lifestyle	250–750	40 franchises	National
Arrow	Classy	200–1,000	30 franchises	National
Double Bull	Party going, colorful fun	250–500	50 franchises; 3 outlets, 60+dealers and multi-brand outlets*	National
Charagh Din	Formal wear, party wear	250–1,000	1 outlet	National

*Multi-brand outlets were shirt and garment stores offering several brands.

Change in Retailing Culture

In the previous 25 years, Indian consumers' preferences shifted from tailor-made to ready-made shirts, the tailor's role was seriously diminished, especially in major cities. Tailored shirt making became mainly limited to rural areas. Income was a direct correlate of ready-made shirt purchases.

Retailers' attitudes followed consumer needs as greater consumer knowledge led purchasing attitudes through a radical change. Contemporary consumers wanted to see products freely; when they entered a shop, they believed themselves more competent than the shopkeeper to select the appropriate style. They also wanted guarantees and higher quality service; observers believed that only fully manufacturer backed products would survive in the market as the consumer movement strengthened. (See Table 3 for data on consumer shopping behavior; see Appendix for results of a consumer shirt study.)

Table 3: Comparison between Tailored and Ready-made Shirts (1993)

Income levels p.m. (Rs '000s)	3–5	5–10	10–15	15 upwards
Ready-mades (%)	74	85	91	94
Tailored (%)	26	15	9	6
No. of store visits p.a.	5.25	3.85	6.67	6.4
No. of shirts per visit	2	2.3	2.5	2.4
No. of shirts p.a.	10.5	9.03	15.56	15.36

Source: SSC&B Lintas Research Group.

Although 70% of ready-made shirt purchases were in major cities, observers believed that rural areas would also be potential markets in the long run as consumers switched from tailored to ready-made garments. Incomes were rising nationwide though with significant regional variation (Table 4).

Table 4: Regional Shares by Income Segment* (1993)

Region	Urban (%)			Rural (%)			Total (%)		
	L-LM†	M	UM-H	L-LM	M	UM-H	L-LM	M	UM-H
North	27.2	24.4	28.6	29.8	25.4	37.2	29.2	25	32.4
South	32.6	23.7	20.8	26.4	19.7	16.8	27.8	21.4	19
East	15.4	23.1	19.9	25.8	37.5	24.9	23.4	31.4	22.1
West	24.7	28.8	30.9	17.9	17.4	21.1	19.5	22.2	26.5

*L = lower income (Rs 18,000); LM = lower middle (Rs 18,001–36,000); M = middle (Rs 36,001–56,000); UM = upper middle (Rs 56,001–78,000); High = high (>Rs 78,000).
†To be interpreted as: of all lower and lower middle income urban families in India, 27.2% are in the north.

Competition

Thadani said it was difficult to assess the full nature and extent of competition because of the complicated industry structure and the unique regionalization of the Indian market. Foreign brands tended to consider each other as direct competitors; national local brands saw local and foreign entrants as direct competitors.

All national companies approached distribution in a roughly similar manner though the specific mix of systems (e.g., own outlets, dealer outlets, franchising, agents) might differ across competitors. Thus, all national competitors had offices in major cities (e.g., Bombay, Delhi, Calcutta, Madras, Bangalore). These cities acted as nuclei for operations that extended to surrounding cities. For example, from Bangalore, vendors sold to customers in Mangalore, Hyderabad; from Delhi, sales were made to Ludhiana, Chandigarh, Jaipur and other cities.

One unusual major competitor was Charagh Din, perceived as a high quality, premium priced brand. Despite having only a single retail outlet, in Bombay, it advertised nationally, was perceived as a national brand and attracted clients from all over India. Quality was integral to Charagh Din shirts, both formal wear and party shirts; executives boasted their shirts lasted six to eight years; growth averaged 25%–30% p.a. Industry observers said Charagh Din customers, mainly flashy businessmen (comparable to Double Bull's consumers), were intensely loyal. In addition to sales in India, Charagh Din had a large customer base outside India.

Double Bull

Called by some "an archetypal example of the Indian entrepreneur," in 1974, Thadani founded Nims Apparel with borrowed money. Previously a sales supervisor in a small garment company, Thadani rose through the ranks by diligence and grit until he established his own company comprising 12 sewing machines and a small team of tailors. Although he had no formal grounding in marketing, Thadani's gut-feel about consumers and the market seemed unerringly accurate. He made all major decisions and deals in creating and establishing the Double Bull brand name, derived from a combination of "Double Band" and "Bull Stripe" from Spain. Thadani was protective and emotional about the brand; he asserted that his three personally owned Double Bull shops in Bombay maintained his involvement with operations while reflecting his personal feelings and confidence in the brand.

Thadani's entry was driven by a desire to provide consumers with something different. He had ideas of new ways to manufacture shirts and introduce new fabrics (e.g., polyknit, stretch) then gaining popularity in India. He designed shirts using Egyptian mummies (front and back) and stitched a small icon to identify the shirts. Initially, he traveled around the country selling by the suitcase and being paid by cash; his first order was Rs 35,000. From the start, Double Bull shirts were advertised; an early medium was Stardust, a popular film magazine commanding nationwide readership.

By mid-1994, Double Bull shirts were sold in 120 shops in 50 cities; annual turnover was Rs 30 crores. Headquartered in the heart of Bombay, where Thadani made all major decisions in concert with director Mr. Rusi Jasawallah, Nims' 50 odd office staff handled quality inspection, orders, office administration and some marketing responsibilities. In addition to Double Bull shirts, Nims also sold unbranded formal-wear shirts through the same distribution outlets.

In the early 1990s, as Double Bull sales revenues increased, sales of designer shirts declined relative to formal shirts (Table 5). This performance corresponded to Thadani's sense of the market where, in an Indian desire for foreign products, formal shirt-wear was growing faster than designer-wear. In the late 1980s, formal wear accounted for only 10%–15% of ready-made shirts; this surged significantly in the early 1990s; Double Bull revenues reflected this trend.

Table 5: Double Bull Sales Revenues

	1989	1990	1991	1992	1993	1994
Total revenue (Rs crores)	20	22.5	24	27	28.5	30
Designer (%)	92	85	80	74	68	58
Formal (%)	8	15	20	26	32	41

Products

Thadani designed all Double Bull shirts; he also purchased all materials and negotiated with cloth producing mills for exclusives on certain materials. Double Bull was described as "a fancy, colorful, exhibitionist shirt made of silk / synthetic materials." Shirt styles were anathema to formal wearers yet commanded near fanatical loyalty among core consumers. Roughly 500 new designs catering to Indian tastes were introduced annually. Double Bull was the only brand providing larger sizes (up to 52-inch collar). Thadani claimed that every design advertised was a hit and that dealers relied on his opinion for next season's fashion.

Nims' production team comprised 900 employees plus 15 "fabricators." Fabricators were manufacturers, paid per shirt plus profit, that produced unfinished shirts from ratios, pieces, designs and cloth.[6] In total, they assembled 2,000 shirts per day. Nims' Bombay main office was responsible for quality control and allocating shirts for distribution.

Distribution

Thadani believed easy access to stores selling his products was critical. Hence, early on, after establishing three successful stores in prime commercial locations in Bombay, he quickly began franchising outlets. Nims had 50 franchisees nationwide. When new cities were approved for expansion, advertisements were placed in local newspapers to solicit prospective franchisees; franchisees typically operated a single store but there were some exceptions. To ensure bidder sincerity, Rs 2,500,000 application deposits were required. Each Double Bull franchise shop was called a "wagon." Wagons were strategically located in highly commercial areas in major cities; shop sizes ranged from 1,000 to 2,000 sq. ft. Typically, wagons had glass fronts and were emblazoned with the Double Bull logo. (See Exhibits 1A, 1B for a selection of competitive distribution outlets.)

Franchising was Nims' preferred geographic expansion method. Typically, franchise arrangements were permanent contracts that could be terminated on three months' notice. Franchisees owned premises and paid all overhead costs; they received a fixed percent of sales subject to guaranteed minima. Wagons received additional incentives: 5% turnover bonus if sales targets were met, 4% cash discount (versus 3% for dealers) and up to 4% of revenues toward advertising (versus 3% for dealers). In addition, they paid no freight charges for goods sent from Bombay. At the

---

[6] Margins ranged from 20% to 22% if Double Bull was the sole customer.

end of each fiscal year, franchisees could return unsold goods at 90% of the original ex-factory price. Nims disposed of these products in sales; franchisees received an agreed percent of the sales price plus 10% of costs to help liquidate stocks. Nims' arrangements differed slightly from Madura Coats (Van Heusen and Louis Philippe brands) that provided minimum guarantees on sale; 25% of retail sales was assured the franchisee.

In the early 1980s, since real estate was expensive for franchisees, common dealers and multi-brand outlets offering formal brands were Double Bull's major distribution channel. Dealers often approached Thadani but he was extremely selective; only one in four dealership proposals was granted. In the mid-1980s, Nims' policy became even more stringent; each dealer was thoroughly examined for commitment and sincerity. Thadani viewed dealers as an integral part of Nims' success; he portrayed the relationship as a "marriage." Nims acted as a wholesaler; it never sold to end-users except for its annual promotion (see next page). On appointment, a Double Bull dealer could place one free 45 cm advertisement in his chosen newspaper; typically the day of product launch. Thereafter, dealers could employ local advertising on a 50/50 basis, up to 3% of total turnover. All such advertising was first cleared by Nims. Nims enjoyed tremendous dealer loyalty because of high quality service and support. For example, if Nims made a design blunder, Thadani did not sell to dealers. Rather, the product was retailed during the sales (see below). Thadani was frequently approached by dealers wishing to sell overseas; he refused these offers by saying that Nims was too busy with the domestic market.

According to Nims' executives, the agency form of distribution was popular in northern India. The ten well-recognized agents carried major brands and exploited their portfolios to add other products; for example, the average Delhi agent carried 8 to 20 items. Agents managed various distribution tasks including collecting bills to assuring prompt payment, handling dealers, booking retailer orders, supplying retailers and generally acting as a conduit between manufacturer and retailer. However, neither Nims nor other national shirt brands used agents.

Advertising

Formal statistics on total advertising expenditures in the ready-made shirt industry were not available; however, industry experts believed expenditure distribution was, roughly: magazines (60%), local newspapers (25%), hoardings and kiosks (15%). In magazines used by ready-made shirt manufacturers, around 75% of advertising tended to be for ready-made garments. Double Bull conducted national advertising in magazines, typically identifying cities and dealers where its products could be purchased. During summer and winter, regional newspaper advertising contained dealers' names and locations (Exhibit 2).

Double Bull used new models in its advertisements; film producers often approached Thadani for models and actors and frequently Nims' models migrated to the thriving Indian film industry. For example, in the 1980s, Jackie Shroff became a superstar movie hero following appearances in Double Bull promotions; other prominent Double Bull alumni were Salman Khan, Mazhar Khan, Chunky Pandey and Rahul Roy. Models were hand-picked by Thadani to ensure their personality appealed to the typical Double Bull customer, described by one analyst as:

An extrovert, party-going creature in metros/mini-metros who is influenced by Hindi feature films. Usually a self-employed businessman, quite wealthy, with the tendency to project wealth. Not very sophisticated in terms of professional education, but successful in life.

Promotion

As an important element of promotion strategy, the Double Bull label was changed every year both to identify the shirt by season and to discourage counterfeiters; buttons, labels and packaging were changed seasonally. Thadani did not believe these changes confused customers; rather, it created customer appeal since they anticipated label changes.

The major promotion activity was the Double Bull annual sale, a highly advertised event spawning much consumer awareness and interest. Each year, the 5,000 to 6,000 sq. ft. rented space in Bombay attracted a huge crowd; queues often extended several miles as loyal customers traveled from nearby cities to purchase products. Merchandise was guaranteed to ensure maximum customer satisfaction and avoid package opening at the sale; confusion was avoided, costs saved and more customers could be served quickly. On average, 30,000 shirts were sold during the three-week period. Two other large sales were held (summer, winter) to ensure economies of scale from large scale shirt manufacture and dispose of inventory. Sale customers constituted a separate segment of "people who appreciate the shirts tremendously but can't afford the regular prices," since they deferred purchases until the sale.

Decisions

Thadani monitored changes in the ready-made shirt industry closely. He believed that by considering formal shirts more as an afterthought and not addressing formal shirt buyers in an aggressive manner he was missing out on a major opportunity. He envisaged a line of formal shirts made on imported machinery and marketed under the "Double Bull Formal" brand name. He took his ideas to SSC&B Lintas, a respected advertising agency and asked for recommendations.

The agency found itself in a dilemma. In-house research indicated that the Double Bull name and image did not correspond to the formal consumer. Rather, the typical formal-wearer (e.g., Louis Philippe, Arrow buyers) considered Double Bull too flashy and over designed. The agency believed formal customers could only be attracted by a brand with an international quality ready-made image.

The challenge for Nims Apparel seemed two-fold:

- To identify a name that actively distanced the new formal line from Double Bull to cater to target audience perceptions (e.g., Louis Philippe, Arrow buyers).
- To create an international image to fight foreign brands at their own game, without losing the "Made in India" label.

Thadani wondered if there were any other issues he had not considered.

Exhibit 1B: Exterior/Interior of Charagh Din Store in Bombay

Exhibit 1A: Exterior of Louis Philippe/Van Heusen Store in Bombay

Exhibit 2: Double Bull Advertisements

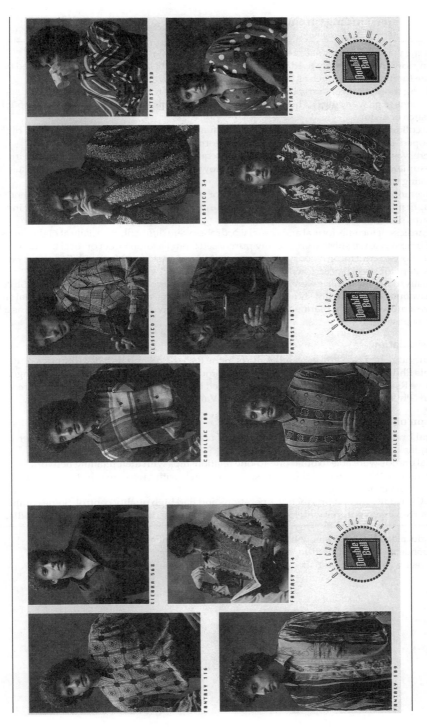

Appendix: Major Findings from Shirt Study (1992)*

- Income was positively related to propensity to buy ready-made shirts.
- Many low-income people used tailored shirts only. They believed tailored shirts offered better value for money inasmuch as they selected cloth design, material and fit.[†]
- Among those who generally bought ready-mades, tailored shirts were reserved for special occasions (e.g., weddings). They believed ready-made shirts did not provide good enough fit for such occasions.
- The collars of tailor-made shirts were inadequate; respondents said they were too high or drooped, giving a very "sorry" image when worn with a suit.
- There was no correlation between purchase frequency and income level. Mid to high income consumers generally purchased more shirts; low income tended to replacement versus augmenting the wardrobe.
- Lower income consumers tended to buy one or two shirts at a time; higher income generally bought more. Shirt buying of the lower income groups was more need-based; higher income groups purchased to own more shirts.
- Regardless of income, formal and casual wardrobes were different, especially at higher income.
- In Bombay, casual shirts were usually purchased from Fashion Street or local brand outlets.[1] Many low-to-mid income consumers possessed a few (one to four) Louis Philippe shirts which they kept for special occasions.
- Usually, daily wear shirts were bought locally; casuals were purchased from Fashion Street or Wearhouse; formals from showrooms such as Cambridge and Louis Philippe. Formal shirts were a more carefully planned purchase; customers traveled specially to purchase as a leisurely pastime.

Brand Assimilation

- Cambridge had maximum recall of shirts in the Rs 3–Rs 5K and Rs 5–Rs 10K price range.
- Louis Philippe and Charagh Din had top of mind recall in the Rs 10–Rs 15K price range.
- Above Rs 15K, Louis Philippe was the preferred brand with highest top of the mind recall.
- Louis Philippe had highest brand awareness; Van Heusen was second most popular.

Comparison of International vs. Local Brands

- Local brands were lower priced; they sold on average for Rs 400 and retain better profit margins.
- Local brands were able to build one-to-one relationships with their retailing network.
- International brands were limited to a specific clientele with a restricted shirt variety, attributed their own vision of image.
- MNCs usually owned production operations and had high quality control. Some companies preferred joint ventures with local firms to avoid labor issues, a sensitive matter in India.

*Study conducted in major cosmopolitan cities with 35 respondents.
[†]These respondents were not used for the remainder of the study.
[1]Fashion Street was the trendiest shopping outlet for modern-day wear in Bombay.

Case 14

Splendor Decorative Laminates India Ltd.: Evaluating Market Research Proposals and Selecting a Market Research Agency

Abraham Koshy
Indian Institute of Management, Ahmedabad

In November 1993, Mr. Vivek Chandra, marketing manager of Splendor Decorative Laminates (SDL) India Ltd. was carefully studying the market research proposals received from three well-known market research agencies. SDL, a newly established company, was in the process of setting up facilities to manufacture decorative laminates and would start trial production within 40 days; marketing activities had to commence by March 1994 at the latest. Chandra had to decide quickly on the agency to carry out the market research project. He was wondering what criteria he should use to evaluate the proposals and what process to follow to choose the agency.

৪০০৪

Decorative Laminates

Decorative laminates (often called *Formica* sheets, a popular brand name) had a wide range of applications in interior decoration in homes, offices, hospitals, railways, ships and aircraft. The more commonly known applications were in houses and offices as table-tops, exterior paneling in built-in storage compartments in kitchens and bedrooms, and for wall paneling.

Decorative laminates, also called high pressure laminates, were basically a form of plastic sheet. The basic raw materials for their manufacture were kraft paper, base paper (providing the design), tissue paper (partly providing the finish), phenol, formaldehyde, melamine and methanol. The manufacturing process was carried out in batches. First, phenol-formaldehyde resin and melamine-formaldehyde resin were applied on kraft paper, tissue paper and base paper through impregnation and dried in a hot air drying system. Several layers of these papers were put together depending on the thickness required. Stainless steel molds were placed on these sheets and a pressure of 3,000 tons applied at a high temperature. The completed laminated sheets were trimmed on all sides and the back of each sheet sanded to make rough for proper bonding. Finished sheets were transported in wooden crates.

Laminated sheet designs depended on the base paper designs. The more popular designs were wood finish, floral and plain color. The top finish depended on the type of stainless steel mold used; gloss finish and matte finish were the most common surfaces. Decorative laminates were available in various thickness, a major determinant of sheet price. Laminated sheets ranged in thickness from 0.6 mm to 1.5 mm; 0.8 mm and 1.0 mm were popular sizes. Prices for 0.6 mm laminated sheet ranged from Rs 300 to Rs 350; for 1.5 mm sheet from Rs 700 to Rs 800.

Various types of high pressure laminates could be made. In developed countries, exterior-grade, floor and solid color laminates were quite popular. However, in India, only decorative laminate sheets were available.

The Company

Splendor Decorative Laminates India Ltd. was established as a public limited company (1992) with an authorized capital of Rs 5 crore.[1] SDL was founded by Sunil Gupta, a young entrepreneur with several years' experience in decorative laminates. Gupta's long-term objective was to grow SDL into a major player in the national and international laminate market. From the start, he staffed SDL with professional managers despite modest goals of achieving Rs 20 crore revenues after three years. Manufacturing facilities were in western India.

The Market and Competition

The market for decorative laminates was estimated at 17 lakh sheets per month.[2] The thickest sheets comprised 30% of market demand, the medium range about 20%; 0.6 mm sheets 50%. In recent years the decorative laminate market grew at a compound annual growth rate of 14%. In the early 1970s, only five manufacturing units produced decorative laminates; by the early 1990s, over 20 establishments were involved. The most intense competition was in low thickness (0.6 mm) laminates, dubbed the "commercial" segment; several, mostly small, manufacturers served limited geographic markets, competing largely on price. In this slowly growing segment, such factors as quality and range appeared to have little influence on purchase decisions. The premium segment (0.8 mm and above; annual growth rate, 15%) attracted branded products from established companies (e.g., Formica, Decolam, Neoluxe, Sungloss, Rammica); new textures, designs and shades were frequently launched.

---

[1] 1 crore = 10 million.
[2] 1 lakh = 100,000.

Need for Market Research

Chandra, well aware of Gupta's vision for SDL, realized it should avoid the crowded commercial segment. However, he possessed little information on which to base a marketing strategy. He had no market data other than his and Gupta's prior knowledge and experience, some opinions from the trade and pure gut feel; he knew that proper planning required better data and decided to hire a professional market research agency to study the market.

As a first step, he wrote to four well-known market research firms inquiring their interest and willingness to conduct a study and requesting a detailed proposal. He sent a brief outlining the research objective and type of information needed. (See Exhibits 1A and 1B for copies of the letter and brief.)

Chandra received quick responses. One agency was fully committed and declined to respond; each of the others submitted a detailed proposal outlining methodology, sample, data collection approach and cost. (See Exhibits 2, 3 and 4 for extracts from the three proposals.) Chandra had some familiarity with the three responding agencies.

Agency A was a relatively new organization, less well-known than the others. It had conducted several studies, mostly for consumer products, but not a syndicated market research study. It had branches in three large cities and was establishing a reputation as a capable market research organization. It appeared to be seriously interested in the project; a senior executive contacted Chandra by telephone to ask for additional information. A few days after submitting the proposal, the same executive inquired about its status and indicated the quoted rate was negotiable. The type of study being planned would be medium-sized for this agency. He had no reservations about the agency's field-level organization, nor its capability to collect primary data from different parts of India.

Agency B was a well-known Indian agency with offices in several major cities. It had conducted many syndicated market research studies. The study would be a small- to medium-sized assignment for this agency. He received two telephone calls from a marketing research executive: one to report interest and confirm a proposal was being sent, the second to inquire if the proposal had been received.

Agency C was a reputable organization with several years' experience; it had ten branch offices in various Indian cities. It had conducted many market research projects and was experienced with syndicated studies. This agency evinced interest in the proposed study; a marketing research executive followed up on the proposal and indicated a willingness to meet with Chandra to clarify any issues.

The Decision

Chandra decided that the price of the study, though important, should not be the major concern. However, he was unclear what other criteria to use, and how he should decide which market research agency to select.

Exhibit 1A: Extract of Letter Sent to Market Research Agencies

To:

Dear Sir:

We introduce ourselves as a newly established company setting up facilities to manufacture and market high pressure plastic decorative laminates. Recently, we entered the capital market with an equity issue which was enthusiastically supported by investors. We are enclosing a brochure and prospectus of our company for your perusal. We are in the process of commissioning the plant and working out the details of our marketing strategies and plans.

The purpose of this letter is to inquire whether, as a professional market research agency, you would be willing and interested to provide us market research support for our marketing decisions. To enable you to assess our requirements better, as well as to arrive at a decision at your end, we are enclosing separately further details of the proposed market research.

After studying the enclosed materials, could you please write to us your clarifications on the following:

(a) Will you be interested in undertaking market research for our company?
(b) If yes, what is the intended methodology (which include the type of studies appropriate and sample size for each sub-study if planned)?
(c) What will be the cost of this research?
(d) Will it be possible for you to complete the study within a period of six to eight weeks from the time the study is commissioned?

Once we hear from you, we wish to have a mutually convenient time for a personal discussion wherein we can clarify several issues, work out the details and firm up further arrangements pertaining to this assignment.

Since we are in the process of planning, we require research inputs rather quickly and hence an immediate reply from you will be a good omen.

Thanking you in advance, we remain,

Exhibit 1B: Brief to Market Research Agencies Sent Along with Covering Letter

---

Requirements for Market Research

During the first phase of our operations, we plan to introduce various types of decorative laminates. The plan is to cover the domestic market first and then enter the export market within a short period of time.

The market for decorative laminates (Formica sheets) can be broadly classified into the "commercial" segment (thickness of 0.6 mm – poor quality and cheaply priced) and the "premium" segment (0.8 mm, 1.0 mm and 1.5 mm thicknesses – higher prices and better qualities). As a policy, we do not wish to operate in the "commercial" segment despite the fact that this segment constitutes the bulk of the market by volume. We would like to obtain an

---

image of a high quality, high profile marketing oriented company. The company has a proposal for certification of its quality systems to international standards ISO 9000 (Series).

The market for conventional laminates is highly competitive. The "commercial" segment is crowded with several players, many of whom are small operators deriving their competitive advantage by excise duty evasion and quality compromises. Even in the premium segment, competition is likely to become more intense – several new players are waiting to enter the field.

The objectives of the proposed market research are the following:

Primary objective: To obtain inputs for deciding critical elements of marketing strategy.

Elements of marketing strategy: Decisions to be based on marketing research inputs are:

a) *Market segments* to concentrate: Which segments to be focused as primary targets? How should the market be segmented (basis for segmenting)? For the above purpose we need to know how the market is segmented at present and what the characteristics of various segments are (e.g., types, sizes, geographic locations, intensity of competition, growth prospects).

b) *Product positioning decision*: How should we position our products and how should we differentiate our products from those of the competitors? For this purpose, we need to know what are the salient attributes that "consumers" and architects/interior decorators (major role players in the consumption chain) look for in decorative laminates? What "dimensions" they use to position various brands and what their perception/evaluation of the major competing brands is.

c) *Product related decisions*: such as quality level, range of designs and colors. We need to know what connotes "quality" from the consumers' point of view, the types of designs preferred by different segments, thickness of laminates preferred by different segments (for various application purposes).

d) *Distribution network and pricing decisions*: Trade practices relating to price, discount, incentives and payment terms.

e) *Advertisement, sales promotion and personal selling*: Decisions include: major "themes" to be advertised, media decisions, specific roles and objectives of advertisements, sales promotion schemes and sales representatives' work. For this purpose, we need to have a good understanding of buying behavior (major role players in product and brand choice, the role played by them in deciding product/brand), nature of competition (major players, their relative market share and size of operations including regional variations in the same), their major competitive strengths and weaknesses, and their image in the market.

Some of the major constituents of the consumption system for decorative laminates are: individual home builders, contractors, furniture makers, carpenters and interior decorators, designers and architects. The proposed market research, in addition to providing information on matters discussed earlier, should also contain a set of considered recommendations for marketing strategy.

Exhibit 2: Extract of the Proposal Submitted by Market Research Agency A

Introduction (industry background, product description, etc.)

Approach

The study is to be done in two phases.

A. Phase I will entail an extensive study of all the segments directly involved/associated with production and consumption of decorative laminates and will provide inputs for a proposed marketing strategy. Keep in mind the (general) marketing objectives of the company, strategic routes/options/choices will have to be developed. This phase will include a study of the current market scenario, market segmentation, "buyer" behavior and trade feedback in this industry.

Though this study will primarily address the "premium" segment of DL (0.8 mm, 1.0 mm and 1.5 mm thickness) we proposed that the study should also include assessment of choices available to the user of decorative laminates, i.e., particle board, synthwood (PVC foam board), prelaminated board, gypsum board.

This would be extremely helpful in providing an assessment of strength and weaknesses of SDL.

Methodology

A. *Target segments:* In this phase, six key segments will be studied:

1) Manufacturers of DL to understand the product, its types and applications. They would also provide inputs on choices/substitutes available for the product.
2) Furniture makers/shops to find out reasons and criteria for selecting DL over other substitutes and within DL, how grades, brands, designs are selected.
3) Carpenters would also provide information on the role of colors, designs, brand names, prices and thickness of laminate in the selection process and buying behavior/decision-making process of the end users.
4) Interior decorators/architects will throw light on primarily institutional and corporate use of laminates. Thus, feedback will be obtained only from those working primarily on commercial projects, like offices, shopping complexes.
5) Homeowners will be studied for product and brand awareness, selection and decision-making process when using laminates (i.e., buying behavior). These homeowners would belong to upper income (Rs 10,000/15,000 per month).
6) Finally, dealers shall provide information on trade channels and practices and enable a SWOT analysis of unbranded versus branded and then, of major brands.

In addition, the key persons from such organizations as the Federation of Indian Plywood/Panel Industry, Laminates Manufacturing Association should be contacted as "Industry Observers."

B. *Centers of conducting study/sample spread:* Despite the fact that "laminated" furniture is making inroads into the rural areas as well, this study will be confined to very urban metros and mini-metros. Each of the above mentioned "segments" will be studied in the five following towns:

Exhibit 2 (cont'd)

1) Bombay;
2) Delhi: Both these metros are trend setters and account for a major proportion of (manufacture and) consumption of furniture/laminates;
3) Madras: Again a major center for manufacturing of laminated and other types of furniture;
4) Ahmedabad;
5) Bangalore/Hyderabad: Large and fast growing mini-metros with increasing use and potential for use of laminates in both domestic and commercial sectors.

This sample spread will also enable us to adequately cover all the major geographical zones.

C. *Techniques of data collection:*

1) Data will be collected separately from each segment;
2) Leading manufacturers of DL will be contacted;
3) The furniture makers, carpenters, designers and dealers will be identified, basis volume of business conducted and minimum criterion will be set for each segment;
4) The homeowners will be those living in premium flats or bungalows only and within each sample town attempt will be made to cover at least five areas/zones;
5) A separate instrument/questionnaire will be designed for each segment to be studied. In-depth interviews will be conducted with the help of structured questionnaires only.

Scope/Objectives

This study will pertain to inputs for marketing decisions and the scope of this phase would be:

1) What the current market scenario with particular reference to 0.8 mm and 1.0 mm thickness laminates is:
   a) Market composition: Organized versus Unorganized and Commercial versus Domestic.
   b) Major players in the market and their shares.
   c) How the market is currently segmented
      - Geographically;
      - By types of laminates (glossy/matte);
      - By grades/thickness of laminates;
      - By application.
   d) Are the needs of each segment different?
   e) To what extent is the DL market "brand led" and/or "commodity" market?

2) What options/substitutes are available to the buyer/end users of DL
   a) What are the obvious substitutes of DL?
   b) How is one option selected over another (strength and weaknesses of each option)?
   c) Who are the decision makers?
   d) Who are the influencers?

3) In the organized sector what distinguishes one brand from another (in the trade segment)?

Exhibit 2 (cont'd)

4) What are the attributes of DL that each "segment" in our sample looks for – are they different between segments?

5) What is the role of the following attributes of DL in each sample segment?
   - Colors;
   - Finish/type;
   - Designs;
   - Branded versus Unbranded;
   - Thickness;
   - Durability;
   - Price;
   - Nature of application.

6) a) Level of awareness of brands of DL among end users;
   b) To what extent do they "ask" for brands;
   c) What "premiums" do brands command?

7) Can end users be segmented based on thickness of DL, that is "Are the 0.8 mm DL users different from 1.0 mm and 1.5 mm DL users?" If yes, what is the buyer profile for each segment.

8) Buyer behavior of end users:
   - Selection of the DL option;
   - Decision-making process;
   - Purchase process.

9) Feedback from DL trade with respect to:
   - Pricing;
   - Discounts/incentives;
   - Distribution system;
   - Payment terms;
   - Advertising and other support from companies.

Sampling – Phase 1

The study will be conducted in six segments in five towns for the following sample size:

Segments	All	Metros*	Mini-metros**	Segments	All	Metros*	Mini-metros**
DL manufacturers	10	6	4	Interior designers	35	25	10
Furniture makers	50	36	14	Dealers	75	60	15
Carpenters	35	25	10	Homeowners	120	80	40
				Total	325		

*Bombay, Delhi-Madras   **Ahmedabad, Bangalore and Hyderabad

Phase II

Segments   **All:** Furniture makers 30; Interior designers 20; Dealers 45; **Total** 95

Time frame: Total time required for Phase I will be seven weeks

Exhibit 2 (cont'd)

Schedule

Questionnaire design and pilot	2 weeks	Data analysis	2 weeks
Fieldwork	2 weeks	Report presentation	1 weeks
		Total	**7 weeks**

Unless done simultaneously Phase II will take another five weeks at the minimum.

Cost: The total cost of:

		Payment schedule	
Phase I will be	Rs 100,000	On completion of study	Rs 90,000
Phase II will be	Rs 25,000	On submission of report	Rs 35,000
Total cost	**Rs 125,000**	**Total**	**Rs 125,000**

Exhibit 3: Extract of the Proposal Submitted by Market Research Agency B

Introduction

(Background information, etc.)

Research Objectives

The key objectives of the study would be to understand the:

- Awareness level of various decorative laminates;
- Usership of different laminates;
- Areas of usage of various materials of interest;
- Comparative rating of decorative laminate vis-à-vis other substitute materials on select attributes;
- Image of various branded laminates – Formica, Decolam, Neoluxe, Sungloss and Rammica;
- Whether uses specific brand or not?
- Level of satisfaction with current brand of laminate;
- Factors considered for purchase of laminates;
- The decision-making process:
  - Who decides on the use?
  - To use and where to use?

  Past exposure to product concept:
  - Like and dislikes;
  - When Influencers?
  - Decision maker?
  - Likelihood of use.

In addition to the above mentioned objectives, we would secure data from industry experts regarding market size, last two years' growth rate, fast moving product segments, trade practices, etc.

Exhibit 3 (cont'd)

Method

1) We propose a study involving the following components:
   a) Group discussion   b) Depth interviews   c) Expert interviews

2) The user segments which would be covered in this study are:
   a) Individual home builders   b) Carpenters and furniture makers
   c) Interior decorators and architects

3) We would conduct group discussions among individual home builders while we would conduct in-depth interviews among the other user segments (carpenters, furniture makers, interior decorators and architects). In addition, we would be contacting ex-employees of some of the large retailers and wholesalers of laminates, etc. and conduct expert interviews. Information about the market size, growth rate, future, etc. would be obtained at this stage. The industry experts however would not be exposed to the Concept Cards.

4) We would conduct 10–15 expert interviews across the study centers. Metros and mini-metros are expected to be the major markets for the client's product. Hence, the coverage would be restricted to these markets. The study centers would be chosen in consultation with the client.

5) The sample size and the coverage proposed for this study are as follows:

   1. Group discussion:

	No. of cities	Individual home builders Number of groups		
		Male	Female	Total
Metro	2	2	1	3
Mini-metro	2	2	1	3
Total	4	4	2	6

   2. In-depth interviews.

Time and Cost

1) We would require a total of seven to eight weeks after the receipt of the Concept Cards to submit the topline findings to the client.

2) The total cost of conducting this study would be Rs 280,000. The terms of payment would be: 50% on commissioning of the study; 30% on completion of fieldwork; and 20% on submission of the report

(Other terms and conditions under which the company undertakes research were appended.)

Exhibit 4:   Extract of the Proposal Submitted by Market Research Agency C

Introduction

(Background information on the company, decisions, etc.)

Primary Objective

The primary objective of this study is to obtain inputs for deciding critical elements of marketing strategy viz.:

a) Basis of segmenting the market;

b) Market segments to concentrate;

c) Position to be adopted for the products;

d) Decisions related to product;

e) Distribution channel decisions;

f) Pricing decisions;

g) Decisions related to product promotions including advertisement and personal selling.

Information Areas

The objectives as spelt out, can be elaborated into specific information areas to be studied.

1) Information relating to the market:
   a) Type of different decorative laminates available in the market;
   b) The total production of decorative laminates by the organized sector;
   c) The number of major players in the market and the type of laminates they deal in;
   d) The projected growth of the market;
   e) The different uses of the laminates.

2) Information relating to the buyer/role influencer:
   a) Buyer profile;
   b) Major influencers in the purchase decision;
   c) Role of the major influencers;
   d) Major attributes sought by buyer/role influencers;
   e) Image in the minds of the influencers towards the different brands existing in the market;
   f) Perception of role influencer towards quality of the product.

3) Information relating to the product:
   a) Various application areas;
   b) Thickness of laminates preferred for each application area;
   c) Patterns/designs preferred for each application area;
   d) Colors sought for each application purpose.

4) Information relating to the dealer:
   a) Distribution channel employed by different manufacturers;
   b) Trade practices followed by different dealers specifically relating to
      - Price;
      - Discounts;
      - Incentives and dealer promotion schemes; and
      - Payment terms.

Exhibit 4 (cont'd)

c) Dealer profile relating to turnover of dealers; number of brands dealing in;
d) Supply and order procedures practiced and desired.

Methodology

We propose to conduct a two-stage research for the above study:
i) Secondary research   ii) Primary research

Secondary research. This will involve data collection from secondary sources such as publications, journals and company literature. This will facilitate the estimation of the market comprising the organized sector.

Primary research. This part of the study involves data collection from the target group. A three-phase study is proposed.

Phase I – preliminary research. To begin with, it is proposed to conduct in-depth interviews among a few interior decorators and carpenters to obtain input so as to facilitate the designing of the questionnaire. These interviews, would be conducted in Bombay and will be carried out using a discussion guide by experienced qualitative researchers. These interviews would provide the specific attributes which are desired in the survey products as well as provide insight into what "quality of laminates" means to the consumer/influencers.

Phase II – retail study. A quantitative survey will be undertaken among a sample set of retailers. The interviews will be carried out using structured questionnaires as an instrument of data collection. The sample size and spread is elaborated later.

Phase III – expert opinion sample survey. It is proposed to undertake a quantitative survey among a sample set of experts or role influencers. The target respondents would be: interior decorators, furniture makers/carpenters, and architects/home builders/contractors.

These interviews will be conducted using a semi-structured questionnaire which will have the flexibility to incorporate the varied opinions of the target respondents. The sample spread and size is elaborated in the following pages.

Sample spread and size. Given on the next page, are two options of sample spread and size for the survey. The first option proposes a study only among the six major metros. We work on the presumption that these towns account for a majority of the market and are thereby fairly representative of the laminate market.

The second option is more intensive and covers 12 metro towns. The option encompasses also those towns which are growing and may become major markets in the near future.

Advertising message. The sample survey that would be undertaken among the retailers and role influencers would reveal the positions occupied by the different brands existing in the market. It would also indicate the vacant positions. Additional information on specific roles played by influencers and dealers would help focus on the target group to whom the communication has to be addressed.

Exhibit 4 (cont'd)

Option 1

Cities	No. of dealers	Segments		
		Interior decorators	Furniture makers/ carpenters	Builders/architects/ contractors
Bombay	40	15	20	15
Delhi	40	15	20	15
Calcutta	30	10	15	10
Madras	30	10	15	10
Bangalore	30	10	15	10
Hyderabad	30	10	15	15
Total	200	70	100	75

Option 2

Cities	No. of dealers	Segments		
		Interior decorators	Furniture makers/ carpenters	Builders/architects/ contractors
Bombay	30	12	15	10
Delhi	30	12	15	10
Calcutta	20	8	10	8
Madras	20	8	10	8
Bangalore	20	8	10	10
Hyderabad	20	8	10	10
Kanpur	10	5	10	5
Lucknow	10	5	10	5
Chandigarh	10	5	10	5
Ahmedabad	10	5	10	5
Pune	10	5	10	5
Jaipur	10	5	10	5
Total	200	86	130	86

Output

The data collected after the fieldwork from our two sets of studies will be analyzed and a set of conclusions and recommendations drawn following specific lines, each of which will be obtained from the various studies proposed. In the list on page 258, reference to the codes are

Exhibit 4 (cont'd)

as follows: SR — Secondary Research; EXR — Exploratory Research; DS — Dealer Study; EOS — Expert Opinion Study; and PAA — Press Advertisement Audit.

1) Basis of segmentation of decorative laminate market – SR
2) Identification of existing market segments – SR/DS
3) Characteristic of each segment – DS/EOS
4) Selection of a specific segment for BDL – DS/EOS
5) Attributes considered during purchase of laminates – EXR
6) Specific platform on which the brands are positioned – EXR/DS/EOS/PAA
7) Identifying existing position of different brands – DS/EOS
8) Evaluation of different brands existing in the market – DS/EOS
9) Meaning of the word quality as it applies to decorative laminates – EOS/EXR
10) Identification of application areas – DS/EOS
11) Patterns preferred for each such area – DS/EOS
12) Thickness preferred for each areas – DS/EOS
13) Identification of specific patterns/thickness for BDL – EOS
14) Specification of quality levels for BDL – EOS
15) Trade practices followed by retailer viz. – DS:
    - Price changes
    - Incentives
    - Discounts
    - Payment terms
16) Major themes that appear in existing advertisements – PAA
17) Total number of insertions and cost of advertisement appearing in the press – PAA
18) Point of purchase promotions by existing manufacturers – DS
19) Sale promotion schemes – DS

Time: The total time required for the study would be eight weeks from the date of commissioning the study to presentation of the research findings and receipt of first installment; for either Option 1 or Option 2.

Cost: The total cost for the study would be as follows:
- Option 1 – Rs 175,000
- Option 2 – Rs 215,000

Terms of payment: The terms of payment for either option would be as follows:
- 40% on commissioning the study
- 40% on completion of field work
- 20% on presentation of report

Validity: The above time and cost estimates will be valid for a period of 75 days from the date of submission of this proposal. All other terms and conditions will be as per the guidelines set by the MRSI.

Map of Indonesia

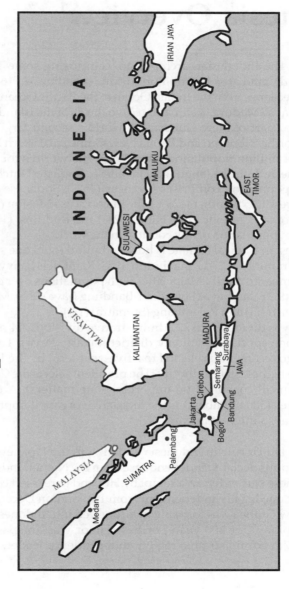

Indonesia Overview[1]

Background. The Indonesian archipelago, comprising some 13,700 islands (about 6,000 inhabited), land area 1.92 million sq. km., coastline 54,716 kilometers is located on the major sea lanes from the Indian Ocean to the Pacific Ocean. Its five major islands are Sumatra, Java/Madura, Kalimantan (two thirds of the island of Borneo), Sulawesi and Irian Jaya (part of New Guinea, the world's second largest island); it borders Malaysia in northern Borneo and Papua New Guinea in eastern New Guinea. Indonesia has a 194.4 million population (Dec. 1995), the world's fourth largest, speaking Bahasa Indonesia (official language), Javanese, English, Dutch and more than 550 dialects. The population comprises Javanese (45%), Sudanese (14%), coastal Malay (7.5%), Madurese (7.5%), others (26%); the majority are Muslim (87%), others are Protestant (6%), Roman Catholic (3%), Hindu (2%) and Buddhist (1%); Indonesia has the largest Muslim population of any country in the world.

The Indonesian tropical climate is hot and humid (only one season); average daily temperatures minimum 23°C, maximum 31°C. Rainfall is heavy during the monsoon season (November to April). Major cities with populations over one million (1995) are: Jakarta (Java) (9.2), Surabaya (Java) (2.7), Bandung (Java) (2.3), Medan (Sumatra) (1.9), Semarang (Java) (1.3) and Palembang (Sumatra) (1.4).

The country is divided into 27 administrative divisions, 24 provinces, two special regions and one special capital city district (Jakarta Raya). The president (head of country and government) is elected to a five-year term by the People's Consultative Assembly, the highest state authority. The president selects the Cabinet and a Supreme Advisory Council (consulted on important state matters). A unicameral House of Representatives (500 members) is the legislative organ; it approves all laws but the president has absolute veto power.

Political. The Dutch rule in Indonesia ended with the Japanese occupation in 1942. Nationalist groups declared independence from the Netherlands in 1945 immediately after the Japanese surrender; an attempt by Holland to reassert colonial rule failed and Indonesia became legally independent from Holland on December 27, 1949. Dutch-held West New Guinea was formally incorporated into Indonesia in 1969; the former Portuguese colony (for 400 years) of East Timor was annexed in 1976 to become Indonesia's 27th administrative region. Independence leader, Dr. Sukarno, elected

---

[1] Republic of Indonesia.

president in late 1945, served as head of state until 1966 when a coup brought General Suharto to power. Suharto was elected president in 1967 and has served five successive five-year terms; in 1998, he was re-elected to his seventh consecutive term. In May 1998, as the result of a faltering economy and social unrest, Suharto resigned. Although incoming President Habibie promised new elections, since he was a close associate of Suharto, Indonesia's political future remained unclear.

Sovereignty over East Timor continues to be disputed with Portugal and is still not recognized by the United Nations. Rebel guerrilla groups resist Indonesian rule and continue to create international embarrassment for the Indonesian government. Indonesia also has territorial disputes with Malaysia (over two islands) and China (Spratly islands); the Natuna gas field (one of the world's largest) is being developed by Indonesia but the territory is also claimed by China.

Social. As 80% of the Indonesian population eats rice, rice cultivation must keep pace with population growth (1994, 1.7%) to maintain self-sufficiency. Once the world's largest rice importer (1984/85), Indonesia is now self-sufficient (1994: 46 million tons produced). The government's current five-year plan is to create at least 500,000 hectares of new rice land by end 1999.

Regional population distribution is very unbalanced; Java, Madura and Bali islands account for about 62% on 7% of total land area. An inter-island transmigration policy aims to open up new land on outer islands by providing basic infrastructure. Income inequality is a cause for social unrest and racial hostility; 3% (mostly ethnic Chinese) of the population control 70% of the wealth. Qualified personnel in hospitals has been increasing, but is largely insufficient; Indonesia has one doctor per 6,786 people. Annual per capita spending on pharmaceuticals (1994) was only US$3.50.

Economy. Indonesia is a member of the United Nations (UN), World Bank (WB), International Monetary Fund (IMF), World Trade Organization (WTO), Organization of Petroleum Exporting Countries (OPEC), Asian Development Bank (ADB) and Association of Southeast Asian Nations (ASEAN). Indonesia is a mixed economy with some central planning but recent emphasis is on deregulation and privatization. Indonesia has extensive natural resources (e.g., oil production of 586 million barrels [1995], over 50% for export; 38% of world natural gas stock [1995]); per capita GNP is only US$880 (1994). On average, 26% of government expenditure pays foreign debt service (1995 foreign debt, US$88 billion; foreign exchange reserves [early 1995], US$13.2 billion). However, Indonesia's real GDP growth (1985–92, 6%) is impressive. Major export destinations (1994) are: Japan (27.4%), U.S. (14.6%), Singapore (10.1%). Major import origins (1994) are: Japan (24.2%), U.S. (11.2%), Germany (7.7%).

Agriculture (including forestry, fishing) accounts for 17% GDP; it employs over 45% of the labor force. Industrial output, based on availability of several natural resources (e.g., oil, natural gas, timber, metal, coal), accounts for 41.5% GDP. Oil products and natural gas dominate exports (1994, 51% total export earnings); the Natuna natural gas field, one of the world's largest fields (estimated reserves, 45 trillion cu. ft.), will be exploited by Exxon and Pertamina (state oil company). To promote tourism, President Suharto declared 1993–2000 a " Visit Indonesia Decade." In 1994, 3.9 million arrivals generated US$4 billion revenues; from 1986 to 1993, tourism's average growth rate was over 20% p.a.

Foreign aid investments are decreasing but foreign direct investments (FDI) are increasing. In 1993, total FDI was US$8 billion; in 1994, US$24 billion (1994 domestic investment was about US$24 billion). In the first four months of 1995 FDI approvals were US$15.6 billion. Foreign companies may hold 100% equity (deregulated 1994) in most Indonesian companies without restrictions; they may invest in strategic sectors such as infrastructure. Tax rates were reduced (corporate tax rate, 30%) and incentives offered for investment in remote regions.

Ethnic Chinese conglomerates dominate the corporate landscape but in the last five years indigenous companies (Pribumi) have begun to flourish as the result of privatization, deregulation, foreign investment and infrastructure development (e.g., Pribumi control the telecommunications sector); some Pribumi are owned by the Suharto family or those with close ties. At the time of President Suharto's downfall, Chinese were targets of riots and reprisals; many left the country.

Bank Indonesia (BI) (central bank) and five large state banks form the banking system's foundation. BI is the sole issuer of currency, holds official reserves and supervises and regulates all financial institutions except insurance companies. BI conducts normal central bank functions and establishes various types of joint-venture financial institutions (e.g., insurance company, venture-capital finance company, two private development finance companies). The five state banks are: Bank Rakyat Indonesia (smallholder agriculture, rural development); Bank Bumi Daya (estate agriculture, forestry); Bank Negara Indonesia 1946 (industry); Bank Dagang Negara (mining); Bank Ekspor–Impor Indonesia (export product producers); all state banks deal in foreign exchange. At end 1993, the state banks accounted for 43% of all bank funds, 49% of outstanding credit; in addition, 158 private national banks (2,926 branches) and 39 foreign banks (75 branches) were in operation.

In March 1996, the Indonesian currency (the rupiah) was valued at US$1 = 2,340 rupiah; rising local interest rates held rupiah depreciation below 5% (1994, 2% to 3%, 1995, 4% to 5% because of a widening current account deficit). However, in summer 1997, Indonesia fell victim to the Asian financial crisis. To help the country, US$40 billion in assistance was pledged (including a US$23 billion IMF bailout package). In 1997, the rupiah lost 55% of its value against the U.S. dollar. Moody's downgraded Indonesia's debt (together with Thailand and South Korea) to junk-bond status in fall 1997. In 1998, 40% of the population were living below the poverty line and the situation was worsening.

Indosat was the first state-owned international telephone company to list simultaneously both domestically (Jakarta) and in New York; it raised over US$1.2 billion, one of Asia's largest stock flotations. More privatizations are expected; 190 companies, including utilities, oil companies, hotels, airlines, mining and industrial firms are on the waiting list. Market capitalization of the Jakarta Stock Exchange's 200 listed companies (1995) (up from under 30, 1990) exceeds US$50 billion.

Infrastructure. Indonesia has 378,000 kilometers of highways (1995) (about 46% paved), 6,458 kilometers of railways (1993), 21,579 kilometers of inland waterways and six airlines. Since Indonesia is an archipelago, sea transport linking the islands is of primary importance. In 1984, a major inter-island development scheme was started; in 1991, the merchant marine, controlled by four state-run port authorities, managed a merchant fleet of 5,490 ships carrying 36 million tons of cargo.

In 1994, less than 5% of homes had a telephone. Several high priority major telecommunication projects are in progress, including the installation of Indonesia's second digital telephone system (1.4 million new lines, a 800-kilometer digital microwave link in central Sumatra.) An estimated US$10.3 billion in official development funds were devoted to transportation and communications infrastructure from 1989 to 1994.

Statistics*	June 1991	June 1997	Statistics*	June 1991	June 1997
Per capita GNP	US$550	US$655	Pop. growth	1.8%	1.6%
GDP growth	7.0%	7.8%	Infant mortality / 1,000	65	66
Savings (GNP)	n/a	37%	Life expectancy (yrs)	n/a	63
Inflation (CPI)	9.1%	5.1%	Literacy rate	74.1%	84.4%
Foreign debt			People per tel.	193	47.7
(in billion)	US$65.7	US$107.8	People per doctor	8,010	6,786
Pop. (million)	182.5	194.4	People per TV	n/a	8.0
Urban pop. (%)	31%**	34%	Calorie intake (cals)	n/a	2,750

*Secured from *Asiaweek*.
**From "A report of the INSEAD Euro-Asia Centre," J. Probert (Sept. 1994), INSEAD.

Case 15

PT Indocipta Pangan Makmur: Snack Food Manufacturing Company

Manuel S. Lizardo, Jr., Buoy Ngadimun
Asian Institute of Management, Makati, the Philippines

In late 1990, Buoy Ngadimun, marketing manager at PT Indocipta Pangan Makmur (IPM) Snack Food Manufacturing Company was reviewing PT IPM's 1990 performance and preparing its 1991 budget. His report would affect spending priorities and marketing efforts and several issues had to be addressed.

PT IPM's modern snack food sales amounted to Rp 36 billion; gross profit margins were 35%. The firm's number one seller was the "Chiki" snack line; consumers readily identified "Chiki" by brand name. However, despite PT IPM's strong industry position, Buoy realized it needed to meet competitive threats, sustain sales growth and expand market share. He contemplated repositioning "Chiki" but was concerned that such a move might effect the brand's strong market position. He wondered whether other options, such as focusing more effort on the company's other products, could be developed.

ဆဎၶ

PT IPM

PT IPM was established in 1984 to form the snacks and confectioneries division of the Indofood Group, Indonesia's leading packaged food manufacturer. Indofood was involved in the production of 140 food items including noodles, baby food, snacks, beverages, and easy-to-cook meals. In addition, it had operations in Malaysia to cater to the Peninsular Malaysia, Singapore and Brunei markets; it also exported products to other parts of the world (e.g., Hong Kong, Holland, U.S., Mexico, Egypt, Australia). Its California-based subsidiary, Indofood USA, marketed products in the U.S.

From 1988 to 1990, PT IPM sales growth (tons) (62.6% p.a.) was higher than the industry (Table 1). Its corporate philosophy emphasized responding to consumer needs and increasing sales volume through an effective marketing system. PT IPM's short-term goal was to maintain dominance of the children's segment and successfully penetrate the teenage and adult markets. For the medium term, it aimed to help increase the modern snack market vis-à-vis traditional types. PT IPM's long-term target was to achieve market leadership in all market segments.

Table 1:   Modern Snack Sales and PT IPM's Share of the Snack Food Market (tons), 1988–90

	1988	1989	1990
Modern snack industry sales	3,005.6	3,426.4	5,400.0
Extrusion	2,164.0	2,227.2	2,701.0
Pellets	541.0	754.0	1,889.0
Solid Chips	300.6	445.2	210.0
PT IPM sales	1,159.2	1,390.0	2,900.0
Extrusion	1,019.2	1,121.3	2,069.5
Pellets	–	116.2	575.5
Solid Chips	140.0	152.5	255.0

Organization

The general manager oversaw all company operations. (See Figure 1 for organization chart.) Personnel policies emphasized equitable compensation, reward for exemplary work, teamwork, adequate training, employee welfare and individual development. PT IPM attempted to create an atmosphere conducive to productivity by cultivation of a harmonious working relationship among company employees, participative management, informal communication to develop teamwork, good work, discipline, synchronization of individual and company goals and regular performance appraisals.

Product Profile

PT IPM produced Extrusion, Solid Chip, and Pellet dry snack products. "Chiki," its biggest seller, was an Extrusion product, packed in 18-gram and 85-gram sachets with three flavors – chocolate, chicken and cheese. The "Chiki" product line also included savories, sweet confectioneries, jellies and chocolate-coated snacks; its target market was 7- to 12-year-old children. "Chiki" was launched in 1984; its almost instant success prompted other companies to manufacture modern snack foods. As a result of the ensuing price war, PT IPM introduced another brand, "Yoyo," to compete with lower-priced brands (e.g., "Maru"); nevertheless, it was priced higher than other competitors (e.g., "Bollo"). PT IPM tried to expand further in the Extrusion category, but its new product, "Chirly," performed less well than the other brands.

Figure 1: PT IPM Organization Chart

PT IPM's line of Solid Chip products offered four varieties: banana, cassava, sweet cassava and potato. However, only "Chitato" potato chips, available in natural, beef barbecue and chicken flavors was successful. This product was marketed for the young, teenage market segment.

In 1989, PT IPM began marketing its "Jetz" product, packed in 18-gram sachets and 85-gram cans, in the Pellet category. It offered additional choices with spicy chicken, paprika, paradiso onion and cheese onion flavors. The 22- to 45-year-old market segment was targeted for this product.

The Company and the Industry

In 1990, Indonesia's snack food industry had monthly sales close to Rp 30 billion; 15% comprised sales of modern, manufactured snacks, the majority was traditional, homemade snacks. However, from 1984 to 1989, sales of modern snacks increased by 750%. In 1990, the market for modern snacks increased faster than traditional snacks in tons sold, total volume consumed and per capita consumption. The rate of increase in per capita consumption of traditional snacks declined in 1990 to 8% from 19% in 1989; by contrast, average per capita consumption of modern snacks increased by 58% in 1990, compared to 14% in the preceding year (Table 2).

Table 2:   Snack Food Consumptions by Category and Weight (1988–90)

Market size	1988	1989	1990
Traditional snacks			
Tonnage	29,761.3	35,416.0	38,250.0
Volume (MIO packs)	1,653.4	1,967.6	2,125.0
Value (MIO packs)	238,090.4	283,328.0	306,000.0
Per capita consumption (grams/population)	165.3	196.7	212.5
% change	–	+19	+8
Modern snacks			
Market size	**1988**	**1989**	**1990**
Tonnage	3005.6	3426.4	5,400.0
Volume (MIO packs)	166.9	190.4	300.0
Value (MIO RP)	30,056.0	34,264.0	54,000.0
Per capita consumption	16.7	19.0	30.0
% change	–	+14	+58

The Market

Indonesians were generally educated and choosy; they searched for quality among the many products that competed intensely for market share. Consumers demanded benefits from products and companies sponsored promotional schemes since preferences were easily influenced by attractive packaging and promotional campaigns.

In 1990, Indonesia's population was 180 million. From 1980 to 1989, population growth was 2.13% p.a.; five-year projections were 2.10% to 2.13%. About 60% of the total population was concentrated in Java, population density – 753 persons per sq. km.; through family planning and government transmigration programs, Javian density was expected to decrease. Java's urban population comprised 26% of the national population. By 2000, Indonesia's urban population was expected to reach 30% of the total population, as increasing numbers of people migrated to urban centers; this could be higher if high economic growth was maintained. Currently, 30% of the population lived in rural areas, mostly at subsistence levels; population growth rate was five times slower than in urban areas.

Consumer Profile

The Indonesian modern snack food market was generally segmented among children, teenagers and adults. Children were most interested in new products, attractive packaging and the products' entertainment value. However, adults (especially mothers) influenced the buying decision. Older segments were more traditional and mature in the values they sought; products were compared on the basis of physical attributes, natural packaging, product affordability and familiarity.

In August 1990, PT IPM conducted a Usage, Attitude, and Image Survey (UAI); respondents included consumers of Extrusion Snacks (322), Pellets (246), and Solid Chips (238). Findings included:

- Snacks were eaten to complement other activities (e.g., watching television, reading books);
- Snack consumption occurred mostly indoors;
- Criteria for snack choice included quality (e.g., taste, shape, crispiness), availability and affordability;
- Children were the biggest snack consumers, followed by teenagers and then by mothers. Snacks were bought at least once a week;
- Overall, snacks were bought on average two sachets at a time. Extrusion snacks were the top sellers;
- Consumers spent on average Rp 791 per purchase for snacks. Solid Chips were most expensive, Rp 977; Pellets and Extrusion Snacks, Rp 788 and Rp 619 respectively. Consumers spent the most on snacks priced below Rp 200.

Product Categories

Two general categories of snacks were recognized in Indonesia, wet and dry:

Wet snacks. Housewives cooked and prepared wet snacks mainly for family consumption. Sold by hawkers, wet snacks included fried bananas, pancakes, fried cassava and many others. Each region of the country had a wet snack popular only within that area.

Dry snacks. Dry light snacks were both traditional and modern. Traditional snacks were usually homemade, conventionally shaped and sold in transparent plastic packaging. Products were generally made from a starchy base with three flavors – salty, sweet, and spicy. Numerous brands were available and each geographic region was identified with a specific traditional snack. Conversely, modern snacks were manufactured in large volumes and distinguished from other snack types by modern packaging; they were available in single packs.

Modern snacks were classified into three groups according to ingredients. Extrusion (or Extrudat) snacks were made of corn, rice and wheat flour; ingredients were mixed together and poured into a die for puff-drying. Pellets were made of natural food flavors, starch and water; manufactured through forming and drying, they were prepared for eating through frying and baking. The main ingredients of Solid Chips, were tuber crops and fruits; ingredients were fried and sold in coated form.

Product Style

Packaging was crucial for building product image. Attractive and unique packaging contributed by conveying product identity to consumers. Snack pack sizes were small, medium and large; small 20-gram packages were common in the industry. Indonesian consumers preferred a variety of snack food flavors. Manufacturers produced snacks with the "Indonesian taste" categorized according to geographic area of origin. The West region produced snacks with chocolate and "rendang" (beef) flavors, the Central region with chicken flavor and the East region with chocolate and chicken flavors.

Pricing

The price of PT IPM's products ranged from Rp 25 to Rp 750. Most Solid Chip products were expensive but Extrusion and Pellet snacks sold for Rp 250 at the most. (See Table 3A for PT IPM price ranges; see Table 3B for industry pricing structure.)

Table 3A: Price Ranges of PT IPM and Competitor Products

Market segment	Product		Price range (Rp)
Children (7–12 years old)	'Chiki' Balls 'Chirly' 'Yoyo' Balls	'Maru' 'Bollo' Balls	25–250
Teenagers (13–21 years old) Adults (22–45 years old)	Potato Chips 'Jetz' 'Chitato' (55 grams) Banana Chips	'Ultra' Chips Cassava Chips Sweet Potato	275–750

Table 3B: Industrial Pricing Structure

Sales to distributors	Rp 100	Distributor margin	15%
Sales to wholesalers	Rp 115	Wholesaler margin	5%
Sales to retailers	Rp 120	Retailer margin	20%
Sales to customers	Rp 140		

Competition

Indonesia's modern snack food industry comprised six companies but two were dominant: PT IPM and PT Rasa Murni Utama. These companies set prices for the industry.

PT Rasa Murni Utama's major brands were "Taro" and "Gaza." "Taro," a Pellet Chips snack, whose main ingredients were wheat flour and tapioca starch, was the second most popular brand in the children's segment. "Taro" was available in barbecue and seaweed flavors; it retailed for Rp 200. Its popularity was attributed to its popular product type and unique flavor (potato barbecue). Moreover, unlike the most popular brand, "Chiki," it did not cause throat irritation.

No specific modern snack brand dominated the teenager segment. PT Mamee Pacific Buana promoted its "Smax" brand for this segment, but it did not perform as well as in the children segment. PT Cipta Rasa Primatama and PT Radiance Food concentrated on the children and teenager segments. However, these companies lacked sufficient distribution and advertising and promotional support to gain significant market share. Sumindo Food Company was a new entrant; its potato tube snack, launched in 1990 with strong promotional support, made the product popular in East Java where the company was located.

Most of the modern snack food companies focused on attracting the children segment. Product positioning was based on attributes such as taste (Table 4). Traditional snacks appealed mostly to the adult market. These snack types were usually bought in bulk in the regions. Traditional snacks maintained their appeal to the older generation, largely because they were homemade, and their conventional packaging provided an image of freshness.

Table 4: Market Positioning of Selected Snack Products in the Industry

Brand	Based on product attributes		
	Flavors	Target market	Snack type
Chiki	chocolate, chicken, cheese	Children	Extrusion
Chitato	starchy, beef barbecue, chicken	Adults	Solid Chip
Jetz	spicy chicken, paradiso onion, paprika, cheese onion	Teenagers	Pellets
Taro	barbecue, seaweed	Children	Pellet sheet
'Smax'	chicken, cheese, cuttlefish	Children	Rice base
Based on prices (Rp)			
High (500–800)	Medium (275–800)	Low (25–250)	
Imported snacks	Smax (big), Taro (big)	Chiki, Smax (small), Tato (small), Jetz, Chitato	

Distribution

Since Indonesians were impulsive snack food buyers, product availability was a key success factor. Two modern distribution systems were present in Indonesia, the conventional distributor system and the wholesaler system.

The distributor system. In this system, manufacturers sold to distributors who maintained their own warehouses in different regions of the country; distributors received a 10% to 13% mark-up. Some manufacturers gave distributors promotional and logistics support; credit terms ranged from one to two months. (Consignment selling was not practiced.) These regional distributors delivered goods to branches in big cities (e.g., Jakarta, Bogor, Bandung, Cirebon). Local offices took orders, assisted in promotions and developed marketing strategies for the localities. Local branches had large warehouses and maintained two-week stock levels. Local distributors shipped products to wholesalers in their regions. Wholesalers had direct contact with and serviced retailers. In addition, they were instrumental in supplying manufacturers with feedback and vital market information. Some distributors bypassed wholesalers and delivered directly to retailers.

The wholesaler system. Most traditional snack producers, largely family-owned businesses, used the wholesaler system. Relying on customer loyalty, business was conducted through wholesalers via telephone and personal contacts. Producers depended heavily on good relations with traders and were strong in their native regions. Scope of operations was typically limited regionally and for established traditional products. Speedy distribution of products through the wholesale system assured product freshness, a crucial issue since most traditional snack items were highly perishable. Wholesalers were responsible for 60% of total industry sales but few modern snack companies were capable of distributing their products through wholesalers. For modern snack manufacturers, only the two leading brands were attractive to wholesalers; other companies gave less margin than the market leaders.

Indonesia comprised 150,000 potential retail outlets; 80,000 (53%) reached through distributors and wholesalers. These outlets comprised three types: 350 supermarkets; P&D grocery shops, smaller than supermarkets; and the "Toko" or "Warung," small neighborhood stores. Retailers sold traditional and modern snacks.

In total, 55 wholesale distributors handled PT IPM products in Indonesian regions; 19 in the West (Sumatra); eight in the Central (Central Java, West Java, and Kalimantan); 28 in the East (East Java, Sulawesi, Maluku, and East Timor). Because of lack of sales teams and wide dispersal of outlets, PT IPM's distribution covered only 13.3% of Indonesia's estimated 150,000 retail outlets. PT IPM offered varying credit terms to distributors: Central region distributors received a 25-day credit term; West and East region distributors received a 35-day credit. In turn, distributors gave traders and wholesalers on average 21 days' credit. PT IPM gave distributors a 10% margin.

Advertising and Promotion

In 1990, PT IPM spent Rp 2.5 billion to promote its products, 40% on brand image building, versus 30% for other modern snack food companies. Of the total budget, 74% was spent to promote "Chiki"; the remainder was divided between "Jetz" and "Chitato." PT IPM used print advertisements and radio commercials together with outdoor advertisements, including billboards, shop signs and banners. Consumer and trade promotions such as game sponsorship and distribution of gifts to consumers were also effective in promoting PT IPM products.

In addition to PT IPM, other big advertising and promotion spenders were PT Rasa Murni Utama (Rp 900 million) and PT Pacific Buana (Rp 600 million). In total, industry advertising and promotion expenditure was Rp 5 billion in 1990. Before 1990, most advertisements were placed in magazines, newspapers, radio, and outdoors (posters and streamers); thereafter, competition intensified with the lifting of the government ban on television advertisements.

The Positioning Decision

PT IPM's best-seller, "Chiki," was strongly positioned only in the children segment. PT IPM's efforts in the two other market segments relied on wholesalers to distribute products; advertising and promotion spending was limited. Buoy believed PT IPM should establish itself in the other market segments. He wondered what marketing effort would be necessary and what priorities should be set for advertising and promotion for all PT IPM products.

Buoy considered recommending either the repositioning of "Chiki," or focusing on PT IPM's other products. He knew top management would examine several factors related to these positioning strategies. For example: What positions did the company's products currently hold against competition? What were the strengths and weaknesses of PT IPM products? In what segment(s) could the company establish strong competitive advantage?

Case 16

Sumber Tehnik

Jose M. Faustino
Asian Institute of Management, Makati, the Philippines

On July 1, 1992, Rony Susanto, president and owner of Sumber Tehnik, reviewed company operations. He concluded that sales performance for the last year and a half was below both his expectations and Sumber's capability. Sumber Tehnik, which bought, reconditioned and sold used cars, operated in Surabaya, East Java's progressive capital city of over three million people. Susanto was dissatisfied because he knew that in the last five years Surabaya had benefited from Indonesia's economic boom; however, Sumber's average unit monthly sales was practically the same, or even a bit lower, than 1989.

εοςεβ

Entrepreneurial Beginnings

In 1979, after working in his father's business for a year, 21-year-old Susanto established Sumber Tehnik (Sumber) to distribute Japanese-made outboard motors used mainly for small fishing boats. Although Sumber also acquired dealerships of sundry machinery (e.g., agricultural, marine) from local distributors, outboard motors remained the main business. Susanto's company enjoyed two profitable years until government credit to fishermen dried up suddenly and sales of outboard motors virtually ceased.

In 1981, Sumber acquired a downtown building and became a dealer for the American-made AMC Jeep. However, when Japanese pick-up trucks were imported business declined and Sumber started buying and selling used cars. This venture was successful and Sumber became the largest used car retailer in Surabaya, against relatively weak competition, selling on average 30 cars a month.

In 1984, Susanto dropped the used car business and all other lines except outboard engines (mostly supplying parts) and became a dealer for Daihatsu, a Japanese brand specializing in minicars that usually sold at the lowest automobile price points. For three years or so, the Daihatsu business was good but introduction of other minicar brands led to fierce price competition and rapidly declining margins. Susanto abandoned the Daihatsu business when the Jakarta-based main distributor began selling cars to Surabaya end users through a local branch at prices below Sumber's acquisition costs.

In 1988–89, Susanto enrolled in a series of courses at the Asian Institute of Management (Manila) culminating in a one-year Master in Management degree. During this period, his wife Vivi managed the business, but took short executive programs at AIM alternately with Susanto. Susanto wrote his master's thesis on Sumber Tehnik's corporate strategy; he concluded that Sumber should re-enter the used car business. His goal was to provide the best quality, value and service in the used car industry.

Current Industry Position

Within months of Susanto's return, Sumber recaptured top position in Surabaya's used car business despite the fact that car showrooms in Surabaya grew from 70 in 1981 to 200 in 1992. (See Table 1 for Sumber's sales and inventory, 1990 to 1992.) Whereas Susanto perceived competition to be relatively weak in 1981, by the early 1990s more competent players operated in the used car business. About ten of these organizations had sizable showrooms that could accommodate five to ten vehicles. Sumber enjoyed several advantages in its current location:

- It has its own premises in the expensive central business area, 2000 sq. m. of land area with parking at the side and 40 meters frontage.
- A ground floor showroom, the biggest in Surabaya, that could display 20 to 25 vehicles ready for sale.
- High housekeeping standards: the showroom was always neat and clean and its white tile well scrubbed. Sumber's potential customers were always surprised to know that the workshop, located at the back of the building, likewise had a neat white-tiled floor despite the grease, oil and cleaning chemicals used for engine reconditioning. The whole operation had an air of neatness and orderliness that surprised visitors.

Table 1:   Sumber Sales and Inventory, 1990–92

		Units sold	Inventory (Month end average)
1990		370	45
1991		342	26
1992			
	January	27	30
	February	31	41
	March	40	43
	April	30	38
	May	35	43
	June	29	50
Total 6 months		192	

Susanto attributed the firm's success to its location, size and several other factors:

- Sumber concentrated on the high volume segment – about 80% of units, 70% of rupiah value. This segment embraced medium-priced sedans and vans with engine displacement ranging from 1300 cc. to 1600 cc. Sumber avoided pick-up trucks for two basic reasons: prices for new products were low and daily use was heavy. As a result, margins for used pick-ups, especially after reconditioning, were unsatisfactory.
- Sumber's inventory and selection of cars was greatest. (See Exhibit 1 for end June 1992 inventory.)
- Sumber had a staff of four knowledgeable buyers, including two expert mechanics (see Figure 1), to scour the market and purchase target used vehicles no older than five years and in reasonably good condition.

Figure 1: Organization Chart

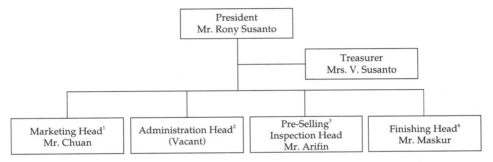

- Sumber had developed a process that reconditioned vehicles in reasonable shape to excellent condition. After purchase, the vehicle came to the Pre-Selling-Inspection (PSI) department; it decided whether body work and/or painting were needed, or just waxing and polishing. For body/painting work, Sumber used one of two competent body/paint contractors. After painting, PSI worked in-house to upgrade vehicle performance: from a simple tune-up, to full overhaul, to replacing brake shoes. From PSI the vehicle moved to the Finishing Department which cleaned and reconditioned every nook and cranny of the engine and passenger cab. No effort was spared in upgrading so the vehicle appeared in first class sparkling condition. Many customers said Sumber cars were more like brand new vehicles than used cars.
- Since it offered a superior product, Sumber provided a six-month guarantee for the engine, transmission and differential. No other used car dealer had any guarantee whatsoever.
- All Sumber vehicles had complete documents; it guaranteed (money-back) that no vehicle was stolen.
- The showroom was open daily from 9:00 am to 8:30 pm except Sunday. No other showroom was open such long hours.

Sumber's Marketing Strategy

Primary Target Market

Susanto identified Sumber customers as professionals, managers and entrepreneurs of small and medium-size businesses. Since automobile prices in Indonesia were among the highest in Southeast Asia, the typical buyer/decision maker was relatively senior in age and career accomplishment. (See Table 2 for Susanto's view of Sumber's primary target market.)

Table 2: Primary Target Market of Sumber Tehnik

Race	60% Chinese, 40% Javanese
Religion	50% Christian, 30% Islam, 20% Buddhist
Socio-economic class	Middle income
Occupation	50% entrepreneurs, 50% managers from both private and government sections
Age	30–45
Location	Urban shops for entrepreneurs and residential estates in urban/suburban areas
Income	Rp 2–5 million monthly for entrepreneurs, Rp 2–4 million monthly for managers
Gender	Male
Civil status	Married, 2 children
Education	Senior high school for entrepreneurs, up to university attainment for managers

Pricing

The construction of prices for Sumber's cars began with the purchase price for the used car. Susanto estimated the average cost to repair the body, paintwork and engine was about Rp 500,000.[1]

The typical body and paint repair by an outside contractor was Rp 200,000 to Rp 300,000; the average cost of engine repair was similar. Since Sumber buyers used relatively high standards in securing used cars, the reconditioning cost was relatively low, typically 2% to 3% of Sumber's selling price. The typical mark-up on acquisition cost was Rp 1,000,000 to Rp 1,500,000; in 1991, average mark-up was Rp 1,200,000. (See Exhibits 2A, 2B for price, cost and margin in May and June 1992.)

Sumber pricing for the same car (i.e., model and year) was the highest in Surabaya. He believed competitors typically invested much less in their cars for both acquisition cost and reconditioning. Often, small scale traders bought and resold with no reconditioning. Susanto estimated that larger-scale competitors typically invested in some

---

[1] In 1992, US$1 was equivalent to Rp 2,040.

reconditioning (but always less than Sumber), and would make almost the same profit margin (i.e., Rp 1,000,000 per car). As a result, Sumber's percent profit margins were lower, even though Sumber listed the same car at Rp 750,000 to Rp 1,000,000 higher than competitors.

Typically, Sumber developed a cellar price according to the system noted above, then added Rp 500,000 to arrive at the list price; this extra margin was used to accommodate customer bargaining. Sumber's list/pre-bargaining price was carried by a sign on the vehicle. Customer attitudes to Sumber's pricing and other attributes were secured from a customer survey conducted from January to May 1992 (Table 3).

Table 3: Results from Customer Survey

Survey results	January	February	March	April	May
1. Sumber Tehnik has					
reasonable pricing	69	73	75	64	78
ST is expensive	31	37	25	36	22
2. Why did they buy ST?					
– due to 6-month guarantee	37	30	33	38	38
– due to good quality	34	32	33	31	38
– due to good service	8	15	7	10	7
– familiar with ST	6	13	10	21	8
3. Reasons they bought a used car:					
– change old car	20	17	27	64	20
– need additional car	47	33	10	14	20
– price lower than new car	7	12	10	0	10
– tired of present old car	26	21	36	22	30

Sales Force

Sumber employed three salesperson, males aged 25, 28 and 29 years. For most of 1991, Sumber had a fourth salesperson, a woman in her mid-30s who started as an accounting clerk. Sometimes she had the highest sales volume per month but Susanto believed she had a "bad attitude ... frequently complaining and criticizing the company." She resigned following disciplinary sanction by Susanto after ten years in the company.

The remaining three salesmen were young looking; they averaged just over two years' experience selling for Sumber. Unlike the buyers, who averaged in the mid-30s, salesmen were not required to have mechanical knowledge of the vehicle. Whatever they knew about cars was picked up on the job on a day-to-day basis. Salesmen had several activities and duties:

- Greet and sell to walk-in customers.
- Respond to telephone inquiries and follow up referrals.
- Follow up potential customers who visited and/or telephoned, by going to their homes or business.
- Accompany the customer on a test drive or, upon request, bring the car to the customer's home or office.

- Handle complaints from customers who bought cars in the previous six months.
- Call on past customers for referral.
- Help to complete reports required by Susanto.
- Participate in customer surveys conducted by Susanto at the rate of one or two per quarter.

The sales department head, Chuan (38), had worked for Sumber for five years. He was a university graduate with a reserved, quiet manner. According to Susanto, Chuan was respected by his team but took little initiative in strategy and discipline. Although he was supposed to train salespeople, Susanto did most of the sales training but even this was not consistent or systematic. Susanto taught salespeople basic skills such as how to answer objections and how to close. However, Susanto did not have time to follow up on a man-to-man basis by observing individual salespeople transacting with potential customers, then correcting and retraining.

Susanto was aware of two chronic problems encountered by Sumber's young sales force. First, potential customers were frequently older and more experienced than Sumber salesmen. As a result, customers were often successful in negotiating a final price lower than the desired level. Second, Sumber salesmen converted a relatively small percent of total potential customers into actual customers (determined from Susanto's control system [Table 4]).

Table 4: Sales Performance, May 1992

Types of negotiation	No. of customers	Actual vehicle sales
1. Customers from referrals	15	5
2. Walk-ins at showroom, 1st negotiation	68	17
3. Negotiation on 2nd, 3rd, etc. occasion	35	13
Total	**118**	**35**

Each Monday, Susanto met with the entire marketing department (salesmen and buyers), all of whom reported to Chuan. In these meetings, the previous week's results and activities for the coming week were discussed. Although Susanto allowed and encouraged everyone to speak out, he was frequently the sole source of new ideas. In problem solving situations, Susanto observed that marketing staff typically behaved as traditional Indonesian subordinates: wait for "Pak (Mister) Rony" to decide and tell them what to do. Susanto was slowly withdrawing from speaking in the weekly meetings and his staff were responding to his urging to contribute to the discussion.

Sumber salesmen were paid monthly salaries; they received no commission on sales. Like other employees, they received year-end bonuses; in the last two years these amounted to:

- Four months' salary for four years or more job tenure;
- Three months' salary for a three-year job tenure;
- Two months' salary for a two-year tenure; one month's salary for a year's tenure.

Three years earlier, Susanto tried sales commissions but observed selfish behavior that practically destroyed teamwork among the sales force. Salespeople on commission would only "look after" first-time customers. A customer who was calling back "belonged" to the salesperson who handled the first call and received little or tepid attention from a second salesperson. As a result, Susanto abandoned the commission scheme.

Advertising and Promotion

Sumber advertised in the local evening paper, the *Surabaya Post;* it carried the majority of classified advertisements for used cars. The morning paper was not as popular for car advertising. Sumber did not advertise among the one-column, usually less than 2.5 cm (one inch) in length, classified advertisements offering to sell a used car. These advertisements were listed by the newspaper in alphabetical order of automobile brand (e.g., Daihatsu, Honda, Kijang, Mazda). Rather, Sumber created its own advertisement featuring an image-building message and a list of cars for sale at its showroom. (See Exhibit 3 for samples of advertisements from January to June 1992.) Sumber's cost per advertisement ranged from Rp 30,000 to Rp 100,000 depending on size. In 1991, Sumber spent Rp 1,200,000 on advertising; since sales volume was not growing, he could justify only budgeting the same amount for 1992.

In June/July 1990, Sumber ran a sales promotion; it gave away a free "genuine Charles Jourdan watch worth Rp 170,000 for the purchase of any car at Sumber." Susanto was disappointed with the results; unit sales were not boosted during the promotion. (See Exhibit 4 for the advertisement announcing the promotion.)

Outdoor and Point-of-sale Advertising

The Sumber showroom comfortably accommodated four rows of ready-to-sell cars with at least two meters between each car. Each row of cars had five to six units such that 20 to 26 cars were displayed at any time. Although the white walls and floor tiles were always neat and clean, the showroom did not have a single picture, poster or sign of any kind, nor any indoor plants or other decoration. The showroom was designed to be open from one end of the frontage to the other. As a result, pedestrians could wander into the showroom and effortlessly examine all the cars that were clearly on sale. Sumber had no sign, poster or advertisement, even at night, to attract pedestrians or motorists, just the car display.

The showroom, sales office and workshop were located in one long and deep building with a narrow driveway on the left side through which two cars could pass with inches to spare. The driveway led to a workshop that could accommodate 20 to 25 vehicles undergoing reconditioning or repair (if a sold car had problems during the six-month guarantee period). Lighting was sufficient but not bright. Susanto discovered that with daylight type illumination even the most minor paint defects could be noticed leading to lost sales or increased price bargaining. Lighting was even dimmer in the two air-conditioned sales offices at the end of the showroom where salespeople conducted negotiations with potential customers; the two sides of these offices were made of glass so that salespeople could see customers walking into the showroom.

Within a five-minute walk of the Sumber showroom was the newest and most popular shopping mall in the city, a modern four-story air-conditioned structure of brightly colored and illuminated shops, including Matahari, the anchor department store and a Hero supermarket. Jalan Tunjungan, the busy one-way street on which Sumber Tehnik was located, was the most prominent downtown street with the highest value per square meter in Surabaya. On either side of Sumber were large branches of established Indonesian banks. Susanto's father had bought the land in 1981; its value escalated through the years and in 1992 was conservatively valued at Rp 6 billion.

Susanto's Marketing Objectives

Rony Susanto was clear about his short-term objectives:

- To maintain leadership in the used car business, in volume, quality and service reputation;
- To raise average sales units monthly to a minimum 40 cars per month on a consistent basis;
- Increase total profit margins overall. (Note: Susanto's estimated monthly cash outflow for overhead was Rp 18 million, not considering lease payments on the property.)
- Increase visitors per month to the showroom from the current 70 units (individuals or groups representing a single potential buyer), to a minimum 100 original units. (An original unit was a first visit; it excluded second, third or more visits by the same original unit. Second or more visits by the same original unit were counted as repeat visits or second / third / fourth, etc. negotiations.)

Susanto began to formulate a marketing strategy to best achieve his objectives.

Exhibit 1: Inventory of Used Cars as at June 30, 1992

	Model/year	Color	Buyer name	List price (Rp '000)
1.	Daihatsu Zebra STW 90	Met. Silver	BIE	12,500
2.	Daihatsu Zebra STW 90	Dark Blue	LUT	12,500
3.	Daihatsu Zebra STW 90	Met. Gray	NAN	12,500
4.	Daihatsu Zebra STW 91	Met. Brown	LUT	13,500
5.	Daihatsu Taft GT 88	White	BIE	22,500
6.	Daihatsu Taft GT 90	White	YEN	27,750
7.	Daihatsu Charade 89	Met. Red	LUT	20,000
8.	Daihatsu Classy 91	White	LUT	31,000
9.	Daihatsu Classy 91	Met. Beige	BIE	30,500
10.	Honda Grand Civic 88	Met. Blue	YEN	34,500
11.	Honda Grand Civic 88	Met. Black	YEN	34,000
12.	Honda Grand Civic 88	White	BIE	34,000
13.	Honda Grand Civic 90	Met. Gray	LUT	42,500
14.	Honda Grand Civic 90	Dark Blue	YEN	42,500
15.	Honda Grand Civic 90	Gray	NAN	42,500
16.	Honda Civic Wonder 86	Blue	YEN	24,900
17.	Honda Civic Wonder 87	White	NAN	28,250
18.	Honda Civic Wonder 87	Green	BIE	28,250
19.	Mazda 323 90	White	NAN	34,000
20.	Mazda 323 INTP.91	Met. Green	NAN	36,500
21.	Suzuki STW 88	Met. Brown	BIE	11,000
22.	Suzuki STW 89	Blue	LUT	12,500
23.	Suzuki STW 89	Green	BIE	12,600
24.	Suzuki STW 90	Red	BIE	13,000
25.	Suzuki STW 90	Gray	BIE	13,250
26.	Suzuki STW 90	Met. Gray	NAN	13,500
27.	Suzuki Katana 89	White	LUT	15,000
28.	Suzuki Katana 89	White	LUT	14,750
29.	Suzuki Katana 90	White	LUT	15,750
30.	Suzuki Katana 90	Blue	NAN	16,750
31.	Suzuki Katana 91	Black	NAN	17,500
32.	Suzuki Forsa 88	Black	YEN	19,600
33.	Suzuki Forsa 89	Met. Blue	BIE	21,250
34.	Suzuki Forsa 89	White	BIE	21,500
35.	Suzuki Forsa 89	White	YEN	21,250
36.	Suzuki Forsa 90	White	NAN	22,000
37.	Suzuki Amenity 90	White	YEN	24,000
38.	Suzuki Amenity 90	Black	LUT	24,000
39.	Suzuki Amenity 91	Blue	LUT	25,500
40.	Suzuki Amenity 91	Black	YEN	25,500
41.	Suzuki Forsa 91	Met. Brown	LUT	22,500
42.	Toyota Kijang STW 89	Blue	BIE	22,500
43.	Toyota Kijang STW 90	Green	NAN	20,000
44.	Toyota Kijang STW 91	Red	LUT	20,000
45.	Toyota Kijang STW 92	Green	NAN	20,000
46.	Toyota Starlet 88	White	YEN	23,250
47.	Toyota Starlet 89	Met. Gray	LUT	27,500
48.	Twincam 87	Met. Brown	YEN	29,000
49.	Twincam 89	White	LUT	34,000
50.	Twincam 90	Met. Black	YEN	38,700

Exhibit 2A: Sales Activity, May 1992 (in Rp)

Model/year	Selling price	Cost of goods sold	Margin
1. Toyota Corolla Twincam 88	30,500,000	30,143,625	356,375
2. Daihatsu Taft GT 90	29,900,000	28,853,525	1,046,475
3. Toyota Corolla Twincam 88	31,000,000	30,506,975	493,025
4. Toyota Starlet 91	31,000,000	30,067,400	932,600
5. Suzuki Forsa 89	20,500,000	19,380,925	1,119,075
6. Suzuki Forsa 89	20,900,000	19,144,450	1,755,550
7. Honda Civic Grand 88	33,600,000	31,727,000	1,873,000
8. Mazda Capella 89	34,000,000	32,980,850	1,019,150
9. Daihatsu Charade 91	19,400,000	18,510,450	889,550
10. Suzuki Forsa 91	31,900,000	30,366,000	1,534,000
11. Suzuki Katana 91	17,200,000	16,484,700	715,300
12. Honda Civic Grand 90	40,500,000	39,555,250	944,750
13. Suzuki Katana 90	16,200,000	15,428,625	771,375
14. Toyota Corolla Twincam 90	38,300,000	36,299,100	2,000,900
15. Honda Civic Wonder 87	27,500,000	27,152,925	347,075
16. Suzuki Carry STW 91	14,000,000	13,488,125	511,875
17. Toyota Starlet 91	31,250,000	30,325,750	924,250
18. Toyota Starlet 91	31,250,000	18,058,950	1,141,050
19. Honda Civic Wonder 87	27,350,000	26,309,025	1,040,975
20. Honda Civic Wonder 87	27,400,000	26,862,400	537,600
21. Suzuki Forsa 89	20,850,000	19,293,300	1,556,700
22. Honda Civic Grand 89	36,150,000	34,961,500	1,188,500
23. Honda Civic Grand 88	33,587,500	32,730,500	857,000
24. Daihatsu Charade 88	18,000,000	15,638,050	2,361,950
25. Toyota Kijang STW 91	20,300,000	19,178,450	1,121,550
26. Honda Civic Grand 91	44,500,000	42,156,000	2,344,000
27. Suzuki Carry STW 89	12,000,000	10,786,500	1,213,500
28. Suzuki Katana 91	17,037,000	16,211,700	825,300
29. Daihatsu Zebra STW 91	7,700,000	7,500,000	200,000
30. Daihatsu Zebra STW 90	11,800,000	10,958,700	841,300
31. Toyota Corolla Twincam 88	31,500,000	29,201,750	2,298,250
32. Daihatsu Charade 91	25,000,000	23,583,750	1,416,250
33. Suzuki Katana 91	17,100,000	16,541,225	558,775
34. Daihatsu Taft GT 91	30,750,000	29,697,725	1,052,275
35. Suzuki Katana 91	17,050,000	16,401,150	648,850
	896,974,500	846,486,350	38,438,150

Exhibit 2B: Sales Activity, June 1992 (in Rp)

Model/year	Selling price	Cost of goods sold	Margin
1. Honda Accord 87	33,725,000	33,276,625	448,375
2. Suzuki Forsa A 90	23,000,000	23,564,450	(564,450)
3. Daihatsu Zebra STW 90	12,500,000	11,722,975	777,025
4. Suzuki Forsa 89	20,500,000	19,265,325	1,234,675
5. Suzuki Katana 90	15,400,000	14,556,200	843,800
6. Honda Accord 87	33,750,000	32,544,425	1,205,575

Exhibit 2B (cont'd)

Model/year	Selling price	Cost of goods sold	Margin
7. Toyota Kijang STW 90	21,300,000	20,139,825	1,160,175
8. Suzuki Katana 91	17,000,000	16,578,450	421,550
9. Suzuki Carry STW 90	13,000,000	12,308,700	691,300
10. Suzuki Carry STW 90	12,900,000	12,416,550	483,450
11. Toyota Kijang STW 89	19,000,000	18,109,900	890,100
12. Toyota Kijang STW 90	19,400,000	18,185,900	1,214,100
13. Toyota Kijang STW 89	18,700,000	17,732,300	967,700
14. Toyota Kijang STW 90	20,150,000	18,938,350	1,211,650
15. Toyota Kijang STW 90	19,250,000	18,578,350	671,650
16. Honda Grand Civic 88	33,000,000	32,233,500	766,500
17. Toyota Kijang STW 87	12,500,000	11,258,250	1,241,750
18. Honda Grand Civic 89	35,800,000	34,701,950	1,098,050
19. Daihatsu Zebra STW 90	12,250,000	11,182,600	1,067,400
20. Suzuki Katana 91	17,075,000	15,964,900	1,110,100
21. Suzuki Carry STW 91	13,750,000	13,033,100	716,900
22. Toyota Starlet 88	23,500,000	21,079,500	2,420,500
23. Honda Grand Civic 90	41,750,000	40,020,500	1,729,500
24. Honda Civic Wonder 87	26,250,000	24,454,000	1,796,000
25. Suzuki Forsa Amenity 90	23,550,000	21,186,250	2,363,750
26. Mazda Interplay 90	32,990,000	31,708,750	1,281,250
27. Daihatsu Taft GT 91	38,100,000	29,935,275	1,064,725
28. Toyota Corolla Twincam 90	38,100,000	36,705,000	1,395,000
29. Suzuki Carry STW 88	9,600,000	9,600,000	–
	657,790,000	620,981,900	29,708,100

Exhibit 3: Sample Advertisements, 1991–92

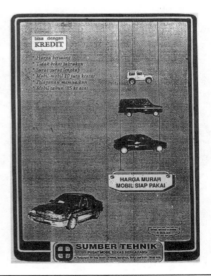

English translation:

Gratis. Free
Jam tangan ekslusif "Charles Jourdan".
One exclusive "Charles Jourdan" watch.
Asli (bergaransi). Guaranteed genuine.
Bagi setiap pembelian 1 unit mobil bekas (Tanpa kenaikan harga.) For every purchase of one used car without increasing the price of the same.
Semua penjual mobil bekas sama. All second hand car dealers are the same.
Tapi hanya kami yang mengutamakan rasa aman & kemudahan. But only we guarantee your security and peace of mind.
Qua faktor utama ini bisa ada karena ditunjang Tim QC (pengawasan Mutu) meliputi/ terdiri dari Cat PSI/Tehnisi – Finishing – Final Control). This is made possible by quality center team support.

Map of Japan

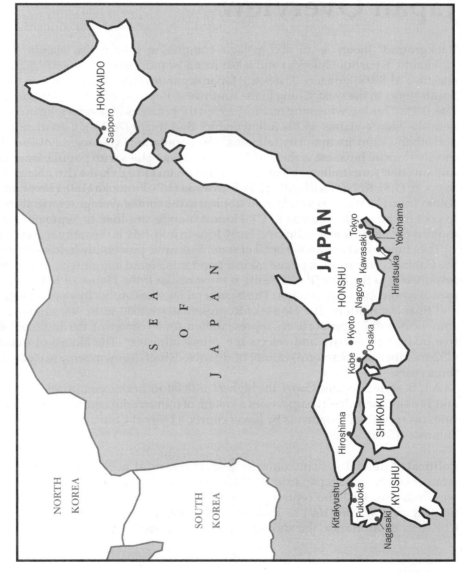

Japan Overview

Background. Japan is an archipelago comprising four main islands (Honshu, Hokkaido, Kyushu, Shikoku) and 6,848 small islands; land area is 377,835 sq. km., coastline 33,889 kilometers. The Sea of Japan separates Japan from Russia in the north; South Korea in the west, China in the southwest. Population is 126.0 million; growth rate, 0.3%. The overwhelming majority adopt the practices of several religions simultaneously. Shinto claims 95.8% followership, Buddhism (76.3%); Christianity (1.4%) and others (12%) are minority religions. The population is Japanese (99.4%), the rest mostly Korean; Japanese is the only language. Major cities with populations over one million (1995) are (millions): Tokyo (8.0), Yokohama (3.3), Osaka (2.6), Nagoya (2.2), Sapporo (1.8), Kobe (1.4), Kyoto (1.5), Kawasaki (1.2), Fukuoka (1.3), Hiroshima (1.1), Kitakyushu (1). Weather varies from tropical in the south (average temperature 16° C) to cool in the north (average 8° C). Hottest months are June to September; coldest months are January and February. Early June to mid-July is the rainy season.

The emperor is ceremonial head of state. Executive powers are held exclusively by the Cabinet comprising a prime minister and ministerial appointees. The Cabinet is responsible to the Diet (Parliament); it must resign if the House of Representatives passes a no-confidence motion. The bicameral Diet has authority over all legislative and financial matters. The House of Representatives (500 seats: 300 single-seat constituencies and 200 proportional representation, four-year term), the dominant legislative body, enacts laws and selects the prime minister.[1] The House of Councilors (252-member, six-year term) cannot be dissolved; half the members are elected every three years.

A U.S.-style Supreme Court, the highest judicial authority, comprises a chief justice and 14 associate judges; it supervises a system of four inferior courts: a High Court that rules on appeals of judgments by lower courts, a District Court, a Family Court and a Summary Court.

Political. A feudal system comprising local powerful noble families and warrior retainers dominated Japan from 1192 to 1867. After a "warring states" period, Japan was unified in 1603 and central power held by the Tokugawa shogunate (family of military rulers) from 1603 to 1867. Fearful of the influence of western traders and Christian missionaries, the shogun adopted a "closed nation" policy in 1637. The

---

[1] This new electoral system replaces single vote, multi-member districts.

country was "walled-off" from all but minor (mainly Chinese and Dutch) intercourse until the arrival of Commodore Perry's "black ships" began a gradual opening policy. External pressure combined with domestic discontent to overthrow the shogunate and restore the emperor (Meiji) to power. The so-called Meiji Restoration initiated a period of drastic reform in political, economic and social institutions including introduction of a modern military, capitalism, universal education and limited democracy. In the late 1920s, Japan became militaristic and authoritarian; it annexed Manchuria (1931), invaded China (1937), pulled the U.S. into World War II by attacking Pearl Harbor (1941) and occupied several Asian countries. After its surrender in 1945 (following atomic bombs dropped on Hiroshima and Nagasaki), Japan was occupied by the Allies (led by the U.S.) for seven years; in this period it adopted amendments to the Meiji Constitution that made the emperor ceremonial head of state and renounced war as a right of the nation. Land reform was implemented and the giant *zaibatsu* industrial conglomerates were broken up. The U.S.-Japan Security Treaty forms the basis for Japan's security, although it maintains land, sea and air defense forces. The conservative Liberal Democratic Party (LDP) effectively dominated government since the War; the principal opposition parties (e.g., Socialist, Clean Government, Communist) were chronically weak. However, 38 years of LDP rule came to an end in July 1993 when a series of scandals led to election of a reformist coalition. The reform government lasted only one year (but changed the electoral system); it was replaced by an LDP/Socialist coalition.

Social. Japan has an aging population and low population growth rate. The 65-plus group is 14% of the population; life expectancy, 80 years, is among the highest in the world. The population growth rate, 0.3% (1995), is among the lowest. Infant mortality, 5 per 1,000 births, is one of the lowest in OECD countries.

Economy. After World War II, several factors led to Japan's emergence as one of the most powerful world economies: high investment demand by business funded by rising savings rates, technology imports and a highly skilled labor force. In the mid-1950s, Japan entered a high growth era that lasted until the early 1970s; it enjoyed more moderate growth throughout the 1980s and entered a virtual zero growth period in the early 1990s. By mid-1990s, modest growth had reappeared. Japan's economy is the world's second largest (after the U.S.), estimated per capita GNP US$36,315. Japan is a member of the Organization of Economic Cooperation and Development (OECD), Group of Seven, United Nations (UN), International Monetary Fund (IMF), World Bank (WB), World Trade Organization (WTO), Asian Development Bank (ADB) and the Asia Pacific Economic Cooperation (APEC) Forum.

In recent years, high surpluses have led to strains with trading partners, notably the U.S. Currently, annual export earnings are US$411 billion; the current account surplus, US$66.1 billion, has dropped from a high of US$126.1, mitigating the problem somewhat. Major export destinations (1995) are: U.S. (27.3%), Taiwan (6.5%), Hong Kong (6.3%). Major import origins (1995) are: U.S. (22.4%), China (10.7%), Australia (4.3%), South Korea (5.1%). From 1970–89, Japan provided US$83.2 billion of foreign aid and is the world's largest aid donor.

Domestic oil and natural gas deposits exist but are negligible. Virtually all Japan's petroleum needs are met by imports. Average real GDP growth 1986 to 1990 was 4.6%, slowing to under 3% in the early mid-1990s. Sectoral labor force employment (1996) was: tertiary industry (60.3%), secondary industry (22.5%), primary industry (6%). From 1985 to 1993, Japanese property investments in the U.S. were US$77.3 billion, concentrated in New York, California and Hawaii; in 1993, US$18 billion were financially restructured or sold. In 1993, Japan invested US$36 billion abroad: U.S., US$14.7 billion; U.K., US$2.5 billion; Netherlands, US$2.2 billion. Japanese direct investment in Asia (total: US$6.64 billion) is increasing. In 1993, direct investment was: China, US$1.7 billion; Hong Kong, US$1.2 billion; Indonesia, US$813 million; Malaysia, US$800 million. In 1994, Japan's foreign equity portfolio comprised: Southeast Asia 40.3%, U.S. 38.8%, Continental Europe 15.1%, U.K. 5.8%.

A unique characteristic of Japan's industrial structure is the Keiretsu system, an intricate web of financial and non-financial relationships between companies linking them in a pattern of formal and informal obligation. The Keiretsu nature of Japanese business has made it difficult for foreign companies to penetrate the Japanese market.

Banks played a dominant role in post-war Japan, especially in the high growth era when business need for external financing was strong and credit markets were not well developed. Large Japanese banks developed close relationships with large industrial clients; client costs were reduced and the quality of monitoring increased.

Japan has different types of specialized banks: city banks, regional banks, long-term banks and trust banks. The Bank of Japan's (central bank) official discount rate is the key interest rate on small amounts. In January 1989, new prime rates, reflecting market rates, were established for short-term loans. Interest rates on time deposits (June 1993) and demand deposits (October 1993) have been liberalized. Liberalization of previously strict controls on capital movements has opened domestic financial markets to foreign participation and to a structural change in financing away from bank-financed debt for large firms.

Nonetheless, the banking sector still remains a powerful factor in Japan's economy and for mid-sized firms. At end 1993, seven of the top ten Tokyo Stock Exchange-listed companies (highest market capitalization) were banks. Market capitalization of the 1,667 listed companies was 324,357 billion yen. Japan's equity market is one of the broadest and most widely diversified in the world. The ten largest firms account for just over 20% of total market capitalization (1993); telecommunications company, NTT, is 3.6% of total. In the early 1990s, Japan's stock market surged rapidly; it passed the New York Stock Exchange in total capitalization, surpassed the major European markets combined and at one stage accounted for almost 40% of world stock market capitalization. Later, the speculative bubble burst and the Nikkei index dove.

Since 1994, Japan has been slowly recovering from a serious recession; economic recovery is closely linked to the US$/yen exchange rate. Yen appreciation (1993, 10.2%; 1994, 10.8%; early 1995, 20%) had many concerned that the U.S. would push to correct its trade imbalance with Japan by driving the yen higher, hence, affecting Japan's international competitiveness. However, from April 1995 to March 1996, the yen depreciated 22% as Japan's current account peaked and U.S. interest rates moved ahead of Japan.

At end 1997, Japan remained over-regulated and cluttered with troubled financial institutions. However, as a creditor nation with a huge current account surplus, it was under no pressure to defend its currency in the Asian financial turmoil. Observers wondered if the Japanese government had the political will to make the necessary reforms to address its economic difficulties. So long as resolute action and commitment to pull the economy out of the recessionary trend was not taken, the yen was expected to continue losing value relative to the U.S. dollar, putting pressure on other Asian currencies and keeping Asian stock markets depressed. Many viewed the Japanese economy as the locomotive that could pull the Asian economies out of recession; as a result, action or inaction by the Japanese government was viewed as having broad implications. Unfortunately, Japan's actions were in sharp contrast to the resolute commitment of the Chinese government not to devalue its currency. Geopolitically, this resoluteness contrast between the Japanese and Chinese governments gave China more respect in Asia and the world."

Relatedly, concern has been expressed over the "Hollowing out" (Kudoka) of Japan's industry as increasing numbers of companies move production off-shore to maintain international competitiveness. So far, domestic economic growth has been maintained via a shift to technology and capital intensive, high value-added production at home. As Japan's population ages, productivity growth will be necessary to keep output growing.

Infrastructure. In March 1992, Japan had 67.0 million motor vehicles, up three-fold from 1970. Car ownership grew from 21.5 million (1980) to 44.7 million (1995). Japan's road system comprises 1,130,892 kilometers of highway, 7,754,102 kilometers paved. The rail network comprises 27,327 kilometers. In fiscal year 1991–92, Japan Railways (formed from privatization and splitting up of stated-owned Japan National Railways [1987]) and other private railways delivered about 400 billion passenger-kilometer. In 1992, total electric energy production stood at 895 billion kWh.

Japan's international and domestic airline industry has prospered from the high yen and strength of the domestic economy. In 1995, Japanese airlines carried 78.8 million passengers on international routes. Japan Airlines (JAL) was privatized in 1987; two other Japanese carriers also operate international routes. All Nippon Airways (ANA) is in direct competition with JAL on many routes.

Japan has excellent domestic and international worldwide telecom service; it has four Pacific Ocean INTELSAT satellites and one Indian Ocean INTELSAT satellite for international transmission. In Japan, there are two phones for every three persons.

Statistics*	June 1991	june 1997	Statistics*	June 1991	June 1997
Per capita GNP	US$23,570	US$36,315	Pop. growth	0.4%	0.3%
GDP growth	4.9%	0.6%	Infant mortality / 1,000	5	5
Savings (GNP)	n/a	34%	Life expectancy (yrs)	78	80
Inflation (CPI)	3.3%	0.5%	Literacy rate	100%	100%
Foreign debt			People per tel.	1.8	1.5
(in US$ billion)	0	0	People per doctor	635	545
Pop. (million)	124.2	126.0	People per TV	n/a	1.6
Urban pop.	77%**	78%	Calorie intake (cals)	n/a	2,956

*Secured from *Asiaweek*.
**From "A report of the INSEAD Euro-Asia Centre," J. Probert (Sept. 1994), INSEAD.

Case 17

Club Med, Japan[1]

Hellmut Schutte, Eriko Ishida
INSEAD, Fontainebleau, France

In winter 1989, Alexis Agnello, Chairman of Club Mediterranee Asia-Pacific-Indian Ocean was sipping wine at the Club's ski resort in Sahoro, Hokkaido, contented with Club Med's progress in Japan. Sahoro, Japan's first vacation village was running at nearly full capacity; membership growth was far greater than the rapidly increasing industry average. However, since many large Japanese companies were entering the leisure industry and expected to offer Club Med-style holidays, maintaining or enhancing Club Med's position required long-term strategic decisions. The unofficial target for Club Med members in Japan was ambitious: 200,000 by 1999, up from 49,300 in fiscal 1989. To achieve this goal, Club Med had to

---

[1] This case was prepared by Hellmut Schutte, Professor at INSEAD and Eriko Ishida, Research Associate. It is intended to be used as a basis for class discussion rather than to illustrate either effective or ineffective handling of an administrative situation. Reprinted with the permission of INSEAD. Copyright © 1994 INSEAD-EAC, Fontainebleau, France.

establish more villages in Japan or elsewhere in Asia. Other potential growth options were new types of Club Med products catering to the booming Japanese leisure market and target groups beyond the young, urban, cosmopolitan clientele Club Med dealt with around the world.

𝄢𝄢

Background

Club Mediterranee (Club Med) was founded (1950) as a non-profit sports association in France by Gerard Blitz, a former member of the Belgian Olympic Team and some friends. As the association grew, the informal, loose organization became increasingly difficult to manage. In 1954, Blitz invited close friend Gilbert Trigano to join the association on a full-time basis; Trigano saw commercial potential, became managing director and transformed Club Med into a profitable organization.

As Club Med grew, geographic expansion was structured more formally. In 1972, Club Med Inc. was formed as a U.S. subsidiary to sell package tours and operate resorts in areas outside Europe/Africa. North America quickly became Club Med's second largest market (Table 1). In 1982, Club Med established four autonomous geographical zones: Europe and Africa run by Club Mediterranee S.A. from Paris; South America run from Rio de Janeiro; North America, run by Club Med Inc. from New York which also directed Asian, South Pacific and Indian Ocean business from Tokyo and Hong Kong. Club Med regarded the European market as mature, U.S. close to mature, Japanese and other Asian markets growing.

By end 1988, Club Med offered 120,837 beds in 243 locations. In addition to traditional Club Med villages, the group managed various holiday villages and residences under different names, some acquired over the years. Valtur targeted the Italian market; OCCAJ operated and marketed vacation villages and rental packages in France; Maeva handled leisure property rentals for Clubhotel, Utoring and Locarev. Club Med villas were traditional hotels enhanced by the Club's own special savoir-faire; City Club combined hotel accommodation in/near downtown areas with conventional premises and fully equipped sports and leisure complexes. There were 96 Club Med villages, 15 Valtur villages, 29 OCCAJ villages and residences, 88 Maeva vacation residences, 12 villas and one City Club. Club Med was by far the world's largest holiday resort operator; in 1987/88 it catered to over 1.6 million holiday-makers. It was the leading tour operator in France, ranking third in Europe in both clients and revenues. Club Med was Europe's fourth largest hotel chain, 12th place worldwide.

Club Mediterranee's Philosophy and Club Formula

Club Mediterranee's main concept was "back to nature": escape from everyday pressures and urban hassles. Guests paid one price, including room, air fare, airport transfers, meals and sports, in advance. To eliminate money, guests wore prepaid bead necklaces used as currency for spending in the village. For many years, rooms did not have telephones, locks or TVs but this policy was recently changed. Telephones were considered a means to connect guests to hassles of the outside world.

Table 1: Composition of Members by Nationality

	1986/87	%	1987/88	%
EUROPE/AFRICA				
France	382,200	38.52	391,100	35.88
Italy	59,100	5.96	76,800	7.05
West Germany	57,400	5.79	66,400	6.09
Belgium	45,400	4.58	53,300	4.89
Israel	23,000	2.32	33,500	3.07
Switzerland	26,800	2.70	29,700	2.73
U.K.	14,600	1.47	15,800	1.45
Other	44,600	4.50	40,400	3.71
Sub-total	653,100	65.84	707,000	64.87
SOUTH AMERICA				
Sub-total	26,000	2.62	33,200	3.05
NORTH AMERICA				
U.S./Canada	215,700	21.74	228,900	21.00
Other	16,800	1.69	17,000	1.56
Sub-total	232,500	23.43	245,900	22.56
ASIA/PACIFIC/INDIA				
Japan	25,100	2.53	37,100	3.40
Australia	21,200	2.14	23,000	2.11
Other	34,300	3.46	43,700	4.01
Sub-total	80,600	8.13	103,800	9.52
Total	992,200	100.00	1,089,900	100.00

Source: Club Med annual report.

What made the Club unique was the staff, "GOs" (gentils organizateurs), who ran the villages; guests were referred to as "GMs" (gentils membres). The GOs (one per eight GMs) mixed with GMs, taught sports and entertained each night after dinner. GOs created a special atmosphere in the village; they were enthusiastic young people working long hours and available for GMs most of the day. Club Med employed 6,400 GOs around the world. GOs turned over frequently, but each year over 30,000 people applied for 2,000 openings. GOs had to be good communicators and have special skills (e.g., music, sports). Club Med spent substantial resources on GO training and moved them from one village to another every six months to keep motivation high.

Each village was designed to maximize social interaction. For example, the bar was centrally located to be a meeting place; GMs and GOs were randomly seated at meals in groups of six or eight; single rooms were not usually available. Shy guests were encouraged, but not obliged, to participate in various Club sports and social activities during the day and might be asked to dance by a GO in the discotheque at night.

History of Club Mediterranee in Japan

Gilbert Trigano identified the Japanese market as attractive when he visited Japan for the Tokyo Olympic Games (1964). In 1973, the large trading house C. Itoh became Club

Med's sales representative in Japan; however, this relationship ended after a few years because of Club Med's dissatisfaction with C. Itoh's commitment to marketing and village development. In 1979, Club Mediterranee K.K. Japan was established to market Club Med products. In 1984, Club Med formed a joint venture with Seiyo Ltd., the leisure branch of Seibu Saison Group, a major Japanese distributor; Trigano had known Seibu Saison Group Chairman, Seiji Tsutsumi, for 20 years. Tsutsumi said his Group had perfected its retail business and wanted to concentrate on leisure activities; it sought expertise from Club Med in resort facility management and the art of entertaining, to supplement Seibu's experience. The alliance would put Seibu Saison one step ahead of other Japanese competitors for whom leisure development meant just building nice facilities. The agreement foresaw marketing Club Med holidays in Seibu Saison's stores and opening vacation villages in Japan.

This relationship was not exclusive for either side. For example, Seibu Saison had numerous joint ventures with other foreign companies including a venture with Accor, a French hotel group, to introduce "sea therapy" and an investment in St. Andrew's golf course in Scotland. Although Club Med considered various projects with other Japanese companies, the Seibu Saison collaboration was very special. In addition to the Japanese collaboration, Seibu Saison owned 3% of Club Med S.A.'s shares. Tsutsumi was a member of the Board of Directors and his sister, who lived in Paris, was invited to join the President's Special Advisory Committee. Japan's largest life insurance company, Nippon Life, held 4.9% of Club Med S.A.'s shares but its role was limited to investment.

In December 1987, Club Med opened its first Japanese Club Med village at the Sahoro ski resort, 140 kilometers east of Sapporo, as a "showroom" village; Japanese clients could experience Club Med's offerings first hand. The village was in a Seibu Saison subsidiary's hotel (acquired 1985) suffering from low occupancy rate, especially in summer. The village was managed by a 50/50 (Club Med/Seibu Saison) joint venture; Club Med's first major move was to transform the hotel's interior. Membership increased substantially since its opening (Table 2); occupancy doubled the first year to 96% in winter, 56% in summer. Despite this success, difficulties in finding suitable sites and very high land prices delayed opening other villages.

Table 2: Membership Growth in Japan

1980/81	6,706	38%	1983/84	11,700	−3%	1986/87	25,100	19%
1981/82	9,300	39%	1984/85	17,200	47%	1987/88	37,100	48%
1982/83	12,100	30%	1985/86	21,100	23%	1988/89	49,300	33%

Club Med (Japan) pioneered other new ideas. In winter 1989/90, it created a "floating Club Med Village" by chartering the cruise vessel Fuji Maru in cooperation with Mitsui OSK, the Japanese liner operator and ship owner. For 26 days, 1,000 Japanese were entertained by GOs from other villages and Club Med's reserve staff. Most guests were married couples, aged 45 to 60, with cruise experience. Few remained on board the whole trip (to Hong Kong, Singapore, Bangkok) but the ship was fully booked at prices ranging from US$1,800 for six days to US$8,000 for 26 days. Club Med was also considering construction of a City Club for corporate use; several real estate developers approached Club Med to discuss a venture close to Tokyo or Osaka.

Recent Trends of Japanese Overseas Travel

The number of Japanese traveling abroad grew from 5.5 million (1985) to 9.7 million (1989) (Table 3). Observers said the "910 million program," established by the Ministry of Transport in September 1987 to increase the number of Japanese traveling overseas by 1991, would be attained in 1990. The sharp yen appreciation made foreign travel economically feasible; some overseas tours were cheaper than domestic tours. For example, a five-day package tour from Tokyo to Guam cost about 90,000 yen; a similar trip to Okinawa, Japan's southernmost island, cost about 110,000 yen. Even so, fewer than 10% of Japanese left the country each year versus the U.K. (44%, 1986), U.S. (15%, 1987). In 1987, 83% Japanese overseas travel was for pleasure, 15% business.

Table 3: Growth of Japanese Tourists Overseas

Year		Year		Year		Year	
1964	128,000	1985	4,948,000	1980	3,909,000	1988	8,430,000
1970	663,000	1986	5,516,000	1984	4,659,000	1989	9,662,000
1974	2,336,000	1987	6,829,000				

Source: Ministry of Justice.

A breakdown of overseas travelers by age and sex showed a rapid increase in young women traveling abroad (Table 4). In 1988, 1.3 million of 8.4 million travelers were women between 20 and 30. The majority were "Office Ladies" (OLs). OLs usually worked for big companies, lived with parents and had few financial and family obligations; they liked to travel as often as possible before marriage. Honeymooners (not classified separately in the statistics) and people over 60 were important segments.

Package tours were popular, used by 90% of Japanese honeymooners and 78% sightseeing tourists. Use of well-known package tours (e.g., Jalpak) offering high service with higher prices remained constant, but less well-known, cheaper package tours were gaining in popularity. All Japanese tour organizers introduced "second brand" tours to meet this growing demand. Increasingly, young people requested only round trip air tickets and hotel reservations for first and last days in destination countries. They preferred deciding their own itineraries.

Favorite Japanese destinations were shifting from Southeast Asia to North America, Australia and more distant regions in line with changing vacation expectations. According to a survey by Mainichi Newspaper, most tourists spent time shopping, sightseeing and eating (Table 5); relatedly, Hong Kong and Singapore were the most popular destinations. However, answers to the question: What type of overseas travel do people like to do? were quite different. Both men and women chose leisure-stay tours first, sightseeing tours second (Table 6). Places like Australia and the South Pacific Islands were closely associated with leisure-stay tours.

Table 4: Composition of Japanese Overseas Travelers by Age and Sex (1988)

Male	Over 50	16.0%
Female	20s	15.9%
Male	40s	15.6%
Male	30s	15.2%
Male	20s	12.0%
Female (38%)	**% of total**	**% of female**
Over 50	8.5%	22.5%
40s	4.6%	12.1%
30s	5.3%	14.1%
20s	15.9%	42.0%
Under 20	3.5%	9.2%
Male (62%)	**% of total**	**% of male**
Over 50	16.0%	25.9%
40s	15.6%	25.3%
30s	15.2%	24.6%
20s	12.0%	19.5%
Under 20	2.9%	4.8%

Table 5: Activities During Overseas Travel

Activities during travel	Men	Women
Shopping	81.3%	86.8%
Sightseeing in cities	78.8%	81.4%
Sightseeing at other noted places	62.0%	60.1%
Eating at various restaurants	42.1%	37.9%
Swimming	30.6%	31.1%
Visits to art galleries and museums	29.5%	31.6%
Pure leisure	29.9%	30.3%
Night tour	17.1%	19.7%
Theaters, concerts, movies	11.2%	12.1%
Drive	11.4%	11.3%

Source: A survey by Mainichi Newspaper (on Japanese overseas air travelers).

Growth in overseas travel was expected to continue if the economy was strong. However, airport capacities limited growth since overseas travel was seasonal; peak seasons were March, July–August and end of the year (Table 7). Although other international airports were available, Narita (Tokyo) and Osaka airports operated close to capacity. The new Kansai Airport was scheduled to open in 1993.

Japanese Attitudes to Leisure

Westerners regarded the Japanese as workaholics whose work days were seldom interrupted by holidays. However, a recent survey for the Prime Minister's Office showed that more than half those polled preferred more free time to extra pay. They also preferred to spend more money on leisure activities than consumer durables. Both leisure and work were important in the lives of 39% of respondents; only 33% said work was more important and that the purpose of leisure time was to prepare for work; 8% said leisure was more important than work (Table 8). The survey demonstrated considerable differences in attitude to work among different age groups; 45% of people in their 50s said work was more important than leisure versus 21% in their 20s.

Generally speaking, the younger generation (especially the "Shinjinnrui" [new breed]) had a more individualistic, western attitude to corporate life and work and tended to take longer holidays. Their preference for spending money versus saving and having fun versus working long hours was frowned on by older generations. Within the same age group, women tended to spend more on holidays than men; they did not view corporate life as a life-long commitment.

Nevertheless, compared with other societies, Japanese worked hard. Although workers received an average of 14.9 days annual paid holiday, the average taken by workers was 7.5 days (1986), down from 8.8 days (1980). Japanese did not take holidays for several reasons. First, leisure infrastructure was lacking in Japan; the long journey to airports, road congestion and high transportation and lodging costs made trips very difficult. Second, Japanese were not used to "active" leisure activities (e.g., sports). Only 20% to 30% of leisure time was spent on "active" leisure (e.g., sports); the remainder on "passive" activities (e.g., reading magazines, watching TV (Figure 1)). Third, most Japanese felt guilty taking long holidays since colleagues had additional work; to avoid friction, they preferred not to take long holidays.

The Japanese government was encouraging more holiday taking. The new five-year Economic Plan (May 1988) called for reducing Japanese average annual working hours from 2,111 hours (1987) to 1,800 hours (1993). (French and Germans worked 1,650 hours [1986]). Until recently, only 30% of the workforce worked a five-day week. In February 1989, the five-day work week went into effect in financial institutions; the government and industries were expected to follow. If the percent of employees working a five-day week grew 10% p. a., it would reach 70% (current level in the U.S. and Europe) in 1992. Extra time, plus increased propensity to spend on leisure, were expected to create high demand for leisure industries. The Economic Planning Agency estimated that extending the five-day work week to all the workforce would boost consumer spending substantially. If salaried Japanese used all their paid leave, leisure consumption would be even higher.

Marketing Club Med in Japan

Segmentation Strategy

When Club Med was first marketed in Japan, nearly 100% of customers were honeymooners. The price, romantic image, destination (New Caledonia) and length of stay (two weeks) appealed especially to this group. As overseas travel patterns changed and the number of experienced travelers increased, other customer segments became important. By 1987/88, the honeymooner ratio reduced to 40% (Table 9).

Table 6: Overseas Travel Tours One Would Like to Make

Preferred overseas activity	Male	Female	Choice				
			1st	2nd	3rd	4th	5th
Leisurely stay	62.5%	70.9%	Hawaii	Australia	U.S.	Switzerland	S. Pacific Isles
Representative sightseeing, sports	38.4%	48.6%	Australia	France	Switzerland	England	W. Germany/Italy
Historical and ancient ruins	36.1%	41.9%	China	Greece	Italy	Spain	France
Shopping	27.0%	48.7%	Hong Kong	Singapore	France	Hawaii	Italy
Local life and customs familiarization	26.8%	36.4%	China	Australia	Spain	England	U.S. (West Coast)
Sports	27.5%	31.7%	Hawaii	Australia	Guam	Canada	S. Pacific Isles
Gourmet	26.6%	28.6%	Hong Kong	France	Taiwan	China	Italy
Folklore	18.3%	28.5%	France	Austria	Italy	W. Germany	Spain
Mountain and sea	17.3%	21.4%	Hawaii	Switzerland	Australia	S. Pacific	Canada
Adventure and remote places	12.2%	14.3%	Other, Latin America	China	N. Africa	E. Africa	Brazil

Source: A survey by Mainichi Newspaper (on Japanese overseas travelers).

Table 7: Number of Japanese Overseas Travelers by Month

Month	1988 ('000)	1987 ('000)	1986 ('000)	Month	1988 ('000)	1987 ('000)	1986 ('000)
January	600	462	381	July	797	655	482
February	647	531	423	August	898	771	616
March	716	572	474	September	744	612	484
April	634	448	414	October	670	557	464
May	617	493	395	November	664	562	461
June	724	569	439	December	706	598	485

Source: Ministry of Justice.

Table 8: Attitudes toward Work and Leisure

Age group	A	B	C	D	E	Age group	A	B	C	D	E
15–19	14	10	53	12	12	50–59	45	7	29	14	7
20–29	21	11	53	11	5	Over 60	34	7	24	16	18
30–39	30	8	46	14	3	Total	33	8	39	13	8
40–49	42	8	36	12	2						

A – Work is more important than leisure.
B – Leisure is more important than work.
C – Both work and leisure are important.
D – Work and leisure are important and no distinction is made between the two.
E – Don't know.
Source: Prime Minister's Office, Public Relations Section – Opinion Poll On Leisure, Time, and Traveling.

Table 9: Japanese Members by Segment

	1984/85	1987/88	Average stay
Honeymooners	72%	40%	7 days
OLs	16%	35%	4.5 days
Families	10%	15%	7 days
Corporate clients	0%	7%	2.5 days
Others	2%	3%	n/a

Source: Club Méditerranée.

Currently, the major target group was the OL segment, 35% of customers, to whom Club Med's image as a young, international, fun-loving organization had great appeal. They were frequent travelers, quite price sensitive, with lower budgets than honeymooners. Observers estimated the budget of an average sightseeing tourist was about 274,000 yen, honeymooners 387,000. Club Med hoped unmarried young women would become repeat clients, as honeymooners and later with families.

In 1987/88, families with children comprised 15% of Japanese GMs. Club Med was surprised to find so many Japanese families traveled with children. As a result, most regional villages were equipped with Mini Clubs where children were taken care of by GOs, participating in various activities, while parents enjoyed themselves on their own. Club Med Sahoro opened a Mini Club in summer 1989.

Although corporate business represented only a small proportion of total business (1987/88, 7%), it was expected to grow rapidly. Club Med provided conference or training packages in exotic locations in the Club Med ambiance complete with meeting facilities and office equipment. Large firms (e.g., Sony, Toshiba) used these facilities. A new village at Opio (French Riviera), opened 1989, specially designed for this purpose, was strongly marketed towards Japanese corporate clients. A contributing factor to increased corporate sector importance was the Government's extension of tax-deductible company trips from two to three nights. Since company trips were a common way of rewarding employees and increasing loyalty, the change from two to three nights meant company trips could take place further afield or even overseas. Club Med Sahoro was focusing marketing efforts for the summer season on corporate clients; in summer 1989, 40% of GMs were corporate clients.

Figure 1: Breakdown of Leisure Hours by Activity

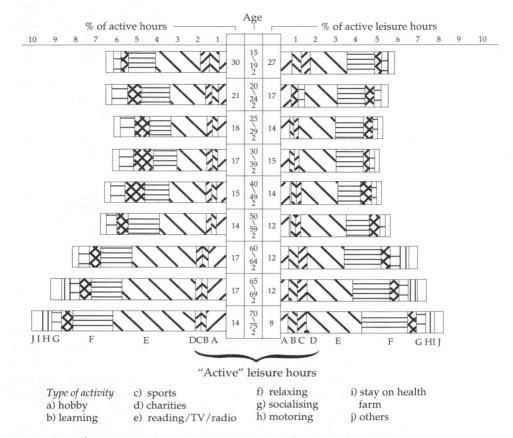

"Active" leisure hours

Type of activity	c) sports	f) relaxing	i) stay on health
a) hobby	d) charities	g) socialising	farm
b) learning	e) reading/TV/radio	h) motoring	j) others

Source: Somucho, Basic Survey on Social Life (Interim Report) October 1987.

Product Strategy

In general, Club Med believed that since the Club Med concept appealed to the French, it would also appeal to other nationalities once the language barrier was removed. However, in Japan, a more flexible approach was introduced by Trigano. He stated: "We have tried very hard to improve products for the Japanese. It seems they need an alibi to go on holiday, so we offer them courses on how to use the computer, or speak French or English, or whatever they want."

To cater to Japanese demand, Club Med shortened length of stay. Club Med's standard packages were designed for European customers where four or five weeks' holiday plus a week or more of public holiday was the norm. Instead of two-week packages, common in the European market, one-week tours were developed for Japan. More recently, three-night package tours to Club Med villages were launched, aimed at the OL segment. The average stay of Japanese GMs was 5 to 5.5 days; the average stay in

France was 15 days. Industry observers believed long vacations might never be common in Japan since the Japanese preferred three- to four-day holidays each season.

Second, utmost care was taken to arrange the most convenient departure schedule. For example, departure on Mondays was essential for honeymooners since wedding ceremonies were typically on Sundays. Third, villages in Asia Pacific were designed to be more luxurious than in the Mediterranean (e.g., telephone in each room, air-conditioning). Even so, accommodation quality did not fully meet Japanese requirements. Instead of sleeping under thatched roofs in rooms decorated with bamboo and other local materials, Japanese preferred more neutral hotel-like environments verging on antiseptic. Announcements and signs in villages were in English, French and Japanese.

Club Med successfully recruited Japanese GOs speaking two or three languages, prepared to work long hours for the standard US$600 monthly salary; almost 200 Japanese GOs, mostly female, were on the payroll. However, some Japanese guests found Japanese GOs too westernized; also, Japanese GOs wanted to be assigned not only to regional villages with large numbers of Japanese but also to Europe and the U.S. or the Caribbean.

Club Med was known for good food. Local dishes and French cuisine were served in buffet-style restaurants. Japanese dishes were added in villages catering to Japanese tourists. Separate dining rooms were available for guests preferring quieter surroundings (e.g., honeymooners). Club Med made extensive use of comment cards filled out by GMs; Analyses were fed back to product development and operations.

Promotion

Club Med's advertising expenses in Japan were approximately 8% of sales. About 40% of expenditures were for printing and mailing brochures; these contained detailed information since Japanese liked extensive knowledge about a tour before departure. Club Med had high awareness among Japanese tourists (Table 10). A poll of Japanese holiday-makers by *AB Road Magazine* awarded Club Med top marks as the tour operator they were most willing to try.

Table 10: Most Well-known and Popular Japanese Tours

Most well-known*		Most popular**	
Look	98.8%	Club Med	62.9%
Jalpak	97.5%	Jalpak	51.7%
Holiday Tours	90.1%	Look	51.5%
Club Med	82.2%	Holiday Tours	25.5%

*Percentage of respondents who recognized the brand name.
**Respondents are asked to name three package tours they would like to try.
Source: A survey by *AB Road Magazine*.

Repeat business in Japan was 20% versus Club Med's worldwide average 70%. In part this low repeat level was due to large numbers of additional members joining Club Med who had had no opportunity for a return visit. In addition, honeymooners, whose time at Club Med was a special occasion, were a high percent of visitors. A regular newsletter and invitations to parties and events given by the Club were designed to promote a Club spirit among GMs and increase repeats. To encourage positive word-of-mouth, Club Med was considering offering free one-day village stays to those successfully introducing new GMs.

Club Med's advertising made extensive use of a "European" image, including photographs of beautifully tanned, smiling Westerners on the beach. Even for Sahoro, where only 8% of GMs were from outside of Japan (mainly from nearby Asian countries) the brochure showed several Westerners. In Sahoro, about half the GOs were non-Japanese. Because of high cost, Club Med rarely used TV advertising in Japan.

Distribution

Since Club Med's holidays appealed mainly to urban dwellers, distribution was concentrated in Tokyo and Osaka. Approximately 90% of overseas travelers booked trips through the 700 Japanese travel agents (7,000 sales outlets). Major tour operators sold products through either their own sales outlets, independent outlets or competitors' outlets. Initially, Club Med depended entirely on other agents; however, to promote sales more aggressively, it developed its own direct sales channels. Direct sales accounted for 15% to 17% of Japanese sales.

Since Club Med's products were different from other package tours they required a fairly detailed explanation. To help people understand Club Med, beautiful videos on Club Med village life were shown at Club Med sales counters; video tapes were also available for home viewing. Club Med had sales outlets in Tokyo, Osaka, Nagoya, Sapporo and Fukuoka. In addition, it had eight sales outlets in Seibu Department Stores, staffed by Japanese GOs. Of the 700 travel agencies, 500 dealt with Club Med; 3,000 of the 7,000 outlets sold Club Med packages.

Price

Price was not of prime importance for the Japanese because vacation failure carried a high opportunity cost; they preferred well-proven products. Although Club Med was a "European product" with an upmarket image, prices were competitive compared to other well-known Japanese package tours (e.g., Jalpak). Price was determined by length of stay, departure date/season and destination; competitor prices and Club Med's internal cost structure were important pricing factors. Typically, prices for tours ex-Japan were higher than tours leaving from other countries.

According to internal statistics, the average Japanese GM paid US$380 per vacation day versus US$140 in Australia, US$70 in Malaysia (including transportation). The Sahoro price (US$200 per night) was much higher than average ski package tours offered by Japanese competitors. Nevertheless, Club Med personnel believed GMs were satisfied since high quality ski lessons using Ecole de Ski Francaise methods and unlimited lift and gondola access, with no waiting time, rare at Japanese ski resorts, were included.

The Future

Although it took Club Med many years to penetrate the Japanese market, Alexis Agnello was pleased with recent progress. He believed the "Club Med magic," close GO-GM interaction in an informal, pleasant environment cut off from everyday life, was finally accepted by the Japanese; moreover, it was not easily imitated. Sahoro worked well, as did other regional villages (e.g., Bali [Indonesia], Phuket [Thailand]). Club Med had no problem finding enough multilingual GOs willing to work very long hours for low salaries. In addition, Club Med's growing traffic volume increasingly enabled it to secure favorable terms from airlines. Although the business seemed to be carried forward almost automatically by the Japanese leisure and travel boom, the 49,300 GMs annually was only 0.04% of Japan's population versus 0.66% in France. Was it correct to cling to a concept different from anything else in Japan?

In addition, virtually every local government was drawing up plans to develop resort complexes in accord with the Law for Development of Comprehensive Resort Areas (1987); 70 projects were already under way. Major private companies in search of growth were entering the leisure industry; firms in heavy manufacturing, recently extensively restructured, had started to convert closed factories into leisure sites, so providing jobs for excess employees. Club Mediterranee K.K. (Japan) was taking part in this development, though on a limited scale. It had already announced a 5% share in a newly formed company, Asahi Kaiyo, which would convert former shipyards into marinas and leisure centers; other partners were Seibu Saison (35%) and Japan Air Lines, Mitsui and Nippon Steel (5% each).

The overseas travel boom also accelerated resort development where land prices and labor costs were comparatively low and government approval was fast. Large-scale leisure facilities (e.g., golf courses, resort condominiums) were under construction by various Japanese consortia in Hawaii, Guam, Saipan, Australia and the U.S. West Coast. In Australia, Japanese capital funded 20 major projects.

To cope with this development, Club Med would have to open up more villages in and out of Japan rapidly and broaden its product range to reach a more general Japanese public. Sites were being considered along the sea in Japan, on Okinawa, in Tokyo, Osaka, the Philippines and Australia. Agnello thought uniqueness was positive but wondered if this was sufficient to be attractive? Perhaps he should start a club without an international flavor, without informality and without too much activity, a Club exclusively for Japanese where learning and shopping would be a major concern. Another concept might be a Club that moved around; its purpose would be to get to know five countries in three days, with a duty free shop in the center of the resort....

Agnello knew he was dreaming. Back in Paris, they would never allow modification of Club Med's recipe for success, the organization's pride. And even if he could follow his instincts, was 200,000 Japanese GMs in ten years a reasonable target?

Case 18

Delissa in Japan

Dominique V. Turpin, Juliet Burdet-Taylor
International Management Development Institute, Lausanne,
Switzerland

"We can maintain our presence in Japan or pull out ..." In fall 1991, Bjorn Robertson, recently named Managing Director of Agria, Sweden's leading dairy products cooperative, met with his team (Peter Borg, Stefan Gustafsson, Lars Karlsson) to review Agria's international business. Delissa fresh dairy products were sold worldwide through franchise agreements; several were up for review, most urgently in Japan. "In the light of these results, there are several things we can do in Japan. We can maintain our presence and stay with Nikko, our present franchisee, we can change our franchisee, or we can pull out. But, let's look first at how badly we are really doing in Japan."

Robertson read out loud a list of Agria's major foreign ventures featuring the Delissa yogurt brand: "U.S. launch 1977, market share, 12.5%; Germany launch 1980, market share, 14%; U.K. launch 1982, market share, 13.8%; France launch 1983, market share, 95%; Japan launch 1982, market share, 2.3%." Robertson circled marked last figure and looked up. "Under 3% after 10 years! What happened?"

∞∞∞

History

Agria was founded in 1967 when several Swedish dairy cooperatives, comprising 20,000 dairy farmers, created a united organization to develop and sell a line of fresh dairy products. In 1970, individual cooperatives dropped their own trademarks and the Delissa line, comprising yogurts, desserts, fresh cheese and fresh cream, was launched, one of few "national" lines of dairy products in Sweden. In the following two decades, guided by founders Rolf Anderen and Bo Ekman, Agria's share of Swedish fresh milk products rose to 25%; Agria developed into a powerful national and international organization. By 1991, over 1.1 billion Delissa yogurts and desserts per annum were consumed worldwide. In fiscal year 1990, Delissa sales were $1.6 billion; it employed 4,400 people in and outside Sweden.

306

Industrial franchising was rare in the 1970s and Swedish dairy products firms did not usually invest abroad. However, Mr. Ekman's idea of know-how transfer ventures, whereby a local licensee manufactured yogurt using Swedish technology, then marketed and distributed products with its own distribution network, enabled Delissa to penetrate over 13 foreign markets with considerable success and minimal capital outlay. By contrast, Delissa's biggest competitor worldwide, BSN – a French food conglomerate marketing yogurt under the "Danone" brand name – entered foreign markets, by buying into or creating local companies, or by forming regular joint ventures.

By the time Bjorn Robertson took over as European marketing director in 1985, the Delissa trademark (the white cow symbol), so familiar in Sweden, was known in many countries worldwide. Delissa was very active in sponsoring sports events and Bjorn Robertson, a keen cross-country skier and sailor, offered personal support to Delissa's teams around the world. In 1991, when he reviewed the international business, Robertson was surprised by the poor results of Agria's Japanese joint venture. Before calling together his international marketing team Robertson perused the history of the alliance.

Proposal for Entry into the Japanese Market

In early 1979, the decision was made to enter the Japanese market. An Agria team is currently in Japan conducting market feasibility research and searching for a suitable franchisee.

Objectives. The Japanese yogurt market (1980), estimated at approximately 600 million cups (100 million ml.), is expected to grow at no less than 8% p.a. for the next five years. Our launch strategy would be based on an expected market growth rate of 10% or 15%. We would develop a high quality range of yogurts with the goal of becoming well known to the Japanese consumer. We aim to secure 5% market share in year one, 10% in three years. In the first two years we plan to cover the three main metropolitan areas, Tokyo, Osaka and Nagoya; the rest of the country will follow within three years.

Robertson circled the 10% with a red pen. He understood management had hesitated to set too high a market share goal since Japan was believed to be a difficult market to enter. But, in 1987, six years after launch, the three-year target was not reached. In 1991, Delissa's share of the total yogurt market, never reaching 3%, fell to 2%. He wondered why the Japanese results were so different from other countries.

Consumption. Per capita yogurt consumption in Japan is low compared to Scandinavian countries: estimated 5.3 cups per person per annum versus 110 in Sweden and 120 in Finland. Yogurt sales in Japan are seasonal, peak period March to July. Highest sales are in June, so end February is the ideal launch date.

Yogurt sales fall loosely into three major categories (volume %):

- Plain (39%): Called "plain" in Japan because the color is white, but flavored with vanilla; generally sold in 500 ml. pure pack cups; sugared or sometimes with a sugar bag attached.
- Flavored (45%): Differentiated from "plain" by the presence of coloring and *gelifiers*; not a wide variety, mainly vanilla, strawberry, almond and citrus.
- Fruit (16%): Similar to the typical Swedish fruit yogurt but with more pulp than real fruit; contains some coloring and flavoring.

Western-type yogurts also compete directly in the same price bracket with local desserts (e.g., puddings, jellies) produced by Japanese competitors.

Competition. Three major Japanese manufacturers account for half the total real yogurt market:

- Snowbrand Milk Products, the largest manufacturer of dairy products in Japan, produces drinking milk, cheeses, frozen foods, biochemicals and pharmaceuticals; 1980 revenues, Y293,322 million.[1]
- Meiji Milk Products, Japan's second largest dairy foods producer, particularly dried milk for babies, ice cream and cheese. An alliance with the Bulgarian government helped start Japan's yogurt boom; 1980 revenues, Y410,674 million.
- Morinaga Milk Industry, Japan's third largest milk products producer, processes drinking milk, ice cream and instant coffee and has a joint venture with Kraft U.S. for cheeses; 1980 revenues, Y250,783 million.

Market share of these three producers has remained stable for years and is approximately: Yukijirushi (Snowbrand) 25%; Meiji 19%; Morinaga 10%.

The Japanese also consume a yogurt drink, "Yakult Honsha," based on milk reconstituted from powder or fresh milk acidified with lactic acid and glucose. Yakult is often included in statistics on total yogurt consumption since it competes with normal yogurt; 31% market share on a total market base of yogurt and yogurt drink. Yakult is sold door-to-door and by women who sell direct to workers in offices in the afternoon; it is not sold in shops.

Robertson found a report on Uppsala meetings when members of Agria's negotiating team presented their findings:

Selecting a franchisee. We have just returned from our third visit to Japan. We again had discussions with the agricultural cooperative, Nikko, Japan's second largest association of agricultural cooperatives, the Japanese equivalent of Agria. Nikko is a significant political force but less strong than Zennoh, the National Federation of Agricultural Cooperatives which is negotiating with Sodima, a French competitor. Nikko is price leader for various food products (e.g., milk, fruit juice, rice) and actively

---

[1] In 1980, US$1 = Y254.

lobbies on behalf of agricultural producers. Nikko has two parts: manufacturing and distribution. It processes and distributes milk and dairy products, and also distributes raw rice and vegetables.

We met several other candidates, but Nikko is the first that seems prepared to join us. We believe Nikko is the most appropriate distributor for Agria; it is big and its credentials seem perfect. Its strong supermarket distribution system for milk in the three main metropolitan areas is ideally suited for yogurt (80% of yogurt is sold through supermarkets). We are, however, frustrated that, after prolonged discussions and several Japan trips, Nikko has not yet signed an agreement. We believe management wants to act but needs to be absolutely sure before signing. We are anxious to get this project under way before Danone, Sodima or Chambourcy[2] enter Japan.

Background information on the Japanese consumer. Traditionally, Japan is not a dairy products consumer, but locally-produced yogurt is sold with milk-based items such as puddings and coffee cream.

Many aspects of Japanese life are miniaturized due to lack of space: 60% of the 120 million population is concentrated on 3% of the islands' surface; the rest of the land mass is mountainous. In Japan, 85% of the population lives in towns; more than one third have over half a million people. High urban density naturally affects lifestyle, tastes and habits. Restricted living space and lack of storage means most Japanese housewives shop daily and consequently expect fresh milk products in the stores every day; they rarely purchase long-life foods or drinks. Japan has a fairly homogeneous culture as far as wealth distribution is concerned. Disposable income is high; Japanese spend over 30% of total household budgets on food (greatest single item); clothing is second (10%).

The market for dairy products is not comparable to Scandinavia or the U.S. Mothers of young housewives purchasing yogurt today barely knew it existed; their mothers would not even have kept milk in the house. At one time it was believed that the Japanese were deficient in enzymes to digest milk; only a generation ago, when children were given milk, it was more likely goat's than cow's. However, with rapid market evolution to "westernization," the Japanese are interested in U.S. and European products, including yogurt.

Although yogurt consumption per capita is still low, research shows high growth potential. When we launch, correct positioning will be key to Delissa's success as a new foreign brand. We must differentiate it from existing Japanese brands and go beyond the rather standardized "freshness" theme.

Distribution. Traditional Japanese distribution was complex, comprising multi-layered chains so costs were high. Distribution of refrigerated products is more direct and slightly simpler than dry goods. The Japanese daily-purchase habit means Delissa's

---

[2] Chambourcy was a brand name for yogurt produced and distributed by Nestle in various countries. Nestle, 1990 sales $27 billion, was the world's largest food company; headquarters were in Vevey (Switzerland).

delivery system must be fast and efficient. Our basic distribution goal would be to secure mass sales retail distribution. Initially, items would be sold through outlets selling Nikko's drinking milk, "Nikkodo." Milk-related products and dessert foods would be sold based on distribution to mass sales retailers. The objective would be to make efficient use of existing distribution channels with daily delivery schedules and enjoy lower distribution costs for new products.

The Japanese retail market. The retail market is extremely fragmented; independent outlets account for 57% of sales (versus 3% in the U.S.). Japan has twice as many outlets per capita as most European countries, 1,350 shops per 100,000 people. Tradition, economics, government regulations and service demands affect the Japanese retail system. Housewives typically shop daily; most select smaller local stores that keep longer hours, deliver orders, offer credit and provide a meeting place for shoppers. Opening western-style supermarkets is expensive and complicated, so small independent, or family business comprise most retailing.

Japan has three major metropolitan areas: Tokyo, Osaka and Nagoya, populations are 11, 3 and 2 million respectively. Nikko's Nikkodo (15% market share) is market leader, ahead of many other suppliers. Nikko feels Nikkodo's milk distribution chain would be ideal for yogurt. Each metropolitan area has a separate distribution system with several depots and branches. For instance, Greater Tokyo – the largest area with over 40 million people – has five Nikko depots and five Nikko branches.

Most physical distribution (drivers and delivery vans) is carried out by a Nikko subsidiary with wholesaler support. Refrigerated milk vans must be fairly small (less than two tons) to drive down the narrow streets. The same routes are used for milk delivery, puddings and juices. Our initial strategy would accept Nikko's milk distribution system but adopt shifting distribution routes. Japan's complicated street identification system (numbers, not names) makes great demands on the distribution system and the drivers.

The Franchise Contract

Bjorn Robertson opened a report by Ole Bobek, head of the Japan project from the start, and responsible for the joint venture's early years; he left the company in 1985. This report contained details of the Agria/Nikko industrial franchise agreement (November 1979) permitting Nikko to manufacture and distribute Delissa products under license. The contract was Agria's standard Delissa franchisee agreement covering technology transfer and trademark exploitation. Agria provided manufacturing and product know-how, and marketing, technical, commercial and sales support. Agria received royalties for every pot of yogurt sold. The Nikko cooperative formed a separate company for distributing, marketing and promoting Delissa products. In the pre-launch phase, Per Bergman, Senior Area Brand Manager, was to train the sales and marketing team, Agria's technicians would supply know-how.

By 1980, a factory to produce Delissa yogurt, milk and dairy products was constructed in Mijima, 60 miles northwest of Tokyo. Agria provided Nikko with advice on technology, machinery, tanks, fermentation processes, etc. Equipment from the U.S., Sweden, Germany and Japan was selected, including a European-style Erka filling machine that filled two, four or six cups at a time; it was considered economical and fast.

Robertson opened another report by Bobek, "Delissa Japan – Pre-Launch Data." This report covered the market, positioning, advertising and media plan, minutes of meetings with Nikko executives and the SRT International Advertising Agency that handled the launch, analysis of market research findings and competitive analysis.

Robertson closed the file and thought about the Japanese market. During pre-launch planning phase, everything looked so promising. In its usual methodical fashion, Agria had prepared its traditional launch campaign to ensure the new Agria/Nikko venture was successful ... "Why then were sales so low after nine years of business?"

The next day, Bjorn Robertson lunched with Rolf Anderen. Although retired, Anderen still took an active interest in the business he had created and directed. Over coffee, Robertson broached the subject of the Japanese joint venture, expressing surprise that Delissa was so slow in taking off. Rolf Anderen nodded his understanding:

Yes, it has been disappointing. I remember those early meetings before we signed with Nikko. Our team was very frustrated with the negotiations. Bobek made several trips and had endless meetings with the Japanese, but things still dragged on. We had so much good foreign business by the time we decided to enter Japan, I guess we thought we could just walk in wherever we wanted. Our Taiwanese franchise business took off and I think we assumed Japan would do likewise. Then, although we knew Japan was different, Wisenborn, our international marketing manager, and Bobek believed something was wrong. They did a very conscientious job, yet blamed themselves for the delays. I told them to be patient ... to remember Asians have different customs and likely need time to decide. Our guys secured enormous amounts of data; they returned from a second or third trip to Japan with a mass of information, media costs, distribution data, socio-economic breakdowns, detailed assessment of competition, positioning statements, etc. ... but no contract. [Rolf Anderen chuckled as he spoke.] Of course, Nikko finally signed, but we never were sure what they really thought about us ... or what they really expected from the deal.

The whole story was interesting. When you enter a market like Japan, you are on your own. If you don't speak the language, you can't find your way around. So you become totally dependent on the locals and your partner. In this respect, the Japanese were extremely helpful, but let's face it, the cultural gap is wide. Another fascinating aspect was the rite of passage. In Japan, as in most Asian countries, you feel you are observing a kind of ritual, their ritual. This can destabilize the solid Viking manager. Of course, they were probably thinking we have our rituals, too. On top of that, the Nikko people were particularly reserved and, of course, few of them spoke anything but Japanese.

There was much tension in those first months, partly because France's two major brands, "Yoplait" and "Danone," were about to enter Japan, confirming Bobek's fear during negotiations. If it's any consolation, Bjorn, these two international brands are doing no better than we are in Japan today.

The European Competitors

Robertson spoke with Peter Borg, a young Danish manager who replaced Bergman and supervised Agria's Japan business for several years. He asked why "Danone" and "Yoplait" were doing no better than Delissa. Borg said:

> I can explain how these two brands were handled in Japan. First, Sodima, the French dairy firm, whose Yoplait line is sold through franchise agreements all over the world, took a similar approach to ours. In 1981, Yoplait tied up with Zennoh, the National Federation of Agricultural Cooperative Association, the Japanese equivalent of Sodima. Zennoh is huge and politically very powerful; total sales are double Nikko's. Yoplait probably has about 3% market share, much less than their usual 15% to 20% share in foreign markets. However, Zennoh had no previous experience in marketing yogurt.
>
> Danone took a different approach; it signed an agreement with a Japanese partner, Ajinomoto. The joint venture, Ajinomoto-Danone Co. Ltd., is run by a French expatriate and several Japanese directors. A prominent French baker, based in Tokyo, is also on the board. Ajinomoto is Japan's largest integrated food processor (sales, $3 billion). About 45% of its business is in amino acids, 20% in fats, 15% in oil. Ajinomoto has a very successful joint venture with General Foods for "Maxwell House" instant coffee, but had no experience with fresh dairy products.
>
> So, for both Japanese partners, Ajinomoto and Zennoh, the yogurt business was completely new; they were probably diversification moves. The Danone venture had a tough time initially since it built a dairy products distribution network from scratch; also, distribution problems discouraged Nestle from re-introducing Chambourcy in Japan. Japanese distribution costs are very high compared to the West. I suspect the Danone-Ajinomoto joint venture probably reached break-even only last year.

"Thanks Peter," Robertson said. "Fascinating story. I hear you just married a Japanese girl. Congratulations!"

Entry Strategy

The SRT International Advertising Agency helped develop Delissa's entry into the "new milk-related products" market. Agria and Nikko approved substantial advertising and sales promotion budgets. SRT confirmed that since Nikko was a major producer in "drinking milk," entry into processed milk or "eating milk," a rapidly growing segment where added-value was high, was appropriate.

Bjorn Robertson studied the SRT's pre-launch rationale which emphasized the strategy proposed for Delissa. The campaign, translated from Japanese, proposed:

> Agria will saturate the market and establish the Delissa brand as distinct from competitor products. We propose "natural dairy food is good to taste" as the basic message for product planning, distribution and advertising. Nikko must distinguish its products from early-entry dairy producers and other competitors by

stressing its yogurt is "new and natural and quite different from any other yogurts." The core target group is families with babies; housewives will be the principal purchasers. However, it will be consumed by a wider age bracket from young children to high school students.

Advertising and point-of-sale will address housewives, particularly the younger ones. In Japan, these consumers tend to shop in convenience stores (small supermarkets), older women prefer traditional supermarkets. Housewives are increasingly insistent that all foods be absolutely fresh so Delissa must be perceived as coming direct from the manufacturer that day. "Freshness," Nikko products' main selling point, will capture consumer interest and differentiate Delissa from competitors. As Nikko is a new entrant, advertising must be attractive and stand out. Delissa should be positioned as a luxurious mass communication product.

SRT also proposed that, since Japanese housewives were increasingly diet conscious, Delissa's dietary value might be mentioned in the launch rationale. Agria preferred to stress that Delissa was a Swedish product made in Japan under license from Agria Co., Uppsala. It felt this would appeal to Japanese housewives, who associated Sweden with healthy food and "sophisticated" taste. Primary messages were: "Healthy products direct from the farm," and "sophisticated taste from Sweden." Although, "good for health and beauty" was another argument in Delissa's favor, it would not differentiate Delissa from other brands, all of which projected a similar image.

To reinforce the product image and increase brand awareness, SRT proposed specific visual and verbal messages be used throughout the campaign. A Swedish girl in typical folk costume was shown with a dairy farm in the background. The agency said: "We feel that using this scene as an eye catcher will successfully create a warm-hearted image of naturalness, simplicity, friendliness and fanciful taste for the product coming from Sweden." The accompanying text was: "Refreshing nature of Delissa Swedish yogurt; it's so fresh when made at the farm."

Also included in the SRT proposal:

Advertising. To maximize advertising effort within the available budget, the campaign should run intensively for a short period of time rather than successively all year. TV ads will be used for immediate impact and make a strong impression through frequent repetition. The TV message will be reinforced in the press. The budget will be comparable to Delissa's U.S. launch.

Pricing. Pricing should follow top brands Yukijirushi, Meiji and Morinaga to reflect a high-class image, but should be affordable. Price sensitivity analysis shows Delissa's price can be 15% above competitors.

Launch

In January 1982, Delissa's product line was presented to distributors prior to launch in Tokyo, Osaka and Nagoya. Three different types of yogurt were selected for simultaneous launch: plain (packs of two and four); plain with sugar (packs of two and four); flavored with vanilla, strawberry and pineapple (packs of two). (Fruit yogurt,

Delissa's most successful offering at home and in other foreign markets, would be launched a year or two later.)

All three types were to be sold in 120 ml. cups. A major promotional campaign was scheduled for the month before launch: strong TV, newspaper and magazine support, street shows, in-store promotions and test trials in and outside retail stores. On March 1, 1982, Delissa was launched in Tokyo; on May 1, in Osaka and Nagoya.

1985: Delissa after Three Years in Japan

Three years after launch, Delissa's 2% market share was a fraction of target. Concerned with the slow progress, Agria formed a special task force to investigate and continue monitoring the Japanese market regularly; its research lay on Robertson's desk. The Uppsala task force included Stefan Gustafsson (marketing), Per Bergman (sales and distribution) and Peter Borg (entire operation and training Nikko's sales force). It spent long periods in Tokyo conducting regular audits of Delissa/Nikko operations, analyzing and monitoring the Japanese market and generating lengthy reports. Borg, eager to excel at his new assignment, sent back his first report to headquarters:

Distribution/ordering system. Delissa's distribution is not satisfactory; it should be improved. The ordering system is overcomplicated and slow; it may be the cause of serious delivery bottlenecks. Stores order milk and juice by telephone but Delissa products are ordered on forms using following procedure:

Day 1 am:	Each salesman sent an order to his depot.
Day 1 pm:	Each depot's orders went to the Yokohama depot.
Day 2 am:	The Yokohama depot transmitted yogurt orders to the factory.
Day 2 pm:	Yogurt was produced at Nikko Milk Processing.
Day 3:	Delivery to each depot.
Day 4:	Delivery to stores.

Gustafsson agrees the delivery procedure is too long for fresh food products, particularly as the yogurt cup date is so important to Japanese consumers. The way we operate, yogurt arrives in the sales outlet two or three days after production; this should be shortened to one day. Traditionally, Japanese distribution is more complex and multi-layered than in the West; in addition, Tokyo and Osaka have no street names. So, a system of primary, secondary and sometimes tertiary wholesalers serves supermarkets and retailers. Since smaller outlets have little storage space, wholesalers often visit them more than once a day.

I wonder if Nikko is seriously behind Delissa; 80 Nikko salesmen sell Delissa, but spend only 5% of their time on it, preferring to push other products. This is not uncommon in many countries but in Japan it is typical – high costs prohibit separate sales forces for each line.

Advertising. Since we launched Delissa in 1982, advertising has not been successful. I wonder how well we pre-tested our launch campaign and follow-up. The agency seems keen on Delissa but I wonder if our advertising messages are not too cluttered.

Recent consumer research surveys show 4% unaided awareness and 16% with any recall at all; 55% of respondents did not know what our TV commercials were saying.

An advertising effectiveness survey by Oka Market Research indicated we should stress that Delissa tastes good ... delicious. But, consumers believe all brands taste good so this message would not differentiate Delissa. Research shows Delissa has a strong "fashionable image"; perhaps this can differentiate Delissa from other yogurts in the next TV commercial.

Delissa in Japan – Situation in and Leading up to 1991

In spite of careful pre-launch preparations, in 1991, Delissa had only 3% of the total yogurt market. Although Agria executives took a long-term view of the Japanese business, they agreed results were far below expectations. A serious setback was the discovery of Nikko's limited distribution network outside major metropolitan areas. When Agria proposed selling Delissa in small cities, towns and rural areas, as agreed in the launch plan, it discovered Nikko's coverage was very thin in many of these regions. In the heat of planning the regional launch, had a misunderstanding on Nikko's range occurred? In 1988, a despondent Borg wrote:

> The Japanese market is tough; competition is very strong. Consumer brand loyalty seems low but market potential is high, particularly among younger people. Nikko has the size and manpower to increase penetration substantially by 1990 but its Delissa organization needs strengthening quickly. Lack of a real marketing function in Nikko is a great handicap.
>
> Distribution is one of our most serious problems. Delissa distribution costs are excessive (1988: 27% of sales versus competition, 19%). Comparing distribution costs, production costs and average unit selling price to distributors, Y54.86 (US$1 = Y145 in 1988), we clearly cannot make money on the whole Delissa range. These costs must be reduced and existing store coverage improved. Distribution levels of 40% are still too low and contribute to Delissa's poor performance in a major way.
>
> 1989: Delissa's strategy in Japan is being redefined (once more). The Swedish advertising image will be dropped; a consumer survey showed some consumers believed "fresh from the farm" meant directly imported from Sweden, questioning its freshness! Ads will now show happy blond children eating yogurt ... Over time, the product line has grown significantly and a line of puddings has recently been added. Nikko asks us for new products every three months and blames unsatisfactory results on our limited line.
>
> By 1991, plain yogurt should represent almost half of Delissa's sales and account for 43% of the total Japanese market; the plain segment grew almost 50% in the past three years. However, our real strength should be in fruit yogurt; it increased by 25% since 1988; it should have 23% of the market in 1992. Delissa's results in fruit yogurt have been disappointing. On the other hand, a new segment – yogurt with jelly – has sold well: 1.2 million cups three months after introduction. Custard and chocolate pudding sales are disappointing; plain yogurt drink sales have been very good.

Bjorn Robertson came across a more recent memo from Stefan Gustafsson:

Mid-year results. Sales to mid-year 1991 are below forecast; we are unlikely to meet our 55 million 120 ml. cup objective for 1992. At the present rate, we should reach 42 million cups by year end.

Stores covered. In 1991, Delissa yogurt was sold mainly in large and super large stores; Delissa products were sold in 71% of total stores selling Nikko dairy products. We think about 7,000 stores are covered in the Greater Tokyo area, but Nikko is somewhat unreliable with retailer information.

Product returns. Delissa product returns are very high compared to other countries. Average return rate (April 1990 to March 1991) was 5.06% versus almost 0% in Scandinavia and 2% to 3% internationally. The average shelf life of yogurt in Japan is 14 days. Does the high return level stem from consumers' perceptions of when a product is too old (i.e., five days)? Level of return varies greatly by product: "healthy mix" and fruit yogurt are highest, plain yogurt and yogurt with jelly are lowest.

Media planning. Oka's latest results suggest Delissa's primary target should be young people between the ages of 13 and 24; the secondary target should be children. Budget limitations demand that money be spent on advertising to actual consumers (children), rather than trying to reach the purchasers (mothers) as well.

However, on our recent visit, we found Nikko and the agency running TV spots intended for young people and children from 11:15 pm to 12:15 am. We said far more consumers would be reached earlier in the evening; with a limited budget, careful media planning is essential. Nikko was probably trying to reach consumers and distributors with these late night spots. Why else would they run spots at midnight when the real target group is children? Another question is whether TV spots are really what we need.

Examining figures on TV advertising rates in Japan, Robertson found a 15-second spot in Tokyo ranged from Y750,000 to Y1,500,000 (1990), depending on when it was run. This seemed expensive compared to European rates (1991: US$1 = Y144). Robertson continued reading Gustafsson's memo:

Positioning. I seriously wonder whom we are trying to reach and with what product. Nielsen and Oka research findings show plain yogurt is the largest segment in Japan; flavored and fruit are second and third. We recommend regular advertising concentrate on plain yogurt with periodic spots for the other two categories. Nikko says it makes only a marginal profit on plain yogurt and prefers to advertise fruit yogurt.

We suggest plain yogurt be advertised using the existing "brand image" commercial (building up the cow on the screen) and develop a new commercial for fruit yogurt based on the "fashion concept." We also believe that, if plain yogurt is clearly differentiated through advertising, sales will improve, production costs will drop, and Nikko will start making money on the product.

Last year, to help understand where we may have erred with positioning and promotional activities, which have changed rather often, we asked the Oka agency for an in-home personal interview survey with a structured questionnaire; 394 respondents in the Keihin (Tokyo-Yokohama) metropolitan area were interviewed between April 11 and April 27, 1990. Some findings are:

Brand awareness. Meiji Bulgaria yogurt had highest unaided brand awareness: 27% respondents recalled Bulgaria first, 47% mentioned without any aid; Morinaga Bifidus was second. Then came Yoplait and Danone – 4% unaided awareness and 14% and 16% recall at any time. For Delissa, unaided awareness, 3%, recall 16%. In a photo-aided test, Delissa plain yogurt scored closer to Bulgaria, 71% recognition; for fruit yogurt, 78%, same as Bulgaria. Delissa awareness was higher than Bifidus and Danone, lower than Yoplait. For yogurt drink, 99% of respondents were aware of Yakult Joy; 44% recognized Delissa (close to Bulgaria).

Interestingly, Meiji Bulgaria's brand image was highest of plain yogurt brands for all attributes except "fashionability." At the lower end (after Bulgaria, Bifidus and Natulait), Delissa was close to Danone and Yoplait in brand image. Delissa was less desirable than the top three, especially regarding taste, availability for daily shoppers, frequency of price discounting, reliability of manufacturer, good for health. Delissa's image was "fashionable." "Is this good or bad?" Gustafsson had scribbled. "Should this be our new platform??? We've tried everything else!"

Advertising awareness. In the advertising awareness test, half the respondents reported seeing no advertising for any yogurt brand in the past six months. For those noticing, top rankings were Bifidus (43%), Bulgaria (41%), Delissa was third (36%), Danone fifth (28%), Yoplait sixth (26%). Respondents noticed Delissa ads mainly on TV (94%), in-store promotion (6%), newspapers (4%), magazines (4%); 65% Delissa noticers recalled some current ad content, 9% recalled previous ads. Regarding message content, 55% did not know what it was trying to say.

Consumption. Altogether, 77% of respondents consumed plain yogurt in the past month: Bulgaria (28%), Bifidus (15%), Yoplait (5%), Danone (4%), Delissa (3%). Only 22% had at least tried Delissa; Bulgaria was first (66%). In the plain category, Delissa was third of brands mainly consumed by respondents; Bulgaria first, Bifidus second. In the fruit segment (consumed the past month), Delissa was third (5%) after Yoplait (10%) and Bulgaria (8%). Danone was fourth with 3%. ["So where do we go from here?" Gustafsson had scrawled across the bottom of the page.]

Robertson closed the file on Gustafsson's question.

Case 19

Levi Strauss Japan K.K.

David B. Montgomery, Elizabeth Carducci, Akiko Horiawa
Graduate School of Business, Stanford University

In May 1993, Mr. A. John Chappell, President and Representative Director, Levi Strauss Japan K.K. (LSJ), was contemplating a recent conversation with the National Sales Manager and Managing Director, Mr. Masafumi Ohki. They were discussing the most recent information regarding the size of the Japanese jeans market. It appeared that after two years of shrinkage (1990, 1991), the market contracted further in 1992. Although LSJ was still increasing market share, this trend disturbed Chappell and he wondered what new strategies, if any, LSJ should pursue.

In addition, Ohki brought up the issue of selection criteria for retailers and sales agents. The distribution channel was undergoing structural changes and Ohki believed LSJ needed to evaluate and possibly revise its distribution. LSJ was highly selective in choosing retailers and historically focused distribution on traditional urban jeans specialty shops. However, many new, large stores, opening in the suburbs, were carrying jeans, among other items. Although LSJ sold jeans in some of these new stores, it had not pursued this new channel as aggressively as some competitors. As a result, Edwin, LSJ's largest competitor was represented in twice as many stores as LSJ.

Chappell realized that increasing numbers of stores would improve LSJ's reach and help stimulate the overall market. However, LSJ's image could be seriously impacted inasmuch as it spent years developing the premium product image that had catapulted it to market leadership. Besides product and advertising strategies, LSJ's image had been cultivated by selectivity in choosing retail outlets and sales agents. Not only did distribution ensure a good image for Levi's with consumers, it was the only way LSJ could influence retail prices. Chappell feared that expanding the number of retail outlets would have a negative impact on LEVI's prices and could lead to discounting, seriously affecting the premium product image LSJ had worked hard to foster. He wondered what new strategies might be pursued to deal with these issues, or whether to continue the strategy that made Levi's Japan's leading jeans brand.

めぐる

Levi Strauss Associates

Overview

Levi Strauss invented jeans in San Francisco in the 19th century gold rush by making pants for gold miners that did not rip. The company bearing the founder's name had been faithful to the guiding principle, "Quality Never Goes Out of Style," and had built a strong reputation and broad customer base. Levi Strauss Associates (Levi Strauss) designed, manufactured and marketed apparel for men, women and children, including jeans, slacks, jackets and skirts. Most products were marketed under the Levi's and Dockers trademarks and sold in North and South America, Europe, Asia and Australia. In 1992, Levi Strauss was the world's largest brand name apparel manufacturer; in 1991, sales of jeans-related products accounted for 73% of revenues.

Levi Strauss International

Levi Strauss International (LSI) marketed jeans and related apparel outside the U.S.; it was organized geographically into four divisions – Europe, Asia Pacific, Canada and Latin America. In sales and profits, Europe was the largest international division; Asia Pacific was second due to the strong performance in Japan and Australia. Sales growth in LSI was faster than in the domestic division (Table 1); in 1991, LSI was more profitable (per unit) than domestic operations.

Table 1: Levi Strauss: Domestic and International Sales (US$ millions)

	1989	1990	1991
Domestic	$2,395 (66.0%)	$2,560 (60.3%)	$2,997 (61.1%)
LSI	$1,233 (34.0%)	$1,686 (39.7%)	$1,906 (38.9%)
Total	$3,628	$4,246	$4,903

Organization and Products

LSI was generally organized by country; manufacturing and distribution activities were independent of domestic operations. For example, each country's operations within the European division were generally responsible for sales, distribution, finance and marketing activities. In addition, with few exceptions, Canada, Latin America and the Asia-Pacific divisions were staffed with their own merchandising, production, sales and finance personnel. In addition to self-manufacture, in 1991, LSI purchased $117.7 million of jeans products from the domestic division.

Sales were primarily from basic lines of jeans, shirts and jackets. LSI resold directly to retailers in established markets, although other distribution agreements were made elsewhere. Retail accounts were serviced by around 300 sales representatives.

Markets, Competition and Strategy

The jeans market varied from region to region and from country to country. Demand for jeans outside the U.S. was affected by several factors of varying importance in different countries: general economic conditions (e.g., unemployment, recession, inflation) and consumer spending rates. Non-U.S. jeans markets were more sensitive to fashion trends and more volatile than the U.S. market. In many countries, jeans were generally perceived as a fashion item rather than a basic functional product, and were priced higher relative to the U.S. Sales in Japan increased in recent years due primarily to increased consumer spending and population growth. Internationally, LSI's advertising programs were similar to domestic, modified as required by market conditions and applicable laws. In 1991, LSI advertising expenditures were $108.4 million (5.7% of sales), up 21% from 1990.

The worldwide apparel market was affected by demographic changes in the consumer population, frequent shifts in prevailing fashions and styles, international trade and economic developments and retailer practices. With the maturation of Levi's target market, "the baby boomer" generation, its future success was expected to become more dependent on its ability to respond to changes in fashion and other customer preferences, quickly and effectively.

Japanese Jeans: Industry Environment and Trends

The Jeans Market

Jeans were introduced into Japan before World War II, yet the first market boom occurred right after the war when U.S. forces brought a large supply of jeans into the country. The second growth spurt (mid-1970s) was concurrent with the U.S. bicentennial when being American was in vogue and the demand for American culture and products was greatly enhanced. The third boom (1986) was fueled by the increasing popularity of the casual look among Japanese youth. This fashion trend, along with more leisure time, greatly increased the market for jeans; output doubled between 1985 (26 million pairs) and 1990 (over 50 million pairs). However, in 1991, the market actually shrunk. (See Exhibits 1A and 1B for jeans production from 1987 to 1991.)

Although 1992 financial results for major jeans manufacturers indicated continued market shrinkage, at year-end, some companies were seeing a revival. Industry changes, including new dying techniques (e.g., antique look jeans) and jeans made of new fabrics (e.g., light ounce denim, rayon) were believed responsible for this revitalization. In addition, some smaller jeans manufacturers, concentrating on the women's market, were experiencing double digit sales growth.

Competitive Environment

During the period of rapid expansion, LSJ sales grew 35% p.a., twice as fast as the market, securing it leadership at 16% market share. Still, LSJ was locked in fierce competition with five other large jeans brands – Lee, Wrangler, Edwin, Big John, Bobson – each offering similar product lines (basic blue denim jeans, other basic jeans, fashion jeans, chino pants) targeted at essentially the same customer segment. All American brands emphasized an Americana image. (See Exhibit 2 for sales of the six largest jeans manufacturers.)

Edwin. In addition to marketing its own brand of jeans, Edwin, the largest domestic manufacturer, marketed Lee jeans under license from VF Corporation (U.S. owner of the Lee brand). Edwin's goals were to increase share of its own brand; Lee was supposed to compete with Levi's but seemed to be cannibalizing Edwin. In 1992, LSJ sales exceeded total Edwin sales for the first time. Edwin also marketed Liberto and was planning (fall 1992) to introduce a new Italian brand, Fiorucci.

Big John. Because of the success of its new "antique" collection, sales and net income were expected to increase after two consecutive years of decrease. Since blue jeans was Big John's major product line, it was believed to be well positioned for growth in 1993. Completion of a new headquarters (May 1993) would enable the firm to concentrate cutting, distribution, trading and kids clothing sections into one location.

Wrangler Japan. Wrangler, a second VF jeans brand, was produced and sold through a license agreement with Wrangler Japan, a joint venture between Mitsubishi and Toyo Boseki. In September 1992, sales, especially women's jeans, were picking up.

Bobson. Bobson's 1993 sales target was Y20,000 million. It was highly successful in women's jeans; from October 1992 to January 1993 sales increased 40% over the prior year and 1993 was expected to be a growth year.

Hitherto, VF Corporation operated in Japan solely by licensing. However, industry observers believed VF was planning to shift to direct sales, a move that would affect market structure. Experts predicted the Japanese market would eventually be dominated by the three major American brands: Levi's, Lee and Wrangler.

New Emerging Markets

In 1990, Wrangler Japan Inc. attempted to reinforce its traditional image by marketing "revival jeans," featuring natural dye extracted from the indigo plant. These indigo blue jeans, named Vintage Wrangler, made of 100% denim and hand dyed, were priced at Y30,000 (approximately $240), but sold well. In September 1991, LSJ introduced reproductions of its 5033BSXX and 701SXX styles, popular in the 1950s and 1960s, priced at Y48,000 ($384). The trade press reported that LSJ was unable to satisfy demand.

In addition, new well-preserved second-hand jeans were also in high demand; some sold for over Y500,000 ($4,000). About 30 to 40 new stores specialized in selling used jeans from the U.S. made in the 1940s, 1950s and 1960s. One store reported its most popular items were priced slightly below Y100,000 ($800). However, slowing growth indicated the market was close to saturation and that oversupply was a problem. According to LSJ's National Sales Manager, this trend was supported primarily by jeans enthusiasts and would be short-lived.

Sales of women's blue jeans grew from 8.5 million to 17.8 million pairs per annum between 1985 and 1989. Since the young men's market was forecast to stabilize, all companies were examining the potential of the women's jeans market, creating fierce competition in that segment.

Changing Distribution Channels

Unlike the U.S., Europe and other countries in Southeast Asia, jeans sales in Japan were predominately through jeans specialty stores. In other countries, jeans specialty stores had already lost market share to large national chains (e.g., Sears, J.C. Penney) and to discounters (e.g., Wal-Mart, Kmart). Successful specialty stores in the U.S. were those with their own brands (e.g., The Gap, The Limited).

Although a similar shift had not occurred in Japan, structural changes were occurring in the jeans specialty shop channel per se and a new type of jeans shop was emerging. Traditionally, jeans shops were located in urban areas and sold only jeans (both factors placed a constraint on store size). Recently, new chain stores, five to seven times larger and carrying other products, were being built in the suburbs. These jeans stores proliferated, increasing revenues at the expense of the smaller jeans stores. In part, their success resulted from an emphasis on sales promotions, the ability to stock a full product line and unique store designs. Two such chains, Marutomi and Chiyoda (the two largest shoe store chains), entered the jeans retail market four to five years earlier and boasted in excess of 200 stores each.

In 1992, approximately 250 new stores were opened, mostly large scale suburban stores described above. Even though the peak was over, industry observers believed an additional 230 stores were likely to open in 1993: 75 to 85 "Mac House" stores by Chiyoda, and 100 "From USA" stores by Marutomi. In some suburban areas, the increased number of stores stimulated competition for local market share. For example, in Tsukuba, a growing suburban area outside of Tokyo, ten jeans stores (including several under construction), ranging up to 4,500 sq. ft. were clustered in 3.1 sq. m. Many retailers were attempting to differentiate their offers by increasing customer service and being more selective in product line choice. Yet, with the jeans market slowing, partly a recessionary effect, the increase in jeans retail space was negatively affecting inventory turnover.

As a result, the ability to develop low cost operations and effective inventory control systems were important competitive advantages. Jeans manufacturers and retailers were believed to be entering a new era of competition where capital strength and efficient inventory management and distribution systems would have a significant impact on company success. Moreover, to provide extensive customer service, recruiting and training employees was an increasingly important point of differentiation.

In the U.S., Canada and Europe, the shift in jeans distribution to discount stores negatively affected the overall image of jeans. Thus, jeans manufacturers had invested heavily to revive their former images. Observers believed that the future of the Japanese jeans industry would depend on how manufacturers, retailers and customers reacted to changes in the retail environment.

Potential Impact on Pricing

Most distribution channels, including jeans specialty stores, department stores and even national chain stores, maintained suggested retail prices. Since national chain stores (e.g., Daei and Itoh Yokado) had discount stores as affiliates, using different supply routes and selling different products, they maintained jeans manufacturers' suggested retail prices.

A similar change in channel structure had occurred in the distribution of business suits; city-based department store and specialty store sales suffered from the emergence of larger men's shops in the suburbs. Price competition increased among discount stores, but not among national chain stores as previously. National chain stores did not enter the price war, but were stuck in the middle between discount stores (low end) and specialty and department stores (high end).

If the jeans industry followed a similar pattern, national chain stores would not compete on price. Also, department stores and traditional jeans specialty stores were unlikely to discount. However, industry observers believed that the new jeans specialty stores with many outlets had strong purchasing power against manufacturers and might begin competing on price. These rapidly expanding stores had experienced increasing competition and inventory surpluses, thus creating a ripe environment for price competition. The eventual outcome depended on how jeans manufacturers would react to discounting if it occurred, and on the policies of traditional jeans specialty stores.

Levi Strauss, Japan

History

In April 1971, Levi Strauss entered Japan by opening a branch office of Levi Strauss (Far East) Ltd. (Hong Kong); previously, its presence was limited to minimal sales generated by importers. The Hiratsuka Distribution Center was opened in November 1973; in June 1974, Levi Strauss began local production of jeans products. In December 1975, Levi Strauss began selling through wholesale agencies, in addition to direct sales to retailers. In 1978, it began importing products from the U.S. and the Japanese reporting line was changed from Hong Kong to LSI headquarters in San Francisco. In 1982, Levi Strauss Japan K.K. (LSJ) was established as an independent operating company. In June 1989, 4.1 million (15%) LSJ shares were listed on the Tokyo OTC market in an initial public offering; proceeds were $80 million.

LSJ's strategy was to maintain consistency and a long-term view. Advertising and new product introductions were heavily emphasized. In addition to traditional styles, systems development, good relationships with suppliers, contractors, wholesalers and retailers, and personnel training, LSJ successfully built a strong position in Japan. LSJ's marketing strategy was to:

- Target young male customers and advertise extensively through TV commercials and men's magazines, creating the image that Levi's jeans were cool American casual wear;
- Have extensive accessibility by contracting with various kinds of sales outlets: from small specialty jeans shops, mainly in urban areas, to national chain stores with larger sales space, mainly in suburbs;

- Provide not only traditional jeans imported from the U.S., but also new jeans in line with current fashion, sewn to fit Japanese physical features.

Performance

LSJ experienced sluggish sales until around 1984. Year-on-year sales then increased by 35% p.a., slowing to 20% in 1991. This slower growth was expected to continue in the short term. In 1991, LSJ sales were Y35,056 billion; profits, Y7,058 billion. LSJ was planning to raise market share to over 20% by fiscal year 1995.

Profits dropped in 1992 due to increases in indirect marketing costs (e.g., depreciation from investment in the distribution center and systems development). Regardless, LSJ's 17.4% return-on-sales was far higher than competitors and nearly three times the industry average. In 1993, net income was expected to fall on moderate sales growth.

LSJ's increased sales volume resulted from stimulating the jeans market. Demand for LEVI's was not subject to fashion whims or changing seasons since LSJ had successfully established a reputation for high quality products and brand image; as a result, it could sell higher-end products than competitors (capitalizing on the strong Japanese economy).

LSJ's operations were extremely efficient. Rather than building a factory, it contracted out all Japanese production, thus freeing itself from potential costs associated with downtime, equipment improvement, workers compensation and so forth. Moreover, LSJ's sales force was small; sales-to-employee ratio was Y180 million ($1.4 million), roughly three times its rivals' average. LSJ had no debt; its stock traded with a P/E ratio over 50.

Products

LSJ sold tops (shirts, jackets, sweatshirts), men's and women's basic jeans, other basic jeans and fashion jeans. Its product assortment included 18 kinds of men's basic jeans (excluding multiple colors), 10 kinds of women's basic jeans, 20 kinds of other basic jeans (including five for women) and several fashion jeans. Other basic jeans comprised trendy products; fashion jeans comprised cotton (non-denim) pants. The sales breakdown was: tops, 20%; women's jeans, 20%; basic men's jeans, 40%; remainder, 20%.

Belts, accessories, shoes, socks, bags and kids' jeans were sold by another company under a license agreement. Apart from traditional styles, LSJ product managers designed new styles in line with fashion; new products were introduced twice a year, spring and fall. Occasionally, product innovations developed for the Japanese market were later introduced in other markets. For example, "stonewashed" denim jeans and the Dockers line were successfully introduced in the U.S. after being developed and introduced in Japan.

Organization and Human Resources

LSJ employed roughly 500 people in its Tokyo headquarters, sales offices (Tokyo, Osaka, Nagoya, Fukuoka) and the distribution center (Hiratsuka, outside Tokyo) where finished products were stored and distributed. Of these 500, 160 people worked as sales personnel in department stores; 150 people worked at the distribution center. (See Figure 1 for an organization chart.)

Figure 1: Levi Strauss Japan Organization Chart

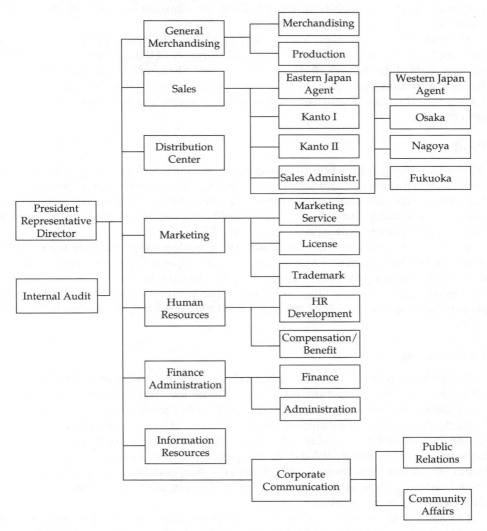

LSJ tended to hire university graduates with one to two years' work experience (not necessarily in the apparel industry) rather than recruiting directly from universities. Although U.S. companies often had difficulty hiring in Japan, LSJ's National Sales Manager claimed no problem since LSJ tended to hire from non-traditional sources (i.e., women and experienced hires) and did not compete directly with traditional Japanese companies.

Approximately 300 of the 500 employees, mostly in the distribution center, worked under contract to LSJ. Although atypical compared to the traditional Japanese lifetime employment system, it was not uncommon in the apparel industry. Furthermore, compensation was based on the employee's job description, not determined according to the traditional Japanese seniority system.

In order to build company loyalty, LSJ provided a complete educational system ranging from teaching new employees the importance of the customer to developing management skills. Many programs were designed to upgrade employee skills. The five major training systems encompassed: training for newly hired employees, correspondence education, English education, various objective training systems and overseas training.

Production

All domestically produced clothing was made by contracted factories producing only Levi Strauss products. Contractors sewed jeans products from denim purchased by LSJ from various domestic textile manufacturers and trading companies. Domestic production accounted for 50% of products sold in Japan; 30% was imported from the U.S. and 20% from Southeast Asia, mainly the Philippines.

Until 1978, LSJ sold only domestic and Asian-made jeans products in Japan. Then, realizing the importance of U.S.-made jeans, it began selling U.S.-made products (specifically the 501 product line). According to Ohki, it was crucial to send customers a message that LSJ was selling "real" American products. Yet, domestically-made jeans fit Japanese bodies better, and partially contributed to LSJ's success in the early years.

Distribution

LSJ's distribution center was established in Hiratsuka in (November 1973). In October 1990, the first reconstruction stage was completed, including installation of a computer-controlled warehouse system AS/RS (Automated Storage and Retrieval System). Automation of picking and shipping areas, along with the automated warehouse, was completed in May 1991. These renovations greatly improved storage capacity and more than doubled daily shipping capability. As a result, LSJ was able to handle small quantity, frequent, short-term delivery orders. LSJ also installed automated ordering systems at some national chain stores, allowing for better inventory control and quicker response.

LSJ employed two distribution channels: direct sales by 40 LSJ sales personnel located in four sales offices (53% of total sales) and wholesale by 13 domestic sales agencies (47%). In 1991, the average LSJ salesperson generated Y464.5 million (approximately $3.7 million).

Sales made by LSJ sales personnel and sales agencies occurred in four kinds of sales outlets: (1) major nationwide jeans shops (e.g., Big American, Eiko) – 70%; (2) major nationwide department stores, ranging from the prestigious Mitsukoshi Department

Store to Marui, a department store specifically targeted to the younger generation – 12%; (3) national chain stores (e.g., Daiei, Itoh Yokado, Seiyu) – 8%; (4) nationwide men's shops (e.g., Iseya) – 8%. (See Table 2 for a listing of LSJ's major sales outlets, suppliers and sales agencies.)

Table 2: Key Sales Agencies, Suppliers and Sales Outlets

Sales agencies	Key suppliers	Key sales outlets
K.K. Daiman Shoten	C. Itoh & Co. Ltd.	*Jeans shops:* Big American, Blue
Daimaru K.K.	Igara Kogyo K.K.	Mate, Eiko, Goshibo, IB Shoji, Joint,
Daiwa K.K.	K.K. Kasuya Shokai	Kyushu Sanshin Group, Marukawa
Eiko Shoji K.K.	K.K. Kisugi Sewing Center	Hachioji, Marukawa Ogawa, Sun
Igarashi K.K.	K.K. Kurabo Apparel	Village, Taro's House, U.S. Sanshin
Ishida Sangyo K.K.	Kurashiki Boseki K.K.	*National chain stores:* Kaiei, Itoh
Maruhon K.K.	Levi Strauss & Co. (U.S.)	Yodado, Jusco, Nichii, Seiyu, Uni
Mori Iroy K.K.	Levi Strauss (Far East) Ltd.	*Department stores:* Daimaru,
Morimen K.K.	Nagao Shoji K.K.	Hankyu, Hanshin, Isetan, Kintestu,
K.K. Ohno Iryo	Nishie Denim Co., Ltd.	Matsuya, Matsuzakaya, Maruei,
Sanwa Iryo K.K.	Nisshim Bouseki K.K.	Marui, Mitsukoshi, Odsakyu, Seibu,
Takaya Shoji K.K.	Scovill Japan Co., Ltd.	Sogo, Takashimaya, Tokyu
K.K. Yamakatsu	Sundia K.K.	*Men's shops:* Iseya, Roughox
	Takahata Co., Ltd.	
	Tentak K.K.	

Currently, Levi's were sold at fewer sales outlets than some domestic competitors. For example, 5,000 stores carried the Levi's brand compared to over 10,000 stores selling Edwin. Although LSJ received a higher percent of sales through traditional jeans shops (70%) than the market overall (60%), distribution patterns were little different from other top brands.

LSJ attempted to be a Japanese company; it attempted to build good relationships with sales outlets by providing various services to each outlet (e.g., from giving advice on product displays and in-store arrangements to organizing seminars and handing out sales manuals). Japanese department stores relied heavily on manufacturers to provide sales staff, hence 160 LSJ employees were placed in department stores as sales clerks.

Pricing

Historically, LSJ was positioned as a price leader, 15% to 20% higher than similar competitors' jeans products. However, in the early 1980s, competitors raised prices to match Levi's, allowing LSJ to greatly increase market share. Currently, LSJ's prices were similar to Edwin, Lee and Wrangler. However, LSJ customers paid on average Y7,900 (approximately $63.20), about 5% to 10% higher than competitors' average prices since LSJ customers purchased more expensive types of jeans.

Because of its rebate system, wholesale prices varied by distributor. However, the average price paid by sales outlets was 55% of retail; sales agents paid on average about 50% of retail. LSJ charged higher wholesale prices to department stores to offset the cost of LSJ employees working as sales clerks. There were no significant differences in retail prices across distribution channels since retail outlets maintained the suggested retail price.

Advertising and Promotion

LSJ employed a similar strategy to Levi Strauss in the U.S. emphasizing heavy advertising spending. Since 1976, LSJ spent approximately 6% of total sales on advertising (TV and print) compared to an industry average of 4%. It used James Dean as an advertising character to establish the image of the young, active American. Its target customer was traditionally young men, 16 to 29, who had grown up with, and maintained, a good image of American products. (See Table 3 for magazine ads.)

Table 3: Levi Strauss Japan Magazine Advertising (1991, 1992)

Magazine	Type	Readership profile	No. of ads
1991 LSJ magazine advertisements			
Popeye	Fashion	Young male, 18–23	22
H.D. Press	Fashion	Young male, 18–23	24
Men's Non No	Fashion	Young male, 18–23	20
Fineboys	Fashion	Young male, 18–23	15
1992 LSJ magazine advertisements			
Popeye	Fashion	Young male, 18–23	18
H.D. Press	Fashion	Young male, 18–23	17
Men's Non No	Fashion	Young male, 18–23	17
Fineboys	Fashion	Young male, 18–23	11
Asahi Weekly	News	White collar males, all ages	1
Shincho Weekly	News	White collar males, all ages	1
Bunshun Weekly	News	White collar males, all ages	1
Bart	News	Young, white collar males	1
Non No	Fashion	Young single females	1
Pia	Entertainment	Young males / females, < 35	1
Dime	New product intro	Affluent males, 30–40	1
Sarai	Housekeeping	Married females, 25–35	1
Number	Sports	Males, all ages	1

When LSJ first launched its campaign in 1984 with the slogan, *"Heroes Wear Levi's,"* its main purpose was to increase awareness of the Levi's brand. The ads showed movie scenes in which James Dean, John Wayne, Steve McQueen and Marilyn Monroe wore jeans, while a famous movie announcer, Mr. Haruo Mizuno, read the slogan. In 1985, the slogan was changed to *"My Mind, Levi's"* and, in 1987, to *"The Original Levi's,"* – both intended to project traditional American values and a pioneering spirit with a more familiar nuance. The current slogan, *"Re-Origin,"* launched in 1989, emphasized the revival of traditional jeans. Since its inception, LSJ recognized the Japanese purchasing mentality towards imported goods – the Japanese were willing to choose imports and even pay more – and had focused on appealing to this psychology.

LSJ's TV commercials (70%) and magazine advertisements (30%) accounted for 65% of its total promotional budget. For TV commercials, LSJ employed an advertising agency to maximize reach and communicate the company's image to a large audience. In contrast, it mostly created magazine advertisements in-house, since its goal was to increase consumer product understanding and to appeal strongly to certain target customer segments. Consistent with other Japanese manufacturers, LSJ used cooperative advertising less than other U.S. companies.

LSJ published seasonal product catalogs, "Levi's Book," placing them in outlet stores to introduce new products. Two million copies, produced twice a year, accounted for 10% of LSJ's promotional expenditures. The remaining 25% promotional expense was used for direct communication with customers at the point-of-purchase. Promotional expenditures were allocated: Television 50%, point-of-purchase 25%, magazines 15%, Levi's Book 10%. LSJ's overall promotional objectives were to increase customer's: (1) awareness of the Levi's brand, (2) understanding of its products, and (3) willingness to buy.

Future Challenges

LSJ's major challenges, resulting from the changing market and retail environment, were to decide:

- How to continue to grow faced with a contracting market;
- How to respond to the changing structure of the distribution channel; and
- How to develop and implement a pricing strategy given the current retail environment.

First, the traditional market for jeans in Japan had peaked and would likely continue to shrink or remain flat as the number of young people decreased due to the lower birth rate and a demographic shift to an older population. For each of the past 12 years, the Japanese birth rate was the lowest on record, a trend that was expected to continue. Also, the average frequency of jeans purchase per person per annum was a meager 0.5 (U.S., 1.5) in part because Japanese high schools required students to wear uniforms; significantly less time was available to wear jeans.

Second, development of the new type of jeans specialty store presented interesting issues for LSJ. This rapid expansion required LSJ to develop a clear distribution strategy: how many and what type of stores (i.e., jeans specialty, department, national chain) should distribute the Levi's brand. Once a strategy was decided, selection criteria for retailers and sales agents needed to be determined. In addition, servicing a growing number of retailers created challenges in delivery and inventory systems, production capacity and sales force expansion.

Finally, increased competition between both manufacturers and retailers raised the possibility of discounting. Price competition might be initiated by manufacturers, or certain retail channels might elect no longer to maintain suggested retail prices and possibly affect LSJ's premium product image. A feasible strategy would have to address the fact that, due to anti-trust laws, LSJ had little direct control over retail pricing. Government intervention was also a concern inasmuch as an international company like LSJ had to be sensitive to trade policies regarding pricing. In addition, since LSJ operated in various countries, it was concerned to limit gray market activities.

Chappell wondered how he should deal with these important strategic and marketing issues.

Exhibit 1A: Size of the Japanese Jeans Market

	Blue jeans		Color jeans		Total jeans	
	Units	Growth	Units	Growth	Units	Growth
1987	36,924		15,186		52,110	
1988	43,274	17.2	12,904	(15.0)	56,178	7.8
1989	45,614	5.4	13,310	3.2	58,924	4.9
1990	45,401	(0.4)	13,238	(0.5)	58,639	(0.5)
1991	43,864	(3.4)	12,946	(2.2)	56,810	(3.1)

Note: These numbers include imports, not exports; there are a proxy for market size. These production quantities exceed LSJ's estimates based on consumer surveys. For example, in 1991, LSJ estimated total market size at 45 million pairs; JJMA indicated 25% more. Since JJMA figures are based on self-reports by jeans manufacturers, they are likely to be inflated.
Source: Japanese Jeans Manufacturing Association (JJMA).

Total jeans production in yen (million)			
	Blue jeans	Color jeans	Total
1988	90,660	27,273	117,933
1989	95,562	28,124	123,686
1990	95,115	27,972	123,087
1991	86,992	24,774	111,766

Source: Yano Institute.

Exhibit 1B: Jean Production by Type

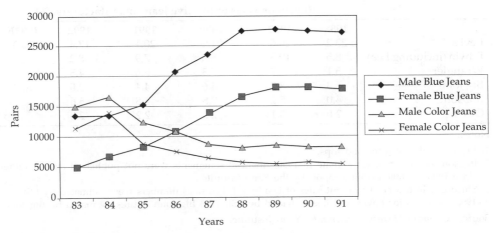

Source: Yano Institute.

Exhibit 2: Sales and Income Data for Jeans Manufacturers

	Sales of top six jeans brands in yen (million)					
	1988	**1989**	**1990**	**1991**	**1992**	**1993E**
Levi's	15,425	21,508	28,855	35,056	37,626	38,600
Edwin (including Lee)	30,342	33,579	38,250	38,534	37,099	
Lee			5,000(e)	6,300(e)	6,500(e)	10,000
Wrangler	11,715	13,550	15,367	16,972	17,847	
Big John	13,939	16,472	18,163	17,684	17,421	18,400
Bobson	13,190	15,578	18,187	18,277	16,403	
Other	90,439	98,674	103,689	108,363	111,327	
Total	**175,050**	**199,361**	**227,511**	**241,186**	**244,223**	

	Net income of top five jeans manufacturers in yen (million)					
	1988	**1989**	**1990**	**1991**	**1992**	**1993E**
Levi's	3,585	4,421	6,124	7,058	6,532	6,280
Edwin (including Lee)	2,592	3,445	3,365	3,045	3,039	
Wrangler	596	631	1,118	1,127	802	
Big John	881	1,358	827	781	346	1,250
Bobson	531	812	1,413	883	925	
Other	1,814	3,023	2,380	2,416	3,141	
Total	**9,999**	**13,690**	**15,227**	**15,310**	**14,785**	

Exhibit 2 (cont'd)

	1988	1989	1990	1991	1992	1993E
Return on sales of top five jeans manufacturers (%)						
Levi's	23.2	20.6	21.2	20.1	17.4	16.3
Edwin (including Lee)	8.5	10.3	8.8	7.9	8.2	
Wrangler	5.1	4.7	7.3	6.6	4.5	
Big John	6.3	8.2	4.6	4.4	2.0	6.8
Bobson	4.0	5.2	7.8	4.8	5.6	
Other	2.0	3.1	2.3	2.2	2.8	

Notes:

1. Includes sales of jeans and tops.
2. Bobson merged its sales affiliate in 1990; financial statements were not publicized since. Figures since 1990 are taken from a report by the Yano Institute.
3. Since Edwin did not break out sales of Lee brand, Lee sales numbers were estimated by LSJ.
4. 1993 estimates for Levi's and Lee provided by LSJ. 1993 Big John figures estimated by Big John.

Source: *Company Financial Statements.* Yano Institute.

Case 20

Lussman-Shizuka Corporation

Dominique V. Turpin, Joyce Miller
International Management Development Institute, Lausanne, Switzerland

At 6:00 pm, June 22, 1991, Rudolf Richter, President of Lussman-Shizuka Corp., could see several photographers and journalists representing Osaka's major newspapers gathered on the street 20 floors below. Richter sighed and glanced nervously at his secretary who was signaling that yet another reporter was on the telephone wanting his view of allegations recently made against the firm. Four hours earlier, Japanese authorities had arrested three of Richter's employees accused of bribing university professors to win orders for company products. In his entire 25-year career with Lussman Pharmaceuticals, Richter had never faced a more difficult situation.

ഇ⊙ര

Lussman in Japan

Located near Osaka, Lussman-Shizuka Corp. was a 50:50 joint venture between Lussman Pharmaceuticals of Dusseldorf, Germany and Shizuka Corp., a Japanese chemical firm. Formed to produce and distribute anti-cancer drugs in Japan, since 1971 the venture operated in what Richter called "one of the toughest, most competitive markets in the world." Richter, the joint venture's only foreigner, headed Lussman-Shizuka for the past six years. Although learning Japanese, his ability to handle business discussions was limited; most meetings were conducted in English. Two Shizuka Corp. executives, Hiroshi Shibuya and Yasumi Kato, who served as Lussman-Shizuka vice presidents, were involved in daily joint-venture operations. Each was reasonably comfortable with English.

For many years, Japan kept foreign products out of its national market with, what Richter described as, "high tariffs and complex production and import procedures." Through negotiations with the European Community, these trade barriers had gradually been dismantled, but Richter believed importing goods into Japan was still cumbersome. Lussman Pharmaceuticals entered the Japanese market by joining with a leading local firm; Lussman-Shizuka was a rare success for a European company in Japan. Lussman-Shizuka sold quality products at competitive prices, serviced through a national distribution network. Technological leadership provided the venture an initial edge in the fight for market share. Currently, 10% of products were manufactured in Japan; the remainder were imported from a Lussman factory in Germany.

In Japan, over-the-counter drugs were primarily available through doctors rather than pharmacists. Japanese physicians typically charged low fees for clinic visits and relied on drug sales for the bulk of their income. Doctors exercised a large influence over both their hospitals' buying decisions and the drug purchases of former students working in other medical institutions.

The Lussman-Shizuka Affair

Three weeks earlier, five doctors at prominent university hospitals in Osaka were arrested for accepting improper cash payments from Lussman-Shizuka. Two doctors, purchasers of Lussman products, reportedly received $22,000 for entertainment expenses. Another was arrested for accepting $31,000 for attending an academic conference in the U.S. Two other professors, whose names had not been released, were each accused of receiving $18,000 from Lussman-Shizuka. Shortly after this incident, the Ministries of Health and Education advised all state university hospitals against purchasing drugs from Lussman-Shizuka for an unspecified period; this action could have devastating consequences for Lussman's business in Japan.

Dr. Yutaka Hayashida, an Osaka physician, observed:

Pharmaceutical companies commonly court doctors to buy their drugs because it is such a competitive market. Salesmen will do almost anything to get access to the most influential practitioners. They'll give them presents, buy drinks, pay for trips, even help their kids get into the best universities.

Dr. Hayashida added that although hospital regulations did not prohibit acceptance of such offers he had made a personal decision not to accept any. He continued:

Low-paid university professors and newly-established doctors are particularly vulnerable to such offers. The Lussman-Shizuka affair is just the tip of the iceberg. Most companies and most doctors do the same thing. In fact, much competitive bidding that does happen in hospitals is meaningless; the doctors decide in advance which drugs to buy and the specifications are set so that only those products will be accepted.

Reaction from Shizuka Corp.

Yasumi Kato, a director in the Japanese parent company and a VP in the joint venture, offered his view:

The fact that Lussman-Shizuka is an outsider makes it especially vulnerable to exposure. Furthermore, in Japan, stability is very important. We brought attention to ourselves by marketing aggressively. Within less than a decade of its founding, Lussman-Shizuka moved to the top ranks in the industry in its particular specialty.

Our share of market did not come cheap. Where most western companies in Japan seek a small position and focus on maintaining high profits, Lussman-Shizuka wanted to be at the top in anti-cancer drugs; it matches Japanese discounts blow for blow. Now we are paying the price.

Richter knew the venture's quick climb had created significant tension among competitors. Indeed, his Japanese partners warned him of the danger of disrupting the market with an aggressive sales policy. Industry leaders frequently complained prices had fallen too low. The venture's Japanese staff speculated that a competitor had leaked inflammatory information to the press. Richter was aware that scandals typically broke in the Japanese press after reporters were fed information aimed at undercutting foreigners viewed as undermining the status quo.

Why was Lussman-Shizuka singled out? According to Richter:

In some respects, we have been too honest. When investigators raided our office last week and demanded to see the company's accounts, we had only one set of books with a straightforward accounting of our activities. Many local companies have two sets of books or, at a minimum, they couch payments to doctors in vague terms, such as cooperative research. The reality in this industry in this country is that you are not a fully-fledged salesman until you have reached the point where a doctor will accept your gifts and agree to meet with you.

Hiroshi Shibuya, another joint-venture VP, felt its difficulties stemmed from efforts to woo university professors. Investigators told the press that Lussman-Shizuka had compiled a list of influential doctors to be regularly targeted by its salesmen.

Where to Go Next

Richter had to decide how to proceed, and quickly. He could not help thinking a scandal would jeopardize his forthcoming retirement. His wife had already moved back to Bavaria; Richter himself was scheduled to leave Japan permanently at end December. Now, the Japanese authorities had forbidden him to leave the country and, if indicted, he could face a long trial.

While his Japanese partners tended to openly blame Richter for the consequences of aggressive selling, Richter felt they shared some responsibility for the current situation. Although he knew "gift-giving" was a long-standing Japanese tradition and standard industry practice, he believed the salespeople may have overdone things.

While Richter mulled over his alternatives, the crowd outside the office building grew considerably. Furthermore, more reporters were likely to be waiting for him at home, all with the same questions. Should he talk to the press and give his own version of the story, or should he try to avoid the media at all costs? Since Japanese doctors and salespeople considered the alleged actions as acceptable industry practice, should he follow one of his managers' advice and meet with competition to work out some common actions? Should he ask for assistance from his government, as a German business associate had suggested? Should he seek help from his European headquarters?

Case 21

See's Candies: Japanese Market Entry

David B. Montgomery, Scott B. Bekemeyer, Keiko Tanada
Graduate School of Business, Stanford University

In July 1991, Charles Huggins read the expansion proposal one last time and inhaled the rich chocolate smell filling his wood-paneled office. Charles (Chuck to the family of employees at See's Candies) knew he and his management team must make a decision before the scheduled telephone call to Japan next evening. He was most concerned about what to tell JAL Trading Company (Japan Airlines' import/export arm) about its proposal to import See's Candies into Japan. A second offer being seriously considered was a marketing and distribution arrangement proposed by M.A.T., a small importer of pineapples, papayas and Hawaiian Host macadamia nut chocolates that had grown with the tourist trade between Hawaii and Japan. Finally, the Bank of Tokyo presented a third entry strategy, encouraging See's to replicate its dedicated candy stores in Japan with help from a local partner. Each proposal offered unique approaches and strengths.

See's Candies was convinced Japan was a significant market opportunity for its premium quality confections but experience demonstrated the market could be confounding. During his long tenure as president, Chuck Huggins had already spearheaded one entry into Japan (1974). That year See's contracted with Nissho Iwai, one of Japan's largest trading companies, to distribute confections at major department stores, but difficulties with the importer led See's Candies to assume direct responsibility for its Japanese operations. See's considered replicating its American dedicated store concept, complete with black and white checkered floors, in Tokyo's fashionable Ginza district and other locations. Despite heartening consumer acceptance of its products, See's operations could not be profitable in Tokyo's high-priced real estate market and Chuck decided to withdraw from Japan.

Huggins was now entering his 41st year as a See's Candies employee; much had changed since that first ill-fated attempt. Indeed, if recent distributor interest guaranteed commercial success, then See's should have no concerns. Unsolicited offers from Far Eastern distributors arrived daily on Marketing Vice President Dick Van Doren's desk. Many addressed the complex distribution and marketing considerations that previously hindered See's Candies in Japan. Chuck followed the chocolate smell from his office to the production floor where he found his favorite snack, chocolate covered almond clusters, cooling at the end of the production line. As he munched a cooling cluster, he asked himself, "Is now the right time to expand to Japan? If so, which partner will offer us the greatest opportunity for success?"

ଈଠଓଃ

See's Candies History

Charles A. See, a Canadian immigrant, founded See's Candies with financial partner John Reed in 1921, choosing central Los Angeles for its first store offering both candies and ice cream. The image of Mary See, Charles' beloved candy making mother, from Gananoque, Ontario was the symbol of home-style goodness and quality; Mary See's image continued to appear on every box of See's Candies (Figure 1). The partnership prospered in California's booming Roaring '20s economy. In the early 1920s, stores were added in downtown Los Angeles and Pasadena; by 1930, See's had over 20 company-owned stores scattered throughout the Los Angeles area. See's mail order service, its first efforts at long-distance distribution, was also introduced in the 1920s. Since breakage was a significant factor in customer quality perceptions and the partners were concerned that candy would arrive smashed or shattered, all mail order candy was packed in reinforced cardboard boxes supplemented with ample cotton padding and insured; damaged deliveries earned full refunds.

Figure 1: Mary See

Challenges of the 1930s and 1940s slowed See's expansion but fortified its uncompromising focus on quality. See's was forced to reduce prices in The Great Depression, but California's relatively strong economy enabled it to expand to San Francisco; nine new shops were opened by end 1936.[1] World War II saw sugar rationing and tested See's strategy of using only superior ingredients. If See's did not substitute inferior ingredients in its recipes it could only produce enough candies to open its stores two or three hours a day; See's never compromised and customers sometimes lined up around the block waiting for stores to open. Purchases were limited to one pound per person; customers were reminded to support the war effort by buying war bonds. Such devotion to principles contributed to See's quality reputation.

On Charles' death, his son Laurance became president and led See's growth in the 1960s and 1970s. See's followed California's population to the suburbs and in 1962 opened its first store outside California, in Phoenix. Successful openings in Seattle (proposed by a young Chuck Huggins), Portland, Salt Lake City and Denver followed. Each new store continued an early (still existing) company tradition: on entering the store all visitors were treated to a candy sample. This tradition both introduced different candies to the buying public and ensured everyone left the store with a smile; it also enabled See's to dispose of end-of-shelf-life inventory yet reinforce consumers' affection for See's.

See's Candies selected Hawaii as the next logical expansion site. Japanese merchants were buying See's candies on the West Coast, then reselling at higher prices in their stores in Honolulu. In turn, Japanese visitors purchased See's candies as gifts for family, friends and co-workers. See's first Honolulu shop, the Kahala Mall store, was the first location where bulk candies in the showcase were labeled in Japanese. Two additional stores were opened in Hawaii and See's achieved high brand awareness among increasing numbers of Japanese tourists visiting the islands.

Dawn of a New Era

See's family ownership ended in early 1972 when Harry See, who assumed company control from his elder brother, sold See's Candies to Blue Chip Stamps. (Blue Chip Stamps was first affiliated with, then fully acquired by, Berkshire Hathaway, Warren Buffett's corporate investment vehicle.) Buffett's first decision was to install Chuck Huggins as President and CEO. Buffett wrote in 1982: "I have at least had the good sense these last 11 years to want See's chief executive, Chuck Huggins, who has spent his working life in its business, to run the company in his and its traditional way. Chuck Huggins is a splendid man and a splendid manager. It is no minor privilege to be associated with him and the kind of quality enterprise he and his predecessors and co-workers have created."

Professional management and sophisticated ownership elevated See's Candies' success standards. Buffett evaluated investments by incremental profits delivered from incremental investment. Capital was available for See's, but only if it could meet Berkshire Hathaway's performance hurdle rate, not just the candy industry's or See's

---

[1] The shops on Polk and Chestnut Streets are still in their original locations!

Candies'. The pressure was on Chuck Huggins to deliver superior financial performance (Table 1).[2]

Table 1: See's Performance Data

Growth ($ millions and millions of lbs)				Growth ($ millions and millions of lbs)			
Year	Revenue	Profit	Shipped volume	Year	Revenue	Profit	Shipped volume
1972	30	1.2	16.5	1982	119	12.5	25
1973	34	1.7	17.6	1983	130	13	25.6
1974	40	2.5	18	1984	131	12.8	25.6
1975	52	5	18.9	1985	149	15.2	25.6
1976	60	5.4	20	1986	152	16.3	25.6
1977	52	6	21	1987	159	17.5	25.6
1978	76	6.2	22.5	1988	170	19.8	25.8
1979	87	7	24	1989	179	21	27
1980	92	7.1	25	1990	194	24	28.5
1981	110	10	25	1991	194	24.5	n/a

Buffett described some of Huggins' operating challenges: "The candy-store business continues to be terrible to mediocre for all other companies, which tend to suffer from a combination of low sales per sq. ft. of retailing space plus the great seasonality of the business which requires staffing and maintenance of stores at minimum levels grossly unjustified by sales about 90% of each year." Buffett also said, "See's seasonal sales peak becomes more extreme each year, causing many operating problems and a growing concentration of See's net income in the single month of December."[3]

"A Grand Scheme"

Marketing studies (1977) evaluated opportunities in several major metropolitan areas (e.g., Houston, Dallas, San Antonio, Austin, St. Louis, Cincinnati, Indianapolis, Minneapolis/St. Paul, Memphis, Louisville). St. Louis was initially the most compelling; several retail shops were planned and it would serve as a distribution hub for the upper Midwest. By end 1978, the first St. Louis shop opened; five others followed

---

[2] Buffett wrote in Berkshire Hathaway's 1991 annual report: "For an increase in profits to be evaluated properly, it must be compared with the incremental capital investment required to produce it. On this score, See's has been astounding: The company now operates comfortably with only $25 million of net worth which means that our beginning base of $7 million has had to be supplemented by only $18 million of reinvested earnings. Meanwhile, See's remaining pre-tax profits of $410 million were distributed to Blue Chip/Berkshire during the 20 years for these companies to deploy (after payment of taxes) in whatever way made most sense."

[3] Berkshire Hathaway's *Letters to Shareholders, 1977–84*.

shortly. See's also rapidly developed in Texas and Colorado; 11 stores opened in Texas and eight in Colorado before the decade's close.

Over-expansion and the 1983 energy industry downturn doomed See's Texas and Colorado operations. The St. Louis ventures failed due to a lackluster economy and intense competition from Chicago-based Fannie May. See's closed all these operations on a staggered schedule from 1986 to 1991, but overall financial performance shone as the core western U.S. operations produced ever stronger earnings. See's clearly possessed a powerful franchise among West Coast consumers and the continued population migration to California continued to boost sales. See's Candies' corporate history summarized the experience: "But the lesson learned had been a good one and strongly indicated that concentration on the operation of a *highly* profitable, regional retail company made a lot more sense for See's than going too far in an attempt to broaden horizons."[4]

Development of the Japanese Chocolate Market

The Japanese consumer chocolate market was unremarkable until the 1970s when sales, primarily of children's treats, steadily blossomed to 200 billion yen (approximately US$616 million). Competition with other confections halted chocolate's growth in the late 1970s, but lower cocoa prices and new product offerings propelled chocolate sales to 250 billion yen by mid-1980s. Soft, melt-in-the-mouth, chocolates and chocolates in the shape of much liked characters became very popular. In 1987, Master Foods[5] challenged the common assumption that chocolate sold poorly in Japan's hot and humid summers by introducing the highly successful M&Ms. Tariff reductions from as high as 35% to 10%–15%[6] in April 1988 increased competition and opened the chocolate market to overseas producers. During the past two decades, Japanese tastes increasingly embraced chocolate. In 1990, chocolate products sales, as snacks for personal consumption and expensive gifts, were approximately 290 billion yen.

A significant event in the Japanese chocolate gift market was St. Valentine's Day. Since the early 1970s, chocolate manufacturers tried to persuade Japanese women to give chocolate to husbands, lovers and office colleagues (or any combination) on this February day. In 1989, 12% of annual chocolate sales were made in the ten days around St. Valentine's Day, even though men did not traditionally purchase chocolates at this time. A uniquely Japanese custom was that men who received St. Valentine's Day chocolates were obliged to reciprocate with similar gifts (e.g., chocolate, candy, cookies) on "White Day," one month later on March 14. Japanese confectioners thus enjoyed an extended selling period compared to the U.S. A prominent industry

---

[4] *Sea Breeze* (the internal publication of See's Candies). "See's Candies: 1921–91."

[5] Master Foods is Mars Corporation's importer in Japan.

[6] See's Candies estimated it faced tariffs of approximately 14% in 1989. Japanese tariff levels varied depending on the type of confections. A further tariff distinction was made for individually wrapped versus bulk shipped confections. The percent tariff varied across similar shipments over time because the tariff was calculated based on CIF (cost, insurance, freight) charges.

source estimated that over 50% of Japan's premium chocolate sales (e.g., Godiva chocolates) occurred in February and March alone. The Bank of Tokyo estimated 25% of all categories of annual chocolate sales at this time.

Approximately 150 domestic manufacturers competed in the Japanese confectionery market, but 75% was controlled by five companies (Table 2). (See Table 3 for company descriptions.)

Table 2: Domestic Japanese Confectioners, 1990

	Sales (yen million)	Market share (%)
Lotte Co. Ltd.	53,000	19.8
Meiji Seika	49,500	18.5
Morinaga	42,600	15.9
Fujiya	31,300	11.7
Ezaki Glico	26,500	9.9

Table 3: Japan's Domestic Competitors

Lotte Co., Ltd. One of Japan's largest confectionery companies, Lotte offered a wide product range; it was the largest manufacturer of chewing gum and chocolates. Lotte was controlled by the Shigemitsu family; it was pursuing a diversification strategy in real estate and restaurant business and also owned a professional baseball team. Its total 1991 sales were 225 billion yen; chocolate represented 35% of sales, chewing gum (35%), ice cream and others (30%).

Meiji Seika. The overall leader in confectionery, pharmaceuticals accounted for 40% of firm sales and approximately 50% of profit. Meiji had technical ties to U.S. drug company Merck & Co., and other firms in confectionery and pharmaceuticals. It engaged in local production in Southeast Asia; 1991 sales were 236 billion yen.

Morinaga & Co. Morinaga, a well-known general confectioner, had a long history and traditional strengths in caramels and biscuits; it was currently branching out to health foods and pharmaceuticals and owned a subsidiary devoted to restaurant operations. Morinaga had a cross-holding relationship with Fujiya; it produced Sunkist-brand products under license. Total 1990 sales were 152 billion yen.

Fujiya. Fujiya operated 1,900 western-style bakery shops and restaurants under both a direct management and franchise system. In addition, it had joint ventures with Nestle for importing confectionery and with Baskin Robbins for its ice cream shop chain. Fujiya was controlled by the Fujii family; 1990 sales were 134 billion yen.

Ezaki Glico. Glico was becoming an integrated food maker, placing increasing emphasis on chocolates and related sweets businesses. The Ezaki family's sizable ownership gave it considerable influence in Glico. Glico also managed almond farms in the U.S. and had a joint venture in France; 1991 sales were 166 billion yen.

Increased demand for imported chocolates stimulated Japanese makers to develop new products. Active technological development led to improved product quality; marketing attention focused on tailoring offerings and flavors to emerging Japanese preferences. Mixed nuts, nut chews and bitter truffles with moderate sweetness were flavor combinations gaining the most consumer acceptance. Technological and marketing efforts resulted in introduction of a variety of new products and expansion of traditional product categories including gourmet chocolates, creme-filled chocolates using new technology and dessert chocolates. Confectioners were loathe to engage in price competition.

Import Trends

Since chocolate bars were introduced over a century earlier, foreign chocolate manufacturers found the Japanese market difficult to penetrate; the key obstacle was always stiff tariffs, 35% at one time. However, chocolate became the best-known imported confection. By the late 1970s, chocolate imports were about 7 billion yen per annum; sales dropped to 5 to 6 billion yen in the early 1980s, but then expanded: 1986, 7.7 billion yen; 1987, 10 billion yen; 1990, 15.3 billion yen. In 1990, U.S. firms had 42.9% import share, Switzerland 9.5%, Germany 7.8%. However, in 1990, import volumes dropped for the second consecutive year to 15,310 tons, down 16.5% from 1989. Low-end products (e.g., chocolate bars) competing directly with Japanese firms sold particularly poorly.

Despite volume reductions, high-quality truffle-type chocolates for Christmas and St. Valentine's Day gifts enjoyed increasing demand. (See Exhibit 1 for a positioning diagram.) Prestigious brand image, high price points and gorgeous packaging were important for success in this segment. Belgian products, typified by Godiva, sold particularly well. Japanese consumers became more accustomed to imported chocolate taste as more traveled abroad and ate richer chocolate. However, not all consumers were wholly satisfied with imported confectioneries. Typical dissatisfaction focused on some candy's inferior quality, a too-sweet taste,[7] absence of Japanese product descriptions, no indication of production dates and anxiety about chemicals and other additives. Quality inspections and continual product improvements appeared necessary for successful sales in Japan.

See's Candies' Experience in Japan

In 1968, See's was approached by Nissho Iwai, one of Japan's largest trading firms, to distribute See's products in Japan. Nissho Iwai proposed selling See's Candies in the Tokyo branches of Takashimaya, a prestigious department store (similar in reputation to Harrod's, London or Nieman Marcus, U.S.). Since See's typically controlled point-of-sale in company-owned stores, this new format represented a break with tradition but, nonetheless, the proposal received serious consideration. During routine due diligence, a trademark search revealed that Nissho Iwai had already registered the See's Candies name in Japan. Only in 1974, after regaining its trademark rights,[8] did See's

---

[7] Kentucky Fried Chicken faced a similar problem with coleslaw; this was solved by nearly eliminating sugar from its secret coleslaw recipe.

[8] The discovery that third parties could register the See's Candies trademark in international markets spurred See's to register its name in likely export markets, including Mexico. In general, international

sign an exclusive Japanese distribution agreement with Nissho Iwai. However, the venture was not successful, largely because it did not circumvent Japan's multiple distribution layers (Figures 2A, 2B). Independent freight forwarders delivered product from the airport to Nissho Iwai's wholesale distribution warehouses. Deliveries were made to retailer warehouses from which candy was distributed to retail outlets. This multi-tiered structure had two serious pitfalls. First, costs of distribution were too high, leading to high retail prices and lower-than-expected demand. Second, central control of the distribution chain was extremely difficult and the product's fragile nature and need for consistent refrigeration led to mishandling and unacceptable damage levels. Two other factors contributed to failure: tariffs on imported chocolate products remained stubbornly high at 35%, and no effort was made to tailor product packaging and assortment selections for Japanese consumer preferences. See's provided its Japanese partner with the same products and packaging used in the U.S.

Disappointing progress of Nissho Iwai's market introduction led See's to explore the possibility of opening its own stores in Japan, replicating its successful U.S. strategy. At the time, land costs and lease rates were exorbitant and no economic argument could be made for direct investment in dedicated Japanese stores.

In 1978, the Fujiya Confectionery Company of Japan approached See's about licensing candy production, thus circumventing imported confection tariffs. Fujiya, one of Japan's largest confectionery producers, would distribute candies in its 1,800 company-owned stores. The owner's son, Shunichi Fujii, studied in the U.S. and was well acquainted with See's products. Fujiya had a highly successful distribution arrangement with U.S. ice cream manufacturer Baskin-Robbins and suggested it was uniquely placed to repeat this success with See's Candies. The Baskin-Robbins experience and Fujiya's solid distribution network prompted interest and Chuck Huggins traveled to Japan to meet Fujiya management. However, his optimism soured when he learned Fujiya marketed a line of confections "based on the good old-fashioned home cooking" of a fictional American matriarch similar to Mary See, using similar packaging, products and promotions. It appeared Fujiya's licensing proposal was a ruse designed to acquire See's proprietary production techniques; even See's quality manager was approached in an apparent effort to learn trade secrets. Obviously Fujiya's objectives did not match See's and the proposal was dismissed.

See's Current Proposals

See's failed domestic expansion east of the Rockies weighed heavily on Chuck Huggins, Dick Van Doren and Chip Huggins (vice president for Purchasing [and

---

(cont'd)

law stipulated that trademarks could be maintained if used lawfully and continually in a country. See's trademark lapsed in Mexico after stiffer trade restrictions made it impossible to export candy. By the time these barriers were reduced and Mexico became an attractive export market, an opportunistic entrepreneur had reregistered the See's trademark for his own use; he then proposed a joint venture with See's. In 1993, despite precautionary measures, See's Candies was again in a legal battle to regain trademark rights in a foreign country.

Figure 2A: Distribution of Imported Confectionery

Figure 2B: Confectionery distribution in Japan

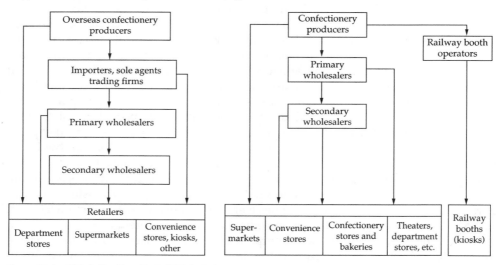

Source: Dodwell Marketing Consultants, BCG Analysis.

Chuck's son]) as they contemplated Japanese confectionery market dynamics. See's had supposedly learned to restrict efforts to its core western region but the western states' population mix was changing. Immigration of Hispanics and Asians, particularly in southern California, was transforming the demographics of See's traditional buying core. Huggins, Van Doren and Huggins were spending increasingly more time trying to market to foreign cultures at home. Perhaps establishing a Japanese operation and gaining the associated market knowledge from developing tailored language displays, packaging and flavor assortments, would enable See's to target Japanese consumers in the U.S. more effectively.

Furthermore, the Japanese market was financially compelling in its own right. The tariff on imported chocolate was a relatively low 10%; See's assortments could be sold at a premium relative to U.S. prices and companies such as Jacob Suchard (Switzerland) and Godiva Chocolates (Belgium) were continuing to increase market share. The three managers knew that if See's Candies did export to Japan, it would partner with JAL Trading, M.A.T. or The Bank of Tokyo. Chuck had studied each company's proposal intensively for the last four months.

JAL Trading could leverage distribution experience from other ventures. It offered a professional presentation and seemed to manage its many other import ventures wisely. JAL Trading would act as an intermediary for See's to local distributors and retail chains. Its superior reputation and extensive partner network ensured that high quality retailers would be attracted. Huggins and Van Doren had met with JAL representatives; they were impressed with their financial sophistication and thorough knowledge of the Japanese confectionery market. Their monthly sales forecasts foreshadowed an aggressive marketing campaign that would immediately capitalize on the expanding premium gift chocolate market.

M.A.T., the second Japanese trading company, operated on a smaller scale than JAL Trading and had bootstrapped its way to success as an importer. M.A.T. was a division of Hawaiian Host; the first product represented in Japan was Hawaiian Host chocolate-covered macadamia nuts, already popular with vacationing Japanese as gifts for family and business associates. M.A.T. methodically developed the Japanese market, increasing distribution piecemeal as word-of-mouth drove market expansion. Chocolate-covered macadamias were M.A.T.'s sole offering until founder Mr. Takitani died. His successor, Sachie Nomura, an energetic and engaging lady, was credited with expanding M.A.T.'s offerings to include pineapples and papayas. M.A.T. storage and distribution facilities were well suited to these perishable commodities, even though fruit represented an entirely different consumer market. M.A.T. was able to deliver directly to retailers, bypassing wholesaler intermediaries, so its products reached consumers more quickly with less handling, minimizing spoilage and damage.

M.A.T.'s proposal might not have been considered were it not for a mutual business contact's introduction. Chip Huggins purchased See's packaging materials from Standard Box Company, a Japanese-owned paper packaging manufacturer in southern California that also supplied Hawaiian Host. When the president of Standard Box gave Nomura his highest personal recommendation, Chip arranged for formal introductions and a presentation. At the South San Francisco meeting, Nomura impressively demonstrated M.A.T.'s capabilities, but she was also regarded as somewhat of an anomaly. For example, she did not include sales and volume forecasts in her presentation. When asked about this omission she replied she did not want to create short-term performance expectations that might compromise the venture's long-term goals.

Bank of Tokyo's research on the Japanese confectionery market highlighted See's marketing opportunities but focused less on transportation and distribution issues (they advised locating a distribution partner). The bank noted there was no precedent for "a widely sold, upper-middle market American-made chocolate. Because there is no precedent, however, there is great potential to position See's Candies as the 'original homemade American chocolate'." An early American style image would capitalize on the "fond, almost nostalgic memories of the Little House on the Prairie television series which ran for many successful seasons on NHK (Japan's national television station)." Their report also advised using the name "See's Chocolates" in Japan rather than See's Candies. Traditionally in Japan, "candy" referred to just hard candy, though most Japanese candy stores carried cakes, ice cream, cookies and confections in addition to hard candy. The Bank of Tokyo recommended that See's expand its product line to include premium ice cream, just as it had in the 1920s. By retaining the traditional facade, interior, and crisp, white employee uniforms of U.S. stores, See's could sustain dedicated stores in Japan by selling "the image of old-fashioned quality and nostalgic late 19th century with its chocolate."

The Decision

See's Candies' revenue and earnings growth were more than acceptable; sales per square foot were two to three times competitors'. However, price increases, reflecting increasing operating costs, accounted for most of this growth;[9] total volume of shipped chocolates was essentially static for years. These real price increases deterred general year round personal consumption, further concentrating sales in the December gift market. That, in turn, heightened the under-utilized capacity issue for much of the year.

Chuck Huggins focused on ensuring continued growth, even as the dynamics of See's principal market changed. Dick Van Doren recently spent time designing a Spanish-language advertising campaign for use in southern California and, possibly in the near future, Mexico. Hispanic consumers were identified as a priority because of their growing purchasing power. Should See's establish export operations to Japan now, even as exporting to Mexico appeared imminent? If so, should See's establish its Japanese operations independently or should it entrust the marketing of its confections, and a quality image cultivated over 70 years, to JAL Trading, M.A.T. or the Bank of Tokyo? How would See's Candies have to adapt its current products and processes to support operations on two sides of the Pacific Ocean?

Chuck broke off a chunk of Victorian toffee and chewed it absent-mindedly as he considered See's options.

---

[9] Raw material costs actually declined but all other operating expenses including rents and labor were increasing.

Exhibit 1: Positioning Diagram for See's Candies in Japan

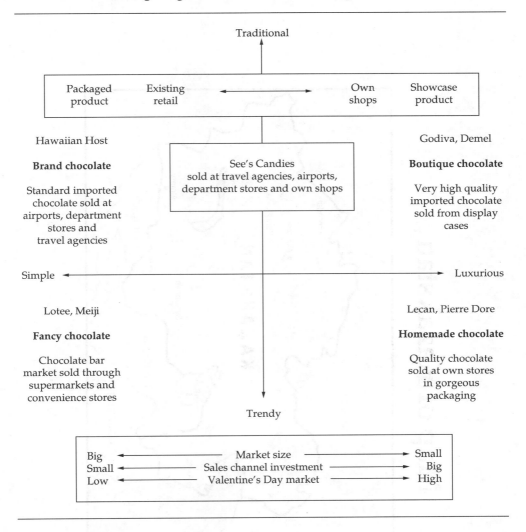

Traditional

| Packaged product | Existing retail | ←——→ | Own shops | Showcase product |

Hawaiian Host

Brand chocolate

Standard imported chocolate sold at airports, department stores and travel agencies

See's Candies sold at travel agencies, airports, department stores and own shops

Godiva, Demel

Boutique chocolate

Very high quality imported chocolate sold from display cases

Simple ←————————————————————————————→ Luxurious

Lotee, Meiji

Fancy chocolate

Chocolate bar market sold through supermarkets and convenience stores

Lecan, Pierre Dore

Homemade chocolate

Quality chocolate sold at own stores in gorgeous packaging

Trendy

Big ←—	Market size	—→ Small
Small ←—	Sales channel investment	—→ Big
Low ←—	Valentine's Day market	—→ High

Map of Kazakstan

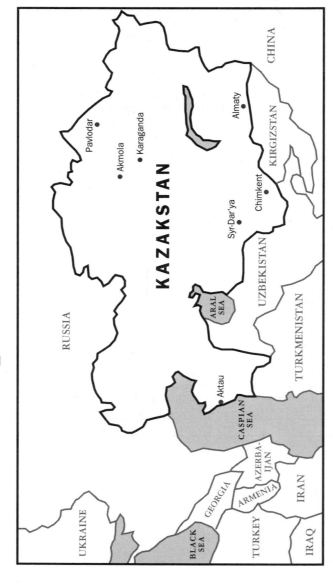

Kazakstan Overview[1]

Background. Kazakstan, comprising 2.772 million sq. km., is at the center of the Eurasian land mass wedged between Russia and China. It stretches from the Caspian Sea and Volga river in the west to China in the east. Kazakstan's land area is 80% of India's, but with only 2% of its population, 16.8 million (1994). Kazakstan is one of five Central Asian republics; other republics are Kirgizstan, Tajikistan, Turkmenistan and Uzbekistan.

Kazakstan comprises 19 regions and two cities (Almaty and Karaganda); the largest city, Almaty located in the deep south, has 1.25 million people, the only city with a population of over one million. Recently, the capital has been moved from Almaty to the more centrally located Akmola, closer to the country's natural resources.

Kazakstan is ethnically diverse. Under Stalin, entire ethnic groups were exiled to Kazakstan; in 1994, 44.3% of the population was Kazak, 35.8% Russian, 5.1% Ukrainian, 3.6% German, 11.2% others. In 1992, 5% of the population was urban. Kazak is the official state language but Russian and other ethnic group languages are widely spoken. The majority of the population is Muslim (47%); the remainder adheres to various other religions (including Eastern Orthodox Christianity) or is atheist.

Of the former USSR's arable land, 20% is in Kazakstan, primarily in the north. The south ranges from desert to semi-desert (100 mm of rain annually). Because of water shortages in the south, several years ago the Syr-Dar'ya river was diverted. The Aral Sea lost one third of its surface (66,000 sq. km.) and affected the climate of the whole region; a major ecological disaster. The climate is noted for wide daily and seasonal temperature fluctuations (summer highs, 35°C to winter lows, – 40°C) with never subsiding winds and violent snow storms. The legal system is based on old Soviet-style civil law; European Union advisors are helping draft a new commercial law.

Political. The Republic of Kazakstan gained independence on December 16, 1991; it adopted a presidential system with three layers of government administration: national, provincial, regional. The directly elected president has extensive powers. In 1995, Kazakstan had seven political parties; President Nursultan Nazarbaev leads the dominant People's Unity Union of Kazakstan; it supports democracy and full participation of Kazakstan's ethnic groups.

---

[1] Republic of Kazakstan.

On March 11, 1995, President Nazarbaev dismissed parliament (the Supremen Kenges, 177 seats). Rebel MPs set up an alternative People's Parliament but Nazarbaev retaliated by ruling by decree. A referendum (April 26) to extend his mandate until 2000 resulted in a landslide victory (95% of the vote) for Nazarbaev.

Social. In 1994, infant mortality was 31 per 1,000, life expectancy, 72 years (1996). Kazakstan has a very young population (1990, 48% under 25 years; 31% under 15). Inter-ethnic marriages are very common; the government actively pursues a policy of preserving and managing the rich ethnic diversity. A key reason for moving the capital from Almaty to Akmola was to integrate ethnic Russians, primarily in the north, in the development of an independent Kazakstan. Despite efforts to retain ethnic variety, economic hardship is taking its toll (per capita GDP 1994, US$3,159 [1990, US$5,698], PPP basis, 75% of neighboring Russia); in 1995, second and third generation Germans were leaving northern Kazakstan for Germany at a reported rate of 300 per day. Several million Kazaks live abroad (mainly forced into exile because of mandatory nationalization in the 1930s); according to the Republic's laws they retain Kazak citizenship.

Economy. Kazakstan is a member of the United Nations (UN), World Bank (WB), International Monetary Fund (IMF) and European Bank of Reconstruction and Development (EBRD); it also has a technological assistance agreement with the European Union (EU). Since 1989, Kazakstan's GDP has dropped (1994: – 11%) to US$53.4 billion and inflation has been very high (1993, 1,400%; 1994, 1,000%; early 1995, 7% per month). Despite a drive to privatize ailing state-owned industries, in 1995, the private sector accounted for only 20% GDP.

Kazakstan's future is linked to its mineral wealth including oil and gas reserves. Kazakstan was responsible for production of 95% of the former USSR's chromium ore, 70% zinc, 40% lead, 30% copper. In 1995, 190 oil fields (total reserves over 2 billion tons) and 75 gas fields (total reserves 2 trillion cubic meters) were operating; some development involves foreign companies (e.g., Chevron in the Tengiz oil field [estimated reserves, 25 billion barrels]). The bulk of western foreign direct investment (1990 to 1993, US$400 million) is in extraction of oil, gas and other resources (including gold). Kazakstan's major oil and gas problem has been transportation; it has faced significant difficulties working out pipeline access to ports in adjacent countries and is a net oil importer despite its large reserves. However, in late 1996, the governments of Russia, Kazakstan and Oman and major oil companies reached an agreement to build a US$1.5 billion pipeline from the Tengiz fields on the Caspian Sea to a new port to be built on the Black Sea near the Russian city of Novorossiysk.

Agriculture accounts for 38% GDP and 16.5% of the working population; 31% work in the industrial sector; the majority (52.5%) work in services (33% state-run). Kazakstan has no foreign debt; it signed the "Zero Option" Agreement with Russia in September 1993 (no former USSR debt [originally assigned 3.8%] but no claim on former USSR foreign assets).

In 1992, total imports were US$9 billion (US$7.5 billion with former socialist states); total exports US$7.5 billion (US$6 billion [mostly oil and gas] with former socialist states). Relative to other Central Asian republics, Kazakstan has an attractive investment climate: up to 90% equity can be bought and owned (49% limits in other former Soviet republics) and no restriction on profit repatriation. Resurrecting the "Silk Road," neighboring China has the most joint ventures, largely trade-related.

Until November 1993, Kazakstan was part of the "Rouble Zone"; it then introduced a national currency, the tenge. The tenge (free floating) has since lost much of its value because of high inflation and given rise to "dollarization" of the economy. The National Bank (NB), Kazakstan's central bank, is trying to prop up the tenge (through increased gold mining) but lack of a tight fiscal policy (because of an ailing state sector and no social security system) makes significant change unlikely in the near future. In June 1996, the exchange rate was US$1 = 67.2 tenge. Kazakstan agreed to form an economic union with Uzbekistan and Kirgizstan; the three countries would share common banking and customs laws.

Infrastructure. In 1993, electric power generation was 79.1 billion kWh, 4,735 kWh per capita. A railroad link with China is being built; it may lead to a trans-Asian railway linking Turkey, Iran, Turkmenistan, Tajikistan, Uzbekistan, Kazakstan and China. Aktau (formerly Shevchenko), on the Caspian Sea, is Kazakstan's only sea port. Kazakstan Airways, the national carrier, has both domestic and international connections; Kazakstan has 20 airports, Almaty airport is adding a second runway.

Statistics*	1991	1994	Statistics*	1991	1994
Per capita GNP	US$5,197	US$3,159	Infant mortality / 1,000	n/a	31
GDP growth	n/a	−11%	Life expectancy (yrs)	n/a	68
Savings (GNP)	n/a	n/a	Literacy rate	n/a	97%
Inflation (CPI)	83%	900%	People per tel.	n/a	58
Foreign debt (US$ billion)	n/a	0	People per doctor	n/a	n/a
Pop. (million)	16.9	n/a	People per TV	n/a	n/a
Urban pop.	57%	n/a	Calorie intake (cals)	n/a	n/a
Pop. growth	0.8%	n/a			

*Secured from K. Charman, Republic of Kazakstan, *Country Report Passport to the New World*, London Business School (March–April 1995), Moscow (Russia). In general, data on Kazakstan is difficult to secure.

ADDITIONAL MATERIAL ON KAZAKSTAN

Since Kazakstan declared independence in December 1991 it has struggled with transformation from a communist to democratic economy. Little published country economic information is readily available and detailed studies are scarce or difficult to locate. This short section, focusing on distribution and prepared by the authors of the Kazakstan cases is, in part, impressionistic and provided for additional insight for study of the cases.

Almaty, Kazakstan's former capital, was often described as "Paris of the East in the 1960s"; in 1995, fashionable cafes were opening up throughout the city. The paved and well-kept streets in the commercial area were lined with trees and the government's deliberate efforts to improve the city were readily noticeable: the water fountains, Grecian architecture, well-manicured gardens, relics and statues symbolizing famous Kazaks were prominently displayed.

Government statistics showed a collapse in retail trade volume post-communist era (1995 = one seventh 1990); however, observers believed these figures were unreliable inasmuch as significant retail activity occurred from roadside trucks, bazaars and many new retail outlets were not captured in government data. In addition, significant black market and gray market activity occurred. In June 1995, the average monthly salary in Kazakstan was US$50 to US$100, double in Almaty; personal income tax rates were progressive (up to 40%). According to a survey in late 1995:

- 62% of Kazaks spent their incomes only on foodstuff and regular bills;
- 3.6% could afford to buy cars during 1995;
- 3.2% had state bank savings accounts;
- 11.2% had commercial bank savings accounts;
- At least 30% of all Kazaks did not trust banks and preferred to pay for purchases using hard currency.

Kazakstan's most striking aspect is its people. Many faces bear the evidence of generations of intermarriage between ethnic Kazaks, Russians, Germans and Koreans. Although the latter two groups contributed only 20% of the population, they appeared to be "Kazak." People seemed to be well-integrated and few believed there were any real racial tensions. Generally, in Almaty, people embraced the latest fashions and were well-dressed. Although several night spots catered to a rising elite that purchased meals at high western prices, poverty was still visible, especially in elderly peasants who may have traveled several hours by bus to sell fruit by the roadside. One Kazak said: "Some elderly are especially affected by the fall of communism as they will no longer receive pensions – the good old days for them are gone."

Many expatriate business persons believed that Central Asia was only just beginning to create professional wholesale and retail distribution. Many world famous brands entered the Commonwealth of Independent States (CIS) through Kazakstan, specifically Almaty since it was the most commercially developed city. However, the western form of fully-stocked supermarkets carrying a variety of goods was still new to Almaty (much less the remainder of the country).

Before independence, the Kazakstan economy was dominated by the Russian economy and much retail trade was conducted at government-run central provision stores. Between independence and May 1995, the volume of business conducted at these stores reduced by 50% as consumers paid higher prices for better quality products at the bazaars. To raise funds and promote capitalism, the Kazak government was privatizing these central stores; the largest concerns were sold to private businesses. One industry observer estimated that approximately 1,000 stores across Kazakstan were being privatized. Some retailers believed bazaars would lose business as newly privatized stores sold wider product assortments in larger quantities.

Traditionally, Kazakstan purchased fresh fruits and vegetables from bazaars; both bazaars and governmental provisional stores were frequented for canned goods and staples (e.g., bread and dairy products) (and consumer durables). According to several

Kazaks, in mid-1995, new supermarkets, aimed at expatriates and upper income segments, were opening on a weekly basis. However, supermarket chains were uncommon. More noticeable were small kiosk-type outlets found throughout Almaty. These "microshops" (25 to 50 sq. ft.) sold a variety of packaged foods, soda, liquor, cigarettes, candy and household products (e.g., detergents). Larger department stores carried consumer goods (e.g., electronics, furniture) along with luxury items including western branded cosmetics.

Bazaars offered wider product variety than the central provision stores (together with illegally-produced vodka and beer). Although some retailers believed bazaar goods were shoddy, after independence, locals generally believed prices were cheaper than in stores and supermarkets. One Kazak shared his recent experience: "I bought a great pair of pants [trousers] for US$40 at a bazaar thinking I was getting a great deal. Then one week later, I saw the same pants hanging in a shop for US$25." In recent years, entrepreneurs traveled to nearby countries (e.g., Pakistan, India) purchasing large product quantities to sell in bazaars. Many retailers believed that import taxes, negotiated at the border, were lower than they paid. Kazak bazaars were cash-based; one observer said that since many Kazaks lacked the means to purchase non-staple goods from stores, the government tended to "turn a blind eye" to VAT avoidance by bazaar stall owners. The four best-known bazaars comprised three wholesale and one minor "entity." One observer said sellers at these bazaars did not pay any government taxes; he believed it was difficult for the government to challenge those who said they were "just reselling old products."

A feature of the Kazakstan economy since independence was evolving demand for high quality goods. Observers believed that as rising income levels spurred Kazaks' buying capacity, chains of shops might be developed catering to varying income levels (e.g., inexpensive shops, prestigious department stores). Some larger retailers believed kiosks and small markets, the main product sources for most consumers, would eventually be replaced by larger specialized shops such as supermarkets.

It was rare to find Kazak-made goods in Almaty stores. Rather, many goods originated from Turkey, Pakistan, Iran and the United Arab Emirates. Major electronic brands suppliers were from Germany and South Korea. Many retailers sought to acquire the status of agent/dealer for established western brands; this was more prestigious than selling Russian products. However, consumers were generally unappreciative of quality differences among international products; "imported" functioned as a "brand name," more important than individual brands.

The major problems for prospective Kazakstan retailers were lack of legislation governing trade and, relatedly, unnecessary "red tape" for importing goods. Since distribution networks were rudimentary, new entrants had to invest significant time and resources to establish their own networks.

Few wholesale companies operated their own retail stores; retail businesses were usually independent of wholesalers. Recent data regarding number of retail establishments was unavailable. Kazakstan's 1995 Yellow Pages recorded 43 Almaty-based advertising agencies. Annual industry advertising expenditures were unavailable. Kazakstan companies were very secretive. Said Alexander Katkov (an attaché at the U.S. & Foreign Commercial Service in Almaty): "It is impossible to get business information from a Kazak company. Their usual reply is 'This is a commercial secret.' It is quite difficult to imagine but due diligence does not exist in Kazakstan!"

Foreign companies entering Kazakstan engaged in a variety of forms of trade. Katkov believed geography played a vital role in determining company participation. He said Turkish companies were most active, mainly involved in trade; German companies were more active than Americans: "Western companies operating in Kazakstan are very cautious because of unpredictable changes in legislation and the economic situation." China, Turkey, Germany and the U.S. were the most important foreign investors outside the energy sector. In early April 1994, 1,400 joint ventures were registered; total capital invested under US$600 million.

Frequently changing and sporadically enforced tax laws added to business climate uncertainty. The Kazak tax office strictly monitored tax compliance by western firms; most foreign companies were equally careful to avoid "illegal" activities (e.g., manipulating invoices) as they did not want to taint their reputations with the government. By contrast, many business professionals believed some Kazak firms, using personal contacts, consistently understated invoice prices to avoid import taxes.

As a result of post-independence banking legislation and the introduction of market reforms (notably bank privatization), a dual level of banking systems evolved, differentiated by customer relations vertically and horizontally. Vertical relations referred to the subordination of commercial and specialized banks to the National Bank of Kazakstan; horizontal relations referred to equal status between different banks at lower levels. The National Bank remained a bank (in the full meaning) except for two categories of customers, commercial and specialized banks and governmental structures, because of a separation of administrative and operational functions serving the Kazak economy.

"Kazcommercebank," one of Kazakstan's largest private banks, provided an array of banking services via its 13 affiliate network throughout CIS which further promoted trading and commercial activities. By May 1995, JSB "Kazcommercebank" had correspondent accounts in 30 foreign banks in 11 countries and correspondent relations without opening accounts in 17 foreign banks. Payments in local currency were performed by payment orders, by telegraph or electronically. Beneficiary receipt of money took five banking days by telegraph, three days electronically. Currency payments were performed by transfer applications in real-time through SWIFT connections.

Case 22

Arthur Andersen, Kazakstan

Samina Seth
The Hong Kong University of Science and Technology

Noel Capon
Graduate School of Business, Columbia University

In August 1995, having been stationed in the Almaty, Kazakstan, office for only ten months, Lisa Gialdini, Arthur Andersen's (AA) new Managing Partner, was assessing the Almaty firm's performance. Lisa previously worked in Russia for several years and was familiar with that region's business environment. However, Kazakstan was a newly formed republic (just over two years old) and legislation and accounting laws were still evolving under a new capitalistic and "democratic" government.

Faced with the challenges of upholding AA's global service levels, yet operating in a country with poor infrastructure, Gialdini wondered how she would be able to justify AA's fees to local companies that currently considered them exorbitant. One goal was to sell value for consulting services to local Kazak companies that currently saw no real benefits. In one month's time, AA would participate in an oil industry exhibition, its first exhibit to promote professional accounting and business consulting services. Gialdini was considering if participation in such events would provide value for the significant financial investment of renting the space.

8003

Arthur Andersen: Worldwide Organization

Arthur Andersen (founded in 1913) was among the world's major international accounting and consulting firms. By 1994, worldwide revenues totaled US$6.7 billion. Rather than operating as a "federation" or group of affiliates, AA was unique among its competitors in its global "one-firm" partnership approach to providing international professional services. AA believed its 2,500 partners (over 80,000 employees), working in over 350 offices worldwide, was the leading integrated professional service organization. AA was determined to maintain leadership as a unique worldwide partnership serving those governments, national and multinational organizations that selected it for its specialist abilities, professionalism and industry knowledge.

355

As a result of its partnership structure, AA maintained a worldwide financial and central management structure with staff solely focused on client needs. The "one-firm" concept enabled AA to bring both specialist competence throughout the firm to consult on each client's problems and the attention of its most senior and experienced practitioners. This concept allowed AA to mobilize resources quickly and effectively.

AA's presence in the former Soviet Union dated to the 1980s when the Moscow office was opened. This office closed a few years later but re-opened in 1991; it presently housed 400 employees. Recently, AA commenced operating elsewhere in the Commonwealth of Independent States (CIS) and had opened offices in St. Petersburg, Russia (50 employees); Kiev, Ukraine (60 to 70); Novosibirsk, Russia (3 to 4); Almaty (30); Tashkent, Uzbekistan (4 to 5); and Minsk, Belorussia (2). Arthur Andersen was the first organization of its kind authorized to perform audits in Russia.

Arthur Andersen, Almaty

Formally registered in October 1993, AA's office in Kazakstan's former capital, Almaty, operated closely with offices in the CIS and elsewhere in the world. The Almaty office also maintained a representative office in Atyrau (3,000 kilometers from Almaty), the center of Kazakstan's oil and gas industry. When first established, the firm supported existing multinational customers with business interests in Kazakstan; consequently it had to build a local client base from zero. As Gialdini explained: "We did not 'follow' any specific clients here but expected those from previous international connections to come to us." Multinational companies paid for services in U.S. dollars; local companies had to pay in tenge.

Organization

By August 1995, the Almaty office, which commenced operations with three professionals, had grown to a staff of 30 including 18 professionals fluent in Kazak, Russian, English, Czech and Turkish. Staff included four resident expatriate professionals together with local professional employees some of whom had prior experience with governmental agencies, enterprises and joint ventures locally. In accord with AA's localization policy, fresh MBA graduates were hired from the Kazakstan International Management Executive Program (KIMEP); others were referrals from current employees. Management preferred to hire those with less than two years' experience so they would better adapt to AA's organizational culture; Gialdini also believed that candidates with more work experience had difficulties in changing negative work habits created under the "old Soviet system." In 1994, five junior staff were hired; by end 1995 a complement of eight to ten juniors was anticipated. Gialdini stressed that recruitment numbers at AA were not fixed; it was always willing to hire high quality, qualified candidates. Some of the Kazak professionals had studied abroad.

AA was the only international professional practice in Kazakstan with both a resident audit and tax partner, and a senior Kazak director. As a result, AA could provide objective and well-informed advice at the highest level. In demonstrating its long-term commitment to Kazakstan, substantial resources were allocated to professional personnel development; Kazak staff underwent the same training as their international counterparts by attending AA-organized training courses in St. Charles (U.S.), Eindhoven (the Netherlands) and Segovia (Spain). CIS-wide courses were offered by other offices in the region; Gialdini believed the variety of international training courses was an ideal recruiting tool. Accordingly, the Almaty office incorporated AA's worldwide culture of client service and, what AA believed, were proven work methodologies.

Gialdini believed AA offered competitive wages and benefits that created strong loyalty; "defections" to competitors were practically zero. Employees that left AA typically won academic scholarships to study abroad. AA's professional staff starting salaries were US$750 monthly; annual increments ranged from 10% to 25% depending on years of AA experience. The average monthly wage in Almaty was US$50, significantly higher than the US$9 paid in rural areas. Kazakstan had a progressive tax income; the ceiling was 40%.

Conduct of Client Services

Teams comprising expatriate and local personnel worked in the Kazak office. These teams, combining local knowledge and experience with international expertise, employed a standardized methodology applied worldwide. All AA's Kazakstan operations were governed by global standards and supervised by the worldwide organization. Regular quality control was performed by senior partners and other visiting AA personnel.

Scope of Services

AA's Almaty office offered the full range of accounting, tax and business advisory services available throughout AA's worldwide organization. In providing these services, AA's goal was to understand client business fully so that its advice was precise and relevant. To help achieve this goal, a full-time qualified local lawyer consulted on registering foreign legal entities' business presence in Kazakstan. Supplementing this service, the local lawyer assisted clients in establishing and registering legal entities under Kazak law. In addition, specially trained staff provided payroll and accounting services.

Business Consulting Division: The recently established Business Consulting Division specialized in the selection and implementation of bilingual multi-currency accounting systems and Local Area Networks (LANs). At Kazakstan's current stage of the economic development, serving international clients was the core of AA's business. Consequently, its organization and services were specifically tailored to serve international companies involved in Kazak joint ventures, joint-stock companies and other business entities. Other services included: corporate and organization restructuring, financial reporting, management information systems, total quality management, market studies, strategic planning, feasibility studies, investment consulting, corporate finance and corporate recovery services.

Professional education: This group regularly offered courses for the accounting staff and for international and local clients. Short seminars, ranging from two to five days, were designed to teach local Kazak accounting, international accounting and the methodology of restating financial statements from local to western standards.

Tax: This division took a full-service approach to tax consulting by counseling clients on both current and emerging tax issues and the business impact on their firms. Since tax laws were still evolving, tax savings were a particular concern to profitable companies. The tax division was also heavily involved in cross-border planning for the most advantageous tax consequences in both home and host countries.

Audit and business advisory: This division offered services designed to help clients meet both their statutory obligations and business objectives. Focusing on business risks and relating accounting principles to business issues helped it offer knowledgeable and practical recommendations. Services included: audit, investment advisory, listing, financial markets, entrepreneurial services and litigation.

The Almaty Market

The Business Climate

In general, foreign investors expressed discontent at "unfair" competitive practices compared to western standards. Many specifically complained about their "partners," and the government's general unwillingness to uphold contracts; some believed this reluctance stemmed from the Kazaks' lack of understanding of business principles. One expatriate worker employed in a joint-venture company stated:

> We had signed a sale of goods contract, but later the Kazak company unilaterally changed the prices. Essentially, since we had paid for the shipment and the goods were physically already in Kazakstan, it was not cost-effective to return them. So, our company had to accept a lower payment than stated on the contract. It was almost like extortion!

Lack of basic infrastructure made it difficult for businesses to operate. Gialdini's major complaint was poor telecommunications services. The process of obtaining additional phone lines was both expensive and time-consuming and line quality was poor. Gialdini complained:

> It's not unusual that when I call a local client, I actually get a "wrong number." The quality of local calls, with static in the background, can be worse than international calls! How does one effectively communicate professional accounting services when the basic phone services are so bad?

Basic office supplies also posed a special problem. Gialdini explained:

> Basic goods and materials to run the office efficiently are difficult to obtain locally; we have to import almost everything, including staplers, paper and pens. But trans-

port costs are very high. For example, the cost of sending each brochure featuring AA's services from London is US$2, excluding printing costs.

Gialdini believed certain items might be sourced locally without compromising overall service levels; the critical question was which items to select. A more serious issue was the lack of basic data on potential markets; essentially, the types of information on the economy, standard in the U.S. and other western countries, just did not exist in Kazakstan. Regardless of these many problems, Gialdini believed demand for setting up both joint venture and local companies continued to remain high.

Competition

The other "Big Six" accounting firms (i.e., Ernst & Young, Price Waterhouse, Coopers & Lybrand, Deloitte Touche and KPMG) each had either branch or representative offices in Almaty. Ernst & Young and Price Waterhouse were early entrants to Kazakstan; other firms followed after winning U.S. government contracts to manage distribution of project aid money to local Kazak companies. Information regarding the relative success of these firms in Kazakstan was not available.

According to industry observers, local accounting companies and the Big Six generally satisfied different clients; as a result, locals were not perceived as AA's direct competitors. Furthermore, whereas AA and its direct competitors advised clients from an international perspective, local analysis was quite different. As a result, Gialdini believed many local companies felt uncomfortable dealing with the "Big Six." In addition, some local firms were well-connected to important business leaders and seemed to operate quite effectively.

Nonetheless, some of AA's international clients required localized investment advice for special projects. In addition, some local companies used AA's services for local accounting advice. Typically, those that sought AA's advice on local accounting matters also sought its advice on international accounting matters. This occurred because AA's clients, mainly foreign companies or local companies with foreign investment, required statements prepared according to GAAP or IAS. Even local companies with no legal requirement for international financial statements might want to have local accounts restated in accord with international standards to attract foreign investment or correspondent relationships with foreign banks. AA did not partner with local firms but they did make referrals on those relatively frequent occasions when potential clients were unable (unwilling) to pay AA's fees.

Sources of Business

An important source of business for AA was multinational clients requiring advice regarding investing in Kazakstan.[1] For example, AA was helping a soft drink manufacturer assess a variety of different start-up arrangements requiring cross-border

---

[1] Some multinationals engaged in business activities in other Central Asian republics made Almaty the center of operations.

planning. Another major source of business was assisting potential investors in those Kazak companies subject to privatization undertake due diligence (i.e., reviewing financial statements) and restating finances in accord with international accounting standards. Gialdini believed accounting statements from the Soviet era were relatively worthless as management tools since they did not indicate organizations' true financial position, net worth, cash flow and profit. Although this business was growing, fees were currently paid on the basis of successful deal making. This practice conflicted with AA's international policy for receiving fee for all services rendered. Regarding client selection, AA had an internal procedure for client acceptance but no specific criterion in terms of revenues, only that the organization be able to pay the fees.[2]

Gialdini said that data sources providing information on numbers of firms of different sizes (by industry, local, joint venture and multinational, including names and locations) from which she might select potential customers would be extremely valuable. Unfortunately, this type of information was simply not available in Kazakstan.

Accounting and Tax Legislation

The transformation of Kazakstan's previous socialist command economy to one based on market principles required a range of legislative amendments to accounting and tax laws. Arthur Andersen's clients received regular updates of these changes through newsletters and personal telephone calls. Important changes in local laws and regulations were regularly summarized in newsletters and / or more comprehensive correspondence distributed to local, international and prospective clients. Meanwhile, copies of finalized laws and decrees were also available upon request. A recent example of service provided by AA related to some clients' non-compliance with tax regulations. The "8th August Amnesty Act" allowed companies to pay overdue taxes immediately and avoid incurred penalties. Gialdini wrote personal letters to clients with complicated tax issues to resolve.

Since independence, the government had introduced voluminous legislation and regulation on various taxes to bolster tax revenues and crack down on tax avoidance. However, Gialdini believed that without strict enforcement, these actions would be ineffective:

> When companies start getting slapped hard with penalties for tax evasion and it's made public, then other companies begin to comply. Only when more and more companies are caught, prosecuted for non-compliance and fined large amounts will people sit up and take notice. From my experience in Russia, news of other firms being caught and penalized for non-compliance will lead them to seek guidance from AA and other professional service firms on how to comply with the law properly.

---

[2] In additon to Lisa Gialdini's responsibilities, Arthur Andersen's Office Government Service (OGS) dealt with aid funded projects (e.g., USAID, World Bank, EBRD) that supported projects of interest to the government of Kazakstan such as legal and accounting reform. These relationships were managed independently of the Almaty office.

In July 1995, a new tax code was introduced to reduce tax avoidance (Exhibit 1). Details regarding practical implementation of the new policies were not yet available.

Tax Avoidance

Multinationals investing long term in Kazakstan were reluctant to avoid taxes both because penalties were high and they did not want to be viewed negatively by the government. Gialdini believed that most multinationals wanted to comply with host country laws but found it difficult to understand and keep up to date on changes.

Currency control regulations were designed to make cash transactions between legal entities next to impossible by requiring that almost all payments be made by bank transfers. However, observers believed many companies continued to make cash payments and various other "off the book" methods for tax avoidance purposes.

Many multinationals believed that local companies avoided taxes through cash payments and other means of concealing income. Moreover, some multinational expatriate employees believed some local companies avoided paying taxes as the result of influential connections with high government officials; in some cases fraudulent tax returns were filed, in other cases returns were just not filed. Gialdini believed tax payment behavior fell into three categories; those who paid no taxes, those who paid some taxes but avoided reporting all of their income and those who tried to comply fully with the law.

The penalty structure for tax evasion was high: late payments were assessed at 0.23% per day; a late filing fee of 10% total tax due was also sanctioned. Gialdini believed the government would eventually begin punishing tax avoiders; it was just a matter of time. Historically, Moscow set the tax structure but Kazakstan's independence shifted these responsibilities to the new republic. Gialdini believed the underlying problem was lack of experience in formulating and implementing tax legislation; the Kazak government needed time to adjust its tax collection system. The heavy penalty structure was aimed at eliminating and punishing tax avoiders.

Arthur Andersen's Marketing Efforts

AA's Goals

Gialdini believed that to enhance and increase its reputation among local Kazak companies, it was essential for AA to attract high profile clients requiring essential accounting services. For example, providing auditing services to a governmental agency at reduced fees could result in referrals to other departments and agencies. In such cases, the "fee discount" was considered an investment in securing long-term clients. Another goal was to maintain and increase the scope and level of services to current clients to ensure long-term loyalty.[3]

---

[3] Because AA was a private partnership, information on Almaty revenues and breakdown among various lines of business was strictly confidential.

Potential Target Market

AA's major target clients were profit-generating multinational companies operating in Kazakstan; these firms already possessed an appreciation of accounting services. A second target was profit-generating local companies. Most new business was secured by current client and other AA referrals both locally and internationally. However, attracting local profitable companies was difficult. Gialdini explained:

> Local companies don't have a lot of money to spend on additional services; their perception is that consulting is a luxury rather than a necessity. Even for companies with money, the problem is acceptance of the value of consultation services. Since services are intangible, it is difficult not only to persuade local companies to pay for value but to understand and accept that there is value in the services provided.

AA also focused on non-profit earning or troubled companies that had potential to earn future profits (e.g., in consumer goods, agriculture, wine and spirits) or that were strategically positioned within an industry (e.g., metal, mining, banking). Gialdini believed servicing such clients represented a long-term investment. AA's client base in Kazakstan increased at 12% per year; the majority of new accounts were non-Kazak companies. The split between foreign and local clients was approximately 80/20.

Marketing Activities

Gialdini believed that Almaty office operations were insufficiently large to support a marketing department with full-time dedicated staff. In other international AA locations, office partners were expected to introduce new clients. Often, they were responsible for initial contacts with potential customers and provided introductions and consultation. They were expected to seek referrals through existing social and business networks. In general, AA attempted to cross-sell services; sometimes an audit client might sign a consulting contract, in other cases the reverse might happen.

AA Almaty's annual budget was approved by the CIS Managing Partner in Moscow and by the regional office in Europe. The total marketing budget for the entire Almaty office for fiscal year 1995 was US$10,000, US$7,000 for the audit department; this was significantly higher than in previous years.

The largest single source of new client recruitment was referrals from existing clients, both internationally and in Almaty. However, occasionally, senior staff would "cold call" local companies if an opportunity was identified to sell services. Gialdini said the success rate was variable:

> People are always willing to talk, so getting your foot in the door is never a problem; whether or not any work comes out of it is another matter. Companies have difficulty in grasping what value our services will add to their businesses.

The Almaty office's monthly newsletter recording changing legislation, tax and legal matters was mailed to approximately 150 prospective and current clients every month.

This newsletter was also distributed to hundreds of multinational companies overseas centrally through the London office.

In addition to publishing newsletters, AA advertised in "Tax & Business," a weekly publication circulated among multinational and Kazak companies. A full page advertisement (A4 size) cost US$700 annually; advertisers were required to provide a hard copy of the final design (Exhibit 2). AA also placed ads (US$100 annually) in "Bookkeepers Bulletin," a Russian language bi-monthly publication.

Although television and radio media were ruled out, Gialdini considered branching into other "innovative" marketing channels by participating in seminars and exhibitions. Participation in a large oil and gas exhibition in Kazakstan during the first week of October was an example of this approach. The rental space and attendance fee for the three-day event was £2,000. In addition, staff from the London office would help promote services to multinational companies outside Kazakstan that had interests within CIS. Many such exhibitions were held in Almaty; for example, the minerals fair was scheduled for later in 1995.

Another marketing activity Gialdini contemplated was the "Hero memo"; she had previously used this method in the U.S. to provide a quick reference to existing clients regarding the value of AA's services. Essentially, the memo contained a comparison of AA's professional advice cost against tax savings. Gialdini wondered if it were feasible to use this approach to demonstrate value to existing clients in Kazakstan.

Decisions

Gialdini was exploring various feasible methods of penetrating the local market. Her major problem was to decide how to persuade local companies to perceive value in AA's services. Furthermore, her main concern was how to formulate a targeted, cogent marketing plan that would allow her to use limited resources to maximum advantage. These resources were both financial, but perhaps more crucial, the limited available time to pursue marketing.

Exhibit 1: Selected Excerpt from Kazakstan's New Tax Code

PRESIDENTIAL DECREE, HAVING THE FORCE OF LAW

On Taxes and Other Mandatory Payments to Revenue*

Authority to enact this Decree is provided by Article 1 of the Extraordinary Powers Act as of December, 10, 1993.

PART I. GENERAL PROVISIONS

Chapter 1. Tax System of the Republic of Kazakstan

Article 1. Tax legislation in the Republic of Kazakstan

1. The Statutory instruments of the Kazak tax legislation shall be the present Decree, to provide for compulsory central and subcentral government revenue payments of the nature of taxes ("taxes") and the incidence of taxation in the Republic of Kazakstan (save in relation to customs law and payments to special purpose funds, which are to be regulated by the statutes of the Republic of Kazakstan; and the edicts by the President or the Government of the Republic of Kazakstan; and acts of the **State Tax Committee agreed with the Ministry of Finance.**

2. This Decree supersedes any previous laws or regulations in contravention with the provisions thereof. Tax or taxation matters shall not be subject of purporting otherwise. **Legislative texts relating to taxation shall be caused to be published.**

3. Provisions of international agreements concluded by Kazakstan shall prevail over the Kazak domestic tax law. Taxation provisions of any of such agreements shall be implemented forthright, unless their application requires adoption of supplementary domestic legislation.

Article 2. Taxes Applicable in the Republic of Kazakstan

1. The taxes in effect in the Republic of Kazakstan are national taxes, representing the modulatory source of general state revenue and subject to allocation envisaged in the annual Budget Law; and local taxes and levies, to provide revenue for local governments.

---

* Including latest amendments and changes introduced under the Law of the RK "On introduction of changes and amendments into the Presidential Degree of the RK having power of Law "On taxes and other mandatory payments into the budget" of 31.12.96 № 61-I as well as the Presidential Degree of the RK of 20.07.95 № 2370, of 21.12.95 № 2703, of 06.01.96 № 2824, of 26.01.96 № 2827 and Laws of the RK of 26.06.96 № 13-I, of 27.09.96 № 37-I RK and of 28.02.97 № 76-I. (Status March 1, 1997)

Latest amendments and changes introduced under the Laws of the RK of 31.12.96 No 61-I and of 28.02.97 № 76-I are given in bold letters.

3

УКАЗ
ПРЕЗИДЕНТА РЕСПУБЛИКИ КАЗАХСТАН, ИМЕЮЩИЙ СИЛУ ЗАКОНА

О НАЛОГАХ И ДРУГИХ ОБЯЗАТЕЛЬНЫХ ПЛАТЕЖАХ В БЮДЖЕТ*

В соответствии со статьей 1 Закона Республики Казахстан от 10 декабря 1993 года "О временном делегировании Президенту Республики Казахстан и главам местных администраций дополнительных полномочий" издаю настоящий Указ.

РАЗДЕЛ I. ОБЩИЕ ПОЛОЖЕНИЯ
ГЛАВА 1. НАЛОГОВАЯ СИСТЕМА РЕСПУБЛИКИ КАЗАХСТАН

Статья 1. Налоговое законодательство Республики Казахстан

1. Налоговое законодательство Республики Казахстан состоит из настоящего Указа, который устанавливает обязательные платежи налогового характера (далее - налоги) в республиканский и местные бюджеты и регулирует налоговые отношения в Республике Казахстан (за исключением вопросов таможенных платежей, регулируемых таможенным законодательством Республики Казахстан, а также платежей в специальные фонды, регулируемых законодательством Республики Казахстан), актов Президента Республики Казахстан и Правительства Республики Казахстан, а также актов *Государственного налогового комитета, согласованных с Министерством финансов.*

2. Законодательные и иные акты, противоречащие положениям настоящего Указа, не имеют юридической силы. Запрещается включение в неналоговое законодательство вопросов, связанных с налогообложением.

---

* *Примечания:*

1. С изменениями и дополнениями, внесенными в соответствии с Законом Республики Казахстан "О внесении изменений и дополнений в Указ Президента Республики Казахстан, имеющий силу Закона, "О налогах и других обязательных платежах в бюджет" от 31.12.96 г. № 61-I ЗРК, а также Указов Президента РК от 20.07.95 г. № 2370, от 21.12.95 г. № 2703, от 6.01.96 г. № 2824, от 26.01.06 г. № 2827 и Законов Республики Казахстан от 26.06.96 г. № 13-I, от 27.09.96 г. № 37-I ЗРК и от 28.02.97 г. № 76-I ЗРК. (По состоянию на 1 марта 1997 г.).

2. Изменения и дополнения, внесенные в Указ на основании Законов Республики Казахстан от 31.12.96 г. № 61-I ЗРК и от 28.02.97 № 76-I ЗРК, выделены в тексте жирным курсивом.

89

Exhibit 1 (cont'd)

PART IX. TAX ON PROPERTY

Chapter 36. *General Provisions on property tax*

Article 131. Payers of the tax

The payers of the property tax are corporations and individuals having ownership rights or trustee, managerial, or operational supervision over taxable objects.

Article 132. Taxable objects

Taxable objects are:

1) capital goods and non-production capital assets of corporations and individuals engaged in business activities, except vehicles taxable with respect to tax on vehicles;

2) houses, apartments, dachas, garages, other structures, facilities and premises in the Republic of Kazakstan, which are in the personal use of individuals, and are not used in business activities.

Chapter 37. *Payment of Tax*

Article 133. Tax rates

1. The tax on capital goods and non-production capital assets of corporations and individuals engaged in business activities shall be payable annually at the rate of 1% percent of the value of the specified assets under the procedure and the terms stipulated in Article 135 of this Decree.

2. The individual tax for property, not used in the entrepreneurial activity shall be paid annually based on the value of real estate, determined by the agency, authorized by the Government of the RK at following rates:
1) up to 1 000 000 tenge – 0.1% of the value
2) 1 000 000–2 000 000 tenge—tax on 1 000 000 value + 0.15% of the balance
3) 2 000 000–3 000 000 —tax on 2 000 000 +0.2% of the balance
4) 3 000 000 —+ —tax on 3 000 000 +0.3% of the balance.

Article 134. Tax exemptions

1. The following shall be exempted from property tax:

1) non-profit and budgetary organizations with respect to property not used in business activities;

2) organizations listed in paragraph 5 of article 129 of this Decree with regards to property used for production purposes and in social sphere;

3) National Bank of Kazakstan and ithes.

4) organizations with regard to state automobile roads of common use and constructions on roads which are given them for operating management.

5) Corporations determined by the Government of the Republic of Kazakstan who are engaged in building in Akmola for the period of their activity with regard to building but no more than 5 years.

6) *Taxpayers under the Contract with the SCI can be assigned:*

55

РАЗДЕЛ IX. НАЛОГ НА ИМУЩЕСТВО

ГЛАВА 36. ОБЩИЕ ПОЛОЖЕНИЯ ПО НАЛОГУ НА ИМУЩЕСТВО

Статья 131. Плательщики налога

Плательщиками налога на имущество являются юридические и физические лица, имеющие объекты обложения на праве собственности, доверительного управления собственностью, хозяйственного ведения или оперативного управления.

Статья 132. Объекты обложения

Объектами обложения налогом являются:

1) основные производственные и непроизводственные фонды юридических и физических лиц, занимающихся предпринимательской деятельностью, кроме транспортных средств, облагаемых налогом на транспортные средства;

2) жилые помещения, дачные строения, гаражи, иные строения, сооружения, помещения физических лиц, не используемые в предпринимательской деятельности, находящиеся в личном пользовании граждан, расположенные на территории Республики Казахстан.

ГЛАВА 37. УПЛАТА НАЛОГА

Статья 133. Ставки налога

1. Налог на основные производственные и непроизводственные фонды юридических и физических лиц, занимающихся предпринимательской деятельностью, уплачивается ежегодно по ставке *1 процент от стоимости* указанных фондов в порядке и на условиях, предусмотренных статьей 135 настоящего Указа.

2. *Налог на имущество физических лиц, не используемое в предпринимательской деятельности, уплачивается ежегодно от стоимости недвижимого имущества, определяемой органом, уполномоченным Правительством Республики Казахстан, по следующим ставкам:*
1) *до 1 000 000 тенге*
2) *от 1 000 000 до 2 000 000 тенге*
сумма налога от стоимости недвижимого имущества 1 000 000 тенге
+ *0,15 процента с суммы, превышающей её;*
3) *от 2 000 000 до 3 000 000 тенге*
сумма налога от стоимости недвижимого имущества 2 000 000 тенге
+ *0,2 процента с суммы, превышающей её;*
4) *3 000 000 тенге и свыше*
сумма налога от стоимости недвижимого имущества 3 000 000 тенге
+ *0,3 процента с суммы, превышающей её.*

Статья 134. Льготы по налогу

1. От уплаты налога на имущество освобождаются:

1) некоммерческие и бюджетные организации по имуществу, не используемому в предпринимательской деятельности;

2) организации, указанные в пункте 5 статьи 129 настоящего Указа, по имуществу, используемому в производственных целях и в социальной сфере;

144

Exhibit 2: Arthur Andersen Print Advertisement

ARTHUR ANDERSEN

Audit and Business Advisory Service	Financial audits Compliance audits Accounting assistance Formation of joint ventures and other entities Business and financial planning Research services
Tax Services	Tax compliance Corporate tax consulting International tax services Compensation and benefits consulting Personal taxation Preparation of income tax returns
Business Systems Consulting	Identification and selection of software EDP reviews Development of strategic business plans Negotiation of software and hardware vendor contracts Installation, training and development of systems procedures
Professional Education Center	Western Accounting for Beginners Intensive Kazak Accounting Restatements of Kazak Accounts and Records into International Standards International Accounting Standards
Corporate Speciality Services	Operational consulting, cost and productivity management Corporate recovery services Contract financial management Bookkeeping and payroll services
Corporate Finance and Privatization Consulting	Assisting Kazak enterprises to restructure through privatization Acquisition search for international companies Investor identification and negotiation for Kazak enterprises Transaction structuring Assistance with the raising of finance Appraisal and valuation services

For more information, please contact:
Lisa A. Gialdini, Managing Partner
Tom Cradock-Watson, Director of Audit
69 Tole Bi Street, 3rd floor
480091 Almaty
Tel: 7 (3272) 69-15-12 or 69-16-19 or 69-49-06
Fax: 7 (3272)-69-15-19
Satellite fax: 7 (327)-581-15-88

Case 23

Astana Foods, Kazakstan

Samina Seth
The Hong Kong University of Science and Technology

Noel Capon
Graduate School of Business, Columbia University

In August 1995, physicist-turned entrepreneur Alexander Garber, sat upright as the eager MBA student from Hong Kong continued to drill him about Astana Foods, his two-year-old Almaty-based business. Specializing in food distribution for the Kazak market, Garber had never created an overall strategy for Astana; rather, he said he ran the business on a daily basis as best he could. His major goal was to establish Astana Foods firmly and quickly as the basis for both short- and long-term growth. He was particularly interested in western marketing techniques to create "competitive advantage," a term learned on an international buying trip. Towards the end of the interview, Garber interrupted the chatty student: "Ms. Seth, these past several hours you have heard everything I could possibly tell you about my business. I have no experience in western business, but in Kazakstan business changes daily. What advice can you give me to increase revenues and profits? How can we improve distribution? Better marketing tools? Improved logistics? Spending more time changing our product mix?"

Surprised at the interview reversal, Seth replied: "I don't really want to respond in haste. May I send you a list of recommendations from Hong Kong in a week or so? I'd like to think things over."

"Certainly!" cried Garber excitedly. "I look forward to your feedback. Let's say September 15? That will give you an extra week and time to recover from your flight on Kazak Air!"

"That's fine," replied Seth, "I'll be sure to give you my honest opinions." With that, she thanked the management team for their time and exited the building to hitch-hike back to her hotel. She had already begun to ponder the issues.

∞∞∞

Company Background

In mid-1993, Alexander Garber approached representatives of the newly-formed Almaty Stock Exchange with a proposal for imported foodstuff distribution in Kazakstan; he believed this could be a high margin business yielding high profits. As

367

a result of these discussions, a joint venture, Astana Foods (AF), was formed: Astana Holdings (AH) (60%), Alexander Garber (40%). By end 1993, Astana Foods operated with three employees and a US$100,000 "loan"[1] from AH in a small office on the third floor of AH's office building in downtown Almaty. Initially, AH wanted to keep a close eye on AF and assess potential profitability by "testing" profits on initial transactions.

AF's first transaction was a trial shipment of champagne and canned vegetables from Hungary. The suppliers were identified by the Kazakstan trade commission, a local organization assisting local companies by recommending prospective international partners. The products sold quickly at very high margins; Astana Foods was officially established.

Garber's process for deciding which products to carry was to examine the Kazak market and import goods not produced locally; as a result, AF did not compete with local producers. During the previous two years, AF imported foodstuffs from many foreign countries (e.g., Israel, Germany, U.S., Holland, Turkey). Garber regularly visited food exhibitions in Europe (e.g., Paris, Frankfurt, Moscow) to meet directly with prospective partners and learn about international food companies. Other sources of potential partners were referrals from AF's sister companies.

The Food Business in Kazakstan

Compared to many western countries, Kazakstan was a small market with low disposable incomes; however, many observers believed it might develop rapidly. Following independence and communism's overthrow, market development was in an early stage; competition was fragmented but expected to increase substantially in the next few years.

Although Almaty's population was only 1.25 million (of 17 million in Kazakstan), it was the largest wholesale food market and many dealers from other Kazak regions visited Almaty to purchase products for resale in home markets. The majority of the population was concentrated in the south and south western regions of the country. Garber identified 11 significant potential markets, each with over 300,000 people (e.g., Karaganda, Chimkent, Pavlodra).

Most goods imported by Astana Foods entered Almaty by air from the supplier's most convenient port although shipments from nearby countries (e.g., Turkey) might arrive overland. Goods were transported to warehouses in the city outskirts where shipping crates were unpacked and boxes stored. Individual orders from distributors, typically comprising a variety of foodstuffs, were then assorted and delivered by company-owned trucks or vans to one of the 11 geographic markets. Some Almaty customers (e.g., bazaars) picked up goods direct from AF warehouses.

Consumer Requirements

Garber was unable to identify any sources of data on consumer foodstuff purchases in Kazakstan. However, based on his experience and perceptions regarding foreign

---

[1] The loan was actually capital contribution; profit was earned in proportion to the 60/40 ownership ratio but no interest was paid.

products, he believed consumers had strong preferences for European or American products, typically those seen in foreign movies and publications. His sense was that locals believed foodstuffs from neighboring countries, where transportation costs to Kazakstan were much lower, were of lesser quality and less prestigious.

Moreover, Garber preferred working with European and U.S. suppliers because of previous problems encountered with several Turkish suppliers. He recounted one incident:

> After securing a bank guarantee on goods from one Turkey supplier, he [the supplier] delayed shipment of the goods. Because of this delay and a national holiday in Turkey, the bank guarantee expired and we had to have it extended. Kazakstan expenses were paid by Astana Holdings; the Turkish suppliers paid all their local costs. However, the Turkish banks demanded extra fees for extending the guarantee. Since we wanted to complete the contract, we had to pay a fine for a 30-day extension!

Competition

AF's major competition was from distributors carrying competing lines: for example, Procter and Gamble and Unilever distributors. Garber had not yet encountered significant direct competition from food distributors carrying the same brands; each firm seemed to specialize in particular products and brands. In general, food distributors requested exclusive rights to distribute foreign partners' products in the Kazakstan market. Moreover, because of working capital requirements, potential direct competitors would need substantially more financial resources than were currently committed to food distribution. However, exceptions did occur; for example, AF was the largest distributor of both Wrigley Chewing Gum and imported sugar, but several other firms distributed identical brands.

Astana Foods

Customer Focus

AF concentrated on wholesale activities. Garber believed inventory turnover was greater at wholesale than retail and that profits could be realized earlier. He believed opening retail stores was too risky and would unnecessarily tie up crucial working capital. In addition, opening AF shops would introduce a conflict of interest with existing retail customers that might seek alternative suppliers.

AF's customers fell into two major categories: private and government operations. Major private customers were ten large wholesalers, with whom Garber was developing close relationships, that supplied foodstuffs and many other products throughout the country to approximately 80% of all Kazak businesses. Almaty customers included small private shops, newly opened supermarkets (some dealing only in U.S. dollars) and small retailers that sold "from boxes" in bazaars. AF's government clients were large central provision stores that sold food and other consumer products. In Almaty, these stores were located in the best commercial locations and comprised 80% (about

100 outlets) of the largest retail shops. Unfortunately, central provision stores were not ideal buyers; they tended to delay payment extensively (or not pay at all). A complicating factor was that these stores were being privatized and Garber did not want to lose potentially good contacts. AF supplied several large central provision stores that paid on time.

Garber did not classify AF's sales according to distribution type. He viewed all customers as resellers and was more interested in unit and currency sales volume per transaction. Nonetheless, he was aware that AF's customers varied by geographic location. For example, in Almaty, AF dealt with individual retail establishments, bazaars and middlemen; goods were either delivered by van (large orders) or collected from the warehouse by customers (small orders). In neighboring cities and towns, AF relied on food resellers to reach retail stores. For distant geographic markets, delivery frequency depended on distance from Almaty and might be from seven to 21 days. AF advertised for new wholesale and retail buyers but was still experimenting to find the best medium; new customers resulted from both advertising efforts and recommendations from AF's sister companies. Regardless of customer type, Garber preferred to move large quantities of goods on a cash basis since credit costs were high.

Business Operations

Garber and members of AF's marketing department used several processes to identify products to extend the product line. Competitors' advertisements were scanned, wholesale markets were visited and shop owners were interviewed to identify products for which a market need might exist. AF attempted to fill market voids before competitors by identifying opportunities with targeted products and prices. Initially, to test market acceptance, only one to two containers were imported; regular orders were placed if the product sold well. However, even a one container purchase might be excessive: Garber recalled a shipment of "Muesli" bars that remained unsold in AF's warehouse. On occasion, AF attempted to purchase a few sample boxes initially; sometimes he was successful but oftentimes manufacturers would not ship in such small quantities. Notwithstanding his "Muesli experience," Garber believed that new products were generally successful if advertised aggressively. He stated: "It's the Soviet mentality. Any product will work if the people have seen it on TV." If an AF customer requested certain goods, prepayment for shipment might be required or bank delivery guarantees arranged.

Product Range

AF management was not interested in offering a wide product assortment, believing that basic staple foods (e.g., sugar, flour and meat) were well supplied. Rather, AF concentrated on high quality, good-selling products with high margins. By August 1995, AF carried 10 to 15 product lines; several were seasonal. Chewing gum and coffee were AF's largest sellers. For all established products, the minimum order size was one container, 160 tons. Garber considered a product launch successful if the product was broadly sold and gross profits were US$50,000 to US$100,000; for branded products, AF was content with profits of US$10,000 to US$20,000. AF's product portfolio included:

- High quality frozen products (e.g., chicken legs): a single delivery cost US$230,000 and would typically be sold within 20 days (from western Europe);
- Coffee and sugar, from Kraft and Jacobs; two containers were imported per month at US$45,000 per container (from Europe);
- Wrigley Chewing Gum: three truckloads imported per month, each truck worth DM 250,000 (from Germany);
- Coffee: from two companies, Kraft and Lite; four containers per month at US$50,000 per container (from Europe);
- Tea: (first trial shipment) $150,000 for one order (from Turkey);
- Sparkling wines (viewed as champagne by consumers) (Italy and Germany); high excise duties led to AF temporarily discontinuing these products;
- Tomato Ketchup: Turkey's largest food company, Koch Holdings, sent one truck every two months at US$25,000 per truck;
- Fruit Juices (seasonal): four containers in summer 1995 at US$15,000 per container; AF believed sales volume was inadequate to import year round (from Holland).

Garber's gross margin realization and price charged varied based on food type, whether Astana was selling it for the first time and perceived popularity. Although competition was steadily increasing, he believed significant margins could still be extracted from imported foodstuffs. For established food products with large distribution and broad market appeal (e.g., sugar, Wrigley's chewing gum), mark-up was approximately 50% of cost. For newer products (e.g., "exotic" fruit drinks) margins ranged from 100% to 150%. Garber believed customers were willing to pay premium prices for western branded products; consequently margins for many products were in the 50% to 100% range.

Garber was reluctant to extend AF's product line beyond foodstuffs as he believed it enjoyed significant first mover advantages in a niche market. He believed substantial opportunities existed to increase sales via promotional activities.

Financing

AF purchased goods from suppliers using U.S. dollar denominated letters of credit; financing costs ranged from 1% to 1.5% per month. To use this payment method, AF had to keep significant U.S. dollar balances as collateral. When reselling products within Kazakstan, regardless of whether customers purchased with Tenge or U.S. dollar, credit facilities were required for at least three months to accommodate slow payers. In mid-1995, because inflation risk was high, financing costs in Tenge were a minimum of 60% p.a.; credit facilities for U.S. dollar were substantially lower, 1.5% per month. The cost for bank guarantees (to ensure AF received payment) ranged up to 80% to 90% p.a. AF offered buyers trade discounts of 2% to 5% based on the product, Astana Holding's required profit margins and whether AF had already paid the foreign supplier for goods.

Working capital consumed most of AF's capital; other investments were low. Other than warehouses (current market value approximately US$45,000) and several trucks (depreciated value US$25,000), Garber was unwilling to invest in fixed assets. Monthly wages, warehouse rental and other recurring expenses ranged from US$20,000 to US$29,000.

The Astana Brand

AF's products were sold under their foreign brand names; Garber had not developed an "Astana" brand. He believed that, in principle, an Astana brand could be created, but did not consider it feasible on a wide scale as AF would have to take full responsibility for correctly managing and sourcing its products. Regardless, AF was experimenting with a new brand "Astana" Tea. Garber wanted to assess results from this effort before considering further developments; he said no Kazak brand launched in the past three years was noticeable in the market.

Promotional Activities

Advertising

Garber budgeted 2% of sales revenue for advertising; he considered this to be very high. He was not particular about advertising to specific market segments but stated: "The more consumers know about a product, the more likely they want to buy it and the greater the chance vendors will want to stock it." Media already tried were:

Radio. By August 1995, radio advertising had been discontinued. The first medium used by AF, Garber described it as "generally ineffective as customers could not see the products."

Television. AF spent between US$4,000 and US$5,000 per month on the six most popular Kazak television channels; each commercial aired cost US$80. Production was fairly inexpensive as foreign partners often contributed completed commercials; AF paid US$100 for each fact-based Russian-language insertion providing details such as store availability. AF did not advertise on those Russian channels widely watched throughout the former Soviet Union and received in Kazakstan. Many observers believed success rates for product launches heavily advertised on these channels were good, but costs were high even by western standards; a one-minute advertisement cost US$45,000. However, AF reaped indirect benefits from products advertised on these channels; for example, Wrigley spent US$3 to US$4 million annually while AF's coffee suppliers spent US$1 million.

Print media. AF's monthly advertising expenditures in newspapers were similar to television. AF also advertised in "Caravan" (See Exhibit 1 for competitive ads), a weekly advertising supplement distributed in Kazakstan and Moscow with a claimed circulation of 0.5 million. Each insertion (500 sq. cm.) cost US$50 to prepare and insert. Garber was also testing advertising in various magazines; each insertion cost US$50.

Garber measured the success of both product and media selection by prospective consumer response rates. All advertisements included AF's telephone number and urged prospective customers to call for more information. The strategic "red telephone" was "monitored" for the number of times it rang. Garber reasoned that if it rang continuously with queries, the product was a hit! The phone response criterion was matched with eventual sales volume to indicate the suitability of product/advertising combinations. One product passing the ringing test was chicken legs, first imported in July 1995.

Although Astana's focus was selling to wholesalers and resellers, advertising attracted responses from both the household and commercial sectors. Consumers that telephoned were advised where a particular product might be found at retail. Garber's aim was to sell goods quickly through any channel.

For the upcoming Astana Tea introduction, AF's tea supplier contributed US$40,000 for advertising. Management was unsure whether this amount was adequate. Garber related a previous experience: "We advertised a new shipment of drumsticks (chicken) for one day on two TV channels and for two days in Caravan. At the time, only Astana Foods could deliver the product; it was very successful."

One American expatriate living in Almaty at the time supported this success differently: "In Almaty, it's impossible to find good chicken that is not old. I wouldn't be surprised if people bought imported chicken, it's got to be better than what you can get here. Do you know where I can get some?"

Another product scheduled for advertising was Elite Classic Coffee; AF planned to spend US$4,000 on launch. Since customers were already very familiar with Jacobs Coffee, also carried by AF, management did not want to encourage cannibalization; rather, it wanted to test consumer response to a new product, especially the effect of adding product variety to the shelves.

Personal Selling

In June 1995, Garber began a merchandising program for Wrigley and Kraft products; a sales manager visited kiosks (small retail sales outlets scattered throughout Almaty) to promote these products. In addition, two part-time van salespeople in Almaty visited kiosks and stores throughout the city selling all AF products direct to owners for cash. Garber believed sales had the potential to grow quickly.

Based on his market knowledge, no other food vendor was using this direct approach. Since initial results of this door-to-door experiment were promising, Garber planned to add two more salespeople on a commission basis. He was unsure what compensation package to offer but was considering some sort of quota, a low base salary and 5% of sales revenue. Garber had no benchmarks to employ, but knew that monthly professional salaries averaged approximately US$300 in Kazakstan.

Organization

By August 1995, AF had 15 permanent employees; Garber said personnel would be added as required, to support sales to Kazakstan and Kirgizstan:

- Director: Head of Astana Foods, Alexander Garber was responsible for seeking new opportunities; as such he was responsible for "strategic planning." Garber made final decisions on controlling the sales process and completed all contracts with both buyers and suppliers.
- Deputy Director: Antoinne assisted the director in all functions.
- Accounting/Finance Department: five employees monitored inventory levels, re-ordered standard items and were responsible for managing all monetary transactions.
- Sales Department: two members were responsible for seeking new clients (wholesale and retail) throughout Kazakstan and nearby regions; the director was looking to increase the number of salespeople.
- Transport Department: three employees were responsible for receiving shipments, clearing customs, breaking bulk and sorting products by client for final delivery.
- Advertising Department: the manager was responsible for posting and selecting print and television advertisements. Final decisions were cleared with both the director and his deputy.
- Warehouse Department: AF operated five warehouses in Almaty; to maximize working capital, four were rented, one was owned. The five warehouse employees were also responsible for security (theft was a potentially serious problem).

Decisions

As her plane neared take-off from Almaty airport, Seth opened her portfolio to confront the challenge provided by Garber. As she contemplated a less than smooth trip to Delhi en route to Hong Kong (on wooden seats, without seat belts, surrounded by entrepreneurs on buying sprees), she decided that intense effort contemplating Astana Foods would keep her occupied and enable the journey to pass more quickly. Almaty was in transition and Garber had to establish his business in a turbulent and changing environment. Many opportunities existed but Astana Foods had to be correctly established and positioned to maximize both short- and long-run returns.

ТОО «Тумар»
продает оптом и мелким оптом со склада:
* **КОНДИТЕРСКИЕ ИЗДЕЛИЯ:**
  - вафли - 2,2-5 тт.;
  - печенье - 2,2-16 тт.;
  - карамель, ирис,
  - конфеты: - 135-168 тт./кг;
  Адрес:
  ул. Байтурсынова, 126,
  Энергетический инст.,
  корпус А, каб. 104.
  Тел. 67-79-55.
* **МАЙОНЕЗ,** 300 г - 42 тт.
* **БЕЛУЮ ГРУНТОВКУ** под различные краски.
  Все пр-ва Ирана.

Продаем сливочное масло по низким ценам. Тел. 29-74-48.

Wholesale cookies, biscuits, candies, mayonaise
Tobacco products (Camel, Winston)
Beverages (Pepsi, Coca-Cola)
Cookies
Vodka
Wine
Beer
Juice
Coffee
Chocolate

Butter
Whisky
Brandy
Rum
Juice
Vermouth
Beer
Gin

Организация реализует:

сигареты Camel	38.50	пиво «Ай-Си премиум», 0.33 л	35.00
сигареты Winston	35.00	пиво «Оранжбуш», 0,33 л, бут.	49.80
«Пепси-Колу», 0,33 л	25.00	пиво «Бавария», 0.33 л, бут.	50.00
«Коко-Колу», 0,33 л	29.00	пиво «Браунштайнер», 0,33 л	33.00
«Фанту», 0,33 л	29.00	печенье «Карнавал», 200 г	55.00
напиток «Топ Дог», 0,33 л	23.00	печенье «Фазер», 160 г	38.00
пирожное «Рафаэлло»	175.00	аперитив «Кампари», 0,7 л	600.00
«Киндер-Сюрприз»	38.00	арахис, 125 г	65.00
«Сникерс»	24.50	бульонные кубики	175.00
«Топик»	23.60	вафли, 275 г	85.00
«Милки Уэй»	16.80	вафли, 350 г	95.00
«Натс»	20.70	сок «Голд», 100%, 1 л	72.00
водку «Абсолют», 0.75 л	460.00	сок «Доул», 100%, 1 л	70.00
водку «Лимон», 0,7 л	120.00	жев. конфеты «Ментос»	19.40
водку «На здоровье», 0,7 л	121.00	жев. конфеты «Фрут-чайс»	19.40
«Финляндия», 1,0 л	790.00	жев. резинку Orbit, пластинка	13.60
водку «Финляндия кувшин., 1,75л	410.00	зажигалку «Крикет»	26.00
шампанское «Бахус»	165.00	конфеты «Рошен»	242.00
пиво «Дон Бадихон»	159.00	конфеты «Фазер», 150 г	80.00
пиво «Сангрия», 1,5 л	215.00	кофе «Якобс», 200 г	280.00
пиво «Петер Мертес» красное	178.00	кофе «Джакин», 100 г	110.00
пиво «Петер Мертес» белое	180.00	кофе «Дисковер Амарилло»,	
пиво «Петер Мертес» белое	164.80	200г	126.00
пиво «Миллер», 0.33 л	36.00	мин. воду «Хайлендр», 1,5 л	68.00
пиво «Холстен», 0.33 л	39.00	мармелад «Орхидея», 264 г	138.00
пиво «Хако Бок», 0,33 л	33.50	чипсы «Таффел», 75 г	43.00
пиво «Хайнекен», 0.33 л, бут.	78.00	шоколад «Фазер», 170 г	92.00

Форма оплаты любая.
Получение товаров на месте. Предусмотрены скидки.
Адрес: ул. Виноградова, 119 (уг. ул. Шагабутдинова).
Тел. 50-95-95.

Компания «МВМ Трейдинг Компани» и Казахстанская фирма OLGA предлагают контрактные поставки ликеро-водочных изделий, пива, соков и продуктов питания европейских производителей.

Сегодня в ассортименте со склада в Алматы:

виски	6 наименов.,
джин	6 наимен.,
бренди	3 наимен.,
ром	3 наимен.,
сок 100%	4 наимен.,
пиво баночное	3 наимен.,
вермут	5 наимен.

Тел. 40-09-48, 40-04-69.
Факс 8(3272) 40-05-19, фирма OLGA.

Tea

ЧАЙ
Ароматный Крупный
ELECOM
Листовой и в гранулах
Тел. 32-58-62.

Case 24

Kazak Enterprises

Samina Seth
The Hong Kong University of Science and Technology

Noel Capon
Graduate School of Business, Columbia University

In September 1995, Sergei Karpov, 35, a Kazak national, was pondering a possible entry into the distribution business in Kazakstan. Educated in Moscow and Paris, Karpov had developed many business contacts in the former USSR, Europe and the U.S. He had recently returned to Almaty, after living many years in Europe, with the goal of developing a successful business enterprise and was fascinated by the success of Kazak Enterprises. In a few short years, Kazak Enterprises had become one of the leading distribution company in Kazakstan. Karpov set out to collect as much information as he could about Kazak Enterprises, in part from its principals, with the goal of identifying both the reasons for its success, which he might hope to replicate, and possible problems that Kazak Enterprises might have had and/or face so that he could avoid them.

∞∞∞

Kazak Enterprises' Growth

Kazak Enterprises Company Ltd. (KE) was incorporated in November 1991, immediately after Kazakstan's independence, with a 15-million rouble loan from Kazcommercebank,[1] by mid-1995 generally rated the best Central Asian bank. KE began humbly; initially its main business was selling garment consignments from small local enterprise to various small and large retail operations in Almaty and to wholesalers serving other areas in Kazakstan. Margins changed daily, the result of runaway inflation; transactions were primarily in the local currency (tenge). (See Exhibit 1 for information on KE's management team.)

---

[1] In recent years, the rouble/U.S. dollar exchange rate fluctuated widely, at the time it was approximately US$1 = 50 roubles.

376

Karpov learned that KE had developed in stages. Soon after its success in selling locally produced garments, KE sought to become a true trading venture. Its directors were keen to make contact with international partners and learn "how to do business." Garments were imported from Turkey; demand far exceeded supply. Because the banking system was undeveloped and ill-equipped for international transactions, KE prepaid cash for all goods. Later, when footwear products were imported, Turkish suppliers cheated KE by substituting inferior products for those ordered and paid for. Disheartened, KE imported goods from Germany; it was similarly cheated.

As a result of these experiences, KE opened a representative buying office in Hamburg, Germany, to ensure that transactions were fair and KE's interests protected. Since KE directors believed the Almaty market comprised two major segments (i.e., low income, high income), it sought high-quality clothing products, automobiles and furniture. In 1992, Autocentre KE was opened in Almaty to sell luxury cars; a second high-profile retail store sold high-quality German and Italian furniture. Initially, both ventures were profitable (100% margins for KE) but as competition increased KE decreased its ownership participation and concentrated on other products. KE developed a strategy of distributing consumer goods (durables and consumables) for everyday use. Thus, KE entered negotiations with such global consumer goods companies as Procter and Gamble (P&G); in mid-1993, KE was granted the exclusive right to sell Adidas products. Initially, KE sourced new products by scouting markets, then approaching companies to be their representative or sole distributor; however, over the past year, international companies were approaching KE. Characteristics of a desirable foreign partner were: stability, international image and potential profitability for business transactions.

Since the distribution system in Kazakstan was poorly developed, KE created a sales department to interface and control relationships with trading agents who worked on a consignment basis and sold mainly in wholesale markets (existing throughout Kazakstan) rather than to commercial stores. Typically, consignments were 14 to 30 days; however, some consignments were as short as seven days, others might stretch to 60 days.[2] Since purchase volumes were frequently substantial, shipment delays were often encountered because loading trucks with the correctly prioritized goods was time-consuming. KE solved this problem temporarily by having a single employee both to assign goods priorities and ensure they were loaded on trucks accordingly. Eventually, KE found it necessary to purchase its own truck fleet; by December 1994, this comprised six Volvo-F12s (three refrigerated, three tented), one Daimler-Benz, two MAZ-64229s, two lorries GAZ 53s, two "Gazel" lorries and four mini vans.

In 1994, KE began heavy advertising with the objective of establishing its name and creating brand loyal customers; for example, it developed its own line of Italian-made suits. In addition, KE sought to improve and expand distribution in Kazakstan, region by region, by selling products on a consignment or margin basis to newly formed

---

[2] In consignment selling, customers could return unsold merchandise.

distributors (private entrepreneurs) and stores. Finally, aware that distributor-level competition was increasing and demand patterns changing, KE began purchasing retail stores. For example, in May 1995 it used its contacts to purchase "Stolich," the highly rated centrally-located food market in Almaty, from the government for US$1.1 million. KE then operated four stores in Almaty and 12 in other major Kazak cities.

The net result of KE's strategy was that revenues increased rapidly: 1992, US$5 million; 1993, US$50 million; 1994, US$120 million; target 1995, US$170 million. Karpov was unable to identify KE's overall profitability; he knew that annual corporate taxes were 30% of profits.

Product and Business Lines

By mid-1995, KE offered around 700 individual product items. Major products and brands represented were:

- Adidas: up to 300 product items;
- Food products: up to 100 products, including Nestle;
- Perfumes: approximately 100 brand names;
- Miscellaneous: almost 60, including Gillette, P&G, Remy Martin, Sony, JVC, Panasonic, Guy Laroche, Cacherel, L'Oreal;
- Cars: Toyota and Renault and BMW (exclusive).

Typically, KE launched new consumer products with a combination of TV, radio and newspaper advertisements. Advertising budgets were developed for individual products and communicated to represented companies as a means of setting appropriate expectations. Some foreign partners agreed to share advertising costs with KE; management based campaign decisions on the willingness of partners to share costs at the product launch stage. KE learned from Gillette executives that constant advertising was not necessary to ensure high sales.

Since 1992, KE had also "lost" distribution rights for several product lines. Karpov identified these products and "fault":

- IBM PC Computers: the marketing and sales system was not properly organized;
- Italian firms — Olivetti (typewriters and personal computers), Zeuro Furniture and a fashion clothes designer: specialized shops for distributing these products were not available;
- Unilever: Unilever did not advertise sufficiently in Kazakstan to assist in selling products. Also, KE personnel perceived Unilever employees to have an arrogant attitude that caused strained relationships.

In addition to wholesale and retail distribution in Kazakstan, KE was involved in several other businesses, many as joint ventures. For example, it exported grain from Kazakstan to Uzbekistan and Tajikistan. In addition, it purchased crude oil in world markets for processing in Russia and Kazakstan; refined products were sold to customers in Kazakstan.

KE Organization

By August 1995, KE's wholesale and retail activities encompassed 70 trading agents and over 1,200 employees: 362 at head office in Almaty (administration [18], sales [39], distribution [315]) and 495 regionally based (administration [38], sales [67], distribution [390]). A further 400 employees worked with KE's "daughter" enterprises (e.g., joint ventures in neighboring republics). All members of the Board of Directors were actively involved in daily operations.

Human Resources

Recruitment. KE's recruitment process followed strict procedures. Applicants for all positions were initially screened on the basis of application forms. The successful applicant completed two interviews: the Chief of the Commercial Department looked for specific traits (e.g., honesty, ambition, dedication, communication skills, initiative); an interview with a director, who made the final decision, followed. New employees had to complete a probationary period. In some cases, foreign specialists were recruited if local candidates were not available.

Training. KE offered many types of training with special emphasis on sales training since making sales was critical to KE's success. Various seminars were offered for branch offices (e.g., managers, salespeople, sales managers), product managers and executives in the Information and Finance departments; training manuals were widely available. Overseas training was also offered for specialized skills. Seminars were also offered by supplier firm executives, notably for sales managers, trading agents, salesmen and product managers.

Sales compensation. Salespersons were compensated in two ways: a fixed monthly salary averaging US$300, plus 0.5% to 1% commission on sales, subject to satisfactory customer debt management and sales returns; average salary / commission splits were 75% : 25%. Sales managers earned salary plus commission; trade agents received either 0.5%, 1% and 3% of sales revenues depending on the product. Typically, salary increases were awarded quarterly; additional bonuses were paid to executives who met performance targets.

Financial Management

KE had several tenge accounts in Kazcommercebank (a Kazakstan joint-stock bank [KJSB]). By May 1995, KE had reduced local currency debts to zero. KJSB offered bank credits on a commercial basis with commonly accepted time, returns, credit conditions at 180% p.a. KE was eligible for low interest loans: below 160% p.a. (13.13% per month).

KE had several foreign currency loan accounts at KJSB and the Almaty Department of Turanbank and a Turkish credit line with the EXIMBANK of Kazakstan. Average interest rates paid on foreign currency credits were 35% to 40% p.a. (3% per month). Since KE deposited substantial cash amounts daily (approximately T17,700,000 per month: T800,000 per day), commission on cashing services was approximately 0.25% rather than the usual 0.75%.

Credit Terms

In 1995, KE's total bad debts in Kazakstan were US$100,000; US$50,000 in Almaty. KE's average 12% gross margin was divided as follows:

Selling	0.005%	Financing	6.3%
Merchandising	0.4%	Profit	5.0%
Administration	0.49%	Total	12.0%
Warehousing and distribution	0.04%		

In May 1995 the financial status of KE's import operations was:

Total assets:	US$12,921,000	Total loan obligations:	US$2,310,000
Amount owed to KE:	US$5,395,000	Total other liabilities:	US$1,025,000

Operations

Meetings among senior KE managers were held twice weekly to resolve operational problems; meetings for all affiliate directors were held bi-annually. Although KE used many media for internal communications (e.g., telephones [regular/cellular], fax, e-mail, pagers), management believed internal communications between branch (affiliate) offices were still poor. As a result, staff from Almaty headquarters often went to branch offices to disseminate information.

In KE's early days, when sales comprised a small product assortment, accounting was fairly straightforward. However, as both volume and product variety increased, the manual tracking of sales and inventory bogged down and backlogs reached over six months. A temporary solution was to increase the number of accountants but, since management believed computerization was essential (and they were fairly inexperienced) seven computer specialists were hired to create, design and implement a comprehensive in-house computer system that tracked inventory and sales. These functions were later expanded to include transportation, commercial operations and other departments dealing with foreign companies (from regional departments to branch relations).

By fall 1994, the LAN NetWare Novell 3.11 system connected 51 workstations and ran comprehensive systems for accounting, revenue tracking and financial planning including budgeting and cash-flow tools. Available off-the-shelf software included Microsoft Office, IC Accounting and a specialized accounting system; "DM," one of the first in-house programs developed, was a real-time editor comprising a database of bills of lading that also formed the basis of a pricing system. "Firm Viewer" analyzed the bills of lading database, planned order processing and monitored stock levels. An internal inspection department monitored quality of imported goods.

Logistics. KE operated 14,000 sq. m. of warehouse space (2,400 sq. m. in Almaty). Outside Almaty, KE owned or leased 18 warehouses (some attached to retail stores) ranging in size from 150 sq. m. to 2,000 sq. m. In Almaty, KE had six separate warehouses ranging in size from 150 sq. m. to 900 sq. m. In total, 50 delivery vehicles serviced 19 branches. KE's physical distribution system ("Bush scheme") had several stages:

- Collect orders from affiliates;
- Sum affiliates' orders to create a final order;
- Receive goods at the central warehouse, send to regional warehouses;
- Distribute goods by the Bush scheme;
- Controlled returned goods and associated payments.

Logistics were the joint responsibility of the commercial, regional and transportation departments. KE used trucks primarily for international collection and long-distance delivery of goods to affiliates in Kazakstan. Smaller lorries delivered goods from central warehouses to retail outlets in Almaty. This system was optimized to reduce delivery costs to remote parts of Kazakstan by considering available truck capacity and location, volume of goods required and delivery time to the final destination. Flexibility was introduced by having small product volumes delivered by sales managers.

Inventory control. Each Stock-keeping Unit (SKU) was individually coded for accounting purposes. Product movement data was transmitted to the computer server from warehouses daily at 9:00 am. Overall inventory updating was performed monthly. Average inventory turnover in the warehouses was 10 to 15 days.

Customers

KE identified five major classes of customers: affiliates, wholesalers, trade (kiosks, wholesale markets [served by trading agents]), cash and carry agents and retail. Affiliates were mainly locally based wholesalers in major regional areas (some partially owned by KE) that agreed to distribute large quantities of KE products; they were especially valuable in regional markets because of Kazakstan's geographic dispersion. KE had the strongest affiliate system of any distributor; management believed sales volume could be increased significantly if a wider product assortment were available. Although KE and its affiliates sold to many types of wholesalers, the majority of sales were to smaller entrepreneurs. KE executives believed that as these smaller distributors grew, its distribution network would be strengthened.

KE had 164 significant customers across Kazakstan. KE's top 20 customers receiving monthly consignments were mostly regionally based affiliates:

1. KE–Akmola	2. KE–Aktau	3. KE–Aktobe
4. KE–Balkhash	5. KE–Zhambul	6. KE–Temirtau
7. KE–Zhezkazgan	8. KE–Karaganda	9. KE–Kokshetau
10. KE–Kizil-Orda	11. KE–Pavlodar	12. KE–Petropavlovsk
13. KE–Semipalatinsk	14. KE–Baikonur	15. KE–Uralsk

				Main customers in Almaty:
16.	KE–Vostok	17.	KE–Shymkent		
18.	"Ai-Tan" Co. Ltd.	19.	"Bulan" Co. Ltd.	20.	"Centre" Co. Ltd.

Distributors offered 7 to 30 days' credit to customers. When bank interest rates were 180% in tenge (70% in hard currency), KE's financial support to distributors was critical for many small businesses to survive. Distributor prices to their customers was based on KE's system; they sought small mark-ups for large volumes according to KE's recommended price lists distributed to all customers every month.

Sourcing and Marketing Activities

Product Management

KE assigned dedicated product managers to specific brand suppliers (e.g., Gillette). They were responsible for creating and establishing business relations with retailers, placing orders on suppliers, securing and disseminating sales information. KE conducted no formal market research. Product managers tended to select those products for which suppliers offered "special deals." In addition, the intricate balance between inventory levels, price and order amounts was difficult to achieve and product managers were unsure how to introduce new products without "upsetting the balance." If KE believed that a potential product was already known to customers through distribution in related countries (e.g., Arabic region) or via regional media (e.g., Star TV) it was more willing to represent the product in Kazakstan. KE did not develop formal marketing plans.

Sales Force

In Almaty, the Chief Sales Manager supervised 51 retail managers, nine merchandising managers and 70 trade agents. For regional operations, the Chief of Regional Department, directed 130 retail managers, 50 merchandising managers and 330 other trade agents. In Almaty, KE sold products to 200 retail stores, restaurants, coffee bars, discotheques and hotels, 15 large wholesalers and in six wholesale markets. By May 1995, KE believed that its fast-moving consumer goods could be sold in over 8,000 retail stores; for a client such as P&G, weekly sales volumes of goods by outlet type might be: over 20 cases, 800 outlets; 5 to 19 cases, 4,500 outlets; under 5 cases, 3,000 outlets. KE.'s sales force covered approximately 10% of Kazakstan's retail market:

	Number	% of business	Calls per week (%)
Chains	5	30	15 (4)
Co-op. groups	–	–	–
Independent retailers	150	40	150 (41)
Pharmacies	–	–	–
Kiosks	200	30	200 (55)
Total	355	100	365 (100)

Salespeople called mostly on retail stores. The average salesperson made six calls per day: three on chain outlets, one each on wholesalers, independent retailers and kiosks; typically, calls were not made on co-op. groups or pharmacies. In addition to making sales, salespeople were responsible for collecting basic marketing data, making pricing recommendations, collecting money from customers, customer debt management, providing service and adding new customers.

Salespeople maintained detailed sales records by brand, item size, account type and region. This data was compared weekly to targets for sales by brand, new retail outlets and other new customers. Sales targets were based on sales in the previous period (week, month, year). However, these targets only functioned as benchmarks since sales varied dramatically from period to period because of the developing nature of Kazakstan's retail markets. As a result, import order planning was difficult, but based on management's belief that sales would generally increase.

KE's major sales policy objective was to cover Kazakstan by joint efforts of its affiliate network, wholesalers and agents. It sought to open new retail outlets and deliver goods to the largest (including private and state-run stores, hotels, kiosks, restaurants and cafes). KE wanted to establish long-term partnerships with customers by offering assistance in advertising, pricing, sales rationalization and stock systems. Strategically, KE aimed for low margins, large turnover and high-quality service delivery.

Sales managers were responsible for maintaining relations with retailers. Salespeople called on retail outlets at least once a week to collect orders, control payments, make pricing proposals, assist in shelving and merchandising, monitor order delivery and receive updates on sales and inventory.

In total, 1,230 distributors' salespeople (372 in Almaty) sold KE's products to retailers, wholesalers and sub-wholesalers.

Trade Support

KE supported distributors and retail clients:

- Merchandising support by distributing stands, boards, posters (to retailers);
- Special discounts for better clients;
- Promoting international partners' trademarks in Kazakstan market by advertising on TV (including locally-produced TV programs), radio, newspapers, magazines;
- Promoted the KE trademark as a high-quality brand supplier;
- Sponsored artist competitions (e.g., general sponsor of the international competition, "Voice of Asia," for young artists "Zhas Kanat"), sports and show business events.

KE made frequently purchased consumer goods available in sufficient volumes and endeavored to have retailers place these strategically at eye level. The watch-word at KE was consumer exposure; executives believed that for sales to increase, exposure had to increase. Said one: "People will only buy the products if they see them." Promoted brands were placed left to right in a priority ranking system; explanatory stickers describing each product were placed next to the price. Management believed large product displays on shelves and in store windows attracted purchasers.

Pricing

Several factors entered into the price for a specific product: supplier's price, customs taxes (0.2%), excise taxes (0% to 50%) and VAT on imports (20% of CIF price + all taxes).[3] An in-house computer program calculated the break-even point and required monthly turnover to achieve a pre-specified profit level. KE had several cost plus pricing formulae depending on customer type:[4]

- retail (KE and other stores)   Cost + 15%
- small wholesale (order volume over $100)   Cost + 10%
- middle wholesale (order volume over $500)   Cost + 8%
- large wholesale (order volume over $2,000)   Cost + 6%
- affiliates   Cost + 6%

Retail prices in KE stores (recommended for other outlets) were set based on competitor prices and statistically-generated forecasts based on previous sales of products.

Advertising and Promotion

In November 1992, KE aired its first TV ads (30 seconds to one minute) on local Kazakstan TV (state and private channels). At the time, advertising cost was for US$20/minute on private channels, slightly under US$100/minute on state stations. Initial advertisements that focused on such goods as shoes and clothes from Italy helped develop awareness of KE. Later, KE commenced in-house production of video and developed motion film quality advertisements at an average cost of US$5,000. Over time, KE shifted its advertising balance to state channels but, on advice from Gillette, continued to advertise on private channels but less frequently.

In 1993, as part of a major transition, KE established an advertising department catering to both in-house needs and private contracts.[5] It offered comprehensive advertising services:

- Identified and expanded original concepts into entire advertising campaigns;
- Produced unique print advertisements for newspapers;
- Produced advertisements using computer graphics and animated cartoons;
- Designed outdoor billboard advertisements.

---

[3] KE was the tax importer for food imports and paid all customs (and excise) taxes. For other products, KE paid customs and excise taxes up to 25% (exporters paid the difference) and import VAT.

[4] The average mark-up for Procter and Gamble products was 8%; of this 8%, fixed expenses, comprising warehouses maintenance, transportation costs, head office upkeep and bank interest averaged 4%.

[5] Advertising accounting functions were handled by this department.

Major KE-produced advertising campaigns were perceived as aggressive. Management believed KE's image advertising was very successful because of high frequency and simultaneous use of all mass media. Resources were optimized by making long-term contracts at reduced rates and using public relations. The "I love KE" slogan was heavily promoted on plastic bags, garments, stationery and lighters. Notable achievements included:

- Over 20 original advertisements and 100 jingles produced;
- Continuous cooperation with international partners, leading to a relationship with a USAID consortium;
- First CIS company to place its logo on a spacecraft.

A difficulty faced by KE was deciding the optimal promotional mix for new product launch. Most western goods were familiar to KE through prospective partner research abroad but few had been promoted as high quality in Kazakstan. Some executives believed it was expensive to promote such new products to an unfamiliar middle class; others argued that such products (e.g., Camay and Lux soaps) were often widely advertised on Moscow-based radio and TV stations received in Kazakstan.

One product manager believed KE should spend at least US$20,000 over two months for a new brand to be successful. He believed the product's name and attributes should be well-communicated before "cluttering" advertisements with KE details (e.g., telephone numbers to avoid consumers shopping at competitor locations). Recently, KE had launched an extremely effective advertising campaign for Vodka Finland (VF), currently the most popular brand. Although, prior to launch, the most popular brands were Absolut and Smirnoff (similar in quality but slightly more expensive) the mainly TV-based campaign (monthly budget, US$30,000; total campaign budget, US$70,000) propelled VF to first place.

Competition

Major competition for KE was at the brand level for the brands it represented. For example, P&G competed with Unilever, L'Oreal and other companies selling frequently purchased consumer goods (e.g., detergents, shampoos, creams). Each of these brands had already established a chain of local distributors; KE believed their market coverage was lower than P&G. KE used share of shelf space as a crude rule-of-thumb rule to evaluate competitor performance. In addition, KE was experiencing increasing competition from distributors offering gray market products.

A specific potential distributor competitor was National Distribution Center Company (NDCC), managed and owned by a U.S. expatriate who placed profits in off-shore accounts. KE believed NDCC's excellent relations with Philip Morris earned it exclusivity. KE believed major sales and profits were earned from cigarettes but significant revenues were also generated by Unilever, P&G and Mars. NDCC was rumored to be expanding to new national markets (e.g., Uzbekistan, Ukraine).

Example of a Supplier

Karpov was able to secure some data on one of KE's multinational suppliers, P&G. P&G sold a variety of consumer products in Kazakstan (e.g., hair care, beauty, detergents). Major outlets for reaching consumers were private stores (e.g., perfumery stores, supermarkets, drugstores) and wholesale markets. Market coverage was:

	Current market coverage	Targeted market coverage
Perfumery shops	40%	100%
Supermarkets	25%	100%
Food stores	3%	80%
Drugstores	15%	60%
Kiosks	1%	50%
Wholesale markets	80%	100%

KE's sales appeared to be increasing, but with some seasonality (Table 1).

Table 1: Sales/shipments of P&G Goods ('000 DM)*

		Sales	Receipts			Sales	Receipts
1994	July	106	178	1994	December	108	213
1994	August	49.5	0	1995	January	345	249
1994	September	64.5	0	1995	February	197	189
1994	October	28.5	35	1995	March	254	464
1994	November	3	0	1995	April	565	387

*Figures include custom taxes.

KE and P&G shared mutually consistent objectives of increasing overall revenue and becoming the leading supplier in Kazakstan from small kiosks to big supermarkets. Eventually KE hoped to build a factory producing P&G products.

KE: August 1995

In conversation with a senior KE executive, Karpov learned about KE's objectives. In the short term, KE wished to:

■ Launch a new food supermarket, "Stolichny," positioned as the most prestigious in Kazakstan;
■ Take over the management of privatized plants including:
a metallurgist factory in Karaganda,
a tea-packaging plant in Almaty (the only one in Kazakstan),
sugar factories in Djibouti and Burundi, and
margarine plants in Almaty and Karaganda;

- Attract foreign investment in a joint venture with Kazcommercebank and Tomen Corporation (without state guarantees) to build a US$95 million business center in Almaty;
- Sell shares of stock company "KE–Kazakstan" to raise funds for new special projects;
- Launch a pension insurance plan for Kazakstan citizens: the "KE" pension fund;
- Launch a series of restaurant and café chains; initially in Almaty but later in other Kazakstan regions;
- Explore the possibility of developing a network of mobile "fast food" units;
- Launch prestigious clothing stores (e.g., Hugo Boss, Versace);
- Develop and extend existing Adidas chains to other regions in Kazakstan; increase sales volume and eventually manufacture Adidas goods in Kazakstan;
- Launch specialized product departments in KE-affiliated shops;
- Establish specialized stores for selling electronics and household appliances.

In the long term, KE wished to:

- Be the foremost professionally-run Kazakstan company by becoming market leader in providing goods used every day (e.g., electronics, household appliances, vehicles, garments, foodstuffs);
- Extend KE's current distribution network to include all Kazakstan markets and supply every geographic population center with goods. Simultaneously, it wished to establish warehouses, cash and carry operations, and KE's own retail network including specialty stores for existing brands (e.g., Adidas, Lancome) and general stores for electronics, garments and footwear (Elite) and foodstuffs. To further establish reliable links with sub-distributors, KE wished to portray the image of a stable company that delivered a wide product assortment promptly.
- After strengthening KE's distribution network, it wished to create a franchising system for KE stores throughout the CIS.

Some executives believed KE's best strategy was to continually introduce business changes. These executives believed KE should continue to establish a country-wide retail network and convert consumers to brand loyals. They said time and financial resources were needed to establish KE better in an environment lacking many elements of basic infrastructure. These executives believed that branch companies not operating competitively should be sold as new management teams to operate them more efficiently. Management believed that unlike other heads of companies spending profits to "up-keep decadent lifestyles" with large cars and houses, KE wisely reinvested profits to continually expand the company. KE's top priorities were:

- To overcome competition from gray markets by providing a superior level of services and stability.
- To establish a system of collecting more and better market and distribution information.
- To create the image of a reliable and stable partner.

Assessment

Sergei Karpov contemplated the extensive material he had collected on KE; he was aware there were significant gaps in his data and knew these needed to be isolated. However, as he thought about KE, several questions came to mind: How well had KE performed? Why had it performed in this manner? What could he learn from the various actions KE had taken? What should/would KE do to ensure its success in the future? And what could he learn that could help him launch a successful enterprise in Kazakstan? If he were to enter a similar business that was competing with KE, he wondered how it would respond.

Exhibit 1: Key Members of KE's Management: August 1995

Position	Years' experience		Chemistry
	Business	KE	
*General Director	16	3.5	friendly
*Deputy Director	13	3.5	friendly
*Finance Director	12	3.5	friendly
*Executive Director	19	3.5	friendly
*Director "Impex"	12	3.5	friendly
*Director "Astyk"	11	3.5	friendly
Deputy Finance Director	4	1	friendly
Chief Acccountant	11	3.5	friendly
Chief Com Department	2	1	friendly
Finance Deputy	12	2.5	friendly
Sales Director	8	1.5	businesslike
Regional Sales Director	10	2	friendly
Information	24	1	just
Warehousing	23	3.5	friendly
Transport	8	2	business
Advertisements	8	1.5	friendly
Lawyers	20	2	just
Builders	21	2	business
Adidas Director	4	1	friendly
Symbat	10	1.7	simple
Food Director	19	2	business
Lancome Director	19	1	friendly
Sales Almaty			
Product Manager	12	1.5	friendly
Product Manager	6	1	friendly
Product Manager	3	1	friendly
Product Manager	2.5	2	friendly
Product Manager	1	0.3	friendly
Product Manager	2.5	0.8	friendly
Sales Manager	8	2	friendly
Sales Manager	8	2	friendly
Sales Manager	4	1	stable
Sales Manager	15	1	business
Sales Manager	2	1	friendly
Sales Manager	2	1	friendly
Sales Manager	3	1	friendly
Sales Manager	5	1	friendly
Sales Manager	9	1	friendly

*Members of the Board of Directors: ages ranged from 30 to 38 years.

Case 25

Philips N.V.: Representative Office in Kazakstan

Samina Seth
The Hong Kong University of Science and Technology

Noel Capon
Graduate School of Business, Columbia University

In July 1995, Arnold Stokking, Philips' Dutch General Manager of the Kazak representative office pondered his next steps. Established in Almaty ten months earlier he was assessing company performance in a business environment he described as the "wild west in the east." His main concern was the potentially lucrative security and communications equipment division; the initial strategy had to be revamped since Philips' major distributor and key contact for prospective sales had died a month earlier. Stokking had to submit feasible alternatives to headquarters and recommend an overall plan of action for activities in Kazakstan that would double first year sales volume next year. The August 30 referendum on Presidential power could alter the already volatile business climate but Stokking would be unable to assess the true impact for at least six months. Meanwhile his report was due August 15.

ഇൻഅ

Company Background

Philips' History[1]

Established in Eindhoven, Holland in 1892 by Gerard Philips and his father (later joined by Gerard's brother, Anton), by 1900, the small light bulb factory grew to be Europe's third largest producer. Philips' single-product focus enabled it to incorporate the latest technology and introduce innovative labor-saving methods. The legendary chemistry and physics laboratories developed many new products, includ-

---

[1] Based on Robert W. Lightfoot and Christopher A. Bartlett, "Philips and Matsushita": A portrait of two evolving companies," Harvard Business School, Case 9-392-156.

ing the highly successful tungsten metal filament light bulb. With the Dutch market well served, Philips expanded to foreign markets (hired its first export manager in 1899) to pursue its mass production strategy. By 1912, Philips had formed many overseas joint ventures with local firms to gain superior market acceptance. Meanwhile, it diversified into new products; in 1926, it produced the first radios and within a decade had 20% world market share; during the 1930s, Philips began producing X-ray tubes.

By mid-1995, the Philips group parent, Philips Electronics N.V. (Philips) was listed on stock exchanges in Amsterdam, London and New York. In 1994, Philips earned NLG (Netherlands Guilders) 2.125 million income[2] on NLG 60.977 million revenues. Share prices increased from NLG 40 (January 1994) to NLG 51.40 (December 1994) reflecting investors' positive outlook. (See Exhibits 1A, 1B for financials.)

Organization Chart

In the early 1930s, in anticipation of World War II, Philips transferred most essential research laboratories to England and management teams to the U.S.; consequently, these individual country organizations enjoyed significant autonomy. After the war, recognizing this strength in responding to country-specific problems, Philips re-built the firm by strengthening the National Organizations (NOs). NOs were responsible for financial, legal and administrative issues; product divisions (in Eindhoven) were responsible for development, production and global distribution. The research division remained independent, expanding internationally with eight separate laboratories in Europe and the U.S.

Philips' Corporate Regional Bureaus (CRB) were traditionally responsible just for consolidating the budgets and accounting data for Philips businesses in individual territories in its various global regions. In addition, the CRBs advised the Board of Management on specific issues regarding territories; in the Philips' geographic/product matrix structure, these bureaus also reported to the product divisions.

In the early 1990s, the Board of Management decided that CRB-1, responsible for Europe, should play a leading role in developing an infrastructure for the emerging markets in East European and CIS countries. Consequently, CRB-1 developed into a sales organization for emerging markets, taking a superior role to the product divisions. A first step was to establish representative offices in strategic locations (Figure 1).

Centurion Program

The Centurion program developed out of Philips' financial loss (over 2 billion NLG) in 1990. The program was formed with two objectives: a short-term focus on return to profitability by downsizing and divesting unprofitable business lines and a long-term objective to revitalize the company. Philips, currently in stage two, commissioned a Corporate Values and Behavior task force; five "Philips Values" were developed:

---

[2] Exchange rate as of January 1, 1995: US$1 = NLG 1.716.

Figure 1: Sample Representative Office Structure

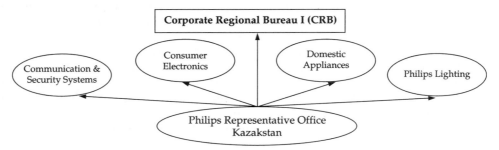

- Delight customers;
- Value people as our greatest resource;
- Deliver quality and excellence in all actions;
- Achieve premium return on equity;
- Encourage entrepreneurial behavior at all levels.

All Philips organizations incorporated these five values in the Centurion handbook, distributed to all employees. These values were expected to drive the organization's culture.

The significance of Philips' financial performance was evident in 1990 when the Berlin Wall came down and international companies were provided with expansion opportunities to new geographic locations. Because of the magnitude of Philips' financial crisis, management believed a focus on internal reorganization was necessary before new projects were initiated. Because of the resulting three-year delay, Philips entered these post-communist emerging markets behind such firms as Sony and Panasonic (Japan) and Samsung and Daewoo (Korea); they entered almost immediately in 1990. Said one observer: "Sony is great; their products are top notch and they have achieved good distribution." Daewoo was especially strong in the ethnic Korean community.

Product Divisions

Philips was organized into major product groups each comprising several product lines of varying profitability levels:

Lighting. World market leader in the development, manufacture and marketing of lighting products, this division offered an extensive range of lamps, luminaries and lighting electronics for indoor and outdoor lighting applications. The division's aim was to satisfy the highest functional and aesthetic requirements.

Consumer electronics. Comprised seven business groups: Television, Video Equipment (e.g., video recorders, camcorders), Audio, Car Systems, Interactive Media Systems (e.g., CD-I, CD-ROM, Photo CD), Business Electronics (e.g., monitors, telephones, fax, cable television) and Key Modules Group (components and technologies).

Domestic appliances and personal care. Effective April 1993, this division, comprising two business groups (Appliances and Personal Care), primarily supplied electrical products for daily personal care and household routines through 60 international sales organizations; development and production was in Europe, South America and the Far East.

Medical systems. This division produced, installed and maintained imaging equipment for hospitals and diagnostic centers worldwide; it also offered radiation therapy (e.g., linear accelerators and simulators). In 1992, focus shifted from individual products to field applications; substantial efforts were devoted to improving service, for example, technical maintenance, user training and financing models.

Communications and security systems. This division supplied telecommunications equipment, systems and solutions for public infrastructure and private use. In recent years, the division pioneered new communication technologies (e.g., Synchronous Digital Hierarchy, Global Systems for Mobile Communication).

Philips in Kazakstan

Philips Almaty Office

As part of Philips' post-communist strategy, management decided to increase activities in the Central Republics, part of the Commonwealth of Independent States (CIS) (former USSR), with a special emphasis on Kazakstan. In August 1994, an Almaty representative office (RO) was established by two medical systems division members and locally hired assistants; by mid-1995, four divisions were represented with a staff of nine (Figure 2).

The RO supported local dealers; it was unable to transact business directly and receive financial payments; organizationally it was a cost center. The RO's major function was to liaise between various international Philips manufacturing enterprises and local dealers (existing and potential). Often, potential dealers would approach the RO regarding product distribution opportunities; for signed-up dealers, RO staff assisted in order selection and quantity. Payment was made direct to the relevant European office by the Kazak distributor before product delivery (mostly by air) was made. (Stokking believed the law might change to allow ROs to open bonded warehouses; this would simplify ordering procedures for local distributors.) The RO provided free product literature, point-of-sale signs, furniture and TV ad copy. In mid-1995, Philips established an Almaty-based service center to provide technical assistance and train distributors' technical staff to repair products in-house. The Almaty RO liaised with three export offices: Dubai (audio / video equipment), Vienna (domestic appliances) and Holland (lighting products, communications and security systems).

Almaty personnel believed that support for the RO from Philips Export Offices could be enhanced. Stokking estimated that 30% of his time was spent on internal lobbying: twice a year he toured Export Offices advocating increased efforts on Kazakstan. However, he believed cost reduction actions throughout Philips made increased hiring extremely difficult and placed real limitations on RO growth.

Figure 2: Philips Almaty Office

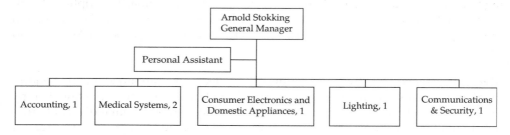

Major Products and Services

Communications and security systems. Stokking said these products were necessary for the communications and security infrastructure for any developed and enterprising city. Philips was generally considered one of the top two suppliers of leading edge security systems; many western corporations appreciated Philips' quality, especially those subject to climatic changes. None of the other 20 to 30 top world players in security systems had entered Kazakstan. Among major potential competitors in communications systems were Ericsson (Sweden) and Kenwood (U.K.).

Communications. Several specialized Philips products were already accepted in the Central Republics. Public address systems led Philips' entry into Kazakstan. The "Conference System" (CS), ideally suited for large-scale meetings, permitted application-wide interactive conversations using microphones. The "Congress System," catering to the government sector, had additional functions for voting and a built-in translation service; it was ideal for parliamentary sessions. Since a Philips Congress System was installed in the Russian Duma,[3] other former USSR republics wanted identical systems for their parliaments. In mid-1995, an advanced digital system was installed in the Bishek's (capital of Kyrgystan, Kazakstan's neighboring republic) presidential palace. Aiming to modernize rapidly, the Kazak government invited Philips to replicate the system in Almaty.

Paging systems (Microware division, Cambridge, U.K.) were also potentially viable in Almaty. On-site systems were useful in places requiring short-distance communication (e.g., construction sites, hospitals). Off-site paging systems (wide-area paging), covered a city and required a paging center. On-site systems were more popular than off-site systems due to the limited number of receiving stations typically required and the higher cost of wide-area paging which provided on- and off-site functionality. According to Stokking, U.S.-based Motorola, offering more receiving stations, was a major threat in both on- and off-site communications.

Security systems. These access control systems were available in large and small versions; as modular systems, they allowed for easy re-configuration. They controlled

---

[3] The Duma was the former Soviet Union's parliament, located in Moscow.

people flow from one location to another and prevented unauthorized individuals gaining access to pre-defined areas.

- Larger systems restricted access by allowing users to designate access rights by specific door remotely; prices ranged from US$5,000 to several million dollars depending on the number of doors controlled. Philips believed the government and large businesses lacked funds to purchase such expensive complicated systems in the short term. However, in two to three years, as more nationalized industries were privatized and funds became available, demand was anticipated from private and public sectors.
- Smaller systems, simply comprising a controller, cost US$300 to US$500; they required users to enter simple PIN codes to unlock one or two doors. Directly competing products from major vendors were unavailable in Almaty, but small substitute systems were sold (US$50) by traders in the black market.

Stokking said that although one particular type of internal security system (an observation system) was not yet popular; he anticipated the market would develop rapidly in the next two to three years. Local private businesses were price conscious but he believed they were almost ready to purchase products.

Major reasons for poor sales among the locals were:

- Financial: Despite high quality system, local businesses generally lacked funds to purchase products they considered both complicated and expensive;
- Quality: Prospective users did not appreciate Philips' quality versus black market alternatives;
- Lack of security concerns: Many businesses (e.g., local banks), did not perceive security as a major problem; in the past four years, only three to four criminal attempts on banks had occurred. Banks and financial institutions preferred to hire security guards, relying on the local mentality that large, intimidating guns were more effective; security guards' salary ranged from US$100 to US$150 per month.

Regardless of poor response from local firms, multinationals considered purchasing security systems; Stokking believed these organizations would pay for good reliable systems. Thus, foreign companies and banks were the initial primary targets; some success had already been made. Stokking believed Philips' camera observation systems were well-positioned overall, but might not be optimally positioned for the professional field (e.g., banks); a critical issue was whether the potential security threat was external or internal. For security systems, including camera observations systems, many traders imported competing products often sold through third parties.

Consumer electronics and domestic appliances. Philips, a late market arrival, trailed Daewoo, Samsung, Sony and Panasonic by two to four years. Consumer electronics was a growth area for Philips in general but success depended on a strong distribution network. Several Philips employees believed positive managerial attitudes resulted in its developing successful distribution in Kazakstan; it had a relatively strong dealer network comprising ten representatives, including Butya, one of the country's largest distributors. Overall, consumer goods were currently Philips' number one activity.

A major logistical problem plaguing Philips was delivering audio, video, telephone and lighting products to dealers in a single container in acceptable delivery times. The problem was caused by the long distance from Philips' overseas central warehouse to Almaty and the necessity of using air freight for the last leg of the journey to Kazakstan. Compared to Europe, where Philips' European warehouses were generally specialized and catered to specialized distribution networks, in Kazakstan, Philips had to deal with "general stores" requiring complex product assortments.

Despite advances in distribution, Stokking believed sales had been initially slow due to limited consumer exposure to Philips' audio/video products. (Sales taxes on consumer electronic products ranged between 10% and 20%.) In June 1995, the "Philips Image Shop" was opened in Almaty in a joint venture with Accept Company; the outlet displayed Philips' comprehensive product range to potential dealers and local retail consumers. The outlet sold products (initially mainly televisions) to the emerging middle class (successful small business persons and employees of multinationals), boosting Philips' revenues.

Stokking was considering selling alarm detectors (security systems) through the audio/video distribution channel. He believed that since competing "black box" systems (ready-to-use) were available cheaply in bazaars, Philips needed to re-position home systems with consumer electronics; he wanted to avoid spending limited resources on difficult-to-move products. He said: "The prices of these systems are not that significant compared to the millions of dollars corporate clients pay."

Lighting products. Philips offered three major types of lighting product in Kazakstan: luminous, outdoor and indoor. Current strategy was to seek new dealers and attempt to secure sales on a project basis (e.g., construction contracts) rather than at retail. Management attributed poor initial retail sales to consumers' lack of appreciation that although Philips' prices were higher; its bulbs lasted significantly longer than domestically produced less expensive alternatives.

Medical systems. Although Philips entered Kazakstan with sales of medical products and continued to support two employees, the potential seemed to be less than originally anticipated. Initially, Philips secured 12 government contracts for medical equipment but, as yet, had received no payments.

Dealing with the Government

In December 1994, the Kazakstan Parliament's chief engineer, interested in establishing his own private enterprise, approached Philips to be its official dealer for communications systems. He had previously installed Philips' systems throughout the former Soviet Union and was familiar with their product features and functions. Since this individual had personal contacts with influential officials and qualified staff, Philips' management believed his enterprise would be an ideal vehicle for entering the Central Asian republics. All necessary documents were signed; Philips Communications and Security Systems Division was ready to solicit prospective clients when, in February 1995, the engineer died. Philips was back to square one; it required another plan for market entry.

Meanwhile, Kazakstan's political situation was changing rapidly. In mid-March 1995, President Nazarbaev dissolved parliament and effectively removed over 100 old-style communist deputies who were obstructing reforms. In a special referendum, 95% of voters (with 90% of the population voting) voted to allow Nazarbaev special powers until 2000. Another referendum was planned for August 30 requesting Kazaks to accept a constitutional change allowing Nazarbaev to define parliamentary powers. In January/February 1996, elections would select a new parliament; an announcement for a double capital was expected to follow. Parliament, parliamentary employees and the capital city would relocate from Almaty to Akmola in the north; embassies and trade commissions were expected to continue functioning in Almaty to service the business community.

Philips identified a second potential agent in parliament with good contacts to parliamentary technical staff; however, he was recently ousted. Stokking described Philips' market entry as "very unlucky"; his faith in the central government had decreased. By mid-1995, the government was thought to be near bankruptcy; its financial position was certainly weak and it had difficulty meeting financial commitments and servicing foreign debt. All Philips' contracts were stipulated in U.S. dollars; for some contracts, especially with medical equipment, prepayment was now required.

Two major problems were evident to Stokking: the governmental decision-making process was complicated and, generally, government commitments to honor contracts were low, especially without prepayment legislation. Stokking was aware that, though contracts were completed, many multinational companies dealing with the government went unpaid. Philips had to lobby actively (parliamentary members and/or other intermediaries) to receive payments. Some expatriate business professionals considered the necessity of such tactics a result of major corruption. Stokking said public versus private interests were being tested; the only solution for successfully receiving payment was to improve personal and professional networks. He believed the government needed to establish a complete infrastructure to provide data on government activities.

Market Segmentation

Stokking used several segmentation procedures. He described one segmentation approach:

> Generally, the provincial governments have financial resources to purchase systems but are difficult to approach; conversely, city administrations have hardly any funds, including for street lighting. New private enterprises are good distributors but selecting appropriate concerns is difficult. Large Kazak enterprises are interested in purchasing Philips' products but many manage their deals the old fashioned way; decision-making processes are not transparent so it is very difficult to find budgetary information.

Foreign companies are Philips' main target for professional activities. A new and emerging group is from donor projects with such sponsors as World Bank (WB), European Bank for Reconstruction and Development (EBRD) and the Asian Development Bank (ADB); these projects are specifically interested in purchasing medical systems.

Consumer goods. Stokking said the consumer goods market was expanding with middle class growth. Despite more Kazaks having increased salaries, progressive tax rates (up to 40%) were considered high and affected disposable income. Stokking believed consumer goods had good potential for Philips.

Communications and security systems. Stokking believed middle class consumers preferred convenient domestic appliances to simple security systems. Kazaks believed that Almaty was generally safe. However, one expatriate living in Almaty claimed: "When I arrived about three years ago, the streets were very safe. However, I'm beginning to hear about knife-point robberies, after dark, more than ever before. I guess it's just a matter of time until they begin robbing homes."

A growing segment comprised foreign companies familiar with the importance of security systems. This segment included foreign banks, rapidly increasing their presence in Kazakstan. Despite the low number of bank robberies, several approached Philips regarding security systems.

Oil and gas companies required security and communications products to monitor expensive equipment. However, pipelines dedicated to Kazak oil fields would take at least two to three years to build. Since Kazakstan was landlocked, making other alternatives to export oil unfeasible, the inadequate pipeline infrastructure was causing a capacity constraint, hindering oil revenues and slowing the industry's (and Kazakstan's) development. The Kazak government was holding discussions with Russia and other nearby countries regarding new pipelines but this was a contentious international issue and observers did not anticipate a resolution in the near term. Oil and gas companies preferred to deal directly with big players for security and communications systems and Philips' management was positive about long term (five to ten years) opportunities when profits were expected and exploration in neighboring countries would commence.

Stokking recently identified a new local segment, the 19 "oblasts" (Russian word for provinces). Many oblasts had mining interests, generated income in U.S. dollars and were considered fairly "rich." Generally, oblast government powers were substantial regarding internal affairs; despite reporting to the central government many Kazaks considered them almost independent. Oblasts were sensitive to traders and intermediaries; these were considered less professional. Stokking believed many oblasts had negative experiences dealing with these "strange" companies, including prepaying for goods that failed to arrive. Almaty had one oblast, but Stokking believed it generated few funds. One southern oblast, 200 kilometers to 500 kilometers from Almaty, purchased Philips' medical equipment through mining corporations required to spend a specified amount (believed by Philips' management a percent of revenue) on social benefits.

Marketing Activities

Philips used several devices to reach target segments. Stokking described Philips' overall marketing strategy in major phases. Phase one: specific targeted segments identified; phase two, targeted segments reached via cost-effective marketing channels. (See Exhibit 2 for excerpts from Philips' brochures.)

For consumer goods, Philips was considering using outdoor banners, advertising on buses and additional neon signs in Almaty. Stokking believed Philips should advertise its brand name on television as distributors tended to sell themselves first rather than their brands. Stokking wondered whether the initial 1996 plan to advertise the company and its products on TV would be as successful as he hoped. Stokking believed that some products (e.g., security systems) would best be sold through professional contacts and word-of-mouth. To reach decision-makers at oblasts, Stokking was considering using an intermediary. However, Philips would need to verify references before compensating intermediaries for successfully negotiating contracts.

Philips' Performance

Philips measured sales at the point of delivery to distributors. It initially entered Kazakstan in October 1994, thereby capturing peak-time Christmas sales and surpassing objectives (Table 1). Stokking believed Philips was one of few profitable foreign companies in Almaty.

Management expected to meet 1996 objectives primarily by increasing the number of distributors; some believed educating distributors on selling techniques could also enhance turnover. A second goal was to divide sales equally between consumers and professional groups.

Table 1: Philips' Revenues*

Target	October–December 1994	1995 (estimated)	1996 (plan)
Consumer	US$250,000	US$2 million	US$4 million
Professional			US$2 million

*Disguised data.

Stokking said deals in Kazakstan were seldom standard; as a result, revenues fluctuated widely. For example, for the oil and gas industry, Philips sold computerized management systems for telemetry camera observation equipment used to send messages regarding pipeline functioning to head offices. It successfully negotiated a sale to one oil and gas company, thus spiking revenues in a particular month.

Philips required all payments in western currencies. Consumer goods distributors were offered a 90-day credit, secured by European bank guarantees; the prevailing interest rate was 8% p.a. All transactions were in U.S. dollars. Distributors were responsible for all bank charges and commissions. For professional goods, Philips used a case-by-case approach.

Decisions

Philips' limited resources in Kazakstan were needed to promote several product sectors. Stokking wondered whether his current strategy of pursuing several different segments was appropriate in these unusual business circumstances. Thus far, no system of priorities had been employed. He believed the key to expanding business lay in sensible marketing but the question remained, "how?" Stokking said that several issues were on his mind:

> Long-term planning is tremendously difficult. The environment is politically unstable and there are potential ethnic problems. Kazak minerals compete with Russian minerals since everything in the ground in Kazakstan is also available in Russia. The oil and gas industry is dependent on Russia for transporting the oil which is vital for Kazakstan's economic growth. This is important to us because we believe success in the oil and gas industry is Philips' major opportunity to make significant profits in Kazakstan.

Exhibit 1A: Philips' Income Statement (million of Netherlands guilders)

	1994	1993	1992
Net sales	60,977	58,825	58,527
Direct cost of sales	44,275	43,066	42,924
Gross income	16,702	15,759	15,603
Selling expenses	11,736	11,975	11,951
General and administrative expense	1,475	1,424	1,504
Other business income	267	205	388
Income from operation (excluding restructuring)	–	–	2,486
Restructuring	–	–	1,200
Income from operations	3,758	2,565	1,268
Net final income and expense	dr866	dr1,039	dr1,784
Income (loss) before taxes	2,892	1,526	d498
Income taxes	598	344	90
Income (loss) after taxes	2,294	1,182	d588
Equity in income of unconsolidated costs	130	dr45	dr34
Group income (loss)	2,424	1,137	622
Shares of other group equity in group income	dr375	dr281	dr278
Income (loss) from normal business operations	2,049	856	900
Extraordinary items, net	76	1,109	–
Net income (loss)	2,125	1,965	d900
Net income (loss) per share	6.39	6.15	d2.91
Year-end shares outstanding	338	328	315

Exhibit 1B: Philips' Balance Sheet (million of Netherlands guilders)

Assets	1994	1993
Intangible fixed assets, net	2,290	2,536
Tangible fixed assets, net	12,954	13,020
Unconsolidated costs	1,218	1,571
Other non-current financial assets	1,763	1,555
Total fixed assets	18,225	18,682
Total inventories	10,443	9,681
Total receivables	16,629	15,599
Cash and cash equivalent	2,824	2,322
Total current assets	29,896	27,602
Total assets	48,121	46,284
Liabilities		
Common shares	3,385	3,280
Priority shares	–	1
Share premium reserve	3,331	3,061
Other reserves	5,967	5,107
Stockholders' equity	12,683	11,449
Other group equity	1,752	1,610
Total group equity	14,435	13,059
Short-term provisions	3,100	3,556
Long-term debt	6,179	7,813
Short-term debt	3,093	3,104
Other liabilities	14,891	13,198
Dividend payable	421	164
Total liabilities and share equity	48,121	46,284

Map of Malaysia

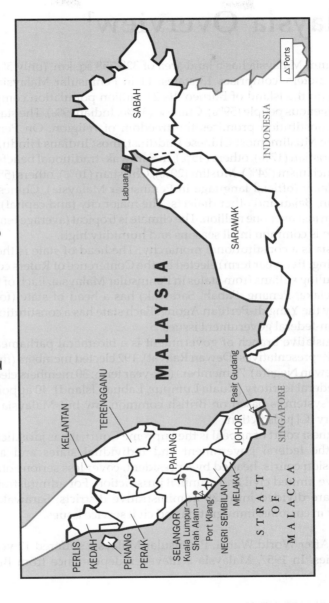

△ Ports

INDONESIA

SABAH

Labuan

SARAWAK

MALAYSIA

PERLIS

KEDAH

PENANG

PERAK

KELANTAN

TERENGGANU

PAHANG

SELANGOR
Kuala Lumpur
Shah Alam
Port Klang

NEGRI SEMBILAN

MELAKA

JOHOR

Pasir Gudang

SINGAPORE

S T R A I T   O F   M A L A C C A

Malaysia Overview[1]

Background. Malaysia has a land area of 329,758 sq. km. (only 3% arable), coastline 4,675 kilometers, comprises 13 states; 11 in Peninsular Malaysia, two (Sabah and Sarawak) on the island of Borneo. Its 21 million population comprises Malays and other indigenous people (59%), Chinese (32%), Indian (9%). The state religion is Islam, but the Constitution promises the freedom of religion. On Peninsular Malaysia, Malays are Muslim, most Chinese Buddhist, most Indians Hindu; in Sabah, Muslim (38%), Christian (17%), others (45%); in Sarawak, traditional beliefs (35%), Buddhism and Confucianism (24%), Muslim (20%), Christian (16%), others (5%). The population speaks Malay (official language in Peninsular Malaysia), Chinese, English, Tamil, Itan Dusan, Bajau and other dialects. The major city (and capital) is Kuala Lumpur, population just over one million. The climate is tropical (average temperatures, 21°C to 32°C); rain is common in all seasons and humidity high.

Malaysia is a constitutional monarchy. The head of state is the Yang di-Pertuan Agong (king, five-year term) elected by the Conference of Rulers comprising nine hereditary ruling sultans from states in Peninsular Malaysia. Each of the four sultanless states (Melaka, Penang, Sabah, Sarawak) has a head of state (four-year term) appointed by the Yang di-Pertuan Agong. Each state has a constitution and assembly to handle non-federal government issues.

The legislative branch of government is a bicameral parliament comprising the House of Representatives (Dewan Rakyat), 192 elected members (five-year term); and Senate (Dewan Negara), 70 members (six-year term; 30 members elected, two per state, two per federal territory [Kuala Lumpur, Labuan Island], 40 appointed by the king). The legal system is based on British common law but Malaysia has not accepted compulsory ICJ jurisdiction.

The highest court of appeal is the Supreme Court; it has jurisdiction over disputes between the federal government and individual states and among individual states. Session courts, headed by a president, cover less serious offenses; magistrate courts have limited civil and criminal jurisdiction. For administrative purposes, the 13 states are divided into 130 administrative districts; Sarawak and Sabah have autonomy in customs, immigration and civil service issues.

Political. After World War II, Peninsular Malaysia suffered 12 years of communist insurgencies. In 1957, Malaysia achieved independence from Britain to form the

---

[1] Federation of Malaysia.

Federation of Malaya. In 1963, the states merged with Singapore, Sabah and Sarawak to form the Federation of Malaysia; in 1965, increasing conflict with the Federal government led Singapore to leave the Federation. The Malay political climate has long been shaped by tensions between indigenous Malays and Chinese; ethnic Chinese generally have greater economic power, Malays dominate the political sphere. Recent years have been marked by intense inter-party power struggles, and proposed constitutional amendments to reduce the sultans' powers. Tension was eased in 1992 when four (of nine) sultans approved a code of ethics for hereditary rulers.

Outspoken Prime Minister Mahathir Mohamad, has governed Malaysia since 1981; he is a staunch supporter of independence and Asian values and has criticized western views on human rights and the environment and the U.S. role in world affairs.

Social. Malaysia's present population is relatively young with 37% in the 0–14 age group; it is targeting 70 million population by 2095, more than triple the current 20 million. The Prime Minister's rationale is that significant population increase will make the domestic market more capable of sustaining the industrial sector.

A far-reaching government initiative is under way to overhaul the higher education system. In 1994, the Prime Minister decreed that Malay should not be the only language of instruction in the universities. Provision of health care and education varies considerably by state.

Economy. Malaysia is a member of the United Nations (UN), World Bank (WB), International Monetary Fund (IMF), World Trade Organization (WTO), Asian Development Bank (ADB), Asia-Pacific Economic Cooperation (APEC) Forum, Islamic Development Bank (IDB) and Association of Southeast Asian Nations (ASEAN). The Malaysian economy, a mixture of private enterprise and a soundly managed public sector, achieved 8.7% p.a. average growth in the early 1990s. Economic growth led to an improved deficit; 1993, 3.8% GNP, down from 5.8%, 1989. Agriculture and manufacturing account for 13.5% and 32.2% of GDP; services and others account for 53.8%. Major agricultural export products are palm oil and rubber; major imports are food and consumer goods. Major export destinations (1994) are: U.S. (21.1%), Singapore (20.7%), Japan (11.9%). Major import origins are (1994): Japan (26.7%), U.S. (16.7%), Singapore (14.1%). Tourism (1993, over 7 million arrivals) is a major foreign exchange earner.

Fast economic growth has caused labor shortages, addressed by relaxing immigration controls and by importing labor from neighboring countries. To encourage investment, foreign companies can own 100% equity in projects exporting over 50% production or employing over 350 people.

Although its foreign debt (about US$30 billion) was less than one third of its Southeast Asian neighbors, Malaysia was quickly drawn into the 1997 Asian financial crisis because its credit expansion as a percent of GDP was highest in the region; in addition, it had the highest credit exposure to the property market (making the stock market very sensitive to changes in interest rates). The Malaysian stock market lost half of its capitalization between July and end 1997. The ringgit lost 35% of its value against the U.S. dollar and remained weak, hurt by successive attacks on the Korean won.

Bank Negara, the central bank, carries out all central banking functions and has responsibility to ensure government goals are attained in the financial sector. Total banking system assets increased substantially in the past two decades: RM6 billion (51% of GNP) in 1970 to RM222 billion in 1993 (135% of GDP).

The Kuala Lumpur Stock Exchange (KLSE) began operations in 1973; a second board opened in November 1988. Automated trading was introduced in 1989 when formal separation of Singapore and Malaysia securities markets occurred.

Infrastructure. Transportation is far more highly developed in Peninsular Malaysia than Sabah and Sarawak; the road network increased from 28,870 kilometers (1980) to 92,545 kilometers (1992). Road transport accounts for almost 90% of Malaysia's total freight and passenger movements. In 1990, private motor vehicle ownership reached 96 per 1,000, highest among Asian countries. Urban traffic congestion is worsening, especially in Kuala Lumpur; improvement plans are in place and work on Kuala Lumpur's Light Rail Transit system has started. In 1993, electric power generation stood at 16.5 billion kWh, 920 kWh per capita; generating capacity was 5.6 million kWh.

Malaysia Airlines, privatized to generate funds for fleet upgrade, operates extensive domestic and international service; the government sold its 42% stake but retains control over fares. An ambitious program of expansion involves 72 new planes, costing RM10.6 billion. In 1992, the government announced plans to construct a new international airport at Sepang (RM20 billion) to replace the existing Subang airport; phase one is completed, planned opening is early 1998.

Malaysia's three largest ports are Port Klang, Penang and Pasir Gudang. Almost 90% of all sea-born trade is carried by foreign ships; Malaysian International Shipping Corporation planned to spend RM1 billion on bulk carriers and tankers in 1992–97. Malaysia has a highly developed telecommunications system (180 telephones per 1,000 population).

Statistics*	June 1991	June 1997	Statistics*	June 1991	June 1997
Per capita GNP	US$2,305	US$3,930	Pop. growth	2.3%	2.4%
GDP growth	10.0%	8.1%	Infant mortality / 1,000	14	12
Savings (GNP)	n/a	41%	Life expectancy (yrs)	n/a	72
Inflation (CPI)	3.1%	2.6%	Literacy rate	72.6%	89.3%
Foreign debt			People per tel.	10.3	5.5
(in billion)	US$15.5	US$27.1	People per doctor	2,656	2,063
Pop. (million)	18.3	21.0	People per TV	n/a	4.7
Urban pop.	44%**	47%	Calorie intake (cals)	n/a	2,884

*Secured from *Asiaweek*.
**From "Vietnam: Open for Business," J. Probert (Sept. 1994), EAC/INSEAD.

Case 26

Edaran Otomobil Nasional Berhad: Challenge of the 1990s

Virginia B. Qunitos, Jacinto C. Gavino, Jr
Asian Institute of Management, Makati, the Philippines

Dato Adzmi Abdul Wahab, Edaran Otomobil Nasional Berhad's (EON) managing director was reviewing the past nine years' growth. Although EON had grown from a car marketing company to a diversified group engaged in other businesses such as property development, banking and financial services, stockbroking, security services, real estate and trading, the motor group was still the cash cow. Adzmi decided to evaluate and assess EON's accomplishments prior to repositioning in the face of new competition. Specifically, he was concerned with introduction of the Perodua, developed by a Malaysian government/Daihatsu Motors (Japan) joint venture. He wondered what entry strategy to expect and how EON should respond.

 howcs

Company Background

Edaran Otomobil Nasional Berhad was incorporated on May 16, 1984 as a private limited company, the sole distributor of Proton Saga vehicles and spare parts in Malaysia. The Proton Saga was the Malaysian national car. All automobile technology, know-how and components came from Mitsubishi Japan. EON was a joint venture of Hicom Berhad (45%), United Motor Works Corporation (35%), United Assembly Sendirian Berhad (15%) and Edaran Pekemans Berhad (5%).

As sole distributor of the Proton Saga, EON developed into a large organization very quickly. It constructed a corporate headquarters at the Hicom Industrial Area in Shah Alam, 35 kilometers from Kuala Lumpur, in 108 days. The complex contained 200,000 sq. ft. of floor space including a Pre-delivery Inspection Outfit, fitment center, parts warehouse, clinic, office space and training facilities. Operations commenced with 200 employees at corporate headquarters; by 1993, EON employed over 400 staff in Shah Alam and 1,600 others across Malaysia. After two years of operations, EON had 40 branches and 19 service centers; by 1994, it had 54 sales branches, 104 dealers, and 143 service outlets.[1]

In 1985, when the Proton Saga was first introduced, the car market was experiencing growth and high demand; also known as the People's Car, the Proton Saga was inaugurated via a nationwide tour. This tour, the Sagarama, lasted 13 days, stopping in many towns throughout Malaysia. In each state, the Proton Saga was welcomed by the Sultan or various ministers. The event was a nationwide festival; Malaysians flocked to see the Saga in each town.

Sales took off in the last quarter of 1985; after eight months, the Proton Saga was market leader in passenger cars. The 1986 recession initially affected Saga sales, but an innovative promotional campaign arrested slipping volume. In 1987, EON introduced three new models – the Proton Saga Aeroback, the Proton Magma and the Proton Magma Aeroback. Although industry sales fell 26%, EON maintained its market share and suffered no losses. In 1988, when the economy improved, EON increased sales by 70%; it started to participate actively in rallies.

Corporate ownership was restructured in 1989; Hicom Berhad maintained 45% ownership; the Ministry of Finance and Kuala Pura secured 25% and 30% ownership, respectively. The Proton Knight, a sportier version of the Aeroback was launched in March 1989.

EON experienced significant growth and development in 1990. It introduced seven-unit car transporter trailers; built Akademi Saga, a technical training school for apprentices and in-service employees, in Shah Alam; and formed its first subsidiary, Automotive Conversion Engineering. Ownership (30%) was opened to the public (36 million shares offered at RM4.3 per share) and shares were listed on the Kuala Lumpur Stock Exchange. After the public offering, ownership was Hicom Berhad (31.5%), Kuala Pura (21%), Ministry of Finance (17.5%), public (30%).

In 1991, the EON "Sogososha" grew with the incorporation of EON Properties Sendirian Berhad, EON Resorts Sendirian Berhad and EON Trading Sendirian Berhad; in addition, a 51% stake was purchased in Jurumuda Sendirian Berhad. Expansion continued in 1992; EON purchased 40% of SRT-EON Security Services, 30% of Leong and Company Securities and 30% of Proton Parts Center. In August, the Proton Iswara, the third cosmetic change of the Proton Saga, was launched by Prime Minister Mahathir Mohamad at Dataran Merdeka.

In May 1993, the Proton Wira, a 1.6 liter sleek, oval sub-compact family sedan offering quality performance, contemporary styling and outstanding comfort was introduced. The Wira Aeroback, launched in the third quarter, offered customers sporty, luxurious styling with impressive performance. The five-door model was available in five-speed or four-speed automatic transmission.

---

[1] In early 1994, EON moved its head office to its new address in Glenmarie, Shah Alam. The new headquarters was a 30-acre square complex that also housed the first 24-hour, seven days a week service center.

The Malaysian Economy

In a widely noted 1991 speech, Mahathir presented his "Vision for Malaysia 2020." The central thrust had nine strategic challenges: national unity, national self-confidence, equity, tolerance, moral ethics, education, technology, human resources and competitiveness. The first six challenges covered social aspects; the last three addressed economic concerns. Mahathir's main point was that social and economic justice were priorities for economic development.

In recent years the Malaysian economy demonstrated substantial growth (8% to 10% annually); it was expected to grow at 7.5% for the foreseeable future. Growth was fueled by an influx of investment for developing the manufacturing sector resulting from Singapore's shifting focus to concentrate on high technology and financial services, relocation of Japanese manufacturing and preparation for expected larger international markets resulting from the ASEAN Free Trade Area (AFTA). The government's privatization projects also played a role; transfer of such state-owned companies as Telekom Malaysia, car-maker Proton and state power monopoly Tenaga Nasional to the private sector was expected to induce investment in the form of technology equipment purchases.

Infrastructure investment such as huge shopping malls and condominiums also made a major contribution to the national economy. Economic growth brought increases in private consumption and changed consumer spending behavior as demand increased for such big-ticket items as housing, appliances and automobiles. The growing economy also increased the need for trained technicians, assembly line and construction workers and others; labor shortages posed bottleneck problems in critical areas such as ports, roads and utility service infrastructure. Labor costs rose sharply; by 9.8% from 1990 to 1991.

Edaran Otomobil Nasional Berhad

Organization

The EON Group comprised five subsidiaries and six associate companies with operations in Malaysia and overseas (Table 1). In 1993, Group revenues were RM3.6 billion; pre-tax profits, RM275 million (Exhibit 1). The company's flagship operation was the motor group. Two divisions reported to Managing Director Dato Adzmi Abdul: Sales, and Finance and Corporate Services. The sales director was responsible for all operations related to marketing Proton Saga vehicles (Figure 1).

Proton Saga Vehicles

EON offered several car models for buyers of 1001 cc. to 1600 cc. vehicles, approximately 85% to 90% of total car sales (Exhibit 2). Major Proton Group products were: the Proton Saga (1300 cc., 1500 cc.), Proton Wira (1300 cc., 1500 cc. and 1600 cc.), Knight, Executive and Iswara. The Proton Saga received several cosmetic changes through the years. (See Exhibit 3 for Proton product specifications versus competition.) EON sold 94,720 Proton Saga vehicles in 1993. (See Exhibit 4 for registered sales per model.) EON's sales network of 158 outlets was distributed throughout Malaysia (Table 2, Exhibit 5).

Table 1: The EON Group

Subsidiaries	
Name	**Activity**
Automotive Conversion Engineering, Selangor (100%)	Conversion and modification of Proton Saga motor vehicles
EON Properties, Selangor (100%)	Investment in and management of properties
EON Trading, Kuala Lumpur (100%)	Trading of car accessories, primary commodities and general trading
EON Resorts, Kuala Lumpur (100%)	Dormant
Jurumuda, Kuala Lumpur (51%)	Rust proofing of motor vehicles
EON Bank Berhad, Kuala Lumpur (61.3%)	Banking and related financial services

Associate companies	
Name	**Activity**
Leong & Company, Kuala Lumpur (30%)	Stockbroking
Cycle & Carriage Limited, Singapore (20.1%)	Vehicles assembly and distribution, property development and investment, and food and retail
Proton Parts Centre, Selangor (40%)	Warehousing and distribution of motor vehicle spare parts and accessories
Mobikom, Kuala Lumpur (30%)	Telecommunication services
SRT-EON Security Services, Selangor (40%)	Security services

Source: EON 1993 Annual Report.

Figure 1: Organization Structure – EON Group

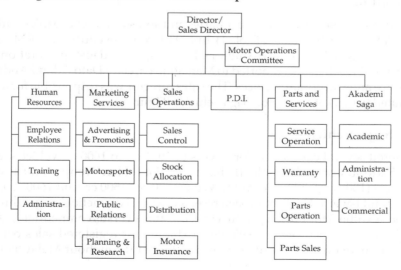

Table 2:   Proton Saga Sales Network Growth

	1985	1986	1987	1988	1989	1990	1991	1992	1993
EON branches	20	42	42	43	44	52	*53	**54	54
Bumiputra*** dealer outlets	–	20	30	29	66	68	68	68	66
Non-bumiputra dealer outlets	–	18	29	27	37	37	37	37	38
Franchise dealer outlets	–	5	5	4	4	–	–	–	–
Total	20	85	106	103	151	157	159	159	158

*Kuching II.
**Langkawi.
***Bumiputras – indigenous to Malaysia, include all native tribes and all Malays (Muslims). The two other ethnic groups were not included.

Competitive Environment

In 1993, sales of all automobiles totaled 127,031 vehicles; the Proton Saga was market leader with 74.6% market share. Major competitors were Toyota, Nissan and Honda (Exhibit 6A). Participants segmented the passenger car market based on the vehicle engine capacity (Exhibit 6B). Other major considerations for customer preference were cosmetics, engine performance and durability, styling, riding comfort and equipment. Since 1986, EON was market leader in the over 1600 cc. market; in 1993, Proton's market share was over 80% (Exhibit 6C). Foreign-made automobiles imported into Malaysia were taxed at about 200%; locally assembled vehicles much less. The Proton Saga was not taxed at all.

Proton's Marketing Strategy

Target Market

The target market for Proton Saga vehicles was the young (21 to 40 years old), male, urban professional, in business or government service, with a monthly income range of RM1,001 to RM2,999. Initially, the bulk of customers were Malays (55.2%); the Chinese population, interested in value for money, generally took a "wait and see" attitude. After two years, when performance was proven, Chinese Malaysians began purchasing Proton Sagas. In 1993, the Chinese comprised 55.8% of Proton Saga customers. (See Table 3 for Proton Saga customer profile.)

Promotion

EON employed two advertising agencies to develop multimedia advertising campaigns. For new product launches (e.g., Wira, 1993) EON's marketing staff met with the two agencies, explained the product and features and requested advertising concepts. Each agency made a creative proposal, EON management made a selection. For 1993, EON spent 50% of its budget on TV, 40% print, 10% radio. Management viewed

Table 3: Proton Saga Customer Profile, 1985–93 (average)

Gender	%	Age	%	Personal income	%	Occupation	%
Male	70	21–30	36	RM1,000–2,999	85	Business/profession/corporate	28
Female	22	31 & above	56	RM3,000 & above	7	Government service	18
Corporate	8	Corporate	8	Corporate	8	Employers/others	54
Total	100		100		100		100

car rallies as a productive method of demonstrating Proton Saga's durability and reliability.

Dealer Management

Individual Proton cars were priced identically regardless of outlet; this policy was designed to protect consumers. In addition, it supported EON's customer service strategy; since dealers could not compete on price, they had to compete on customer service. Dealers and salesmen were paid a fixed commission; salesmen commissions were paid directly by EON and did not pass through the dealers. This policy ensured dealer honesty and prevented use of sales force commissions for their own purposes.

Industry average sales were 2.5 cars per salesman per month; at EON, salesmen were required to sell six cars per month. Bookings required a RM3,000 downpayment, non-refundable if the order was canceled; this policy ensured salesmen only made bookings for actual sales. EON bookings translated 99% to actual sales. In 1993, demand for EON vehicles was larger than supply; Proton cars were delivered two months after the sale closed.

After-sales Service

One EON manager stated: "The salesmen sell the first car, the after-sales service sells the succeeding cars." Over the years, EON built a network of 143 outlets (Table 4). Service centers, classified A, B, C based on equipment sophistication, were scattered throughout Malaysia. Class A service centers (EON had four) used computerized equipment; the most sophisticated was a newly opened 24-hour service center in Glenmarie.

Table 4: EON's Customer Service Network

Outlets	1985	1986	1987	1988	1989	1990	1991	1992	1993
EON service centers	16	23	24	29	30	36	36	35	38
EON service dealers	1	5	8	8	10	18	31	48	62
EON service stations	27	30	31	35	40	40	41	72	43
Total	44	58	63	72	80	94	108	155	143

EON offered a limited 24 months / 50,000 kilometers warranty, whichever occurred sooner. The warranty covered any part of the vehicle manufactured or supplied by Proton found defective in material or workmanship. It did not cover filters (oil and fuel), filter elements, oil seals, gaskets, light bulbs, clutch linings, brake linings, windshield wiper blades, V-belts, bolts and nuts, engine tune-ups, wheel alignment and balancing, spark plugs or fuses.

Each customer received a Delivery Acknowledgment and Warranty Registration, plus a booklet specifying services available at service centers; the centers provided all service needed for maintenance of Proton vehicles. Owners received a checklist reminding them periodically to have their cars checked. EON also offered pre-delivery inspection service, free service at 1,000 kilometers, 5,000 kilometers and 10,000 kilometers, and periodic inspection and maintenance service.

EON service centers were open from 8:00 am to 5:00 pm, Monday to Friday, half day on Saturdays. From 1985 to 1993, EON sold over 550,000 cars; by 1994, all service centers were operating at capacity. Customers made a practice of booking five days ahead. EON budgeted RM100 million in 1994 to expand the number / quality of services offered.

Akademi Saga

Akademi Saga was EON's mechanic training school. Its main objective was to supply trained manpower for EON's service centers and its franchise service dealers; a secondary objective was to upgrade the skills of the existing service labor force. Akademi Saga's main course was a nine-month program (six months theory; three months on-the-job training), the conversion course. This program accepted applicants who finished automotive courses in vocational schools; Akademi Saga trained these graduates on the specifics of Proton cars.

In 1990, Akademi Saga offered a two-year apprenticeship program for students finishing secondary school. The school, which graduated 60 mechanics who worked in various service outlets, was phased out at government request since it competed directly with the government's automotive course.

Akademi Saga employed nine expert trainers; some were sent to Japan for updating on new Mitsubishi technology. These trainers taught EON mechanics so they were better equipped to handle Proton vehicles. Akademi Saga also offered ten modules to upgrade existing mechanics' skills and special courses such as a one-day orientation program for new Proton Saga owners.

Competitive Action

In September 1994, Malaysia's second national car, the Perodua, was launched. The Perodua was a joint venture between the Malaysian government and Japan's Daihatsu Motor. The Perodua was a 660 cc. Kancil minicar selling for RM13,000; it was the least expensive automobile on the market. By early October 1994, pending orders for the car totaled 14,000. Wahab wondered how the new competitor would approach the market, and what strategy EON should develop to deal with this competitive threat.

Exhibit 1: EON Financial Highlights (RM '000)

	1993	1992	1991	1990
Assets				
Cash and short-term funds	495,362	120,836	147,594	268,090
Investments	107,503	500	50,030	–
Loans and advances	1,165,768	–	–	–
Statutory deposit with Bank Negara Malaysia	97,045	–	–	–
Stocks	138,705	115,026	78,892	32,931
Other assets	87,011	72,548	365,787	31,851
Investment in associated companies	534,546	586,618	–	–
Fixed assets	198,348	70,222	55,105	36,155
Goodwill on consolidation	105,290	–	–	–
Total	2,929,578	965,750	697,408	369,027
Liabilities				
Deposits from customers	1,237,923	–	–	–
Deposits and balances of banks and agents	357,691	–	–	–
Bills and acceptances payable	28,325	9,089	1,184	–
Due to associated company	4,038	–	–	–
Other liabilities	475,770	322,855	432,393	187,702
Total	2,103,747	331,944	433,577	187,702
Minority interests	52,963	2,244	1,524	125
Total liabilities and shareholders' funds	2,929,578	965,750	697,408	369,027
Operating revenue	3,642,649	2,683,658	2,569,730	2,076,412
Profit before taxation	275,866	181,046	174,155	112,842
Profit after taxation and minority interests	177,617	108,360	103,991	68,984
Profit available for appropriation	332,945	190,151	165,191	69,000
Bonus issue	–	–	(60,000)	–
Dividend	(36,991)	(32,477)	(23,400)	(7,800)
Retained profit carried forward	295,954	157,674	81,791	61,200

Source: EON 1993 Annual Report.

Proton Saga Aeroback

Proton Saga Aerokit

Proton Saga Sedan (Magma Engine)

Proton Saga Megavalve

Proton Saga Cares

Proton Saga Sedan (Orion Engine)

Proton Knight

Proton Limousine

Proton Saga Iswara

Proton Executive

Exhibit 3A: Proton Wira 1.3 Competitive Comparisons, December 1993*

Identification	Saloon	A/Back	H/Back	H/Back	Saloon	Saloon	Saloon
Insigna ID	1.3S Iswara	1.3S Iswara	1.0 Daihatsu	1.3 Daihatsu	1.3 Nissan S.	1.3 Ford L.	1.3 Toyota C.
Engine model	4G13P	4G13P	3CYL SOHC	16V SOHC	E13S OHC	16V SOHC	OHC 12V
Engine (cc.) displacement	1298	1298	993	1295	1270	1298	1296
Engine power (kw)	62	62	52	56	74	n/a	55
Acceleration 0–100 kph in secs.	13.1	13.1	n/a	n/a	n/a	n/a	10.3
Fuel consumption/100 kms	5.5	5.5	n/a	n/a	n/a	n/a	n/a
Maximum speed km/hr	163	163	n/a	n/a	n/a	n/a	n/a
Vehicle weight (kg)	920	920	740	800	835	n/a	n/a
Shifting	M/T	M/T	M/T	M/T	M/T	M/T	M/T
Price: Solid RM	RM31,694	RM30,544	RM37,605	0	RM37,454	RM52,061	RM60,788
Price: Metallic RM	RM32,339	0	RM38,909	RM47,443	RM37,805	RM52,969	RM61,694

Exhibit 3B: Proton Wira 1.5 Competitive Comparisons, December 1993*

Identification	Saloon	Saloon	Saloon	Saloon	Saloon	Saloon	Saloon	Saloon	Saloon	Saloon
Insigna ID	1.5 Wira	1.5 Wira	1.5 Honda Civic	1.5 Honda Civic	1.5 Ford Laser	1.6 Mazda Familia	1.6 Toyota Corolla	1.6 Nissan Sentra	1.6 Ford Laser	1.6 Honda Civic
Engine model	4GI5	4GI5	SOHC 16V	SOHC 16V	4CYL8V	SOHC 16V	Efi Twin Cam	GA 16DE	SOHC 16V	SOHC 16V
Engine (cc.) displacement	1468	1468	1493	1493	1498	1598	1587	1597	1598	1590
Engine power (kw)	67	67	91	91	n/a	87	81	n/a	n/a	120
Acceleration 1–100 kph in secs.	12.1	14.6	11.6	11.6	n/a	12.7	14.2	14	n/a	14.5
Fuel con./100 kms	5.6	6.6	n/a	n/a	n/a	n/a	n/a	n/a	n/a	n/a
Max. speed km/hr	172	165	n/a	n/a	n/a	n/a	n/a	n/a	n/a	n/a
Vehicle weight (kg)	955	975	985	1015	n/a	995	n/a	1005	n/a	1050
Shifting	M/T	A/T	M/T	A/T	M/T	M/T	M/T	M/T	M/T	M/T
Price: Solid RM	RM39,278	RM42,301	RM68,838	RM64,144	RM40,464	RM56,856	RM75,226	RM54,819	RM58,789	RM74,778
Price: Metallic RM	RM39,971	RM42,995	RM69,564	RM69,870	RM41,344	RM57,732	RM76,152	RM55,535	RM59,696	RM75,504

*None of the cars came with radio, air-conditioner, power lock or power window accessories.

Exhibit 3C: Proton Wira 1.6 Competitive Comparisons, December 1993*

Identification	Saloon	A/Back	A/Back	Saloon	A/Back	Saloon	Saloon	A/Back
Insignia identification	1.6 Wira	1.6 Wira	1.6 Wira	1.6 Honda Civic	1.6 Mazda Astina	1.6 Nissan Sentra	1.6 Toyota Corolla	1.6 Ford Laser
Engine model	4G92	4G92	4G92	SOHC 16V	SOHC 16V	GA 16 DE	Efi Twin Cam	SOHC 16V
Engine (cc.) displacement	1597	1597	1597	1590	1598	1598	1597	1598
Engine power (kw)	88	88	88	120	87	n/a	81	n/a
Acceleration 1–100 kph. in secs.	13.0	10.8	13.0	14.5	12.7	14.0	14.2	n/a
Fuel consumption/100/kms	6.2	5.8	6.2	n/a	n/a	n/a	n/a	n/a
Maximum speed km/hr	175	187	175	n/a	n/a	n/a	n/a	n/a
Vehicle weight (kg)	1075	1065	1095	1140	1010	1030	n/a	n/a
Shifting	A/T	M/T	A/T	A/T	M/T	A/T	A/T	M/T
Price: Solid RM	RM54,308	RM54,336	RM58,436	RM80,821	RM56,923	RM62,102	RM79,330	RM57,219
Price: Metallic RM				RM81,547	RM57,883	RM66,206	RM80,256	RM58,127

*None of the cars came with radio, air-conditioner, power lock or power window accessories.

Exhibit 4: Proton Saga Registered Sales by Model

	1985	%	1986	%	1987	%	1988	%	1989	%	1990	%	1991	%	1992	%	1993	%
1.3S SAL	4,105	55	12,361	51	9,272	37	14,508	34	17,625	34	16,512	23	21,198	25	20,232	25	20,360	22
1.3S A/Back	–	–	–	–	1,018	4	4,132	10	18	–	–	–	–	–	–	–	952	1
1.5S SAL	3,389	45	11,787	49	12,112	49	19,025	45	23,955	46	32,995	46	36,900	44	37,035	46	16,048	17
1.5S A/Back	–	–	–	–	–	–	298	1	6,446	12	8,805	12	7,573	9	4,755	6	3,587	4
1.5I SAL (M)	–	–	27	–	1,532	6	2,648	6	4,416	8	74	–	–	–	–	–	–	–
1.5I SAL (A)	–	–	–	–	–	–	–	–	–	–	12,483	17	15,775	19	15,674	20	8,733	9
1.5I A/Back (M)	–	–	–	–	924	4	1,709	4	197	–	1,653	2	–	–	–	–	–	–
1.5I A/Back (A)	–	–	–	–	–	–	–	–	–	–	–	–	3,382	4	2,752	3	1,859	2
Wira 1.5GL (M)	–	–	–	–	–	–	–	–	–	–	–	–	–	–	–	–	23,195	25
Wira 1.5GL (A)	–	–	–	–	–	–	–	–	–	–	–	–	–	–	–	–	7,911	8
Wira 1.6XLI (A)	–	–	–	–	–	–	–	–	–	–	–	–	–	–	–	–	8,531	9
Wira 1.6XLI AB (M)	–	–	–	–	–	–	–	–	–	–	–	–	–	–	–	–	1,772	2
Wira 1.6XLI AB (A)	–	–	–	–	–	–	–	–	–	–	–	–	–	–	–	–	1,772	2
Total	7,494	100	24,175	100	24,858	100	42,320	100	52,657	100	72,522	100	84,828	100	80,448	100	94,720	100

1 Pudu	12 Rawang	23 Muar	34 Bukit Mertajam	45 K.K. Sinsuran
2 Ampang	13 Klang	24 Kulai	35 Sg Petani	46 Tawau
3 Jln Chan Sow Lin	14 Banting	25 Kluang	36 Alor Star	47 Sandakan
4 Sg Besi	15 Glenmarie	26 Ipoh	37 Langkawi	48 Labuan
5 Segambut	16 Seremban	27 Jln CM Yusuff	38 Kangar	49 Lahad Datu
6 Cheras	17 Bahau	28 Sitiawan	39 Kuantan	50 Kuching
7 Old Kelang Road	18 Malacca	29 Telok Intan	40 Temerloh	51 Kuching II
8 Kepong	19 Segamat	30 Taiping	41 Bentong	52 Sibu
9 SS/2	20 Johor Bahru	31 Georgetown	42 Kuala Terengganu	53 Miri
10 PJ New Town	21 Taman Pelangi	32 Jln Sultan Azlan Shah	43 Kota Bharu	54 Bintulu
11 Kemajuan	22 Batu Pahat	33 Butterworth	44 Kota Kinabalu	

LEGEND: ⚠ EON Branches
△ EON Branches & Services Centers

Exhibit 6A: Total Passenger Car Market Share (units)

Car brand	1985	1986	1987	1988	1989	1990	1991	1992	1993
Proton	7,468	24,193	24,876	42,301	52,695	72,519	84,796	80,487	94,765
Nissan	21,530	11,806	5,225	5,584	9,806	11,450	10,000	8,215	6,279
Toyota	15,439	6,548	1,789	4,879	4,102	9,987	9,513	10,101	9,111
Honda	6,542	3,179	2,451	3,451	8,141	10,575	12,590	9,931	10,009
Volvo	2,790	654	261	254	1,206	1,984	2,106	1,407	1,212
Daihatsu	1,358	1,023	911	299	1,543	2,554	2,987	2,010	1,331
Ford	2,877	1,563	687	125	784	3,849	4,001	3,121	2,287
Mercedes	2,814	988	465	280	547	965	1,101	812	611
Mazda	2,037	422	321	159	422	885	936	711	512
O. Gemini	2,178	216	232	116	261	555	622	365	221
Mitsubishi	1,926	299	368	187	101	654	754	356	272
Others	929	365	568	312	354	800	1,049	500	422
Total units	67,888	51,256	38,154	57,947	79,962	116,777	130,455	118,016	127,031

Exhibit 6B: Market Segment Based on CC. Range from 1985 to 1993 (units)

Model range	1985	1986	1987	1988	1989	1990	1991	1992	1993
1000 cc. and below	8,146	2,934	611	201	1,541	2,547	3,214	2,415	1,874
1001–1400 cc.	31,730	20,000	14,216	23,801	26,789	29,565	33,918	28,146	23,147
1401–1600 cc.	15,687	19,215	15,810	29,587	46,211	68,798	76,112	72,145	86,458
1601–1800 cc.	4,987	6,892	3,262	348	310	1,822	2,212	1,874	1,547
1801 cc. and above	7,338	2,215	4,257	4,010	5,111	14,045	14,999	13,436	14,005
Total units	67,888	51,256	38,155	57,947	79,962	116,777	130,455	118,016	127,031

Exhibit 6C: Passenger Car Market Share < 1600 CC. Market from 1985 to 1993 (units)

Car brand	1985	1986	1987	1988	1989	1990	1991	1992	1993
Proton	7,491	24,186	24,869	42,334	60,203	72,554	84,838	81,547	94,717
Nissan	26,321	7,564	3,214	3,542	10,145	9,789	8,971	9,541	6,790
Toyota	7,899	6,541	1,847	2,896	2,987	8,721	8,896	7,984	6,100
Honda	1,546	1,463	487	1,271	2,731	3,123	4,002	4,166	4,010
Others	9,872	3,590	1,142	2,875	5,731	6,442	6,561	3,081	2,229
Total units	53,129	43,344	31,559	52,918	81,797	100,629	113,268	106,319	113,846

Case 27

Malaysia Airlines: Landing Gear Shop

Mario Lluch Padillas, Francisco L. Roman, Jr., Kim Y. Wolf, Wong Yoon Sung
Asian Institute of Management, Makati, the Philippines

Malaysia Airlines (MAS) executives were evaluating the possibility of transforming its landing gear shop into a profit center whereby it would solicit overhaul business from carriers in the Asia-Pacific region.[1] The entry decision required an evaluation of market demand, production capacity and financial viability, and development of marketing strategy for the proposed overhaul center.[2]

৪০৫৪

Malaysia Airlines

History

In 1937, the Ocean Steamship Company of Liverpool and the Straits Steamship Company of Singapore secured a license for air service and named it Malayan Airways Ltd. (MAL). MAL began modestly in 1947 with three small twin-engine Airspeed Consuls, each with five-person capacity. Business grew rapidly in subsequent years and service was extended throughout Malaysia and major cities in Southeast Asia.

---

[1] Malaysia's main airport was located between Hong Kong in the north (four-hour flight) and Singapore in the south. Operationally, airlines preferred to terminate their flights in these locations and overhaul aircraft component in bases there.
[2] Landing gear comprised the complexity of wheels and struts that provided shock absorption and support to the aircraft during the landing process. For example, the shipset of five landing gear for a B747 supported a weight of 785,000 pounds.

420

In 1958, a year after independence, MAL became a public company owned by BOAC, Qantas and governments of the Federation of Malaya, Singapore and the Borneo territories. When Malaysia was formed in 1963, the airline, whose major aircraft were jets, was renamed Malaysian Airways Ltd. In 1966, the governments of Malaysia and Singapore acquired majority control, changed the name to Malaysia-Singapore Airlines (MSA) and expanded international routes to Tokyo, Madras, Colombo, Bombay, Bahrain and Melbourne using new Boeing 707, 737 and Fokker aircraft. In 1971, the governments of Malaysia and Singapore dissolved the partnership and each country operated its own national carrier.

In 1985, Malaysia Airlines System (MAS) was publicly listed and traded on the Malaysian Stock Exchange with a new name, Malaysia Airlines. According to Managing Director Dato Abdul Aziz, the privatization was positive for MAS inasmuch as the equity injection stabilized its cost of funds and provided a cushion against fluctuations in interest and exchange rates. From six international and 34 domestic points in 1985, by 1988, MAS serviced 25 international and 35 domestic points.

MAS experienced considerable year-to-year growth in many aspects of its system (Exhibit 1). As part of its fleet expansion and modernization program, in 1985, MAS ordered six super long range B747-400's and placed an option on another four. Over the ensuing several years, total investment in fleet development was anticipated to amount to about RM5.5 billion.[3]

Malaysia Airlines Engineering Department

Maintenance of MAS aircraft was the responsibility of the engineering division. Its main objective was to provide airworthy aircraft for commercial service at optimum cost. The division, headed by the director of engineering, comprised seven departments. (See Figure 1 for organization chart including the proposed landing gear workshop organization.)

Workforce. Manpower increased from 630 in 1972 to 2,500 by 1982, when a RM36 million loss led to a company-wide recruitment freeze and the implementation of productivity programs. In 1988, personnel numbered 2,340 but the decision to perform heavy maintenance on wide-body aircraft in-house was expected to raise the number of employees to 4,000 by the year 2000. At that time, MAS would perform all maintenance and overhaul work on all its aircraft, engines, and components. (See Table 1 for distribution of current manpower strength.)

Facilities. Facilities were added when it was financially justified. Over the years, the engineering division developed resources comprising hangars and workshops covering 84,410 sq. m.

---

[3] In September 1992, US$1 = RM2.50.

Table 1: Engineering Staff Manpower Distribution by Department

Department	%	Department	%
Product support	12	Technical training	1
Technical services	2	Workshop	21
Maintenance	48	Engineering development	1
Quality assurance	4	**Total staff strength**	**2,630**
Trainees	11		

Figure 1: Organization Chart

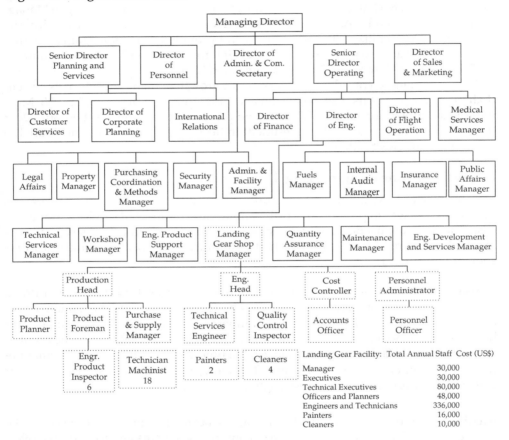

Landing Gear Facility: Total Annual Staff Cost (US$)

Manager	30,000
Executives	30,000
Technical Executives	80,000
Officers and Planners	48,000
Engineers and Technicians	336,000
Painters	16,000
Cleaners	10,000

Engineering capability. Engineering capability ranged from minor servicing to major repair and overhaul of all aircraft (except B747s). The division had about 65% capability level in the overhaul of components and 45% in engines. With a new workshop it would reach 75% for components and 85% for engines. It also successfully secured some contract work from regional airlines as an additional income source. MAS's consistent performance in ensuring high maintenance quality standards and on-time departures was rewarded by the world's leading aircraft manufacturer, Boeing, on three occasions. The first "Pride in Excellence" award was given in 1973 for outstanding efforts in maintaining a near perfect on-schedule operation for B737 aircraft. In 1979, Boeing presented a second award for maintaining a consistent above 99% mechanical dispatch reliability for its B737 fleet since 1972. Third, in 1988, it achieved the best dispatch reliability in the world for B737 aircraft.

The Landing Gear System

Landing Gear

The landing gear was the "legs" of the aircraft used primarily as support while on the ground and during takeoffs and landings. It was designed to be small so it could be tucked under the aircraft wings and body and built extremely strong to be able to withstand the shockload during the landing impact. Materials used in the manufacture of landing gear components were mainly high strength aluminum alloy and chromium steel. Damage limits were very tight to ensure safe operations.

Services and Prices

Basically, repair and overhaul companies offered five types of services:

- Repair and recondition of sub-assembly parts. The airline's maintenance organization would disassemble landing gear in its own workshop and send out parts that failed preliminary inspection. Repair work entailing replating, rebuilding and rebushing, usually had a turnaround time of 30 days. Prices, based on labor time and materials consumed, ranged from 5% to 10% of the price of a new part.
- Complete landing gear overhaul. The airline's maintenance organization would send out the whole landing gear assembly; it would be overhauled and restored to zero life. This process normally took 60 to 90 days and cost 20% to 30% of the price of a new gear.
- Complete landing gear overhaul, plus installation onto aircraft. Many small airlines did not have the capability to remove and install landing gear on aircraft. They would contract the work of removal, installation and gear overhaul to an overhaul company, typically every four years. The removal/installation service, normally provided by airline-based overhaul facilities, cost US$6,000 per gear.[4]
- Exchange program. The customer's landing gear would be transported to the overhaul company and a fully repaired assembly provided as an exchange. The shop charged a fee equivalent to 10% of new landing gear cost, plus the overhaul cost for defective gear. The faulty gear, once repaired, became the property of the overhaul company.

---

[4] Removal/installation required on average 80 man-hours of four skilled personnel. The labor rate used was US$75 per hour.

- Pooling arrangement. For a fixed annual fee, the airline had access to a pool of landing gear owned by the overhaul company. When the airline needed to replace faulty gear, the overhaul company delivered workable gear immediately. The inoperative assembly was repaired and the airline charged an overhauling fee.

All these services were supported by after sales service in the form of warranty against premature failure due to poor workmanship and faulty material. The warranty period typically varied by airline: 180 days to one year, and 1,000 to 3,000 hours.

Expenses incurred in the maintenance and overhaul of airframe, engines and flight equipment were part of an airline's operating expenses. Landing gear repair and overhaul cost accounted for about 12% of total flight equipment maintenance and overhaul costs, or about 0.4% of total airline operating expenses.

Prices of landing gear overhaul were perceived as consistently high, in part because facilities shortages led to little competition. Repairs were considered uneconomical if the overhaul cost estimated during preliminary inspection exceeded 65% of the price of brand new gear; in such cases, the overhaul company might recommend replacement to the customer.

The most significant contributor to the price of landing gear was the material used in its construction. Special chromium steel, whose manufacturing process was still considered a trade secret, was important to the gear manufacture industry and overhaul companies. (See Table 2 for the cost of overhaul for various aircraft models.)

Table 2: Landing Gear Overhaul Costs in 1988*

Aircraft type	Type of landing gear	Unit cost (US$)	No. of units per aircraft	Total cost per aircraft
B747	Body gear	1,080,000	2	2,160,000
	Wing gear	1,272,000	2	2,544,000
	Nose gear	960,000	1	960,000
	Overhaul costs per shipset			1,167,242
DC10	Main gear	1,270,456	2	2,540,912
	Nose gear	633,762	1	633,762
	Center gear	646,788	1	646,788
	Overhaul costs per shipset			803,695
A300	Main gear	1,769,858	2	3,539,716
	Nose gear	770,933	1	770,933
	Overhaul costs per shipset			632,611
B737	Main gear	269,007	2	538,014
	Nose gear	186,238	1	186,238
	Overhaul costs per shipset			144,000

*The unit cost increases by 15% to 25% every year.
Source: Company data.

Landing Gear Repair and Overhaul

Once a landing gear arrived at the shop, visual inspection and identification of necessary services in the overhaul process was provided. Review of the historical record followed. The gear might be transferred to the testing area for simulation of its operation to trouble-shoot for defects. The disassembly process followed: two mechanics took two to three days to disassemble the gear. All parts were transferred to another section for cleaning and other operations. (See Figure 2 for the repair plan process.) The industry standard for internal shop turnaround time was around eight weeks.

Figure 2: Landing Gear Repair Flow Process

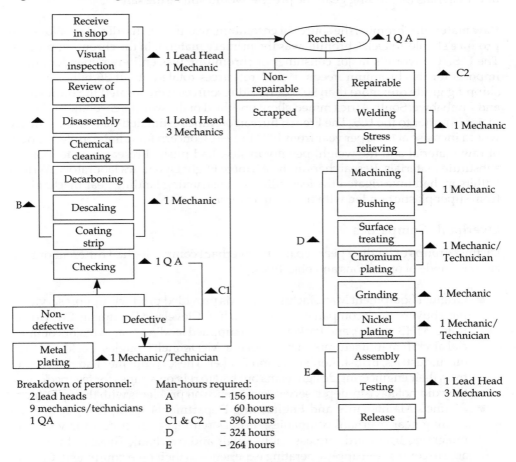

Breakdown of personnel:
2 lead heads
9 mechanics/technicians
1 QA

Man-hours required:
A — 156 hours
B — 60 hours
C1 & C2 — 396 hours
D — 324 hours
E — 264 hours

Manpower. Skill and experience were required in almost all process stages. The inspector had to be competent in using various inspection equipment such as magnetic particle and special x-ray machines and to interpret accurately findings. Expertise was critical in the machining, grinding and shot peening process where operators were involved in handling parts and operating sophisticated machinery. Engineers who conducted tests and analysis on metal had to be fully conversant with the test equipment and knowledgeable in metal properties. Twelve skilled personnel were required to overhaul a single landing gear.

Technology. The landing gear repair and overhaul process involved high technology machines: the universal milling machine, magnaflux inspection equipment, hydraulic test stand and precision measurement equipment. The shop required special jigs supplied by the manufacturer. Investment in machinery, tools and equipment could reach US$9 million for a new shop. Technology obsolescence was not an issue as even with new materials for landing gear, the process would still be the same.

Raw material. Chromite, the source of chromium, was used to harden steel alloys and produce stainless steel. Chromite was the primary material in the chroming process. The U.S., the world's major consumer of chromium, was entirely dependent upon imports for its chromium needs. World resources totaled about 36 billion tons of shipping grade ore; more than 90% of world resources were located in South Africa and Zimbabwe. South Africa mined about one third of the world's chromite and was a major exporter to the U.S. The French Bureau of Mines estimated that chromium use would increase at 6.4% per year from 1983 to 1990. Concern for uninterrupted supply of raw material and the weight penalty in steel had pushed researchers to look for substitute materials. Researchers at the Airforce Flight Dynamics laboratory, Wright Patterson, had investigated the feasibility of constructing landing gear mechanisms from super plastic bonded with titanium materials.

Overhaul Companies

Distinct groups of landing gear repair and overhaul companies had different organizations, mode of operations and objectives:

- Original Equipment Manufacturers. OEMs provided product support service to their buyers. Such companies as Menesco Inc., Cleveland Pneumatic Co., Dowty Rotor, MHB (Spain), and Parker/Bertea supplied landing gear to major commercial aircraft manufacturers such as Boeing, McDonnell Douglas, Lockheed, Airbus Industries, British Aerospace and Fokker. These companies had full backup from their engineering design teams but had to rely on airlines for feedback since they did not have in-depth service experience on problems with their products.
- Airline's Maintenance and Engineering Departments. Comprising 85% of all landing gear overhaul companies, airlines with large aircraft fleets vertically integrated backward into assembly repair and overhaul. These airlines were able to control and apply operating experience to their own equipment. Control took the form of planning the removal of landing gear at convenient times to avoid schedule disruptions. Like OEMs, they sold excess capacity to smaller airlines. However, they did not compete vigorously for this work since their primary purpose was to satisfy their own needs.

- Independent Maintenance Organizations. This group of landing gear repair and overhaul companies were neither airline nor manufacturer based. They were set up by investor groups seeking a share of the aircraft maintenance and overhaul business. Normally staffed by experienced personnel formerly employed by airlines and / or aircraft manufacturers, these companies did not have full overhaul capability. As a result, they had to subcontract some processes, such as chromium plating, to other facilities; this increased turnaround time. Included in this category were Air Asia, Aviation Engineering and Maintenance and Sogema; Sogema was one of the largest independent maintenance and repair companies in Europe. It entered the civil aircraft landing gear overhaul business in early 1984.

The Airline and Landing Gear Industry

Demand and Supply

Passenger air traffic exhibited consistent growth, moderated by important macroeconomic considerations (e.g., oil crises in 1973 and 1978; global recession 1980 to 1983). (See Table 3 for the growth of passenger traffic 1970–87; see Table 4 for the performance of different airlines in the Asia-Pacific region.) Both airline companies and the owners / operators of other aircraft required the services of landing gear overhaul shops. (See Table 5 for the population of commercial aircraft.) The fleets of many airlines in the Asia-Pacific region were among the most modern in the world. Of the 824 aircraft (1985) (Table 6), one third were due for overhaul every year. (See Table 7 for MAS's planned fleet expansion and anticipated landing gear overhaul schedule.)

Landing Gear Life and Services

The life of landing gear depended upon the number of hours flown by the aircraft or the number of cycles (one takeoff and landing constituted a cycle). For example, the landing gear for long haul aircraft (e.g., B747, DC 10, L1011) lasted from four to five years, or 20,000 to 25,000 flight hours. For aircraft used in short haul operations (e.g., B737, B767, A300, F27, DC9 and B727) forecast life was 2.5 to 3 years. Short haul operations involved numerous takeoff and landing cycles; as a result, landing gear wore out sooner. Aircraft had longer operating lives; approximately 15 years based on economic life, or 25 to 30 years based on fatigue life.

Landing Gear Market

The total number of shipsets of landing gear overhauled during 1980 was 2,650; by 1989, this was estimated to have increased by 32.1%, 3,500 shipsets worldwide. During 1988, 1,060 shipsets were available in the Asia-Pacific region; one third underwent an overhauling process. Based on the average four-year life for each landing gear, perhaps 25% to 30% of landing gear would be overhauled every year.

With the exception of Japan, almost all overhaul requirements were completed in overhaul shops owned by airlines from Europe and North America because these were industry leaders with sophisticated technology that entered the overhaul business

Table 3: Total Tonne Kilometers Performed* by the Scheduled Services of Each Region, 1970–87

Year	North America	Europe	Asia & Pacific	Others**	Total
1970	28,345	19,845	4,434	4,044	56,668
1971	29,103	21,835	4,931	4,604	60,473
1972	32,415	24,661	5,859	5,229	68,164
1973	35,006	27,358	7,431	5,988	75,783
1974	35,588	29,346	8,658	7,104	80,696
1975	35,287	31,244	10,225	8,037	84,793
1976	38,257	34,028	11,571	9,401	93,257
1977	40,974	35,800	13,057	10,603	100,434
1978	46,524	39,713	15,348	11,954	113,539
1979	52,525	43,010	17,870	13,451	126,856
1980	51,719	44,756	20,057	14,447	130,979
1981	50,756	46,935	22,335	15,469	135,495
1982	51,674	46,935	23,859	15,988	138,456
1983	55,771	48,766	25,081	16,777	146,395
1984	60,916	52,180	27,941	18,055	159,092
1985	64,683	54,557	29,723	18,571	167,534
1986	70,726	56,579	32,288	19,045	178,638
1987	78,150	61,500	36,900	20,090	196,640

*Product of weight of passengers and freight (tons) and total distance traveled (km).
**Includes Africa, Middle East, and Latin America and Carribean.
Source: *ICAO Digest of Statistics.*

early. Approximately 43% of the world's commercial aircraft operated out of North America; 16 of 30 landing gear overhaul facilities were located in this region.

Europe had nine landing gear repair facilities for approximately 32% of the landing gear market. Airlines in this region pooled their overhaul facilities into two groups, KSSU and ATLAS, to maximize use of resources. Within these groups, each airline had between 85% to 90% capability to conduct maintenance and overhaul on its own fleet. Under the pooling arrangement they shared small components with their partners and had a network of facilities within Europe.

The Japan Airlines (JAL) Center had good location and facilities, and would be the closest competitor for the proposed MAS overhaul shop. Built in 1953, by 1988 it employed 80 engineers and skilled technicians. JAL had total employment strength of 20,896 staff and operated a fleet of 90 wide-body aircraft. Its maintenance and engineering organization had 3,887 staff, 688 in support functions. The JAL Center serviced 32 shipsets or 110 landing gear per year; eight shipsets were non-JAL aircraft. MAS was currently one of JAL's customers. JAL's shop was operating at full capacity and sometimes had to refer clients to European facilities. JAL wished to build a second overhaul shop but faced strong resistance from the Ministry of Environment as the result of potential pollution problems.

Table 4: Financial Data and Traffic for 20 Asia/Pacific Airlines

	Tonne-km performed	Operating revenues per t-km performed	Tonne-km available	Operating expenses per t-km available
	Millions	U.S. cents	Millions	U.S. cents
Merpati Nusantara Airlines	44	109.9	74	68.9
Thai Airways Company	49	100.3	94	40.5
Air Niugini	67	134.3	119	76.1
Bangladesh Biman*	166	72.0	320	33.0
Japan Asia Airways	185	78.5	246	52.5
Air Lanka	245	53.5	397	32.0
Trans Australia Airlines	445	120.7	658	79.3
Indian Airlines	663	76.4	958	44.1
Malaysia Airlines	746	71.1	1,064	42.8
Garuda Indonesia	845	77.5	1,959	33.1
Pakistan Int. Airlines	874	77.2	1,539	38.3
Air New Zealand	1,004	58.6	1,380	36.3
Philippine Airlines	1,056	46.0	1,660	21.1
Thai Airways Int.	1,196	57.8	1,823	31.1
Air India	1,241	56.5	1,964	32.7
All Nippon Airways	1,650	112.3	3,652	48.6
Qantas Airways	2,209	55.7	3,385	34.8
Korean Air	2,561	47.7	3,623	31.9
Singapore Airlines	2,991	45.5	4,184	31.2
Japan Airlines	5,993	54.2	9,171	33.7
Total for 20 airlines	**24,230**	**59.4**	**38,267**	**35.0**
Total estimated for all airlines in the region	**28,100**	**64.8**	**44,250**	**38.4**

*Estimated data.
Source: *ICAO Digest of Statistics.*

Table 5: Commercial Airlines Aircraft Population

Year	Total commercial aircraft	Aircraft delivery backlog	Year	Total commercial aircraft	Aircraft delivery backlog
1973	7,620	n/a	1981	8,770	n/a
1974	7,860	n/a	1982	8,987	1,030
1975	8,110	n/a	1983	9,123	1,042
1976	8,240	n/a	1984	9,167	1,070
1977	8,339	n/a	1985	9,365	1,250
1978	8,380	n/a	1986	9,723	1,555
1979	8,460	n/a	1987	10,070	1,968
1980	8,700	n/a	1988	10,460	2,120

Source: *ICAO Digest of Statistics.*

Table 6: Commercial Aircraft Operated by International Carriers of the Asia-Pacific Region (as of mid-year)

Aircraft category		1979	1985
Wide-body jet		130	287
Narrow-body jet			
	4-engine	142	72
	3-engine	63	53
	2-engine	113	166
Turbo-prop		210	218
Piston engined		84	28
Total		742	824

Table 7: Malaysia Airlines Fleet Projections

	1989	1990	1991	1992	1993	1994	1995	1996	1997	1998	1999	2000
Total aircraft	41	49	51	53	55	55	58	61	65	69	72	72
Total flt hr. per year	14,125	16,863	17,390	18,615	19,491	19,783	21,097	22,411	24,163	25,915	27,083	27,083
Total shipsets of ldg	13	15	15	16	16	17.0	18.0	19	22	22	22	22

	Avg. mhr	Avg. Mat Usd	Trn Time Wks	O/H Price	O/H Cost per year	Mhr per year	Mat per year
F50	2,500	25,000	6	150,000	492,750	8,213	82,125
B737	3,000	40,000	7	220,000	115,632	15,768	210,240
DC10	4,800	90,000	8	739,000	809,205	5,256	98,550
A300	3,600	75,000	8	606,000	884,760	5,256	109,500
A330	3,600	75,000	8	606,000	0	0	0
B747	6,000	11,000	10	107,000	135,843	7,617	13,965

Avg Mhr – Average man-hours
Avg Mat Usd – Average materials used (US$)
Trn Time Wks – Turn time in weeks

O/H Price – Overhead price (US$)
O/H Cost – Overhead Cost (US$)

Landing Gear Repair and Overhaul Facility for MAS

Total new capital outlay was estimated as follows (US$):
1. Land   200,000
2. Building   2,000,000
3. Building equipment   1,000,000
   a. Electric hoist
   b. Air-conditioner
   c. Lighting
   d. Waste water treatment
   e. Paging system
4. Shop equipment   9,200,000
   a. Surface treatment machine
   b. Cleaning machine

c. Measurement equipment
d. Honing machine
e. Plating machine
5. Others   600,000
a. Initial spares provisioning
b. Training
c. Travel allowances

The full complement of equipment was 75% of the total cost of the facility; estimated life of the building and equipment were 40 and 10 years respectively, with zero salvage value.

The facility would be under a manager reporting to the engineering head; main functions would be supervised by four section heads. Total annual staff cost for the facility (excluding marketing costs) comprising salaries and compulsory company contributions was US$550,000. (See Figure 1 for the proposed workshop organization.)

The project would be financed through 50% equity and 50% long-term loan (7% interest). A 10% dividend would be paid annually so long as the facility would make a profit.

Assumptions made in the proposal were:

a. Service fee based on market rates and projected to grow at 5% per annum.
b. Labor rate pegged at US$10 per hour.
c. Internal cost was US$6 per hour.
d. Labor cost, and operating and administration cost escalated at 7% p.a.
e. Materials cost forecasted to increase at 4% p.a.
f. Facility initially on a single shift with an annual capacity to overhaul 20 shipsets of landing gear.
g. Annual available man-hours per man was 1,660.

Construction would cover a two-year period; start-up operations were scheduled for 1990. The number of landing gears due for overhaul in the first year was 15.8 shipsets. Anticipated revenue was US$6.2 million; anticipated profit was US$2 million, doubling by the sixth year (Exhibit 2). Forecast cash flow showed a cash closing of US$2.9 million in the first year and cumulating to US$55.8 million in 2000 (Exhibit 3). (See Exhibit 4 for the pro-forma balance sheet.)

Decision

MAS executives pondered over the material they had accumulated. Should they go ahead with the new facility or continue the status quo. If MAS did invest in a facility, what should be the targeted capacity. Regardless of this capacity, how much of the landing gear overhaul capacity should be allocated for its own aircraft, how much for other airlines' aircraft. Finally, what response might MAS expect from other overhaul shops, notably Japan Airlines.

Exhibit 1: Ten-year Statistical Review, 1980/81–1987/88 (US$)

	1987/88	1986/87	1985/86	1984/85	1983/84	1982/83	1981/82	1980/81
Financial								
Total revenue ($'000)	1,613,910	1,432,770	1,326,003	1,314,437	1,237,302	1,183,514	995,345	824,734
Profit/(loss) after tax ($'000)	151,456	112,211	104,904	131,584	95,190	10,041	(35,168)	6,977
Profit/(loss) as % of revenue	9.38	7.83	7.91	10.01	7.69	0.85	(3.53)	1
Production								
Time flown (hours)	108,589	99,824	94,886	95,025	94,692	95,570	98,547	93,761
Available capacity ('000 tkm)	1,430,429	1,257,844	1,085,170	1,056,419	1,022,806	1,030,229	828,372	763,329
Available passenger capacity ('000 seat km)	10,319,998	9,315,545	8,494,894	8,221,762	7,935,831	7,958,333	6,844,460	6,170,601
Traffic								
Passengers carried ('000)	6,138	5,597	5,520	5,625	5,232	5,018	4,838	4,151
Passengers carried ('000 pax km)	7,828,266	6,589,990	6,195,474	6,134,053	5,624,476	5,588,615	4,810,862	4,206,004
Passenger load factor (%)	75.9	70.8	72.9	74.6	70.9	70.2	70.3	68
Cargo carried ('000 tkm)	352,080	288,283	212,216	196,076	178,519	143,979	132,925	112,693
Mail carried ('000 tkm)	11,886	10,549	8,300	7,361	7,730	7,299	7,403	7,108
Overall load carried ('000 tkm)	1,101,276	916,734	803,513	779,648	713,785	670,603	587,579	513,456
Overall load factor (%)	77.0	72.9	74.0	73.8	69.8	65.1	70.9	67
Staff								
Employee strength (at March 31)	11,249	11,136	10,798	10,632	10,055	10,124	10,248	9,327
Revenue per employee ($'000)	144	129	123	124	123	117	97	89
Available capacity per employee (tkm)	127,160	112,953	100,497	99,362	101,721	101,761	80,833	81,841
Profitability and Efficiency Analysis, 1980/81–1987/88								
Network size ('000 km)	115.9	101.8	91.8	91.3	88.5	87.6	87.5	88
Passenger carried (million pax km)	7,828	6,590	6,195	6,134	5,624	5,589	4,811	4,206
Overall load carried (million tkm)	1,101	917	804	780	714	671	588	513
Load factor								
Passenger	75.9	70.8	72.9	74.6	70.9	70.2	70.3	68
Overall	77.0	72.9	74.0	73.8	69.8	65.1	70.9	67
Breakeven load factor	65%	63%	64%	62%	61%	64%	76%	66

$$= \left(\frac{\text{Fixed cost}}{\text{Revenue yield} - \text{variable cost}} \right) + \text{available capacity} \times 100\%$$

Source: Company Annual Report, 1987/88.

Exhibit 2: Pro Forma Income Statements (US$)

Year	1 (1992)	2	3	4	5	6	7	8	9	10	11	12
Revenue	6,182,802	6,844,665	7,462,127	8,480,166	9,581,354	11,053,760	12,649,454	13,994,792	14,694,532	15,429,258	16,200,721	17,010,757
Cost of sales												
Labor	547,760	611,778	670,039	617,560	692,241	995,506	1,140,641	1,276,752	1,366,125	1,461,753	1,564,076	1,673,561
Material	834,453	909,026	978,755	1,093,255	1,215,249	1,378,767	1,553,313	1,702,863	1,770,978	1,841,817	1,915,490	1,992,106
Depreciation	775,833	775,833	775,833	775,833	775,833	775,833	775,833	775,833	775,833	775,833	775,833	775,833
Overhead	138,221	152,080	164,879	171,081	190,759	237,427	269,395	297,962	313,710	330,357	347,957	366,567
Gross profit	3,886,535	4,395,948	4,872,621	5,822,437	6,707,272	7,666,227	8,910,272	9,941,382	10,467,886	11,019,498	11,597,366	12,202,687
Op.&adm. exp.	90,000	96,300	103,041	110,254	117,972	126,230	135,066	144,520	154,637	165,461	177,044	189,437
Op. profit	3,796,534	4,299,647	4,769,580	5,712,183	6,589,200	7,539,988	8,775,206	9,796,862	10,313,249	10,854,037	11,420,322	12,013,250
Interest	455,000	455,000	420,000	385,000	350,000	315,000	280,000	245,000	210,000	175,000	140,000	105,000
EBT	3,341,534	3,844,647	4,349,580	5,327,183	6,239,200	7,224,998	8,495,206	9,551,862	10,103,249	10,679,037	11,280,322	11,908,250
Prov. tax	1,136,613	1,537,859	1,739,832	2,130,873	2,495,680	2,889,999	3,398,082	3,820,745	4,041,300	4,271,615	4,512,129	4,763,300
Net income	2,004,920	2,306,788	2,609,748	3,196,310	3,743,520	4,334,999	5,097,124	5,731,117	6,061,950	6,407,422	6,768,193	7,144,950
Dividend	200,492	230,679	260,975	319,631	374,352	433,500	509,712	573,112	606,195	640,742	676,809	714,495
Net earnings	1,804,428	2,076,110	2,348,773	2,876,679	3,369,168	3,901,499	4,587,411	5,158,005	5,455,755	5,766,680	6,091,374	6,430,455

Exhibit 3: Pro Forma Cash Flow Statements (US$)

Year	0	1 (1992)	2	3	4	5	6	7	8	9	10	11	12
Inflow													
Paid up	6,500,000												
Load	6,500,000												
Debtor current		5,152,129	5,703,659	6,218,191	7,066,523	7,984,142	9,211,098	10,540,790	11,661,860	12,244,953	12,857,201	113,500,061	14,175,064
Debtor prev. year			1,030,673	1,141,006	1,243,937	1,413,644	1,597,212	1,842,662	2,108,664	2,332,932	2,449,578	2,572,057	2,700,660
Total	13,000,000	5,152,129	6,734,332	7,359,197	8,310,460	9,397,786	10,808,310	12,383,452	13,770,524	14,577,885	15,306,779	16,072,118	16,875,724
Outflow													
Labor		547,760	611,778	670,039	617,560	692,241	995,506	1,140,641	1,276,752	1,366,125	1,461,753	1,564,076	1,673,661
Credit mat. current		695,100	757,219	815,303	910,681	1,012,396	1,148,513	1,293,910	1,418,485	1,475,224	1,534,233	1,595,603	1,659,427
Credit mat. prev.			139,354	151,807	163,452	182,574	202,963	230,254	259,403	284,378	295,753	207,583	319,887
Additional inv.		83,445	3,961	3,085	6,699	6,699	9,436	9,436	6,643	0	0	0	0
Purchase													
Overhead		138,221	152,080	164,879	171,081	190,759	237,427	269,395	297,962	313,710	330,357	347,957	366,567
Op. admin. exp.		90,000	96,300	103,041	110,254	117,972	126,230	135,066	144,520	154,637	165,461	177,044	189,437
Tax			1,336,613	1,537,859	1,739,832	2,130,873	2,495,680	2,889,999	3,398,082	3,820,745	4,041,300	4,271,615	4,512,129
Sub total		1,554,526	3,097,305	3,446,013	3,719,559	4,333,514	5,215,755	5,968,701	6,801,847	7,414,819	7,828,857	8,163,878	8,721,108
Op. surplus		3,597,602	3,637,027	3,913,183	4,590,900	5,064,272	5,592,555	6,414,751	6,968,677	7,163,066	7,477,921	7,908,242	8,154,616
Investment	13,000,000												
Interest		455,000	455,000	420,000	385,000	350,000	315,000	280,000	245,000	210,000	175,000	140,000	105,000
Principal			500,000	500,000	500,000	500,000	500,000	500,000	500,000	500,000	500,000	500,000	500,000
Loan bal.		6,500,000	6,000,000	5,500,000	5,000,000	4,500,000	4,000,000	3,500,000	3,000,000	2,500,000	2,000,000	1,500,000	1,000,000
Dividend		200,492	230,679	260,975	319,631	374,352	433,500	509,712	573,112	606,195	640,742	676,819	714,495
Bal. after loan		2,942,110	2,451,348	2,732,208	3,386,269	3,839,931	4,344,055	5,125,039	5,650,565	5,846,871	6,162,179	6,491,422	6,835,221
Cash opening	0	0	2,942,110	5,393,458	8,125,666	11,511,935	15,351,866	19,695,922	24,820,960	30,471,525	36,318,396	42,480,575	48,971,997
Cash closing	0	2,942,110	5,393,458	8,125,666	11,511,935	15,351,866	19,695,922	24,820,960	30,471,525	36,318,396	42,480,575	48,971,997	55,807,218

Exhibit 4: Pro Forma Balance Sheets (US$)

Year	1 (1992)	2	3	4	5	6	7	8	9	10	11	12
Current assets												
Cash	2,942,110	5,393,458	8,125,666	11,511,935	15,351,866	19,695,922	24,820,960	30,471,525	36,318,396	42,480,575	48,971,997	55,807,218
Trade debtor	1,030,673	1,141,006	1,243,937	1,413,644	1,597,212	1,842,662	2,108,664	2,332,932	2,449,578	2,572,057	2,700,660	2,835,693
Inventory	83,445	87,406	90,491	97,190	103,889	113,325	122,761	129,404	129,404	129,404	129,404	129,404
Total current assets	4,056,228	6,621,870	9,460,094	13,022,769	17,052,967	21,651,908	27,052,385	32,933,861	38,897,378	45,182,036	51,802,061	58,772,315
Fixed assets	12,224,167	11,448,334	10,672,501	9,896,668	9,120,835	8,345,002	7,569,169	6,793,336	6,017,503	5,241,670	4,465,837	3,690,004
Total assets	16,280,395	18,070,204	20,132,595	22,919,437	26,173,802	29,996,910	34,621,554	39,727,197	44,914,881	50,423,706	56,267,898	62,462,319
Liability & equity												
Current liabilities												
Trade creditor	139,354	151,807	163,452	182,574	202,963	230,254	259,403	284,378	295,753	307,583	319,887	332,682
Tax	1,336,613	1,537,859	1,739,832	2,130,873	2,495,680	2,889,999	3,398,082	3,820,745	4,041,300	4,271,615	4,512,129	4,763,300
Total current liability	1,475,967	1,689,666	1,903,284	2,313,447	2,698,643	3,120,253	3,657,485	4,105,123	4,337,053	4,579,198	4,832,016	5,095,982
Other liability												
Long-term loan	6,500,000	6,000,000	5,500,000	5,000,000	4,500,000	4,000,000	3,500,000	3,000,000	2,500,000	2,000,000	1,500,000	1,000,000
Total liabilities	7,975,967	7,689,666	7,403,284	7,313,447	7,198,643	7,120,253	7,157,485	7,105,123	6,837,053	6,579,198	6,332,016	6,095,982
Equities												
Paid-up capital	6,500,000	6,500,000	6,500,000	6,500,000	6,500,000	6,500,000	6,500,000	6,500,000	6,500,000	6,500,000	6,500,000	6,500,000
Ret. earnings	1,804,428	2,076,110	2,348,773	2,876,679	3,369,168	3,901,499	4,587,411	5,158,005	5,455,755	5,766,680	6,091,374	6,430,455
Acc. Ret. earnings	1,804,428	3,880,538	6,229,311	9,105,990	12,475,158	16,376,657	20,964,068	26,122,073	31,577,828	37,344,508	43,435,882	49,866,337
Total equities	8,304,428	10,380,538	12,729,311	15,605,990	18,975,158	22,876,657	27,464,068	32,622,073	38,077,828	43,844,508	49,935,882	56,366,337
Total liabilities & equities	16,280,395	18,070,204	20,132,595	22,919,437	26,173,801	29,996,910	34,621,553	39,727,196	44,914,881	50,423,706	56,267,898	62,462,319

Case 28

Prime Pharmaceuticals Malaysia (M) Sdn. Bhd.

Manuel S. Lizardo, Jr., Lope L. Belardo
Asian Institute of Management, Makati, the Philippines

During the management staff meeting in January 1991, Managing Director Oliver Smith, announced the sales growth objective set by head office for the decade just starting: "With major new product introductions scheduled in our market in the next few years, and with continuing support from the mother company, we are committed to a targeted growth rate of 25% p.a. in the near and medium terms and 30% long term." Smith said that although these numbers appeared optimistic, considering the previous three years' growth rates, he also knew that, given the continuing strong performance of the Malaysian economy and the increasing health care awareness in all sectors of the country, these targets were achievable. He was considering strategic marketing moves to further strengthen Prime Pharmaceuticals Malaysia's competitive position and enable it to meet management expectations.

The first move Smith had in mind was to discontinue Prime's exclusive distribution arrangements with M.T. Rollins (MTR), in favor of self-distribution. He wondered if this move would have the support of the head office. In any event, he knew that his recommendation would weigh heavily in the final decision.

        ✣

Company Background

Prime Pharmaceuticals USA (PPUSA) was established in the early 1900s. Focusing efforts and resources on R&D, it developed a wide array of products. Through the years, PPUSA expanded its operations to different parts of the globe. Prime's organization was functionally structured. Divisions included the major subgroups: marketing, finance, R&D, and manufacturing and logistics. Marketing and R&D were the leading functions; other areas provided support.

    PPUSA's corporate policies reflected its emphasis on R&D; R&D budgets were required to be 20% of sales; thus, growth was pursued by developing new products and identifying new markets. A research area was given priority if it satisfied an urgent medical need. The firm set market leadership in a priority research area as a primary corporate objective.

Rather than enter into licensing agreements, PPUSA preferred to establish operations in other countries especially in Southeast Asia. Expansion of productive capacity and R&D took the bulk of capital expenditures both in the U.S. and abroad. From 1985 to 1990, contributions from foreign operations averaged 24.5% of total revenues.

Prime focused operations and resources in the cardiovascular, respiratory, gastrointestinal, infection and local anesthetics segments. The main thrust of PPUSA and all subsidiaries was to "product/markets" with consistent and uniform product strategies. Introduction of new products and branching into new markets were the main avenues for profitability and growth. These objectives were accomplished by research for new products and innovative projects.

Company Background in Malaysia

Prime Pharmaceuticals Malaysia (M) Sdn. Bhd., wholly owned by PPUSA, formally started its Malaysian operations in 1981 by marketing products imported from its parent. Company objectives included: maintenance of Prime's premier position in ethical pharmaceuticals; concentration on the private sector to increase use of Prime's products; increase use of Prime's products in all sectors of the market; and involvement in doctor training via its educational program.

Several products were launched in the ensuing years; 1984 sales were RM8.7 million, up 40% from 1981. Growth slowed in 1985 (sales: RM9.4 million) but picked up the following year to RM11.28 million. The late 1980s were a slow growth period, but sales spurted to RM20.2 million in 1990 (Table 1).

Table 1: Historical and Targeted Sales

Year	Sales RM million	Increase %	Year	Sales RM million	Increase %
1984	8.70		1989	16.90	9.0
1985	9.40	8.0	1990	20.20	19.5
1986	11.28	20.0	1991*	25.00	25.0
1987	14.50	28.5	1992*	31.25	25.0
1988	15.50	7.0	1993*	40.60	30.0

*Targeted

PPUSA decided on all product launches based on corporate product policies. Decisions made by the local company had to fall within boundaries set by PPUSA's philosophy and policies. International operations emphasized "product marketing" and distribution following strict PPUSA guidelines, including centralization of licensing, finances and investments. Company growth targets were set above industry growth. The company secured market share information from market research conducted by survey organizations but closely guarded this data from competitors. Profits were repatriated largely through transfer pricing; contribution to the parent was pegged at 25% of sales.

The Malaysian Pharmaceutical Industry

In Malaysia, major pharmaceutical companies engaged only in formulation compounding and marketing. The marketing function could be further segregated into promotion, distribution, wholesaling, retailing and the tendering agents in government medical facilities.

The Malaysian pharmaceutical industry was generally divided between the government and private sectors:

- Government purchases were made through General Medical Stores (GMS). The GMS, under the control of the Ministry of Health (MOH), facilitated collective government purchases of medicines.
- Local purchase orders (LPOs) referred to public hospitals' own purchases when demand exceeded GMS supply and/or special drugs were needed. Hospital purchasing committees decided on LPOs subject to GMS regulations.
- The private sector comprised 280 private companies which together vied for the RM488–RM517 million market (including government purchases). Local companies included 23 manufacturers and 59 distributorships. From time to time, distributors also acted as marketing arms. Several tendering agents dealt mainly with government hospitals. The remainder were small firms engaged in minor operations.

Industry Composition

Most pharmaceutical companies were concentrated in Selangor, and Kuala Lumpur, Malaysia's capital.[1] A high percent (37.5%) of all Malaysian doctors were located in Selangor and in the capital; other important areas were Penang and Perak. Customers were concentrated in Selangor and Perak states and Kuala Lumpur. These areas, together with Penang, Johore, Sabah and Sarawak accounted for 80% to 90% of customers.

Clinics. Malaysian doctors dispensed drugs through their clinics; by law, doctors had to be present whenever the clinic was open. In 1990, this channel represented 55% (RM268 million) of total purchases. Stocks were purchased primarily from wholesale pharmacies. Average inventory (RM20,000 to RM30,000) turnover was three times per annum. Revenue estimates for clinics were RM100,000 to RM250,000 annually; profit margins were estimated at almost 50%.

Pharmacies. Pharmacies were either retailers, wholesalers or both; in Malaysia, the majority fulfilled both functions. Together, pharmacies accounted for 7% (RM34.16

---

[1] Although geographically located in Selangor, Kuala Lumpur was part of the Federal Territory.

million) of total industry sales. A pharmacy with RM2.5 million sales volume required RM300,000 equity for its operations.

Distributors. Distribution agreements between pharmaceutical companies and their distributing agents varied. Typically they fell into one of three categories:

- Distribution and promotion of the principal's products. The distributor was responsible for all aspects of distribution (e.g., storage, delivery / physical transfer of goods, receiving orders, order processing, billing, collection of payment, credit handling, providing the principal with sales and market information). Promotion involved detailing calls on doctors and advertising. The principal's role was limited to supply.
- Distribution of the principal's products. The distributor was responsible for all aspects of distribution but the pharmaceutical company promoted its own products.
- Physical transfer of principal's products. The distributor warehoused and delivered the principal's products. Other aspects of distribution and marketing were undertaken by the pharmaceutical company.

Pharmaceutical companies paid from 9% to 21% of sales for distribution services. Although 59 distributors carried pharmaceutical products, 90% of distribution was handled by three distributors; their revenues ranged from RM100 million to RM400 million. Low gross and net margins earned by distributors were compensated by high volume sales. In addition, through licensing and representation of parent companies, these major distributors imported and carried products of other pharmaceutical companies. Payment periods for distributors ranged from 45 to 90 days from receipt of stocks.

Tendering agents. Up to 18% (RM90 million) of industry sales was to tendering agents, middlemen who offered tenders to the GMS, and hospitals authorized to make LPOs on government purchases not exceeding RM10,000. Mark-up averaged 3%; average revenues for tendering agents were RM5 million, net profit, RM27,000.

The flow of goods in the pharmaceutical industry is shown in Figure 1. Competition for profits, market share and brand awareness took place where the arrows meet. Mark-up was highest at the level of clinics, hospitals, druggists and retail pharmacies, lowest between the distributors and its principals.

Marketing Practices

Before 1984, roughly 20,000 different drugs were offered to the Malaysian market; for example, the antibiotic ampicillin alone was offered as 110 different brands. In 1985, the Drug Control Authority (DCA) was established to authorize the use of drugs in Malaysia. By 1990, 4,000 drugs had been approved by the DCA.

Stiff competition limited price increases. Since 1989, prices had risen by 8% to 10%, driven by inflation, rising expenses and the increased cost of manufactured goods.

However, clinic treatment costs had not risen during the previous eight years. Drug prices were not subject to regulation in Malaysia and the medical care and health expenses price index increased only by 5.5% in 1989.

Figure 1: Flow of Goods in the Malaysian Pharmaceutical Industry

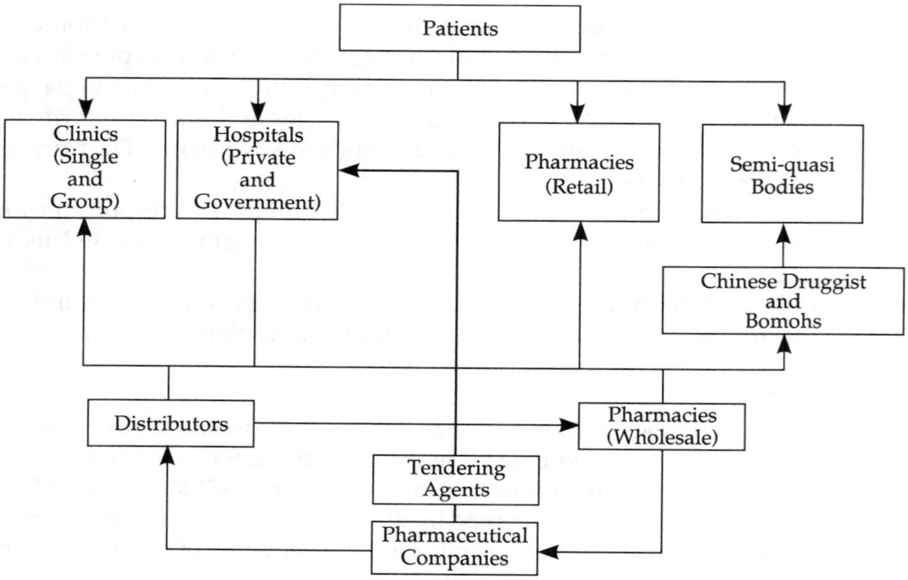

Product advertising in Malaysia was regulated by the Medicine and Advertising Act. Promotional practices included:

- Missionary sales generated by medical representatives;
- Printed promotional materials distributed to customers;
- Discounts given to customers;
- Sample distribution to customers;
- Advertising for over-the-counter products;
- Consumer product education through symposia, congresses and the like;
- Generation of purchases via local and overseas trips;
- In certain cases, direct cash donations to charitable funds.

Manpower. Medical representatives were integral components of the industry. Their primary function was detailing, approaching doctors or pharmacists and introducing the company's products. Signed orders were executed through distributors or pharmacies. Product deliveries were usually made within 72 hours of order placement.

Sales teams cover different product groups. On average, medical representatives visited clients every 60 to 90 days. However, visits were sometimes made twice or three times per month. Detailing coverage ranged from 9.4% to 51.4%; no company reached 100% market coverage since most focused efforts on specific market segments.

Prime Pharmaceuticals Malaysia

Sales Performance

Sales by product segments. The cardiovascular, infection and respiratory product segments were the largest sales contributors to Prime Malaysia, about 77% of total company sales (Table 2). However, in 1990, growth was only significant in infection (47%). Except for cardiovascular products, Prime Malaysia's top sellers registered growth rates higher than the industry. Prime's highest growth rate (376%) was in the gastro-intestinal segment.

Table 2: Sales by Product Segment, 1989, 1990 (RM)

	1989	1990	% of total	% increase
Cardiovascular				
Commerical	1,410,887	1,663,882	8.2	17.9
LPO*	26,787	13,089	0.06	–51.1
Tender	5,574,303	5,545,690	27.4	–0.5
Subtotal	7,011,977	7,222,661	35.7	3.0
Infection				
Commerical	1,411,696	1,720,277	8.5	21.9
LPO	1,453	16,123	0.1	1,000.8
Tender	2,519,569	4,043,785	20.0	60.6
Subtotal	3,932,718	5,780,185	28.5	47.0
Respiratory				
Commerical	1,469,720	1,643,395	8.1	11.1
LPO	104,345	127,299	0.6	22.0
Tender	1,014,292	890,100	4.4	–12.2
Subtotal	2,588,357	2,660,794	13.1	2.4
Local anesthetic medical				
Commerical	660,769	716,666	3.5	7.4
LPO	272,359	414,011	2.0	52.0
Subtotal	933,128	1,130,677	5.6	20.0
Local anesthetic dental				
Commerical	354,032	404,144	2.0	14.2
LPO	8,552	32,511	0.2	280.2
Tender	1,068,603	1,374,075	6.8	28.6
Subtotal	1,431,187	1,810,730	8.9	26.5
Gastro-intestinal				
Commerical	137,017	650,515	3.2	374.8
LPO	311	3,224	0.01	936.7
Subtotal	137,328	653,739	3.2	376.0
Others				
Commerical	554,481	634,429	3.1	14.4
LPO*	167,264	293,135	1.4	75.0
Tender	154,553	81,018	0.4	–47.6
Subtotal	876,298	1,008,582	4.5	15.1
Total commerical	6,004,402	7,422,808	36.6	23.6
Total LPO	581,071	899,392	4.4	54.8
Total tender	10,331,320	11,935,368	58.9	15.5
Total	**16,916,793**	**20,257,568**	**100.0**	**19.7**

*Local purchase orders

Sales by state. In 1990, sales growth varied considerably by state (Table 3). For example, in Selangor, Penang and Perlis, sales increased by over 50%. However, this growth was offset by declines in such areas as Negri Sembilan and Terengganu. Poor performance in these states was attributed to lack of manpower; one person covered several product ranges and segments in several states.

Table 3: Sales by State, 1989, 1990 (RM)

	1989	1990	% of total	% increase	% of industry
East Malaysia					
Sabah	360,035	474,683	2.3	31.8	
Sarawak	475,790	530,906	2.6	11.6	
Brunei	124,403	170,426	0.8	37.0	
Subtotal	960,228	1,176,015	5.8	22.5	15.4
West Malaysia					
Federal Territory	1,349,365	1,842,205	9.1	36.5	
Selangor	1,143,809	1,803,461	8.9	57.7	
Johor	474,772	682,065	3.4	43.7	
Pahang	132,390	148,594	0.7	12.2	
Malacca	158,606	202,572	1.0	27.7	
Negri Sembilan	174,562	171,826	0.8	−1.6	
Kelantan	212,539	265,919	1.3	25.1	
Terengganu	134,038	132,161	0.7	−1.4	
Kedah	277,462	318,177	1.6	14.7	
Perak	752,233	847,199	4.2	12.6	
Perlis	12,351	41,907	0.2	239.3	
Penang	762,129	1,167,955	5.7	53.2	
Subtotal	5,584,256	7,624,041	37.6	36.3	12.5
Tender sales	10,372,818	11,467,510	56.6	10.6	12.5
Total	**16,916,792**	**20,257,566**	**100.0**	**19.7**	**12.7**

Sales and Marketing Organization

Sales teams were divided into Private, Hospital and East Malaysian Divisions and the Prime Task Force (Figure 2).

- Private: responsible for three product categories and divided geographically into North, Central, East Coast and South Malaysia. This division had four area managers and 11 medical representatives.
- Hospital: responsible for two product categories and divided into the Northern Central/South Malaysia areas. This division was managed by two area managers and eight medical representatives.
- East Malaysia: included Sabah, Sarawak and Brunei.[2] This division was respon-

---

[2] Although Brunei was not part of Malaysia, sales were handled by this division.

sible for three product categories covered by two area managers and one medical representative.

- Prime Task Force: a specialist group concentrating on existing selected products that also took charge of other product launches. A single product specialist and six medical representatives comprised this division.

The primary function of Prime's medical representatives was detailing doctors and pharmacists, introducing and promoting Prime's products. They also booked orders; these were turned over to M.T. Rollins for processing, delivery, billing and collection.

Figure 2: Organization Chart

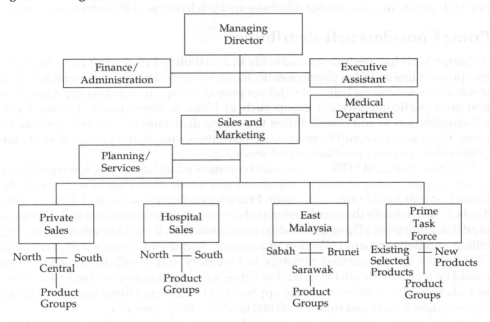

Distribution

Prime Malaysia contracted the services of M.T. Rollins (MTR) for distributing its products. MTR was one of Malaysia's leading distributors of pharmaceutical products; it had five offices and stores across the country.[3] From these offices it handled product distribution for over 100 companies in Malaysia, including Prime. In addition to pharmaceutical products, MTR distributed consumer and agro-chemical goods. It employed

---

[3] In addition to the main office in Kuala Lumpur serving central Malaysia were branches in Johor Bahru (south Malaysia), Perak (north of Kuala Lumpur), Penang (north Malaysia), and Sabah (East Malaysia).

31 sales representatives (supervised by nine sales supervisors) to call on customers for order booking and collection of payment for all purchases.

The distribution arrangement between Prime and MTR called for MTR to provide storage, order taking and processing, delivery, credit, billing and supply of sales and delivery information. MTR's fees averaged 9% of sales. MTR's 1990 purchases from Prime were RM12.4 million. MTR paid Prime within 60 days from receipt of stocks. MTR's customers received 30- to 60-day credit for all purchases; credit limits extended ranged from RM2,500 to RM20,000. MTR's 1990 sales exceeded RM400 million.

Deliveries were made by vans within city limits and in areas covered by MTR branches and stores. If possible, deliveries were made in 48 hours; in some cases, delivery could be delayed up to one week by transport problems. Lorry services (RM2 per package) were available outside these areas: delivery was 48 hours to one week.

Prime Considers Self-distribution

Although MTR had performed creditably in distributing Prime's products, its extensive product line included pharmaceuticals, agro-chemicals and consumer items. As a result, Prime executives believed it did not provide adequate attention and concentration on a particular product group such as Prime's. Moreover, it appeared that self-distribution would enable Prime to save on distribution costs as sales volume grew. These savings could be reinvested in additional medical representatives to improve Prime's market penetration and servicing.

If Prime terminated MTR's services and commenced self-distribution, it would have to set up a minimum of four distribution units across Malaysia, in addition to the Kuala Lumpur-based unit, to maintain Prime's distribution status and delivery standards. (Table 4 details the annual estimated cost of one distribution unit and associated capital requirements.) These distribution units would handle storage, order processing, billing and delivery and collection of accounts. Because of Prime's inexperience in distribution, an experienced manager in inventory and distribution management would be required. Smith believed that Prime's good reputation and industry status would allow him to attract qualified applicants. He estimated that a suitable distribution manager would cost from RM30,000 to RM48,000 per annum.

Smith's tentative plan was to assign outlets covered by MTR to Prime medical representatives for order booking; orders would be passed to distribution units for processing and delivery. Collection of accounts would be handled by Prime's sales force. Since the proposed change would entail additional new responsibilities, particularly credit management and collection, Smith wondered how the sales force would adjust and react. He was also concerned about the degree of orientation and training the sales force would require and who would accept this responsibility. Mostly, since the sales force's primary responsibility was demand creation for Prime products among physicians, he wondered how distribution responsibilities would affect its performance in the physician's clinic.

Smith was also concerned about the reaction the proposed change would have on Prime's working relations with outlets, inasmuch as many had long-term working relationships with MTR. Would they be as cooperative in placing their orders for

Table 4: Estimated Cost of One Distribution Unit, 1991

Cost	RM	Cost	RM
Salary of pharmacist	40,000	Telephone charges	5,000
Salaries of six staff (2 clerks, 2	65,000	Transport charges	5,000
store keepers, 2 delivery men)		Courier charges	3,000
Electricity and water	2,400	**Grand total**	235,610
E.P.F.	13,650		
Insurance premium	55,250	**Capitalization**	
Licence fee	310	Two vans	80,000
Postage	1,000	Deposits	10,000
Petrol and traveling	14,000	Renovations	50,000
Overtime	1,500	Equipment	100,000
Office upkeep	2,500	Miscellaneous	60,000
Rental of warehouse	24,000	**Total**	300,000
Stationery	3,000		

Prime products, maintaining adequate inventories, providing prominent and adequate display space and meeting payment terms as they were with MTR? Based on industry standards and MTR practices, Prime would offer the same terms: 30 days credit with a 30-day grace period. Also in line with industry practice, discount terms would range from 15% to 25%, depending on whether purchases were direct or through wholesalers.

In addition to the economics, Smith believed important qualitative factors had to be considered. For example, greater attention and concentration on Prime's products at the outlet level might be expected if the Prime sales organization was fully responsible for distribution. This issue was particularly important for new product introduction, a major source of growth and profitability for Prime. Prime medical representatives could also provide better in-store support (e.g., maintaining displays, educating retail clerks, assisting inventory tracking of Prime products). Smith also felt that problems in delivery, billing, back orders, cancellations, returns and product quality could be more effectively handled on the spot by a company representative.

Smith believed that the advantages of self-distribution revolved around the greater control it allowed management. He believed Prime medical representatives could provide more and better market information than MTR. Information on competitive activities, new product introductions and trade developments would be fed back to marketing and necessary actions quickly implemented. Finally, self-distribution would present more job opportunities. Existing employees, as well as people outside the company, could fill new openings the distribution units would make available and could contribute to matching the qualifications of some company's personnel to the right job.

As he contemplated the issues, Smith knew that his recommendation would be critical for the Malaysian organization's future. He also knew that head office would scrutinize any plan, so it would have to be backed up by solid economic analysis.

Map of the Middle East

Case 29

Star TV

Winnie Chik, Eddie Chow, Henry Ma, Walter Ngan, Gary Tsang,
Yortie Wong, Samina Seth, Shamza Khan
The Hong Kong University of Science and Technology

Noel Capon
Graduate School of Business, Columbia University

In mid-May 1993, Jane Farrow, newly hired network planning executive, was charged with assessing the potential for Star TV in ten selected Middle East countries and, if necessary, developing a positioning strategy. Working in the Hong Kong headquarters, since funds were limited and consumer surveys expensive, her information was limited predominantly to secondary published sources and local interviews with personnel experienced in the region. By June 12, 1993 she had to present a proposal for viable countries to be further studied to Charles Sampson, Special Project Manager; her recommendations would significantly affect Star TV's 1994 business plan for that region.

"There can be no question, the next ten years will be the most extraordinary period in communications history. A new technological revolution has begun."—Rupert Murdoch

ଓଉଓ

Background

Star TV Network[1] received a broadcasting license from the Hong Kong government on December 22, 1990; transmission commenced on April 15, 1991. This first Asian satellite-based broadcaster was owned by a joint venture between the HutchVision Group and Hutchison Whampoa Ltd., a company controlled by Li Ka-Shing and his family;[2] Li contributed a majority of the US$300 million start-up capital. Growth in leisure time and disposable income accompanying economic growth in the Pacific Rim provided the impetus to launch Star TV.

---

[1] Star TV was an acronym for Satellite Television Asian Region.
[2] Li Ka-Shing was one of Hong Kong's leading businessmen, reputed to have a personal net worth of almost HK$4 billion.

Star TV was run by Richard Li, Li Ka-Shing's son, described by one industry observer as "a passionate man full of youth and vigor who was a frontline soldier taking a hands-on approach to Star TV."[3] Richard believed that providing viewers with access to Madonna, American movies and BBC news would allow him to make money in a few years, justifying his belief that the Asian audience was hungry for variety. He said: "Americans and Europeans have access to, on average, 25 channels. In Asia, including Japan, the average is 2.4 channels – most of them government-controlled and filled with boring propaganda."

By December 1991, Star TV was broadcasting on five channels, almost nine months ahead of schedule (Exhibit 1). Four English language channels were dominated by "western" programming; the fifth broadcast programs in Mandarin. The first "viewership validation" figures showed that 680,000 households were receiving and watching Star TV. One industry analyst believed the fast move to air had advantages of both generating early cash flows and establishing a lead over potential "competitors." In its first full year, Star TV secured US$120 million in advertising revenues.

A study conducted for Star TV by Frank Small and Associates in June 1992 estimated the potential number of households able to view Star TV at 1.8 million (Exhibit 2); within six months of launch, eight million viewers had tuned in. In February 1993, the *Far Eastern Economic Review* reported that 11.4 million households representing 45 million viewers received Star TV, then accessible to three billion people. Across 38 countries, it appeared that viewers were already switching on to the new world of multi-channel television through satellites.

Some industry observers questioned Star TV's ability to substantiate its viewership figures; these data, together with demographic information, were important to potential advertisers. Although other observers applauded Star TV's early, and unprecedented, research activities, the general consensus agreed with Kay Golding:[4] "It (the media research firm used by Star TV) doesn't tell you a lot of information." Observers were also concerned that potential viewer and household research did not adequately address the number of homes that would pay to receive Star TV.

Industry reaction was not unnoticed by Star TV officials. Bob Alter, advisor to Star TV's board of directors stated: "What we are looking at is a prodigy. In one year we have completed five channels and three months after the launch of the last one, people are expecting us to be performing Beethoven's Fifth Piano Concerto without a flaw." Since Star TV offered free-to-air programming, it depended on revenue generated by advertisers. In response to industry "outcries," Star TV began preparation of a new research methodology to address directly concerns of the initial study.

By mid-1993, Star TV's "footprint" encompassed one third of the world's population including many of its fastest growing economies, from Russia in the north to Australia in the south.[5] Star TV delivered program variety, from news and information to entertainment and sports. The planned launch of additional satellites, along with

---

[3] John Dikkenburg, "A star is born," *Asia Magazine*, September 6, 1991, p. 4.
[4] Media Director of McCann-Erickson in Hong Kong.
[5] A satellite footprint (also referred to as a "catchment area") was defined as satellite's reach; the number of viewers theoretically able to receive programming.

introduction of new compression technologies, coincided with Star TV's plans to introduce additional channels and region-specific programming.

Financially, Star TV hoped to achieve operating break-even by end 1994; it forecast pay-back by end 1997. First year operating costs were approximately US$80 million.

Star TV Functioning

Broadcasting

Star TV was a satellite based television network offering programming 24 hours a day, seven days a week. Program signals were sent from Star TV's Clearwater Bay Station in Hong Kong to the AsiaSat Satellite hovering 22,000 miles above the equator. This signal was beamed to earth, potentially viewable by anyone in the "footprint" with a satellite dish. Star TV leased ten of AsiaSat's 24 transponders;[6] 14 were reserved for national telecommunications and relays. Because of this supply constraint, in the short term, competitive entry was blocked to most of Asia and the Middle East.[7]

Viewing

To capture Star TV's broadcasts, a terrestrial satellite dish had to be aimed at AsiaSat. Two types of satellite dish were available: Satellite Master Antenna Television Systems (SMATV) and Television Receive Only Systems (TVRO). SMATVs were large communal satellite receiving dishes usually installed on apartment building roofs or on high elevations near housing communities; TV signals were distributed to individual units by cabling attached to the dish. By contrast, TVROs were much smaller satellite dishes intended for use by single households.

Star TV also broadcast over a special sound system, PANDA, that allowed stereo and multi-lingual broadcasting; it functioned by compressing the broadcast soundtrack which was expanded upon reception. This technique created extra room for stereo broadcasts and as many as four additional languages for each transmission.

Channels

Star TV's sister company, Media Assets Ltd. (established 1991 with US$300 million capital) handled all program acquisition. For the rights to air MTV and Prime Sports, Star TV shared profits 50/50. Since Star TV's broadcasts were designed to appeal to specific audiences with different tastes, Media Assets actively sought links with potential distributors to expand the range of movies and TV programs.[8] By June 1993, Star TV's channels comprised:

---

[6] Transponders were devices to boost and relay microwave signals; they were essentially "amplifiers" for television transmissions. They had limited capacity.

[7] AsiaSat 1 had "leased" its satellite capacity within 18 months of launch; Indonesia's new satellite had a waiting list. Operators were proposing to increase numbers of transponder from 327 to 943 within five years.

[8] This form of programming was often referred as "niche" or "genre specific."

- *Prime Sports*, a non-stop sports station tailored to regional audiences, offering a mix of international programs in conjunction with U.S.-based Prime Network International, the world's largest sports programming and production company.
- The *Music Channel*, a joint venture with music video pioneer MTV, providing both regional and global music selections. Star TV also helped develop MTV's Asia Beat, a program combining regional talent from Thailand, Singapore and Hong Kong with western artists (e.g., Madonna and Michael Jackson).
- The *Chinese Channel*, formed with Hong Kong's Asia Television, provided a library of entertainment programming focused on Taiwan, the People's Republic of China (PRC) and Hong Kong. Additional Mandarin-language programs were sourced worldwide (e.g., North America). In addition to entertainment programs, the Chinese Channel presented pan-Asian financial and economic programs focused on the PRC and Taiwan. A Star TV press release described the Chinese Channel as offering audiences a viewing "alternative" in markets where local terrestrial stations had programming restrictions. However, in Taiwan, the government controlled international satellite TV reception; in the PRC, TVRO use was restricted.
- Programming for the *News and Information Channel* was provided by the British Broadcasting Corporation's (BBC) World Service Television. World headlines were aired at 15-minute intervals between information programs broadcast throughout the day. Richard Li described the content and emphasis of the News Channel:

> News will be very cognizant of religion because much of the 38-country satellite footprint is Muslim. We'll avoid Asian politics because it's hard to keep a common thread and denominator throughout our news content. Breaking news will be beamed in from outside the region but there will be a lot of local economic and business stories, stock market reports and the like, to keep local businessmen up to date. Local emphasis is uppermost. We knocked back CNN because it had too much American content. In the Gulf War, their American bias was all too apparent and a lot of countries were not appreciative.

- *Star Plus Family-Entertainment Channel* programming, supplied by producers from around the world, including feature films, women's and children's programs, and game, variety and chat shows. Programming was carefully scheduled for intended audiences. For example, early morning and after-school hours programming concentrated on animation and live action shows for audiences aged 18 and younger; daytime programming concentrated on cooking, talk shows, fashion, exercise and drama series targeting women; evening programming provided dramas, comedies and movies for a family viewing audience.

Programming at Star TV was conservative; a press release described the program and advertising content:

As invited guests into people's homes we have a duty of care and respect to our audience, a responsibility Star TV takes very seriously. If a broadcaster abuses such trust and encourages people to watch things that will upset them, the broadcaster will quickly go out of business and ought to.

Star TV established a Standards & Practices Department to ensure that programming met the Codes of Practice issued by the Hong Kong Broadcasting Authority. Star TV did not accept advertisements for pornography, cigarette commercials or hard liquor.

PANDA was used to broadcast multi-lingual programs to create a "local" approach. Star TV had plans for a Hindi channel targeting the large potential Indian audience and possibly a Japanese channel. Richard Li encouraged additional partnerships based on Star TV's technological ability and local emphasis: "We would like to join forces with as many partners as possible in the scenario of combining (digital picture) compression with a theoretically limitless number of channels."

Whereas Star TV enthusiastically embraced expansion, some concerns were expressed regarding the need to strengthen its viewing base. One issue was the size of the footprint versus the solidity of viewership. Richard Li addressed this concern: "In terms of programming emphasis, do we go for more homes or do we go for viewership in such homes? Shall we increase this balloon or make sure this balloon is solid? How much time people spend watching these channels may be more important than expanding."

Star TV also planned to offer direct sale programming to 150 terrestrial broadcasters within Star TV's footprint.[9] Deals currently being negotiated in Pakistan, Sri Lanka and Bahrain were designed so that Star TV would share profits of the affiliated re-broadcasting systems.

Free-to-air versus Encrypted Programming

Star TV's free-to-air programming meant consumers were not charged subscriptions. Broadcasts were not scrambled when transmitted and Star TV could be viewed free-of-charge by anyone in the AsiaSat footprint with a satellite dish. Thus, Star TV operated as an advertisement-driven company; advertising provided the firm's revenue base. Introduction of some pay services via encrypted programming had been discussed by Star TV executives[10] but Bob Alter, advisor to the board of directors, clarified that while encrypted programming definitely had a place in Star TV's future it would not replace free-to-air programming: "We are committed to provide a quality free-to-air service. We see that is important to fulfill our compact with the [satellite] dish owners."

One option advocated a "two-tier" system: some programming would be provided free-to-air; other more specialized programming could be scrambled requiring a decoder for viewing.

---

[9] Terrestrial broadcasters would negotiate for the right to re-broadcast Star TV's programming via a land-based network such as cable or VHF signal.

[10] Programming requiring decoders necessary for viewing, provided at an additional cost.

Marketing Activities

Star TV's Asian marketing strategy was based on developing its program distribution business by selling programming to other TV companies, redistributing its signal to SMATVs in hotels and transmitting to land-based cable systems. One industry analyst believed that providing the marketing strategies to exploit Asia region's potential could tempt program suppliers to join with HutchVision and Star TV.

Audience validation was important for advertisers to determine advertising values. The large potential viewing audience, determined by the satellite footprint, offered what one media observer called "very cheap CPM (cost per thousand target audience)." Under Star TV's license, a maximum of four hours of commercials was permitted in a 24-hour period. Numbers of advertisers increased from 60 to 300 from February 1992 to 1993. By June 1993, Asian advertising packages for 4,000 30-second spots over two years were offered for US$2,353,000. Star TV hoped to attract a variety of sponsors to fill its advertising spots; current sponsors included multinationals in the hotel, banking, watch and automobile business. Advertising revenues were estimated to have increased from US$80 million in 1991 to US$100 million for 1992.[11] (Exhibit 3.)

The Middle East Market

Farrow was unsure about the Middle East's viability as a market for Star TV. She had to determine the potential for attracting advertisers by balancing governmental regulatory measures regarding advertising content, based on secondary information compiled by her predecessor. (See Appendices 1 to 4 for material on media and advertising; see Appendix 5 for more general country information.)

Advertising Potential in the Middle East

Advertising expenditures developed by the Gulf Cooperation Council (GCC), measured by media (i.e., press and television), rose from US$336 million in 1991 to US$450 million in 1992;[12] industry experts expected a doubling by end 1993.

Figures for 1989 to 1992 showed an overall 13% increase but this was significantly affected by a decrease in Kuwait's contribution to regional advertising revenues as the result of the Gulf War. Kuwait's 1992 advertising expenditures were up 350% from 1991 but below 1989 levels.

Specific increases recorded from 1991 to 1992 were: Bahrain (33%), Kingdom of Saudi Arabia (22%), Oman (15%) and Pan Arab (12%). The launch of new satellite stations (e.g., MBC) contributed to increases in advertising expenditures.

---

[11] Note HK$120 million was secured as advertising revenues by April 1992, split between calendar years 1991 and 1992.

[12] These figures exclude expenditures in other advertising media i.e., outdoor, exhibitions, point-of-sales, video advertising, etc. If included, the media expenditure in 1992 would be over US$550 million.

Competition

London-based subscription television, Middle East Broadcasting Center (MBC), launched in September 1991, was owned by Sheik Walid al-Ibrahim, a prince and brother-in-law of the King of Saudi Arabia, and Salah Kamal, a Saudi businessman. One observer stated: "So close are its connections to the seat of power in the oil kingdom that for the Saudis, MBC stands for My Broadcasting Company!"

MBC, initiated with a five-year US$200 million budget, broadcast up to 12 hours a day providing news bulletins, drama and women's programs. Its 200-person London staff (one third Arab) produced one third of its daily output. Since the Saudi middle class ran into the millions, MBC guidelines specified social codes to ensure programming was strictly family entertainment.

For viewers in Bahrain, Kuwait and Morocco, MBC was considered a local TV station; however, in other countries satellite dishes were required to view programming. MBC's style was perceived as very different from local channels; one international newspaper reported:

> In the Middle East, MBC's style has proved almost revolutionary. In an area where most news bulletins consist of little more than reports on who the Great Leader or His Highness met today, MBC represents the slickest TV news service available in the Arab world. It looks good, it comes from London and has no obvious social hang-ups. Female presenters appear nightly on the news in true CNN style, lip gloss and bouncy long hair, without the obligatory head-scarf or view required by so many stations in the Arab world. In Saudi Arabia, there are no women presenters let alone fashion shows on television. More importantly, it is in Arabic and costs a fraction of the expense of a satellite dish [needed] to receive BBC World Service Television.

MBC's programming motives were hotly debated. Some said the station represented a Saudi Arabian effort to cover the Arab world with carefully sanitized news and debate. However, Managing Director Abdullah Masri denied "any grand Saudi conspiracy to dominate TV programming in the Arab world"; rather, the station promoted Arab unity and moderation, a commodity he felt, was in short supply in the region. MBC proved popular for western-educated Saudis familiar with the freedom of televised political debate. One observer said that MBC was positioned against powerful Islamic groups that believed television should broadcast prayers, the Koran and nothing else. For the government, MBC was a useful means by which the elite could have "watchable" television in a country where public entertainment (e.g., theaters, cinemas) were banned.

By December 1992, revenues from its single television channel covered about 45% of total costs; income was expected to increase and operating break-even reached by 1996. Said Masri:

> After 15 months of operation, we are well ahead of our target. We are getting a very satisfying response from advertisers and all our advertising spots are full to the

brim for the first and second quarters of 1993. However, we will not be relying totally on advertising income; we are going into subscription in 1994.

In Kuwait and Bahrain, where MBC had agreements for its satellite service to be re-broadcast by terrestrial stations, it planned to replace direct transmission with an encrypted service available only to viewers paying the subscription fee. Masri elaborated: "We are going to have different broadcast policies for different areas. In some, we rely on subscription, in others the service will be free. Saudi Arabia is a market where encrypted MBC service might be applicable."

In addition to the two Gulf states, Morocco was the only Arab country to have reached a re-broadcast agreement with MBC. After signing a protocol agreement with Tunis Radio and Television Corporation (TRTC), Tunisian service was started in early 1993. Under the agreement, MBC supplied TRTC with news reports generated from its London newsroom in exchange for light entertainment, documentary films and children's programming. Masri was in discussion with TV Libyan but believed an agreement was not close. MBC was already available in most of Europe and the Middle East for viewers with satellite dishes.

MBC's mission to reach as many Arab communities as possible led it to expand aggressively in other geographies. For example, MBC was targeting the two million-strong Arab community in the U.S.; in mid-1992, it acquired United Press International (UPI), a U.S. news agency, and planned to inject US$25 to US$35 million. Masri explained the stimulus for this purchase was US$400,000 monthly savings normally paid to Visnews. MBC's plan (cost: US$16.5 to US$23 million) would transform UPI into a TV news supply service for the Middle East, Africa and the Muslim republics in Central Asia. Because of the significant financial commitment, MBC was negotiating with other Arab partners (e.g., Kuwait, Egyptian Middle East news agencies) to join the venture.

By December 1992, MBC was negotiating a cable television acquisition or joint venture in North America. It was also planning to launch an Arabic FM radio music and news-based service carried on the same signal as MBC's satellite television to be re-broadcast from local radio stations. MBC was also planning to open a bureau in Jerusalem, the first ever official presence established by an Arab media organization in Israeli-occupied territory. One critic noted: "The Saudi agenda is to get us used to dealing with Israel."

Political and Cultural Factors

In addition to traditional market-based issues, Jane Farrow knew that political and cultural factors would have to enter into her decision-making process. Perhaps the major political issue was the relationship between Israel and her Arab neighbors. Despite ongoing discussions on Israeli-Palestinian relationships, deep-rooted political problems were unlikely to be solved in the short term because of seemingly intractable nationalistic and ethnic discord. Middle East experts believed that even if peace agreements were reached at governmental levels, the danger remained that hard-liners opposed to reconciliation (on either side) could sabotage them. (See Exhibit 4 for a selection of risk profiles.)

Whereas Israel practiced a form of western-style democracy, in most Middle East countries representative government was neither in place nor likely to be instituted in the near future. Indeed, the Arab Middle East was a complex mix of peoples, religious sects, styles of government, interests and loyalties. The painful instability and turbulence encouraged many people to attach primary loyalties to the family, tribe and broader aspirations of regional identity (e.g., pan-Arabism, Islamic unity) rather than nation-states. The region was predominantly Muslim and political/legal structures were governed by strict Islamic laws. Social customs were based on the societal and familial dominance of males and it was unusual for women to participate in business transactions.

Many foreign companies found it difficult to operate in the region because of strict Islamic laws. For example, cultural differences were an important aspect of project management for multinational construction firms and incidents of social-cultural mishaps (e.g., misinterpretations, frustrations, conflicts) were not unusual. In addition, severe restrictions were imposed on emotional expression; in particular, advertising campaigns had to be executed and tested with special care. Advertising agencies had to consider the complex social rules, sensitivities and taboos affecting media use in the Arab world. For example, it was unacceptable to depict women in western-style dress; advertising in the holy month of Ramadan should not depict eating or drinking; and music and dancing were offensive during the Haj period.

Notwithstanding the traditionalism in most of the Middle East countries, significant quantities of commercial and residential satellite TV equipment were being imported. For example, since 1990, Hoosier Satellite, an Indiana-based distributor, sold satellite hardware to distributors and brokers in every Middle Eastern country except Iran and Iraq; the region currently represented 70% of Hoosier's business. To achieve success, Hoosier tailored its equipment to meet the region's special requirements. CEO Steve Bland predicted ultimate market penetration at 1,000 times higher than the U.S. since most towns had neither cable nor TV stations.

In addition, Orbitron (Spring Green, Wisconsin) had shipped four 20-foot containers of satellite equipment per month to the region since 1991 but claimed it had spent years establishing its presence and that only recently had the customer mix become increasingly diverse. Orbitron executives said that Bahrain and the United Arab Emirates were countries where it conducted brisk business and that, although sales had yet to reach mass-market proportions, reforms in several countries were increasing market size. In particular, Saudi resistance was expected to decrease as the availability of technology and programming became more pervasive. Some industry experts believed the ready availability of racy western programs via satellite was an underlying barrier to a more liberalized regulatory environment.

Recommendations

Jane Farrow gathered together the mountain of secondary data prepared by her predecessor. She believed her task was two-fold; first, to decide whether the Middle East in general was an attractive market for Star TV; second, to formulate an entry strategy focusing specifically on which countries to enter and which to avoid. For those countries that might be entered she had to make decisions on form of entry and positioning strategy.

Exhibit 1: Star TV History (1990 to 1991)

1990	
April 7:	Launch of AsiaSat 1.
December 22:	Non-exclusive broadcasting license awarded by Hong Hong Government.
1991	
April 2:	Broadcasts first test signal from 11-meter transportable disk in Fanling (New Territories, Hong Kong).
April 15:	Broadcasts of Preview Channel begin.
July 1:	Uplink transferred from Fanling to Clearwater Bay Station (Kowloon).
August 26:	Prime Sports channel launched.
September 15:	MTV launched.
October 14:	BBC-World Service TV soft launch.
October 21:	Chinese Channel launched.
November 15:	BBC-WSTV begins full 24-hour broadcasts.
December 15:	StarPlus launched to replace Preview Channel.

Source: Asia-Pacific Broadcasting, June 1992, p. 5.

Exhibit 2: Star TV Potential Penetration, Selected Countries (1992)

	No. of homes able to view Star TV	Percent of total TV homes	Total potential audience
Hong Kong	116,925	8%	412,745
India	412,500	4%	2,103,750
Indonesia	14,335	*	57,340
Israel	198,500	20%	794,000
Taiwan	1,059,369	23%	5,084,970
Total	**1,801,629**		**8,452,805**

Exhibit 3: Star TV Advertisers, 1992

Academy of Arts (San Francisco)	Lippo Group
Ambassador Hotel	Lotto Sports Shoes
Bank of China Group	Mandarin Singapore Hotel
Banque Paribuas	Mars Inc.
Brand's Essence of Chicken	Mastercard International
Cadbury's Chocolate Candy	McDonald's Restaurant Ltd.
Canadian Imperial Bank of Commerce	Mitsui & Company
Canon	Mobil Oil
Cathay Pacific Airways	Movado Watch
Chase Manhattan Bank	MRF Tyres
Chee Shing Foundation	New World Hotels Int'l
Chia Hsin Cement Corp.	Nike International Ltd.
China Resources Holdings	Nikko Securities
China Travel Service	Nishimatsu Construction
Citibank	Northwest Airline
Citizen Watches	Pepsi Cola
Coca-Cola	Peregrine
Dah Chong Hong	Pioneer
Dao Hen Bank	Reebok International
Deutsche Bank	Remy Nicholas Fine Wines
Durffee Watch	Royal Pacific Hotels
Forum Restaurant	Satch Leather Products
Fuji	Shell Oil

Source: Asia-Pacific Broadcasting, June 1992, p. 15.

Exhibit 4: Selected Country Risk Profiles

Country regimes & probabilities of holding power*	Turmoil	Transfer	Investment	Export	Date	Real GDP growth (%)	Inflation (%)	Current account (%)
EGYPT	Feb 93				1988–92	2.6	19.1	0.94
Mubarak 65%	High	C+	B	C+	1993	1.8	20	-0.12
Mubarak 50%	Moderate	B–	C–	C–	1994–98	2.6	24	-0.15
ISRAEL	Oct 92				1988–92	4.3	16.3	-0.31
Labor Coalition 55%	V. High	C+	B+	C+	1993	6	18	-1
Labor Coalition 40%	High	C+	B+	B	1994–98	5	15	-0.5
KUWAIT	Nov 92				1988–92	-1.4	13	-1.17
Al Sabbath Family 65%	Low	B+	B–	B+	1993	-4	40	-1
Al Sabbath Family 50%	Low	B–	C–	C–	1994–98	-1	30	1
OMAN	Aug 92				1988–92	8.9	2.9	0.15
Qaboos 85%	Low	A+	B	A+	1993	8	5	0.1
Qaboos 60%	Low	A+	B–	B+	1994–98	6	5.5	0.25
SAUDI ARABIA	Feb 93				1988–92	5.6	2.2	-10.16
Fahd 80%	Low	A	B	A+	1993	5	2	-5
Fahd 50%	Low	A	C+	B–	1994–98	3.5	3	-2.5

*Next to each country name is the date of the last update, followed by the 18-month (2nd line) and 5-year (3rd line) political forecasts: the regimes most likely to hold power and their probabilities, risk ratings (A+ the least to D– the most) for financial transfer, direct investment, and export to the country. Parentheses indicate a changed forecast.
Source: Planning Review.

Appendix 1: Media Regulation in the Middle East

Jordan, Israel: Regulatory – Media
Advertising regulation: n/a
Main regulation by medium: n/a

Bahrain, Egypt, Kuwait, Oman, Qatar: Regulatory – Media
Beverage/alcohol: no restrictions/regulations for non-alcohol beverages. Alcohol advertising is banned.
Cigarettes: tobacco advertising is permitted only in the print media and on video.
Pharmaceuticals/drugs: banned.

Main Regulation by Medium
Television: all commercials are subject to approval by the local Censorship Committees. Alcohol and tobacco are banned.
Print: alcohol and related products are banned.
Outdoor: alcohol and related products are banned.
Non-traditional: any media vehicle or medium will adhere to the laws of the land.
  – Any form/content which is culturally revealing is not allowed.
  – Public representation of Gulf women should conform to strict tradition.
  – Exaggeration is seen as the most unacceptable trend in advertising and indeed is interpreted as a form of lying with the intention of misleading the consumer.
  – No wild dancing, revealing dress, violent dreams, intimate scenes, etc., are allowed.

Oman (additional)
Cigarettes: restricted to print media and some outdoor advertisements. Statutory to incorporate a government health warning.
Pharmaceuticals/drugs: prior approval from Ministry of Health is required.
Financial advertising: prior approval from the Central Bank of Oman is required for all media.

Main Regulation by Medium
Print: cigarette/tobacco related advertising is permitted in the press.
Outdoor: cigarette/tobacco related advertising is permitted and is subject to prior approval from the municipality.

United Arab Emirates (additional)
Cigarettes: restricted to print media, video and some outdoor advertisements. Statutory to incorporate a government health warning.
Pharmaceuticals/drugs: prior approval from Ministry of Health is required.

Saudi Arabia: Regulatory – Media
Beverage/alcohol: prohibited
Cigarettes: strictly prohibited in TV and local press but indirect advertising is always possible.
Pharmaceuticals/drugs: not allowed as long as it is registered at the Ministry of Health.
Advertising to children: no false claims are allowed. No "dangerous" scenes for kids to imitate.
Commercial production: same rates apply to in-country productions.

Main Regulation by Medium
Television: no cigarettes. No alcoholic beverages. No females (if hair uncovered).
Print: no cigarettes. No alcoholic beverages.
Outdoor: faces are not allowed to show. No cigarettes and no alcoholic beverages are allowed.

Appendix 2: Advertising in the Middle East

BAHRAIN	1988	1989	1990	1991
% advertising spending (national) by medium:				
Total advertising expenditure (US$ million):	10.1	10.9	10.8	12.5
Television (US$ million):	5.2	4.6	5.1	6.3
Newspapers (US$ million):	n/a	n/a	5.2	5.6
Magazine (US$ million):	n/a	n/a	0.5	0.6
Historical household TV penetration:	n/a	90%	n/a	n/a

Main broadcast language: Arabic

Remarks: Basically advertising agencies dealt with media but some small advertisers approached the media directly.

Media pricing is generally non-negotiable. Structured media buying services are not available. Ownership is diversified. Government normally owns TV in addition to one or two print media vehicles. Others are enterprise-driven.

EGYPT	1988	1989	1990	1991
% advertising spending (national) by medium:				
Total advertising expenditure (US$ million):	86	98	114.7	121.2
Television (US$ million):	34	42	54.7	65.1
Newspapers (US$ million):	n/a	n/a	35	31.4
Magazine (US$ million):	n/a	n/a	9	8.7
Cinema (US$ million):	n/a	n/a	2	3
Radio (US$ million):	n/a	n/a	5	3
Outdoor (US$ million):	n/a	n/a	9	10

Media broadcasting

Television (1992): Sets in use – 4,150,000 (1987); 83 per 1,000 population (1987)/Number of TV stations: 47 (1990)/Primary broadcast language: Arabic. Secondary: English

Historical household TV penetration			90%	90%	90%

Network stations	Ownership	Station profile	Commercial Min/Day	Coverage
Channel 1	National	General	90	95%
Channel 2	National	General (EDU)	30	65%
Channel 3	National	General (Greater Cairo)	20	20%
Channel 4	National	Local (Canal Zone)	10	10%
Channel 5	National	Local (Alexandria)	10	10%

ISRAEL	1988	1989	1990	1991
% advertising spending (national) by medium:				
Total advertising expenditure (US$ million):	523.1	588	646.8	
Television (US$ million):	20	n/a	n/a	n/a
Newspapers (US$ million):	313.9	379.3	n/a	n/a
Historical household TV penetration	n/a	n/a	n/a	n/a

Media broadcasting

Television (1992): Sets in use – 1,150,000; 263 per 1,000 population (1987)/Number of TV stations: 54 (1990)/Primary broadcast language: Hebrew. Secondary: English

Appendix 2 (cont'd)

Network stations	Ownership	No. of channels	Programming Hours/week	Coverage
Israel TV	Govt.	1	55	100%
Channel 2 TV	P.M's Special Committee	1	26	n/a
Educational TV	Public	1	56	n/a
Arabic TV	Public	1	14	n/a

JORDAN

Media – non-broadcasting
Newspapers: n/a / Magazines: n/a / % advertising spending (national) by medium: n/a

Media broadcasting
Television (1992): Sets in use – 260,000 (1988); 69 per 1,000 population (1988)/Number of TV stations: 24 (1991)/Primary broadcast language: Arabic. Secondary: English/Historical household TV penetration: n/a

Network stations	Ownership	No. of stations	Station profile	Coverage
Channel 1	Govt.	1	n/a	National
Channel 2	Govt.	1	n/a	National

Programming hours per week: 112

KUWAIT	1988	1989	1990	1991
% advertising spending (national) by medium:				
Total advertising expenditure (US$ million):	93.5	98.9	67	24.2
Television (US$ million):	18.7	21.8	13.4	2.2
Newspapers (US$ million):	40.2	19.6	n/a	n/a
Magazine (US$ million):	13.4	2.4	n/a	n/a
Historical household penetration	98%	n/a	n/a	n/a

Media – Broadcasting
Television (1992): Sets in use – 810,000 (1989); 410 per 1,000 population (1989)/Number of TV stations: 3 (1990)

Network stations	No. of stations	Ownership	Commercial (Min/day)
1	2	Govt.	I Arabic channel

Remarks: Commercials aired only in specific time block and aired only at the start and end but never during programs.

LEBANON	1988	1989	1990	1991
% advertising spending (national) by medium:				
Total advertising expenditure (US$ million):	11.3	23.2	18.6	27.8
Television (US$ million):	6.8	15	13	19
Newspapers (US$ million):	1	1.8	n/a	n/a
Magazine (US$ million):	0.4	0.6	n/a	n/a
Cinema (US$ million):	0.2	0.4	n/a	n/a
Radio (US$ million):	2	3	n/a	n/a
Historical household penetration:	n/a	98%	n/a	n/a

Appendix 2 (cont'd)

Media – broadcasting

Television (1992): Sets in use – 325,000 (1985); 305 per 1,000 population (1985)/Number of TV stations: 15 (1989)/Primary broadcast language: n/a

Network	No. of stations	Ownership	Station profile	Coverage
Tele Liban	2	State	General	National
LBC	1	Private	General	National
C33	1	Private	Francophone	National
Mashrek	1	Private	General	National
NTV	1	Private	General	
ICN	1	Private	General	
MURR TV	1	Private	General	
BTC	1	Private	General	
Ehden TV	1	Private	General	
Bekaa TV	1	Private	General	
Baalbeck TV	1	Private	General	

QATAR	1988	1989	1990	1991
% advertising spending (national) by medium:				
Total advertising expenditure (US$ million):	10.5	10.9	10.8	9.9
Television (US$ million):	2.8	2.7	3.8	3.6
Newspapers (US$ million):	6	5.4	n/a	n/a
Magazine (US$ million):	1	0.9	n/a	n/a
Historical household penetration:	n/a	95%	n/a	n/a

Media – Broadcasting

Television (1992): Sets in use – 1,000,000 (1989); 452 per 1,000 population (1989)/Number of TV stations: 3 (1990)/Primary language used to broadcast TV: Arabic

Network	No. of stations	Ownership	Commercial (Min/day)	Station
	12	Govt.	5.2	General

Remarks: Commercials aired only in specified time block; only at the beginning and end of programming.

OMAN	1988	1989	1990	1991
% advertising spending (national) by medium:				
Total advertising expenditure (US$ million):	n/a	n/a	12.3	12.8
Television (US$ million):	n/a	n/a	4.4	4.6
Newspapers (US$ million):	n/a	n/a	6.7	7
Magazine (US$ million):	n/a	n/a	1.2	1.2
Historical household penetration:	n/a	n/a	90%	n/a

Media – broadcasting

Television (1992): Sets in use – 1,000,000 (1989); 703 per 1,000 population (1989)/Number of TV stations: 11 (1990)

Network	No. of stations	Ownership	Commercial Min/day	Station profile
	12	Govt.	8.8	General

Appendix 2 (cont'd)

SAUDI ARABIA	1988	1989	1990	1991
% advertising spending (national) by medium:				
Total advertising expenditure (US$ million):	155	170	174	188.3
Television (US$ million):	46	48	46	45.5
Magazine (US$ million):	116	129.8	n/a	n/a
Outdoor (US$ million):	12	13	n/a	n/a
Historical household penetration:	96%	n/a	n/a	n/a

Media – broadcasting
Television (1992): Sets in use – 4,000,000 (1990); 283 per 1,000 population (1990)/Number of TV stations: 97 (1991)

Network	No. of stations	Ownership	Commercial Min/day	Station profile
Channel 1 (Arabic)	1	Govt.	30 (ave)	Religious/educational
Channel 2 (English)	1	Govt.	2 (ave)	entertainment/

Remarks: Commercials aired only in specified time block; only at the beginning and end of programming.

U.A.E	1988	1989	1990	1991
% advertising spending (national) by medium:				
Total advertising expenditure (US$ million):	58.2	70.6	69.9	85.9
Television (US$ million):	17.5	22.6	21.7	21.7
Newspapers (US$ million):	41.9	58.6	n/a	n/a
Magazine (US$ million):	6.3	5.6	n/a	n/a
Historical household penetration:	n/a	93%	n/a	n/a

Media – broadcasting
Television (1992): Sets in use – 150,000 (1987); 103 per 1,000 population (1987)/Number of TV stations: 12 (1989)/Primary broadcast language: n/a

Network	No. of stations	Ownership	Commercial Min/day	Station profile
Dubai	2	Govt.	14.6	General
Abu Dubai	2	Govt.	14.6	General
Sharjah	1	Govt.	14.6	General

Remarks: Basically advertising agencies deal with media but some small advertisers approach the media directly. Media pricing is generally non-negotiable. Structured media buying services are not available. Ownership is diversified. Government normally owns TV in addition to one or two print media vehicles. Others are enterprise-driven.

Appendix 3: Top 10 Advertisers by Parent Company in 1991 (US$ million)*

	Parent company	Product category/s	Total spending		Parent company	Product category/s	Total spending
BAHRAIN	Pampers	Baby diapers	1.1	OMAN	Toyota	Passenger cars	1.8
	Rothmans	Cigarettes	1.08		Minara	Sunflower oil	0.8
	Hilal	Computer service	1.08		Al Jamil	Baby diapers	0.4
	Australian Meat	Fresh/frozen meat	1.05		Solar	Corn oil	0.4
	Alia	Corn oil	0.93		Honda	Passenger cars	0.4
	Dunhill	Cigarettes	0.9		Nivea	Skin care – oil and lotion	0.3
	Fairy	Dishwashing L/P	0.89		Pert Plus	Hair care	0.2
	Clorox	Bleach powder	0.8		Rothmans	Cigarettes	0.2
	Bridgestone	Cars/truck tires	0.78		Ford	Passenger cars	0.2
			–		Benson & Hedges	Cigarettes	0.2
EGYPT	National	Bank	1.2	QATAR	BMW	Passenger cars	0.12
	Procter and Gamble	Toiletries	1.1		Philip Morris	Cigarettes	0.10
	Al Shamadan	Biscuits	0.8		Rothmans	Cigarettes	0.10
	Miar	Bank	0.8		General Motors	Passenger cars	0.09
	ParficC (Unilever)	Toiletries	0.7		Shabab El Yom	Magazines/newspapers	0.08
	Egypt Air	Airline	0.6		Gulf Air	Airline	0.08
	Pepsi International	Soft drinks	0.5		Bridgestone	Cars/truck tires	0.08
	Fine Foods	Food	0.5		Concord	Watches	0.08
	CAC	Air conditioning	0.5		Pampers	Baby diapers	0.08
	Lecico	Sanitary wares	0.3		Dunhill	Cigarettes	0.08
KUWAIT	Marlboro	Cigarettes	0.9	SAUDI ARABIA	Toyota	Passenger cars	1.81
	Al Anba	Magazines	0.4		Alali	Food	0.93
	Kuwait Airways	Airline	0.3		Afia	Cooking oil	0.88
	NBK	Banks	0.3		Kraft	Cheese	0.86
	Mis. Prof. Services	Mis. Prof. Services	0.3		Pampers	Diaper	0.81
	Rothmans	Cigarettes	0.3		Tide	Washing powder	0.68
	Sawf. Al Kuwait	Magazines	0.2		Head & Shoulders	Shampoo	0.67

Parent company	Product category/s	Total spending
B.K.M.E	Banks	0.2
Merit U Lights	Cigarettes	0.2
Nissan	Passenger cars	0.2
LEBANON		
n/a	Cigarettes	2.6
n/a	Alcoholic drinks	1.9
n/a	Soft drinks	1.9
n/a	Chocolates	1.3
n/a	Perfumes/cosmetics	1.2
–	–	–
–	–	–
–	–	–
–	–	–
–	–	–

U.A.E

Parent company	Product category/s	Total spending
Fairy Liquid	Dishwashing liquid	0.61
Mobil	Motor oil	0.56
Nido	Powder milk	0.49
Crest	Toothpaste	0.49
Kit Kat	Chocolate	0.48
Philips	H/H kitchen appliances	0.47
Riyadha Al Shabab	Magazines/newspapers	4.71
Toyota	Passenger cars	3.79
Benson & Hedges	Cigarettes	3.76
Citizen	Watches	3.41
Dubai I. Duty Free	Department stores	3.33
Sony	Video cameras	3.16
Al Ghurair Center	Department store	3.14
Lipton	Tea bags	3.02
Fairy	Dishwashing L/P	2.93
Citibank	Special accounts	2.85

*Data on Israel and Jordan not available.

Appendix 4: Non-media Broadcasting; Magazines*

	Name	Type	Circulation	Average issue Adult audience	Cost (1PG US$)	Frequency
BAHRAIN	Gulf Panorama (E)	General/leisure	15,000	/	1,700	Monthly
	This is Bahrain	General/leisure	15,000	/	1,165	Quarterly
EGYPT	Hawaa	Women	220,000	1,316,000	2,000	Weekly
	Aljer Saa	Sports	400,000	1,452,000	3,200	Weekly
	Radio & TV	Weekly guide	100,000	1,115,000	2,200	Weekly
	Al Mussawar	Political	220,000	816,000	4,600	Weekly
	October	Social	300,000	1,590,000	3,300	Weekly
	Kawakeb	Entertainment	120,000	825,000	2,500	Weekly
	Sabah El Eheir	General interest	600,000	618,000	4,400	Weekly
	Rose El Youssef	General news	600,000	578,000	5,300	Weekly
	Koleanms	General news	120,000	252,000	13,300	Weekly
	Al Ahram El Iktissadi	Business	170,000	104,000	20,700	Weekly
	Nisf El Donia	Women	400,000	1,504,000	2,200	Weekly
	Al Ahram El Riyadhi	Sports	320,000	579,000	4,800	Weekly
	Horriyati	General news	120,000	751,000	4,400	Weekly
	Akhbar El Hawades	Hawades	70,000	200,000	2,200	Weekly
KUWAIT	Al Nahda	Social/political	148,000	/	4,510	Weekly
	Al Yagza	Social/political	128,000	/	4,677	Weekly
	Al Riyadhi	Social/political	102,000	/	4,009	Weekly
	Al Majales	Social/political	111,000	/	1,832	Weekly
	Hayatuna	General	55,000	/	/	Weekly
	Al Arab	Social/political	25,000	/	/	Weekly
	Kuwait TV/Radio Guide	Guide	60,000	/	/	Quarterly
LEBANON	Magazine	General interest	12,000	56,000	850	Weekly
	Chabaka	Soc/fem	20,000	100,000	850	Weekly
	Hasna'	Soc/fem	15,000	65,000	750	Weekly
OMAN	Al Adnan	News	10,000	/	386	Weekly
	Al Akidah	News	10,000	/	429	Weekly
	Al Nahda	News	10,000	/	429	Weekly

Appendix 4 (cont'd)

	Name	Type	Circulation	Average issue Adult audience	Cost (1PG US$)	Frequency
OMAN	Al Omaneya	News	21,500	/	429	Weekly
	Oman	News	10,500	/	859	Weekly
QATAR	Akhbar Al Ousbou (A)	Pan Arab news	21,000	5,000	485	Weekly
	Al Adh	General news	15,000	11,000	567	/
	Al Jawhara (A)	Women	23,000	10,000	567	Monthly
	Al Ouraba (A)	General interest	35,000	19,000	408	Weekly
	Al Saquer (Al) Riyadhi	Sports	5,000	3,000	Non-commercial	.
	Al Vmmah (A)	General interest	80,000	/	386	Monthly
	Al Mourshed (A/E)	Maps, guides	5,000	/	794	Bi-monthly
	Diaruna Wal Alam (A/E)	Energy, oil, gas	5,000	/	Non-commercial	Monthly
	This is Qatar	Local business	10,000	/	970	Bi-monthly
SAUDI ARABIA	Majalla	Social/political	172,000	10,800	5,734	/
	Al Sharq Al Awsat	General	184,000	31,700	4,667	/
	Sayidati	Women	154,000	17,900	5,000	/
	Oqraa	Social/political	45,000	3,300	2,000	/
	Baseem	Children	34,000		2,134	/
	Al yaahmah	Social/political	40,000	4,700	2,400	/
	Ahlan Wasahlan	Leisure & holiday	150,000	40,000	5,915	/
U.A.E	Arriyadan Walschabab	Sports/social	66,000	117,000	1,335	Weekly
	Zahrat Al Khaleej	Socio Feminine	69,000	186,000	1,144	Weekly
	Htatt Annas	Feminine	35,000	/	1,989	Monthly
	Al Sahruq	Political	n/a	/	2,800	Weekly
	What's On	General interest	22,000	53,000	1,022	Monthly
	Emirates Woman	Women	8,000	/	1,090	Quarterly
	Gulf Weekly	General interest	43,000	242,000	1,022	Weekly
	Weekend	General interest	46,600	250,000	1,158	Weekly
	Gulf Commercial	Business	5,000		625	Monthly
	Trade & Industry	Business	5,000	34,000	1,090	Weekly
	U.A.E. Digest	Business		10,000	/	Monthly

*Data on Israel and Jordan not available.

Appendix 5: Country Profiles

	Bahrain	Egypt	Israel
		Social aspects	
Total population	503,000 (Mar 1993)	55,000,000 (Mar 1993)	4,837,000 (Mar 1993)
Urban population (% of total)	83	46.7	91.6
% by sex: male, female	Nationals 50%, 50% (1992) Non-national 68%, 32%	51%, 49% (1992)	n/a
Official population projections	601,000 (1995) 682,000 (2000) 823,000 (2010)	60,470,000 (1995) 66,710,000 (2000) 78,456,000 (2010)	7,920,000 (1995) 5,280,000 (2000) 6,009,000 (2010)
Life expectancy	71.9 yrs. (1990–95 proj.)	63.1 yrs. (1990–95 proj.)	76.3 yrs. (1990–95 proj.)
Population projections by age	**1995** **2000**	**1995** **2000**	**1995** **2000**
0–14 years	31.9% 29.6%	39.0% 35.8%	29.1% 27.5%
15–64 years	66% 68.2%	57.0% 60.0%	62.2% 63.9%
65+ years	2.1% 2.2%	4.0% 4.2%	8.7% 8.6%
Total households	108,000 (Mar 1993)	6,667,000 (Mar 1993)	1,248,000 (Mar 1993)
Average household size	3.5 (Mar 1993)	5.5 (Mar 1993)	4.9 (Mar 1993)
Home ownership level	67% (1985)	n/a	72% (1985)
Literacy rate	n/a	45%	n/a
Durables ownership (% households)	Car: 77% Phone: 97%	Car: n/a Phone: n/a	Car: n/a Phone: n/a
Media penetration (1992):			
TV households	115,000 (Mar 1993)	4,300,000 (Mar 1993)	1,175,000 (Mar 1993)
Cable penetration	n/a	n/a	25–30% linked to private cable TV
Satellite: # channels	2 satellite channels	n/a	n/a
Viewers	227,000 adults	n/a	n/a
Star TV penetration	0 homes (Mar 1993)	500 homes (Mar 1993)	460,000 homes
MBC penetration	65,000 homes	n/a	n/a
Remarks	Recently, Star TV joined Bahrain TV to use "Split Run" advertising		n/a
VCR penetration (by total households)	70%	7%	91.6%

Appendix 5 (cont'd)

	Bahrain	Egypt	Israel
Economic			
Monetary unit	Bahraini Dinar (BD)	Egyptian Pound (LE) LE	New Shekel (NIS) = 100 Argot
Exchange rate	BD 0.38 per US$ (1991)	3.32 per US$ (Jan 1992)	NIS 2.3734 per US$ (May 1992)
Gross National Product (US$)	2.912 billion (1988)	34.22 billion (1991)	38 billion (1989)
Per capita (US$)	6,054 (1988)	665 (1988)	8,422 (1989)
Gross Domestic Product (US$)	3.61 billion (1991)	29.9 billion (1991)	51.2 billion (1990)
Per capita (US$)	6,940 (1991)	615 (1991)	10,622 (1990)
Per household (US$)	25,522	4,142 (Mar 1993)	22,197 (Mar 1993)
Growth	8%(1991)	2.3% (1991)	5% (1990)
Inflation	3% (1991)	20% (1991)	18% (1990)
Economic forecasts			
GDP growth	2.5% (1994), 1% (1995)	2.3% (1994), 1.3% (1995)	7% (1994), 2.9% (1995)
H/H growth	3.8% (1994), 2% (1994)	2.2% (1994), 2.2% (1994)	4.4% (1994), 4.4% (1995)
Inflation	n/a	18% (1993–1997)	15.0% (1993–1997)
Labor force indicators (total)	74,000 (1987)	13,273,000 (1985)	1,494,100 (1987)
Unemployment rate	n/a	6% (1990)	n/a
Cultural			
Predominant language	Arabic (official), Eng. (commerce)	Arabic	Hebrew (primary), Arabic and English
Literacy rate national language	60%	45%	
Literacy rate in English	20–25%	3%	
% ethnic groups	Bahrain's 63%, Asian 13%, other Arab 10%, Iranian 8%, Other 6%	Eastern Hametic 90%, other 10% (including Greek, Italian, Syro-Lebanese)	Jewish 83%, non-Jewish (mainly Arab) 17%
% religious groups	Shiite Moslem 70%, Sunni Moslem 30%	Sunni Moslem 94%, Coptic Christian & Other 6%	Jewish 83%, Moslem (mostly Sunni) 13.1%, Christian 2.3%, Druze (Moslem) 1.6%

	Jordan	Kuwait	Lebanon
Social aspects			
Total population	3,900,000 (Mar 1993)	2,143,000 (Mar 1993)	2,800,00 (Mar 1993)

Appendix 5 (cont'd)

	Jordan	Kuwait	Lebanon
		Social aspects	
% by sex: male, female	n/a	Nationals 49%, 51% Non-nationals 60%, 40%	48%, 52% (1992)
Urban population (% of total)	61% (1990 est.)	95.6% (1990 est.)	83.74%
Official population projections	5,218,000 (1995) 6,329,000 (2000) 8,941,000 (2010)	2,438,000 (1995) 2,782,000 (2000) 3,451,000 (2010)	3,286,000 (1995) 3,603,000 (2000) 4,170,000 (2010)
Life expectancy	67.9 yrs. (1990–95 proj.)	73.9 yrs. (1990–95 proj.)	68.5 yrs. (1990–95 proj.)
Population projections by age	**1995 2000**	**1995 2000**	**1995 2000**
0–14 years	48.5% 48.5%	36.8% 34.7%	34.7% 33.7%
15–64 years	49.0% 49.0%	61.4% 62.8%	59.8% 60.6%
65+ years	2.5% 2.5%	1.8% 2.5%	5.5% 5.7%
Total households	523,000 (Mar 1993)	227,000 (Mar 1993)	583,000 (Mar 1993)
Average household size	6.5 (Mar 1993)	6.5 (Mar 1993)	4.8 (Mar 1993)
Home ownership level	66%	/	36%
Literacy rate	80%	71% (1990)	75%
Durables ownership (% house holds)	n/a	n/a	n/a
Media penetration (1992)			
TV households	285,000 (Mar 1993)	225,000 (Mar 1993)	560,000 (Mar 1993)
Cable penetration	n/a	n/a	n/a
Satellite: # channels	n/a	3 (2 com., 1 non-com.)	n/a
Viewers	n/a	550,000 adults	
Star TV penetration	1,000 homes (Mar 1993)	17,500 homes (Mar 1993)	2,000 homes (Mar 1993)
MBC penetration		200,000	
Remarks		Kuwait Space Channel (KSC), controlled by Ministry of Information; main purpose to support national cause	
VCR penetration (by total households)	35.8% + (1993 est.)	90%	66% + (1993 est.)

Appendix 5 (cont'd)

	Jordan	Kuwait	Lebanon
Economic			
Monetary unit	Jord. Dinar (JD = 1000 fils)	Ku Dinar (KD = 1000 fils)	Leban. Pound (LL) = 100 piastres
Exchange rate	JD 0.64 per US $	KD 0.295 per US$ (9/92)	LL 828 per US $ (12/90)
Gross National Product (US$)	3.819 billion (1989)	31.3525 billion (1989)	6.05 billion (1990)
Per capita (US$)	931 (1989)	15,500 (1989)	2,292 (1984)
Social aspects			
Gross Domestic Product (US$)	4.3 billion (1991 est.)	23.1 billion (89), 13.3 billion (90)	3.6 billion (1990)
Per capita (US$)	950 (1991 est.)	12,500 (Jun 1990)	1,000 (1989)
Per household (US$)	6,650 (Mar 1993)	40,000 (Mar 1993)	6,000 (Mar 1993)
Growth	1% (1991 est.)	11% (Jan–Jun 1990)	0% (1990)
Inflation	5% (1991 est.)	2% (1990)	60% (1990)
Economic forecasts			
GDP growth	3% (1994), 1.6 (1995)	8.7% (1994), 3.7% (1995)	8.2% (1994), 4.3% (1995)
H/H growth	4% (199$), 3.2 (1995)	4.2% (1994), 2% (1995)	4.1% (1994), 3.0% (1995)
Inflation	n/a	10% (1993–1997)	n/a
Labor force indicators (total)	446,300 (1979)	670,400 (1985)	n/a
Unemployment rate	n/a	4.2% nationals	n/a
Cultural			
Predominant language	Arabic	Arabic	Lebanese
Literacy rate national language	n/a	86%	85%
Literacy rate English	n/a	70%	50%
% ethnic groups	Arab 98%, Circassian 1%, Armenian 1%	Ku 27.9%, Other Arab 39%, South Asian 9%, Iranian 4%, Other 20.1%	Lebanese 93%, Armenian 5%, Other 2%
% religious groups	Sunni Moslem 92%, Christian 8%	Sunni Moslem 45%, Shiite Moslem 30%, other Moslem 10%, Christian Hindu, Parsi & Other 15%	Moslem & Druze 57%, Christian (mostly Catholic) 42%, Other 1%

Appendix 5 (cont'd)

	Oman	Qatar	Saudi Arabia
		Social aspects	
Total population	2,000,000 (Mar 1993)	387,000 (Mar 1993)	12,000,000
% by sex: male, female	Nationals 51%, 49% (1992) Non-nationals 81%, 19%	Nationals 50%, 50% (1992) Non-nationals 67%, 33%	55%, 45% (1992)
Urban population (% of total)	10.6%	89.65 (1990)	77.3%
Official population projections	1,735,000 (1995) 2,057,000 (2000) 2,772,000 (2010)	426,000 (1995) 499,000 (2000) 632,000 (2010)	17,118,000 (1995) 20,686,000 (2000) 29,551,000 (2010)
Life expectancy	58.4 yrs. (1990–95 proj.)	70.8 yrs. (1990–95 proj.)	65.8 yrs. (1990–95 proj.)
Population projections by age	1995 2000	1995 2000	1995 2000
0–14 years	46.0% 45.9%	36.1% 3.0%	45.4% 45.7%
15–64 years	51.3% 51.3%	61.5% 62.4%	52.0% 51.7%
65+ years	2.7% 2.8%	2.4% 3.0%	2.6% 2.6%
Total households	308,000 (Mar 1993)	100,000 (Mar 1993)	5,642,000 (Mar 1993)
Average household size	6.5 (Mar 1993)	2.2 (Mar 1993)	9.2 (Mar 1993)
Home ownership level	n/a	n/a	n/a
Literacy rate	10% (1990)	50% (1990)	62% (1991)
Durables ownership (% households)	n/a	n/a	n/a
Media penetration (1992):			
TV households	277,000 (Mar 1993)	95,000 (Mar) 1993	3,950,000 (Mar 1993)
Cable penetration	n/a	n/a	n/a
Satellite: # channels	n/a	2 (commercial)	none, but foreign transmission received
Viewers	n/a	n/a	n/a
Star TV penetration	13,000 homes (Mar 1993)	0 homes (Mar 1993)	300,000 homes (Mar 1993)
MBC penetration	n/a	53,000 homes	n/a
Remarks	n/a	New satellite entrants (e.g., MBC, Star TV) making forays in Arabia peninsula	
VCR penetration (by total households)	78%	70%	80%

Appendix 5 (cont'd)

	Oman	Qatar	Saudi Arabia
Economic			
Monetary unit	OM Riv. (RO = 1000 biaza)	Qatari Rival (QR)	Saudi Rival (SR)
Exchange rate	RO 0.38 per US$ (12/90)	QR 3.61 per US$ (12/90)	SR 3.75 per US$ (91)
Gross National Product (US$)	10.6 billion (1990)	4.12 billion (1988)	86.90 billion (1989)
Per capita (US$)	7,100 (1990)	12,118 (1988)	6,020 (1989)
Growth	9.9% (1990)		
Gross Domestic Product (US$)	8.402 billion (1990)	6.7 billion (1989)	106 billion (1991)
Per capita (US$)	5,170 (1989)	15,800 (1989)	7,180 (1991)
Per household (US$)	25,525 (Mar 1993)	34,835 (Mar 1993)	20,000 (Mar 1993)
Growth	n/a	n/a	3% (1991)
Inflation	10.4%	n/a	3%
Economic forecasts			
GDP growth	−2.8% (1994), −6.1% (1995)	10.1% (1994), 4.1% (1995)	9.5% (1994), 4.8% (1995)
Household growth	3.8% (1994), 2.9% (1995)	4.2% (1994), 3.6% (1995)	3.8% (1994), 3.8% (1995)
Inflation	7.5% (1993–97)	n/a	3.5% (1993–97)
Labor force indicators (total)	n/a	n/a	2,751,000
Unemployment rate	3.6%	n/a	n/a
Cultural			
Predominant language	Arabic	Arabic	Arabic
Literacy rate national language	n/a	60%	70%
Literacy rate English language	n/a	25%	60%
% ethnic groups	Arabs 88%, Baluchi 4%, Persian 3%, Indian 2%, African 2%, Other 1%	Arabs 40%, Pakistanis 18%, Indians 18%, Iranian 10%, Other 14%	Saudis 70%, Other Arabs 10%, South East Asians 5%, Anglo Saxons 10%, Africans 5%
% religious groups	Ibadhi Moslem 75%, Sunni Moslem, Shiite Moslem, and Hindu 25%	Moslem 95%	Sunni Moslem 85%, Shiite Moslem 15%

United Arab Emirates

Social aspects

Total population	1,900,000 (Mar 1993)
% by sex: male, female	Nationals 50%, 50% (1992) Non-nationals 66%, 34%
Urban population (% of total)	77.8%
Population projections by age	1995 2000
0–14 years	29.1% 27.1%
15–64 years	68.7% 69.8%
65+ years	2.2% 3.1%
Total households	350,000 (Mar 1993)
Average household size	4.7 (Mar 1993)
Home ownership level	12%
Literacy rate	53.5%–68%
Durables ownership (% household)	Car 65%, Phone 64%, Washers 93%

Economic

Monetary unit	Dirham
Exchange rate	Dirham 3.671 per US$ (fixed since 1988)
Gross National Product (US$)	27.76 billion (1989)
Per capita (US$)	17,959 (1989)
Gross Domestic Product (US$)	35 billion (1991)
Per capita (US$)	18,400 (1991)
Per household (US$)	60,000 (Mar 1993)
Growth	–2%
Inflation	9% (1991)
Economic forecasts	
GDP growth	23.5% (1994), 7.5% (1995)
Household growth	4.1% (1994), 3.5% (1995)
Inflation	7.0% (1993–97)
Labor force indicators (total)	560,000 (1980)
Unemployment rate	9%

Cultural

Predominant language	Arabic
Literacy rate national language	75.5%
Literacy rate English language	n/a
% ethnic groups	Emirian 19%, Other Arabic 23%, South Asian 50%, Other 8%

Media penetration (1992):

TV households	315,000 (Mar 1993)
Cable penetration	Feasibility study conducted by U.S. firm early 1990
Satellite: # channels	2 (commercial)
Viewers	n/a
Star TV penetration	100,000 homes (Mar 1993)

Appendix 5 (cont'd)

	United Arab Emirates		
	Social aspects	Religious groups	Cultural
Media penetration (1992):			
MBC penetration	n/a		Moslem 96%, Christian, Hindu, Other 4%
Remarks	New satellite entrants like MBC and Star TV making forays in the Arabia peninsula. A buoyant audio visual medium might become a dominant audio visual buy in a TV mix strategy. All satellite-imported programs and commercials are confined to domestic law.		
VCR penetration (by total households/ (by TV households)	78% / 84%		

Map of Pakistan

Pakistan Overview[1]

Background. Pakistan has a land area of 803,940 sq. km. and a 1,046-kilometer coastline on the Arabian Sea. It is bounded by India in the east, China in the northeast, Afghanistan in the northwest, Iran in the west. Pakistan is divided into four provinces: Punjab, Sind, Baluchistan and the Northwest Frontier Province (Peshawar); it also controls a portion of the Indian states of Jammu and Kashmir. The 134.2 million population comprising Punjabi, Sindhi, Pashtun (Pathan), Baloch and Muhajir adhere to Islam (97%) (Sunni: 77%, Shiite: 20%); others follow Christianity, Hindu and other religions. Languages are Punjabi (48.2%), Sindhi (11.8%), Pashtu (13.1%), Balochi and others (9%); Urdu (7.6%) and English are the official languages. Major cities are (million): Karachi (9.9), Lahore (5.1), Faisalabad (1.9), Rawalpindi (0.93); the capital is Islamabad. The climate is mostly hot, dry desert; temperate in the northwest; arctic in the north; temperatures average 15°C (January) to 37°C (May to July); monsoon season is from mid-July to September.

Under Pakistan's constitution, the president, a Muslim, is head of state and must be elected (five-year term) by a joint session of both houses of the Federal Legislature and the four provincial assemblies. The president has certain exclusive powers such as appointment of the Chief Justice, heads of the armed forces and provincial governors; the country's chief executive is the prime minister who governs under a parliamentary system. The bicameral Federal Legislature (parliament or Majlis-e-Shoora) comprises a 217-member National Assembly (lower house) and an 87-member Senate (upper house); 10 of 217 National Assembly seats are reserved for non-Muslim minorities, 20 seats for women selected by elected members. Legislation originating in either house must be approved by the president. Each province has a legislative assembly and presidentially appointed governor. The Supreme Court is final authority in a judicial system comprising high courts in each province and subordinate district and sessions courts. The legal system is mainly based on the English Common Law with provisions to accommodate Pakistan's status as an Islamic state (e.g., the Federal Shari'a Court enforces traditional Islamic law). Recently, Islamic Law has been taking precedence over the Common Law in several areas (e.g., women's rights).

Political. The Islamic Republic of Pakistan became independent in 1947 when Britain partitioned India in response to massive public pressure to create a separate Muslim

---

[1] Islamic Republic of Pakistan.

state. The first free elections were held in 1970; Ali Bhutto's Pakistan People's Party (PPP) dominated the west; Sheikh Mujibur Rehman's Awami League swept the east. In March 1971, East Pakistan seceded to become Bangladesh. In 1977, Bhutto was deposed by Gen. Zia-ul-Haq; he was hanged (1979), charged with abetting a political opponent's murder. In 1988, a plane carrying President Zia crashed under suspicious circumstances. Democracy returned to Pakistan in 1988 when the PPP won a legislative majority and Benazir Bhutto (Bhutto's daughter) was appointed prime minister, the first female minister in an Islamic country. Bhutto lost power in the early 1990s, but returned to power in 1993.

In recent years, Pakistan's relations with India have deteriorated as conflicts over Kashmir continue to surface. In an effort to win support, Pakistan has sought to internationalize the Kashmir conflict and has mounted a campaign against Indian human rights abuses in the state. Open militancy by both nations remains a major source of tension. This tension increased markedly in May 1998 when Pakistan conducted nuclear tests in retaliation for similar tests conducted by India.

Social. Pakistan has a low literacy rate (38%) (1995) and high infant mortality rate (97 per 1,000) (1996). Life expectancy at birth is 62 years (1996); Pakistan has a relatively young population, 41% under 15 years. Education and health expenditures are low, together accounting for only 3% of total government expenditures.

Pakistani society is split along ethnic, tribal, caste and economic lines, all of which impact daily life. The five major ethnic groups reveal a mix of Arab, Mongol, Indian and European features; all ethnic groups (particularly the smaller ones) are slightly suspicious of the majority Punjabis (50%–60% of the population). The class system is a legacy of the Hindu tradition; Pakistanis are very class-conscious.

In recent years, Karachi (former capital and business center) has suffered a wave of terrorism blamed on Indian Muslim immigrants (Muhajirs) who settled in Sind cities following partition. Militant threats and army crackdowns have affected business, and many people and businesses have left Karachi for Lahore.

Pakistan's efforts to stabilize the political situation in neighboring Afghanistan has had severe consequences: in particular, increased numbers of Afghan refugees put pressure on an already fragile economy and arms and ammunition supply (especially in Peshawar) and drug trafficking cause problems.

Economy. Pakistan is a member of the United Nations (UN), World Bank (WB), International Monetary Fund (IMF), World Trade Organization (WTO), Asian Development Bank (ADB) and Islamic Development Bank (IDB). Pakistan is a developing country, per capita GNP US$465. In the late 1980s, the economy grew on average 6% p.a. but slowed to 3% p.a. in the early 1990s largely because of high debt service and defense spending, together amounting to almost two thirds of the government budget. In 1994, the budget deficit was 26.4% of total expenditure; to comply with IMF conditions, the deficit was reduced to 5.4% of GDP in 1994 (down from 7.9% [1993]). Labor force distribution was 1994: agriculture (47.6%); manufacturing (including mining, quarrying) (18.9%), other (36%). Pakistan is largely an agricultural country; almost 60% of exports are directly or indirectly derived from cotton. In 1995, major export destinations were: U.S. (16.8%), Hong Kong (6.3%), Japan (5.7%). Major import origins were: Japan (9.5%), Malaysia (9.1%), Germany (6.7%), Britain (5.1%), U.S. (4.2%).

Pakistan seeks foreign investment. A new (1989) Board of Investment (BOI), headed by the prime minister, was charged to cut red tape and make decisions on investment applications in 45 days. In 1991, a major economic reform package lifted all controls on foreign exchange movement in Pakistan and on repatriation of private and corporate profits and capital. The Investment Promotion Board (1992), established 12 additional industrial investment zones (IIZ) with favorable tax status. Privatization is ongoing (from 1991); by June 1994, 65 of 118 state-owned factories were sold.

The Pakistan rupee (PR) became fully convertible on July 1, 1994; in early 1996, the exchange rate was 34 PR = US$1 (November 1994, 30 PR = US$1). A tight monetary policy has been implemented to control inflation (1994, 11.5%). Despite decreasing tax revenues, since 1991, the budget deficit has declined as a percentage of GDP but the 4% target for 1994/1995 was not achieved.

The State Bank of Pakistan (the central bank) implements government monetary policies; the Pakistan Banking Council acts as watchdog over the banking system. Before 1991, all domestic banks (except a few locally incorporated private investment banks) were state-owned;[2] in recent years, some banks (e.g., 51% of the Muslim Commercial Bank [MCB] was sold to 12 local companies; a majority of shares of Allied Bank were offered to employees) were returned to private sector ownership. The new liberalized banking system allows Pakistanis to open foreign currency accounts with local banks; unrestricted conversion of any amount of foreign exchange is permitted. About 23 foreign banks operate in Pakistan, mainly focused on foreign trade financing; they must operate according to Islamic banking rules but are subject to the same credit constraints and reserves as domestic banks.

Pakistan has three stock exchanges (i.e., Karachi, Lahore, Islamabad [opened 1992]); the Karachi Stock Exchange (KSE) is the most important. Removal of exchange controls boosted KSE average daily share turnover to 9 million from 3.3 million. In 1994, market capitalization reached US$13 billion.

Infrastructure. Pakistan has a 171,000-kilometer road network (35% of good quality). The 805 kilometers Karakorum Highway permits entry to northern areas (including China's Xinjiang province [northwest]), otherwise accessible only by four-wheel drive or goat caravan. The railway system is extensive (8,850 kilometers of track) but has changed little since British rule; it is slow and somewhat dilapidated. The main route runs from Karachi to Peshawar, passing through Lahore and Rawalpindi. Following privatization and deregulation (commenced late 1993), the

---

[2] The government nationalized all private banks and insurance companies in the early 1970s; subsequently all important industries were also nationalized. In this process, firms with foreign shareholdings were exempt from acquisition.

major state-owned Pakistan International Airlines (PIA) competes with private airlines on domestic and international routes.

Pakistan is energy deficient. In 1992, electric power generation (including one nuclear power plant) was 43 billion kWh, 350 kWh per capita. By early 1995, Pakistan's power generation capacity was about 11,200 megawatts (MW), a 2,000 MW shortage; an additional 54,000 megawatts are needed in the next two decades. Investments in the power sector are estimated to reach $3 billion by 1998; by early 1995, 30 projects under consideration would develop 7,000 MW.

Pakistan's major port facilities are in Karachi; it intends to expand its new Port Qasim (in the Arabian Sea) into a major deep-sea port. The domestic telephone system is poor (less than 20 telephones per 1,000 persons); international telecommunication is better and employs microwave radio and satellite relay. Privatization of the country's telephone company, the Pakistan Telecommunications Corporation, began in August 1994.

Statistics*	June 1991	June 1997	Statistics*	June 1991	June 1997
Per capita GNP	US$365	US$465	Infant mortality/1,000	98	97
GDP growth	5.6%	6.1%	Life expectancy (yrs)	n/a	62
Savings (GNP)	n/a	12%	Literacy rate	25.6%	37.8%
Inflation (CPI)	6.0%	13.8%	People per tel.	159	56.1
Foreign debt (in billion)	US$19.5	US$30.2	People per doctor	2,086	2,000
Pop. (million)	114.8	134.2	People per TV	n/a	45.2
Urban pop.	n/a	35%	Calorie intake (cals)	n/a	2,377
Pop. growth	2.9%	2.9%			

*Secured from *Asiaweek*.

Case 30

Allied Marketing (Private) Ltd., Lahore

Irfan Amir, Wasim Azhar
Lahore University of Management Sciences, Lahore

Since January 1992, Ahmad Hasnain, Director of Allied Marketing (Private) Ltd. (AML), one of the Lahore distributors of Pakistan Tobacco Company Ltd. (PTC), was under constant pressure from PTC to increase sales. During the past few years, AML sales of PTC brands had shown signs of stagnation, and PTC management wanted AML to increase sales force size to boost sales. However, Hasnain was not certain such an increase would improve company profits. He was also concerned about the effect an increase in sales force size would have on average salesman compensation. In June 1992, Hasnain decided to make a detailed assessment of the optimal sales force size for PTC distribution.

Another issue occupying Hasnain's attention was reducing his company's dependence on the wholesaler. By December 1991, after considerable effort, only 90% of PTC brands' distribution was through the wholesaler; the remaining went through retailers. Hasnain treated the wholesaler as a "necessary evil," but wished to reduce AML's dependence even further. However, as with the sales force size issue, Hasnain knew there were tradeoffs to be made. Less wholesaler dependence would minimize the adverse effect of some wholesaler practices on AML's trade, but significant costs would be incurred in increasing retail distribution channel penetration. Hasnain wondered how far wholesaler dependence should be reduced.

ജ്ഞാ

Background

Originally founded as a chinaware business in 1898 by Hasnain's great grandfather, what became S.M. Ilyas and Sons was granted the agency business (1905) for Scissors brand cigarettes for the entire Punjab province by Bakhsh Elahi and Company, Delhi, the sole agent of the Imperial Tobacco Company Ltd. of India. In 1914, it secured distribution of Sunlight soap for the Lahore market from Lever Brothers; subsequently it added other Lever products (e.g., soap, toiletries, vegetable oil) and, in 1927, several Imperial Tobacco brands. After independence (1947), both Imperial Tobacco Company

481

and Lever Brothers, trading as Pakistan Tobacco Company Ltd. (PTC) and Lever Brothers Pakistan Ltd. (LBP) respectively, established separate distribution arrangements in Pakistan.[1] S.M. Ilyas and Sons handled distribution for both companies. However, over the years, the area assigned for distribution decreased as the result of population increases, changes in manufacturer policies regarding coverage and productivity.

S.M. Ilyas and Sons had also managed distribution for several other popular products and international firms in Lahore: Lipton Tea, Ovaltine, Abbott Pharmaceuticals, ICI Pharmaceuticals, Pakistan Industrial Development Corporation (PIDC) cement and fertilizer and Fauji Cereals. However, distribution for these products and organizations had ceased as the result of policy changes by the manufacturers and / or S.M. Ilyas and Sons.

In 1984, S.M. Ilyas and Sons was divided into two companies: Allied Marketing (Private) Ltd. (AML) and United Marketing Ltd. (UML). AML was given distribution rights for part of the Lahore market by PTC. (UML was assigned distribution of PTC brands for part of the Lahore market not covered by AML.) Distribution of all LBP products for part of the Lahore market was also given to AML. Two separate sales departments, headed by sales managers, were developed for PTC and LBP (Figure 1). AML management concentrated on developing its allotted sales territory, especially new areas like Defense, Faisal Town and Green Town.

In 1992, AML handled distribution for part of the Lahore market for all products and brands of PTC, LBP and Mohsin Matches (MM). Distribution of MM was awarded in 1988; salesmen for PTC brands carried MM cartons on field visits. According to Hasnain, match distribution used minimal warehouse space and other resources. The total cost of supporting the sales force (including salesmen salaries and commission, vehicles and other direct selling expenses) for distribution of LBP products was shared equally by AML and LBP. However, for PTC brands, all selling costs were borne by AML.[2]

PTC Distribution

PTC sold all its brands including Gold Leaf, Capstan, Wills, Player's No. 6, Gold Flake, Embassy and Scissors entirely through distributors. PTC had three distributors for the Lahore market: AML, UML and Fair Marketing Ltd. (FML). In 1991, market share by volume of these distributors was: AML, 37%, UML, 33%, FML, 30%.

As a PTC distributor, AML worked on commission. AML's main responsibilities were: proper market coverage; achieving sales targets; providing distribution logistics such as godown (warehousing) and vehicles; and maintaining a trained and motivated sales force. PTC was responsible for product quality, advertising and promotion, pricing and safeguarding AML against trade malpractice such as cross-territory sales

---

[1] In August 1947, the Indian subcontinent was divided into two sovereign states, India and Pakistan. Later, East Pakistan became Bangladesh.
[2] Selling costs did not include advertising and promotion costs; all such costs were borne by PTC.

Figure 1: Organization Chart (December 1991)

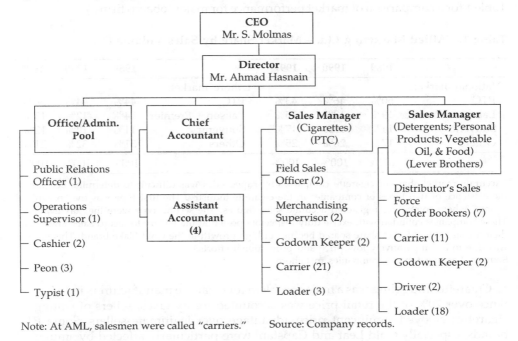

```
                          CEO
                       Mr. S. Molmas

                        Director
                     Mr. Ahmad Hasnain
```

Office/Admin. Pool	Chief Accountant	Sales Manager (Cigarettes) (PTC)	Sales Manager (Detergents; Personal Products; Vegetable Oil, & Food) (Lever Brothers)
Public Relations Officer (1)		Field Sales Officer (2)	Distributor's Sales Force (Order Bookers) (7)
Operations Supervisor (1)	Assistant Accountant (4)	Merchandising Supervisor (2)	Carrier (11)
Cashier (2)		Godown Keeper (2)	Godown Keeper (2)
Peon (3)		Carrier (21)	Driver (2)
Typist (1)		Loader (3)	Loader (18)

Note: At AML, salesmen were called "carriers."   Source: Company records.

and smuggling. Cross-territory sales was a major problem.[3] If a distributor whose territory had been infiltrated obtained proof, such as cash memos, he could complain to the manufacturer.

PTC put significant pressure on distributors to meet sales targets. According to Hasnain, though the primary basis of distributor performance evaluation was sales volume, other criteria included target market coverage and maintenance of adequate stock levels.

Open price competition among distributors did not occur as prices were set by PTC. However, according to Hasnain, the distributor who operated in the cigarette "mandi,"[4] delivered products to wholesalers at rates lower than PTC's scheduled wholesale rates. This practice was a concern for PTC's other two distributors. PTC knew of this practice but was unable to eliminate or reduce it due to difficulty in securing proof of cut-rate deliveries. Salesmen using this practice issued cash memos at the scheduled selling price but passed discounts "under the counter."

A second level of competition was distributors of other tobacco companies. PTC competed with Lakson Tobacco Company, Premier Tobacco Industries, Souvenir Tobacco Company, Saleem Cigarette Industries, Sarhad Cigarette Industries and

---

[3] One distributor making sales in another distributor's territory.
[4] A wholesale market.

United Tobacco Industries.[5] All these manufacturers sold through distributors. (See Table 1 for a comparison of market performance for major tobacco firms.)

Table 1: Allied Marketing Ltd. – Market Share by Sales Volume (%)

	1989	1990	1991		1989	1990	1991
National market:				Lahore market:			
PTC	50%	46%	43%	PTC	44%	44%	54%*
Lakson + Premier	19%	13%	15%	Lakson + Premier	14%	12%	13%
Souvenir	14%	15%	17%	Souvenir	11%	12%	12%
Others	17%	26%	25%	Others	31%	32%	21%
	100%	100%	100%		100%	100%	100%

*Accurate market share of cigarette companies by rupee sales was difficult to determine because of the existence of two types of companies in the cigarette industry. The first type was the "organized sector," where companies registered accurate sales figures. The second type were the "tax evaders." These companies colluded with excise duty inspectors posted at the factory to record sales lower than their actual value. Market share soared because of high growth in the Gold Flake brand. This growth was due to a comparatively low price and promotional efforts.
Sources: Leading tobacco companies in Lahore.

Cigarette smuggling was a major problem for cigarette manufacturers in Pakistan. Since over 70% of the retail price was accounted for by taxes, sellers of smuggled cigarettes enjoyed significant price advantage over legitimate sellers. Some PTC brands, especially Gold Leaf and Capstan, were particularly affected by smuggled brands such as Dunhill, Rothmans, Marlboro, Benson and Hedges, State Express 555 and some Japanese brands (especially Mild Seven). According to Hasnain, the industry had lobbied the government to stop the flow of smuggled brands but to no avail. Although the government had once announced a fine of Rs 5,000 for trading in foreign cigarettes, lack of enforcement allowed smuggled cigarettes to be widely available on the open market. According to one cigarette industry estimate, in 1990, distributors lost 20% of higher-priced brand sales to smuggled cigarettes.

The Sales Force

Salesmen Compensation

By 1990, AML increased its PTC sales force size from 14 salesmen (carriers) in 1986, to 21. During this period, total sales territory remained the same, but was reorganized to accommodate the additional salesmen. As a result, average carrier compensation dropped. By late 1990, carriers expressed serious concern about the decrease in take-home pay. AML decided to review the carrier compensation system and claims made by carriers regarding decline in take-home pay were evaluated (Table 2). Sales-

---

[5] Lakson Tobacco Company and Premier Tobacco Industries had been under single management since 1986. The new company was called the Lakson Premier Group.

men's total take-home had two components: "token money" and commission. Each carrier was paid a fixed sum of Rs 500 per month token money, plus commission. Commission rates varied by brand.

According to the Labor Laws, employers had extensive obligations for regular employees. AML had a legal agreement with the carriers stipulating that they were not AML employees. Rather, they acted as carriers with limited AML obligations. The agreement stated that carriers were only entitled to commission. There was no mention of any fixed token money; legally, token money could be treated as a salary.

Table 2:   Monthly Average Compensation by Carrier (rupees)

Year	Number of DD* carriers	Monthly average compensation per carrier
1986	14	2,786
1987	15	2,472
1988	18	2,292
1989	21	2,003
1990	21	2,346

*Direct delivery.
Source: Company records.

In early 1991, AML abolished token money and increased carriers' commission rates. Different commission rates were set across carriers for the same brand based on factors such as carrier seniority and brand potential in the area. Management believed this change was necessary as it relieved AML of the obligation to pay carriers a fixed monthly amount. Management also believed the increase in commission rates would raise both carriers' average commission and AML sales. Average monthly compensation for carriers increased from Rs 2,346 in 1990 to Rs 2,688 in 1991.

In addition to commission payments, two incentive schemes operated at AML. First, a fixed sum of money, typically Rs 0.50, was paid for each productive sales call. The objective of this incentive was to increase brand availability, particularly for new brands. Second, incentives were given to carriers who exceeded sales targets. Performance above allocated sales targets for all 21 carriers was ranked each month and cash awards given to the top three positions. Monthly sales targets for carriers were set by adding one percentage point to the previous three months' average performance. Some adjustments were made for seasonal and market trends in cigarette sales.

Optimal Sales Force Size

Having restructured carriers' compensation system, Hasnain was not sure AML had the optimal number of salesmen. Since he was under constant pressure from PTC to increase the number of carriers, ideally, he wanted to identify the sales force level that would achieve three objectives simultaneously: higher sales, higher profits and higher average carrier compensation. In an attempt to determine the optimal number of carriers, Hasnain asked his sales manager to gather data about sales territories, carrier performance and selling costs (Exhibits 1 to 5).

The Wholesale-retail Split

AML distributed PTC cigarettes through two main distribution channels, retailers and wholesalers. Retail channels included direct delivery (DD) outlets, army canteens and outlets in villages. Through considerable effort, by December 1991, Hasnain had managed to achieve about 80% distribution through the retail channel and 20% through the wholesale channel (Exhibit 6). Retail market coverage was achieved by increasing the direct delivery sales force. Only one salesman was used for the wholesale trade. Hasnain wondered whether or not he could eliminate the wholesaler from his distribution network.

Hasnain also felt strongly about two specific wholesaler malpractices. First, PTC scheduled rates were not stable; the wholesaler engaged in cut-rate selling by offering products to retailers at rates lower than PTC's scheduled prices. Second, "cross-territory" sales took place through the wholesale trade.

While Hasnain was critical of these activities, he acknowledged that increasing retail channel emphasis was not easy. Retailers were inclined to contact wholesalers because of the lower rates, availability of different brands, credit facilities and longer wholesaler working hours. Hasnain remarked:

> To cater to retail trade is tough in that you need more resources such as carriers and vehicles, and the overheads are high. However, retail margins are better than wholesale margins and perhaps it is worth the extra effort required to manage the retail trade. (See Exhibit 7 for margins by channel member.)

Hasnain wondered whether or not, and to what extent, he could bypass the wholesaler.

Exhibit 1: Monthly Average Sales by Carrier (1991) ('000 rupees)

S. No	Carrier	Monthly average	S. No	Carrier	Monthly average
1	Abdul Razzak	1,213	11	Nazir Ahmad	784
2	Mohammad Boota	1,301	12	Mohammad Shafiq	922
3	Mohammad Ayyaz	1,244	13	Ghulam Rasool	887
4	Zahoor Ahmed	1,389	14	Mohammad Ilyas	976
5	Mohammadusman	550	15	Sadiq Hussain	903
6	Mohammad Riaz	1,282	16	Shafiq Ahmed	796
7	Mohammad Akmal	664	17	Khalid Mehmood	869
8	Zahid Ali	1,136	18	Ejaz Ahmad	905
9	Ehsan Baig	901	19	M. Saeed Asghar	473
10	Mohammad Ashraf	842	20	Tariq Javed	487
			21	Mehtab Ahmad Khan	784

Source: Company records.

Exhibit 2: Monthly Coverage, Sales Staff, Vehicles in Lahore (December 1991)

		Number of outlets	Frequency of coverage	
		Daily	Thrice per week	Twice per week
Retailers	4,089	240	160	3,689
Wholesalers	58	–	38	20

Sales staff:		Vehicles:	
Sales manager	1	Suzuki pick-up	16
Field sales officers	2	Tri-vans	5
Merchandising supervisors	2	Van for wholesale	1
Direct delivery (DD) carriers	21	Spare vehicle	2
Spare carrier	1	Motorcycles	4
Incharge for wholesale	1		
Godown keepers	2		
Loaders	3		

Notes:
1. The retail trade comprised 21 sections, one direct delivery carrier per section.
2. Retail outlets averaged 195 per section. An average carrier made 65 calls a day.
3. The total retail outlets included 84 army canteens and 350 outlets in 35 small villages (called "Pinds"). Both army canteens and village outlets were covered twice a week.
4. Except for about 50 small retail outlets, all retail and wholesale outlets in the assigned area were covered.
Source: Company records.

Exhibit 3: Monthly Average Sales by Brand ('000)

Brand[1]	Packing[2]	1987	1988	1989	1990	1991
Gold Leaf Int.	20EP	37	36	42	25	19
Gold Leaf Ks Ft	20HL	9,599	9,824	10,833	11,004	11,803
Gold Leaf Mild	20HL	4	–	–	–	–
Gold Leaf Lights	20HL	–	–	–	–	288
Capstan Ks Ft	20HL	22	39	8	–	–
Capstan Int.	20HL	–	–	100	157	169
Capstan Int.	10HL	–	–	150	126	73
Capstan Ls Ft	10SS	2,614	1,969	1,822	1,606	1,437
Wills Kings	20HL	919	696	648	660	676
Wills N/C Ft	20SS	1,741	1,248	995	885	812
Player's No.6	20HL	603	442	414	344	299
Gold Flake Ks Ft	20SC	12,952	15,247	17,987	20,910	24,025
Gold Flake Ks Ft	20HL	–	–	548	1,329	449
Wood Bine Ft	10SS	9	–	–	–	–
Wood Bine Vir.	10SS	61	–	–	–	–
Embassy Ft	10SS	11,509	14,554	12,369	11,105	8,991
Embassy N/C	10SS	244	156	110	60	47
Embassy Kings	20HL	–	–	–	–	–
King Stork	10SS	27	–	–	–	–
Scissors Ft	10SS	3,016	1,515	256	19	–
Others	–	–	–	22	–	–
	Total	43,357	45,726	46,304	48,230	49,088

[1] INT.: International; KS FT: King Size, filter tipped; LS: Long Size; N/C: Navy Cut Vir.: Viriginia.
[2] EP: Empra Pack; HL: Hinge Lid; SS: Shell and Slide; SC: Soft Cup.
Source: Company records.

Exhibit 4:   Carrier Commission Rates (December 1991) (rupees per 1,000 cigarettes)

S. No.	Carrier	Gold Leaf 20EP	Gold Leaf 20HL	Gold Leaf Light 20HL	Capstan 20HL	Capstan 10HL	Capstan 10SS	Wills Kings 20HL	Wills N/C 20SS	Gold Flake 20SC	Gold Flake 20HL	Player's #6 20HL	Embassy 10SS	Embassy N/C 10SS	Embassy Kings 20HL
1	Abdul Razzak	2.00	1.40	1.40	1.00	1.00	1.00	1.00	1.00	1.60	1.00	1.00	0.75	1.00	1.00
2	Mohammad Boota	2.00	1.40	1.40	1.00	1.00	1.00	1.00	1.00	1.60	1.00	1.00	0.60	1.00	1.00
3	Mohammad Ayyaz	2.00	1.40	1.40	1.00	1.00	1.00	1.00	1.00	1.50	1.00	1.00	0.75	1.00	1.00
4	Zahoor Ahmed	2.00	1.45	1.45	1.00	1.00	1.00	1.00	1.00	1.40	1.00	1.00	0.75	1.00	1.00
5	Mohammadusman	1.80	1.60	1.60	1.25	1.25	1.25	1.25	1.25	1.80	1.25	1.25	1.35	1.25	1.00
6	Mohammad Riaz	2.00	1.40	1.40	1.00	1.00	1.00	1.00	1.00	1.50	1.00	1.00	0.60	1.00	1.00
7	Mohammad Akmal	2.00	1.40	1.40	1.00	1.00	1.00	1.00	1.00	1.50	1.00	1.00	0.60	1.00	1.00
8	Zahid Ali	2.00	1.50	1.50	1.00	1.00	1.00	1.00	1.00	1.50	1.00	1.00	0.65	1.00	1.00
9	Ehsan Baig	1.80	1.55	1.55	1.25	1.25	1.25	1.25	1.25	1.60	1.25	1.25	0.90	1.25	1.00
10	Mohammad Ashraf	1.80	1.50	1.50	1.25	1.25	1.25	1.25	1.25	1.65	1.25	1.25	1.05	1.25	1.00
11	Nazir Ahmad	1.80	1.70	1.70	1.25	1.25	1.25	1.25	1.25	1.80	1.25	1.25	1.05	1.25	1.00
12	Mohammad Shafiq	1.80	1.50	1.50	1.25	1.25	1.25	1.25	1.25	1.60	1.25	1.25	0.75	1.25	1.00
13	Ghulam Rasool	2.00	1.50	1.50	1.00	1.00	1.00	1.00	1.00	1.60	1.00	1.00	0.95	1.00	1.00
14	Mohammad Ilyas	2.00	1.60	1.60	1.00	1.00	1.00	1.00	1.00	1.60	1.00	1.00	0.75	1.00	1.00
15	Sadiq Hussain	2.00	1.60	1.60	1.00	1.00	1.00	1.00	1.00	1.60	1.00	1.00	0.75	1.00	1.00
16	Shafiq Ahmed	2.00	1.60	1.60	1.00	1.00	1.00	1.00	1.00	1.60	1.00	1.00	0.75	1.00	1.00
17	Khalid Mehmood	1.80	1.60	1.60	1.25	1.25	1.25	1.25	1.25	1.70	1.25	1.25	1.00	1.25	1.00
18	Ejaz Ahmad	2.00	1.40	1.40	1.00	1.00	1.00	1.00	1.00	1.50	1.00	1.00	0.65	1.00	1.00
19	M. Saeed Asghar	1.80	1.50	1.50	1.25	1.25	1.25	1.25	1.25	1.60	1.25	1.25	0.75	1.25	1.00
20	Tariq Javed	1.80	1.70	1.70	1.25	1.25	1.25	1.25	1.25	1.80	1.25	1.25	1.35	1.25	1.00
21	Mehtab Ahmad Khan	1.80	1.50	1.50	1.25	1.25	1.25	1.25	1.25	1.60	1.25	1.25	0.90	1.25	1.00

Source: Company records.

Exhibit 5: Direct Expenses for Incremental Direct Delivery Carrier (rupees)

Initial investment of 1 Suzuki pick-up:	Rs 120,000	Repair and maintenance	10,000
Yearly operational expenses:		Depreciation	24,000
Interest expenses on initial		Carrier commission	
investment (Rs 120,000, 18%)	21,600	(Rs 2,590 per month)	31,080
Taxes (token tax, registration fee, etc.)	1,687	Printing and stationery	2,600
Insurance premium (car, stock, cash)	9,303	Total yearly operational	
Petrol, oil and lubricants	16,500	expenses	Rs 116,770

Notes:

1. The above costs are direct costs only.
2. Salesman commission excludes incentives passed on for meeting sales targets expenses incurred for their entertainment and welfare.
3. Increase in the cost of loading, godown incharge, and cashier not included.
4. The cost sheet has been prepared according to the situation prevailing in December 1991. The costs will obviously rise on account of inflation.

Exhibit 6: Monthly Average Sales by Market Segment ('000 cigarettes)

	1987	1988	1989	1990	1991
Direct delivery	28,040 (65%)	30,771 (67%)	33,066 (71%)	34,618 (72%)	34,769 (71%)
Wholesale	12,954 (30%)	11,632 (25%)	10,367 (22%)	10,575 (22%)	11,044 (23%)
Army canteens	621 (1%)	732 (2%)	290 (1%)	275	189
Villages	1,742 (4%)	2,591 (6%)	2,581 (6%)	2,762 (6%)	3,086 (6%)
Total	43,357	45,726	46,304	48,230	49,088

Source: Company records.

Exhibit 7: Trade Margins (%) (December 1991)

Brand	Packing	Distributor margin		Wholesaler margin	Retailer margin
		Wholesale	Retail		
		%	%	%	%
Gold Leaf Int.	20EP	1.21	1.60	0.43	2.12
Gold Leaf Ks Ft	20HL	1.20	1.64	0.43	2.14
Capstan Ks Ft	20HL	1.24	1.69	0.45	2.13
Capstan Int.	10HL	1.24	1.69	0.45	2.13
Capstan Ls Ft	10SS	1.24	1.69	0.45	2.13
Wills Kings	20HL	1.27	1.75	0.47	2.18
Player's No. 6	20HL	1.27	1.75	0.47	2.18
Gold Flake Ks Ft	20SC	1.26	1.72	0.45	2.33
Gold Flake Ks Ft	20HL	1.26	1.72	0.45	2.33
Embassy Ft	10SS	1.34	1.83	0.49	2.10
Embassy N/C	10SS	1.34	1.83	0.49	2.10

PTC price to distributor = 100 percent.   Source: Company records.

Case 31

Atlas Honda Ltd.: Communication Plan 1993

Ehsan ul Haque
Lahore University of Management Sciences, Lahore

At end October 1992, Mr. Zamir Haider, General Manager Marketing and Mr. Nurul Huda, National Sales Manager of Atlas Honda Ltd. (AHL) were busy developing the 1993 marketing communication plan for Honda motorcycles. Mr. Haider was scheduled to present his plan to Mr. Aamir Shirazi, CEO of AHL for final approval at end November. Mr. Shirazi became CEO in early 1992 when Mr. Danishmand, the previous CEO who had served the Atlas Group for 15 years, left AHL to head Suzuki Motorcycles. Mr. Haider was fully aware that Mr. Shirazi, new to the position, would scrutinize the plan in great detail and ask some basic questions: the rationale behind allocating X% of communication rupees to consumer versus dealer promotion; the role/need of print and TV advertising for Honda; the cost-benefit of any sales promotion programs, and so forth.

In addition, Mr. Haider had his own concerns regarding the 1993 plan. He was particularly frustrated that, despite AHL's efforts, customers in some markets were still not convinced of the benefits of four-stroke versus two-stroke engines. A more urgent concern was the aggressive stance Suzuki had taken since Mr. Danishmand's arrival. Some AHL managers were concerned that it might lose market share if it did not respond effectively. Mr. Haider decided to review the market situation and previous AHL marketing communication activities to prepare a sound 1993 plan.

૪૦૭જી

Company Background

AHL was part of the Atlas Group of companies (founded 1962). By 1992, the Group comprised six public limited and five private companies; assets were Rs 1.6 billion and sales over Rs 3 billion. In 1992, Mr. Yusuf H. Shirazi, the Group's founder was chairman.

AHL was formed on January 1, 1991 when Atlas Autos Ltd. and Panjdarya Ltd., sister units of the Atlas Group, merged. Atlas Autos was incorporated in 1962; in

1963 it started assembly of, then progressively manufacture of, motorcycles in Karachi with technical collaboration from Honda Motor Company Ltd., Japan. In 1978, Atlas Group established Panjdarya Ltd., in Sheikhupura near Lahore, as a private limited company for motorcycle manufacture, to avoid government restrictions on capacity expansion at Atlas Autos. The merger rationalized operations and provided economies of scale; Pakistan's political and economic environment was conducive to this action. Honda acquired 20% of AHL and appointed two directors to the board. (See Table 1 for income statements.)

Aamir Shirazi, Mr. Yusuf H. Shirazi's son, was educated in Pakistan, England and the U.S. He worked for Honda of America (Ohio), returning to Pakistan in 1987 as Assistant Manager Marketing, Multan; later, he moved to Lahore as General Manager, Panjdarya Ltd. With the merger, Aamir became Managing Director at AHL, CEO on Mr. Danishmand's departure. Mr. Zamir Haider, educated in Pakistan, worked for Atlas for 16 years; prior to becoming General Manager Marketing in early 1992 he was Manager Spare Parts.

Honda Products and the Four-stroke Technology

AHL manufactured/assembled two Honda motorbike models in Pakistan: CD 70 (74 cc.), nearly 80% of AHL revenues (1992), and CG 125 (125 cc.).[1] AHL was the only manufacturer in Pakistan to use four-stroke engine technology exclusively; all competitors used two-stroke technology. Honda introduced a two-stroke model, MB-100, in 1980, but technical problems negatively affected market acceptance.

AHL top management believed four-stroke engines were well-suited to customer needs in developing countries like Pakistan. They maintained this technology gave

Table 1: Atlas Honda Income Statements ('000 rupees)

	1992 (projected)	1991	1990	1989	1988
Sales	1,650,000	1,562,577	1,305,480	1,106,650	919,716
Cost of sales	1,520,000	1,458,826	1,174,565	1,021,108	843,495
Gross profit	130,000	103,751	130,915	85,542	76,221
Operating expenses:					
Administrative	39,000	40,160	31,970	18,832	14,889
Selling & dist.	45,000	37,525	34,076	26,278	22,272
Adv. & publicity	11,600	6,790	8,467	5,816	4,005
Sales promotion	2,400	4,145	1,456	925	1,812
Distribution*	31,000	26,590	24,153	19,537	16,455
Operating profit	46,000	26,066	64,869	40,432	39,060

*Distribution expenses included salaries, freight and travel charges among others.
Source: Corporate documents.

---

[1] The cc. specification indicated the power of the motorbike engine; more ccs implied more power.

Honda a unique competitive advantage inasmuch as four-stroke engines had significantly lower fuel consumption. In addition, Honda products had better resale value, fetching almost the same price as a year earlier whereas most competitive motorcycles depreciated 4,000 to 5,000 rupees. Furthermore, four-stroke engines required less maintenance than two-stroke engines.

However, four-stroke engines were more complicated; thus, repair and service, when needed, were more difficult. According to AHL, four-stroke engine repair required better trained and more experienced mechanics than two-stroke engines. Four-stroke technology also resulted in higher manufacturing costs, leading to premium prices for Hondas: the Honda CD 70 was a few thousand rupees more expensive than competitors' more powerful products.

Competition

In 1992, Pakistan's motorcycle industry comprised five main competitors:

Honda was the leader with 56% market share (Exhibit 1). Combined annual production capacity in its Karachi and Sheikhupura plants was 80,000 units. According to AHL executives, Honda had a strong brand image; its motorcycles were perceived as high quality, very reliable and durable, but somewhat expensive.

Honda's market position was traditionally very strong in southern Pakistan.[2] According to AHL executives, this dominance resulted because consumers preferred four-stroke over two-stroke engines. Two-stroke technology was well-entrenched in northern Pakistan, particularly in rural Punjab. However, whereas four-stroke technology received concentrated marketing efforts in southern Pakistan in the 1960s and 1970s, Yamaha focused marketing activities in the Punjab since the late 1960s.

Yamaha was manufactured by Dawood Yamaha Ltd., a private limited company that started operations in 1968 by establishing an assembly plant in Uthal, Baluchistan. Manufacturing capabilities were progressively added over the years and by 1990 annual production capacity was 37,000 units. In September 1991, a second Yamaha plant opened in Islamabad bringing annual capacity to 60,000 units. Yamaha sold two well-received models in Pakistan: YB 100 "Royale" and YB 80 "Special."

Yamaha traditionally spent little on advertising and promotion, restricting efforts to distributing posters and leaflets to dealers (Exhibit 2). Zamir Haider believed this strategy was due to the entrenchment of two-stroke technology in the Punjab, Yamaha's major market. He believed Yamaha did not even need to train mechanics as servicing two-stroke engines was not complicated. In 1990 and earlier, all Yamaha output was pre-sold since demand exceeded supply; this situation changed when the Islamabad plant came on stream. Zamir noticed a few print ads in newspapers; Yamaha also introduced some field service camps.

Suzuki motorcycles were assembled / manufactured in Karachi by Sind Engineering Ltd. Capacity was 15,000 units but production fluctuated considerably in prior

---

[2] The southern region was defined as south and inclusive of Sukkur; the rest of the country was the northern region.

years. In 1991, Suzuki Corporation of Japan took a more active interest and in late 1991, Danishmand, highly regarded in the motorcycle industry, was appointed CEO. Danishmand introduced an aggressive marketing strategy for Suzuki. In 1992, it spent heavily to promote its two models Samurai and Ninja Master; four 15-second spots were run on national television daily for three months, an expenditure unheard of in the industry. In addition, Suzuki increased its number of print and radio ads, banners, hoardings, dealer and consumer leaflets and brochures (Exhibit 3).

Suzuki offered special incentives to customers and dealers. For a brief period, customers were given wrist watches (retail value Rs 500) with purchase of any Suzuki model. The "friend gets 20 liters free" campaign provided 20 liters of fuel (retail value of Rs 160) to the friend whose recommendation was instrumental in a Suzuki sale. Life size posters depicting attractive foreign females standing by Suzuki motorcycles with the tag line, "Suzuki meri Jaan hai,"[3] were distributed to dealers who also received promotional items (e.g., key chains, wall clocks).

Suzuki improved market share considerably. Some AHL executives believed Suzuki's strategy was beneficial to Honda as it would increase primary demand and give consumers more choice; others believed Suzuki was becoming a formidable threat. According to Aamir Shirazi, the impact on Honda sales was negligible.

Kawasaki was one of two smaller players. Models were produced by Saif Nadeem Kawasaki Motors Ltd. at an assembly/manufacturing plant (capacity 10,000 units) in Abbotabad. Kawasaki offered two models – 100 cc. and 125 cc. The 125 cc. model, very popular among young people, had been unavailable in the past two to three years. Honda executives believed the motivation and commitment of Kawasaki for future support of its models were low.

Vespa scooters (145 cc.), manufactured by Khwaja Autos, were not seen as a competitor by AHL executives. In any case, over the years, increasing plant capacity was allocated to auto-rickshaws and scooter sales declined.

Motorcycles prices in Pakistan were influenced heavily by the rupee–yen exchange rate, firm dependence on import of critical parts from Japan and government policies. In the late 1980s, motorcycle prices gradually moved upwards as the rupee declined consistently against the yen. In 1988, the Pakistan government imposed a 12.5% sales tax on motorcycles, raising taxes to 36% of total motorcycle costs. Between 1990 and 1992, the rupee devalued at an average annual rate of 23% against the yen; motorcycle prices rose sharply. In 1992, CD 70s sold at approximately Rs 31,000; CG 125s at Rs 37,000 (Table 2). AHL executives believed price rises dampened motorcycle demand.

Motorcycle Customers

"In Pakistan the motorcycle is no longer a luxury item. For a vast section of the society it is now a necessity," said Aamir Shirazi: "All kinds of people, students, hawkers, office workers, milkmen, etc., need motorcycles for commuting." Motorcycles were the

---

[3] Suzuki is my life.

Table 2: Competitive Prices for Motorcycles (September 1992)

Brands/models	Price (Rs)	Brands/models	Price (Rs)
Honda		Kawasaki	
CD70	31,000	GT 100 cc.	32,000
CG125	37,000	GT 100 cc.	n/a
Yamaha		Suzuki	
YB 80 Special	29,000	Samurai 80 cc.	29,200
YB 100 Special	33,300	Ninja Master 100 cc.	30,300

Source: Corporate documents.

prime mode of transportation for Pakistan's lower middle and middle class. Motorcycles were not just vehicles for the individual, but more of a family transport. A family of four or five persons riding one bike was not uncommon.

AHL divided customers into two broad categories – Students and Non-students (those past the student stage). Management believed different kinds of people bought CD 70s and CG 125s. CD 70 customers were generally lower to middle income (up to 10,000 rupees per month); they ranged in age from 17 to 45 years; about 70% were salaried office workers or self-employed; they were predominantly urban and the basic motivation for purchasing motorcycles was transportation. Students comprised the remaining 30% of CD 70 customers; for some, motorcycles represented personal freedom and coming of age; for others it was transportation.

CG 125 customers were relatively higher income (10,000–15,000 rupees per month); aged 17 to 35 years. Students and Non-students were more equally split but the CG 125 was more popular with younger Students and heavier-built Non-students. These users were not worried about petrol prices or maintenance costs; rather, the motorcycle was an expression of prestige, thrill seeking and adventure.

Although AHL had done no specific research, top management believed customers were generally influenced by five factors when considering a motorcycle purchase: maintenance costs, resale value, availability of mechanics, availability of spare parts and brand name. Management did not know the relative importance of these factors, nor did it understand the customer decision-making process. It believed parents played a critical role for Student customers; they financed, and therefore decided, when a motorcycle was purchased. Sometimes parents influenced the selection of engine power; for example, they might force their sons to purchase a 70 cc. or 80 cc. motorbike (versus 125 cc.) if they believed less powerful engines meant slower speeds and reduced safety hazards. However, parental influence on dealer selection and brand choice was not known.

Similarly, little was known about Non-student motorcycle purchases. For almost all customers, motorcycles required major cash outlays of six months to five years savings.[4] It seemed a long, well thoughtout purchase; customers talked to friends,

---

[4] By comparison, an inexpensive automobile would cost four to six times more.

other motorcycle owners, mechanics, as well as different motorcycle dealers before purchasing, but the relative influence of these sources on brand choice was not known.

AHL top management believed objective information on motorcycle customers was important to run a successful business. In 1991, it commissioned a consumer perception study from a local management consulting firm. Study objectives included consumer profiles of Honda, Yamaha and Kawasaki users, consumer opinions of Honda and feedback on Honda dealers. In total, 1,400 motorbike users were interviewed in Lahore, Karachi and Multan. Owner demographics (Exhibit 4) and reasons for purchase/non-purchase of Honda were tabulated (Exhibit 5).

Honda Dealers

Honda motorcycles were sold all over Pakistan through company-appointed dealers, an industry-wide practice. AHL divided the country into four regions for sales force dealer coverage: south of and including Sukkur (Karachi sales office); Rahim Yar Khan to Multan (Multan); cities like Sahiwal, Faisalabad, Gujrat and Sialkot (Lahore); northern Pakistan (Rawalpindi). AHL salespersons visited all dealers at least once a week to take orders, receive cash payments and discuss dealer concerns; some dealers were visited almost daily.

AHL dealers had to estimate future sales and/or inventory requirements and place advance orders on AHL; payment terms were cash with order. Generally, delay occurred between order placing and order delivery; in 1992, orders were pending for about 45 days. Financial risk from a drop in market prices was borne by dealers; financial losses from AHL cost increases were absorbed by the company.

In 1992, AHL's suggested retail prices allowed dealers to earn about Rs 1,800 per motorcycle, the industry norm. Suggested retail price was strictly maintained. In each major city, a committee comprising two dealers and one territory in-charge from AHL monitored dealer compliance. Dealers found discounting prices were fined. However, at times, some dealers indulged in price-cutting to attract customers.

Dealers were categorized according to provision of add-on services. Three-in-One dealers sold Honda motorcycles, carried a reasonable parts and supplies inventory (i.e., authorized Honda parts dealers) and had motorcycle maintenance and service facilities (i.e., in-house Honda authorized mechanics). Two-in-One dealers had one of the additional facilities; One-in-One dealers only sold motorcycles. AHL management believed Three-in-One dealers were better positioned to make sales. (See Table 3 for competitive position of motorcycle dealers.)

AHL management believed dealers played a key role in motorcycle sales. Since most dealers for the different brands were concentrated in few city locations, comparison shopping was easy. Multiple dealers were typically appointed for one brand in the same city (e.g., Lahore, 27 Honda dealers; Karachi, 16). Not all dealers were equally successful: good location, stock availability and a pleasant store environment determined dealer success. Regarding the store environment, Aamir Shirazi observed: "There was a perception that dealerships with air-conditioned showrooms and big mirrors merely attracted browsers rather than serious purchasers. This myth has been exposed."

Company	Three-in-One	Two-in-One	One-in-One	Total
Honda	64	53	96	213
Yamaha	46	11	69	126
Suzuki	–	8	64	72
Kawasaki	–	4	35	39
Vespa	–	1	10	11

Source: Corporate documents.

Shirazi believed good product knowledge, a more "humanistic" approach to sell-ing (i.e., good eye contact, more refined interpersonal skills) and high personal involvement by dealers could sway potential customers; he believed dealer trustwor-thiness was important for customers. According to Haider, because of the product's complex nature and high financial outlay, a majority of customers purchased only from dealers they knew directly or through extended friendship networks; the 1991 survey secured important data on dealers (Exhibit 6).

Marketing Communications at AHL

At AHL, marketing communication activities were broadly divided into two catego-ries. Electronic or print media advertising, poster, banners, hoardings and cinema ads were funded through the advertising and publicity budget; activities such as me-chanic training camps, competitions for best fuel mileage ("Econo-Runs"), free service camps, free T-shirts, key chains and other dealer premiums were funded through the sales promotion budget.

Traditionally, AHL relied more on hoardings, banners, print and cinema advertis-ing than television advertising; it was unsure of returns to high cost television. In 1992, a few national television spots (cost Rs 1.72 million), depicting an older Honda model, were used to move showroom stocks, make room for new models and reassure dealers of Honda's support of older models. In prior years, Honda promoted the four-stroke engine's fuel efficiency in various media including television. According to Aamir Shirazi, the slogan, "Aik litre main Suttar kilometre,"[5] was popular among customers. In 1992, AHL spent Rs 970,000 on radio advertising but none in the cinema.

Other advertising and publicity activities were print ads in various media (Rs 2.5 million). In addition, 10,000 large four-color posters on various aspects of Honda mo-torbikes were distributed to dealers; each cost Rs 100. Mechanics found the blow-ups of Honda motorcycles and engines depicted very useful; posters showing the advan-tages of four-stroke over two-stroke engines were also popular. About 250,000 leaflets (cost, Rs 5 each) of CG125 and CD70 printed in four colors on glossy paper were also

---

[5] 70 kilometers in 1 liter.

distributed to dealers who placed them in store dispensers for potential customers (Exhibit 7).

The motorcycle industry relied heavily on hoardings, boards and banners to develop and reinforce customer awareness of brands. About 130 Honda hoardings (cost, Rs 8,000 to Rs 15,000 each) were strategically placed across Pakistan. These were augmented by 5,000 banners (cost, Rs 500 each) displaying Honda motorbikes.

Consumer promotions were not viewed favorably by AHL executives. Aamir observed: "Free helmets or watches do not generate sales for a Rs 40,000 item." Price discounts were also believed futile since Honda's previous experience with discount schemes was unsuccessful. In 1983, AHL had problems selling Honda's two-stroke motorcycles (MB 100, H100 S) because market perception of model quality was poor and sales were dwindling. To boost sales, a special Rs 500 discount was given during the month of Eid-ul-Fitr (Ramadhan); sales completely collapsed. Aamir believed the discount scheme was the proverbial last straw.

Nonetheless, two events aimed at consumer education and appreciation were held quite regularly. The annual "Econo-Run" promoted the better fuel efficiency of Honda's four-stroke engine; about 15 Econo-Run events took place annually in different Pakistan cities. Banners, print ads (Exhibit 8) and radio invited motorcyclists to take part; typically, 30 to 40 motorcyclists participated in each Econo-Run, open to all brands of motorcycles. A measured amount of petrol was provided to each contestant; the person covering the maximum distance was the winner. Since the Econo-Run was instituted, Honda motorcycles had won top honors. The results and photographs of winners appeared in the press (Exhibit 9). In addition, attractive prizes (Rs 100 to Rs 2,000) were distributed among all contestants. Every third year, an "All Pakistan" Econo-Run was held; the previous years' winners competed for top honors. Prizes ranged from free return tickets to Singapore to Rs 1,000 cash awards. In 1992, an All Pakistan Econo-Run would have cost about Rs 800,000; actual 1992 expenditures were about Rs 200,000. The second event was "Free Service Clinics" for Honda motorcycle owners. Ten to 15 clinics/camps were held in various parts of Pakistan each year; mobile teams of Honda mechanics tested/evaluated customer motorcycles for free. The 1992 cost of these events was about Rs 100,000.

Dealer and mechanic education and training were important activities. About 50 one-to-three day "Mechanic Training Camps" were held each year in different parts of Pakistan. Senior Honda mechanics imparted the latest knowledge in maintenance and repair to mechanics. At times, Japanese mechanics, specially flown in from Japan, assisted Pakistani mechanics. In 1992, AHL spent around Rs 600,000 on these camps. Dealers were also educated on technical aspects of Honda motorcycles and Honda technology; posters, leaflets and other printed material were distributed. AHL management was not satisfied with the technical knowledge possessed by some dealers.

No special incentives were provided to dealers except the margins from selling motorcycles. AHL top management did not believe dealer contests were useful in promoting sales. A few years previously, the dealer with maximum bookings in a specific month was to be awarded a free one-week trip to Japan. Because of personal rivalries, winning this contest became a matter of great prestige for several dealers and massive price-cutting occurred. Because of the close proximity of dealer locations, even non-interested dealers were forced to cut prices and suffer, what they considered, unnecessary losses. Much ill-will was generated among the dealers and with AHL.

Each year, an all-Pakistan convention of Honda dealers (1992 cost, Rs 1 million) enabled dealers to get to know AHL management, each other, and to discuss mutual problems. Dealers were provided Rs 100,000 worth of give-aways and prizes to pass on to customers.

The Task Ahead

Haider gathered his papers and began outlining marketing communication activities he wanted AHL to undertake in 1993. He decided to focus first on customer buying behavior; he believed a good understanding of the decision-making process would provide him with guidelines as to "when" to communicate "what" to "whom." The roles of parents, friends, mechanics and dealers all needed to be considered.

Then there were decisions regarding budgets, budget allocations and various "events." Honda could continue past activities or make changes. He grabbed several media tariff and circulation sheets (Exhibits 10 to 14) provided by the advertising agency and started entering numbers on his calculator. "But this is not the end," he mused. "After this exercise, I still have to sell the plan to Aamir Shirazi."

Exhibit 1: Motorcycle Sales and Market Shares

Total

Year	Honda Units	%	Yamaha Units	%	Suzuki Units	%	Kawasaki Units	%	Vespa Units	%	Total Units	%
1987	33,579	61.0	15,723	28.0	3,364	6.0	1,310	2.0	1,419	3.0	55,395	100.0
1988	33,842	59.0	18,214	32.0	1,201	2.0	2,891	5.0	1,331	2.0	57,479	100.0
1989	39,973	60.0	22,728	34.0	243	0.0	3,022	4.0	1,215	2.0	67,181	100.0
1990	52,170	60.0	28,690	33.0	384	0.0	4,733	5.0	1,106	1.0	87,083	100.0
1991	57,729	60.0	32,832	34.0	1,872	2.0	3,634	4.0	667	0.0	96,734	100.0
1992*	52,300	56.0	35,500	38.0	3,500	4.0	1,900	2.0	550	0.0	93,750	100.0

Northern region

Year	Honda Units	%	Yamaha Units	%	Suzuki Units	%	Kawasaki Units	%	Vespa Units	%	Total Units
1990	37,814	55.0	25,569	38.0	356	0.5	3,689	5.0	816	1.0	68,244
1991	40,237	54.0	29,429	40.0	1,729	2.0	2,417	3.0	480	0.5	74,292
1992*	36,400	49.0	32,800	44.0	3,000	4.0	1,200	2.0	400	0.5	73,800

Southern region

Year	Honda Units	%	Yamaha Units	%	Suzuki Units	%	Kawasaki Units	%	Vespa Units	%	Total Units
1990	14,356	76.0	3,121	17.0	78	0	1,044	5.5	290	1.5	18,889
1991	17,492	78.0	3,403	15.0	143	0.5	1,217	5.5	187	1.0	22,442
1992	15,900	80.0	2,700	13.5	500	2.5	700	3.5	150	0.5	19,950

*1992 figures are on AHL projections.
Source: Corporate documents based on motorcycle registrations in major towns.

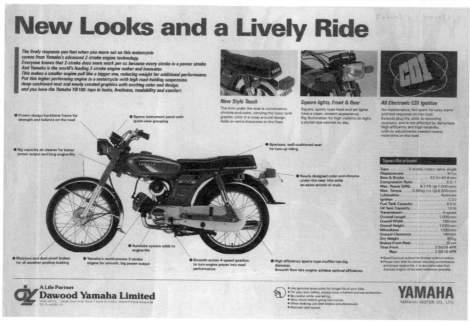

Exhibit 4: Selected Consumer Demographics and Usage Data*

	Honda owners	Yamaha owners	Kawasaki owners
Age			
Less than 20	8.0%	8.0%	7.0%
21–30	59.5	49.0	67.0
31–40	25.5	28.0	17.0
41–50	6.0	12.5	7.5
More than 50	1.0	2.5	1.5
Income			
Less than 3,000	19.0%	27.0%	19.5%
3,001–5,000	35.0	35.0	25.0
5,001–7,000	29.0	21.0	26.5
7,001–9,000	10.5	8.5	8.5
9,001–11,000	4.5	5.5	13.5
More than 11,000	2.0	3.0	7.0
Profession			
Student	30.0%	24.0%	37.0%
Own business	25.0	30.0	38.0
Govt/private service	35.0	29.0	18.0
Blue collar workers	4.0	13.0	2.0
Professionals	4.0	3.0	5.0
Farmers	1.0	1.0	0.0
Period of ownership			
Less than one year	24.7%	26.2%	40.0%
1–4 years	56.1	58.7	48.3
5–10 years	15.5	18.3	4.8
Over 10 years	1.4	3.7	6.4

	Honda owners	Yamaha owners	Kawasaki owners
Terms of purchase			
On installment	6.7%	9.9%	4.8%
Cash	93.3	90.1	95.2
Sources of funds			
Self	55.3%	60.9%	51.6%
Father	31.9	28.1	40.0
Brother	10.7	6.2	4.8
Others	5.5	4.6	6.4
Use/purpose			
Personal use	62.1%	54.2%	64.9%
Business	12.8	15.8	20.7
Load carrying	1.6	3.7	2.6
Pleasure	5.0	9.9	2.6
Family transport	17.0	15.5	9.9
Other	1.3	0.7	0.0
Fuel consumption			
Satisfied	71.2%	69.7%	61.0%
Dissatisfied	28.7	30.0	39.0
No. of respondents	907	435	60

*Some series do not sum to 100%.
Source: Consumer survey.

Exhibit 5: Reasons for Purchasing/Not Purchasing Honda Motorcycles

Reasons for purchasing Honda motorcycle
CD 70 owners

	Karachi	Lahore	Multan
1. Low fuel consumption*	94.0%	99.0%	90.0%
2. Four-stroke engine – no plug problem	16.0	23.0	7.0
3. Attractive design	18.0	22.0	31.0
4. Engine durability	38.0	0.0	9.0
5. Reasonable price	53.0	11.0	28.0
No. of respondents	**255**	**203**	**176**

CG 125 owners

	Karachi	Lahore	Multan
1. Low fuel consumption*	27.0%	7.0%	13.0%
2. Four-stroke engine – no plug problem	0.0	28.0	9.0
3. Attractive design	38.0	31.0	53.0
4. Engine durability	25.0	6.0	1.0
5. Reasonable price	46.0	5.0	9.0
No. of respondents	**110**	**87**	**76**

*94% of CD70 owners gave low fuel consumption as one reason for buying Honda.
Figures do not add up to 100 because of multiple answers.

Reasons for not purchasing Honda motorcycle

	Karachi	Lahore	Multan
1. High price	48.9%*	56.7%	18.2%
2. Unattractive design	35.6	33.8	14.2
3. Limited color range	13.3	20.5	1.4
4. Expensive spare parts	16.3	24.3	6.1
5. Poor road grip	43.7	27.6	40.5
6. Cannot carry load	5.2	20.0	39.9
7. Poor brakes	15.6	15.7	4.7
8. Not suitable for rough terrain	5.9	11.4	20.9
9. Low speed performance	17.8	14.8	11.5
No. of respondents	**135**	**210**	**148**

*Figures do not add up to 100 because of multiple answers.
Source: Consumer survey.

Exhibit 6: Dealership Survey

Reasons for buying motorcycle from a particular dealer

CD 70 owners

	Karachi	Lahore	Multan
1. Convenient location	42.0%	1.0%	42.0%
2. Polite staff	27.0	40.0	24.0
3. Knowledgeable staff	32.0	10.0	15.0
4. Dealer provided registration documents	30.0	35.0	14.0
5. Friends' recommendation	0.5	12.0	0.5
6. Dealer known	4.0	5.0	28.0
7. Credit/guarantee facility	62.0	4.0	42.0
8. Other reasons	53.0	10.0	26.0
9. No specific reason	8.0	21.0	7.0
No. of respondents	**255**	**203**	**176**

CD 125 owners

	Karachi	Lahore	Multan
1. Convenient location	23.0%	1.0%	30.0%
2. Polite staff	23.0	29.0	17.0
3. Knowledgeable staff	19.0	7.0	11.0
4. Dealer provided registration documents	18.0	24.0	18.0
5. Friends' recommendation	0.0	7.0	1.0
6. Dealer known	5.0	9.0	30.0
7. Credit/guarantee facility	44.0	8.0	24.0
8. Other reasons	45.0	9.0	28.0
9. No specific reason	22.0	32.0	11.0
No. of respondents	**110**	**87**	**76**

Customer suggestions for dealership improvements*

CD 70 owners

	Karachi	Lahore	Multan
1. Location to be convenient	56.9%	12.8%	5.7%
2. Sales and service available at one shop	14.6	14.3	9.7
3. Sales and spare parts available in one shop	11.0	19.2	11.4
4. Sales/service/spares available in one shop	56.5	55.2	21.6
5. Prices to be low	1.0	0.0	21.0
6. None	13.3	9.4	21.0

CD 125 owners

	Karachi	Lahore	Multan
1. Location to be convenient	41.8%	18.4%	10.5%
2. Sales and service available at one shop	10.9	19.5	6.6
3. Sales and spare parts available in one shop	13.6	18.4	9.2
4. Sales/service/spares available in one shop	44.5	40.2	28.9
5. Prices to be low	0.0	0.0	11.8
6. None	12.7	12.6	15.8

*These answers are in response to a close-ended question. Figures do not add up to 100 because of multiple answers.
Source: Consumer survey.

Exhibit 9: Honda Econo-Run Winners

Exhibit 8: Honda Print Advertisement for the Econo-Run

Exhibit 10:   Tariff Rates on Pakistan Television Corporation Ltd.

Spot Rates (in Rs)*

Duration of spot	Karachi Center	Lahore Center	Islamabad Center	Peshawar Center	Quetta Center	National** Center
7 sec	1,820	1,750	1,050	250	150	4,760
15 sec	3,510	3,380	2,030	480	280	9,180
30 sec	6,240	6,000	3,600	850	480	16,320
60 sec	9,360	9,000	5,400	1,280	720	24,480

Sponsorship charges for PTV and film programs (in Rs)*

Duration of programme	Com. time allowed***	Karachi Center	Lahore Center	Islamabad Center	Peshawar Center	Quetta Center	National** Center
5 min	15 sec	13,800	13,130	7,880	1,430	750	36,980
15 min	45 sec	39,330	37,410	22,440	4,060	2,140	105,380
25–30 min	90 sec	70,380	66,940	40,160	7,270	3,830	188,570
50–60 min	180 sec	107,640	102,380	61,430	11,120	5,850	299,500

Discounts

1. Sponsorship of foreign films: 30%
2. Advertisement of books: 75%
3. The advertisements of institutions
   promoting art and culture: 15%

4. (a) Films/spots, produced by an advertiser, in the national interest on health hygiene and social/civic problems for educating and informing the general public and, (b) sponsorships of PTV's public service and educational programs: 30%

5. A bulk purchase discount will be applicable according to the following scales:

Aggregate billing in a year	Rate of discount
Rs 1.2 million to Rs 3.6 million	1%
Rs 3.6 million to Rs 7.2 million	Rs 36,000 + 1.5% on business exceeding Rs 3.6 million
Rs 7.2 million to Rs 10.8 million	Rs 90,000 + 2% on business exceeding Rs 7.2 million

The above discount will be admissible to advertising agencies, and will be first adjusted against the late payment surcharge and other dues, if any, outstanding against the agency concerned.

Surcharges

Special position:
1. Before or after specified program: 200% of the rates
2. Spots inserted in the mid-break in films: 200% of the rates
3. Mid-break in live or VTR programs: 225% of the rates
4. Mid-break in the news: 225% of the rates

*Rates for single transmission.
**Inclusive of station discount.
***In addition to free station announcements.
Source: Excerpts from PTV tariff sheet effective July 1, 1992.

Exhibit 11:   Advertising Rates on NTM (rupees)

Karachi Station

Duration (seconds)	Before 7:00 pm	7:00 pm to 7:59 pm	8:00 pm to 8:59 pm	English feature film	Urdu feature film
7	1,200*	1,500	2,700	3,900	5,400
10	1,590	2,010	3,590	5,160	7,140
15	2,200	2,800	5,000	7,200	10,000
30	4,000	5,000	9,000	13,000	18,000
45	5,100	6,400	11,500	16,700	23,100
60	6,000	7,500	13,500	19,500	27,000

Islamabad Station

Duration (seconds)	Before 7:00 pm	7:00 pm to 7:59 pm	8:00 pm to 8:59 pm	English feature film	Urdu feature film
7	600	750	1,350	1,950	2,700
10	795	1,005	1,795	2,580	3,570
15	1,100	1,400	2,500	3,600	5,000
30	2,000	2,500	4,500	6,500	9,000
45	2,550	3,200	5,750	8,350	11,550
60	3,000	3,750	6,750	9,750	13,500

Lahore Station

Duration (seconds)	Before 7:00 pm	7:00 pm to 7:59 pm	8:00 pm to 8:59 pm	English feature film	Urdu feature film
7	1,003	1,254	2,257	3,260	4,514
10	1,329	1,680	3,001	4,314	5,969
15	1,839	2,341	4,180	6,019	8,360
30	3,344	4,180	7,524	10,868	15,048
45	4,264	5,350	9,614	13,961	19,312
60	5,016	6,270	11,286	16,302	22,572

Source: NTM tariff sheet (1992).

Exhibit 12:   Circulation Figures and Advertising Rates for Selected Newspapers

Newspaper	Language	Circulation	Rate per square column cm		
			Front page	Back page	Inside page
Dawn	English	75,000	812	650	325
Muslim	English	10,000	575	460	230
PakistanTimes	English	40,000	520	520	260
Jang	Urdu	500,000	3,440	1,720	860
Nawa-i-Waqt	Urdu	375,000	2,000	1,000	500
FrontierPost	English	15,000	450	315	180
News	English	25,000	1,400	1,120	560

Source: Company records.

Exhibit 13: Advertising Rates on Radio Pakistan

Stations	Spot advertisement				
	7 sec.	15 sec.	30 sec.	45 sec.	60 sec.
World Service / Islambad / Karachi / Lahore	560	960	1,500	1,800	2,000
Rawalpindi / Multan / Hyderabad / Peshawar / Muzaffarabad	280	480	750	900	1,000
Quetta / Bahawalpur / Faisalabad / Khaipur / D.I.Khan	140	240	375	450	500
Gilgit / Skardu / Turbat / Sibi / Abbottabad	70	120	188	225	250

Program duration	Program sponsorship					
	5 min	7 min	10 min	15 min	20 min	30 min
Commercial Time	20"	30"	45"	75"	90"	150"
World Service / Islambad / Karachi / Lahore	2,200	3,080	3,960	5,280	7,040	10,560
Rawalpindi / Multan / Hyderabad / Peshawar / Muzaffarabad	1,250	1,750	2,250	3,000	4,000	6,000
Quetta / Bahawalpur / Faisalabad / Khaipur / D.I.Khan	750	1,050	1,350	1,800	2,400	3,600
Gilgit / Skardu / Turbat / Sibi / Abbottabad	500	700	900	1,200	1,600	2,400

Radio or film songs up to 5 minutes duration

World Service / Islamabad / Karachi / Lahore	1,000
Rawalpindi / Multan / Hyderabad / Peshawar / Muzaffarabad	500
Quetta / Bahawalpur / Faisalabad / Khaipur / D.I.Khan	300
Gilgit / Skardu / Khuzdar / Turbat / Sibi / Abbottabad	150

Above charges include sponsorship announcements at opening and closing of item and one 7-second spot.

Source: Excerpts from Radio Pakistan Tariff Sheet (1992).

Exhibit 14: Circulation Figures and Advertising Rates of Magazines

Magazine	Language	Frequency	Circulation	Rate for full page (in rupees) Black and White	Color
Category I:					
Herald	English	Monthly	15,000	7,000	17,500
Women's Own	English	Monthly	12,000	2,500	7,500
Category II:					
TV Times	Urdu	Monthly	17,000	2,000	5,000
MAG	English	Weekly	25,000	13,000	15,000
TV Times	English	Monthly	12,000	2,000	5,000
Category III:					
Akhbar-e-Watan	Urdu	Monthly	10,000	2,500	6,000
Cricketer	Urdu	Monthly	10,000	2,000	5,000
Cricketer	English	Monthly	8,000	2,000	5,000
Category IV:					
Sub-Rang Digest	Urdu	Monthly	125,000	4,000	6,000
Suspense Digest	Urdu	Monthly	45,000	4,000	16,000*
Urdu Digest	Urdu	Monthly	40,000	5,000	–
Jasoosi Digest	Urdu	Monthly	30,000	4,000	16,000*
Khawateen Digest	Urdu	Monthly	25,000	4,000	12,000*
Category V:					
Akhbar-e-Jehan	Urdu	Weekly	200,000	36,000	42,000
Khawateen	Urdu	Weekly	20,000	7,000	8,500

*Back cover.
Source: Company records.

Case 32

Excel Engineering: Accelerating into the Future

Kara Isert, Irfan Amir
Lahore University of Management Sciences, Lahore

For more than ten years, until summer of 1994, business had gone well for Excel Engineering, one of the larger producers of tractor components in Pakistan. Excel was gradually expanding its product line, income and earnings were steady, production flowed well, and employment levels were stable. However, in July, the Pakistan government announced the Awami Tractor Scheme; suddenly future prospects for all tractor suppliers, including Excel, looked grim.

By mid-December, Excel CEO Adil Mansoor, felt cautiously hopeful. The previous week's conversations with government officials promised yet another change to the Awami Tractor Scheme, designed to provide cheap tractors to small farmers. Rather than importing 60,000 tractors and unlimited spare parts in the current fiscal year, the government offered to include local production of 18,000 tractors and only 20,000 imports. In addition, strict limits were promised on duty-free imports of spare parts. These modifications would ensure some protection for the local tractor industry and its suppliers.

Adil Mansoor had been active lobbying the government for Scheme changes to salvage Excel's future. This latest modification offered a reprieve; it allowed time to examine the situation and provided an incentive to plan Excel's long-term strategic options. However, since the Scheme would not be officially launched for several weeks, further surprises were still possible. Excel was a captive supplier to the tractor industry. As Adil contemplated its future he wondered: What were Excel's alternatives? How should it respond to this changing environment to remain competitive and profitable?

ଚ୍ଚଜ୍ଞ

Adil Enterprises

Excel Engineering was established (1982) by Adil Mansoor, an entrepreneur who had run his own firms since 1974. Adil's career began (1970) as a senior clerk in a foundry, earning only Rs 175 per month. Within four years he was deputy managing director of

511

the 250-employee enterprise. In 1974, Adil resigned to start his own company, Adil Enterprises. He planned to export carpets to Europe but on his first sales trip to London he was sidetracked during a stopover in Abu Dhabi. During a chance meeting he learned of material needs in the construction industry. He returned home straight-away with a US$20,000 order to supply pipe fittings to the United Arab Emirates.

Adil's first venture was strictly trading, purchasing products from Pakistani manu-facturers for export to the Middle East. Later ventures were both similar and unrelated: importing reconditioned cars from Japan to Pakistan; supplying construction materi-als to domestic Pakistani organizations (e.g., municipal development authorities); speculating in real estate and establishing a cooperative banking society.

At end 1981, Adil Enterprises was offered a large contract to supply footrests to Millat Tractors Ltd. Adil jumped at this opportunity and the firm's primary focus switched to developing the tractor parts division, eventually named Excel Engineer-ing. In 1990, Adil purchased Ferrocrafts, a tractor parts company making sheet metal components.

Supplying the Tractor Industry

In 1981, Millat Tractors was a state-owned enterprise assembling Massey Ferguson tractors, nationalized ten years earlier, along with Al-Ghazi Tractors Ltd., producer of Fiat tractors. In 1980, the Pakistan government's "Deletion" policy was introduced, designed to hasten local manufacture of tractors and other automotive vehicles and shift from assembling completely knocked-down (CKD) kits imported from foreign manufacturers. Under this policy, local manufacturers were encouraged to develop locally-made components and gradually increase the percentage of local parts. The mandated target was 75% of tractor component costs to be accounted for by local parts within five years. The percentage of local parts deleted or removed from the permissi-ble import list was known as the "deletion rate."

In 1983, to further develop the tractor industry, the Pakistan government gave approval for five firms to assemble tractors: the long-established Millat Tractors (Massey Ferguson) and Al-Ghazi Tractors (Fiat), both public sector companies; and three new private sector entrants: Allied Tractors (Ford), IMT (from Yugoslavia) and Fecto (Belarus brand, Russia). Each firm received permission to manufacture so long as it achieved 75% deletion within five years. Millat and Al-Ghazi achieved this goal; the others did not. In the next decade, many changes occurred: IMT closed its Pakistani operations (1990); Allied Tractors did not establish Ford as a market leader, was bought out and renamed Khyber Tractors (late 1980s). Fecto and Khyber continued assembling small numbers of tractors with low deletion levels into the 1990s.

By 1994, the Pakistani tractor industry comprised two significant players, Al-Ghazi and Millat; each was privatized in the early 1990s and together made over 90% of tractors sold. During the past five years, 10,000 to 20,000 new tractors were sold annu-ally: Millat, 60% market share, Al-Ghazi over 35% (Table 1). Adil believed the natural demand for tractors in Pakistan was about 25,000 per year with liberal financing. In 1994, supplying locally-made tractor components was a Rs 1.75 billion industry. Excel was a medium-sized player, Millat is the 17th largest supplier of 153 local parts supply companies, comprising 0.87% of local purchases.

Table 1: Tractor Production and Government Financed Sales

Fiscal year	Millat	Al-Ghazi	ADBP* Financed	Fiscal year	Millat	Al-Ghazi	ADBP* Financed
1982/83	11,180	n/a	17,497	1988/89	14,064	8,169	19,725
1983/84	13,298	n/a	22,766	1989/90	11,472	6,607	20,290
1984/85	13,581	4,236	25,500	1990/91	7,344	5,664	12,468
1985/86	10,195	8,500	20,603	1991/92	6,269	3,328	8,823
1986/87	9,987	7,175	23,648	1992/93	10,025	6,182	16,574
1987/88	11,014	6,532	20,288	1993/94	8,768	5,547	17,552

*ADBP is the Agricultural Development Bank of Pakistan. Very few tractors were purchased outside of ADBP financing, particularly for agricultural use.
Sources: Annual reports of Millat Tractor Limited, Al-Ghazi Tractors Limited and the Agricultural Development Bank of Pakistan.

Government policy regarding tractor manufacture was difficult to predict. In the past 15 years, it had protected engineering industries and tried to build them up, but this might not continue. Pakistan signed the General Agreement on Tariffs and Trade (GATT) and was under increasing pressure from the International Monetary Fund (IMF) and other influential agencies to abandon "deletion" and other protectionist measures. In other sectors, the government was moving more towards trade liberalization policies and away from import substitution initiatives. These changes seemed likely to impact the entire engineering sector and related industries such as steel.

Tractor sales depended on subsidized financing, mainly provided through the Agricultural Development Bank of Pakistan (ADBP); annual sales (industry and Excel) fluctuated widely reflecting the availability of tractor financing. Each year, the ADBP determined a tractor financing budget; this determined the number of tractors purchased through ADBP. For financing, farmers had to meet certain landholding criteria and make 10% down payments; 90% loans (eight to ten years) were granted at lower than market interest rates. Land could be held as collateral.

Excel Engineering

Millat's push to achieve higher deletion created a demand for engineering firms to develop and supply parts to Massey Ferguson specifications. The early 1980s were a good time for entrepreneurs such as Adil Mansoor to enter the tractor supply industry. According to Adil, when Adil Enterprises received its first tractor parts order: "Millat Tractors was owned by the government. But, by a miracle, it was run by some honest people. They were hardworking and capable engineers and bureaucrats. They did not take bribes or commissions. It was one of the very few companies in the Pakistan government custody that was profitable."

For Adil, working with a well-managed company that dealt with its suppliers in a straightforward manner was a clear advantage; as a result, he changed his focus from trading to supplying Millat with tractor components.

Supplying components to Millat, rather than trading, was a different type of business for Adil Enterprises. The first tractor components procured locally were heavy, simpler, non-precision pieces such as frame parts made from iron or steel molded to manufacturer specifications for each production model. Adil Mansoor's first career experience in the early 1970s, managing a foundry, gave him knowledge of metal products; he was convinced he could supply this new and promising industry. His family invested Rs 600,000 in the new venture, an old foundry and facilities were rented, and in 1982 Excel Engineering, a division of Adil Enterprises, was established. The new company's first product was footrests, a simple part to manufacture. In the second full year of operations, sales reached almost Rs 10 million (Table 2, Exhibits 1A, 1B); the initial investment capital was repaid in full.

Table 2: Excel Sales (million rupees)

Fiscal year	Millat	Others	Total	Fiscal year	Millat	Others	Total
1982/83	1.067	0.000	1.067	1989/90	10.817	4.157	14.974
1983/84	9.587	0.306	9.890	1990/91	6.141	5.391	11.532
1984/85	4.005	0.000	4.005	1991/92	3.399	2.099	5.498
1985/86	4.209	1.467	5.676	1992/93	8.373	9.063	17.436
1986/87	6.122	1.464	7.586	1993/94	7.215	10.143	17.358
1987/88	5.234	0.000	5.234	1/7–31/12/94	3.621	11.443	15.064
1988/89	6.971	6.001	12.972				

Additional information: In 1983/84 Excel was the sole supplier to Millat of two components. The following year Millat developed two other suppliers for those parts. Millat was privatized in fiscal year 1991/92 and its factory was shut down for several months during the transition period. The price of a Massey Ferguson tractor in 1984 was approximately Rs 65,000; this had increased to Rs 250,000 by 1994.
Source: Company documents.

Products

Gradually, new parts were introduced; older parts earning small contributions were phased out. After a few years, Excel developed and produced parts for Ford tractors assembled by Allied Tractors. Ford secured small market share, so Excel discontinued production of Ford components; it began producing Fiat parts for A1-Ghazi. In 1994, Excel produced seven tractor components (Table 3). The newest parts, the final drive casing and cover (for Al-Ghazi), were the most expensive; they contributed the most profit. In fiscal 1994, 43% of Excel sales were to Millat Tractors; 57% to Al-Ghazi. The predominance of Fiat parts, related to development of the casing side final drive, was a new development inasmuch as Millat was traditionally Excel's major customer.

No Excel parts were sold in the "aftermarket" (spare parts), in part because of contractual obligations; Millat and Al-Ghazi insisted they sell branded parts exclusively. Also, Excel's components were generally big, solid tractor frame parts. Commented Adil: "That's a mistake I've made. These parts don't wear out and don't ever need to be replaced." On the other hand, they were also relatively expensive pieces, integral to the assembly of new tractors.

Although Excel was not an exclusive supplier for any product, it had no single direct competitor. Millat listed over 200 possible suppliers, Al-Ghazi 120. For each of

Table 3: Parts Produced and Price List (December 1994)

For Millat Tractor Ltd.

Part	Production commenced	Current price (Rs)	Unit sold 1992/93	Unit sold 1993/94
Fly wheel	1990	1,125	2,762	2,811
Front weight frame	1985	655	3,984	4,577
Lower link assembly	1990	500	7,577	5,475
Footrest	1983	48	7,835	4,494

For Al-Ghazi Tractors Ltd.

Part	Production commenced	Current price (Rs)	Unit sold 1992/93	Unit sold 1993/94
Casing side final drive (2-piece set)	1992	3,200	2,440	2,095
Cover side final drive	1992	495	4,302	6,381
Lower link assembly	1986	410	2,395	2,308

Source: Company documents.

Excel's parts, another supplier manufactured the same part. Typically, the other supplier was a much smaller company manufacturing only one or two parts.

Developing and maintaining good relationships with customers were very important to Excel Engineering. Supplier and customer knew implicitly that the relationship was long term and stable, each relying on the other. Tractor manufacturers needed reliable suppliers of locally-produced parts to meet mandated deletion levels; Excel expected stable order levels and fair prices so developing new components for this small, specialized market was worthwhile. Since the market for each part was about 17,000 units per annum, economies of scale were difficult to achieve; development costs were relatively high. Adil was the main contact between Excel and Millat and Al-Ghazi; he met with key persons frequently, and was personally responsible for developing and maintaining good rapport.

Product Development

Adil saw product development as the most crucial element of the customer relationship. Development of new components was undertaken when customers issued letters of intent for parts they wished to source locally. Development costs, involving much time, money and machinery, were borne by suppliers; developers anticipated regular orders when the part was ready for production. Each major manufacturer preferred two suppliers for each part. Dependable suppliers, such as Excel, were often approached for new components.

Excel seriously began new product development after discussions between Adil and tractor company representatives and issue of a letter of intent. Excel began prototype production following discussions with Excel engineers and production managers and tractor company R&D people. The customer provided drawings and specifications; engineers visited Excel regularly to provide technical assistance during development. A key step was obtaining the customer's First Piece Approval (FPA); a prototype piece was examined and assessed by its quality team. If FPA was received, a 50- to 100-piece pilot batch was produced. If this batch met specifications at a price agreeable to both parties, a final order was given and regular parts production began. New part development could take from two months to three or four years, depending on the specific component and the production complexity involved.

Pricing and Contracts

Component prices, negotiated between Excel and Millat, and Excel and Al-Ghazi, were based on production costs. Detailed breakdowns were provided to customers. Standard overhead rates for product rejects and profits were used; materials and labor were costed at market rates. Adil negotiated profit rates for Excel products, at most, 15% of costs; overhead was generally calculated at 5% of material plus labor, 2% of gross costs was added for product rejects.

Since imported versions of Excel products were not available in Pakistan, Adil could not make direct price comparisons between its products and imports. However, he was confident Excel's parts would be competitive in an open market, despite high material costs, as long as taxes and import duties on inputs were changed to make the market truly open and competitive. (See Table 4 for cost breakdowns for Excel products.)

Table 4: Per Item Product Costs

Fiat components		Massey Ferguson components			
Casing side final drive		**Fly wheel**		**Lower link assembly**	
Raw material	Rs 890	Raw material	Rs 685	Raw material	Rs 324
Direct labor	270	Direct labor	70	Direct labor	90
Overheads	320	Overheads	225	Overheads	100
Profit (loss)	120	Profit (loss)	145	Profit (loss)	(14)
Covering side final drive		**Front weight frame**		**Footrest**	
Raw material	Rs 227	Raw material	Rs 492	Raw material	Rs 19
Direct labor	54	Direct labor	65	Direct labor	11
Overheads	99	Overheads	131	Overheads	10
Profit (loss)	115	Profit (loss)	(33)	Profit (loss)	8
Lower link assembly					
Raw material	Rs 275	Overheads	82		
Direct labor	60	Profit (loss)	(7)		

Note that both the lower link assemblies and the Massey Ferguson front weight frame were near the end of their contract terms, thus were due for renegotiation with the customers. Overheads were allocated proportionately to sales based on projected annual sales of Rs 18 million.
Source: Company documents.

Parts contracts were awarded for one year; prices could be renegotiated during the year, but only in exceptional circumstances. Typically, contracts were renewed at year-end when prices and other terms were renegotiated. Contract talks took place between Adil and the customers' cost and supply committee, including engineering, finance and marketing representatives. Both Al-Ghazi and Millat had standard contracts for all suppliers, making most terms and conditions non-negotiable. Where the tractor company maintained several suppliers, a price would often be negotiated with one and the other(s) asked to match.

As former state-owned enterprises, Al-Ghazi and Millat provided accurate revenue and taxation reports to the government. Income taxes were deducted from suppliers such as Excel, directly from sales orders. Taxes were reported and remitted to the government by tractor manufacturers on the suppliers' behalf; Excel had 2.5% of sales deducted at source as income tax. As a result, Excel did not deal directly with government collection departments until the fiscal year end when it prepared income statements and filed tax returns. This arrangement formalized, and in some ways simplified, relations between even small manufacturers and the government.

Production and Facilities

In 1987, Excel shifted operations from a leased site to its own property next to Millat Tractors, a few kilometers from Al-Ghazi's Lahore operations. In 1994, Excel employed 200, mainly semi-skilled, laborers. In fiscal 1994, capacity utilization was 60%; by December 1994, in response to the Awami Tractor Scheme, it was only 40%.

Excel Engineering was involved in five of six basic metal-working processes. The factory's backbone was the foundry; cast iron and automotive steel scrap were melted into molten steel, the basic production material. The use of scrap metal reflected insufficient supply of new steel. Government-owned Pakistan Steel Mills could not meet local demands for new steel; its prices were higher than international and sometimes product quality was too low for the engineering industry. Most metal fabricating companies, such as Excel, used scrap metal in their foundries.

Excel used several processes and machinery in production:

- Casting: shaping parts by pouring molten iron or steel into a mold. Excel used oil-fired rotary furnaces, cupola furnaces and pit furnaces. To cast the molten steel, jolt squeezing pneumatic molding machines were used with molds created in the in-house sand-making plant.
- Forging: metal is heated until soft so it can be converted to a desired shape through hammering and use of dyes. Excel owned a forging hammer, three presses and some butt-welding machines.
- Fabrication: creating a new part out of various sub-components or semi-processed pieces. Excel used arc welders and argon welders in this process.
- Heat treatment: changing physical characteristics of metal parts by heating in an oil-fired furnace and cooling in water and/or oil baths. For example, to give different surface effects or harden metal.
- Machining: using lathes, drills and other precision tools to refine metal pieces. Some equipment used to make necessary refinements were boring, milling, shaving, slot-making and various drilling machines. Of all Excel's processes, machining used the most precise and expensive equipment.

Over Rs 12 million was invested in Excel's equipment; Rs 8 million in land and plant. Most processes were basic metalworking techniques, but some parts machining equipment was specific for automotive parts production.

Production scheduling was quite simple; Al-Ghazi and Millat provided suppliers with delivery schedules that broke annual requirements into monthly orders. Delivery schedules were updated quarterly; since parts were shipped immediately after production, Excel generally had no finished goods inventory.

Organization

Excel Engineering shareholders were nominees designated by Adil Mansoor to keep his various business enterprises distinct. His responsibilities as CEO involved marketing, business development and finance; he also had several business activities outside Excel. Adil's brother was general manager and an executive director of Excel in charge of production and day-to-day company operations (Figure 1).

Excel employed two engineers, responsible for developing new products and ensuring quality standards were met. Adil was proud that most workers came from the first foundry where he worked in the early 1970s; most workers were semi-skilled and had been trained by their employers. Excel did not have a union; Adil strongly believed an excellent relationship existed between workers and management. Said Adil: "We have so good human relationships with our workers; I have never dismissed any worker in my career up to now."

Awami Tractor Scheme

In July 1994, the Pakistan government announced the Awami Tractor Scheme (also the People's or Green Tractor Scheme). First floated by the previous government, the idea was to distribute locally-made tractors at low prices to poorer farmers. The proposal was renamed and modified to distribute cheaper imported tractors by Prime Minister Benazir Bhutto's government; it was due to be implemented in fiscal 1995. Outside the scheme, Millat and Al-Ghazi tractors were sold at Rs 250,000 to Rs 300,000 per tractor with ADBP financing.

Under the Awami Scheme, duty and tax-free imports of 120,000 tractors were to be sold at Rs 150,000 each for the next two years. Soft credit terms for imported tractors would be available through ADBP. Down payments of Rs 20,000 were required; purchasers would receive ten-year loans for Rs 130,000 at 13.5% (market rate 17.5%). (A further 1.5% discount was granted for timely payments.) Although ADBP raised interest rates relative to market rates in the previous few years, the new rates still offered attractive subsidies. Tractors from Russia (Belarus) and Poland (Ursus) conformed to the scheme; they would be imported and sold by Fecto and Khyber Tractors, established Pakistan firms. In addition to tractor imports, unlimited amounts of tractor parts could be imported in the two-year period. According to the commerce minister:

> Local manufacturers have been pampered for a very long time; the time has come for them to prepare for competition ... In the new budget, equal opportunities have been

Figure 1: Organization Chart

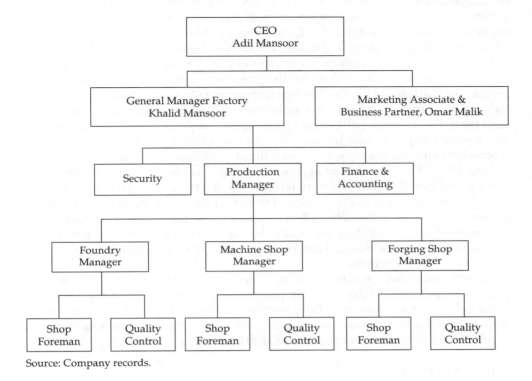

Source: Company records.

offered to local manufacturers – 10% duty on CKD units with sales tax while there is no sales tax on spares manufactured in the country.

Tractor industry response was quick but uncoordinated. Millat and Al-Ghazi each lobbied the government to discontinue or alter the scheme, or at least include locally-built tractors. They argued that tax and duty exemptions granted to imported tractors should also be available to local tractor assemblers, allowing them to reduce prices to customers and that the same soft financing terms should be available.

Tractor suppliers had no formal organization. The larger firms belonged to industry associations (e.g., Pakistan Association of Automotive Parts & Accessories Manufacturers [PAAPAM], local chambers of commerce). PAAPAM immediately began working with Millat and Al-Ghazi to lobby against the Awami Tractor Scheme. However, since PAAPAM represented suppliers to all automotive sectors, it was cautious about jeopardizing its position for other automotive suppliers and did not take a confrontational stance.

In September 1994, Millat Tractors organized a vendor meeting to discuss the Awami Scheme. The suppliers recognized the need for a lobbying group to represent their interests. Adil Mansoor and Omar Malik (business associate, fellow vendor), were nominated leaders of the Pakistan Tractor Vendors Association (PTVA), an ad hoc action committee formed to address issues raised by the Scheme. The PTVA began a publicity campaign to raise public interest and persuade the government and its supporters it should be altered. (See Exhibit 2 for a publicity statement.) Adil and Omar Malik met with government and industry leaders to discuss tractor supplier concerns.

Under pressure from various forces including the PTVA, Millat managers and the foreign owners of Al-Ghazi Tractors, the government modified the Awami Tractor Scheme. For parts suppliers, the first big change was a limit of 8% of a tractor's value on the amount of spare parts that could be imported. This move promised to preserve, at least partially, the local parts manufacturing industry, but was less than suppliers and tractor companies had hoped. Pressure was maintained and, after months of discussions and negotiations, more significant modifications were announced (December 1994). The government agreed to include locally-assembled tractors in the Scheme and to reduce its scale from 60,000 to 38,000 tractors in the first year; 20,000 imports, the remaining 18,000 produced locally. In addition, the limit on spare part imports was further reduced to a 4% maximum of a tractor's value. These parts could be imported exempt of duty and taxes. Negotiations continued; the government delayed the Scheme's official launch so that further modifications could be fully discussed before implementation.

In these uncertain conditions, Millat and Al-Ghazi decreased production to prepare for expected lost sales. Work in progress was completed, but further orders, passed along to the tractor suppliers, were minimized. Excel's orders decreased and its production schedule was reduced. By December 1994, business had slowed so much that Adil expected that month's sales to be the worst of the year.

Adil's Alternatives

Although the proposed December changes relieved Adil from initial despair, the tractor supply industry's future was still uncertain. Since Millat and Al-Ghazi expected to be included in the new scheme, production continued and orders trickled into Excel and other suppliers. Adil contemplated Excel's prospects.

After 20 years as an entrepreneur, Adil had ambitious goals for himself and Excel. Attracted by recent government deregulation moves in financial services, he wanted to return to banking, but with a chartered bank. He also had political aspirations; he had met many influential people and become knowledgeable of the local political scene. Adil believed Excel was important in helping to achieve these goals; income from Excel could be relied on to finance other ventures. Adil eventually expected to hand Excel over to his son and brother to ensure they had interesting careers and a reliable income source. He also wanted to build a completely Pakistani tractor, 100% from local components. Expansion of Excel business and continuing current production were necessary to achieve this goal.

Option 1: Maintain Status Quo

Excel could continue on the same path. Until announcement of the Awami Tractor Scheme, the fiscal year's business was exceptionally good; sales for the first five months were Rs 13 million versus Rs 18 million for the entire previous year. Adil was sure that Excel would not stop any of its current products. The Awami Scheme had slowed down sales for this year, but he believed the tractor supply industry would be solid in the long run. He said: "This country is still very reliant on agriculture and farmers won't go back to hand plows after having tractors." He estimated the replacement market for old tractors being retired at 20,000 to 25,000 per year.

Supplying tractor manufacturers had been a good, reliable business for over ten years, providing steady income, while also giving Adil the freedom to pursue other interests and business activities. Making tractor parts was a good business decision. He noted:

> It's a very nice business in Pakistan. I don't have to pay any bribes or commissions. I don't have to save for income tax because two and a half percent is deducted directly from orders to Millat and Al-Ghazi. At the start this was a very difficult business, but now that it is streamlined, it's very easy. I can keep very loose control on the business. I just get reports on sales, orders, inventory, banking and so on.

Now that the Awami Tractor Scheme was modified to include local tractors, Adil believed Excel could continue without a major strategy evaluation.

Option 2: More Tractor Components

Adil considered the advantages of adding new tractor components; indeed, the final drive casing for Al-Ghazi was the main cause of recent increases in sales and earnings. Adil believed money could be made by adding components and better using Excel's capacity and equipment. Millat approached Excel to develop more complex and expensive components (e.g., clutch assembly), giving the opportunity to expand into higher value-added products.

Adding more sophisticated products involved considerable development costs. In early 1994, Excel began developing new components; these activities were on hold because of the Awami Tractor Scheme. The clutch assembly for Millat had been developed and Rs 3.6 million invested in equipment changes and extensions but Excel could not begin production until it obtained a test rig. This computerized equipment checked heat emissions, materials, reliability and other clutch features. It was not available locally, so Excel would have to import the test rig at a cost of Rs 5 million to Rs 6.25 million. Clutch assemblies could be sold to Millat at Rs 5,000 per set; Adil anticipated 600 sets per month production. Since clutches wore out, the assemblies could be sold through Millat to the aftermarket. Another supplier was already producing clutches locally, but Millat had approached Excel because of its two-supplier policy. The other supplier had a test rig, but was unwilling to share with a direct competitor such as Excel. In introducing the clutch assembly, Adil believed a best case scenario was annual sales of Rs 70 million within two years, topping Rs 100 million in five years.

Excel had begun development of an engine bracket assembly for Al-Ghazi, a less complicated part used to hold the engine in place. Development took six months and a prototype was sent to Al-Ghazi for FPA. Adil expected approval; he could then decide if Excel should enter production. To date, Rs 200,000 was invested in jigs, fixtures and patterns.[1] There was no aftermarket demand for this component, but Adil expected Excel could sell 400 sets per month at Rs 500 per set. Excel expected profit margins of 15% on all tractor components.

Al-Ghazi and Millat were licensed by Fiat and Massey Ferguson respectively to manufacture and sell tractors in Pakistan. Neither firm could export tractors or tractor parts without principal manufacturer's permission. However, parts developed locally could be purchased by Massey Ferguson or Fiat dealers in any country. Excel's export possibilities were limited unless it developed a clutch assembly or other part suited for these tractors on its own.

Option 3: Looking to New Markets

Other paths were open to Excel. The tractor aftermarket was difficult for Excel as its products were mostly rarely replaced or rebuilt frame parts. However, adapting these parts for other automotive sectors was feasible; an obvious choice was other automotive parts markets. Adil was less enthusiastic about prospects in the main automotive sectors; years previously he had approached automobile companies about being a supplier but was discouraged by their response. The aftermarket was open to Excel, but in Adil's view, would represent a difficult challenge.

Supplying the automotive aftermarket would mean hiring a sales team, developing relationships with distributors, perhaps paying commissions throughout the channel and extending credit to small and less reliable customers. Adil estimated a basic sales team would comprise a marketing manager and three salespeople based in major centers (e.g., Karachi, Lahore, Rawalpindi). Each would receive a salary and commissions accounting for about 7% of an item's price. Accounts receivable and bad debt costs would increase because of dealing with small wholesalers rather than major manufacturers. Buyers in the parts market were not very quality conscious; they tended to purchase the cheapest brand so margins were leaner than Excel typically earned. Retail prices of Millat or Fiat branded parts were about 50% higher than the cost to the tractor manufacturers; these prices incorporated all increased sales costs.

Excel had the expertise, capacity and general ability to manufacture parts for cars, buses, trucks, auto rickshaws and other vehicles. Adil had not ruled out other automotive sectors but had not investigated them in depth.

Option 4: Something Completely Different

Adil considered developing completely new products. Excel was skilled at producing tractor parts, but its production processes were not limited to that sector; other metalworking applications were feasible. For example, Adil learned of an opportunity to manufacture pumps for a Chinese company. He began talks with the Chinese manufacturer to learn more about the pumps and opportunities to produce and sell them in Pakistan.

---

[1] Jigs and fixtures were extensions added to machines to modify them for different uses.

Adil was considering centrifugal and submersible pumps designed to move domestic water and deep water (tubewells), and for commercial use by service stations. Other pump families were available in Pakistan, but Excel was investigating just one type of relatively small pump using simple technology that could be produced on existing equipment. Some investment in jigs and fixtures would be needed to modify machines for these new products but not major capital investments. Adil estimated development costs of Rs 1 million to Rs 1.5 million. Some small R&D activities would be necessary and a sales force would be needed. The pumps would be targeted at the private market, not government agencies. Adil foresaw opening his own sales outlets in larger cities where the majority (60% to 70%) of sales could be expected. Non-exclusive dealers could be used in smaller communities.

Currently, three companies made similar pumps in Pakistan: KSB, PECO and Golden Pumps. KSB was a subsidiary of a German company; it sold expensive high quality products and had 64% pump market share. PECO (government-owned) and Golden Pumps (private) each had annual sales of Rs 100 million, 18% market share. Total pump sales were Rs 550 million per year. Adil estimated Excel could develop and begin production of a submersible pump in six months, but spending 18 months on development and introduction of a six to eight pump full product line, with a goal of securing 25% market share in the first full year, might be advisable. Prices would be slightly higher than other local products, Rs 1,500 per pump versus Rs 1,300 for PECO/Golden Pumps, but less than foreign branded alternatives or imports. Adil believed pumps would provide gross profits of 18% to 20% after deducting selling expenses. Since the technology was not very sophisticated, Adil believed he could position Excel pumps as high quality, backed with lifetime performance guarantees. Based on his projections, Adil was confident pump production could be profitable by the second year, after first year losses.

Decisions

Adil believed many possibilities were open to Excel but only a few were being seriously considered. He could see almost limitless opportunities for diversifying even in the engineering industry. The problem was identifying the best and in choosing among them. He meditated:

> The nice thing about engineering is its flexibility. It is different from textiles, agriculture and other industries Pakistan is so reliant on. The engineering industry can diversify. Numerous options are open with only small changes in equipment and Excel has all the facilities of a good engineering workshop.

Without taking on any very new technological capabilities, Excel could use its machinery to produce products as diverse as bombshells (defense industry); rough castings (export); pumps, pipe fittings and other equipment (textile, sugar mills); and, of course, tractor and other automotive parts. He wondered the best way to drive Excel into the future, maintaining current momentum and capitalizing on its strengths.

Exhibit 1A: Profit and Loss Account for Year Ended June 30, 1994 (rupees)

Sales		18,013,657
Cost of sales		14,320,806
Gross profit		3,692,851
Operating expenses:		
Administrative	2,422,970	
Selling	283,168	
Financial	441,550	
		3,147,688
Operating profit (loss)		545,163
Other income		589,426
Profit (loss) before taxation		1,134,589
Provision for taxation		450,341
Profit (loss) after taxation		684,248
Profit (loss) brought forward		1,394,873
Unappropriated profit		2,079,121

Exhibit 1B: Balance Sheet for Year Ended June 30, 1994 (rupees)

Share capital and liabilities		
Share capital and reserves		
Authorized share capital		
15,000 ordinary shares of Rs 1,000 each	1,500,000	
Issued, subscribed and paid up share capital		
12,710 ordinary shares of Rs 1,000 each	12,710,000	
Unappropriated profit	2,079,121	
Total share capital		14,789,121
Current liabilities		
Short-term running finance	70,212	
Creditors and accruals	685,053	
Bill discounting	1,781,000	
Provision for taxation	450,341	
Total current liabilities		2,986,606
Share capital and liabilities		17,775,727
Property and assets		
Operating fixed assets		8,927,656
Long-term securities		10,000
Current assets		
Stock in trade	3,043,061	
Stores and spares	850,950	
Debtors – considered good	2,610,768	
Advances and deposits	1,671,775	
Cash and bank balances	661,517	
Total current assets		8,838,071
Property and assets		17,775,727

Pakistan Tractor Vendors Association

Prime Minister Awami Tractor Scheme – How It will Destroy Pakistan's Tractor Industry

1. World over governments, even in developed countries like the U.S., Japan, European countries, etc., protect the interests of national industries against unfair imports. Recently, the EEC has imposed penal duties against dumping of electronic products originating from Far Eastern countries. U.S. has all along been protecting its industry through quotas for various categories of imports. Similarly, Japan has restricted its market through various means to protect their own industry. It is unfortunate that in Pakistan the local manufacturing industry is being made to suffer at the hand of dumping from Socialist Block countries. It is even more regrettable that our own government, instead of protecting the industry is a party to this dumping of tractors to spoil the local tractor industry. The tractors which are normally sold at around US$6,500* Ex-Works, are being offered at Rs 150,000 retail anywhere in Pakistan. Assuming a cost of around Rs 16,000 from C&F to retail and allowing for the freight and FOB costs in the country of origin, this would mean an Ex-Works price of US$3,500 for the same product. This is a clear cut case of dumping which is being encouraged by our government and is against International Fair Trade and the GATT agreement to which Pakistan is signatory. Instead of imposing penal duties on such offers, the government is waiving the normal duties irrespective of the crippling effect which it will have on the local industry.

2. An impression is being created that the local tractor manufacturers are not willing to participate in the Awami Tractor Scheme. On the contrary, the local industry has been in negotiation with the Government for over six months to try and determine the parameters under which the scheme is to be run in terms of volume, withdrawal of duties and sales tax on raw material and CKD components, financial aspects, etc. While up to now no confirmation of the rules of the game have been made to the local industry, the scheme has been launched to two particular makes of imported tractors. SROs have also been issued for these two tractors exempting them from the Custom Duty and Sales Tax, not only for the CBU tractors but also for unlimited spare parts. Details of financial support for the imported CBUs in terms of opening Letters of Credit, mode of payment, insurance, clearance charges, etc., are up to now not known.

3. If the Yellow Cab and the Yellow Tractor Schemes of the previous government were bad, the Awami Tractor Scheme can by no yardstick be called a healthy scheme for the country. The Yellow Cab Scheme crippled the automobile sector, which has still not recovered from the setback despite special concessions provided by the government. The Yellow Tractor Scheme launched but not implemented by the previous government had provisioned for supply of locally built tractors only, whereas the Awami Tractor Scheme has not even given the chance to the local industry to participate in the scheme which is based on imported tractors only.

4. The local industry has the capacity to meet the entire requirement of the government for the Awami Tractor Scheme but instead of utilizing the local industry and offering only additional requirements for import, the scheme is being launched the other way round.

Exhibit 2 (cont'd)

5. The Government of Pakistan had approved the indigenisation programme under which tractors were to be manufactured. Based on the enforcement of this indigenisation programme, vendor industry developed by making huge investments and today over 80% of the tractor is locally manufactured to achieve self-sufficiency to a large extent. At this stage if the deletion programmes are done away with or CBU imports are allowed duty-free, it will be a disservice to the local industry.

6. In case the local industry is ignored in trying to make the Awami Tractor Scheme a success, hundreds of companies will become bankrupt and will not be in a position to survive or repay loans taken by them from banks.

7. Under the Awami Tractor Scheme, the ADBP has booked 122,000 tractors which are to be supplied by import from ex-Socialist countries. The present sales per year of tractors in Pakistan are 17,000 – the market will be flooded with inferior tractors and the market will collapse which will result in the following:

    i)   Shall destroy Pakistani tractor industry which has developed 80% local content over a period of 15 years.

    ii)   Shall render 100,000 skilled workers jobless.

    iii)   Shall close down 502 manufacturing units of tractor parts and accessories and billions of rupees industry investment shall be wasted.

    iv)   Shall incur revenue loss of Rs 540 crores** to the Government of Pakistan.

    v)   Shall cost Government of Pakistan Rs 900 crores in precious foreign exchange on import of these tractors.

    vi)   Shall cost huge amounts in foreign exchange on import of spare parts of imported tractors.

    vii) Shall increase the miseries of the farming community on account of frequent break-downs of inferior imported tractors.

8. If only Pakistani manufacturers are allowed in the Awami Tractor Scheme and no tractor is imported this will have the following benefits:

    a)   Pakistan capacity of world famous tractors is 50,000 per year. This will generate 300 thousand jobs for skilled and unskilled workers.

    b)   Booked tractors can easily be supplied in 2½ years and the farmer will get instead of inferior tractors, high grade technology tractors.

    c)   Revenue loss of 540 crores will be saved by the Government.

    d)   Crores in precious foreign exchange shall be saved.

Omar Malik (Chairman)

---

* In 1994 the exchange rate was Rs 30 per US$1.
** Crore is an Urdu term for ten million.

Case 33

Pearl Continental Hotel, Lahore

Zehra Saced Mahoon, Wasim Azhar
Lahore University of Management Sciences, Lahore

As he skillfully steered his car out of the hotel driveway into the fast moving evening traffic along the Mall, Syed Qasim Jafri, general manager of the Pearl Continental Hotel, Lahore, Pakistan, ruminated over the pricing decisions confronting him. It was January 12, 1990 and he had to make decisions regarding three pricing issues. His most immediate concern was a quotation to the organizers of the World Hockey Tournament in Lahore who wanted 100 double rooms for 11 days starting February 19, 1990. He also had to review, and possibly revise, the discount policy for group accounts such as the Pakistan International Airlines (PIA) and foreign tour groups. Finally, he had to submit recommendations concerning room rates for fiscal 1991 to head office within a week; he had to decide whether or not to recommend an alteration in the five-year pattern of increasing room rates by 10% to 12% p.a. Qasim Jafri considered Pearl Continental (Pearl) Lahore to be the price leader not only among five-star hotels in Lahore, but of the four hotels that made up the Pearl Continental hotel chain in Pakistan. He wanted to retain that leadership.

ജാ

The Hotel Business in Pakistan

Hotels were generally rated on quality, at either an international or national level, by an assigned number of stars; a five-star hotel was considered top of the line. At the international level, the rating was granted by an association of hotel managers and operators. At the national level in Pakistan, the rating was given by the Ministry of Tourism. The Ministry established criteria for evaluation, of which the hotel managers were aware, and usually informed the hotels prior to an inspection for rating evaluation. To some, these ratings appeared subjective and arbitrary.

Many foreign business persons and tourists visited Pakistan but there existed a marked difference between the hotel business in Lahore and Karachi, Pakistan's two major cities. Karachi's hotel industry flourished during the 1970s as Karachi had the country's only international airport. All foreign tourists and business people, as well as Pakistanis traveling abroad, had to pass through Karachi. In the late 1980s, airports in Lahore, Islamabad and Peshawar also became international, but the frequency of foreign flights to and from these cities remained lower than Karachi's. Most export deals were consummated in Karachi and it continued to be the most significant business city of Pakistan. However, since it was a relatively new city compared to Lahore, it offered few tourist attractions, just the beach and a few modern monuments.

In the past, Karachi had been the center of trade and commerce in the country. However, many businesses had transferred headquarters to Lahore due to political uncertainty and ethnic unrest in the 1980s. Airline traffic in Lahore had grown substantially as the result of increased commercial activity and the promotion of tourist attractions in and around the city. Development of the Sheikhupura and Chunian industrial areas led to increased numbers of Pakistani executives traveling to Lahore.[1]

Lahore was the center of several cultural and athletic events such as the annual Horse and Cattle Show and international cricket, hockey, and squash tournaments.[2] During these events hotel rooms were scarce. Rooms were reserved in advance for contract customers and hotels frequently refused walk-ins, resulting in "closed dates" for room reservations.

Many Pakistanis traveled for business and pleasure; in general, executive travel was financed by companies. Qasim Jafri believed 85% of Pearl guests were company financed. He also believed executives who traveled frequently were more inclined to stay at five-star hotels; those traveling infrequently preferred staying with relatives or friends. Companies generally reimbursed salespersons up to Rs 500 per day for actual expenses; alternatively, salespersons might, and frequently did, take a daily traveling allowance of about Rs 300 and stay with friends or relatives; as a result, they supplemented their incomes with the traveling allowance. Some large companies maintained guest houses that were available for employees and their families.

India was a major tourist competitor; the Indian government heavily subsidized the tourist industry and was more aggressive in advertising tourist attractions. Hotel rates in India were lower than in Pakistan; hence, Indian tour rates were appreciably lower. Most tourists did not differentiate between the cultural heritage and traditions of the two countries since before independence (1947), Pakistan was part of India. In addition, since Delhi was only 35 minutes' flying time from Lahore, the Pakistani tourist industry was under pressure to lower rates to be competitive.

The Pearl Chain

The Pearl Continental and the Holiday Inn chains in Pakistan were owned by the Hashwani group through its holding company Pakistan Services Ltd. (PSL) and

---

[1] The Sheikhupura and Chunian industrial areas, comprising various manufacturing plants, were located west and south of Lahore respectively. The government made special provisions for utilities in these areas and offered several tax advantages.

[2] The Horse and Cattle Show had evolved from the traditional system of market fares, when traders from all over the Punjab would gather in Lahore with their livestock and other produce for barter. Currently, the show lasted one week and farmers from all over Pakistan participated. The event was celebrated with folk song, dance and other cultural events.

Hashwani Hotels Ltd. respectively. The Hotel Inter-Continental chain was acquired in 1985, when the hotel's image was deteriorating due to service inefficiencies. The name was changed to Pearl Continental and several improvements were made: new decor, fresh landscaping of hotel grounds, and upgrading of food and service by training relevant personnel.

As a result of political uncertainty in Karachi, the chain's head office was recently shifted to Islamabad. The general managers of the chain's hotels reported to the Director of Operations, who was responsible to the Chairman of the Board, Mr. Hashwani (Figure 1).

Figure 1:   The Pearl Continental Organization Chart

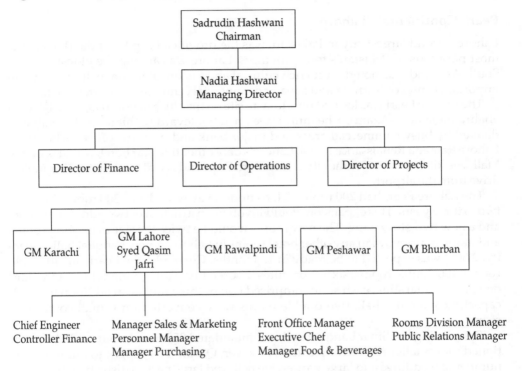

The board of directors decided that future PSL expansion should not focus solely on the hotel industry, but should also be related to tour operations, rent-a-car services and travel agencies. Accordingly, a travel agency, Trans Air Travel, based in Karachi was recently acquired. The group was considering expanding internationally and Pearl Continental Hotels (Overseas) Ltd. had been incorporated in the U.K. PSL had 60% equity participation, 40% was mainly from Pakistanis settled abroad.

Pearl's annual budgeting process (January to December) commenced in June. (See Exhibit 1 for financial results.) By October, hotels submitted targets for review: occupancy levels (ratio of room nights occupied divided by total room nights available); average room rate (total room rental revenue divided by total room nights occupied);

revenues by department; staffing levels and costs. Final targets were negotiated between general managers and head office staff; budget revisions were rare. Annual evaluation of general managers was based on several comparisons: actuals versus budgeted targets, competitors' performance and Pearl's previous year's performance.

The Pearl at Lahore was the second of the four hotels in the Pearl Continental chain; other Pearl locations were Karachi, Peshawar and Rawalpindi. The Pearl in Rawalpindi was a half-hour drive from the federal capital of Islamabad. The newest member of the Pearl chain would be the Bhurban Resort, due to open in 1991 in the popular Murree hills in northern Pakistan, about 350 kilometers from Lahore. The Pearl chain's current capacity was 1,000 rooms. Completion of Bhurban Resort and planned expansion in Lahore would add 410 rooms.

Pearl Continental, Lahore

Lahore, second largest city in Pakistan, was the provincial capital of the Punjab, the most populous of Pakistan's four provinces. Lahore was among the oldest cities in South Asia and was noted for its rich cultural and historical heritage. It was both an important center of learning and a major commercial center in northern Pakistan.

The Lahore Pearl was located on a 13-acre site on the city's major road, the Mall (aka Shahra-e-Quaid-e-Azam), a beautiful tree lined boulevard (Exhibit 2). The Mall was flanked by busy commercial areas and major bank and business offices. The Avari Lahore Ramada Renaissance Hotel, Lahore's only other five-star hotel, was also on the Mall, one kilometer nearer the city center. Both Pearl and Avari were about 15 minutes' drive from the airport.

The Lahore Pearl had 200 rooms. Plans under way would add 300 rooms in about two to three years. This expansion would involve construction of two additional floors and a new two-story wing. The new rooms would be twice the size of existing rooms and more luxurious than any other hotel rooms in Lahore. A new banquet hall (capacity: 2,500) was expected to be ready in 12 months. Currently, the Pearl had 40 single rooms, 100 double rooms, six junior suites, 12 executive suites, four deluxe suites and one presidential suite; each suite comprised two or three rooms. In addition to a 850-capacity conference hall, two double rooms were converted into small conference rooms.

The existing Shalimar banquet hall accommodated 850 people, but could be partitioned into smaller rooms for parties. However, Qasim Jafri sought to minimize the number of weddings and large parties. He believed large parties disturbed the hotel's normal routine and reduced service efficiency to hotel guests. Owing to increased demand on rooms, soon after becoming general manager, he eliminated the program under which a complimentary double room (one night) was given to couples whose wedding party was at the hotel.

Seasonality played an important role in demand for hotel accommodation in Lahore; high from October to April, when many business travelers and foreign tourists came to Lahore, slow during the summer. Qasim Jafri thought the basic reason was climatic; people liked to travel in the cooler months, even for business purposes. He believed that during the summer vacation most holiday makers in his target segment preferred either to go abroad or travel to the cooler northern parts of the country. The Pearl Bhurban Resort was being built to cater to this need. (See Table 1 for a breakdown of guest composition by nationality at the Pearl.)

Table 1: Guest Composition

Country of residence	Percent occupancy	Country of residence	Percent occupancy	Country of residence	Percent occupancy
Africa	1.78	Indonesia	0.11	Singapore	0.21
Australia	1.28	Italy	1.00	Spain	1.30
Bahrain & Gulf States	0.42	Japan	6.44	Sri Lanka	0.15
Canada	1.07	Korea	1.06	Sweden	0.88
China	0.38	Kuwait	0.31	Switzerland	1.94
Denmark	0.61	Malaysia	0.10	Thailand	0.24
England	4.23	New Zealand	0.38	U.A.E.	0.64
France	2.14	Norway	0.16	U.S.	4.29
Germany	3.63	Pakistan	35.10	Other countries	14.05
Greece	0.07	Philippines	0.08	Airline crew	14.00
Hong Kong	0.38	Portugal	0.02		100.00
India	1.48	Saudi Arabia	0.09		

Source: Company records.

Qasim Jafri believed the Pearl's success was due to timely service and quality. He placed his department heads under great pressure to maintain the quality image and monitored them closely. He believed better service was provided at lower occupancy levels inasmuch as the telephone and elevator were less busy, more parking spaces were available, the lobby was less crowded and the hotel staff able to extend better care to guests. During previous years, the Pearl's average occupancy levels were 80% and 85% (Tables 2A, 2B).

When a large tour group or Pakistan International Airlines (PIA) crew left the hotel, a significant number of rooms were vacated; it took several days to reach average occupancy levels. Airline crew and in-transit passengers accounted for 10% to 15% of hotel occupancy. At times, PIA sent more people than were scheduled and the front office manager accommodated them at other hotels (e.g., the Avari or one of the city's four-star hotels). The Pearl had reciprocal arrangements for dealing with such exigencies.

Pearl Lahore's General Manager: Syed Qasim Jafri

Qasim Jafri had been with the Pearl Lahore for just over two years; he was the first Pakistani general manager. Most of his career was with the Hilton International chain of hotels, both in Pakistan and abroad. Having obtained his bachelor's degree from the University of the Punjab (1974), Qasim Jafri completed a one-year course in hotel management in Austria. He graduated top of the class and was offered a one-year training program at the Hilton in Vienna. He became a regular member of the Vienna Hilton staff and was sponsored by Hilton to take courses in Hotel Management at Cornell (U.S.) and at the Hilton's Career Development Institute in Montreal. In 1977, he was

Table 2A: Occupancy Rates (1989)

Category	October–April	May–September
Rack rate	12.45%	9.75%
Corporate rate	39.10	25.80
Tour groups	10.65	7.80
Airline crew	12.85	10.20
Preferred rate	17.85	11.70
Total occupancy	92.80	65.25

Table 2B: Room Statistics (1989)

	December Actual	Budget	Total 1989
Room nights available	5,890	5,890	69,350
Room nights occupied	5,411	4,567	55,987
Percentage occupancy	91.87%	77.54%	80.73%
Number of guests	6,509	5,199	64,310
Avg. room rate (Rs)	1,067	1,181	1,133

Source: Company records.

transferred to the newly opened Lahore Hilton. He remained for two years, then became Sales Director at the Abu Dhabi Hilton. Believing his career was blocked in Sales, Jafri requested a transfer to Operations. He accepted a lower-level position as Front Desk Manager in Lahore; within six months he was promoted to Rooms Division Manager. When he left the Hilton he was Assistant General Manager in charge of Sales and Marketing.

According to Qasim Jafri, personal contacts were very important in securing business in the hotel industry. For example, members of cricket teams customarily stayed at the Inter-Continental during tours. However, when Qasim Jafri joined the Lahore Hilton, his personal friend Arif Abbasi in the Pakistan Board of Cricket Control diverted this business to the Hilton. This arrangement continued until Qasim Jafri left the Hilton to join the Pearl; then, Mr. Abbasi canceled his Hilton contract and took his business to the Pearl. Qasim Jafri believed he had brought over 30% of the hotel's business with him when he joined. He was convinced, however, that even with friends, such business would only remain if customers received good value for money.

On joining the Pearl, Qasim Jafri was careful to cultivate a good working relationship with his counterpart at the Avari. As a result, an understanding developed that neither hotel would quote prices lower than a specified amount. Qasim Jafri took pride in his work and personal track record, especially his achievements at the Pearl. Since joining in 1988, several changes were made in lobby decor and room furnishings. He was involved in details of daily operations (e.g., choice of fragrances for towels and artwork for wall hangings). He often said to his staff: "The devil lies in the details."

As general manager, he introduced a regular monthly newsletter, "The Pearl Flash," containing information on current and planned promotional events at the Pearl that was regularly mailed to guests who frequently stayed or dined at the hotel and contract customers. The corporate office published a quarterly magazine, "Bonjour," for guests staying at the hotel. Containing articles of tourist interest, Bonjour was subsidized by various advertisers. Qasim Jafri believed that most problems at the hotel occurred when occupancy dropped below 50%: "Employee morale falls, since people are happier when they are busy. They have less time for gossip and stirring up union problems. Besides, the number of tips is related directly with the volume of business."

Qasim Jafri was interested in classical music and literature and believed that diversions from work were important … "there was more to life than work." Although the general manager had a hotel apartment, Qasim Jafri preferred to live outside the hotel. However, he often visited the hotel at night and stayed several hours on weekends.

The Competition

The Lahore Avari had 172 rooms and 15 suites of two to three rooms each. The rooms were less spacious than at the Pearl and offered somewhat less pleasant views. The Avari started operations in Lahore on October 1, 1988, having previously been leased by the owner, Mr. Byre Avari, to the Hilton Hotel chain for 23 years. Although Mr. Avari had been in the hotel business since 1944, his operations were mainly in Karachi, where he ran Avari Towers and Hotel Beach Luxury. Recently, management turnover at the Avari Lahore had increased; the French general manager left and the position had been vacant for some weeks. In the past three years, the Avari had three general managers, all expatriates. Qasim Jafri did not regard the Avari as a significant threat to the Pearl. He believed the Avari always followed the Pearl's actions. For example, the Avari also planned a hillside resort at Malamjabba to compete with Pearl's Bhurban resort.

Sheraton and Holiday Inn, each with 200 rooms, were expected to enter Lahore in 1993. The Holiday Inn Lahore franchise was not controlled by the Hashwani group but by a prominent local businessman. Both the Sheraton and the Holiday Inn were ranked as five-star hotels in Pakistan; the Sheraton was the price leader in Karachi. The new Sheraton Lahore would be located closer to the airport, about seven kilometers from the Pearl; the new Holiday Inn would be located on the Mall next to Avari, behind the Al Hamra Arts Centre.

At the Pearl, average contribution margins were 85% on rooms, 30% to 45% on food and beverages. (See Exhibit 2 for revenue breakdown.) Hotel guests accounted for 60% to 65% of total food and beverage revenue. Qasim Jafri believed that Avari had similar contribution margins.

Pricing at the Pearl Lahore

Room rates at the Pearl Lahore were the highest in the chain. Established practice at both the Pearl and Avari was to review room rates twice a year; the first price increase was implemented in January, the second in late September. Until late 1988, room rates at the Pearl were lower than the Avari's; for the past two years Pearl room rates were Rs 100 to Rs 200 higher than the Avari's. Rooms were priced on the basis of past performance, required growth rate and expected inflation rates. Rates for the different categories of rooms were listed in the "Rack rate." Various categories of customers were given discounts off these rates. Hence, rates varied among guests staying at the hotel. The main categories of rates were:

- **Rack rate** was the list price of rooms displayed at check-in counters (Table 3) and quoted to walk-in customers who would only stay for a few nights. Mostly, these customers were not regular guests.
- **Corporate rate** was charged to those organizations that guaranteed a certain number of nights per month, generally contracted on an annual basis. It comprised two categories: customers who guaranteed 50 to 100 nights per month (up to 25% discount); those guaranteeing 100 or more nights per month (up to 60% discount). Each contract was negotiated independently so that two corporate customers might have different rates, even if they guaranteed the same number of nights per month.
- **Tour groups rate** discounts (up to 60% to be competitive with Indian tour rates) were provided for travel arrangements handled by a tour operator. Two other tourist categories, arrangements made personally with the hotel on or before arrival in Pakistan and walk-in customers did not receive discounts.
- **Airline crew rate** (up to 70% discount) was given the crew of international airlines staying at the hotel in transit. PIA, the Pearl's largest customer had a contract for 1,000 nights per month, although it took a long time to clear its bills.
- **Preferred rate** (up to 40% discount) was a special rate for frequent business travelers, diplomats and government officials. (See Table 4 for occupancy rates.)

Negotiated Rates

Since room rates at the Avari were in general lower than at Pearl, Qasim Jafri would often be approached by people attempting to use these lower rates as a bargaining device. At such times, Qasim Jafri would listen but would hold his rates firm and advise acceptance of the lower quote. Once, when the New Zealand cricket team was touring Pakistan, the Avari quoted 30% lower than the Pearl; the Board of Cricket Control of Pakistan (BCCP) threatened to cancel its Pearl contract. Since the contract covered the entire Pearl chain, Qasim Jafri informed the BCCP that if their business went to Avari, the Pearl would not entertain them in Rawalpindi and Peshawar, where the Avari had no branches. After several rounds of negotiation, involving his superiors, Qasim Jafri retained the BCCP account by lowering rates by only 10%.

Corporate customers often approached the chairman or the director of operations at Pearl to put pressure on Qasim Jafri during price negotiations. Qasim Jafri would keep a margin of Rs 200 to Rs 300 when he submitted a quote. He also informed his superiors regarding this margin so the hotel would not accept a non-profitable contract.

Qasim Jafri was particularly concerned about discounts given to PIA and tour groups. PIA was one of the Pearl's oldest customers. It provided the Pearl with three

Table 3: Rack Rates

Rack	Rs	Corporate	Rs	Groups	Rs
Single	2,060	Single	1,210	Single	1,450
Double	2,360	Double	1,510	Double	1,750
Commercial		**Preferred**		Junior suite	2,840
Single	1,810	Single	1,050	Executive suite	4,000
Double	2,110	Double	1,350	Deluxe suite	5,700
Preferred commercial		**Official/DIP**		**PIA crew**	
Single	1,450	Single	1,050	Cockpit	580
Double	1,750	Double	1,350	Cabin	465
				PIA layover	
				Single	750
				Double	950
				Extra bed	300

Source: Company records.

Table 4: Occupancy Rates (%) at Pearl and Avari

Months	1988		1989		Average room rate Pearl 1989 (Rs)
	Avari	Pearl	Avari	Pearl	
January	72	80	63	82	1,130
February	94	94	93	97	1,185
March	93	92	88	94	1,106
April	71	73	54	59	952
May	50	52	56	71	1,055
June	65	71	61	77	1,092
July	62	50	51	77	1,105
August	63	75	54	71	1,074
September	70	68	65	74	1,072
October	97	78	75	85	1,144
November	70	80	90	96	1,245
December	n/a	84	86	92	1,180

Source: Company records.

categories of business: airline crew (regular guests at the hotel), in-transit passengers (mostly foreign) and airlines catering. Jafri described PIA crew as "finicky at best," as they were often "out of sorts" and intolerant of small service lapses. The standard hotel practice was not to guarantee a room if the crew's arrival time was not stated on the reservation sheet. The Pearl did not follow this practice. Occasionally a "no show" occurred when a guest failed to arrive, even though an airline had made a reservation.

The tour group business was generated mainly through travel agencies and tour group operators, local or abroad. Foreign guests' unfamiliarity with the local language and Lahore often put additional pressure on hotel staff.

The Pricing Issues

Qasim Jafri's most immediate problem was the quote for the World Hockey Tournament. The tournament was only seven weeks away and hotel arrangements had to be finalized within the next few days. In previous years, hockey teams had stayed at the Hilton; Qasim Jafri knew that the International Hockey Federation had sent inspection teams to both the Avari and the Pearl before asking for bids. He was also aware that his predecessor had at times quoted up to 65% discount for the International Hockey Federation account. He also had to consider that the tournament would be close in time for the annual kite-flying (Basant) festival and followed closely by the Horse and Cattle Show and the Industrial Exhibition.[3] These latter two events were held at Fortress Stadium and many guests would stay at the Pearl.

In 1989, many people stayed at the Pearl for the Basant festival. Members of the diplomatic corps and other foreigners stayed in and around Lahore, and prominent businessmen in the area were invited by Qasim Jafri to participate in the festival; hotel guests also participated. The entire hotel lobby was decorated with colorful kites and streamers. The Basant festival at the Pearl was "by-invitation only"; it was not uncommon for Lahore's business, political and official elite to solicit invitations up to two months before the event. Qasim Jafri planned to celebrate the more important traditional festivals at the hotel since he believed it was effective promotion.

Field hockey was extremely popular in Pakistan. Pakistan won the World Hockey Cup twice (1978, 1982) before losing the title to England in 1986. Pakistan was Olympic champion in 1984 but lost that title to Australia in 1988. The World Hockey Cup was held every four years; Lahore was the 1990 venue and many sports enthusiasts were expected to flock there.

Qasim Jafri was pleased with the Pearl's performance under his management; he considered room pricing to be a key to continued successful management. He had been thinking intensely for some days about the pricing issues. He wondered what pricing options were available and how these would trigger changes in other strategic elements. A major consideration was the quality image he was trying to promote; this had to be balanced against occupancy. Time for submitting an International Hockey Federation quote was running out. In addition, soon he would have to submit recommendations for rack rates and discount structures to company management.

---

[3] The Industrial Exhibition was an annual event in which major manufacturers of consumer goods participated. The exhibition lasted several weeks; it commenced at the same time as the Horse and Cattle Show, at an adjacent location.

Exhibit 1: Pakistan Services Ltd. – Profit and Loss Account

	Total		Head Office		Karachi		Lahore		Rawalpindi		Peshawar	
	1988	1989	1988	1989	1988	1989	1988	1989	1988	1989	1988	1989
Sales and services	338,275	455,462	0	0	112,767	149,826	115,923	152,219	67,557	88,641	42,038	64,776
Cost of sales	219,882	289,079	0	0	79,741	102,627	67,638	89,569	43,370	54,856	29,073	42,027
Gross profit	118,393	166,373	0	0	33,026	47,199	48,285	62,650	24,187	33,785	12,965	22,749
Administration & selling expenses	68,156	73,949	5,067	6,380	22,729	26,862	18,355	20,052	12,952	12,284	9,053	8,371
Operating profit/loss	50,237	92,424	(5,067)	(6,380)	10,287	20,337	29,930	42,598	11,235	21,501	3,912	14,378
Allocation of H.O. expense	50,237	92,424	5,067	6,380	(1,789)	(2,252)	(1,192)	(1,501)	(1,192)	(1,501)	(894)	(1,126)
Total income	50,237	92,424	0	0	8,498	18,085	28,738	41,097	10,043	19,990	3,018	13,252
Other income	2,586	5,214	1,372	1,059	338	909	383	1,563	322	622	171	1,161
Total income	52,823	97,638	1,372	1,059	8,836	18,994	29,121	42,660	10,365	20,512	3,189	14,413
Financial charges	11,091	40,534	2,009	3,862	3,847	12,559	2,183	9,700	2,015	8,614	1,037	5,799
Net profit/loss	41,732	57,104	(637)	(2,803)	4,989	6,435	26,938	32,960	8,350	11,898	2,152	8,614
Additional information												
Occupancy rate					69%	73%	78%	81%	72%	75%	53%	72%
Average single room rate (SGL)						2,000		2,500		2,100		2,000
Average double room rate (DBL)						2,300		2,900		2,400		2,300
SGL Avari (1990)		2,200										
DBL Avari (1990)		2,300										

Source: Pakistan Services Ltd. (holding company for the Pearl Continental Hotel Chain), *Annual Report 1989.*

Exhibit 2: Revenue Report 1989

	Revenue (December) Actual (Rs)	Total revenue Budgeted (Rs)	1989 (Rs)
Revenues			
Rooms	6,389,025	4,874,000	63,434,271
Food	4,582,704	2,613,000	48,460,163
Beverage	2,233,933	997,000	20,999,077
Telefax	43,843	0	401,772
Telephone/telex	731,778	602,000	7,989,219
Guest laundry	105,532	82,000	1,061,572
O/S laundry	53,875	46,000	579,037
Barber shop	3,725	4,000	41,210
Pool	0	0	79,145
Guest valet	2,245	35,000	511,112
O/S valet	9,181	165,000	1,214,552
Airline catering	1,645,394	1,308,000	9,314,085
Other income	295,906	59,000	335,695
Total	16,097,141	10,785,000	154,420,910
Food revenue			
Brasserie	1,273,914	966,000	12,601,092
Pan	63,962	0	58,860
Pool terrace	3,682	0	147,646
Pastry shop	56,560	3,300	524,361
Room service	412,762	332,000	3,872,097
Banquets & parties	2,637,823	1,282,000	19,209,799
Airline catering	0	0	9,518,979
Others	144,001	0	2,567,329
Total	4,592,704	2,583,300	48,500,163
Beverages			
Brasserie	7,226	39,000	394,338
Pool terrace	21	0	29,757
Room service	1,888	8,000	34,413
Permit room	2,055,606	840,000	18,535,131
Banquets & parties	26,493	20,000	330,556
Mini bar	133,736	82,000	1,472,922
Others	8,663	8,000	201,660
Total	2,233,633	997,000	20,998,777

Map of People's Republic of China (PRC)

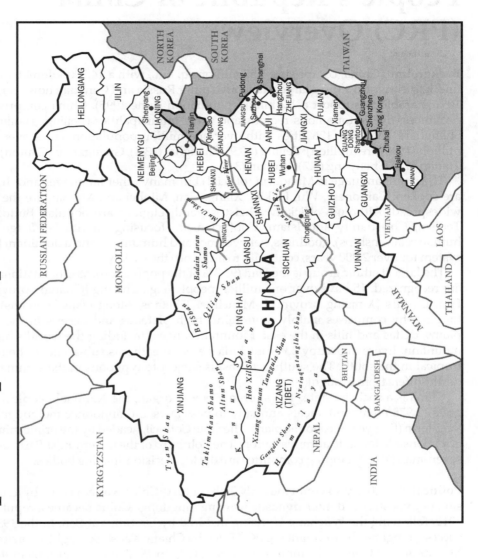

People's Republic of China (PRC) Overview

Background. China, comprising 9.57 million sq. km., with a 14,500-kilometer coastline, has the world's third largest land area (after Russia and Canada); however, only 10% is arable to support a 1.2 billion population (June 1995). China comprises 22 provinces, five autonomous regions and three municipalities (Beijing, Tianjin and Shanghai). There are 126 cities with over one million population; cities over three million (1990) are (million): Beijing (10.9), Shanghai (13.4), Guangzhou (Canton) (9.1), Tianjin (4.5), Shenyang (3.7), Wuhan (3.5).

The main language is Mandarin (official) but many other languages and dialects are spoken: Cantonese, Wu, Hakka, Xiang, Gan, Minbei and Minnan are the most widespread. Although officially atheist, several religions are popular: Buddhism, Taoism, Christianity and Islam. Confucianism, focusing on rituals – *li* (governs human relationships), goodness, benevolence and humanity – and a dominant belief system for over 2,000 years, continues to influence the society.

The largest ethnic group is the Han (93.3% of the population); 55 other nationalities are recognized, 15 have over one million people (e.g., Zhuang [Guangxi province], Hui, Uygurs [Xinjiang province], Manchus, Tibetans, Mongolians, Koreans). The topography comprises mainly mountains, high plateaus and deserts in the west, plains, deltas and hills in the east. Mountain ranges (including the world's highest mountain, Everest) occupy 33% of China's area. Weather is sub-arctic in the north, tropical in the south. The southeast coast is subject to typhoons in the summer, the north suffers from drought.

China is a socialist state. The supreme power organ, the National People's Congress (2,978 members), meets annually to pass laws and announce the budget and long-term (five-year) economic plans. The State Council, headed by the prime minister, is responsible for state administration. The Politburo of the Communist Party and its seven-man (1995) standing committee are the top decision-making bodies.

Political. For 2,000 years until the early 20th century, China was governed by a succession of dynasties and inter-dynastic warring kingdoms. China became a republic in 1912, following the Wuchang Uprising inspired by Dr. Sun Yat-Sen. In the 1930s, a successor regime, the Kuomintang (KMT) led by Chiang Kai-shek fought incursions by Mao Zedong's Chinese Communist Party (CCP). In 1937, the two groups united to fight the Japanese invasion but resumed hostilities after Japan's surrender in 1945. In

1949, the Communists seized power and proclaimed the People's Republic of China; the KMT fled to Taiwan but acted as China's government in major international bodies (e.g., the UN) until 1971 when it was replaced by the PRC. The PRC pursues a major goal of reunifying all of China. It negotiated the return of Hong Kong (1997) and Macau (1999) under the "one country two systems" doctrine. Little progress has been made regarding Taiwan; in 1996, coinciding with the first direct presidential elections in Taiwan, China conducted intimidating military exercises off Taiwan's coast.

Major events under the Communist government were the Great Leap Forward (1958 to 1960), a failed attempt at rapid industrialization leading to famine in which many millions died; and the Cultural Revolution (1966 to 1976) in which followers of Mao Zedong overthrew the Communist Party apparatus. Only Mao's death (1976) and the arrest of the "Gang of Four" (headed by Mao's widow Jiang Qing) allowed Deng Xiaoping to assume power and follow pragmatic economic reform policies. Deng legitimized free market forces, de-collectivized agriculture and permitted private ownership under the umbrella of the "Socialist Market Economy." China's increasing openness was stalled by use of massive military force to crush the student-led democracy movement in Tiananmen Square in 1989. China has been widely criticized for human rights violations but nonetheless secured most-favored-nation (MFN) treatment from the U.S. under President Clinton's policy of separating human rights and economic issues (1994).

Social. China has 20% of the world's population, but only 7% of its arable land. As the population has increased, birth control has become less a social problem than a survival problem. To ameliorate the situation, the government operates a one-child policy but infanticide is reportedly prevalent, leading to abnormal sex ratios. In five of 30 provinces, the sex ratio is over 1.2 : 1 (boys : girls). Three quarters of the population live in rural areas; despite controls, substantial migration to urban areas occurs. Although the literacy rate is 80%, most people receive only primary schooling; about 1% receives post-secondary or higher education. The crime rate is low, two cases per 1,000 (1990), but is reportedly rising, notably corruption involving senior government officials.

Economy. China is a member of the United Nations (UN), World Bank (WB), International Monetary Fund (IMF), Asian Development Bank (ADB) and Asia-Pacific Economic Cooperation (APEC) Forum; it has applied for World Trade Organization (WTO) membership but faces opposition from the U.S. In recent years, as the result of Deng's reforms, the Chinese economy, including the five coastal Special Economic Zones (SEZs) (Shenzhen, Xiamen, Zhuhai, Shantou, Hainan), has grown rapidly (industrial output grew an average 19% p.a. in the early 1990s). Most growth has been driven by the vibrant private sector. Many state-owned enterprises (SOEs) continue to make significant losses; in fall 1997, the Chinese government announced plans to sell shares in these organizations. GDP by sector is (1995): agriculture (20.6%), industry (48.4%), services (31.1%). China accounts for 2.5% of world trade and is the tenth largest exporter (US$151 billion [1996], up from US$90.3 billion [1993/94]). China's major markets are (1995): Hong Kong (24.1%), Japan (19%), U.S. (16.6%); major import origins are (1995): Japan (21.9%), U.S. (12.2%), Taiwan (11%), Korea (7.8%). Inflation has averaged 20% in urban areas in recent years. Foreign companies have made significant investments in China, mostly through joint-venture arrangements. China is strongly protectionist; a long list of commodities (mainly luxuries) have high import duties.

In the last decade, China has received a significant fraction of total world foreign direct investment; by 1995, over US$300 billion was committed to China (slightly less than US$100 billion spent). Most investment (about 80%) is from overseas Chinese (primarily Hong Kong), mostly in the form of equity joint ventures and primarily in the coastal provinces. Since its domestic market is very large, the Chinese are in a strong bargaining position; they request (and increasingly receive) more and advanced technology transfers as part of foreign direct investment projects. Lax enforcement of patent and intellectual property rights (and laws and regulations in general) has been a major concern to companies transferring (often proprietary) technology to China; this issue together with the semi-convertibility of the renminbi, excessively high import tariffs on many products and poor regulatory enforcement is a major reason why the U.S. has opposed China's entry to the WTO.

Since 1978, the People's Bank of China (PBC) has been the country's central bank, directly under control of the State Council and not fully independent. The four major state banks are controlled by the PBC: The Bank of China (specializes in foreign exchange and international trade transactions), People's Construction Bank of China (manages state budgeted expenditures for capital construction), Industrial and Commercial Bank of China (specializes in lending to industrial enterprises) and Agricultural Bank of China (specializes in rural business loans).

Foreign banks may open representative offices and branches in certain coastal cities and SEZs (where foreign investors receive favorable taxation and other treatment) with approval from the PBC; in late 1995, about 120 foreign banks operated in China. In June 1987, a money market comprising 74 banks and other financial institutions opened in Shanghai; other cities followed suit. The official exchange rate for the Chinese currency, the renminbi (yuan), was abolished in 1994; in response, the Shanghai-based interbank currency market started trading. This market consolidates the renminbi exchange rate based on Forex trading in the country's three SWAP centers (i.e., Beijing, Shanghai, Guangzhou). The U.S. dollar exchange rate (Sept. 1996, US$1 = 8.3 renminbi) has been relatively unchanged since Forex currency exchanges at SWAP centers are tightly controlled (government approval is needed); temporary renminbi (RMB) shortage has occurred, implying that the currency is not fully convertible. Reforms are expected to lead to full renminbi convertibility (before the year 2000).

The Shanghai Stock Exchange (before 1949, the largest in East Asia) reopened in 1986; the Shenzhen Stock Exchange opened in 1991, offering "A" shares for Chinese citizens, "B" shares for foreigners. In 1994, 17 Chinese firms were listed on the Hong Kong Stock Exchange and two on the New York Stock Exchange.

Beijing stood serenely by during the 1997 Asian currency turmoil. However, the PRC faced competitive pressures and observers believed a devaluation of the renminbi, widely expected as economic growth and foreign investment slowed, might trigger a further round of competitive devaluations in Southeast Asia. China required a growing economy to absorb excess labor as it restructured its state-owned enterprises; it was feared that the Asian crisis might delay this process. Another damper came from the beating "red chips" (mainland companies listed in Hong Kong) took in the Hong Kong Stock Exchange (the Hang Seng lost 20% of its value in 1997). Observers expected that other initial public offerings, anticipated as part of the SOE restructuring, would probably be postponed. Nonetheless, staunch support by Premier Zhu Rongji not to devalue the renminbi has positioned the PRC as the most stable factor in Asia and earned widespread recognition from the U.S. and major international organizations (eg., IMF, WB).

Infrastructure. Electricity, transportation (rail, air, road, water) and telecommunications have historically been weak in China but the government is committed to significant infrastructure improvement. For example, although China is the world's largest coal producer (1989) and estimated the world's sixth largest oil producer, much of the Chinese countryside has no electricity. The world's largest hydroelectric project, Three Gorges Dam (estimated cost US$11.2 billion, completion in 2009) on the Yangtze River, will ameliorate the situation for southeast and central China by producing 18,200 megawatts. In 1993, total electric energy production was 746 billion kWh.

Transportation is a top investment priority, particularly the railway network and seaports; reportedly one third of Shanghai's container capacity is idle due to poor road links. Car ownership is very low; many people use bicycles (270 million) and motorcycles (2.2 million). Since 1984, the authorities have been decentralizing the Civil Aviation Administration of China (CAAC) by separating airline operations from administration of civil aviation and by forming six state-owned airlines. Small regional airlines serve various domestic markets.

China is gradually modernizing its telephone and communication network, spending US$10 billion annually until 2000. Telephone penetration will then be eight per 100 people. Telephone shortages have created a large market for mobile phones and radio pagers; in Beijing 70 private paging firms operate with around 300,000 users.

Statistics*	June 1991	June 1997	Statistics*	June 1991	June 1997
Per capita GNP	US$325	US$540	Pop. growth	1.4%	1.2%
GDP growth	5.0%	9.9%	Infant mortality / 1,000	27	31
Savings (GNP)	n/a	40%	Life expectancy (yrs)	n/a	71
Inflation (CPI)	2.1%	5.6%	Literacy rate	72.6%	81.5%
Foreign debt			People per tel.	134	29.8
(in billion)	US$45.4	US$116.3	People per doctor	724	1,034
Pop. (million)	1,150	1,228	People per TV	n/a	4.9
Urban pop.	n/a	30%	Calorie intake (cals)	n/a	2,703

*Secured from *Asiaweek.*

Case 34

Shanghai Chlor-Alkali Chemical Company Ltd.: PVC

Ho Yuen Ching, Michelle
The Hong Kong University of Science and Technology

Noel Capon
Graduate School of Business, Columbia University

Product marketing where competition is keen and supply exceeds demand is a familiar experience for most marketing professionals. The challenge is no less great when demand exceeds supply. Senior executives at Shanghai Chlor-Alkali Chemical Company (SCAC) faced that problem with their PVC product line.

On December 4, 1994, in the spacious conference room at Hua Nan Hotel, a wholly owned subsidiary of SCAC, key executives met to discuss the company's "fist" (representative) product, PVC. Mr. Gu Wei-liang (Marketing Director) was joined by Mr. Wang Zhong-yang (Chief Economist), Mr. Wu Da-yuan (Deputy General Manager, International Trade Department) and Mr. Wang Zu-de (Business Division, International Trade Department). Excess demand and lucrative development potential for PVC led management to review past marketing strategy for the local China market.

8003

Company Background

Formerly The Shanghai Electrochemical Plant, SCAC was established in 1959. Originally a state-owned enterprise under the supervision of the Shanghai Chemical Industry Bureau, SCAC's principal business was the production of industrial chemicals. In 1984, SCAC underwent a major expansion and modernization program; capacity expansion via modern facilities then continued steadily. SCAC was the largest producer of chlorine-based alkaline products in the Far East, employing about 9,000 people. In recent years, SCAC's revenues and profits had increased steadily (Table 1). In June

1992, SCAC received government permission to convert to a limited liability joint stock company; its shares were listed on the Shanghai Stock Exchange.[1]

Location. SCAC was located on the banks of the Huangpu River, approximately 20 kilometers south of downtown Shanghai, in an industrial area (Wu Jing) specifically zoned for chemical production. It was readily accessible by rail and sea; a branch railway line linked the plant site to the main railway line and SCAC owned two pur-pose-built wharves on the Huangpu River. SCAC plants were linked by pipeline to its principal supplier of ethylene, a key raw material in PVC production.

Products. SCAC manufactured a wide range of industrial chemicals, including caustic soda (sodium hydroxide), bleaching powder (calcium hypochlorite), tetra-chlorocarbon (CCl_4), perchloroethylene (PCE), fluorine refrigerants (F11, F12, F13, F22) and polymers such as polyvinylchloride (PVC) and polytetrafluorethylene (PTFE). Some products were sold in their crude manufactured state; others were used as raw materials in a variety of primary and secondary industrial and manufacturing appli-cations. (See Exhibit 1 for major products, uses and sales volumes.)

Table 1: Summary of SCAC Accounting and Business Data

		1991	1992	1993	1994 (projected)
Sales	RMB '000	931,310	1,105,300	1,396,550	1,778,530
Profit before tax	RMB '000	150,400	185,590	194,410	237,930
Profit after tax	RMB '000	105,260	179,910	192,040	200,680
Foreign exchange generated	US$ '000	36,890	31,160	27,440	37,310
Total assets	RMB '000	–	4,030,950	4,270,990	4,669,920
Equity	RMB '000	–	2,285,610	2,411,410	2,717,530
Caustic soda production	Ton '000	221	235	249	269
PVC production	Ton '000	100	110	143	171
Income per share	RMB	–	0.216	0.231	0.209
Net asset per share	RMB	–	2.75	2.90	2.82
Dividend per share	RMB	–	0.10	0.15	0.15
Ratio of income for net assets	%	–	7.87	7.96	7.93

Organization structure. SCAC's organization structure comprised five major areas:

- Meeting of shareholders;
- Subsidiaries;
- Production plants and research and development facilities;
- Management offices;
- Administrative departments.

---

[1] In 1993, SCAC's share capital was RMB831,8100,700; 60.8% was owned by the state, 10.3% (A shares) by local Chinese investors, and 28.9% (B shares) by investors outside the PRC. In 1994, share capital was RMB962,382,700; state, 52.51%, local investors, 12.58%, foreign investors, 34.91%.

Wang Zu-de explained SCAC's organization:

We arranged the constituent units as a network, rather than a hierarchy, to illustrate our concept that all departments and subsidiaries are at the same level. Our view is that each unit supports the others rather than the traditional approach of top-down bureaucratic management. Operating SCAC requires collaboration of personnel with different skill; they have equal standing inside the company.

Local Chinese versus International Sales

SCAC's sales function was the responsibility of two separate departments: the Sales and Supplies Department and the International Sales Department.

Sales and Supplies Department

This 824-strong department had four major roles:

- Overall planning. Planning the supply and raw materials requirements for SCAC's various production systems and coordinating local sales and production functions; this department was also responsible for environmental scanning (e.g., interfacing with environmental protection agencies).
- Local sales. Totaling 230 staff persons, this group included the 30-person sales force plus order-placing and warehouse personnel. The sales force was organized first by product, second by geographic location. For each of SCAC's product groups (e.g., PVC, freons, caustic soda) one or two persons were responsible for each of three geographic areas: Shanghai Urban, Shanghai Suburban and Other Provinces. Three persons in the sales team were responsible for ensuring that overall product mix sales were balanced.

  Sales efforts were usually increased when a downward market trend was predicted or observed. Six other representatives solicited additional businesses from existing customers; they also contacted potential customers referred by current customers.

  Sales representatives were remunerated in one of two ways: a fixed salary or based on an "underwriters" scheme; the choice was mutually agreed between the sales representative and management. In the "underwriters" scheme, salespeople were evaluated on three criteria: ability to sell (based on quantity sold), ability to sell at good prices and customers' promptness in payment. Only when all three criteria were reached did management consider a sale had actually been made.
- Raw materials supply. Employing 250 people, this group was responsible for purchasing, storage and requisition approval for raw materials.
- Transportation. This group of 130 people was responsible for all product transportation; it managed SCAC wharves and rail transportation system and supervised a separate transportation subsidiary.

International Sales Department

The International Sales Department, established in December 1991, comprised 37 staff in four major subdivisions:

- Business Office. Supervised by Wang Zu-de, this office was responsible for sales of SCAC products to overseas markets. It also administered overseas representative offices, including Sydney, Hong Kong and Vietnam.
- Technology Office. This office was responsible for importing technology and negotiating joint ventures with overseas companies. Existing joint-venture partners included the major German company, Bayer.
- Financial Planning Office. This group was responsible for budgeting, accounting, exchange balancing and other financial functions relating to international trade.
- Manager's Office. This office supervised the department's work.

Because its products sold at low prices and transportation costs were high, the domestic market accounted for 80% of SCAC sales. But management believed it was important to explore the overseas market and that SCAC should, "Grasp both markets at the same time." Wang Zhong-yang explained:

> Currently, sales of most products rely heavily on the domestic market. Our international market presence is still relatively small. Nevertheless, we are not ignoring the overseas market. Rather, we know that we must be in the international market as early as possible. As a successful enterprise, going international is the only end. International market pressure drives us towards improvements and makes us more competitive. With the China market gradually opening to foreign businesses, especially as China is trying to comply with the World Trade Organization's free trade requirements, international competition is getting more intense; it is wiser to learn the hard lessons at an early stage.

PVC (Polyvinyl Chloride)[2]

Historical Development

PVC was a plastic raw material with several important properties including good electrical insulation and heat resistance. Many daily necessities were produced with PVC (e.g., artificial leather, outer sheathing of wires and cables, bottles, flexible pipes, flooring, wall paper and communication cables); the construction industry was also a heavy user. PVC was manufactured both as powder and paste.[3] Two production

---

[2] The formula for PVC was $[CH_2 - CH]_n$.
$$\underset{Cl}{|}$$

[3] In each case PVC was produced in several different grades for different end-use application.

methods were commonly used. Large PVC producers such as SCAC employed the ethylene method involving the pressurized reaction of ethylene with chlorine and oxygen to produce VCM (vinyl chloride monomer); VCM was then polymerized into PVC (Figure 1). Smaller manufacturers typically used the electrification method, a lower capital investment but outdated technology that produced lower-quality PVC resins. SCAC emphasized quality control not only for PVC production but also in packaging, transportation and customer communications.

Figure 1: The PVC Production Process

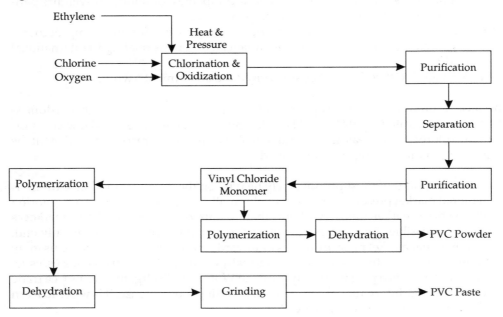

Following initial PVC production (1932), the PVC industry experienced steady growth modulated by periodic demand cycles linked to macroeconomic changes. By 1994, world PVC production capacity was about 20 million tons; actual production reached 18.53 million tons.

PVC Demand in China

Before 1983, consumption and production of PVC was basically balanced. However, rapid development of PVC applications caused demand to outstrip supply. Excess demand was satisfied by imports (Table 2). Recently, Chinese demand for PVC continued to rise as the quality of raw materials for PVC production improved quickly; new technologies for manufacturing products from PVC came on stream and high potential markets for PVC products were identified requiring small initial investments that could quickly be made operational.

Table 2: Demand/Supply of PVC Resin in China (tons p.a.)

Year	1991	1992	1993	1994	1995*
Production	880.20	898.00	1,008.30	1,161.00	1,323.80
Import	194.00	232.10	285.70	358.83	338.90
Export	(85.10)	(12.50)	(17.90)	(82.70)	(97.40)
Consumption	989.10	1,117.60	1,276.10	1,437.13	1,565.30

*Forecast.

In the early 1980s, the government's focus on PVC applications switched from a quantity orientation to improvements in quality standards for PVC products and new application developments. A particularly noticeable trend was the transition from soft to hard PVC products. As a result, local market conditions were aligned with those in other countries. (Table 3 displays global application patterns; see Appendix for application details.)

According to market research conducted by SCAC (1992/1993), about 40 new PVC-user manufacturers, local and joint ventures were starting production. In addition, existing factories were continually enhancing production capacities and broadening product lines. In late 1993, the assistant general manager of SCAC's Marketing Division visited 27 major customers in different provinces to understand their operating situations and PVC usage (see Table 4).

Local Competition

In 1994, China boasted 73 PVC resin producers, total production capacity, 1.45 million tons. Nationally, 20 producers had annual production in excess of 10,000 tons, mostly located in northern and eastern China; most PVC finished goods producers were concentrated in southern China (e.g., Guangzhou, Shenzhen). (See Table 5 for top ten PVC resin producers.) Only three companies employed the ethylene production method: Beijing No. 2 Chemical Factory, Qilu Petroleum Chemical Company and SCAC. (See Exhibit 2 for SCAC and major competitors' production history and forecasts.)

From 1989 to 1992, ten projects (capacity 1,820,000 tons) for new PVC (ethylene method) production facilities were started. Except for Shanghai Chemical, Qihua and Pankeng whose facilities were on stream, all others were expected to be completed in 1995 to 1996. New projects with alternative production technologies were estimated to add 400,000 tons capacity. In total, about 130,000 tons of capacity was expected to come on stream in 1995. Expansion plans of major producers (including SCAC) involved expanding existing systems rather than opening new plants. In 1994, production from the three plants (including SCAC) using advanced ethylene technology (capacity 480,000 tons) was 360,000 tons, 36% of national production.

International Competition

Under China's currency control measures, PVC products manufacturers seeking raw materials abroad had to have hard currency (typically earned from exports). In

Table 3: PVC Consumption Patterns by Country

Country/region	Pipes and bearings	Molded plastics and soft pipes	Bottles and containers	Plastic sheets and membranes	Others	Soft*	Hard
World	33%	15%	6%	23%	24%		
U.S.	44%	20%	3%	15%	19%	69%	31%
Canada	36%	30%	1%	12%	22%		
Mexico	20%	5%	19%	19%	37%		
South America	32%	5%	13%	22%	27%		
Western Europe	26%	19%	9%	19%	28%	65%	35%
Eastern Europe	40%	14%	9%	13%	25%		
Africa and Middle East	42%	9%	10%	16%	23%		
Israel	43%	12%	10%	12%	24%		
Saudi Arabia	47%	18%		34%			
South Africa	36%	12%	14%	12%	27%		
Turkey	44%	9%	5%	8%	35%		
Asia Pacific	30%	10%	2%	36%	23%		
Japan	30%	12%	3%	28%	27%	60%	40%
Korea	31%	6%		39%	24%		
Taiwan	27%	13%	1%	44%	15%		
Thailand	46%	7%		24%	24%		
Other Asian countries	29%	7%	3%	39%	21%		
China							
Year 1985	5%	6%		20%	70%	18%	82%
Year 1990	6%	7%		25%	62%	26%	74%
Year 2000	25%	9%	3%	29%	34%	42%	58%

*Soft articles include plastic shoes, plastic membranes, artificial leather, etc. which have a soft texture. Hard articles include plastic pipings; floorings; plastic sheets, etc.
**Including China.

Table 4:   PVC Use by 27 Major SCAC Customers

Year	Use ('000 tons)	Percent increase over prior year	Purchases from SCAC ('000 tons)	Percent increase over prior year
1992	62	–	26	–
1993	85	37%	33	27%
1994 (F)	119	40%	49	48%

Table 5:   Top Ten PVC Resin Producers in China (1993)

Company	Output (tons)	Production share (%)	Company	Output (tons)	Production share (%)
Qilu Petroleum Chemical Co.	152,062	15.2	Dagu Chemical Works	47,000	4.7
SCAC	136,286	13.6	Fuzhou No. 2 Chemical Works	32,699	3.3
Tianjin Bohai Chemicals Group Ltd.	115,290	11.5	Shanghai Tian Yuan Chemical Works	32,732	3.2
Tianjin Chemical Works	67,862	6.8	Jingxi Chemical Complex	28,778	2.9
Beijing No. 2 Chemical Factory	68,000	6.8	Jilin Chemical Industrial Co.	24,440	2.4
				705,149	70.4

addition, they had to pay transportation costs and accept delays that might hinder smooth production. As a result, imported PVC resins were not considered a material threat to local PVC resin producers even though international prices might be lower than that of domestically produced resins.

Pricing

Local China market prices for SCAC products were determined by the firm on a monthly basis. These prices had to be filed with the Shanghai Chemical Industry Bureau but were no longer subject to approval as in earlier years. Rather, filing served as a governmental control device to prevent unfair pricing practices. Several factors affected PVC market prices in China: international PVC prices, readily observable through arbitrage activities in the open market, and fluctuations in the PVC raw material prices, typically secured through futures contracts in the U.S.

SCAC's PVC pricing policy allowed a time lag before fully adjusting to market prices. This approach enhanced raw material price stability for customers and was believed to be mutually advantageous to both supplier and customers. When PVC prices rose, SCAC adjusted prices upwards slowly; when prices fell, SCAC enjoyed a slightly longer period of higher-than-market prices. In July 1994, contract execution rate was 98%. In early 1994, when the PVC market relaxed slightly and prices adjusted downwards, SCAC prices were maintained at RMB6,700; contract execution was still over 90% (Exhibit 3).

Production and Marketing at SCAC

SCAC production of PVC resin (initial annual capacity 200,000 tons) commenced in March 1990 using ethylene oxidization technology (secured from Japan); product quality was comparable to the well-known Japanese TK brand. The facility converted liquefied VCM produced by SCAC's organic plant into PVC powder by the suspension method. A similar capacity plant using identical technology was established by Qilu Petroleum Chemical Company shortly after. Later, Beijing No. 2 Chemical Factory acquired a similar technology plant, 80,000 tons capacity. In mid-1994, no other Chinese company possessed this technology. In 1991, SCAC imported a production facility for manufacturing PVC paste (capacity 20,000 tons) from the U.S. This new product was used in textiles and floor coverings; sales efforts, which posed a new challenge for SCAC, concentrated on a dozen major customers.

Projected 1994 PVC production was 170,000 to 180,000 tons, below SCAC's 200,000 tons capacity due primarily to raw material supply problems (i.e., ethylene) and synchronization issues. (See Table 6A for SCAC sales history; see Table 6B for sales by end-use application.) However, the government's efforts to develop local ethylene production was expected to ease these problems in future years. In accord with firm policy, export volumes were expected to be maintained at 20% despite product shortages and lower international prices. Furthermore, SCAC had commenced, or entered into negotiations for, several joint ventures for processing PVC resins into consumer and other industrial products in addition to wholly owned operations (Table 7).

For 1994, SCAC had 255 contracted customers; 31 (12%) each contracted for over 1,000 tons, 80,000 tons in total, around half of SCAC's total production. These customers were mainly final product manufacturers whose long-term relationships with SCAC largely predated its 1990 entry into PVC production. Overall, 177 (70%) of SCAC's PVC customers were direct purchasers and users of PVC, accounting for 78% of domestic sales. Besides these manufacturing customers, SCAC sold to 78 distributors (serving small customers) accounting for 22% of sales; purchases to individual distributors tended to be small and fluctuating. Each year, sales to existing customers accounted for over 85% of total production; the remainder was for new customers.

SCAC sold PVC both to industrial users making such consumer products as PVC plastic shoes and transparent plastic sheets and for industrial products such as artificial leather where further processing was required. In the early 1990s, SCAC expended substantial effort in marketing PVC. Sales representatives visited, and actively sold PVC to, manufacturing companies. Gradually, a stable market base of around 10% market share was established. Gross profit on PVC was currently about 30%; revenues accounted for about 65% of total firm revenues.

In 1993, local market conditions improved substantially; demand outstripped supply and SCAC focused efforts on consumer product applications where PVC cost represented a small percent of final product value (e.g., transparent plastic sheets and

Table 6A: Export and Local PVC Sales at SCAC (tons)

Year	1990	1991	1992	1993	1994 (projected)
Export sales	15,993	30,866	26,446	28,144	34,000
Local sales	32,713	69,142	65,651	78,096	104,000
Used by subsidiary enterprises	–	–	17,050	30,046	32,000
Total production	48,706	100,008	109,147	136,286	170,000

Table 6B: PVC Applications by SCAC Customers

Application	Nationwide composition	SCAC contracted customers (%)	SCAC contracted customers Number
Pipings, remolding	30%	39%	83
Membrane and transparent plastic sheets	30%	27%	46
Artificial leather	15%	14%	24
Other (e.g., electric cables)	25%	20%	24
Total	100%	100%	177

Table 7: SCAC Downstream PVC Processing Plants

Enterprise	Ownership	Production capacities	Expected completion
Shanghai Guochen Plastics Co. Ltd.	Sino-foreign joint venture, 10% ownership	4,600,000 sq. m./yr. PVC louvers	1997
Shanghai Da Kai Plastics Co. Ltd.	Sino-foreign joint venture, 25% ownership	12,000 tons/yr. plastic cards (credit card basis)	1996
Shanghai Lu Wei Plastics Co. Ltd.	Sino-foreign joint venture, 50% ownership	6,100 tons/yr. PVC special pipe material	1996
Shanghai Bai Shi Gao Plastic and Rubber Co. Ltd.	Sino-foreign joint venture, 70% ownership	4,200 tons/yr. PVC core layer of bubble pipe	Commenced in 1995
Shanghai Xinlu Plastic and Rubber Co. Ltd.	Wholly owned	2,500 tons/yr. construction drain pipe and fittings	1996
Shanghai Chlor-Alkali Plastic Works	Wholly owned	2,000 tons/yr. various kinds of PVC chemical compounds	Commenced in 1992
PVC Chemical Compound Works	Wholly owned	30,000 tons/yr. PVC chemical compounds	Commenced in 1992

growth markets such as domestic automobiles); management viewed past attention to low-end applications as a start-up phase necessity. SCAC could not satisfy all customers' needs; management's challenge was to develop a methodology for allocating PVC output among its 255 current customers and potential new customers. Shen said SCAC should take care not to offend old customers and jeopardize long-term relationships; at the same time, formal guidelines were required to evaluate potential new customers.

Sales Planning and Contracting

SCAC's motto was: "Production to follow sales, and sales to follow the market." Each October, sales forecasts were developed by SCAC's planning department in cooperation with the sales department. Discussion drafts were prepared by the various departments concerned. After considering sales/production balancing issues and various market situations, sales forecasts were adjusted and worked into production planning.

In November, about 20 major existing customers were invited to a "Contract Discussion Meeting" in which PVC sales contracts for the upcoming year were negotiated. Customer business situations were discussed and PVC quantities agreed. All other customers submitted applications that were evaluated on an individual basis. Major criteria in setting contract amounts were: past payment, contract execution records and business prospects. To provide customers with flexibility, contract quantities were best estimates adjusted upwards by 15% to 20%. Annual volumes were broken down into monthly offtake plans. Prices were not specified but agreements allowed adjustment to market prices, communicated monthly to customers. Customers were not required to execute 100% of contracts and purchase amounts might vary from monthly plans.

Sales and Service Activities

Dragon service. To better serve customers outside Shanghai, SCAC established "Dragon Service." A customer could, for a fee, "employ" an SCAC sales and service center staff person as purchasing agent to make arrangements for contracts, place purchase orders, follow up on PVC deliveries, plan contract executions, perform accounting tasks and arrange for after-sales service and other requirements.

Facilitating demand smoothing. Sometimes customers needed to place urgent PVC orders, yet contracts did not provide for these sudden increases. SCAC would attempt to assist customers if excess inventory was available after considering allocations to all contracted users. If no product could be shipped, Sales and Supplies Department staff would try to explain the difficulties, with sympathy and courtesy, seeking customer understanding.

In some cases the problem might be solved by contacting customers with excess contracted PVC that was not immediately needed and shifting excess quantities. SCAC attempted to facilitate this demand balancing as all parties could benefit. Although slightly higher prices were usually charged to cover administrative expenses, many customers appreciated SCAC's efforts.

Promotion

Because of the demand/supply imbalance, PVC sales were not really solicited. Nevertheless, a six-person sales team in the Sales and Supplies Department was allocated to PVC because of its importance. In addition to three persons assigned to three Chinese regions, three others were assigned to the large number of customers in Shenzhen and Guangzhou. The sales representatives' role was to evaluate current and future PVC use.

SCAC had a long-established tradition of not placing resources into advertising; for PVC, customers proactively approached SCAC. However, management agreed the market situation could change and SCAC might need to consider promotional spending. It believed SCAC enjoyed considerable recognition from its long history and reputation among long-term customers that spread SCAC's name to potential customers. In addition, its Shanghai Stock Exchange listing provided many opportunities for SCAC's name to appear in newspapers and magazines.

New Orders for 1995

In the previous few weeks, 1995 contract discussion meetings were concluded. Recognizing SCAC could not satisfy all requests for PVC, management decided to satisfy the 25 largest customers first. Together, these customers contracted for 59,000 tons of SCAC's 1995 production out of a planned volume of 120,000 to 130,000 tons for all non-export customers. Shen explained the importance of prioritizing these customers favorably:

- First, they have very good credibility. No matter what fluctuations occur in their market environments, they still consider our PVC or other products as their major, or even only, source of raw materials.
- Second, most of these customers, local or joint ventures, have imported advanced technologies.
- Third, they are mainly high-end product producers (e.g., artificial leather, modern construction and decorative materials).
- Fourth, they are financially sound. Basically they can honor payments on all deliveries. Some even pay before the PVC is delivered.
- Fifth, they are competitive. Their production systems make quality products; this affords them good reputations and economic benefits among competitors. They have better abilities to absorb price fluctuations in raw materials and are better able to survive.

The difficult question for SCAC management was how to allocate remaining PVC production among other existing customers and potential new customers. In previous years, 15% of sales were to new customers. The sales department compiled a log of new requests for next year's PVC contracts from some of its larger manufacturing and distribution customers (Exhibits 4A, 4B).

Various views surfaced on how to perform allocations. Shen suggested limiting growth of the distributor segment; he said these customers tended to execute their contracts only when market conditions were good; they defaulted when market conditions were poor. They were involved in simple trading and did not have the commitment to PVC production exhibited by manufacturing customers.

Another approach was suggested by a fluoro-products executive. The process-flow manufacturing system produced many chemical by-products along with PVC; SCAC attempted to synchronize PVC sales with other products since excessive storage increased inventory costs and posed serious physical hazards. This executive was annoyed that some customers did not execute contracts promptly. He proposed that PVC contracts not be awarded to customers who "misbehaved" in other SCAC dealings, even though they might be good PVC customers.

Marketing Strategy for PVC Local Sales

Following Shen's presentation, the executives vigorously discussed how to develop the SCAC's PVC marketing system for future years. Questions particularly rigorously debated were: how to control fluctuations in contract execution rates; how to allocate limited output among customers; whether the company's "lag" pricing strategy should be continued; whether the amount of PVC sold through distributors should be reduced; whether SCAC should rely on a small number of major customers. In addition, executives were concerned about promotion planning in anticipation that, in the future, PVC supply would exceed demand.

Exhibit 1: SCAC's Major Product Lines and Sales Volume

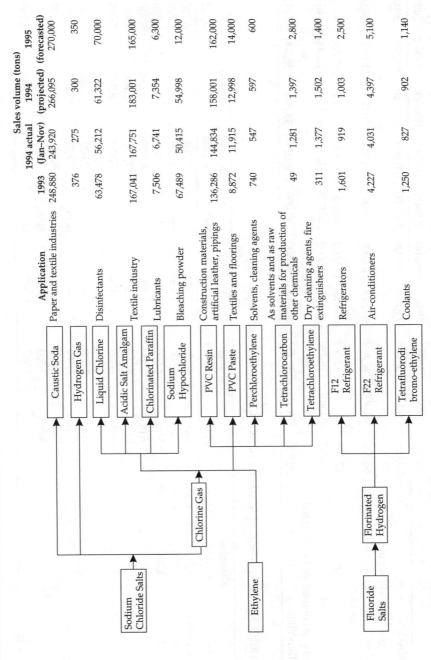

		Sales volume (tons)			
Product	Application	1993	1994 actual (Jan–Nov)	1994 (projected)	1995 (forecasted)
Caustic Soda	Paper and textile industries	248,880	243,920	266,095	270,000
Hydrogen Gas		376	275	300	350
Liquid Chlorine	Disinfectants	63,478	56,212	61,322	70,000
Acidic Salt Amalgam	Textile industry	167,041	167,751	183,001	165,000
Chlorinated Paraffin	Lubricants	7,506	6,741	7,354	6,300
Sodium Hypochloride	Bleaching powder	67,489	50,415	54,998	12,000
PVC Resin	Construction materials, artificial leather, pipings	136,286	144,834	158,001	162,000
PVC Paste	Textiles and floorings	8,872	11,915	12,998	14,000
Perchloroethylene	Solvents, cleaning agents	740	547	597	600
Tetrachlorocarbon	As solvents and as raw materials for production of other chemicals	49	1,281	1,397	2,800
Tetrachloroethylene	Dry cleaning agents, fire extinguishers	311	1,377	1,502	1,400
F12 Refrigerant	Refrigerators	1,601	919	1,003	2,500
F22 Refrigerant	Air-conditioners	4,227	4,031	4,397	5,100
Tetrafluorodi bromo-ethylene	Coolants	1,250	827	902	1,140

Feedstocks shown in the flow diagram: Sodium Chloride Salts, Chlorine Gas, Ethylene, Fluoride Salts, Florinated Hydrogen.

PVC resin is a relatively minor product; this case focuses on PVC paste.

Exhibit 2: PVC Production and Development Among Major Competitors (tons)

	1991	1992	1993	1994	1995(e)	1996(e)	1997(e)	1998(e)	1999(e)	2000(e)
SCAC	100,008	109,147	136,286	171,199	170,000	180,000	180,000	250,000	280,000	300,000
Largest competitors in China										
Beijing No. 2 Chemical Factory Qilu Petroleum	66,332	61,405	67,862	60,319	65,000	65,000	70,000	120,000	140,000	140,000
Chemical Company	117,509	145,155	152,062	160,016	170,000	180,000	180,000	200,000	280,000	300,000
Tianjin Bohai	105,543	94,407	115,290	118,476	115,000	120,000	140,000	140,000	140,000	140,000
Largest competitor in Shanghai										
Tian Yuan	30,920	26,823	32,732	38,089	38,000	38,000	38,000	38,000	38,000	38,000

Exhibit 3: Comparison of Market and SCAC PVC Prices (RMB per ton)

Year	Shanghai market	SCAC
Mar 1990	4,200	4,200
1991	4,200	4,200
1992	4,200	4,200

1993	Shanghai market	SCAC
Jan	4,250	4,400
Feb	4,300	4,450
Mar	4,500	4,450
Apr	4,550	4,500
May	5,100	5,250
Jun	7,700	6,150
July	8,350	6,150
Aug	7,500	6,450
Sept	7,500	6,450
Oct	7,750	6,450
Nov	7,300	6,600
Dec	7,300	6,600

1994	Shanghai market	China CIF	SCAC
Jan	7,280		6,700
Feb	7,200		6,700
Mar	6,875	5,120	6,700
Apr	6,875	5,280	6,700
May	7,150	5,800	6,800
June	7,550	6,240	7,000
July	7,625	6,880	7,000
Aug	7,600	6,880	7,100
Sept	7,850	7,880	7,100
Oct	8,500	7,880	7,500
Nov	8,900	7,880	8,000
Dec	9,080	7,880	8,200

Exhibit 4A: Sales History of a Selection of 12 SCAC Manufacturing Customers

Industry	Customer	1990 Contracted	1990 Actual	1991 Contracted	1991 Actual	1992 Contracted	1992 Actual	1993 Contracted	1993 Actual	1994 (Jan–Jun) Contracted	1994 (Jan–Jun) Actual	Requested
1. Artificial leather	Shanghai Plastics No. 1 Factory	2,900.4	1,484.4	1,800	148.8	480	432	960	722.4	960	342	960
2. Artificial leather	Qunshan Ziafeng Company	240	108	1,800	1,946.4	2,400	3,396	3,600	3,516	3,360	1,380	3,600
3. Pipings	Zumbu Plastics Company	240	240	1,692	1,644	2,400	1,092	2,400	300	840	360	1,200
4. Pipings	Shanghai Chemicals Luodian Branch			1,320	1,383.6	1,800	1,947.6	1,800	1,440	1,680	732	1,800
5. Transparent plastic sheets	Changzhou Qioye Plastic Materials Factory	288	288	1,800	1,284	3,600	2,730	3,000	1,812	2,400	792	1,800
6. Transparent plastic sheets	Zigong Nainhua Plastic Materials Factory			360	60	480	360	480	492	480	240	600
7. Construction materials	Bolu Plastics Company					360	396	600	456	600	264	600
8. Electric wires	Shanghai Chemicals Factory	6,800.4	6,800.4	11,400	8,707.8	7,200	5,481.6	4,800	2,892	4,560	1,440	2,400
9. Plastic membranes	Kururcing Plastic Materials Factory			360	348	480	354	360	360	360	180	600
10. Plastic membranes	Xinjiang Shibezi Plastic Materials Main Factory					360	372	240	360	360	180	480
11. Semi-finished plastic material	Hangzhou Plastic Materials Factory	2,280	2,059.2	3,360	1,956	7,200	6,162	7,200	6,300	6,600	2,820	7,200
12. Medicines	Yangzhou Huakang Medical Plastic Materials Factory	480	276	1,560	1,308	1,800	1,578	1,200	1,320	1,200	552	1,200

Exhibit 4B: Sales History of a Section of 10 SCAC Distribution Customers

Customer	1992 Contracted	1992 Actual	1993 Contracted	1993 Actual	1994 (Jan–Jun) Contracted	1994 (Jan–Jun) Actual	1995 Requested
1. Shanghai Chemicals Division No. 1	1,200	815	800	590	800	290	1,000
2. Yanchang Chemicals	800	670	400	380	400	170	500
3. Haining Economic Cooperation Co.	1,500	1,095	1,000	530	800	330	1,000
4. Haining Chemical Materials Development Ltd.	800	720	600	600	500	185	500
5. Huzhou Chemical Supplies Co.	400	300	400	310	300	140	500
6. Anhui Chemical Supplies Co.	300	110	100	30	50	30	100
7. Fuzhou Chemicals and Construction Materials Co.	300	150	100	90	100	120	300
8. Chienzhou Chemicals and Construction Materials Co.	300	250	300	290	300	150	400
9. Shantou Chemicals	1,000	530	500	750	500	250	600
10. Shantou Chemicals and Construction Materials Co.	1,000	300	500	500	500	30	400

Appendix: Future Trends in PVC Demand*

For at least the next five years, total Chinese consumption of PVC will sustain high growth (estimated 8% to 10% p.a.). Major reasons are:

- Construction of residential apartments will reach 200 million sq. m. annually, demanding large quantities of PVC construction and decoration materials.
- Large-scale rebuilding of infrastructure and buildings in old cities will fuel enormous growth for PVC piping.
- Agriculture is still very primitive in many parts of China; additional use of plastic membranes to wrap fruit in plantations and plastic pipes (hard and soft) for better productivity can be foreseen.
- PVC artificial leather has entered high-end markets; prospects are promising.
- Explosive credit card growth will lead to similar growth for plastic card manufacturers.

PVC processing industries developing most rapidly include:

Construction materials: In the past several years, property development in China has grown at 18% p.a. In urban areas, annual construction area of residential apartments is about 200 million sq. m.; annual demand for door and window materials is each 150 million sq. m. If 1/15 of construction and decoration materials were PVC, annual consumption would amount to over 100,000 tons. PVC applications in construction materials include wallpaper, flooring tiles, partitions, doors and windows, piping and mending. Much PVC would be in the form of hard plastic sheets or molded plastics. Production of molded plastic materials in China soared in the early 1980s; currently over 200 production lines have total annual capacity exceeding 150,000 tons. Annual assembly capacity for plastic doors and windows is about 150,000,000 sq. m. In recent years, promotion activities combined with more advanced technology for manufacturing better quality plastic doors and windows at lower costs have led to increased acceptance from the general public. High quality plastic compound doors now cost only RMB60 to 80 per sq. m., comparable to wooden doors but with additional qualities of sound resistance and higher durability (up to 40 to 50 years).

Piping: In 1991, Chinese PVC pipe production was about 60,000 tons. In recent years, new PVC products have proliferated, fueling industry growth (e.g., aluminum PVC electric wire tubing, foamed PVC pipes, double tube pipes, high pressure endurance pipes). UPVC (underground PVC) construction water pipes have been installed in over 20 provinces and over 300 miles of public water supply pipe has been connected. Based on estimated construction of 200 million sq. m. residential properties yearly in urban areas; assuming 30% of apartments use UPVC plastic pipe, annual demand should be over 50,000 tons.

Packaging materials: PVC plastic sheets are used in packaging food, drinks, apparatus, clothes and agriculture. PVC transparent membranes are used in cigarette packaging. Current Chinese demand for transparent plastic sheets is about 100,000 tons p.a., expected to grow to 150,000 tons in 1995.

Insulating materials: PVC is widely used as an insulator in electric wires and cables. Current Chinese production capacity of PVC insulating materials is about 150,000 tons p.a. In 1988, consumption for PVC electric cable insulating materials was 140,000 tons; current demand is 160,000 tons, expected to increase to 220,000 tons in 1995.

* Prepared by the Sales and Supplies Department.

Case 35

Shanghai Chlor-Alkali Chemical Company Ltd.: F12 (A)

Ho Yuen Ching, Michelle
The Hong Kong University of Science and Technology

Noel Capon
Graduate School of Business, Columbia University

In August 1994, key executives of Shanghai Chlor-Alkali Chemical Company (SCAC) had just finished the semi-annual performance review. Net profit, driven by good performance in caustic soda and PVC, reached a historic high of US$12 million. As the group anticipated the evening's champagne celebration, Mr. Gu Wei-liang, Director of Marketing, initiated a discussion on future strategy for freon refrigerant F12, a long-neglected small volume product. Facing unfavorable market conditions and environmental protection pressures, Gu said SCAC should decide whether to continue with F12 or kill it.[1]

✾✽✾✽

Fluoro Products at SCAC

The fluoro products line was one of four chemical systems (i.e., chlorine, fluorine, alkaline, plastics) produced at SCAC. It comprised fluorine refrigerants F11, F12, F13, F22,[2] hydrofluoric acid (HF) and tetrafluoro-dibromo-ethane; revenues were approximately 5% of total firm revenues.

Production of F12 was a multi-stage process. During production of one of SCAC's "fist" (major profit producer) products, caustic soda, a large quantity of chlorine gas (Cl_2) was produced. Some chlorine was pressurized into liquid chlorine for sale; most

---

[1] For extra background data on SCAC, see Shanghai Chlor-Alkali Chemical Company Ltd.: PVC; certain numerical data have been disguised.

[2] Chemically, these products were: F12, dichloro-difluorocarbon, aka Freon 12; F22, difluoro-chloro-hydrocarbon, aka Freon 22; F11, trichlor-fluorocarbon, aka Freon 11.

was used to produce PVC, another "fist product." A by-product of PVC manufacture, produced in substantial quantities, was tetrachloro-carbon (CCl_4); the subsequent reaction of CCl_4 with hydrofluoric acid (HF) produced F12. (Figure 1). Production of F12 fulfilled the valuable function of balancing chemical flows among systems; one ton of HF produced 380 kg of F12. Alternatively, HF might be reacted with "lufang" (hydro-trichloro-methane, $CHCl_3$), a product that SCAC outsourced, to make F22. One ton of HF produced 560 kg of F22. (See Exhibit 1 for a direct cost analysis for F12 production.)

Figure 1: The Production Process for Freon Products, F12 and F22

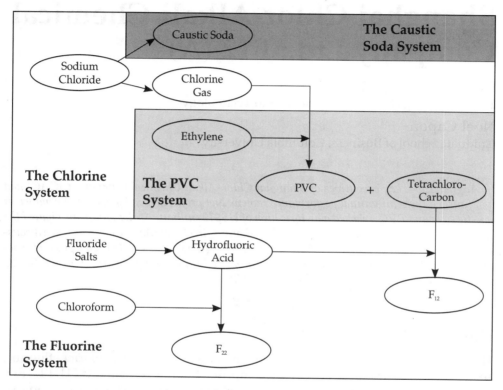

F12 and F22 (aka Freons),[3] invented in 1931, were used as refrigerants in a variety of electrical appliances and machinery (e.g., refrigerators, air-conditioners, electrical cleaning systems); F12 was used in refrigerators, F22 in air-conditioners. Product substitution was not possible in these applications because of physical properties related to temperature and pressure. SCAC had manufactured F12 and F22 for over 30 years; about 100 workers were currently employed in these operations.

---

[3] Freon is a registered trademark of E.I. Du Pont de Nemours. The name was used for many products in the chemical family of halogentated hydrocarbons including F11, F12 and F22.

Market trends differed for F12 and F22. F12 use in China was being phased out due to environmental concerns; conversely, demand for F22 was growing with increased air-conditioner purchases as living standards improved. Previously considered a luxury, in 1993 air-conditioner ownership was less than six per 100 households in China's major cities, but 1993 sales were up 92% over 1992. In addition, automobile ownership was increasing, leading to demand for vehicle air-conditioning systems. For both F12 and F22, two major market segments could be identified, the direct market (for use in new products) and the aftermarket (for servicing existing products).

Chinese F22 production in 1992 was 18,000 tons; 1993, 21,000 tons. SCAC's F22 production was close to its 6,000 tons annual capacity; one third consumed by SCAC-related enterprises. F22 demand was expected to grow at 15% to 20% p.a. In addition to traditional air-conditioning manufacturers, new entrants with various production capacities were proliferating throughout China.

Freon 12 (F12)

Historically, SCAC was China's market leader for F12 (1965 share, 25%); annual profit margins averaged about 30%. Then, China's economy was centrally planned; large state-owned enterprises such as SCAC were protected from market fluctuations by government price controls and product flow planning mechanisms among major enterprises. As a result, SCAC was highly production oriented. However, as the economy opened up in the early 1980s, SCAC experienced competitive pressures from "laoxiang" (county collective enterprises). These small agile competitors were more able to adapt to changing market conditions. SCAC also faced competition from "laowai" (Sino-foreign joint ventures). SCAC lost market share; by 1992 profit margins had fallen to 11%; by end 1993, SCAC's market share was 10% and dropping. Annual production was 1,600 tons, down from 7,000 tons in the mid-1980s; F12 barely escaped joining the "money losers" category.[4]

Product Quality

F12 quality was measured by two criteria: purity level and water content. In 1986, SCAC was awarded the Silver Medal for Quality (best in China) for F12 by the State Chemical Industry Bureau. (There was no gold medal for this award.) Standards for different quality classes were set by the bureau; it also sampled and inspected output quality of regulated chemicals manufacturers. Three acceptable F12 grades were recognized: excellent – purity level 99.9%, water content less than 10 parts per million (ppm); first class – purity level 99.5%, water content less than 30 ppm; and pass – purity level between 99.0% and 99.5%. Although SCAC's F12 was endorsed by customers and compared favorably in quality to many overseas producers, it did not reach the level of such multinational giants as Du Pont. SCAC was in the process of applying for ISO 9000 certification.

---

[4] Raw material costs for F12 and F22 were quite low; much of the manufacturing cost was allocated overhead.

Since the early 1990s, prices for chemicals were no longer controlled by the State but were negotiated between buyers and sellers. Nonetheless, certain industry norms continued; in particular, excellent class products were 20% to 25% more expensive than pass products and 10% to 15% more expensive than first class products. SCAC's process tended to produce the higher grades of F12.

The F12 Market in 1993

Until 1992, F12 was a profitable business for many suppliers; demand consistently exceeded supply. (See Exhibit 2 for China's capacity, production and sales volumes.) However, during the economic boom from 1990 to 1992, several new F12 factories were planned and/or entered production, despite signing of the Montreal Protocol by the Chinese government (see below) to cease all F12 production by the year 2000. From 1990 onward, supply increased but demand decreased by about 10% p.a.; demand was forecast at 20,000 tons for 1994, 17,000 tons in 1995. In 1993, supply exceeded demand for the first time (by 5%); this imbalance was expected to increase when Juzhou Chemical's long-planned plant came on stream in 1994. The majority of F12 use was in southern China (especially Guangzhou); it accounted for around 50% of China's refrigerator and air-conditioner production.

The Montreal Protocol

Signed on September 16, 1987 (effective 1989), the Montreal Protocol on Ozone-Depleting Substances (ODS) was an international agreement among 46 nations, including most European countries, Canada, the U.S. and Japan, that required signatories to control the production and consumption of substances that can cause ozone depletion. In subsequent meetings (London 1990, Copenhagen 1992) the signatories agreed to accelerate the phaseout schedules for controlled substances (i.e., chlorofluorocarbons [CFCs], halons, carbontetrachloride, methylchloroform, hydrochlorofluorocarbons [HCFCs], hydrobromofluorocarbons [HBFCs] and methylbromide). In developed countries, phaseouts of CFCs and carbon tetrachloride were required by January 1, 1996. Phaseout schedules for HCFCs were slower and would proceed according to a fixed schedule based on calculated baselines for each country (i.e., 2004, 35% reduction; 2010, 65% reduction; 2015, 90% reduction; 2020, 99.5% reduction; 2030, 100%).[5, 6] (See Exhibits 3A, 3B for annual production of various fluorocarbons.[7])

---

[5] Individual countries were free to accelerate these schedules; several had.

[6] F12 belonged to a class of chemical compounds termed chlorofluorocarbons (CFCs); F22 belonged to a class of compounds termed hydrochlorofluorocarbons (HCFCs). Unlike CFCs, HCFCs broke down readily in the lower atmosphere and caused less ozone depletion. In particular, when the ozone-depleting potential (ODP) of F12 was indexed at 1.0, the ODP of F22 was 0.055. (The difference between individual CFCs related to the number and position of chlorine, fluorine and carbon atoms in the chemical compound; the difference between individual HCFCs related to the number and position of hydrogen, chlorine, fluorine and carbon atoms in the chemical compound.) The ozone-depleting potential of hydrofluorocarbons (HFCs) was zero.

[7] It was common industry knowledge that the U.S. was an active market for smuggled F12; it entered via West Indian countries such as Grenada and Trinidad and Tobago. India was rumored to be the production center for this trade.

China and many developing countries that were not signatories accounted for only 10% of world ODS consumption in 1987 (1.2 million tons p.a.). However, rapid economic growth from 1988 to 1990 and consequent increased demand for home appliances and aerosol products increased China's F12 annual demand from slightly over 1,000 tons to more than 10,000 tons; 1991 demand was 20,000 tons. In 1989, a senior National Environmental Protection Agency (NEPA) official acknowledged the problem, but explained that unless technical and financial assistance were provided to China, it would be forced to use ODS like F12 to meet pressing development objectives. In 1990, the Montreal Protocol signatories responded to such concerns from developing countries (e.g., China, India) and formed the Multilateral Fund (MLF) to assist the 40 developing countries that agreed to abide by the Protocol's terms.

From 1992 to date, the MLF provided $22 million to China, mainly for the foam industry; the refrigerant industry received less funding as substitute technologies were immature. Indeed, no substitute technologies for F12 were available in China. Since overseas buyers of refrigerators banned F12 use, local manufacturers interested in exporting had to convert production facilities to use the more expensive Forane 134a, only available abroad. In 1990, the Chinese Ministry of Machinery and Electronics Industry assisted the Jingdenezhen Huayi Electric Appliance General Company in negotiating the foreign purchase of a household compressor line that used Forane 134a. In 1993, refrigerator exports (free of F12) were only 370,000. By 1993, several major refrigerator manufacturers had successfully converted their manufacturing processes to use limited quantities of F12. Simultaneously, Guangzhou's Wan Bao and Qing Dao's Hai Er, Chang Ling and Hua Yi began emphasizing "Green" (environmentally friendly) refrigerators using 20% to 40% less F12.

SCAC and Chinese government officials embarked on serious discussions with the MLF to convert F12 production facilities to make F22. MLF officials made several visits to SCAC but technical uncertainties held up approval. Concurrently, the MLF was considering funding production facility conversion for F12 users (e.g., a Guangdong aerosol maker and six large domestic refrigerator manufacturers).

Competition

In August 1994, the 16 Chinese Freon producers had total F12 capacity of 31,400 tons (Exhibit 4); addition of Juzhou's new plant would increase national capacity to 40,000 tons p.a.; competition was increasingly keen. In the early 1990s, industry prices increased from less than RMB7,000 (US$1,000) to RMB19,000 (US$2,710) per ton in spring 1993. By late 1994, prices had dropped to around RMB10,500 (US$1,500) (Table 1). Furthermore, SCAC management believed several smaller competitors used illegal means to sell F12 such as offering procurement personnel rebates for F12 purchases; concerned with image and reputation, SCAC would not use these practices.

Customers

Heavy F12 users were typically large joint-venture refrigerator manufacturers and chemical wholesalers serving the needs of smaller users; 14 customers nationally accounted for around 75% of F12 sales. Medium users were smaller local refrigerator

1992	China	SCAC	1993	China	SCAC	1994	China	SCAC
Jan	7,050	8,150	Jan	13,500	13,750	Jan	13,800	14,500
Feb	7,780	8,560	Feb	16,000	16,600	Feb	13,700	14,550
Mar	9,000	8,850	Mar	18,000	18,800	Mar	14,900	14,600
Apr	9,200	9,360	Apr	18,050	18,650	Apr	14,000	14,600
May	9,500	9,985	May	19,000	18,250	May	13,220	14,300
Jun	9,700	10,050	Jun	18,000	18,300	Jun	13,110	14,210
Jul	9,750	10,090	Jul	17,500	17,800	Jul	13,050	14,168
Aug	10,875	9,070	Aug	16,500	17,150			
Sep	10,925	8,000	Sep	15,000	15,500			
Oct	10,000	9,900	Oct	14,000	15,200			
Nov	11,000	9,557	Nov	13,900	13,800			
Dec	10,500	11,500	Dec	13,800	14,400			

manufacturers, relatively well dispersed throughout China, light users were typically the tens of thousands of repair and maintenance shops that replaced exhausted refrigerants in both commercial and domestic refrigerators.

Over 70% of SCAC's F12 sales were made around Shanghai and Guangdong, mainly to heavy F12 users for refrigerators, largely consistent with previous state planning system directives. Individual F12 use by most of its over 50 customers was small: 30 to 40 tons p.a. for large customers, 5 to 20 tons p.a. (medium), 3 to 5 tons p.a. (small). Typically, SCAC received payment when customers received the product.

Most single refrigerators used 200 g to 390 g of F12. China's retail price for refrigerators averaged RMB6,000 (US$860). In 1993, 6.2 million refrigerators were manufactured in China; sales in major cities were 4.2 million. Over 50% of Chinese households in major cities had refrigerators and growth was expected to slow in the next five years. In addition, domestic refrigerator demand was seasonal (for F12 also); sales usually increased from March to July and dropped from November to February. Between the peak and slack seasons, 10% price fluctuations were typical. Because of low winter demand, SCAC ceased F12 production from December to March. Excess CCl_4 was sold to competitors for F12 manufacture or for use in the pharmaceutical industry.

Raw Materials and Packaging

Currently, SCAC and competitors used two types of packaging: one ton (800 kg) and half ton (400 kg) steel tanks. The cost of 400 kg tanks was RMB3,200 (US$460), RMB5,200 (US$740) for 800 kg tanks; SCAC maintained about 2,000 tanks in approximately equal proportions. For about one third of SCAC's sales, customers provided their own storage facilities; however, for the majority, SCAC loaned tanks and customers placed deposits equal to the tank cost. The factory retained 20% of tanks as a reserve for inventory and for loans to upcoming customers. Average turnaround time for a tank was two to three months; average useful tank life was about ten years.

Since many customers used small amounts of F12, turnaround time for large tanks was considered too slow. Small purchasers (e.g., repair and maintenance units) found large F12 tanks inflexible and impractical for their purposes. SCAC knew international chemical companies (e.g., Du Pont) offered F12 in containers as small as 13.5 kg. However, since the international F12 price was 25% more than the local China price, imports were not a threat.

Alternatives

It was apparent to SCAC management that if trends in market demand and F12 sales performance continued, SCAC would soon start to lose money. The situation was complicated by the upcoming ban (2000) on F12, severe competition and synchronization problems with the production processes for caustic soda and PVC. Because of environmental regulations, SCAC was unable to dispose of CCl_4, Cl_2 or F12 in rivers or the sea.

Let It Be

One set of opinions at SCAC was to leave F12 alone and accept that sales would continue to fall, in essence continuing the current strategy. All possible F12 would be sold before 2000; inventory would be used as an interim solution for production balancing in the short term. Unfortunately, owing to complexity of the production processes and disputes over production forecasts for various products germane to the situation, it was impossible to make informed estimates of year-end inventories before 2000.

Opponents argued that as production and sales of PVC increased, huge quantities of F12 would have to be produced for synchronization: new steel tanks specific to F12 would be required; dumping F12 inventory could not be countenanced and avoiding the F12 problem might attract public accusations that could hurt SCAC's reputation for other fluoro products and damage the expected bright future for F22.

Aggressive Marketing

Advocates of aggressive marketing wanted to increase market share through intensified marketing efforts. They argued that, although the market was weakening, it would not disappear overnight as substitute technologies would not be available for several years. In any event, refrigerator manufacturers would not be able to convert that quickly and the market would be sufficiently large to support the current capacity of major players like SCAC. This strategy assumed SCAC could squeeze out small competitors through economies of scale, establish reputation and customer loyalty. These executives believed satisfactory profitability was attainable.

In addition, SCAC was optimistic about sales of F22 for air-conditioning. Many large refrigerator manufacturers (70% to 80%) also made air-conditioners. Abruptly ceasing F12 supply could adversely affect long-run client relationships and affect SCAC's F22 prospects. By contrast, aggressive F12 marketing would provide the opportunity to establish a far-reaching reputation for SCAC's fluoro products and develop a comprehensive distribution system throughout the country. This strategy would require significant investments in market development; in addition, implementation would have to commence shortly because of F12's limited life span.

Stop F12 Production

Some executives argued for stopping F12 production right away. They argued that the product was a money loser and that since production was halted in the winter months alternative means to dispose of CCl_4 and Cl_2 already existed. Opponents argued that storage capacity for CCl_4 and Cl_2 was limited to 300 tons and that maintaining excessive inventories was dangerous. This solution only appeared practical for short production halts.

The Decision

While Gu recognized that other alternatives might emerge, he asked his Executive Secretary Mr. Chang Quing and Marketing Executive Mr. Da Su-hua, for fluoro products, to prepare detailed analyses of the alternatives and to present recommendations including marketing plans (if appropriate).

Exhibit 1: SCAC Production and Overhead Cost Analysis for F12 (per ton) (data of April to July 1994 operations, total actual production was 950 tons)

Item	Unit	Unit cost (RMB*)		Quantities consumed**		Total itemized cost (RMB)	
		Target	Actual	Target**	Actual	Target	Actual
Raw materials							
Hydrofluoric acid	ton	5,059.16	4,785.31	0.48	0.48	2,428.40	2,273.02
Carbon tetrachloride	ton	8,112.86	5,396.21	1.73	1.72	13,994.69	9,301.72
Utilities							
Water	ton					128.81	75.00
Electricity	unit	0.41	0.51	730.00	550.00	237.08	223.74
Steam	ton	65.63	46.33	1.88	1.00	95.85	37.06
Salaries and staff benefits						73.25	67.00
Factory overhead						967.65	625.00
Production costs						17,925.73	12,602.54
Company management						925.24	646.88
Overhead						0.00	0.00
Total costs						18,850.97	13,249.42

*RMB1 approximate US$0.125.
**The quantities used per ton of F12 production was based on prior year figures for the same period.

Exhibit 2: F12 Production Capacity, Actual Production and Demand in China

	1988	1990	1991	1992	1993	1994 (F)	1995 (F)	1996 (F)	1997 (F)	1998 (F)	1999 (F)	2000 (F)
Capacity	n/a	n/a	n/a	29,600	31,400	35,400	40,000	40,000	40,000	40,000	40,000	40,000
Production	n/a	n/a	n/a	14,300	13,100	17,500	20,000	n/a	n/a	n/a	n/a	n/a
Demand	1,000	10,000	20,000	15,000	12,500	15,000	13,000	11,700	10,530	9,477	8529.3	7676.37
SCAC sales	n/a	6,500	5,500	4,100	1,600	956	2,500	n/a	n/a	n/a	n/a	n/a
SCAC market share	n/a	0.22	0.22	0.28	0.08	0.05	0.15	n/a	n/a	n/a	n/a	n/a

Exhibit 3A: Annual Global Production of Selected Fluorocarbons[1]

1994 production (est.) (metric tons)		Change (1993 to 1994) (metric tons, %)	
CFC11	60,232	86,899	decrease (–59%)
CFC12	133,600	81,064	decrease (–38%)
CFC113	29,547	18,490	decrease (–38%)
CFC114	3,207	1,369	decrease (–30%)
CFC115	6,834	4,577	decrease (–40%)
HCFC22	239,444	1,175	decrease (–0.5%)
HCFC142b	39,522	4,866	increase (+14%)

Exhibit 3B: Annual Global Production of Selected Fluorocarbons Reported to AFEAS (1980–1994 est.)

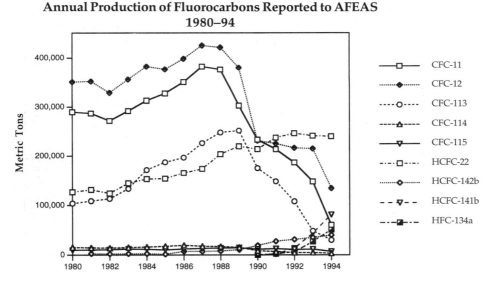

**Annual Production of Fluorocarbons Reported to AFEAS
1980–94**

Notes: 1. Production (as defined in the Montreal Protocol) does not include feedstock uses.
2. CFC-11 = F11; HCFC-22 = F22, etc.

Source: Reported to AFEAS, an industry association of American, European and Japanese fluoro-carbon producers (U.S.: AlliedSignal, Du Pont, LaRoche; Italy: Ausimont; France: Elf Atochem, Rhone-Poulenc; Greece: SICNG; Germany: Hoechst; U.K.: ICI; Belgium: Solvay); Japan Fluorocarbon Manufacturers Association.

Exhibit 4: Competitors in the F12 Industry*

Chemical companies	Production capacity (ton/year)	Production (tons)	Sales (tons)	Average price (RMB/ton)	Production cost (RMB/ton)	Production value (constant price) (RMB/'0000)	No. of employees at year end	Raw material usage		Quality of products			GP%
								AHF (tons)	CC14 (tons)	Excellent (tons)	First class (tons)	Pass (tons)	
1992													
1. SCAC	7,000	3,444	3,442	8,000	7,118	3,443	116	384	1,366	2,089	1,354		
2. Wuhan Changjiang	4,500	1,442	1,277	8,600	6,790	1,422	99	424	1,378	78	869	475	
3. Jinan	3,000	2,468	2,950	8,500	7,195	2,468		441	1,462	21	332	2,115	
4. Weiyang	3,000	1,320	1,435	8,555	6,982	1,320	30	424	1,447		1,175	145	
5. Hebeishi Factory No.1	3,000	844	897	8,000	10,200	844		431	1,471		844		
6. Chaowushi Fluoro	2,000	457	413	8,320	8,303		236	428	1,489		100	357	
7. State-owned Factory 3414	1,500	1,220			7,055					94			
8. Taizhou Electric Factory	1,000	509	740	8,912	8,295	509	42	450	1,440			509	
9. Changshou Refrigerants	800	613	420	8,765	7,315	613		373	1,324	613			
10. Jiangxi Stars Fluoro Co.	700	224											
11. Tungyang	700	258			7,488		35	359	1,385				
12. Hunan Yiyangshi Jiangnan	600	393	445	90,000	8,434	393		489	1,545			393	
13. Baotoushi No.1	500	241	307	12,000	8,200		77	449	1,451	241			
14. Linhai Jianshen	500	369	417	8,965	9,762	369		417	1,446		19	350	
15. Zigongshi Fugiang	500	428	395	9,000	7,543		50	408	1,423		163	266	
16. Chongxing Tianyuan	300	117	120	9,200	8,604			521	1,707	18	78	22	
1993													
1. SCAC	7,000	1,601	1,601	18,227	11,717	1,601	93	385	1,380	683	918		35.7
2. Wuhan Changjiang	4,500	1,446	1,596	17,467	13,133	1,446	94	420	1,405		255	1,446	24.8
3. Jinan	3,500	2,369	2,269	17,090	12,258	2,369		443	1,447		82	2,297	28.2
4. Weiyang	3,000	1,696	1,480	18,000		1,696		462	1,481		1,696		
5. Hebeishi Factory No.1	3,000	714	670	19,657	11,949	714	34	630	1,494		655	59	39.2
6. Chaowushi Fluoro	2,000	876	919	17,000	13,500	876	236	395	1,400	359	517		20.9
7. State-owned Factory 3414	1,500	1,023	1,174	19,243	17,322	1,023	670	458	1,528	417	606		10.0
8. Taizhou Electric Factory	1,500	442	432	16,197	16,657	442	24	479	1,668			442	
9. Changshou Refrigerants	1,000	952	800	16,000	11,443	952		437	1,447	952			28.8
10. Jiangxi Stars Fluoro Co.	1,000	383	370	18,000	18,275	383	34	446	1,416			383	
11. Tungyang	800	1,023	891	18,091	11,358	1,023	45	382	1,347	1,023			37.2
12. Hunan Yiyangshi Jiangnan	700	182			11,076	182		418	1,286				
13. Baotoushi No.1	500	93	136		10,741	93	29	560	1,671			93	69.0
14. Linhai Jianshen	700	92			12,512	92		384	1,381				
15. Zigongshi Fugiang	500	94			13,787	94		390	1,549				
16. Chongxing Tianyuan	200	158	158	16,000	11,462	158	44	490	1,679	24	154	80	28.3

*Blanks imply data unavailable.

Case 36

Shanghai Chlor-Alkali Chemical Company Ltd.: F12 (B)

Ho Yuen Ching, Michelle
The Hong Kong University of Science and Technology

Noel Capon
Graduate School of Business, Columbia University

SCAC's 1995 half year report concluded: "Moving against the current of shrinking market size, our marketing efforts on F12 have effectively turned around a small long-neglected by-product into a profit maker." Mr. Gu Wei-liang recalled all that he and his F12 team had gone through in the past year. After much heated debate with the Board of Directors, in September 1994, the decision had been made to continue production and start actively marketing F12.

ঙOৎেঙB

Re-establishing Market Leadership

On the decision to retain F12, Gu said: "The characteristic of chemical enterprises is that once you start your car, you cannot brake as you like." SCAC's chemicals' production was intertwined; engineers believed adjustments to production processes would be expensive and could take years to implement; furthermore, no satisfactory disposal method had been identified for CCl_4.

During the transition period to 2000, SCAC would relentlessly pursue substitute development and conversion studies for transitioning the F12 facility into F22 manufacture. In the interim, it would actively market F12 to re-establish a position as the "big brother" in fluoro products to lay the groundwork for F22 market development. A 25% market share objective was set for F12 in 1996.

As soon as the F12 decision was made, Gu formed an F12 marketing team comprising Mr. Chang Quing and Mr. Da Su-hua. Chang, a Gu's protégé, was a university graduate studying for an MBA at a local university; Da, also a college graduate, joined SCAC 20 years earlier, shortly after the Cultural Revolution; Gu was one of China's senior economists. This group decided that in the cut-throat competitive environment,

572

reforming any single aspect of F12 distribution would not suffice, a thorough overhaul of all aspects of F12 marketing was required. As a first step, the SCAC marketing group segmented the F12 market on the basis of annual F12 consumption: heavy (over 20 tons), medium (5 to 20 tons) and light (less than 5 tons).

Product Management

SCAC focused on three different elements of product improvement:

- Actual product (core benefits). SCAC recognized that although F12 quality was among the best in China, it lagged prestigious overseas giants like Du Pont. SCAC decided to use Du Pont's standards as benchmarks and strengthen quality controls based on Du Pont's model. It guaranteed F12 product quality by offering free replacement of unsatisfactory product even though SCAC had not received any quality complaints from customers.
- Packaging. Besides packaging F12 in large tanks for heavy industrial users, Du Pont provided F12 in small tanks, 13.6 kg and 22.7 kg and even 390 g for individual refrigerators. SCAC purchased 13.6 kg ($100) and 22.7 kg ($140) tanks from the U.S. to add to the current one ton (800 kg) and 0.5 ton (400 kg) tanks. By mid-1995, small tank sales of F12 averaged 2.5 tons to 3 tons per month. Initially, customers purchased these small tanks full; for subsequent F12 purchases they returned these "private" tanks for refilling. SCAC did not purchase any new large tanks but, by more frequent customer calling, reduced turnaround time for large tanks (two thirds loaned to customers) to one month. Before refilling tanks, SCAC implemented a process for cleaning tanks of chemical residuals and thoroughly drying them out.
- Branding. In 1994, SCAC started branding its products, including F12. Chang observed: "Before 1993, SCAC was a state-owned company, focusing on serving an allotted group of large enterprises. It did not have to market its products and did not believe it necessary to brand products since suppliers and customers knew each other. Now that customers have much more autonomy in choosing suppliers and competition is cut-throat, we need ways to differentiate ourselves, including a smart, sharp contrast brand name. We have to establish a brand name that can specifically associate itself with chemical products of exceptional quality and reliability that customers can easily remember and speak of."

SCAC selected the name "Shen-Feng," embracing Chinese characters for "Shen" (Chinese abbreviation for Shanghai), and "Feng" (meaning peak, height). A six-person brand management division was formed within the sales department. Two persons visited prestigious refrigerator manufacturers to secure associations with, and complimentary references from, these firms to enhance F12 confidence in other potential customers. SCAC secured business with 15 dominant manufacturers in Guangzhou. (See Table 1 for F12 sales to refrigerator manufacturers in Guangdong province.) Total 1994 F12 demand in Guangdong was estimated at 7,500 tons, slightly over half the national demand.

Table 1:   SCAC Sales and Distribution in Guangdong, 1994

Company	Volume (tons)	Company	Volume (tons)
Wanbao Group	60	Oceanic Boats Materials Supplies	24
Hualing Group	96	Chongshan Chemicals	96
Zhujiang Group	120	Puhua Repackaging Station	36
Lingbao Group	18	Chunghua Repackaging Station	18
Fushan Refrigerating Facilities Factory	24	Other repackaging station	84
Guangzhou Coolant engines Factory	36	Other manufacturers of the 390 g tubes	360
Ocean Packaging Company	120		
		Total	**1,092**

Transportation and Distribution

F12 transportation costs to Guangzhou, borne by customers, could account for 15% of the ex-factory price. SCAC ensured timely delivery service through its own transportation subsidiary; ready access to wharves and rail transportation allowed SCAC to secure a 10% to 12% freight cost advantage over most competitors.

In addition to direct sales to large accounts, SCAC began selling large tanks of fluoro products to its traditional wholesalers. Wholesalers repackaged F12 into small tanks (e.g., 390 g containers) for sale to small users; they also provided refill services but SCAC had some concerns over their ability to clean empty tanks appropriately.

SCAC also began building an alternative distribution system for fluoro products by targeting major cities and forming partnerships with reputable chemical distributors. Cities were selected on the basis of strategic geographical location (e.g., good transportation infrastructure) and high concentration of fluoro product users; Guangzhou, Haikou, Shantou, Beijing, Qingdao and Hangzhou were selected (see Exhibit 1). In each city, SCAC identified one or two distributors with good connections to fluoro product users. Distributors conducted research on local markets, visited fluoro product users to understand demand patterns and requirements for extra services; they reported these findings to SCAC. As a result, SCAC was able to deliver F12 in the most desirable manner and offer needed services (e.g., container cleaning at client sites). In turn, SCAC was able to provide continuous supply, assist distributors' marketing efforts and provide lower prices via higher discounts on bulk purchases.

Development of this network was considered a major factor in the F12 revitalization campaign; by mid-1995, sales through the network reached 55% of F12 total sales. SCAC placed most emphasis on Guangdong (mainly Guangzhou) where refrigerator users were highly concentrated and where significant potential for other products such as F22 existed. In particular, it worked closely with distributors on client purchasing negotiations, market forecasts and product quality feedback from client procurement personnel. By 1995, SCAC's F12 sales by region were: Hainan (Haikou), 10%; Guangdong, 35%; Beijing, 25%; Hangzhou, 25% and Shantou, Qingdao, Zhuhai – 5%.

Pricing and Promotion

Previously, SCAC's prices were based on production cost plus mark-up. However, after corporate overhead allocation, "cost" exceeded F12's market price. SCAC recognized that sunk costs allocated as factory overhead (e.g., depreciation) were irrelevant and that any margin above variable cost would contribute positively to earnings. Furthermore, a pricing analysis conducted in October 1994 revealed that a production increase of 500 tons per month would reduce F12 costs by 15%, allowing SCAC's price to be competitive at RMB12,000 (US$1,710) per ton. As a result, SCAC adopted a variable-cost pricing scheme; F12 prices were adjusted downwards from RMB14,000 to RMB12,000 in November 1994.

Since SCAC was a firm believer in establishing customer loyalty through product quality, historically it spent few resources on promotion. Even in the new strategy no budget was allocated for promotion and potential campaigns were considered on their merits in an incremental fashion.

Direct mailers. SCAC continued to communicate with customers via telephone and face-to-face personal contacts. However, for first time new customer purchasers, SCAC prepared direct mailers comprising technical details that played an informational rather than a promotional role. No mailers were sent to potential or continuing customers.

The Haikou conference. In mid-November 1994, SCAC organized a fluoro products conference at Haikou on Hainan Island attended by 58 potential and continuing customers. SCAC introduced its fluoro products line and secured contracts for 2,500 tons of fluoro products.

Newspaper advertising. SCAC had never advertised in the mass media, not even in industry or trade magazines; TV commercials were considered both unprofessional and unable to target industrial customers effectively. However, as part of the F12 relaunch, in November 1994, SCAC published a newspaper advertisement (7 cm × 4.5 cm) entitled "hao shue zhong" (good refrigerant) and promoting the "Shen Feng" brand name in *Liberation Daily*, next to the headline on the front page, for five continuous days. Total cost was RMB120,000 (US$17,140) (Exhibit 2).

SCAC received 20 inquiries from prospective customers resulting in increased business of about RMB110,000 (US$15,710). SCAC also received several letters from readers complaining that the advertisement for ozone-depleting substances was promotion for a "gong hai" (public hazard).

F12 Performance

In 1994, SCAC's F12 production was 1,121 tons; sales slid from 1,601 tons in 1993 to 956 tons in 1994. However, in the first six months on 1995, sales were 1,800 tons; inventory was cleared and production was 1,655 tons. SCAC estimated 1995 market share would approximate 20% of the 15,000 tons market demand. In late 1994, profit margins turned positive, reaching 8% by year end, and 9.5% in early 1995.

New Competition

In mid-1994, Juzhou Chemical's new 8,000-ton capacity plant came on stream. Located in rural Zhejiang, Juzhou was a state-owned enterprise whose facilities were planned in the rosy early 1990s. Despite Juzhou's short history, SCAC considered it a major competitor. First, the scale of operations was similar to SCAC in terms of number of employees, investment and chemical production capacities. Second, it used the most up-to-date production technology. Third, it produced "lufang," a key raw material for F22 production that suffered from wide market fluctuations; over a two-year period from 1993 to 1995, market prices rose from RMB5,000 (US$710) per ton to RMB10,000 (US$1,420). Fourth, in a short time, Juzhou built a customer base comparable to SCAC's by making product delivery before payment.

However, as a state-owned enterprise, Juzhou suffered from insufficient working capital whenever, as currently, the Chinese government tightened credit; it also lacked technical and administrative experience. Furthermore, it was required to depreciate fixed asset investment of RMB540 million (US$64 million) in ten years; as a result costs and prices would likely be high. In addition, relationships with customers were tense as Juzhou required timely payment at the end of the credit period. Also, it relied on an in-house sales force and did not have an established distribution network like SCAC. Finally, located deep in a mountainous area, transportation costs were high; it had to rely on China's relatively undeveloped road and rail system. For delivery to Guangzhou, SCAC's transportation costs were one third of Juzhou's.

New Challenges

The F12 market was expected to continue shrinking until December 2000 when F12 would be banned and the market would cease altogether. During the next few years, SCAC's challenge was to sustain market position while weaker competitors exited; SCAC management anticipated that Juzhou would be the major competitor. In addition to dealing with this specific competitive challenge, SCAC had to consider what additional marketing efforts could be made to outperform other competitors in China's many provinces, to sustain and improve market position and what additional information was needed to make the appropriate decisions.

Exhibit 1:   SCAC Distribution Network for Fluoro Products

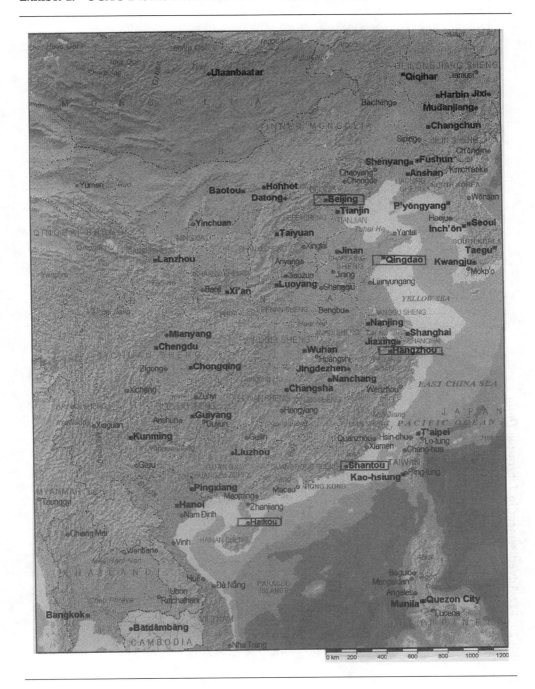

F12 Good Freezing Machine, Best Price

Case 37

Shanghai Honggong Advanced Instrument Co. Ltd. (SHAIC): Marketing Electromagnetic Flowmeters in China

Wilfried Vanhonacker
The Hong Kong University of Science and Technology

上海香江特仪器有限公司

Looking from his office window, Mr. E. J. Broekers, General Manager of Shanghai Honggong Advanced Instrument Co. Ltd. (SHAIC), a Sino-German joint venture (JV) in the Minhang Economic and Technological Development Zone (ETDZ) southwest of Shanghai (Exhibit 1), noticed the two large smokestacks of the main Shanghai electric power station spitting huge clouds of smoke into the hot summer air.[1] "Despite continued growth in revenue and profits, some clouds have appeared on SHAIC's horizon as well," he thought to himself.

SHAIC was established in 1986 as an equity JV between the Shanghai-based Honggong Instrument Works (HIW) (60%) and Krüger, SHAIC's German parent (40%). Since its establishment, the JV had developed a profitable China business selling various size electromagnetic (magnetic) inductive flowmeters. Revenues in 1994 were ¥48 million (including VAT); net profit margins, 17%.[2] But market development had been a rollercoaster. Since 1993, orders were increasingly from southern China (primarily Guangdong Province) and from sectors other than the steel industry that represented the bulk of SHAIC's business in its early years. As a result, the Ministry of Nuclear Energy's role (to which HIW belonged administratively) in opening up markets waned. As new opportunities fell increasingly outside MNE's sphere, Broekers believed its Chinese partner would face increasing difficulty executing its sales and marketing responsibilities. A more aggressive market development approach was needed.

However, deciding where to focus was not easy. Specific problems were: lack of liquidity in the economy due to the central government's tight monetary policy (since August 1993); complex differences in the various industrial ministries to which clients reported (particularly extent of central control and information exchange); and general lack of experience with electromagnetic flowmeters among potential Chinese customers. Broekers had to decide how to access and develop virgin applications, how to secure efficient entry, and how to preempt foreign competitors busy finalizing their own JV arrangements. Broekers also wondered how to maintain motivation among Chinese employees; the enthusiasm and aggressiveness in the JV's initial years would have to be maintained, even increased, to tackle successfully new market opportunities.

୧୦୪୫

Company Background

SHAIC, located in the Minhang ETDZ, southwest of Shanghai, was formed in 1986 after two years of negotiation with the central government in Beijing. Chinese parent HIW (Shanghai) was a centrally-controlled state-owned enterprise (SOE) based in Shanghai, administratively belonging to the Ministry of Nuclear Energy (MNE), one of China's smaller industrial ministries. Krüger was a family-owned German company headquartered in Duisburg, Germany. Established over 70 years earlier, it grew to become an international force in measurement technology; in flowmeters, Krüger was synonymous with quality and reliability. In 1994, worldwide revenues were about DM500 million. In the early 1980s, as China opened its door to foreign direct invest-

---

[1] Company names and some confidential data have been disguised.
[2] ¥ or RMB stands for renminbi, the Chinese currency. In October 1995, the renminbi was semi-convertible at about ¥8.6 = US$1.

ment, Krüger saw enormous opportunities. Although electromagnetic flowmeters were new to China, many overseas clients (e.g., Bayer, BASF, Ciba-Geigy), required flowmeters for Chinese production facilities. To secure broader penetration in the local market and educate potential customers on its advanced technology, Krüger decided to form an equity JV and transfer flowmeter product and production technology to China. Initial contacts with the central government were made in 1984; the JV contract with HIW was formally signed in 1986.

Under the agreement, Krüger contributed technology and a DM11.7 million equity investment for a 40% stake in SHAIC; HIW took the majority 60% stake. Krüger was responsible for production, HIW for marketing and sales. By September 1995, SHAIC operated two production plants in Shanghai's Minhang ETDZ and a sales office in downtown Shanghai. One Minhang facility was equipped with a large flow calibration rig capable of handling a wide range of flowmeters, up to 3 meters in diameter – the only flow calibration system in China (see page 579). In 1995, 122 people were employed at the three sites; Broekers and the production manager were the only expatriate managers. (See Figure 1 for SHAIC's organizational structure.)

Figure 1: SHAIC Organization Chart*

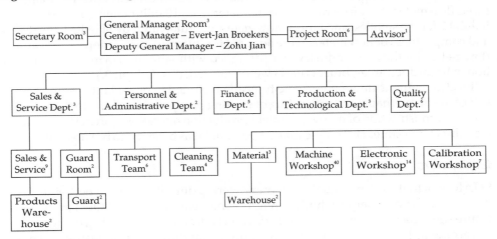

*Number indicates number of personnel.

Administratively, SHAIC (through Chinese partner HIW) belonged to the MNE. Located in Shanghai and working in instrumentation, it also reported to the Shanghai Measurement Instrument Bureau (SMIB) of the Shanghai Municipal Government. These administrative arrangements meant that SHAIC was required to report periodically performance statistics to MNE in Beijing (central government link) and SMIB in Shanghai (municipal government link). The SMIB link was an increasing concern since SMIB recently established JVs (at the local, Shanghai Municipal Government level) with two of Krüger's international competitors.

In addition to JV production, Krüger imported electromagnetic flowmeters and occupied a representative office in Beijing.[3] Although typically more advanced in design than SHAIC-manufactured flowmeters, from time to time SHAIC competed with Krüger on orders originating outside China. In 1994, SHAIC's revenues were ¥48 million; cost of goods sold – 67%; net profit – 17% (down from 20% in 1993), 2% higher than the average of 112 foreign-funded enterprises operating in Minhang at end 1994.[4] Broekers believed that by September 1995, 60% of flowmeters installed in China were SHAIC products; of the remaining 40%, about 8% were Krüger flowmeters. In September 1995, Krüger was negotiating with MNE and HIW to increase its equity stake from 40% to 52% and transfer more advanced technology to SHAIC.

The Market

Products

Electromagnetic (or magnetic inductive) flowmeters measured mass flow in pipes. They were installed and used as process control instruments in a wide range of industrial applications including water cooling systems for the steel industry, drinking water supply, mining, chemical, power and beverage industries. SHAIC manufactured flowmeters for pipes ranging in diameter from 10 millimeters to 3 meters. (See Exhibit 2 for the smallest and largest flowmeters manufactured by SHAIC.) The design and compactness of flowmeters were adapted for different applications. For example, flowmeters for the dairy industry were designed with sanitation in mind; for installation in hazardous areas, other criteria were required. (See Exhibit 3.)

Electromagnetic flowmeters were typically included in new plant design. As a result of major overhauls and upgrading of existing production facilities in many industries, and construction of many greenfield production operations (often involving foreign direct investment), Chinese market potential was believed to be substantial.

Customers

SHAIC's actual and potential customers were primarily state-owned enterprises (SOEs). As the number of wholly foreign-owned enterprises (WFOEs) grew, in the future some customers might fall outside direct administrative control of the Chinese government. In the near term, however, understanding the administrative control mechanisms operating at different government levels, and identifying important actors and gatekeepers, were crucial for successful marketing and selling to China's state-owned sector.

Under the old planned economy system (until the late 1970s), all enterprises belonged administratively to a central government ministry and/or a more local (pro-

---

[3] Under Chinese government regulations, representative offices could not transact business in China (i.e., solicit orders); they did not have business licenses.

[4] As a high-tech company, SHAIC had preferential tax status; income tax rate was 10% versus the normal 33% corporate tax rate.

vincial or municipal) government bureau. The central government link typically involved administrative reporting to, and control by, a central ministry; for the local link, provincial authorities and local representative organizations or administrative bureaus were involved. Since SOEs were essentially manufacturing sites, responsible for both production output and social welfare of all employees, decision-making authority for many important managerial decisions (e.g., distribution) fell outside the SOE and rested (or was shared) with one or more administrative units in the complex governmental control mechanism.

One Chinese government objective for industrial reform (commenced 1984) was clearly to separate ownership from management. By 1995, government decentralization and reorganization (including ministry restructuring) was partially (to varying degrees in different sectors) achieved but the objective was not fully reached. Recently, since many SOEs were in difficulties (two thirds were reportedly making losses in 1995) and the central government was concerned about social stability (the state-owned sector was the largest industrial employer), some signs indicated a policy reversal and tightening of government control. As a result, expatriate managers (and often Chinese colleagues) were at a loss to identify loci of authority in this complex, evolving decision-making nexus.

In 1995, SOEs (and JV partners) continued to report to local, provincial and central government authorities, creating the impression among foreign JV managers that a shadow management structure influenced their operations. For companies such as SHAIC selling to SOEs, it was difficult to identify where, and with whom, decision-making authority rested. Bureaucratic control seemed to be exercised by government officials via vague regulations (often without clear implementation rules or publicly unknown – the so-called "neibu" regulations). Cultivating personal relations with such officials at various levels was critical to understanding the system and potentially important for exercising influence. Broekers and foreign colleagues in other JVs realized that China "was governed by men, not by laws." In this context, design institutes and their engineers were critically important to SHAIC's business.

Design Institutes

Design institutes, typically responsible for technical design of new domestic plants, developed specifications for equipment to be installed. Historically, design institutes were part of state-owned enterprises, but were gradually separated in the industrial reform process. By 1991, most were "engineering bureaus," no longer dependent on, nor directly supervised by, either the industrial ministry or enterprise to which they once belonged. Finding, pretty much overnight, the need to fend for themselves drastically changed the way they operated. Understanding the critical role they played, enterprises and industrial ministries were rebuilding relations with design institutes.

SHAIC understood the critical role of design institutes in its business. If an institute included electromagnetic flowmeters in technical drawings and specified SHAIC as preferred supplier, the likelihood of clinching the order was very high. Since flowmeters were relatively new, and Krüger's advanced technology unfamiliar to Chinese customers, the design institute's recommendations were typically followed in building new production facilities.

SHAIC paid particular attention to design institutes. Understanding the critical importance of "guanxi,"[5] it spent significant time and effort cultivating good relationships both with the institutes, and industrial ministries and enterprises where strong links or influence still existed. SHAIC developed a system whereby it hired as "advisors" key decision makers in design institutes (and other influential units). It negotiated annual contracts with these advisors; if they were useful and helpful, contracts were extended. A fixed advisory fee of 1% to 1.5% commission on clinched orders was provided to advisors working for design institutes.

By contrast, in greenfield operations involving foreign direct investment, Chinese design institutes played an insignificant role. Major multinational firms making plant investments in China typically executed plant designs using in-house engineering bureaus. These bureaus were familiar with flowmeters and flowmeter technology; they typically specified equipment used in plants elsewhere in the world. European multinationals (e.g., Bayer, BASF, Ciba-Geigy) used Krüger technology; American multinationals (e.g., Coca-Cola, Johnson and Johnson) used American technology; Japanese multinationals (e.g., Marubeni, Itochu) used Japanese technology. SHAIC was often quoted by Krüger as a reliable and quality domestic supplier but Krüger Beijing sales representatives preferred to import equipment from outside China for U.S. dollars; this led to conflict between SHAIC and the Beijing office. However, if plant investments were partially financed in renminbi, SHAIC stood a chance to get orders.

Application Industries

SHAIC's industry breakdown of direct orders was (1995): steel (18%), drinking water (19%), sewage (0.4%), chemical (5.5%) and petrochemical (5.0%). Another 30% of SHAIC's orders came from instrument companies functioning either as original equipment manufacturers (OEMs) or distributors. In 1995, average order size was four flowmeters; orders ranged from ¥10,000 to ¥200,000. The average list price for a flowmeter was about ¥20,000. To assist customers in budget proposals, and design institutes with cost estimates, specific list prices were developed for all equipment. Competitors relied on these list prices as reference points for the domestic market. The domestic order cycle was highly seasonal. Typically, no orders came until March; in subsequent months, orders picked up and peaked in July, August or September. From October on, orders fell rapidly to the end of the year.

Steel. The Chinese steel industry was dominated by very large SOEs (e.g., Shougang [aka Capital Iron and Steel], Magang, Baohang); some had ministerial status. Steel, considered a backbone industry, was tightly controlled by the central government. Because of this heritage, a "planned economy" mentality haunted many steel giants in 1993. Because of huge production capacities, these enterprises, historically targeting well-defined geographic areas, expanded geographic market areas in attempts to sell steel output. In these new geographic markets, dominated by smaller, more aggressive

---

[5] Guanxi is the Chinese term for network or relationship.

and flexible competitors controlling strong local guanxi networks, the steel giants did not have the contacts (or guanxi) to develop orders. The central government's economic retrenchment program (primarily designed to slow rapid expansion of SOEs' capital construction projects) shook the market; as steel imports drove prices down, steel giants became short of cash and highly indebted. For example, by 1995, Shougang was SHAIC's largest customer and largest debtor. The central government continued a tight monetary policy to control inflation; funds were not allocated to the steel sector.

The steel giant mentality was demonstrated by Shougang's reaction to SHAIC's 1995 request to settle outstanding debts. By end 1993, accounts receivable from Shougang were ¥ 6.7 million. Orders continued but Shougang did not pay and SHAIC stopped delivering. As the tight monetary policy worsened the triangular debt problem, SHAIC required cash on delivery, then unheard of in the industry. To avoid debt write-off (done in 1995), SHAIC approached Shougang to settle with a steel delivery. However, Shougang's production and sales department could not agree, in part because the requested delivery was small compared to Shougang's typical order size.

Drinking water. As deliveries to the steel sector dropped, drinking water became a new and promising application. Under the administrative control of the Ministry of Water Resources (MWR), local water supply companies were traditionally quite independent and essentially local (regional) monopolies. Recently, as the central government (and MWR) became concerned about drinking water, a re-centralization process to bring the companies under central coordination and control was occurring. Water supply companies now met three times a year to exchange information and discuss development plans (including infrastructure investment). Recognizing opportunities in this sector, SHAIC bought "speaking time" at these meetings and recently engaged two "advisors" from the MWR.

Sewage industry. Opportunities in the sewage industry (also under MWR) were not aggressively pursued until recently because they required a radically different approach. Sewage projects were typically large; they often involved financing through international institutions (e.g., Asian Development Bank, World Bank, Japanese funds) and involved international tendering, a process relatively new both to China and SHAIC. In early 1995, SHAIC received a very large tender order (the largest ever for flowmeters) for a project in Chongqing. Inexplicably and surprisingly, the order was received six months after the official granting date. In a recent Shanghai project, SHAIC was listed as the preferred supplier in the tender document, a highly unusual practice. Developing opportunities in this sector required a lot of personal involvement by Broekers. However, despite his efforts, Broekers was uneasy and unsure about the tendering process in China; who controlled it and who made the key decisions. The Chongqing project required SHAIC to pay 8% commission before the order was firmly placed; Broekers was concerned about how to pursue opportunities in this sector efficiently and effectively.

Chemical and petrochemical industries. These industries offered great opportunities for SHAIC; in 1995, each was responsible for about 5% of orders. The chemical industry, administered by the Ministry of Chemical Industry (MCI), was vast and quite decentralized; some sectors were expanding very rapidly (e.g., dyestuffs for the textile industry). The large number of chemical industry enterprises constituted great potential, but only small inroads had been made, mostly in the many JV projects. Apart from projects involving foreign direct investment and production expertise, SHAIC, its products and technology were unknown.

Increased use of water in oil refining led the petrochemical sector to show interest in flowmeters. In contrast to the chemical industry, the petrochemical industry was highly concentrated in a few large petrochemical sites, mostly majority-owned and controlled by SINOPEC, a ministry-level organization in charge of petroleum production. Broekers believed that orders could be secured if effort was expended.

Paper industry. Potentially new market opportunities were anticipated in this centrally-controlled sector (which used large amounts of water) inasmuch as the ninth five-year plan (1996–2000) highlighted paper as a priority. Several projects, some involving foreign direct investment, were under negotiation. Noting China's dismal paper quality (e.g., the paper of the *China Daily*, the English-language newspaper) and low usage levels (25 kg per head annually versus Germany [195 kg], U.S. [400 kg]), Broekers saw a market with much potential but requiring educational efforts because of lack of knowledge and use of flowmeters.

Food industry. This industry offered significant opportunities. The dairy industry was small but concentrated and China was rapidly becoming the world's largest beer market. Broekers estimated about 860 breweries in China (1995); most were small regional breweries needing substantial upgrading in production equipment and technology. Process control measures (e.g., flowmeters) were needed; SHAIC estimated about 20% of beer was lost in production. Compared to many Chinese industries, the beer industry was extremely competitive; Qingdao was the only national brand, exports were substantial. SHAIC received some small, repetitive orders from breweries, but Broekers felt that JVs, bringing in their own technology, were an increasing factor. As a method of exploring potential, Broekers instigated a policy allowing traveling salespeople to drink beer at SHAIC's expense provided they recorded the name and address of the brewery marked on the bottle. As Chinese consumers developed a liking for Coca-Cola and other western sodas, the soft drink industry was another big and growing market. However, SHAIC saw little immediate potential as U.S. multinationals using U.S. technology dominated the industry.

Sales and Distribution

SHAIC sold flowmeters through various channels. Instrumentation companies functioning both as wholesalers and OEMs, were typically involved in large projects. In 1995, 30% to 40% of orders came from these companies whose trained engineers knew flowmeter technology. SHAIC considered selling to them rather easy. Instrumentation companies claimed a 4% to 6% discount off SHAIC's price in the form of a credit note.

SHAIC was also developing a direct sales channel. Broekers had increasingly emphasized use of a direct sales force to keep "the channel as short as possible." In 1995, six sales engineers and three service engineers had direct contact with customers. Working out of the Shanghai sales office, salary and commission placed them above the level of other JVs. This was a SHAIC concern because of high turnover rates for personnel employed by foreign-invested enterprises. The sales and service engineers enjoyed traveling and developing new contacts across China. Often, salespeople followed up leads established by the general manager; Broekers complained that salespeople were hesitant to make "cold calls"; he used expatriate contacts to open up new accounts, particularly with JVs. Service people primarily provided installation help and support.

Sales engineers were supported by locally-based representatives. In 1995, SHAIC employed seven regional representatives; SHAIC was actively developing export opportunities and had two foreign representatives (South Korea, Hong Kong). Initially, Broekers was reluctant to use representatives as the Chinese side was responsible for sales and marketing; it believed its guanxi network within MNE was more than adequate to clinch orders. However, since MNE was a small industrial ministry, its network was quite limited; furthermore, SHAIC increasingly realized that MNE could not keep up with its various opportunities. As SHAIC operated in broader geographic markets, its Shanghainese sales engineers (with their dialect and customs) had increasing difficulty cultivating contacts in remote, regional markets. SHAIC supplemented its direct sales force with representatives; they signed one-year contracts and received 6% commission. The JV provided technical support and conducted all invoicing. Representatives had product but not territory exclusivity. In selecting new representatives, careful attention was paid to product expertise, financial soundness and market access.

As a result of the split in responsibilities determined in JV negotiations, HIW also functioned as a selling organization. As an established instrument manufacturing firm, HIW had good contacts upon which Krüger was determined to capitalize. HIW received 12% commission for orders generated. However, some of SHAIC's sales engineers and representatives complained that HIW was undercutting their efforts by selling at 6% below SHAIC's list prices.

A final sales channel was the Shanghai Measurement Instrumentation Corp. (SMIC), part of the Shanghai Measurement Instrumentation Bureau (SMIB). SMIC's sales and distribution network sold a broad range of instruments to industrial clients all over China. SHAIC viewed SMIC's network as a quick, efficient way to gain national presence; SMIC received 8% commission on SHAIC flowmeter sales.

Developments in 1995

Despite many opportunities, Broekers was concerned about several developments. The continued tight monetary policy created a degree of industry havoc; lack of liquidity in the economy and triangular debt problems were becoming serious. To maintain cash flow, Broekers, against the objections of sales engineers, required cash on delivery (1993). More recently, he required pre-payments with orders; in 1995 these were 30% to

50% of the order. Such policies, new to China, took the wind out of domestic sales, particularly to existing customers. In September 1995, SHAIC's warehouse was almost filled with finished orders waiting to be paid for and shipped.

To maintain revenues, new opportunities were pursued aggressively; the geographic mix of orders shifted.

	1993	1995
Beijing	20%	8%
Guangdong	0%	16%
Shanghai (including exports)	25%	25%

Furthermore, large projects in areas such as sewage were increasingly being specified outside China. Thus, Broekers spent increasing effort on sales development. (The deputy GM was responsible for domestic sales and market development.) Specifically, projects involving tendering required his increasing involvement and attention.

Although Krüger stood for quality and reliability, Broekers felt SHAIC was at a disadvantage relative to Krüger and other international competitors for orders originating outside China. Chinese enterprises typically preferred to import equipment despite difficulties in securing foreign exchange.[6] Although the excuse was quality assurance, Broekers believed the reason was pocketing commissions. JVs found it difficult to hide cash payments in the books or inflate invoices, practices importers resorted to more easily. He recalled a recent instance at a neighboring U.S. JV: a US$1 million equipment order, increased by a ¥1 million "fee," was only discovered at a board meeting when the assistant GM became suspicious about the invoice amount given the nature of the delivered equipment.

With competitors actively negotiating JVs, Broekers was concerned about future domestic competition. Broekers was especially concerned with the two international competitors engaged with SMIB, SMIC's local parent and the local government link to which SHAIC periodically had to report financial performance results. These links worried Krüger since it was considering transferring more technology to SHAIC. Internally, Broekers worried that Chinese employees were becoming relaxed about the JV's performance and were showing signs of losing eagerness and motivation when new opportunities required even more aggressive actions.

---

[6] All imports and exports had to be conducted through Chinese import/export companies. SOEs were typically not allowed foreign exchange and had to apply to the government for allocations.

Exhibit 1: Shanghai's Minhang ETDZ

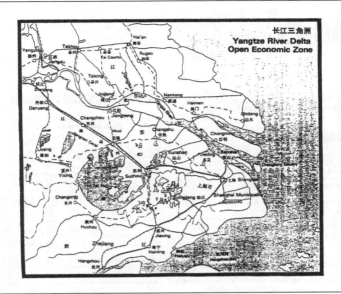

Exhibit 2: Electromagnetic Flowmeters

The largest and smallest flowmeters produced at SHAIC.

K 300-Ex

Meter size DN 10 to 300. Compact flowmeter for use in hazardous areas. **The electronics are enclosed in an exchangeable housing. Functional and technical data, see K 300.**

Safety data

Approval in accordance with European Standard	EEx eq [ib] IIC T3 to T6 (PTB No. Ex-81/2069)
Ambient temperatures	≦ 40° (VDE 0165/6.80, Section 5.2.4)
Type of enclosure	IP 65
Electrode circuit	In protection category:
	Intrinsic Safety "ib" (internal connection only)
Mains circuit, output circuits	In protection category: Increased Safety "e"
Coil circuit	In protection category: Increased Safety "e" (internal connection only)

Dimensions and weights

Meter size DN mm	Dimensions mm							Weight
	a	b	c	d	e	f	j	kg
10, 15, 20	200	342	–	66	92	–	70	22
25, 32	200	364	–	77	96	–	94	23
40	200	408	264	99	184	785	94	32
50	200	408	264	99	184	775	94	32
65	200	428	264	109	184	765	94	32
80	200	428	264	109	184	745	94	36
100	250	488	314	139	234	830	125	44
125	250	488	314	139	234	805	125	60
150	300	508	346	149	266	835	172	60
200	350	568	434	179	354	965	210	73
250	400	628	514	209	434	1070	244	93
300	500	704	570	247	490	1305	280	130

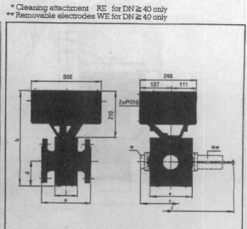

* Cleaning attachment RE for DN ≥ 40 only
** Removable electrodes WE for DN ≥ 40 only

Case 38

Shanghai Zheng Zhang Textiles Factory

Ho Yuen Ching, Michelle
The Hong Kong University of Science and Technology

Noel Capon
Graduate School of Business, Columbia University

Late one afternoon in July 1995, Mr. Li Yi Ming, director of the Shanghai Zheng Zhang Textiles Factory met with his management staff, Mr. Xia Yu, executive director and Mr. Sun Bo Liang, supervisor of the Local Marketing Team. At week's end, they had to report the firm's recent performance in the local market to the Board of Supervisors (BOS). Although Zheng Zhang had experienced considerable success as a textile exporter, the previous six months marked its first venture into the domestic Chinese patchwork quilt market. Li knew the BOS was concerned whether this directional shift was justified. The meeting would determine if Zheng Zhang would attempt to develop a viable long-term marketing plan for the domestic market or whether the venture would be scrapped in favor of increased export efforts.

৪৩৫৪

Company Background

In the early 1980s, Shanghai Zheng Zhang Textiles Factory (ZZ) was formed by a neighborhood committee as a county collective enterprise to export textile goods.[1] (See Exhibit 1 for information on Shanghai.) When factory supervisor Mr. Li Yi Ming assumed the manager role in 1986, ZZ had debts of RMB400,000 (US$47,000) and empty order books. Li took out a small bank loan, bought a few new sewing machines and

---

[1] County collective enterprises belonged to the "non-state" sector; they were owned by the local or municipal government. Under collectivization, people in villages and counties were organized into groups (collectives) responsible for assigned production targets. In the post-Mao environment, they still remained an important form of business in China.

stitched together sample tablecloths that he "hawked" around Shanghai's export companies. Soon he started to win contracts for tablecloths, quilts and other patchwork products from the U.S. Consistent good quality and credibility in meeting deadlines won ZZ an outstanding reputation among overseas merchandisers. Within eight years, Li's leadership turned the company from "hopeless" factory to a little "kingdom" of five subsidiaries and eight plants. Steadily growing export business was established in the U.S., Canada, Europe, Southeast Asia, Hong Kong and Macao. Li's contributions to the domestic economy led to his receiving both the Shanghai "model worker" prize and the all-China "May First"[2] labor medal from Beijing.

Congruent with China's privatization reforms, in 1994, ZZ was reorganized into a joint-stock company; ownership was vested in its 500 employees, the neighborhood committee's stake dropped to 10%. Employees were provided free shares based on length of service and seniority; additional shares could also be purchased.

By end 1994, ZZ was China's largest manufacturer of hand-made patchwork products. For several successive years, ZZ was a member of China's top 500 industrial enterprises, providing optimum economic benefit to China by generating substantial export revenues; it was also one of the top 500 industrial enterprises in the Shanghai area. In 1994, annual sales were RMB112 million (US$14 million) (Exhibits 2, 3); Li expected sales to double in 1995. ZZ had secured government approval for listing on the Shanghai Securities Exchange in early 1996.

Company Organization

Li said that ZZ's corporate strategy was: "One business to lead the way and allow other supporting businesses to prosper under its umbrella." Over the years, ZZ's business expanded from the original patchwork quilts focus to such related activities as manufacturing lace and bed skirtings, packaging for quilts (i.e., large transparent plastic bags) and joint ventures on developing textile factories. ZZ thus diversified its risk by broadening product range and reducing reliance on outside suppliers.

ZZ was a group company comprising five constituents (Figure 1); the mother company earned the majority of revenues by producing hand-made patchwork products. Wholly owned subsidiary Zheng Dong operated a computerized lace-making and embroidery plant; Zheng Zhu (also 100% owned) was a trading company providing supporting export services. A 51%-owned joint venture with Taiwanese partner Zheng Li focused on factory development for other bedroom products for export. Curtain maker, Xin Hua, was a 60%-owned joint-venture subsidiary with a local partner.

ZZ's eight production plants (including subsidiaries) were scattered around Pudong, Shanghai's industrial development zone; three plants operated by the mother company focused on quilt production. ZZ also maintained close working relationships with over 40 manufacturing enterprises in Jiangsu, Zhejiang, Anhui and Shandong provinces. ZZ held shares (15% to 30% ownership) in six small textile

---

[2] Each year China celebrated Labor Day on May 1.

product workshops for extra production capacity. Relationships with other firms were mainly contractual for special orders and technical support.

Figure 1: Shanghai Zheng Zhang Textiles Factory Organization Chart

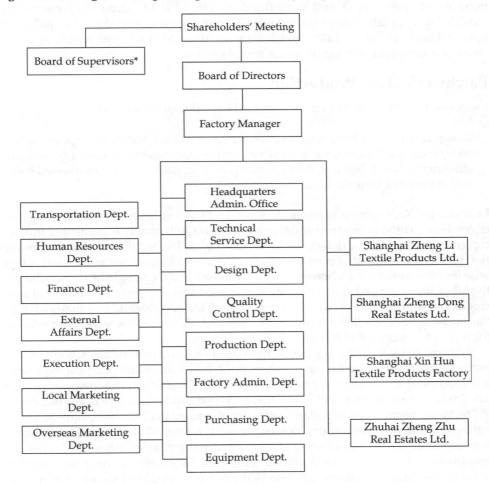

For control purposes, each ZZ plant was considered a separate cost center. ZZ maintained two sales teams; each was evaluated as a profit center, responsible for both revenue generation and costs. Li believed this approach reduced conflict between sales and production personnel and deterred sales teams from accepting urgent orders that might be expensive to fill.

Products and Production Processes

ZZ's initial business was as an upper-end manufacturer and exporter of high quality patchwork quilts, napkins, tablecloths, cushions, bed skirtings, curtains and lace.

Characterized by an artistic flavor and labor intensive production processes, ZZ's products commanded premium prices in overseas markets.

ZZ's bread and butter products were patchwork quilts made by stitching together many small pieces of cloth. The combination of different colors, shapes and combinations of cloth pieces produced many floral and other kaleidoscope-like patterns. The outside layers of fabric were stuffed with high-quality cotton making the quilts soft, light and heat-retaining. Quilts, which were usually sold in sets with matching pillow cases, accounted for 85% to 90% of ZZ's total revenues.

Patchwork Quilt Production

Executive Director, Mr. Xia Yu, emphasized the value of ZZ's quilts:

> Zheng Zhang's patchwork quilts are not merely artistic, something appreciated as an art piece. Each quilt is unique in that complicated patterns require a good deal of stitching by hand. Besides, they are also practical, good for air-conditioned rooms and at the same time durable.

Li attributed ZZ's success to its emphasis of, and strict adherence to, three basic principles: best quality, high speed and top new design. Quilt quality was ensured through rigorous quality control; defect checking points were located throughout the production process ensuring that problems were caught and corrections made early; otherwise if errors were found when the product was finished they might be irreversible and the labor input wasted. Currently, defective products were sent for rework at prior stages; non-remarkable products were scrapped. Defect rates and raw material usage variances were controlled at under 0.5%; any and all exceptions were reported daily for timely evaluation and action.

ZZ boasted high ability in meeting tight deadlines and production schedules. Factory managers, promoted from the shop floor, had substantial practical experience with technical aspects of the production process. Production processes were separated into skilled and non-skilled elements. When production schedules were tight, ZZ factories might employ freelance workers, abundant in China, who came to Shanghai from throughout the country looking for work, for non-skilled tasks. This flexibility was especially important in view of China's recently enacted labor law to ease unemployment: from May 1, 1995, workers could only work eight hours a day, five days a week. Overtime was allowed, but had to be compensated at triple the regular wage. Currently, ZZ employed roughly 700 full-time skilled workers, each trained intensively for one to two months.

ZZ recruited designers only from China's most prestigious design colleges. Designers were placed in close contact with buyers so as to understand their special needs and interests. New quilt designs were developed at a rate of about six per month. Draft designs were sent to the production department; typically one day was required to "test-make" a new product by sticking pieces of cloth together to evaluate design effects. This procedure also enabled management to estimate material requirements, the technical skill necessary to make the quilt and production time. If the new design was satisfactory on these criteria, management granted approval, detailed technical specifications were issued and workers were trained and assigned to production. The period from new design approval to full-scale production was typically about two weeks; however, for some complicated designs, 40 to 50 days were required. ZZ maintained a wide-ranging portfolio of over 300 quilt designs.

The Overseas Market

ZZ exported products under 15 different labels, six ZZ labels and nine buyer-supplied (private) labels. For patchwork quilts, ZZ used its own labels. Sales of quilts and tablecloths to a few wholesalers in the U.S. and Canada represented most own label sales. ZZ manufactured garments and other textile products for special orders to exclusive buyer-supplied designs (e.g., large U.S. department store chains such as JC Penney and Wal-Mart). For products other than quilts and tablecloths, private labels were 85% of sales.

In 1993, favorable trade arrangements for finished consumer textile products into the European Economic Community (EEC) led ZZ to place efforts in the European market. ZZ management also believed that cold weather, especially in northern Europe, might prove an attractive market for a wide variety of ZZ's quilts. In 1994, about 86% (1993, more than 90%) of all exports were to North America (U.S., Canada), 7% to France and Britain, the remainder to Southeast Asia.

Despite this recent geographic diversification, ZZ executives believed an exclusive focus on exports involved considerable risk. Sino-U.S. relationships were worsening and results of negotiations on textile products were uncertain. Furthermore, erection of trade barriers by the EEC could not be ruled out.

The Local Market

ZZ executives were proud of its status as China's largest patchwork quilt producer, notwithstanding more or less exclusive focus on export markets. Exporting was attractive for it led to large batch purchases by overseas buyers leading to economies of scale in production, transportation and administration; in addition, payments were timely, easing working capital concerns. Since consumer purchasing power in overseas markets was generally higher than in China, ZZ could charge highly satisfactory wholesale prices ranging from RMB260 (US$33) to RMB400 (US$50) for an average patchwork quilt.

Despite this export focus, ZZ management had not totally overlooked local market developments. In recent years, annual income in several large cities reached RMB24,000 (US$3,000) to RMB32,000 (US$4,000); living standards were rapidly improving. In the more prosperous cities (e.g., Shanghai, Guangzhou), retail outlets offering prestigious brand products from around the world crowded the streets. Shanghainese, in particular, were the most fashion- and brand-conscious of Chinese citizens; they were willing and able to pay premium prices for high quality products. ZZ knew several competitors that imitated ZZ products in the past had started tapping the local market. If ZZ delayed too long, or did not invest sufficiently, one of these competitors might secure a dominant position.

In November 1994, senior management decided ZZ should attempt to develop the domestic China market; Shanghai was selected the test site and quilts as the test product. A new local marketing team would operate parallel to the well-established export marketing team. Said Li about local market strategy:

> Zheng Zhang's strategy in China is to sustain its reputation for exceptional high quality. To succeed locally, we are going to position ourselves as a premium producer. Product quality for local sales should be even higher than exports. The Chinese don't need ordinary products; they have lots. They are actively seeking better products to improve living standards.

Li talked about the opportunity of building the Zheng Zhang brand in China:

> Currently in China, there are three ways to build a brand. First, a joint venture may be established with an overseas brand. Second, a brand may be "bought" from an overseas company and used on locally-produced products; in reality this is franchising. In both these cases, the Chinese company uses brand names established by others. Zheng Zhang has elected a third strategy, to build its own brand name. This method takes time, but it's the way to go.
>
> Chinese consumers are clever. They used to believe in foreign brands, blindly. They are now more and more aware that most of these products are actually manufactured locally. They are starting to recognize that local brand quality can be as good as foreign brands. I think the first two approaches are not good long-term strategies.

Li also maintained that foreign brand users were concerned with immediate profits, but ZZ had a longer term interest in establishing relationships with local retailers. Much patience and deep pockets were required, including continuous improvement of production capabilities through facilities investment.

However, notwithstanding this long-run view, Li said the road to building local brands was fraught with difficulties. In part, the current Chinese legislative system was to blame. First, copycats were a problem, in particular the stealing of product designs by competing enterprises. Although the legal system embraced patent protection, experience in enforcement was lacking and piracy was rampant. Relatedly, competitors employing fake labels were also a problem. In addition, Li said many local manufacturers were too inclined towards immediate profits, overlooked the importance of continual adherence to strict quality control, and did not possess a long-term vision. As a result, one or two bad sheep might spoil the confidence of consumers in local brands altogether.

The Local Marketing Team

Xia Yu discussed ZZ's approach to the local quilt market:

> We apply experience from overseas sales in production, quality control and other daily functional operations. The difference is to consider our local marketing team

as the wholesalers; we are used to overseas buyers playing these roles. They are now inside ZZ. On the one hand they are buying from our production department; on the other they are selling to local consumers and retailers. They are interfacing both parties, making them essentially a separate business.

The 18-strong local marketing team was headed by former plant manager, supervisor Mr. Sun Bo Liang, reporting directly to Li. Two staff types reported to Sun: 12 "salesladies" sold direct to consumers at special ZZ counters in contracted department stores; six staff were responsible for dealing with retailers. Sun formulated local marketing plans according to Li's directions; similar to its export strategy, in China, ZZ also focused on the upper-end market. Li explained:

> To start building a brand, we will target high-end consumers first. It is much easier to establish a brand with a high-end target group, then penetrate the middle class, rather than the other way round. As a result, we shall sell the same products to local consumers as to overseas buyers.

Quality was ZZ's highest priority criterion in local marketing decisions. In Shanghai, locally-manufactured products (for local and export sales) had to pass quality inspection by the Technical Supervision Bureau, a branch of the Central Government's Business and Commerce Department. Products for local sale were also subject to scrutiny by the Shanghai Consumers Society, a social organization sponsored by the provincial government to protect consumer rights. Quality problems would gain unwanted publicity, widely and rapidly, through newspapers and other mass media. Because of these dangers, ZZ management continually told its workers that "the reputation of the factory is your fate," and that product quality was paramount to establishing a good reputation.

To build its reputation for quality, ZZ provided a complete satisfaction guarantee. It emphasized a "complete sales service," embracing both before-sales and after-sales service, in addition to offering high quality products (the same designs as sold in export markets) through its strict quality control standards. Before a sale was made, ZZ salesladies patiently introduced the buyer to the characteristics and care instructions for ZZ quilts; they also answered queries and provided suggestions for home decoration. If, after purchase, a customer discovered a defect, the quilt could be returned; the customer received a replacement quilt or a refund. If a customer purchased a quilt but later decided the colors or style did not match furniture and/or other decorations in the home, s/he could exchange the quilt for another. This practice was very different from many other local manufacturers that operated under a "buyer beware" philosophy and did not accept returns.

Consumer and Retail Markets in Shanghai

With a 13.2 million population, Shanghai was China's largest city; about half lived downtown, half were scattered in the suburbs. With its famous Huangpu River harbor and strategic geographic location, Shanghai was the heart of China's commercial and industrial activities for decades.

"Shanghainese" stood out from other Chinese; annual income levels were much higher (US$3,000 per capita versus US$400 [national average]), citizens were more receptive to western trends, were highly fashion- and brand-conscious and spent more on entertainment and betterment of living standards. One Shanghai retailer noted: "Once a batch of garments manufactured in Shanghai was exported to Hong Kong and then re-imported to Shanghai, just to earn a foreign label. Compared to similar garments without the label, they sell for triple their prices!" (See Table 1A for comparative statistics on China's two major cities, Shanghai and Beijing [the country's cultural center]; see Table 1B for data on other Chinese cities.)

Table 1A: Beijing and Shanghai, Comparative Data

	Shanghai	Beijing
No. of households	4,443,800	3,603,000
Population	12,988,100	11,643,000
Non-agricultural population	9,104,900	6,838,000
Household composition	Household size mainly 3–4 persons with 1.82 income earners	40% of households consist of 3 persons with 1.41 income earners
Per capita living area	7.5 sq. m.	8.3 sq. m.
No. of air-conditioners	20 per 100 households	5 per 100 households
Area	6,340.5 sq. m.	16,807.8 sq. m.
Temperature	$-2.1°C$ to $37.9°C$	$-11.5°C$ to $37.2°C$
Average worker's wages	RMB7,401	RMB6,540
Per capita income	RMB5,566	RMB4,731
Retail sales	77.07 billion	66.7 billion
No. of retail stores	145,000	???

Table 1B: Per Capita Annual Disposable Income Data (RMB)*

City/province	Income	City/province	Income	City/province	Income
Beijing	100	Zhejiang	116	Hainan	95
Tianjin	99	Anhui	80	Sichuan	89
Hebei	83	Fujian	101	Guizhou	84
Shanxi	74	Jiangxi	68	Yunnan	92
Neimenygu	66	Shandong	88	Xizang	114
Liaoning	86	Henan	71	Shaanxi	76
Jilin	73	Hubei	83	Gansu	76
Heilongiang	72	Hunan	93	Qinghai	80
Shanghai	134	Guangdong	154	Ningxia	81
Jiangsu	95	Guanxi	93	Xinjiang	87

*For selected Chinese cities and provinces indexed on Beijing = 100.

Shanghai retailers were China's largest and most profitable. Garment companies from Hong Kong and many other countries sold products in Shanghai; some had opened retail outlets. Among the more well known were: Benetton, Giordano, Episode and LaCoste. Large department stores (e.g., Dongfang, Liubai, Shanghai First Department Store) were Sino-foreign joint ventures. In 1994, Shanghai had 145,000 retail outlets; total retail sales were RMB77 billion, 11% of consumer income.

Market Segmentation

ZZ segmented the domestic market by occasion of use; it identified four basic segments:

- The "Yuppies." This segment comprised younger, better educated and higher income people. Aged 30 to 40 years, they were both concerned about living standards and able to appreciate the artistic value of ZZ's products. The critical buying occasion was typically a major renovation of their apartments. To ensure that bedding was well matched with the new decoration, they considered a complete renewal of bedroom fabrics.
- People moving to new houses. Improving living standards led to a general trend for urban Chinese to move from smaller to larger apartments (hopefully with stable electricity supply and air-conditioning). When moving to new houses, they usually discarded old furniture and accouterments and purchased replacements. As Xia Yu observed:

In the past, many Chinese were squeezed into a small room with folding beds. Things are different now. The government has been rapidly building better public housing for lower income people; for the better off, more and more are buying their own flats. The increasing popularity of air-conditioning in residential flats makes quilts indispensable throughout the year and opens up a market for Zheng Zhang's products.

An average household in Shanghai comprised five or six persons, on average two bedrooms; air-conditioner density was 20 per 100 households (see Table 2 for data on living conditions).

- Wedding purchases or gifts. Traditionally, after marriage, Chinese couples used bright red bedding and pillow sets for a few weeks to bring good luck (e.g., getting pregnant, having lovely babies, good husband/wife relationship). However, with newer thinking and western influence, more and more young Chinese were attracted to fashionable furnishings that could be used longer and whose style matched the decoration and furnishings in their apartments. According to feedback from local customers, young Chinese couples appreciated ZZ's elegant yet practical patchwork quilts as wedding purchases or gifts.[3]

---

[3] In 1994, marriages in Shanghai averaged 7,465 monthly.

- People buying gifts for overseas relatives and friends, ethnic Chinese and others.[4] The Chinese considered such gifts as quilts and bedding as meaningful signs of personal concern. Purchases by this segment were expected to be more seasonal than the other segments; for example, the Chinese usually sent gifts to relatives before the Lunar New Year (late January to early February), the most important festival, when propensity to purchase was highest. The period immediately after Chinese New Year was "low" season since many Chinese spent excess disposable income in preparation for, and during, the festival.

Table 2: Living Conditions in Shanghai*

Per capita living area (sq. m.)	Percent	No. of rooms in apartment	Percent
less than 4	9.4	1	43.8
4 to 6	31.2	2	48.8
6 to 8	25.4	3	6.9
8 to 10	15.8	4 or more	0.5
10 to 12	6.4		
12 to 14	5.2		
more than 14	6.6		

*Per capita annual expenditures on room furnishings and furniture were RMB18.88 (US$2.36).

A final segment targeted by ZZ was tourists; in 1994, Shanghai welcomed 1,321,800 persons. Tourists might purchase for own use or as gifts for overseas friends. Traditionally, Chinese labor-intensive handicrafts were considered inexpensive but nice presents and welcomed by tourists; however, quilts might be bulky to carry. ZZ estimated that 10% of tourists might be in the potential market.

Competition

ZZ was the first Chinese organization to make patchwork quilts in a factory. Hitherto, quilt manufacturing was a cottage industry; many Chinese made patchwork quilts by hand in their homes, often from scrap materials. Following ZZ's success, many local textile factories imitated its products. Sun estimated that in Shanghai alone eight to ten local manufacturers produced and sold similar products, generally low to medium quality (Exhibit 4). Some firms attempted to secure cost advantage by shifting production from Shanghai to Jiangsu where labor costs were significantly lower. However, they suffered problems of lower skilled labor and excessive design stealing in these less developed areas.[5]

In addition to these domestic Shanghai-based quilt manufacturers, ZZ was concerned about the threat from a Sino-Hong Kong joint venture, Jiali Textiles. This

---

[4] Estimates of ethnic Chinese living overseas were 57 million.
[5] ZZ had relationships with small manufacturers in Jiangsu, limited to occasional special orders and technical research and development.

organization mainly produced patchwork quilts in the medium-quality category, yet was increasingly targeting high-end customers.

A particular concern of ZZ's domestic marketing team was that consumers purchasing patchwork quilts might be insufficiently careful (or concerned) in the buying process to distinguish ZZ's quality from competitors'. Although no government statistics were available for patchwork quilts, ZZ executives estimated it achieved 11% to 12% market share in targeted market segments in Shanghai.

ZZ's Quilt Strategy in China

Pricing

The Chinese government no longer maintained price controls on consumer goods; it would not intervene so long as the Prices Supervision Authority considered prices reasonable for the quality level. However, ZZ management found the price-setting process difficult as it had not previously sold products in the local market, nor to ultimate customers. ZZ was not certain whether local consumers should be charged the same final price as ultimate customers in foreign countries by ZZ's overseas buyers. It knew that the purchasing power of local and overseas consumers differed considerably; management knew it should also be concerned with competitors' prices.

When it first offered goods for sale in Shanghai, ZZ decided that the local and export market consumer price differential should be maintained at a relatively low level to avoid potential gray market problems. Management also believed high local prices would assist high-end brand-building efforts. Considering these factors, ZZ set prices 18% lower than overseas consumer prices for the same goods; in general, ZZ quilts were around 20% more expensive than competitor products at retail price. Sun remarked:

> Of course we have to adjust for the affordability of local people and the local market situation. We look at people's disposable income and competitors' prices. At this initial stage of our local market entry we are really testing our hand at pricing. Given our ambition to establish Zheng Zhang as a premium brand, we should start off charging premium prices, yet we do not have any data on price elasticities for these products. Our only guideline is that we do not have to undercut our competitors in terms of prices; they are for reference only.

Distribution

ZZ did not have its own local retail outlets, in part because of high rents charged for prime retail space; management also believed establishment of outlets would be premature. It believed brand-building efforts were better pursued through association with high-end retailers with good reputations. In July 1995, ZZ's local sales network comprised ten sales "spots" in Shanghai: six special sales counters rented at major department stores and four stores operating on a consignment basis (Table 3).

Table 3: Zheng Zhang Patchwork Quilt Sales History in Top Ten Retail Sales Spots in Shanghai

Spot	Type*	1994		1995					
		Nov	Dec	Jan	Feb	Mar	Apr	May	Jun
1	c	54	49	60	66	82	107	135	150
2	c	59	71	55	89	101	119	141	162
3	c			50	44	47	75	57	34
4	c				77	93	101	139	121
5	c				67	79	98	85	87
6	s						215	224	235
7	c						216	240	211
8	s						198	146	201
9	s								188
10	s								97
		113	120	165	343	402	1,129	1,167	1,486
Sales revenue (RMB '000)						320			1,118

*s = special sales counters, c = consignment sales.

Legend:
1. Knittings Center
2. Yu Yuan Shopping Mall
3. North Wing Shopping Mall
4. Hua Qiao Company
5. Tung Yi Company
6. Xin Wai Tan Shopping Mall
7. Shanghai First Department Store
8. Friendship Shop (Hong Qiao Development Area)
9. Friendship Shop (Wi Tan)
10. Golden Shopping Mall

The special sales counters in department stores averaged about 120 to 200 sq. ft.; each was the responsibility of a ZZ saleslady supervised by the local marketing team. Each counter might stock about 70 to 80 quilt sets; one or two beds were usually set up to display quilts and pillow sets. Rents, negotiated separately with each store, typically on annual contract, ranged from RMB8,500 to RMB28,000 per month, averaging slightly over RMB100 per sq. ft.

In selecting retailers, reputation and location were dominant criteria. Once ZZ management selected a particular retailer as a prospective outlet, a sales representative from the local marketing team approached the department store manager with ZZ's promotional leaflets (Exhibit 5), brochures and product samples. Thoroughly trained in ZZ product offerings and distribution strategies, he explained the sales counter proposal. Retail store management was invited to visit ZZ's headquarters showroom. Comprising 1,500 sq. ft., the showroom was partitioned into 12 bedrooms where ZZ products were displayed with accompanying furniture and other decorations. According to Mr. Xia, only two other local manufacturers maintained such exhibition rooms in Shanghai.

Retailers for consignment sales were approached in a similar manner but fewer details had to be negotiated. Consignment sale contracts usually allowed for a 30% to 35% retail margin mark-up over factory prices, similar to competing products. Currently payment terms were net 30 days after the product was sold at retail. ZZ's experience with large high-end retailers was very good and payments were prompt;

however, it believed that as distribution expanded to smaller retailers, greater flexibility in payment terms would be required. At its own sales counters in department stores, where ZZ received all retail revenues, ZZ was assured of negotiated shelf space and could control the arrangement of displays and conditions under which its quilts were sold. However, when sales were by consignment, ZZ invariably found its products placed adjacent to competing products sold at lower prices.

ZZ's reputation won it contracts with popular and prestigious retail shops in Shanghai. Currently, several new contracts were under negotiation and retail chains such as Watson's (a renowned retail chain store in Hong Kong) had approached ZZ to carry its products. ZZ management anticipated that by end 1995, over 20 retail spots in Shanghai would carry its products.

ZZ management believed personal relationships between its personnel and retail distributors, a typical requirement for doing business in China, were critical. As a result, sales representatives both paid frequent visits to the shop floor and met with retail management to discuss inventory turnover and sales performance. Because several manufacturers competed for shelf space, department stores had significant bargaining power in selecting consignment products and/or manufacturers to whom shop space would be rented, as well as negotiating payment terms.

Promotion

ZZ seldom advertised in local media. Occasionally, it responded to solicitations from local government-owned media and advertising companies by placing small ads in newspapers (cost per week, RMB50,000 [US$6,250] to RMB100,000 [US$12,500]) or renting light boxes (special billboards) (RMB1,700 per month) and regular billboards (costs varied). Such advertising was considered "helping" other government enterprises and economic benefits were not evaluated. Although management believed current local sales did not justify a regular advertising budget, ZZ was ready "to open its wallet ... if sufficient evidence appears that benefits will exceed costs." In general, management decided to rely on word-of-mouth to spread ZZ's name. Although this approach was inexpensive, it took time and management was considering whether other economical promotion methods were available to speed sales.

Sun was also considering how to attract new retailers. Currently, personal selling by ZZ sales representatives was the only method used. Since the local marketing team was small and had an extremely heavy workload (e.g., new retailer solicitation, new orders, order placements, liaison with production), he was considering the possibility of direct mail for solicitation.

Sales Force Management

Both the marketing staff and shop floor salesladies were trained by an experienced local marketing team. Most team members were selected from production because of outstanding performance and product experience. Several others recruited outside had marketing experience with local retailers.

Salesladies selling at ZZ's special department store counters worked alternate days because of long working hours and industry practice for all retail salespersons in

Shanghai. As a result, two salesladies were responsible for each site. Women were appointed to these retail positions because ZZ management considered them more patient, more used to talking to the decision makers (typically female) and in general more familiar with soft furnishings. Owing to wide variations in traffic among stores, exclusive commission-based incentive schemes were considered unfair; ZZ salesladies were each paid salaries of roughly RMB11,000 annually.

To pave the way for smooth negotiations with potential retailers and help manage its employees, ZZ management articulated detailed guidelines and incentive schemes for shop floor salespersons. Both rewards and penalties were used to encourage positive behaviors while simultaneously discouraging negative behaviors. Details of these schemes and guidelines were contained in a five-page booklet distributed to each staff member. (See Figure 2 for major provisions.)

Marketing staff selling to retailers were evaluated on total quantity of sales orders per month; they were paid basic salaries based on sales performance versus quota. However, sales quotas acted as guidelines rather than strict goals. Management believed that strict adherence to a sales-volume incentive system was an unfair performance indicator, given the limited number of outlets and wide variation of sales volume among stores. Special bonuses were paid for successful establishment of new sales spots.

Figure 2: Shanghai Zheng Zhang Textiles Factory Salesperson Handbook

Chapter 4: Rewards and Penalties

Section 1: Rewards

Salespersons achieving the following will be awarded incentives of RMB50 to RMB500:

- Significant achievement in attaining sales targets, improving revenues or service qualities.
- Significant achievement in improving company operations, raising local sales operating standards or raising economic benefits of the enterprise or the society.
- Protecting products from substantial loss under unusual circumstances.
- Outstanding performance in being responsible and honest.

Section 2: Penalties

- During performance of duties, salespersons who do not stand up in servicing customers or do not wear namecards will be penalized RMB10 for each observed occurrence.
- Each offense of the "10 Don'ts on counter" will be penalized RMB10.
- Impolite or insulting words to customers will result in being fired.
- Salespersons guilty of embezzlement or theft will be fired and have to pay a penalty of five to ten times the product price.
- Leaves must be approved by the supervisor in advance, or the monthly bonus will be canceled.

Performance Review

Li examined the local marketing team's performance report. During the first five months' operations (November 1994 to March 1995) when the number of sales spots reached five, sales were 1,143 quilts, RMB320,000 (US$38,000). In April to June 1995, the number of sales spots expanded to ten; total sales were 3,782 quilts, RMB1,180,000

(US$141,000). Projected 1995 sales were RMB4 million (US$500,000). Four more sales spots would open shortly and business was growing at an accelerating rate. However, sales performance was still far below his goal of RMB2 million (US$250,000) sales per month, RMB20 million (US$2,500,000) annually.

Next Steps

Li considered his report to the Board of Supervisors. Was current performance significantly encouraging to continue efforts in the local market? If the decision was made to continue, it seemed two major issues had to be addressed. First, was the current distribution strategy the most effective means to reach the target market segments or were other channels available? Second, instead of passively relying on word-of-mouth, should ZZ use other methods to build ZZ's brand name and promote its products? If so, how large a promotion budget should be authorized and how should it be allocated? Finally, was ZZ's overall marketing strategy the most appropriate in view of intensifying competition?

Exhibit 1: The City of Shanghai

Situated along the mainland's central coastline, Shanghai is China's largest economic, financial and trade center; it is also one of the world's famous port cities and an important industrial base. Shanghai's dimensions are 120 kilometers from north to south, 100 kilometers east to west. Shanghai's weather is congenial as it belongs to the north subtropical marine monsoon climate. Annual average temperature is about 16°C; monthly average temperature is lowest in January (about 3°C), highest in July and August (about 28°C). Frost-free days are 230 p.a.; annual rainfall averages 1200 mm.

As China's largest transport hub, Shanghai has good air, land and water communications. Two trunk rail lines, Shanghai-Nanjing and Shanghai-Hangzhou, link with the Hangzhou-Nanchang and Beijing-Guangzhou lines, thus connecting Shanghai with 28 provinces and municipalities throughout China. International rail lines link China with 18 countries and regions (e.g., Russia, Korea, Iran, eastern Europe, northwest Europe). Two expressways, Shanghai-Hangzhou and Shanghai-Nanjing, link to the national highway network. Shanghai Hongqiao International Airport has direct and indirect flights to and from other important world cities. Besides CAAC (Civil Aviation Administration of China), Japan Airlines, United Airlines, Northwest Orient, Canada Air, Singapore Airlines and Cathay Pacific operate charter flights; 37 domestic air lines link Shanghai with 36 cities. Airport capacity is eight million passengers p.a.

Shanghai has ocean shipping links with over 400 ports in more than 160 countries and regions; it is also linked by 25 domestic coastal shipping lines to such ports as Qingdao, Dalian, Ningbo, Wenzhou, Xiamen, Fuxhou, Hong Kong and Haikou. The Yangtze River shipping line links Shanghai with such cities as Jiangsu, Anhui, Hunan, Hubei and Sichuan. In 1993, the volume of freight handled in Shanghai Port was 180 million tons, making it one the world's ten largest ports; as a river-seaport, it is ice-free all year round. Two great bridges, Nanpu and Yangpu, span the Huangpu River; a second cross-river tunnel at Yanan Road East is under construction. Shanghai Metro No. 1 Route was planned to open by end 1994; in 1995, a Metro extension to Shanghai Minhang Economic and Technological Development Zone was planned and part of the elevated inner-ring road would open to traffic.

Shanghai is a major Chinese hub of international and domestic post and telecommunication. Telephone exchange capacity is 1.6 million lines; long distance capacity (domestic and international) has reached 70,000 terminals and 30,000 lines. Yearly postal delivery capacity is 160 billion PCs per kilometer.

Exhibit 1 (cont'd)

As one of China's most important industrial bases, Shanghai is home to over 30,000 industrial enterprises, employing 3.8 million workers, in over 400 industrial sectors. Long-standing sectors include light industry, textiles, machinery, shipbuilding, metallurgy, chemicals, electronics, instruments and meters. In the last decade, high-tech industries (e.g., new metallurgical materials, high polymer compounds, cars, airplanes, computers, precision instruments, aviation and space) have emerged. Shanghai contains a fairly complete range of industrial sectors offering advantages for cooperation, advanced production technologies, competent management and good economic results; gross industrial output value for 1993 was RMB330 billion. Shanghai has 145,000 retail stores.

Shanghai is a major financial center. Financial institutions include the Industrial and Commercial Bank of China, People's Construction Bank of China, Agriculture Bank of China, Bank of China, the Bank of Communications, CITIC Industrial Bank, China Merchants Bank, the Pudong Development Bank, credit cooperatives and non-banking financial institutions (e.g., trust and investment, insurance, finance, securities and leasing companies). In addition, 23 banks are under overseas Chinese or foreign ownership; one is a Sino-foreign owned bank.

Shanghai is rich in intellectual resources including many scientific, technical and management personnel as well as experts in international finance and trade; it is a base for training cadres for important positions. Shanghai boasts 50 colleges and universities with total enrollment over 130,000 students and graduate students; 36,000 students graduate each year. In addition, over 130,000 adults receive higher education at colleges and universities. Shanghai has more than 1,600 R&D institutes employing over 900,000 scientific and technical personnel. Shanghai is also rich in well-trained labor resources, many of whom are young and have received at least a high school education.

As China's most open-to-the-world coastal city, Shanghai provides a better environment for investment than elsewhere in China, particularly in recent years. The opening and development of Pudong has broadened development throughout Shanghai. By 1993, 7,000 foreign investment projects from 54 countries and regions were approved; pledged foreign investment totaled US$14 billion.

Exhibit 2: Shanghai Zheng Zhang Textiles Factory – Income Statement (RMB '000)

Item	1992	1993	1994
1. Sales	100,899	127,633	111,757
Less: Production costs	66,604	94,899	89,010
2. Gross profit	34,295	32,734	22,747
Less: Operating expenses	5,482	5,523	5,436
Finance charges (income)		(421)	136
Loss (income) from other operations	243	1,835	440
Add: Other income	4	164	142
Investment income			(4,322)
Less: Other expenses	2,769	838	18
Retirement funds and efficiency wages	5,252	3,102	
Net income	20,545	21,693	20,897

Note: RMB1 approx. US$0.125.

Exhibit 3: Shanghai Zheng Zhang Textiles Factory – Balance Sheet (RMB '000)

Item	1992	1993	1994
Current Assets: Cash	12,711	16,251	10,492
Accounts receivable	112	3,033	8,751
Less: Provision for bad debts		(9)	(26)
Net accounts receivable	112	3,024	8,725
Other receivable	641	7,177	6,143
Inventory: Raw materials	1,324	13,646	15,037
Work in process	8,054	14,979	16,513
Finished goods	16,812	23,516	31,960
Consignment goods	76	83	215
Total	26,266	52,244	63,725
Loss on current assets	(2)		
Current portion of long-term bond invest.	15,507		
Total current assets	55,235	78,696	89,085
Long-term investment		10,305	8,269
Fixed Assets: Cost	14,816	21,363	21,386
Less: Accumulated depreciation	(2,381)	(4,325)	(9,281)
Net fixed assets	12,435	17,038	12,105
Construction in progress	4,549	203	123
Total fixed assets	16,984	17,241	12,228
Total Assets	72,219	106,242	109,582
Current Liabilities: Short-term borrowing			4,500
Bills payable			10,832
Accounts payable	1,740	13,709	14,336
Unearned revenues	21,214	32,656	3,259
Other payable	3,257	5,431	3,061
Wages payable	8,213	8,535	
Welfare fee payable	610	1,318	24
Taxes payable		3,486	184
Other unpaids		521	2,213
Miscellaneous payable	10	7	
Total current liabilities: Short-term borrowing	35,044	65,663	38,409
Long-term liabilities: Long-term borrowing	8,714	3,135	135
Stockholders' equity: Capital	14,007	23,749	47,500
Additional paid-in-capital			686
Appropriation for welfare fund		8,934	13,127
Retained earnings	14,454	4,761	9,725
Total stockholders' equity	28,461	37,444	71,038
Total liabilities and stockholders' equity	72,219	106,242	109,582

Exhibit 4: Competitor Analysis

Name	Location	Ownership	Export coverage	Geographic coverage	Estimated 1994 sales (RMB)		Target market
					China	Shanghai	
Jia Li	Shanghai	Sino-Taiwan JV	U.S., Taiwan	Shanghai, Beijing, Guangzhou	240,000	180,000	Young couples
Xin Yi	U.S., Canada, Shanghai	Collective	n/a	Shanghai, Beijing, Jiangsu, Qingdao	450,000	300,000	Middle-aged
Hui Cheng	Shanghai	Collective	n/a	Shanghai	100,000	100,000	Lower income
Jian Kang Bao	Zhejian	Sino-HK JV	U.S., Australia, Hong Kong	Shanghai, Beijing, Guangzhou	150,000	100,000	Children
Emerald	Beijing	Private	n/a	Shanghai, Beijing, Tianjin	550,000	400,000	Various
Zheng Zhang	Shanghai	Collective	U.S., Canada, Europe	Shanghai	200,000	200,000	n/a

Jia Li: Image – New & innovative. Aggressive designs and promotions. **Distribution network in Shanghai** – 12–13 specialty shops and four major department stores. All sales on consignment. **Strengths** – Eye-catching innovative designs, patterns often mirroring latest European fashion trends. Deepest pocket for promotion spending (set at about 5% of sales p.a.). Fair amount of brand awareness achieved. **Weaknesses** – Perceived lower value for money and practicality.

Xin Yi: Image – Established brand-name for quality and luxury in China since 1980s. **Distribution network in Shanghai** – Apparently all high-end department stores in Shanghai (about 60 sales spots). Estimated 80% of sales through company trained personnel at sales sites. Remainder on consignment. **Strengths** – Established distribution network and good relationship with channel members. Quality image of brand name. Strong export background. **Weaknesses** – Very traditional designs.

Hui Cheng: Image – Traditional small-scale workshop. Lower end manufacturer. **Distribution network in Shanghai** – Mainly through small specialty shops. Number of spots about 30. **Strengths** – Successful in catering for the lower end quilt market, meeting the purchasing power of the public mass. **Weaknesses** – Perceived lower quality and durability.

Jian Kang Bao: Image – Children-oriented. **Distribution network in Shanghai** – Mainly through small specialty shops. Number of spots around 12. **Strengths** – Use mostly imported fabrics for quality. Cartoons and funny patterns catering specifically to the child segment. **Weaknesses** – Relatively new to the market (company only started production mid-1994). Perceived expensive.

Emerald: Image –Renowned company selling wide-ranging products. **Distribution network in Shanghai** – Sole distribution through 17 outlets of bedding items. **Strengths** – Variety of quilts sold. Variety of bedding products. Outlets recognized as providing comprehensive range of choices. Convenient one-stop shopping. Low prices. **Weaknesses** – Designs relatively conventional.

Zheng Zhang: Image – Renowned export company. **Distribution network in Shanghai** – Six specialty counters at department stores; four other consignment sales spots. **Strengths** – Strong export background for financial and production viability. **Weaknesses** – Relatively new to the market (company only started local sales end 1994).

Map of the Philippines

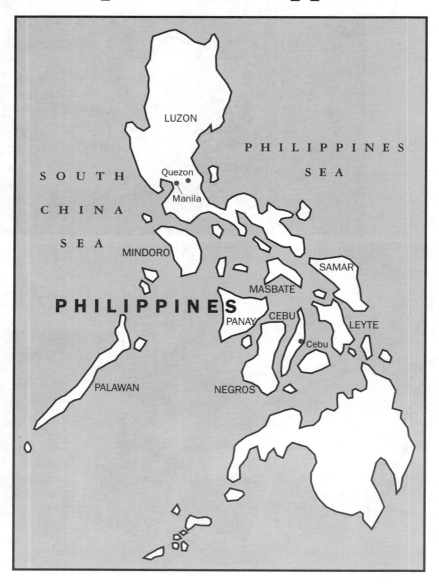

The Philippines Overview

Background. The Philippines comprises a land area of 300,000 sq. km. contained in a 7,100-island archipelago; the 11 largest islands encompass 95% of its total land mass. Its 70 million population (1994), growing at 2.2% p.a., speaks mainly Filipino (based on Tagalog) and English, both official languages, and also a variety of other native languages. The majority of the people are Roman Catholic (83%), followed by Protestant (9%), Muslim (5%), Buddhist and others (3%). Major cities and populations (million) are Manila (2) and Quezon (1.5), Luzon; and Cebu (0.6), Cebu. Weather is tropical marine (range: 21° C to 32° C) with both Northeast (November to April) and Southwest Monsoons (May to October). The legal system is based on Spanish and Anglo-American law.

Political. Colonized by the Spanish, a U.S. possession since 1898, occupied by the Japanese in World War II, the Philippines formally became a republic in 1946. From 1965 onwards, the Philippines was governed by an increasingly corrupt president, Ferdinand Marcos. Following Marcos' ouster (1986), the Philippines has struggled with some success to achieve political stability in the face of attempted military coups, first under Corazon Aquino (widow of the assassinated [1983] opposition leader Benigno S. Aquino), later under former military leader Fidel Ramos and currently under President Joseph Estrada (elected June 1998). In recent years, the Philippines has suffered from domestic insurgency movements. However, internecine struggles within the Communist Party of the Philippines and transition of some rebel leaders to civilian status have diminished these threats. In 1992, leases on the Subic Bay and Clark bases were terminated, ending the U.S.'s long-standing military presence in the Philippines. The executive branch of government comprises a directly elected president (six-year term), vice-president and Cabinet; the legislative branch comprises a bicameral Congress (the Senate, 24 seats; the House of Representatives, 204 seats).

Social. The government operates an aggressive population control program that has brought it into conflict with the powerful Catholic Church. President Ramos is Protestant; in 1994, the population growth rate was 2.2%. The literacy rate is 95% (1995); 15.2% of the 25+ age group has post-secondary level education. Under Ramos, crime has decreased, in part the result of some success in disarming "private-armies," long fixtures of the political structure in rural areas, but kidnapping for ransom continues to be a problem allegedly involving corrupt police.

Economy. The Philippines is a member of the United Nations (UN), World Bank (WB), International Monetary Fund (IMF), World Trade Organization (WTO), Asian Development Bank (ADB) (based in Manila) and Asia-Pacific Economic Cooperation (APEC) Forum. It is also a founding member of the Association of Southeast Asian Nations (ASEAN). Economic reforms, launched by the Aquino government, accelerated under Ramos, have positively impacted the economy; Ramos has set a goal of turning the Philippines into a Newly Industrialized Country (NIC) by 2000. The economy is structured (1992) as: primary, 24.1%; secondary, 30.4%; tertiary, 45.5%. GNP growth, reaching 5% in 1994, has been broadly based: agricultural, 2%; industry, 6%; services, 3.5%; results are evident throughout the country. In the 1990s, despite a strengthening peso, export growth was strong (over 15% p.a.), but import growth of both capital and consumption goods has been even sharper (over 25%). Some economists believe the "underground economy," comprising countless unregistered small businesses, may account for almost one third of the Philippines' output of goods and services. Many of these unlisted and untaxed enterprises are built on wages sent home by four million Filipinos working abroad, each estimated to remit on average US$500 a month.

The Philippines has restructured its monetary system by forming a new Central Bank (New Central Bank Act, 1994) and liberalized its policy on investment of foreign capital. Foreign banks may enter the local banking system and joint ventures have become popular vehicles for new foreign direct investment. Another recent optimistic signal was the share listing of 15 major Philippine companies (including oil-refiner Petron, P20 billion offering), on the Philippine Stock Exchange (1994: 187 stocks listed and 292 issues listed) providing a venue for investment of foreign funds. These new listings raised stock market capitalization to US$60 billion (1994) from US$39 billion (1993).

In 1994, the Philippine peso strengthened significantly due to an influx of foreign exchange (investor optimism about the country) and interest rate reductions (triggered by a reduction in bank reserve requirements by the central bank). Lower interest rates and a reduction in inflation (October 1994, 7.8%) eased the budget deficit; however, increasing tax revenue is a serious issue since tax evasion is rampant.

The Philippines did not escape the 1997 Asian financial crisis; the peso lost 35% of its value against the U.S. dollar by year's end. The economy was headed for a sharp downturn (IMF forecasts of 4% growth in 1998). Newly elected President Estrada has promised to give priority to fighting poverty, guaranteeing food security, revitalizing the agricultural sector, and restoring peace and order in the country.

Infrastructure. Long-standing electric power crises (in 1993, electric energy production equalled only 20 billion kWh) have led the government to pursue private-sector involvement in infrastructure development through build-operate-transfer (BOT) arrangements: several "fast-track" power plants have already been completed. Expanding this policy, the government has identified almost 100 priority infrastructure projects (total US$9 billion) for transportation, industrial estates, roads, railways, water systems, tourism ventures and other public utilities. For example, a US$450 million light railway mass transit system will be built in Manila by a consortium of mostly foreign companies. In addition, to improve telephone service, the Philippine Long

Distance Telephone monopoly is being freed for competition; in 1994, telephone density was only 12 per 1,000 people.

Statistics*	June 1991	June 1997	Statistics*	June 1991	June 1997
Per capita GNP	US$727	US$1,265	Pop. growth	2.3%	2.3%
GDP growth	3.0%	5.0%	Infant mortality/1,000	40	40
Savings (GNP)	n/a	16%	Life expectancy (yrs)	n/a	67
Inflation (CPI)	14.9%	4.6%	Literacy rate	88.7%	93.5%
Foreign debt			People per tel.	67	38.6
(in billion)	US$28.6	US$39.4	People per doctor	1,090	1,016
Pop. (million)	62.8	69.7	People per TV	n/a	9.2
Urban pop.	n/a	46%	Calorie intake (cals)	n/a	2,452

*Secured from *Asiaweek*.

Case 39

Barclay International Manufacturing Corporation: Gruff Aircon Maintenance Fluid

Jose M. Faustino
Asian Institute of Management, Makati, the Philippines

In the first week of January 1993, Rafael "Arbie" Bonifacio, president of Barclay International Manufacturing Corporation, studied the marketing strategy and 1992 sales record for Gruff Aircon Maintenance Fluid. Bonifacio believed that among the products emerging from Barclay's product development efforts in the last three years Gruff had the best potential. However, he wondered how dramatically faster sales growth for Gruff could be achieved from 1993 to 1995.

ഇരുൻ

Company History

The deep recession of the mid-1980s had just started when, in 1983, brothers Rafael "Arbie" Bonifacio, 27, and Joey, 25, started Barclay in a tiny apartment in Mandaluyong, Metro Manila. The Bonifacios had a great incentive to succeed in their new business: P2.4 million in debts from a previously failed business venture. The brothers were attracted to network or direct sales marketing because of:

- Their study of successful network marketing firm, AMWAY, and subsequent studies of several direct selling organizations (e.g., Tupperware, Avon, Mondragon);
- The limited investment needed to enter (actual initial investment was just P50,000.00);
- The cash nature of transactions, versus 90 to 120 days terms for the typical retailer;
- The ability to sell consumer products to the mass market without mass media advertising.

Barclay's first 12 products were for household and personal use; the two brothers batched these products in plastic and aluminum tubs used by housewives for their washing.

After mixing and packaging the products, the brothers sold door-to-door and office-to-office. It was hard work but tenacity and their do-it-yourself approach were amply rewarded. Indeed, they discovered the recession could be positive. The middle and lower income classes reacted to the long recession by reducing, and often ceasing, purchases, not only of imported items but also of higher-priced household goods. Barclay products were priced significantly below multinational brands; as a result, Barclay gradually grew and picked up strength in the 1980s.

Having experienced the selling task first hand, the brothers developed their own systems for recruiting, training and commissioning. Their corporate vision was "to research, develop and manufacture superior quality products for Filipinos using as much local raw material as possible; and to provide Filipinos a better way of life through networking." Barclay's avowed corporate mission was:

> To operate as a top Filipino network company, ascribing Christian values and providing business opportunities and incentives through the development, manufacture and distribution of superior quality products and services worldwide.

Barclay Direct Sales Force

By January 1993, Barclay had an estimated direct sales force of 130,000 distributors; roughly 20,000 sold at least one item per quarter. About 80% of active Barclay distributors were female; the majority considered themselves full-time housewives working part-time with Barclay.

To become qualified as a Barclay distributor, the applicant had to complete several steps:

1. Go to the Barclay office to complete distributor application form;
2. Attend the two-hour distributor orientation seminar;
3. Pay the P500.00 registration fee;
4. Receive the free distributor kit, complete with product samples and brochures.

Once the distributor had qualified, as above, s/he had to operate within three sales policies:

- Products were not advertised. Distributors using product brochures were the sole communication vehicle with target customers.
- Distributors purchased any and all products on a cash basis only. Likewise, they were expected to sell to customers on cash on delivery (COD) basis.
- Barclay did not sell its products to retailers; distributors were likewise forbidden to sell to retailers. Distributors who violated this policy were subject to termination.

Each distributor earned discounts from the customer's price according to her/his monthly volume in sales points (Table 1). (See Exhibits 1A, 1B for the distributors' price list.)

Table 1: Performance Discount Chart[1]

Monthly point value	Discount (%)	Monthly point value	Discount (%)
7,500 or more	21	1,000–1,499	11
6,000–7,499	19	600–999	9
4,000–5,999	17	300–599	6
2,500–3,999	15	100–299	3
1,500–2,499	13	Below 100	0

Barclay Product Line

Barclay's price list carried 95 items from four different product categories. Not all products Barclay sold were self-manufactured; some items were sales aids to be bought and used by the sales force.

The four product categories and constituent elements were:

- Personal care (21 items): shampoo, lotion, skin condition, health soap, hand soap, baby care products, men's/women's cologne, luxury soap, deodorant, hand cleaner, foot powder;
- Home care (32): bath soap, detergent bar/powder, cologne furniture polish, toilet bowl cleaner, disinfectant, dishwashing detergent, dog shampoo, garden fertilizer, Gruff, organic cleaner, air fresheners;
- Traded items (28): business briefcase, cameras, film, photo album, plastic bags, rubber gloves, casual/collared shirts, sprayer bottles;
- Printed materials (14): calling cards, order forms, gate signs, product brochures, price lists.

Gruff Cleaning Fluid

Gruff Product and Use

Gruff was available in four packages: 500 ml. (half-liter) plastic bottle; kit form containing the half-liter bottle plus a manual sprayer; four-liter plastic jug; plastic carboy containing 20 liters. When sprayed on the evaporator coil at the back of a room air-conditioner, Gruff's cleaning chemicals loosened stuck-up dirt and other foreign deposits due to corrosion, encrustation, oxidation, scaling and industrial fallout. Directions for use were easy to follow:

---

[1] Each point was worth approximately 10% of the sales value in pesos.

1. Dilute Gruff with water in different ratios depending on the severity of the dirt and other foreign deposits (i.e., full strength for heavy dirt, 1:2 for average condition, 1:5 to 1:10 for less severe dirt).
2. Apply with low pressure sprayer. When frothing stops, rinse with moderate water pressure.

Gruff User Benefits

Gruff offered strong benefits (Exhibits 2A and 2B) for air-conditioning users. According to Barclay, Gruff:

- Needed no scrubbing or drying time, often the window unit need not be pulled out;
- Provided 50% to 70% savings over conventional cleaning methods;
- Reduced the load on compressors and cut energy consumption costs by 15% to 20%;
- Prolonged the life of air-conditioner coils and the air-conditioner itself by as much as 300%;
- Worked fast in removing dirt deposits found between aluminum fins of the evaporator coils;
- Frothing action pushed out dirt and deposits from air-conditioner coils for easy cleaning;
- Rinsed out easily without leaving traces of the chemicals which, in any event, were 100% biodegradable;
- Safer on aluminum than the alkaline type of cleaners;
- Concentrated, could be diluted up to a ratio of 1:10 with water.

There was no other product like Gruff on the market. Most institutional users applied simple chemicals in cleaning their units. Cleaning the evaporator coil took a significant amount of manual labor and care was essential to prevent damage to the fragile aluminum fins.

Institutional Users

In January 1992, Philippine cities included thousands of office buildings and hundreds of thousands of air-conditioners. Barclay's conservative market estimate for Gruff was P1 billion to P1.2 billion.

An informal survey conducted for Barclay by a student team (Exhibit 3) revealed that for institutional air-conditioning users (i.e., building supervisors) the most common cleaning materials for the evaporator coil were soap and water, or lye and water. Roughly one third of institutional respondents replied that they used "cleaning chemicals" like lye, acid based cleaners for cleaning window air-conditioning units even though the possibility that strong chemicals might damage the surrounding surface or structure was present. According to Barclay, this potential damage was not a problem with Gruff since it was not corrosive and could be washed away with water.

The main challenge in selling Gruff was that virtually all air-conditioning users interviewed were "generally satisfied" with the maintenance of their air-conditioning units. Indeed most users were not even conscious of power savings available from cleaning the evaporator coil. Barclay managers reasoned that key decision makers or influencers were physically located a good distance away from their large air-conditioner units. Second, use of Gruff dramatically increased the cost of cleaning the evaporator coil and fins compared to lye and water; the cost differential was even more dramatic for soap and water.

A third problem was that many institutional air-conditioning users contracted out air-conditioner maintenance to service companies, usually the unit installers. Typically, institutional air-conditioning users were unconcerned with the method or materials used to clean the air-conditioning unit, so long as it was cleaned. The researchers found that the few air-conditioning maintenance companies using Gruff, usually small to medium enterprises, purchased sporadically since they had to pay cash compared to 30 to 60 days' credit for most other parts and materials.

Gruff Sales Record

When Bonifacio analyzed Gruff's sales performance he found little satisfaction with the trends (Table 2). Although sales had grown since the February 1992 launch, they were erratic and seemed to have leveled off at around P400,000 per month. A study of invoices revealed only about 100 distributors regularly selling Gruff, virtually all in Greater Manila. (See Figure 1 for Barclay's organization structure.)

Table 2: Monthly Sales Revenues, 1992 ('000 pesos)

	House-hold	Institu-tional	Total		House-hold	Institu-tional	Total
February	24.5	69.7	94.2	July	330.0	199.2	529.2
March	295.8	96.7	392.5	August	269.7	79.1	348.8
April	324.0	104.4	428.4	September	200.6	207.5	408.1
May	319.9	158.2	478.1	October	125.0	273.4	398.4
June	317.8	96.9	414.7				

Gruff Sales Policy

Barclay's current policy for Gruff was the same as for all Barclay products: Gruff was only sold to qualified Barclay distributors, not to retailers. Any air-conditioning equipment or service company wishing to buy Gruff had to buy it from a qualified distributor. Barclay president Bonifacio preferred distributors with institutional selling experience. He thought that in institutional selling a salesperson would have to deal with many levels (e.g., actual user, maintenance engineer, purchasing people).

Structure

Training for selling Gruff was three to four classroom hours conducted by the training director, an experienced engineer. In addition, two hours on professional salesmanship

Figure 1: Barclay Organization Structure

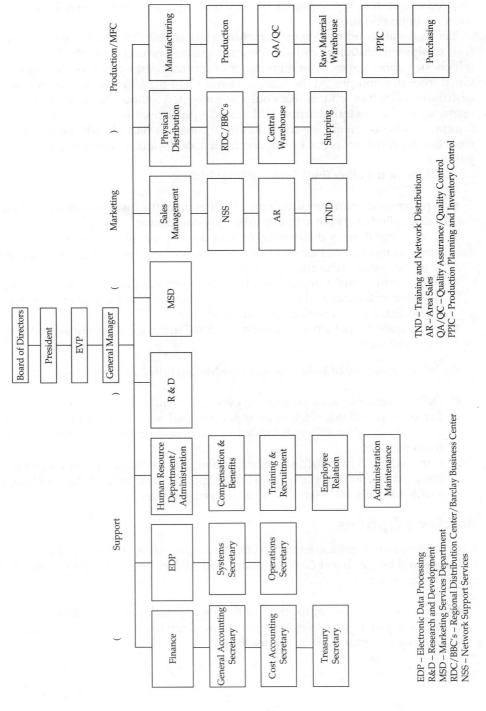

EDP – Electronic Data Processing
R&D – Research and Development
MSD – Marketing Services Department
RDC/BBC's – Regional Distribution Center/Barclay Business Center
NSS – Network Support Services

TND – Training and Network Distribution
AR – Area Sales
QA/QC – Quality Assurance/Quality Control
PPIC – Production Planning and Inventory Control

was recommended. Remaining distributor training was experience on the job, "hit or miss" as Bonifacio surmised.

Ten major air-conditioning manufacturers and at least 50 air-conditioning contractors, equipment installers and servicing companies were listed in the Metro Manila telephone yellow pages. A small number of service companies was already buying Gruff from distributors. At the launch, Barclay had made available (i.e., for sale) to distributors Gruff brochures that could be presented to household and institutional users, as well as manufacturing and servicing air-conditioning companies. Thus, Bonifacio believed many air-conditioning companies had already heard of Gruff, since Barclay distributors had been going from door-to-door, and office-to-office for the past year.

Bonifacio noted other findings on selling Gruff:

- An increasing number of high profile, high potential institutional accounts were being called on by more than one Barclay distributor.
- The typical Barclay distributor (female, 30–45 years of age, housewife) did not know as much about air-conditioning as service contractor/maintenance engineers or even purchasing managers.
- Some institutional buyers asked Barclay to serve orders directly, skipping the distributor. Barclay had politely refused so far and continued to refer customers to the distributor who had opened the account.
- When institutional accounts inquired about Gruff, they were referred to the nearest distributor.

An informal survey of 14 buildings in the Makati office area revealed that:

- Only two maintenance people had ever used Gruff;
- For most buildings, maintenance people used soap and water or lye or acid based chemicals with water for cleaning air-conditioning units; they were relatively satisfied;
- Prices charged by outside air-conditioning service firms for cleaning each unit were (labor and materials): P300 to P350 per window unit; P1,200 to P1,500 per 7 to 20 ton unit; P3,300 to P4,400 per large centralized unit.

Barclay's Options

Barclay president Bonifacio examined the available data and wondered what action Barclay could take to boost Gruff sales dramatically in 1993 to 1995. Options he was considering included:

- Continue the same approach of 100% sales through Barclay distributors;
- Develop a dedicated sales team for selling Gruff to institutional accounts;
- Develop a mixture of both approaches.

Exhibit 1A: Distributors' Price List, Barclay Manufactured Products (pesos)

Product description	Size	Division	Prod. code	Dist. price	Cust. price	Basic disc	Bus vol.	PT. value
Affini Conditioning Shampoo	200ml	PC	ASA	42.35	50.80	8.45	42.35	4.23
Affinity Astringent Lotion	125ml	PC	AAL	32.50	40.60	8.10	32.25	3.25
Affinity Skin Conditioner	100g	PC	ASC	75.00	93.75	18.75	68.15	6.81
Barclay Family Health Soap	360g	PC	BFC	44.00	52.80	8.80	5.28	4.06
Bright Days Detergent Bar	480g	HC	BDB	21.00	23.70	2.70	4.20	1.80
Bright Days Liquid Detergent	500ml	HC	BDL	52.85	66.05	13.20	48.04	4.74
	1000ml	HC	BDL-L	89.90	112.35	22.45	81.73	8.16
	4000ml	HC	BDL-G	263.70	329.60	65.90	239.73	26.12
	carboy	HC	BDL-C	1,050.00	1,312.50	262.50	954.54	100.00
Catharsis Women's Cologne	125ml	PC	CWC	106.00	132.50	26.50	96.30	8.83
Clean Scene Toilet Bowl Cleaner	500ml	HC	CST	37.95	47.40	9.45	37.95	3.79
	1000ml	HC	CST-L	61.60	77.00	15.40	61.60	6.16
	4000ml	HC	CST-G	203.10	253.90	50.80	203.10	20.13
	carboy	HC	CST-C	779.50	974.50	195.00	779.50	77.95
Deep Shine Furniture Polish	500ml	HC	DSP	78.60	98.25	19.65	78.60	7.86
	4000ml	HC	DSP-G	325.00	406.25	81.25	325.00	32.50
	carboy	HC	DSP-C	1,200.00	1,500.00	300.00	1,200.00	120.00
Dexan Disinfectant Cleaner	4000ml	HC	DDC-G	233.35	291.00	58.35	133.35	23.33
	carboy	HC	DDC-C	849.00	1,061.50	212.50	849.00	84.90
Dixie Dishwashing Liquid	500ml	HC	DDL-L	46.20	57.75	11.55	42.00	4.26
	1000ml	HC	DDL-L	82.40	103.00	20.60	74.91	7.18
	4000ml	HC	DDL-G	266.55	333.15	66.50	242.32	20.41
	carboy	HC	DDL-C	757.20	946.50	189.30	688.36	65.20
Eureka Waterless Hand Cleaner	30ml	PC	EHL-LX	15.20	19.00	3.80	15.20	1.52
First Price Dog Shampoo	250ml	HC	FP-DS	52.80	66.00	13.20	52.80	5.28
Garden Liquid Fertilizer	250ml	HC	GOF-X	35.10	43.90	8.80	35.10	3.51
Maintenance Fluid	500ml	HC	GOF	56.65	70.80	14.15	56.65	5.66
Gruff A/C Maintenance Fluid	500ml	HC	BCC	124.35	155.45	31.10	113.05	11.30

Product description	Size	Division	Prod. code	Dist. price	Cust. price	Basic disc	Bus vol.	PT. value
	Kit	HC	BCC-K	200.00	250.00	50.00	181.82	1,831.00
	4000ml	HC	BCC-G	856.00	1,070.00	214.00	778.18	77.82
	carboy	HC	BCC-C	4,000.00	5,000.00	1,000.00	3,636.36	363.64
Happy Habit Liquid Hand Soap	500ml	PC	HHS	60.00	75.00	15.00	60.00	6.00
	4000ml	PC	HHS-G	292.60	365.75	73.15	292.60	29.60
	carboy	PC	HHS-C	951.00	1,189.00	238.00	951.00	95.10
Innocence Baby Bath	250ml	PC	IBB-X	40.70	509.90	10.20	40.70	4.07
Baby Cologne	250ml	PC	IBC-X	51.75	64.70	12.95	51.75	5.17
Baby Lotion	250ml	PC	IBL-X	39.00	48.75	9.75	39.00	3.90
Baby Oil	250ml	PC	IBO-X	39.60	49.50	9.90	19.80	3.96
Baby Powder	75g	PC		33.55	41.90	8.35	33.55	3.35
Joyance Women's Cologne	125ml	PC	JWC	83.60	104.50	20.90	76.00	5.97
Kareva Men's Cologne	125ml	PC	KMC	85.70	107.10	21.40	77.91	6.12
Neige Luxury Bar Soap	360g	PC	NLS	49.50	61.90	12.40	5.44	4.40
Seasons Anti-Perspirant Deodorant	60ml	PC	SDS	44.20	55.25	11.05	44.20	4.42
Spick N' Speedy Organic Cleaner	500ml	HC	SNS	46.25	57.80	11.55	46.25	4.62
	4000ml	HC	SNS-G	206.05	257.60	51.55	206.05	20.60
	carboy	HC	SNS-C	660.00	825.00	165.00	660.00	66.00
Spring Breeze Air Freshener	190g	HC	SBL	59.40	74.25	14.85	59.40	5.94
	4000ml	HC	SBL-G	237.90	297.40	59.50	237.90	23.79
	carboy	HC	SBL-C	801.00	1,001.50	200.50	801.00	80.10
Spring Breeze Air Sanitizer	90g	HC	SBL	75.00	93.75	18.75	68.18	5.90
Talver Men's Cologne	125ml	PC	TMC	120.00	150.00	30.00	109.09	8.56
Time Out Foot Powder	100g	PC	TFP	37.40	46.75	9.35	37.40	3.74
Virtue Women's Cologne	125ml	PC	VWC	95.90	119.85	23.95	87.18	6.85

Exhibit 1B: Distributors' Price List, Barclay Non-manufactured Products (pesos)

Product description	Division	Prod. code	Dist. price	Cust. price	Basic disc	Bus vol.	PT. value
Business Portfolio	TI	NP-033	40.00	50.00	10.00	0.00	4.00
Business Portfolio New	TI	NO033A	50.00	62.50			
Kodak							
A. Camera							
Ektralite 10	TI	EKT-10	1,000.00	1,078.00	78.00	90.91	9.09
Model 237	TI	M-235	1,120.00	1,177.00	57.00	101.82	10.18
Model 335	TI	M-335	1,475.00	1,562.00	87.00	134.09	13.40
Model 735*	TI	M-735	2,199.00	2,309.00	110.00	199.91	19.99
S10 (Promo only)	TI	S10-P	847.50	890.00	42.50	77.04	7.70
B. Film							
GA 135-24 ISO 150 Gold Film	TI	GA-24	75.60	79.40	3.80	3.44	0.34
GA 135-36 ISO 150 Gold Film	TI	GA-36	91.55	96.15	4.60	4.16	0.41
GA 135-24 ISO 200 Gold Film	TI	G-24	61.30	64.40	3.10	2.79	0.27
Photo Album	TI	PN-ALB	234.60	293.35	58.75	58.65	23.46
Plastic Bag – Big	TI	PR-W23	1.85	0.00	0.00	0.00	0.18
Medium	TI	PR-W24	1.10	0.00	0.00	0.00	0.11
Small	TI	PR-W25	0.70	0.00	0.00	0.00	0.07
Extra Small	TI	PR-W26	0.60	0.00	0.00	0.00	0.06
Rubber Gloves	TI	AC-GLO	28.60	35.75	7.15	0.00	2.86
SAC	TI	PR-W027	84.65	105.80	21.15	3.85	0.04
Southwind Casual Shirts:							
Traditional Style							
Dark Colors – DC	TI	SW1-DC	215.00	268.75	53.75	78.18	7.81
Light Colors – LC	TI	SW1-LC	215.00	268.75	53.75	78.18	7.81
White Colors – WC	TI	SW1-WC	215.00	268.75	53.75	78.18	7.81
Dark Colors – 1DL	TI	SW1-DL	215.00	268.75	53.75	86.00	8.60

Product description	Division	Prod. code	Dist. price	Cust. price	Basic disc	Bus. vol.	PT. value
(Desert Green, Manne Blue, Deep Rouge & Classic Yellow) Dark Colors – 2DL	TI	SW2-DL	210.00	252.00	42.00	42.00	4.20
(Burgundy, Basic Mustard & Antique Rose) White Colors – 2WL (Tux White)	TI	SW2-WL	200.00	240.00	40.00	40.00	4.00
Sprayer Bottle	TI	AC-BTL	9.00	11.25	2.25	0.00	0.90
Sprayer Only	TI	AC-SPR	40.50	50.60	10.10	0.00	4.05
Sprayer Set	TI	AC-SET	47.10	58.85	11.75	0.00	4.71
Southwind			175.00 per piece			0.00	0.00
Collared Shirts	TI	SW1-PR	1,020.00 in packs of six			0.00	0.00
Southwind			105.00 per piece			0.00	0.00
Round Neck Shirts	TI	SW2-PR	630.00 in packs of six			0.00	0.00

Exhibit 2A: **Gruff Product Brochure**

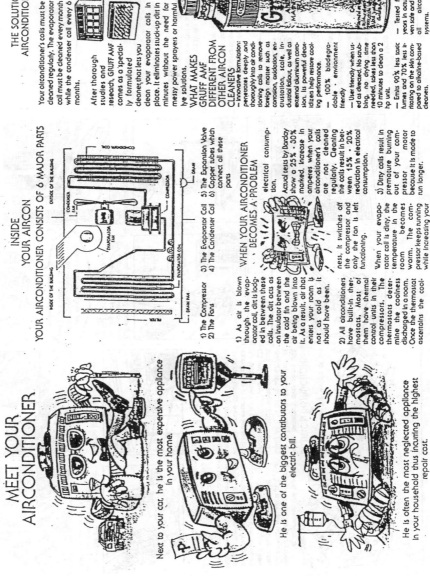

Exhibit 2B: Gruff Product Brochure

HOW TO USE GRUFF AMF

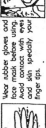

Pre-Application:

If the condenser coil is within reach then there is no need to pull-out the aircon unit. Just unplug your aircon then spray GRUFF AMF and rinse it with water. However, if the condenser coil is beyond one's reach then unplug your airconditioner and remove the unit from its place. Make sure that you have some old newspaper and a wooden crate on hand to carry the weight of the aircon.

DILUTION INSTRUCTIONS:

For an extremely dirty aircon unit, use full-strength concentrate of GRUFF AMF. For an average dirty aircon unit, simply dilute one (1) part concentrated GRUFF AMF to two (2) up to five (5) parts water (depending on the extent of dirt); and for easy to remove dirt on your unit, use one (1) part GRUFF AMF to ten (10) parts water.

DIRECTIONS FOR USE:

For an extremely dirty aircon (First Time Use)

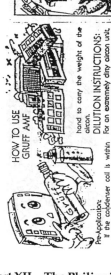

1. Assemble the dip tube on the sprayer. Be sure that the white gasket is in place.

2. Fill the sprayer bottle with water.

3. Wear rubber gloves.

4. Unplug the Gruff bottle.

5. Install the sprayer on the Gruff bottle.

6. Spray the aircon coil from top to bottom.

7. Detach the sprayer from the Gruff bottle. Make sure that you discharge all ingrained liquid in the dip tube by spraying it on the coil.

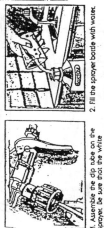

For average dirt in your aircon, follow dilution instructions and procedures 1 to 9

8. Install the sprayer on the sprayer bottle.

9. Rinse the coil by spraying it with water from bottom to top.

Note Additional Maintenance Tip

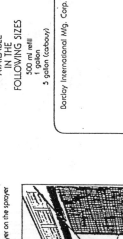

Make sure you give your unit/s an annual/once a year/ general cleaning of all parts by a qualified airconditioner maintenance/ repair shop.

PRECAUTIONARY MEASURES

Wear rubber gloves and face mask before using. Avoid contact with eyes and skin specially your finger tips.

IMPORTANT

To prolong the life of the sprayer, clear off all contents on dip tube by continuously spraying water until chemical contents have disappeared. Rinse with water.

When using other similar sprayers other than those found in the GRUFF AMF kit, make sure that it is clean and free from water or other chemicals before squeezing GRUFF AMF into the dip tube. Always rinse with water after usage.

Never leave the sprayer installed on the Gruff bottle.

AVAILABLE
IN THE
FOLLOWING SIZES

500 ml refill
1 gallon
5 gallon (cabouy)

Barclay International Mfg. Corp.

Exhibit 3: Opinion Survey of Gruff Users and Non-users

I. NON-USERS

A. Maintenance of air-conditioner	Household	Institutional
1. Who cleans your air-conditioner		
– Contracted a servicemen	100%	43%
– Employees	0%	42%
– From the seller (service)	0%	
2. Materials used:		
– Water and soap	42%	25%
– Lye and water	18%	32%
– Water only	10%	0%
– Chemicals	0%	33%
– Don't know	30%	10%
3. Frequency of cleaning		
– quarterly	37%	0%
– 3 × a year	23%	0%
– 2 × a year	25%	0%
– monthly	15%	31%
– 2 × a month	0%	32%
– Weekly	0%	37%

B. Satisfied? Generally, most of the consumers are satisfied

C. Problems encountered

Institutional
– Inconvenient to take down for window type air-conditioners
– Brushing ruins the grill
– Improper placement

II. USERS

A. How would you compare Gruff to other cleaners?

Institutional
– It is less messy
– Convenient – handling is easier
– Cheaper

Household
– It is less messy
– Convenient
– Cheaper
– Saves time

B. Suggestions for improvement

Household
– Improve the scent
– Improve the sprayer
– Need to clean the inside and back portion of air-conditioner

C. Frequency of usage

Household
– Depends on the weather – seasonal (affects usage of air-conditioner)
– One bottle lasts 2 to 3 weeks
– If diluted, 1.5 months

D. Old method

Institutional
– Pressurized water and chemicals problems?
  1. Parts deformed – fins bent

Exhibit 3 (cont'd)

I. NON-USERS

Household
  – It is hard to find servicemen
  – Ruins the wood, dirties the floor
  – Suspicious of strangers
  – Improper placement

D. Attributes they are looking for:

Institutional
  – Not noisy
  – Cooling ability
  – Physical appearance
  – Safety of the air-conditioner unit

Household
  – Convenience, fast and hassle-free
  – Physical appearance of the air-conditioner
  – Less noise
  – Must not contain toxic chemicals

II. USERS

  2. Metal fins get thinner (perception)

E. Attributes consumers are looking for:

Institutional
  – No acid vapors
  – Scent
  – Physical appearance
  – Dust-free grill

F. How did you learn about Gruff?

Institutional
  – Recommendation
  – Product demonstration
  – Through salesmen

¹This survey was conducted by a group of AIM students using convenience sampling. The MBM students personally interviewed 40 to 50 users and non-users of Gruff.

Case 40

Basic/Black Zale Youngman Advertising, Inc.[1]

John R. Kennedy
University of Western Ontario, London, Ontario, Canada

Francisco L. Roman Jr., Marjorie Poblador
Asian Institute of Management, Makati, the Philippines

Maritess B. "Tess" De Leon arrived at her office shortly after 8:00 am on Tuesday, March 1, 1994. The previous few days had been special for Tess. In a senior management reorganization she was appointed agency president and CEO of Basic/Black Zale Youngman, Inc. (BZY), an advertising agency in Manila. Announcement of the changes was part of the agency's annual client reception held the previous evening at a five-star hotel; the news was warmly received by guests, virtually all BZY's 50 plus clients. That morning Tess noticed an unusually large fax machine output. She gathered the sheets, sat down and read. Page one was a memo from BZY New York dated February 28, 1994:

> *Last Friday, Colgate-Palmolive announced a consolidation of worldwide advertising responsibilities to Black Zale Youngman and Young & Rubicam. The attached press release spells out details (Exhibit 1).*
>
> *Clearly, changes of this magnitude will have a profound impact on many of our agencies around the world; we in New York will be working with each of you to ensure smooth transitions and a clear understanding of the financial ramifications. Coincident with the changes in agency alignment and assignments will be changes in agency compensation practices. These too will be explained in greater detail in the next few weeks.*

---

[1] This case was written by Professor John R. Kennedy of the Western Business School, in collaboration with Professor Francisco L. Roman and Research Assistant Marjorie Poblador of the Asian Institute of Management (AIM). Copyright (1994) the University of Western Ontario. This material is not covered under authorization from CanCopy or any reproduction rights organization. Any form of reproduction, storage or transmittal of this material is prohibited without written permission of Western Business School, The University of Western Ontario, London, Canada N6A 3K7. Reprinted with permission, Western Business School.

Colgate-Palmolive wishes these transitions to be completed no later than March 31, 1994. The primary objective is to ensure the service we provide to Colgate continues at its high level and that all assignments are handled impeccably. The preliminary announcement is just that, preliminary. We will be in touch quite a bit over the next few weeks.

Tess was stunned! She had no idea such decisions were being considered, but she understood clearly the meaning for BZY. Colgate-Palmolive billings in 1993 were P250 million;[2] a 20% to 30% increase was expected in 1994. The New York decision meant that approximately 90% of this business was moving out of the agency; planned 1994 billings would drop substantially.

ഇറ

The Philippines Advertising Agency Industry

Gross advertising billings in the Philippines grew substantially in recent years (Table 1). Although billings increased dramatically, proportionate expenditures across media remained quite stable (Table 2).

Table 1: Gross Media Billings

Year	Gross billings	
	Million pesos	**Previous year**
1992	9,415	34.5
1991	7,001	13.1
1990	6,189	19.6
1989	5.175	23.4
1988	4,194	33.2

Source: National Statistics Coordination Board.

Table 2: Percent of Billings by Media

	% change over		
TV	**Radio**	**Print**	**Others**
65.1	15.6	18.4	0.9
64.3	15.5	19.1	1.1
60.6	15.6	22.6	1.2
59.2	15.8	23.7	1.3
65.9	14.9	17.2	2.0

Source: Association of Accredited Agencies – Philippines (4 As-P).

Basic/Black Zale Youngman, Inc.

In 1977, Basic Advertising, Inc., later transitioned into Basic/Black Zale Youngman, Inc. (1984), was founded by five partners formerly employees at Ace Compton. From the start, the partners decided the environment would be different from their working experience in other advertising agencies. Said Ricardo "Carding" Francisco, Basic's Group Chairman, "In many agencies the creative work is very often characterized by huge egos, arrogance and obstinacy. We decided the predominant character at Basic would be a servant culture; the core value, client delight." He identified four contributing factors: organization structure, employee empowerment, organizational feedback mechanism, propagation of a fetish for quality.

---

[2] Fall 1993: US$1 = P28.48.

Organization structure. Basic's structure was flat, a mosaic of small business units called foxholes (Exhibit 2). "A foxhole is a World War II term referring to a trench," said Carding. "In a foxhole, there is no room for an armchair general. There are no specific job descriptions. The general had better shoot a rifle himself or the foxhole will fall. Each member of a foxhole should be able to shoot a rifle, a bazooka and use a machine gun, or use a bayonet. Work is seamless. There is no room for primadonnas!" (Exhibit 3.) The behavior and character of each foxhole reflected the client; thus, foxholes could be, and were, different in expertise, pace, size and average member age. Competition among foxholes was encouraged; transfers of people among foxholes did occur, decisions were settled in the Management Committee operating as a federation of independent states.

Employee empowerment. People empowerment was real; decisions were made collegially at the foxhole level. The Management and Executive Committees met only to team up for common tasks, solve general problems and share learning across foxholes about agency successes and failures. Turnaround of assigned work was widely perceived inside and outside the agency as the fastest in the industry.

Organization feedback mechanism. The agency used a feedback mechanism called "Feedback-an."[3] When one told a fellow Basic partner: "Feedback-an tayo," it meant: "Let's pause for a moment; you tell me what's wrong with what I am doing or how I am doing it and I will mirror to you your good and bad points." Feedback occurred face-to-face at all levels, including the chairman, peer to peer, subordinate to supervisor, supervisor to subordinate. The same "feedback-an" culture was brought to the client side; agency personnel believed working relationships with clients were better. Said Gabriel "Gabby" Faylona, agency Chairman and Chief Creative Officer: "The feedback-an philosophy is the Christian value of Fraternal correction; correction by a caring brother who loves you is valuable and should be treasured."

Early in the agency's life, there was concern that the traditional non-confrontational Filipino nature would not be receptive to a "feedback-an" culture. Believing Filipinos tried anything in a party or fiesta atmosphere in the spirit of fun, the founding partners hired a dance floor and band for a "feedback-an" party for all employees. When the party started, each person listed five persons to whom they wanted to give feedback and five persons from whom they wanted feedback. When the band began to play, each person found a person on their list and gave or received feedback. Said Carding: "After a while there were lots of tears, a lot of crying; there was laughter and crying into the night, even after the band had left. But, oh, what honesty! What deep feelings! What catharsis! Everyone ended up as great friends, a fabulous team!"

At bi-weekly agency-wide staff meetings foxholes shared information on client activities and asked for and received assistance on unsolved issues. Foxholes reported

---

[3] The Philippines was multilingual; these words were Filipino, the official language, based on the Tagalog dialect. Filipino was spoken by approximately 60% of the population. English, taught in schools as a second language and widely used in business, was spoken by 50% of the population.

financial results monthly in a rally-like atmosphere with much public pride and shame: wild cheers and foot stomping for foxhole profits; dead silence for losses. An annual offsite "Corplan" meeting involved every individual, from chairmen to messengers. Meetings were held at foxhole-level, then agency-wide, to develop, present and refine annual foxhole business plans, including financial outcomes.

Propagation of a fetish for quality. Basic's two-year Vision Statement development illustrated this fetish. First, Asian Institute of Management faculty (at a seminar) outlined features of an effective Vision Statement. Second, each employee was asked to write his/her version of a Vision Statement. Third, each foxhole conducted workshops to develop common versions. Fourth, the foxhole federation agreed on common values. After 20 drafts, a corporate-wide referendum confirmed Vision Statement agreement:

This agency will think, eat, breathe quality.
Quality as defined by our clients.
In Creative, in Media, in Fiscal and Account Management.
To deliver quality the first time every time.
We will only hire people with strong bias for quality.
Who will not compromise. Who will not
surrender an inch to mediocrity. People who
will welcome the opportunity to improve themselves.
To improve the work of their team.
To improve their partnership with suppliers.
To improve the quality output of the agency.
Quality will be our culture, our work style,
our behavior. It's our commitment to the community.
It's our commitment to our Creator.
We will be a quality team.
We will set our business goals together.
We will share equitably the fruits of our endeavors.
And we will have fun!
Quality will spring from our minds.
Quality will seep from our pores.
Quality will be our aura.
Our clients will see it. Feel it.
And they will be delighted.

Supporting Agency Activities

Profit sharing. The profit-sharing plan included all employees; annual "kitty" distributions were based on salaries. In December 1993, each employee received the equivalent of almost three months' salary.[4]

---

[4] Employee compensation was the largest cost item for an advertising agency. Basic/BZY's compensation costs, including bonuses, were just under 50% of revenues, substantially lower than North American averages and reflecting the lower Philippine wage scales.

The Adschool. "People with experience in work environments different from ours often found it difficult to fit in," said Tess De Leon. "Therefore, we evolved to hiring mostly young people with no business experience and training them our way. However, we found it difficult to attract the best minds because college students tended not to hold advertising agencies in high regard. Our solution, in 1988, was to start an advertising school." The Adschool offered college graduates (classes of 10 to 15), a six-month program in all phases of advertising agency operations including hands-on experience. Trainees received a monthly salary plus the same benefits as Basic/BZY employees. At the program's end, a rigorous oral examination was conducted; Basic/BZY typically hired 80% of graduates, the remainder found other jobs in the industry. In recent years, course offerings attracted 300-plus applicants for the bi-annual offering.

Physical fitness and team sports. Basic/BZY encouraged physical fitness among employees. It employed a staff athletic director, used a large multi-purpose room in the agency as a gymnasium in the afternoons and offered subsidized membership in a nearby fitness club. Finally, a strong agency culture developed to compete and win annual inter-agency competitive meets (e.g., track and field, swimming, golf, darts).

Broadening the mind. For several years, Basic/BZY sponsored the approximately 100 creative employees for a weekend in an artistic community outside Manila; specialists in acupuncture, martial arts, music and origami demonstrated their specialties. Employee response to this Lawak Utak (Broadening the mind) experience was so positive that for the past two years it was made available to accounts people.

Agency Internationalization

By the early 1980s, it was apparent that Philippine advertising growth was driven by international packaged goods manufacturers; many had Philippine subsidiaries. However, country managers frequently did not make advertising agency decisions. Head offices, encouraged by large international agencies, frequently assigned worldwide brand responsibility to a single agency. Basic Advertising management perceived this trend as an opportunity to develop billings and employee skills. In 1984, Black Zale Youngman, a Chicago-based agency that recently secured a worldwide mandate for several Colgate-Palmolive brands, visited the Philippines and other East Asian countries seeking to build a network. The two organizations negotiated an agreement: BZY secured 30% ownership[5] in a renamed Basic/Black Zale Youngman, Inc. The new agency gained immediate responsibility for: Palmolive Soap, Palmolive Shampoo, the Tender Care baby products line, and Ola, a detergent.

Compensation was the same as other agency accounts; 15% commission on media billings, 17.65% mark-up on production costs. In addition to share of agency profits, BZY was paid a 1% commission on Colgate-Palmolive billings. The contract between Basic/BZY and Colgate-Palmolive (Philippines) contained the standard clause that, if

---

[5] The maximum permitted by Philippine law.

the client terminated the contract, the agency was entitled to commission on media billings for a further 90 days. This clause ensured an agency received compensation for advertising it created that ran after termination.

Prior to Basic/BZY securing Colgate-Palmolive business, all Colgate Philippine agency business went to DYR;[6] Basic/BZY brands represented under 10% of Colgate's Philippine billings. For Basic/BZY, Palmolive Soap and Palmolive Shampoo were considered major brands but both lagged category leaders: Palmolive Soap was a poor third, 8% market share. In 1985, Palmolive Shampoo was withdrawn from Basic/BZY and returned to DYR.

In late 1987, Colgate-Palmolive moved to "equity management"; all Colgate brands went to a single agency, similarly for all Palmolive brands. In the Philippines, DYR retained all Colgate brands; Basic/BZY received all Palmolive brands. Basic/BZY retained Tender Care,[7] a strong number two behind Johnson & Johnson's Baby Care, and Protex, a detergent soap. Although immediate billing gains were minimal, Basic/BZY considered itself a winner, both because of Colgate-Palmolive's stated intention to place increased attention worldwide on personal care and the explosive category growth potential in the Philippines.

Agency Growth

The following years saw great agency growth fueled by award-winning creative advertising that increased client sales (Table 3). Business increases came from new clients and existing client billings increases. Basic/BZY's television use increased substantially; 73% by 1993.

The relationship developed between Basic/BZY and Colgate-Palmolive was excellent; over time agency staff worked ever more closely with Colgate product development personnel to create effective advertising. This advertising produced market results that, in turn, led to increased advertising budgets. For several years, growth in Colgate-Palmolive budgets was double the agency as a whole; by 1994, Basic/BZY had 60% of Colgate-Palmolive billings. Three foxholes, comprising 68 of 279 agency staff, worked full-time on Colgate-Palmolive business.

Palmolive Soap. Prior to Basic/BZY's work, Palmolive Soap (8% market share) was a poor third to Lux (Lever) and Camay (P&G). Following Basic/BZY recommendations, based on focus groups, the brand was repositioned to the teenage market. Vibrant advertising helped move Palmolive to first in beauty soaps, 17% market share.

Palmolive Naturals. Palmolive Shampoo (1988: 16% market share) was a weak second to Sunsilk (Lever). A new improved product, renamed Palmolive Naturals, was introduced with advertising based on *hiyang* (compatibility). Later advertising featured

---

[6] This agency had several names over the years; it was known in the trade as DYR, initials for Dentsu, Young & Rubicam, the previous corporate name and part of the current name.

[7] The Tender Care line was sold in only two countries: the Philippines and Thailand (where it was called Care).

Table 3: Basic/BZY Billings and Agency Rankings

Basic/BZY billings		Agency billing	Basic/BZY billings		Agency billing
Year	Million pesos	Rankings	Year	Million pesos	Rankings
1993	1,132	n/a	1988	245	–
1992	957	1	1987	199	–
1991	573	2	1986	129	–
1990	434	2	1985	120	–
1989	280	4	1984	79	–

Source: Basic/BZY records.

Filipino Lea Salonga, the original female lead in the New York musical production of "Miss Saigon." By 1994, market share grew to 38%.

Tender Care Soap. Tender Care Soap was the flagship of Tender Care. In the late 1980s, Basic/BZY developed a pool of material called "Babies in adult situations"; faced with strong competitive activity the brand maintained market position and won the agency several creative awards.

Palmolive Optima Shampoo. Palmolive Optima Shampoo entered the shampoo and conditioner (2-in-1) market in November 1991, almost two years after P&G's Rejoice pioneered the category in the Philippines. Soon after introduction, several Colgate subsidiaries used Philippine creatives for their introductions. By 1994, Optima had a respectable 9% market share.

Axion dishwashing paste/gel. Axion dishwashing paste was the first advertised dishwashing product in the Philippines. After three months, shipments increased seven times, leading to a gel line extension early in 1994.

By 1994, the Philippine Colgate-Palmolive organization was acknowledged as the Asian center for excellence in body care by the worldwide organization. In turn, the Philippine organization credited Basic/BZY as the agency instrumental in sales and profit success for its brands.

After the Fax

Tess De Leon had little time to digest Colgate-Palmolive's news. At 9:30 am, she, Gabby and Carding were meeting the new president of a major client firm for the first time. Tess made copies of the letter and news release; her companions read the material in silence on the 30-minute drive. On the way back they agreed to meet later that day with Ernesto Carpio, agency Vice President for Finance and Administration to discuss the situation and formulate a plan of action. At the afternoon meeting, Ernesto said the realignment would reduce Basic/BZY's share of Colgate-Palmolive billings from 60% to 6% or 7%, virtually all on Axion. The agency would gain Ajax detergent; however, this mature brand had significant market share, was not advertised now, nor likely to be in the future. The loss of Colgate-Palmolive billings would reduce Basic/BZY's planned 1994 billings by about 20%.

Exhibit 1:   Colgate-Palmolive Press Release

February 25, 1994   Colgate-Palmolive Realigns Global Advertising Agency Assignments

New York, N.Y. – Colgate-Palmolive announced today that it is realigning its worldwide advertising agency assignments, to improve global advertising effectiveness and generate savings to be used for additional media spending. This new move gives worldwide responsibility for an entire product category to the same agency and changes agency compensation from a fixed fee to a variable pay-for-performance formula.

Young & Rubicam will now assume global responsibility for all Oral Care and Personal Care advertising. The brands include Colgate Toothpaste, Colgate Toothbrushes, Palmolive Soap and Shampoo, Irish Spring, Softsoap, Protex and Neutro Balance. The Mennen line of deodorants/anti-perspirants, baby products and men's toiletries currently being handled by McCann Erickson and Lowe & Partners, will be assigned on a global basis to Black Zale Youngman. In addition, BZY will be responsible for worldwide advertising for all household surface cleansers and fabric care brands. Equities in these categories include Ajax cleansers, Palmolive dishwashing products, Murphy's Oil Soap and the company's various detergent, bleach and fabric softener brands. Murphy's Oil Soap was previously handled by Genova, Hartwick and Juliano. BZY's Siboney unit will continue to have responsibility for all Colgate U.S. Hispanic advertising.

In announcing these changes, Colgate CEO, Reuben Mark, stated "Our very wide global presence, and the strength of our business in developing countries demand that our best advertising ideas spread as rapidly as possible around the world. This is best accomplished with the same agency work on a brand everywhere. The pay-for-performance elements being introduced will reward the agency that delivers truly great advertising ideas. Together with the strong increases in media spending we have budgeted for 1994, both in the U.S. and abroad, these changes will add profitable growth momentum to our consumer businesses worldwide." He went on to say "This was an especially difficult choice because we had to balance the benefits of this move with the loss of the services of McCann Erickson, Lowe and Genova, Hartwick & Juliano who had done outstanding work for Colgate in the U.S. and around the world. However, in the interest of global focus and efficiency, we must concentrate our brands in two agencies which will service us everywhere we are in the world."

Young & Rubicam Chairman Alex Kroll said, "We are very proud to be entrusted with the two great trademarks, Colgate and Palmolive worldwide, plus the additional assignments in the oral care and personal care categories. In our ten years with Colgate, we've always been proud of this partnership with a company with a true global orientation to its brands, that's constantly pushing for creative excellence. This new global alignment will take us to a new level of performance. And what a terrific way to celebrate an anniversary."

Bruce Mason, Chairman and CEO BZY Communications said, "We are delighted that Colgate is again expressing confidence in our worldwide creative partnership. This consolidation will help us generate even more effective advertising for Colgate Global brands. The change to pay-for-performance will certainly motivate our people to put forth even more effort to achieve positive results."

Exhibit 1 (cont'd)

Colgate measured media expenditures in 1993 on a global basis exceeded $500 million. The company did not disclose the total billings assigned to each agency. There will be an orderly transition over the next few months for those brands that change from one agency to another.

Colgate is a $7 billion global consumer products company, with core businesses in oral care, body care, household surface care and fabric care. The company markets its products in 170 countries under such internationally recognized brand names as Colgate, Palmolive, Mennen, Ajax and Fab.

Exhibit 2: Basic's Foxhole Organization Structure

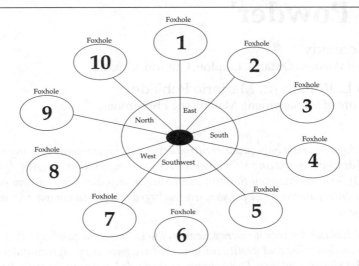

Exhibit 3: The Organization of a Foxhole

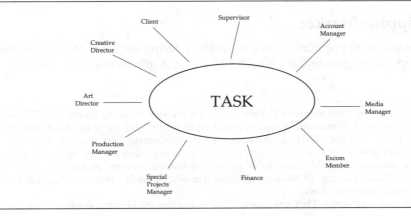

Case 41

J&J (Philippines), Inc.: Johnson's Face Powder[1]

John R. Kennedy
University of Western Ontario, London, Ontario, Canada

Francisco L. Roman Jr., Marjorie Poblador
Asian Institute of Management, Makati, the Philippines

"We have decided we must have product introductions if this company is going to grow," said P.M. "Boy"[2] de Claro, marketing VP for Johnson & Johnson (Philippines), Inc. It was Tuesday, August 21, 1990; next Monday the firm would begin shipping a brand new product to the trade. The product, Johnson's face powder, was packaged in a plastic compact for use outside the home. Said Boy:

> *We're not looking for rocket science new products; we want products that may provide relatively modest sales and profits initially, but we have very high confidence regarding their market place acceptance. Those successes are needed, not only for our bottom line, but to instill confidence in our employees that we are doing our part to make the country grow.*

ಬಿಂದ

The Philippine Market

The Philippines' 1990 population was 61 million, living on 2,000 of 7,100 islands; estimated population growth, 2.3% p.a. Of 42% living in urban areas, only half were in

---

[2] Many Filipinos had nicknames. They commonly used nicknames on business cards.

the dozen cities with populations over 250,000. Metro Manila, estimated 1990 population 7.9 million, was by far the dominant urban area. The country's age distribution was skewed towards youth; just under 50% of the population was under 20 years (Table 1A).

Table 1A: Age Distribution of the Philippine Population, 1989

Age	% of population	Cumulative %
under 5	14.0	14.0
5–9	12.9	26.9
10–14	12.2	39.1
15–19	10.7	49.8
20–24	9.6	59.4
25–29	8.4	67.8
30–39	13.2	81.0
40–49	8.3	89.3
50–59	5.5	94.8
60 and over	5.2	100.0

The Philippines' 1989 GDP per head of US$708 lagged all but one of its major ASEAN partners (Table 1B). Not only was 1989 GDP growth behind its partners, so also was forecast 1990 growth. Many attributed this poor performance to political instability and unrest, as well as a severe power shortage resulting in brownouts that created substantial reductions in industrial output.

Table 1B: Economic Performance of ASEAN Countries

Country	1989 GDP per head (US$)	1989 GDP % growth rate	Estimated 1990 GDP growth rate
Indonesia	527	13.1	7.1
Malaysia	2,159	8.7	9.8
Philippines	708	6.0	2.7
Singapore	10,875	9.4	8.2
Thailand	1,252	12.0	10.0

Johnson and Johnson, Inc.

Johnson & Johnson (J&J), founded in the U.S. in the mid-1880s to produce antiseptic bandages for wound care, grew to become the leading manufacturer of babycare, first-aid and hospital supplies. Its first foreign subsidiary was established in Canada (1916) followed by Great Britain (1923). J&J expanded at home and abroad in its traditional business until 1959 when it entered the pharmaceutical industry by acquiring both U.S. and Swiss pharmaceutical firms. By 1989, J&J sold products in over 150 countries and had operations in over 50. Its broad product line comprised three segments: consumer products, pharmaceuticals and medical/professional products. Worldwide sales in 1989 were US$9.75 billion, 50% outside the U.S.

Johnson and Johnson (Philippines), Inc.

Johnson & Johnson (Philippines), Inc. started business in 1956 as a manufacturer/distributor of baby products. J&J (Philippines) grew by a combination of growth in existing product lines plus addition of new products. In 1989, J&J's (Philippines) sales of P1.03 billion exceeded one billion pesos for the first time, making it the 90th largest firm in the Philippines. The firm reported to the U.S. parent through a VP International, who had responsibility for ten Asian countries. In 1989, the product line included several product groups and brands:

- Baby products: Johnson's baby powder, baby oil, baby shampoo, baby lotion and baby soap, buds, cottonette, Johnson & Johnson Disposable Diapers;
- Feminine hygiene products: Modess, Carefree, Stayfree and Feminex;
- Personal care products: Bandaids, Johnson & Johnson Dental Floss, Reach Toothbrushes, Shower to Shower Soap, powder, shampoo and conditioner;
- Over-the-counter drug products: Tylenol tablets and capsules, Co-Tylenol tablets.

Products were sold by a company sales force direct to retailers and through wholesalers. J&J's distribution channels were: supermarkets, wholesalers, van dealers, grocery stores, drug chains, independent drug stores, market stalls, "sari-sari" stores (downscale corner variety stores), department stores and institutions. Direct accounts included department and large general merchandise stores, supermarkets and some drug outlets. Most drug outlets had not evolved from traditional pharmacy-oriented products to the same extent in North America. In contrast, supermarkets were well developed relative to their North American counterparts. They occupied large square footage, carried a broad range of product categories and, with retail margins of 5% to 8%, priced aggressively. Several supermarkets were owned by department stores and located on their basement floors. Many supermarkets were reached by passing through large expanses of fast food operations, occupying space leased from the supermarkets.

Department stores carried a broad range of merchandise categories, comparable to North American department store operations of the 1960s and early 1970s, before the development of "category killer" specialty stores and price clubs. Each store or chain operated in a narrow range of price points, but there were some noticeable price point differences across chains. Retail margins ranged from 10% to 15%; high price point stores earned even higher margins. Department stores and supermarkets usually purchased goods direct from manufacturers.

Wholesalers sold to a range of smaller stores in both larger and smaller urban areas. They generally bought at the same price as large direct accounts and worked on margins of 3% to 5% of their selling prices. There was not always a clear distinction between retail and wholesale inasmuch as some retailers acted as wholesalers for some lines and some wholesalers sold at retail. Van dealers sold to downscale corner variety stores and small market stalls. They sold in very small quantities (e.g., three to six pieces) ex-truck on a cash basis.

In 1989, roughly 65% of J&J's sales were direct to retailers, 15% to wholesalers, 20% to van dealers. Sales to van dealers were made at prices averaging 5% higher than for large direct accounts and wholesalers.

Organizational Change

In 1989, several senior management changes took place at J&J (Philippines), in particular the arrival of a new president and two VPs. The president was a former J&J (Philippines) marketing VP who spent the previous seven years as country manager in three Caribbean countries. Both new VPs of sales and marketing had substantial packaged goods experience, but neither worked previously for J&J. All three were Filipino by birth and upbringing.

Political instability in the Philippines was exacerbated by an attempted coup in December 1989; this had a negative effect on business results and executives' morale. Within J&J (Philippines), over several months, the future of country and company was frequently discussed at board meetings. Board members finally concluded that, while they could have absolutely no impact on the country's politics, they would work to improve the country's business performance by devoting their efforts to increasing J&J's business performance.

P.M. "Boy" de Claro was the new vice president for marketing. His background included extensive Colgate-Palmolive experience, including three and a half years in New York. Said Boy:

> Johnson & Johnson is a quality brand name in this country. However, the firm itself has been very conservative. Sales and profits have increased only marginally in real terms in recent years. The one big product introduction in the 1980s was not successful, although the problem was more in execution than concept. While there was planning within marketing, it was more of an exercise than an integral part of operations. Yearly plans were made but they were put on the shelf while business went on as usual.

Boy set out to change the marketing group's perspective. A series of meetings developed a strategic vision of J&J's growth for the next decade. The marketing group was reorganized from an individual brand orientation into strategic product groups with clearly delineated growth opportunities, both new products and product line extensions. Boy also appointed a senior marketing staff member to the new position of product development manager. He commented: "That was not an easy sell. Given our history, his initial reaction was that I was putting him in the freezer! It took time before I could convince him that his success or failure was going to be my success or failure."

Although the firm was not active in product introductions, the R&D department had several "ready-to-go" products and others close to completion. The first product selected for introduction was Johnson's baby bath, a tear-free bath shampoo that was a new product to the worldwide J&J organization. Introduced in spring 1990, it achieved very satisfactory trade acceptance; by mid-summer it topped management's modest yet realistic goals.

Johnson's Face Powder

In the discussion and analysis leading to the development of strategic product groups, it became apparent that use of Johnson's baby powder among teens and young adults was much lower than for mothers. However, among teens and young adults who used talcum powder, over 80% reportedly applied it to their faces. Said Boy:

> In retrospect, that should have been very easy to spot. Young Filipinos are no different from their counterparts in many other countries. They want to put distance between themselves and their childhood on some dimensions, yet maintain comfort and security on others. A brand with the word "baby" just doesn't cut it with them, even though they may really like the benefits of the physical product. That got us thinking about how we could develop this market with its very sizable potential.

Market research confirmed a strong interest among female teens and young adults in the physical performance of several J&J's baby products, including powder. Further research produced several findings:

- Teen and young adult females used face powder far more as a skin freshener than as "cosmetic" makeup.
- Mothers exerted strong pressure on teenage daughters not to use "cosmetic" face powder from compacts.
- Young female adults put baby powder in a handkerchief or tissue, put the package in their purse, and applied the powder on their face outside the home.
- Adult women often refilled their "cosmetic" compacts with Johnson's baby powder.
- No face powder was currently being sold in compacts in supermarkets.
- Face powder in compacts currently sold in department stores had retail prices ranging from P60 to P150; most were priced at P100 and above. The lowest-priced face powder packaged in compact form was Angel Face by Pond's; it typically retailed at P59.95.

Within J&J, a strategy for a toiletry product carrying the name Johnson's face powder emerged, primary target urban females, 16–25 years old, from B and C category economic households (Table 2). A limited line of shades would include white to give emphasis to the toiletry concept; no other firm sold white face powder in compact form.

Key distribution would be in supermarkets, critical for two reasons. First, it was believed supermarkets would be a key factor in creating a new "everyday beauty care" market, allowing J&J to address a currently untapped young female market. Second, J&J had strong distribution strength among supermarkets: traditional cosmetic firms

Table 2: Distribution of the Philippine Households by Economic Classification (1990)

Economic class	Number ('000s)	%
AB (upper)	125	1.1
C (middle)	764	6.7
D (lower)	5,932	52.0
E (extremely low)	4,586	40.2
Total	11,407	100.0

Source: Pulse Research Group.

had no existing strength and were perceived as unlikely to attempt to build any. Preliminary discussions with large supermarkets indicated they would be very supportive of a product retailing under P50, with a launch supported by advertising. Such a launch would have the product "everyday"-priced with a 10% retail margin.

Initial costing revealed that a quality face powder product in compact form, selling in supermarkets for P39.95, would yield J&J a gross margin of approximately 60%. Later detailed cost estimates for two product shades gave a gross margin figure of 60.8%. Comparable estimates for two refill stock-keeping units (SKUs), retailing at a parity-priced P24.95, gave a gross margin of 57.6%. Production costs would vary no more than 10% for production volumes plus or minus 50% of the preliminary 15-month sales forecast of P6,500,000 in a unit ratio of 1.5 refills per compact sale.

Starting the Johnson's Face Powder Launch

The decision was made to introduce Johnson's face powder with four SKUs, two shades in each of the compact and refill packs, at ex-factory prices of P35.96 and P22.46, designed to retail at P39.95 and P24.95 respectively in the supermarkets (Exhibit 1).

An advertising budget of P700,000 was developed for a three-month introductory television campaign, to be followed by a P2,000,000 budget for the following 12 months. Of the initial budget, P500,000 were allocated for production of a 30-second commercial with the tag line: "Because the baby is now a lady."

The initial 40,000-unit production run commenced in August; shipment to the trade would start in late September for a mid-November media launch. As for Johnson's baby bath, early production units were sent to J&J headquarters in New Jersey, U.S. for quality testing and worldwide brand registration. Recalled Boy de Claro:

"We knew we would do well in supermarkets but had serious initial concerns regarding department store reaction. Our position going in was that we were pioneering a new product category. They understood and bought our thinking. What's more, most were opting for supermarket-level pricing, both to keep business from the supermarkets and to establish an image of value pricing against food stores. When the media campaign breaks in November, we shall have very good distribution in virtually all urban centers."

Johnson's Face Powder: Part Two

Three days later, August 24, 1990 at about 8:00 am, shortly after Boy arrived at his office, he received a telephone call from a senior manager in J&J's International Division at the New Jersey head office. He told Boy that the Philippine introduction of Johnson's face powder was to be canceled. If introduction had already started, the product was to be recalled.

When Boy asked the reason for this decision, he was told there were two: first, "Johnson & Johnson is not in the cosmetics business"; second, the word "Johnson's," appearing on the package, was in gold, in clear violation of company policy that the Johnson name should always appear in a standard blue shade.

At the conclusion of a relatively brief call, Boy sat for what he described as "a very long time," first digesting the phone message, then starting to think about what he should do next.

Exhibit 1:   The Johnson's Face Powder Compact and Refill

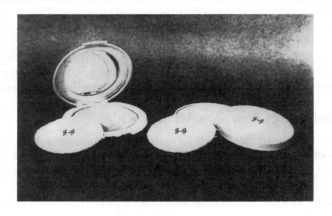

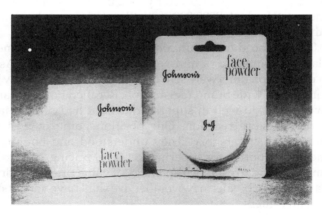

Case 42

SAE Products Marketing Corporation: The Air Compressor Company

Pallevi Gupta, Jose M. Faustino
Asian Institute of Management, Makati, the Philippines

In October 1993, CEO Noel Risos was reading reports prepared by the Sales and Marketing Director of SAE Products Marketing Corporation. The leading competitor had increased market share as the result of new promotions and Risos had implemented several strategic and organizational changes. However, he was unsure that these moves were the best actions and wondered if other moves might strengthen his position. He realized that if SAE did not act expeditiously, leading competitor Atlas Copco would gain even more market share.

ଛୠ୯ଓ

Company Background

SAE Products Marketing Corporation (SAE) was incorporated by Noel Risos, his brother-in-law and two university classmates in June 1980. Risos became CEO and the company, initially focusing on sales and servicing of air compressors and boilers, started operations in July 1980.

Risos, a mechanical engineer, previously worked as assistant vice president for Commercial Exponent (Commex) selling air compressors and other industrial equipment. Commex was the Philippine distributor for CompAir Broomwade (U.K.) and other foreign brands such as Clayton, Black & Decker, Rockwell, Graco, O&K and Bea, each different brands of industrial equipment. Commex subsequently declared bankruptcy (closed operations in 1982) and in late 1980, CompAir Broomwade gave its distributorship to SAE.

SAE's sales were initially slow but it remained profitable by selling parts and servicing air compressors sold by both Commex and SAE. An early breakthrough came when San Miguel's Beer Division gave SAE an important order for two units of 370 HP oil-free piston compressors for its San Fernando plant; an additional unit of the same model was ordered for the Polo Brewery Plant in 1981. Shortly thereafter SAE dropped its boiler product line since the sale of parts and service was insufficiently profitable and competition was very keen.

The Air Compressor Market

Types of Machine

Air compressors were devices that caused air to flow against pressure and convert mechanical force and motion into pneumatic fluid power. Generally, manufacturing and assembly plants required air compressors to operate their pneumatic equipment and devices. In 1993, three types of air compressor were available in the Philippine market: piston, screw and centrifugal. Piston and screw type were available in low and medium capacities; centrifugal compressors were high capacity devices.

Piston and screw type compressors were available in both lubricated and oil-free types. Lubricated compressors discharged compressed air containing several parts per million (ppm) of oil; oil-free compressors discharged air with no oil traces. Oil-free air compressors were used in industries such as food, pharmaceutical and beverage where oil contamination could damage the products. Oil-free air compressors cost 20% to 40% more than the lubricated type.

Piston compressors operated by positive displacement. Air, drawn in during the piston's suction stroke, was compressed by decreasing its volume when the piston moved in the opposite direction, then discharged when the air pressure exceeded the pressure acting on the outlet valve.

Industries needing to compress air from low to very high pressure used piston air compressors. However, in the Philippines, these machines were slowly becoming obsolete. Since they had many moving parts, maintenance costs were high. However, manufacturers were adding new features to piston compressors to delay obsolescence.

Screw compressors also operated by positive displacement. In these rotary, positive displacement machines, two inter-meshing rotors, each in a helical configuration, displaced and compressed the air. The two rotating elements, male and female rotors, were housed in a body called the stator. Rotary screws were the most popular type of air compressors and were fast replacing piston compressors in many manufacturing industries. Screw compressors were used for all applications in all industries where medium pressure was required. They had fewer wearable parts, low noise level and less weight and volume than piston air compressors.

Centrifugal air compressors were commonly known as the dynamic type. Dynamic compressors were rotary continuous flow machines in which the rapidly rotating element accelerated air as it passed through, converting the velocity head into pressure, partially in the rotary elements and partially in the stationary diffusers or blades. Centrifugal air compressors were suited for compressing large volumes of air where low to medium pressure was required. Because of their high capacities, few companies had uses for these machines.

Air compressors had an average life of ten years. Generally, if air compressors were properly used and maintained, large repairs were not needed in the first three to five years. However, if a major component (e.g., the air end for the screw type) were damaged, repair could cost 30% to 40% of the total packaged screw air compressor cost.

Costs

With the assistance and approval of CompAir Broomwade, SAE started assembling rotary screw air compressors locally in early 1992. Finished products were priced 30% to 40% lower than similar air compressor brands imported from the U.K. and other countries. SAE believed that prices could be even lower if non-major components were manufactured locally.

SAE priced its 15 horsepower (hp) heavy duty piston lube at P345,000; a 30 hp heavy duty piston lube at approximately P515,000. A locally-assembled 15 hp heavy duty screw lube was priced at P282,000; a 30 hp heavy duty screw lube at P360,000. A 40 hp heavy duty screw lube was priced at approximately P525,000. If discounts were to be offered, SAE could only afford 5%, otherwise sales would be unprofitable.

SAE only reported invoiced sales. As many as 60% of clients ordered from SAE, but received air compressors direct from Broomwade "by indent." SAE earned only 5% to 7% margin on these sales. In 1993, SAE sold 70 air compressors; 28 in Philippine pesos, reported in the financial statements (Exhibit 1), the balance on an indent basis.

Competition

SAE had three major competitors: Atlas Copco, Ingersoll-Rand and Koppel. Atlas Copco and Ingersoll-Rand carried their own brands; Koppel carried Sullair and SAE carried CompAir Broomwade. (See Table 1 for the firm brands and product ranges.)

Table 1: Brands and Products Carried by Air Compressor Firms

Firm	Atlas Copco	Ingersoll-Rand	SAE	Koppel
Brand name	Atlas Copco	Ingersoll-Rand	CompAir Broomwade	Sullair
Product range				
Piston Lube				
Low capacity	x (Inactive)	x	x	
Medium capacity		x	x	
High capacity		x	x	
Piston Oil-free				
Low capacity		x	x	
Medium capacity		x	x	
High capacity		x	x	
Screw Lube				
Low capacity	x	x	x	x
Medium capacity	x	x	x	x
High capacity	x	x	x	x
Screw Oil-free				
Low capacity	x			
Medium capacity	x		x	
High capacity	x			
Centrifugal		x	x (Joy)	

SAE was the only firm without other product lines; all other firms offered products unrelated to air compressors. In particular, compressors were a small part of Ingersoll-Rand's product offerings.

Although all firms added features to the slowly becoming obsolete piston compressors, each concentrated on screw air compressors; the main competition was in screw lubes. In late 1993, Atlas Copco was overall market share leader (38%) followed by Ingersoll-Rand (26%) and SAE (26%); remaining players held 10% market share.

Atlas Copco became market share leader in the early 1980s. The quality of Sullair's (represented by Engineering Equipment from mid-1970s to mid-1980s) after sales service dropped, and former leader, Ingersoll-Rand, became complacent when customers did not return for after sales service and parts. Financial backing from its Belgian parent and aggressive marketing allowed Atlas Copco to capture the leadership position.

In the late 1980s, Atlas Copco developed the "Exchange Deal"; customers could exchange old air compressors for a new Atlas Copco compressor at a minimal price. Air compressor customers availed themselves of this deal; Atlas Copco's market share increased sharply and was maintained.

Competitive Moves in the 1990s

SAE

In 1991, SAE made the decision to attempt to secure second-place market share via extensive marketing. It introduced a five-year warranty, the Screw Compressor Breakdown Protection Plan (SCBP), exclusively for screw air compressors. This warranty contrasted sharply with one- to two-year warranties typical in the industry. Clients paid a fixed charge of 1% of the FOB air compressor price per year for this benefit.

For this "insurance premium," SAE replaced and repaired any damaged element free of charge including defects in materials and casing, faulty design and bad workmanship, lack of operator skill and negligence and carelessness. SAE derived several benefits: clients perceived SAE's compressors to be reliable, durable and of the highest standard and quality inasmuch as only a firm with excellent products could afford such a long warranty period.

Regardless, the promotion was not highly successful since clients saw no reason to pay the 1% charge on a product they believed should need no repairs for at least five years. Second, competitors offered better promotions and prices that provided short-term benefits.

Atlas Copco's Promotion

In early 1992, Atlas Copco countered SAE's offer. It offered a 30% to 40% discount on all products, regardless of significant losses it would incur. SAE management believed Atlas Copco could afford these losses, since headquarters' policy was market share maintenance and its actions had the parent company's blessing. SAE believed a second reason for Atlas Copco's action was its lack of piston air compressors; SAE and

Ingersoll-Rand carried the piston, screw and centrifugal air compressor lines. It believed Atlas Copco had to offer large discounts to compete with SAE and Ingersoll-Rand.

In addition to its drastic price-cutting action, Atlas Copco offered a free supply of wearable parts and, depending on the particular customer, free service maintenance for two to three years. It also offered free air receivers, a supplementary part, that provided immediate air to the compressor (priced at about P150,000).

SAE thought that Atlas Copco believed it could make money by supplying more expensive spare parts and service. In the air compressor industry, spare parts were specific to individual models; each firm manufactured its own spare parts and usually sold them at excellent profit margins. In addition, SAE believed Atlas Copco was assuming that items provided free would be used indiscriminately, hence needing new parts or service sooner. This situation was beneficial to Atlas Copco since no other air compressor firm could match its offer.

SAE's Countermove

Rather than fight Atlas Copco directly, SAE decided to target another market. Until October 1992, air compressor firms targeted the top 700 corporations in the Philippines; as a result, most sales were made to these prestigious accounts and smaller organizations were not being serviced.

The top 700 corporations needed high horsepower air compressors. Hence, even though sales volume per customer was low, the value of each transaction was high. These clients tended to have fairly sophisticated purchasing departments and frequently secured compressors from the lowest price supplier.

Because SAE believed it could not match Atlas Copco's 30% to 40% discount offer, it decided to target smaller corporations, the top 700 to 1,500. SAE secured names from published lists and generated additional leads from the Securities and Exchange Commission, Board of Investments and the business dailies; referrals from current customers were secured by salespeople. In general, smaller companies needed small air compressors (0.5 hp to 40 hp). The sales value of each transaction would be smaller but Risos believed that large volumes might compensate.

The possibility of selling to smaller corporations led Risos to decide on local assembly of air compressors; costs were reduced so that these products were more affordable for smaller firms. In general, these firms purchased reconditioned air compressors from hardware shops and, before being approached by SAE, were unaware of the new product technology. Although SAE generally received a warm reception in initial meetings, it was difficult to convince these firms to buy its air compressors. Payment terms of 50% down and balance on delivery contrasted with 30-day terms for larger corporations.

In October 1993, SAE removed the insurance premium on the SCBP and made the five-year warranty a standard feature for all screw air compressors. SAE management believed this strategic initiative generated significant customer interest and that CompAir Broomwade air compressors were perceived as superior, durable and reliable.

SAE Reorganization

To implement its new schemes, SAE reorganized its sales force of five salesmen and one sales director. In 1992, SAE's sales force was divided into five segments according to groups of industries served. Each salesman (applications engineer) was responsible for keeping abreast of activities in his assigned industries. (See Table 2 for industry division by salesman; see Table 3 for sales force information.[1])

Table 2:   Sales Force Allocation by Industry

Name	Age	Education	Years w/SAE	Basic salary (P)	Commission (P)
A	32	B.S.M.E.	7	$199,200	$312,640
B	30	B.S.M.E.	5	$83,850	$9,290
C	29	B.S.M.E.	4	$75,820	$126,430
D	25	B.S.M.E.	2	$67,500	$161,554
E	25	B.S.M.E.	1	$72,250	$18,168
F	25	B.S.M.E.	1	$70,250	n/a

Table 3:   SAE's Sales Force

Salesman	Industry group
1	Food, pharmaceuticals, soap
2	Steel vehicles, Non-metal
3	Semiconductor, electronics, building materials
4	Sugar mills, provincial dealers
5	Textiles, plastic, rubber

When the application engineer system seemed successful, SAE's management ventured further. In 1993, each Product Engineering Unit became a Business Unit (BU) profit center run by a product manager. From July 1993, each business manager prepared his own sales, profit and expense forecast and marketing plans and was responsible for hiring his own sales force. BU managers became very cost-conscious but more people could be hired if justified to senior management; the sales force had expanded to ten. (By contrast, both Atlas Copco and Ingersoll-Rand each had five salespeople dedicated to the air compressor market.) BU managers reported directly to the sales and marketing director, who in turn reported to the CEO.

---

[1] The Sales Director (A in Table 2) received a 2% override on the sales team's sales. In 1993, his commissions also included those earned from several direct accounts. Salesman B handled provincial dealers, considered virgin territory for air compressors.

The Future

As a result of the reorganization, Risos hoped slowly to overcome moves made by his major competitor. He knew the SCBP was a competitive advantage for SAE, that SAE now had more salesmen than its competitors and was more flexible in decision-making. Risos wanted to use these advantages to secure industry leadership but was unsure whether SAE's actions would enable it to achieve this objective. Also, he wondered what actions competitors might take if SAE were successful.

Exhibit 1: Income Statement (million pesos)

Year	1993	1992	1991
Net sales	21.5	18.2	13.6
Cost of sales			
Merchandise inventory, beginning	6.9	4.0	3.3
Purchase	13.0	12.9	9.4
Merchandise inventory, ending	(8.8)	(6.8)	(4.0)
Cost of sales	11.1	10.0	8.7
Gross income on sales	10.4	8.2	4.9
Operation expenses			
Salaries, wages and bonuses	2.1	1.7	1.1
Selling expenses	1.9	1.0	0.9
Transportation and gasoline	0.5	0.5	0.3
Depreciation	0.6	0.5	0.2
Car repairs and maintenance	0.3	0.3	0.3
Installation and commission	0.3	0.3	0.1
Advertising and promotion	0.3	0.3	0.2
Office rental / warehouse	0.7	0.5	0.2
Employee benefit	0.3	0.2	0.1
Telex, telephone and postage	0.3	0.2	0.2
Entertainment	0.3	0.2	0.1
Insurance	0.2	0.2	0.1
Office supplies	0.1	0.1	0.1
Office expenses	0.3	0.1	0.1
Charitable contributions	0.1	0.1	
Professional fees	0.1	0.1	0.1
Miscellaneous	0.3	0.2	0.1
Total expenses	8.7	6.6	4.1
Income before income tax	1.8	1.6	0.7
Provision for income tax	0.6	0.6	0.2
Net income	1.1	1.0	0.4
Retained earnings, beginning	0.4	0.4	10.0
Stock dividend		1.0	(1.0)
Retained earnings, ending	1.6	0.4	0.4

Map of Singapore

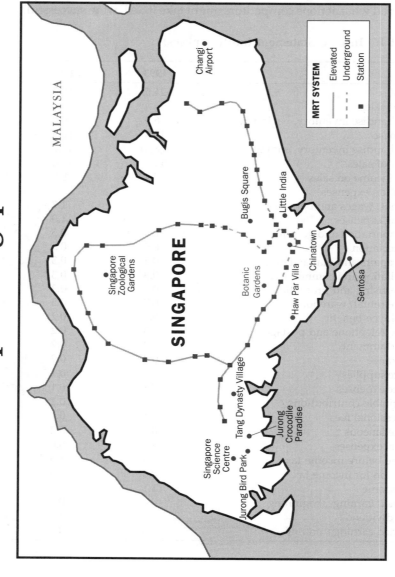

MALAYSIA

SINGAPORE

Changi Airport

Bugis Square

Little India

Chinatown

Sentosa

Singapore Zoological Gardens

Botanic Gardens

Haw Par Villa

Tang Dynasty Village

Jurong Crocodile Paradise

Singapore Science Centre

Jurong Bird Park

MRT SYSTEM

Elevated
Underground
Station

Singapore Overview[1]

Background. Singapore is a city state; land area of 641 sq. km. with a coastline of 193 kilometers. Singapore comprises the island of Singapore and 57 smaller islands; Peninsular Malaysia is to the north and east, Indonesia to the south. Its 3.1 million population is Chinese (78%), Malay (14%), Indian (7%), other (1%). The Chinese are Buddhist or atheist, the Malays generally Muslim; others are Hindu, Christian, Taoist, Sikh, Confucianist.

Singapore's official languages are English (language of administration), Malay (national language), Mandarin and Tamil. The government encourages the use of Mandarin rather than other Chinese dialects (e.g., Hokkien, Teochew, Cantonese, Hainanese, Hakka, Foochow). Singapore's climate is tropical, warm with high relative humidity, moderated by prevailing cool sea breezes; heaviest rainfalls are from November to January. Temperatures average 31°C in the day and seldom fall below 23°C at night.

Political. Singapore was under British rule (and Japanese wartime occupation) from 1867 to 1955, when a constitution introducing limited self-government was adopted. Singapore achieved self-government in 1959; in 1963, it joined the Federation of Malaysian States. In 1965, conflicts with the Malaysian government led Singapore to withdraw from the federation and become an independent country. The People's Action Party (PAP) won the 1966 election; there were no major opposition parties from 1968 to 1981 and Singapore was effectively a one-party state. Lee Kuan Yew, Singapore's first prime minister (1959–90), was succeeded by his deputy Goh Chok Tong in November 1990. Singapore held its first direct presidential elections on August 28, 1993; Ong Teng Cheong became Singapore's first ever directly elected president.

The president is the head of state (six-year term, previously ceremonial), now elected by universal adult suffrage (citizens over 21 years of age). Executive authority rests with the Cabinet, led by the prime minister, appointed by the president. Advised by the prime minister, the president appoints ministers to form a Cabinet. In January 1991, Parliament passed a constitutional amendment giving the president veto over senior civil servant appointments and custodial power over Singapore's financial reserves and religious matters.

The Singapore Constitution ensures a unicameral parliamentary system based on universal adult suffrage. In September 1988, the number of Members of Parliament was increased from 79 to 81. For the 1991 general elections, 60 constituencies were reorgan-

---

[1] The Republic of Singapore.

ized into 15-group representation constituencies; each elects four representatives, one must be a member of an ethnic minority group.

The judicial structure comprises 10 district courts, 11 magistrate courts, one juvenile court and one coroner court. The Supreme Court, presided over by the Chief Justice, comprises the High Court, the Court of Appeal and the Court of Criminal Appeal. Singapore's laws are based mainly on the British judicial system. Parliamentary bills become laws when passed by Parliament and approved by the president.

Social. Since 1987, to achieve its goal of four million population, the government has encouraged Singaporeans to have three or more children per family by offering comprehensive and generous tax incentives. The number of Singaporeans aged 64 and above will rise four-fold by 2030 to comprise 20% of the population. The government discourages dependence on the state; rather, workers and employers each contribute 20% of the employee's wage to a compulsory savings scheme, the Central Provident Fund (CPF); this covers retirement, home ownership and health needs. Members can withdraw savings at age 55 but must set aside at least S$33,800 to provide for retirement.

All males 18 and above must complete 24 or 30 months of national service; the period varies according to rank attained; the army is 45,000 strong. Children receive ten years' formal education from age six at 220 primary and 141 secondary schools. Singapore has two universities and three polytechnics.

Despite its informal atmosphere, Singapore has tough laws against drug trafficking and abuse (convicted offenders trafficking in over 15 grams of heroin face the death penalty), littering, spitting, chewing gum, vandalism (convicted offenders face flogging with a cane) and jay walking. The Singaporean government has expressed concern over the corrosion of Singapore's "Core Values" (duty to family and to state) and economic performance by unthinking absorption of western values. The government's response to an increasingly educated and volatile electorate, and challenges to authoritarian ways, has been to stress loyalty and a sense of order. Singapore streets are much safer than other Asian cities.

Economy. Singapore is a member of the United Nations (UN), World Bank (WB), International Monetary Fund (IMF), World Trade Organization (WTO), Asian Development Bank (ADB), Asia-Pacific Economic Cooperation (APEC) Forum and Association of Southeast Asian Nations (ASEAN). Singapore has the largest per capita foreign exchange reserves (US$24,000); total foreign exchange reserves (1997) were US$76 billion, fifth in the world. GNP per capita was US$26,400, among the largest in the world; real GDP growth was 5.8% p.a.

The Singaporean government pursues a highly interventionist economic policy; it has deep involvement in many sectors via firm ownership and policy making. Singapore has few natural resources; it is a major oil refining and trading center, importing crude oil and refining for domestic consumption and export. International companies like Shell, Mobil, British Petroleum, Exxon and Caltex are all involved in refining operations.

In 1994, manufacturing accounted for 27% GDP; the electronics sector was Singapore's largest single industry (over 40% industrial output). Financial and business services was the largest sector (29.5% GDP). Major export destinations are (1994): U.S. (19.1%), Malaysia (18.8%), Hong Kong (8.7%). Major import origins are (1994): Japan (22%), Malaysia (16.4%), U.S. (15.3%). The tourism industry is important economically as a source of domestic employment and foreign exchange earner; 1994 arrivals were 6.89 million (more than twice the population).

Singapore encourages foreign investment; it offers a comprehensive range of tax incentives to spur investment, particularly in high-technology industries. However, limits are placed on foreign investment in certain key industries (e.g., four major local banks, Singapore Airlines, Singapore Press Holdings).

The Monetary Authority of Singapore (MAS) (established in 1971) performs many functions normally associated with a central bank; it regulates the offshore financial (relatively liberal) and domestic (tightly controlled) systems. Currency issue is the responsibility of the Board of Commissioners of Currency. Banks are classified as: full-license (transact all types of banking business); restricted-license (restricted to a single banking office) and offshore-license (prohibited from accepting Singapore dollar deposits from residents).

Despite high economic growth rates, tight monetary and fiscal policies (eased somewhat in 1995) have controlled inflation. In the mid-1990s, a strengthening Singapore dollar somewhat affected international competitiveness, but this was partly offset by productivity gains.

Singapore weathered the Asian financial crisis well. As it competed directly with Korea (and Taiwan) in value-added manufacturing, it let its currency slide 16% (relative to the Korean won's 50% drop) to protect export markets. The Taiwanese dollar kept pace with the Singapore dollar and lost 15.5% against the U.S. dollar by year's end.

In June 1993, 195 domestic companies (capitalization S$97.5 billion) were listed on the main Stock Exchange Singapore (SES). SES's electronic over-the-counter market (SESDAQ) listed 30 companies (capitalization S$2.1 billion); Singapore Telecom, listed October 1993, increased market capitalization by 43%. The Singapore International Monetary Exchange (SIMEX) trades futures and options contracts; it has grown over four-fold since 1992 and is one of the world's top three foreign exchange markets. Since the Barings' collapse (March 1995), affecting SIMEX's international reputation, stricter rules to control recklessness in future trading have been implemented.

Infrastructure. Singapore has excellent infrastructure; its 2,989 kilometers of roads (1994), over 95% asphalt-paved, include a 109-kilometer network of eight expressways. An "area licensing scheme" (begun 1975) requires passenger vehicles with less than four people in the busy commercial district to have a license (S$5 per day; S$100 per month). In 1991, a weekend car scheme was introduced to encourage weekend-only use. The 67-kilometer Mass Rapid Transit (MRT) system (operational 1990: cost S$5 billion) has two lines and 48 stations; it carries 600,000 passengers daily.

Singapore's Changi Airport is one of the busiest in the world; it handles over 18 million passengers and almost 700,000 tons of cargo annually. When the third (year

2000) and fourth terminals are completed, handling capacity will reach 50 million passengers p.a. Singapore Airlines (SIA) (part government owned) is a major international air carrier; pre-tax profits (year ending March 1994) were S$871 million (US$555 million). Singapore typically has 700 ships in port; vessels arrive and depart on average every three minutes; it claims to be the world's busiest port in shipping tonnage handled; it vies with Hong Kong to be the largest container port.

Singapore is a major telecommunications center linked to other countries by satellite and submarine cable communications, facsimile, telegraph and telegram services. Singapore Telecom (ST), a local monopoly until 2007, plans a five-year S$2 billion investment to extend satellite transmission and submarine cables, including linking ASEAN members with optical cable submarine systems. Telephone use is universal in Singapore; in 1994 there were 6.2 mobile telephone subscribers per 100 inhabitants.

Power generation (four power stations) and distribution facilities, run by Singapore Power Pte are very efficient; electricity generation (1993) was 18 billion kWh, 6,420 kWh per capita.

Statistics*	June 1991	June 1997	Statistics*	June 1991	June 1997
Per capita GNP	US$11,575	US$23,565	Infant mortality / 1,000	8	5
GDP growth	8.3%	5.8%	Life expectancy (yrs)	n/a	76
Savings (GNP)	n/a	51%	Literacy rate	90.1%	91.6%
Inflation (CPI)	3.4%	1.6%	People per tel.	2.3	2.0
Foreign debt (US$ billion)	0	0	People per doctor	888	667
Pop. (million)	3.0	3.1	People per TV	n/a	2.6
Urban pop.	n/a	100%	Calorie intake (cals)	n/a	3,198
Pop. growth	1.1%	2.0%			

*Secured from *Asiaweek*.

Case 43

Haw Par Villa Dragon World

Clare Chow, Wee Chow Hou
National University of Singapore

In mid-May 1991, Mr. Goh, General Manager of International Theme Parks Pte. Ltd. (ITP), was wondering how to market Haw Par Villa Dragon World (HPVDW), a newly revamped world-class oriental theme park in Singapore, to achieve higher growth. Although ITP was profitable after just eight months' operations, Mr. Goh was worried that attendance rates for locals might reduce when the Park's novelty wore off. He faced two important questions:

- *What strategy he should adopt to maintain and increase long-run visitorship to HPVDW.*
- *How should he deal with threats posed by modernization and/or new opening of competitive parks: Bugis Square, Telok Ayer Market, Sentosa Underwater World and Tang Dynasty Village. Goh had several meetings with his managers; they developed two alternative courses of action:*
  1. *Turn Haw Par Villa into a showpark by adding more shows.*
  2. *Add more rides to the park, thus slanting the theme park to an amusement park.*

Mr. Goh was not sure which alternative to pursue or whether other courses of action should be investigated. He asked Mr. Lee, division manager and Mr. Sim, entertainment manager to make a thorough analysis and report back.

৪୦୯୪

Origin of Haw Par Villa

Haw Par Villa (HPV) aka Tiger Balm Gardens was built in 1931 by the Aw brothers, local businessmen, as part of their private residence; the original HPV occupied 1.9 hectares. Design and construction took over two years and cost $1.2 million,[1] a huge sum in 1931. HPV took its name from the Aw brothers, Boon Haw, the tiger (Haw), and Boon Par, the leopard (Par).

---

[1]All figures in Singapore dollars.

In 1937, the villa was opened free to the public on a regular basis; previously it was opened only during the first three days of Chinese New Year. The villa was renamed "Tiger Balm Gardens"– the namesake of the brothers' flagship product, Tiger Balm, a Chinese herbal ointment. The public was able to enjoy many displays portraying legends in Chinese mythology and ancient folklore. Most themes centered on filial piety, righteousness and obedience to authority, cornerstones of the Confucian ethical system. Opening the park enabled the Aw brothers both to provide the public with a place for relaxation and enjoyment and to promote Tiger Balm. Throughout the park, statues and figures could be seen holding Tiger Balm ointment.

HPV was destroyed in World War II; in 1952, it was revamped (cost: $800,000). In 1954, the Aw brothers dedicated the villa to the public; it became a favorite attraction for foreign and local visitors. Most guide books listed HPV as a must-see showpiece. In 1984, a Singapore Tourist Promotion Board (STPB) survey placed HPV as the fifth most visited tourist attraction; its redevelopment was believed critical in the growth of Singapore's tourist industry. In 1985, HPV was leased to STPB; it invited private-sector proposals for redevelopment. In 1986, the redevelopment project was awarded to International Theme Parks Pte. Ltd. (ITP) on a 40-year lease.

Corporate Background

The new Haw Par Villa was developed by ITP, a 75%/25% joint venture between two local corporate giants, Fraser & Neave Ltd. and Times Publishing Ltd. Fraser & Neave, founded in 1883, had business concerns in beer, soft drinks, ice cream, dairy products, packaging and property development; Times Publishing was a leading publisher. In fiscal year 1990, Fraser & Neave earned $54.3 million profits: Times Publishing, $45.4 million.

HPVDW's debut marked the entry of these two conglomerates into the leisure industry; as major investor, Fraser & Neave appointed the managing agent. ITP was confident HPVDW would continue to be profitable; daily attendance since opening was encouraging. However, management realized that to maintain current success, park attractions had to be continually enhanced.

The new HPVDW design was undertaken by American Theme Park Consultants (ATPC); credits included Knotts Berry Farm (U.S.), Lotte World (Korea) and Expo '86 (Vancouver, Canada). Because of ATPC's creative influence, HPVDW had the ambiance of Disneyland with a generous dose of oriental flavor.

By May 1991, ITP had a full-time cast of 450. The term "cast member" was applied to all park employees, instead of the usual "staff" or "worker." Mr. Lee explained this term was chosen since every member of the company was cast to perform a task, just as if performing in one of the various live shows. The main idea was to promote HPVDW as a "show" rather than a "park." Most cast members were hired one month prior to the Park's official opening (October 1990). Top management received training from major theme parks in the U.S.

New Haw Par Villa Dragon World

Singapore's new first-class theme park opened on October 2, 1990 as Haw Par Villa

Dragon World (HPVDW); the appendage "Dragon World" was intended to distinguish the new park from its predecessor. Redeveloped over two years for $80 million, HPVDW, occupying 9.5 hectares, encompassed land adjacent to the old park ground. Located in Pasir Panjang, on the west coast of Singapore, it was five times larger than the original park (see Exhibit 1 for scenes from HPVDW).

HPVDW was easily accessible by bus or taxi. It had ample parking, over 300 carpark lots and 25 coach lots, directly opposite the main entrance. Carpark charges were $4.00 per entry. Management was considering converting these facilities into a $20 million theme, retail, food and beverage and entertainment complex.

The only Chinese mythology theme and showpark in Singapore, HPVDW attracted over 4,000 visitors the first day. Major draws for visitors were shows and exhibits on Chinese culture, history and traditions. The Park offered unique displays reminiscent of the Aw brothers' collections of colorful statues and figures together with a selection of rides, shows and displays that distinguished HPVDW from other theme parks around the world.

Visitors were greeted with bursts of color from every possible source; even footpaths and waste bins were brightly colored. Live shows, staged at scheduled times, presented Chinese mythology and legends using the latest electronic gadgetry, laser, smoke machines and stereo sound equipment.

The nine major attractions included three theaters with special laser, sound and visual effects: *Creation of the World Theater, Legends and Heroes Theater, Spirits of the Orient Theater*, three open-air theaters for live performances: *South China Sea Amphitheater, Puppet Theater, Four Seasons Theater*; two fun rides: the *Tales of China Boat Ride* – a leisurely cruise through the belly of the 60-meter long giant dragon sculpture – and the *Wrath of the Water Gods Flume Ride* – a faster-paced ride, and the *Xu Mu Kong Plaza*, an area where visitors were entertained with stunts and dance.

Park operating hours were 9:00 am to 6:00 pm; in February 1991, operating hours were extended to 10:00 pm for Sundays and public holidays, the most popular times for local visitors. Extending operating hours increased operating costs marginally. Peak time for park attendance varied: weekdays, 9:00 am to 1:00 pm; weekends, 10:00 am to 2:30 pm. Hourly attendance figures were computed from ticket stub numbers and turnstile counters.

The entrance fee included all rides and shows. In May 1991, entrance fees were $16.00 for adults, $10.00 for children 3 to 12 years; children under 3 years were admitted free. Initially, a majority of the public believed the $16.00 admission fee was too high since entrance was free before the expansion. Management explained the $16.00 included five shows and two rides, $2.29 per show/ride on average. Later, a visitor survey showed the vast majority believed $16.00 was reasonable and that they got their money's worth. Tickets could be purchased at the entrance or at selected retail outlets.

Besides rides and shows, the Park provided food and beverage facilities, souvenir and gift shops, Hospitality and Lost and Found Centers, First Aid Stations and a "Lost-parents" Center (a term chosen to dispel parental anxieties about losing contact with their children that was believed congruent with identifying the Park as a "Fun Place").

The four major food and beverages outlets were: The Artisan Eating House, Bamboo Tea House, The Golden Nest and the Water Gardens Seafood Palace. Both western and Chinese cuisine were served; the food was rated favorably. The Water Gardens Seafood Palace was the only air-conditioned restaurant; refreshment kiosks/carts serving drinks and light snacks were located throughout the park.

Games stalls at *Xu Mu Kong Plaza*, introduced in February 1991, were viewed as a new revenue source. They featured games of skill common to any amusement park. Souvenir shops selling gift items and handicrafts formed an integral element of the Park. Kiosks outside the main park grounds provided similar amenities; some were concessioned to non-HPVDW retail owners but ITP maintained control over prices and items for sale.

HPVDW Attractions

Theaters offered a variety of different entertainment:

- Creation of the World Theater (capacity 240 seats) had 3D multi-image and 2D mixed media presentations. The 17-minute show told tales of earthly creation according to early mythology.
- Legends and Heroes Theater (capacity 240 visitors) was an 18-minute multi-image mixed media presentation featuring a life-sized robotics old man figure who told tales of past heroes and warriors.
- Spirit of the Orient Theater (capacity 500 visitors) highlighted the stories behind many Chinese traditions and practices in a 17-minute multi-screen slide show presentation.
- Four Seasons Theater had open-air seating capacity for 100. Its story telling session, presented by four character actors – Spring, Summer, Autumn, Winter – lasted about 20 minutes.
- The open-air Puppet Theater catered to younger visitors with a fully computerized 20-minute puppet show.
- The South China Sea Amphitheater (capacity 240 seats), an open-air theater with a huge sun shade, was the largest in the park. Its live entertainment included cast members representing elements of nature such as Father Sun, Mother Earth, Fire, Water, Wind and Cloud. Audience members were invited to the stage to mimic the actions of the cast members and to put on impromptu shows; response was generally favorable.

Several park entertainers (e.g., Jazzo, Da-Long, Toh Be, Lee Ming) performed for visitors waiting for shows/rides. Like the Mickey Mouse and Donald Duck characters at Disney Theme Parks, they mingled with visitors.

The *Tales of China Boat Ride* and the *Wrath of the Water Gods Flume Ride* were the most popular rides.

- The *Tales of China Boat Ride* (10 minutes) took visitors on a 16-seater ancient Chinese journey through the belly of a 60-meter long dragon. Visitors witnessed the adventures of the legendary Eight Immortals, tale of Lady White Snake and scenes from the fabled Ten Courts of Hell.

- The *Wrath of the Water Gods Flume Ride* (8 minutes) was a favorite with the young at heart. The most energetic ride available, at its climax, riders plunged about 15 meters down a waterfall.

Park Physical Constraints

It was estimated to take about 4.3 hours for visitors to enjoy all attractions; longer on weekends due to larger crowds and queuing. The park attracted 2,000 to 7,000 visitors daily since its opening; an average of 3,000. HPVDW could accommodate 7,000 visitors at any one time, an average of 12,000 visitors per day. Park capacity was constrained both by actual physical space and kitchen capacity. During the 1991 Chinese Lunar New Year, an uncommonly large number of visitors boosted daily attendance level past 17,000 and entry had to be controlled.

Mr. Lee thought that outside caterers might supply food when kitchen capacities were exceeded; he also considered tendering out food and beverage outlets. He preferred the former option since ITP would exercise direct supervision to maintain food and customer service quality, even though the latter option assured a fixed income stream.

Park Operations

Visitor attendance levels were closely monitored via an on-line reporting system. This information was primarily used to ensure manageable visitor levels so that enjoyment of shows and rides was not hampered by unnecessary long queues. Whenever park attendance was sufficiently high to warrant action, messages were relayed to all managers and key personnel who carried transceivers when on duty. Managers constantly moving in the Park had to decide what, if any, action to take. For example, if the queue for the *Tales of China Boat Ride* was longer then usual, they might call for pocket entertainments (impromptu shows) at the queuing site.

Duty managers were responsible for keeping Park operations running smoothly; standard operating procedure manuals were available for reference. These manuals detailed how particular jobs or actions should be undertaken. For example, all maintenance jobs were to be carried out at night, after operating hours.

Since the Park was positioned as a show, interruptions or distractions were strongly discouraged. As a result, all servicing, clearing and repair work was kept out of view and normally done when the Park was closed. When work had to be done immediately or during operating hours, for example, repainting statues, a sign read "Artists at work." Thus, a job was turned into a performance and the worker presented as a cast member.

The main administrative building was located at the rear of the park grounds. It housed administrative offices, staff canteen, restrooms, rehearsal halls, costume and props rooms and computer facilities.

ITP was organized into two divisions (Finance and Administration comprising two sub-groupings – Administration and Finance and Purchasing; and Park Operations) and five departments (Human Resources, Retail and Merchandise, Advertising and Promotion, Food and Beverage, Sales). A division manager was responsible for day-to-day operations of the sub-departments (see Figure 1). In turn, each department had its own manager.

Figure 1: Organization Structure

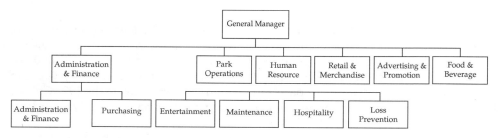

- The Administration and Finance Department was responsible for administration, including finance.
- The Purchasing Department secured all materials; it purchased office supplies, sourced for goods, secured tender quotations and worked closely with Administration and Finance in supply contract negotiations.

The Park Operations division supervised four departments: Entertainment, Maintenance, Hospitality, Loss Prevention and the Radio Control Room.

- The Entertainment Department ensured that all shows and performances were carried out as scheduled. The entertainment manager was responsible for cast member availability, props, support staff and functioning equipment to stage shows. The most important job was to ensure that visitors received good value from the professional and efficient presentation of shows, displays and rides with as little disruption and inconvenience as possible. The basic tenet at HPVDW was that visitors came to enjoy themselves and all possible actions were taken to ensure a memorable and pleasant visit. Certain occurrences were to be avoided at all costs: power failures, malfunctioning light bulbs, non-working sound systems, too long queues and shows canceled because cast members were unavailable. In striving for high degrees of professionalism, certain things could not be done once and forgotten; rather, constant monitoring was the watch-word.
- The Maintenance Department was responsible for ensuring park grounds were litter-free at all times. Every employee, from kiosk helpers to division managers, helped keep the park clean. This department was also accountable for making sure that every piece of equipment was performing efficiently and repairing faulty equipment.
- The Hospitality Department was responsible for visitor queries, missing person

reports, maintaining theater grounds, ticket selling, and overseeing admission, car park, rides and theaters.

- The Loss Prevention Department was responsible for internal and external theft investigations. Fire prevention and safety measures also fell under its jurisdiction.
- The Radio Control Room operated as a message service center. The operator monitored, executed and coordinated messages sent by cast members among themselves. It also monitored Park attendance levels and prepared hourly reports on PAE – Park Attendance Entered; PAL – Park Attendance Left; PAS – Park Attendance Status.

Key personnel in the park were in constant contact with each other via transceivers ("walkie-talkies"). Conversations through these transceivers were kept short and to the point. After several months' operations, a convention concerning call-signs evolved; for example, the duty manager was referred to as "Happy Dragon." Grammar and syntax were not high priorities; rather, messages were passed quickly, clearly, with as few words as possible. In 1991, 53 transceiver sets were available for staff use.

Cast Members

In May 1991, the Park was expanding its pool of 39 full-time performers; the majority had singing and/or acting experience. Most were hired after passing an audition where skills and talents were tested. Once hired, HPVDW provided coaching in a series of dance, vocal and acting classes to polish performers' abilities. HPVDW aimed to have each performer capable of playing all roles she/he might be called upon to assume. HPVDW engaged professional artists, some involved in the selection process, to coach its performers. Successful applicants were awarded generous remuneration, vacation, medical benefits and insurance coverage.

Target Market

HPVDW was designed to appeal to tourists and locals. The local target market comprised families, the younger generations and corporate groups. ITP's business review revealed an adult/child attendance ratio of 9 to 1.

In 1990, despite its small population, Singapore attracted a record 5,322,854 foreign visitors, an average monthly arrivals of 440,000 (Table 1); visitor arrivals were increasing steadily. Mr. Goh, realizing Singapore's large tourist base, wanted to capture a substantial portion of this market. He also realized attendance would decline unless locals made repeat visits or the tourist participation rate increased. STPB's annual report showed that the majority of tourists were female, arrived by air, were on holiday and stayed in hotels. By studying tourist characteristics, HPVDW management hoped to market more effectively.

Before HPVDW operations commenced, ITP projected a visitor profile comprising 60% tourists, 30% residents (Singaporean or permanent residents) and 10% Malaysian. However, in mid-May 1991, an in-park survey showed a visitor profile of 30% tourists, 60% residents and 10% Malaysians. Mr. Goh wondered why more tourists were not visiting the Park; he estimated attendance included only 0.27% of arriving tourists. Furthermore, there was no evidence of repeat visits from local residents.

The vast majority of tourists were free, independent travelers (FIT or non-group tours). (See Exhibit 2 for a detailed breakdown of visitor arrivals by purpose of visit; see Exhibit 3 for Singapore arrivals by residence.) An ITP survey disclosed that 80% of HPVDW visitors were satisfied and rated the park favorably; foreign visitors tended to rate the Park more favorably than locals.

Table 1:   Total Visitors to Singapore

Visitor arrivals (1981–90) (millions)

1981	2.83	1986	3.19
1982	2.96	1987	3.68
1983	2.85	1988	4.10
1984	2.99	1989	4.83
1985	3.03	1990	5.32

Visitor arrivals (January 1990 to April 1991)

Month	Total	Month	Total
January, 1990	433,549	September, 1990	492,569
February, 1990	425,093	October, 1990	435,285
March, 1990	445,492	November, 1990	448,583
April, 1990	430,812	December, 1990	488,784
May, 1990	410,356	January, 1991	432,286
June, 1990	409,917	February, 1991	363,560
July, 1990	409,917	March, 1991	403,170
August, 1990	474,880	April, 1991	418,318

Promotion

HPVDW forecast first-year (end September 1991) total attendance of 1.7 million. To meet this target, a conscious effort was made to capitalize on the Park's unique displays, rides and shows. Promotions included press releases and advertisements in news dailies, travel trade magazines, life style magazines and selected news agencies.

To maximize exposure to Singapore visitors, HPVDW worked closely with other tourist industry sectors. HPVDW attractions were advertised in 61 hotels; tour agencies offered packages for HPVDW visits. Admission tickets were sold to tour agents at wholesale price, then resold to visitors in packaged tours, inclusive of hotel / HPVDW transportation, at a higher price. Unlike other tourist attractions, HPVDW did not offer incentives to tour guides; as a result, many tour guides were reluctant to bring clients to HPVDW.

HPVDW was featured in "Variety Tonight," a regular TV show. Promotional advertisements were also placed regularly in both English and Mandarin daily newspapers. Besides newspaper, television and radio advertisements, extensive additional efforts were made to promote the park locally. HPVDW was involved in community work; in December 1990, 259 under-privileged children were invited for a free visit. In February 1991, a promotion scheme motivating taxi drivers to bring passengers to the park was introduced. ITP had just initiated a coloring contest for children. (See Exhibit 4 for an HPVDW advertisement in *The Straits Times*.)

HPVDW catered to a demand for theme parties. Some corporations were interested in having parties where staff could be involved in a play or act (e.g., dress up in ancient Chinese costumes). ITP created unique theme parties, minimum charge of $50.00 per person for a 100-person minimum. Advertisements were placed in Teleview, a local information channel.

STPB played a significant role in promoting HPVDW abroad. ITP also sent several members overseas to market HPVDW. Recently, a giant poster featuring the Park was erected at the Marriot Marquis Hotel in New York City.

Financial Performance

ITP was fully self-funding, not subsidized by any public funds. Performance was measured by per capita cost and per capita spending. Per capita cost was the total operating cost divided by the total number of visitors; per capita spending was total visitor spending divided by the total number of visitors. Total visitor spending included admission fees plus all revenues from sale of souvenirs, games stalls, car park charges and food outlets. Total operating cost comprised both fixed and variable costs.

From HPVDW opening to May 1991, average per capita spending was greater than estimated per capita cost. Mr. Lee was satisfied that per capita spending and per capita cost met his projected figures. Data available to management indicated that locals spent less on souvenirs, food and beverages than tourists.

In addition to revenues related to park attendance, HPVDW received sponsorship revenues. For example, the *Spirits of the Orient* theater was sponsored by Kodak; the flume ride by Fraser & Neave. Sponsorship was announced at the beginning of each sponsored show. ITP planned to seek corporate sponsors for its other attractions.

For fiscal year 1991, operating costs were 20% below budget; Mr. Lee was unsure of the cause, insufficient spending or efficient cost control? He preferred high variable costs to high fixed costs since variable costs changed with attendance levels. Unit per capita expense, used to evaluate each department, provided Mr. Goh with better control over operating expenses. He was able to identify which shows, exhibits or kiosks were profitable.

Other Tourist Attractions in Singapore

According to a 1990 STPB report, 55.15% of tourists stayed for two days or less; the average length of stay was 3.44 days. HPVDW faced competition from other tourist attractions for visitors' limited time in Singapore:

Tang Dynasty Village: A theme park highlighting the legends, folklore and tales of the Tang Dynasty, was scheduled to open in September 1991 (cost: $70 million). It was publicized in the *Sunday Times* (February 3, 1991) (Exhibit 5). Tang Dynasty Village was the closest competitor on two counts: first, it was located nearby; second, its theme was the Tang dynasty period, a subset of the legends, tales and mythology of ancient China receiving close attention at HPVDW.

In 1991, **Bugis Square**, historically a tourist favorite, was in the initial stages of redevelopment; whether it would regain its past popularity was unclear. The most germane competitive dimension was its evening hours. Bugis Square hoped to rekindle a 1950s/1960s ambiance with cabaret-style entertainment, complete with hostesses. Bugis of yesteryear was a showpiece, due in part to its unforgettable transvestite population. These "Ladies of the Night" were a tremendous draw, a "show" in their own right.

Redevelopment plans for the new Bugis Square included a 150-seat theaterette featuring shows unique to the Bugis sub-culture. Two to three shows per night were planned on two spot-lit stages. Other features included 105 stalls, hawker food fare, six retail shops and an English style pub with a live band. When complete, Bugis would compete with HPVDW's shows, decor and cuisine, but not rides.

Sentosa, a 375-hectare island, was a stone's throw from HPVDW. By 1991, Sentosa had invested several million dollars to upgrade many facilities and undertake new construction. In 1990, Sentosa had 2.62 million visitors (45% foreign); increases over 1989 were, 12% – local and 41% – foreign. Major attractions were a man-made swimming lagoon, an elaborate musical fountain, corallarium, Fort Siloso, butterfly park, wax museum and rare stones museum. Sentosa used differential pricing: normal tickets, inclusive of ferry ride, musical fountain shows, unlimited monorail and bus rides, access to lagoon and playground were $3.50 for adults ($3.00 after 5:00 pm), $2.00 for children under 12; major attractions were additional. A second, composite ticket, also included admission to the Pioneers of Singapore and Surrender Chambers, Corallarium, Nature Ramble and Fort Siloso. Ferry services operated from 7:30 am to 11:00 pm (Friday to Sunday – midnight).

The five-star Beaufort Sentosa Resort Hotel, under construction, would allow visitors to stay on the island after operating hours. More late night activities were planned (e.g., concerts, variety and fashion shows). Visitorship increase in 1991 was projected at 12.3%. In the latest Sentosa attraction, Underwater World, visitors secured an undersea view of marine life through a see-through tunnel, unique in the region.

Jurong Bird Park, open daily from 9:00 am to 6:00 pm, was a 20-hectare park featuring 4,000 birds from 400 species, the largest bird collection in Southeast Asia. Admission $5.00 per adult, $2.00 per child, allowed entry to all shows (once daily). A tram ride ($1.00 per adult: $0.50 per child) took visitors around the park. Jurong Bird Park's operations was subsidized by public funds and corporate donations.

Singapore Zoological Gardens, occupying 28 hectares, was home to 1,700 animals from 170 species. Enclosures in the Gardens were designed to resemble closely the animals' actual habitats. In 1990, pandas came from China on a promotional tour; monthly visitor attendance was boosted to well over 200,000, a 46% increase over the previous month's. Admission, including primate, reptile, elephant and sea lion shows (twice daily), was $5.00 per adult and $2.50 per child. The zoo, open daily from 8:30 am to 6:30 pm, offered such other attractions as tram ($2.50 per adult, $1.50 per child), pony and elephant rides. The zoo was highly subsidized by public funds and corporate donations.

The Singapore Science Center displayed well over 500 exhibits covering the physical, life and health sciences. Admission – $2.00 per adult, $0.50 per child – exclusive of shows at the planetarium or OMNI theater (one of few installations worldwide able to screen panoramic omnimax movies). Daily planetarium hours were 10:00 am and 11:00 am; omnimax movies were screened at noon, 1:30 pm, 3:00 pm, 4:30 pm, 7:00 pm and 8:30 pm.

The 47-hectare **Botanic Gardens**, a natural habitat for plants, comprising almost half a million species ranging from orchids to trees, was open daily from 5:50 am to 11:00 pm; at weekends it closed at midnight. There was no admission fee and many tourists visited the garden to enjoy its natural beauty.

Jurong Crocodile Paradise, showcasing 2,500 crocodiles, was open daily from 9:00 am to 6:00 pm; crocodile wrestling shows were at 11:30 am and 3:00 pm. Admission was $4.50 for an adult, $2.50 for a child under 12 years. Besides Jurong, there were two other crocodile farms in Singapore; entry to the farm at Serangoon was free but it had no wrestling shows.

Little India, at Serangoon Road, offered an insight to Indian culture (e.g., Hindu temples, flower garland vendors, shops selling Indian items and exotic Indian food).

Chinatown, encompassing a two-sq. km. area, comprised pre-war shophouses, some still engaged in ancient trades such as traditional medical halls, handicrafts stores and old-fashioned tea houses. Amidst the old and traditional were shopping complexes offering electronic goods, from compact disc players to stereo televisions. Shoppers bargained for the best prices, sometimes 50% off the initial quoted price. Although the decor was shabby, Chinatown was probably Singapore's best place for bargains.

In addition, over 30 other local tourist spots competed with HPVDW for tourist time and resources. Since the tourist trade was very lucrative and contributed significantly to Singapore's GNP, both the Economic Development Board and STPB actively promoted its attractions to potential visitors. All attractions featured above received equal promotional exposure. (For average lengths of stay, see Table 2.)

Major Management Concerns

Management was determined to resolve several issues, many of a teething nature. First, visitors complained about the weather and indicated that HPVDW should offer protection from the scorching heat and occasional downpours. In several instances, visitors demanded refunds because heavy rain resulted in cancellation of shows. HPVDW was considering installing a fogging system to cool the entire park; also, trees were being planted to provide shade but these would take time to grow. The South China Sea Amphitheater's giant canopy provided some protection against the sun. In January 1991, in a pilot scheme, 5,000 umbrellas were purchased for visitor use during adverse weather. After three months, HPVDW found only 10% were returned; visitors kept them when they left the park.

Table 2:   Average Length of Stay at Tourist Attractions

Attractions	Average no. of hours needed to visit all the sites
Tang Dynasty Village	Not accessible
Bugis Square	Not accessible
Sentosa	12
Jurong Bird Park	3.5
Singapore Zoological Gardens	3.5
Singapore Science Center	2
Botanic Gardens	1
Jurong Crocodile Paradise	1
Chinatown	3
Little India	1.5

Source: Singapore Tourist Promotion Board (STPB).

The second major concern was the recruitment of talented performers and instructors; there was a high turnover of part-timers. Good performers and instructors were difficult to identify in Singapore even though, unlike other establishments, HPVDW paid overtime compensation according to National Wages Council (NWC) guidelines. Basic pay was also very competitive. HPVDW found that movie companies and TV stations offered actors and actresses broader audience coverage and exposure. Mr. Lee wondered how to resolve this problem.

Decision to Add More Shows or More Rides

HPVDW management believed the Park's success depended primarily in its "product content." For HPVDW to continue to attract visitors, a certain degree of fluidity or change had to occur. A ride's lifespan was normally three to five years; statue displays provided very little flexibility and were neither easily moved nor could their content change. As a result, emphasis was on live performances and shows; these provided more flexibility and management was confident of HPVDW's success as a show park. Currently, five scheduled shows were offered in five different theaters (Table 3). Showtimes for automated performances were fixed; showtimes for live performances varied. Schedules were updated as and when necessary and distributed to visitors at the entrance.

In seven months of operation, none of the live shows had changed; although change was believed necessary to attract repeat visitors, the lifespan of individual shows had not been established. In February, two new shows were staged in conjunction with the Chinese New Year; visitorship jumped considerably.

All shows were performed in English; local senior citizens who could not understand were disappointed. Shows were choreographed to involve as much audience participation as possible. Costumes were designed to be colorful and vibrant. Songs and musical scores were a unique blend of western and oriental sounds. All shows,

Table 3: Show Schedule

| | No. of shows per day | | Showtimes (weekend, if different) | |
	Weekday	Weekend	First show	Last show
Spirits of the Orient	17	25	9:30 am	5:30 pm (9:30 pm)
Legends and Heroes	17	25	9:30 am	5:30 pm (9:30 pm)
Creation of the World	16	24	10:00 am	5:30 pm (9:30 pm)
South China Sea Amphitheater	4	5	11:00 am (10:30 am)	4:00 pm (7:45 pm)
Four Seasons Theater	3	4	11:30 am (11:00 am)	3:30 pm (7:30 pm)
Artisan's Plaza	2	3	11:00 am	3:00 pm (4:00 pm)
Phototaking sessions with park characters AM	5	5	9:00 am	11:00 am
PM	1	3	5:20 pm (5:30 pm)	5:00 pm (6:30 pm)

musical scores and park characters, were copyrighted and specially tailored to the Park's theme.

Mr. Lee investigated the possibility of contracting shows from abroad and sent Mr. Sim to China to identify some Mandarin shows comprising a mixture of acrobatics, opera and play. If he should pursue this route, Mr. Goh wondered what level of Chinese tradition should be offered; Beijing shows were more traditional than in Shanghai. At present, HPVDW found it more cost-effective to produce shows in-house than to contract with outside performers. The cost to produce a live show in-house ranged from $5,000 (simple show, four performers) to $200,000 (full scale live show with special effects). Management was concerned that relatively few experienced and talented performers and instructors were available in Singapore.

Considering Mr. Lee and Mr. Sim's information, Mr. Goh had to consider carefully the alternatives available to ITP. He had to decide whether to maintain the status quo or to implement change. If changes were to be made, he had to decide what sort of changes were appropriate to ensure HPVDW's continued success.

Exhibit 1: Scenes from Haw Par Villa Dragon World

Exhibit 2: Summary of Characteristics of Visitor Arrivals from Major Markets – January 1991 (%)

Characteristic	Total	ASEAN	Japan	India	Taiwan	HK.	Korea	U.K.	Germany	Scandi-navia	Nether-lands	France	Australia	N.Z.	U.S.
Mode of arrival	100.00	100.00	100.00	100.00	100.00	100.00	100.00	100.00	100.00	100.00	100.00	100.00	100.00	100.00	100.00
Air	79.95	65.71	88.60	86.88	78.03	83.57	87.59	82.94	80.61	75.34	83.97	83.65	8.94	83.25	85.92
Sea	7.53	19.33	2.35	2.59	3.28	1.97	6.25	3.50	5.68	4.48	5.59	3.11	2.40	2.04	5.17
Land	12.53	14.96	9.06	10.53	18.69	14.46	6.16	13.56	13.71	20.17	10.45	13.24	12.66	14.72	8.91
Sex	100.00	100.00	100.00	100.00	100.00	100.00	100.00	100.00	100.00	100.00	100.00	100.00	100.00	100.00	100.00
Male	61.88	63.57	57.12	76.76	61.82	68.59	55.07	59.74	60.66	60.39	62.11	64.87	54.63	54.75	66.34
Female	38.12	36.43	42.88	23.24	38.18	31.41	44.93	40.26	39.34	39.61	37.89	35.13	45.37	45.25	33.66
Age group (years)	100.00	100.00	100.00	100.00	100.00	100.00	100.00	100.00	100.00	100.00	100.00	100.00	100.00	100.00	100.00
14 and below	5.75	5.64	3.06	6.08	3.99	3.53	3.78	5.65	2.44	4.20	2.67	4.96	13.13	9.99	4.75
15–19	2.66	2.97	1.61	2.17	1.12	0.91	0.99	2.01	0.88	2.00	0.77	1.32	7.80	6.31	1.31
20–24	8.61	10.86	8.90	9.37	6.25	6.32	3.87	7.14	5.84	12.08	6.24	5.20	8.92	10.62	6.15
25–34	26.14	29.57	21.39	35.48	28.27	34.60	16.04	23.83	28.97	27.87	25.24	28.07	19.91	26.31	21.28
35–44	24.15	27.69	21.10	25.14	28.65	29.94	25.65	18.88	21.67	16.84	19.12	25.75	22.31	19.64	23.93
45–54	17.32	14.18	20.40	11.90	14.41	13.52	24.52	18.79	23.46	20.22	21.33	18.16	17.87	16.04	20.37
55–64	9.93	5.70	16.00	6.42	10.43	7.50	18.42	14.08	10.63	10.75	14.91	10.15	6.75	7.44	12.14
65–& above	4.72	2.25	7.14	2.41	6.29	3.32	6.03	9.14	5.69	5.57	9.16	5.87	2.86	3.11	9.49
Not stated	0.71	1.14	0.39	1.03	0.58	0.36	0.70	0.48	0.42	0.47	0.57	0.53	0.45	0.55	0.57
Average age (years)	37.82	35.22	41.51	34.89	39.16	37.27	43.47	40.61	40.52	38.37	42.31	39.22	33.77	34.20	41.35
Purpose of visit	100.00	100.00	100.00	100.00	100.00	100.00	100.00	100.00	100.00	100.00	100.00	100.00	100.00	100.00	100.00
Holiday	61.94	46.31	87.78	43.33	65.64	47.46	72.86	67.56	68.61	75.61	61.39	58.04	67.50	62.48	45.03
Business and pleasure	11.44	14.83	6.47	14.94	14.78	28.60	6.07	10.36	8.76	7.21	11.10	16.57	6.45	5.72	18.51
Business	3.51	4.48	0.86	4.24	3.27	5.97	6.50	3.60	2.53	2.89	3.53	3.43	2.20	2.18	7.01
In transit	9.76	9.81	2.21	9.49	6.54	6.76	4.86	11.05	12.06	8.15	15.76	12.77	15.86	20.02	19.36
Convention	0.35	0.71	0.06	0.32	0.28	0.62	0.42	0.10	0.11	0.13	0.12	0.24	0.23	0.10	0.20
Official mission	2.85	3.90	0.32	9.65	1.76	5.16	1.41	2.54	1.06	1.49	2.43	1.75	3.37	3.84	4.24
Education	0.43	0.93	0.03	0.59	0.24	0.33	0.59	0.13	0.06	0.15	0.22	1.12	0.19	0.04	0.36
Others	4.79	9.71	1.10	7.73	3.05	2.84	3.87	2.34	2.73	2.39	2.61	3.21	1.93	2.81	2.65

Exhibit 2 (cont'd)

Characteristic	Total	ASEAN	Japan	India	Taiwan	H.K.	Korea	U.K.	Germany	Scandinavia	Netherlands	France	Australia	N.Z.	U.S.
Type of accommodation	100.00	100.00	100.00	100.00	100.00	100.00	100.00	100.00	100.00	100.00	100.00	100.00	100.00	100.00	100.00
Hotel	73.04	52.08	93.27	54.95	82.88	76.52	89.13	76.77	76.95	81.11	76.34	77.52	74.19	72.25	76.97
Residence of friends/relatives	12.25	20.40	2.02	26.50	7.71	15.79	3.33	12.72	5.91	6.84	10.11	9.85	14.77	16.51	13.03
Others	3.78	7.21	1.53	6.03	2.54	1.77	3.06	2.46	2.96	2.72	2.53	2.50	1.59	2.10	1.96
No accommodation required	5.84	10.09	1.78	3.82	2.35	3.18	1.74	1.83	7.49	5.91	7.76	5.50	7.82	7.20	6.08
Frequency of visit	100.00	100.00	100.00	100.00	100.00	100.00	100.00	100.00	100.00	100.00	100.00	100.00	100.00	100.00	100.00
First visit	38.96	11.90	61.55	37.53	51.12	31.07	73.78	47.51	49.34	53.18	40.03	42.38	31.78	31.69	38.68
Re-visit	53.86	77.27	25.76	52.63	44.02	66.24	22.49	51.06	46.84	44.95	57.50	53.29	67.24	67.46	59.38
Travel arrangement	100.00	100.00	100.00	100.00	100.00	100.00	100.00	100.00	100.00	100.00	100.00	100.00	100.00	100.00	100.00
Package/group travel	26.79	7.32	75.53	13.60	38.55	17.10	74.12	8.22	21.66	18.44	12.97	17.10	8.83	8.35	13.05
Non-package/group travel	65.01	78.56	22.16	70.75	54.19	78.45	21.84	86.33	71.06	77.02	81.28	73.07	87.03	86.47	83.29
Length of stay (days)	100.00	100.00	100.00	100.00	100.00	100.00	100.00	100.00	100.00	100.00	100.00	100.00	100.00	100.00	100.00
Under 1	12.08	21.38	5.10	9.06	9.61	7.41	4.89	8.57	13.46	8.67	14.97	12.00	10.96	10.27	14.57
1	19.68	19.75	15.69	12.78	23.75	22.12	22.54	18.66	25.63	20.38	26.34	24.06	20.27	23.49	24.96
2	22.49	15.42	27.54	13.10	37.67	27.74	58.18	23.81	23.75	21.11	22.54	21.49	18.56	21.17	19.08
3	17.46	10.74	35.97	14.85	10.93	14.99	6.26	20.21	15.96	16.88	14.63	15.75	13.76	14.58	12.88
4	8.17	6.11	10.13	11.08	5.60	8.03	3.38	9.57	7.76	14.08	6.53	7.43	8.86	8.10	7.42
5	4.09	3.98	2.32	6.49	2.97	4.72	1.19	4.36	3.15	6.03	3.30	5.26	5.87	5.18	4.29
6	2.82	2.99	0.78	5.40	1.70	2.49	0.57	2.57	4.50	3.55	2.45	2.32	5.21	3.77	2.88
7	2.25	2.57	0.58	3.95	1.31	3.00	0.59	2.04	1.47	2.16	1.60	2.56	3.31	2.65	2.85
8–10	3.27	4.14	0.77	5.20	2.42	3.39	0.52	2.97	1.51	2.94	2.79	3.52	5.57	3.32	4.09
11–14	3.97	7.03	0.62	9.15	2.26	2.93	0.91	3.12	1.38	2.18	2.14	2.76	3.72	3.35	3.19
15–29	2.26	2.84	0.37	5.15	1.32	2.04	0.66	3.25	1.17	1.64	1.90	2.11	2.86	3.07	2.83
30 and over	1.46	3.06	0.13	3.78	0.85	0.86	0.30	0.86	0.27	0.37	0.81	0.75	1.06	1.05	0.97
Average length of stay (days)	3.44	3.87	2.64	5.20	2.76	3.30	2.18	3.48	2.64	3.24	2.84	3.17	3.79	3.48	3.31

Exhibit 3: Visitor Arrivals by Country or Residence (1970, 1980, 1987–90)

Country of residence	Thousands						Annual percentage change			
	1970	1980	1987	1988	1989	1990*	1978–1988	1988	1989	1990
Total	521.7	2,562.1	3,678.8	4,186.1	4,830.0	4,375.9	7.4	13.8	15.4	10.7
Asia										
ASEAN	172.2	1,028.0	1,074.0	1,158.0	1,257.0	1,146.4	3.1	7.8	8.5	14.0
Japan	33.6	287.4	541.4	682.4	841.4	816.2	12.5	26.0	23.3	17.3
Hong Kong	16.9	82.5	125.1	124.1	147.5	161.5	9.1	(0.8)	18.3	31.7
India	20.0	85.5	243.5	203.7	194.1	178.7	13.8	(16.3)	(4.7)	10.1
China and Taiwan	4.8	57.0	165.0	173.5	248.3	210.2	18.9	5.2	43.1	5.5
Other countries	18.0	105.9	195.4	244.9	308.0	288.1	13.9	25.3	25.8	14.5
Australia and New Zealand										
Australia	77.0	239.2	330.2	361.5	450.2	386.5	4.7	9.5	24.5	2.6
New Zealand	8.8	63.0	76.5	79.1	86.7	62.3	4.3	3.4	9.6	(15.7)
Europe										
U.K.	37.1	128.4	195.2	253.6	281.3	244.2	9.8	29.9	10.9	6.9
Germany	7.5	73.0	93.3	118.5	140.6	114.9	8.0	27.0	18.6	(0.8)
Netherlands	6.3	47.1	48.2	63.9	70.9	62.7	5.7	32.6	10.9	4.8
France	5.9	40.2	47.5	63.1	68.8	62.3	5.5	32.8	9.0	5.3
Italy	4.4	26.3	37.3	53.5	55.0	48.9	9.9	43.4	2.9	3.3
Other countries	17.2	98.4	197.7	258.1	284.5	244.5	13.7	30.6	10.2	6.3
America										
U.S.	76.6	135.8	211.4	226.8	248.0	217.1	6.0	7.3	9.4	5.2
Canada	6.8	20.9	36.6	42.6	55.3	49.5	8.9	16.4	29.6	12.6
Other countries	4.6	15.4	12.6	12.4	12.8	12.3	2.4	(1.6)	3.2	10.3
Africa	1.1	10.5	31.5	46.6	55.0	44.0	19.9	47.9	18.0	(0.5)
Others and not stated	2.9	17.6	16.4	19.8	24.6	25.5	3.2	20.7	24.2	30.7

*Jan–Oct data.

Note: Figures exclude Malaysian arrivals by land. For 1970, they excluded other arrivals by land and Malaysian arrivals by air and sea.

Source: Department of Statistics.

Tang Dynasty to Open at Night

SINGAPORE'S S$70 million Tang Dynasty Village, scheduled to open on target some time between July and September, will operate at night to cater to incentive groups, tourists and local visitors.

TDV is looking at evening operating hours up to 22.00, which may be extended to midnight on weekends, said a spokesman from the company.

Night-time activities being planned include light and sound shows and laser and firework displays on festive occasions.

Entrance fees to TDV are now being finalized and it is likely that a multi-tiered pricing system will be adopted.

"We are looking at several packages because the high-end user may want a guide, meals and shows, whereas others may not want everything," the spokesman noted.

He revealed that the range of prices will be around S$15 (US$9) to S$45 depending on the options.

"We will be in a better position to announce our pricing policy closer to the opening date," he said.

To beef up the marketing strength of the attraction, TDV has appointed industry veteran and former chief of the Singapore Tourist Promotion Board Mr. K.C. Yuen as advisor, and Ms. Lynn Tan and Mr. David Tan as sales managers.

Flexible

Said Mr. Yen, who is president of Meeting Management: "We want to, and it's important for us to work very closely with the industry. Our basic philosophy is to be market oriented. We will be flexible and package whatever the market wants."

TDV's participation in major trade shows and the STPB's recent promotions to Taiwan and Australia has resulted in several enquires from companies interested in representing the village.

TDV appointed a Japanese representative in mid-1990.

Source: *The Sunday Times*, February 3, 1991.

Case 44

Procter and Gamble:
Always/Whisper

Lau Geok Theng
National University of Singapore

In early 1988, executives from Procter and Gamble's (P&G) Singapore office were pondering what strategy to adopt in introducing a name change for P&G's feminine pad products, from Always to Whisper. Since the Singapore operation increasingly depended on P&G Japan (which used Whisper for its feminine pad products) for product supply, the time seemed ripe for a name change.

One strategy being considered was to introduce the name change swiftly and rapidly by replacing Always with Whisper products immediately. A second possibility was a phased introduction of Whisper for different product items at different times. For example, the name change could be introduced first for regular Maxi pads, later for thin Maxi pads and still later for pantyliners. A third strategy was to introduce Whisper products into the market side-by-side with Always for a limited period before taking Always products off the market. P&G executives wondered how consumers would react to these strategies and which would result in greatest consumer acceptance of the name change.

∞∞∞

The Company

Procter and Gamble, head office in Cincinnati, manufactured and marketed consumer and household products, many of which were household names; it had operations in 60 U.S. cities and 24 foreign countries. It ranked 14th in the *Fortune* 500 and 42nd among industrial companies worldwide; its products were sold in 123 countries. For year ending June 30, 1987, P&G had US$17 billion in revenues and US$786 million net earnings. Its success was attributed to a commitment to develop and market products that satisfied real consumer needs, continuous innovation even to well-established brands and generating the most profitable returns for shareholders.

P&G's Asia-Pacific regional headquarters, overseeing subsidiary operations in Australia, New Zealand, India, Pakistan, the Philippines, Indonesia, Taiwan, Japan,

676

Thailand, Singapore and Malaysia was in Hong Kong. Its major brands in the region included *Pampers, Always, Head and Shoulders, Rejoice, Oil of Ulan, Clearasil, Camay, Zest* and *Vicks* (Exhibit 1).

Annually at the regional meeting, budgeted and targeted sales and other performance indicators were discussed and set for each product category (e.g., disposables, hair care, soap, health), for each country. Increasingly, P&G employed a strategy of cooperation and coordination among regional operations.

The Singapore Office

Procter and Gamble's Singapore office (70 staff), headed by a managing director, was also responsible for Malaysian operations. The marketing group developed and implemented marketing strategies for P&G's brands in Singapore. Specific tasks included monitoring strategies and actions of competitors, examining consumer profiles and changing tastes and making marketing strategy and marketing mix decisions for each brand. P&G's ultimate goal was to lead competition in market share and profitability.

The sales section was responsible for recruiting and motivating wholesalers and retailers to carry and promote P&G's products. The market research department provided relevant information to aid marketing and sales decisions; research activities were conducted by departmental staff or market research consultants. The finance-accounting department was responsible for accounting matters, personnel department was responsible for staffing.

The Product and the Market

Feminine pads / napkins had been used by women for over 50 years. Their basic functions were to absorb wetness and protect clothing and undergarments. Over the years, many improvements had made the product easier to use. For example, present-day feminine pads could be held in place by being attached to panties rather than by a string. In addition, more highly absorbent materials led to thinner pads offering greater comfort.

The feminine pad or catamenial market in Singapore, valued at $15 million (1987), was larger than for shampoo or disposables; market growth was projected at 2.0% p.a. Feminine pads were typically used by women aged 15 to 50. The market was affected by demographic trends and social values since women bought and used the product discreetly. Product variety was important since women had different experiences with their menstrual cycles.

Always

Always feminine pads were test marketed and introduced in three lead markets (i.e., U.S., Saudi Arabia, Singapore) in 1983. The brand was an initial success: Singapore, 25% market share; Saudi Arabia, 35%; U.S., 25%). In Japan, for trademark reasons, P&G was blocked from using *Always*; *Whisper* was used instead and was successful.

In 1987, *Always* enjoyed 25% of the catamenial market in Singapore. P&G's product range included both maxi (thick) and slim (thin) products; the market was split fairly evenly between these two types. *Always'* unique feature was its "Dri-Weave" topsheet, funnel-shaped holes that drew in wetness quickly and the absorbent material that trapped it. *Always-Plus* had wings (panty protectors) to prevent side leakage and staining.

Competition

In 1988, the feminine pad market in Singapore had three major competitors. Kimberly-Clark's Kotex, introduced 30 years earlier, was market leader with 35% market share. P&G's *Always* (25%) was second; Kao Laurier had 20% market share. Eight other brands competed for the remaining market share.

P&G was the largest media spender; in 1989, it outspent Kotex five times, Kao four times. Kotex spent heavily on media advertising in certain quarters, often associated with new product launches; Kao invested in media advertising year round. All three companies placed two thirds of their media budgets in television, one third in print. *Always* was premium priced: 30% to 50% above Kotex (on a per pad basis) and 50% to 60% above Kao Laurier.

The three major competitors were about evenly matched in product line breadth. However, P&G executives believed *Always* was superior in absorption capability, protection and comfort. *Always* and Kao tended to be used by younger women, Kotex by older women. Kotex tended to be purchased by higher proportions of Malays and Indians. *Always* and Laurier appealed more to highly educated women; Kotex to the less well educated. Kotex was strong in lower income segments; *Always* and Laurier were stronger in higher income segments.

Strategies for a Name Change

Executives in the Singapore office believed introduction of the name change from *Always* to *Whisper* could be used to P&G's advantage by securing media attention; the news value should lead to increased market share. Many strategies were suggested to introduce the name change; three in particular were being favored:

- The name change could be introduced swiftly. Consumers could be informed through four to six weeks of intensive media advertising plus some promotional programs (e.g., inserting *Whisper* name change pamphlets into existing *Always* products). *Whisper* would be introduced to retailer shelves and minimal stocks of *Always* supplied. Consumer attention would be focused intensively on *Whisper* since *Always* products would be phased out. This strategy involved the highest risk since customers who did not understand or accept the name change and continued to request *Always* products might switch to competitor products.
- The name change could be phased in for different items at different times. For example, *Whisper* could be introduced first for regular Maxi pads, then for super-thin pads, later for pantyliners. Sales could be monitored to examine consumer acceptance of the name change. Consumer attention might not be focused only

on *Whisper* as some *Always* products would still be featured. Thus, when *Whisper* regular Maxi pads were introduced, super-thin pads would only be available as *Always*. The danger of this strategy was consumer confusion since individual items would only be available under different brand names.

■ *Whisper* products could be introduced and co-exist with *Always*; consumer acceptance of the name change could be monitored. Consumer attention would not be focused totally on *Whisper* since *Always* products would be available until they were discontinued. This strategy would require the most resources since both brands would have to be stocked, and retailer shelf space would have to accommodate both brands.

The Decision

P&G executives had to make a decision shortly to introduce the name change around March 1989. Once a general strategy was decided, detailed programs (e.g., product packaging, advertising, promotion, retailing and pricing) would have to be planned and implemented.

Exhibit 1: Procter and Gamble's Product Selection

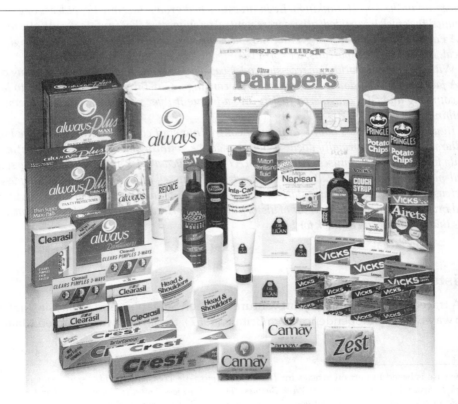

Case 45

Singapore Airlines[1]

Lim Gaik Eng, Ng Seo Hui
National University of Singapore

On October 23, 1992, the Business Times announced that Singapore Airlines (SIA) was losing its status as the airline with highest net earnings, to British Airways. And while SIA slipped to second place, Asian competitors such as Taiwan's China Airlines and Indonesia's Garuda moved up in the Top 10 rankings. Even investors had grown pessimistic; at least one recommended the stock be avoided; others were neutral or suggested that investors continue to hold. SIA Foreign, available to foreign investors, was off more than a third from its 1992 high; SIA Local, limited to Singaporeans, was off 11%.

With the current worldwide recession, over-capacity in the airline industry and rising costs, SIA faced continued downward pressure on earnings. Cut-throat competition led to heavy discounting and SIA considered instituting a frequent flyer program, an action previously unthinkable.

In addition, SIA was having difficulty controlling staff costs; these exceeded one billion dollars in 1992. Its normally docile union was active, winning an agreement for a better formula for calculating bonuses. Although SIA once enjoyed a brisk and profitable trade selling well-maintained used aircraft, in 1992, it was unable to sell any because of a worldwide glut. Increased fuel expenses, greater start-up costs for new routes and an expected decline in interest and investment income as a result of historically low worldwide interest rates, combined for a less than rosy interim outlook for SIA.

History

SIA traced its roots to a 1947 joint venture between Singapore and Malaysia, Malayan Airways. After independence from Britain (1957), the airline was renamed Malaysia

---

[1]The case is based in part on articles in: *The Straits Times, Air Transport World, Asian Business, Aviation Week & Space Technology, Business Week Business Times, Business Traveller, Euromoney, Far Eastern Economic Review, Financial World, Forbes, SIA Annual Report, The Economist, Travel.*

Singapore Airlines. Singapore's separation from Malaysia (1965) eventually led to differences in goals and priorities for the joint airline. Malaysia wanted to build a domestic and regional airline to serve its much larger population scattered across a wide geographic area; Singapore, only 641 sq. km. in area, wanted to build a profitable international airline. The two parted ways in 1972; Singapore inherited most of the long-haul fleet, the international route network and most overseas offices.

Since 1972, SIA was continuously profitable, riding out fuel increases, recessions and world events that discouraged travel. Although listed on the Singapore Stock Exchange since 1985, the airline was still 54% owned by the Singapore government; 12% owned by Singapore Airlines' employees. Strategic alliance partners, SwissAir (0.62%) and Delta Airlines (2.74%) both had ownership stakes; the remaining shares were publicly traded.

In 1992, SIA produced 4.3% of Singapore's GDP, was its largest employer and accounted for 12% of local stock market capitalization. Because of its importance to the national economy, rivals claimed SIA's performance was helped by the Singapore government; it made Changi International Airport one of the world's most efficient and ensured that the unions were docile. By offering foreign airlines use of Changi as a hub, the Singapore government directly helped SIA win overseas landing rights.

Management

Chairman Joseph Pillay stated:

> Our mission remains inviolable: offer the customer the best service we can provide; cut our costs to the bone; and generate a surplus to continue the unending process of renewal.

Top management comprised Chairman Pillay, Deputy Chairman Lim Chin Beng and Managing Director Cheong Choong Kong. Mr. Pillay, a non-executive chairman, was also Singapore's Minister for National Development; Mr. Cheong, an employee since 1984, was a former mathematics professor. According to Deputy Chairman Lim, they worked as a team with no hard and fast rules demarcating lines of communication or even allocation of duties and authority. Although the Singapore government was majority shareholder, top management had full autonomy. This situation was unlike any faced by top management in counterpart national carriers where many decisions, from aircraft purchases to route development and commercial agreements, were referred to boards of directors. By contrast, SIA's board was only involved in key decisions involving the allocation of major resources and the development of business through new investment. Five working committees dealt with General Policy, Management, Staff, International Relations and Investment (Figure 1).

Employee training was a core element of management philosophy, viewed as an investment central to SIA's goal of superior service. All employees, from office assistant and baggage handler to the managing director underwent periodic training. Management believed training was a necessity, not an option. According to Managing Director Cheong, training was not something:

Figure 1: Singapore Airlines Working Committees

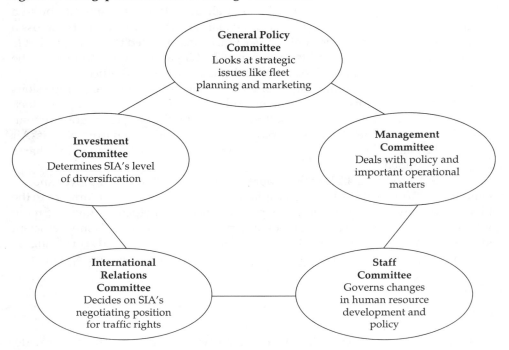

... to be dispensed with at the first sign of a downturn, nor something that can be postponed for operational expediency.... To defer the scheduled training of a subordinate because he cannot be released from a project is a sign of poor planning.... We do not stint on training. We don't waste, but we don't penny-pinch and we'll use the best in training software and hardware that money can buy.

Top management was not only preoccupied with employee training; it paid a great deal of attention to detail. For example, it was involved in the scrutiny and evaluation of toothpicks, napkins and chopsticks.

The Singapore Girl

Gentle hostess in your sarong, you care for me as only you know how. Singapore Girl, you're a great way to fly (SIA advertising slogan).

"The Singapore Girl is the image that makes or breaks us," said Suan Seng Tan, a steward who led in-flight training courses: "The passengers love it." The Singapore Girl was created in the early 1970s as a means to attract passengers, particularly male business passengers, with attentive and high-quality in-flight service from pretty young women in their figure-hugging trademark uniform, the *kebaya*. Although advertisements often featured good-looking, curvaceous young stewardesses, nearly half of the cabin crew were stewards. When the airline began service to New York in 1992, Singapore Girls were featured perching atop the Chrysler Building and the Statue of Liberty. The Singapore Girl campaign was tremendously successful with high recall rates. However, it was not without critics. Said Meana Shivdas of Singapore's Association of Women for Action and Research: "It perpetuates this image of Asian women that we all have almond-shaped eyes, are svelte and never answer back."

Hiring rules stipulated that applicants could not be over 26 years and must speak fluent English; recruitment advertisements asked for applicants who were: "slim and attractive with a good complexion and a warm personality." An air stewardess' five-year contract could only be renewed three times unless she was willing to take a ground job. She could be married, but would have to leave if she became pregnant. SIA's cabin crew salaries started at US$1,200 per month, similar to entry-level salaries on U.S. airlines. However, American salaries rose quickly with seniority; on average, SIA's cabin crew wages were half those for U.S. and European international carriers.

Despite limits placed on stewardesses' job duration, the glamour attached to being a Singapore Girl ensured these jobs were in demand, not only in Singapore, but in countries where SIA recruited, such as Korea and Japan. SIA cabin crew went through one of the longest training programs in the industry, three months. The airline had a cabin crew of 19 for each Boeing 747 versus 15 for U.S. carriers.

Human Resources

Staff Training

Most of SIA's 14,000 employees were retrained annually to maintain high service levels. Airline flight crews were frequently checked for skills and knowledge; pilots went through three mandatory base checks annually. SIA spent an annual average of S$40 million on staff training, yet earned an enviable S$350,000 revenue per employee.

Industrial Relations

SIA subscribed to a flexible wage policy whereby a relatively large portion of employee compensation was tied to company performance, thus reducing operating leverage. However, unions were successful in winning an agreement to base bonuses on returns to non-cash assets; these were historically higher than returns to investment assets.

In March 1992, the Industrial Arbitration Court ordered SIA to negotiate a new salary structure for cabin crew executives (CCEs). SIA's Air Transport Executive Staff Union claimed that CCEs were paid $1,200 per month less than their immediate subordinates. CCEs, who were ground-based and flew only periodically to monitor the standard of in-flight service, were originally in-flight supervisors; they suffered a drop in income when promoted to their present positions. Part of the income loss was salary-structure related; part was a loss of in-flight allowances (e.g., cost of hotel meals). The union sought an increase in basic salary and a ground allowance.

However, SIA's industrial relations manager, Mr. Chew, said, there were no grounds for payment in lieu of in-flight allowances because "they are meant to defray the cost of meals at hotels where cabin crew stay" (away from Singapore). If CCEs did not have to buy such meals in the first place, they should not seek compensation. Before accepting promotions, CCEs were assured by SIA management that half their time would be spend on ground training and appraising cabin crew and that they would work a five-day week. According to the union, CCEs spent annual leaves and days off working on SIA flights to make up income lost after promotion.

Subsidiaries

SIA had 21 subsidiaries including Singapore Airlines Company, Singapore Airport Terminal Services (SATS) Group, Service Quality Center, SIA Properties, SilkAir, Singapore Engineering Company Pte. Ltd. and Singapore Flying College.

SATS Group. In 1992, the SATS Group, comprising three companies – SATS Airport Services, SATS Catering, and SATS Security Services – handled 13.9 million passengers on 46,510 flights at Singapore Changi Airport, a 22.6% increase over 1991. This growth reflected additional capacity from a new, second terminal at Changi Airport that doubled previous passenger handling capacity. SATS serviced 47 scheduled airlines operating out of Changi.

SATS Airport Services combined SATS Apron Services, SATS Cargo Services and SATS Passenger Services. SATS Cargo Services opened Asia's first dedicated express cargo and courier facility in March 1992. The $18 million center processed time-sensitive cargo and provided a base for nine courier companies. SATS Passenger Services opened a new Premier Lounge at Changi Airport Terminal One for First and Business Class passengers.

SATS Catering expanded meal preparation areas and added in-flight catering at Kansai International Airport (Osaka) as part of a consortium. In Singapore, SATS Catering prepared 29,200 airline meals daily.

SATS Security invested over $1.6 million in X-ray screening equipment as part of a continued effort to upgrade services.

Service Quality Center, a joint venture with the National Productivity Board of Singapore, trained over 7,000 employees from more than 100 service and manufacturing firms from July 1991 (opening) to July 1992.

SIA Properties undertook a major investment in Indonesian tourism by acquiring a 20% stake in a hotel project (1992). SIA Properties was involved in 14 Singapore projects valued at $443 million and 26 overseas projects valued at $8 million. Overseas, SIA Properties managed development of three new offices (i.e., Kota Kinabalu [Malaysia], Surabaya and Sendai [Indonesia]) and three new Silver Kris lounges for premier travelers (i.e., Bangkok, Hong Kong and Penang [Malaysia]).

SilkAir. This regional subsidiary (formerly Tradewinds), established in the 1970s, was created to handle inbound tours to Singapore and organize outbound holidays in the Asia-Pacific region as SIA Holidays. On April 1, 1992, Tradewinds took to the skies as SilkAir. In 1992, SilkAir scheduled operations to 14 destinations in Asia Pacific including Malaysia, Burma, Thailand, Taiwan and Indonesia. Its two divisions were an air services division responsible for flight operations and a tours and travel division handling the wholesale marketing of holiday packages. SilkAir took advantage of such parent company resources as SIA hangers for aircraft technical support but maintained its own reservations system. Although its first two years of jet operations resulted in losses, general manager, Mr. Chan claimed it was about to break even.

Singapore Engineering Company Pte. Ltd., formerly, the Singapore Engine Overhaul Pte. Ltd., provided engine overhaul and related services such as aircraft modification; clients were 62 airlines.

Singapore Flying College offered pilot training courses; it averaged 70 trainees in 1992.

Financial Performance[2]

For year ending March 1992, SIA Company's operating profit rose $22 million (2.6%) to reach $864 million; profit after tax was up $34 million (3.8%) at $921 million (Exhibits 1, 2). SIA Company accounted for 92.3% of SIA Group's revenue, 88.5% of operating profit, 97.9% of profit before tax, and 99% of profit after tax; the remainder was contributed by subsidiary companies. Company revenue grew $411 million (8.9%) to $5.013 billion. However, the strength of the Singapore dollar against a basket of major currencies resulted in foreign exchange losses of $224 million. SIA's expenses rose $389 million (10.3%) to $4,149 million, primarily due to higher staff costs (+$205 million [24.5%]), depreciation charges (+$101 million [19.8%]), handling charges (+$49 million [15.6%]), landing and parking fees (+$27 million [13.3%]) and aircraft maintenance and overhaul costs (+$16 million [6.4%]). SIA maintained a conservative depreciation policy; its fleet was depreciated to 20% residual value over ten years. This policy strengthened its balance sheet while lowering profits.

SIA operated the youngest fleet in the world; average plane age was five years, one month versus thirteen and a half years industry-wide. Airplanes were sold after ten years and new planes added at the rate of four to five annually. Fleet expansion, continued even in downturns, was made possible by a cash reserve of $2.1 billion. In 1991, SIA drew $720 million from these reserves to purchase its 10th, 11th and 12th Boeing 747-400 jetliners, dubbed MegaTops. The greater range of MegaTops allowed SIA to fly non-stop to Europe and across the Pacific to North America with fewer stopovers, hence cutting traveling time; they also used 35% less fuel. (See Table 1 for operations summary.)

---

[2]All figures in Singapore dollars.

Table 1: Statistical Summary of Operations

	1991–92	1990–91	1989–90	1988–89
Employee productivity				
Average number of employees	14,113	13,354	12,407	11,485
Revenue per employee ($)	355,183	344,593	381,293	371,946
Value added per employee ($)	193,800	184,858	231,831	195,960
Capacity per employee (tonne-km.)	540,239	497,551	506,190	494,793
Load carried per employee (tonne-km.)	377,751	353,078	374,265	367,723
Yield (cts/ctk)	90.8	95.2	99.2	99.2
Unit cost (cts/ctk)	54.9	58.4	57.8	58.3
Break-even load factor (%)	60.5	61.3	58.3	58.8
Fleet				
Aircraft (no.)	48	43	40	37
Average age (months)	61	57	55	54
Production				
Destination cities (no.)	67	63	57	57
Distance flown (million km.)	142.3	123.6	117	105.8
Time flown (hours)	180,744	157,039	149,355	136,632
Network size (km.)			641,308	615,160
Overall capacity (million tonne-km.)	7,624.4	6,644.3	6,280.3	5,682.7
Passenger capacity (million seat-km.)	47,454.3	41,791.2	39,236.4	36,461.6
Cargo capacity (million tonne-km.)	2,898.3	2,494.5	2,380.7	2,080.8
Traffic				
Passengers carried ('000)	8,131	7,065	6,793	6,182
Passengers carried (million pax-km.)	34,893.5	31,332.2	30,773.7	28,785.1
Passenger seat factor (%)	73.5	75.1	78.3	78.9
Cargo carried (million kg.)	342.8	295.7	278.1	241.3
Cargo carried (million tonne-km.)	1,954.8	1,705.7	1,679.5	1,448.6
Cargo load factor (%)	67.4	68.4	70.5	69.6
Mail carried (million tonne-km.)	55.0	41.8	50.3	42.1
Overall load carried (million tonne-km.)	5,331.2	71.4	4,643.5	4,223.3
Overall load factor (%)	69.9	71.0	73.9	74.3

Operations

SIA was well-known for cabin service and amenities; high-quality in-flight service was a cornerstone of its success. SIA offered greater meal variety per flight and more cabin crew than competitors. In 1992, an information system was installed to advise flight attendants of the preferences of frequent business travelers (e.g., drinks). It also adopted an inertial navigation expert system that allowed technicians to detect navigational faults more quickly.

However, as senior VP for American operations, T.A. Hwang, acknowledged, it was increasingly difficult to distinguish SIA's service from strong competitors such as Japan Airlines, United and Northwest. The airplane's restricted space constrained what could be offered after more obvious amenities such as telephones and extra leg room were added. "You can have the little gimmicks," said Managing Director Mr. Cheong of nonservice changes to airline travel, "but you will find that very soon others will have them."

In 1989, SIA committed $4 million to Outstanding Service on the Ground (OSG), a new program to complement its highly-rated in-flight service. SIA's 3,000 ground staff – customer sales, reservations, ticketing and airport operations – around the world were urged to show a warm interest in customers and to look beyond procedures and problems in helping passengers, in order to turn ground service into a competitive advantage. SIA also developed a Service and Performance Index, used for further organizational improvements, based on passenger feedback.

Singapore Airlines Route Network

Since SIA's home nation of 2.7 million population supplied only 20% of its traffic, SIA always looked abroad to support its growth and large size. It aimed for network growth of 8% p.a. with a commensurate increase in fleet size: 1990, 39 aircraft; 1994, 50; 1997, 71. Projected route expansion involved opening new markets, increasing service to major markets, having more non-stop operations and increasing flight frequencies and capacity. However, route expansion posed more problems than expected; for example, in 1991, Canada abrogated an agreement that would have allowed SIA to fly the Singapore–Toronto route for fear its national carrier Air Canada would be at a disadvantage competing with such a strong carrier. In 1992, SIA and Garuda (Indonesia) renegotiated a December 1990 memorandum of understanding (MOU) governing the busy Jakarta–Singapore route. The memorandum allowed each airline to increase the frequency of its flights and permitted SIA to fly direct to other Indonesian cities. Upon implementation, Garuda's share of traffic plummeted to 27% (1991) from 43% (1990) and SIA swiftly secured over 50% market share. Garuda alleged that SIA's use of larger planes – Boeing 747-400 (capacity: over 400) versus Garuda's Airbuses (capacity: 200–250) – affected its market share. SIA was also allowed to pick up passengers in Indonesia for travel both to Singapore and further destinations. Under the new MOU, SIA ceased using Boeing 747-400s and Garuda and other Indonesian airlines were allowed to fly from any Indonesian city (not just Jakarta) to Singapore and beyond. In 1987, relations with the Malaysian government were strained when Malaysia Airlines claimed unfair competition on the Singapore–Kuala Lumpur route, dominated by SIA largely because of heavy interlining through Singapore.

In order to ensure the carrier was not overly dependent on any single market or route, SIA planned to continue route network diversification so that no country or route accounted for more than 15% of total revenue. SIA hoped to secure a larger presence in the U.S. with flights to more major cities, particularly on the east coast. Service from Singapore to New York via Frankfurt was planned to commence in 1993.

In late 1989, SIA entered a global alliance with Delta and SwissAir that allowed the three airlines to integrate routes and schedules and share ground facilities. As a result, SIA could offer passengers travel to final destinations that SIA itself did not serve, but on carriers that shared SIA's commitment to quality and service. Delta gained a pipeline of Asian passengers that SIA brought to the U.S. mainland, while SwissAir gained passengers for transatlantic flights, brought to Europe by SIA, whose final destination was the U.S.

The International Airline Industry

Besides high levels of capital expenditures, intense rivalry on several routes and customer price sensitivity, particularly in economy class, several factors beyond the airlines' control made the industry a tough challenge.

An international airline's main asset was its route network. For every international route, an airline had to secure the right to fly that route from the government(s) involved. This was accomplished through bilateral negotiations between governments of the involved states; these agreements also covered traffic rights and air freedoms. As a result, many routes were duopolistic; governments typically tried to ensure that distribution of capacity, traffic between countries and airline competitiveness were not heavily tilted in favor of the other country's airline. However, since the distribution of passengers could not be precisely forecast in advance, governments sometimes abrogated these agreements when their national carriers failed to compete effectively.

An airline's route network determined the size and type of its aircraft fleet. For example, it might be more cost-efficient to use larger planes on heavily trafficked routes because fixed costs could be spread effectively. Or, longer routes might require planes with large fuel capacity and/or fuel-efficiency so that refueling time was low.

The high capital expenditures necessary to match aircraft to routes, and potential long lead times to procure aircraft, meant that airlines had to plan capacity well in advance. Such forecasting, based on forecast customer demand, was difficult. Quite frequently, airlines canceled contracts with aircraft manufacturers when an unexpected downturn or recession was less tractable than predicted, particularly if an airline was short of cash. The drawback of canceling contracts was that when demand picked up, airlines might be faced with insufficient capacity.

In some cases, airline management had less than full control over income structures since fares on some international routes were subject to approval from the involved governments. About half an airline's costs comprised direct and/or variable costs; fuel costs and wages were the major components. In high-wage locations, up to 25% of total operating costs could be wage costs. Airlines such as SIA and Cathay Pacific, operating in countries with relatively low labor cost structures and high productivity, were at an advantage. European wage costs were higher; U.S. airlines faced the highest wage costs.

The airline industry was susceptible to unexpected events such as the OPEC oil price increases in the 1970s, the U.S. attack on Libya in the 1980s and the Gulf War in the 1990s; the first event led to increased industry costs, the second and third events led to decreased air travel.

Overall, the industry did not have a profitable history; many airlines showed significant losses in recessions and bankruptcies were frequent. In 1991, the industry as a whole lost US$4 billion. Overall industry growth in passenger traffic, estimated at 5.7% worldwide, hid regional differences; for example, growth in Asia Pacific averaged 9.7% as the result of strong regional economies and a trend towards deregulation, new airports and the opening of new destinations. New airlines such as Asian Airlines (South Korea), EVA Air (Taiwan) and Bangkok Airways (Thailand) were established. These new airlines used lower fares to challenge established carriers. In addition, large U.S. carriers such as United and Northwest were expected to make rivalry more intense.

There was also a growing trend towards strategic alliances in the form of equity tie-ups: KLM joined with Northwest; British Airways planned to invest in USAir; Air China, the People's Republic of China's state-owned international carrier asked SIA to take an equity stake; and Shanghai Airlines(SAL) and United Airways were planning a joint venture.

Competitors

Cathay Pacific was one of the world's most profitable airlines. Like SIA, it was an international carrier from a small territory (Hong Kong) with a similar wide-bodied fleet. However, the roots of its success lay in a very different corporate philosophy. Historically, as the result of Hong Kong's colonial status, Cathay's international interests had always been subordinate to BOAC (now British Airways). Only in 1980, after a lengthy fight with British regulators, did Britain grant Cathay the right to fly to London. This concession implicitly acknowledged that Cathay should have greater freedom to expand, particularly across the Pacific and to Europe. As a result of political constraints on its expansion plans, Cathay became a strong regional carrier. It earned twice as much revenue from Asia than SIA; SIA earned twice as much as Cathay outside Asia. Since travel in Asia was expected to grow at 9.7% p.a. until 2000, Cathay would benefit. However, in 1992, the Japanese recession hurt Cathay more than SIA.

There was much uncertainty regarding Cathay's future when Hong Kong reverted to China in 1997. A key question was whether China would interfere with Cathay's long-range plans and operations. The China factor already had a negative impact as Beijing was delaying several new bilateral air agreements and objections to plans for Hong Kong's new airport were threatening Cathay's expansion.

United Airlines, which purchased Pan American Airline's (Pan Am) Pacific Division in 1986, grew faster than both Northwest and Japan Airlines. United Airlines rivaled Northwest as the largest trans-Pacific airline. Its success resulted from a combination of routes acquired from Pan Am, expansion of operations and aggressive discounting. Aggressive discounting enabled it to win market share from Japan Airlines. Because of its stronger financial position, United grew its Pacific fleet faster than Northwest while simultaneously expanding to Europe. Owning Pan Am's Pacific routes effectively shut out major domestic competitors Delta and Northwest from lucrative opportunities because of tightly controlled route capacity. Its frequent flyer program for international passengers made it a formidable competitor to many Asian counterparts (whose frequent flyer programs, if any, were primarily limited to first- or business-class passengers), because of enhanced ability to maintain/attract customers.

United's plans for a joint venture with Shanghai Airlines (SAL) would provide it with valuable access to the growing Chinese market. Despite these positive factors, United's recent performance (1991, 1992) was not sterling, largely because of the prolonged Japanese recession and destructive domestic (U.S.) fare wars in 1992. United was cutting staff and reducing payroll expenses.

British Airways ranked in the top three international carriers in profitability and traveler ratings. Privatization (1987) was pivotal to British Airway's turnaround, spurring the airline to set goals carefully and achieve overall team effort. The airline plied Europe–Asia routes; it spent more than US$80 million upgrading business- and first-class accommodations. In late 1992, British Airways gained access to critical Asian, South Pacific and Western U.S. markets by outbidding SIA for a stake in Qantas.

Qantas, originally Australia's international carrier, merged with Australian Airlines to give it both international and domestic connections. New air agreements reached by Australia with New Zealand and Hong Kong opened up markets for Qantas, but exposed it to increased competition. The Australian government decided to privatize Qantas by selling 35% of its stake to foreigner buyers; SIA contemplated buying a 10% to 35% stake, even though it was heavily unionized and had an aging fleet, because Australia represented an important market. However, SIA lost to British Airways which secured a 25% stake. The Qantas/British Airways link-up provided benefits to each airline; British Airways secured access to the Asia-Pacific market; Qantas gained access to Europe.

Japan Airlines (JAL), the world's seventh largest airline, suffered heavy losses in 1992 as intense competition exposed weaknesses in its cost structure; JAL recently revised its corporate plans. Since increased competition was anticipated when the new Kansai International Airport (Osaka) opened in 1994, JAL took steps to slash costs and cut down on high expenses; even so, pilots were still driven in chauffeured cars between airport and home and flight attendants received at least US$150 for taxi expenses per trip.

In spite of its cost disadvantage vis-à-vis many leading Asian airlines, Japan Airlines was financially attractive. It had a strong balance sheet (cash-on-hand, US$2.9 billion), a modern fleet, a reputation for good service and access to low-cost loans from Japan's Export-Import Bank. Running counter to a growing industry trend of airlines entering operational or equity tie-ups, JAL had no such plans; Chairman Yamaji believed that it could become more flexible through investment commitments.

Frequent Flier Programs

Frequent flyer programs offering priority and exclusivity privileges in wait-listing, checking, seating preferences, upgrades and lounge access had long existed (e.g., Cathay Pacific's Marco Polo Club). However, free-travel-for-miles-accumulated frequent flyer programs were pioneered in 1981 by American Airlines. The U.S.-style frequent flyer programs, open to passengers in all countries, offering free trips through any of the airline's route networks, were long resisted by Asian and European airlines. These airlines feared future multi-billion dollar liabilities on their balance sheets, even though redemption rates for U.S. plans were less than 30%. However, as a result of competitive pressure from U.S. carriers, British Airways, SwissAir and KLM launched their own frequent flyer programs: "A U.K.-based business person signed up with British Airways is likely to be loyal, rather than choose one of the Asian airlines," admitted SIA's London-based sales chief Gerry Stevens in a reference to British Airways' Air Miles program which had made considerable inroads in the U.K. market.

Diversification

Singapore Airlines had long-term plans to diversify into catering, freight services, engineering and hotels. Mr. Lim Chin Beng, Deputy Chairman, said: "Generally, companies diversify when their core business is a sunset industry. The airline industry is vigorous and expanding. The other reason to diversify is to protect your flanks.... If we diversify, it will be because it is profitable and supports the core business."

Mr. Lim said that he wanted SIA to be more active in the catering business. "We have the expertise." On engineering, he added: "Engineering is another good area; not only for day-to-day maintenance of aircraft but there are also a lot of older aircraft that need to be modified."

SIA wanted to turn its cargo subsidiary into a separate profit center, believing it could soon lose market share to freighter companies like Federal Express, as well as to passenger airlines such as All Nippon Airways (Japan) and Lufthansa (Germany), both of which had large market shares in freight.

As SIA had no experience in the hotel business, it planned to enter joint ventures with maximum 20% equity stakes. "Our partner has to be world class in keeping with our image," said Mr. Lim. If SIA moved into the hotel business it would not be the first time for an airline. United Airlines purchased Western International (1970), and American Airlines operated its Flagship Hotels; the now bankrupt TWA acquired Hilton International (1967) and Pan Am had operated Intercontinental Hotels.

The Future

As other airlines realized the importance of in-flight service and sought to improve, SIA believed it would have to find other means of differentiation. "A competitive edge can be eroded very soon," said Managing Director Mr. Cheong; Deputy Chairman Mr. Lim saw the internationalization of U.S. airlines as SIA's biggest challenge for the 1990s:

> I can see U.S. carriers moving out internationally in a very big way as they realize that more money is to be made on international rather than domestic operations. I can foresee them going to Europe and then on to Singapore. If I were them, I would tap the very rich Europe–Asia market. Air Canada has shown that they can make money from day one.

Exhibit 1: Singapore Airlines Company's Income Statement, 1988–92 (year ending March 31)

Profit and Loss Accounts	1991–92	1990–91	1989–90	1988–89
	(Singapore dollars in millions)			
Total revenue				
Revenue on scheduled services	4,842.00	4,488.00	4,606.20	4,190.20
Passenger	3,925.00	3,594.00	3,644.10	3,249.70
Cargo	851.00	836.00	898.50	878.20
Mail	40.00	35.00	40.80	40.00
Excess baggage	26.00	23.00	22.80	22.30
Non-scheduled services and incidental	171.00	114.00	124.50	81.60
Total revenue	5,013.00	4,602.00	4,730.70	4,271.80
Total expenditure				
Staff costs	1,036.00	831.00	816.40	674.90
Fuel and oil costs	704.00	780.00	613.50	507.80
Depreciation charges	614.00	513.00	438.80	550.30
Handling charges	365.00	316.00	278.50	248.20
Aircraft maintenance and overhaul costs	279.00	263.00	240.00	193.50
In-flight meals costs	235.00	220.00	227.90	207.80
Landing and parking fees	231.00	204.00	184.50	172.50
Others	685.00	633.00	802.20	851.70
Total expenditure	4,149.00	3,760.00	3,601.80	3,406.70
Operating profit	864.00	842.00	1,128.90	865.10
Surplus on sale of aircraft and spares	129.00	207.60	195.20	96.00
Dividends from unquoted subsidiaries, gross	92.50	75.10	73.70	64.30
Profit before taxation	1,085.50	1,124.70	1,397.80	1,025.40
Provision for taxation	164.50	237.40	221.00	97.00
Profit after taxation	921.00	887.30	1,176.80	928.40
Minority interests				
Profit after taxation and minority interests	921.00	887.30	1,176.80	928.40
Unappropriated profit brought forward	0.90	0.90	1.10	0.50
Profit available for appropriation	921.90	888.20	1,177.90	928.90
Appropriations				
General reserves	720.00	708.00	1.025.00	833.00
Dividends	201.10	178.80	152.00	94.80
Unappropriated profit carried forward	0.50	0.90	0.90	1.10
Earnings per share ($)	1.44	1.39	1.89	1.50
Dividend rate, before tax (%)	45.00	40.00	35.00	22.50

Exhibit 2: Singapore Airlines Company's Balance Sheet, 1988–92 (year ending March 31)

Profit and Loss Accounts	1991–92	1990–91	1989–90	1988–89
	(Singapore dollars in millions)			
Share capital				
Authorized	1,000.00	1,000.00	1,000.00	1,000.00
Issued and fully paid	641.30	637.30	637.30	619.70
Reserves	6,027.80	5,227.00	4,519.00	3,158.80
Shareholders' funds = share capital and reserves	6,669.10	5,864.30	5,156.30	3,778.50
Minority interests	103.90	134.40	154.90	185.30
Deferred accounts	326.10	271.80	215.60	145.60
Deferred taxation	421.20	450.10	517.70	642.40
Long-term liabilities	7,520.30	6,720.60	6,044.50	4,751.80
Fixed assets				
Aircraft, spares and spare engines	4,483.30	4,053.50	3,582.20	2,888.90
Land and buildings	259.60	281.80	304.50	306.50
Others	1,132.80	624.50	628.50	730.40
Fixed assets	5,875.70	4,959.80	4,515.20	3,925.80
Interests in subsidiaries				
Investment in subsidiaries	276.30	218.30	224.40	222.00
Amount owing by subsidiaries	232.20	241.20	(318.20)	(263.80)
	508.50	459.50	(93.80)	(41.80)
Long-term investments	486.60	420.90	407.30	37.60
Current assets				
Trade debtors	717.00	699.60	660.70	622.60
Stocks	47.70	46.40	36.90	25.60
Investments			292.00	224.30
Cash and bank balances	1,730.10	1,930.40	1,890.70	1,570.20
Current assets	2,494.80	2,676.40	2,880.30	2,442.70
Total assets	8,857.10	8,057.10	7,802.20	6,406.10
Current liabilities				
Loans – repayable within one year	0.90	11.00	3.30	66.60
Bank overdrafts – unsecured	22.20	10.30	23.90	15.20
Trade creditors	1,063.20	952.90	944.60	880.80
Sales in advance of carriage	405.60	482.70	449.40	499.70
Provision for taxation	218.70	229.20	133.40	55.40
Proposed final dividend, less tax	134.70	109.90	109.90	94.80
Current liabilities	1,845.30	1,796.00	1,664.50	1,612.50
Total liabilities	2,266.50	2,246.10	2,182.20	2,254.90
New current assets	649.50	880.40	1,215.80	830.20
	7,520.30	6,720.60	6,044.50	4,751.80

Map of South Korea

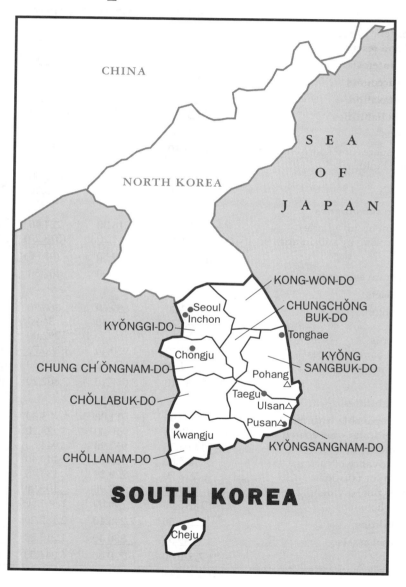

CHINA

NORTH KOREA

S E A

O F

J A P A N

KONG-WON-DO

CHUNGCHŎNG
BUK-DO

Seoul
Inchon

KYŎNGGI-DO

Tonghae

Chongju

KYŎNG
SANGBUK-DO

CHUNG CH´ŎNGNAM-DO

Pohang

CHŎLLABUK-DO

Taegu
Ulsan△

Pusan△

Kwangju

KYŎNGSANGNAM-DO

CHŎLLANAM-DO

SOUTH KOREA

Cheju

South Korea Overview[1]

Background. South Korea, located on the southern part of the Korean peninsula, is separated from North Korea by the 38th parallel; land mass is 99,314 sq. km., coastline 2,413 kilometers. South Korea's 45.5 million population is Christian (48.6%), Buddhist (47.4%); a minority are Confucianist (3%) and Shamanist (0.2%). South Korea is ethnically homogenous (except for 20,000 well-assimilated Chinese); the official language is Korean but English is widely taught in middle school and high school. Major cities (1995) are (million population): Seoul (11.6), Pusan (4.1), Taegu (2.4), Inchon (2.3), Kwangju (1.4). South Korea has a temperate climate and four distinct seasons; winter is dry (average temperature – 5°C); summer is humid (25°C). South Korea has nine provinces and six urban areas called Special Cities (e.g., Seoul Special City), treated as provinces. Under the 1987 constitution, the president is head of state, elected to a five-year (non-renewable) term. The president appoints the prime minister and State Council (13- to 30-member Cabinet). Most seats in the unicameral National Assembly (299-member, four-year term) are elected; remaining seats are allocated to parties (winning five or more elected seats) according to percent of popular vote. The Supreme Court supervises appellate, district and local courts; it also reviews military court (jurisdiction over the armed forces and military personnel) decisions. Provincial governors and mayors are appointed by the president.

Political. The 35-year Japanese rule in Korea ended after World War II; the country was divided into two; the western allies held the South, the former Soviet Union the North. In 1948, South Korea was proclaimed an independent state, capital Seoul, bordering North Korea at the 38th parallel. In June 1950, war broke out between South and North Korea. A United Nations approved, U.S.-led expeditionary force aided South Korea; China aided North Korea. Following a 1961 army coup, Korean military leaders ruled by fiat; a pro-democracy movement was increasingly significant. Coup leader General Park Chung Hee (president 1963), assassinated in 1979, was succeeded by another military leader, General Chun Doo Hwan; in 1987, following large-scale demonstrations, government-backed candidate Roh Tae Woo (military classmate of Chun Doo Hwan) succeeded Chun. In 1992, Kim Young-Sam became the first directly elected civilian president. In 1996, former presidents Chun Doo Hwan and Roh Tae Woo were placed on trial for corruption, staging the 1979 coup and

---

[1] Republic of Korea.

massacring pro-democracy demonstrators in Kwangju (1980); they were found guilty and sentenced to life imprisonment.

Social. The geographic population distribution has shifted markedly to towns: 1965, 32%; 1997, 78%. Roughly 10.6 million (25%) (1990) live in Seoul; such a large concentration close to the North Korean border is a matter of concern to the government. Military service is compulsory and extends beyond two years, since the end of the Korean War (1953), U.S. troops have been stationed in Korea (1992 U.S. troop strength, 35,500); primary school enrollment has been virtually 100% since mid-1960s; secondary school enrollment rose from 30% to about 88% (1994). Enrollment in higher education institutions by the 20 to 24 age group rose from 6% (1965) to about 40% (1994) (higher than Germany and Japan). In 1994, education spending was 15.5% of the government budget. Korea claims the world's largest number of PhDs per capita; PhDs trained in the U.S. and Europe are returning to key positions in companies, financial institutions, universities and think tanks. A national welfare pension scheme was implemented in 1988; those paying into the scheme for 20 years will receive an average 40% of final salary on retirement at 55 or 60.

Economy. South Korea's economy is the 11th largest in the world. South Korea is a member of the United Nations (UN), World Bank (WB), International Monetary Fund (IMF), World Trade Organization (WTO), Asian Development Bank (ADB), European Bank of Reconstruction and Development (EBRD) and Organization for Economic Cooperation and Development (OECD). South Korea's real GDP growth rate has averaged over 7% in the 1990s; per capita GNP is US$10,076.

South Korea is the world's fifth largest auto manufacturer. The industrial sector employs just over one third of the labor force; it accounts for one third of GDP and is the most important source of economic growth. Agriculture and services account for 12.5% (7% GDP) and 48.4% (46.1% GDP) of total employment. Manufacturing is expected to lead overall growth in the seventh Five-Year Plan (1992–96), averaging 8.5% p.a. The government has invested W1.55 trillion in small and medium-sized manufacturing firms (1991–96) to develop 919 production technologies. Exports for year ending June 1995 were US$98.8 billion. Major export destinations (1995) are: U.S. (19.3%), Japan (13.6%), Hong Kong (8.5%). All imports, divided into automatic and restricted categories, require licenses, granted only to registered traders. Major import origins (1995) are: Japan (24.1%), U.S. (22.5%), China (5.3%).

The Korean economy is dominated by chaebols, large business conglomerates, many still family owned and operated. The relationship between the government and the chaebols remains close (special privileges and lending rates for promoting national development goals) despite President Kim's (1993) anti-chaebol drive. Investigations into the complex system of cross-shareholding among parent companies and their operations have slowed amid concern that harsh treatment could hinder international competitiveness. Chaebol strength in a still largely regulated economy is exemplified by Samsung's move into the automobile industry to become the sixth business group to make cars.[2]

Effective January 1994, foreign companies can borrow up to 75% of investment capital abroad (especially for financing imports of raw materials and high technology equipment). They can buy land for factories and employee residences (effective March 1994). The approval process for setting up a business has been simplified; it now requires at most five days (effective July 1994).

The Finance Ministry controls the banking and financial system; it sets bank interest rates, regulates financial instruments and approves all external borrowing. Banking regulations allow commercial banks to invest in equity-linked securities and provide more equality for foreign banks. Banking institutions include 14 nationwide commercial banks, 10 local banks and 52 foreign banks (with 72 branches [end 1994]). The Korea Development Bank, Export-Import Bank of Korea and the Korea Long-Term Credit Bank are state-run development banks. The currency (won) floats according to a rate determined by a composite weighted basket of currencies of the nation's major trading partners with reference to the IMF's Special Drawing Rights (SDRs). The won/ U.S. dollar exchange rate was quite stable in 1994 but has risen slightly due to an influx of foreign capital and improved balance of payments.

The Korea Stock Exchange opened in 1956 with W3 billion capital, government (70%), 25 member firms (30%). Stock exchange listing requires government approval; in September 1994, 692 companies were listed. Foreign participation (up to 15% market value) is allowed in member firms providing the firm has over W20 billion capital. At end August 1994, foreign investors controlled 8.6% of market capitalization (total US$9.2 billion).

South Korea was the most damaged victim of the 1997 Asian financial crisis. As the world's 11th largest economy, the economic crisis came as an absolute shock to Koreans. Hugely leveraged balance sheets of most companies (average debt levels of the chaebols were three to four times assets), massive over-investments in key industries, lack of market incentives after years of command capitalism and the unquestioning confidence of foreign investors in Korean debtors came to haunt the country as Asian currencies plummeted. In a matter of months, the Korean won lost 50% of its value against the U.S. dollar; the crisis deepened as balance sheets froze and money markets were paralyzed. As export earnings and domestic demand dropped, South Korea was forced to agree to a US$57 billion IMF bailout (the largest in IMF history) to prevent a serious recession. However, the bailout did not calm the markets and, in an attempt to throw the country a lifeline, international banks rolled over outstanding debt positions (half of South Korea's total foreign debt, or about US$100 billion, was short term). In late December 1997, Moody's downgraded South Korea's debt (along with Thailand and Indonesia) to junk-bond status. National pride was severely damaged and the IMF bailout was seen by many Koreans as an intervention in Korea's sovereignty; the IMF pushed for open capital markets and allowing near-solvent

---

[2] The combined sales of South Korea's four largest chaebols – Hyundai, Samsung, LG (formerly GoldStar), Daewoo – represent 84% of GDP and 60% of exports. *The Economist*, May 18, 1996.

banks to collapse. The worst of the crisis hit in the presidential election campaign which saw an opposition victory. The new government's challenge was to demonstrate at home and to the markets its ability to lead in tough times and regain the Korean people's self-confidence. It was clear that the chaebols would have to restructure significantly to survive; many suffered from overlapped investments in crowded industries. Apart from the leading firms, many others faced collapse if interest rates remained high (68 publicly-traded firms became insolvent in 1997). The crisis is culminating in a major economic downturn and unemployment previously unseen in postwar Korea.

Infrastructure. The 1988 Seoul Olympic Games encouraged the government to increase investment in the transportation system and general facilities. The road network is 61,296 kilometers (1993); by 2030, over 300,000 kilometers of new roads will be built. By end of 2000, 6.68 million motor vehicles will be in use. The rail system is 6,500 kilometers linking all major towns. Underground rail networks operate in Seoul (177 kilometers) and Pusan (26 kilometers). A Seoul–Pusan high-speed electrified railway is planned, at a cost of US$8 billion.

Seoul, Pusan and Cheju have airports; a second Seoul airport (on Youngjong island) and an airport at Chongju are planned. Before 1988, privately owned Korean Airlines Company was the only airline; a second, Asiana Airlines, now operates domestic and international routes. Among 24 ports for ocean-going ships, the largest port is at Pusan; other major ports are Pohang, Ulsan and Tonghae. Satellites contribute greatly to international communications; high quality telegraph, telephone and television connections connect Pacific Coast and Indian Ocean countries. Telephone facilities from South Korea to Japan have been improved by "tropo scatter system A."

Electric power generated was 137 billion kWh (1993), 2,460 kWh (1991) per capita. Diversification from fossil fuel plants to nuclear has received top priority. South Korea has nine nuclear plants (1991); in 1994, it announced a tripling of nuclear capacity to 20,000 MW by 2006.

Statistics*	June 1991	June 1997	Statistics*	June 1991	June 1997
Per capita GNP	US$5,569	US$10,076	Infant mortality / 1,000	24	8
GDP growth	8.6%	7.2%	Life expectancy (yrs)	n/a	72
Savings (GNP)	n/a	37%	Literacy rate	92.7%	97.4%
Inflation (CPI)	12.0%	3.8%	People per tel.	3.3	2.1
Foreign debt			People per doctor	1,216	855
(in billion)	US$30.4	US$54.2	People per TV	n/a	3.4
Pop. (million)	43.1	45.5	Calorie intake (cals)	n/a	3,296
Urban pop.	73%**	78%			
Pop. growth	0.9%	0.9%			

*Secured from *Asiaweek.*
**From "A report of the INSEAD Euro-Asia Centre," J. Probert (Sept. 1994), INSEAD.

Case 46

A President is Made: The Three Parties' Political Marketing in the Presidential Election[1]

Doo Hee Lee
Korea University, Seoul

Late Sunday evening December 13, 1992, just five days before the Korea's 14th presidential election, each of the three candidates – Kim Young-Sam, Min-Ja Party; Kim Dae-Jung, Min-Ju Party; Chung Ju-Young, Kook-Min Party – met with their advisors to plan strategy for the final week of the campaign. Each had campaigned hard in this first presidential election that permitted television advertising and each was evaluating his strategy and poll standings. Only a few days before the polls, decisions that each made would be critical for their candidacies.

৪০৫৪

The History of Political Marketing in Korea

Political marketing commenced in 1947 in Korea with the first election for the National Assembly. In 1947, the national election law stated that, "Registered candidates can promote themselves freely for campaign purposes." Guidelines for election campaigning were established in the 1960s. In 1963, new presidential election laws declared specific media policies: candidates were allowed to advertise five times in each daily newspaper; each party could advertise its candidate and policies ten times in each daily newspaper. Advertisement sizes were also specified; each candidate advertisement could be no larger than 15 cm × 19 cm (later increased to 20 cm × 38 cm) and party advertisements could not exceed 20 cm × 38 cm.

---

[1] Translated by Theresa Seung Ho, Graduate School of Business, Columbia University.

In 1987 (13th presidential election), following years of military rule, voters directly elected the president (largest number of votes wins) for the first time in 16 years. Political marketing was more active; large advertising companies participated directly in campaigns and consistent election strategies (e.g., developing candidates' image) were instituted. (Previously, a simple campaign motto or slogan comprised most campaign efforts.) For the first time, polls were conducted; candidate images managed, campaign strategy set and different promotional materials and political advertisements developed.

Seasoned observers believed successful image-making was critical to Roh Tae-Woo's 1987 victory. Early on, polls showed Roh with a negative image because of his military background, his major role in the previous coup d'etat and his close friendship with previous president, Chun Doo-Hwan, disliked by many voters. Roh's campaign team developed a new slogan, "The Great Era for Ordinary People," and created the image of "Ordinary Roh Tae-Woo." Elaborately scheduled, heavily publicized events (e.g., visits to communes, epilepsy patients, inner cities) and emphasis on Roh's large ears as a metaphor for ability to listen to others were believed critical factors in his success.

For the 14th presidential election, political marketing advanced to a higher level. Commercial advertising firms were involved; compared to previous campaigns that simply stated candidate positions, advertising reflected voter views. Election strategy shifted to active political advertising from simple promotional events; however, advertising companies contributed only to the technicalities of image-making, not overall strategy (see Appendix for components of political marketing).

Min-Ja Party

As the presidential campaign commenced, the Min-Ja Party and candidate Kim Young-Sam had two obstacles to overcome. First, voters might feel betrayed by the former opposition party leader's (Min-Ju Party) switch to become the dominant party's candidate; second, Kim Young-Sam was attacked for lack of experience and competence. Kim's "expressive" strategy to convince voters his party switch was legitimate and that he was fully competent was the theme, "reform politics." "Reform" was chosen despite Kim's being the incumbent party candidate because of his background as opposition party leader. The paradox resulting from his "betrayal" was actively delineated by the campaign of "Creating New Korea" (instead of "jumping the boat"); "Curing the Korean Disease" by "Reform through stability" offered the vision of a brighter future.

The Min-Ja Party sought to differentiate itself from the main opposition parties. It avoided ads on controversial issues, yet set up the "0303 direct phone line" campaign to emphasize its interest in ordinary citizens lives.[2] The party implied it promised feasible policies whereas opposition parties only generated impossible ideas.

---

[2] 0303 in Korean reads young-sam-young-sam.

The Min-Ja Party used the slogan "leading the reform" early in the campaign; it later switched to "led by Kim Young-Sam" after realizing that the candidate was more popular than the party. Another slogan, "Let us create the New Korea with Kim Young-Sam" and related symbol (the bear) were selected in a national contest. The winning slogan, announced in nine major and three sports newspapers (October 13, 14), "Koreans are going forth again; Kim Young-Sam now leads them," was slightly revised for the campaign.

The bear symbol embodied two meanings. First, the bear was the crucial benefactor that built the first Korea (Tan-Kun mythology); it symbolized the will to "create the new Korea." Second, the bear was traditionally viewed as a patient, lasting animal; it was an appropriate metaphor for Kim Young-Sam, demonstrating his will to build a new Korea with patience and diligence (Exhibit 1). The slogan and mascot were used consistently in newspapers, magazines and publicity materials (Exhibits 2, 3).

The Min-Ja Party's promotional strategy was implemented by advertisements in newspapers, TV, magazines and publicity materials; publicity was secured via interviews and spokespersons. The major emphasis was newspapers; the party's goal was two-fold: to establish the candidate's image and convince voters of its policies. Four legal newspaper advertisements were developed, two focused on building the image, the other two elaborated on policies given the candidate's image.[3]

In legal advertisements, the Min-Ja Party clearly distinguished establishing candidate image from promoting policies. In policy advertisements, these two foci merged. Thus, policy ads (e.g., "0303 direct line," "building New Korea" [Exhibit 4]) promoted Kim's friendly image and will to reform; they simultaneously showed the party's vision. The "0303 direct line" series especially, using Kim Young-Sam's name, asked voter opinions and advertised party responses, firmly building the image of an open minded president. In addition to replying to most-asked questions or suggestions, the "0303 direct line" also served a polling purpose (similar to the Min-Ju Party's "7070" or Kook-Min Party's "9090"). Although not a systematically conducted poll, many important issues were identified. Issues from the direct line were more often reflected in advertisements than those from official polls.

Kim Young-Sam advertisements evolved during the campaign. Initially, emphasis was placed on policy and image; later advertising focused on specific issues. More recently, advertising attacked rivals or responded to attacks (Exhibit 5). The first attack advertisements focused on the Kook-Min party candidate (in particular campaign expenses) since the Min-Ja and Kook-Min parties were targeting similar voters. When the Min-Ju Party unexpectedly gained benefit from this focus, the attack switched to the Min-Ju Party candidate's "background issue," his image as a political martyr from an oppressed region of the country.

Two series of magazine advertising were placed in current-event periodicals popular among educated voters (e.g., SiSa Journal, Newsweek, Weekly Korea). "Our Future" publicized the Min-Ja Party's intention to promote science yet preserve

---

[3] In legal advertisements, only the candidate's symbols and name could be explicitly stated; in policy advertisements, only the party's policy could be publicized, the candidate could not be mentioned.

traditional culture, provide welfare for the disabled and reform the political system. Science endorsement was advertised when the first Korean space orbiter was launched; culture preservation was advertised at Harvest Moon holidays. The "Korean Disease" series followed, focusing on the undesirable characteristics of regional conflicts, materialism and in-group bias, using the slogan "Curing the Korean Disease: We are leading it." The large differences between magazine (mainly to promote party policies) and newspaper (emphasize candidate's image) advertisements related to magazine readers who tend to be more highly educated.

For the first time in a presidential election TV advertising could be used;[4] each party was allowed five one-minute spots. The Min-Ja Party produced five advertisements (three by advertising agencies, two in-house); four were used (or planned) (Table 1). In "The Voters' Wishes" interactive ad, voters offered their views on issues; the candidate expressed his will to implement these positions in his policies; the 60 seconds was divided by economy, politics and Kim Young-Sam's image. By having voters express Kim's positions, the party sought to have voters accept its views. The "Man Who Starts the Dawn" emphasized Kim Young-Sam's "clean politician" image; the unpretentious Kim taking his usual morning jog with neighbors. He commented, "even if I become the president, I will come back to this house to live with an empty pocket." This advertisement was aired twice to establish Kim's clean image (Exhibit 6). The other two advertisements developed were "The Girl" and "New Korea." TV ads targeted undecided voters; late in the campaign one third were undecided, including 60% in their 20s and 30s. The party also believed that short exposure in five one-minute spots was unlikely to change "decideds."

Table 1: Min-Ja Party – Television Advertising Schedule

Date	Time	Channel	Content
November 27	20:58	KBS1	Voters' Wishes
December 12	20:54	SBS	The Man Who Starts the Dawn
December 13	19:55	MBC	The Man Who Starts the Dawn
December 16 planned	20:52	MBC	The Girl
December 16 planned	20:58	KBS1	New Korea

Finally, promotional pamphlets were delivered to voters by direct mail and passed out on the streets. Nine pamphlets were designed before the campaign; eventually, five legal promotional pamphlets were printed mainly promoting party policies. An easily understood cartoon book, "Policy or Comedy?" by popular cartoonist Koh Woo-Young, in typical virulent tone, compared the three parties' policies, criticizing the others' campaign promises and emphasizing the Min-Ja Party's superiority. Four-page pamphlets depicted Kim's human side "Kim Young-Sam's Way"; elaborated

---

[4] In the 13th presidential election (1987), Min-Ja Party and Min-Ju Party produced ads but were not allowed to air them.

party policies, "New Korea in Reform"; covered economic policies, "Kim Young-Sam's New Theory of Economics"; and focused on education, environment, culture, art and the worker and disabled's welfare.

Min-Ju Party

The Min-Ju Party candidate Kim Dae-Jung's image was a strong opposition leader who fought against dictatorial regimes. On the verge of death five times, including a death sentence and a kidnapping, he was often called the "resentful politician" based on these dramatic political experiences; he came from Chon-La Province, the most oppressed and disparaged area in Korea. Polls indicated two weaknesses, radical image and strong local roots; Kim Dae-Jung had to convince voters these two points were untrue. Kim was framed as the "new leader for the great reconcilia-tion." To address concerns that the abused party would take revenge when given power, this theme implied Kim Dae-Jung would accommodate everyone rather than execute radical reforms. An "expressive strategy" was developed to respond to these key issues. To counteract the radical image, Kim was portrayed as having "a subdued, soft image" and as a believer in the market economy and democracy; for background, he was emphasized as the "leader of the nationwide party, not a regional leader." The overall image of Kim Dae-Jung and Min-Ju Party was "the leader and party appropri-ate for the progress of democracy and unification."

To form a soft image, Kim Dae-Jung developed a conversational speaking style and smiled in campaign posters. On economic issues, supported by wide knowledge from avid book reading and successful entrepreneurial experiences, he emphasized belief in capitalism and the market economy. His overall strategy was to convince voters that electing Kim Dae-Jung would not bring drastic changes since he was knowledgeable in theory and practice. As the major opposition, the Min-Ju Party focused attacks on Kim Young-Sam, his party-switching background and lack of competence, while accentuating Kim Dae-Jung's positive qualities.

The Min-Ju Party's motto "New Era of Great Reconciliation and Change ... "; was an extension of the campaign theme "Leading the New Era of Great Reconciliation ..." "Great Reconciliation" referred to Kim Dae-Jung's image; "New Era of Change" em-bodied the party's will for reform. The "New Era of Great Reconciliation and Change" slogan was symbolized by a rabbit and tortoise, based on the fable. However, rather than compete, the rabbit and tortoise ran side-by-side and gave each other piggy-back rides, symbolizing reconciliation and progressive spirit; and urging everyone to help one another in solid unity.

The party's original slogan, "Let Us Change This Time," was modified to "Let Us Change on Friday"; the election was Friday, December 18. This slogan was selected from a nationwide contest, providing voters the chance to express the Min-Ju Party's will for peaceful overturn of the establishment for true democracy (Exhibit 7). The meaning was two-fold: change and reform in society and change political power (similar to the party's slogan in the 1950s, "We Cannot Live Any Longer. Let Us Try Changing!"). The slogan was used in all promotional materials (e.g., newspapers, television, publicity pamphlets) like a symbol.

The Min-Ju Party's planning office and publicity team each conducted polls before the campaign commenced (Tables 2, 3; Exhibit 8). Observers believed that although the party merely tracked support for each candidate and did not tap into voters' desired change, it provided basic information to build strategy. Thus, the November 27 poll by the publicity team catalyzed a decision not to attack the Kook-Min Party and candidate Chung Ju-Young. According to this survey, the maximum (minimum) support for the three parties was: Kook-Min Party 21% (12%), Min-Ju Party 32% (24%), Min-Ja Party 37% (24%). The Min-Ju Party determined that because the Kook-Min Party's maximum support was less than the Min-Ju Party's minimum support, it need not consider it a primary competitor.

The proposed cabinet system (similar to the British system) was an important electoral issue; for the statement, "democracy is affirmed," 63% favored the proposal, only 11% opposed. Although party policy was against the change, the survey raised a need for reconsideration. Polls also targeted regional issues. Around November 27, Kim Dae-Jung was behind Kim Young-Sam in several areas: 840,000 votes in metro Seoul, 500,000 central region, 2,600,000 Kyung-Sang Provinces; he led only in Ho-Nam Provinces, by 3,000,000 votes. In total, Kim Dae-Jung trailed Kim Young-Sam by 980,000 votes; the need to concentrate efforts in metro Seoul was raised. In addition, a simulated poll-based experiment showed that if Chung Ju-Young secured 18% rather than 12% and Kim Dae-Jung support held, Kim Dae-Jung would be even with Kim Young-Sam; if Chung secured 19%, Kim Dae-Jung would lead. Finally, polls revealed 47% of Kim Young-Sam's supporters voted for Roh Tae-Woo (Min-Ja Party) in the 13th presidential election, 30% were "pure" loyalists for Kim Dae-Jung, 62% were loyal supporters, 16% had just acquired the right to vote. In short, Kim Young-Sam's support base was conservative tending to the incumbent party. ("Other" made up 23% and 22%.)

Table 2: Min-Ju Party, Polls Conducted by the Planning Office: Trends in Voter Support (%)

Poll #/Date	Min-Ja Party	Min-Ju Party	Poll #/Date	Min-Ja Party	Min-Ju Party	Kook-Min Party
1 August	25	21	4 November 11	30.0	25.0	n/a
2 October	35	26	5 December 4	30.5	25.4	14.1
3 November	33	27	6 December 9	28.3	25.3	10.3

Table 3: Min-Ju Party, Polls Conducted by the Publicity Team: Trends in Voter Support (%)

Date	Min-Ja Party	Min-Ju Party	Kook-Min Party	Date	Min-Ja Party	Min-Ju Party	Kook-Min Party
November 2	33	27	n/a	November 27	30.2	26.9	12.2
November 20	35.0	29.8	15.8	December 5	31.4	24.6	10.7

The Min-Ju Party promoted via newspapers, TV, radio, magazines, promotional pamphlets, interviews with reporters, spokesperson interviews and party periodicals (e.g., Min-Ju Party News, Min-Ju Forum); unlike other parties, the Min-Ju Party used magazines geared to women. In the November issues of 15 women's magazines, policy ads targeted mainly homemakers; the eight-page "participation" and "policy" series demonstrated party emphasis on female voters. Advertising goals were two-fold: to form the candidate's image (60%) and to elaborate its post-election vision (40%). Early in the campaign, the party wished to target different voter classes; budget constraints led to two targets: overall voting population (targets varied modestly over time) and female voters.

In four types of newspaper legal advertisements, the Min-Ju Party focused on a change in power, distinguishing image, issues and policies, consistently using the slogan, "New Era of Great Reconciliation and Change." Congruent with Kim Dae-Jung's image, the party responded to voter frustration with the long period of military rule using such catch-phrases as "We promise an independent president," "We will give you back the Blue House (presidential residence)." Economic uncertainty, addressed under the headline, "We really need a true Economy President," was a response to rival Chung Ju-Young's slogan, "Economy President, Unification President." At the campaign's height, when direct confrontation between the Min-Ja and Kook-Min parties produced unexpected favorable polls for the Min-Ju Party, the Min-Ja Party attacked Kim Dae-Jung's background.[5] Counter-attacking, the Min-Ju Party retorted, "How can you paint your 30-year colleague in the Min-Ju movement as a pro-Communist, even if you are about to lose?" The Min-Ju Party reaffirmed its will for political change with such slogans as "If we change, the world will change like this," "Min-Ju Party's promises are definitely different," and "Let us change this time." (Exhibit 9). General advertisements, alternating general policy and candidate image-making, were run mostly in national papers, only once regionally. Regional newspaper advertising focused mainly on policies to resolve local problems (Exhibit 10). The party did not conduct polls on advertising effectiveness; it believed effectiveness was a function of frequency.

The Min-Ju Party produced three TV advertisements: "Power Replacement" I and II, and "The True Economy President"; five spots were aired (or planned) (Table 4). The "Power Replacement" theme, derived from Washington Times' reporter Michael Bryn's article "Kim Dae-Jung's election would be the first true power replacement in East Asia," was targeted at "undecideds," politically apathetic, those antagonistic to Kim Dae-Jung and new undecided voters. Only five one-minute advertisements were allowed; it was believed this narrow target would maximize benefit.

The expressive strategy was changed slightly to appeal to this group; it focused on power replacement, rather than candidate's character; its goal was to persuade those disliking Kim Dae-Jung that the important issue was to change political power not the candidate per se. To convince apathetic voters, a clear simple message was designed to convince voters that a power change-over was legitimate.

---

[5] In some quarters, Kim Young-Sam gained the reputation as an opportunist for overly zealous attacks on Kim Dae-Jung.

Table 4: Min-Ju Party – Television Advertising Schedule

Date	Time	Channel	Content
December 4	20:58	KBS1	Power Replacement I
December 11	19:53	SBS	Power Replacement II
December 13 planned	20:55	MBC	Power Replacement II
December 16 planned	20:58	KBS1	True Economy President
December 16 planned	20:54	MBC	Power Replacement I

The "Power Replacement" advertisements comprised three people: one apathetic, one who disliked Kim Dae-Jung, one just eligible to vote. The three discussed their election views, then formed a consensus to vote for Kim Dae-Jung. The advertising rationale was that when undecided voters articulated why they would vote for Kim, mobile voters would rethink their choices. Although some campaign members disliked these ads for not accentuating Kim Dae-Jung directly, converting 10% of the 20% undecided votes would be a success. Moreover, Kim Dae-Jung decided that, "focusing on me would please my loyal supporters but not the undecided voters." Kim Dae-Jung never appeared; some observers believed the ads were refreshingly different from the other parties' by radically and honestly declaring, "We don't like Kim Dae-Jung, but are willing to support a promising candidate for power replacement." The "Power Replacement" ads were produced in two parts. In Part I (Exhibit 11), new models were used to build a fresh image; in Part II, popular entertainers were used.[6]

The "True Economy President" advertisement targeted homemakers. Chung Han-Yong, a radio personality believed popular among homemakers, saw numerous worn-out books on the shelves in Kim Dae-Jung's study. He explained Kim's theoretical and practical abilities; Kim was a studious politician who wrote "Dae-Jung (General) Economic Theory" published by Harvard University, was a successful businessman and had significant accomplishments in the National Assembly. Kim Dae-Jung was the truly deserving Economy President.

Six promotional pamphlets were published before the campaign; later, five more were published, including the "Cartoon Dae-Jung Economic Theory." These were delivered to voters via direct mail or on the street. The pamphlets comprised three main content branches: the Min-Ju Party's policy when in power; Kim Dae-Jung's character and response to the Min-Ja Party's attack on Kim's background. In the "Why Kim Dae-Jung?" section, Kim Dae-Jung was introduced, "Voters want a competent, loyal and internationally renowned president with a vision and warm heart." In the "Let Us Change This Time. If We Change, Our Country Would Improve Like This" section, the Min-Ja Party's 34 months and the new era promised by the Min-Ju Party were compared: correction of political corruption, reconciliation, economic power, quality education and better life in the agricultural and fishing sectors. Finally, the "Spies from North Korea" incident and his distorted pro-Communist image was explained in

---

[6] Only the Min-Ju Party used popular entertainers in its television advertisements.

the "How can you paint your 30-year colleague in the Min-Ju movement as pro-Communist, even if you are about to lose?" section. The Min-Ju Party also published and distributed a separate pamphlet listing its policies; voters could easily compare them after the election and have faith in their face value. In another pamphlet, agricultural sector issues, the working environment of taxi drivers and quality education accentuated main Min-Ju Party issues.

The Min-Ju Party also used promotional events. The "Let's Begin: the Wave of 20s and 30s" event, sponsored as a cultural project by the Min-Ju Party Youth Special Committee, opened in the Olympic Park's Gymnastic Stadium. Many events with "reconciliation" and "progress" themes followed all over the country. The Special Committee on Environment sponsored a "Let Us Save Han River" event. In addition, several popular young entertainers formed a mobile promotional group; they received favorable responses for giving instant photos to voters.

Kook-Min Party

Kook-Min Party candidate Chung Ju-Young entered politics when he determined voters were tired of the "Two Kim Period." As head of major chaebol, Hyundai, Chung believed his background as business entrepreneur would satisfy voters anxious for economic reform. However, voters were uncomfortable with his old age (77) and lack of political experience. Thus, candidate Chung competed with two strategic opportunities and two weaknesses.

To use his strengths, Chung denounced Kim Young-Sam and the "Two Kim Period" to lure voters bored with the two Kims. To attract conservative voters, he selected Kim Young-Sam as his primary target, Kim Dae-Jung as the second. Despite being conservative, at times Chung sided with Kim Dae-Jung on political issues to enhance his opposition credentials. In response to economic change desired by voters, Chung claimed the mantle of the "Economy President" who had created a modern fairy tale from zero. His old age weaknesses was addressed by excellent health and stamina; his lack of experience by visits to Russia and North Korea as the "Unification President." The party motto, "Clean Politics, Clean Economy," embodied Chung's themes of economic revival and fresh and clean politics. Along with this motto, the slogan "Economy President, Unification President" aimed to resolve economic renewal and the pain of separation from North Korea. (Chung was born in North Korea.[7])

The first candidate to select a mascot, Chung chose the tiger, often regarded as Korea's representative animal and mascot for the Seoul Olympics (1988). Viewed favorably by Koreans, the tiger embodied Chung's mobility and propulsion and expressed Korea's leap into the future (Exhibit 12). As an industrialist, Chung Ju-Young used management techniques and led his campaign to the highest use of political advertising in Korean history. Before March 1992, Chung consistently built the Kook-

---

[7] Chung Ju-Young campaigned heavily in Kang-Won Province claiming that it was almost his hometown.

Min Party's image via its policy advertising series. Voter response was surprisingly favorable and helped the party rank third.

The Kook-Min Party mostly used newspapers, magazines, television and promotional pamphlets; Chung also conducted interviews with reporters and a spokesperson. Kook-Min Party advertising objectives were to establish Chung's image as the "Economy President." Most legal newspaper advertisements related to economic issues and included such slogans as: "The Great World Economic Competition, Chung Ju-Young Can Lead," "He Will Compensate for the 11-Year-Old Grudge of the 1.4 Million Home Buyers in National Savings System," "Victimization of the Small and Medium Companies: Chung Ju-Young Will Take Care of It." In an advertisement planned for December 15, the Kook-Min Party's headline would be: "Chung Ju-Young, Candidate Number 3, Promises the Voters the Following." To address Chung's negative chaebol background, it declared Chung will "donate all his net worth to society," while reaffirming his promises to "supply apartments at half the current price," "improve the traffic situation with two-level roads," and "eradicate regional conflict through a cabinet system." To express his strong will, at the beginning of the advertisement he would ask readers to "store this newspaper and compare later" (Exhibit 13).

Starting September 15, the Citizen Party began a "Policy Reform" series of advertisements mainly elaborating reform policies in 15 areas: administrative, politics, education, environment, unification, welfare, tax system, labor, agricultural and fishing sector, science and technology, small and medium companies, transportation, women, culture and housing. These were discontinued on November 17, observers believed, to concentrate directly against the Min-Ja Party. Later, advertisements were run demanding that criticism of the Kook-Min Party (for its impractical policies and plutocracy) cease.

Periodicals carried advertisements related to their specific characteristics: those in economic periodicals focused on economic policies; sports periodicals on Chung's background as President of the Korean Physical Fitness Association with headlines, "Development of Physical Fitness, Leave It to Chung Ju-Young," and "Everyone Becomes a Coach on December 18."

For television, the Kook-Min Party produced the "Candlelight" advertisement, aired (or planned) all five times. (Advertisements on national welfare and the economy were planned but not executed due to lack of time.) Content of the "Candlelight" series focused on reviving the Korean economy; the party used Chung's strength as a businessman to show his ability to save the economy as the main campaign goal, rather than power, fame or wealth (Table 5). Chung was portrayed as the man who successfully completed dam construction for the first time in history and who possessed extraordinary leadership in Korean economic development. The 60-second advertisement comprised three 20-second segments: first, the dark realities of the agricultural and fishing sectors and small and medium companies; second, a brief Chung biography as accomplished businessman; third, an optimistic message on economic revival (Exhibit 14). To focus completely on Chung, only Chung and a candle light were used. When the screen depicted dark economic realities, the light flickered and died; for optimistic messages, it lit brightly. The last scene, a map of Korea, was delineated with candlelight; Chung's face was juxtaposed to show that his leadership would make the country's future bright.

Table 5: Kook-Min Party – Television Advertising Schedule

Date	Time	Channel	Content
December 5	20:58	KBS1	Candlelight
December 13 planned	20:55	SBS	Candlelight
December 16 planned	20:52	MBC	Candlelight
December 16 planned	20:51	MBC	Candlelight
December 16 planned	20:57	KBS 1	Candlelight

Comparison of the Three Parties

Election Strategy

Several observers commented on the presidential election. One said political marketing, although of questionable caliber, played a more important role than in any previous election; however, concerns focused more on candidate than voter reactions. All three parties attempted to listen to voters; the candidates used diverse expressive strategies to overcome weaknesses. Campaign strategies are summarized in Table 6. However, reflecting critical economic concerns, all put greatest emphasis on economic revival. Chung Ju-Young concentrated most on the economy, hoping to take leadership based on business experience and offering such radical ideas as "apartments at half price," and "two-level roads." Kim Young-Sam used results from detailed surveys very effectively. When the Kook-Min Party gained, he attacked it as materialistic; when the Min-Ju Party gained, he attacked Kim Dae-Jung's background.

The campaign contributed to a "festivalization of the election." In some cases, election songs were critical of a candidate, indicating their importance in dictating campaign mood. The Min-Ja Party revised the song "End of Military Rule" (1987) and developed "Koreans Run Again": "Koreans run again / Kim Young-Sam leads / Our choice Kim Young-Sam / For your honest mind / We trust you." The words embodied the image Kim Young-Sam sought to build. On December 1, The Min-Ju Party introduced the song "Let Us Change This Friday" similar to a commercial theme song: "Let us get together for our country / Let us change this Friday, to Kim Dae-Jung / Let us get together for tomorrow / Let us change this Friday, to Kim Dae-Jung." By repeating the main theme, the song delivered the strong message that voters should replace the political power on Friday. The Min-Ju Party also revised folk songs "Oh, Fox, Fox" into "Oh, Rabbit, Rabbit"; "Hurrah" into "Hurrah for the Great Reconciliation / Hurrah for the New Era"; and "Youthful Age of 18" into Kim Dae-Jung of Min-Ju Party." The Kook-Min Party developed 16 songs used at different campaign stages: for example, "The Candidate's Song"; "The Big Road, Chung Ju-Young"; "Chung Ju-Young, Tatata"; "Let's Change the Whole Country"; "Wealthy Country"; "Let's Go toward Unification" and "Who?"

Table 6: Comparison of the Three Parties' Election Strategies

	Min-Ja Party	Min-Ju Party	Kook-Min Party
Candidate	Kim Young-Sam	Kim Dae-Jung	Chung Ju-Young
Weaknesses	Merging with the opposition party, competence	Background issue, too regional	Old age, absence of political experience
Strategy	Reform through stability	New politician for reconciliation	Economy President
Concept	I will create New Korea by curing the "Korean Disease" through reform	Let's bring Min-Ju progress, unification and economic progress through power replacement	I will become the Economy President who will resurrect the economy of this country ruined by politics
Motto	Kim Young-Sam leads the reform	New era of great reconciliation and change	Clean politics, prosperous national economy
Slogan	Let's create the New Korea with Kim Young-Sam	Let's change this time	Economy President, Unification President
Mascot	Bear	Rabbit and Turtle	Tiger
Election Song	Koreans Run Again (revised version of the song celebrating the end of military regime), You (Koreana)	Let Us Change on Friday; Oh, Rabbit, Rabbit; Hurrah for the Great Reconciliation; Kim Dae-Jung of Min-Ju Party	16 songs (12 new, 4 revised): The Candidate's Song; Chung Ju-Young, Tatata; The Big Road, Chung Ju-Young …

According to the new election law, campaign ads could run only during the month before election day. In this period, a candidate could air five television and radio advertisements and run four newspaper advertisements per paper; television ads could be no longer than one minute; a newspaper ad could be no larger than five columns, 37 cm long. However, if the ad did not contain the name and number of the candidate, it was regarded as a normal party promotional ad. Thus, the political campaign really started in August; Kim Young-Sam's "0303 Direct Line" series, his name disguised as numbers, was advertised throughout the campaign. One analyst compared the parties' newspapers advertisements (Table 7). Content analysis demonstrated similar numbers of policy and legal ads for the Min-Ja Party; however, policy ads were run three times more frequently than legal ads (712 versus 256), 80% of ads were five columns. The Min-Ju Party developed twice as many policy ads as legal ads.

The candidates used many different media: videotapes, answering machines, computer networks and promotional events; cartoons and logo songs played an important role. Videotapes were distributed primarily to party members: the Min-Ja Party produced four versions on the character of Kim Young-Sam: "People Who Start the Dawn

Table 7: Analysis of Types of Newspaper Advertisements for Min-Ja Party and Min-Ju Party by Content (post October, 1992)

Content	Min-Ja Party*	Min-Ju Party
Introductory, including contest announcement	4	7
policy	27	26
legal	26	12
others	2	5

*Forty-nine of Min-Ja Party advertisements were five-column, one was ten-column.

(16 minutes)," "The Great Mountain Kim Young-Sam: His Biography," "The Door to the Great Way," and "The People of this Country and Kim Young-Sam." The Min-Ju Party distributed three videotapes on Kim Dae-Jung: "Kim Dae-Jung Speaks," "This is the Truth" (clarifying rumors of Spokesman Hong Sa-Duk's ownership of a Chinese restaurant [the Lee Geun-Hee incident], and existence of an underground library safe) and "The Party Convention" featuring the party's convention. Featuring Bong Doo-Hwan, widely known as anchor of the "Nine O'clock News," the Kook-Min Party made 15 versions of "Kook-Min Party News" and "Kwang Hwa Moon Discussion," comprising Chung Ju-Young's activities along with "What is that?" "The Newspaper," "The Family Law Forum" and "This is the Answer." Using computer networks, the Min-Ja Party offered the program "The Leader Kim Young-Sam" and other news; Kim Dae-Jung used a computer graphic disk file, "Do You Know Kim Dae-Jung?"

Promotional cartoons were very popular, especially among young voters. The Min-Ja Party published "The Man Who Starts the Dawn of New Korea," a 64-page cartoon story elaborating Kim Young-Sam's political experiences and 77 policies (structure and content were loose and feedback was disappointing) and "Is that a Policy or a Comedy?" comparing the major parties' policies. The Min-Ju Party developed "Even the Falling Dragon Has a Wing," a 68-page cartoon depicting the Korean economy's guardian dragon, hurt by falling; it went to the Min-Ju and Kook-Min hospitals to no avail; it was finally cured by doctor Kim Dae-Jung at the Min-Ja General Hospital and returned to heaven. The Kook-Min Party had a 220-page cartoon, "The Potato Flower Tractor" based on Chung Ju-Young's "There May Be Hardship but Never Give Up." For promotional events, the Min-Ju Party's Special Youth Committee sponsored "Let's Go, the Wave of 20s and 30s" and "The Citizen's Cultural Festival to Save the Han River" using an environmental protection theme. To boost patriotism and confirm the will to unification, the Kook-Min Party sponsored the "4325 Festival" race, marking the 4325th year of Tan-Kun's establishment of Korea.

Numerous advertisements from private groups illegally supported candidates; none named a specific candidate or party but content made obvious who was supported. The Min-Ja Party was supported by "The Committee on the Elementary Educational System in Korea," "Korea-US Friendship Committee," "Korean Anti-Communist Youth Group" and "Seoul Elementary School Parent Association." The Min-Ju Party was supported by "Seoul National University Association," "The National Association for Patriotic Will," "National Forum for Min-Ju Reform and the Establishment of Min-Ju Government" and "Election Campaign Committee for

Working People." The Kook-Min Party was supported by various subsidiaries of Hyundai Group; "The Association of Employees at Hyundai Family and Contractors" participated in ads against government intervention and stalking. In general, these advertisements resulted in adverse publicity for their respective parties; illegal support for the Min-Ju Party fueled "background criticism"; Kook-Min Party advertisements from the Hyundai Group led to "monetary campaign" criticisms.

Advertising Expenditures

Tables 8, 9 track newspaper advertising expenditures before and during the campaign. Because election law only allowed four advertisements in each newspaper, in some cases advertising quantity decreased during the campaign. Total advertising quantity was Min-Ja Party 1,061, Min-Ju Party 372, Kook-Min Party 1,331; the Min-Ja Party concentrated advertising in October and November; the Min-Ju and Kook-Min parties increased advertising in September and August respectively. By end November, the Min-Ja, Min-Ju and Kook-Min parties spent 4.6, 2.8 and 7.7 billion won, respectively on newspaper advertising; observers believed each party spent similar proportions of available resources. Each party's spending was expected to peak in the final few days.

Table 8: Newspaper Ads (#) and Expenses ('000 won) by Party Before the Final Campaign

Party	June		July		August	
	Freq.	Expense	Freq.	Expense	Freq.	Expense
Min-Ja	28	333,169	8	325,000	99	693,924
Min-Ju	14	135,999	14	131,384	20	136,235
Kook-Min	12	104,123	54	292,724	210	1,146,697

Party	September		October		November		Total	
	Freq.	Expense	Freq.	Expense	Freq.	Expense	Freq.	Expense
Min-Ja	38	282,399	209	1,592,638	598	1,712,244	980	4,939,374
Min-Ju	52	323,370	95	588,396	177	1,529,539	372	2,844,923
Kook-Min	274	1,465,708	306	1,354,100	475	3,289,543	1331	7,652,895

Table 9: Legal Newspaper Ads (#) and Expenses ('000 won) by Party During the Campaign

Party	11/20–11/30	
	Frequency	Expense
Min-Ja	64	323,872
Min-Ju	48	261,232
Kook-Min	20	104,738

Decisions

Each of the three candidates, Kim Young-Sam (Min-Ja Party), Kim Dae-Jung (Min-Ju Party) and Chung Ju-Young (Kook-Min Party) sat with his advisors to plan strategy for the final week of the campaign. Each had campaigned hard, yet each knew that the final week was crucial. Each reflected on his campaign thus far, wondering if mistakes had been made and how they might be addressed.

Exhibit 1: Min-Ja Party, Announcement of the Solicitation of Slogan and Symbol

Headline translation:
   "We will start the era of change from your wisdom."
   " We are soliciting the slogan and symbol to be used for the presidential election." Min-Ja Party

Exhibit 2: Min-Ja Party, Newspaper Advertisement

Headline translation:
Candidate No. 1, Kim Young-Sam
"'Kim Young-Sam's Reform' will begin with the economy."
"Only clean politics and courageous reform will save our economy." Min-Ja Party

Exhibit 3: Min-Ja Party, Newspaper Advertisement

Headline translation:
"Korea that is running again, Kim Young-Sam the leader."

Exhibit 4: Min-Ja Party, Policy Advertisement: "Building New Korea"

Headline translation:

"Declaration of the Creation of New Korea! The country where diligent workers live happily, and the honest own the country." Min-Ja Party

1. New Koreans ... can walk safely even in late evening.
2. New Koreans ... are diligent and thrifty; even the ministers and the vice-ministers take the subway.
3. New Koreans ... freely talk over the phone and write letters to North Koreans ... and share the joy of unification eventually.
4. New Koreans ... love the traditional taste and prepare dinner with domestically grown vegetables.

론조사보다는 직통전화에 의한 안건을 광고에 더 많이 반영하였다.

김영삼 후보의 광고는 선거단계별로 그 내용을 달리하였는데 선거초반에는 정책광고와 이미지광고에 치중한 데 반하여 중반에는 상

Exhibit 5: Min-Ja Party, Advertisements Attacking Other Parties

Headline translation:
   "Candidate No. 1, Kim Young-Sam: Let's Create New Korea with Kim Young-Sam!"
   "How can we trust the fate of this country to someone who rides on the back of the radical opposition forces?" Min-Ja Party

   "The fantasy that presidency can be bought,
   Let's eradicate with the force of our people." Min-Ja Party

Translation:
  Number 7, Sang-Do Town in the city of Seoul, Kim Young-Sam has lived here for the past 30 years. His dawns are all the same.
  Child: Good morning.
  Kim Young-Sam: Good morning.
  He has lived here for 30 out of his 40 years in politics, but never bought an additional space or land for his house.
  Kim Young-Sam is such a man!
  An honest man, Kim Young-Sam!
  Kim Young-Sam: Even if I become the president, I will come back to this house to live with an empty pocket, after my tenure is over.
  Narrator: Creation of New Korea: Our choice is only Kim Young-Sam.

서울 상도동 7번지, 이곳에서만 30년을 살아온 김영삼 후보
그의 새벽은 언제나 같다.
꼬마/안녕하세요.
김영삼/안녕하세요.
정치경력 40년 그중 30년을 이곳에서 살면서 집 한칸 땅 한평 늘려 본 적이 없다.
이러한 김영삼!
정직한 사람 김영삼!
김영삼/제가 만일에 대통령이 된다 해도 임기를 마치면 빈손으로 다시 이 집에
돌아와 살 겁니다.
성우/신한국 창조 우리의 선택은 오직 김영삼뿐입니다.

Exhibit 7: Min-Ju Party, Announcement of Solicitation of Slogan and Symbol

Headline translation:
"Min-Ju Party is searching for the slogan for the presidential election."

〈그림 17〉 민주당의 구호공모광고

Exhibit 8: Min-Ju Party, Poll Results: Trends in Voter Support

(Conducted by external sources, publicity teams, planning offices and telephone polls)
Month/Day
   Min-Ja Party (solid black bar)
   Min-Ju Party (striped bar)
   Kook-Min Party (gray bar)

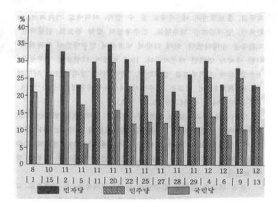

Exhibit 9: Min-Ju Party, Legal Newspaper Advertisement

Headline translation:
Candidate No. 2 Kim Dae-Jung
"'92 our choice ... Change or stall?

Let's change this time!"
"How can you paint your 30-year colleague in the Min-Ju movement as a pro-Communist, even if you are about to lose?"

Headline translation:
   "The worst traffic situation in the country, the worst water supply situation in the country."
   "After 33 months since the merge of the three parties, how much has Inchon improved?"
   "7070 'Democracy Phone Line'." Min-Ju Party

   "The weakest industrial structure in the country, the least-developed region in the country."
   "Do the farmers and fishermen in Kyung-Book Province live better than those in other regions?"
   Min-Ju Party

Exhibit 11: Min-Ju Party, Television Advertisement: "Power Replacement I"

Translation:

Man 1: Who should I vote for this time?

Man 2: What do you mean, vote? Even if we vote, they will again merge with other parties or do some in-fighting

Woman: That's why we have to vote and make changes!

Man 1: Who are you going to vote for, Kim Hye-Ryung?

Woman: Kim Dae-Jung.

Men 1, 2: Who?

Woman: Kim Dae-Jung!

Man 2: You used to dislike Kim Dae-Jung?

Woman: Yes, I used to, before.

Man 2: But you are still voting for him?

Woman: Does individual sentiment matter in a presidential election? The issue for this election is not whom I like, but the question of changing the power!

Man 1: Yeah, Korea is the only country where the incumbent and the opposition parties never changed during 40 years.

Woman: Yes, we should change them this time. We should teach the politicians that if they do poorly, they will be replaced.

Man 2: Would things change if we replace the hands of power?

Woman: Then, they will fear the common people. If they do poorly again, we should change again!

Man 2: Now that I listen to you, you are right!

Man 1: Yeah, Let's try changing this time!

Woman: We will make a change on Friday.

Please make a change on Friday! (on one of the screens appears "2, Kim Dae-Jung")

Exhibit 12: Kook-Min Party's Mascot Advertisement, Tiger

Headline translation:
  "The cabinet system is the culmination of democracy."
  "We, Kook-Min Party, will begin the new era of change with the cabinet system."

Exhibit 13: Kook-Min Party, Legal Newspaper Advertisement

Headline translation:
  "Candidate No. 3 Chung Ju-Young promises the following to the people of Korea."

Exhibit 14: Kook-Min Party, Television Advertisement: "Candlelight"

(On screen, in order: "Who will save this country?" "Total foreign deficit, 42 billion dollars," "Economy President, Unification President")

Background music

Narration: Our economy is dimming. Our future is getting dark. Series of defaults of small and medium companies; 40,000 unemployed in a month; 9.5 trillion won in deficit for agricultural and fishing sector. Who will save this country? Chung Ju-Young; we have Chung Ju-Young. The man who has run vigorously changing numerous impossibilities into possibilities. The man whose heart still thumps with the start of dawn. This is Chung Ju-Young, a specialist in the economy. Tell us your dreams of tomorrow. Chung Ju-Young will accomplish them with you. Let us save the economy. Let us light up our future.

Appendix: Political Marketing

Political marketing applies the methods of traditional marketing, effectively managing financial, human, material and time-related resources for maximum effect in political purposes. Because election campaigns can be viewed as marketing, the term "political marketing" is widely accepted.

Election Strategy

Election is a political activity in which several candidates compete for a limited number of positions. In modern elections, candidates strive to persuade voters of their policies and characters. Choice of candidate should be based on voter interests and voters should use rational processes to select only competent candidates. However, because human beings are not always perfectly rational and sometimes rely on other means to judge candidates, image is an important electoral factor. Because voters cannot easily have personal contact with candidates, they often rely on images stored in their cognitive schemata. Thus, modern election strategy can be summarized as image-making.

Image Strategy

Image is an amalgamation of belief, concept and impression one person holds for another. In an election, a candidate's image refers to the unique characteristics s/he conveys to voters. As such, it can form the basis of differentiation from other candidates. A candidate's image comprises seven dimensions: generosity, quality, morality, seniority, distance, personality, dynamics (Appendix Table 1). All interact to form a candidate's image; good images comprise positive directions on the seven dimensions.

Appendix Table 1: The Seven Dimensions of Image

Dimension	Expression
Generosity	understanding, broad-minded, "large bowl"
Quality	smart, superior, incompetent, dull
Morality	honest, immoral, unfair
Seniority	young, old, experienced
Distance	friendly, kind, unkind, detached
Personality	cheerful, active, moody, intellectual, responsible
Dynamics	active, passive, healthy, aggressive

Developing a positive image requires identifying the positive and negative factors held by voters. Image is constructed around these chosen factors, accentuating the positive, counteracting the negative. An image strategy refers to the process of creating and emphasizing the positive image to voters.

In an election, position, theme, symbol and slogans are used to create an image. Position signals the candidate's ideological standing. (Because Korean political parties all tend to the conservative, position has not been an important image element; this is expected to change as political consciousness grows.) Whereas position is short-term oriented, theme is long-term and more inclusive. Korean themes include "Building an efficient welfare society," "Creating an advanced country"; U.S. examples include "The New Deal" and "Frontier." These themes, based on the candidate's political philosophy or party ideology, are the specific mechanisms through which long-term directions are presented.

A symbol stands for abstract or specific objects that relate to the candidate or party. In previous Korean campaigns, parties used such symbols as "oxen," "bear," "rabbit," "turtle" and "tiger." In addition, colors on the party's flag, shirt or cap can serve as symbols. Symbols help maintain a sense of unity among supporters and display party/candidate power to opposition or neutral voters. A slogan is a message communicated between candidate and voters. It can serve as a concentrated message conveying the candidate's image, opinion, policy, position and symbol. It should be selected carefully.

Managing an image is as important as its establishment. Image management, eliminating negative factors and promoting positive factors comprises three facets: image replacement – negative factors discarded, replaced with positive factors; image enlargement – established image stabilized and promoted; image enhancement – parts of an image constantly changed and evolved for improvement. A candidate's image-making should be based on a general advertising strategy; it should consider voters' political tendencies and preferences and incorporate the candidate's personality, background and political philosophy.

In Korean politics, specific image management issues are crucial. First, a negative image related to financial matters is fatal and should be solved immediately; second, voters tend not to forgive candidates with morally negative images. Finally, since voters tend to side with winners, a loser image can be fatal.

Promotional Strategy

Because neither candidate nor campaign workers can contact all voters personally, different media are used for indirect contact. Promotional strategy informs voters of the candidate's image through different media (e.g., advertising, direct mail, telephone, promotional pamphlets, posters, events).

Promotion target. The key to promotional strategy is market segmentation. Based on polls, information on each district should be used to decide the proportion of campaign resources to be allocated. Second, among the five types of voters – active supporters, supporters, neutral, dissent – active dissent, supporters and neutral voters should be targeted extensively. Data for this decision comes from polls.

Promotional route. Different methods should be identified for approaching promotional targets. Human and material resources should be allocated efficiently to distribute promotional materials. Since house-to-house calls and telephone campaigns are prohibited in Korea, direct mail or trips to different regions should be considered. By constantly monitoring success (through polls), particular routes can be supplemented and improved.

Political advertisements. Political advertisements are one element in promotional strategy: "(a) communication process through which a candidate or a party conveys political messages using general media to affect voters' political beliefs, attitudes and behavior." Similar to commercial advertisements, political ads package the candidate in favorable light, hoping for voter support.

For several reasons, political advertisements are popular in many democratic countries. First, the structure of the political environment has changed: since campaigns last longer and party functions are weaker, a strong candidate image and policies are necessary. To gain the attention of voters amid much competitive information, only advertisements that vividly emphasize candidate's character can effectively persuade and formulate a strong image. Second, as the number of eligible voters has grown, traditional methods such as political rallies have become inefficient; advertising appealing to a greater audience has emerged as the preferred choice.

Finally, general media (e.g., television) have changed the form of political communication. Emergence of television and growth of political advertising are closely related. Political ads in prime time can potentially influence election results since "undecided" mobile voters tend not to pursue information through newspapers, political magazines or interpersonal communications actively. Since they tend to favor entertainment rather than news, ads targeting them can be most effectively delivered via television, between entertainment programs.

Case 47

Cheil Jedang Corporation's Seasoning[1]

Doo Hee Lee
Korea University, Seoul

In January 1992, Taek-Kyung Im, Executive Vice President of Marketing for Cheil Jedang Corporation, was reviewing the history of the Korean Seasoning Market with new employees of the Samsung Group. He discussed the various market shifts and competitive moves that led to Cheil Jedang's current position in seasonings. As he introduced Cheil Jedang's new venture, entry in the new Instant Food category, he challenged his audience to see what lessons might be learned from seasonings that could be applied to instant food.

৪৩৫৪৪

Summary of Development of the Seasoning Market in Korea

Monosodium glutamate (MSG), discovered by Dr. Ikeda in Japan (1908) became the basis for the so-called "culture of seasoning"; the essence of savory taste, MSG lessened saltiness, softened and heightened the flavor in food. Chemical seasoning (also called fermentation seasoning), composed mainly of MSG was introduced into Korea under the brand name "Ajinomoto." By the 1960s, the Korean market for chemical seasoning was highly competitive involving such brands as Mannani, Miwon, Mipoong, Miwang and Ilmiso.

From the 1960s to the early 1980s, the chemical seasoning market was characterized by Cheil Jedang's endless attempts to challenge the market leader, Mi-Won Corp. (Mi-Won). Cheil Jedang introduced a series of products under both the Mipoong and Ayimi brand names but, despite spending significant resources, was unable to reverse consumers' perceptions that "seasoning equals Miwon." After many years' effort in

---

[1] Translated by Theresa Seung Ho, Graduate School of Business, Columbia University.

chemical seasonings, in 1975, Cheil Jedang introduced Dashida, based on natural ingredients, in an attempt to revolutionize the seasoning market.

In the early post-introduction years, consumers did not respond favorably to Dashida and it was close to being discontinued. However, in the early 1980s, growing public concern with potential harmful effects of chemical seasoning worked in Cheil Jedang's favor. As a result, sales of chemical seasoning peaked and sales of Dashida grew rapidly. In response, rival Mi-Won introduced Manna, also based on natural ingredients. Despite extensive efforts, Manna was unable to dislodge Dashida from leadership in natural seasonings. Subsequently, Mi-Won reduced marketing resources for natural seasonings, preferring to defend its position in chemical seasonings. The dynamic competition between Cheil Jedang and Mi-Won was creating a new market structure: Miwon led in chemical seasonings, Dashida in natural seasonings.

By 1985, as competitive pressure from Miwon eased, Cheil Jedang strove to maintain its natural seasonings leadership by consistently promoting Dashida as the "symbol for taste." However, realizing the growth potential for natural seasonings, Mi-Won introduced a new high-quality natural seasoning, Gamchimi, and shifted marketing resources from Manna to Gamchimi. In response, Cheil Jedang introduced Dashida Gold. By the early 1990s, the new market structure had further developed; in 1991, the ratio of chemical to natural seasoning unit sales was 6:3 (Exhibit 1). Miwon continued to lead in chemical seasonings, Dashida in natural seasonings. (See Table 1 for major products, 1964 to 1991.)

Table 1: Major Competitive Products, 1964–91

Year/company	Cheil Jedang	Mi-Won Corp.
1964 to 1976	Mipoong Series	Miwon
1976 to 1982	Mipoong, Ayimi series*	Miwon, Complex Miwon
1982 to 1991	2.5, Dashida, Dashida Gold	Miwon, Manna, Gamchimi

*Yo-In Mipoong, Baek-Sul Mipoong, No. 100 Mipoong, Gook-Ja Mipoong, RBTC Mipoong, Ayimi, Ayimi Gold, Baek-Sul Ayimi.

The Competitive Period in Chemical Seasoning (1964–82)

Miwon was developed by Dong-A Hwa-Sung Industry in 1956. In September 1958, Dong-A Hwa-Sung changed its name to Mi-Won Corp. and entered the food industry; it dominated the seasoning market in the 1960s. In 1964, Cheil Jedang Manufacturer, a producer of sugar, flour and oil, acquired Won-Soon Industry, the third ranking seasoning firm; it attacked Mi-Won with its Mipoong brand. In response, Mi-Won developed a new fermentation method for successful large-scale production, established national distribution and generally confirmed Mi-Won's superior market position.

The intense Mi-Won versus Cheil Jedang competition drove small firms from the seasoning business and, from 1972 on, the two rivals dominated the market. In the 1970s, Cheil Jedang launched aggressive efforts in attempts to displace Mi-Won as market leader. The natural seasoning, Dashida was introduced in 1975; chemical seasoning RBTC Mipoong in 1976.

Historically, Cheil Jedang distributed its products to small retailers and restaurants through exclusive regional distributors; it serviced large retailers (e.g., supermarkets, department stores) and food establishments directly. When seasonings were added to the product line, they had to compete for shelf space and distributors' attention with large-scale products such as sugar and flour.[2] In part because of this problem, when Dashida was introduced, Cheil Jedang added a new system of seasoning-only specialty outlets.

In general, marketing efforts concentrated on a "push" strategy through incentive plans for wholesalers and retailers. Despite these efforts, consumers' strong brand loyalty for Miwon impeded Cheil Jedang from significantly increasing market share.

Realizing the limitations of attacking Miwon with its various Mipoong products, Cheil Jedang introduced and strongly supported a nucleic acid-based chemical seasoning brand, Ayimi, based on new technology. Since sales of Mipoong were concentrated in restaurants, Ayimi was launched with energetic advertising and sales activities aimed at households. In addition, Cheil Jedang introduced a brand management system for guiding its efforts with seasoning products. Mi-Won quickly responded by introducing Complex Miwon based on similar nucleic acid technology. However, most consumer purchases were habitual (Miwon, 46%) and buying patterns did not change significantly; Cheil Jedang made little headway with Ayimi.

In sum, Cheil Jedang's quantity-driven "push" strategy for increasing market share resulted in greater inventory and unstable prices. Frequent brand name changes failed to install a brand concept in consumers' minds; rather, the variety of different, evolving products seemed to be regarded as "just another one similar to Miwon." (See Exhibit 2 for sales of Mi-Won and Cheil Jedang products, 1964 to 1982.) Nonetheless, sales of both companies grew as the seasoning market developed; growth averaged 13% p.a. in the early 1970s, 10% p.a. subsequently. By 1982, Mi-Won outsold Cheil Jedang by a ratio of roughly 7:3.

The Period of Natural Seasoning Competition

Recognition of Natural Seasoning

In the mid-1970s, realizing that its various attempts to dislodge Mi-Won from its leadership position were largely unsuccessful, Cheil Jedang executives turned attention to natural seasoning. The rationale was several-fold: first, consumer loyalty to Miwon was extremely strong and Cheil Jedang's various efforts in chemical seasoning had been largely unsuccessful; second, although chemical seasoning improved the taste of food, its ability to enhance taste was limited and Cheil Jedang executives believed that consumers were potentially willing to switch to a higher quality, higher price alternative; third, in the 1970s, the Korean economy grew rapidly and by the mid-1970s annual per capita income reached US$590 – consumers were beginning to seek

---

[2] As time progressed, both Cheil Jedang and Mi-Won products were available in similar distribution outlets, from small grocery stores to large department stores.

natural and healthy food; fourth, by comparison, natural seasoning was introduced in Japan in the early 1960s when per capita income was between US$500 and US$600; finally, market leader Mi-Won appeared content with its current market position and seemed to be in a defensive posture.

Development of Dashida and Introductory Marketing Strategy

Cheil Jedang conducted diverse studies to identify ideal characteristics for its natural seasoning prototype product "X." First, favorite dishes in households were researched; consumers were found mainly to prefer soup or stew rather than steamed/sauteed vegetable dishes and fried cakes. Also, they tended to use natural condiments such as beef, scallion and garlic when cooking soup or stew. Based on this research, the concept for product "X" was determined to be "a natural seasoning, with an ideal blend of natural condiments such as beef, scallion, garlic and onion, that will enhance the taste of traditional soup stock." (See Exhibit 3 for a positioning map.) Benefits to consumers were asserted to be: "Enhanced the taste of beef stock, easy to use, economical, safe due to its natural ingredients." Unlike chemical seasonings such as Miwon and Mipoong, product "X" fell into the natural/seasoning food quadrant in which the product had a taste of its own, rather than merely "assisting" flavor enhancement. The target market was "middle-class, highly educated and urban homemakers in their 30s."

In naming the new product, Cheil Jedang deviated from the tradition of using the "Mi" syllable (signifying taste) as in Miwon and Mipoong. Top executives decided on "Dashida," meaning "the act of smacking lips after a taste of good food" such that consumers would understand it was a natural seasoning that enhanced the taste of soup stock. Packaging was also different. Whereas chemical seasoning was packaged in transparent tubes with simple graphics such as a traditional pot or soup dipper, Dashida was packaged in aluminum-coated paper with a simplified picture of a cow. Based on taste preference research, 12 different types of Dashida (e.g., fish, anchovy, lunch-box, beef-stock, beef) were introduced to satisfy consumers' diverse taste preferences.

Dashida was priced to be about 10% of the total cost of making beef broth from scratch, roughly double chemical seasoning. In addition to selling Dashida through its traditional multi-product system also handling sugar, flour and oil, the seasoning-only specialty outlet system was introduced.

Cheil Jedang advertised on radio and in print and simultaneously staged "consumer-participation events." The advertising concept was based on consumer preferences for natural, good quality and traditional taste; this concept was tailored to customer convenience and characteristics of the target market (Exhibit 4). Advertisements for Dashida, especially on radio, were considered highly original. Popular entertainers promoted Dashida by personally handing out samples to consumers. A radio advertisement would typically announce that "Today, Hye-Ja Kim goes to Bo-Moon Market in Sung-Book district." (See Table 2 for summary radio advertisements accompanying consumer-participation events.)

Despite large marketing investments, Dashida made little headway in the seasoning market until the late 1970s. First, Dashida contained small quantities of salt and

Table 2: Summary of Radio Advertisements

Theme	Contents
No. 1 Lucky Dashida Gift Hunt	The "Lucky Gift Van" visited one of ten selected residential areas with middle-class homemakers everyday. The location was announced through radio. Eligibility limited to homemakers only.
No. 2 Quiz for Dashida Family	Three popular entertainers announced messages such as "high in nutrients," "easy to cook with," and "used in all types of dishes." Participants who sent in postcards with correct identification were selected through lottery and given rewards. The program sought to increase product knowledge and program participation.
No. 3 Short Prose for Dashida	"Have you tried Dashida yet?" was the theme-phrase. Responses to the product were sent in short prose and announced, promoting consumer participation.
No. 4 Year's Dashida Gift	Consumers cut and paste Cheil Jedang's logo on postcards that were sent with a neighbor or relative's address, name and a short Message. Selected messages were announced in advertisements; senders received awards.

chemical seasoning (< 20%); some sensitive consumers complained about its salty and greasy taste, doubting the ingredients were natural. (Nonetheless, Dashida was much less greasy than 100% chemical seasoning.) Second, many products other than Dashida offered convenience, time saving and versatility. Third, many homemakers were sensitive to price and believed Dashida was simply too expensive.

Cheil Jedang executives believed that a lower price was needed for Dashida to be successful; prices were reduced by about 5%. In addition, simplifying the product line, improving the packaging and subdividing package units was necessary.[3] Finally, product defects were solved as it was believed that these, rather than advertising or other marketing programs, were having a fatal effect on Dashida sales.

Executives believed the greatest accomplishment of Dashida's marketing strategy between 1975 and 1982, when rival product Manna was first introduced, was the consistent use of the catchy phrase "just like the taste of beef broth, Beef Dashida." This slogan was perceived to have effectively increased product recognition and almost changed the conventions of food usage. Dashida sales grew from 100 tons (1975) to 3,000 tons (1982) as consumer-eating patterns began to favor natural foods (Exhibit 5).

Introduction of Rival Product, Manna, and Cheil Jedang's Defensive Strategy (1982–85)

From 1982 to 1986, the seasoning market's trajectory was uncertain as chemical seasonings were increasingly believed to be harmful to health. Recognizing the negative impact on chemical seasoning demand, in October 1982, Mi-Won announced the birth

---

[3] Initially, Dashida was offered in few, generally large, package sizes.

of its new natural seasoning: "Mi-Won Corp., the originator of seasoning, introduces a new compound seasoning, Miwon Beef Manna." Mi-Won attempted to use the halo of its formidable predecessor, Miwon, to overcome the disadvantage of being a late entrant. Marketing expenditures were heavy: in 1983, advertising spending was 1.8 times Dashida; by 1985 it secured 40% share of natural seasonings. (See Table 3 for Manna's message strategy promoting the simulated taste of beef broth as its major strength.)

Table 3: Message Strategy for Manna

• Taste	–	"rich taste of broth, beef Manna"
• Versatility	–	"any dishes, soup or stew ..."
• Economics	–	"just one teaspoon for a serving ..."
• Natural	–	"fresh beef, garlic, onion ... 85%"
• Legitimization	–	organizing events such as sampling parties

Cheil Jedang's response to Manna's natural seasoning entry initially focused on advertising that told consumers: "It is the era of Dashida," and "No matter what, it is Dashida." In addition, Cheil Jedang attacked the chemical seasoning market with catchy phrases such as "From the era of chemical seasoning to the era of Dashida," and "It is the era of natural seasoning."

When first introduced, Dashida's "natural" seasoning quality was sufficient to distinguish it from traditional chemical seasonings. However, Manna's introduction made this differentiation insufficient and Cheil Jedang executives determined that Dashida needed to create "a culture of taste." Many research studies were conducted.

Research on Dashida's target market focused on the profiles of homemakers, the dominant users of Dashida (Table 4). In particular, Cheil Jedang determined that Dashida's target market was urban homemakers who had left their hometowns and enjoyed "soupy" dishes or traditional dishes such as stew. These urban citizens were nostalgic for the taste of the past, mother's home-cooked meals. This study led to a new advertising strategy promoting "delightful taste of hometown," "our taste," "taste of Korea," "sound of hometown," and "taste of hometown."

A comparative Dashida/Manna brand loyalty study demonstrated that consumers preferred Dashida (42.7%) over Manna (19.3%); undecided consumers ("I don't know" [22.5%] and "The two are about the same" [11%]) reached 33.5%. Cheil Jedang divided the factors driving loyalty into "inherent" quality and "peripheral" factors (Table 5). Not unexpectedly, since seasoning was a frequently used item, satisfaction after use was the most important and pervasive factor, with consistent emphasis on taste as the main value. However, Cheil Jedang executives were concerned with the weak (9.4%) level of "habit" for choosing Dashida (compared to 46% for Miwon). They reasoned that if "habitual loyalty" due to taste-related characteristics was a strong factor, market share could be sustained even though other marketing factors were inferior. Conversely, if Dashida, with its weak habitual element, were not better in quality, advertising and promotion, risk of market share loss was significant.

Table 4: Characteristics of Dashida's Target Market

Item	Characteristics
Demographics	Urban homemakers between the ages of 25–39 Above high school education with 1–2 children Either or both of the couple had left their respective hometown
Lifestyle	Plan menu around husbands' taste, dine out at times Favor apartments as housing Favor advertised products
Usage	Use both natural and chemical seasonings Use seasoning to enhance the taste of soup and stew
Buying pattern	Buy own at supermarkets Buy at least once a month, in 100 grams
Contact with media	Watch television a lot (especially sitcoms and hit-song programs) Listen to women-, homemaker-, and hit-song programs on radio Read newspapers for about 20 minutes a day

Table 5: Reasons for Buying Different Brands

Reasons	Dashida	Manna
Characteristics for the product quality		
1. Has good taste	26.2	24.9
2. Has beef flavor	23.4	22.9
3. Is not greasy (refreshing taste)	17.1	10.8
4. Is good quality	2.6	6.4
5. Has unique taste	1.3	4.5
Subtotal	**70.6**	**69.5**
Other reasons		
1. Is from an established company	10.9	5.1
2. Has been used habitually	9.4	3.2
3. Has good advertisements	3.9	1.3
4. Others	5.8	5.0
Subtotal	**30.0**	**14.6**

Product studies indicated that about 30% of consumers used neither brand; among users, Dashida use (74.4%) was superior to Manna (22.6%) (use of both, 1.8%; other, 1.2%). Thus, nationally, 52.6% of consumers used Dashida (61.2% in Seoul). (See Table 6 for geographic distribution results, later used to restructure Dashida's distribution system; see Table 7 for use of different types of seasoning.)

Brand recognition and familiarity studies (Exhibit 6) showed that brand recognition was higher for Manna's advertisements; more people indicated seeing or hearing key scenes or phrases in advertisements. However, measurement of brand familiarity by writing the name of the brand in key phrases showed Dashida and Manna to be about the same. In a brand image analysis study, consumers were asked to express their subjective views of both Dashida and Manna. Dashida was viewed favorably by 2.5 times as many respondents as Manna (Exhibit 7).

Table 6: Product Usage by Geography (%)

	Total	Seoul	Pusan	Kwangju
Dashida	52.6	61.1	47.8	37.1
Manna	15.9	18.4	12.1	14.7
Dashida + Manna	1.2	1.2	1.3	0.4
Other	0.9	0.9	1.3	1.3
None	29.4	18.4	37.5	46.5
Total	100.0	100.0	100.0	100.0

Table 7: Use of Different Seasonings

Use	Proportion (%)	Number of households
Chemical seasoning	27.1%	313
Chemical + Natural	69.4%	802
Natural seasoning	1.1%	13
None	2.4%	27

In 1985, Cheil Jedang executives believed that future Mi-Won strategy for Manna would be to use fully Miwon's halo effect. It was expected to maintain its advertising slogan, "rich soupy taste, Beef Manna," as a direct attack on Dashida's advertising phrase, "just like the taste of beef broth, beef Dashida." Regarding distribution, Dashida's wholesale channels were restructured from the traditional multi-product system to specialized wholesalers handling only seasoning. In addition, since Dashida sales were concentrated in households, especially in Seoul, a newly-formed sales department managed supermarkets in Seoul.

Finally, in 1984, Cheil Jedang introduced the "Musical" advertising series to sustain and emphasize Dashida's advertising concept as "the taste of beef soup, Beef Dashida." It also sought to fragment Mi-Won's efforts by targeting the chemical seasoning market and in February 1985 introduced the brand, "2.5," with the catchy phrase, "nucleid-seasoning you use only a little."

Dashida, an Attempt to Symbolize Taste (1985–90)

Debates on "The Theory of Harmful Chemical Seasoning" that commenced in the early 1980s increased by the mid-1980s to embrace many different consumer organizations. These environmental forces adversely affected chemical seasonings and favorably affected natural seasonings. By this time, consumer dissatisfaction with Dashida's product features were much diminished and Manna's attacks were somewhat curtailed. Cheil Jedang began a serious effort to install a critical advertising concept in consumers' minds: "We search for the root of our culinary culture in which our tradition still breathes."

Starting in 1985, a series of related advertising campaigns was launched: "Taste of Season, the Sounds of Four Seasons" (1985, 1986), "Taste of Hometown" (recreation of taste) (1987), "Our Taste, Korea's Taste" (common taste, culture of taste) (1988) and "Taste of Hometown," "Sound of Hometown" (symbolization of taste) (1989, 1990). Over time, the concept of "taste" was gradually magnified.

The campaign, "Taste of Season, the Sounds of Four Seasons" was Cheil Jedang's first attempt to symbolize Dashida as a synonym for taste, by linking Dashida to seasonal delicacies. This campaign paved the way for "The Taste of Hometown" that established Dashida as the "Taste of Our Folkway Tradition." It emphasized that such taste was of mothers' homemade meals, the taste of hometown. Advertising executions comprised dishes typically associated with rural hometowns such as vegetable soup, cold cucumber soup, handmade noodles and zucchini stew. A soap opera star, Kim Hye-Ja, popular for her homely role in the rural family drama "Rural Diary," appeared exclusively to link the drama's image with the concept of Dashida (Table 8).

Table 8: Advertising Expressions for Dashida (1988)

"Rural Market" series	"New Year's Day" series
Taste of Hometown, the Rich Flavor It is a generous harvest this year, and generous minds Do I feel so good, oh so good This is the very taste of genuine soybean soup Yes, this is our bountiful taste, the taste of Dashida Taste of beef broth, Beef Dashida	Taste of our hometown, it is so good and rich It is a cold winter day, but my mind has warmed up Neighbors here and there make rice cakes The sound of mill is everywhere Laughter everywhere Grandmothers sit around with their grandchildren And shape dough into dumplings together The night deepens with overflowing love Wow – The taste is so rich – The taste of hometown has not changed at all Dashida

Consistent emphasis throughout 1987 on the concept of "Taste of Hometown, Dashida" led Cheil Jedang executives to believe Dashida had changed the value and use traditionally associated with seasoning and promoted a new genre for taste. Advertisements were systematically featured in the four major media (i.e., television, radio, newspapers, magazines) to maximize reach and frequency. (See Table 9 for a typical radio advertisement, "Returning Home.") Other executions aired nationally were: "Morning Greeting," "Harvest Moon Festival," "Grandmother," "Maternal Grandmother," "Father," "Grinding Mill" and "Bean Soup on Dong Ji" (traditional celebration of the 11th lunar month). In other media (i.e., television, newspapers, magazines) executions differed from season to season while consistently using the theme "Dashida, the Taste of Deep, Hometown Flavor."

Table 9: "Returning Home" Series for Dashida

I still have far to go but I am already back in my hometown in my mind; I have almost become a Seoul person, but how can I forget the homemade taste; Of the squash stew and just-made tofu, cooked in homely clay pot? The taste of hometown; Still the same today; Beef Dashida

"Our Taste" (1988) was a further evolution of the advertising strategy that broadened beyond "hometown taste like mother's cooking." The target market was enlarged as Dashida evolved to represent the traditional and simple taste of hometown. Subsequently, advertising executions comprised food in settings such as traditional wedding celebrations, simple rice-soup in rural markets and rice cake-soup on New Year's day, appreciated by any Korean.

Whereas 1987 advertisements emphasized the purpose and use of Dashida, in 1988, the focus shifted to scenes of everyday life (e.g., Korean traditions and lifestyle) enhancing the breadth of expression. At a time of national pride (the 1988 Summer Olympic Games were held in Seoul), the Dashida advertisements emphasized the characteristic lightheartedness of Koreans: "Wedding Festival" featured simple and playful townspeople at a wedding; "Rural Market" described rural generosity.

The Sound of Hometown, embodying elements of traditional Korean taste, changed from season to season; Dashida advertisements in 1989 and 1990 sought to symbolize those tastes. Because television could not convey all different taste of hometown sounds, other media were used; "visible sounds" were featured in newspapers and magazines, and "audible sounds" in radio (Figures 1, 2).

While Cheil Jedang worked on symbolization of Dashida's taste, rival Mi-Won introduced Gamchimi (1988), an improved version of Manna containing 20% beef (Figure 3). Cheil Jedang executives believed Mi-Won was attempting to segment natural seasonings into high- and low-classes; Gamchimi would secure leadership as a high-class product. In response, Cheil Jedang introduced Dashida Gold; its beef component was five times Dashida's.

Figure 1: "Summer Series" for Dashida

- Background: A peaceful scene in the country in which farmer attends to his cow while children fish.
- Concept: The taste of hometown – Dashida.
- Phrase: Moo – Rich flavor, the taste of hometown.
    Cold cucumber soup and handmade noodles, they taste like my mother's cooking.
    Wow! How long has it been since I tasted something like this?
    Yes – It is still the taste of hometown. Has not changed a bit.
    Beef Dashida, Dashida.
(*Top left scene: "The Taste of Hometown, Dashida." Bottom right scene: "Beef Dashida," "Cheil Jedang Sugar Manufacturer."*)

Figure 2: "Autumn Sounds Series" for Dashida

- Background: Rice is almost ready for harvest; a woman is shouting to chase sparrows away.
- Concept: Sounds of Hometown, Taste of Hometown – Dashida.
- Phrase: Bang, bang, bang, hurrah – (sound of chasing birds away).
     In the hometown's autumn, there is a sound, there is a taste
     Hurrah –
     Sound of hometown, taste of hometown, Dashida (sound of soup boiling)
     Yes, this is the taste –
     Taste of beef broth, Beef Dashida, Dashida!
     (Top left scene: "Dashida's Autumn." Bottom left scene: "Taste of beef broth, Beef Dashida" (partial view).)

Figure 3: Print Advertisements for Gamchimi

Top Quality Seasoning Beef Gamchimi, with 20% beef
The Taste is Really Different.
"Why have so many homemakers switched to Gamchimi with 20% beef?"
- Composition is different, with 20% beef
- Taste is different
- Seasoning particles are different
- Packaging is different
Miwon Gamchimi (on both the package and bottom right hand corner)

736   Part XIV   South Korea

With stalling aggregate demand for chemical seasoning post 1987 and continued growth anticipated in natural seasonings, in 1989, Cheil Jedang shifted marketing resources from brand "2.5" to Dashida. (See Exhibit 8 for advertising expenditures in natural seasonings.) Overall spending patterns for Cheil Jedang (Mi-Won) were: television, 69% (78%); radio, 19% (10%); magazines, 6% (5%); newspapers, 5% (6%). From 1989 onwards, Cheil Jedang maintained advertising expenditures for Dashida; Mi-Won drastically reduced spending. Mi-Won's reductions were believed to have two major causes: first, it had successfully increased brand familiarity of Gamchimi; second, market shares of Manna and Gamchimi increased only marginally (Exhibit 9).

Results from Cheil Jedang's Advertising Strategy

A 1989 survey (Korea Gallup) demonstrated Dashida's high brand loyalty. In recall tests for natural seasonings, 49% recalled Dashida first (Manna, 11%); 91% recalled at least one of Dashida's advertisements (Manna, 80%); 81% used Dashida frequently (Manna, 17%) and 78% indicated a willingness to purchase Dashida again in the future (Manna, 17%).

By 1989, Dashida was the clear leader in natural seasonings. Although Manna's market share reached 40% in 1985, it subsequently lost position. By contrast, Dashida's market share increased from 60% (1985) to 68% (1991). In 1991, the seasoning market was partitioned between chemical and natural seasonings in a 6:4 ratio. Cheil Jedang retained 37% of chemical seasonings for about 50% of the total seasoning market.

Rival Mi-Won Corp.'s Overall Advertising Strategy

In the mid- to late 1980s, Mi-Won's advertising had two goals. First, it attempted to re-develop the chemical seasoning market through a "recycling" strategy. The "source campaign" reminded consumers that Mi-Won was a "fermented" seasoning made by refining sugar cane, a natural source; thus, Mi-Won supposedly differed from regular chemical seasonings (Figure 4). Second, since Mi-Won was found popular among middle-aged consumers (40s and 50s) but less so among younger consumers (20s and 30s), the "Mi-Won in Your Life" campaign was launched.

In 1990, Mi-Won developed a new natural seasoning strategy in an attempt to sustain its superior position in the overall seasoning market. Unlike previous approaches that positioned Manna as a substitute for Dashida, the new strategy sought to present an urban and modern image that differentiated Manna in product and advertising concept. (See Exhibit 10 for the construction of Manna's new advertising concept, "refreshing taste – Manna," highlighting greasy taste, the chronic complaint of Dashida users, while accentuating Manna's "fresh source" image.)

Manna's advertising concepts were promoted in all major media (i.e., television, radio, newspapers, magazines). On television and radio, an emotional approach announced "refreshing taste – Manna"; in newspapers and magazines, the reason for the refreshing taste was explained, an impossible task on television. In sum, Mi-Won attempted to build a sympathetic relationship with homemakers in their everyday lives, then connect Manna and "refreshing taste" (Figure 5). On radio, differentiation from Dashida was sought by expanding the refreshing taste theme to the whole family's favorite (Table 10).

Figure 4: Print Advertisement for Mi-Won

"Mi-Won's Taste Begins from Sugarcanes"

Figure 5: Manna "Autumn" Series

- Background: Actress Doo-Shim Goh, seeming angry, is lying down waiting for her husband, who is late from work.
- Concept: Refreshing taste – Manna
- Phrase: Men are so selfish
  - But men leave every day so that they can return home later
  - Do as you please but I am waiting and hungry
  - For this autumn, make some refreshing soup
  - Beef Manna, its soup is so refreshing
  - Yumm, so refreshing
  - Beef Manna, from Mi-Won.

Predicting Trends in the Seasoning Market

In the early 1990s, the seasoning market demonstrated consistent growth: demand for chemical seasoning plateaued in response to changes in eating patterns and consumer needs; natural seasoning continued to expand. Both Manna and Dashida

Table 10: Radio Advertisement for Manna

Background:	Sound of soup boiling
Woman:	Women make refreshing taste
Background:	Sound of soup boiling
Man:	Men just love refreshing taste
Background:	Sound of soup boiling, getting louder
Woman and Man:	The whole family loves refreshing taste
Background:	Sound of laughter
Woman:	Now, enjoy refreshing taste of broth
Narrator:	Refreshing taste loved by the whole family – (song) Beef Manna

continued to pursue attachment-oriented advertisements emphasizing the emotional aspects of their products. Dashida employed themes such as "Leaving the Hometown" in pursuit of "The Taste of Hometown," Manna responded with its "Waiting" series featuring a middle-aged couple's sentiments and episodes.

Cheil Jedang executives believed that although overall seasoning market shares of Cheil Jedang and Mi-Won were comparable, neither firm's products were distinctive. Nonetheless, Miwon continued to dominate chemical seasonings; Dashida dominated natural seasonings. The market seemed to be so structured that reversal of market positions was impossible. Mi-Won was expected to continue to focus on chemical seasoning's advantages through its re-development strategy. However, if the natural seasoning market continued to grow, Mi-Won would surely not concentrate only on chemical seasonings!

Instant Food

Executive Vice President, Taek-Kyung Im, paused in his address:

O.K. Now I am almost done with the story of the long and tumultuous war in the seasoning market. But, let us go back to 1991 when Cheil Jedang was pursuing brand expansion through "Instant Food." We agonized over how to utilize the Dashida brand. Now I'll tell you more about that.

Instant Food is a product whose strengths are convenience and economy. For example, seaweed soup can be prepared by placing the contents of an "Instant Seaweed Soup" into boiling water. However, because Dashida's image is based on the "Taste of Hometown," characterized by long simmering, calling a brand "Instant Food Dashida" seemed somehow awkward and could cause confusion in product concept. Moreover, if the whole class of Instant Food failed, Dashida's established image could be damaged. Conversely, Dashida's product concept was already well established in consumers' minds and the name Instant Food Dashida could penetrate the market for Gamchimi and Manna whose images were very close to instant food. Also, Instant Food Dashida could accommodate changes in consumers' lifestyles.

Through this session, you all have had a chance to learn the characteristics of the seasoning market. Now, as marketing strategists, what decisions would you make in this situation?

Exhibit 1: Total Consumption of Chemical and Natural Seasonings

Year	Chemical seasoning	Natural seasoning	Year	Chemical seasoning	Natural seasoning
1964	1,500	–	1978	35,000	800
1966	3,500	–	1980	42,000	1,200
1968	8,000	–	1982	39,000	2,000
1970	13,000	–	1984	47,000	7,000
1972	20,000	–	1986	52,000	11,000
1974	25,000	–	1988	52,500	16,500
1976	31,500	–	1990	57,000	23,000
			1991	60,500	29,000

Exhibit 2: Total Sales during the Competitive Period in Chemical Seasoning

Year	Mi-Won Corp.	Cheil Jedang Mfg.	Year	Mi-Won Corp.	Cheil Jedang Mfg.
1964	1,000	0	1974	17,000	6,800
1966	3,000	800	1976	22,000	8,000
1968	6,000	2,000	1977	25,000	10,500
1970	105,000	2,300	1979	27,500	13,500
1972	15,000	4,500	1981	28,000	10,000

Exhibit 3: Product Positioning Map

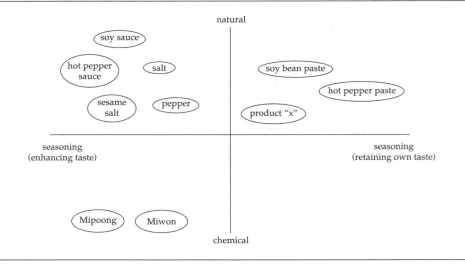

Exhibit 4: The Advertising Concept for Dashida

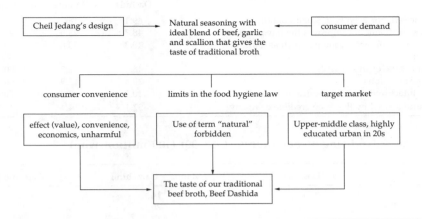

Exhibit 5: Sales of Dashida in the Early Period (1975–82) (tons)

Year	Sales	Year	Sales
1975	120,000	1979	500,000
1976	200,000	1980	750,000
1977	260,000	1981	1,300,000
1978	380,000	1982	3,010,000

Exhibit 6: Recall from Advertising (%)

	Recall brands	Does not recall	Recall the ad
Beef Dashida			
• "For greater flavor, of course it is _____."	42.4	39.7	(82.1)
• Several dishes appearing on TV screen.	23.9	22.3	(46.2)
• "Devotion of 9 years, the taste of _____."	15.9	18.2	(34.1)
Miwon Beef Manna			
• "Rich flavor of beef, Beef _____."	45.5	37.7	(83.2)
• Model Eunah Ko, holding the product, explains it.	28.9	48.3	(77.2)
• Because Beef ____ is so rich, just use a little for a serving ..."	15.4	42.2	(56.6)

Exhibit 7: Brand Image (%)

	Dashida	Manna	No response
• Enhances flavor even with small quantity	49.1	18.7	32.3
• Even a small amount improves the flavor or taste	48.7	23.9	27.4
• Has many different seasonings such as garlic and scallion	40.3	20.6	39.9
• Enhances flavor in any dish	46.8	22.7	30.6
• Is more nutritious	29.6	13.9	56.5
• Is manufactured more hygienically	20.3	9.5	70.1
• Is manufactured by the more credible company	37.1	14.4	48.5

Exhibit 8: Advertising Expenditures (1988–90) (100 million won)

Year	Dashida	Manna + Gamchimi	Gamchimi
1988	18	14	12
1989	28	26	13
1990	27	17	7

Exhibit 9: Market Shares in the Natural Seasoning Market (1982–91) (100 million won)

	Dashida	Mi-Won and Gamchimi		Dashida	Mi-Won and Gamchimi
1982	80	20	1987	66	34
1983	70	30	1988	67	33
1984	68	32	1989	66	34
1985	60	40	1990	69	31
1986	65	35	1991	70	30

Exhibit 10: The Advertising Concept for Manna

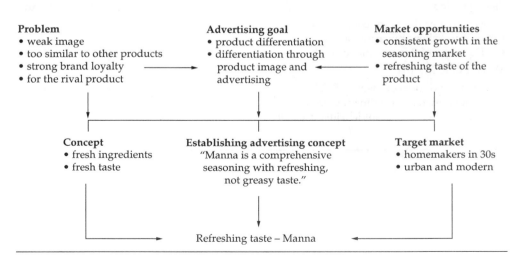

Case 48

Super Miracle CC: Marketing and Advertising for the Large-screen TV Market[1]

Doo Hee Lee
Korea University, Seoul

Late one afternoon in November 1990, Kim Sun-Min, director of sales promotion and advertising at GoldStar Electronics (LG Electronics) was summoned to Executive Kim Yongwook's office. Executive Kim expressed his concerns about GoldStar's position in large-screen TVs.

GoldStar, founded in the difficult days of the Japanese colonial regime, and financed solely by non-Japanese sources, was a leader in Korea's electronics industry. GoldStar had pursued a strategy of independent technology development, a humane corporate culture and customer-centered corporate management to establish its position. In television, GoldStar manufactured Korea's first black and white television (1966) and secured a technological and manufacturing leadership position. However, in the 1980s and 1990s, it faced increasingly strong competition from Samsung and Daewoo.

In particular, GoldStar did not lead in new large-screen TVs, nor did management have confidence the situation would be quickly reversed. Since increasing demand for these products was expected, GoldStar's position was a matter of serious concern. Executive Kim Yongwook charged the Sales Promotion and Advertising Department (SPAD) to remedy the situation. Director Kim assigned section managers Im Gab-Young and Chun Yeon-Sung the task of researching the market and developing strategic alternatives.

⧉

Technological Background

Development of color TV was driven by a desire to outgrow the limits of black and white television and achieve life-like color vision. First demonstrated by CBS (U.S.), in

---

[1] Translated by Theresa Seung Ho, Graduate School of Business, Columbia University.

1947 RCA (U.S.) announced the format of its color television; this led eventually to the current NTSC format. Other nations selected different formats: France (1966) chose SECAM, the rest of Western Europe chose PAL. Japan began broadcasting color TV in 1960; Korea started color-TV programming in the NTSC format in December 1980.

In the mid-1980s, industry observers believed that consumers were no longer satisfied with conventional color TV. At the 1985 Tsukuba Expo, Japan's NHK announced its concept of "Hi-Vision," HDTV. NHK broadcast its first HDTV programming for the Seoul Olympics (1988). HDTV technology represented continued progress through realization of ultra-fine vision and adding new and varied functions.

Market Research Findings

Section managers Im Gab-Young and Chun Yeon-Sung collected various types of TV market data.

Attribute Importance

Among the set of elements considered important by consumers, 50% were related to visual; about 30% related to added functions (Gallup Poll). Audio-related functions rated low, apparently consumers had low expectations of high-quality audio enjoyment (Table 1).

Table 1: Attributes Considered Important in Purchasing a Television Set (%)

Visual quality	Screen size	Functions	Design	Price	Audio quality	Others
29	21	15	14	9.5	4.2	7.3

Source: Gallup Poll.

Market Situation

The three pillars of Korea's electronics industry, "the electronics three," were GoldStar (LG Electronics), Samsung Electronics, and Daewoo Electronics. Table 2 shows 1990 domestic and export sales (Association for Promotion of Electronics Industries).

Table 2: Sales Figures for Major Electronics Product Manufacturers (1990) (100 million won)

	GoldStar	Samsung Electronics	Daewoo Electronics
Domestic	15,054	18,662	5,632
Export	14,786	26,455	7,478
Total sales	29,840	45,117	13,110

Source: Association for Promotion of Electronics Industries.

According to GoldStar executives, Samsung's greater sales owed much to the inclusion of computer products, semi-conductors and telecommunications, in addition to electronic products. However, just as Samsung could not be said to lead GoldStar, neither could GoldStar claim leadership over Samsung. Daewoo, pursuing an innovative growth-strategy through creative advertising and "group-wide" support could not be underestimated.

Among electronic products, TV had special status in Korea; it had a close relationship to the culture and exerted a strong influence over consumers; competition for market share was fierce. By 1980, color televisions were mass produced. Sales grew to over 2 million per annum; 95% of households had at least one color TV. Tables 3 and 4 show sales and market share figures for televisions.

Table 3: Domestic TV Sales, 1981–90 (number of sets [million won])

Item	1981	1982	1983	1984	1985
Color	(1,256) 357,481	(1,288) 361,593	(1,514) 464,613	(1,715) 425,976	(1,117) 263,372
Black & White	(257) 16,233	(136) 8,380	(53) 3,301	(28) 2,072	(31) 1,998
	1986	**1987**	**1988**	**1989**	**1990**
Color	(1,368) 323,832	(1,583) 281,572	(2,149) 367,747	(1,912) 359,659	(2,010) 460,901
Black & White	(33) 1,967	(47) 2,992	(94) 4,605	(36) 1,823	(48) 1,921

Source: Association for Promotion of Electronics Industries.

Table 4: Market Shares for Top Three TV Producers

	1988	1989	1990
GoldStar	37%	35%	39%
Samsung	38%	39%	40%
Daewoo	15%	16%	10%
Others	10%	10%	11%

Source: Electronics News.

Samsung and GoldStar competed for top position, currently held by Samsung by a close margin; Daewoo's market share trend was generally downward. For a short while, Anam held higher market share than Daewoo, possibly because of its early entry in large-screen TV based on assembling imported parts.

Advertising Spending

The four main media for advertising in Korea were television, radio, newspapers and magazines. Typically, advertising in TV and radio used emotional approaches; print media used rationally-driven appeals. (See Table 5 for advertising expenditures [Korea Advertising Data].)

Trends in Demand for TV Products

In recent years, significant changes occurred in the TV market. Until 1987, demand was highest for compact television sets, around 14" screen size; at the time of the Seoul Olympics (1988), demand underwent abrupt changes. Rising living standards led to a

Table 5: Product Advertising, Top Three TV Producers (million won)

		GoldStar	Samsung	Daewoo
1988	TV	1,443	1,751	906
	Radio	110	371	46
	Newspaper	643	1,257	121
	Magazines	32	31	–
	Total	2,228	3,410	1,073
1989	TV	1,666	756	627
	Radio	189	33	110
	Newspaper	1,398	1,525	251
	Magazines	45	14	41
	Total	3,298	2,328	1,029
1990	TV	675	1,311	579
	Radio	173	217	92
	Newspaper	1,356	2,932	361
	Magazines	31	59	49
	Total	2,235	4,519	1,081

Source: Korea Advertising Data.

shift from simple sight and sound to a requirement for vivid and realistic pictures. In addition, functional devices such as remote control and "one-touch sensors" were demanded, concurrent with the growing supply of VCRs (Table 6).

Table 6: Demand for Color TV According to Screen Size

	Less than 16 ins.	16 to 20 ins.	Greater than 20 ins.
1988	81.3%	18.0%	0.7%
1990	54.8%	34.9%	11.1%
1991 (expected)	39.0%	37.0%	24.0%

Other notable phenomena were increased demand for replacement TVs and multiple purchases. The proportion of first-time purchases was decreasing steadily; additional purchases and replacements were rising as consumer tastes shifted to higher-quality, large-screen TVs (Table 7). Accordingly, the three leading suppliers focused major efforts on large-screen TVs (monitor size 20" and over), targeting multiple and replacement purchases.

Table 7: Demand for Color TV According to Purchase Type

Year	Total demand ('000 units)	New	Additional purchase	Replacement
1988	1,350	52%	25%	23%
1990	2,288	32%	29%	32%
1991 (expected)	2,388	26%	32%	41%

Emergence of Large-screen TV

The first large-screen TV, the "Excellent Max," was introduced by Samsung in February 1990; Daewoo followed with "Super-vision Pro" (April 1990); GoldStar introduced "Super Miracle" in October 1990. GoldStar's third placed entry was ill planned; conscious of its late entry, it overly extended production and leapfrogged from 20" screens to 29" screens (ignoring 25"). Although consumer demand trends were for large-screen products, GoldStar failed to match adequately consumers' purchasing power. Retail prices for 29" TVs were about one million won, 400 thousand won for a 20" screen TV. In comparison, Samsung introduced 20", 25" and 29" screens; it also offered medium-priced products. As a result, GoldStar lost lead position. (See Figure 1 for predictions of TV demand.)

Figure 1: Television Product Life Cycles

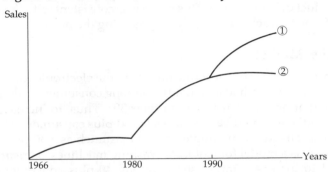

GoldStar Conference

Director Kim Sun-Min summoned a conference in early December 1990 to discuss the market research data. The participants concluded that GoldStar could not significantly improve its position in large-screen TV with the 29" TV alone; a new product that broadened consumers' choice of screen size was necessary. In addition, an effective advertising strategy was needed to bring GoldStar's products closer to consumers. Efforts shifted to developing a new product and new advertising strategy.

Marketing and Advertising Strategy for Introduction of the "Super Miracle CC"

On a group-wide scale, GoldStar emphasized the "Consumer-Oriented Value System," setting a high priority on understanding consumer wants, making these a group-wide ideal and applying them from product manufacturing to sales in a unified cooperative process. GoldStar emphasized the change from an existing "sales-mentality" to a more marketing-oriented perspective. Based on this philosophy, in early 1991, GoldStar TV executives raced to redress their poor market position in large-screen TV. (See Exhibit 1 for the new product development process.)

Following analyses of the market, competitors and GoldStar itself, a strategy agenda was established. Central to the agenda was introduction of a 25" large-screen HDTV; a second key element was the need for a product distinctive from competitors. Vision quality was selected and the concept of a "black screen" was introduced. The screen's surface was given a black finish to increase color delivery quality; this non-glare (NG) function prevented light reflection from the screen. In addition, the screen received an anti-static (AS) coating that reduced dust movement when the TV was turned on and off. Dust movement was unhealthy for viewers and decreased vision quality. Vision coordinating functions were also added.

Naming the Product

Various product names were considered to deliver the product image effectively. "CC (Clean & Clear) Black Screen," was selected, highlighting the black-colored screen and achieving product differentiation. This name was consistent with the existing 29" TV; it also used "Super Miracle," pointedly emphasizing the product's screen.

Targeting the Market

A comprehensive analysis of corporate images in the electronics industry concluded that GoldStar, the pioneer, had a high rating among consumers in their 40s; Samsung was more popular among consumers in their 30s. Thus, to increase market share, GoldStar's advertising would have to appeal to 30-plus consumers. This general strategy analysis was already being implemented inasmuch as a 30-plus former actress, mother of two, was a model for GoldStar washing machines. Samsung, on the other hand, needed to increase market share among 40-plus consumers; it hired Kim Changsook, an actress in her 40s for a series of advertisements posing as a weekend home keeper.

GoldStar executives concluded that, despite being able to break the overall electronics market into rather clear distinctions, these were difficult to draw for television alone since consumers did not believe TVs differed much in practical functions and design. Furthermore, consumer expectations and requirements did not vary greatly. Although market differentiation was extremely important to GoldStar, it was difficult to achieve for TV products.

Developing the Advertising Concept

Message elements for TVs were categorized broadly as visual (e.g., visual quality, screen size, screen shape, screen manipulability), audio (e.g., speaker capability, method of audio recreation) and miscellaneous functions for manipulation (e.g., remote control, one-touch sensor, satellite reception). The importance of audio quality was comparatively lower than for audio equipment.

In 1988 and 1989, advertisements by the three major manufacturers (i.e., GoldStar, Samsung, Daewoo) centered on audio quality. However, GoldStar executives now believed that only after consumers received a certain level of visual satisfaction did increased audio quality and other functions become important. As a result, new advertising was oriented around visual quality. Samsung also refocused its advertising on visual quality; Daewoo Electronics continued with audio quality, believing consumers saw little difference in visual qualities among domestically produced TVs (Table 8). In addition, in 1990 all three manufacturers sought product differentiation via artificial intelligence-related advertisements.

Table 8: Summary of Competitive Advertising

	1988	1989		1990	
GoldStar	Misc. function (secret code)	Audio (stereo)		Audio (revolving sound system)	Visual quality (high density)
Samsung		Audio (stereo)	Visual quality (screen in the screen)	Supplementary function (digital control)	Visual quality (flat screen)
Daewoo	Audio (stereo)			Audio (Dolby stereo system)	

Advertising Concept for Super Miracle CC

A black-colored TV screen that eliminated light reflection and static was expected to appeal to consumers as refreshing and novel while also having a distinct appearance. However, the IQ color-coordinated control, offering a wider range of color recreation providing a greater degree of delicate hues, required specialized knowledge that was difficult to convey to consumers. After much discussion, GoldStar chose "The black-colored screen of GoldStar TV is high-definition vision" for its advertising concept. The basic technological concept was "Black-colored screen and IQ color coordinated control" (Table 9).

Table 9: Advertising Concept for Super Miracle CC

Function		Differentiation		Application for advertisement
Features	Direction	Competitive	Consumer recognition	
Black monitor • no glare • no statics		Yes	visible and refreshing	main concept
IQ color coordination	visual quality	Yes	logical (difficult to understand)	supplementary concept
Artificial intelligence • Viewing distance control		weak	hackneyed	not critical, but would benefit from having one
• Automated screen-sound		weak	hackneyed	not critical, but would benefit from having one
Aero dome speakers	audio quality	No	hackneyed	not critical, but would benefit from having one

Advertising Strategy

Advertising that simply delineated product functions rarely yielded the desired customer response. In addition, advertising experts believed many factors led commercials for visual and audio enhancement to have less than the desired effect.

As a result, LG Ad GoldStar's advertising agency affiliate sought a more visual orientation for advertising Super Miracle CC; it planned a campaign based strongly on analogy and fantasy. It also concluded that emphasis should focus on emotional rather than functional elements. The themes would be used for all visual and in-print advertising. For print advertisements, a serialized product concept was employed as a means to induce logical and consistent interests through varied expressive means (Table 10).

Table 10: Summary of Advertising Concepts for Super Miracle CC

Advertising concept	High visual quality of CC black screen TV
Approach	analogy, fantasy
Strategy for each medium	• a unified image for print, radio and TV commercials
	• visual and emotional approach
	• newspaper ads: stage-by-stage approach
	• May 1: black-color image (woman in a black veil) publicize introduction of the new product
	June 2: differentiation of TV screen (emphasis on monitor) – product differentiation
	• July 3: high visual quality as product's image (fish) suggests product's utility to consumer
Brand	Super Miracle CC

Unfolding the Advertisements

TV and newspaper advertisements began appearing on TV and in print in May 1991. GoldStar's agency developed a plan of strategic advertising to counteract competitor advertising. Advertising for Super Miracle CC comprised:

TV commercials. The television commercial for Super Miracle CC was based on delivering its main advantages and securing product awareness (Table 11, Exhibit 2). An observer commented:

> The commercial opened with the image of a woman shrouded in a dark veil (to conjure up the product's black screen). Mystery and curiosity about the woman's identity is contrasted to maximize the effects of high-quality vision. The next scene showed a yellow fish leaping free from a palm into the TV screen; the screen's solid is transformed into a liquid one, thereby inducing life-like imagery.
>
> Later, the woman is shown standing in front of the TV screen, her veil in the wind, emphasizing the product's screen and the TV itself. The commercial ends with the woman's sharp gaze and the fish's liberating leap, placing conclusive emphasis on life-like imagery.

Table 11: Contents of Super Miracle CC TV Commercial

Background: a woman in a dark veil and a bright yellow fish are seen on the TV screen's surface
Concept: life-like rendition of high quality vision
Voice: The desire for live vision. GoldStar's Super Miracle CC
High-sensation, CC Black Screen
GoldStar Super Miracle CC

Printed advertisements. These advertisements, closely related to those on TV but restricted because of medium limitations, were based on three stages (Exhibit 3): stage 1, "The woman in a dark veil"; stage 2, "The woman and the screen"; stage 3, "The fish and the woman." The observer commented:

> Stage 1 introduces the new product and emphasizes its distinctive black screen by using the image of a woman in a dark veil. The woman's large eyes draw the reader's attention; the vivid eye make-up color implies the advertising concept of high visual quality. Stage 2 strives for product differentiation by emphasizing the black TV monitor, the basis for stage one's black-color concept and the basic functional difference from competitors' products. In stage 3, the image of the bright yellow fish is juxtaposed with the veiled woman to induce the concept of high visual quality. For added emphasis of the black color concept, the background is in black.

Competitor Advertising

When GoldStar's advertising campaign was launched, competitors responded: Samsung with the "parakeet," Daewoo with its "Impact" series.

Samsung Electronics

Samsung's advertisements for Cinema TV employed a parakeet and an eagle (Table 12, Exhibit 4). An observer interpreted its advertising:

> The parakeet's wings exude color extravagance; together with the enlarged image of an eagle they represent color clarity and the product's large-size screen. The commercial begins with the TV showing the image of the parakeet; its extravagance and life-like wing coloring lead the eagle to mistake it for real. At the mid-point of the commercial, the eagle heads straight for the parakeet into the screen; the TV screen then becomes real, emphasizing the life-like visual quality of the product. The scene in which the eagle flies into the TV screen employs the same special effect as GoldStar's "Super Miracle CC" commercial in which a fish is floating in the monitor and makes the screen vivid for consumers. The last portion shows the parakeet flying out of the TV screen; it turns off the TV and escapes the eagle's threat. This mini-suspense enhances customers' product interest. The commercial finishes with

the parakeet repeating, "cinema, cinema," leaving the strong impression of an entertaining commercial and raising consumer awareness for Samsung Cinema.[2]

Table 12: Contents of Samsung's Cinema TV Commercials

Background: A multicolored parakeet is flying in circular motions while being targeted by an eagle
Concept: High quality TV of live images
Voice: Masterpiece in large-screen TV, Cinema TV
Color is alive, sound is alive
High quality Cinema TV
Samsung Excellence
Parakeet: Cinema, cinema

Daewoo Electronics

In response to Samsung "parakeet" and GoldStar's "tropical fish," Daewoo developed computer graphic-enhanced commercials for its Impact TV. An observer interpreted its advertising:

> In the commercial's initial scene, a man stands with arms crossed surrounded by several TV sets. From the background, green laser beams, representing precision of visual quality, shoot forth in vivid display. Concurrently, the TV screens show light movements in an electronic circuit pattern. The next scene zooms on one TV screen; it shows a range of hues, emphasizing clarity of the visual quality. (Thus far the emphasis is visual quality, suggesting that Daewoo, whose TV ads traditionally focused on audio capabilities, decided that visual quality should no longer be ignored.) The commercial then goes on to present Daewoo's distinct advertising concept emphasizing audio capabilities: several heavy-duty speakers are shown inside one of the TV sets and added emphasis placed on audio quality via medium and low sound. Finally, the man from the start of the commercial reappears and raises his hands toward the sky. Several beams of light emerge from the TV screens around him, rising from bottom to top of the male figure. The beams converge to create the word "Impact."

These commercials seem to create an anticipation of a new level of TV audio/visual capabilities. Whereas Samsung and GoldStar focused only on visual clarity, Daewoo centered its message on superior audio. To this essentially unchanged advertising strategy, visual quality was added; Daewoo's distinctive feature was the concurrent emphasis on both audio and visual qualities (Table 13, Exhibit 5). (See Table 14 for a summary of competitor ads.)

---

[2] This commercial won the grand prize in a major Korean advertising competition.

Table 13: Commercial Contents for Super Vision Impact TV

Background: A man stands, surrounded by several television sets.
Concept: Large-scale visual shock, medium/low sound speakers
Voice: Visual shock – Daewoo Super Vision Impact
        Even clearer. Even grander. The wait was for a TV like this.
        Now the choice for large-screen TV is Daewoo's Super Vision Impact.

Table 14: Summary of Product Advertisements

	GoldStar's Super Miracle CC	Samsung's Cinema	Daewoo's Super Vision Impact
Advertising concept	• live image • ultra-sensitive TV	• visual quality • audio quality • high quality TV	• audio quality • visual quality
Functions	• black-colored screen • IQ color-coordinated visual quality • artificial intelligence • aero dome speakers	• RGB visual quality • CCD's comb filter • Dome speakers • Artificial intelligence	• Horizontal 800 • Dome sound system • mid-to-low frequency woofer
Advertising medium	TV, radio, printed	TV, radio, printed	TV, radio, printed
Subject material	fish (long nose-butterfly), woman in a black veil	parakeet, eagle	computer graphics

Effect of Advertising

GoldStar's agency conducted a study of advertising effects (i.e., consumer response, ratings of commercials) via market research firms and broadcast station data. The following summarizes data collected until December 1991:

The highest responses related to the image of visual quality such as "vivid and clear," "true to life," "clean" (Table 15). Since over 50% of viewers' impressions related to visual quality, GoldStar executives believed the strategy of emphasizing visual clarity was successful.

Table 15: Impressions of the Super Miracle CC TV Commercial

Impressions		Areas of impressions
Vivid and clear*	13%	image of high visual quality
Life-like	12%	image of high visual quality
Fantasy-like	11%	image of high visual quality
True to life	7%	image of high visual quality
Clean	7%	image of high visual quality
Vivid color of the fish	9%	subject material

*13% of all respondents viewing the commercials stated strongly that its image was "vivid and clear."

Subject materials making the most impression on viewers were model-related contents (e.g., model's eyes, fantasy-like model's face, female model); the tropical fish was

Table 16: Viewers' Recollection of the Contents (%)

On model (18)	Model's eyes	12.6	On scenery (17)	Fish	7.8
	Female model	3.4		Tropical fish (in water)	5.4
	Fantasy-like model's face	2.0		Tropical fish (eyes)	3.8
			Announcement/BGM	Background sound	4.0

also rated highly (Table 16). GoldStar executives believed the commercial's use of a model and tropical fish succeeded in effectively delivering the image of high visual quality.

Tables 17 through 20 show research data on the commercials for Super Miracle CC and competitor products.[3] Table 17 shows that Super Miracle CC commercial's emphasis on visual clarity was well received by consumers. Table 18 shows the percent of respondents replying that a certain TV product commercial made an impression (June to October 1991); 26.5% of respondents picked GoldStar's Super Miracle CC commercial as having made an impression, higher than Cinema and Super Vision Impact.

Table 17: Viewers' Content Retention

Super Miracle	%
Emphasis on clarity	47.4
Vividness	16.3
Live vision	15.7
Clean vision	6.8
Life-like vision	4.2

Table 18: Impressionable TV Commercials (1991) (%)

Company/month	6	7	8	9	10
GoldStar	21.4	26.7	29.8	28.3	26.1
Samsung	15.2	15.3	24.9	–	–
Daewoo	–	–	9.3	11.9	–

The rates of recognition for TV and newspaper commercials (1991) show that in Seoul and Daejon, GoldStar's Super Miracle CC commercials were a greater success than those of competitors (Tables 19 and 20).

Table 19: Rate of Recognition for Newspaper Advertisements (1991)

	Super Miracle CC	Cinema	Super Vision Impact
Seoul	33.0%	22.7%	18.9%
Daejon	32.2%	20.5%	21.2%

Table 20: TV Commercial that Left an Impression (1991)

	Super Miracle CC	Cinema	Super Vision Impact
Seoul	26.8%	20.8%	13.4%
Daejon	28.6%	16.7%	16.0%

---

[3] Conducted by Korea Marketing Research & Public Opinion Poll Center (KMR); KMR conducted surveys of approximately 800 respondents monthly.

Lee's PR, a professional research agency specializing in domestic advertising, surveyed a 1,400 respondent panel monthly; it investigated the rate of recognition, preference and dislike for the commercials (Table 21).[4]

Table 21: Responses to the TV Commercials

	Super Miracle CC			Cinema	Super Vision Impact	
	September	October	November	November	October	November
"I saw it"	30.6%	36.5%	33.8%	25.1%	29.6%	26.0%
"I liked it"	12.6%	13.6%	13.0%	10.4%	8.6%	7.9%
"I hated it"	1.5%	1.4%	2.7%	1.4%	2.4%	1.6%

Sales Results

By late 1991, GoldStar's 25" and over screen TV sales increased four-fold since the start of the advertising campaign. In part this was due to a dramatic increase in demand for large-screen television products; sales rose from 9% to over 20% between the second and third quarters of 1991; in part due to focus on the 25" product, providing a wider range of choices (20", 25", 29").

In late 1991, GoldStar's agency assessed market shares for large-screen TV, 25" and over in screen size (Table 22).

Table 22: Market Shares for Large-screen TV, 25" and Over (1991) (%)

	Quarter 1	Quarter 2	Quarter 3	Quarter 4 (expected)
GoldStar	29	33	34	35
Samsung	37	30	33	33
Anam	27	28	24	22
Daewoo	7	9	8	10

GoldStar Evaluation

In January 1992, Kim Sun-Min, head of GoldStar's agency met with his subordinates and representatives LG Ad:

> As you are aware, Super Miracle CC's advertising ended last month. It is appropriate to say it has been a success. First, the increase in sales can be considered a result of the emphasis on 25" screen. In any case, our sales have increased four-fold following the advertising campaign and we have surpassed our competitors in advertising recognition. Today, I would like us to examine the lessons learned from this advertising campaign, begin to plan future campaigns.

---

[4] In the category, newspaper advertisements, GoldStar won the grand prize in the 1991 Korea Advertising Competition; it also won for the color category in the Chosun Daily's 28th advertising competition.

A representative from the agency opened the discussion: "As far as advertising TVs are concerned, I think the main focus should remain aspects of visual quality. I don't think consumers yet expect sound quality like that of an audio system." Section head Im Gab-Young said: "I think use of the color black to emphasize visual quality was a great success. In future, the black color concept should be used continuously to differentiate GoldStar's product from competitors in large-screen TVs." Section head Chun Yeon-Sung added: "Realistically, it appears that consumers do not feel there is a great difference in quality among domestic TV products. Sales can be increased greatly if we succeed in convincing consumers of even a slight superiority in product quality. Investment in R&D is crucial, so is an advertising strategy stressing our superior product quality.

One suggestion was that, in addition to advertising GoldStar's individual products, a campaign for the overall firm would maintain and improve GoldStar's image. Since consumers had low product-differentiation (i.e., did not consider products different in quality) corporate image was an important factor in deciding which products to purchase. Someone noted that Daewoo launched its "New Daewoo Family" campaign in September 1991 for this reason. Other suggestions were for promotional efforts (e.g., brand-wide exhibitions at dealer locations, special discount sales) in addition to advertising.

Director Kim Sun-Min concluded the meeting:

Based on various data, our advertising efforts were a success. But, we must remember that competitors' advertising had innovative elements and they are putting in great efforts. Future competition in advertising is sure to be fierce and unpredictable. Let us pat ourselves on the back for now but make efforts for a new advertisement that will continue Super Miracle CC's success. I commend you all for your efforts.

After the meeting, a celebration of dinner and karaoke was planned. As the staff got ready to leave in an atmosphere of anticipation, the telephone rang. "Director! Executive Director Kim wants to see you immediately."

Exhibit 1: New Product Development Process

Market analysis
Color TV's market saturation/maturation point
(with major supply starting in 1980)
Consumer preference for large-screen TV
Consumer preference for high-definition
Demand for replacement and multi-purchases

Competitor analysis
Popularization of artificial intelligence
Increased production line of large-size products
Trend towards high-definition, high-audio
performance

Self-analysis
Preference for artificial intelligence
Preference for superior audio performance
Main product: 20" and 29" TV

Strategy agenda
High-definition vision (product differentiation from competition)
Strengthening of main product's production line
Emphasis on 25" products

Product: CNR-2590 AI (25")
Functions:
1. Black screen
2. IQ color in parallel circuit
3. Artificial Intelligence
4. AERO DOME speakers
Production Line: 20", 21", and 25"

Exhibit 2: TV Advertising for Super Miracle CC

Exhibit 3: Print Advertising for Super Miracle CC

Exhibit 4: Print Advertising for Samsung's Cinema TV

Exhibit 5: Print Advertising for Daewoo's Super Vision Impact TV

Map of Sri Lanka

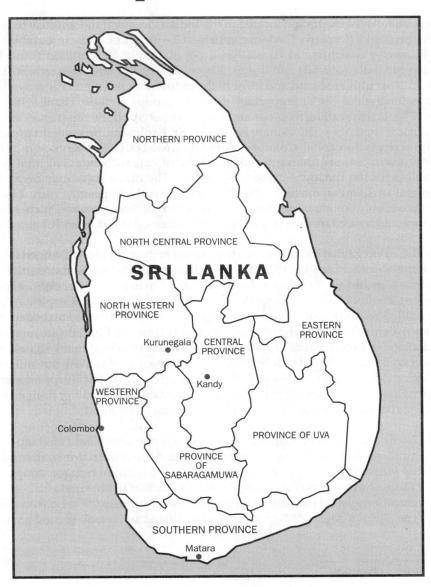

NORTHERN PROVINCE

NORTH CENTRAL PROVINCE

SRI LANKA

NORTH WESTERN
PROVINCE

EASTERN
PROVINCE

Kurunegala

CENTRAL
PROVINCE

Kandy

WESTERN
PROVINCE

Colombo

PROVINCE OF UVA

PROVINCE
OF
SABARAGAMUWA

SOUTHERN PROVINCE

Matara

Sri Lanka Overview[1]

Background. An island nation located in the Indian Ocean off the southeastern coast of India, Sri Lanka (formerly Ceylon) comprises 65,610 sq. km. (only 16% arable) and a 1,340-kilometer coastline. Sri Lanka has a population of 17.9 million (June 1995), speaking Singhala (official) and Tamil. About 70% live in southwestern Sri Lanka where 75% of cultivated land and most of the industries are found. The major ethnic group is Singhalese (74%); important minority groups include Tamils (18%) and Moors (7%). The prevailing religions are Buddhism (69%), Hinduism (15%), Christianity and Islam (both 8%). The climate is tropical. Sri Lanka comprises eight provinces; the largest city is the capital, Colombo, population 615,000 (1990). Revised in 1978, Sri Lanka's constitution embraces a president as head of state with the prime minister and the Cabinet having the highest executive power. The major legislative organ is the unicameral Parliament; the highest judicial agency is the Supreme Court. The legal system is a highly complex mixture of English common law, Roman-Dutch, Muslim, Singhalese and customary law; Sri Lanka has not accepted compulsory ICJ jurisdiction.

Political. Ceylon gained independence from Great Britain in 1948. It changed its name to the Republic of Sri Lanka in 1972. The president assumed dominant executive powers and the constitution was changed to its current form in 1978. Major political parties are the pro-market United National Party (UNP) and the left-wing People's Alliance. Having ruled Sri Lanka for 17 years, in August 1994, the UNP was succeeded by the People's Alliance. Tamil separatists (i.e., Liberation Tigers of Tamil Eelam) and others have demanded independence for the Tamil community in northern and eastern Sri Lanka. A civil war broke out in July 1983, reached a peak in mid-1991, but still continues. Having defied solution for several decades, meeting the political aspirations of the minority Tamils is as daunting as it is urgent. Sri Lanka's costly and prolonged ethnic conflict has been a major obstacle to increased foreign investment.

Social. Since the outbreak of hostilities between the government and Tamil separatists, several hundred thousands Tamil civilians have fled the country for southern India, populated largely by a similar ethnic group; many remain in refugee camps. Over 200,000 Tamils have successfully sought political asylum in the West.

The education system has historically been a major priority of Sri Lankan governments. The literacy rate is 90%; primary schooling is universal; secondary school

---

[1] The Republic of Sri Lanka.

enrollment comprises 74% of the relevant age group; 5% receive tertiary education. Medical treatment, provided by government-employed physicians is free. Life expectancy at birth is 72 (1995).

Economy. Sri Lanka is a member of the United Nations (UN), World Bank (WB), International Monetary Fund (IMF), World Trade Organization (WTO) and Asian Development Bank (ADB). In the mid-1990s, the Sri Lankan economy grew between 5%–6% p.a.: the U.S. (35%), Germany (8%), U.K. (7%) are the main export destinations. Imports come mostly from Japan (12%), India (9%) and Hong Kong (8%) (1993). Sri Lanka's current account deficit, driven by deficit budgeting and foreign debt interest, reached over 7% of GDP in 1994. Foreign debt interest accounts for almost 25% of the total government expenditure. In 1993, net foreign debt was US$77.8 billion versus US$9.4 billion GDP.

In 1994, agriculture contributed 24% GDP (46% employment), industry 25.4% (20.9% employment), services 50.6%, (33.2% employment). Tea (US$413 million), rubber (US$64 million) and coconuts (US$58 million) are the main agricultural exports. Key industrial exports are textiles and garments (US$1.5 billion). In recent years, the government has attempted to diversify the economy to generate new sources of foreign exchange especially in manufacturing and services, notably tourism and banking. A rigorous liberalization program was only put in place in 1989; by end 1993, 33 state-owned enterprises had been privatized. However, roughly half of the industrial base remains in the public sector.

In 1993, private investment grew 10% in real terms and now accounts for more than 85% of total investment; elimination of foreign exchange controls (1994) is expected to further stimulate foreign investment. In 1993, foreign direct investment reached US$188 million. Import controls have been reduced and corporate taxes cut to 35%; the initial 40% limit on foreign ownership for most companies has been removed. The Sri Lankan Board of Investment, acting as a "one-stop shop" for foreign investors, is legally empowered to make decisions in respect of foreign investment.

The official currency, the Sri Lankan rupee (SLR) was allowed to float freely against a basket of foreign currencies in 1978. The overall trend has been downward reflecting persistent current account deficits and relatively high rates of inflation (1988, US$1 = 33 SLRs; December 1995, US$1 = 54.05 SLRs). The Central Bank of Sri Lanka (formed 1950) implements monetary policy and regulates the money supply. The commercial banking system comprises 23 banks (six local, 17 foreign-owned) and 14 rural development banks; by end 1994, Sri Lanka had over 1,100 domestic and foreign commercial bank branches. The Colombo Stock Exchange is relatively small but growing; average daily trading is less than US$10 million; at end 1994, market capitalization was US$2.857 billion.

Infrastructure. Sri Lanka's infrastructure is inadequate and generally poor quality. Sri Lanka has 775,749 kilometers of roads, 27,637 kilometers paved; inter- and intra-city public transport is overcrowded. The government-owned Sri Lanka Railways has 1,944 kilometers of track and operates at a loss. Sri Lanka has three ports to accommodate deep sea vessels: Colombo (largest), Trincomalee and Galle. Colombo ranks 26th among world harbors in tonnage handled (over 800,000, 20-foot equivalent units in 1993). Colombo is an important way station on international air routes; the national airline, Air Lanka (60% government-owned), has flights to Europe, the Middle East, West and Southeast Asia.

In 1993, electricity generating capacity was 1.3 million kWh; production was 3.2 billion kWh, 200 kWh per capita. Sri Lanka has 9.3 telephones per 1,000 population (1993). International direct dialing was introduced in 1980 by the government-owned monopoly, Sri Lanka Telecom; by 1995 the backlog for telephone line requests exceeded 100,000. Since 1992, private operators have been able to provide value-added services such as mobile phones, paging, cardphone and data transfer; Sri Lanka has four cellular telephone operators.

Statistics*	June 1991	June 1997	Statistics*	June 1991	June 1997
Per capita GNP	US$430	US$660	Pop. growth	1.3%	1.2%
GDP growth	5.1%	5.6%	Infant mortality / 1,000	24	14
Savings (GNP)	n/a	16%	Life expectancy (yrs)	n/a	72
Inflation (CPI)	21.3%	16.7%	Literacy rate	86%	89%
Foreign debt (in billion)	US$5.3	US$8.2	People per tel.	124	88
Pop. (million)	17.4	18.3	People per doctor	7,253	5,888
Urban pop.	n/a	22%	People per TV	n/a	19.2
			Calorie intake (cals)	n/a	2,286

*Secured from *Asiaweek*.

Case 49

Keells Food Products Ltd.

Samina Seth
The Hong Kong University of Science and Technology

Noel Capon
Graduate School of Business, Columbia University

Ranjan de Silva, Director of Jaykay Marketing Services Ltd. (JMS), was contemplating a key branding decision. JMS distributed food products for sister company Keells Food Products (KFP) whose 1995 results showed a significant rebound from a 1994 loss. With increased funding for product expansion now available, a crucial point was reached regarding the Keells name; in particular, decisions had to be made about new lines of vegetables and canned meats. "Keells" was strongly associated with meat products but was also used by other group companies; some employees believed the brand would be "over-used" if more "Keells" products were added. De Silva wondered if KFP should adopt an umbrella branding strategy in the food division or create sub-brands with different names for new products to cater to specific segments. A sub-brand strategy would require the Sector Committee's approval. The next meeting was August 15, 1995, only two weeks away; de Silva had to work fast to identify key issues and make recommendations.

കൗ

Background to Keells Food Products Ltd.

By the early 1980s, John Keells was Sri Lanka's market leader in tourism, primarily via hotel ownership. Since quality meat products were critical to hotel food and beverage activities and imported foodstuffs were not cost-effective (duties and taxes on a variety of food items reached as much as 70%) processing meats locally became a priority.

In 1983, John Keells Holdings (JKH) launched Keells Food Products (KFP) to manufacture and market processed meat for the Sri Lankan hotel and catering industries; to improve economies of scale, the target market was expanded to include local retailers. JKH engaged a German entrepreneur to set up a quality-oriented meat processing plant in Sri Lanka; German personnel trained local staff in food technology. JMS controlled all KFP's marketing functions; it earned revenues based on a percent of KFP sales.[1]

In 1987, Sri Lankan ethnic violence escalated, affecting JKH's core tourism industry. The Board of Directors reassessed the group's exposure to tourism and decided to focus more on local industries. One result was increased emphasis on building the food division whose vision was to be the leading food manufacturer and marketer in Sri Lanka; JKH's food and beverage sector grew rapidly (see Figure 1 for organization chart). KFP developed and launched a range of meat products incorporating many innovative features with the goal of increasing sales five-fold by 1995; several sub-brands were launched including "Farm House" (1990), "Krest" (1992) and "Kirata/Mirisata" (1993).

By August 1995, KFP was the dominant marketer of processed meat products in Sri Lanka, employing 250 people.[2] In addition to local sales, significant exports went to the United Arab Emirates and the Maldives, an island chain forty five minutes by air from Sri Lanka. Management's top priorities were to increase Keells product range and market coverage, locally and overseas. By mid-1995, food import duties decreased to 35%.

Overall, Keells Food Products demonstrated significant growth and profitability (Exhibits 1A, 1B). De Silva attributed a 1993 sales reduction to a temporary government-imposed advertising ban. Local companies believed this ban resulted from lobbying by Buddhist and Muslim politicians and clergymen (observers said that sections of the Buddhist clergy had always opposed the sale of meat); however, the information minister blamed the ban on creation of unwanted needs.[3] Intense industry lobbying led to a lifting of the ban after six months; during this period, Keells screened a television commercial without showing any meat but this was not effective.

The Sri Lankan Food Market

The Sri Lankan food market differed from the West in several ways. First, although Sri Lankans did not generally pay premium prices for good meat sections (e.g., chicken breast), more recently premium cuts were offered at higher prices; industry observers believed Sri Lankans would increasingly become more discriminating in meat quality. Second, unlike the West, processed food (e.g., sausages) was not considered negatively from a nutritional perspective as a large percent of "good meat" was often included. A significant portion of the population (Buddhist and Hindu) were vegetarians and were more inclined to eat fish. One meat producer believed that pork was not considered bad by the general population and that beef consumption was in decline.

---

[1] KFP was listed on the Colombo Stock Exchange; JMS was a private company. In both cases, JKH had a controlling interest.

[2] In 1993, at the Sri Lankan government's request (many jobs were at stake), JKH acquired Ceylon Cold Stores (CCS) whose meat division manufacturing "Elephant House" brand frozen meats was running at a loss. CCS operated autonomously as a competitor to KFP; JMS serviced only KFP, not CCS.

[3] The right wing United National Party government also halted the import of films with an adult rating in an alleged bid to safeguard the country's youth from corruption and violence.

Figure 1: Organization Chart for John Keells Holdings' Food and Beverage Sector

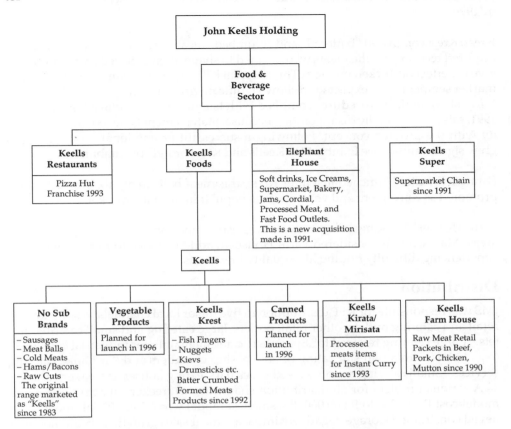

Source: Jaykay Marketing Services (Pvt.) Ltd.

Keells Food Products

KFP's initial (1983) market entry was with beef and pork products, "pre-cooked and hygienically vacuum packed for retaining freshness," marketed under the "Atlas" name. In September 1985, when management believed the products were "perfected," they were re-launched under the Keells name with an aggressive promotional and marketing campaign. As new products were added, they were marketed under the Keells brand and categorized by product type (e.g., sausages, cold meats, processed and raw meat, meat types [e.g., chicken, beef]).

"Keells" was largely promoted as a processed meat brand. In 1991, KFP's widening customer base led to a strategic reassessment and this complex approach was scrapped; by July 1995, four major product groups were offered – Keells, Krest, Kirata/ Mirisata and Farm House (Exhibit 2). "Keells" continued to function as the brand name for a range of sausages, meat balls, hams, bacons and cold cuts; it also functioned as an umbrella brand supporting newly introduced sub-brands (Exhibits 3A, 3B, 3C). New lines of vegetable products and canned meats were scheduled for launch in 1996.

Krest: Krest comprised "battered" and "crumbed" meat products produced via newly acquired technology; the meats were formed to shape, then battered and crumbed to give the effect of chicken nuggets. This first real KFP diversification, targeting the up-market segment, was expected to show significant growth. All Krest products were *halal*;[4] slaughtering procedures complied with Islamic law. Introduced in December 1991, sales were initially disappointing because, management believed, of unfamiliarity with the product concept. Following a successful promotional campaign sales grew significantly. (See Exhibit 4 for Keells and Krest brands profitability.)

Kirata/Mirisata: Launched just after Krest, this meat ball curry mix product range, promoted as convenient and versatile, was popular in the mass market.

Farm House: This range of raw meats was especially popular in highly urbanized areas. Management considered Farm House an added service to Keells consumers experiencing difficulty finding high quality raw meats.

Distribution

JMS was responsible for KFP distribution in five major local channels: wholly owned retail and catering outlets, other retail outlets, large catering and small catering outlets.[5] Large catering referred to "Specialist" catering mainly for industrial customers (e.g., hotels with a two-star rating or above, ship chandlers and Air Lanka catering services). Small catering mainly served snack bars, eating houses and bakeries.

A serious problem for all distribution channels was freezer capacity: a 26 cu. ft. model cost Rs 40,000 to Rs 60,000, the smallest model was 4.5 cu. ft. Salespeople believed constrained storage negatively impacted meat sales growth; JMS did not offer loaner freezers, although the idea had been proposed at a strategy session.

Retail Distribution

Wholly owned retail distribution. The first Keells Delicatessen opened in September 1986 in Colombo. In 1991, JKH launched "Keells Super," its own supermarket chain as a division of JKH's food and beverage sector. Said de Silva: "It was a compulsive marketing exercise for us. Until then, no single vendor displayed the entire Keells food range so it was a logical distribution step. We also identified the supermarket business as a profitable line."

---

[4] *Halal* refers to the Islamic methods of "correctly" slaughtering animals for consumption.
[5] Management had considered and rejected door-to-door distribution for larger volume consumers because of poor road infrastructure and a concern for cost effectiveness.

By 1995, JMS operated four Keells Super supermarkets (two outside Colombo); the larger "Keells Super" versions averaged 6,000 sq. ft. and carried a full range of supermarket products. The smaller "Super K" versions averaged 2,000 sq. ft. and carried a limited range of assorted products. Keells Super assisted with introduction of new products by setting up taste-testing booths. Like the "Pepsi Challenge," also staged in Sri Lanka, free trials of new food products were widely used throughout Sri Lanka.[6]

By mid-1995, other high-end supermarket chains operated in Sri Lanka (e.g., Cargills Food City). These supermarkets, opened before Keells Super, had locations in Colombo and other towns (Table 1). Generally, Keells processed meat products were not carried by supermarkets with their own meat processing operations (e.g., Cargills). De Silva believed that since supermarkets were a new concept in Sri Lanka, substantial growth opportunities existed; he believed current outlets were "just a drop in the ocean." All supermarkets stressed quality by guaranteeing products; these commanded generally higher prices.

Table 1: Sri Lankan Supermarkets

Supermarket chains	Area	No. of outlets
Cargills Food City	5,000 sq. ft., 2,000 sq. ft.	3, 6
Safemart	over 3,000 sq. ft.	3
Premasiri	2,000 sq. ft.	1
Crystal	over 1,500 sq. ft.	2
Park 'N Shop	400 sq. ft.	1
Luminex	1,500 sq. ft.	1

Independent retail distribution. Mr. Wickramage, JMS' sales manager, identified approximately 18,000 potential retail distribution outlets in Sri Lanka (4,000 to 5,000 in Colombo) that could sell meat products; 8,000 outlets were deemed "no man's land" as they either had no freezer facilities or management considered their locations too low in income to sell KFP products. Although Keells products were distributed islandwide, 40% of retail sales were through Colombo outlets. Retailers earned 10% to 12% margins.

Distributors

Distribution was contracted to 20 geographically appointed distributors that established retail accounts in specific areas; JMS distributors often held agencies for other foodstuffs.[7] Assigned areas were based on estimated potential profitability rather than

---

[6] Keells Super was part of JMS with its own management team; its managing director, marketing director and finance director served on the boards of JMS and KFP. From the perspective of food products distribution it was treated more or less like another customer; however, it gave preferential treatment to Keells, Krest, Kirata/Mirisata and Farmhouse products.

[7] Since inception, four urban-based agents that could not meet sales quotas left because of financial difficulties; no agent defected to competitors.

by a systematic approach. Wickramage explained: "One area could be five streets, another could be three to four cities. We assign areas on a case-by-case approach."

Distributors, working on 5% margins, stocked goods in their own warehouses equipped with freezers purchased via bank guarantees with JMS' assistance. They were responsible for seeking out prospective retailers, offering financial assistance, servicing existing clients, maintaining stock levels and collecting payment. Distributors purchased products from JMS on credit; discounts were offered for cash. Typically, distributors were expected to generate monthly revenues over Rs 1 million. JMS had no immediate plans to increase the number of distributors but cases were evaluated individually.

Assisting distributors were 50 JMS-paid salespeople responsible for servicing shops currently carrying Keells food products and approaching prospective retailers. Wickramage was willing to hire more salespeople if necessary. New salespeople were typically fresh high school graduates involved in sports, possessing management-determined attitude, ability, friendly manner and personality. From the last newspaper advertisement, 350 qualified potential recruits responded, 47 were shortlisted and seven hired. New salespeople underwent one month factory training, then accompanied senior sales representatives for six months for on-the-job training; they also attended grooming classes. In the previous 18 months, no salespeople had left, despite threats from multinationals poaching staff with higher salaries. Monthly salary and commissions ranged from Rs 4,500 to Rs 10,000, depending on experience and performance. JMS remuneration placed better paid salespeople in the top 25% of Sri Lankan income earners. Sales managers believed sales targets were realistic and achievable.

At least weekly, salespeople in company service vans visited retailers purchasing over Rs 20,000 to Rs 25,000 KFP products per month. Salespeople played several roles: quality control by replacing expired products on shelves; increasing retail market coverage and identifying changes in market conditions. On the last day of each month, salespeople submitted formal reports to Wickramage, including any interesting marketing-related data; this was forwarded to the in-house marketing research team. Since salespeople built rapport with retailers rather than distributors, JMS maintained retailer control by ensuring continuity, thus minimizing the possibility of distributor defection to competitors or breaking contracts.

Nominated direct buyers. JMS also sold directly to 20 specially chosen large volume purchasers. With monthly purchases over Rs 50,000, these customers earned regular retailer bulk discounts plus an additional 2%. These were typically the largest retailers in a town (generally one per town); they sold Keells as the exclusive processed meat brand in addition to other non-competitive items.

Catering

Small catering (aka mass catering). By mid-1995, six JMS service representatives supported 2,000 of 20,000 mass catering outlets (not bakeries) islandwide (7,000 to 10,000 in Colombo). Marino de Silva, Area Sales Manager for Catering said penetration was low because JMS only began focusing on catering channels at end 1993. JMS identified three segments (plus bakeries) based on monthly purchase values:

- Group 1: Eating houses (e.g., snack bars, small hotels) purchased on average Rs 15,000 per month; JMS serviced almost 700 in Colombo.
- Group 2: "Tea boutiques" (like tea cafes) and small catering houses selling snacks purchased Rs 1,500 to Rs 15,000 per month.
- Group 3: A small number of caterers that used Keells products but also distributed them to other stores, acting like sub-distributors, spent up to Rs 100,000 per month.
- Bakeries: JMS sold to a maximum of 50 (out of 2,700 bakeries, 1,500 in Colombo); monthly purchases averaged Rs 5,000 to Rs 10,000.

Large catering (specialized catering). Of 149 registered Sri Lankan hotels, ten were owned by JKH. JMS distributed to six Colombo-located five-star and two four-star hotels purchasing on average Rs 250,000 and Rs 125,000 respectively per month, and five Colombo-located two-star hotels buying approximately Rs 70,000 per month. Total monthly revenues from JKH's 120 hotel customers were Rs 5 to Rs 6 million. Four salespeople visited hotels on a weekly basis. Daily deliveries, direct from the factory, were made to the Colombo-based hotels; weekly deliveries were made to hotels outside Colombo.[8]

Large catering (industrialized catering). JMS supplied its major industrial customer, Air Lanka Catering Services (ALCS), with Rs 300,000 processed meat products per month. Managed in accordance with international airline standards, ALCS provided in-flight meals to all airlines operating through Sri Lanka's international airport. Duty-free provisions enjoyed by airlines allowed cost-effective import of chickens from Singapore and beef from Australia; shortages were sourced by JMS. Maldives Flight Kitchen also purchased KFP processed meats; KFP was the only approved Sri Lankan manufacturing facility.

Exports

In 1993, JMS was unable to meet sales targets because of legislation banning advertising of meat products. Concerned at over-reliance on domestic sales, de Silva explored potential overseas markets. Initial focus was on the newly introduced Halal Krest products. Distributors appointed in Dubai (United Arab Emirates) and Oman operated in similar capacities to Sri Lankan distributors. Distribution networks were set up by hiring salespeople through affiliated companies in Oman and Dubai to assist appointed distributors. Dubai was the "trading base" to other Middle East countries; pork products could be re-exported to expatriate populations in Oman and Bahrain. Halal sales were expanded to Doha (capital of Qatar) where response was positive.

---

[8] The non-Colombo located hotels were resort hotels.

Early success was attributed to unique product spicing, not used by other international competitors; European sausages were considered bland compared with spicy Keells. The Maldives resorts had been serviced through indirect exports since the company's inception. Keell's products were launched in the Male (capital of Maldives) retail market in 1994 with the appointment of a distributor and TV-advertising support.

Production

KFP controlled two plants; one (opened 1983) manufactured the Keells range and part of the Farm House range. Annual capacity of this plant was increased from 2,000 tons in 1992/93 to 2,400 tons in 1993/94; capacity utilization from 1992/93 to 1995/96 was 89%, 66%, 85%, 99% (estimated) respectively. The second plant (opened in 1991) manufactured the Krest, Kirata/Mirisata and rest of the Farm House range; it was separately located and produced halal products. Annual capacity of the Krest plant (from inception) was 750 tons; capacity utilization from 1991/92 to 1995/96 was 6%, 9%, 25%, 41%, 55% (estimated) respectively.[9] In this plant, an Australian-trained Muslim veterinary consultant oversaw animal slaughtering procedures to ensure compliance with Muslim rites and requirements. De Silva emphasized the importance of Islamic procedures as Muslim housewives frequently called KFP to ensure meat products were correctly prepared under Islamic laws.

Control Measures

KFP was unique in having a modern, well-equipped laboratory for its processed meat business. State-of-the-art equipment ensured products conformed to predetermined and regulatory standards. All products were tested for taste, smell, chemical composition and microbiological assay to maintain consistent quality levels. Key factory staff were regularly sent overseas to learn the latest machinery and equipment.

To ensure high quality raw materials, KFP made agreements with reputable local farmers who received advice, guidance and support from company consultants. KFP consultants regularly visited farmers to ensure proper feeding and breeding of animals. All animals were inspected by KFP's veterinary surgeon; pre- and post-mortem tests were conducted to ensure animals were healthy and fit for processing. Regular inspections and tests were completed at every stage of processing and packaging.

Marketing Keells Food Products

JMS controlled all marketing aspects of KFP products: marketing budgets, distribution, advertising, promotions, product development and market research. KFP focused on manufacturing at the highest quality and lowest cost. Marketing expenditures rose continuously (Exhibit 5).

---

[9] In 1994/95, the Keells plant has 200 employees, the Krest plant, 35.

Brand Issues

"Now we seriously want to export and expand to non-meat areas. In the last monthly 'strategic thinking' meeting, the question was how to value our brands. JMS equates 'Keells' to Coca-Cola in Sri Lanka in terms of image, awareness, positions we enjoy, position most firms aspire to. In fact our advertising briefs state we should make Keells the Coca-Cola of Sri Lanka." – Sriomal de Silva, Product Manager.

Initially sold under the "Atlas" name, from September 1985 all products were marketed under the Keells name. By June 1986, Keells achieved market leadership in Colombo and by year-end, Keells was the dominant market leader for processed refrigerated meats, distributed country-wide. Management believed the reason for Keells' success was that "Keells" became synonymous with quality, making it a major selling point.

In the mid-1980s, several other companies in JKH adopted the Keells name (e.g., Keells Computer, Keells Aquariums, Keells Ago, Keells Homes, Keells Transport); however, Keells was not the only brand name used in the 65 company Keells Group. KFP management believed that in food, the Keells name was most strongly associated with sausages, meat balls, hams, bacons and similar meat products, stronger even than JKH, the mother company. At the JKH level, senior management had such a high regard for the Keells name it believed it should be associated with every aspect of Keells' food business.

By July 1995, Keells Foods had an 80% share of the entire Sri Lankan processed meat market. Some observers believed "Keells" had stronger brand equity than Coca-Cola in Sri Lanka. (Sri Lanka ranked 13th in Coke consumption of all Asian countries!) JMS management associated "Keells" with quality, convenience and versatility: quality, illustrated by KFP's commitment to quality control and its two-year effort to secure ISO 9000 certification; convenience, illustrated via easy-to-buy, quick-to-prepare processed meat products; versatility, referred to the wide product assortment for different occasions (e.g., lunch-meat, meals, snacks, parties, BBQs, picnics).

JMS sales managers believed they could successfully distribute food products without the Keells name. Said Wickramage: "Yes, for the moment, we can distribute successfully as we have a strong and established sales force. With the rapport our salespeople have in the field, everyone knows he's a Keells sales rep. So, even if he sells a product without the Keells name, as long as the product is good, the retailers will still know it's by Keells."

However, the sales force conceded that advertising support had to accompany sales efforts. Wickramage said that competitor J.L. Morrisson and Sons tried to sell a high quality food product line but was unsuccessful; the products were not promoted or sold to outlets in the "proper manner," so most people were unaware of their existence. Similarly, JMS managers felt a product with a Keells logo would not "sell itself."

Sales managers also faced the issue of how to sell products to a broader customer base; they believed management should introduce more broadly targeted products, rather than for just the upper income group. In their opinion, the only way to increase revenues was to introduce new products. Wickramage said: "It's tough to increase sales when you have 80% of the market. We don't think we can get the 20% balance easily!"

Another manager commented: "For the past few years Keells has been targeting the top end of the market. For the next five years, we shall try to broaden the market base. Kirata/Mirisata was introduced to gain a wider market."

Superior Keells Quality Logo

In some cases, sub-brands were associated with the specially developed "Keells Quality Assurance" logo (Exhibit 6). This logo was established both to make Keells Foods synonymous with high quality products and to make the umbrella branding concept more meaningful. As Sriomal de Silva explained:

> Keells has been in the market for about 10 years. When we started, Keells was a manufacturer of processed meats for basic products such as hams and sausages. Over the years, we evolved new products using new technology and new features; for example, products with new protective packaging. We've built an image of concern for quality and Keells has grown to carry other brands. All sub-brands were initially associated with Keells but some are now on their own. When Farmhouse was launched, it had a line saying "Keells quality frozen meats and Farmhouse fresh." We needed the Keells name to create common credibility. So, today, Keells is both an umbrella brand plus the original product line still continues so Keells acts as a sub-brand in some people's view.

A potential problem for Keells products the Quality logo might dispel was possible association with junk food. According to Vasantha Chandrapala, product manager:

> In sophisticated health conscious markets like the U.S., certain people associate sausages with junk food. But that is not the case in Sri Lanka. True, some forms of unsaturated oils are very bad for you, but in Sri Lanka the real concern is whether customers get value for money. In the West, good meats are sold at a premium in specific outlets; in Sri Lanka, we don't have enough of those outlets so a lot of good meat goes into sausages. We don't have the same ratios as the West for "bad meat to good meat" so we can charge slightly higher prices. We must counter the junk food problem before we encounter it; it's on its way. We have already taken the Asian diet angle by advertising that all one needs is just a little meat, but good meat, at every meal.

JMS introduced a nutritional press campaign focusing on Keells food facts.

Market Research

JMS maintained a small in-house market research team comprising two fresh mathematics and science graduates. On an on-going basis, the team collected brand awareness and competitor performance data. At Keells Super and independent supermarkets, it collected data on users' and non-users' perceptions of Keells' and competitors' processed meat products; occasionally, it conducted "mini" surveys to secure quantitative data on purchase behavior (Appendices A, B, C, D). At competitor supermarkets, the team simply observed customers' meat products purchasing behavior; telephone interviewing, uncommon in Sri Lanka, was not used. The team was also responsible for dealing with customer complaints for all Keells products; this assignment was not time consuming. External research agencies were used periodically (about every 18 months) for strategically important studies; each project cost between US$1,000 to $6,000.[10]

Advertising Activities

Management believed television was a very effective advertising medium for Keells. Technically, although only one channel reached the entire population, Chandrapala believed all channels aired different programs aimed at different target markets simultaneously. Consequently, the cost was unnecessarily high to reach specific segments; JMS advertised on all television channels.

To reach the mass market, commercials were scheduled heavily on ETV[11] channels. In 1992, an advertisement's video production cost was approximately Rs 300,000 per commercial; de Silva believed it was currently at least 50% higher. Ideas for television advertisements originated from focus group feedback; these often featured national sports players, considered "heroes," in conjunction with sponsoring popular sports (e.g., cricket, volleyball, soccer). Since inception, JMS used 15 base advertisements to launch 56 marketing campaigns. Examples included:

- July 1994 to present: Keells Rock 'n Roll BBQ, dubbed in English and Sinhalese, aired to improve brand image among 15- to 24-year-olds; core message, be trendy and young.
- 1994: Launched "Krest Golden Goodness from Keells, fry some" series of ads featuring Mrs. Sri Lanka World 1984 as the mother figure, a well-known role portrayed in milk advertisements, the campaign was successful; sales increased significantly.
- 1993: Keells Krest range targeted at 15- to 24-year-olds.
- 1993: Introduced the skinless sausage as an economical product to the mass market; specifically targeted the Muslim population who generally believed that sausage skin was made from pork.
- April 1993: Aired for six months during the ban on meat products, this advertisement promoted meat balls. The product was not shown, just a plain bowl of rice without any meat products.

---

[10] JMS believed Sri Lanka had only three "really professional" marketing research companies, one of international repute.

[11] ETV stood for extra-terrestrial vision, a local channel comprising two channels: ETV 1 showed BBC 24 hours per day; ETV 2 showed a mix of Star Sports and Star Plus from the Hong Kong-based Star TV network, 24 hours per day.

- Mid-1992 to present: Three cricketers in the Sri Lankan national team endorsed Keells food products at a cheerful BBQ event. Management claimed the ads were among the most successful; sales increased.
- 1992: Children eating sandwiches, made with Keells lunch-meat, at school; targeted at housewives to increase daily consumption.
- December 1991: Introduced the first Keells Super in Liberty Plaza, Colombo.
- Late 1980s: Commercials, featuring chefs preparing Keells' meats, built image by associating Keells food products with five-star hotels.
- 1988: The "Surprise" series featured facial expressions of people tasting Keells sausages; some of the oldest but most successful ads.

KFP's Rs 500,000 ten-minute corporate video was screened at international food exhibitions and the Sri Lankan Expo fair 1992; 1993 feedback was generally positive.

Competition

Although KFP identified four major competitors in the retail, institutional and supermarket segments (Table 2), by March 1995, it enjoyed almost 80% market share in processed meat. All competitors actively advertised using a combination of press, TV and radio. JMS used SRL Media Scan services to track competitor marketing expenditures (Table 3).

Elephant House. In the early 1980s, Ceylon Cold Stores (CCS) was the uncontested market leader, focusing mainly on raw (and pre-cooked) sausages under the Elephant House brand name.[12] KFP managers believed CCS's management allowed sales of the "Elephant House" brand meat products to stagnate thereby enabling Keells to steal market share and eventually expand the entire market. As one employee recalled:

> In five years the market has grown substantially. When Keells entered, Elephant House was the true market leader; they sold raw sausages, which spoilt quickly, according to grocers at the time. Keells developed a new convenience market (for meats) and were not really competing with Elephant House. Elephant House's sales have stagnated, virtually remaining the same since the early 1980s.

Since JKH acquired CCS in 1991, no major new initiatives were made; management focused on restructuring the current business. CCS offered both processed meat and raw meat generated in the manufacturing process.[13]

Cargills. Founded in the 1890s as a department store, Cargills, a privately owned family business, was legendary throughout Sri Lanka. In the mid-1980s, Cargills opened Sri Lanka's first supermarket, "Food City"; by mid-1995 it had nine urban

---

[12] CCS was also involved in a variety of other food product activities.
[13] All CCS meat revenues are considered in market share calculations.

locations throughout Colombo. In 1993, Cargills purchased a meat processing plant equipped with similar machinery to KFP from Goldi (KFP's competitor). However, de Silva believed Cargills was inexperienced in meat processing and undercapitalized; he believed suppliers funded the supermarkets through credit. Although promoted as one-stop shopping, de Silva believed Cargills supermarkets did not live up to their claims relying instead on sales gimmicks and compromising on product mix and quality. KFP's marketing team did not believe Cargills would open more supermarkets in the near term.

Table 2: Sri Lankan Meat Market Share by Brand

Brand market share %	83/84	84/85	85/86	86/87	87/88	88/89
Keells Food Products*	5%	34%	66%	70%	70%	81%
Elephant House	87%	60%	29%	25%	25%	15%
Cargills	–	–	–	–	–	–
Bairaha Norfolk	–	–	–	–	–	–
Goldi	8%	6%	5%	5%	5%	4%
Deal	–	–	–	–	–	1%
	100%	100%	100%	100%	100%	101%
Total market size by tons	980	1,203	1,408	1,440	1,460	1,475
Brand market share %	**89/90**	**90/91**	**91/92**	**92/93**	**93/94**	**94/95**
Keells Food Products*	83%	85%	87%	79%	73%	79%
Elephant House	11%	11%	10%	15%	14%	12%
Cargills	–	–	–	2%	11%	8%
Bairaha Norfolk	–	–	–	4%	2%	1%
Goldi	5%	3%	2%	–	–	–
Deal	1%	1%	–	–	–	–
Total market size by tons	100%	100%	99%	100%	100%	100%

*Includes Krest, Kirata-Mirisata, Farmhouse and Keells.
Source: Jaykay Marketing Services (Pvt.) Ltd.

Cargills produced and sold a similar meat product range to Keells (except for halal products), distributed similarly. Keells' in-house marketing research indicated Cargills consistently ranked in the first three when consumers were asked to name processed meat producers. Keells management could not identify any consistent Cargills positioning; from prior marketing campaigns they could only interpret, "Cargills is new." Keells management believed Cargills' main weakness was staff quality; JKH was seen as a reputable firm offering better opportunities than Cargills.

Marketing efforts intensified during seasonal periods (e.g., Christmas, Sinhalese New Year). Off-season, Cargills did not regularly use TV or radio; it focused on the press for new product launches and point-of-sale materials (e.g., price lists, informational leaflets with recipes); mailers were not used. Cargills recently introduced a qual-

Table 3: Press, TV and Radio Expenditures by Meat Manufacturers

Period from: 12/01/94 to 12/31/94

Brand name	This month				Total year to date			
	Press	TV	Radio	Total	Press	TV	Radio	Total
Bairaha	–	–	–	–	113,531	–	–	113,531
Cargills	280,550	223,550	120,200	624,300	280,550	988,650	120,200	1,389,400
Elephant	–	10,500	–	10,500	14,300	78,600	–	92,900
Keells	187,440	523,325	67,525	778,290	321,575	7,075,141	751,274	8,147,990
Keells Krest	15,120	168,538	75,675	259,333	51,840	2,431,171	145,975	2,628,986
Product total	483,110	925,913	263,400	1,672,423	781,796	10,573,562	1,017,449	12,372,807

Period from: 01/01/95 to 01/31/95

Brand name	This month				Total year to date			
	Press	TV	Radio	Total	Press	TV	Radio	Total
Cargills	–	42,500	–	42,500	–	42,500	–	42,500
Elephant	–	2,000	–	2,000	–	2,000	–	2,000
Keells	6,900	464,575	77,450	548,925	6,900	464,575	77,450	548,925
Keells Krest	–	99,000	700	99,700	–	99,000	700	99,700
Product total	6,900	608,075	78,150	693,125	6,900	608,075	78,150	693,125

Period from: 01/01/95 to 01/31/95

Brand name	This month				Total year to date			
	Press	TV	Radio	Total	Press	TV	Radio	Total
Cargills	–	–	12,500	12,500	–	42,500	12,500	55,000
Elephant	–	49,700	–	49,700	–	51,700	–	51,700
Keells	–	451,175	2,300	453,475	6,900	915,750	79,750	1,002,400
Keells Krest	–	45,450	2,100	47,550	–	144,450	2,800	147,250
Product total	–	546,325	16,900	563,225	6,900	1,154,400	95,050	1,256,350

Source: SLH, Mediascan.

ity seal, imitating Keells' Quality logo. De Silva was unsure how customers perceived this logo and whether any importance was attached to it (Exhibit 7).

Bairaha Norfolk (BN). Bairaha Norfolk was a Sri Lankan Muslim organization established in the late 1980s and well-known locally. BN was a subsidiary (established 1992) of Bairaha Farms manufacturing processed meat. BN's single halal factory concentrated on halal chickens, sold as parts (dressed or processed) to the same distribution outlets as Keells and Cargills; BN also exclusively supplied its own Colombo-based fast food outlet. De Silva believed BN was the only competitor to Krest; it was thought to be under capacity constraints and unlikely to expand in the near term.

Deal. Considered an insignificant player with less than 1% market share in raw and processed meats, de Silva described Deal as a "one-man show"; it focused on raw meats.

Decisions

Since KFP's vision was to be the leading manufacturer and marketer of food in Sri Lanka, the branding decision was a strategic matter. De Silva had to plan branding strategy for future product introductions that would seamlessly integrate with the current portfolio. In particular, he had to decide a branding strategy for the soon-to-be-launched lines of vegetables and canned meats. Several questions had to be answered: How should sub-brands be developed in the future? Should the current Keells product line be sub-branded? If yes, how could it be sub-branded without causing confusion? De Silva wondered if more strategic issues should be resolved before the branding question was addressed.

Exhibit 1: John Keells Holdings' Food and Beverage Sector

A. Ownership data

Company name & year of incorporation		JKH exposure %		Number of shareholders		Group holding % (gross)		Issued share capital Rs '000s		Shareholders funds Rs '000s	
		1995	1994	1995	1994	1995	1994	1995	1994	1995	1994
Ceylon Cold Stores Ltd.	1941	7.48	9.43	1,408	1,344	53	53	50,600	50,600	388,755	372,143
Ceylon Cold Stores (Distributors) Ltd.	1928	0.30	0.23	8	8	100	100	90	90	15,676	8,965
Elephant House Farms Ltd.	1983	0.08	0.10	8	8	100	100	400	4,000	(16,140)	(17,397)
Jaykay Marketing Services (Pvt.) Ltd.	1980	2.59	0.95	14	14	100	100	70,000	20,000	71,902	20,488
Keells Food Products Ltd.	1982	2.01	2.44	1,058	1,073	56	56	50,000	50,000	113,071	107,136
Keells Restaurants (Pvt.) Ltd.	1993	1.37	0.39	3	3	100	100	36,000	11,000	37,731	8,241
Sector total		13.83	13.54								

B. Operating performance

Company	Gross revenue Rs '000s		Net profit for year Rs '000s		Net profit after tax Rs '000s		Number of employees	
	1995	1994	1995	1994	1995	1994	1995	1994
Ceylon Cold Stores Ltd.	648,429	637,276	30,072	10,213	16,610	10,213	1,956	2,269
Ceylon Cold Stores (Distributors) Ltd.	940,247	655,793	10,962	3,736	6,712	2,435	–	–
Elephant House Farms Ltd.	636	1,909	1,797	(2,139)	1,797	(2,139)	–	–
Jaykay Marketing Services (Pvt.) Ltd.	846,710	599,505	721	1,718	1,443	566	400	136
Keells Food Products Ltd.	283,261	211,218	5,935	(3,376)	4,435	(4,876)	297	245
Keells Restaurants Pvt. Ltd.	56,916	20,657	5,238	2,175	2,752	2,175	61	61
Sector total	2,776,199	2,126,358	54,725	12,327	33,749	8,374	2,714	2,711
Intra group sales	859,576	461,460						
Unrealized profit thereon								
As per profit and loss account	1,916,623	1,664,898	54,725	12,327	33,749	8,374		
John Keells' % of group total	41.69%	41.21%						

Exhibit 2: John Keells Food Product Range

- Pork Sausage
- Cocktail Sausage
- Garlic Sausage
- Luncheon Meat
- Bier Sausage
- Paprika Mortadella
- Back Bacon
- Cooked Ham (special)

- Honey Roast Ham
- Salami Bratwurst
- Bacon Sausage
- Frankfurters
- Chicken & Ham Aspic
- Smoked Leg of Ham
- Baked Meat Loaf

- Roast Pork with Stuffing
- Streaky Bacon
- Hot Dogs
- Gammon Steak
- Smoked Dry Salami
- Kassler
- Pork Meat Balls

Keells Pork Raw

- Pork Belly
- Pork Leg
- Pork Knuckle

- Pork Shoulder
- Schnitzel
- Pork for Roasting

- Pork Shoulder Chops
- Pork Fillet
- Pork Cubes

Keells Beef Processed

- Beef Sausage
- Chipolatas

- Bockwurst
- Beef Meat Balls

- Smoked Beef
- Beef Frankfurters

Keells Chicken Processed

- Chicken Sausage
- Chicken Meat Balls
- Chicken Roll

- Chicken & Shiitake Roll
- Chicken Mortadella
- Chicken Liver Pate

- Chicken Bockwurst
- Chicken Ham Roll
- Chicken Steak Gammon Style

- Chicken Ham

- Chicken Frankfurters

Keells Imported Meats

- Steer Tenderloin
- Steer Sirloin
- Beef Shortloin
- T-Bone Steak

- Rib eye
- Veal HQ's (Rump)
- Veal HQ's (Topside)
- Veal Knuckle

- Lamb Leg (Whole)
- Lamb, Chops, Loin, Rack
- Lamb Shoulder/Chops
- Lamb Shortloin

Keells "Krest" Snack Range

- Fish Finger
- Chinese Rolls (Croquette in Chicken, Beef, Fish, Vegetable)

- Kiev-Mini (Chicken)
- Nuggets (Chicken, Beef, Fish)

- Cutlets (Crumbed Patty in Chicken, Beef, Fish, Vegetable)

Keells "Krest" Meal Range

- Jumbo Patty Stuffed with Cheese Sauce (Chicken)
- Fish Cake

- Crumbed Chicken Drumstick (Boneless)
- Potato Croquettes

- Jumbo Patty with Garlic Butter (Chicken)

Keells "Kirata-Mirisata"

- Chicken Meat Balls with Curry Mix

- Beef Meat Balls with Curry Mix

- Fish Meat Balls with Curry Mix

Keells "Farm House"

- Assorted Chicken Pieces

- Curry Pork

- Chicken Thighs

- Chicken Drumstick

- Fish Meat Balls with Curry Mix
- Mutton Cubes
- Beef Cubes

Exhibit 3A: Sales Volumes of Keells Food Products, by Meat Type (1983 to 1996 est.) (tons)

Brand segments	83/84	84/85	85/86	86/87	87/88	88/89	89/90	90/91	91/92	92/93	93/94	94/95	95/96 est.
Keells													
Processed	39	326	779	857	877	984	970	945	1,283	1,300	1,051	1,313	1,519
Raw	10	83	150	150	146	211	225	340	471	485	532	738	855
Krest													
Processed	–	–	–	–	–	–	–	–	47	68	80	218	297
Kirata/Mirisata													
Processed	–	–	–	–	–	–	–	–	–	–	38	51	64
Farmhouse													
Raw	–	–	–	–	–	–	–	–	–	–	70	36	47
Total	49	409	929	1,007	1,023	1,195	1,195	1,285	1,801	1,853	1,771	2,356	2,782

Exhibit 3B: Sales Volumes of Keells Food Products, by Distribution Outlets and Brands (1983 to 1996 est.) (tons)

Brand segments	83/84	84/85	85/86	86/87	87/88	88/89	89/90	90/91	91/92	92/93	93/94	94/95	95/96 est.
Keells (Sausages, Cold Meats, Ham, Bacon)													
Retail – own outlets	–	–	–	–	68	196	220	263	340	413	470	631	747
Retail – other outlets	31	336	847	906	846	868	812	782	1,109	973	752	922	955
Catering – own outlets	–	–	–	–	–	–	–	–	2	5	2	5	22
Catering – large	18	66	73	93	98	118	140	175	219	269	232	264	291
Catering – small	–	–	–	–	–	–	–	32	39	68	67	139	173
Exports	–	6	8	9	10	13	25	33	46	57	60	90	186
Krest (Batter Crumbed Products)													
Retail – own outlets	–	–	–	–	–	–	–	–	3	22	24	45	56
Retail – other outlets	–	–	–	–	–	–	–	–	44	33	14	24	29
Catering – own outlets	–	–	–	–	–	–	–	–	–	3	8	18	22
Catering – large	–	–	–	–	–	–	–	–	–	7	5	4	7
Catering – small	–	–	–	–	–	–	–	–	–	1	27	115	142
Exports	–	–	–	–	–	–	–	–	–	2	2	12	43
Mikirata Risata (Meatballs with Curry Mix)													
Retail – other outlets	–	–	–	–	–	–	–	–	–	–	38	51	64
Farmhouse (Raw Meat Retail Packs)													
Retail – other outlets	–	–	–	–	–	–	–	–	–	–	70	36	47
Total output	49	408	928	1,008	1,022	1,195	1,197	1,285	1,802	1,853	1,771	2,356	2,784

Exhibit 3C: Actual Sales Volumes of Processed Keells' Raw Meats (tons)

Product Segment	87/88	88/89	89/90	90/91	91/92	92/93	93/94	94/95
Products western in nature*	798	829	903	887	1,026	1,051	878	1,151
Products localized in nature#	224	265	292	398	728	735	704	900
Total Keells	1,022	1,094	1,195	1,285	1,754	1,785	1,582	2,051

Exhibit 4: Index of Financial Results for Keells (1983/84 = 100) and Krest Brands (1991/92 = 100) for Each Indicator

Indicator	83/84	84/85	85/86	86/87	87/88	88/89	89/90	90/91	91/92	92/93	93/94	94/95	95/96 est.
Revenues													
Keells	100	700	1,400	2,267	2,567	3,367	4,133	5,167	8,233	9,900	9,433	12,000	14,733
Krest	–	–	–	–	–	–	–	–	100	157	214	586	800
Revenues net of taxes													
Keells	100	667	1,267	2,067	2,330	3,033	3,600	4,400	7,133	8,400	8,267	10,900	13,476
Krest	–	–	–	–	–	–	–	–	100	150	250	617	867
Gross profit													
Keells	100	690	1,260	2,550	2,820	3,650	4,310	4,440	7,930	9,420	9,290	12,490	15,810
Krest	–	–	–	–	–	–	–	–	100	153	221	353	505
Net profit													
Keells	–100	–219	–8	211	250	300	256	236	586	147	14	311	589
Krest	–	–	–	–	–	–	–	–	–100	–758	–850	–475	350

Note: In 1991/92, the ratio of Keells' figure to Krest's were: Revenues, 35.3:1; revenues net of taxes, 35.3:1; gross profit, 41.7:1; net profit, 17.5:1 (absolute numbers).
Source: Jaykay Marketing Services (Pvt.) Ltd.

Exhibit 5: Index of JMS' Marketing Expenses (1983/84 = 100)

Year	Keells	Krest	Year	Keells	Krest
1983/1984	100	–	1989/1990	614	–
1984/1985	143	–	1990/1991	443	–
1985/1986	257	–	1991/1992	1386	100
1986/1987	371	–	1992/1993	2114	425
1987/1988	386	–	1993/1994	2400	463
1988/1989	543	–	1994/1995	2957	288
			1995/1996 est.	4043	338

Appendix

Appendix A: Conclusion from meat balls – home placement test (May–June 1993)

- Meatballs were a welcome food item among working and non-working housewives. Both groups found meat balls convenient and useful.
- Spiced meat balls were favored because they were easier to prepare with the addition of only water or milk.
- Milk seemed to be generally preferred; it probably helped subdue the hot and spicy taste.
- The common complaint: the spiced product was too hot, particularly for children.
- Respondents cooked meat balls in various ways; tempering was one of the more popular methods.
- Reducing product versatility did not seem very important to housewives; meat balls were not a frequent or daily food item.
- The quantity of gravy required depended on what meat balls were eaten with (e.g., bread needed more gravy).
- According to respondents, a little less chili and spices and addition of milk could make the new spiced meat balls concept more acceptable to the consumer, particularly households with younger children.

Appendix B: Observation from Krest's survey (August–September 1993)

- For a sample of 106 households that used Krest products in the past three months, 323 households were contacted.
- 119% of households had not heard of "Krest."
- Of the 81% that knew Krest: 19% had not eaten its products; 29% were not currently eating them or had stopped altogether.
- Only 33% had eaten Krest products within the previous three months.
- The highest Krest usage was among Colombo Inners, households with total monthly income over Rs 10,000.
- Nugget was the most popular variety.
- Two main reasons for not eating Krest products: the items could be prepared at home and dislike for processed foods.
- Krest-eating homes had marginally more children from 6 to 15 years and more housewives were employed.
- Krest products were considered tasty and convenient, especially liked by children.
- Krest's foods were too expensive to eat frequently. Consumers commented on increased pack quantity or a price reduction.
- Some respondents had an experience of stale and mildewed packs.
- Consumers complained the taste of all products was the same, regardless of whether it was chicken, pork, beef or mutton, probably because there was very little meat content.
- There was some confusion regarding the Krest range and processed foods (e.g., sausages, meat balls). Respondents did not differentiate one from the other.

Appendix (cont'd)

Appendix C: Observation from processed meat range survey (December 1993)

- Though considered a convenience food, only 23% of housewives were employed, 88% ate processed meats.
- 91% of households had children.
- Monthly household income of 97% of respondents was over Rs 5,000, seemingly the general income level for processed meat-product eaters.
- Keells (81%) was most popular, over 50% above competitors: Elephant House (36%), Cargills (12%), Bairaha (4%).
- The main types were sausages (83%) followed by meat balls (64%).
- Chicken was the favorite meat.
- Taste and quality were important factors in choosing a processed meat. Children seemed to influence choice.
- Parties seemed important as a venue for processed meat.
- The purchase of processed meats seemed more a question of availability than preference.
- For 56% of consumers, the product was not consumed immediately after purchase.
- Processed meats were generally considered expensive.
- Consumers were anxious to know more about each type's composition. If composition were clarified to disprove current disagreeable information, processed meats could be a more desired food.
- More information dealing with composition (e.g., quantity of soya, meat) and best preparation methods in the least time could be a plus for the product and a boon to housewives.

Appendix D: Observation from fish curry home placement test (November 1994)

- Generally fish was eaten in all homes; the majority ate fish at least once a week.
- Popular fish varieties were tuna, para, seer and thalapath (large fish) in Colombo, hurulla and salaya (small fish) in Kandy. If the popularity of small fish in Kandy was due to non-availability or difficulty in keeping large fish, a product like Fish Curry could find a ready market.
- Consumers considered fish red or white. Main red fish, tuna and balaya; main white fish, seer and para. Thalapath was mentioned in both categories; kelawalla was not mentioned at all. Consumers seemed to believe red fish was "meaty," white fish not.
- Main methods of preparing fish was *kirata* (milk added to curry, with gravy) or *mirisata* (cooked in water, dry). Addition of less liquid could be recommended for mirisata curry.
- The curry sample was well received by respondents. However, on the second visit, some commented it was unlike real fish because it lacked flavor and texture. Regarding shape, more 'kutti' pieces were desirable.
- Consumers expected a product called "Fish Curry" to contain real fish pieces; they were disappointed to taste, in their opinions, a composition of soya and a little fish. Calling the product Fish Curry might mislead consumers; they might not be repeat purchasers.
- The convenience and usefulness of the product was a positive feature but it is questionable if this could compensate for lack of fish flavor and texture.

Source: Jaykay Marketing Services (Pvt.) Ltd.

Case 50

Mackinnon & Keells Financial Services Ltd.

Samina Seth
The Hong Kong University of Science and Technology

Noel Capon
Graduate School of Business, Columbia University

In July 1994, Ralph de Lanerolle, newly appointed head of Investment Banking at Mackinnon & Keells Financial Services Ltd. (MKFSL) (formerly with National Development Bank) was contemplating the firm's relaunch strategy. MKFSL was a diversified organization offering a limited number of financial products with moderate success in a fast-growing financial services market. Formed in 1986, management believed that in the public's mind the Keells name was usually associated with Keells Food Products and that, after broadening its investment portfolio, a relaunch campaign for MKFSL should be planned and implemented. The Financial Sector Management Committee, supervising all John Keells Holdings (JKH) financial services activities, was charged with creating a comprehensive marketing strategy to build and establish brand equity in the local and international financial markets. Ralph de Lanerolle stated the firm's mission: "To make our name known as a major player in an 'overbanked' environment." His recommendations to JKH's Board were due October 25.

୨୦୬୫

Company Background

In 1986, Ajit Gunewardene, Managing Director of John Keells Holdings money broking operations, approached Mr. Blackler, John Keells Holdings Deputy Director, for a change in responsibilities. Growth in Colombo Stock Exchange's volume and the influx of foreign financial institutions to Sri Lanka, led Blackler to believe John Keells Holdings (JKH) could seize the opportunity to become a leading Sri Lankan investment house, locally and internationally. Mackinnon & Keells Financial Services Ltd. was established with two employees headed by Gunewardene, initially to provide financial services to Sri Lankan companies.[1] MKFSL's initial emphasis was on clients in the capital city, Colombo.[2] At inception, MKFSL made several Colombo property investments for which it received monthly income rental.

By mid-1994, MKFSL comprised four major operating entities, responsible for different investment banking lines, physically separated in head office: capital markets, fixed income securities, corporate finance and margin trading. (See Exhibits 1, 2 for income statement and balance sheet.)

MKFSL Services

In its eight-year life, MKFSL secured several "firsts": it was one of the first Sri Lankan firms to offer selected investment banking services (e.g., financial instruments, hedging instruments, asset swaps); it was first to coordinate a Global Depository Receipt issue jointly with internationally renowned investment banks; it was the forerunner in introducing margin trading, far ahead of the Colombo stock market's "takeoff" (early 1990s). By mid-1994, MKFSL's four major services achieved varying degrees of success. In general, de Lanerolle did not believe that price competition was a serious woe.

Capital markets: MKFSL was the market leader in new issue underwriting and management, market share about 50%. The majority of clients were large corporate entities interested in raising capital via equity, long-term debt and related products.

Fixed income securities: MKFSL only recently entered this market; management considered its operations in infancy along with the Sri Lankan market as a whole. Fixed income securities were mainly treasury bills, government bonds and commercial paper; MKFSL took positions at weekly auctions and traded with a well-established corporate and retail client base. The firm was still developing products and had under 5% market share.[3] (See Table 1 for recent fixed income business.)

Corporate finance: Like fixed income securities, corporate finance was a fairly new MKFSL area. Management believed that MKFSL could play an important role in providing financial advisory services to clients. It placed emphasis on this division and believed an important position had been secured.

---

[1] Keells entered share broking in 1960 when E. John Thompson White & Company merged with Keells and Waldock. In 1986, another Keells subsidiary, Mackinnon Mackenzie & Company of Ceylon Ltd. linked with Keells and Waldock to form Mackinnon & Keells Financial Services Ltd.

[2] Despite being focused on quality products and services, a mission statement was never drafted.

[3] MKFSL's Treasury Bills department was one of 16 financial institutions (four non-banking organizations) appointed by the government (1992) to place government securities in the primary market. Lanerolle believed banks received higher margins in other areas and minimized resources and marketing efforts. MKFSL actively traded treasury bills in the secondary market via repurchase agreements (REPOs) and reverse REPOs.

Table 1: Recent Business in Fixed Income Securities

Company	Year	Value (Rs)
Commercial paper		
Aiken Spence & Co.	1993	50,000,000
John Keells Holding	1993	25,000,000
Singer (Sri Lanka)	1994	250,000,000
Shaw Wallace & Hedges	1994	25,000,000
United Motors	1994	45,000,000
Associated Motorways	1994	50,000,000
Kelani Tyres	1994	60,000,000
Metal Packaging	1994	25,000,000
Pugoda Textile Mills	1994	75,000,000
John Keells	1994	235,000,000
Keells Food Products	1994	40,000,000
Keells Developments	1994	50,000,000
Ceylon Cold Stores	1994	100,000,000
Walkers Tours	1994	225,000,000
Keells Food Products	1994	10,000,000
Lanka Orix Leasing Co.	1994	50,000,000
Forward rate agreements		
Singer (Sri Lanka)	1994	35,000,000
Singer (Sri Lanka)	1994	100,000,000
Other		
Talawakele Plantation – Treasury Bill Backed Securities	1994	192,000,000

Source: Mackinnon & Keells Financial Services Ltd.

Margin trading: MKFSL was the first Sri Lankan firm to introduce margin trading. By 1994, MKFSL secured a dominant leadership position with 30% market share, mainly from high net worth individuals.

Market Segments

MKFSL segmented its market by retail and corporate customers; in mid-1994 approximately 50% of revenues came from each. MKFSL had about 100 corporate and retail accounts, almost 40% originating from John Keells Holdings (i.e., companies in the group or companies/high net worth individuals [> Rs 5 million] sourced through JKH contacts).

The remainder (i.e., 60%) comprised medium size (revenues < Rs 100 million) and large companies (revenues > Rs 100 million) and high net worth individuals. Of the 100 accounts, 15 to 20 accounted for 90% to 95% of all business. Of these 15 to 20, approximately 90% were corporate clients, 10% retail.

Customer targets for retail business were high net worth individuals (over Rs 5 million); de Lanerolle believed these people were approximately 4% of the Sri Lankan population. Management further segmented this group by professionals and small unlisted businesses; de Lanerolle believed small businesses were easier to contact. In total, MKFSL had 75 margin trading accounts, all retail; de Lanerolle believed margin trading was very lucrative.

Investment Consultants

Professional employees in each of the four operating entities were termed investment consultants; they averaged about 30 years and generally had a degree in Economics, Business, Engineering or a CIMA qualification.[4] Work experience was not mandatory, but was preferred. Management wondered whether more stringent and streamlined hiring requirements should be introduced. Turnover was not a serious problem (three to four employees anually) due to small staff size; new recruits were generally fresh university graduates who tended to stay longer than more experienced personnel.

Recruitment. In the financial services industry, poaching professional staff from competitors was fairly common practice for "a fairly inexperienced industry workforce." Most locals considered JKH an excellent employer, hiring young staff, quickly promoting them to managerial levels, and providing, on average, higher benefits and salaries than other firms. Recruitment took place year round but little effort was placed on attracting new employees as job advertisements yielded high response rates. From April to August, de Lanerolle received hundreds of inquiries for potential entry-level jobs from graduates of overseas educational programs returning home; he believed 30 to 40 annually were "potential MKFSL material."

Training. Career paths were neither set nor identified for new employees. Management provided on-the-job training but believed high investment in staff development was risky because of poaching, especially by the increasing numbers of foreign firms willing to pay premium prices for local "qualified and experienced" analysts.

Compensation. New recruits were paid market rate (Rs 12,000 to 15,000) based on professional qualifications and work experience. Employees were salaried because MKFSL wanted to reduce the possibility of investment consultants resorting to hard sell tactics for short-term commission gains. Generally, competitors offered comparable remuneration practices for similar reasons.

Technology

De Lanerolle described technology at other Sri Lankan financial service providers as very basic; for example, one major competitor was computerized only in the early 1990s. Although MKFSL management believed it was as technologically advanced as competitors much remained to be done and it was unsure whether to increase in-house expertise or to source products and services from Keells Computers or from foreign firms. Keells Computers developed a comprehensive customer database for MKFSL to

---

[4] CIMA was the acronym for "Certified Institute of Management Accounting," a U.K.-based accreditation.

maintain customer accounts but de Lanerolle said this data was not available for JKH-group use due to the client confidentiality requirements.

Promotional Efforts

MKFSL employed print advertisements and editorial coverage to generate awareness of the firm and its activities. Most efforts were on personal selling activities conducted mainly through networking, typically by directors at senior levels targeting directors of other companies, often through the cocktail circuit. De Lanerolle said that since Colombo was relatively small (locally referred to as "the village"), "everyone knows everyone else." Networking was also practiced by executives at operational levels in potential client firms and with local business organizations (e.g., Chamber of Commerce, Board of Investment, Export Development Board) to secure leads. MKFSL also followed up with firms in the news, often by telephone perhaps followed by a personal visit. From time to time, MKFSL held focused seminars and workshops for targeted groups (e.g., firms potentially able to secure stock exchange listings) on advantages of listing, the listing process, legal issues and so forth.

One employee believed customers developed in this manner demanded higher service levels: "Once we had a complaint from a person regarding a transaction. Instead of dealing with the personnel involved, he went straight to Mr. Ajit Gunewardene in the Sector Management Committee." Customer turnover was low and confined to the more junior levels; customers were seldom, if ever, poached by competitors.

MKFSL was the first firm to publish locally academic research papers (written by in-house analysts) about Sri Lankan financial markets. These were used to solicit business by tapping John Keells Holdings' vast network of foreign investors for potential business opportunities.

The Sri Lankan Economy

For many years, the Sri Lankan economy operated under the shadow of a civil war; from 1983 to 1989, hostilities initiated by Tamil separatists, involving escalating civil disturbance and security operations, adversely affected several economic sectors (e.g., agriculture, trading, tourism, transportation). Foreign investment decelerated, GDP growth dropped to 2.2% (1987 to 1989) and unemployment increased due to setbacks in the government's ambitious investment program. Tourism was most adversely affected: arrivals, 400,000 in 1982, dipped to 180,000 (1987), but manufacturing grew at 3.5% due to expansion of industrial exports, mainly textiles and apparel.

Post 1989 economic liberalization (e.g., incentives, concessions, removal of trade and exchange controls) led to much better economic performance (Table 2). Export processing zones, modern banking networks, upgraded telecommunications, transportation and road networks stimulated foreign and local investment and increased economic activity (GDP growth 1993, 6.9%; 1994 [forecast], 5.6%). Favorable weather and reduction in civil strife improved agricultural; industrial exports advanced significantly, driven by availability of a skilled, relatively low cost labor force. Gunewardene believed that although a small area in north and northeast Sri Lanka was held by Tamil separatists, this did not significantly impact daily business:

Table 2: Basic Economic Indicators

		1993	1994
Population			
Mid-year estimate (million)		17.6	17.9
Growth rate %		1.2	1.4
National income			
Rate of growth of GDP % (real)		7.7	5.3
Per capita GNP (current factor cost prices)			
	Rs	25,377	28,843
	US$	526	584
Per capita GNP (market prices)	Rs	28,357	32,231
	US$	588	652
Sectoral growth rates (%)			
Agriculture, forestry, and fishing		4.9	3.3
Mining and quarrying		11.9	6.0
Manufacturing		10.5	9.1
Construction		6.5	6.0
Services		6.3	5.2
Investment and savings			
As a percentage of GDP (current market prices)			
Investment		25.6	27.0
Government		4.2	3.2
Domestic savings		16.0	15.2
National savings		20.3	19.1
Prices			
Colombo Consumer Price Index			
% change Dec.–Dec.		10.3	4.2
Average annual % change		11.7	8.4
% change in implicit GNP deflator		9.5	9.4
Trade*			
Imports	Rs million	193,550	236,030
	SDR million	2,870	3,328
Exports	Rs million	138,175	158,544
	SDR million	2,046	2,235
Tea	"	295	296
Rubber	"	46	51
Coconut	"	41	53
Garments and textiles	"	1,009	1,080
Petroleum products	"	57	56
Other industrial exports	"	422	540

Table 2 (cont'd)

	1993	1994
Balance of payments (SDR million)		
Trade balance	−825	−1,095
Service account	28	12
Private transfers (net)	402	438
Official transfers	115	115
Current account balance	−281	−531
Overall balance	375	173
Overall debt service ratio %	13.8	13.0
Government finance		
As a percentage of GDP		
Government expenditure	28.1	29.0
Government revenue	19.7	19.0
Current account surplus/deficit (−)	−0.8	−2.9
Budget deficit (before grants)	−8.4	−10.0
Budget deficit (after grants)	−6.8	−8.6
Money and credit		
% change M1	19.0	19.0
% change M2	23.5	19.6
Money and credit		
% change in domestic credit	3.5	14.7
% change in external banking assets (net)	87.9	37.7
Exchange rate (average)		
Rs/USD	48.25	49.42
Rs/SDR	67.39	70.75

*The published SDR values in the 1993 annual report differ from these values due to a change in the conversion method based on monthly SDR values.
Source: Central Bank of Sri Lanka, *Annual Report 1994*.

Business and commerce carry on regardless and, except for isolated incidents in the rest of the country, there is no direct impact on the average citizen. However, the big and often overlooked impact on all of us is the cost, which slows development. About one quarter of the national budget is spent on the war.[5]

Gunewardene believed international markets were maturing about the extent of political violence:

Foreigners finally accepted that with the exception of very rare episodes, political violence is confined to the north and that this remained a safe place for investment. The stock market barely blinked when the president was blown to smithereens

---

[5] Chris Pritchard, "Sri Lanka's Tide of Economic Change," *Business Review Weekly*, February 25, 1994.

and continued its upward path. Malaysian and Singapore interests concluded Colombo's biggest property purchase in several years, only a few days after the assassination.

Increased stock market activity via a large number of initial public offerings (almost US$70 million) and development of an active secondary market provided investment banking opportunities (Table 3). By 1993, market capitalization increased three-fold since 1990 to reach Rs 123.8 billion as increasing numbers of Sri Lankan companies sought market listings. Fueling this growth were major financial institutions entering Sri Lanka. Foreigners could purchase unlimited numbers of shares except for banking and insurance stocks (40% limit); some observers estimated international buyers owned about 40% of all Sri Lankan stocks. In June 1994, the *Wall Street Journal* ranked the Colombo Stock Exchange (CSE) first in greatest stock value growth potential in Asia.

Table 3:   Stock Market Indicators (1991–93)

	1991	1992	1993
1. Market capitalization (Rs million) at 31 Dec.	81,840	66,200	123,789
2. Number of new issues	6	12	12
3. Total number of shares issued (million)	13	78	49
4. Value of shares issued (Rs million)	326	1,370	1,247
5. Number of shares traded (million)	79	88	351
6. Value of shares traded (Rs million)	4,304	4,969	18,579
7. Price indices – CSE all as at 31 Dec.	838	605	979
CSE sensitive at 31 Dec.	1,199	827	1,442
8. Total listed	178	190	200
9. Annual turnover (Rs million)	4,302	4,974	18,568

Sources: Central Bank of Sri Lanka, *Annual Report 1994*; Colombo Stock Exchange.

Future prospects for the economy were driven by increasingly liberal economic policies enacted by the new government based on private sector expansion, indigenous industry development and encouragement of foreign investment; the new government was also committed to eliminating corruption. GDP growth rates were expected to increase, especially if political turmoil were eliminated. Prominent businessmen and economists believed that redirecting substantial defense funds (20% of total budget) to more productive uses (e.g., infrastructure development) could provide Sri Lanka with double digit growth rates. Gunewardene believed that 10% p.a. economic growth would enable Sri Lanka to achieve newly industrialized country status by 2000.

Banking and Finance

Entry in investment banking was straightforward; the industry was not regulated and neither licensing nor minimal capital requirements were necessary. The only restriction was use of "bank" in the firm's name; many new entrants used the term "financial services." De Lanerolle believed that apart from perhaps three players, most were neither professional nor offered wide product ranges; he said it was not uncommon to hear of "fly-by-night" operations that swindled investors. However, tightening government supervision led to a reduction in players from 60 (end 1989) to 24 (end 1993). MKFSL believed the proposed Banking Act, expected to be drafted and passed in two years, would make it more difficult for small players to enter the market.

In 1994, several financial institutions (e.g., the two major development banks [Development Finance Corporation of Ceylon {DFCC} and National Development Bank], five merchant banks, 24 finance firms, seven venture capital firms, four leasing firms) offered flexible financing methods.[6] Revenues for the five merchant banks were expected to grow 117% in 1994 (1993 growth, 69%) (Table 4). Business for the three registered leasing companies was also growing: combined total assets in 1993, Rs 1.134 million were expected to be almost Rs 2 million in 1994. Major fund users were: commercial vehicles (over Rs 1 million), passenger vehicles and plant and machinery (each Rs 300 million to Rs 400 million).

The Colombo Stock Exchange

The Sri Lankan stock market was administered by the Colombo Stock Exchange (CSE) and regulated by the Securities and Exchange Commission (SEC); substantial trading did not begin until 1985. Ranked the world's tenth fastest-growing market, it trailed India and South Korea. Current market capitalization (Rs $123.8 billion) equaled a quarter of Sri Lanka's GDP. Since 1993, "the CSE Sensitive Index grew from 827 to 1,442; improved economic and trading prospects recorded Rs 5.1 billion through new listings, rights issues and three privatizations."[7]

Table 4: Merchant Bank Activities (1993–94)

	1993	1994*
1. Earned income on leasing	168.5	289.9
2. Interest on discounting trade bills	168.4	275.5
3. Financial and marketing consultancy	13.3	7.2
4. Underwriting commissions	10.6	18.3
5. Insurance commission	3.1	1.5
6. Interest on margin trading	11.9	52.9
7. Profit on investment in shares	35.9	175.9
8. Interest on treasury bills	11.1	85.4
9. Other	106.8	243.9
Total	**529.6**	**1,150.5**

*Provisional.
Sources: Central Bank of Sri Lanka, *Annual Report 1994*; Merchant Bank of Sri Lanka Ltd.; People's Merchant Bank Ltd.; Seylan Merchant Bank Ltd.; Vanik Incorporation Ltd.; Asia Capital Ltd.

---

[6] In addition, Sri Lanka had five insurance companies; Sri Lanka Insurance Corporation and National Insurance Corporation were state-owned.
[7] Anonymous, "Small but powerful," *The Financial Times*, October 1994.

In 1992, the CSE computerized its clearing operation. In 1994, it introduced scriptless trading with installation of the Central Depository System (CDS) to eliminate backlogs and delays; the 300% share volume increase (since 1992) was well handled. In 1994, the planned screen-based system to facilitate trading volume expansion was delayed. Some foreign analysts believed the new system would be far more advanced than competing regional exchanges in Bangladesh, Pakistan and India.

To list on the CSE, a firm had to fulfill minimum capital requirements (i.e., one million rupees) and other criteria (e.g., staffing); the capital requirement was considered outdated and government revisions were expected within one year. The government regulated retail customer commissions; these were based on transaction values. However, there were no regulations restricting advertising in investment banking.[8]

In mid-1994, the Sri Lankan investment industry comprised no cartels nor associations. Through informal conversations with key financial leaders, de Lanerolle believed major market players were interested in forming a united body to protect financial firms' interests. He also believed professional standards should be set to ensure higher quality firms, protect consumer interests and eliminate unnecessary and possibly destructive price practices. However, neither private nor government financial bodies had initiated action to form an association. Currently, the Colombo Stock Exchange was developing regulations for specific financial transactions.

Capital Market Growth

The first CSE's first "real growth" period commenced in 1985; a second, fueled mainly by initial public offerings (IPOs) occurred between 1987 to 1990. As a result, several international financial institutions (e.g., Jardine Fleming, Crosby Securities, Development Bank of Singapore) placed Sri Lanka in the favorable emerging markets category; they entered aggressively by forming alliances with local institutions. These partnerships partly resulted from regulations stipulating majority Sri Lankan ownership of local firms. Active participation by domestic investors and portfolio investment by these non-nationals led to increased stock market volume. In 1993, 11 new firms received exchange listings (total 201); in mid-1994, CSE executives believed 36 more firms would be listed in the next 12 months. MKFSL management believed the entry of seasoned organizations into Sri Lanka would stimulate both local and international demand for more professional investment banking services.

Trading Volume

In the early 1980s, average daily volume was less than Rs 1 million; on occasion in the mid-1990s, it exceeded Rs 300 million (Exhibit 3). Annual volume in 1988 was Rs 62 million; it was expected to reach over Rs 30 billion by 2000. Observers believed over 50% of shares traded in 1994 (versus 37%, 1992) were bought by foreigners, largely for European and North American institutions. Said Isuru Tillakawardana, the SEC's assistant general manager: "We got rid of our public gallery. We needed the space for the trading floor, we couldn't control the bigger and bigger crowds."

---

[8] In fact, there were no formalized advertising laws in Sri Lanka!

Customers

Sri Lankans traditionally considered fixed deposit savings at state banks the preferred form of investment, partly because of familiarity, partly because of lack of knowledge of investment alternatives. Those in urban areas (e.g., Colombo) tended to be more sophisticated in banking decisions, for example, considering opening foreign bank accounts. However, Devapriya Ellepola, manager of stockbroking and sales at HDF Securities, believed more investors were entering the market: "There's been a sharp rise in local investor confidence. But with only 17,000 active Sri Lankan investors, there's plenty of educational and promotional work to be done." Sri Lankans had several other investment alternatives (Table 5):

Table 5: Interest Rates on Various Investment Alternatives (1990–94 est.)

	1990	1991	1992	1993	1994
TBills/primary	18.36	17.43	18.99	19.38	
TBills/secondary	18.34	17.30	18.06	19.13	
Fixed deposit (com. banks – 1 year)	16.00	15.00	16.75	15.50	13.60*
Fixed deposit (NSB – 1 year)	17.00	17.00	17.00	16.00	15.38
Savings deposit (com. banks)	9.50	10.25	10.25	10.50	9.65*
Savings deposit (NSB)	16.20	14.00	14.00	14.00	14.00

*Average.
Source: Colombo Stock Exchange.

- Real estate. Sri Lankan real estate construction was quite active. In 1990, construction accounted for 6.8% of GDP (6.7%, 1991; 6.9%, 1992). Annual growth in construction output rose from 1990 (2.9%) to 1993 (7%).
- Gold. Traditionally, Sri Lankans believed gold held value; they continued to purchase significant quantities.
- Bypassing commercial banks. By mid-1994, the commercial paper market (established 1993), was valued at Rs 2.5 billion and increasing fast.[9]
- Mutual funds and unit trusts. Mutual funds were introduced in the early 1990s by DFCC, a state-owned commercial bank. Colombo Stock Exchange approval was required to launch a new fund; it was currently drafting new (and updating old) legislation on mutual funds. Most funds were open-ended vehicles investing in equities. By 1994, investors had nine fund options.
- Foreign investment. This was not a legal option for Sri Lankan investors; legislation prohibited unauthorized overseas investment; Sri Lankan citizens could not maintain bank accounts in other countries.

---

[9] Commercial paper, mediated by investment banks was a financial instrument whereby corporations loaned and borrowed from each other; it was directly competitive with traditional corporate loans from commercial banks.

Competition

Stockbroking

By February 1994, 15 stockbroking firms (1990, 11) had licenses to trade shares in 201 listed companies (1990, 175).[10] In 1992, four new brokers entered the market in joint ventures with international brokerage houses (e.g., HDF [Jardine Fleming, Hong Kong], City Smith [Smith New Court, U.K.]. By 1994, City Smith and HDF were considered among Sri Lanka's top three brokers.

Merchant Banks

MKFSL competed against Sri Lanka's five merchant banks; it had the fewest staff and was the least experienced in leasing and trade finance where it was a late entrant. Most other investment banks were associated with commercial banks that provided needed sources of funds. MKFSL identified two major competitors (i.e., Vanik, Merchant Bank of Sri Lanka) offering a similar range of financial products and services.

Vanik. By mid-1994, Vanik (Sanskrit for merchant) Incorporated, founded by Justin Meegoda, 48, with three other merchant bankers (January 1993), had over 100 employees. Initially working with a borrowed computer, rented furniture and no carpets, car or photocopier, its makeshift office looked nothing like an investment bank. However, by mid-1994, Vanik had arranged three times as many new share issues as its nearest competitor.

In the Sri Lankan business community, Meegoda was considered a seasoned banker and serious in his new venture; he claimed to have staked everything except his wife's jewelry and the family home. Previously, with the Central Bank, in 1979 he helped establish the National Development Bank; ten years later, he helped set up the Merchant Bank of Sri Lanka and was CEO from 1989 to February 1992. He resigned when a bank's client was adversely affected by political interference (Table 6). Meegoda's professionalism and personal integrity were incorporated in Vanik's mission statement:

> Our mission is to be an efficient and effective facilitator in creating wealth through innovative financial products and services. We endeavor to achieve this by providing the best investment banking services to business enterprises at the highest professional and ethical levels, in an entrepreneurial environment.

In October 1993, a successful promotion campaign (print and television) led Vanik's initial public offering of Rs 170 million (US$ 3.4 million) to be 22 times oversubscribed. Institutional backing was strong: Canadian-based Forbes & Walker and Delmege Forsyth each held 8%; Commonwealth Development Corporation held 9%. In early 1994, Asian Finance & Investment Corporation (affiliated with Asian Development Bank) bought 9%. Vanik's foreign affiliated banks included: Deutsche Bank

---

[10] Central Bank of Sri Lanka, *Annual Report 1994*.

Table 6:   Extract from a News Report Regarding Justin Meegoda's Resignation

Quietly spoken and portly, banker Justin Meegoda is hardly the image of a man renowned in Sri Lanka for taking the fight against political interference to the country's ruling elite. But two years ago, when Meegoda was managing director of Sri Lanka's premier merchant bank he showed that his soft spoken manner concealed a rock-hard determination which would not yield to all but the most violent threats. Now a successful private banker, Meegoda resigned from the Merchant Bank of Sri Lanka in 1992 only after other board members said they feared for his life if he kept resisting political interference against one of the bank's clients. The bank, an associate of the state-run Bank of Ceylon, had been structuring a financial package for a client bidding for control of Kelani Tyres under a government scheme to privatize state companies. But another investor with powerful connections to the ruling United National Party also wanted control. Meegoda resisted the political intrusion which followed – a rare thing in either the government or private sector – and angered powerful politicians, including the late president Ranasinghe Premadasa. It was suggested through a Premadasa appointee that Meegoda go on medical leave and charges of insider dealing were planned against him. Finally, threats were made against Meegoda and his family, but ceased after his resignation. "I know it was to do with the privatisation of Kelani Tyres, a state-owned firm," said Meegoda, now president and chief executive officer of Vanik Incorporation, a new merchant bank in Sri Lanka. "I also know the president was involved because some senior cabinet ministers said the order to get rid of me came from the very top."

"People should stand up for what they believe in. I think professionals and the business community should stand up and be counted," he added. Meegoda had been managing director of Merchant Bank for about three years when he quit in February 1992. He quickly sought private sector backing for a new merchant bank and, with a group of professionals, set up Vanik Incorporation in early 1993. The local and international business community admire Meegoda for the stand he took at Merchant Bank.

Source: Prithi Kodagoda, "Soft Spoken Sri Lankan Banker Speaks Out," *Reuter Asia-Pacific Business Report,* June 9, 1994.

(Germany), Hatton National Bank, People's Bank, Public Bank, Sampath Bank, Seylan Bank and Standard Chartered Bank (Hong Kong).

Vanik offered several financial services: short- and medium-term financing, corporate finance, capital market operations, money market operations and company secretarial services. Vanik department heads averaged 32 years:

- Capital Markets and Investment Department: Main activities were share issue underwriting, margin trading, portfolio management and managing Vanik's portfolio. Other activities included underwriting, placement and management of equity and debt issues, dealing in shares and securities and investment advisory services.
- Corporate Finance Department: Primarily involved in providing Vanik and clients fundamental analysis including daily project analysis and corporate mergers and acquisitions. Products included short- to medium-term finance and equity finance. Main activities include privatizations, mergers, acquisitions, restructuring, syndication, bridging loans and venture capital investments.

- Leasing Department: Vanik syndicated leases for large-scale projects, structured leases to meet clients' needs and ventured into vendor leasing.
- Legal, Secretarial and Issue Management Department: Played an advisory role to all departments, subsidiaries and clients on all legal matters pertaining to business transactions.
- Trade Paper Department: Vanik's Trade Paper portfolio was the second largest among institutions holding such portfolios; it pioneered "Invoice Discounting."
- Treasury and Money Broking Department: Impacted the Fixed Income Securities Market by pioneering the structuring and placements of Sri Lanka's first Lease Securitization Certificates.
- Finance Department: Responsible for financial control, financial accounting, preparing and publishing financial statements and providing management information. Corporate planning was recently added to strengthen the Vanik's planning process.
- Information Technology Department: Activities included maintaining the computer network (over 60 computers) and integrating all departments to a centralized data base. A separate software unit developed Vanik's software needs.
- L.B. Finance Company Ltd.: Vanik acquired L.B. Finance to facilitate entry into hire purchase, leasing, trade bills discounting and land sales. It provided geographic diversification via its Kandy office.

Vanik was profitable from the start (1993, Rs 44.5 million [US$900,000]; first quarter 1994, Rs 41.3 million [US$843,000]). Industry observers expected increases in fee and fund-based activity to cause 1995 profits to be three times greater than 1994. Vanik's shares traded at several times the issue price; analysts contended there was still substantial upside potential.

De Lanerolle considered Vanik MKFSL's most serious competitor. Its many accomplishments included: lead underwriter for Forbes Ceylon's Rs 625 million IPO (Sri Lanka's largest issue); a Rs 850 million IPO for Puttalam Cement (involving Sri Lanka's first convertible bonds); and raising US$41 million for the government's privatization efforts. Despite these major deals, Meegoda considered Sri Lanka's capital markets in infancy; in 1993, total assets of the four investment banks doubled, new financial products were being introduced rapidly.

Merchant Bank of Sri Lanka (MBSL). MKFSL considered MBSL, Sri Lanka's first merchant bank (formed 1982, originally owned by Bank of Ceylon [49% stake] another strong competitor. Changa Samaraweera, MBSL's new managing director said it was looking for potential partnerships with foreign players: "We are looking East and West, and will decide what sort of marriage before the end of the year." Like Vanik, MBSL comprised several functional departments: Corporate Finance, Capital Markets, Leasing (MBSL's main business), Trade Finance, Business Development and Management, Corporate Secretarial, Money Market, Finance Company and Stock Broking. MBSL's after-tax profit for year ending March 31, 1994 was Rs 554 million; its first overseas branch was scheduled to open in Katmandu, Nepal (early 1996).

Forbes Capital. Forbes was wholly-owned by Canadian-based Ondaatje Corporation; in October 1993, it purchased Forbes & Walker, a 113-year-old commodity and stockbroking firm. Sri Lanka-born Christopher Ondaatje split the firm into Forbes Capital, stockbroking and investment banking operations, and Forbes Ceylon Ltd., for real estate investment, food and tourism.

Asia Capital. Established in 1991, Asia Capital Ltd. owned Asia Securities, Asia Fort Asset Management (Pvt.) Ltd., Asia Growth Fund (Pvt.) Ltd. and Asia Fort Sri Lanka Direct Investment Fund Ltd. In years ended March 31, 1993 and 1994, Asia Securities outperformed CSE's 14 other brokerages in commissions earned. It was considered aggressive in direct equity investments, asset management, corporate finance, under-writing and loan financing.

People's Merchant Bank. Incorporated in 1983, People's Merchant Bank offered basic services: company secretarial, share and debenture issue management, issue manage-ment for other equity and quasi-equity instruments, registrars and managers to share issues, trustee and trust related services and investment portfolio management. By mid-1994, main activities were finance leasing, bills discounting, commercial paper, share issue underwriting and stock exchange activities. For year ended March 31, 1994, net income was Rs 62 million.

Commercial Banks

Development and Finance Corporation of Ceylon (DFCC). Founded in 1955, by mid-1994, DFCC had three branches (i.e., Kandy, Matara, Kurunegala), each a strategic business unit and profit center, and five associate companies: HDF Securities (securi-ties broking), Lanka Industrial Estates (only private sector industrial estate), Lanka Ventures Ltd. (largest specialized venture capital firm), National Asset Management and Development Insurance Broking Company Pvt. Ltd. (institutional fund manager).

DFCC's core business was project financing and investment banking. It offered a variety of financial products including: long- and medium-term loans, working capi-tal loans, finance leasing, equity investments, technology financing, bills discounting, factoring, consultancy services, underwriting, venture capital finance, fund manage-ment, securities broking, industrial estate development, insurance broking, property development and wholesale commercial banking. DFCC's mission statement said:

> DFCC will be a catalyst in national development by promoting and assisting pri-vate sector enterprises in Sri Lanka. It will provide finance as well as a range of services including the identification and development projects, financial services and consultancy. DFCC will maintain a dedicated and highly motivated team committed to the achievement of excellence in service, leading to realization of the twin goals of improvement of overall economic prosperity of the country and growth with financial viability of the corporation.

DFCC Newslink was believed to be planning a quarterly newsletter to add value to customer services. Contents would include articles on topical issues and research findings on business and finance related subjects.

National Development Bank (NDB). Established in 1979 as a state-owned institution, NDB was privatized (61%, a majority held by leading local and international institutions) in 1993. NDB's main purpose was to promote Sri Lanka's industrial, agricultural and commercial development by providing medium- and long-term credit to development projects and by mobilizing internal and external capital for investment in such projects. In mid-1994, NDB was Sri Lanka's largest development bank; 1994 after-tax profits were expected to exceed Rs 500 million. NDB was diversifying; it entered new areas by forming associate / subsidiary companies with technical partners. It gave special emphasis to export-oriented projects and those capable of generating substantial employment.

Relaunch Strategy

During a strategy session in early 1994, JKH's Board of Directors decided to reassess its entire Financial Services sector. Supervising development of MKFSL's relaunch strategy were the Financial Services Sector Committee and several key MKFSL personnel: Roshni Fernando (capital markets analyst), Ralph de Lanerolle (MKFSL Director), Prasantha Fernando (Corporate Finance Manager) and Ajit Gunewardene (Managing Director). This group was assisted by Donna Christie, a New Zealand expatriate account manager, assigned by McCann-Erickson.[11] Grant McCann-Erickson was one of the six largest and oldest advertising agencies in Sri Lanka. De Lanerolle gave Christie significant creative freedom in proposing an entire advertising campaign; the final budget, likely to range between Rs 1 million and Rs 5 million, was based on a Rs 10 million benchmark for a successful consumer product relaunch. Issues under consideration were:

Company positioning. Historically, the only positioning within JKH was to be market leader. Management wonder if a detailed, focused positioning strategy was necessary for a successful campaign. One suggestion was "to be the fully-fledged financial services provider"; management was undecided since the firm would have to offer a wider product range.

Product development. The team knew MKFSL would probably have to offer a more comprehensive product mix. One member proposed the following regroupings:

- Fixed income securities and treasury management
- Corporate finance and advisory services

---

[11] MKFSL did not have a full-time marketing staff. However, de Lanerolle had previous work experience with renowned international advertising agencies (e.g., J. Walter Thompson); he assigned several staff into a "marketing team" to brainstorm marketing ideas.

- Capital markets and investor services
- Trade finance and leasing
- Project financing and venture capital funding
- Management consultancy services

Advisory and management consulting services, project financing and venture capital funding would be new services. The team believed the mix was ideal; hiring additional expertise could be accomplished at fairly short notice since de Lanerolle had a substantial network of potential hires.

The Sector Committee believed MKFSL was well-established in insurance, fund management, stock and money broking. Under the influence of major international firms (e.g., Merrill Lynch) de Lanerolle wanted to establish a wider spectrum of professional investment banking services.

Reorganization. The committee agreed early on that Financial Services group personnel should be assessed and better organized; each service division should be located apart from the others. Currently the group employed 15 to 18 people, including support staff; management wondered which areas needed additional personnel and how the organization could be regrouped to form synergies between various financial activities. Prasantha proposed a new organizational chart related to new product introductions (Figure 1).

Figure 1: Mackinnon & Keells Operations Division

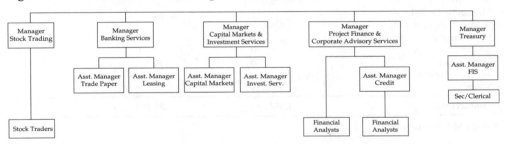

Name change. All members agreed a name change should be seriously considered. "Keells" was connected with a well-established and prestigious organization. However, the association with meat products seemed to cheapen its professional services. Fernando believed there was an associated problem: "Saying Mackinnon & Keells Financial Services Ltd. really is a mouthful. Even when we abbreviate it to MKFSL, it still seems too long and complicated. I really think our full name is difficult enough to be remembered by locals, let alone foreigners."

The major consideration was whether any association with "Keells" should remain. One member argued: "Is a name change feasible at all? After building our reputation over a number of years and then changing it to a new name, will it jeopardize MKFSL in a growing and lucrative market?"

Customer segmentation. The committee wondered whether current customer segmentation was adequate. Since MKFSL was predominantly financially-, rather than marketing-focused, strategic segmentation was not considered earlier. Generally, members felt the current segments worked but agreed other possibilities might be better.

Advertising media. MKFSL had to determine an appropriate advertising budget and media mix. Other financial service providers used a combination of press, TV and radio. De Lanerolle secured several historic reports (October to December 1993) (Table 7). One item: currently used press items were informational and often used color.

Table 7: Total Press, TV and Radio Expenditure for Selected Finance Companies (Oct–Dec 1993, in rupees)

Finance company	October	November	December
Arpico Finance	111,713	88,425	107,740
Bartleet	0	0	15,000
Central Finance	626,080	274,826	98,510
Central Investments			
Ceylinco Securities			
Colombo Credit Ltd.			
Fin. & Land Sale	3,780	7,960	17,310
HDFC	47,576	41,984	0
Industrial Finance			
LOFAC			66,420
Mackinnon & Keells	12,150	0	0
MB. Financial			
Mercantile In. Ltd.			
N M & G Finance Ltd.			
Senkadagala			
Singaputzu	0	0	0
The Finance	0	15,300	52,050
Toho Investments			
Vanik	863,024	0	0
Product total	1,664,323	428,495	357,030

Source: SRL Media Scan.

Television: Since several business-related programs were aired, management believed TV was essential in any relaunch campaign. In 1987, an estimated 520,000 television sets received two state-controlled channels; three private channels began operating in 1992 and 1993. Prime time rates (7:00 pm to 9:00 pm) commanded a 20% premium. Advertising costs were vastly affected by channel choice. Rates for the most popular television stations were:

TV station	Time period	Language	Cost (Rs)
ETV1	7:00 am to 8:00 am	English	3,000
	7:00 pm to 9:00 pm		3,500
	9:00 pm to 11:00 pm		2,000
ETV2	3:00 pm to 4:00 pm	English	1,000
	7:00 pm to 9:00 pm		3,500
	9:00 pm to 11:00 pm		2,000

TV station	Time period	Language	Cost (Rs)
MTV	7:00 pm to 9:00 pm	English	8,400
	9:00 pm to 11:00 pm		6,300
Rupavahina	8:00 pm to 9:00 pm	Singhalese	15,000
	9:00 pm to 11:00 pm		12,500

Print: Seventy percent of English newspapers' circulation was in Colombo; Singhalese newspapers reached wider audiences. Although over 20 newspapers were published, the *Daily Island, Daily News, Sri Lanka Times* and *Sri Lanka Observer* were considered the most important. Advertising rates varied by size, color usage and location in the paper. Selected newspapers with advertisement sizes were:

Newspaper	Size of ad and color	Location	Language	Cost (Rs)
Daily News	5 cm × 54 cm (B/W)	Inside	English	24,300
	10 cm × 38 cm (col.)			54,340
	10 cm × 39 cm (col.)			55,770
Dinamina	2 cm × 20 cm (col.)	Front	Singhalese	5,160
Silumina	8 cm × 27 cm (col.)	Inside	Singhalese	61,776 (Sunday only)
	4 cm × 27 cm (col.)			19,440
Island	10 cm × 38 cm (col.)	Inside	English	22,275
	5 cm × 27 cm (B/W)			7,425
Divaina	2 cm × 20 cm (col.)	Front	Singhalese	3,600
	4 cm × 26 cm (B/W)	Inside		7,800
Lanka Deeba	2 cm × 20 cm (col.)	Front	Singhalese	5,400
	8 cm × 27 cm (col.)	Inside		23,760
Leader	10 cm × 27 cm (col.)	Inside	English	40,500 (Sunday only)
	4 cm × 27 cm (B/W)			18,900
Sri Lankan Observer	3 cm × 25 cm (col.)	Inside	English	11,325 (Sunday only)
	6 cm × 30 cm (col.)			24,480
Sri Lankan Times	3 cm × 25 cm (col.)	Inside	English	10,950
	6 cm × 30 cm (col.)			23,760
	10 cm × 38 cm (col.)			61,560
	10 cm × 39 cm (col.)			63,180

A limited number of local and international business publications was also available; cost differences between the two could be substantial. The team also considered printing more comprehensive and attractive brochures; it believed Keells printing company's quality was relatively inferior and secured quotes from two printing houses:

Description: One thousand copies of 16 pages (9.5 ins. × 8.25 ins.), 2 colors on 100 grams Conqueror Contour White Embossed Paper.

- Aitken Spence Printing (Pvt) Ltd.: Rs 85.50 per copy (additional charge for laminating cover on one side only, Rs 3.50 per copy).
- Gunarantne Offset Limited: Unit cost Rs 75.00 per copy.

Radio: The team was unsure whether radio was effective, few financial services firms advertised on radio. Both English and Singhalese channels were available, the latter had wider audiences. Advertising rates varied widely by language station. A sample of radio stations, with possible advertising periods:

Radio station	Time period	Language	Cost (30 sec.)
FM 99	5:00 am to 10:00 am	English	Rs 600
	6:00 pm to 9:00 pm		Rs 500
Sirasa FM	6:00 am to 8:00 am	Singhalese	Rs 3,000
	8:00 am to 9:00 am		Rs 2,000
SLBC – Ruhunu	Anytime	Singhalese	Rs 400
Sri Lankan Broadcasting Corporation (English Service)	6:00 am to 7:00 am	English	Rs 2,000
	7:00 am to 8:00 am		Rs 1,800
Sri Lankan Broadcasting Corporation (Singhalese Service)	6:00 am to 7:00 am	Singhalese	Rs 2,500
TNL Radio	7:00 am to 8:00 am	English	Rs 900
	8:00 am to 9:00 am		Rs 650
	5:00 pm to 6:00 pm		Rs 650
YES FM	10:00 am to 2:00 pm	English	Rs 600

Outdoor Advertising: It was uncommon for financial institutions to advertise on billboards. Some firms had a group policy against such advertising as it "obstructed the scenery" and made the city look ugly.

Mailers: Management wondered if mailers were viable for potential business and whether they should be included in a relaunch strategy. Postage per brochure was estimated at Rs 10. This task would have to be assigned to employees, but none had slack time available. Management wondered if full-time marketing staff should be hired.

Decisions

The relaunch team had to assess how MKFSL should be positioned in the fast-growing financial services market. Many issues remained to be decided; final decisions would have to be based on a clear understanding of MKFSL's strengths and weaknesses. A relaunch strategy would have to set the course for long-term growth and gain the interest of multinational firms entering Sri Lanka.

Exhibit 1: Mackinnon & Keells Financial Services Ltd., Income Statement

	1992 (Rs)	1993 (Rs)
Turnover	26,109,557	36,706,142
Operating profit	7,853,083	14,349,563
Other income	3,383,179	1,764,946
	11,236,262	16,114,509
Interest charges	7,055,386	9,696,067
Profit on ordinary activities before taxation	4,180,876	6,418,442
Tax on profit on ordinary activities	1,200,056	1,939,454
Profit on ordinary activities after taxation	2,980,820	4,478,988
Extraordinary items after taxation	31,304,939	840,212
Profit for the year	34,285,759	5,319,200
Dividends	2,204,280	2,850,896
Transfer to reserves	34,044,308	
Profit/(loss) retained for the year	−1,962,829	2,468,304
Statement of retained earnings/(accumulated losses)		
At the beginning of the year as previously stated	1,501,516	389,319
Adjustments in respect of prior years	−1,275,633	−2,126,265
Adjusted balance brought forward	225,883	−1,736,946
Profit retained for the year	−1,962,829	2,468,304
At the end of the year	−1,736,946	731,358

Exhibit 2: Mackinnon & Keells Financial Services Ltd., Balance Sheet

	1992 (Rs)	1993 (Rs)
Fixed assets		
Tangible assets	113,821,760	113,538,300
Investments	10,315,843	17,416,055
Non-current assets		
Loans		
	124,137,603	130,954,355
Current assets		
Stocks	246,702	211,470
Debtors	71,996,078	56,620,912
Amounts due from related companies	40,128,428	66,028,939
Investment in treasury bills		243,166
Commercial paper		
Bank balances & cash	24,435	584,853
	112,395,643	123,689,340
Current liabilities		
Trade creditors		
Creditors & accruals	2,875,412	5,902,324
Taxation		
Dividends	1,080,000	
Bank overdrafts	16,072,134	26,203,921
Loans repayable within one year	1,101,408	1,237,541
Amounts due to related companies	58,540,791	63,292,793
	79,666,745	96,636,579
Net current assets	32,728,898	27,052,761
Total assets less current liabilities	156,866,501	158,007,116

Exhibit 2 (cont'd)

	1992 (Rs)	1993 (Rs)
Long-term liabilities	(7,918,343)	(6,680,802)
Deferred liabilities	(1,283,871)	(1,193,723)
Net assets	147,664,287	150,132,591
Capital & reserves		
Share capital	10,800,000	10,800,000
Revaluation reserve	120,601,233	120,601,233
Other reserves	18,000,000	18,000,000
Profit retained	(1,736,946)	731,358
	147,664,287	150,132,591

Source: Mackinnon & Keells Financial Services Ltd.

Exhibit 3: Stock Market Volume

		Total turnover	Daily average turnover	Non-national transactions	
				Purchases	Sales
Period		Rs million	Rs million	Rs million	Rs million
1986		140.4	0.6	–	–
1987		289.5	1.5	–	–
1988		62.0	1.1	–	–
1989		65.0	1.0	–	–
1990*	1st quarter	172.0	2.8	–	–
	2nd quarter	508.0	9.0	–	–
	3rd quarter	715.9	8.5	366.0	3.1
	4th quarter	165.3	8.2	31.9	4.2
1991	1st quarter	306.0	5.4	94.9	21.2
	2nd quarter	1,308.0	22.5	468.3	183.7
	3rd quarter	169.9	8.9	38.4	12.4
	4th quarter	558.9	60.9	166.8	46.5
1992	1st quarter	519.2	24.7	233.2	57.8
	2nd quarter	413.5	18.8	130.5	122.3
	3rd quarter	335.0	16.7	93.8	72.0
	4th quarter	250.3	11.9	87.1	41.5
1993	1st quarter	494.3	21.5	259.2	109.4
	2nd quarter	1,266.1	60.3	613.9	335.7
	July	2,227.0	101.2	1,046.7	527.5
	August	2,016.1	100.8	658.0	843.4
	Sept.	1,913.0	91.1	1,218.7	632.8
	Oct.	1,931.2	92.0	1,195.1	745.5
	Nov.	3,971.5	180.5	1,936.9	1,308.6
	Dec.	3,209.4	160.5	1,429.8	1,128.6
1994	Jan.	4,499.9	236.8	2,316.5	1,028.9
	Feb.	5,510.3	306.1	2,178.6	1,804.6
	Mar.	5,467.9	237.7	2,345.6	2,852.3
	April	2,106.2	131.6	796.9	922.4
	May	1,585.8	88.0	661.3	564.7
	June	2,334.7	111.2	1,242.1	847.8

*Including extraordinary items.

Source: Central Bank of Sri Lanka, *Annual Report 1994*. (Information from Colombo Stock Exchange.)

Case 51

Waldock Mackenzie

Samina Seth
The Hong Kong University of Science and Technology

Noel Capon
Graduate School of Business, Columbia University

By end May 1995, the first stage relaunch, renaming Mackinnon & Keells Financial Services Ltd. as Waldock Mackenzie (WM), was complete. The relaunch committee believed the advertising campaign was highly successful inasmuch as its themes generated wide response in both the investment banking community and general public. In particular, WM received a prestigious award for the best corporate advertising campaign. Numerous copy-cat commercials by non-financial companies appeared subsequently; direct competitors fought back with print and television ads addressing WM's core message. While the investment banking community speculated wildly about its next campaign, WM's cross-functional team, responsible for the first campaign, was uncertain how to maintain momentum. The advertising agency was developing a new print advertising campaign continuing the "zany and radical" theme but WM had not accepted its recommendations because of negative stock market conditions. A presentation laying out future marketing strategy, to John Keells Group directors was due on June 30, a few weeks away.

಄಄಄

The New Strategy

By end October 1994, a radical strategy for Mackinnon & Keells was finalized by Ralph de Lanerolle (Investment Banking Head), Ajit Gunewardene (JKH Director) and Prasantha Fernando (Corporate Finance Manager); approval was secured from the Financial Management Committee Sector. The strategy comprised major operational and marketing phases. De Lanerolle believed the "financial product" had to be intact and fully functional before a comprehensive advertising campaign was conducted.

807

Phase 1: Operational Changes

Name change. On November 1, 1994, Mackinnon & Keells Financial Services Ltd. was officially renamed Waldock Mackenzie. This more Anglicized version was an attempt to be more "user-friendly" and easily remembered while simultaneously reducing negative associations with the John Keells group. Both "Waldock" and "Mackenzie" were derived from earlier JKH financial subsidiaries; de Lanerolle did not want the "new company" completely disassociated from the parent as many advantages continued to exist, especially in recruitment.

Mission statement. After unanimously agreeing to become a fully-fledged financial service provider, the following mission statement was accepted:

> At Waldock Mackenzie, our vision is to be the market leader in investment banking in Sri Lanka by offering a quality service with a high degree of professionalism and integrity. We shall strive to make a significant contribution to the financial services industry and the Sri Lankan economy in general, by offering innovative financial products and setting industry standards.

Company reorganization. The geographically separated businesses were consolidated in a new centrally located headquarters in Colombo. De Lanerolle's proposed organization chart (Mackinnon & Keells case, Figure 1, page 801) was accepted; staff size was set at approximately 50. Five core financial areas were established. Following relocation, creating a comprehensive in-house computer network to link all departments and increase productivity was a high priority. De Lanerolle wanted to invest heavily in technology to provide timely and accurate financial information throughout the firm while also improving customer service. All professional staff would have access to computer terminals by mid-1996. A separate dealing room was set up for the expected increase in equity-based transactions both from the international and domestic markets.

The five core business areas (35 professionals) were established as independent operating departments:

Fixed Income Securities (FIS) & Treasury Division: This eight-member group managed FIS portfolios via investment in treasury bills, government securities, commercial paper and other short-term money-market products. Cash management concerned the structuring of FIS instruments and raising short/long-term funding by securitization; it also offered advisory services for treasury management and related areas.

Corporate Finance & Investment Banking Services: This six-person group provided the full range of debt and equity financing including project valuation and structuring equity and/or debt issues: private placement, syndication arrangements for equity and debt, advice on mergers, acquisitions and buy-outs, project funding, Build Operate Transfer (BOT)/Build Own Operate (BOO) projects, project formulation, feasibility studies and company turnarounds.

Capital Markets & Investor Services: This 15-person group was responsible for managing the equity/debt issue process including preparation of statutory documents, registrar services, underwriting share issues, formulating underwriting consortia, marketing new issues (jointly with Corporate Finance) and so forth. Investor services included fund/portfolio management, advisory services, securities research and margin trading.

Trade Finance: This six-person group offered leasing, bill discounting and other banking services for short-term trade finance.

Management Consultancy Services: This new 10-person group provided consulting services; it specialized in strategic and corporate planning, business process re-engineering, total quality management, management reorganization and system studies.

WM pioneered introduction of several derivative instruments despite concerns that the firm might not be sufficiently mature to take on such complex products. In 1995, the FIS group introduced several new products: Forward Rate Agreements, Treasury Bill Backed Securities, Asset Swaps and a Securities Index-linked commercial paper. WM was in the process of launching a new open-ended mutual fund and was aggressively advertising a close-ended mutual fund based on Sri Lankan securities.

Staff recruitment. High priority was given to staff recruitment. Before the official relaunch campaign employee headcount was increased by 150%. An intensive search was conducted among top management's banking networks to "fill in missing positions"; priority was given to high-level hire. For example, two primary dealers were poached from Bank of Ceylon for the Treasury Bills Unit (in Fixed Income Securities) and appointed head of leasing and head of treasury bills to create secondary market competence.

WM upgraded hiring requirements to embrace multiple professional and academic qualifications and candidates with several years' work experience; de Lanerolle would consider fresh graduates from reputable U.S. universities with little to no experience, but only in rare cases. Annual salaries rose to match this greater professionalism; WM paid new hires from Rs 15,000 to over Rs 40,000 per month. De Lanerolle was keen to "create seasoned and professional staff" from entry-level hires; unlike previously, career paths were identified for junior employees who would receive regular annual reviews. One specific growth area was consultancy; this division anticipated near-term heavy recruiting. Management's average age was approximately 30 years.

Although WM significantly expanded and upgraded professional staff, de Lanerolle believed full-time marketing staff were unnecessary; rather, he decided to rely on cross-functional teams.

Staff training. An on-going training plan was being devised and continually improved; all new employees were assigned a unique program for their professional career paths. Some employees were sent to seminars overseas for updating on the latest products (e.g., derivatives). More broadly, the entire employee base would participate in in-house training programs for familiarization with WM's products (e.g., a Fixed Income Securities course on specialized services currently provided to clients). As a result of WM's greater professionalism, higher ranked WM employees were susceptible to poaching by competitors. Management was developing human resource strategies to instill firm loyalty.[1]

Phase 2: Marketing Activities

An innovative marketing campaign was launched to position WM as a high quality financial service provider with a view to it becoming the Sri Lankan market leader. De Lanerolle stated WM's specific strategic positioning as: "If you don't know your business, don't talk to us!"

Customer segmentation. Previously, Mackinnon & Keells retail focus was on professionals and small business people with net worth over Rs 5 million. Since some WM employees believed these targets were difficult to identify, a new and broader segmentation approach focused on education level, believed directly correlated to earnings; management wanted to approach various professional organizations (e.g., Rotary Assembly). Corporate segmentation was altered slightly: segments were reclassified into three major groups: large listed companies, medium unlisted companies (up to Rs 100 million revenues annually), and middle-range unlisted companies (under Rs 100 million revenues annually).

Advertising strategy. Advertising agency Grant McCann-Erickson proposed a six-stage advertising campaign; four stages were accepted with minor modifications (Exhibit 1):

- Cost-effective and concentrated "teaser" campaign (Exhibit 2) to introduce the "Ant," followed in one week by "The Launch Ad";
- Press conference to introduce Waldock Mackenzie;
- Direct marketing campaign inviting existing and prospective clients to a "Launch Cocktail Party" to view the television campaign, begun that evening; and
- Brand campaign relying heavily on TV, radio and print media (Exhibit 3).

Three million rupees were allocated for the entire launch, including agency services, print and media time. For consistency, and to promote a slightly "foreign" tone, English was used for advertising; all advertising was in print and television.[2]

Print: Only black and white "classical and simple" advertisements were used. After the first intense launch week, frequency was twice per week for three months. WM

---

[1] Sri Lankan law made it illegal for private sector companies to "sign bonds" or restrictive contracts disallowing employees to work for competitors shortly after leaving their jobs.
[2] The agency believed radio would be ineffective for reaching WM's target audience.

advertised in three financial magazines, including *Lanka Monthly Digest*, Sri Lanka's most reputable business magazine. Since WM was positioned as a fully-fledged financial services provider, all major divisions were included in the print advertising campaign.

Television: All television commercials were aired daily at peak time after 9:30 pm for three weeks on three stations, Star TV, BBC and Rupavahina. Commercials were generally aired immediately before or after the English/Singhalese News Bulletin or the Business News.

Seminars: In February 1995, WM held its first seminar (half-day) at a local five-star hotel to promote the new management consultancy division; a Sri Lankan speaker from London spoke on Business Process Re-engineering. The chairman of John Keells Group invited 100 carefully selected firms from the industrial sector; 50 participated. WM offered reduced prices for professional services; it secured six projects (Rs 600,000) from the event (cost Rs 150,000). De Lanerolle said these projects filled the department's schedule for several months; since few Sri Lankan firms offered consulting services, reduced prices were consistent with WM's penetration strategy. De Lanerolle had not decided whether to organize more events: "I don't know if more such events should be organized, it really depends. Right now we're not planning seminars for other areas. Seminars are not for all products."

Sponsorship: WM hosted a Rotary Club meeting at the National Assembly in exchange for the opportunity to speak. The meeting (cost Rs 150,000) was attended by 350 leading Sri Lankan business figures; despite the promising clientele, no business leads were generated.

Publicity: WM's upper-level management were often quoted as experts on Sri Lankan financial markets in leading business publications. De Lanerolle believed such opportunities gave WM credibility in the financial community.

Newsletter: Various methods of maintaining relationships with current customers were considered. A newsletter was suggested, but the Margin Trading group already sent customers weekly updates to keep them informed of market performance and trends. Indeed, most brokerage firms, especially those focusing on margin trading, sent such materials regularly. WM wondered whether and how newsletters might be further exploited as a promotional tool.

Phase 3: New Marketing Techniques

The third and current phase was identifying new marketing techniques to reach targeted clients cost-effectively. De Lanerolle was willing to consider any approach that would not tarnish the brand equity built in the launch campaign.

Mailers: Lanerolle wanted WM to become more aggressive in marketing but with a quality strategy: He urged: "Go after quality and not volume. We don't want to run after accounts that could default on payments." WM experimented with direct marketing for a fixed income retail product: flyers were mailed to 160 doctors (Doctors'

Association members), 80 employees in revenue-earning government departments, 35 lawyers and 12 randomly selected corporate business people. Only a handful responded but business was secured from several clients of competitors. Executives in charge, Isuru Pethiyagoda and Chandima Desinghe, took the initiative: "You cannot expect to just send a mailer and then sit on your laurels!" They began contacting recipients regarding receipt of the package and any questions they might have.

Relaunch Campaign Results

WM's relaunch was judged successful. Roshni Fernando said response to the advertising campaign was "excellent," many telephone calls were received each day; she believed any reaction, negative or positive, met WM's objectives. Revenues jumped sharply in early 1995 despite a slowdown in the capital markets. In particular, WM handled eight public offerings including the People's Merchant Bank that attracted the largest number of applications ever for a single issue; in addition, it recently clinched a contract to privately place abroad a US$10 million Sri Lankan telecommunications fund. De Lanerolle stated: "The company had been so impressed with our advertising campaign that they signed us on!"

However, there was some concern regarding interaction of the advertising campaign with direct mail activities. Although Desinghe believed WM's press advertisements were "unique and off-the-wall with a cheeky attitude," many direct mailer recipients had not heard of Waldock Mackenzie, implying the launch campaign achieved limited success. Pethiyagoda said:

> Many people were surprised WM was a primary dealer in the treasury market; it kind of reflects that credibility counts. I'm not convinced that we're well-known; Vanik is well-known because of its retail campaign. When Vanik tries to sell IPOs to the public, it also builds its name in the retail market. So, I tell customers to shop around for a great rate; it's to their advantage to compare the best rates.

Although he did not maintain detailed records on follow-up telephone calls, Desinghe said respondents generally had limited understanding of materials they received. They often requested more information but the relaunch team was unsure whether a second round of mailers should be sent to the first group or whether new prospective clients should be targeted. He opined: "Perhaps the first mailers did not hit the people with the finger on the button to make decisions. No point in just hitting the top people. Better just to send materials to the finance directors, accountants and CFOs. Finance managers are the ones that want more details."

Furthermore, Desinghe identified other approaches:

> Spending money on a larger sales force will get better results. Just familiarizing prospective customers with the company name is good but now we need product specific marketing. It's time to target the retail market. Since nearly all WM's business is in Colombo, we should plan something outside; except for Kandy we don't have any real presence. There's not much competition so margins could be higher.

Competitor Reactions

Most competitors retaliated immediately by running more advertisements; one merchant bank even copied the tone of WM's ads. Total industry advertising expenditures in late 1994 were: November, Rs 1,774,944; December, Rs 1,480,235 versus Rs 428,495 and Rs 357,030 respectively (1993). WM's costs were growing; management wondered if more advertising was necessary.

Financial Market Conditions[3]

The economy: GDP growth (1994, 6%) slowed to 5.7% in 1995 as the government tackled a rising budget deficit and uncomfortably high inflation. Experts predicted 6.5% growth in 1996 if good progress were made to reduce inflation and the budget deficit and foreign investment continued. The government promised to accelerate privatization and reduce defense expenditures and subsidies.[4] Many observers expected manufacturing and distribution would be the two fastest growing sectors.

Inflation: Inflation in 1994 (8.4%) was much lower than anticipated. Experts believed increased spending on pensions, government salaries and many welfare measures would lead to Sri Lankan rupee depreciation and 1995 inflation over 10%. They also believed a decrease to 8% was possible in 1996.

Rupee: Net capital inflow increases in early 1995 caused modest rupee appreciation against the U.S. dollar; some believed the currency was overvalued. Exporters pressed for devaluation to retain and/or regain price competitiveness. The Economic Intelligence Unit forecast rupee depreciation from Rs 50 to Rs 54.50 per US$1.

Stock market: From August to November 1994, the Colombo Stock Exchange (CSE) All-share Index moved in a 200-point band between 1,000 and 1,200; in December, increasing labor unrest caused the market to slip below 1,000. On December 30, the index was 986.7 versus 1,122 in mid-November.[5] This fall was correlated with a drop in foreign activity from a high of 60% of volume, to 50% in September/October, 30% in November and a virtual absence in January 1995. Despite this fall, in 1994, CSE activity was much higher overall than in 1993; in December 1994, CSE daily turnover averaged US$4.7 million. In February, the index reached a 16-month low (791.98); it rose to 867 in March but fell below 750 by end April.

---

[3] This section is based on "Sri Lanka Country Report," *The Economist Intelligence Unit Limited*, 1st quarter 1995.

[4] In early 1995, the President announced the government would retain at least 51% of shares in privatized state banks and insurance corporations; the remainder would be sold to the public. Some observers believed such a partial sell-off would reduce attractiveness to potential buyers and raised doubts about the government's enthusiasm for privatization.

[5] The all-time high, 1,378.82, was reached on March 1; the 1994 low was 909, in June.

Competitors

New financial institutions continued to enter Sri Lanka. The Central Bank formally approved the Korean Exchange Bank's request to set up in Sri Lanka 72 hours after receiving its application, an indication of the value monetary authorities attached to the South Korean connection. Three new domestic commercial banks were also approved (each was expected to list on the CSE) bringing the number of Sri Lankan banks to 26, 18 foreign. The PRC was planning to open a fully-fledged commercial bank at end 1995 to bolster its growing trade and investment, believed related to the increasing number of overseas Chinese firms doing business in Sri Lanka. Waldock Mackenzie's emergence as a fully-fledged investment bank plus new entrants increased the number of merchant/investment banks to seven; de Lanerolle said that Vanik and Merchant Bank of Sri Lanka continued to be WM's closest competitors. Competitor information secured included:

Merchant Bank of Sri Lanka. Changa Samaraweera, Managing Director and CEO of Merchant Bank of Sri Lanka (MBSL) said of market conditions and his own bank:

> Merchant banks anywhere are very sensitive to stock market conditions. But we are confident that our main strength in making medium- to long-term investments will see us through. We can stand on our own feet. The balance sheet of Merchant Bank, a Colombo blue chip, and its human resources put us in a good position to negotiate medium- and long-term funding.

MBSL successfully sourced medium- and long-term funding in excess of Rs 2 billion since its last published balance sheet, December 1994. It earned net profits of Rs 200 million in 1994, but 1995 performance was poor due to a bearish stock market and high domestic interest rates. Leasing continued to provide the backbone of the company's net earnings.

Forbes Capital. Forbes Capital (FC) earned Rs 51.9 million on Rs 78.9 million revenues in its first six months of operations ended March 31, 1995; pre-tax ROI was approximately 8.6%. Revenue from Sri Lankan operations included Rs 22.8 million interest on Government of Sri Lanka Treasury Bills, Rs 20.7 million from its lending portfolio to Forbes & Walker Ltd. companies, Rs 2.8 million on sale of quoted investments and Rs 1 million in dividends from marketable securities.

Development Finance Corporation of Ceylon. By end March 1995, DFCC had 199 staff including 98 executives (33 with multi-disciplinary qualifications); in 1995, 40 staff would be trained overseas. DFCC was the largest source of term financing for private sector projects in Sri Lanka; in 1995, gross approvals for financing facilities were expected to exceed Rs 9 billion; it financed the first ever private sector mini hydro-electric power plant. DFCC maintained its position as highest in market capitalization on the CSE; Rs 10.4 billion on March 31, 1995, 8.1% of the total market. Associate company HDF Securities was ranked the leading institution in research for 1994 by *Asiamoney Journal.*

Second Advertising Campaign Proposal for Waldock Mackenzie

Grant McCann-Erickson was in the process of developing new print press advertisements for Waldock Mackenzie; they discussed their ideas with several employees at varying organizational levels. Chandima believed the campaign should continue in the same tone since brand equity was achieved in the first campaign. However, he believed more funds should be devoted to sales force expansion. Isuru believed that if the second campaign had a different tone, customers might become confused; he believed the campaign should target customers with large commercial bank deposits outside Colombo suggesting they consider alternative financial instruments. Meanwhile, a separate series of Singhalese print advertisements for leasing products was approved and published in local newspapers; these ads simply stated that prospective customers should consider WM when shopping for leases.

At a management meeting, Roshni Fernando commented on the agency's print media ideas for the second campaign (amusing faces with accompanying copy text), she kept in mind de Lanerolle's decision that WM would not heavily target the retail sector.

> You know, we really must think through our strategy. The banking industry is generally conservative and most state banks are still under some colonial influence. Of course, we are really focusing on newer banks that are noticeably more innovative. But the stock market has really taken a downturn and a serious look at our image is important. I don't think the direction the new print advertising is going is appropriate.

Prasantha Fernando retorted skeptically: "What do you mean a serious look at our image? The first campaign used a rather unconventional and humorous approach which obviously worked to our advantage. We even won an award and ..." Roshni interrupted: "True, but let me finish. Our first campaign was to get noticed, which we did. Now it's time to establish ourselves. I would hate Waldock Mackenzie to be treated as, or considered, a joke within the investment community. It might be an ideal occasion to state that Waldock is a serious player." De Lanerolle, seated at the head of the table, began jotting some questions that needed to be resolved:

- Was Waldock Mackenzie's image an issue?
- Should he encourage the agency to pursue its ideas for the new print advertising proposal? Why or why not?
- What other marketing methods should WM consider; which should be implemented?
- What should WM's long-term strategy be?

Grant McCann-Erickson Advertising Strategy

Date - 22 September 1994

The following proposals for MKFSL (formerly known as) will be presented, initially for discussion, and then if need be, fine tuned to the point of mutual agreement between Client and Agency.

Firstly, the name.
After some discussion, I feel we have *all* agreed on the name ;

Waldock & Mackenzie

This is a name that both partners feel comfortable with.
Appealing to Client are the solid, strong, traditional connotations, mixed with the actual founders/shareholders.
Agency also feel the name is appropriate *if* we take advantage of the seriousness of the name, and combine it with a 'twist' or a 'modern direction'.
Bringing together the two aspects ~ **old and new, tradition and innovation, past and future.**
These elements should be an underlying element of our total communication programme.

So, we have the name. The payoff line **'The Art of Investment'**, follows the Classic, Sophisticated tone of the 'name'.

Waldock & Mackenzie
The Art of Investment

The Logo. We have (internally) discussed this at great length. The pros of having 'Just Type' as opposed to developing a mnemonic or logo for Waldock ~ Mackenzie.

The importance of theTypeface should not be underestimated, as this will be the 'first impression'/ at-a-glance,/ take out, of the Bank.

We wanted something that was contemporary yet timeless, something that represented solidity but was also innovative and the typeface which represented these qualities in our opinion, was the face 'ONYX'.

It has a lovely feel. It is modern but has a traditional base.
It is also rarely seen. This, mixed with the strap line 'The Art of Investment' in 'SABON ROMAN' whilst quite different from Onyx, compliments it very nicely. It has double kerning and the 'of' is used subtly in italics as simply a design element. So, that's the scoop on the recommended logo typeface.

The next stage was deciding whether or not to find a graphic device or logo representative of our Bank.
How did we arrive at our solution?
We experimented with various symbols but our overall feeling was that if we could find a 'graphic' or representative logo for the bank, it would work even harder for us.

We started with logos and followed with graphics, then we looked for 'something' be it man, mineral or animal, which represented who we are, as accurately as possible.

Graphics such as the 'eye' representing vision and foresight, -Thumbprint representing individuality, uniqueness, - Lightbulb representing new ideas etc.

Finally we went through our 'animal' lists. The Lion, Panther, Elephant, etc

Until we discovered......

Exhibit 1 (cont'd)

The Ant

The Ant. One of the world's tiniest creatures. Yet it can lift 450 times its own weight. And its diligent, non-stop work at moving soil is vital to the earth's ecological balance.

Efficient and determined, Methodical and Flexible, Motivated and Nurturing, Enterprising and Creative, the Ant symbolises so perfectly, the many qualities we possess, it's almost unbelievable!

We have researched the Ant indepth and it lends itself beautifully to our campaign and moreover, corporate image.
Our intention is to introduce it slowly by way of 'very subtle' teaser - (See Exhibit A.)

We build up a curiosity through the introduction of small Ants crawling throughout the 'finanzial' pages in the press and in between the weather report and the financial new report on TV, using the 'crawler' device. All very subtle but unusual - arousing interest.

Finally on the 'Launch day' we run a double page spread with the Ant on the left page and the copy on the right hand page. We explain the new philosophy and the give significance to the Ant mnemonic.

The information is interesting enough to educate people and will give us an intellectual yet different angle to talk about ourselves, helping us stand apart from every other financial institution in Sri Lanka.

Waldock & Mackenzie
The Art *of* Investment

*I must stress at this point, that once we all agree on the name,logo, typeface, point size and colours.

It will be absolutely vital to the success of the entire advertising campaign, to give *everybody* involved in the advertising, or even those involved in producing internal newsletters, business cards or stationary, a set of corporate guidelines which will contain all the information needed for using the logo, Pantone color, 4 colour breakdown, typeface, proportions, etc

---

I stress this because I have, very unfortunately, seen a lot of very hard work and successful identity branding be totally misused and as a result set back the entire campaign by a long way.

It may seem like a very small issue, but infact, it's extremely important. Always treat your corporate identity with the utmost respect.
You'd never see Merryl-Lynch use a different (but similar) typeface, or change the bull to a cow. It just means exercising a bit of discipline.

I guess I've regressed!.

At this point I really should go back to our 'overall plan' to give you an overview of how it will all work *together*.

Exhibit 1 (cont'd)

Advertising Plan

The idea here, is to set enthusiastic but realistic and achievable goals for both the Agency and Client.

1- We have to introduce our new name, logo and philosophy as part of a launch campaign. This should consist of (as above) a relatively cost effective but concentrated teaser campaign to introduce the Ant.
Followed approximately 7 days later by the biggie - 'The Launch Ad.'

2- We need to come in with a huge noise and a press conference is the best way of getting mileage in the press.

3- A 'Direct Marketing' Campaign, inviting existing clients/prospects to a 'Launch Cocktail Party to take place on the same day as the TVC.

4- Now we go into the 'Brand Campaign' which will be used to instil and build on, our image. Once our logo has been qualified, there is no need to harp on this any longer if we don't want to. We can then go straight into our brand.This will be using multi-media quite heavily for the first 3 months.
Each Medium will support and strengthen the preceding and following piece, adding weight to our overall image. (N.B for maximum benefit, this should, in theory, run consistently in the background for the first 9-12 months).

5- After we have established clearly and strongly our 'Brand Personality', the 'Tactical campaign' will follow. We will develop this in order to become more specific and focussed on our actual products/services or any targeted messages we wish to relay.

6- Direct Marketing. We would like to propose a special plastic membership card for all privileged 'Waldock-Mackenzie' valued clients.
The idea is to link with it, certain discounts and benefits, tied up with exclusive or appropriate suppliers/hotels/clubs/shops/airlines...........
Kind of a 'membership has it's special rewards' type of thing.

Actual Media Recommendations
As per the Advertising Plan

1~ The new launch teaser would be launched via use of **Print and TV**.
The print would be either buying small space spots and running 'dummy' financial editorial and running the ants on top of the actual copy.
Or by buying 'gutter space' (we're making enquiries) and running them in between and around other material.
Or thirdly, by buying small narrow 'Strip Ads' without using borders, and running our ants either vertically or horizontally across the financial/stock pages.
They should start off as just a few then each day build up more and more until the day of the launch ad.
The Tv will run as a (5 sec) crawler between the weather and the financial news or the stock report. Again they will appear intermittently just for the week prior to the launch.

2~ We send out 'Ant **Invitations**' to the press, inviting them to hear about our new launch and the exciting changes and we give them a sneak preview of the new television.
(Basically, we do some major schmoozing)

3~ The Direct Marketing will involve an **invitation** using either your existing lists of valued clientele or adding a new list of hot prospects, inviting them to attend the launch cocktail party where they will be shown the new ads and the new materials (**Product/Corporate Brochures**) whilst listening to a guest speaker from the bank and sipping G and T's.
We can also get them to sign up to join the 'Waldock § Mackenzie' - **Risks & Rewards Club**. We will need to develop some pre requisites which they will have to meet to qualify.
An **enrolment form** will have to be designed.

4~ Brand Campaign would be **2 X 45"s TVC's and 4 or 5 Print Ad's** (size to depend on executional decision) also recommended would be to make a monthly appearance in the new 'Sri Lankan Business Digest Monthly'.
Strategically placed **Billboards** could be very effective if placed in highly prominent, business areas.
Advertising Cards placed on restaurant tables at lunch times - Hilton, Intercon, Oberoi, Royal Golf Club, etc. Brand **Radio** produced to enhance/support the Tv and to be expanded into a tactical campaign further down the line.

Exhibit 1 (cont'd)

5- Tactical Campaign should ideally run in **Print** (the number will depend on actual number of tactical messages), but be supported by Radio and **Direct Mail** (follow up on the 'Risks and Rewards' Club thing).

6- Direct Marketing. By now we have already (in our tactical advertising) introduced the 'Membership Card'.
This would ideally encourage a feeling of Status, Superiority, Recognition, Loyalty, Achievement, Success.
It would be a chance to gain the Loyalty of existing clients and entice prospects through incentive. There is unlimited opportunity here. The card could be quite simply an elegant plastic credit card style job.
Nice corporate branding, something they would be proud to flash, something that says something about *who* they are, something that allows them entry without payment or special benefits or privileges etc.
Basically something that makes them feel they have 'made it', they have been recognised for their outstanding financial business prowess.
Women will flock to them, Men will envy them etc etc - you know the deal...

Advertising
Tone and Manner

Ok. Having generally agreed with the initial strategic direction - (the words we used to describe who you are etc) and taking the liberty of assuming we know fairly accurately what form the strategic executional direction should take, I'd like to give you several 'image sketches' some of them original, some of them borrowed but all of them have the same kind of 'tone and manner'. (Exhibit B).I want to discuss this and make sure we are all in agreement of the tone and manner of our material because we will be staying very close to this throughout all the material we produce, for a very long time.

1/ Not an actual mainstream ad. but wow, what leadership, what confidence!. There is a market out there who have not been tapped into yet, who really want to feel 'superior', 'the best', respected etc. There's nothing wrong with going this route. It's gutsy, confident and inturn builds confidence. No one has been this bold so far.

2/ Another 'slightly arrogant' ad. This one goes for the 'kill'. It says that other banks treat their clients like they have brains the size of peas. (without actually saying it!) It's quite subtly humerous and reeks of superiority.
It makes us sound more intelligent and moreover respectful of our clients intelligence.
Executionally lovely with just a small green pea as the central focus.

3/ This approach uses a very different execution to any other bank. It uses a very intelligent style of cartoon like illustration. It mixes an important moral with a light hearted traditional saying "You can't teach an old dog new tricks" This plays on our tradition and history while saying that we have a new way of doing things.

4/ The 'Shark'. A favorite of mine. Using a well known symbol of untrust-worthy financial institutions. Playing on the common perception that most banks cannot be trusted. This is, again, humerous but seriously appropriate. It brings out in the open what most people already think.

5/ Using superb old photographs to highlight the old versus the new. This direction can be extended extemely well. Again humerous in an endearing way. It highlights the same moral " *you can* teach an old dog new tricks" It brings to light the tradition of the bank with a new approach.

6/ Using the strap line 'The Art of Investment' This 'striking' takes actual Art Old Masters - and focuses on appropriate qualities in each ad to our advantage.

The Bank, the Ant and the connection

THE COMMON ANT. IT IS ONE OF THE WORLD'S TINIEST CREATURES AND YET, INCREDIBLY, IT CAN LIFT 450 TIMES ITS OWN WEIGHT. IT IS DILIGENT, ENTHUSIASTIC AND ITS NON-STOP WORK AT MOVING SOIL IS *vital* TO THE EARTH'S ECOLOGICAL BALANCE. EFFICIENT AND DETERMINED, METHODICAL AND FLEXIBLE, MOTIVATED YET NURTURING, ENTERPRISING AND CREATIVE, THE ANT REPRESENTS WHO WE *are* IN EVERY SENSE. IT IS A BRILLIANT, INNOVATIVE INSECT WHICH SYMBOLISES PERFECTLY ALL OF THE QUALITIES WE POSSESS. ~ SO WHO *are* WE? WE ARE THE LATEST HOT INVESTMENT BANK. WALDOCK MACKENZIE HAVE CONNECTIONS WITH THE ESTABLISHED JOHN KEELLS GROUP, FOUNDED IN 1870. IN FACT, ALONG THE WAY, WE'VE BEEN ASSOCIATED WITH *many* OF THE PIONEERS IN THE FINANCIAL AND BROKING BUSINESS IN SRI LANKA - E. JOHN, THOMPSON, WALDOCK, WHITE, AND KEELL. MOST RECENTLY, SINCE 1986, YOU WOULD HAVE KNOWN US AS: MACKINNON AND KEELLS FINANCIAL SERVICES LIMITED OR MKFSL.

OUR BACKGROUND AND HISTORY SPEAK FOR THEMSELVES BUT OUR FUTURE IS *far* MORE EXCITING. WE HAVE ESTABLISHED AN APPROACH TO INVESTMENT BANKING, NEVER BEFORE EXPERIENCED IN SRI LANKA. WE ARE AN INVESTMENT BANK BEYOND THE USUAL. OUR PHILOSOPHY IS BUILT ON TEAM WORK, DEDICATION AND CREATIVITY. ~ WE MAKE THINGS HAPPEN.

CALL US. 342451 - 60 OR MEET US AT 80 NAVAM MAWATHA, COLOMBO 2.

FIG A. THE ANT

Waldock Mackenzie
THE *Art* OF INVESTMENT BANKING

Exhibit 3: Brand Campaign, Print Advertisement

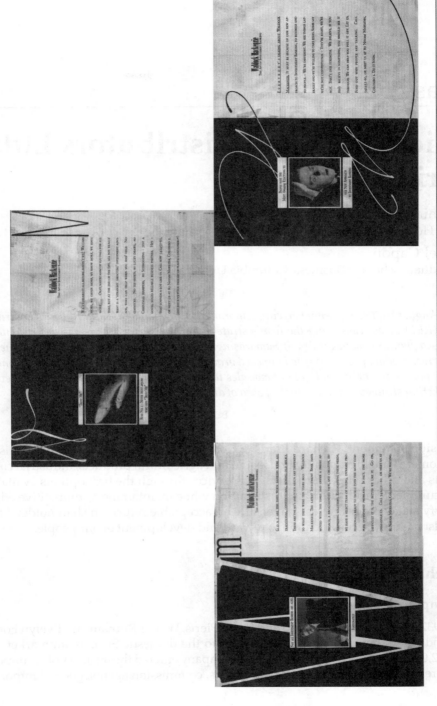

Case 52

Richard Pieris Distributors Ltd., Sri Lanka

Samina Seth
The Hong Kong University of Science and Technology

Noel Capon
Graduate School of Business, Columbia University

On August 10, 1995, Jeremy Ferreira, senior marketing manager, Richard Pieris Distributors Ltd.(RPD), was reassessing the firm's strategy for latex foam mattresses in Sri Lanka. He advised planning manager Pravir Samarasinghe that inconsistent quality, low awareness and incorrect product positioning had impeded growth and that Pieris was accessing only one third of its potential market. In light of new sales targets for mattresses, Ferreira had to develop a marketing strategy to present to the board of directors in one month's time.

৪০ᄚ৪

Mission statement, Richard Pieris & Co. Ltd.: To strive for excellence by satisfying customers with high-quality household and agricultural products, industrial components and other related products and services through the best options available in procurement, production and distribution while maintaining a competitive edge, to satisfy stakeholder interests, to ensure an acceptable return on shareholders' funds whilst paying special attention to reward and development of our people.

Richard Pieris & Co. Ltd.

Company Background

In 1932, entrepreneurs Richard and Percy Pieris, Walter Rutnam and Evelyn Fonseka introduced a new rubber product range to the domestic Sri Lankan market. With Rs 12,000 capital and four staff, the new company entered the business of "... importers and repairers of motor cars, tires and tubes, commission agents, general import and export merchants and dealers in cars, tires, tubes, petrol, oil, motor accessories and estate supplies." In the first seven months, net profit was Rs 1,770 on Rs 72,000 revenues. By 1995, Richard Pieris & Co. Ltd. (RPC) comprised 11 subsidiary and five associate companies (Table 1). In 1994, revenues were Rs 1,073 million compared to Rs 1,517 million in 1993 (Exhibit 1); the decline was attributed to the divestment of Richard Pieris Motor Co. (via a management buy-out) integral to the group's overall reorganization plan.[1] By contrast, after-tax profits increased, from Rs 29.4 million (1993) to Rs 110.3 million (1994).[2]

Table 1: Richard Pieris Group's Annual Divisional Turnover, 1991 to 1993 (Rs million)

	Revenues		
	1991/92	1992/93	1993/94
1. Richard Pieris Distributors Ltd.	471	581	656
2. Richard Pieris Motor Company Ltd.	289	596	–
3. RP Agricultural Enterprises Ltd.	33	45	49
4. Arpidag International Ltd.	6	25	53
5. Plastishells Ltd.	–	1	15
6. Dry Rubber	103	123	117
7. Compounding	–	–	29
8. Foam Rubber	12	18	35
9. Steel Furniture	64	80	85
10. Plastics	179	206	220
11. Retreading	89	136	192
Total turnover	1,246	1,811	1,451
Inter-company sales/adjustments	–244	–294	–377
Consolidated turnover	1,002	1,517	1,074
Average annual growth rate	–4%	51%	–27%

Over the years, RPC pursued several strategies, mainly manufacturing and trading, that achieved steady and sustained expansion. Richard Pieris was Sri Lanka's pioneer manufacturer of rubber-based products including latex foam, expanded rigid polystyrene, artificial leather cloth and polyurethane. In 1995, its core business lines were:

- Manufactured rubber-related goods;[3]
- Joint venture for retreading tires, mainly commercial vehicles, sold through 1,000 dealers;

---

[1] In each year, export sales were comparable: 1993, Rs 46.5 million; 1994, Rs 47.6 million.

[2] Much of this profit increase was a capital gain through sale of shares in an associate company.

[3] Rubber products were sold both domestically and for export. They included master batch compound (tires and others), molded (e.g., industrial mats, domestic mats, vehicle mats, automotive spares, floor tiles), extruded (e.g., rubber bands, sealing rings, beading, dock fenders, garden hoses) and latex (e.g., balloons, mattresses, pillows, cushions, veterinary rings, fishing tackle).

- Plastic products for the domestic market, including polyurethane foam for mattresses, PVC cloth for upholstery, shoes, handbags, rigid polystyrene to transport ice cream containers and hoses and tubing;
- Steel furniture for the low- to middle-income class domestic and office markets. A new steel furniture factory anticipated increased demand as wood scarcity led to increasingly expensive wooden furniture;
- Distribution – to the domestic market through 29 showrooms (nine company-owned, 20 franchised), in 4,500 dealer outlets, one mall and through interior decorators.

Future Focus

The board of directors aimed aggressively to expand all businesses, emphasizing exports;[4] recent projects included:

- A US$2 million loan from the Development Bank to build a new foam rubber mattresses factory (Rs 90 million). RPC's Dutch representative office (current annual distribution of rubber-related products to Europe and North America, Rs 100 to Rs 200 million) would sell these mattresses.
- Collaboration with three banks for a US$13 million joint venture to manufacture shoe soles, RPC's single largest investment in any project (Rs 650 million).
- Aggressive expansion of retreading capacity to keep pace with higher market penetration (committed investment, Rs 57 million); by mid-1995, RPC's market share had doubled from 12% three years earlier. RPC also secured new technology through an information transfer agreement with an American company.
- Commitment of Rs 85 million by subsidiary Arpico Industrial Development Co. to polyurethane production.
- Greater focus on polystyrene (Rs 22 million) and steel furniture production (Rs 50 million).

Richard Pieris Distributors Ltd.

By 1995, Richard Pieris Distributors (RPD) was distributing and retailing a wide range of products, including RPC group manufactured, imported and locally-purchased items.[5] Included in this assortment was the "Arpico" line of mattresses produced by sister companies. In 1994, these mattresses accounted for 15% of RPD sales; management's goal was to raise this share to 18% in two years. In 1994, RPD revenues were Rs 656 million, up from Rs 581 million (1993); pre-tax profits were Rs 38.4 million versus Rs 18 million (1993).

The generally young marketing department for the trading division was headed by senior marketing manager Jeremy Ferreira, assisted by two product managers

---

[4] Major export markets were Europe, North America and Australasia.
[5] Household products distributed by RPD included: glassware, plastics, kitchenware, gardenware, houseware, domestics and linen, interior decor, stationery, furniture, giftware, toys and table tops.

(furniture, miscellaneous), two merchandizing managers for third party products and a marketing services manager.

The Sri Lankan Mattress Market

Four major types of mattresses were available to Sri Lankan consumers: coir, rubberized coir, polyurethane and latex. (See Table 2 for retail price ranges.) Ferreira believed almost half the domestic population slept on reed or plastic mats placed on the floor. Foldable cots were also available but these were uncomfortable and not popular. Typically, coir mattresses represented the first shift from mats as disposable income increased; folding beds, with two-inch rubberized coir mattresses, were fairly popular, especially as "second beds" for vacations. Moving up the quality spectrum were polyurethane mattresses followed by the more expensive latex mattresses. Generally, as disposable income increased, children received beds before parents. RPD executives were unsure either of total mattress sales or of the sales distribution of mattresses by type; however, they believed increasing disposable income favored a trend toward more expensive products.

Table 2: Prices (in Rs) of Bedding Alternatives in Sri Lanka

Mats (used on floor)	100	——>	250
Coir mattresses	450	——>	750
Rubberized coir mattresses	600	——>	2,000
Arpifoam (polyurethane mattress)	1,800	——>	3,000
Latex mattress	2,990	——>	7,000

Spring mattresses, recently reintroduced to Sri Lanka, imported by entrepreneurs in container loads were priced 50% above the highest priced local mattresses. Ferreira said it was too early to judge if these would be popular. One customer group using spring mattresses was large Sri Lankan hotels, granted tax benefits by reduced import duties. Another possible market was expatriates working in Sri Lanka; Ferreira estimated these numbered 5,000. (Sofa beds were uncommon.)

Consumer Behavior

The only "known" bed purchasing characteristic was that in Sri Lanka, children traditionally slept with their parents until ages five to seven. In early 1995, RPD conducted a Rs 70,000 consumer survey in a Colombo residential suburb; it investigated mattress decision making according to age, income level and spoken language. The major finding was that for high income consumers (monthly earnings, over Rs 25,000), who tended to be English-speaking and spanned the age spectrum, the mattress purchase decision was joint husband/wife. For lower income and Singhalese speaking consumers, who tended to buy inexpensive mattresses, the decision was typically made by the husband. RPD also discovered that mattresses tended to be purchased at distinct life stages (e.g., getting married, moving house).

Ferriera agreed it was important to conduct more in-depth research on consumer behavior to develop better tailored products and marketing strategies. However, he said securing honest feedback was difficult:

Among other factors and partly due to the civil war, people have become increasingly suspicious of one another; this attitude has permeated into every aspect of their lives and it is difficult to determine what people really mean. Since it's not easy to collect reliable consumer data, we have to conduct our business with a fair amount of gut instinct.

Richard Pieris Mattress Products

RPC manufactured two major mattress-types for the domestic market: latex foam, where it was the clear leader, and specially constructed (four inches) Arpifoam.[6] The unbranded latex foam mattress was targeted at the Sri Lankan upper middle class; Arpifoam was sold to middle income households. In addition, foam toppings for mattresses were exported, mainly to the U.S. through Richard Pieris Exports Ltd.; RPC also produced cushions (average monthly cushion sales, 100,000 units).[7] RPC did not make rubberized coir or coir-based mattresses.[8]

Historically, RPC was production- rather than market-driven, a natural result of the government's (1970s) production restrictions; limited supply meant limited choice for Sri Lankans who had to buy what was available. In the mid-1980s, government suspension of quota policies led to expanded competition. Richard Pieris began branding products (Arpifoam was an early example) to distinguish itself from competitors. By the 1990s, RPD was concentrating on marketing activities, rather than just distribution that hitherto dominated selling mattresses.

Distribution

RPD distributed latex mattresses through 29, 2,000 to 14,000 sq. ft. outlets,[9] located in key Sri Lankan cities. (The northeast region was excluded because of ethnic violence.) These outlets were company controlled showrooms where latex mattresses were sold exclusively (not available in any other retail outlets), along with the entire range of products from RPC factories (e.g., rubber mats, garden hoses, crockery, linen and other household requisites). RPD owned nine outlets outright; the remainder were franchised. Approximately 100,000 consumers per month visited RPD-owned showrooms; all outlets were profitable.

RPD estimated that 30,000 other dealers (retail stores nationwide) were potentially available for selling RPD products; many of these were small corner stores which RPD

---

[6] Most competitive polyurethane mattresses were three inches thick.
[7] Latex and polyurethane cushions were made as a by-product of mattress production, leftovers when mattresses were cut to size.
[8] Coir was a by-product of coconut, one of Sri Lanka's largest crops.
[9] Household outlets sold products such as furniture, crockery, linen and lighting.

was attempting to access through 30 to 50 selected distributors for such items as playballs, balloons and other rubber products. The number of stores available for selling mattresses was much smaller; in mid-1995, of 4,000 furniture outlets in Sri Lanka, 400 sold mattresses. RPD was actively trying to improve and expand its dealer network; 500 dealers (mostly also selling furniture) currently sold Arpifoam mattresses; 4,500 dealers sold a variety of other Richard Pieris produced products. Ferreira believed accessibility to distribution channels, which were increasing slowly, was an important criterion for consumers buying mattresses. Dealers were visited by RPD's geographically organized sales force; individual salesmen carried a full line of RPD products but were incentivized separately for individual product groups (e.g., mattresses, rubber products, furniture). Ferreira believed that the incentive scheme in place for mattresses was sufficient to encourage the sales force to put significant effort on these products. Arpico Industrial Development Co. was in the process of building a large central warehouse (57,000 sq. ft., Rs 50 million) to provide logistical support for improving distribution.

RPD's Arpifoam and other polyurethane mattresses were sold to consumers at 40% mark-up on cost: 6% was earned by distributors (interfacing between Arpico and the dealers), 17% by dealers and the remaining 17% by RPD. For latex mattresses, Arpico earned a 20% mark-up on cost of which 10% went to franchisees. Twice a year, RPD conducted two islandwide discount sales for Arpifoam through its 500 dealers; an additional discount was provided for dealers to pass on to consumers.

RPD recently initiated an experiment to sell mattresses at Arpico's own 2,000 sq. ft. "furniture-only" store outside Colombo; results would be assessed after six months. If successful, management planned to open 20 more furniture and bedding outlets throughout Sri Lanka. Since adding outlets and improving current retail space was costly in the Colombo area, management was attempting to substitute smaller shops with mini malls to tap higher consumer purchasing power. RPC invested Rs 15 million in a mini mall at Nawinna and committed Rs 250 million to create a five-mall network. Samarasinghe was also considering joint ventures to manage shops with other trading parties.

Latex Foam Mattresses by Arpico

Four-inch thick latex foam mattresses, manufactured and marketed in Sri Lanka for over 30 years, were available in various dimensions; standard sizes, 72" × 36" × 4"; 75" × 48" × 4". These mattresses, 90% natural, manufactured in two days from latex sourced from rubber trees, "set" in special molds of different sizes, lasted 10 to 15 years. Arpico's initial success was due to poor quality and the uncomfortable nature of coir-based mattress alternatives. Rubberized coir mattresses lasted only a few years but management believed sales, mainly to low income groups, were growing by 20% per annum. Although quality had improved over the years, coir-based mattresses were still considered inferior to latex mattresses.

Annual latex mattress sales were unchanged in the last few years; Ferreira believed they were incorrectly positioned as alternatives to coir-based products. Management focused on production issues, reducing per unit cost by substituting lower quality input materials, leading to inconsistent quality. Ferreira believed current R&D investment (Rs 500,000) would produce a completely re-engineered product, with better designs, based on higher quality/priced inputs; in particular, mattress covers could be vastly improved. Richard Pieris Exports Ltd. would contribute cash; RPD would contribute management time for the entire product development process.

In mid-1995, latex foam mattresses were the most expensive locally-produced mattresses; management believed consumers perceived them as expensive but also very comfortable. Arpico sold about 350 units per month country-wide, over 90% of latex-based luxury mattresses. Prices for raw materials increased sharply in the past three years; 40% on average for rubber imports and other raw materials. Latex mattress prices rose 25% in this period; since gross profit was 20% (10% to franchised dealers), management wondered if prices should be further increased.

Arpifoam Mattresses by Arpico

In the mid-1980s, Richard Pieris launched Arpifoam, a polyurethane foam mattress with five to eight years' life; it retailed for half the retail price of a latex foam mattress. Manufactured in about two hours, the core product was sliced to fit the required mattress dimensions. Customers perceived Arpifoam as fairly comfortable and providing good value. Ferreira commented: "Since there was a void in the market for such a product and consumers were just waiting for someone to introduce a product like this, sales took off immediately!"

By mid-1995, Arpifoam was selling over 7,000 units per month. Management believed Arpifoam had captured about 60% of the mid-priced mattress market. Retail list prices ranged from Rs 1,800 to Rs 3,000.

Marketing Mattresses in Sri Lanka

For "best selling" products, RPD allocated 2% of revenues for marketing programs; new and relaunched products were assigned 5% to 6%. Product relaunch campaigns spanned one to three years. In the 1990s, RPD began using several marketing activities emphasizing "hard sell" tactics. For example, one tactic was an incentive package for staff selling latex mattresses. After selling ten mattresses per month, salespersons earned monthly commissions: Rs 10 per mattress for 11 to 20 mattresses; Rs 20 per mattress for 21 to 30 mattresses; Rs 30 for 31 to 40 mattresses; Rs 40 for over 40 mattresses.[10]

Latex foam mattresses: Management was considering branding its latex foam mattresses. Since consumers referred to these products by generic description, copy-cat products could enter the market and take advantage of years of RPD's effort. Historically, advertising spending was low; sales were primarily stimulated through point-of-sale materials at showrooms, print and electronic media and word-of-mouth.

---

[10] For example, if 32 mattresses were sold over one month then commission earned would be: $(10 \times Rs\ 10) + (10 \times Rs\ 20) + (2 \times Rs\ 30) = Rs\ 360$.

Management was contemplating "re-naming" its latex mattresses "Realfoam"; the annual advertising budget would be increased to Rs 1.2 million.

Arpifoam mattresses: Management believed Arpifoam mattresses were effectively advertised within the 2% budget constraint. Mailers targeted specific organizations and associations (e.g., all MasterCard holders) that Ferreira believed could achieve high response rates. In general, RPD did not conduct in-store activities at dealers stocking Arpifoam mattresses.

Major Marketing Campaigns

Although mattresses were generally purchased throughout the year, management believed March to April (Sri Lankan new year) and November to December were seasonal bands for major campaigns. The first major annual campaign extended to all stores began in December (budget Rs 500,000); no discounts were given but typically incremental sales far exceeded promotional costs. The second major "mid-year" campaign was typically price-focused; discounts ranged from 10% to 60% off retail price for mattresses and bedding (Table 3).

Table 3: Sales Prices (in Rs) for Latex Mattresses

Item code*	Retail price	Sale price	Savings Rs	Item code*	Retail price	Sale price	Savings Rs
LM75364PC	2,990	2,691	299	LM75364QC	3,490	3,141	349
LM85424PC	3,790	3,411	379	LM85424QC	4,290	3,861	429
LM75484PC	4,390	3,951	439	LM75484QC	4,990	4,491	499
LM75544PC	4,790	4,311	479	LM75544QC	5,490	4941	549
LM75604PC	5,390	5,851	539	LM75604QC	6,190	5,571	619

*PC = Plain cotton cover – increase in price by 50% after relaunch.
LM = Latex mattress   QC = Quilted cotton cover

Displays: Ferreira believed in-store displays lacked sophistication and appeal; RPD traditionally copied displays from European and American bedding catalogs (e.g., Target, U.S.; IKEA, Sweden) rather than using unique layouts for local tastes. Unfortunately, specialized professionals/organizations concentrating on displays were not available in Sri Lanka. Two options were available: recruit and train local staff overseas in layout, displays and lighting or contract an experienced Singapore-based firm to be responsible for setting up displays in existing showrooms while training local staff. Option 1 would cost Rs 100,000 per person; total cost for option 2 was Rs 300,000 to Rs 500,000. Ferreira wondered which would be a better long-term option for Arpico.

Print advertising: For print advertising, major national newspapers were used featuring advertisements that emphasized Arpifoam's product attributes. This media was used only during seasonal periods with advertisements appearing, on average, three times per week, costing Rs 14,000 per insertion.

Television advertising: Sri Lanka had about one million televisions, one in every three households. Although six television channels were available, the state-run channel, "Rupavahini," had the widest audience coverage. Broadcasts were divided into morning and evening belts with a combined daily air-time of 12 hours. The morning belt began at 6:00 am, the evening belt ended at 12:00 pm. Prime time, 6:30 pm to 8:30 pm, featured local "teledramas," similar to American soap operas. Star TV, a satellite network television station, was beamed through local TV stations and was received universally.

National television advertising campaigns, using 20-second ads, varied according to season; during off-peak periods, advertisements were shown twice a month versus four to seven times per week during peak periods. Arpico ads were featured only during prime time on "Rupavahini"; each screening cost Rs 8,000.

Outdoor advertising: RPD's managing director strongly opposed large billboard advertising; he believed it damaged the "view" environmentally. RPD was unable to use this advertising medium.

Point-of-sale materials and displays: Historically, RPD relied heavily on point-of-sale materials, mainly handwritten mattress descriptions on styrofoam signboards placed by merchandise. Although not ugly, Ferreira believed they were not professional either. Point-of-sale signs were used mostly for latex mattresses (approximate annual expenditure Rs 5,000); on average, three to four displays were used for a large store, two at smaller outlets. Point-of-sale materials were not provided to Arpifoam dealers. (See Exhibit 2 for a brochure.)

Customer databases: The marketing staff had begun to compile a comprehensive database for sending mailers for all RPD products. Recently, RPD sent mailers three times as part of regional marketing campaigns but incremental sales due to mailers had not been measured.

Leaflets: Leaflets were distributed on the streets by two "RPD propaganda people" during peak seasons at company-controlled outlets having "sales." For regional campaigns, 5,000 pieces were distributed; islandwide campaigns used approximately 50,000. No coupons were attached; like mailers, RPD had no method to determine effectiveness.

Bonanza competition: The annual year-end "Bonanza competition," begun in 1988, was timed to coincide with the peak Christmas season. Customer information was systematically collected by lucky draw coupons entitling participants, including latex mattress buyers, a chance to win 20 cash prizes (first prize, Rs 150,000). By mid-1995, almost 60,000 names had been collected.

Promotions: Most in-store promotions were concentrated during peak periods. Historically, gift-with-purchase promotions included pillow or bedding set gift or a bed set (including bed frames) with a mattress purchase. In 1994, the "Lucky Dip" campaign was introduced in all RPD showrooms; customers could win prizes, valued between Rs 20 to Rs 1,500, as stated on the chit picked from the lucky draw box. Ferreira believed this promotional method was popular with customers.

Competition

Latex foam mattresses: Management believed there was no serious direct competition for latex foam mattresses due to high raw material prices and the perceived small size of the niche market. Arpico considered itself the dominant market leader.

Arpifoam mattresses: Management believed competition was strong but largely regional; all competitors were privately-owned. It also believed all competitors competed primarily on distribution and price. Arpico's mid-1995 market share of polyurethane mattresses was 60% (target 65%); the board's goal for 2000 was 80%. Ferreira had to create a growth strategy!

Specific Competitors

Damro. Ferreira believed Damro, historically a furniture manufacturer, was the most serious competitor. Six years earlier, Damro entered the polyurethane cushion market but withdrew when Arpico cut prices. In recent years, Damro expanded its product line to include polyurethane mattresses, a strategic fit with its core business. It distributed directly through 50 to 100 selective independent outlets in major towns. Prices were generally 10% to 15% lower than Arpifoam for comparable quality. Ferreira believed Damro mattress outlets earned 12% to 15% margins. Despite its 15% market share in polyurethane, RPD believed the Damro brand was weak and its financial position precarious because of the "cushion blunder." Damro was the only competitor that advertised, but just in high season on outdoor billboards on busy routes.

Pentform. Pentform was a holding company whose main business was fiber glass products (e.g., marine boats, water tanks); it entered the mattress market at the same time as Damro. Ferreira called Pentform managers opportunists inasmuch as product launch occurred in the peak mattress sales season when demand sometimes outstripped supply. Pentform manufactured and sold basic polyurethane mattresses priced 15% to 20% lower than Arpifoam; distribution was through 20 regionally-located dealers. Pentform manufactured mattresses intermittently using a non-dedicated production line; Ferreira believed this practice affected product quality. He believed Pentform was beginning to withdraw from the mattress market to concentrate on its core activities. For marketing efforts, Pentform depended on dealers "hard sales tactics." Pentform also supported low dealer prices.

Lionco. Lionco sold both cushions and mattresses; RPD believed it could be a serious threat. Since entering the mattress market in 1990, Lionco consistently undercut Arpico's prices; it used similar distribution outlets. RPD believed Lionco's share of polyurethane mattresses was 4% in October 1994 but had since dropped to 1% to 2%. Lionco did not advertise but relied on dealers to promote its mattresses.

Product Evaluation Issues

Three marketing department members and the factory general manager formed a task force on the mattress production process. (Richard Pieris Exports Ltd. was also involved as it was interested in development of higher quality mattresses for export.) RPD executives believed that a greater marketing focus combined with modern management tools were necessary for success. As a result, latex mattresses were being completely re-evaluated; one specific "packaging" question was: how should an Arpico mattress be delivered to the final customer?

The advertising agency made three recommendations:

- Brand latex mattresses, "Realfoam," using an aqua blue logo; Realfoam should be integral to the communication strategy. Local markets should view an association with Arpifoam positively.
- The communications strategy should emphasize to customers that price was unimportant. If the mattress was improved to be more expensive-looking, the agency could create associations of Realfoam as an important durable product for a targeted lifestyle. It proposed that consumers should be told not to accept "less than the best." All advertising would concentrate on educating customers to the benefits of real mattresses. The agency director wanted advertisements to invoke a sense of family consciousness by focusing the concern with children: "Only quality and care in manufacturing can support even the bed-wetting years."
- Offer customers a five-year guarantee; RPD would repair/replace mattresses for defective workmanship or materials, excluding mattress cover damage.

Decisions

Since RPD maintained such a dominant position in latex mattresses, Ferreira believed it was only a matter of time before new entrants entered the market. Furthermore, he believed that Arpico had not captured the full potential for these luxury mattresses; he was also confident that RPD could enhance its position in polyurethane mattresses. Although he believed that the new aggressive sales targets could be achieved, many issues had to be resolved before an overall marketing plan was ready for the board of directors.

Exhibit 1: Richard Pieris Group's Annual Divisional Turnover (Rs '000)

Year ended March 31	1990	1991	1992	1993	1994
Trading results					
Turnover	756,023	1,058,828	1,017,169	1,517,367	1,073,117
Other income	3,574	8,789	5,679	4,730	72,323
	759,597	1,067,617	1,022,848	1,522,097	1,145,440
Turnover tax, excise duty &					
defense levy	37,112	48,211	57,258	104,608	208,704
Raw materials	467,374	683,046	625,514	969,449	506,435
Remuneration to employees	91,010	112,083	117,882	141,887	135,645
Other operating costs	89,597	107,915	118,313	163,233	121,819
Financial changes	25,818	34,490	45,437	70,082	27,569
Depreciation	9,365	12,231	18,269	21,116	17,268
Profit before taxation (excluding					
the profit of associate companies)	39,321	69,641	40,175	51,722	128,000
Provision for taxation	17,218	25,114	13,988	20,185	18,689
Deferred tax	–	–	–	2,120	–719
Profit after taxation	22,103	44,527	26,187	29,417	110,030
Minority interest	289	672	1,442	–1,725	–6,229
	22,392	45,199	27,629	27,692	103,801
Share capital & reserves					
Share capital	22,110	32,259	32,259	83,939	85,277
Capital & revenue reserves	139,960	182,765	257,351	387,189	480,700
Shareholders' funds	162,070	215,024	289,610	471,128	565,977
Minority interest	–51	9,769	9,885	16,105	31,841
	162,019	224,793	299,495	487,233	597,818
Assets & liabilities					
Current assets	253,096	318,093	366,995	509,370	480,150
Current liabilities	228,098	281,070	337,930	327,586	277,475
Working capital	24,998	37,023	29,065	181,784	202,675
Fixed assets	103,304	146,754	273,408	294,868	342,508
Investments (associates & other)	67,460	82,698	97,422	112,540	140,590
Deferred taxation &					
deferred expenditure	–1,160	–475	–14,750	–14,020	–14,010
Long-term liabilities & provisions	–32,583	–41,207	–85,650	–87,939	–73,945
	162,019	224,793	299,495	487,233	597,818
Other data					
Capital expenditure					
(including W.I.P.)	26,178	56,315	92,780	43,752	80,718
Ordinary dividends	8,251	9,283	7,735	13,354	18,799
No. of employees	2,060	2,053	1,970	1,887	1,709

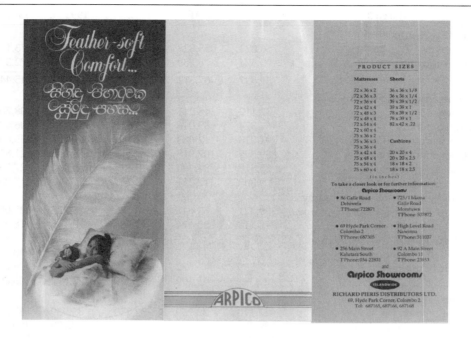

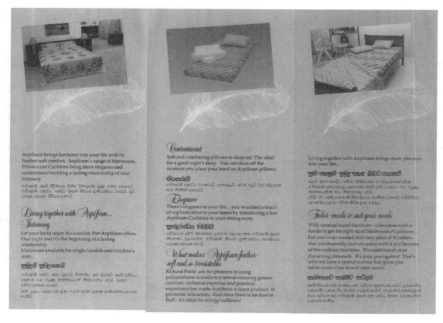

Map of Taiwan

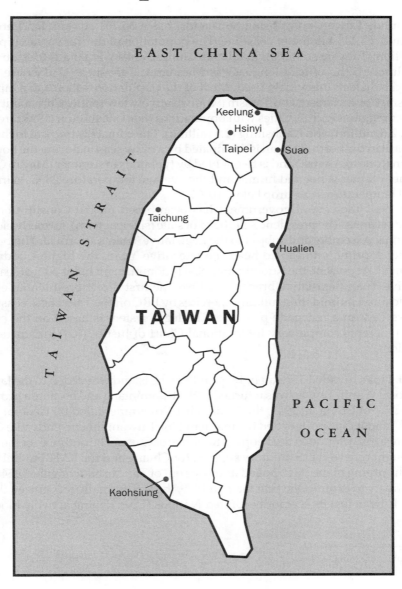

Taiwan Overview[1]

Background. Taiwan, comprising 86 islands, has a 35,751 sq. km. land area (24% arable) and a 1,448-kilometer coastline. The population of the Taiwan archipelago is 21.3 million; Taiwanese (70%), mainland Chinese (14%), Hakka (14%), aborigines (2%). Although the official language is Mandarin, Taiwanese (Fukienese dialect) and Hakka dialects are widely used. Most of the population adheres to a mixture of Buddhism, Confucianism and Taoism (93%); relatively few follow Christianity (4.5%) and other religions (2.5%). Cities with populations over one million (1995) are: Taipei (capital, 2.6 million) and Kaohsiung (1.4 million). The climate is tropical in the south, subtropical in the north. Taiwan is dominated by a rainy season during the Southwest Monsoon (June to August) and is frequented by typhoons in summer (May to October) when the weather is hot and humid and the average temperature 28°C. Winters are mild but temperatures can drop below 10°C.

Since 1947, the central government has been based on the Constitution of the Republic of China. The president is the head of state (six-year term), formerly elected by the National Assembly and subject to the Legislative Yuan's approval. The president nominates a prime minister to head the Executive Yuan, the highest body in the government. At present, the Kuomintang (KMT) dominates; it holds 60% of seats in the Legislative Yuan (legislative branch). In 1996, the first direct presidential elections were held amid intimidating military exercises by PRC off the Taiwanese coast; China considers Taiwan a renegade province. The legal system is based on the civil law system; it accepts compulsory International Court of Justice (ICJ) jurisdiction with reservations.

Political. Japan invaded Taiwan in 1874; in 1895 the island was ceded to the Japanese. After World War II, Taiwan was returned to the Kuomintang and became a province of the Republic of China. In 1949, the Nationalist Government (led by General Chiang Kai-shek) and its supporters fled the mainland for Taiwan; concurrently, the Chinese Communist Party founded the People's Republic of China. The outbreak of the Korean War brought renewed U.S. military support for Chiang and the KMT but in 1978, the U.S., at the urging of the PRC, pulled its troops out of Taiwan allowing the 1954 mutual defense treaty to expire. One year later, in 1979, the U.S. formally recognized the PRC. In 1971, Taiwan lost its seat in the United Nations (UN); Beijing actively blocks any

---

[1] The Republic of China.

attempts by Taiwan to re-enter. Only a handful of countries forgo relations with the PRC to maintain diplomatic ties with Taiwan but several have mutual defense treaties. Taiwan is a member of the Asian Development Bank (ADB) and the Asia-Pacific Economic Cooperation (APEC) Forum; similarly to the PRC, Taiwan is attempting to enter the World Trade Organization (WTO).

In 1987, the Taiwan government, led by President Chiang Ching-kuo (Chiang Kai-shek's son), relaxed restrictions on travel to mainland China; about three million Taiwan residents have since visited the mainland. In 1990, the National Unification Council, headed by President Lee Teng-hui, was inaugurated to take charge of all issues relating to reunification with mainland China. On May 1, 1991, the "Period of National Mobilization for the Suppression of the Communist Rebellion" was terminated, opening the way to improve relations with the mainland. Semi-official talks are held regularly between the two sides to promote closer cooperation but with interruptions, notably military exercises and missile tests by the PRC. Following the first missile tests in 1996, the Taiwan bourse fell 17% relative to June 1995; the government intervened to prop up the jittery stock market. Although future political clashes with PRC are likely, economic and business interests are expected to move forward.

Social. At the end of 1995, 24% of the population was under 15 years of age; 7% was over 65 years. The government's firm commitment to education is reflected in the relatively high level of spending on education, science and culture (1995/96, 13%). As a result, 12.5% and 88.8% of the population respectively has received higher and secondary education (1995). Taiwan's literacy rate is 94%; life expectancy at birth is 75.

Economy. In the 1990s, Taiwan's economy grew on average over 6% p.a.; per capita GNP is US$13,130. The government has promoted a revised Six-Year National Development Plan (1991–96) comprising 556 projects (total investment NT$5 trillion) comprising industry zones, business parks, power stations (including a fourth nuclear plant), reservoirs, waste disposal centers, housing units, new universities and a high-speed train system between Taipei and Kaohsiung.

Taiwan has no foreign debt problem (foreign exchange reserves are close to US$90 billion), but a serious defense problem fearing an attack from mainland China. At its peak (1954/55), defense accounted for 63.6% of government spending; in the 1989/90 budget, defense, security and police expenditure had dropped to 29.1%.

Because of the buoyant economy and a dwindling youth population, unemployment has remained below 2% since 1987, creating a labor shortage. In 1995, agriculture (including forestry and fishing) was 3.4% of GDP; manufacturing 27.4%, banking and insurance 20%. Manufacturing continues to be the economy's driving force although its share of GNP declined from 40% (1987) to 32% (1992). Major export destinations are (1995): U.S. (23.6%), Hong Kong (23.4%), Japan (11.8%). Major import origins (1995) are: Japan (29.2%), U.S. (20.1%), Korea (4.2%). Three export processing zones (EPZs) in Kaohsiung, Nantze and Taichung promote development of export industries; low-interest loans for factory purchases are available.

In most industries, enterprises may be 100% foreign owned but some restrictions exist in certain financial, leasing and navigation services. In high technology industries, profits and interest payments can be remitted freely. The corporate tax rate is a favorable 25%; companies may not form partnerships.

Taiwanese high average propensity to save (25% [estimated] 1991) enables local firms to invest elsewhere. Recently, Taiwanese firms have switched investment focus from the U.S. to Southeast Asia. Taiwan firms are also major investors in mainland China despite lack of direct communication links (all contact is conducted through a third country, usually Hong Kong).

Both the Ministry of Finance (MOF) and the Central Bank of China (CBC) supervise the banking industry. The MOF implements banking and fiscal policies; the CBC carries out most functions of a typical central bank. Recently, the New Taiwan Dollar (NT$), has been appreciating against the U.S. dollar.

To ensure banking sector stability, applicants for new banking licenses are subject to tight restrictions, including NT$10 billion (US$380 million) capitalization. In September 1993, 41 domestic banks had 1,312 branches; 42 foreign banks had 65 branches and 20 representative offices.

In recent years the Taipei stock market has significantly reduced in value in part due to the government's reimposition of a capital gains tax on share-dealing profits. In February 1990, the Taipei weighted Stock Price Index was 12,495; by September 1994, the index had almost halved to 6,890. At end 1994, market capitalization was over US$247 billion.

Taiwan weathered the 1997 Asian financial crisis well. Relative to its Southeast Asian neighbors, it had no banking or external debt problems. However, to remain competitive (particularly with Singapore and South Korea in the value-added manufacturing sector), the Taiwan dollar devalued 15.5% to the U.S. dollar in late 1997. Although this made exports more competitive, it raised import costs and U.S. dollar denominated debt.

Infrastructure. Taiwan has 20,041 kilometers of roads, 17,095 kilometers (85.3%) paved. In 1995, 14.5 million motor vehicles were registered, 8.5 million motorcycles, 3.9 million automobiles for private use. The state-owned rail network has 2,439 kilometers of track (1993).

International air services operate from Kaohsiung Airport in the south and Chiang Kai-shek International Airport outside Taipei. The latter's annual capacity is scheduled to reach 20 million passengers and 1 million tons of freight by 2000. China Airlines (CAL) enjoyed a monopoly as Taiwan's only international airline until privately owned EVA Air emerged in 1991. CAL has begun to create distance from its semi-official status as Taiwan's national carrier. In 1995, as part of a corporate image make-over designed in part to keep open the possibility of flying to mainland China, it dropped the Republic of China flag.

In 1993, Taiwan's five major ports (i.e., Kaohsiung, Keelung, Hualien, Taichung, Suao) handled 384 million tons of freight. Kaohsiung (63.5%) is the world's third largest container port; Taiwan has the largest cargo container fleet in the world.

Taiwan has Asia's best developed telecommunications system outside Japan (one telephone per 2.4 persons [1994]), 1.2 million radio-paging subscribers and 424,000 mobile phone subscribers [1993]. Telecommunications is considered a key technology in the Six-Year National Development Plan. There is international direct dialing (IDD) and direct dialing to the Chinese mainland.

In 1993, Taiwan's electricity generation was 101.8 billion kWh; 38% nuclear.

Statistics*	June 1991	June 1995	Statistics*	June 1991	June 1995
Per capita GNP	US$7,990	US$13,130	Pop. growth	1.2%	1.0%
GDP growth	5.2%	6.6%	Infant mortality/1,000	5	5
Savings (GNP)	n/a	25%	Life expectancy (yrs)	n/a	75
Inflation (CPI)	4.1%	0.8%	Literacy rate	91.2%	94%
Foreign debt			People per tel.	3	2.3
(US$ billion)	0	0	People per doctor	1,010	903
Pop. (million)	20.6	21.7	People per TV	n/a	3.1
Urban pop.	n/a	58%	Calorie intake (cals)	n/a	3,036

*Secured from *Asiaweek*.

Case 53

Carrefour in Asia (A) Taiwan: A Bridgehead to Asia[1]

Pierre Courbon, Philippe Lasserre
INSEAD, Fontainebleau, France

In June 1993, leaving Taiwan for Hong Kong, Gerard Clerc, Carrefour's new CEO for Asia, considered Carrefour's first Asian operations. He had started from scratch in Taiwan; five stores were open, two larger stores would open by December. Results of his formula were satisfactory but competition was fierce. Reflecting on six years' experience, Clerc wondered if

---

[1] This case was prepared by Pierre Courbon, MBA participant, under the supervision of Philippe Lasserre, Professor of Strategy and Management at INSEAD. It is intended to be used as a basis for class discussion rather than to illustrate either effective or ineffective handling of an administrative situation. Reprinted with the permission of INSEAD. Copyright 1994 INSEAD-EAC, Fontainebleau, France.

Carrefour could continue its success in the face of increasing competition from well-established mass retailers like Makro and newcomers from the U.S., Europe and locally. Should he have done things differently and would his Taiwan experience be applicable elsewhere in Asia?

৪৩০৫৪

First Steps

A Carrefour Missionary

In summer 1986, Gerard Clerc was sent to prospect the Taiwan market. Largely unknown to the French public, Jacques Fournier (Carrefour's founder, chairman) and partners, Denis and Jacques Defforey, thought this island had great potential.

Business graduate Clerc was formerly an auditor with L'Express, a French news magazine. Since joining Carrefour in 1971, his experience was: store manager (six years), some headquarters responsibility for five- to ten-year development plans, then regional manager (five years) in Paris and Bordeaux.

The Feasibility Study

Clerc, accompanied by two department heads, conducted a 1.5 month feasibility study in Taiwan. He analyzed local conditions against Carrefour's criteria for assessing new markets. In favor of entry were the embryonic nature of retailing, openness to foreign investment, political stability and low inflation; against were a less than satisfactory legal environment and the language barrier.

Clerc gathered facts and figures about population, GNP per capita growth, road network, motorization rate and so on, although data were often unreliable. He believed the 20 million population could support development of many stores; food consumption sophistication was low but GNP per capita (US$4,000) implied high growth potential. The key criterion of motorization rate was low but motorcycles and scooters abounded. Clerc checked real estate prices; he evaluated expected price differentials with local competitors and payment terms to develop income and cash flow projections.

At first glance, other countries offered favorable conditions; however, Hong Kong and Singapore were too small and urbanized for Carrefour's ambitions; Korea's GNP per capita was lower; Japan seemed largely closed to foreign retailers and much too difficult a country to initiate an Asian strategy.

In spite of uncertainty inherent in any overseas investment, Clerc had a good feeling about Taiwan. He presented his study to the Executive Board in October 1986; one month later, Clerc was appointed head of Carrefour's development in Taiwan.

PresiCarre Corporation, a Partnership

Clerc settled in Taipei in February, 1987; his first task was to find a local partner. Carrefour management believed entering a country like Taiwan, far from home and so culturally different, required a partnership. Clerc met with President Enterprises,

Taiwan's largest foodstuff manufacturer; President had a foothold in retailing and was interested in securing preferential outlets via vertical integration.[2]

PresiCarre Corp. was formed in August 1986; FF120 million (US$20 million) invested capital, 40% President Enterprises, 60% Carrefour; Clerc was appointed president. President was a sleeping partner; Clerc avoided requests of President so as not to develop obligations. Still, President's visibility and Chairman Kao's stature as head of the local union of industrialists assisted Carrefour's integration in local networks.

Carrefour

Carrefour Supermarches S.A. was a hypermarket pioneer in France. Hypermarkets were self-service mass retail stores but on a much larger scale than supermarkets. Typical supermarkets had sales areas 400 to 2,500 sq. m. and carried 5,000 to 10,000 items. Hypermarket sales areas were over 2,500 sq. m.; they carried 40,000 to 50,000 items. Large Carrefour stores in France had over 20,000 sq. m. sales areas offering such diverse products as fresh vegetables, PCs and mountain bikes; often, sales assistants on roller skates assisted customers (Exhibit 1)!

Carrefour's first store opened in 1963 in a Paris suburb; currently it was France's largest retail organization with 114 stores, averaging 9,400 sq. m., in total over one million sq. m. Consolidated worldwide sales were FF123 billion (US$20 billion). Carrefour's original principles continued to underpin the company: one-stop shopping, self service, discount, quality products and free car park.

Carrefour's international expansion started in the late 1960s in Europe. Its most successful foreign operations were in Spain (its Pryca chain was Spain's second largest retailer) and Brazil (Table 1).

Table 1: Carrefour in the World

Country	Number of stores	Net turnover (MF)	Net turnover (%)
France	114	81,991	66.5
Spain	43	21,226	17.2
Brazil	29	10,191	8.3
Argentina	7	5,545	4.5
Taiwan	7	1,752	1.4
Portugal	2	1,657	1.3
Italy/Turkey	2	–	0.7

Source: Carrefour 1993 annual report.

Carrefour had withdrawn from the U.K., Belgium and Switzerland (lack of expansion space) and from the U.S. where results were poor. It was relatively unsuccessful in mature markets, compared to entry in markets with potential for dramatic changes in consumer buying habits (e.g., 1960s France), high GNP per capita growth,

---

[2] Introduced to Clerc by the Credit Lyonnais branch in Taiwan; President assisted Clerc with his feasibility study.

suburbanization, increased labor force participation by women and large increases in car and refrigerator ownership.

President Enterprise Corporation

Founded in 1967, President initially produced flour and animal feed. By mid-1980s, it was Taiwan's largest agribusiness firm, tenth largest firm in total and fifth largest employer (Exhibit 2). In 1992, the President group had consolidated NT$49.7 billion[3] (over US$1.7 billion) gross revenues. President's strengths were food and beverage products and its distribution network. In addition to bakeries and automatic vending machines, President cooperated with Southland Inc. to manage 824 7-Eleven convenience stores, Taiwan's largest chain store.

Much of President's power stemmed from a sustained strategy of partnership with foreign groups; as Taiwanese agent-importer (e.g., Budweiser beer, Anheuser Busch; Lu biscuits, BSN, Welsh fruit juice, National Grape-Coop), as shareholder in local joint ventures (e.g., PepsiCo, Frito Lay, Kentucky Fried Chicken, Kikkoman) or abroad with major Filipino agribusiness firm, San Miguel, to which President was transferring technology.

President had ambitions to become a world leader by 2010; it had numerous investments in mainland China. Its latest annual report noted that President Enterprises pursued a long-term goal of establishing a Food Kingdom, thus achieving once again a new miracle in the history of the President Enterprises operations.

A Slow Start

Initial plans to build 10,000 sq. m. stores with over 1,000 car park spaces were quickly scaled down. In February 1987, a large plot of land offered by government tender was sold for double the expected price. Clerc had underestimated land price increases in Taiwan; in the next two years, prices increased five to ten times. Carrefour was negotiating land purchases but prices increased 20% to 30% every two to three months. Because most negotiations were lengthy, prices were becoming too high; revaluation of the New Taiwan dollar made prices in French francs even higher. Clerc decided to rent rather than buy land, an action without precedent for Carrefour. Annual rents were 1% to 2% of land prices; this was affordable and minimized financial risk. After 19 months, Clerc finally found a good location in Kaohsiung, southern Taiwan. He negotiated a ten-year contract, later increased to twenty years. Carrefour could only build on 3,500 of 7,000 sq. m. available; car parking took the rest.

Clerc's assistant Monique Thirion, two expatriate section heads, plus three Taiwanese staff hired in France a year earlier arrived in Kaohsiung to assist Clerc in opening the store. Unlike France, the store's 3,500 sq. m. sales area was on two floors, partly in a basement, quite different from large French stores. Some French managers, committed to single floor rectangular Carrefour stores with car park on proprietary

---

[3] NT$ stands for New Taiwan dollar.

land, were reluctant to accept the Taiwan model. Clerc argued the essence of Carrefour's concept worldwide was discount, freshness, car park; nothing else.

The first store opened in December 1989 (Table 2); it was immediately successful (first year break-even). A second Kaohsiung store (same landlord) opened a year later concurrent with Taipei's first store. The initial phase was difficult, with general distrust from suppliers, real estate promoters and local government authorities. Said Clerc of the local retail industry, "It was as if the Huns had arrived in Taiwan."

Table 2:   Carrefour Stores in Taiwan

Opening date	Location	Type	Sales area	Parking
December 1989	Ta-Shun (Kaohsiung)	Store	4,500m²	220 car spaces
January 1991	Nan-Kang (Taipei)	Store	5,600m²	240 car spaces
February 1991	Shih-Chuan (Kaohsiung)	Store	5,400m²	370 car spaces
October 1991	Tien-Mou (Taipei)	Store	4,300m²	350 car spaces
July 1992	Pan-Chiao (Taipei)	Store	5,200m²	300 car spaces
November 1993 (planned)	Chung-Hua (Tainan)	Store	7,500m²	390 car spaces
November 1993 (planned)	San-Chung (Taipei)	Warehouse	9,600m²	720 car spaces
March 1994 (planned)	Tao-Yuan (Taipei)	Warehouse	12,400m²	720 car spaces
Extension 84	To other		6,000m²	400 car spaces

	Net revenues (MF)	Net income (MF)	Investments (MF)
1990	100	(−9)	38
1991	600	(−14)	50
1992	1150	26	40
1993	1750	39	110

Source: PresiCarre Corp.

The Carrefour Adaptation in Taiwan

Clerc wanted to avoid simply transferring to Taiwan a successful French concept proven in other countries; he wanted to adapt the Carrefour concept, accounting for the local environment.

Adapting the Store

A critical, difficult, early problem was store location. Because of complicated regulations regarding land use, and distinctions between industrial use and commercial use land, Carrefour could not build in the suburbs. It had to operate in urban areas, on rented land; new stores were not located on flat open land, but in buildings, basements or ground floors in high population density areas.

In most Taiwanese stores, investment in decoration and layout was limited. In contrast to France, shelves were standard, none was product-specific. Floors were usually plain painted cement, white tiles in the most luxurious stores. Carrefour managers tried to create a familiar atmosphere for Taiwanese. For example, lamps above food stalls in fresh products sections were the same as those found in traditional "wet markets." On their first visit to Taiwan, Carrefour's founding fathers said the stores were similar to the first basic stores built in France 30 years earlier.

Adapting the Offer

Carrefour's Taiwan policy was to leverage its decision to limit product assortment (more than in Makro's [major competitor] larger stores) and buy greater volumes; more competitive prices could thus be secured from suppliers. Carrefour mineral water and wines were imported from France; wines were sold only in one store near expatriate apartments. Since securing regular quality supply from local manufacturers was difficult, Carrefour did not sell locally produced labels for fear of damaging its reputation. However, generics were launched (1991); these were very successful, especially rice (top selling item), and diapers (NT$159 per pack versus Pampers, NT$459).

Carrefour promotions (announced with flyers or print advertising) were held regularly at individual stores or nationwide. In contrast to France, few promotions were launched by local manufacturers, even large companies (e.g., Weichuan, I-Mei Foods, Foremost, President) unless Carrefour requested. Large multinationals (e.g., Procter and Gamble, Unilever) promoted products heavily. L'Oreal recently introduced some products at Carrefour.

Tracking Rapidly Changing Shopping Habits and Educating Customers

Taiwan's population density, heavy street traffic and Carrefour's urban store locations meant that customers came from a three-kilometer radius, rather than from larger distances as in France. Carrefour studies showed that store visits averaged twice a week in Taiwan versus 1.2 times monthly in France. The average client basket value was NT$680,700 (FF150) versus FF500 in France.[4] Most Taiwanese customers made frequent, smaller value proximity purchases in line with traditional buying patterns.

The Taiwanese market changed rapidly. In 1991, favorite flavors in food products were peanut and lemon; in 1994, top selling flavors were vanilla, chocolate and strawberry, practically unsaleable a few years earlier. Retailers exercised an important role in educating consumers about service and products. Some degree of westernization of local tastes was occurring. Whereas previously purchasing was for necessities, impulse buying was increasing. For many families, visits to the "French" hypermarket were like a Sunday "day trip"; buying for pleasure was normal. All Carrefour stores had pilot departments continually introducing new product ranges. Successful local

---

[4] FF 1 = NT$ 4.6, May 1994.

introductions were taken national at all Carrefour stores. This cross learning spread know-how; managers learned about the market, and followed its evolution.

Keeping close to the client, Carrefour's new product promotions contributed increasingly to total revenues. In France, sales increases from year-to-year were purely incremental. By contrast, in Taiwan, big sales increases came from introducing new product categories. Carrefour recently promoted such articles as barbecue equipment, home decoration, cars, gear for swimming, camping and all kinds of outdoor sports, hi-fi equipment, microwave ovens and large screen TVs. By following the market very closely, Carrefour identified under-exploited products; top selling products changed at least every six months. French patterns had to be forgotten and the market learned from scratch. Nonetheless, Carrefour's Virtuous Circle was unchanged:

Management Adaptation

Carrefour had to adapt traditional French store management.

Human resource management. Store management was highly decentralized in Taiwan. Department heads were much more autonomous; they were entirely responsible for handling supplier relationships, selecting products and negotiating prices; they fixed retail prices, recruited employees, negotiated salaries (a human resource function in France), presented paychecks, determined promotion possibilities for staff and had input into bonus decisions. They faced significant sales and profit pressure. Initially, all store managers were French expatriates; by mid-1993, three of eight were Taiwanese; two were women.

Carrefour had a reputation for good pay: department heads earned 20% more than at other supermarkets; section heads 25% to 40% more. Monthly salaries for local store managers ranged from NT$120,000 to NT$200,000 (FF26,000 to FF43,500; US$4,400 to US$7,400), similar to U.S.-educated financial managers in large firms. Cashiers were paid NT$17,000 monthly (FF3,600, US$625) per 48-hour week versus FF7,000 (NT$32,500, US$1,200) per 39-hour week in France. In France, employees made additional earnings from a participation scheme; bonuses were linked to individual store results. In Taiwan, a maximum of three months' salary was available for all employees at Chinese New Year; payouts were based on store, section and department results. Carrefour's Taiwanese growth provided significant potential for internal promotions.

In Taiwan, human resource management was a serious problem for all firms. Unemployment was low (1993: 1.15%) and young unskilled people preferred to work in clean services (karaoke bars, coffee shops, restaurants). Carrefour's average staff turnover was 65% per annum; 40% of staff was under 18 years old, mostly part-timers.

The sense of belonging to the organization was limited and training efforts, technical and personal development, were central to store management policy.

Managing the relationship with suppliers. Managing relations with suppliers was different from French standard practice; Carrefour's experience was that Taiwanese suppliers lacked rigor, organization, equipment and aggressiveness, but flexibility was much higher. Typically, suppliers lacked such basic data as sales (volume or value), inventory levels and simple accounting or invoicing information. List prices were not based on cost but on an ideal selling price; some suppliers lost money. Frequently, selling conditions were different from one retailer to another. When Procter and Gamble acquired its former agent (1992), it discovered 123 different conditions were being offered. Suppliers neither sought productivity gains nor had development strategies; the only clear preoccupation was retail price. Suppliers wanted stability and consistency in all retail outlets in competitive chain stores. A few foreign-owned firms were starting to segment their customer bases, offering different package sizes to different retailers.

Equipment was a problem; only 10% of suppliers delivered goods on pallets and pallet sizes were not standardized. Although Taiwan was a world-leading plastics producer, blister-pack was hard to find locally. Manufacturers were starting to realize local market potential as firms like Carrefour approached them. Salespeople visiting Carrefour with samples typically had no catalogs, no product reference numbers and sometimes no order forms.

In contrast to Taiwanese exporters (and western practice), local suppliers were not aggressive. Retailers often had to solicit products; innovation was limited but could be initiated by Carrefour. Many local manufacturers focused solely on exporting and ignored the local market; it offered lower margins, required smaller and more frequent deliveries and obligated acceptance of unsold products.

However, suppliers were very flexible on delivery terms (next day was never a problem) and payment terms. Establishing good relationships with suppliers (and all stakeholders including foreign-owned firms) was important; the best business deals were seldom made in offices, but in karaoke bars with some XO Cognac or local liquor.

Taiwan specific management problems. For French expatriate managers, communication was the most serious problem. For Carrefour, Taiwan was the only country where the working and local languages were not the same, and where all documents were written in two languages (i.e., Chinese and English); minutes of all meetings, performance reports, all other documents (including company policy) were bilingual. Foreign managers could not learn Chinese as fast as Portuguese, Spanish or English; most did not even try since it was very difficult and working hours were long.

Communication problems between foreign managers and local employees had important consequences; competent department heads who could not communicate in basic English with expatriate store managers had difficulty being promoted to section head. This problem might ease as Taiwanese earned more store manager positions, but promotion from section head to store manager was possible only for English speaking staff. It was also difficult to communicate company policy and corporate culture. Mass retailing was a new concept in Taiwan and the language barrier made it difficult to communicate goals, strategy and the reasons for Carrefour's way of doing things. It was extremely difficult for foreign managers to communicate the central message that the smaller the assortment, the higher the turnover, and that fewer products implied more sales per product, better buying prices, lower selling prices, more sales and less chance of being out of stock.

A second problem was the cultural gap. Philippe Ravelli, a local French store manager, said the key difference between French and Chinese cultures was priority given to three basic elements of daily life. Chinese priority order was emotion (qing), reason (li), law (fa); for the French, law was first (implying Carrefour policy was the golden rule), then reason and emotion. This inverse order was a source of misunderstanding in managing local operations. In the French distribution sector, staff training was a managerial duty; in Taiwan, managers were more concerned to retain information than share knowledge. They received much more autonomy than Carrefour practice but delegated little power to subordinates.

A third problem was relationships with new stakeholders, neighbors (since most of Carrefour stores were in urban areas) and local triads.[5] "Protection" had to be negotiated and strict client circulation and delivery scheduling organized for each store in cooperation with suppliers. Taiwanese suppliers, unused to such constraints in normal operations with less demanding clients, had to be educated. Clerc remarked: "What Carrefour has done in Taiwan is learning how to walk by walking."

Carrefour has been Successful in Taiwan but is not Alone

Key Success Factors in Taiwan

In addition to its successful financial performance, Carrefour and other retailers were shaping Taiwanese consumer habits. Executives had differing views on the reasons for Carrefour's success. Philippe Ravelli said Carrefour's real competitive advantage in Taiwan was its basic concept – free parking, one-stop shopping, competitive prices. Jean-Luc Chereau, Clerc's replacement (1993) in Taiwan, believed three different key factors were important and that implementation was critical: entry when the consumer market was developing, fast increasing disposable income and the country opening up to the outside world; choice of people to constitute the backbone of the operation, including the French-Chinese mix in local management; and adaptation of a successful concept to a local environment very different from France.

Customer Satisfaction

Based on repurchasing behavior, Carrefour believed customers were satisfied. But executives thought these data were insufficient to measure actual satisfaction. In

---

[5] Triads were secret societies that became powerful in central and southern China in the 18th century; currently they exercised wide influence among Chinese communities worldwide. They were sworn brotherhood groups, sharing a common tradition, initiation rites, secret signs and languages. Activities ranged from mutual aid organizations to gang-related businesses.

March 1993, Carrefour conducted a nationwide survey to understand better consumer perceptions. To the question: "What is your main reason for shopping at Carrefour?" price was the unprompted first answer (51%), followed by freshness (25%) and one-stop shopping (24%). Carrefour surveyed a 1,000 customer panel twice a year.

After the first survey, Carrefour designed a Customer Suggestion Form, available at each store's information desk. Department heads had to address any suggestion or complaint within 48 hours. Complaints and inquiries were filed regularly; Carrefour believed this system provided excellent, continuous customer feedback.

Competition is Tough

Carrefour was not alone in Taiwan; the growth of western-style supermarkets was dramatic. In 1989, Taiwan had 199 supermarkets, 600 were projected by 1995. Although only six years old, Taiwan's mass retailing industry was dominated by foreign companies but local firms were showing an increasingly strong interest:[6]

- The supermarket league was very active in Taiwan.
- *Wellcome* opened its first Taiwan store in 1987; in 1993 it had 72 stores. An independent study found that 95% of Taiwanese recognized the Wellcome name; it was Taiwan's best known supermarket chain.
- *Park 'N Shop* was the second largest player. Its first store opened in 1989; it had plans to open 12 new stores per year for the next four to five years.
- Hypermarkets were capturing increasing market share among Taiwan supermarkets. Two major players emerged, Carrefour and Makro.
- *Makro* was Taiwan's largest retailing operation.

Makro's five outlets were all much larger than Carrefour's downtown stores; turnover per store was higher than Carrefour; sales were greater than all other mass retailers. Makro recently had to close its Kaohsiung and Wuku stores; according to local regulations, these were illegally located in an industrial area unsuited for commercial activities. Makro's five remaining stores, warehouses that clients could access only with membership cards, were similarly located. Anticipated zoning changes (July 1994) were expected to solve this problem and open up more largely industrial areas for all competitors. Carrefour was building two warehouse stores ("green stores").

Continent (French) had a joint venture with the Far Eastern Group; its first Taiwan store should open at end 1994.

Carrefour managers said they welcomed competitors. Since the market was far from saturated, competitors would contribute to educating consumers to shopping in hypermarkets rather than traditional wet markets or small stores.

---

[6] See Retailing in Taiwan.

Increasing the Pace

In 1993, Gerard Clerc was promoted to CEO for Asia and nominated to the Carrefour Board in France. He moved to Hong Kong to oversee Carrefour's Asian activities. Jean-Luc Chereau took Clerc's position in Taipei.

Coordination of the Existing Operations

In April 1993, Taiwan operations were divided into two regions (North, South), each headed by a French regional director. Regional managers coordinated store activities; human resource management, including training, was a central activity, followed by more centralized merchandising. Carrefour's goal was to limit the number of wholesalers, concentrate same product purchases with one or a few suppliers, reduce buying prices and pass savings to consumers. However, as total sales increased, some suppliers could no longer supply the quantities Carrefour demanded. Diversification of sourcing, possibly via imports, was the only way Carrefour could cope with these problems; it was instituting more centralized buying to improve purchase terms and compensate for large staff turnover that often disrupted operations. Drawing up expansion plans was a regional director responsibility; it accounted for 50% of their time.

Development: "Green Stores"

Since inception, Carrefour operated smaller urban stores in commercial (and legal) areas, compared to Makro's real hypermarkets in industrial suburban areas. Carrefour's response, "to clients, not Makro," said a Carrefour executive, was the soon-to-be opened Warehouse, with a new distinctive red and green logo, in San-Chung, sales area 9,600 sq. m. A second Warehouse would open in 1994, sales area 12,400 sq. m. Both outlets were in industrial areas where local zoning regulations prohibited retailers from opening stores. Although Carrefour had business and factory licenses, membership cards were required to enter these outlets (similar to Makro) and the fiction of a Carrefour Warehouse Club instead of a standard hypermarket was maintained. The San-Chung store distributed over 200,000 cards. Carrefour's trend in Taiwan was large hypermarkets, its real area of expertise, rather than large supermarkets currently being operated. Further large stores were planned for Tamshui, Taichung and Tainan but smaller urban stores would be opened at good locations.

Nonetheless, despite good results, in 1993 Taiwan operations were only 1.4% of Carrefour revenues, similar to Portugal. The limited size of Taiwan stores led to low sales per store, but sales were expected to surge ahead as new stores opened.

Questions for Gerard Clerc

As he settled into his new position as Asia CEO, Clerc posed himself two questions. First, what should he expect from Jean-Luc Chereau in Taiwan? Second, learning from Taiwan could help develop Carrefour business in other Asian countries. He had faced many difficulties, especially at the beginning, a combination of legal, relational, cultural, communication and other problems. Mistakes had been made, but many things had been learned. How could he put that learning to good use?

Exhibit 1:   The Hypermarket Concept

The difference between a supermarket and a hypermarket is not always clear. The term "hypermarket" was introduced in 1969 by Jacques Pictet, founder of Libre Service Actualites (LSA), a self-service retail trade publication, to describe large supermarkets with a sales area of more than 2,500 sq. m., or the exact surface of Carrefour's store in Sainte Geneviève at that time.

A hypermarket was supposed to have the following characteristics:

- sales area of at least 2,500 sq. m. – large variety of food and general merchandise
- large free car park (minimum 1,000 cars) – self-service and payment at central checkouts

The term hypermarket imposed itself very rapidly but for 25 years its definition did not change while large chain retailers like Carrefour were building larger stores with a sales area of over 10,000 sq. m. or even 15,000 sq. m. According to René Brillet, CEO for Carrefour in North Europe (including France), a hypermarket should supply 80% of consumers' needs. Below 5,000 sq. m., this would be impossible: under these conditions, a store could only offer a few home appliances and a limited textile assortment. Only dry and fresh foodstuffs would be handled reasonably well. To take into account the changes in the trade, in 1993 LSA decided to change the definition and to retain as hypermarkets in its figures only the stores with sales areas of more than 5,000 sq. m. Stores with an area of 2,500 to 5,000 sq. m. were considered as "large supermarkets."

Following is a paper written in 1969 by Marcel Fournier, founder and President of Carrefour, explaining his money-making discounting strategy.

"In front of those clients who want to get the best prices to increase their living standard, what do we find? Old fashioned shopkeepers with medieval thinking who want to sell as high as possible and are so happy when they can take very high margins. It was maybe the best way to build a fortune when goods were scarce, but it is not the case anymore when modern industries can supply so many different articles and so much of them on the market. But there is a barrier between the flow of merchandises and the clients. It is the barrier of brains ridiculously blurred by the absurd and antiquated concept of gross profit margin. U.S. retailers accomplished a great step the day discounters replaced this traditional concept by the modern idea of return on invested capital. When we understood the importance of the change, we got rid of the formula:

$$\frac{gross\ profit}{sales\ turnover}$$

to replace it with the new formula

$$\frac{net\ profit}{invested\ capital}$$

For the operation to be profitable, this ratio has to be as high as possible. Both terms of the ratio have to be acted upon: net profit will have to be maximized, while invested capital will have to be minimized. To obtain a high net profit while selling at discount rates, it is imperative to sell a lot and to limit overheads. Selling huge volumes, that is our first law at Carrefour ... "

Source: LSA, April 29, 1993.

Exhibit 2: President Enterprises Organization Chart

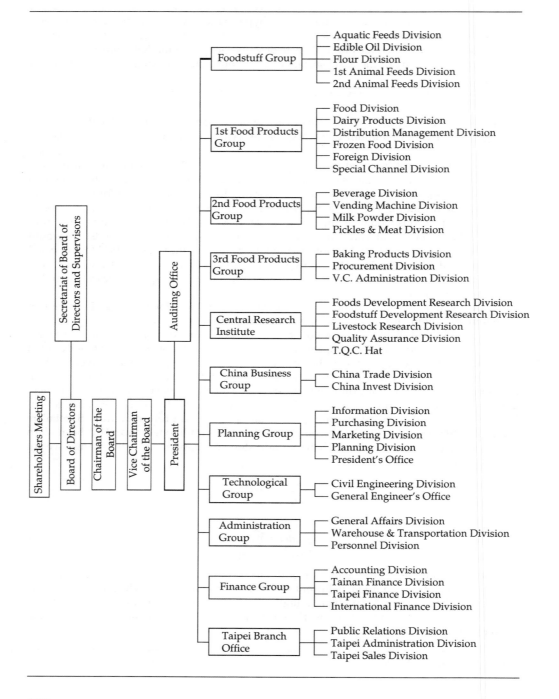

Case 54

Retailing in Taiwan[1]

Pierre Courbon, Philippe Lasserre
INSEAD, Fontainebleau, France

As Taiwan became a high consumption country, its retail network evolved rapidly. The 1980s saw explosive growth in the retail industry; new outlet types slowly continued to replace traditional bazaar style family stores.

ജഇഓ

How the Economic Environment Influences the Retail Market: Demand Factors

Rapid increase in per capita income. In 1989, per capita income reached US$6,048, up 18-fold from 1960; the "Gini" coefficient decreased to 0.303, indicating a more equal income distribution. Standards of living increased; consumption was more sophisticated (Exhibit 1). Along with rapid industrialization, supermarkets provided the population with convenience and cleanliness; convenience stores offered accessible hours, locations and product ranges. Department stores served as cultural and purchasing centers.

Upgrading education. In 1988, about 9.5% of Taiwan residents above age six were college students or graduates; 15% were senior high school students or graduates. Education level improved upward mobility and created demand for better living standards.

---

[1] This case was prepared by Pierre Courbon, MBA participant, under the supervision of Philippe Lasserre, Professor of Strategy and Management at INSEAD. It is intended to be used as a basis for class discussion rather than to illustrate either effective or ineffective handling of an administrative situation. Reprinted with the permission of INSEAD. Copyright 1994 INSEAD-EAC, Fontainebleau, France.

Diminishing traditional family and growth of working women. The traditional extended family was gradually replaced by the nuclear family; average family membership dropped to 4.14 (1988). Most, especially urban families were two-income. Housewives had less time to manage household work; they sought more convenient stores and patronized new retailer types for cleanliness and convenience, even though prices were higher.

High percentage of appliance owners, but a low percentage of car owners. Most families had full home appliance sets. In 1988, 98% owned refrigerators; by contrast, only 20% owned cars. This low ratio made it preferable to shop at convenience stores rather than supermarkets.

How the Economic Environment Influences the Retail Market: Supply Factors

Infrastructure improvement. During the 1980s, traffic and communication infrastructure improved throughout the island. As a result, new retailer types had much lower costs. Furthermore, package standardization and classification of major commodities were conducive to greater retailer efficiency.

Decrease in the relative cost of facilities. Costs of vehicles and electrical/mechanical facilities reduced because of declining tariffs and Taiwan's industrialization. Research indicated that facility costs for more convenient retailers decreased significantly, strengthening their competitive advantage.

Refining of management knowledge. At the end of the1970s, more educated people entered retail marketing; updated management concepts spread widely. Moreover, implementation of management information systems enabled managerial decision making to be more rapid and precise. Chain store management became feasible in Taiwan.

The Retail Market Considerably Changed in Taiwan

Historically, the Taiwan retail market was characterized by many small operators. However, because no real statistics existed, not only was gauging market shares accurately impossible, but the fast pace of change made tracking developments even more difficult. Regardless, the underlying trend was towards larger sales areas, driven mostly by development of department stores and, more recently, supermarket and hypermarket chains (Exhibit 2). Supermarkets, hypermarkets and convenience stores accounted for 30% of food expenditures in Taiwan.

Wet markets. Although 80% of Taiwanese still used traditional wet markets for fresh produce, latest research showed a discernible trend away from wet markets to supermarkets. For most Taipei residents, two jobs was the norm, making it impossible to shop at the local wet market, usually open only in the morning.

Mom-and-pop shops. In 1989, Taiwan had over 330,000 retail outlets, mostly small traditional family-owned firms. These stores handled the largest share of food sales, even though the first large food store opened in 1965. Since 1987, entry of large foreign-invested chain stores and local followers made competition very fierce.

Modern retailing. The biggest battle fought by large retail chains was less against themselves than tradition; many consumers still shopped at traditional markets or ate outside the home. Taipei supermarkets were in the awkward position of fighting to bring back the family tradition of eating at home. Classification of modern retailing depended on the goods and services offered: Department stores: environment + choice + service; Supermarkets: proximity + price; Hypermarkets: price + choice; Convenience stores: proximity + time.

Department stores. These stores developed greatly in quantity and quality under guidance of major Japanese department stores. They brought professional management and merchandising to Taiwan and were often linked to real estate investments by large construction or insurance companies. Previously, Taiwan department stores operated by "consignment," stores leased space to "brands" (manufacturers or sole importers) providing merchandise for commissions paid to the store. However, department stores increasingly developed purchasing policies and no longer relied exclusively on consignment. They also tended to concentrate on fashion, accessories, cosmetics and expensive imported goods from Europe, Japan and the U.S. Most department stores contained a basement floor supermarket, typically just-profitable high-price outlets not particularly geared for department store shoppers. Observers believed these supermarkets would gradually evolve into such stores as delicatessens and health food. These supermarkets would thus find a niche beside expanding neighborhood supermarkets and large hypermarkets.

Supermarkets and hypermarkets. Although the main difference between these two outlet types was size, many other differences existed. Hypermarkets had larger sales areas, usually offered free parking and required large development sites; high real estate costs led to locations outside city centers. Supermarkets were centrally located downtown in densely populated areas, were much smaller and rarely had parking lots. Although hindered by high land prices and zoning regulations, hypermarkets were expected to develop further, favored by the "automobile" population that enjoyed weekly one-stop shopping sprees and picked up forgotten items at convenience stores.

Convenience stores. The retailing sector that typified development of the entire industry was convenience stores. In just a few years, they mushroomed at many street corners and changed the face of Taiwan streets. Convenience stores offered: convenience of time, open 24 hours a day; convenience of distance, within 250 meters of every home; convenience of checkout, convenience of self-service. Convenience stores offered limited choice of goods, mainly food (65% of total sales); other goods were magazines and personal products. They targeted mainly students, night owls and young hard-working adults not wishing to waste time shopping but prepared to pay extra. A survey by Dr. Ripley (CEO Wellcome, Taiwan) (sample, 250 students) revealed less than 1% of grandparents and 10% of parents patronized convenience chain stores but 85% of students were regular customers. (Comparable U.S. figures were 20%, 40% and 45%.) Convenience chains' chief objectives were quickly to establish many outlets to increase buying power. Food manufacturers set up convenience store chains to increase control over product distribution.

Impact of Large Food Stores on Taiwan's Distribution System

Taiwan's food distribution system, as in most countries, was strongly influenced by the retail sector. As retail changes occurred, the distribution system tried to adjust to meet retailers' changing needs. Retailing changes in Taiwan created shock waves throughout the distribution system.

As major supermarket chains developed new and larger stores, they placed different demands on supplying wholesalers and manufacturers. Small retailers with low sales volume might find one delivery per week adequate; larger supermarkets might require two or three deliveries per week for packaged goods, daily deliveries for fresh and frozen products. Supermarket firms with new warehouse facilities demanded that suppliers ship in large quantities and reduce wholesale prices by 3% to 5% to reflect retailer warehousing activities and wholesaler delivery cost savings. These price reductions placed increased pressure on suppliers to be efficient low-cost distributors. Many small manufacturers and wholesalers found such price competition a serious problem; they were unable to reduce costs by introducing efficiencies in their distribution systems.

Very large supermarkets placed additional demands on suppliers since merchandising programs demanded products be sold in large sizes or quantities; manufacturers were frequently required to provide special packages. In addition, suppliers might be asked to deliver products directly to hypermarkets and cash-and-carry stores, bypassing distribution centers and other middlemen. Some large retail chains imported directly, bypassing import agents.

Since Taiwan's food retailing system was in transition, wholesalers and manufacturers faced challenges of meeting the needs of new supermarket customers, yet continuing to provide services and products for the many small food retailers making up the majority of Taiwan's food markets. Observers said small retail stores would continue to play an important food distribution role for many years, in spite of numbers declines. Because wholesalers and distributors provided special services to small food retailers, they would also play important roles in the food distribution system.

Future Challenges for Taiwan's Retail Industry

Warehousing facilities. Lack of adequate warehouse facilities was a critical problem faced by fast growing retail chains; it undermined efficient food distribution. Most retail chains had inadequate central warehousing; they relied on small in-store stocks and frequent supplier deliveries (e.g., Carrefour); facilities were usually too small and often multi-level. By contrast, Wellcome and 7-Eleven set up centralized warehousing and distribution systems early. Central warehousing allowed retailers to consolidate a wide assortment of products in a single shipment and make single deliveries to stores. This system was important as retailers typically received products from many suppliers (up to 400); furthermore, located in urban areas, frequent deliveries were inconvenient for the neighborhood.

Centralized purchasing. Large food retailers mostly bypassed traditional wholesalers; they were too small and disorganized to provide needed services. High wholesaler operating costs prevented price discounts requested by retail chains; offering quantity discounts was not their practice. Most large retail chains preferred to purchase fresh fruits and vegetables via direct negotiation with farmer groups or importers to secure low bulk prices.

Bar coding. Smaller manufacturers gave only lukewarm acceptance to bar code scanning technology, provided by major food product suppliers to increase productivity, performance and profits. About 60% of products in supermarkets and 75% in convenience stores were barcoded. However, this technology concept did not fit well with small suppliers that traditionally sold products through small grocery stores and food shops. Not all retailers agreed on bar coding system advantages.

Palletization. Large retail chains requested suppliers to ship all products to distribution centers or stores on pallets to speed handling. However, pallet sizes were not standardized and retailers were trying to achieve uniformity. Products delivered in bulk had to be palletized by retailers; this took time and slowed truck rotations and distribution of other deliveries waiting at the docks.

Customer Service should Adapt to the Local Environment[2]

There were significant differences between Taiwanese and American experiences and expressions of good customer service (Table 1). Some major themes were similar: polite/friendly salespeople, knowledgeable salespeople, no pressure sales, pleasant store. Differences included: Taiwanese defined good customer service by a feeling of respect (second most important theme) but no U.S. respondent mentioned this; conversely, merchandise-related aspects of customer service (e.g., good merchandise, quality, good prices) were important to U.S. consumers, not Taiwanese. The similarity in importance of impolite/impersonal salespeople affecting the service experience masked many differences. Taiwanese defined bad experiences by reference to respect: being ignored, followed around, embarrassed, hurried and subject to abusive language; in the U.S., bad experience was characterized by merchandise (e.g., not having required products, badly informed staff) and price (higher than expected) considerations.

---

[2] Based on "Cross-cultural similarities and differences in definitions of customer service in retailing settings," Richard A. Feinberh, Ko de Ruyter, Charles Trappey, Tzai-Zang Lee, World Marketing Congress, Academy of Marketing Science, Istanbul, Turkey, July 1993.

Table 1: Taiwan and U.S. Service Differences

Taiwan		U.S.	
Polite/friendly	19%	Good merchandise/what I want	18%
Felt important/respected	12%	Friendly	11%
Competent/knowledgeable salespeople	10%	Good prices	10%
Smile	7%	Knowledgeable salespeople	9%
Patient/paid attention	6%	Pleasant interior	9%
No pressure	5%	Convenient	8%
Went out of way/special service	4%	No pressure	7%
Pleasant/comfortable store	4%	Quality merchandise	4%
Good merchandise presentation	4%		
Prompt/quick	4%		
25 total themes	75%	30 total themes	76%
Taiwan		**U.S.**	
Impolite/impersonal	16%	Doesn't have what I wanted	19%
Ignored	12%	Impolite/impersonal	12%
Problems in delivery	8%	Not knowledgeable	11%
Long delay/lines	6%	Little selection	10%
Followed around	6%	Paid more than expected	9%
No attention/help	5%	Left feeling angry/disappointed	6%
Abusive language	5%	Dirty store	5%
Embarrassed me	5%	Inconvenient	4%
Sales pressure	4%	Long delay/lines	4%
Hurried me	4%		
29 total themes	71%	53 total themes	80%

As consumer-oriented businesses face problems and opportunities of internation-alization, they must also face the challenge of delivering excellent customer service. If international results mirror U.S. experience, a direct link exists between customer satisfaction, sales and profits. Understanding how customers define and experience good and bad customer service must precede its delivery. Dr. Feinberg's results show that despite similarities in how consumers in different countries define good and bad customer service experiences, significant differences require special approaches to delivering customer service and satisfaction at retail. Training employees and deliver-ing customer satisfaction must consider the country's unique experiences, history and culture, and the unique experiences of that market place.

Delivery of good customer service in Taiwan is based on the process by which goods are delivered and how the person is treated in the stores. The respect issue seem to conform to the West's view of the Asian personality. There seems to be less of a merchandise/price orientation to defining good and poor customer service. Notwith-standing these findings, consumer habits and attitudes to customer service were rapidly changing in Taiwan. The limited importance of price in customer service could partly be explained by the separation of price and service in consumers' minds. Taiwan remained a very price-oriented market, especially in the food sector.

Regulations Slowly Adapt to the De facto Situation

Although Taiwanese trends clearly favored mass merchandising, regulations and laws failed to keep pace with this rapid development. Some large supermarkets established on industrial land conducted marketing and sales operations in conspicuous violation of land use laws prohibiting profit-driven warehousing or commercial distribution centers in industrial zones. Despite assistance from the central government, local county governments were reluctant to approve land conversion to supermarkets, notably because of opposition from many other business stores. Some argued that use of industrial land for commercial purpose gave large supermarket chains an unfair competitive edge against smaller stores with high land costs in commercial districts.

In May 1994, the Taiwan Provincial Government notified Makro Taiwan that it should change operations at two stores or face closure. A few days later, two stores (Kaohsiung and Wuku, near Taipei) were shut down by local county authorities. Makro claimed to be a victim of conflicting policies of the central and municipal governments; it argued that central government instructions to allow Makro stores to operate on industrial land were being defied locally. An additional political dimension concerned the conflict between fully democratically elected local governments (often run by the DPP opposition party) and the not-yet-entirely legitimate central government, still controlled by the KMT. Makro decided not to open its latest store (planned opening, May) in Chungho, a southern Taipei suburb. Makro temporarily froze new investments in Taiwan until the situation was resolved.

Some changes were occurring. In March 1994, the regulation restricting retail stores to a maximum 500 sq. m. was partly abolished. Basements and ground floors of buildings in residential areas of Taipei City and Taiwan County could be used for commercial purposes without size limitations. A July 25 decision of the Ministry of Economic Affairs (MOEA) began the process of regulating warehousing and wholesale industries; more complete regulations were expected after the December county elections.

According to one western executive: "It is difficult to be 100% legal in this country." Foreign firms were advised to be as pragmatic as the Taiwanese and accept that sometimes situations were slightly illegal, especially when no specific regulations applied. A compromising fiction had to be maintained; operators should keep a low profile, simply to give authorities face. These situations could last many years and might result in de facto situations slowly being accepted, if not entirely legal, until a new law endorsed the status quo. This process occurred for discos before the lifting of Martial Law in 1987.

The Number of Actors in the Retail Market was Increasing

Large foreign chains expanding operations in Taiwan competed with traditional retail outlets.

Government stores. The government operated about ten supermarkets in Taipei, more in other cities. These stores faced competition from new foreign chains (e.g., Wellcome, Park 'N Shop) that offered better prices and service. The Ministry of National Defense operated PX Stores (MNDPX), the only really hard discounters in Taiwan. Initially designed for military personnel only, in 1971, the franchise was broadened to allow access to government employees, dependants and retired military and government staff, as compensation for poor public sector wages. As a result, 18% of the population had access to PX Stores causing significant problems, especially with purchases for resale. In 1988, the PX was split in two (50/50), the old PX and the United Cooperative Association (UCA): the UCA took over some urban PX supermarket outlets.

With sales over NT$17 billion, the 110 small MNDPX stores were too big for suppliers to ignore. However, they had to sign particularly onerous contracts guaranteeing not to sell at lower prices and facing penalty clauses for non-delivery and out-of-stocks. Product listing was by invitation only; typically via announcements in newspapers, usually once a year. Price negotiations were conducted across a table from three uniformed men; potential suppliers had three opportunities to write out their best price! For certain product categories, MNDPX were essential outlets, responsible for large percent sales of shampoo (50%); milk powder (60%) and tissue paper (50%). The more commodity-oriented product categories had higher percent MNDPX sales.

MNDPX policies requiring suppliers not to sell at lower prices was of greater concern since the National Fair Trade Law came into effect (January 1, 1992). Large retailers were expected to test the law if MNDPX stores could buy at lower wholesale prices. As large supermarkets developed greater sales and more efficient distribution systems, suppliers would find it difficult to justify selling at lower wholesale prices to MNDPX stores than to large privately owned firms. MNDPX prices were still 10% to 15% lower than large retail stores.

Supermarkets. Wellcome was positioning itself as the "convenient neighborhood supermarket." "We're not trying to be all things to all people," said Jeffrey Shaw, CEO of Wellcome Taiwan. "We just want to be the friendly, low-cost supermarket around the corner." A recent independent study found that 95% Taiwanese recognized the Wellcome name, making it Taiwan's best known supermarket chain.

Wellcome was 97% owned by Dairy Farm International; local firm, Ding Hao Acme Ltd. owned 3%. Wellcome opened its first Taiwan outlet in 1987; it operated 72 stores, 15 more were scheduled before end 1994. It targeted 200 stores in five years, 400 before 2005. The average store had approximately 1,025 sq. m. floor space. Wellcome offered a wide range of products: 4,000 dry food, 1,000 perishable, 2,500 non-food. Carrefour considered Wellcome a possible threat because of fully centralized purchasing but believed its profit margins were a problem. Wellcome measured price competitiveness against hypermarkets to stay ahead among the supermarkets. According to Shaw, when Wellcome opened in Taiwan it put in the most modern and efficient system possible. All stores had scanning devices and would soon be on-line with the new distribution center that receive consolidated orders each day. The 1995 target, "to be more fresh than anyone," counted on opening a new ultra-modern frozen and chilled center and a new produce distribution center.

Wellcome operated in Hong Kong, Taiwan, New Zealand, Australia, Spain and the U.K.; its first Malaysian store would open in September 1994; it was actively examining Indonesia, Thailand and Japan. Wellcome signed joint-venture agreements in four different Chinese cities; the Dairy Farm Group managed 15 7-Eleven stores in Shenzhen.

The second largest player, Park 'N Shop (wholly owned by A.S. Watson, Hong Kong) opened its first store in 1989; it operated 30 stores and planned to open approximately 12 new stores per annum in the next four to five years. The average store contained approximately 560 sq. m. of trading area. A firm official said it would attempt to change public habits. "Conversion of wet market shoppers to supermarket shoppers will be our first priority. Considerable work is needed as more than 80% of Taiwan shoppers still prefer to purchase fresh produce in the market."

Locally-owned supermarket chains were emerging. Wang Teh Fu Supermarket Company operated eight full-size outlets in northern Taiwan; floor space, 335 to 700 sq. m. It also operated three mini-marts, 33 sq. m. shopping area; future outlets were planned as suitable sites were located. Other chains were developing networks; for example, Kasumi, controlled by local manufacturer Wei Chuan and Sun-Ching, each had ten supermarkets in Taipei.

Hypermarkets. Capturing increasing market share among Taiwan's supermarkets were hypermarkets, huge outlets providing 10 to 15 times typical supermarket floor space. Taiwan had two major players, Makro and Carrefour.

Makro emerged as Taiwan's largest retailer, sales about NT$21 billion per annum. Said Carlos Perez, President of Makro Taiwan: "We are the leader, we have no challenger, we need to challenge ourselves." Makro defined itself as a wholesaler rather than a retailer; it targeted professional customers, often food retailers. However, analysts regarded Makro as a retailer because it employed a tiered price structure; individuals purchased products at higher prices than *bona fide* resellers. The largest share of company sales were to individual buyers.

Makro was owned by SHV Holding (Holland) (55%); Charoen Pokphand (Thailand) (10%), Taiwan's Holinsgreen Group (35%); Makro in Thailand had the same partners. Although the Taiwanese partner helped considerably with legal and political issues, management was left entirely to SHV. Perez (who took a crash Chinese course before taking up his position) was the only foreigner in Makro Taiwan; local management will succeed him. (By contrast, Carrefour had a large staff of expatriate managers.) For Makro, the human factor was key to managing retailing operations. Finding good profiles, picking the winners and teaching them the Makro way of doing things was central to Makro management. At Makro, "Buying is central, decision making is local," said Perez. "This often leaves a grey area with which managers must deal. It is a situation of 'managers who manage without definitions.'"

Makro operated seven stores, floor space, 10,200 to 13,475 sq. m.; each store provided parking for 700 to 1,000 cars. Makro claimed it was Taiwan's price setter; it sold both local products and a wide range of imported goods, as well as generics and own labels under the Aro name. In mid-1994, Makro was forced to close two stores in industrial areas not zoned for commercial activities; all other stores were in similar situations. Makro treated its huge outlets as warehouses; clients could enter only with membership cards. In the legislative vacuum, Makro preferred to wait for the December municipal elections results when, it believed, political decisions would be made.

Makro recently caused controversy among suppliers by making a clean break with standard price fixing. To attract customers, Makro offered best selling merchandise at cut-throat prices for a limited period. It sold Proton brand TV sets at NT$1,000 less than the fixed wholesale price, popular Hey-Song soft drinks at NT$265 per carton (standard wholesale price, NT$310) and offered 25% discounts on all products supplied by President Enterprises, Carrefour's partner. Makro's cut-throat competition irritated other buyers and supplier company agents. Many Proton Electronics agents filed complaints with their supplier; Carrefour threatened to stop purchases from President Enterprises. Insiders said Makro should not destroy the market order and hurt other competitors just to promote itself. Some Makro suppliers decided to limit supplies if Makro did not cease its oligopoly-busting activities.

Makro also operated in Indonesia, Malaysia and Thailand; it was seriously considering entry in South Korea, the Philippines, and Beijing and Guangdong province in China. Makro's next Asian move would build regional purchasing power using synergies from different countries, a possible future advantage when competitiveness would be more based on retailer margins.

Carrefour entered Taiwan at the same time as Makro (1989) and expanded rapidly. It had eight stores and planned to open more in 1995 (see Carrefour in Asia (A)).

Convenience stores. The omnipresent 7-Eleven convenience store chain was managed in Taiwan by President Enterprises in cooperation with the Southland Company. It added 60 stores in 1992, 100 in 1993 to total 809; 1993 revenues were NT$17.6 billion, pre-tax profits NT$815 million, up 57% from 1992. 7-Eleven planned 910 stores by end 1994 and purchased real estate for 30 more, posing a threat to competitors having to pay rent. 7-Eleven was also planning to open over 500 outlets at gas stations owned by China Petroleum Corporation. On opening (1979), 7-Eleven targeted housewives; results were disappointing. It changed strategy and switched attention to the workforce, adolescents, working women and night owls, by opening 24 hours per day. All stores were near large people flows; product ranges catered to the target markets needs.

Increasing competition from other convenience chains led 7-Eleven to develop new business strategies. In 1992, it launched a fast-growing mail order operation; in stores, it planned more service item expansion, offering magazines, transportation tickets and installing automatic teller machines. It also planned banking, postal and telecom services, classified ads and ticket agency services. A second direction was upgrading information systems by installing an electronic ordering system to eliminate slow moving items and improve inventory control. The final axis was adopting the franchise system for rapid expansion and broad distribution at relatively low cost.

Although 7-Eleven tried franchising earlier with poor results, it believed its success would facilitate this development. President was also eyeing mainland China, competing with Hong Kong's Dairy Farm Group to negotiate retailing rights.

President also managed a chain of over 650 President Bakery stores focusing primarily on selling food items produced by President Enterprises. It also oversaw a franchise program; independents operated stores similar to President Bakery shops under the name President 3Q Shops. President also managed many vending machines.

Another rapidly growing company was Niko Mart, operating 84 shops; the most noticeable difference from other players was in imported foods. Because of ties to the Japanese Niko chain, it relied heavily on Japan as a source of imported products; most other convenience stores obtained the bulk of imports from the U.S. One of the largest convenience chain store firms with no ties to either a foreign chain or major local industrial group was Green Bean. It opened its first outlet in 1986 and currently operated 50 company-owned stores; it oversaw another 130 franchised outlets. It planned 250 stores by end 1996.

Among the dozens of other convenience store operators, some of the largest players included The Best, B&D, AM-PM Mini-Market, OK and Family Mart, a large completely independent distributor. Local food manufacturers Hsin Tung Yang, Wei Chuan and I-Mei also operated convenience stores under their own names, mainly to distribute their own manufactured products.

Department stores. The most successful and ambitious department store chain was a recent market entry; Shin Kong Mitsokushi, a joint venture between Shin Kong Insurance Group (Taiwan) and Japan's Mitsukoshi department store. The first store opened in October 1991, a second in December 1993 (in the new 52-story Shin Kong Life Tower [Taiwan's tallest building]), another in Kaohsiung City. By end 1993, it was Taiwan's largest department store and one of the few to report expansion plans in the nearly saturated market. Branches were expected to open in Taiwan (1996), subsequently in Taichung and in Taipei's Hsinyi district. Other main department store chains were Far Eastern (11 stores); Lai Lai and Tokyu Evergreen (three stores each). President Group had two Isetan stores, Sunrise (two stores) and Sogo (one store). Ming Yao and Tonlin (one store each) had management contracts with the Japanese group Keio. Most recently, Dayeh Takashimaya opened in Taipei.

Local Operators Teamed up with Foreign Firms on New Projects

Promodes, one of Carrefour's largest competitors in France operated hypermarket chains, Continei and Champion. After several years' examination (first Taiwan mission, 1986), Promodes (35%) formed a NT$700 million joint venture with a large local company, the Far Eastern Group (65%). Far Eastern operated department stores and three hypermarkets. Observers speculated the balance of power would be different from Carrefour's joint venture PresiCarre; President was only a sleeping partner. The new venture, Far Eastern Continent, would use Promodes management technology to open a hypermarket in southern Taiwan, the first of a planned hypermarket chain. Originally planned to open in July, the store would open at end 1994. Observers believed Continent was awaiting resolution of the Makro situation to avoid antagonizing local authorities by opening a new hypermarket as others were being closed. The Far Eastern Group was a serious competitor; it had a track record as a developer, operating department stores in urban areas; it also had land available in industrial areas following overseas delocalization of most plants of its Far Eastern Textile affiliate. Continent had a reputation for very aggressive promotions.

The President Department Store Group (Kaohsiung City) (unrelated to Carrefour's partner) (49%) planned a NT$5 billion joint venture with Price-Costco Group (U.S.) (51%) for 25 large-scale discount wholesale stores. President entered retailing 19 years previously; annual sales exceeded NT$10 billion. It operated the Dollar hypermarket chain, a serious competitor to Carrefour in southern Taiwan. The three Dollar warehouse clubs were directly inspired by Makro; they offered the lowest Taiwan prices on beverages but did not promote these too strongly because of warehouse regulations. President also cooperated with the Isetan Department Store Group of Japan.

The Price Club (U.S.), the U.S.'s sixth largest discount wholesale store group recently acquired the Costco Group. Price-Costco operated over 100 outlets around the world; it would open in South Korea in September 1994. Price Club's headquarters were in the same building as the Carrefour Sanchung store, clearly an aggressive act towards Carrefour that actually owned 25% of Price Club. One marketing analyst noted, "If Price Club sells products in Taiwan at U.S. prices, it will probably bury any competitor on the island."

A Large Number of Domestic Construction Firms Entered the Hypermarket and Department Store Markets

The Tuntex Group recently opened its first hypermarket (10,000 sq. m.) in Keelung, north of Taipei; managed by a former Makro employee, very good results were reported. Far Eastern Construction (unrelated to the Far Eastern Group) was building its first store (planned opening, September 1994) in Hshichi, an eastern Taipei suburb.

J & Y Huang Land Development and Construction Company signed a contract (April 1994) with Standa, Italy's largest department store, to establish the first Sino-Italian department in Taiwan. Located in Neihu, a northern Taipei suburb, it planned to offer Italian imports at 40% to 60% of average Taiwan prices. Construction would begin in September, the new store was expected to open by end 1994.

Despite increasing competition from these new chains, most retailers did not feel threatened because of their expertise and lead acquired in the last few years. They believed the market was far from saturation and that room existed for many. Official declarations were of the form: "We welcome more companies to join the business line, so Taiwan consumers can enjoy lower prices."

Projected Trends in the Taiwan Retail Market

In the past few years, the Taiwan retail market changed quickly under pressure of modern retailing forms, but more change was expected. Douglas Hsu, Chairman of Far Eastern Department Stores, made the following predictions: independent stores (e.g., old fashioned convenience stores) will be replaced by convenience stores; new selling space will become larger; new commerical areas will develop in the suburbs in conjunction with construction of Taipei's Mass Rapid Transit System; government policy will encourage establishment of fully functioning shopping centers; operational efficiency will improve with advanced computer techniques and usage.

Exhibit 1: Taiwan Background Data

Economic data of Taiwan R.O.C.			
Year	Population '000	GNP growth %	GNP per capita US$
1985	19,258	5.0	3,144
1986	19,455	10.8	3,784
1987	19,673	11.9	4,989
1988	19,904	7.8	6,048
1989	20,107	7.3	7,571
1990	20,353	5.0	7,954
1991	20,557	7.2	8,788
1992	20,752	6.0	10,215
1993	20,944	5.9	10,566

Motorization in Taiwan		
Year	No. of sedans registered for private use	No. of registered motorcycles
1985	830,315	6,588,854
1986	956,625	7,194,202
1987	1,159,701	5,958,754
1988	1,480,478	6,810,540
1989	1,868,389	7,619,038
1990	2,225,174	8,460,138
1991	2,535,174	9,232,889
1992	2,932,796	10,057,307
1993	3,317,580	10,948,972

Change of household expenditures in Taiwan				
Expenditure (%/year)	1964	1976	1987	1991
Food, beverages & tobacco	59.7	46.4	36.5	31.1
Clothes & footwear	6.3	6.8	6.0	5.9
Rent, fuel & power	17.2	21.5	23.0	25.7
Family furniture & equipment	3.4	3.9	4.4	4.3
Transportation & communication	2.0	5.0	8.5	8.9
Education & recreation	1.2	6.4	10.6	12.8
Medical care & health expenses	–	4.6	5.3	5.4
Others	4.9	5.5	5.6	5.9

Source: *Statistical Yearbook of the Republic of China.*

Exhibit 2: Taiwan Retailing Data

Monthly food expenses in 1989		
Store type	NT$ billion	Market share
Super & hypermarket	1.1	10
Traditional wet market	3.2	30
Street vendors	2.5	24
Mom-and-pop shops	2.2	21
Convenience stores	0.66	6
Government & military stores	0.66	6
Others	–	3

Changes in the number of food retail stores by type				
Store type	1988	%	1991	%
Large supermarkets	130	0.3	313	1.0
Small supermarkets	1,041	3.0	1,164	4.0
Large traditional	1,466	4.0	1,582	5.0
Medium traditional	7,279	18.7	12,346	40.9
Small traditional	19,627	51.0	12,604	42.0
Pure food	8,195	25.0	2,352	8.0
Total	37,738	100.0	30,361	100.0

Source: Government statistics.

No. of food stores operated by major chains, by type (1992)	
Type of format	No. of stores
Convenience stores	887
Supermarkets	161
Hypermarkets	7
Cash and carry	7
Total	1,062

No. of convenience stores operated by the major food chains	
Company	No. of stores (1992)
7-Eleven	680 (vs 420 in 1988 and 809 in 1993)
Family Mart	80
Nesun	55
AM/PM	38
OK	17
High Life	17

Sources: AC Nielsen Taiwan/Investec Taiwan Ltd./survey data by Gene German.

Exhibit 2 (cont'd)

No. of supermarkets operated by major food chains

Company	No. of stores (1992)
National Co-op.	60
Wellcome	40
Far Eastern	13
Taipei Ag	12
President	11
Kasumi	11
Sung-Ching	8
Park 'N Shop	7
Makro	6
Carrefour	4
Homey	3
Total	175

Sources: AC Nielsen/Investec/survey data by Gene German.

No. of supermarkets and convenience stores

Year	Supermarket	Convenience store
1986	404	122
1987	69	18
1988	121	378
1989	213	795
1990	343	1,229
1991	438	1,617
1992	491	1,914
1993	541	2,289
1994 March	n/a	2,310

Source: Investec Coopers & Lybrand.

Case 55

Carrefour in Asia (B): The Expansion in Asia[1]

Pierre Courbon, Philippe Lasserre
INSEAD, Fontainebleau, France

By late 1994, Gerard Clerc, Carrefour's new CEO for Asia, based in Hong Kong, was pondering his next moves. In Taiwan, Clerc built Carrefour's operations in Asia from scratch,[2] but company ambitions were now much higher. Based on his Taiwan experience, Clerc was appointed to lead Carrefour's Asian expansion. In the past year he had taken several actions; he wondered what his next steps should be....

৪০৫৪

A Context of Dramatic Growth

Annual growth rate of food consumption in the Asia-Pacific region was estimated at 2% to 6%, or even higher. In addition to population growth, consumers were buying more sophisticated products with higher added value. Experts believed consumers began modifying food consumption patterns at US$3,000 to US$4,000 per capita GNP (Exhibit 1). In Asia Pacific, households with annual disposable incomes over US$3,000 were expected to increase from 96 million (1990) to 217 million (2000). The trend for families with disposable incomes over US$10,000 was similar: from 38 million (1990) to 93 million (2000) (Japan excluded). In Taiwan, average disposable household income would shortly exceed US$10,000! All economic indicators were up;

---

[1] This case was prepared by Pierre Courbon, MBA participant, under the supervision of Philippe Lasserre, Professor of Strategy and Management at INSEAD. It is intended to be used as a basis for class discussion rather than to illustrate either effective or ineffective handling of an administrative situation. Reprinted with the permission of INSEAD. Copyright 1994 INSEAD-EAC, Fontainebleau, France.

[2] See Carrefour in Asia (A), page 840.

in addition, increased urbanization made most countries potential markets for Carrefour (Exhibit 2).

Carrefour's Commitment to Asia

In 1993, Gerard Clerc was promoted to Carrefour's Board of Directors, demonstrating Carrefour's strong commitment to Asia since Asian operations represented only 1.4% of global revenues. Notwithstanding Taiwan's role as a bridgehead for further Asian expansion, Clerc decided to move to Hong Kong since local operations in Taiwan might have consumed his time. The British colony was centrally located in Asia Pacific; many multinationals made it their Asia-Pacific headquarters. Clerc contemplated various options for Carrefour expansion.

Malaysia

British influence in Malaysia made the local legal environment much easier to deal with than in Taiwan. Although Carrefour had not found a *bumiputra* partner as required by the law, a significant grace period was allowed for foreign firms after operations commenced. Carrefour's maximum stake in the joint venture would be 30%.

Carrefour's first Malaysian store was opened (October 1994) in a suburb of Kuala Lumpur; floor area 6,000 sq. m. on one level with a second level for future expansion. In accord with Carrefour's typical worldwide practice, Carrefour purchased the land; annual rents were 8% to 10% of land value versus 1% to 2% in Taiwan. Carrefour's Malaysian concept was similar to other countries: prices, freshness and free parking. Future managers, mostly ethnic Chinese, were being trained in Taiwan to become Carrefour's first section-department heads in Malaysia.

Malaysia was considered a high potential market; land was cheaper than Taiwan, vehicle ownership was greater and economic growth was high. If the first store succeeded, Carrefour planned six stores by 2000.

Thailand

In late 1993, during a short trip to Thailand, the French Embassy's Trade Promotion Department informed Clerc that Central Group top management was trying to contact Carrefour. Clerc accepted a dinner invitation that evening; two days later Thai representatives flew to Taiwan to visit local Carrefour operations and a joint venture was quickly arranged. Since majority ownership had to be Thai, the ownership structure was: Carrefour 40%, Central 40% and a local holding company 20%; Carrefour owned 49% of the holding company.

Central was a family-owned company controlled by the Chirathivat family, wealthy overseas Chinese entrepreneurs. It was the largest retailer (70% of group revenues) in Thailand, operating 11 department stores, 13 supermarkets, two hypermarkets, 30 convenience stores and some specialized chain stores (e.g., Marks & Spencer); it also had franchises for Burger King, Kentucky Fried Chicken and Baskin Robbins. Other business interests were real estate, hotels (partner with the Accor group for Sofitel in Thailand), branded product imports (e.g., Wrangler, Adidas), industry and catering.

Clerc was aware Central's long-term interests might diverge from Carrefour and that Central was interested in management know-how. Nonetheless, he believed in long-term development of the Carrefour concept with Central. Land was sought in anticipation of an initial end 1995 store opening; Thai employees were being trained in Taiwan.

China

From 1980 to 1990, Chinese food market growth exceeded 27%; size estimates for 2000 were US$200 billion. Several Carrefour teams conducted fact finding missions to mainland China in the last few years; they found China well behind most Asian countries in objective economic terms; disposable income was low and private cars rare. However, some Carrefour officials believed these aggregate figures were misleading; they reasoned the market was ripe in some east coast cities and Carrefour should move ahead straightaway. According to Clerc, "China is for Carrefour a step into the unknown."

Carrefour met with government organizations over several months; the possibility of a further alliance between Carrefour and Taiwan partner President Enterprises was raised but no agreements made. In August 1994, Carrefour signed a joint-venture agreement (55% Carrefour ownership) with the Lin Hua Group from Shanghai. Lin Hua managed 15 supermarkets (500 to 1,000 sq. m.) in Shanghai; it was looking for a partner to help develop its activities. Lin Hua initially wanted Carrefour to take over its 15 stores; Carrefour agreed only to manage a 4,500 sq. m. store, commencing 1995.

Other projects were in preparation in Beijing; Monique Thirion, Clerc's Taiwan assistant, was working with Taiwan-trained French managers to develop further activities in China. Carrefour's most important problems were not land (as in Taiwan) but finding the right partners. Anticipated problems were organization and human resource management. Carrefour's goal in China was not immediate profit but to be ready, competent, well known and accepted when the market was really ripe in a few years' time. Carrefour's investment was currently quite limited; the Chinese partner supplied the store.

Other Countries in Asia

In 1993, a Carrefour mission spent two months in Indonesia; it concluded that the country was not yet ripe for Carrefour. Since significant potential was identified in other countries, Indonesia did not justify the investment of money, time and human resources. Nevertheless, Carrefour was contacted by Indonesian groups. Korea was pretty much closed to foreign retailers but Carrefour and Makro were making studies. In Japan, the market was highly concentrated upstream, making discount activities difficult to manage.

Clerc knew that, regardless of the opportunities, Carrefour could not expand to all Asian countries simultaneously because of human resource constraints. For Carrefour in Asia, 1993 was spent researching the best countries for entry, 1994 was the year for signing contracts with partners and landowners, 1995 the year of store openings.

As the European market became saturated with big retail chains, Carrefour and other large retailers were moving to emerging economies in search of development opportunities. Carrefour's increasing revenues were largely driven by international expansion. Although Asia represented a small portion, Carrefour perceived an enormous potential. According to its 1993 Annual Report: the development of Carrefour's presence in Asia was one of the main goals.

Said Paul Halley, President of Promodes, Carrefour's new French competitor in Asia: "Asia will be in the 21st century what the U.S. has been in the 20th: The reference. We will have to be there and react as soon as possible, even though the cultural and language diversity seems to us so complex and difficult to manage."

Decisions

Now fully responsible for Asia, Clerc had to plan a regional development strategy. Investments had been made in Malaysia and Thailand; Carrefour's China projects were a bet on development of a real consumer society. Clerc believed a key competitive advantage was early mover advantage and preemption of available space. Now he had to place these moves in the context of a development plan for the entire region including country choice, market entry timelines, trigger events and so forth.

Exhibit 1: Food Consumption Growth Rate in Asia

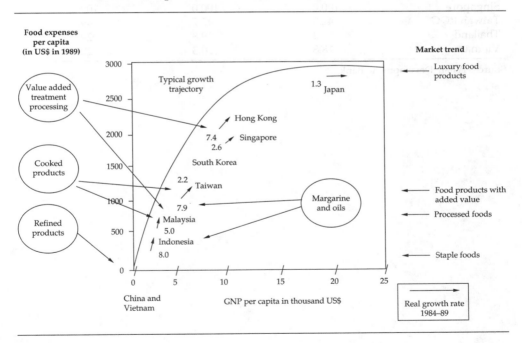

Exhibit 2: Country Economic Indicators

Per capita GNP in Asian economies (US$)				Growth rate of real GDP (%)			
Countries	1989	1990	1991	1989	1990	1991	1992
China PRC	360	370	370	3.7	5.1	7.7	14.4
Hong Kong	10,420	11,700	13,20	2.8	3.2	4.2	5.0
Indonesia	510	560	610	7.5	7.1	6.6	5.8
Korea	4,450	5,450	6,340	6.2	9.2	8.5	4.8
Malaysia	2,120	2,330	2,490	9.2	9.7	8.7	8.5
Singapore	9,540	11,200	12,890	9.2	8.3	6.7	5.8
Taiwan ROC	7,571	7,954	8,788	7.6	4.9	7.2	6.6
Thailand	1,220	1,420	1,580	12.3	11.6	7.9	–
Vietnam	230	150	110	2.7	2.3	4.8	7.5

Urban population as a percentage of the total population			
Countries	1975	1985	1992
China PRC	17.3	25.8	29.4
Hong Kong	90.6	92.9	94.5
Indonesia	19.4	26.2	30.9
Korea	48.0	64.8	74.1
Malaysia	30.7	38.8	44.7
Singapore	100.0	100.0	100.0
Taiwan ROC	42.8	47.7	49.3
Thailand	15.2	19.8	29.0
Vietnam	18.8	20.3	22.8

Source: Asian Development Bank.

Map of Thailand

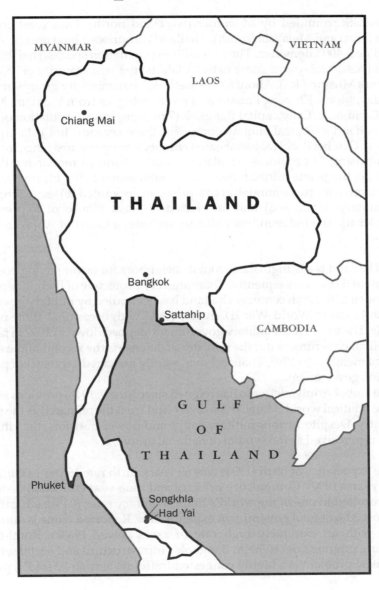

Thailand Overview

Background. Surrounded by Myanmar (west and north), Laos (east and north), Cambodia (east) and Malaysia (south), Thailand comprises a land area of 513,115 sq. km., coastline 2,400 kilometers. The 61.4 million population speaks Thai (official language), Chinese, Malay and some native dialects; the vast majority (95%) are Buddhists, others Muslim (4%). About 82% are ethnic Thai; minority groups are Chinese (14%), Malay, Mons, Khmers, Phuans and recent refugees from Vietnam, Myanmar, Laos and Cambodia. Only capital Bangkok (9 million) has a population of over one million. Thailand's tropical climate comprises three seasons: hot (March to May), rainy (June to October), cool (November to February); temperatures range from 17°C to 36°C. Comprising 73 provinces, Thailand is a constitutional monarchy; the king is head of state, the prime minister head of the government. The bicameral National Assembly (convenes twice annually) comprises an appointed 270-seat Senate (traditionally military-dominated) and an elected 360-seat House of Representatives (four-year term). The independent judiciary includes a Court of Appeals and a Supreme Court.

Political. Thailand is distinguished from its neighbors for never having come under western colonial rule; consequently, Thais are very protective of their independence. Through much of the 20th century, Thailand has been ruled by military governments (allied with Japan in World War II), interspersed with occasional short periods of civilian rule. The most recent military government stepped down in 1992 in favor of an elected civilian government but the minister of defense is the second highest ranking government member. In 1995, Thailand successfully managed a transfer of power to a new coalition government.

King Bhumibol Adulyadej, who has reigned since June 9, 1946, provides stability in an unstable political world. Many Thais revere and trust the monarch as the true ruler of the country. Despite various military coups and power transfers, the king has endured and is perceived as the symbol of national unity.

Social. Life expectancy at birth (1994) was 69 years, birth rate 19 per 1,000; 32.7% are aged 0–14 years (1990). Compulsory primary and nine-year education (extended in 1996) has resulted in one of the world's highest literacy rates (94%); education comprises almost 20% of total government expenditures. Reported crime is quite low (14 per 1,000) with an extremely high rate of cases solved (96%). Rural-to-urban, work-seeking migrants overwhelm Bangkok's infrastructure and social services; its single greatest problem is a highly congested traffic system. In 70 (of 73) provinces, firms with over 20 workers are required to contribute to a compensation fund, financed by payments from employees, employers and the state.

Economy. Thailand is a member of the United Nations (UN), World Bank (WB), International Monetary Fund (IMF), World Trade Organization (WTO), Asia-Pacific Economic Cooperation (APEC) Forum, Asian Development Bank (ADB) and Association of Southeast Asian Nations (ASEAN). GDP per capita is over US$2,500 as the result of fast economic growth, averaging over 8% p.a. for several years, making Thailand one of the leading Asian Tigers and the world's eighth fastest growing economy. About 45% of the labor force works in agriculture, manufacturing 25% and services 30% (1994). In the 1980s, roughly 70% of large-scale investment (30% to 40% from Japan) was concentrated in and around Bangkok.

Regulations on foreign investment relate to product destination. If production is mainly for domestic consumption, foreign ownership is a maximum of 49%; if over 50% of output is for export, foreign ownership can be a majority. If 100% of production is for export, 100% foreign ownership is permitted.

Exports increased rapidly to US$56.9 billion (1996) versus US$20 billion (1989); the government's growth target is 15.5% p.a. until 2000. Rice is the major exported agriculture commodity but Thailand has diversified into products such as rubber, kenaf, maize, sugar and cassava. In part because of significant direct investment (in particular Japanese), the structure of exports has shifted from commodities and labor-intensive products to more high technology and capital-intensive products. Thailand is the largest producer of automobiles and motorcycles in ASEAN. Major export destinations are (1994): U.S. (21%), Japan (16.9%), Singapore (12%). Major import origins are (1994): Japan (30.2%), U.S. (11.6%), Singapore (6.4%). Tourism is also fast growing: 6.6 million visitors in 1994, up from 5.8 million (1993).

In the mid-1990s Thailand's chronic, and increasing, current account deficits (US$13.5 billion [1996], US$8.5 billion [1994]), led to concern of a possible run on the Thai baht.

The Bank of Thailand has functions and responsibilities similar to other central banks (e.g., note-issuing, monetary policy, exchange controls, bank of last resort). In 1993, Thailand granted offshore banking licenses to 47 local and foreign banks. Further liberalization (1994) increased competition for deposits. Foreign banks with offshore licenses under the Bangkok International Banking Facility (BIBF) may open two branches outside Bangkok.

In 1990, Thailand liberalized foreign exchange controls; foreign investors could then transfer dividend and capital gains abroad (up to US$500,000) without central bank approval. In 1994, a second round of liberalization removed most remaining controls. The Securities Exchange of Thailand (SET) began operations in 1975; by mid-1993, 323 companies were listed.

Thailand was the first major victim of the Asian financial crisis. On July 2, it was forced to devalue the baht, leading to a sharp decline in imports (and a current account surplus for the first time in 11 years). At the heart of its deteriorating economic situation were troubled financial institutions and a cash strapped banking system. In August, Thailand agreed to a US$17.2 billion bailout package from the IMF. It immediately suspended 58 finance companies, cut budgets, and raised the external debt ceiling. The financial crisis was compounded by a political crisis and in November, a new government was sworn in, pledging to make economic recovery its primary focus. An economic task force was put together to deal with the IMF as it became clear that the deepening financial crisis might force a request for relaxation of rescue package terms. By late December, Moody's downgraded Thailand's debt (together with Indonesia and South Korea) to junk-bond status. The stock market closed 1997 down 55% from its January 1 level (82% from its peak in 1995); the baht lost 45% of its value against the U.S. dollar in one year.

Infrastructure. Infrastructure development accounts for about 25% of total government expenditure. Thailand has over 18,500 kilometers of national highways and about 34,000 kilometers of provincial highways for its 12.7 million registered motor vehicles (1994). The 2.4 million vehicles registered in Bangkok are the major cause of its traffic nightmare. Bangkok has no mass transit rail system and the future of three planned mass projects remains uncertain. The State Railway operates a 4,600-kilometer rail system (1994); the Port Authority manages the country's five major ports (i.e., Klong Toey [Bangkok], Sattahip and Laem Chabang [Eastern Seaboard], Songkhla and Phuket [in the south]). Bangkok's (Don Muang) airport, used by over 60 scheduled airlines, can handle around 15 million passengers per annum; other international airports are in Chiang Mai, Phuket and Had Yai.

In 1989, electric power generation reached 28 billion kWh, about 500 kWh per capita; generating capacity was 7.1 million kWh. In 1994, Thailand had one telephone per 36 persons; demand for telecommunication services has outpaced the capacity of the Telephone Organization of Thailand (TOT) and the Communication Authority of Thailand. The three million lines in use were insufficient to meet the anticipated requirement of 13.5 million by 2001. By 1997, a joint venture between Charoen Pokphand (CP) and British Telecom increased availability to one telephone per 13.5 persons.

An important project, on the "drawing board" for many years, is the Kra Canal, labeled "Asia's Suez or Panama Canal." The Kra Canal would cut across Thailand (from the Indian Ocean to the Gulf of Thailand), cost about US$20 billion. The canal would bypass the congested Straits of Malacca and reduce the sea voyage from West to East Asia by up to 3,000 kilometers (three days sailing each way). It would cause a major realignment of economic power in Southeast Asia inasmuch as trade would also bypass one of the region's major trading hubs, Singapore, port of call for 70% of strait traffic. Less ambitious plans embracing a "Land bridge" concept (two ports on opposite sides of the Kra Isthmus linked by road, rail and an oil pipeline) are also under consideration.

Statistics*	June 1991	June 1997	Statistics*	June 1991	June 1997
Per capita GNP	US$1,418	US$2,680	Infant mortality/1,000	24	26
GDP growth	10.0%	8.5%	Life expectancy (yrs)	n/a	69
Savings (GNP)	n/a	36%	Literacy rate	8.88%	93.8%
Inflation (CPI)	6.0%	4.3%	People per tel.	53.0	13.5
Foreign debt (in billion)	US$27.3	US$88	People per doctor	5,564	4,361
Pop. (million)	54.6	61.4%	People per TV	n/a	8.8
Urban pop.	n/a	36%	Calorie intake (cals)	n/a	2,443
Pop. growth	1.4%	1.5%			

*Secured from *Asiaweek*.

Case 56

Gilman Office Automation, Bangkok, Thailand[1]

Jake Vigoda, Hellmut Schutte
INSEAD, Fontainebleau, France

Now that we have successfully rebuilt the business from its poor image under the previous distributor, we need to move from third to first in market share ... June 29, 1990.

Charnchai Leelawatanasuk (41) CEO Gilman Office Automation (Thailand) believed gaining market leadership was critical for his business, distribution of Ricoh copiers in Thailand. Julian Fryett, marketing manager, agreed: "New firms continue to enter and gaining market share is difficult. We should at least achieve Gilman's Hong Kong market share for Ricoh copiers. After all, Ricoh is market leader in Japan."

Charnchai had to define his overall strategy for the Thai market: "We have to decide on our product lines, the principals to work with and which network of agents and dealers to use ..." Fryett and Charnchai each stated: "We are approaching a B250 million firm; in five years we must be B1 billion."[2] Each knew his promotion in the Inchcape Group largely depended on creating a large and profitable company. Charnchai might expect a more important role in Inchcape Thailand; Fryett could expect to continue receiving high profile assignments in Hong Kong and Asia Pacific with Inchcape Pacific.

୫୦୪୬

Ricoh in Thailand

For over 20 years, Ricoh copiers were distributed in Thailand by Fantaract Ltd., a tightly-held, Chinese family-owned firm. In the early 1980s, Ricoh was market leader.

---

[1] This case was prepared by Jake Vigoda, MBA participant, under the supervision of Hellmut Schutte, Professor at INSEAD. It is intended to be used as a basis for class discussion rather than to illustrate either effective or ineffective handling of an administrative situation. Reprinted with the permission of INSEAD. Copyright 1994 INSEAD-EAC, Fontainebleau, France.
[2] US$1 was roughly equivalent to 25 baht.

However, as both Fantaract and the copier business expanded, the Thai market became more competitive and some Fantaract management practices were no longer appropriate. Most notable, the family patriarch did not trust outside family members, accept distribution of power or share company information with non-family associates.

Unknown to Ricoh, in addition to a sizable business distributing Canon cameras, Fantaract distributed Minolta copiers through a wholly owned subsidiary. Ricoh also believed Fantaract may have been involved in other questionable distributorship practices. Fantaract could not retain good management and well-trained staff; thus, although it handled import logistics, little real value was added in distribution. Ricoh sustained market leadership because of early entry advantages and technical copier leadership. As these advantages eroded, so did market share.

Over time, the Fantaract family lost control of its staff and business procedures. By 1984, accounts receivable were out of control; often, it was unable to find buyers and collect on invoices. "Hiding buyers" was a service offered by some sales staff! In addition, technical service staff sold parts and consumables to Fantaract customers from non-Fantaract distributors for personal profit; imitation parts were sold at prices set for Ricoh parts and consumables produced in Japan. By 1985, Fantaract faced bankruptcy; copier sales declined from 608 (1982) to 273 (1985).

Gilman Office Machines (Hong Kong), a wholly owned subsidiary of the Inchcape Group, had successfully sold Ricoh copiers in Hong Kong for almost 20 years. Inchcape heard about the Thai situation from Ricoh contacts and offered to buy the distribution rights for Ricoh copiers from Fantaract. Fantaract refused.

In the first ten months of 1986, Fantaract failed to sell a single machine; in October 1986, it filed for bankruptcy. In November 1986, Gilman acquired the distribution contract for free. Peter Bond, an expatriate Inchcape manager from Hong Kong, moved to Thailand to build up the business.

Growth of Gilman in Thailand

In November 1986, Gilman Office Automation was formed to take over distribution of Ricoh copiers in Thailand. Although legally a subsidiary company of Anglo-Thai, a wholly owned subsidiary of Inchcape Thailand, Gilman Office Automation reported to Inchcape Pacific in Hong Kong through the Business Machines Group. Affiliate companies included Gilman Office Machines and Repromac (also a distributor of office machines) in Hong Kong, Dodwell Business Machines in Hong Kong and Japan, and DBE in Australia.

Inchcape PLC., an international services and marketing group headquartered in London, was the largest European trading company. Organized into ten business streams and regional sectors, Business Machines was one of the smallest business streams. The Business Machines group, headquartered in Hong Kong, marketed and distributed office equipment in the Asia-Pacific region. The Business Machines director reported to the Chairman of Inchcape Pacific Limited, Inchcape's regional subsidiary (Figure 1).

Figure 1: Inchcape Organization Chart

Inchcape's corporate philosophy was to use local management wherever possible. Qualified Thai management was not available when Gilman took over Ricoh in Thailand; Gilman believed Peter Bond's experience in copier products would shorten the time required to restore the company to profitability. In January 1987, Gilman sold the first Ricoh copier in Thailand in over a year; in the next 12 months, sales averaged 40 machines per month.

Most new staff were recruited from Fantaract; Bond decided to leverage customer contacts and Ricoh experience from the previous sales and technical service staffs. Simultaneously, Gilman benefited from introduction of a new line of Ricoh dry toner copiers. Ricoh was late in matching competitors' switch to dry toner copiers. Indeed, in its final years, Fantaract had to sell Ricoh's liquid type toner machines against competitors' dry toner machines.

Charnchai joined Inchcape (Thailand) in 1971; he previously ran Fuji Film distribution for another Inchcape (Thailand) subsidiary, Borneo (Thailand) Co. Ltd. In June 1988, he was promoted to CEO of Gilman Office Automation; Bond returned to Hong Kong as Inchcape felt that Gilman could be run by local management.

In June 1989, Julian Fryett, 26, was recruited from Inchcape's management training program. Half Thai, half English, Fryett was raised in England since age three but had visited Thailand on several occasions. On joining Gilman, he could neither speak nor read Thai; within one year he could speak Thai well and read marginally.

Charnchai's initial strategy was to build the leading service organization in Thailand: he believed service reputation sold machines and that service contracts, including spare parts and machine maintenance, added to revenues. As business growth slowed, he believed service would represent a growing fraction of total revenues. In his first 18 months, Charnchai added Pitney Bowes facsimile machines, GBC binding machines and 3M overhead projectors to Gilman's product line. Staff expanded to 28 salesmen, 45 servicemen; a sales and service outlet was opened in Had Yai (800 kilometers south of Bangkok).

Charnchai also rebuilt a network of agents throughout Thailand by improving communication and contacts with company staff, increasing availability of spare parts and consumables inventory, faster delivery, improving point of sale and promotional support and faster response time to service requests. He and Fryett met regularly with dealers seeking to anticipate the evolution of distribution channels. Many agents previously sold Ricoh machines in affiliation with Fantaract but, in the final years of Fantaract's tenure, switched to other suppliers because of inability to secure spare parts, service or reliable deliveries. Charnchai and Fryett kept a close eye on shipments per dealer and accounts receivables, actively supported dealers that moved machines and paid bills promptly, and paid close attention to delivery, promotion and service requirements.

Charnchai and Fryett closely studied salesman and technical service staff performance; they charted salesman performance in unit and baht sales per month, and service staff performance by number of daily service calls, time per call and the time to next machine failure after the service call. They released salesmen and servicemen who consistently under-performed, regardless of length of tenure. They also attempted to instill a service and customer first mentality throughout Gilman by example, training, reminders and reprimands. They were very conscious of targets and were quick to reward staff who exceeded them.

Gilman was also seeking to improve communications with Ricoh. It was lobbying Ricoh aggressively for shorter lead times on orders and lower transfer prices on certain machine models. It was trying to identify unique characteristics of the Thai market that could be better served with modified products, including a high quality/low speed copier for copy service centers. In 1990, Charnchai estimated Gilman would deliver an average of over 120 machines per month, 14% market share. He expected Gilman's profit to grow substantially (Table 1).

Table 1: Profit and Loss Statement, Gilman Office Automation (millions baht)

	1987	1988	1989	1990 (Jan–June)
Sales	59.3	124.9	165.6	110.0
Cost of sales				
Cost of goods	37.1	77.0	94.7	59.4
Warranty costs	0.1	0.1	0.2	–
Stock depreciation	0.4	7.8	5.9	3.0
Others	0.1	1.2	1.1	1.1
Total	37.7	86.1	101.9	63.5
Gross profit	21.6	38.8	63.7	46.5
Overheads				
Staff commission	2.3	4.6	7.3	5.8
Direct overheads	20.3	26.3	33.0	22.0
Depreciation (fixed assets)	2.4	3.4	5.6	4.6
Total	25.0	34.3	45.9	32.4
Trading profit	−3.4	4.5	17.8	14.1

Relationship with Ricoh

Charnchai believed Gilman's position as Ricoh distributor was safe for the next five years. Gilman successfully rebuilt Ricoh's reputation in Thailand and developed a close network of agents and a dedicated customer base. Although Ricoh was unlikely to revoke the distribution agreement in the short term, Charnchai believed he needed to secure leading market share for Ricoh to reinforce sustainability of the contract. He felt Ricoh would remain highly committed to distributors that performed. However, Gilman was unable to win distribution rights for Ricoh facsimile machines. Under Fantaract's tenure, Ricoh awarded the facsimile contract to a competitor. As long as the competitor continued to perform well, Charnchai did not expect to secure this contract.

Charnchai knew from experience that distributors always ran the risk of losing distribution rights. For example, if Ricoh wanted greater control and stability with its product lines, it might establish a subsidiary company. However, if Ricoh wanted to form a joint venture, Gilman would be the most likely candidate for local partner. Personally, Charnchai preferred the independence, flexibility and control over cash flow that Gilman enjoyed as an independent company and was disinclined to change. Should Ricoh opt to start manufacturing locally, it might approach one of Inchcape's holding companies to be a local partner. Under current Thai investment promotion law, Ricoh, if deemed eligible by the Board of Investment, could only establish a distribution, sales and service subsidiary, or a manufacturing facility restricted to 49% ownership.

Ricoh was one of Japan's leading office equipment makers; it was market share leader in both copiers and fax machines. Although it performed well in Hong Kong, Ricoh failed to match its domestic performance elsewhere in the world. Of its $5.2 billion 1989 sales, 63% was domestic; 50% of export sales was to OEMs, but 100% of Asian sales was brand-name products.

Affiliation with Inchcape Ltd.

Inchcape subsidiaries had operated in Thailand for over 130 years; in revenue terms, the Inchcape Group was the largest multinational in Thailand. Because of its long-standing presence and establishment prior to most laws regulating foreign ownership of businesses and properties, it benefited from several privileges and exemptions under Thai law. Essentially, it operated with both the benefits of a foreign company and the rights of a local company. It also had a deep in-house knowledge of the Thai business community and government machinery.

Inchcape (Thailand) had significant in-house management expertise. It introduced western business practices and theory into local businesses: from mission statements and customer feedback to work scheduling and working capital management. When appropriate, it encouraged local and expatriate managers to adapt to local business practices. Inchcape (Thailand) provided access to capital. Gilman could secure short- or long-term funds easily and quickly at the lowest prime rates, a significant advantage in Thailand where local money markets were quite tight.

As part of Inchcape Pacific Business Machines Group, Gilman benefited from specific business stream expertise encompassing setting up businesses, training sales and service staff, marketing, product knowledge, administration and compensation schemes. Gilman continued to benefit from Inchcape's ability to reach potential principals around the world, to train staff at all levels and to share knowledge. Inchcape distributed Mita copiers in Hong Kong, Konica copiers in Hong Kong and Singapore and Ricoh copiers in Australia, Thailand and Hong Kong. Thai executives were in continuous contact with counterparts in these firms and were open to sharing new ideas and performance benchmarks (e.g., market share, profitability, sales per salesman). Inchcape recently approached Charnchai with several new products including check handling equipment for banks and letter handling equipment for post offices and large corporations. As Fryett explained:

> We benefit from being part of Inchcape. We get together; they're good lads, we help each other out. In Hong Kong, Gilman also distributes Ricoh copiers and we share ideas. We can also take advantage of other Inchcape businesses, like shipping. They also use our copiers; Inchcape (Thailand) is a large rental customer.

Although the Inchcape Pacific and Gilman philosophy was supportive of entrepreneurial, locally-driven country groups, Inchcape sought to bind the different companies in a cohesive, focused direction in Business Machines. As Charnchai considered his options, he knew few boundaries would be imposed by Inchcape Pacific (Exhibit 1).

The Thai Copier Market, 1990

Market size, based on MITI export statistics and revised upward to account for copiers shipped through Singapore and Hong Kong, assumed that 100% of copiers sold in Thailand were imported from Japan (Table 2). Ricoh 1982 sales represented a decline from an estimated 20% market share peak. This decline corresponded to increasing financial and managerial difficulties at Fantaract and the late introduction of new copier models. Charnchai attributed the 1984 market decline to saturation of the copy service center market and slow initial growth in the private business market resulting, in part, from a short recession following devaluation of the baht.

In 1987, Ricoh sales responded to initiation of the Gilman distribution contract and introduction of dry toner copiers (Table 3). In 1990, sales were projected from estimates of total growth in the Thai industrial sector (13%) and Thai real GNP growth (9%). In 1989, sales fluctuated on average 49% from month-to-month, up from 1988's 23% monthly variation. Sales forecasting was therefore a very difficult task. Gilman sold from inventory and re-ordered from Ricoh once a month. Current lead time on orders was five months: four months' advance orders on shipments from Ricoh and one month to clear customs and port backlogs. Gilman had been unable to model sales fluctuations in total or unit sales, or to correlate expected sales to supporting data (e.g., previous months' sales calls).

Table 2: Market Size and Growth

Year	Exports from Japan	Market growth	Ricoh	Market share
1982	3,743		608	16.2%
1983	5,389	44.0%	542	10.1%
1984	4,021	25.4%	493	12.3%
1985	3,662	−8.9%	273	7.5%
1986	3,736	2.0%	0	0.0%
1987	5,740	53.6%	482	8.4%
1988	8,110	41.3%	926	11.4%
1989	9,300	14.7%	1,148	12.3%
1990 (est.)	10,700	15.1%	1,500	14.0%

Table 3: Gilman Sales by Copier Type

Product type	Revenue (millions of baht and % of total)							
	1987		1988		1989		1990 (est.)	
Copier sales	40	62%	75	65%	91	60%	139	63%
Rental copy charge	4	6%	8	7%	14	9%	18	8%
Supplies	13	21%	22	19%	30	19%	47	21%
Service/maintenance fees	7	11%	10	9%	17	11%	18	8%
Total	64		115		152		222	

Market shares in Japan were Ricoh (35%), Canon (27%), Fuji-Xerox (21%), Sharp (7%) based on an estimated 2,550,000 machines in the field. In Thailand, Ricoh's largest market share was in mid-range copiers (Table 4). In Japan, Ricoh dominated the high end of the market; most of these machines had almost no market potential in Thailand.

Table 4: Unit Market Share Estimates

Brand	1988	1989	1990	In the field	Brand	1988	1989	1990	In the field
Fuji-Xerox	24%	26%	25%	26%	Sharp	5%	5%	5%	5%
Mita	22%	21%	20%	21%	Toshiba	3%	4%	4%	4%
Canon	16%	14%	14%	14%	Panasonic	2%	1%	1%	1%
Ricoh	11%	12%	14%	13%	Others[3]	5%	4%	3%	3%
Minolta	6%	8%	8%	8%	Total	100%	100%	100%	100%
Konica	6%	5%	6%	5%	Units	8,110	9,300	10,700	30,500

---

[3] Primarily included OEMs, Selex, Gestetner and Rex Rotary.

In 1989, Gilman's Ricoh sales were 56% in Bangkok, 44% upcountry (Table 5); most upcountry purchases were made directly from Bangkok outlets. In general, Thais believed merchandise could always be purchased more cheaply in Bangkok and would often order direct from the capital without checking local prices or attempting to identify local agents. Gilman's policy was to quote upcountry customers' rates set by Gilman agents in provinces where agents were established. However, Gilman had not decided how to credit sales made directly by Gilman salesmen in an agent's territory. Competitor Canon allowed salesmen to quote rates in competition with local agents; in contrast, Fuji-Xerox directed all sales through the authorized Xerox branch in each customer's region.

Gilman used a network of agents/dealers in the north (9), northeast (10), central (8), south (7), east (4). Annual sales per agent varied from five to forty copiers for agents in major cities; from three to twenty copiers for agents in smaller provincial towns (Table 6). In addition to carrying Ricoh machines, agents might also represent two to five different manufacturers. Mita was the dominant competitor in government sales, typically secured by tender offer. Price was usually the most critical purchase decision factor; service quality was not considered significant in this market.

Table 5: Market Segmentation

	1989	1990	1991	1992	End user	1989	1990	1991	1992
Bangkok	50	47	44	40	Private	70%	80%	82%	84%
Upcountry	50	53	56	60	Government	30%	20%	18%	16%

Table 6: Purchase Patterns by End User

Customer size	Preferred finance mode	Machine size (cpm)[4]	Estimated market growth
Large corporations B500m+	1) rent 2) buy	20–45	15%
Medium corporations B500m–B500m	1) buy 2) rent	15–30	20%
Small offices < B100m	1) buy 2) lease	12–20	15%
Copy service centers < B100m	1) lease 2) buy	30–45	5%
Government sector	1) tender	12–20	5%

Rental: No installation and service charge; machines installed with a meter and charged on a copies per month basis.
Lease: Machines purchased by a finance company and lent to the customer; monthly payments.
Sale: Machines bought outright by the customer; financing arranged independently.

---

[4] cpm-copies per minute. As machine capacity increased, other features increased also: e.g., size, image clarity, job processing capabilities.

Competitors believed Fuji-Xerox had an advantage in rental. As a joint venture, it was easier to finance inventory costs for rental machines. Fuji-Xerox was also believed to have more flexible evaluation criteria than Gilman; for example, it was apparently not as concerned to maximize return on average business assets (ROABA) (Table 7).

Table 7:   Competitor Profiles

Brand	Distributor and product portfolio
Fuji-Xerox (26%)	• Thai Xerographic System Ltd.: Joint venture of Fuji-Xerox (49%) and local partnership (51%). Incorporated, 1978. Previously a wholly owned subsidiary of Fuji-Xerox. Fuji-Xerox had never used distributors in Thailand. • Distributes all Fuji-Xerox products, predominantly copiers and fax machines. • Dominates high end copier market, measured by copy quality and speed; perhaps as much as 70% high end market share.
Mita (21%)	• Mita (Thailand) Ltd.: Joint venture of Mita (49%) and partner from previous distributor (51%). Established, 1984. Previously used local distributor. Distributes all Mita products, specifically copiers and fax machines. • Dominates low end copier market. Poor service reputation.
Canon (14%)	• FMA Corporation: Fully independent Thai distributor of Canon for over 20 years. Won contract from previous Ricoh distributor. Exploring joint venture with Canon. • Distributes all Canon business machines, including copiers, typewriters, computers, printers, fax machines and calculators. • Dominates the personal copier market.
Minolta (8%)	• Bangkok Business Equipment Ltd.: Fully independent distributor of office equipment. Believed to be currently exploring a joint venture with Minolta.
Konica (5%)	• Inter Far East Engineering: Public company, major shareholder Saha Patanapibul Group, a major Thai conglomerate with holdings in computer and telecommunication companies.
Sharp (5%)	• The Bangkok Trading Company Ltd.: Joint venture (1987) between Sharp (49%) and previous distributor of same name for over 60 years (51%). • Distributes all Sharp consumer electronics (excluding white goods).
Toshiba (4%)	• Chevalier Office Automation (COA): Wholly owned subsidiary of COA (Hong Kong). • Distributes most Toshiba business/office machines. Handled Toshiba copiers since late 1988.
Panasonic (1%)	• Siew National Sales & Service Ltd.: Joint venture of Matsushita (49%) and previous distributor of National products (51%). Established 21 years ago. • Distributes all Matsushita products, including Panasonic, National and Technics brand names.

Gilman salesmen's take-home pay, 30% to 50% salary, 50% to 70% commission and bonus, averaged B15,000 per month. Gilman technicians' salary, 50% to 70% salary, 30% to 50% commission and bonus, averaged B10,000.

Average monthly sales per salesman was three units per month in Bangkok, nine units per month upcountry; Gilman believed it led the Thai market in salesman efficiency. By contrast, Thai Xerographic was estimated to average two sales per month per salesman. Charnchai planned to continue increasing targets; in Hong Kong, Gilman achieved 15 sales per month per salesman (Table 8).

Gilman believed it led in response to emergency maintenance calls; average six hours, 80% of calls two to eight hours, matching Fuji-Xerox. However, Fuji-Xerox segmented customers, offering varying grades of service. Class A customers had access to standby service, one to four hours; class B, four to eight hours; class C, six to 12 hours. Customers did not choose a service class; Fuji-Xerox assigned customers based on price sensitivity, service requirements and customer importance. Charnchai believed service response time should be reduced further. However, should he build capacity to reduce average service time or differentiate customers like Fuji-Xerox?

Except for Fuji-Xerox, all companies sold in Bangkok from a central office location. Fuji-Xerox had four wholly owned sales and service outlets throughout Bangkok set up as upscale copy service centers, with an open receiving area to display models. These centers carried large inventories of consumables and spare parts.

For upcountry sales, Fuji-Xerox was building a network of wholly owned outlets, identical in structure to those in Bangkok. Sharp and Matsushita sold via established electric appliance stores throughout Thailand; inventory and display space were usually tight. All other companies sold through a combination of dedicated upcountry salesmen for direct sales, limited branch networks and independent agents. Independent agents carried competing models but offered an intimate knowledge of the business community, fast service and access to consumables.

Estimated Media Spending, 1989

Mita made the most extensive use of media, 36% of total copier advertising expenditures in print, radio and television. Minolta, Ricoh, Toshiba and Sharp spent one third to one half as much. Mita also used paste-up advertising: stickers and A4 size posters were placed on telephone booths, light poles, rain shelters, above urinals and on construction facades.

Table 8: Sales and Distribution Channels

Brand	No. of offices	Sales staff	Service staff	Brand	No. of offices	Sales staff	Service staff
Fuji-Xerox	10	45	120	Minolta	1	25	35
Mita	2	50	75	Konika	1	20	25
Canon	1	30	65	Sharp	1	15	30
Ricoh	2	28	45	Toshiba	1	10	20
				Panasonic	1	8	10

The Thai media responded well to press releases; however, only Fuji-Xerox and Mita made routine use of this channel for copiers. Fuji-Xerox was widely cited for new product releases, exhibitions, promotions, appointments, training, seminars and financial results. It was recognized as one of the best run local multinationals. Mita's periodic donations of copiers to the Royal Family and selected government groups were widely reported by all television networks on prime-time news.

The officially quoted list price was far above the prices at which the copiers were actually sold to business, dealers or the government. Contribution margins per copier were 45%, based on a commercial price of 57.0 baht; for sales to the government margins dropped to 33%. Although these margins were roughly comparable for all models, service costs decreased and sales costs increased, as a percent of total cost, as machine size increased. Contribution margins averaged 46% on spare parts, 60% on rental machines and 44% on machine service (Table 9).

Table 9: Tax and Cost Data Per Machine

Line item	Copier cost	Line item	Copier cost
FOB	Y 98.5	List price	B 115.0
	1.5		
Freight charge CIF	100.0	Commercial price	B 57.0
Import duty	40.0	Dealer price	B 52.0
B&M taxes	28.9	Government price	B 47.0
Clearing charge	1.0		
Landed cost	Y 170.0 = B 31.4 (100 yen = 18.5 baht)		

The Thai Office Automation Market, 1990

Paralleling double digit economic growth for the previous three years, and close to 9% average in the 1980s, office automation equipment sales in Thailand boomed. The largest categories were electronic machines (e.g., calculators, key punches, typewriters, computers, key telephones, mobile telephones, computer systems, facsimile machines, data processing, data support services and local communications exchanges) and accessories (e.g., stands, furniture, binders, laminators). Growth in office automation equipment sales was expected to exceed 20% for 1989–90; projected growth rates in the U.S., Europe and Japan were under 10%. In recent years, growth of personal computers and related products exceeded 40% p.a. Thailand was often referred to as the fastest growing office automation market in the world. Analysts expected high growth to continue for at least the next three years and perhaps through the 1990s. These forecasts were based on new office space and plant construction coming on stream, anticipated steady demand and Thailand's ability to absorb this new investment.

All major principals were represented by distributors, joint ventures or wholly owned subsidiaries. Some (e.g., IBM, Kodak, Philips) were active in Thailand for over 20 years through wholly owned subsidiaries. In addition, Thailand had long-standing ties with business communities in South Korea, Taiwan, Hong Kong and Singapore. Companies from these countries, especially those dealing in personal computers and telecommunications equipment, were well represented; Thailand was one of the world's fastest growing markets and one of the most competitive.

The Thai government had not yet resolved various issues concerning intellectual property rights, subscription to international copyright agreements and breach of faith contract disputes. Pending resolution, several principals avoided direct investment leading to technology transfer. However, the government was under pressure to ease regulations on data communication.

Observers believed that infrastructure problems, notably lack of cellular and key telephone exchanges, were holding up market development; the waiting list for telephone lines was measured in years, not months. The government was taking a leading role and installing a nationwide network of fiber optic cable and microwave transmission-receiving towers, together with state-of-the-art satellite data communication capabilities. The goal: make Bangkok the Indo-Chinese subcontinent's service/information center, matching many of Singapore's features.

Taxation on fully built-up electronic machines, 35% to over 70%, restricted buyers to larger firms and those involved in international transactions. Following current GATT negotiations, analysts expected the government to lower taxes, possibly to 20% to 35%. Such action would broaden the market in all segments, most significantly in small- to medium-sized internationally competitive firms.

The industry suffered a serious lack of skilled staff. Firms had to be willing to invest in expatriates (e.g., programmers, software and data support system developers) and overseas training of technicians, maintenance and repairmen, as well as systems and applications installers.

Several local firms sought to build strong positions in office automation equipment distribution by developing applications and service staff, making binding contracts with principals, local manufacturing and captive retail outlets. The most powerful, eight-year old Sahaviriya, was projected to reach 1 billion baht revenues in 1990. Its estimated market share in computers, peripherals and data communication devices was 15% to 20%. It took a leading role in developing standards for the Thai market, increased support staff to 400 and was building an extensive upcountry distribution network.

The Thai Economic Outlook, 1990

Economists predicted the current economic expansion would continue; Bangkok Bank (the largest local bank) estimated 10% economic growth, 14% manufacturing, 4% agricultural. Neither inflation nor pressure on wage rates was a significant concern; however, land prices were increasing dramatically. The Consumer Price Index was expected to increase by 6% in 1990, up from a ten-year average of 2.2%.

The Thai government had managed foreign debt well; despite a historically low savings rate, the current account deficit was only 3.5% of GDP; debt service ratio, 13.8%; external debt, 39.6% of GDP. The government ran a balanced budget for fiscal years 1987 to 1989; a small budget surplus was projected in fiscal 1991. There was no external pressure for structural reform of the economy nor for currency revaluation. Exchange rates were fixed to a basket of currencies, predominantly the U.S. dollar and the yen. The Bank of Thailand maintained a consistent policy; exchange rates only moved in a marginal band around the dollar, mostly in response to dollar/yen changes. Interest rates on deposits were controlled, effectively capping commercial lending rates at 16% to 17%.

The most serious threat to the economy was strain on the existing infrastructure: rail, road and port facilities, industrial and municipal facilities, wastewater disposal and telecommunications. Of equal concern was lack of skilled labor and educational facilities. Nonetheless, foreign investment remained strong. Recent polls of Japanese business indicated Thailand was the leading destination for foreign investment in Southeast Asia. Of over 1,000 foreign investment projects in new industries approved by the Board of Investment from 1988 to 1989, only a few hundred had commenced implementation. Total foreign investment in new projects was expected to grow by 150%; net direct investment in existing projects would expand by 45%.

The Tactical Plan for Copiers, July 1990

Charnchai wanted his staff to aim to "be better than our competitors." He laid out a tactical plan to "encircle them" and "pick at their business, one copier at a time." Charnchai evaluated opportunities for competitive advantage over market leaders in Thailand. Gilman had little control over hardware, price, availability, features and the Ricoh brand name. It had greater control over availability and breadth of consumables. It had complete control over service and maintenance; Charnchai decided Gilman should excel by distinguishing its distribution network and retail concept. He had many ideas, but had to decide which activities to prioritize.

The Strategic Questions for Gilman, July 1990

Charnchai's first goal was to achieve lead market share in copiers; he knew he should also consider long-term product line development and market position. Gilman could lose the Ricoh business at any time since it could not influence the competitiveness of Ricoh machines. Ricoh currently represented over 90% of Gilman revenues.

Charnchai developed a long-range vision for Gilman: "To be the best office equipment supplier in Thailand for service quality, distinguished by exceptional responsiveness to customer needs." He broadened his description of potential product mix to "anything that goes into an office." He considered typewriters, printers, computers, key telephones even office furniture. He expected to examine acquiring computer distribution within two years.

No growth possibilities outside Ricoh were worked out in detail. Charnchai mostly struggled with copiers: what niche should it fill in the market; how should upcountry sales channels be built; who should be its dealers/agents; how should they be bound to Gilman; what they should look like; what should be their range of products and services? Charnchai believed long-term strategy could evolve in several directions. Gilman could become involved in the distribution of unrelated products through

Inchcape (e.g., check handling and mail handling equipment); it could also move further into retail.

Fryett's first priority, like Charnchai, was to overtake Gilman's competitors. However, he was continually examining Gilman's long-range vision and formula for the entire Business Stream Group. Should it invest resources to dominate the copier business and plan on an eventual joint venture with Ricoh? Should it build a flexible distribution and retail network to allow it to pick and switch among principals as the dominant business machines marketing and distribution firm in all Inchcape Pacific's countries?

Charnchai concluded: "First we beat our competitors, then we beat Sahaviriya ..."

Exhibit 1: Inchcape Pacific – Mission and Goals

Statement:

1. Inchcape Pacific will be the clear market leader in specialized marketing and services in the Pacific region.
2. We shall be judged to be the most successful organization in our chosen markets by our customers, our principals, our staff and our shareholders.
3. We shall differentiate ourselves as a successful organization, by the value we add to our products and services and by the quality of our people.

Our goals:

1. To consolidate our leading position in Hong Kong and to expand each of our business streams regionally, to achieve a significant position in all of the other major markets.
2. To be recognized as a highly commercial organization which creates market opportunities, achieves above average growth and enhances value within our five core businesses.
3. To respond to new markets, products and technology in our core businesses so that change and improvement is synonymous with the Inchcape style.
4. To achieve success through individual and team excellence rather than the application of added cost.
5. To be known for the high caliber, dynamism and integrity of our people. We shall encourage and develop their talents, recognize and reward our people's achievements, and ensure that they share in the company's success.
6. To develop decentralized and accountable business unit management thus reducing the reliance on central controls.
7. To listen to our customers, principals and employees and seek to satisfy their needs as they relate to our business.

Our core values:

1. We care about our customers and the way in which we satisfy their needs.
2. We care about our principals and the way in which we represent them.
3. We care about our people and the way in which we manage them.

Case 57

Maverick Bank

Ho Yuen Ching, Michelle
The Hong Kong University of Science and Technology

Noel Capon
Graduate School of Business, Columbia University

On a cool humid night in May 1995, Mr. Joseph Poon gazed from his window in Maverick Bank's Hopewell Center office overlooking Victoria Harbor in Hong Kong, contemplating the Bank's Asian expansion strategy. His exhausting four-hour conference with key bank executives to discuss the feasibility of Hong Kong banks entering the emerging credit card Chinese market finished only one hour ago. On his desk was the Thailand Credit Card Report, commissioned in mid-1994, just received from the Bank's Research Department. Poon was considering how to assess the attractiveness of each country's credit card market for potential Maverick Bank entry; how prepared the bank should be to expand to less mature markets; and what priorities should be placed on China and Thailand if entry seemed warranted. In the near term, entry would have to be limited to at most one of the two countries.

๛

Company Background

Maverick Bank, headquartered in New York, was a powerful international bank. As Maverick's Asian Regional Head stationed in Hong Kong, Poon was responsible for bank operations in Hong Kong, Taiwan, China, Thailand and Singapore. Established in the 1940s, present in over 80 countries, Maverick was a leader in developing and using sophisticated information technology systems for both retail and corporate sectors. Maverick's well-earned reputation was for "excellent quality banking services and credit products around the world."

Maverick Bank's mission was: "To provide the best quality financial services to our customers and the best value to our investors." Over the decades, an enviable reputation and loyalty among depositors and investors were earned by its conservative approach. Nevertheless, to survive intensifying competitive pressure worldwide, the board of directors issued directives for a more aggressive stance to market expansion.

Despite strong presence in the West, Maverick had a relatively low profile in Asian markets. As a result, Poon spent much effort scouting for new, lucrative opportunities in the region.

Maverick's fastest growing sector was credit card operations; it was affiliated with both Visa and MasterCard. In 1994, it issued 18% more cards worldwide than in 1993. Maverick had card operations in several Asian countries (e.g., Hong Kong, Japan, Taiwan) but was a follower, slow to enter; as a result, market shares in these countries were relatively small. Considering China and Thailand, Maverick had the opportunity to be among the first credit card issuers entering these potentially lucrative markets. Maverick currently had two branches in China (Shanghai and Shenzhen) and one in Thailand (Bangkok) serving corporate customers. Poon examined the materials on his desk. The night was young ...

China Background

Formerly recognized as a "poor third-world country," as the result of economic reforms in the 1980s and early 1990s, China evolved into a versatile, rapidly growing economy. Its 1.2 billion population enjoyed an ever increasing per capita income. Commentators consistently predicted that China would become the world's largest economy within the next decade (Exhibit 1).

Consumers

Traditionally in China, living without saving money was considered shameful, so people tended to save; the younger generation mainly for marriage, middle-aged and older people for retirement. However, the desire for better living standards led young people, especially those in cities, to spend rather than save. Installment payments were gaining increased acceptance for durables (e.g., air-conditioners, refrigerators).

A January 1995 study conducted by the Beijing City Statistics Bureau found the average financial assets of an average household in Beijing was RMB17,000 (US$1,910) comprising: bank savings 73%, securities 19.3%, cash-in-hand 7.3%, other 0.4%.

Although official statistics indicated average Chinese annual income at approximately US$320 (1994), many felt this did not indicate real earnings and buying power, in part due to large urban/rural differences. McKinsey & Co., which believed Chinese with annual per capita incomes over US$1,000 represented China's real consumer market, estimated average Chinese purchasing power almost 30% above published figures, indicating a potential "consumer credit market" of 70 million. McKinsey defined as "rich people" those with incomes over US$2,400, 28 million in 1993, forecast to grow to 66 million by 2003; the US$1,000 to US$2,400 earners were projected to grow to 240 million.

The Retail Market

According to Dun and Bradstreet, in April 1995 only 3.9 million of China's 12.9 million stores were located in cities. In 1994, retail sales of consumer goods were

RMB1,600 billion (US$179.8 billion), up 30% (7% in real terms) from 1993. Rapid income growth and large savings underpinned the spending surge. For sheer volume, only a few world stores could match Shanghai Hualian Department Store; on a peak shopping day an estimated 300,000 customers spent RMB7 million (US$790,000).

The Banking Industry

Historically, China's banking industry was limited to local banks. In the early 1980s, China allowed foreign bank entry to encourage foreign investment and competition in the local banking industry; foreign banks could set up representative offices and branches in specific regions. After running a representative office for three years, foreign banks might register the entity as a bank, capital requirement RMB10 billion; to register a branch required RMB20 billion. By end 1993, over 220 representative offices were opened by foreign financial enterprises; over 50 foreign bank branches were opened. Maverick had two branches: one in Beijing, one in Shenzhen. In May 1995, the Chinese government announced that local banks could act as separate commercial entities, minimizing government interference. This new autonomy would allow local banks to operate with fully profit-oriented initiatives; improved efficiency and increased competitiveness against foreign banks was anticipated. This government action was believed to presage further opening of the industry to foreign banks.

Foreign bank representative offices were subject to many restrictions; they could engage only in information gathering, head office coordination and research, but not solicit customers. Foreign bank branches were restricted to foreign exchange dealings and generally could not deal in renminbi. As a result, trade bills discounting and trade document processing for importers and exporters accounted for up to 90% of revenues. Regarding credit card operations, foreign banks provided clearing services for merchants.

According to an early 1995 report in the Japanese press, 31 foreign banks learned about the risks of doing business in China; "they have asked the Chinese authorities to help them recover about HK$600 million (US$68 million) in loans to Chinese state enterprises."

Regarding current renminbi restrictions on foreign banks, one respected observer believed that, in accord with China's policy of protecting its currency and ultimately national security, the government would not fully open up renminbi business to foreign banks for at least 10 or 15 years. However, another equally respected observer expected renminbi restrictions to be relaxed in a few years in line with China's open door policy to economic development. In addition, China was determined to enter the World Trade Organization (WTO); complete renminbi convertibility was required. In January 1995, the People's Bank of China (PBOC) announced that some foreign banks with "sound business performance" in Shanghai would be allowed to deal in renminbi by end 1995, seemingly supporting the optimistic view.

Government Policies and Regulations

China's transition from a socialist to a market economy in the 1980s and 1990s was characterized by rapid growth and high inflation. The government planned to develop the nation's economy in stages, the so called "point-line-surface" development plans. First, coastal cities were opened up for rapid development (e.g., Guangzhou, Shanghai); second, more coastal cities were opened, together forming a "line." It was hoped that economic successes in these coastal cities would bring prosperity to the inner areas, forming a "surface." However, to avoid an overheated economy, in 1993 the government took measures to check inflation and tighten credit control; both corporate and personal lending were discouraged. These actions hindered development of the increasingly popular debit (or transfer) cards into fully functioning credit cards. In February 1995, the government announced completion of a draft for the first credit card bill. The contents were not yet released, but the optimistic observer (see page 894) stated:

> I don't think the regulations will be relaxed in this bill and I expect it will still be quite restrictive. But it will be relaxed as plastic money develops in China. There is a demand though not a trend yet. The PRC in a few years can be compared to Hong Kong ten years ago. The card issuing policy won't be relaxed shortly because it is against the government's overall policy of credit control. I think they're right. They cannot relax the consumer lending market now, especially as the multiplying lending effect is difficult to measure. However, in a couple of years' time we will have relaxation.

The Credit Card Industry

Industry Infrastructure

A major obstacle to foreign banks entering the Chinese credit card market was the under-developed banking infrastructure. Foreign banks viewed credit cards as a "computer business," dependent on efficient card payment and processing systems. Furthermore, information networking among banks was necessary to broaden service distribution and facilitate sharing cardholder credit information.

Branches in different Chinese regions were not electronically inter-linked; they operated as single independent local banks. Primitive inter- and intra-bank information networking made communication between branches extremely difficult; it could take local banks as long as two weeks to clear credit card transactions. Another problem was scarcity of cash withdrawal facilities, i.e., automatic teller machines (ATMs). Chinese citizens found it difficult to withdraw cash with credit cards in areas other than major cities. Said one observer:

> Currently, the four big state banks issue their own cards in Shanghai. The Shanghai branch of the People's Bank of China is developing a unified card clearing system to consolidate these independent banks system into one network by pooling efforts and resources to encourage growth of the credit card industry. In early 1995, when the network is scheduled to go on-line, cardholders will be able to deposit or withdraw money at any ATM in Shanghai and enjoy more flexibility in shopping.

Visa member banks in Beijing, Shanghai, Guangzhou and Shenzhen had electronic connections needed to issue Minternational standard cards; it linked Chinese banks with over 20,000 overseas banks. Visa was designing its own fiber-optic gateways for future expansion of its credit card network (VisaNet). MasterCard was installing a communications network nationwide and adding computers at member sites to improve technical system support. Expected project completion was in two to three years.

The Golden Card Project. In 1993, China launched the ambitious "Golden Card Project," to develop a nationwide electronic card payment system. This program was a concerted effort by the Ministry of Electronic Industry, the PBOC and the Ministry of Posts and Telecommunications. Visa was actively involved.

System security and fraud issues. The pessimistic observer said China's current card transaction system had many security problems; fraud issues were the "thorniest." Because of name similarity and passwords in a vast customer base, Chinese systems lack specific functions to detect and report fraudulent transactions. For foreign banks considering linking these systems to their own international networks, he warned:

> The problem is that all pin-numbers of the foreign bank's system will be exposed to the local bank's system during integration. So there is a huge risk involved, not only on the technical side but also on security concerns of the foreign bank's existing system. Thus, during the negotiation process for system integration, it is important who you send and take as the negotiator – a general manager or a security analyst.

Owing to poor information networks across provinces, credit card authorization could involve long distance calls to the card issuing center for payment authorization, and take at least 20 minutes. This caused inconvenience for both merchant and customer and was prone to fraudulent activities by merchants (e.g., stealing card numbers, signatures) and consumers (e.g., using fake cards). Said one Hong Kong banker:

> I won't use my credit card in China except at five-star hotels. When you use your credit card in China, hotel employees can hold it for 10 or 15 minutes, saying they are "checking" the information. Then you go and park your car, come back and take back your card. During this 10 or 15 minutes, all your card information might have been "tapped" should the hotel employees be dishonest. I know Visa and MasterCard are working on fraud detection systems. Nevertheless, the merchant side is critical and difficult to control. I don't think they would send people to every merchant to monitor them. They won't send people to train merchant employees to detect fraud in customers using credit cards either.

Market Size and Growth

In the West, a credit card referred to a card system (revolving credit); consumers paid for purchases over an extended period and chose how much of the outstanding balance to pay each month. In China, the credit card concept was different. Usually a consumer had to deposit a minimum balance (e.g., RMB1,000 [US$112]) before a card was issued; s/he could then spend up to the deposited amount.[1]

By end 1994, the combined number of Chinese and western-type credit cards issued was 8.4 million (110% increase over 1993). The majority of new cards issued were denominated in renminbi, although most transactions processed were in U.S. dollars. Overall card penetration rates were still low in major cities (e.g., Beijing 2% versus Hong Kong [1.5 to 1.8 cards per person] and the West [2 to 3 cards per person]).

In 1994, billings were RMB51.69 billion (US$5.8 billion); numbers of participating stores and businesses rose to 135,900. Credit card usage expanded to more than 30 cities. The Bank of China forecast that by the year 2000, over 200 million credit cards would be issued, a 30-fold increase. The PBOC outlined a program to expand credit card use to over 400 cities and counties by 2000, providing access to over 300 million people.

Since Chinese-type credit cards offered significant payment convenience, many consumers opted for credit cards over bank accounts. McKinsey forecast that retail credit card purchases would account for 56% of payment volume in 2000 versus 9.4% in 1993 (Table 1); check use was expected to increase from 1.3% (1993) to 9.4% (2000). Essentially, consumers would shift from cash to cards, largely avoiding the check stage of development.

Table 1: China Payment Profiles

Purchase payment method	1993	2000 (F)	% Change
Credit cards	9.4%	56.3%	498.9%
Installment loans	2.8%	41.3%	1,375.0%
Cash purchases	97.8%	28.4%	−71.0%
Checks	1.3%	9.4%	623.1%

Source: 1993 McKinsey Report.

Local Card Issuers

Several Chinese banks issued credit cards, mostly affiliated with MasterCard and Visa. Observers believed China's banks, lacking technology, telecommunications and basic fraud prevention knowledge would be unable to set up even the most basic credit card infrastructure without Visa or MasterCard. (See Tables 2 and 3.)

Major International Card Players

American Express. U.S. based American Express (AMEX) was a major international player in card payment systems; for example, of the world's 100 largest companies 87 used the AMEX corporate card. Currently, American Express International was making a concerted effort to penetrate China's credit card business. It opened its first China

---

[1] The Chinese credit card was like a debit card in the West; it was also similar to credit cards issued to consumers with poor credit records.

Table 2: China's Selected Card Issuers

Mou Dan Card: As early as 1989, the Industrial and Commercial Bank of China started issuing its Mou Dan credit card in Beijing, Shanghai, Tianjin and Guangzhou. In the last five years, the Mou Dan Card has expanded from major cities and prosperous coastal areas to other smaller cities and towns. Currently, Mou Dan Card cardholders can use cards at over 30,000 member retail shops, and withdraw cash from the bank in over 1.4 million network locations throughout China. At end 1994, the cardholder base was over three million, 50% of issued cards in China.

Golden Harvest Card: The Golden Harvest Card was first issued by the Agricultural Bank in 1990. Although the bank had an extensive network throughout local villages, Chinese peasants provided insufficient market potential for credit cards. As a result, the Golden Harvest Card turned to major cities for further development.

Dragon Card: At end 1994, the card base of Dragon Card, issued by the People's Construction Bank, reached one million in 360 issuing cities. Cards could be used at over 800 ATMs and 20,000 merchants. Annual transactions were RMB30 billion.

Pacific Visa Cards: Pacific Visa credit cards, issued by the Shanghai-based Bank of Communications (BOCom), premiered in September 1994. However, the bank began its credit card business in 1993 in cooperation with MasterCard; in one year, 58,000 cards were issued. Bank officials said approximately 3,000 businesses throughout China were authorized to accept the card; annual billings topped RMB1 billion.

Guangdong Development Bank: The Guangdong Development Bank, claiming to be the first "real" credit card in China, was jointly owned by the Guangdong Finance Bureau, specialized banks, Guangdong Enterprises and Bank of China Hong Kong Group. In 1994, it earned RMB700 million (US$83.3 million) on RMB43.1 billion (US$5.1 billion) assets, making it the third largest of China's nine commercial banks.

Table 3: China's Credit Card Issuers, VISA and MasterCard

Banks	Members	Issuing cards	Acquiring	Significant player
PRC Banks				
People's Bank of China (PBOC)	Yes			No
People's Construction Bank of China (PCBOC)	Yes	Yes	Yes	No
Bank of China (BOC)	Yes	Yes	Yes	Yes
Industrial & Commercial Bank of China (ICBC)	Yes	Yes	Yes	Yes
Agricultural Bank of China	Yes	Yes	Yes	No
Communication Bank of China	Yes	Yes	Yes	No
CITIC Industrial Bank	Yes		Yes	No
Foreign Banks				
HongKong Bank	Yes		Yes	Yes
Nanyang Commercial Bank	Yes		Yes	Yes
Bank of East Asia	Yes		Yes	No
Standard Chartered Bank	Yes		Yes	No

Source: Maverick Bank, July 1993 Board Meeting.

office in Beijing in 1982; over a decade later offices were opened in Shanghai and Guangzhou.

In 1994, AMEX established offices in Shenzhen and Xiamen; currently other potential locations were being scouted (e.g., Wuhan, Hubei Province; Chengdu, Sichuan Province). AMEX hoped to expand branch offices throughout China; in addition, 20 China International Travel Service offices were converted to American Express agents. Services offered by these offices included: direct purchasing of traveler's checks, U.S. currency sales, issuing and re-issuing AMEX cards, traveler's check refunds, customer mail provision and other tourist support.

Like major foreign banks, AMEX could not issue renminbi denominated cards. An AMEX China spokesperson said that AMEX continued to seize all available opportunities to issue foreign currency denominated cards to expatriates. Although its corporate card base, comprising local Chinese and western expatriates, numbered in the thousands (tiny compared to 36 million cards issued worldwide) (AMEX did not disclose exact numbers), growth in the previous two years was over 50%.

In addition, AMEX was establishing and building brand equity among Chinese, in part by encouraging visitors to China to use AMEX cards. In March 1994, the China National Tourism Administration named the American Express card as the official tourist card in China, an honorary title with no real privileges. However, the two parties invested US$1.5 million to launch a series of marketing and advertising programs in North America promoting tourism to China. In addition, information centers, established in major cities to assist tourists, promoted AMEX.

AMEX's Asian headquarters in Hong Kong claimed the AMEX card, currently accepted at almost 7,000 establishments in more than 130 cities across China, would grow to 8,500 by early 1996. It also claimed that AMEX business represented approximately 50% of the foreign credit card market in China. In 1993, business volume rose 45% (over 1992), 20% in 1994. According to Jeremy Ng, marketing services manager for China, AMEX forecast continued compound annual growth of 20%. AMEX payment volume was 88% hotel-related, average per person payment was about US$200, double other cards. According to Eugene Xi, AMEX International Beijing Representative Office Chief, Beijing, Shanghai and Guangzhou accounted for the majority of Chinese billings.

Since the AMEX card was a charge card, AMEX was both card issuer and clearing house. One observer noted:

> Since merchants must go to AMEX for clearing, merchant acceptance cannot be as powerful as for Visa and MasterCard. These organizations accept credit card slips from any merchant's banker whereas for AMEX, only specified AMEX offices can be used; these are severely limited in number and location.

MasterCard. MasterCard International Inc. (MC), headquartered in New York, was one of the world's leading payment service franchises. By end 1993, 210 million MasterCards were issued by member banks worldwide; annual transaction volume over US$320 billion.

MC entered China in 1987; it opened its Beijing office in 1988. Since the early 1990s, cardholder activity enjoyed triple digit growth. In 1993, MC issued 3.5 million cards in China, 137% year-to-year growth; receipts registered US$30.4 billion, up 257%. By end 1993, 76,386 acceptance locations were established across China, 125% year-to-year increase. According to Mr. Tse, director of MC's China operations, by end 1994: six million MC cards were issued, over 100,000 merchant locations accepted MC, annual billings were over US$50 billion. Annual per card billing (1994) was US$287. China accounted for over 40% of MC's business volume in Asia Pacific. Member banks included: Bank of China, Industrial and Commercial Bank of China, Bank of Communications, People's Construction Bank of China and Agricultural Bank of China.

Visa. Visa International, based in San Francisco, was the world's largest credit card company; 54% of worldwide charges were Visa. Visa cards were accepted at over 11 million commercial locations in over 200 countries; cash could be secured from over 200,000 ATMs. In early 1995, annual charge volume was US$560 billion; 380 million cards were issued worldwide through 20,000 member banks.[2]

In 1988, Visa International introduced Visa cards to China; in one year, 481,600 cards were issued. By end 1994, over three million Visa cards were issued, 50% more than 1993; by mid-1995, over 45,000 merchant locations in China accepted Visa cards. Average per Chinese-issued card billing for 1994 was US$441 (RMB3,700) (versus US$2,000 in Japan).

According to the Chief Representative of Visa's Beijing Office, Visa was further raising its China profile. In early 1995, it applied to open a representative office in Shanghai; opening was expected in mid-year following final approval from the central bank's head office. Visa member banks included: Bank of China, Industrial and Commercial Bank of China, Bank of Communications, Guangdong Development Bank, People's Construction Bank of China, Agricultural Bank of China, CITIC Industrial Bank.

Income Sources from Credit Cards

Banks could secure three issuing types of income from credit card activity:

- Card subscription fee: Issuing banks that issued credit cards could charge annual fees to cardholders.[3]
- Interest: Income from unpaid cardholder balances at the end of the interest-free period.

---

[2] Note that, whereas AMEX issued its own cards, neither MasterCard or Visa issued cards directly. Rather, these member-owned (bank parents) organizations provided infrastructure, brand name awareness and marketing support for MasterCard and Visa cards issued by member banks. These member banks, not MasterCard and Visa, thus incurred the risks associated with providing credit.

[3] In the Chinese "debit" system, card issuing banks earned interest income on the required consumer balances.

Table 4: Minimum Mandated Merchant Fees on Credit Cards in China

Merchant business type	Fee as % of transaction/amount	Merchant business type	Fee as % of transaction/amount
Food catering, service industry (restaurants, entertainment)	2.5	Rail operations	1
		Flight operations	1
Hotels, hostels	3	Handicrafts, decorations, art pieces	4
Department stores	1	Others	1

■ Merchant fee: Merchant fees (percent of transaction amount) were paid by merchants for processing credit card transactions (Table 4). Merchant fee revenue was usually split equally between the card issuer and the transaction clearing bank (which need not be a card issuing bank).[4]

Potential Credit Card Entrants

Hong Kong. Hong Kong's proximity and eventual return (June 1, 1997) to China made the British colony's card-issuing banks (currently over 35) the most logical entrants. Possessing technology, marketing expertise, some brand awareness (among frequent cross-border travelers) and language ability, led some observers to believe that Hong Kong banks were set for a full-scale assault on China's infant credit card market. For many multinational banks (e.g., Chase Manhattan, Citibank, Maverick), Hong Kong was the beach-head for Asian expansion; all major Chinese cities could be reached in less than four hours. Many of these banks were believed to be continually monitoring the Chinese market and formulating entry strategies. The optimistic observer (page 894) believed the "end-is-near" and that entry was likely as early as 2000.

Japanese banks: the JCB company. Attempting to enter the infant China market, the Tokyo-based bank opened a Chinese office in mid-1994; China business was restricted to Japanese cardholders. In anticipation of local card ownership, JCB was boosting promotional activities and introducing value-added services, hoping to gain competitive advantage over other card issuers. JCB planned to install 3,000 on-line terminals in China by fall 1995. According to its president, Masaaki Ikeuchi, JCB anticipated issuing cards in China within two to three years.

Credit Card Substitutes

In China, consumers historically paid in cash for goods and services; however, since the early 1990s, consumers had more credit options available (e.g., mortgages, personal installment loans). Real estate developers were taking the lead in offering installment payments; in addition, household electronic appliance sellers were offer-

---

[4] Part of the merchant fee was earned by MasterCard and Visa for "interchange" services.

ing credit to certain customers. Since most Chinese citizens had relatively low incomes and free housing provided by the state, spending on big-ticket capital items, such as buying a house on mortgage, was not common. One observer said that since only 10% of housing was private, and since increasing numbers of multinationals were vying for limited accommodations, housing prices tend to be very high, beyond the reach of most Chinese consumers.

The first firm specializing in consumer credit services, the Shanghai Yintong Trust and Credit Service Co. Ltd. (a joint-venture private company), opened in Shanghai in November 1993. By end 1994, it had received 2,700 requests for installment loans (RMB14.6 million [US$2 million]). Cooperating stores reported sales of household electronic appliances surged (upwards of 30%) when the installment service was introduced.

Strategies to Start Credit Card Operations

Currently, foreign banks in China could only provide merchant clearing services. Some foreign banks were investigating joint-venture alliances with merchants, government and local banks as a means to overcome (wholly or partly) obstacles posed by restrictions on renminbi dealing and distribution.

With merchants: One observer suggested forming an alliance with a specific merchant(s) to launch a "private label" card(s). He suggested Giordano (garment retailer) and Lane Crawford (prestigious department store) as possible partners. These firms had information on potential card users from analysis of store data so easing marketing effort; joint promotion efforts might be made. This observer estimated the potential card user base for Lane Crawford at 200,000 to 300,000.

With government: AMEX early success in establishing a China presence emphasized the importance of "guanxi" with the government. Although central government decisions and regulations were final, regional and local governments, especially in special economic zones, had much discretion regarding action with certain high profile foreign investors; rules could be bent when it suited officials' guanxi. Foreign banks brought capital, technology, managerial expertise and employment opportunities; Chinese government provided market access. A strategic alliance could be beneficial to both parties.

With local banks: Chinese local banks had the background, relationships, branch networks, customer base and basic infrastructure but not high service levels. Foreign banks might make good use of Chinese bank partners' strengths; local banks could expand correspondent bank bases and acquire greater entree to international markets.

Another observer suggested an ideal joint venture would include three players: merchant (to handle marketing); Chinese local bank (renminbi dealings); foreign bank (experienced in credit cards, information technology, building links to international systems).

Marketing Decisions

Consumers. Existing cardholders were proprietors, owners of private enterprises and management level personnel in stock companies or state-owned enterprises. One observer suggested the key target market would be the emerging middle class in key cities. McKinsey reports suggested Chinese consumers currently using credit cards were predominantly the "rich" class, annual incomes, RMB12,000 to RMB21,600 (US$1,348 to US$2,427) (Table 5).

Table 5: Consumer Profiles

Consumer profiles	Characteristics
Credit card users	Annual income RMB12,000 to RMB 21,600
Younger consumers (18 to 24 years)	Annual income under RMB6,000
Older consumers (over 55 years)	Tend to pay with cash
Higher income earners	Annual income over RMB21,600

Source: 1993 McKinsey Report.

Another observer said:

> An ordinary consumer in China (middle class) has around RMB2,000 to RMB3,000 disposable income. The target segment for credit cards can be senior executives in large state-owned enterprises. They have high salaries, expense accounts and other fringe benefits. And, they incur significant entertainment expenses.

Distribution. Key cities often cited were Beijing, Shanghai, Guangzhou and Shenzhen. Should Maverick enter China, it would have to decide which city(ies) to enter initially. A critical restraining factor would be limited distribution coverage due to small branch networks.

Products and pricing. Critical decisions would include: positioning, classes of cards to be issued (regular, gold, platinum), interest-free period, savings guarantees required, annual subscription fees and so forth.

Initially, foreign bank card issuers would have difficulty competing with local Chinese banks in facilities and network coverage, they had better access to worldwide networks (unavailable to most local banks) and ability to take advantage of foreign exchange flexibility. Foreign card issuers might emphasize "prestige." (In a Beijing cardholder survey [Table 6] almost 10% of respondents cited "social status" as the reason for holding a credit card.) An aggressive, well-funded brand-promotion campaign aimed at a "prestigious, high status" positioning might be effective (see Table 7 for data on the Mou Dan card).

Promotion. TV, radio, print, posters and brochures were common advertising media in China. Rates for joint-venture firms and foreign advertisers with local manufacturing partner were double locally owned advertisers; fully foreign-owned marketers paid double joint-venture rates.

Thailand Background[5]

The Banking Industry

Until the 1990s, regulations in Thailand's banking sector were hostile to foreign banks. For example, only one branch was allowed (an ATM machine constituted a branch) in Bangkok, thus hindering foreign banks' ability to tap the local Thai deposit base, the cheapest available source of funds. As a result, foreign banks had a significantly higher cost of capital than local banks. Under pressure from the General Agreements on Trade and Tariffs (GATT), Thailand liberalized its banking sector. In 1992, the Bangkok International Banking Facilities (BIBF) was established; foreign banks could bring in foreign currencies from abroad more freely and both local and foreign banks could more effectively tap international money markets for cheaper fund sources. The new Securities and Exchange Commission (SEC) (May 1992) provided for extra liquidity in Thai financial markets by making available venues for companies (including banks) to issue debt within well-defined guidelines and efficient controls.[6] Furthermore, interest rate ceilings on loan products, 19% for loan products including credit card loans were removed.

The new regulations allowed foreign banks to open branches in provinces outside Bangkok. However, this change had little impact on their ability to tap Thailand's retail banking market as Bangkok was still the major (if not the only) financial center in Thailand. In particular, most credit card users were in the Bangkok area. A seasoned observer noted that only when foreign banks were allowed to open more branches in Bangkok would they be on the same playing level as local banks. However, foreign banks had significantly more expertise in foreign exchange transactions and risk management than local banks and observers believed they would continue to develop their growing foreign currency deposit bases, surpassing local banks despite each having only a single branch in Bangkok.

Thailand's banking sector comprised 15 commercial banks (classified by size in Table 8), 61 foreign banks with a single branch or representative office and four specialized state banks focusing on housing, savings and agriculture. The Ministry of Finance and the Bank of Thailand (the central bank) acted as supervisor and regulator of the banking industry. The commercial banking sector was dominated by the four large commercial banks controlling approximately two thirds of Thai banking business; the other 11 local banks shared 31% of the market, foreign banks 5%. The 29 commercial banks incorporated in Thailand comprised the 15 local and 14 foreign banks, over 2,500 branches in total. (For more information on Thailand, see the country synopsis.)

---

[5] The following section is taken mainly from a Maverick Bank Research Department report exploring entry into Thailand.

[6] Previously, companies could not issue debt and banks, seeking to maintain appropriate Capital Adequacy Ratios (total assets [distinguishing among risk characteristics of assets by assigning weights divided by capital to measure banks' financial viability) were seriously limited in their ability to expand.

Table 6: Survey of Credit Cardholders in Beijing

Reasons for holding a credit card	Safety	Convenience of clearing & transfer	Quick cash withdrawal	Social status	Others
	48.8%	69.2%	31.5%	10.0%	2.6%
Problems with credit card	Tedious application procedures	Low acceptance	Inadequate functions	Inapplicability due to poor data network	Inadequate fraud prevention measures
	28.0%	48.0%	39.5%	26.5%	4.3%
Monthly income level vs. percent of cardholding households	Below RMB500	RMB500–RMB1,000	RMB1,000–RMB1,500	RMB1,500–RMB2,000	Over RMB2,000
	1.7%	17.2%	39.8%	12.9%	28.5%
Card brand held	Mao Dan	Great Wall	Dragon	Golden Harvest	Pacific
	48.8%	28.7%	24.2%	23.2%	0.8%

Note: Sample size not published. Multiple responses cause percents not to sum to 100.
Source: *Chinese Industrial and Commercial Times*, November 28, 1994.

Table 7: Information on the Mou Dan Card

Terms	Mou Dan regular card	Mou Dan gold card
Annual subscription fee	RMB20	RMB80
Initial deposit required	From RMB1,000 up	Nil or to be negotiated
Overdraft (OD) limit	RMB1,000	RMB5,000
Interest on OD	• First 15 days, calculated at 0.05% per day on OD balance. • 16–30 days, calculated at 0.10% per day on OD balance. • Over 30 days or for OD exceeding OD limit, interest calculated at 0.20% per day on OD balance.	
Charge for transfer to non-merchant cross-provincial service charge	For transfers to enterprises not affiliated with the bank as merchants, service fee 0.5% charged on transfer amount. Minimum and maximum charges set at RMB10 and RMB500 respectively. Deposits or cash withdrawals over RMB1,000, service fee 1%. For deposits less than RMB1,000, service fee RMB10.	

Table 8: Thai Commercial Banks Categorized by Size

Large commercials (> US$8 billion assets)	Medium commercials (> US$2 billion assets)	Small commercials (< US$2 billion assets)
Bangkok Bank	Bank of Ayudhya	Thai Danu Bank
Thai Farmer Bank	Thai Military Bank	Union Bank of Bangkok
Krung Thai Bank	First Bangkok City Bank	Nakornthon Nabk
(government-owned)	Siam City Bank	Laemthong Bank
Siam Commercial Bank	Bangkok Bank of Commerce	
	Bangkok Metropolitan Bank	
	Bank of Asia	

Consumers in Thailand

Despite recent economic growth, Thailand remained an agrarian society; three quarters of the population were connected with agriculture. The population was young; 50% of its 60 million people were aged 20 to 54, 38% were under 20. Virtually all major commercial, financial and industrial activity was concentrated in Bangkok, home to over 10% of the population. In general, Thais preferred saving to high private consumption and were accustomed to cash transactions. Although private consumption was increasing, consumers seldom used all available credit facilities in their everyday lives. Among the new western-educated elite, sexual equality was occasionally accepted, otherwise such acceptance was very rare. However, women, whose purchasing power was growing, were more respected as economically independent in Bangkok than elsewhere in Thailand.

The social environment in Bangkok was very different from the rest of Thailand. Bangkok was an urban center with an increasingly westernized, class-structured (by wealth) society; in urban areas (Bangkok and the largest provincial towns), where private consumption and personal wealth were expanding, social values associated with this class differentiation were foreign to rural concepts. Thais distinguished Bangkok Thais from those in other places. Thais' attitudes toward things western were generally favorable although some ambivalence was present. Most Thais, particularly in rural areas, were satisfied with their way of life and had no urge to change. Observers said it was not easy to change Thais' personal values, that Thais were reluctant to reveal their true feelings and that most Thais preferred established relationships.

Private Consumption

Thai economic growth experienced a slowdown post 1993. GDP was affected by a reduction in private investment and political instability. Some observers attributed the slowdown in private investment to over-investment in the late 1980s. Thailand was experiencing over-supply in the manufacturing, construction, property and even agricultural sectors. As the result of falling agricultural prices, private consumption of farmers and related workers diminished as purchasing power and incomes were reduced. (See Table 9 for private consumption expenditure growth.)

Table 9: Private Consumption Expenditure Growth in Thailand

Year	1986	1987	1988	1989	1990	1991	1992	1993	1994(F)
Growth (%)	3.6	8.7	8.8	12	11.5	7.2	6.5	6.3	5.5

Credit Cards in Thailand

Market Penetration

Credit card penetration in Thailand was 0.02 cards per person (0.2 cards in Bangkok), low compared to Hong Kong and Singapore, two of the more developed Asian markets (Table 10). However, Visa cardholders in Thailand spend more on average than cardholders in other countries, despite lower per capita savings rates. These differences implied a different customer profile of Visa cardholders in Thailand; middle upper class, higher earnings, higher education levels. The major demographic difference between local and international cardholders was that most local cardholders had secondary education; most international cardholders had tertiary education. In 1992, Thailand had 0.88 million university graduates, almost all in Bangkok.

Table 10: Financial Data of Selected Asian Countries

	Thailand	H.K.	Singapore	Taiwan
		1993		
Visa card penetration rate	0.8%	48.0%	27.0%	6.7%
Average use per Visa card (US$)	2,040	1,600	2,020	1,490
Per capital savings (US$)	1,790	6,130	7,880	2,640
Per capital GDP (US$)	5,670	1,945	1,667	9,830
	1992 education level (million people)			
Primary	7.20	0.52	0.54	2.29
Secondary	2.30	0.44	0.15	1.87
University	0.88	0.05	0.06	0.51

Competition

The Thai banking industry was favorable to credit cards inasmuch as fund sources from customer deposits were inexpensive and the general public's reception to local banks was positive. By December 1993, 1.2 million credit cards were issued in Thailand; 0.61 million international branded credit cards (e.g., Visa, MasterCard), 0.65 million locally branded credit cards issued by Thai commercial banks (Tables 11A, 11B). (See Table 12 for credit card and charge card issuers [AMEX and Diners Club] in Thailand.)

Credit card terms varied from international to local brands. Most local credit card issuers required applicants to hold current or savings bank accounts with the bank. Until recently, most also required credit card applicants to pledge deposits equal to credit on the card (similar to China currently). Increased competition led some local banks to lower the pledged deposit requirement; some waived it completely.

Table 11A: Credit Card Growth in Thailand ('000s)

	Year	Local cards	International cards	Total
December	1986	80	100	180
June	1988	90	120	210
December	1989	200	210	410
June	1991	600	440	1,040
December	1992	700	710	1,410
December	1993	650	610	1,260

Table 11B: Credit Card Expense Growth in Thailand (millions of baht)

	Year	Local cards	International cards	Total
December	1986	0	0	0
June	1988	100	900	1,000
December	1989	900	1,200	2,100
June	1991	2,000	2,600	4,600
December	1992	1,900	4,200	6,100
December	1993	1,984	4,332	6,316

Table 12: Credit Card and Charge Card Issuers in Thailand

Bank	Visa card issuers	Master-Card issuers	Local credit card issuers	AMEX participating banks	Diners Club
Bangkok Bank	Y	Y	Y	Y	
Thai Farmer Bank	Y		Y	Y	
Krung Thai Bank	Y	Y	Y	Y	
Siam Commercial Bank	Y	Y	Y		
Bank of Ayudhya	Y	Y	Y		
First Bangkok City Bank	Y	Y	Y		
Nakornthon Bank	Y		Y		
Union Bank of Bangkok	Y				
Bangkok Metropolitan Bank	Y	Y	Y		
Thai Military Bank		Y	Y		
Citibank	Y	Y			Y
Bangkok Bank of Commerce			Y		
Thai Dhanu Bank				Y	

The major international credit card issuer in Thailand was Citibank (Visa and MasterCard). Application requirements differed from most local commercial banks (international and locally branded). For example, Citibank did not require a pledged deposit; each applicant was assessed on age, profession, salary and personal liabilities. Citibank's additional risk was compensated by a high interest rate on unpaid credit balances, 26.08% p.a. (Competitor rates for local credit cards were: Bangkok Bank 18%; Siam City Bank 19%; Thai Farmer Bank 23.6%.) (See Table 13 for competitive fee structures.) Currently, foreign banks had 32% market share; cards issued by local banks (mainly the four largest Thai banks) had 68%. (Maverick Bank was unable to secure market share data by bank.)

Table 13:   Various Costs of Possessing Credit Cards

Credit card issuers	Subscription fee	Annual fee	Supplementary card fee
International credit cards	Bahts	Bahts	Bahts
Thai Farmer Visa Classic	600	1,000	500
Citibank Visa Classic	500	750	750
Citibank MasterCard	1,250	750	750
Bangkok Bank Visa	500	500	500
Siam Commercial Visa	500	1,000	1,000
Bangkok Bank Visa Gold	1,000	1,000	800
Thai Farmer Visa Gold	600	1,500	750
Siam Commercial Visa Gold	–	1,500	1,500
Krung Thai Visa	300	700	300
Diners Club	1,000	2,000	1,000
American Express	1,000	2,000	1,000
Local credit cards			
Thai Farmer Local Card	300	600	300
Bangkok Bank Robinson Card	200	400	200
Siam Commercial Robinson	300	600	600
Krung Thai Robinson Card	300	400	300
Siam City Card	200	400	200
Bangkok Bank Robinson Gold	300	700	350
Siam City Gold Card	300	700	300

Technology

Telecommunications services were provided primarily by two state-owned companies, the Telecommunications Organization of Thailand (TOT) and the Communications Authority of Thailand (CAT). TOT provided domestic service and connection to neighboring countries; CAT provided all other international service. In 1990, 70% of total line capacity was in metropolitan areas, telephone density 14% per 100 inhabitants, 2% or less in rural areas (Table 14).

Table 14:   Telecommunications Environment in Thailand

Population	57 million	Cellular subscribers per 1,000 inhabitants	3.7
Waiting time for tel. lines	8.6 years	Pagers per 100 inhabitants	0.4
Tel. lines per 100 inhabitants	2		

Source: Telecommunications Sector Reform/World Bank Discussion Paper 1994.

In satellite applications, the highly competitive VSAT (Very Small Aperture Terminal) market developed swiftly in recent years. Four private companies competed fiercely providing point-to-point and point-to-multipoint data communication services to computer system users (e.g., hotels, banks, manufacturing firms, petroleum, finance and other sectors).

Credit Card Fraud

Credit card fraud was common largely because the legal system was lenient to offenders. Offenders were typically punished by a B500 to B1,000 fine and repayment of all fraudulent balances. Observers believed fraud would be a serious consideration for foreign banks. (In 1993, globally, MasterCard fraud was 0.14% of charged volume.) Similar to China, poor technology in Thailand, especially in communication systems, exacerbated the problem since it was often impossible to secure real-time authorization and clearance from card issuers.

Legislative protections for both card issuers and cardholders were expected to improve with enactment of Thailand's Civil and Commercial Act; this Act attempted to close existing loopholes in credit card facilities and protect card users from unfair treatment by card issuers.

Starting Credit Card Operations

Thailand's credit card business, free of Bank of Thailand monitoring (e.g., no limits on interest rates charged by issuers), was relatively easy to enter. No specific regulations governed the credit card industry and the Bank of Thailand intervened very little in the operations of credit card issuers. As a result, many local issuers entered the credit card business in recent years; these issuers came in many different forms. For example, the Volvo dealership (with Siam Commercial Bank) issued a MasterCard; cardholders received a 5% discount on purchases of Volvo spare parts. According to observers, most local credit card issuers were less concerned with interest profits than they were with increasing deposit bases to improve liquidity.

Potential entrants. Currently 20 foreign banks in Thailand (including Maverick) and four small local banks had not entered the credit card market. Though small, the local banks had retail networks in Bangkok and would be partner candidates for a foreign entrant. The 19 other foreign banks would be more serious competitors. For example, the Hongkong and Shanghai Banking Corp., already with strong credit card operations in other Asian countries, could be a direct threat.

Substitute Products

In Thailand, credit cards were mainly used for extraordinary items and emergencies. Both credit cards and charge cards were available. Young people, with a few years' work experience, limited income and a high urge to spend favored credit cards; older, higher earners were more concerned with convenience and might use either a charge or credit card. Preferential cards (e.g., issued by large department stores) were popular substitutes for frequent shoppers. However, the major purchase medium was still cash, welcomed by all merchants and readily available because of ATM proliferation. Most Thai merchants were conservative and preferred cash (Table 15).

Table 15: Number of Thai Merchants Accepting MasterCard

Year	1989	1990	1991	1992	1993
Number	18,000	31,500	36,000	43,000	49,000

Market Survey

In a market survey conducted by Maverick Bank's research department, 44% of existing cardholders had more than one card; of multiple cardholders 85% had experience in canceling a card, implying some lack of satisfaction with services provided. Most cardholders perceived convenient and emergency use as the major card benefit; corresponding costs were interest charges and the merchant fees inasmuch as many merchants charged customers commission charges paid the banks; this merchant fee was the major resistance to card use (Appendix).

About 15% of cardholders used the rollover credit facility; observers said this was much below the break-even threshold. These observers said that unless the borrower mix in the bank's cardholder portfolio grew significantly credit card entry would not be profitable.

The merchant survey revealed three market types in Thailand: the buyers' market, the competitive market and the sellers' market. It concluded that most of the Thailand market was still a seller's market; this conclusion was supported by the high percent of shops transferring the merchant fee discount to consumers.

Decisions

Poon contemplated his knowledge of the two markets. Maverick's research department had secured significant information on China and Thailand, but it was fragmented, incomplete and sometimes contradictory; nevertheless, he believed it was the best available. He returned to the questions he set himself: how should the attractiveness of each country's credit card market be assessed for potential Maverick Bank entry; how prepared should Maverick be to expand to less mature markets and what priority should be placed on China and Thailand if entry seemed warranted. He wondered if more information should be collected; if so, he wanted to be sure he developed precise data requirements, there was no time for undirected fishing expeditions. He had to make decisions quickly.

Exhibit 1:   China by Numbers

Population	1.2 bn
GNP per capita	$470
Gross Domestic Savings (% of GNP)	35.50%

Major exports: Machinery and electronics, garments and accessories, textile yarns and products, shoes, toys

Major imports: Machinery and electronics, steel, aircraft, automobiles, textile machinery

	1993	1994F	1995F
Gross Domestic Products (% growth)			
State Statistical Bureau	13.4%	11.0%	n/a
W.I. Carr (Far East) Ltd.	13.4%	11.0%	9.0%
Nomura Research Institute (HK)	13.4%	10.5%	9.5%
General Retail Price Index (% rise)			
State Statistical Bureau	13.2%	n/a	n/a
W.I. Carr (Far East) Ltd.	13.2%	20.5%	17.0%
Nomura Research Institute (HK)	13.2%	19.5%	13.9%
Prime Interest Rate (%)			
Peregrine Brokerage Ltd.	11.0%	11.0%	12.0%
W.I. Carr (Far East) Ltd.	9.3%	11.0%	11.0%
Nomura Research Institute (HK)	9.00%*	9.00%*	9.00%*
Average Dollar Exchange Rate (RMB/$)			
Peregrine Brokerage Ltd.	8.70	8.70	9.10
W.I. Carr (Far East) Ltd.	8.70	8.70	8.90
Nomura Research Institute (HK)	8.70	9.00	n/a
Trade			
Total exports ($bn/% change)	$91.76 bn	28.0%	17.0%
Imports ($bn/% change)	$103.95 bn	19.0%	15.0%
Current account deficit (% of GDP)	2.2%	1.0%	0.6%
Foreign exchange reserves ($bn)		$31.86 bn**	n/a
Number of months of import cover	2.5	3.4	n/a
Debt-service ratio (% of export earnings)	9.5%	n/a	n/a
Direction of trade (% of total)			
Exports			
U.S.	18.5%	17.8%	n/a
Japan	17.2%	16.8%	n/a
EU	12.7%	12.7%	n/a
Asia (excluding Japan)	33.9%	37.9%	n/a
Imports			
U.S.	10.3%	11.7%	n/a
Japan	22.4%	22.6%	n/a
EU	13.9%	15.6%	n/a
Asia (excluding Japan)	33.4%	33.1%	n/a

*Six-month working capital loan.
**People's Bank of China, 1st half.
Source: Asian Economic Survey 1994: China, *Asian Wall Street Journal*, October 24, 1994.

Purpose and Methodology

The research study comprised three separate elements: focus group studies, field surveys (consumer and merchant) and on-site observations. The objectives of the study were to:

- examine credit card market shares;
- profile existing cardholders;
- assess individual card transactions across personal spending;
- study the added-value of credit card ownership;
- identify resisting forces for credit card ownership;
- establish key success factors for card operations;
- examine merchant attitudes to card transaction purchases;
- examine consumers' purchasing behavior.

The focus group study and the customer field survey addressed the first six objectives; the merchant field survey focused on the seventh objective; site observation covered the final objective. Personal interviews and discussions to supplement research findings were conducted with representatives from the Bank of Thailand and Maverick Bank in Bangkok. Questionnaires were sent to leading card issuing banks in Bangkok but no responses were received.

The researchers believed the study would enable the customer profile and corresponding market size to be constructed; the income structure of running a card business could be predicted from customer spending behavior and hypothetical operations patterns. The merchant attitude survey would provide the magnitude of resisting forces on card acceptability; the rationale would be revealed through informal discussions with local Thai people. Overall, the research was expected to provide direction for marketing and launch strategies if a "go" decision were made.

Customer Analysis

Focus Group Study

Two separate focus groups were conducted in early April 1994 to help to formulate the scope and hypotheses for the subsequent field survey. The first focus group was conducted in Thailand with six Thai nationals (four females, two males; age 28 to 36), all educated above secondary level and holding white collar jobs; four possessed credit cards. The second focus group was conducted in Hong Kong with five Thai nationals (three females, two males; age 25 to 38) working in Hong Kong, educated to university level or above; all possessed credit cards. Several preliminary hypotheses were developed:

Cardholders, first focus group

- People prefer cash transactions;
- People have limited understanding about financial concepts like credit facilities and interest rates;
- Credit limits are secured by pledged deposits;
- Only middle to higher class people use cards frequently;
- Card transactions are only popular in purchasing luxury goods;
- Card authorization process takes too long.

Common to both groups

- People spend little on unnecessary items and save most of their disposable income;
- People's consumption is usually small in amounts;
- People settle balances before due.

Non-cardholders

- Do not understand the functions of credit cards;
- Are not comfortable disclosing secrets in the application;
- Do not feel the need for credit cards;
- Do not want to pay the annual fee;
- Feel that credit cards are not widely accepted;
- Merchants unwilling to accept cards;
- Merchants charge the 2%–3% merchant fee to customers.

Cardholders, second focus group

- Educated people have some understanding about financial concepts like credit cards features and facilities;
- Credit cards are less widely accepted and popular in Thailand;
- Credit cards are for emergency use and payment of last resort.

Based on the above hypotheses, the following were assumed during questionnaire construction.

Customer behavior

- Frequent travelers are typical card customers;
- Emergency is the major reason for possessing credit cards;
- Local credit cards are more popular;
- Existing cardholders do not use overdraft or cash advance facilities; they are reluctant to use the card because of the merchant-imposed surcharge.

Merchants

- Prefer cash because of the merchant fee and the time lag in getting payment from the bank;
- Do not believe card transactions can significantly increase sales.

Card issuers

- Local banks offer credit cards because they bring in pledge deposits;
- Default rate is high.

Field survey

The survey aimed to examine credit card ownership patterns in specified age, education, income and occupation class, reasons for credit card ownership and repayment patterns through field interview of 100 cardholders and 100 non-card holders. Samples were randomly selected from those meeting the prescribed selection criteria established to assist selecting reliable and quality samples.

Target group

- Age range, 20 to 45;
- Income: use minimum salary point for Citibank credit cardholders;
- Sample size, 100+100 good survey results;
- Default rate is high.

Interview locations

- Central business office district in Bangkok;
- Shopping area in central district and outskirts (surveys evenly divided among different locations).

Merchant Analysis

Hypotheses from the Focus Group Study

- Customers prefer paying in cash rather than by credit cards;
- Resisting forces are merchant fee and time lag in receiving payment;
- Accepting credit cards cannot increase sales;
- Merchant fees will be charged to customers.

Field survey

The merchant survey was conducted in a shopping complex (38 upper high end, 19 middle and 3 lower end) by local Thai people. Of the 60 shops visited, 46 accepted credit cards

Type of business	Sample	Type of business	Sample
Department store	1	Electrical appliance	10
Restaurant	6	Supermarket	1
Boutique	15	Miscellaneous – randomly selected	18
Household and furniture	9	Total	60

Of those shops accepting cards, 54% had card business below 30%, 39% from 30% to 60%; 6.5% over 60%. Generally, there were few restrictions of card usage based on amount of sales; 500 baht was an appropriate benchmark for the minimum sales for credit card acceptance.

Case 58

RAA (Thailand)

Benjamin V. Carino, Lope L. Belardo
Asian Institute of Management, Makati, the Philippines

Porntip Lyimapun, a Thai MBA student at the Asian Institute of Management, Manila, the Philippines, noticed that the Classified Advertisements (Ads) sections of Bangkok daily newspapers were crammed with advertisements. She observed that many advertisements were homogenous and seemed neither exciting nor attention-grabbing. She investigated the industry and identified a successful recruitment agency that assisted clients advertising for personnel in newspapers, in Malaysia. She believed a similar agency might be successful in Thailand and was currently in discussions with the Malaysian agency regarding some form of joint approach to the Thai market. However, before the venture could move ahead, she would have to develop a well-thought out marketing strategy that would attract clients and a total business plan, including marketing, operations, organization and finance that would be satisfactory to the Malaysian agency.

❧❧❧

Background

Recruitment advertisements were specifically directed at prospective personnel in the labor market. They usually appeared in the Classified Ads sections of newspapers. Most advertisers were the personnel departments of companies seeking employees. Typically, advertisements were prepared by company personnel department staff or by newspaper employees in the Classified Advertisement department. In many countries, companies seldom used advertising agencies for this purpose, mostly because they did not want to pay additional fees for a task they believed was straightforward; conversely, few advertising agencies were interested in accepting small advertisement placements. Small companies typically had to design their own recruitment ads as agencies were not interested in their business. As a result of these factors, most recruitment advertisements tended to look alike (Exhibit 1).

Practices in Malaysia

Porntip's discussions in Malaysia taught her that companies placed classified advertisements in one of three ways:

- Their own personnel departments designed an advertisement,
- The publishers would be contacted directly to design an advertisement, or
- A mainstream or recruitment advertising agency (RAA) would design and place advertisements.

RAAs saved clients' time and money in preparing materials and producing attractive and distinctive recruitment advertisements (Exhibit 2). They provided services that enabled clients to receive greater value for recruitment expenditures at no additional cost since agency fees were paid by publishers. Publishers were willing to pay agency fees since RAA personnel provided expertise in the production of recruitment advertisements. This arrangement simplified the publisher's printing requirements and saved the time and effort typically required in dealing directly with clients.

Practices in the Philippines

There were no RAAs in the Philippines; clients contacted newspapers directly. Advertisers did not work with mainstream advertising agencies since these organizations made only commercial advertisements for clients. Newspapers took responsibility for the design, size, layout, frequency, production and publication of recruitment advertisements. Sometimes clients gave newspapers a finished advertisement for publication. Clients received a discount if an advertisement was displayed frequently.

Manila Bulletin, a local newspaper with approximately 80% of the classified ads market, had a separate division for recruitment advertisements. This section was further divided into two areas: classified recruitment advertisements and display advertisements. The former group handled all employment advertisements.

Mr. Ding Reyes, a branch manager for Manila Bulletin, stated there might not be a place for RAAs in the Philippines since newspapers were capable of laying out and producing advertisements themselves. He said this arrangement was also convenient for clients. Indeed, he argued, large publishers (e.g., Manila Bulletin) served as RAAs inasmuch as they had separate divisions to take responsibility for these advertisements.

Advertising in Thailand

Total advertising expenditures in Thailand reached 13 billion baht in 1990 (Table 1); television advertising generated the largest advertising revenues. However, share of newspaper advertising increased from 1986 (22%) to 1990 (28%). In this period, total advertising expenditures in newspapers increased 37%, 3.6 billion baht in 1990.

From 1989 to 1990, the classified advertisement sections in most major newspapers grew between 80% and 100%, driven largely by the increased demand for employees. In 1990, the net volume of recruitment advertising was about 4 million baht per day

Table 1:   Advertising Expenditure Share by Medium (%)

	1986	1987	1988	1989	1990
TV	50	50	51	51	51
Radio	19	18	16	15	14
Magazine	9	10	10	8	7
Newspaper	22	22	23	26	28
	100	100	100	100	100

(1.5 billion baht per annum) (Table 2). Paralleling the growth of classified ads, newspaper classified advertising rates also increased.

In Thailand, the majority of recruitment advertising clients were company personnel departments: 60% multinational companies, 40% domestic. Most companies placing recruitment advertisements were newly establishing business or expanding operations.[1]

The Thai advertising agency industry was also displaying a period of rapid growth. Billings increased significantly in recent years: 1988, 25%; 1989, 29%; 1990, 30%. The Thai advertising agency industry was the largest among ASEAN countries; it was expected to surpass Hong Kong in five years.

Mainstream Advertising Agencies

Thailand supported about 120 mainstream advertising agencies; however, the top ten accounted for approximately 55% market share. Most mainstream advertising agencies were growing fast and operating at full capacity; new home-grown agencies were springing up, existing international agencies were expanding operations and unrepresented international agencies were seeking local partners. In all cases, the major business of advertising agencies was product advertising. In general, advertising agencies did not have a separate division for recruitment advertisements but were fully capable of developing a recruitment practice should they believe it worthwhile.

Similarly to other sectors of the economy, the advertising industry was frustrated by Thailand's over-stretched infrastructure. The country's continuing fast economic growth, especially in the past two years, created severe strains on transportation, communications and other basic services. Many advertising agencies claimed these problems increased operating costs. Long-term solutions did not seem likely in the near future.

Rudiger Reinecke, managing director of DDB Needham's Bangkok operation said:

> You could say the advertising industry is the pulse of the economy. When things go bad, agencies are the first to feel it inasmuch as companies believe cutting advertising and promotion budgets is the easiest way to improve the bottom line. As soon as sales take a turn for the better, we see advertising budgets go up.

---

[1] In 1990, 1,511 companies were newly registered in Thailand; all required employees.

Table 2: **Recruitment Advertising in Thailand**

Selected publications	Circulation '000s	Cost per col. inch (baht)	Cost per page (baht)	No. ad pages	Total per day*
English newspapers:					
Bangkok Post	45	620	106,000	6	636,000
The Nation	40	560	99,000	9	891,000
Thai daily newspapers:					
Thai Rath	900	850	216,005	0.5	108,000
Daily News	500	650	156,000	0.25	39,000
Matichon	160	360	86,400	4	345,600
Naew Nah	100	300	72,000	0.1	7,200
Wata Jak	60	250	60,000	10	600,000
Smakduan	–	250	60,000	15	900,000
Turakij Kam-ngang	–	200	48,000	20	960,000
Thai business newspapers:					
Tharn Settakij	100	350	84,000	7	**588,000 (168,000)
Prachachart Turakij	90	400	96,000	7	**672,000 (192,000)
Poojadkarn	90	380	90,000	6.5	**585,000 (167,000)
Krungthep Turakij	90	370	93,240	8	745,920
Koo Kaeng	85	345	82,800	2	165,600
Chinese daily newspapers:					
Sing Sian	50	110	29,648	0.25	7,412
Tong Hua	50	120	29,648	0.25	7,412
Total volume per day					5,940,144

*In baht.
**Newspapers published only twice a week; daily average per week.

The basic characteristics common to many of the top mainstream advertising agencies were as follows:

- Well-established in the market;
- Had good relationships with clients and media;
- Had strong financial support;
- Were well-connected with local and international companies;
- Had an existing track record;
- Had well-trained staff and technical know-how;
- Had advanced equipment and tools;
- Offered a variety of services;
- Emphasized product advertising and charged clients 17.65% of advertising expenditures.

In 1990, the top ten Thai agencies grew about 20% to 25%, lower than the industry growth rate due to new entrants. Demand for mainstream advertising agencies was increasing, but the industry was also becoming more competitive.

Newspaper Publishers

Newspaper publishers controlled the amount of recruitment advertising in the Classified Ads section. They were capable of producing advertisements and were often commissioned to do so. The over 30 newspapers in Thailand could be categorized as follows:[2]

Thai daily newspapers (TDN)	20	English daily newspapers (EDN)	2
Thai business newspapers (TBN)	5	Thai recruitment advertising newspapers (RAN)	2

Market shares of daily newspapers were:

Bangkok Post (EDN)	30%	Matichorn (TDN)	10%
The Nation (EDN)	20%	Wattajak (TDN)	10%
Poojadkarn (TBN)	15%	Others	15%

The most popular newspapers for recruitment advertising were English daily and Thai business newspapers; these publications were popular among young, educated, business-oriented people. Market shares of recruitment advertising in several newspaper categories were:

English daily newspapers	26%	Thai daily newspapers	9%
Thai business newspapers	24%	Thai recruitment advertising newspapers	41%

Twenty percent of the orders placed in newspapers were from mainstream advertisers; 80% directly from clients.

The Classified Ads section was a major source of income for newspaper publishers. Most publishers increased personnel levels to deal with increased demand and generally invested in this section to increase revenues. In particular, publishers provided in-house training programs to salespeople and added computer systems to improve service quality. Direct telephone sales saved time and transportation expenses.

Individual newspapers offered different rates and promotional programs. Major newspapers did not offer discounts to direct clients but offered 15% discounts to advertising agencies. Some publishers offered 10% to 20% discounts to direct clients and agencies based on the relationship between newspaper and client and the

---

[2] Chinese and Japanese daily newspapers were also available.

monthly volume of advertising placements by clients (and agencies). Some newspapers also offered bonuses (e.g., making an advertisement free) on its third run.

Thailand

Thailand is strategically positioned in Southeast Asia. Over 10% of the population lived in the capital, Bangkok, the country's second major seaport. Bangkok is also the country's legislative, industrial and economic center. In 1990, Thailand was ranked as one of the world's fastest growing economies (1990 economic growth estimated at 10%). Improvements in economic and social conditions were largely due to increases in foreign investment, tourism, exports and gains in real estate and construction.

According to National Economic and Social Developments Board projections, Thailand's GDP would increase to US$280 billion by 2000, more than double 1990's. Thailand would then be the largest economy in Southeast Asia (larger than Indonesia). The IMF predicted the Thai economy would average an annual growth rate of 7.6% between 1990–95, making it eighth among the world's fastest growing economies. From 1986 to 1990, Thailand saw great acceleration in gross domestic and foreign direct investment. The number of registered companies increased to 25,771 in 1990, a 36% increase from 1989. The construction section expanded by approximately 10% in 1990 in spite of the higher cost of materials, tight money and high interest rates. The sector was expected to expand at a strong rate for five succeeding years. Investment expenditures by the government in fiscal 1990 was 82 billion baht.[3]

Several other factors combined to make Thailand an attractive investment target:

- Political stability;
- Generous Board of Investment (BOI) incentives;
- Cost-effective and cooperative labor abundant natural resources;
- Abundant natural resources;
- Diverse supplier resources;
- Central location (Southeast Asian mainland);
- High priority infrastructure development;
- Low cost of living;
- A large, progressive, and growing domestic market; and
- Generalized System of Preferences (GSP) privileges.

The number of international tourists visiting Thailand increased in the mid- to late 1980s: 1986, 2.8 million; 1987, 3.5 million; 1988, 4.2 million; 1989, 4.9 million; 1990, 5.8 million due to both promotion of Thailand as a tourist destination and a general government policy to open the country to foreigners. This openness was reflected in the government allowing 100% foreign ownership of corporations.

---

[3] In 1990, one U.S. dollar was equivalent to 25.59 baht.

Labor Market Situation

In 1990, Thailand's labor force was 31,129,000; 29,951,000 were employed. Rapid economic growth led to a significant demand/supply imbalance in the Thai labor market. Private corporations and government entities faced serious human resource shortages, especially engineers, scientists, professional managers, secretaries and other highly skilled workers. Basically, foreign and domestic companies found it difficult to hire professionals to conduct local operations. Comparatively, however, government institutions were in greater difficulty. For example, at a state university, Chulalongkorn, professors with doctorates earned about US$360 per month (dictated by a rigid civil service schedule); in the private sector, engineers with similar qualifications could earn three times as much.

Previously, industries employing the largest numbers of worker were textiles, garments and leather products. In recent years, however, employment in services and commerce had grown rapidly; some industry analysts were skeptical about the labor problem easing in the future. Said one expert:

> The industrial workforce is only beginning to stabilize. Commitment to wage employment and factory discipline remains low and many of the urban workforce has a rural base to which they may return if they are not retrained or cannot find jobs that suit them.

Simultaneously, salaries were increasing dramatically. A representative of a foreign electrical company operating in Bangkok claimed his firm originally moved operations from Taiwan because Thailand offered a competitive edge due to cheap labor, but that advantage soon began to fade. The minimum wage in Thailand rose from 70 baht a day (1986) to 73 baht a day (1987, 1988), 78 baht a day (1989), 90 baht a day (1990) and was expected to increase rapidly "When we moved to Thailand, we didn't expect wages would rise so fast," he said.

The domestic labor market was evolving to a buyers' market; there were many opportunities for employees to research, compare and choose jobs that best suited them. Most companies had no choice but to increase salaries, incentives and training to maintain current employees and attract qualified personnel. Because of fierce competition for university graduates, companies were paying salaries of 13,000 baht per month for new engineers with bachelor degrees; double the salary of a few years ago. According to a report by Thai Farmers Bank, larger firms attracted recruits with the required expertise since they offered a full range of incentives and benefits and higher salaries than smaller firms. The bank reported trends of employees migrating from small, to medium, to large firms and from the public sector to the private sector.

Human resources were important contributors to Thailand's dynamic economy. The availability of low wages and hardworking laborers had previously allowed the country to take advantage of favorable external market conditions. In addition, prudent macroeconomic management enabled the country to grow rapidly and in a relatively organized fashion. However, rapid structural changes and the need for Thailand to upgrade the technological and skill base of its production sectors led human resources to become the key constraint to sustained growth (Table 3).

Table 3: Work Status of Economically Active Population in Thailand (%)

Category	1960	1990	Category	1960	1990
Professional and technical	1.3	3.4	Service industries	2	3.6
Administrative, executive and managerial	0.2	1.5	Agriculture and fishing	82.6	64.0
Clerical	1.1	2.8	Production and related workers	7.1	13.2
Sales	5.3	8.8	Others	0.7	0.1

Industry experts believed investment growth was seriously affected by labor market shortages; some Thai experts blamed the labor market imbalance on the failure of the educational system to adjust to the changed composition of demand in the labor market. Although the Permanent Secretary of State for University Affairs predicted the bottleneck would last until 1993, when a gradual return to a balance between supply and demand for engineers was expected, many observers remained unconvinced. The Secretary said the demand for new graduates in engineering grew from about 1,700 yearly in the mid-1980s to over 4,000 yearly currently; studies by his Ministry and Thailand Development and Research Institute predicted demand would almost double in the next few years.

The Labor Department reported that several enterprises were forced to import foreign engineers and offer higher salaries. In the past three years, the Department gave work permits to 4,000 to 5,000 foreign engineers to work in Thailand. Private firms continued to file applications requesting permission to bring in even more foreign engineers. Corporations also offered scholarships to Thai students in prestigious educational institutions in order to recruit them upon graduation. Most companies were extremely protective about recruited employees and paid close attention to human resource policies. They sought to keep their present employees satisfied while simultaneously attracting qualified applicants.

Almost every sector of the Thai economy was concerned about the shortage of manpower since this affected growth and profitability. The government sector faced an acute shortage of workers in several engineering fields, especially civil engineers for construction and related projects. In the short term, engineers were recruited from abroad; a long-term solution was being debated by the Ministry of University Affairs, responsible for producing engineering graduates. One group of organizations in difficulty were the many firms participating in national petrochemical projects; they were unable to secure sufficient qualified personnel. Some companies (e.g., National Petrochemical Corporation) invested in training programs to upgrade current human resources to meet their requirements.

A Recruitment Advertising Agency

Careful review of the Thai market led Porntip to the conclusion that, at present, no agency specifically offered production and placement services to recruitment advertising clients. As in the Philippines, recruitment advertisements were produced and placed by clients through mainstream advertising agencies or directly with the Classified Ads sections of newspapers. In her search for a model, Porntip found a successful RAA in Kuala Lumpur, Malaysia. She arranged an interview with Robert Chen, the agency CEO to determine what requirements would be necessary to start and operate a RAA. She discovered that strategic office and plant location was critical; travel time and retail costs were also important considerations. Since publishers would have to be visited frequently, and Bangkok had a serious traffic problem, the agency would save time and expense if located near the major publishers (Exhibit 3).

The average office rental cost in the center of Bangkok was around 400–700 baht per sq. m. (excluding utilities); RAA would require 144 sq. m. for equipment and personnel. Provision would also have to be made for office furniture, fixtures and renovation. Porntip learned that production and placement of distinctive and attractive recruitment advertisements quickly would require:

Five Macintosh computers
One Laser Writer IINTX
One ScanMaker (Microtek)
One PC computer
One photocopy machine

One electric typewriter
One camera and dark room facility
Five telephone lines and ten telephones
Two fax machines
One car
Two motorcycles

(See Table 4 for prices; if leased, initial payments would be equivalent to 30% of the purchase price, the balance payable in two years at 15% interest p.a.)

Table 4: RAA (Thailand) – Prices of Start-up Materials

Equipment and tools	Purchase (baht)	Equipment and tools	Purchase (baht)
Macintosh IFsi	130,000	Photocopy machine	150,000
Macintosh LC	100,000	Electric typewriter	15,000
Macintosh SE/30	110,000	Camera	60,000
2 Macintosh Classic	110,000	10 telephones	20,000
Laser Writer IINTX	210,000	2 fax machines	40,000
Scanmaker (Microtek)	70,000	2 motorcycles	60,000
PC Computer	20,000	Car (second hand)	250,000
		Total	1,345,000

In discussions with Mr. Chen, Porntip proposed the idea of establishing a joint venture between the Malaysian RAA and a new Thai RAA. Mr. Chen expressed interest but was concerned about the size of the Thai market for classified advertising and whether it was ready for a specialized RAA. He asked Porntip to look carefully into these issues and submit a proposal that included a market and sales forecast; a business strategy and a framework for the proposed relationship between the Malaysian and Thai agencies.

Exhibit 1: Sample Recruitment Advertisements

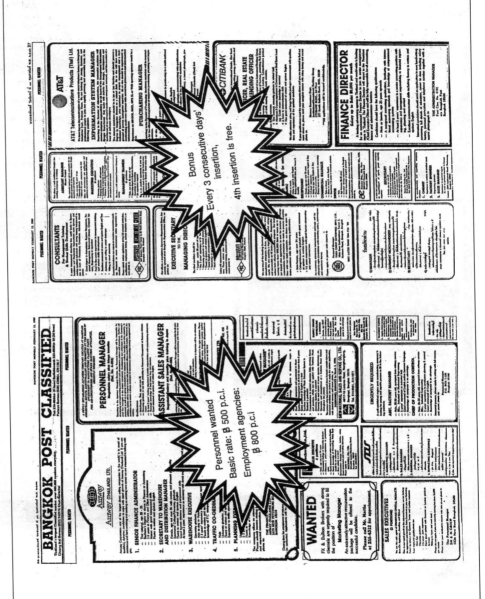

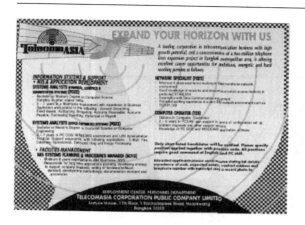

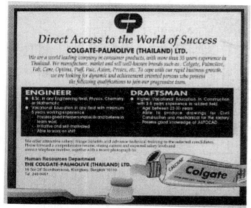

Exhibit 3: Map of Bangkok

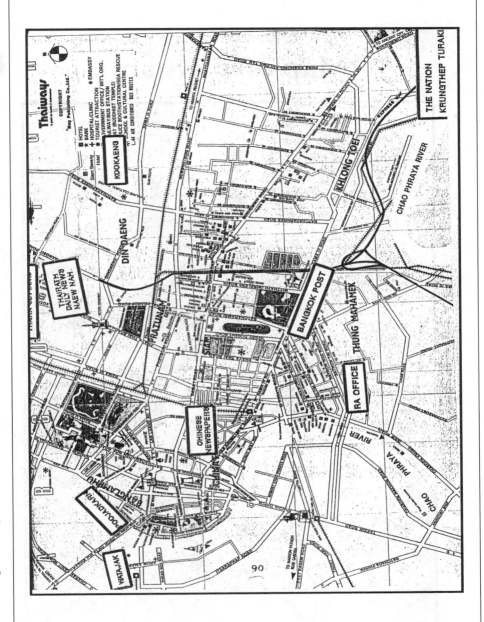

Map of Vietnam

Vietnam Overview[1]

Background. Vietnam's long and narrow land mass (330,000 sq. km.) is 75% mountainous or forested; coastline is 3,818 kilometers. The 76.7 million population (2.3% p.a. growth rate) speaks Vietnamese (official), French, Chinese and English; it comprises 85% Vietnamese, 3% Chinese and small numbers of Thai, Mao, Muong, Man, Khmer and Cham. Major religions are Buddhism, Taoism and Confucianism. Vietnam's landscape is dominated by two large river systems: the Red River in the north, flowing through Hanoi; and the Mekong River forming the Mekong delta in the south (south of Ho Chi Minh City). Climate is subtropical in the south (warm to hot throughout the year, rainy from May to November), and temperate in the north (cool and cold, rainy from October to March). Average temperatures range from 17°C to 30°C. Vietnam comprises 50 provinces, three municipalities and one special economic zone. Three cities are of political and economic importance (million population): Ho Chi Minh (4.3), Hanoi (2.2) and Haiphong (1.5). The unicameral National Assembly (Quoc-Hoi) with 395 members (Vietnam Communist Party [VCP] or VCP approved), the legislative branch of government, meets twice a year. The Communist Party's 12-member Political Bureau (Politburo) is Vietnam's most powerful institution; it supervises the Party's day-to-day functioning and issues directives to the government. The Party Congress makes major policy decisions (e.g., five-year plan thrusts) after long, behind-the-scenes, discussions.

The legal system is based on Communist legal theory and French Civil Law. Legal property ownership is ensured in all economic sectors for all citizens. On October 14, 1994, National Assembly President, Ngo Duc Manh signed two state ordinances on land use rights and land leasing in Vietnam previously ratified by the sixth session of the ninth National Assembly; the Law on Foreign Investment in Vietnam enables foreign investors to build and own the structures on the leased land within the scope and terms of the lease.

Political. Conquered by France (1858), occupied by Japan (1940) in World War II, Vietnam became independent in September 1945. Although the French quickly re-established colonial rule, they were finally defeated by nationalist/communist forces in 1954. The subsequent Geneva agreements formed North and South Vietnam giving the Communists control of the area north of the 17th parallel. When South Vietnam backed

---

[1] Socialist Republic of Vietnam.

by the U.S., refused to abide by Geneva agreements calling for nationwide elections, North Vietnam sought reunification by force. In the early 1960s, fighting between the Soviet-Chinese-supported communist North and the U.S.-backed South intensified. In 1964, the U.S. began air strikes against North Vietnam; in 1965 it committed ground forces. The 1973 Paris Peace Agreement ended direct U.S. involvement; with the later defeat of South Vietnam, the Socialist Republic of Vietnam emerged (July 1976) as a unitary state comprising the Democratic Republic of Vietnam (previously North Vietnam) and the defeated Republic of Vietnam (previously South Vietnam).

Social. Vietnam's population growth is 2.3%, life expectancy 67 years; the literacy rate of the over-15 years population is 92%. Relative to other poor nations (e.g., Bangladesh, India, Indonesia), Vietnam's health and education indicators are good. Vietnamese tend to be very entrepreneurial and hardworking; many hold a second private job in addition to their official state job. Since the South has received most foreign direct investment, a North–South rivalry has been developing. Since the Communists came to power, many Vietnamese have fled the country. In addition to those with political refugee status, 57,000 boat people are in camps in various Asian countries (e.g., Hong Kong, Malaysia, Thailand, Indonesia, the Philippines). The vast majority are being repatriated to Vietnam, many forcibly.

Economy. Vietnam is a member of the United Nations (UN), World Bank (WB) and International Monetary Fund (IMF). In July 1995, U.S. President Clinton announced normalization of relationships with Vietnam, ending the prolonged stagnant Hanoi–Washington relationship and opening the way for granting most favored nation (MFN) trading status. In 1995, Vietnam joined ASEAN; it wishes to become a full member of the World Trade Organization (WTO). The Communist Party launched free-market reforms in 1986; its goal is to double per capita GDP to US$450 by 2000. Per capita GNP is currently US$250 (1989, US$200); GDP growth is 9.5%, exports are US$5.2 billion p.a. The economy is structured as (1995): agriculture, 36%; industry, 25%; services, 37%. Vietnam's top three trading partners (imports and exports) are Japan, Singapore and Thailand. Largest foreign investment in Vietnam is from Hong Kong and Taiwan.

Almost three quarters of Vietnam's export earnings are generated by commodities, in particular, rice and crude oil; many multinational companies are drilling for oil on the Vietnamese continental shelf. Vietnamese industry is in infancy and generally weak, burdened by uncompetitive state-owned enterprises. Privatization efforts continue; the 12,000 (1990) state-owned firms have been reduced to 7,000 (early 1995). In 1994, moves were taken to establish enterprise groups modeled after the Korean chaebol. Unemployment is well over 25%; prime lending rates (%) hover in the mid-20s.

A serious government concern has been a growing budget deficit (end 1994, about US$800 million) following a sharp deterioration in fiscal policy after 1992. Although extremely high in the early 1990s, attempts to control inflation have brought the inflation rate to 8.4% in April 1996. The government is addressing dollarization of the economy (1995 estimates of U.S. dollars in circulation ranged from US$600 million to US$2 billion) to protect and build a strong Vietnamese currency (the dong).

In response to the Asian currency crisis and an attempt to stimulate exports, Vietnam devalued its currency on October 14. By end 1997, exports were down; the World Bank projected a 5% growth rate in 1998, lower than the officially anticipated 9%.

Infrastructure. In 1993, Vietnam Airlines was established as a state enterprise under the supervision of the Civil Aviation Authority of Vietnam; it flies modern aircraft on both domestic and international routes. On the ground, the inter-city road system is underdeveloped; much is unpaved (1994, only 9,400 kilometers of 85,000 kilometers highways paved). Roads in major cities are badly in need of repair; in particular, lack of working traffic lights at major intersections is a serious problem. Roads are very congested and traffic jams are frequent; for example, Ho Chi Minh City has 88,000 cars, but over three million motorcycles and bicycles. The inadequacy of telephone switching equipment and cable systems is a serious constraint on the business sector; access to international links is restricted. Telephones are rare; six telephones for each 1,000 people. In 1992, electricity production was 130 kWh per capita; total capacity was 3.3 million kWh (1993). A 1,500-kilometer north-south 500 kilovolt power line (switched on May 27, 1995) supplies 1.7 billion kWh annually from the power-rich North to the power-hungry South.

Statistics*	June 1991	June 1997	Statistics*	June 1991	June 1997
Per capita GNP	US$200	US$250	Infant mortality / 1,000	54	34
GDP growth	2.4%	9.5%	Life expectancy (yrs)	n/a	67
Savings (GNP)	n/a	16%	Literacy rate	94.0%	91.9%
Inflation (CPI)	90.0%	3.6%	People per tel.	537	157
Foreign debt			People per doctor	3,140	2,298
(in billion)	US$14.6	US$26.5	People per TV	n/a	9.2
Pop. (million)	68	76.7	Calorie intake (cals)	n/a	2,250
Urban pop.	20%**	21%			
Pop. growth	2.2%	2.3%			

*Secured from *Asiaweek.*
**From "Vietnam: Open for Business," J. Probert (Sept. 1994), EAC/INSEAD.

Case 59

European Liquors, Vietnam[1]

Noel Capon
Graduate School of Business, Columbia University

Samina Seth
The Hong Kong University of Science and Technology

In September 1995, Alberto Moses, newly appointed Asian region V.P. for European Liquors, a major producer of top quality (and top priced) cognac, scotch, gin and vodka was contemplating sales and distribution of products in Vietnam. Based in Singapore, Moses' responsibilities embraced sales of entire product line to all Far-Eastern countries but he was particularly concerned about Vietnam because of information gained on a recent visit.

೮೦೦೮3

Vietnam was one of the first countries Moses visited because, across the product line, sales were low, yet stable. However, when he visited Hanoi and Ho Chi Minh City, in the days before meeting with Nguyen Tan Nam, European's exclusive distributor, casual observation suggested European's brands overall were well stocked and displayed. Conversations with bartenders and store owners revealed that generally, not only were European's products well respected, people purchased them.

When questioned about the apparent discrepancy between Nguyen's low level of purchases from European and his own market research efforts, Nguyen explained that the Vietnamese government imposed prohibitive tariffs on liquor imports. The government was most concerned about the development of basic industries and viewed liquor products, virtually all of which were produced outside the country, as incompatible with its economic goals.

Nguyen said the discrepancy Moses had noted was easily explained – smuggling! He explained that not only did Vietnam have a very long coastline, but that both Cambodian and Chinese borders were leaky. (Liquor import duties for these countries

---

[1] Based on an article in the *Far Eastern Economic Review*, June 8, 1995.

were often less than half Vietnam's.) Despite government efforts, smuggling for several product types, especially liquor, was rampant; he estimated 80% to 90% of premium spirits sold in Vietnam were smuggled. Furthermore, law enforcement officers often turned a blind eye to liquor smuggling if given a couple of bottles for personal consumption. One bottle of top-of-the-line Scotch was the equivalent of a month's salary for many policemen.

Nguyen said European's line of liquor products was not profitable; if business did not improve he would have to reduce his commitment to European's brands. Sales were low, yet inventories had to be maintained. This cost money, used scarce warehouse space and selling effort was diverted to profitable non-competing products.

In other meetings, Moses discovered that not all liquor companies viewed smuggling as a problem. Said the Vietnam representative of a U.S. distiller: "We don't know how our stuff gets in here, but as long as it does, we want to develop awareness of our brands."

Indeed, Moses discovered that in April, Martell (Seagrams) spent around US$30,000 to sponsor the Martell Golden Cup 95 at the Phu Tho Turf Club in Ho Chi Minh City for several thousand horse racing enthusiasts. As reported the *Far Eastern Economic Review*: "Few in the VIP boxes seemed to mind that the horses (ponies, really) didn't run straight, that the jockeys looked barely old enough to walk, much less ride, and that the pre-race favorites occasionally finished dead last." For Martell, apparently, the event was a "big success." Jacques Mernier, Martell's France-based export manager for Asia Pacific said that horse racing, aided by enormous Martell banners, was: "A great way to build brand recognition." Relatedly, J&B Scotch, a Grand Metropolitan brand, had commitments to sponsor Vietnam's National Tennis Championship each year to 2000. Apparently, J&B viewed the 1995 sponsorship as worthwhile: "It gets us a lot of coverage," said senior executive, John Rowley.

Moses discovered that alcohol advertisements were barred from TV and that similar bans on billboards and other outdoor advertising were anticipated as part of a campaign against social evils (e.g., gambling, prostitution, pornography, drug addiction) accompanying economic reform. Some shops in Ho Chi Minh City had been told to remove point-of-sale promotions for liquor. David Bell, Bates Worldwide advertising agency, provided some basic data on Vietnam: advertising expenditures were roughly US$30 million p.a., mean per capita income was about US$200. Most of European's brands sold at retail for US$10 to US$30 per bottle in Hong Kong.

As he returned to Singapore, Moses contemplated his options. He could do nothing, but he might lose his distributor and allow competitors to move ahead. If he commenced promotion, sales might increase, but his distributor might gain little benefit. He also wondered what the government's reaction might be. Perhaps he should attempt to identify the source of smuggled goods and take steps to stop this activity for European's brands. He wondered about other options and if he had fully considered all implications of the identified options. Regardless, the potential size of the Vietnam market as economic growth continued made it clear he should make some affirmative decisions.

Case 60

Vinataxi[1]

Noel Capon
Graduate School of Business, Columbia University

Samina Seth
The Hong Kong University of Science and Technology

In July 1995, Allan Ho, founder of Vinataxi, Vietnam's first radio taxi service in Ho Chi Minh City, had just been informed by the Ministry of Transportation that a third competitor, Saigon Taxi-cabs, was to begin operations within one week. Despite enjoying 75% market share in Ho Chi Minh, Ho had to reassess Vinataxi's current operations to predict the new competitor's impact on the taxi market. Operating in a country with little law enforcement history, growing demand for taxi services and historically unfair competitive practices, Ho decided Vinataxi should revisit its marketing strategy and quickly decide if changes were necessary. At the same time, private investors were urging Ho to begin a new taxi service in Hanoi; he wondered also if Vinataxi should begin service in other major cities. Since Vinataxi would likely be listed on a Southeast Asian stock exchange within a year, his decisions would be important for Vinataxi's future and his own financial well-being.

৪০৫৪

The whole affair, as it turned out was not worth more than a paragraph, and a humorous paragraph at that. It bore no relation to the sad and heavy war in the north, those canals in Phat Diem choked with the grey days-old bodies, the pounding of the mortars, the white glare of napalm. I had been waiting for about a quarter of an hour by a stall of flowers when a truck-load of police drove up with a grinding of brakes and a squeal of rubber from the direction of Surete Headquarters in the rue Catinat; the men disembarked and ran for the store, as though they were charging a mob, but there was no mob – only a zareba of bicycles. Every large building in Saigon is fenced in by them – no university city in the West contains so many bicycle owners. Before I had time to

---

[1] Certain financial data in the case have been disguised.

adjust my camera, the comic and inexplicable action had been accomplished. The police had forced their way among the bicycles and emerged with three which they carried over their heads into the boulevard and dropped into the decorative fountain. Before I could intercept a single policeman, they were back in their truck and driving hard down the Boulevard Bonnard. Graham Greene, *The Quiet American*.

Background

On a business trip to Ho Chi Minh City in the late 1980s, Allan Ho concluded that better, more reliable and convenient transportation services were needed.[2] His initial impressions of transportation in Ho Chi Minh were:

- Public transportation was poor and non-existent in many parts of the city. Public buses were old, ran infrequently and were very crowded. Ho Chi Minh had no fixed rail (underground) system such as many western cities, Singapore and Hong Kong.
- Rather than travel by bicycle as in the 1950s, many Ho Chi Minh residents used motorized bicycles, motor scooters or small motorcycles. Lack of traffic lights in many areas, the primitive design of in-place traffic lights and large traffic volume made crossing four-way intersections particularly dangerous.
- Taxis were American and French (1950s, 1960s) and Russian (1970s) cars (Exhibit 1) described by one writer as: "Running by creative roadside mechanics and the will-power of the drivers." Ho recalled that: "The taxis had no meters, no air-conditioning, no radio paging (services) and no headlights."
- Taxi service was negotiated on a per fare basis; requested payments varied greatly depending on time of day, location and whether the traveler was a local resident or visiting foreigner. Since many taxi drivers did not speak English, identifying the final destination and completing the financial negotiations were always difficult and sometimes impossible!
- Hiring a rental (or private) car was relatively expensive: US$25 to US$80 per day[3] included a driver, necessary in Ho Chi Minh's chaotic traffic. This was not cost-effective for a business person requiring a few short trips a day.
- Pedal-powered "cyclos" (Exhibit 2) were inconvenient and dangerous, especially in the rainy season. Many cyclo drivers were unwilling to go to the city center because of the risk of being fined by police; they frequently dropped customers one or two blocks from the desired destination. Problems of fares and destinations were the same as for taxis; fares for short distances ranged from US$0.50 to US$0.90.

---

[2] Ho, formerly a successful Hong Kong property developer, also invested HK$1.8 million in Pacific Airlines, through his Hong Kong-based company, Golden Class International, Ltd., to fly the lucrative route from Ho Chi Minh City to Taipei. However, when relations between these countries improved, both Vietnam Airlines and China Airlines began flying the route; Golden Class lost roughly US$1.2 million.

[3] One day's car hire comprised eight hours and travel within 100 kilometers.

- Bus service was limited and buses were considered "user-unfriendly." Decent bus maps were unavailable and many bus stops were unmarked. Many locals who could not afford cyclos opted for the bus.
- Honda Om, or motorbike, was a quick way to travel around the city. Drivers waited at popular pick-up points and passengers rode on the back; prices were comparable to cyclos. Motorbikes could also be rented: US$4 to US$10 per day plus US$3 for a guide.
- Passengers and drivers were sometimes stopped by police who requested protection money.

Vinataxi

Start-up

In 1991, Hong Kong native Ho, a newly-minted MBA (his second) from the University of Macau, approached the Ministry of Transportation (MOT) with plans for improving Vietnam's transportation system. He was initially attracted by the lack of taxi-industry regulation and poor transportation alternatives in Ho Chi Minh City. His immediate plan was to offer superior taxi service with the best taxi environment and quickest response time for visiting foreigners; he thought to follow up with comprehensive bus service between major cities (like U.S. Greyhound service), the Trans-Vietnam Express.

Ho proposed a joint venture, licensed and incorporated in Vietnam, between the Transport and Communication Development Investment Corporation (TRACODI),[4] Ho Chi Minh City People's Committee and the Department of Public Works and Transport (30%) and Tecobest Investment Ltd. (70%). Operations began in an unused government aircraft hangar near the city's Tan Son Nhat Airport; Ho was responsible for all operational aspects. The joint venture was granted a ten-year license (from May 1992) to operate taxis exclusively in Ho Chi Minh City. In May 1994, Tecobest sold a 70% stake to British-based Beta Vietnam Fund for US$3.5 million (leaving its ownership position at 21%); it was guaranteed US$1.5 million in loans for working capital and fleet expansion.

Operations

In January 1995, Vinataxi's fleet comprised 147 cars; by summer 1995, 200: 90 Nissan Sunnys, 60 Toyota Coronas and 50 Mazda 323s. Delivery of an additional 100 taxis was expected by September. Since the car import tax had increased to 200% of delivered price and Vinataxi's tax-free car import quota was exhausted, Ho sourced the new fleet of 100 cars locally. The locally-made taxis were "Kia cars" (Mazda engine, Ford body), small four-door sedans with spacious trunks. Ho visited the Philippines,

---

[4] Since the government could not "directly engage" in commercial transactions for profit, TRACODI was an MOT subsidiary company used for joint ventures. The Vietnamese side's contribution was US$300,000; Tecobest, jointly owned by three Vietnamese partners (70%) and Allan Ho (30%), invested US$700,000.

where Kias had been used as taxis for five years, to determine quality and durability. Ho believed Kias (US$14,000) were better value than Mazda 323s (US$26,500). All taxis were painted a distinctive bright yellow, modeled after U.S. "Yellow cabs" and were air-conditioned.

Customers requiring taxi service called a central telephone number; taxis were dispatched by radio. On an average day's shift, 5,000 calls were received by eight paging operators. However, because all taxi companies used the same radio frequency, several potential drivers heard information for an individual pick-up and raced to the pick-up location. Passengers typically engaged the first arrival. Ho believed 8% of paging business was lost to competitors. To ensure the best service, Ho personally handled all customer complaints and followed up with the appropriate drivers. Courtesy was extremely important to Ho: two passenger complaints and the taxi driver was dismissed.

Ho employed eight "FBI-type" motorcycle patrol teams of two persons to ensure that taxi drivers' meters were on when transporting passengers, the cardinal rule at Vinataxi. These potential Vinataxi drivers spent three months as agents before starting work full-time. If drivers were caught, passengers were asked to sign a document stating the meter was off. Patrol teams were not paid a salary; they received US$100 for each successful "collar" resulting from management information or "tip-offs," US$200 for using their own initiative. Management refunded all petrol and maintenance expenses. Ho believed this system was very successful and reduced free rides drivers gave to friends and relatives. Since beginning the program, no disputes had arisen regarding the validity of FBI-team accusations from Vinataxi drivers caught "red-handed." Moreover, Ho believed the FBI agents learned a valuable lesson about "stealing" from the company.

Ho's immediate operational goal was to increase the taxi efficiency ratings ratio (passenger miles divided by miles traveled) from 60% to 80%. Ho paid US$400 to US$500 monthly protection money, split among numerous police districts, to ensure taxis were safe from unscrupulous police officers, especially during night shifts. Ho viewed this problem as serious in Ho Chi Minh but did not foresee similar serious corruption in other Vietnamese cities. In contrast to competitors, Vinataxi fully insured cars, drivers and passengers. Ho attributed high premiums not to Vinataxi accident rates (actually very low) but to potential operations-disrupting arson and bombing by competitors.

Organization

Ho ran Vinataxi on a day-by-day basis. Oversight was provided by a six-member board; primary responsibilities were to oversee Vinataxi's strategy, approve major capital expenditures and accept year-end financial statements.[5]

Vinataxi was organized hierarchically (Figure 1). A large detailed organization chart was prominently displayed to guide all employees (especially drivers) for the

---

[5] When Beta Vietnam Fund acquired a majority interest, it replaced three board members with its own staff.

Figure 1: Vinataxi Organization Chart

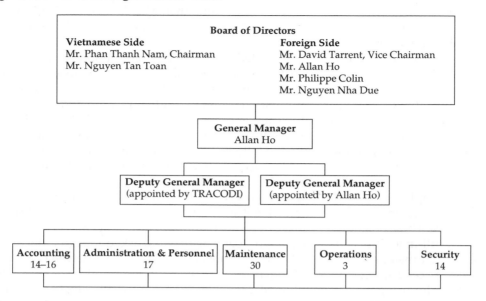

correct person to approach with complaints. Ho believed the chart created a sense of unity among employees. As general manager, Ho had two direct reports; these deputy general managers, one each appointed by Ho and the Vietnam Beta Fund, oversaw all departments.

Accounting Department had four meter checkers, six or seven cashiers and six accountants. When taxis returned at the end of each shift, meter checkers verified fares collected; they recorded figures on a chit that was submitted, along with the cash, by drivers to the cashiers.

Administration and Personnel Department had 25 employees; 16 were paging operators. Ho monitored each operator's performance by calls successfully answered relative to other operators. Each week, the highest ranked person received a US$10 bonus. Ho believed the winning operator enjoyed the prestige of being the most efficient member; operators who consistently ranked at the bottom were dismissed. Other employees handled general administrative tasks and Ho's "ad-hoc" experimental marketing projects.

Maintenance Department with 30 employees is responsible for taxi maintenance and repairs.

Operations (3 employees) was the smallest department. It oversaw scheduling and assigning; substitute drivers when drivers could not perform. Ho described these employees as drivers' "team captains."

Security Department oversaw security for taxis parked on premises. Since Ho was fearful of thefts and arson, he viewed this department as vital to Vinataxi's survival. Moreover, although all cars were fully insured, Ho feared loss or disruption of regular business would cause long-term harm.

Notwithstanding confidence in his direct reports, Ho was concerned about others learning too much detail about running Vinataxi. Initially, Ho employed an executive assistant for taxi operations and special projects for his consulting business, mainly for translation.[6] Once this person learned the intricate operations of each, he began "stealing Ho's business." As a result, Ho dealt with all sensitive and confidential matters personally.

Taxi Drivers

Vinataxi employed over 600 drivers; increasing to 800 in September. His target driver / taxi ratio was 2.2. Drivers typically worked 11 hours per shift; shift times were staggered. The first (morning) shift started from 3 am to 5 am; the second (night) shift from 3 pm to 5 pm. Ho allowed drivers to begin shifts early if taxis were available.

Initially, Ho had no difficulty attracting drivers; they were hired in batches and assigned a team number. All drivers in the first batch (1991 hires) were personally interviewed by Ho. (Between 40 and 50 of these most senior drivers still worked for Vinataxi.) Eight more teams were subsequently created. The teams engaged in friendly monthly competition for highest team revenue and per driver income; each victorious team member received a US$5 bonus. Ho believed the prestige attached to winning was more important to drivers than the financial gain. Additional benefits for senior drivers were preference for holidays, new taxis and more lenient treatment of offenses.

By 1995, each newspaper advertisement yielded at least 200 applicants, many were working for competitors. Criteria for Vinataxi drivers were: driving competence (at least five years' experience), speak English well enough to know the city's major buildings and sites, have no criminal record and be pleasant looking (to Ho's standards). Potential drivers had to pass tests personally conducted by Ho. Recently, only three of 140 applicants passed Ho's driving test; Ho believed it was becoming more difficult to hire qualified drivers. Unsuccessful candidates with potential were offered places in Vinataxi's three-month old driving school (VDS) located behind the office. Ho said:

> If I underestimate their ability and they become excellent drivers tomorrow, then these people could work for my competitors and become my enemy! I don't want to risk it! This way I can guarantee that someday, after passing all the tests, they can become Vinataxi drivers.

VDS offered Chinese (Cantonese) and English language courses; practical driving courses cost US$20. Driving courses were taught at basic, intermediary and advanced

---

[6] Ho's Hong Kong-based consulting business catered to Hong Kong organizations considering large investment projects in Vietnam.

levels; four hours per day, six days per week, for two to four weeks. Despite not advertising for students, VDS ran at full capacity of almost 50 students per month. The two teachers, former Vinataxi drivers whose licenses were revoked by the government, were paid US$100 to US$120 per class. The student-instructor ratio was 1:14, but several classes might be conducted simultaneously. Instructors referenced the Hong Kong Driving School's learner manual and adapted instruction material to suit local driving conditions and culture. Students practiced driving on taxis undergoing body work or other non-mechanical repairs. Vinataxi subsidized the school by US$400 to US$500 per month.

When a successful applicant was hired, he attended a half hour, one-on-one, personal grooming session to ensure personal hygiene and cleanliness on the job. A company handbook, including all personal grooming information and other rules and regulations was provided to each driver. While waiting to become a full-fledged, full-time Vinataxi driver, he either worked as an "FBI-agent," or as a substitute for drivers who were sick or late for work. All on-duty drivers were required to wear a smart company-provided uniform: white T-shirt, yellow cap with Vinataxi's logo, dark trousers and shoes. (Many Vietnamese wore sandals; Ho considered these dangerous for driving.)

When new drivers were assigned cars, Vinataxi collected US$300 security deposits, increased to US$500 in six months. (Since operations began, one driver's taxi was stolen "at gun point"; he forfeited his entire deposit.) These funds paid deductibles for driver-responsible accidents and payments for the "FBI motorcycle patrol"; funds were deposited in interest-bearing accounts. When drivers resigned they were reimbursed, principal and interest; drivers dismissed for carrying passengers with the meter off forfeited deposits. Ho reasoned that Vinataxi did not know delinquency levels and could not assess revenue loss.

Ho used western-style human resource practices. Unlike other taxi companies, all Vinataxi drivers took compulsory holidays each seven working days to avoid fatigue. Ho regarded driver safety as a matter of utmost importance.

The points system. To measure driver performance, Ho set up a points system. When drivers were hired, they received 20 points. Ho added points for exceptional performance such as good deeds (e.g., returning wallets and personal belongings left in taxis) and customer testimonials (e.g., calling in appreciation of excellent service). Conversely, customer complaints and damages attributable to driver carelessness led to point deductions.

Initially, if drivers were over 15 minutes late for work, they lost their cars to substitute drivers for that shift and were fined two points. Later, Ho reduced this to one point; drivers insisted the two-point penalty was overly harsh. For behavior issues affecting Vinataxi's reputation, five to ten points were added or subtracted; ten points were deducted for being caught with the meter off. Ho was particularly incensed by this behavior: "It's like a soldier going into battle without his gun!" he said; in other words, customers had to pay for Vinataxi to survive. On average, eight to ten cases per month were brought to "court"; about half were customer complaints.

The points system at work. A lady made a written complaint to Ho claiming harassment by a Vinataxi driver. Apparently, during the ten-minute journey, the cab driver continually pestered her for a date. Despite telling the driver she was married, he continued to insist she meet with him. When Ho received the complaint letter, he sent for the driver who admitted his misbehavior. Ho took the driver to the unhappy passenger's office to personally apologize for his conduct. Ho deducted five points from the driver's points total for behaving in such a way as to damage the company's reputation.

At year end, drivers with high points were rewarded with larger bonuses; drivers with less than ten points were dismissed. However, Ho was willing to rehire dismissed drivers based on previous behavior, work history and experience. If successfully reinstated, drivers lost entitlements: holiday allowance, end-of-year bonus and seniority.

Drivers paid for gasoline but earned one third of the metered fare; Vinataxi retained two thirds. Fare income plus tips ranged from US$270 to US$900 per month, comparable to executive salaries at large local corporations. Foreign tourists tipped 10% to 20% of metered fares. At year end, management allocated 5% profits to a welfare fund for medical purposes for all taxi drivers. Bonuses of US$5 to US$20 were distributed on Vietnam Independence Day, Chinese New Year and Christmas; amounts depended on driver performance, accumulated points and seniority.

Maintenance

Vinataxi's attention to taxi maintenance was distinctive; the technical repair shop housed 14 mechanics and 18 body work experts. Cars were inspected after each shift for properly functioning meters, cleanliness and basic mechanical operations. Mechanics sprayed interiors with perfumed air deodorizers. The entire process from recording daily fares to car inspection, assuming no body or mechanical problems, lasted 10 to 15 minutes.

Any interior/exterior damage was recorded in driver log books. A "jury," comprising all department heads, met monthly to assess driver payments for negligence-related damage; the jury was required to state reasons for its decisions. As chairman, Ho made final decisions on apportioning blame (e.g., 40%). Although fully insured, Ho wished to avoid the moral hazard of lack of driver responsibility for taxi welfare.

Poaching

Ho was considering a custom-designed Motorola system (cost US$150,000) to block radio calls from being received by taxi drivers with other companies. Proposed to the board of directors, specially designed frequency senders and receivers would allow calls to be isolated to specific drivers. Vinataxi's benefit for this project would be two-fold: regain lost paging business from competitors' drivers and send paging business to drivers on a priority ranking based on least metered fares for the day, thus distributing calls fairly based on driver earnings.

Marketing Decisions

Pricing. When Vinataxi started operations its price was US$2 flag fall (first two kilometers), US$0.30 for each additional 300 meters. When competitor Airport Taxi introduced service (1993), the fare was reduced to US$1.60 flag fall (first two kilometers), US$0.20 for each additional 300 meters. Vinataxi announced the reduced fares "to thank customers for their support during the past year." By mid-1995, the price was progressively reduced to US$0.60 flag fall (first kilometer), US$0.14 for each additional 200 meters.[7] Ho stated: "My aim is to make Vinataxi affordable for all Vietnamese people." All fare changes were matched exactly by competitors.

In 1994, government regulations required commercial transactions, including taxi fares, be paid in dong (VND). Vinataxi meters were changed to dong; Ho encouraged taxi drivers to remind customers that "00" should be subtracted from metered fares to translate from dong to U.S. dollars/cents (ignoring the decimal point). Ho said: Some foreigners believe the (meter) charge is U.S. dollars/cents (they are actually displayed in VND). They pay in hard currency and lose money to the greedy taxi driver (who does not explain the new system). Regardless of the new regulations, taxi drivers accepted payment in both VND and U.S. dollars.

Advertising and promotion. Ho recognized the importance of advertising, but spent less than half a percent of revenues. When Vinataxi was first launched, Ho paid US$3,000 for the production and rental of a centrally-located downtown billboard, one kilometer from the Rex Hotel. Concurrently, leaflets were distributed on streets (Figure 2); both media used the same picture of Vinataxi with telephone number. Ho felt billboard advertising was too expensive; company resources could be better used with other media such as TV advertising.

In early June 1995, Vinataxi aired a locally produced 35-second TV commercial (production cost: US$2,000) in prime time (7:00 pm before movies) 12 times per week for 10 weeks; each screening cost US$300. The directors agreed to spend more to establish Vinataxi's name in Ho Chi Minh; Ho had not decided how much.

The TV campaign focused on safety, comfort, affordability and time-saving. One particular advertisement Ho planned to air in September, after arrival of the new fleet was constructed as follows:

> Three groups of people are headed for the same party. The first couple take the cheapest transportation, the cyclo. The second man decides to ride his bicycle; the third group travels by Vinataxi. Later, the party is in full swing with all Vinataxi passengers enjoying themselves. The first couple arrives drenched from the rain; the second man, traveling by bicycle, arrives even later. The Vinataxi passengers all begin laughing when they discover they paid the least per passenger, yet arrived most quickly and comfortably.

---

[7] In mid-1995, the exchange rate was US$1 = 11,300 VND (Vietnamese dong).

Figure 2: Vinataxi Promotion

To target foreign travelers, especially business visitors, Vinataxi advertised in Cathay Pacific's in-flight magazine, *China Paper* (Chinese newspaper), *Vietnam Week* (daily Vietnamese newspaper), *Vietnam Economic Times* (weekly English magazine) and *Investment Review* (only English newspaper). When solicited for advertising, Ho usually agreed; as a result, small Vinataxi advertisements appeared in a variety of local publications (Exhibit 3). Ho also focused on the local market via advertisements on beer mats in local bars: "Don't drive drunk, call Vinataxi!" Ho did not advertise on radio; he believed it was too cheap and inappropriate for his target audience.

In early June 1995, Ho began targeting major multinational firms in Ho Chi Minh. The scheme invited (by mail) 200 prestigious companies to use a credit system; customers could pay by coupons which served as company receipts. At month end, a tabulated statement would be sent to each firm. Ho believed the convenient payment advantage of issuing receipts for tax purposes was a major incentive for companies. To encourage participation, Ho offered 10% discount for the first month. Fifty companies responded to the assigned employee from Administration and Personnel. Ho contemplated hiring a dedicated sales force but faced two dilemmas: because of a shortage of qualified salespeople in Ho Chi Minh, Vinataxi would have to train new recruits who might then be poached by competitors; and, he was reluctant to overpromote a system that might result in bad debts.

A major source of Vinataxi business was hotels. Ho contemplated paying commissions of 5% to 10% of metered fares attributable to business called in by concierge desks. Hotels would receive a check at the end of each month.

In Asia, Ho was frequently interviewed as a successful entrepreneur in Vietnam. This publicity improved Vinataxi's image and increased interest in Vinataxi as a target buyout by potential investors. Interviewed in *Asia Inc.* (June 1995), Philippe Colin, executive director of Beta Vietnam Fund said: "Ho is truly entrepreneurial, and even though he has faced adversities and problems, he has turned his operation into a highly successful company."

Performance

In 1994, Vinataxi's revenues reached US$3.5 million; Ho anticipated much higher revenues in 1995 but was unsure of the level: his fleet would be larger, but competition was increasing. (See Exhibit 4 and Table 1 for income statements and balance sheets.) Ho used Hong Kong's internationally accepted accounting system to record profits. Although profitability continued to increase, Ho wondered if he could improve revenues further (Exhibits 5, 6). Over the years, Ho noticed several trends affecting revenues, notably increases on weekends and rainy days (Table 2).

Table 1: Vinataxi's Financial Statements (December 31)

	1993	1994		1993	1994
	US$	US$		US$	US$
Revenues	1,815,427	4,297,628	Fixed assets	1,536,929	1,783,160
Profit before tax	698,581	2,131,929	Net current assets	234,344	1,236,020
Profit tax	152,735	385,953			
Profit after tax	545,846	1,745,976		1,771,273	3,019,180
			Financed by:		
Transfer to legal reserve	27,293	68,000	Legal capital	1,225,426	1,250,000
Profit available for distribution	518,554	1,677,976	Legal reserve	27,293	95,293
Interim dividends	–	522,643	Retain profits	518,554	1,673,888
Profit for the year retained	518,554	1,155,334		1,771,273	3,019,180

Table 2: Typical Weather Patterns in Ho Chi Minh City and Hanoi

Weather for a typical year in Ho Chi Minh City

Month	Jan	Feb	Mar	Apr	May	Jun	Jul	Aug	Sep
Temperature (Celsius)	25	26	27	28	28	27	26	27	26
Rain (mm)	16	3	13	42	220	331	314	269	336
Probability of dry day	97%	99%	97%	91%	63%	46%	44%	52%	44%
Hours of sunshine	6.7	7.6	7.5	6.5	4.6	3.9	3.2	3.9	3.2

Weather for a typical year in Hanoi

Month	Jan	Feb	Mar	Apr	May	Jun	Jul	Aug	Sep
Temperature (Celsius)	15	17	19	23	27	29	28	28	27
Rain (mm)	22	36	45	89	216	254	335	339	276
Probability of dry day	92%	85%	80%	74%	66%	60%	49%	52%	60%
Hours of sunshine	1.5	1.5	1.4	2.1	4.1	5.0	4.8	4.1	4.4

Ho Chi Minh City and the Taxi Market

When the Vietnam War ended (1975), Saigon, its largest city (2,029 sq. km., population 6 million [25% rural]), was renamed Ho Chi Minh. The city comprised 12 urban districts including Cholon (district 11), the huge Chinatown west of downtown Saigon (district 1) (Figure 3). Districts 1, 11 and the immediate surrounding area, the most densely populated area in Ho Chi Minh, had 3 million population, 21,500 people per sq. km. About 4.5 million people had resident permits to live in Ho Chi Minh, the remainder were residents without government permission. Periodically, police made house calls to examine residence documents (one per family); they compared numbers on the document with those staying in the house. Positive variances could usually be smoothed over by financial transactions with the individual policeman; traffic problems were often dealt with in a similar fashion.

Figure 3: Map of Downtown Ho Chi Minh City

Despite constant efforts by municipal authorities to upgrade roads, bridges and traffic signals, road accidents in Ho Chi Minh continued to increase: a mid-July 1995 report showed a 17% increase over the previous year (Figure 4). Precipitation in the rainy season added to driving difficulties. One report noted that of the city's 941 streets (1,600 kilometers), 25% were heavily damaged; the lighting system met only half the traffic demand. Worse, overloaded trucks threatened many of the 227 bridges with collapse.

Figure 4: Traffic Conditions in Ho Chi Minh City

Alarming rise in traffic accidents

Maybe such dense traffic jams are a deterrent to the huge increase in the number of traffic accidents!

Source: *Vietnam News*, July 15, 1995.

Ho Chi Minh accounted for 30% of nationwide road transport. Vehicles numbered: 458 buses;[8] 88,000 cars; 1 million mopeds, motorized bicycles and motorcycles; 40,000 cyclos and 2 million bicycles. Road space for driving dropped dramatically from 1975 to 1995 resulting in dangerous and congested driving conditions. One factor was encroachment on roads by coffee shops, street restaurants and retail sellers. A survey in the first inner precinct (early 1995) revealed 4,400 sq. m. of road surface was illegally occupied. Rush hour traffic density at some major intersections reached 12,000 vehicles per hour; major traffic jams were endemic. Road accidents in Ho Chi Minh rose from 1,300 in 1993 to 1,600 in 1994; in 1994, 1,500 people were killed and 2,600 injured.

---

[8] In early July 1995, the *Vietnam News* reported that 60 30-seat air-conditioned buses would enter service on four main routes later in the year.

In 1993, 670,000 visitors arrived in Vietnam. Although government data did not break down business versus tourist, one observer believed numbers of business visitors were currently, and would continue to be, greater in number. Taiwanese were most numerous, but fastest growth was by westerners. By 1995, Vietnam expected to receive 1 million visitors, growing to 3 million by 2000. In 1993, 480,000 foreigners arrived in Ho Chi Minh.

Little data was available regarding income distribution. Preliminary results from a government survey suggested two thirds of the most wealthy lived in cities, nine tenths of the poorest in rural areas. Another survey showed 68.5% of all households monthly income was VND 150,000 (US$13.75) or less. In the northern and central highlands, earned incomes were one third the national average; Mekong delta farmers earned 25% more.

Although, in 1945, over 3,000 taxis operated in Saigon, in early 1995, only 500 taxis were active: Vinataxi 120 cars, Saigon Tourist 70, Airport Taxi 51; the remainder were private. By comparison, Bangkok (Thailand) and Hong Kong, two cities similar in size and population, each had over 45,000 taxis. Singapore (population 2.6 million) had 3,000 public buses and 15,000 taxis. The Vietnamese deputy minister stated: "Ho Chi Minh City not only needs more cabs, but more cab companies as well."

Few Ho Chi Minh residents could afford to buy a new car; in 1994, only 2,500 were purchased in Vietnam. Foreign-made cars were extremely expensive; import duties were raised from 50% to 200% in the previous two years; right-hand drive cars could not be imported. Ho believed more new cars would be purchased in ensuing years as foreign car manufacturers (e.g., Ford, Chrysler) entered joint ventures to build affordable cars domestically. Parking was also a problem for car owners; many houses had no garages and street parking was unsafe.

Government Regulation

Taxi fares were not regulated; taxi companies set fares and could change them quickly. Bui Van Suong, Deputy Minister of Transport and Communication said a union of taxi companies was needed to deal with fares, areas of operation and related matters (*Vietnam Investment Review*). Ho believed taxi prices would eventually be regulated.

In October 1994, when the government required customer payments in dong, all foreign currency earnings had to be kept in bank accounts. In addition, all taxi firms, including foreign-owned ventures, were required to reapply for new licenses to deal in foreign currencies.

Competition

Airport Taxi. Airport Taxi was launched in October 1993 by Southern Airports Services Co. (SASCO), a subsidiary of Tan Son Nhat Airport (Ho Chi Minh) and Dong Nai Ceramics Company. Airport Taxi aimed to monopolize the market for passengers arriving at Tan Son Nhat Airport, seven kilometers from downtown. Ho bitterly complained about the unfair competitive practice that excluded Vinataxi from airport pick-ups; he believed Vinataxi could easily capture 80% to 85% market share in Ho Chi Minh if allowed to pick up airport passengers.

Ho said the airport authority was unfair in allocating only two parking spaces for Vinataxi. In January 1994, as a result of Vinataxi's complaints and after meeting with Vinataxi, Airport Taxi and the City's Public Transport Service (PTS),[9] Bui Van Suong ruled that Vinataxi could enter the airport and bring arriving passengers to the city. When the ruling was announced, Vinataxi was licensed by the PTS; Airport Taxi had neither registered with the City Business Arbitration Bureau, nor received an operating license. The deputy minister stated Tan Son Nhat had parking area for at least 600 cars; Airport Taxi's 51 cars could not occupy the entire area. Despite this ruling, Ho claimed Airport Taxi used unscrupulous methods (e.g., street gangs) to scare Vinataxi drivers. Since Ho was concerned with his drivers' well-being, he advised them not to pick up airport passengers.

Airport Taxi's operations were modeled after Vinataxi (e.g., price, service, radio frequency); the white taxi color was different. Airport Taxi abandoned a monthly salary scheme (US$80 per month) in favor of Vinataxi's meter-based plan. Ho believed the major operational difference was the shift system; Airport Taxi required drivers to work two continuous 12-hour shifts, then take an entire day's break between the 24-hour workdays. Ho felt this system was ineffective; he had seen many Airport Taxi drivers sleeping in parked cabs outside hotels, often during Vinataxi's 2:00 am to 5:00 am shift change over when few cabs were available.

Shortly after Airport Taxi started service, some hotels were threatened with having airport pick-up booths removed if Vinataxi serviced their clients. Ho complained bitterly about such unfair practices. However, by January 1994, he was receiving daily complaints from foreigners about Airport Taxi's service. Cabs were described as "outdated, unreasonably priced, unsafe and uncomfortable."

By summer 1995, Airport Taxi's fleet included almost 70 Japanese gift-donated, second-hand cars, 50 Daewoos, 50 Mazda 323s and some limousines. The initially donated fleet was a gift from Dong Nai Ceramics; it imported the Japanese right-hand drive cars tax-free and converted them to left-hand drive (49 were later sold).

Airport Taxi did not advertise. Ho believed it relied on being the sole airport taxi service. First-time visitors tended to use the taxi service with which they were most familiar – the first used, Airport Taxi. Airport Taxi had arrangements with hotel concierge staff: staff members calling Airport Taxi for hotel guests were paid 5,000 VND for each trip. Ho complained that hotels were forced to promote Airport Taxi to retain their airport booths.

Saigon Taxi/Airport Taxi. In April 1995, Airport Taxi, under a joint business agreement between SASCO and Viet Ha & Kai Nam Company, repainted 38 taxis solemn blue and branded them Saigon Taxi; 100 more cars were ordered. However, Saigon Taxi seemed to have a severe driver shortage. Flag fall for Saigon Taxi/Airport Taxi was US$0.80 for 1 kilometer, then US$0.80 per kilometer; drivers communicated with the central control station via a paging system.

---

[9] The Public Transport Service was the sole body entrusted with the state management of public places, including airports.

Saigon Tourist. State-owned Saigon Tourist Group owned almost 70% (53 total) of all hotels in Ho Chi Minh. Ho believed its fleet comprised 200 cars, 40 leased from British Petroleum. Drivers were salaried at US$120 per month; US$1 per hour overtime; customers paid US$4 per hour for car and driver. Member hotels used the Saigon Tourist Taxi like a rental car for clients; multinational companies could lease cars and drivers.

Saigon Taxi. Newcomer Saigon Taxi (owned by Mai Linh Company Ltd.), painted the firm's green logo on its 20-taxi fleet of white-bodied Kia cars. Flag fall was US$0.60 for the first kilometer, then US$1.00 per kilometer; it had no radio paging but relied on mobile phones. Ho perceived no threat.

Taxi Feuds

As competition for taxi business increased in Ho Chi Minh, periodically violent feuds between drivers flared up:

> According to a police source, the incident began with a minor dispute between two taxi drivers at one o'clock in the morning on January 5, 1995, and soon turned into a fierce struggle between the two taxi camps. Having received a request from a fare at the Shangri La Hotel Complex, Vinataxi dispatchers sent a car to make the pick-up, but on arrival at the hotel, the Vinataxi driver found an Airport Taxi already present, preparing to load the customers. The Vinataxi driver, believing the Airport Taxi driver had stolen his fare by eavesdropping (on the Vinataxi radio frequency), called his colleagues for help. Two yellow taxis in the vicinity came and the three proceeded to chase the white cab through the city streets until one of them (drivers) hit the white cab. The two cars were severely damaged. Both were seized by the police. Informed by radio of the incident, more taxis from both camps came to the police station where the taxis and drivers were being detained. After being dispersed by the police, the drivers resumed the fight at a nearby park. Police forces interfered and seized two more taxis, one from each side. "Vietnam Taxi Feud Flares Up," *Vietnam Investment Review*, January 12, 1995.

Expansion Considerations

In July 1995, Vinataxi's directors considered increasing capital for expansion to other Vietnamese cities. In addition to Can Tho, Nha Trang, Da Nang and Dalat (licenses applied for), Ho was interested in Haiphong, Hue and Hanoi.

Hanoi and the Taxi Market

Greater Hanoi embraced 400 sq. km., population about 3 million. The central city's 342 streets comprising 200 kilometers, mostly built under French colonial rule, were not designed to support mid-1990s traffic. Since 1991, car population increased from 40,000 to 60,000, motorcycle (including mopeds and motorized bicycles) ownership from 250,000 to 450,000. Bicycles, cyclos and other forms of transportation were estimated at 1.5 million.

Beginning July 1, 1995, by ministerial decree, a police operation sought to restore order and safety (300 people killed in 1994) to Hanoi's streets. Police made random vehicle checks in efforts to reduce the number of dangerous cars, motorcycles and trucks; various illegal street markets were moved to official sites to reduce congestion. The Public Works Service altered many city pavements; plans were made to improve public transportation to reduce bicycle and motorcycle traffic. By end 1996, 300 extra buses and 1,000 extra taxis were supposed to be in operation. The city's combined fleet would then stand at 500 buses and 2,000 taxis.[10]

In 1990–91, 50,000 visitors arrived in Hanoi; 1993, 300,000; the first six months of 1994, 430,000.

Taxi and Other Car Services in Hanoi

Hanoi's Department of Public Works and Transport of the Hanoi People's Committee had stakes in all local taxi companies and influenced their strategies.[11] According to Ho, management from several Hanoi Taxi firms visited Ho Chi Minh to conduct in-depth research on Vinataxi's operations so as to replicate its success. If Vinataxi were to expand to Hanoi, service delivery competition might be greater than in Ho Chi Minh.

Fujicab. Fujicab was the only car rental service before metered taxis. It operated a large fleet of small cars.

Hanoi Car Service. Hanoi Car Service (HCS), owned by the business arm of the Department of Public Works and Transport of the Hanoi People's Committee established three metered taxi services in Hanoi (i.e., Hanoi Taxi, PT Taxi, Red Taxi) (Figure 5). In early 1995, it asked the government to license no more foreign joint-venture taxi services. It argued it had to pay 200% import tax for each vehicle; joint ventures (e.g., Vinataxi) were exempted under the foreign investment law. The government had yet to act on this request; a decision was expected soon.

Taxi fares in Hanoi were higher than in Ho Chi Minh. HCS conceded it received many requests to cut fares, but had no plans to do so in 1995. Company officials argued (incorrectly) that since Vinataxi (in Ho Chi Minh) imported vehicles tax-free, it could offer cheaper fares. HCS management believed demand for taxi service was greater than supply; it had plans to add 50 metered cabs to each of its three fleets. Toyota had several business deals with HCS; it sold excess inventories (Toyota Corolla) from overseas plants at very competitive prices, net 80 days payment. However, with car import duties at 200%, HCS was looking to source cars locally.

---

[10] Some residents were cynical regarding government commitment to air-conditioned buses. They said in the past, new air-conditioned buses were positively received but a combination of heavy use and concern to save fuel led to an atrophying of the air-conditioning benefit.

[11] In Vietnam's decentralized governmental system each major city had its own People's Committee.

Figure 5:   Taxi Service in Hanoi

Hanoi Taxi. Hanoi Taxi service was launched in May 1993; the People's Committee invested US$1 million in 100 white Toyotas, targeting foreigners. In January 1995, Hanoi Taxi had 75 cars; passengers could phone from 6:00 am to 1:00 am. Flag fall was US$2 (first 2 kilometers), US$0.60 per kilometer subsequently. The trip from Noi Bai Airport, 35 kilometers to downtown Hanoi cost about US$24. Ho believed the firm was not financially successful and resorted to copying elements of Vinataxi's operations (e.g., Vinataxi's launch leaflets, distinctive color [blue]).

PT Taxi. PT or Pho Thong ("general") Taxis fleet of 50 second-hand blue or white Toyotas, targeted affluent Vietnamese; the entire fleet was older than Hanoi Taxis. PT was a favorite with expatriates; its flag fall (first 2 kilometers) was US$1.50, US$0.40 per kilometer subsequently. The Noi Bai Airport/downtown Hanoi trip was US$16.

Red Taxi. Red Taxi was the third HCS offspring. Pricing and service was identical to Hanoi Taxi; only its red color was different.

Mansfield Toserco. Mansfield Toserco (MT), a joint venture of the Hanoi People's Committee and a Malaysian firm, operated a limousine service targeting the upper-end market. It had facilities for bookings outside Vietnam and engaged in long-term leasing. General Director, Vincent Ho, said: "It was not true that foreign ventures in transport services could import vehicles tax-free. The government is not that stupid. How can they grant tax breaks for joint ventures and tax their own people 200%?"

Mansfield paid import tax on each of its 26 limousines, acquired in 1992 when the tax was 50%. In response to complaints to government departments that Mansfield stole taxi business, Ho said that taxi and limousine services were different, there was no direct competition. Limousines rented for US$36 per day from 7:30 am to 5:00 pm in a 100-kilometer radius; beyond 100 kilometers, extra charges applied, overtime rates were US$6 per hour. Ho stated that: "In the evenings our clients now use taxis instead of limousines, so they (metered taxis) affect our business in a way. But every city should have a taxi service." Ho said that Mansfield Toserco had no plans to cut fares since operational costs were high; it was considering adding ten vehicles to its fleet.

Private cars as part-time taxis. Unlike Ho Chi Minh, almost 2,200 private cars moonlighted as taxis in Hanoi: most popular was the Noi Bai Airport/central Hanoi trip, cost around US$20. In October 1994, city authorities ruled these part-timers register to be taxed properly; few car owners complied. For passengers arriving at Noi Bai Airport, getting into town could be a nightmare. Said one visitor whose travel agent failed to show up at the airport:

> My wife and I emerged from immigration and customs looking for our driver. We were greeted by a mass of bodies jumping up and down behind a barrier yelling taxi service. We stepped into the car park to look for our car and were immediately surrounded by 8 to 10 youths grabbing and trying to steer us to a vehicle. Eventually we made a deal with the 21-year-old who seemed to be the boss. But, as we left the airport in a 20-year-old vehicle, without a taxi sign, we were concerned that we would end up, not in Hanoi, but ...

Indirect Competition in Hanoi

Cyclos. Priced slightly cheaper than in Ho Chi Minh, cyclos were wider; they allowed two people to sit comfortably. However, one visitor noted: "Cyclo drivers in Hanoi are far more rapacious than their Saigon counterparts. I had a fingers bargaining session with one, only to discover at the end of the ride he was bargaining dollars and I was bargaining dong! He got 5,000 dong not U.S. dollar – much to his disappointment – but I had to be very forceful."

Bicycles. Many hotels offered daily bike rentals, about US$1 per day, but these were easily stolen.

Other Major Cities in Vietnam

No Vietnamese city other than Ho Chi Minh and Hanoi had modern taxi-cab service.

Can Tho, Can Tho Province's capital, in the Mekong delta had a population over 150,000. It was the political, economic, cultural and transportation center; the main local industry was rice-husking mills. It was connected to most other cities in the Mekong by a system of rivers and canals.

Nha Trang, a coastal city of over 200,000 inhabitants, was situated 448 kilometers north of Ho Chi Minh by car. The transparent turquoise waters around Nha Trang made fishing, snorkeling and scuba diving popular activities for tourists. With more parlor signs appearing, visitors were expected to increase. Fishing was the major industry.

Da Nang, population over 400,000, was Vietnam's fourth largest city; it served as the main seaport for southern Laos and Thailand. It was 972 kilometers by car from Ho Chi Minh.

Dalat. Once called Le Petit Paris, Dalat was a picturesque city, elevated at 1,475 meters, of 125,000 inhabitants. Tourism was the largest industry; over 300,000 domestic tourists made the annual pilgrimage, foreign visitors were increasing at a steady rate. Dalat was 308 kilometers by car from Ho Chi Minh, 205 kilometers from Nha Trang.

Hai Phong, an industrial city, Vietnam's third most populous (1.5 million) was a major seaport. Greater Hai Phong encompassed 1,515 sq. km.; central Hai Phong covered 21 sq. km. (population 370,000). Located 103 kilometers by car from Hanoi, one travel writer described it as a sleepy place with little traffic and many dilapidated buildings.

Hue, historically Vietnam's political capital (1802 to 1945), was a cultural, religious and educational center. Population 200,000, Hue was 689 kilometers from Hanoi, 1,097 kilometers from Ho Chi Minh.

Ho's Current Decisions

Ho was the key advocate for aggressively expanding Vinataxi operations in Ho Chi Minh; he wondered how long he could sustain the momentum. The Board had to make critical decisions: Should Vinataxi concentrate solely in Ho Chi Minh or expand elsewhere? If so where? How should profitability be increased at current growth rates? What marketing strategies should be followed?

Exhibit 1:   Russian Volgas and French Cars Still Going Strong in Vietnam

Exhibit 1 (cont'd)

Exhibit 2:   Mode of Transport ... Cyclos

Saigon still whirls with cyclists and rickshaws

Exhibit 3:   Vinataxi Advertisement

Exhibit 4: Vinataxi's Monthly Income Statements

Monthly Income Statements from January to April 1995

	1995 Jan.	Feb.	Mar.	Apr.
Revenue				
Income	456,564	494,904	561,949	554,138
Less income tax	4,565	5,660	6,274	6,250
Net income	451,998	489,244	555,675	547,889
Bank interest	1,345	3,611	1,804	1,286
Exchange rate				
Sundry income	450	463	14,022	714
Total income	453,793	493,318	571,501	549,889
Less: Operating expenses				
Payment to drivers	141,092	155,665	166,466	164,043
Workshop/repair expense	617	1,711	1,420	5,018
Spare parts	21,551	3,370	2,503	6,735
Car parking site expense	3,182	2,955	2,727	3,182
License and registration	12,679	10,931	260	160
Insurance	15,092	17,092	17,092	17,092
Depreciation – MV and equipment	44,388	45,909	50,265	50,265
Bridge and road fee		4,895	5,475	–
Parking fee	1,941		–	5,474
Parking site upgrade expense				
Rental of land	1,941	1,941	1,941	1,941
Advertising/marketing expense	1,176	618	–	17,025
Entertainment	459	85	996	292
Office furniture expense	356	74		90
Labor protection tariff		76		
Gross profit	207,432	247,996	322,356	278,573
Less: Administration expense				
Salary	9,229	9,302	9,661	9,503
Bonus and allowances	41,834	8,528	3,285	27,497
Electricity and water	462	365	367	1,197
Social security insurance	6,258	6,360	6,520	6,626
Printing and stationery	2,241	845	1,363	1,503
Overseas traveling	1,140	1,945		1,133
Meeting fee	15,000	8,125		
Local traveling	37	184	54	141
Company formation expenses	623	623	623	623
Bank charge	415	397	623	544
Telephone, fax and postage	1,990	2,001	5,023	16,036
Sundry expenses/overhead	2,060	442	2,175	3,729
Fuel for director's car	138	71	123	184
Total expenses	81,428	39,188	29,817	68,715
Gross profit before taxation	126,004	208,808	292,539	209,859
Less: profit tax (21%)	26,461	43,850	61,433	44,070
Profit/loss after taxation	99,543	164,959	231,106	165,788
Retained profit	99,543	164,959	231,106	165,788

Note: US$1 = 11,000 VND.

Exhibit 5: Vinataxi's Revenue by Month

	Vinataxi revenue by month (October 1992 to June 1995)			
	Revenues (US$)	Taxis	Coefficient (%)*	Average income per taxi
1992				
October	21,613.13	25		864.53
November	50,176.56	29	28.09	1,714.27
December	58,264.06	29	27.19	2,025.17
1993				
January	66,239.06	29	31.73	2,300.77
February	73,113.13	28	35.80	2,602.82
March	90,981.88	28	36.87	3,219.46
April	93,542.19	30	37.27	3,068.97
May	129,654.38	52	31.61	2,496.23
June	154,532.81	54	34.76	2,872.36
July	176,208.44	56	35.72	3,158.42
August	187,156.56	62	38.40	3,023.53
September	195,375.31	74	39.35	2,653.83
October	217,159.69	82	42.00	2,644.10
November	223,522.50	85	42.92	2,635.88
December	207,941.56	83	36.31	2,519.89
1994				
January	208,377.50	82	40.90	2,546.16
February	236,405.00	101	38.91	2,351.82
March	327,526.25	103	45.34	3,170.94
April	333,940.00	105	43.71	3,181.90
May	365,818.00	110	44.07	3,325.01
June	354,857.25	109	45.26	3,254.68
July	388,128.75	125	43.55	3,107.76
August	403,332.75	126	44.29	3,204.87
September	393,015.00	130	44.41	3,034.86
October	466,192.75	130	47.88	3,589.14
November	400,251.21	136	47.59	2,941.29
December	419,784.00	136	48.69	3,086.19
1995				
January	456,549.25	138	50.37	3,307.61
February	485,982.51	144	52.85	3,373.94
March	552,314.60	152	51.94	3,634.13
April	543,809.50	152	52.36	3,574.06
May	530,551.55	158	50.32	3,365.38
June	564,352.68	174	50.30	3,235.04

*Number of passenger miles divided by number of miles traveled.

Exhibit 6: Vinataxi's Daily Revenue for Selected Months

Date	November 1994 Income US$	Coefficient (%)	No. of taxis	April 1995 Income US$	Coefficient (%)	No. of taxis	May 1995 Income US$	Coefficient (%)	No. of taxis
1	13,098.00	44.48	137	18,496.94	52.64	152	20,160.91	55.55	150
2	11,676.75	41.22	135	18,268.53	51.32	154	18,348.29	52.69	153
3	12,342.00	41.90	137	16,498.75	51.23	151	17,198.98	51.95	153
4	13,204.00	43.25	137	16,739.20	50.97	151	16,201.70	50.25	153
5	13,587.75	43.33	140	16,899.31	51.42	149	16,339.78	49.91	153
6	14,343.00	44.32	136	17,185.23	50.61	150	17,276.70	51.90	151
7	12,530.75	43.97	134	16,593.86	48.97	151	17,963.88	51.36	152
8	11,043.75	45.49	128	18,603.41	51.81	155	15,472.50	49.07	152
9	10,624.88	43.29	132	18,408.06	50.94	154	16,125.23	49.71	151
10	11,433.75	44.92	130	16,063.64	48.47	154	15,930.00	48.92	151
11	12,036.13	46.99	132	17,280.11	51.41	152	16,134.89	48.73	152
12	13,683.98	48.40	137	16,291.14	49.61	154	17,299.09	50.98	151
13	15,270.91	50.13	136	17,065.91	50.79	152	18,260.45	51.63	151
14	13,139.09	48.83	137	17,690.56	51.98	153	20,039.31	53.55	153
15	13,568.88	49.08	139	18,604.20	52.52	152	15,485.69	49.22	150
16	12,854.66	47.76	140	17,611.36	52.00	148	15,957.73	49.73	150
17	13,852.95	49.66	140	16,716.36	52.03	151	15,831.48	48.34	149
18	13,918.98	49.72	138	17,444.20	51.33	153	17,495.91	51.54	152
19	14,134.31	49.59	137	17,425.00	52.14	152	17,026.03	50.25	154
20	14,383.88	48.89	135	19,163.30	53.39	151	16,975.34	50.90	151
21	12,846.14	47.43	137	18,086.59	52.17	149	17,990.23	51.64	151
22	13,629.44	48.33	139	18,954.89	54.47	151	15,506.48	48.04	167
23	13,782.39	49.24	139	19,915.90	53.70	152	16,103.19	46.68	170
24	14,268.19	48.99	137	17,004.43	51.47	152	17,050.23	48.45	173
25	14,212.95	48.59	138	18,425.23	52.50	153	16,871.36	47.00	171
26	15,389.31	51.34	138	18,382.50	52.06	153	18,231.81	49.07	176
27	15,926.25	53.00	134	20,034.20	54.88	155			
28	13,424.78	49.05	138	19,706.70	54.32	154			
29	13,310.56	48.12	136	21,667.73	56.30	156			
30	12,732.84	47.51	137	22,582.28	59.39	146			
31	400,251.21	45.70	132	543,809.50	52.34	152	443,277.14	50.32	155